THE CONFLICT OF LAWS

AUSTRALIA
LBC Information Services Ltd
Sydney

CANADA AND USA
Carswell
Toronto

NEW ZEALAND
Brooker's
Auckland

SINGAPORE and MALAYSIA
Sweet & Maxwell Asia
Singapore and Kuala Lumpur

DICEY AND MORRIS

ON

THE CONFLICT OF LAWS

THIRTEENTH EDITION

UNDER THE GENERAL EDITORSHIP OF

LAWRENCE COLLINS
Q.C., LL.D. (Cantab.), F.B.A.

WITH

SPECIALIST EDITORS

VOLUME 1

LONDON
SWEET & MAXWELL
2000

First Edition	1896	By A.V. Dicey
Second Edition	1908	By A.V. Dicey
Third Edition	1922	By A.V. Dicey and A. Berriedale Keith
Fourth Edition	1927	By A. Berriedale Keith
Fifth Edition	1932	By A. Berriedale Keith
Sixth Edition	1949	By J.H.C. Morris and Others
Seventh Edition	1958	By J.H.C. Morris and Others
Eighth Edition	1967	By J.H.C. Morris and Others
Ninth Edition	1973	By J.H.C. Morris and Others
Tenth Edition	1980	By J.H.C. Morris and Others
Eleventh Edition	1987	By Lawrence Collins and Others
Second Impression	1992	By Lawrence Collins and Others
Twelfth Edition	1993	By Lawrence Collins and Others
Second Impression	1994	By Lawrence Collins and Others
Thirteenth Edition	2000	By Lawrence Collins and Others

Published in 2000 by
Sweet & Maxwell Limited
100 Avenue Road
London NW3 3PF

Computerset by Interactive Sciences Ltd, Gloucester
Printed in Great Britain by Clay's Limited, St Ives Plc

No natural forests were destroyed to make this product. Only farmed timber
was used and re-planted.

ISBN: 0 421 661 402

British Library Cataloguing in Publication Data
A catalogue record for this book is available from the British Library.

CONTENTS

VOLUME 1

Part One
PRELIMINARY MATTERS

Contents

PART TWO
PROCEDURE

PART THREE
JURISDICTION AND FOREIGN JUDGMENTS

VOLUME TWO

PART FOUR
FAMILY LAW

Contents

Contents

PART FIVE
LAW OF PROPERTY

Contents

Contents

PREFACE

The editorial team has the formidable responsibility of ensuring that the standard of a work generously described by Lord Goff of Chieveley as "the prince of legal textbooks" (H.L. Deb. Vol. 515, col. 1482, February 15, 1990) is maintained, and that a work first published more than 100 years ago keeps pace with modern developments in law and practice. For this edition, we welcome Mr Briggs and Professor Hill to the team, and they replace Professor Hartley, who made a significant contribution to the two previous editions.

Since the last edition in 1993 there have been major statutory developments, including the Private International Law (Miscellaneous Provisions) Act 1995 (which affects the law on polygamous marriages, and introduces modern choice of law rules in tort) and the Arbitration Act 1996. The bringing into force of Part II of the Family Law Act 1996, which affects jurisdiction in matrimonial proceedings (or marital proceedings, as they are to be called), has been delayed, and it is unlikely to be in force (if at all) before the year 2001.

Other developments, or the growing importance of certain topics in practice, have led to new passages on comity (Chapter 1), injunctions to restrain foreign proceedings in breach of arbitration agreements, and on foreign judgments rendered in breach of arbitration agreements (Chapters 12 and 14), banking contracts (Chapter 33), and to substantial revisions of the material on *Mareva* injunctions (Chapter 8), the taking of evidence abroad (Chapter 8), *forum non conveniens* and *lis alibi pendens* (Chapter 12), arbitration (Chapter 16), child abduction (Chapter 19), the assignment of intangibles (Chapter 24), restitution (Chapter 34) and torts (Chapter 35).

One development is the enormous increase in the use of the internet, both for electronic mail and electronic commerce (if, which is doubtful, a sharp distinction can be made between them). It is plain that in the next few years electronic commerce will revolutionise cross-border trade. A very distinguished former Law Lord recently expressed in a public lecture the view that the internet meant the end of private international law. That is certainly an exaggeration, but it is true that rules previously based on a "place", such as the place of a contract or place of a tort or the country in which a consumer is invited to make purchases, are difficult, and perhaps impossible, to apply where websites have no, or no identifiable, location. There is no doubt that, by the time of the next edition, the internet will have had a major impact on some areas of the conflict of laws.

The European Court has continued to give important rulings on the Brussels Convention, which now number more than 100, but the continuing delay in the giving of rulings is still very great. Two cases of considerable commercial importance, both decided in the last year, illustrate the point. In *Van Uden Maritime B.V. v. Firma Deco-Line*, on the question of the relationship between the Brussels Convention and abitration proceedings, three years elapsed between the reference from the Dutch Supreme Court and the ruling of the European Court; and in *Castelletti v. Hugo Trumpy*, on jurisdiction clauses in bills of lading, the period was two years from the reference by the Italian Supreme Court.

The number of reported decisions continues to reflect the great practical importance of conflicts over jurisdiction. Questions of jurisdiction and foreign judgments now take up more than three times the space devoted to them by Professor Dicey in the first edition, and more than twice the amount which Dr Morris first devoted to them in 1949. A tendency in some (but by no means all) judicial quarters to deprecate satellite litigation about where disputes should be decided overlooks the point that in many cases the results of that satellite litigation determine whether a case is to be fought at all. The significance of the subject is underlined by the fact that the Government is actively participating in negotiations for the revision of the Brussels and Lugano Conventions, and for a worldwide jurisdiction and judgments Convention under the auspices of the Hague Conference on Private International Law.

The responsibility of the editors for this edition is as follows: Mr Briggs is responsible for Chapters 9, 12 (jointly with the General Editor), 14, 24, 26 to 28, and 34; Professor Hill is responsible for Chapters 2 to 4, 7, 13, 15, 16 (jointly with the General Editor), 22 to 23, and 36; Professor McClean is responsible for Chapters 6, 8 (the sections on judicial assistance and security for costs), Chapters 17 to 21, 29 and Rule 189; Professor Morse is responsible for Chapters 30 to 31, 33 (except for Rule 189), and 35; in addition to my overall responsibility as General Editor, I am responsible for Chapters 1, 5, 8 (the section on *Mareva* injunctions), 10 to 11, 12 (jointly with Mr Briggs), 16 (jointly with Professor Hill), 25 and 32.

As before, we have had the benefit of much advice and information. We should mention, in particular, Dame Mary Arden, Xolisa Beja, Charles Booth, Sir Anthony Colman, Gilles Cuniberti, Andrew Dickinson, Professor Ian Fletcher, Steven Gee Q.C., Professor A.G. Guest, Sir Peter North, Oliver Parker, Sir Bernard Rix, Professor P. Schlosser, Philip Smart, and Dr H.D. Tebbens. I remain grateful to my partners in Herbert Smith for their encouragement of my involvement in this book over the last 25 years.

We also express our thanks for secretarial assistance to Carole Flowerday and Liz Haigh. Thanks are also due to the publishers, and in particular to the tablers and indexer for their excellent work.

The work on this edition was substantially completed early in 1999, but we were able to take account of major subsequent developments, so that the law is stated as at May 3, 1999. In particular, we have been able to take account of the Woolf Reforms to the English civil justice system introduced in April 1999. The main thrust of the reforms has not substantially affected this work, since they relate mainly to case management, the simplification of the civil justice system, and the saving of costs. The new Civil Procedure Rules have not yet altered Order 11, which remains, now embodied in Schedule 1 to the new Rules. But as part of the reforms, in order (it is said) to make the civil justice system more accessible, old and familiar legal terminology has been abandoned. Writs are now claim forms, plaintiffs have become claimants, third party claims are now Part 20 claims, and *Mareva* injunctions are to be called freezing injunctions. We have, where the context allowed, endeavoured to use the new terminology.

Lawrence Collins
October 1999

BIOGRAPHICAL NOTE

ALBERT VENN DICEY, the author of this book, was born on February 4, 1835. He was educated at Balliol College, Oxford, where he took a first in Honour Moderations in 1856 and a first in Greats in 1858; he was also President of the Union. He was elected a Fellow of Trinity College, Oxford, in 1860, and held his Fellowship until his marriage in 1872.

He was called to the Bar by the Inner Temple in 1863 and for some years "devilled" for Sir John Coleridge, afterwards Solicitor-General and Attorney-General. In 1870 he published his first law book, *Parties to Actions*, which (it is interesting to observe) was arranged in the form of rules and illustrations. His practice at the Bar was never very lucrative, though in 1876 he was appointed Junior Counsel to the Commissioners of Inland Revenue, a position which he held until 1890, when he took silk. In 1879 he published his second law book, on Domicil.

From a very early age he was intensely interested in politics. From family tradition and associations he belonged to the Whig as opposed to the Radical wing of the Liberal party. He was a convinced Free Trader. He ardently supported the cause of the North in the American Civil War, and the cause of Italian unity. He disliked the autocratic pretensions of Louis Napoleon and rejoiced in his fall. When Mr. Gladstone split the Liberal party in two over the Home Rule question in 1885–1886, Dicey identified himself with the Unionist cause, and was prominent in its support from then until 1921. He wrote many pamphlets against Home Rule, and was an active speaker on Unionist platforms. This—the ruling political passion of his later years—naturally brought him into association with leading Conservative statesmen, whom hitherto he had tended to regard with suspicion. But he never lost his faith in Liberalism. "I am an old, an unconverted, and an impenitent Benthamite" he declared in 1913.

In 1881 the Vinerian Professorship of English law in the University of Oxford fell vacant, and after some hesitation Dicey resolved to become a candidate. He was duly elected in the following year. This Chair, of which Blackstone had been the first occupant, carried with it a Fellowship at All Souls College, and it was here that Dicey's most lasting work was done. He chose as the subject of his inaugural lecture the question "Can English law be taught at the Universities?" to which he replied with a vehement if closely reasoned affirmative. He admitted the immense advantages of reading in chambers, but argued that at the universities "a student can be taught to regard law as a whole, and to consider the relation of one part of English law to another"; that at the universities "can be taught the habit of looking upon law as a series of rules and exceptions, and of carefully marking off the exact limits of ascertained principles." In 1885 he published his *Law of the Constitution*, a book which was based on his Oxford lectures, and made his fame, not only in England but also in France and the United States, as the leading constitutional lawyer of the day. In 1898 he was invited to deliver a course of lectures at the Harvard Law School, the fruit of which was published in 1905 as *Law and Opinion in England*.

His *magnum opus*, however, was *The Conflict of Laws*, at which he was working from 1882 onwards, and which was first published in 1896. In a letter to a friend he declared in 1922 that "a successor of Blackstone should show that of one branch of English Law at least he could speak with authority." Shortly after the publication of the first edition, he thus described the book in a characteristic letter to his friend James Bryce: "In outward look it is like Story. I cannot flatter myself there is much other resemblance. For after reading much on the Conflict of Laws, I am well assured that Story and Savigny have written the only great books on the subject and, considering the state of legal speculation in Story's time and country, I am not sure that his is not the greater achievement of the two. If I had Westlake's knowledge, or if Westlake could have expressed himself as clearly as I can, a considerable book might have been produced. As it is, my clearness makes patent my errors. He has, I must add, acted with great generosity in giving me help when asked for and, if I had had more impudence, I believe I might have asked for and obtained much more. . . . My Introduction I like and some of the appendices. I doubt if there is much else really good which is not to be found in my *Domicil*, but I am tired and not quite a fair judge. Still, my impression is that the 'practical' man will prefer Foote, and the theorist Story or Savigny. What a queer thing life is. Why should I ever have become involved in this conflict of laws?" Four years later he wrote: "It is unlucky that the endless labour expended on the *Conflict of Law* cannot, from the nature of things, ever be visible to my Oxford friends to whom I principally wish, so to speak, to vindicate my work. If they say the labour was misspent, I more than half, though not completely, agree with them. My faith in digests has declined."

In 1907 the University of Oxford conferred on Dicey the degree of Honorary D.C.L., and in 1909 he resigned the Vinerian Chair, having unquestionably brought more lustre to it than any of his predecessors since Blackstone. He still retained his interest in teaching and in the Conflict of Laws, and in the following year All Souls College created especially for him a Lectureship in Private International Law, which he held until 1913. The duties of the post included giving informal instruction as well as lecturing, and he was thus brought into close contact with a number of under-graduates, largely Rhodes scholars, whose society he greatly enjoyed. Many of the Rhodes scholars were Americans, and he felt that his teaching created a new link with the United States. He died on April 7, 1922, at the age of 87, a few days after the publication of the third edition of this book.

J. H. C. M.

BIOGRAPHICAL NOTE

JOHN HUMPHREY CARLILE MORRIS, "whose contribution to the conflict of laws has excelled even that of his great predecessor. A. V. Dicey" (Lord Denning M.R.[1]), the General Editor of the 6th to 10th editions of this book and whose name appeared as co-author from the 8th edition in 1967, was born in 1910. He was an undergraduate of Christ Church, Oxford, and took firsts in the Final Honour School of Jurisprudence and in the B.C.L. and was elected Eldon Scholar. In 1934 he was called to the Bar by Gray's Inn, and following pupillage he practised for a short time in the chambers of Sir Andrew Clark before taking up a Fellowship at Magdalen College, Oxford in 1936, which he retained until his retirement in 1977, when the College elected him to an Honorary Fellowship. From 1951 to 1977 he was Reader in the Conflict of Laws at Oxford University. During that time, and until his death, he achieved and retained a distinction in teaching and scholarship, particularly in the conflict of laws, which earned him worldwide renown and respect and the devotion of generations of his Oxford pupils.

Dicey's great work on the Conflict of Laws, which had, following his death in 1922, suffered a considerable decline, was revived under John Morris' general editorship in 1949. In 1945 he was invited to undertake the sole editorship but (as he put it in the preface to the 6th edition) by October 1946 he felt that the task was beyond his strength and he therefore invited seven learned friends to help him. Those friends were Zelman (later Sir Zelman) Cowen, Rupert (later Sir Rupert) Cross, Otto (later Sir Otto) Kahn-Freund, Dr. (later Professor) K. Lipstein, Dr. (later Professor) Clive Parry, Mr. R.S. Welsh and Professor Ben Wortley. In the preface to the 6th edition he regretted that no practitioner had felt able to accept his invitation to be an editor; but this deficiency was remedied in later editions, among whose editors were two practising barristers (who subsequently became High Court judges, and then members of the Court of Appeal, and one of whom became a distinguished Law Lord) and one practising solicitor. His wife, whom, as Jane Kinch, he had married in 1939, was a great support to him and had the unique experience of contributing to the accuracy of the work by reading successive editions aloud to the general editor.

There is no doubt that, even among these distinguished co-editors, it was John Morris' influence as general editor which was paramount in re-establishing the book as the leading work on the subject in the Commonwealth. In succeeding editions the influence of Dicey (from 1967, Dicey and Morris) grew, because under his guidance it kept up with, and anticipated, the great changes in the law caused by the 20th century revolution in communication and travel, and by new social attitudes to family life. As Lord Scarman put it in the foreword to an entire issue of the International and Comparative Law Quarterly in 1977 devoted to essays in honour of John

---

[1] *The Hollandia* [1982] Q.B. 872, 884 (C.A.). See for an appreciation of his life and work, Professor G. Treitel in (1984) 55 B.Y.I.L. p. ix–xiv; Dr. P. M. North in (1988) 74 *Proceedings of the British Academy*, pp. 443–482.

Morris, "the depth and range of his learning coupled with his gift of critical analysis brought the flattering consequence that what Dicey said on a point mattered as much to the judges who made the case law as did their case law to the editor of Dicey".[2]

He was also the author of several important articles in the conflict of laws and in property law. Among the most influential in the former field were those on the proper law of contract in 1940, which was co-authored by Professor Cheshire, who acknowledged, however, that it was conceived and written by John Morris[3]; on the choice of law clause in statutes[4]; on family law, especially polygamy[5] and recognition of foreign divorces[6]; on property, especially transfer of chattels[7] and intestate succession to land.[8] No article was more influential than "The Proper Law of a Tort",[9] which had a profound effect on American case law and the American Law Institute Restatement (Second) of the Conflict of Laws.

In addition to his articles and work on this book, John Morris produced four editions of a case-book on the conflict of laws first published in 1939, a book of cases and materials (with Dr. P. M. North, now Sir Peter North) in the year of his death, and an influential students' text book on the Conflict of Laws in 1971, the third edition of which was also prohibited in the year of his death. He was editor of three editions of *Theobald on Wills* and the general editor of one edition of *Chitty on Contracts*, as well as co-author (with W. Barton Leach) of a well-known book on the Rule against Perpetuities.

Although he was no seeker of honours, the excellence of his work, and his influence on the law, was marked by a series of distinctions: he was awarded the degree of Doctor of Civil Law by Oxford in 1949; he was elected an Associate Member of the Institute of International Law (1954); Associate Member of the American Academy of Arts and Sciences (1960); Fellow of the British Academy (1966); Honorary Bencher of Gray's Inn (1980); Queen's Counsel (1981). But unlike Dicey, he never became Vinerian Professor at Oxford. As the author (rumoured to be a highly reliable source) of his obituary in *The Times* put it, "in 1964 the Vinerian Chair of English Law at All Souls College fell vacant, and Morris was strongly tipped for the succession. The Chair was offered to him, but to the surprise of his friends and many academic lawyers he declined it. He was devoted to Magdalen, which he served long and faithfully as a Fellow, Clerk to the College and (for one year) as Vice-President and could not bear the thought of migrating to All Souls, for which he had a life-long antipathy." As a result John Morris was entitled to the title of professor only twice, once when he was visiting professor at Harvard Law School in 1950–1951, and latterly when, despite his life-long devotion to Oxford, he spent a happy year in 1978–1979 as Goodhart Professor at Cambridge University and Fellow of Gonville and Caius College.

---

[2] (1977) 26 I.C.L.Q. 701.

[3] (1940) 56 L.Q.R. 320, 339. See also (1950) 3 Int. L.Q. 197.

[4] (1946) 62 L.Q.R. 170. See also (1979) 95 L.Q.R. 59.

[5] (1953) 66 Harv. L.Rev. 691, first published in *Festschrift für Martin Wolff* (1952), p. 287.

[6] (1946) 24 Can. Bar Rev. 73; (1952) 29 B.Y.I.L. 283; (1975) 14 I.C.L.Q. 635.

[7] (1945) 22 B.Y.I.L. 232.

[8] (1969) 85 L.Q.R. 339. See also (1937) 18 B.Y.I.L. 32 (renvoi); (1938) 54 L.Q.R. 78 (marriage settlements).

[9] (1951) 64 Harv. L.Rev. 884. See also (1949) 12 M.L.R. 248.

He completed work on the last supplement to the 10th edition only a few days before his death on September 29, 1984, and on September 19 he wrote "It is with relief, not untinged with emotion, that I lay down the burden of the task I assumed as long ago as January 1945. I have improved the book—no question about that—and perhaps prevented it from dying a natural death."

L. A. C.

TABLE OF STATUTES

Chapters 1 to 16 will be found in Volume 1; Chapters 17 to 36 will be found in Volume 2.

Table of Statutes

TABLE OF CASES

Chapters 1 to 16 will be found in Volume 1; Chapters 17 to 36 will be found in Volume 2

lxxi

Table of Cases

Table of Cases

Table of Cases

Table of Cases

Table of Cases

Table of Cases

Table of Cases

Table of Cases

Table of Cases

Table of Cases

Table of Cases

Table of Cases

Table of Cases

Table of Cases

Table of Cases

Table of Cases

Table of Cases

Table of Cases

Table of Cases

Table of Cases

Table of Cases

Table of Cases

Table of Cases

Table of Cases

Table of Cases

Table of Cases

Table of Cases

Table of Cases

Table of Cases

Table of Cases

Table of Cases

Table of Cases

Table of Cases

Table of Cases

Table of Cases

Table of Cases

Table of Cases

Table of Cases

Table of Cases

Table of Cases

Table of Cases

Table of Cases

Table of Cases

Table of Cases

Table of Cases

Table of Cases

Table of Cases

Table of Cases

Table of Cases

Table of Cases

Table of Cases

Table of Cases

Table of Cases

Table of Cases

Table of Cases

clxxvi

Table of Cases

Table of Cases

Table of Cases

Table of Cases

Table of Cases

Table of Cases

Table of Cases

Table of Cases

Table of Cases

Table of Cases

Table of Cases

Table of Cases

Table of Cases

Table of Cases

Table of Cases

Table of Cases

Table of Cases

Decisions of the European Court of Justice are listed below numerically. These decisions are also included in the preceding alphabetical table.

Table of Cases

Table of Cases

Table of Cases

Table of Cases

TABLE OF STATUTORY INSTRUMENTS

Chapters 1 to 16 will be found in Volume 1; Chapters 17 to 36 will be found in Volume 2.

TABLE OF CIVIL PROCEDURE RULES

Chapters 1 to 16 will be found in Volume 1; Chapters 17 to 36 will be found in Volume 2.

TABLE OF FOREIGN CASE REFERENCES

A.	Atlantic Reporter (U.S.A.)
Abb.N.C.	Abbott's New Cases, New York (U.S.A.)
A.D.	Appellate Division (South Africa)
A.I.R.(All).	All India Reports (Allahabad)
Ala.	Alabama Reports (U.S.A.)
A.L.R.	American Law Reports
A.L.R.	Australian Law Reports
Alta.L.R.	Alberta Law Reports (Canada)
Argus L.R.	Argus Law Reports (Australia)
Ariz.	Arizona Reports (U.S.A.)
Atl.	Atlantic Reporter (U.S.A.)
A.T.P.R.	Australian Trade Practices Reports
B.C.R.	British Columbia Reports (Canada)
Cal.	California Reports (U.S.A.)
Cal.App.	California Appellate Reports (U.S.A.)
Can.S.C.R.	Canada Supreme Court Reports
C.B.R.	Canadian Bankruptcy Reports
C.L.R.	Commonwealth Law Reports (Australia)
Conn.	Connecticut Reports (U.S.A.)
C.P.D.	Cape Provincial Division (South Africa)
D.	Session Cases, 2nd Series (Dunlop) (Scotland)
Del.Ch.	Delaware Chancery Reports (U.S.A.)
D.L.R.	Dominion Law Reports (Canada)
E.A.	East African Law Reports
E.D.C.	Eastern Districts Court (South Africa)
E.D.L.	Eastern Districts Local Division (South Africa)
Ex.C.R.	Exchequer Court Reports (Canada)
F.	Session Cases, 5th Series (Fraser) (Scotland)
F.	Federal Reporter (U.S.A.)
F.L.C.	Family Law Cases (Australia)
F.L.R.	Federal Law Reports (Australia)
F.Supp.	Federal Supplement (U.S.A.)
Fam.L.R.	Family Law Reports (Australia)
H.K.C.	Hong Kong Cases
H.K.L.R.	Hong Kong Law Reports
Hill	Hill's New York Reports (U.S.A.)
Ill.	Illinois Reports (U.S.A.)
Ill.App.	Illinois Appeal Reports (U.S.A.)
I.L.R.Bom.	Indian Law Reports (Bombay)
I.L.R.Calc.	Indian Law Reports (Calcutta)
I.L.R.M.	Irish Law Reports Monthly
Iowa	Iowa Reports (U.S.A.)
I.R.	Irish Reports
Ir.C.L.	Irish Common Law Reports
Ir.L.T.	Irish Law Times Reports
Kan.	Kansas Reports (U.S.A.)
L.C.J.	Lower Canada Jurist
L.C.R.	Lower Canada Reports
L.R.I.A.	Law Reports Indian Appeals
L.R.Ir.	Law Reports Ireland
M.	Session Cases, 3rd Series (Macpherson) (Scotland)
Macq.	Macqueen's Reports (Scotland)
Man.L.R.	Manitoba Reports (Canada)
Mass.	Massachusetts Reports (U.S.A.)
Md.	Maryland Reports (U.S.A.)

Mich.	Michigan Reports (U.S.A.)
Milw.	Milward's Ecclesiastical Reports (Ireland)
Minn.	Minnesota Reports (U.S.A.)
Misc.	Miscellaneous Reports, New York (U.S.A.)
N.B.Eq.	New Brunswick Equity Reports (Canada)
N.B.R.	New Brunswick Reports (Canada)
N.E.	Northeastern Reporter (U.S.A.)
N.H.	New Hampshire Reports (U.S.A.)
N.Ir.	Northern Ireland Reports
N.J.	New Jersey Reports (U.S.A.)
N.L.R.	Natal Law Reports (South Africa)
N.P.D.	Natal Provincial Division (South Africa)
N.S.R.	Nova Scotia Reports (Canada)
N.S.W.L.R.	New South Wales Law Reports (Australia)
N.S.W.R.	New South Wales Reports (Australia)
N.W.	Northwestern Reporter (U.S.A.)
N.Y.	New York Court of Appeals Reports (U.S.A.)
N.Y.S.	New York Supplement (U.S.A.)
N.Z.L.R.	New Zealand Law Reports
O.A.R.	Ontario Appeal Reports (Canada)
O.B. & F.	Ollivier, Bell and Fitzgerald (New Zealand)
Ohio App.	Ohio Appellate Reports (U.S.A.)
O.L.R.	Ontario Law Reports (Canada)
O.R.	Ontario Reports (Canada)
P.	Pacific Reporter (U.S.A.)
Pa.	Pennsylvania Reports (U.S.A.)
Qd.R.	Queensland Reports (Australia)
Q.L.R.	Quebec Law Reports
Qu.K.B.	Quebec Reports King's Bench
Q.R.S.C.	Quebec Reports Superior Court
Que.S.C.	Quebec Superior Court Reports
R.	Session Cases, 4th Series (Rettie) (Scotland)
R. & N.	Rhodesia and Nyasaland Reports
R.F.L.	Reports of Family Law (Canada)
R.I.	Rhode Island Reports (U.S.A.)
S.	Session Cases, 1st Series (Shaw) (Scotland)
S.A.	South Africa Law Reports
S.A.R.	South African Republic Supreme Court Reports
Sask.L.R.	Saskatchewan Law Reports (Canada)
S.A.S.R.	South Australian State Reports
S.C.	Session Cases (Scotland)
S.C.	Supreme Court Reports (Cape of Good Hope)
S.C.R.	Canadian Supreme Court Reports
S.E.	Southeastern Reporter (U.S.A.)
Sing.L.R.	Singapore Law Reports
S.L.R.	Scottish Law Reporter
S.L.T.	Scots Law Times
So.	Southern Reporter (U.S.A.)
S.R.N.S.W.	State Reports New South Wales (Australia)
St.R.Qd.	State Reports Queensland (Australia)
S.W.	Southwestern Reporter (U.S.A.)
Terr.L.R.	Territories Law Reports (Canada)
T.P.D.	Transvaal Provincial Division (South Africa)
T.S.	Transvaal Supreme Court (South Africa)
U.C.C.P.	Upper Canada Common Pleas
U.C.Q.B., U.C.R.	Upper Canada Queen's Bench
U.S.	United States Supreme Court Reports
V.L.R.	Victoria Law Reports (Australia)
V.R.	Victoria Reports (Australia)
Wall.	Wallace's United States Supreme Court Reports
W.A.L.R.	Western Australian Law Reports
W.A.R.	Western Australia Reports
Wheat	Wheaton's United States Supreme Court Reports
W.I.R.	West Indian Reports

Table of Foreign Case References

TABLE OF BOOKS REFERRED TO[1]

Anton	Private International Law (A treatise from the stand-point of Scots law) (2nd ed. 1990) (as "Anton")
	Civil Jurisdiction in Scotland (1984)
Bate	Notes on the Doctrine of Renvoi (1904)
Batiffol and Lagarde	Droit International Privé (7th ed. 1981–1983)
Beale	Treatise on the Conflict of Laws (1935)
Blom-Cooper	Bankruptcy in Private International Law (1954)
Briggs & Rees	Civil Jurisdiction and Judgments (2nd ed. 1997)
Castel	Canadian Conflict of Laws (4th ed. 1998)
Cavers	The Choice of Law Process (1965)
Cheshire and North	Private International Law (13th ed. 1999)
Collier	Conflict of Laws (2nd ed. 1994)
Collins	Civil Jurisdiction and Judgments Act 1982 (1983) (as "Collins")
	Essays in International Litigation and the Conflict of Laws (1994) (as "Collins, *Essays*")
Cook	Logical and Legal Bases of the Conflict of Laws (1942)
Currie	Selected Essays on the Conflict of Laws (1963)
de Almeida, Desantes Real, Jenard	Report on the Convention on the accession of the Kingdom of Spain and the Portuguese Republic to the 1968 Convention on jurisdiction and the enforcement of judgments in civil and commercial matters and to the Protocol on its interpretation by the Court of Justice: Official Journal of the European Communities, 1990, C189, p. 35
Ehrenzweig	Treatise on the Conflict of Laws (1962)
Falconbridge	Selected Essays on the Conflict of Laws (2nd ed. 1954)
Fawcett	Declining Jurisdiction in Private International Law (1995)
Fawcett and Torremans	Intellectual Property and Private International Law (1998)
Fentiman	Foreign Law in English Courts (1998)
Fletcher	Insolvency in Private International Law (1999)
Foote	Private International Law (5th ed. 1925)
Giuliano-Lagarde	Report on the Convention on the law applicable to contractual obligations: Official Journal of the European Communities, 1980, C282, p. 1
Hancock	Torts in the Conflict of Laws (1942)
Hartley	Civil Jurisdiction and Judgments (1984)
Hertz	Jurisdiction in Contract and Tort under the Brussels Convention (1998)
Hill	International Commercial Disputes (2nd ed. 1998)
Jenard	Report on the Convention of 27 September 1968 on jurisdiction and the enforcement of judgments in civil and commercial matters: Official Journal of the European Communities, 1979, C59, p. 1
Jenard-Möller	Report on the Convention on jurisdiction and the enforcement of judgments in civil and commercial matters done at Lugano on 16 September 1988: Official Journal of the European Communities, 1990, C189, p. 57
Johnson	Conflict of Laws with special reference to the law of Quebec (1933–1937)
Kaye	Civil Jurisdiction and the Enforcement of Foreign Judgments (1987)
	European Case Law on the Judgments Convention (1998)
	The New Private International Law of Contract of the European Community (1993)

---

[1] The only books listed in this Table are books on the Conflict of Laws which are cited by the name of the author alone. Where more than one book is listed, the context will indicate which work is being cited.

Table of Books Referred To

Lalive	The Transfer of Chattels in the Conflict of Laws (1955)
Lando	International Encyclopaedia of Comparative Law, Vol. III, Chapter 24 (1976)
Lauterpacht	Recognition in International Law (1947)
Leflar, McDougal and Felix	American Conflicts Law (4th ed. 1986)
Lipsfein	Harmonisation of Private International Law by the EEC (1978)
Lorenzen	Selected Articles on the Conflict of Laws (1947)
McClean	International Judicial Assistance (1992)
	Recognition of Family Judgments in the Commonwealth (1983)
Mann F.A.	Foreign Affairs in English Courts (1986)
	Further Studies in International Law (1990)
	Legal Aspects of Money (5th ed. 1992) (as "Mann")
	Studies in International Law (1973)
Mendelssohn-Bartholdy	Renvoi in Modern English Law (1937)
Morris	Conflict of Laws (3rd ed. 1984)
Morse	Torts in Private International Law (1978)
Mustill and Boyd	Commercial Arbitration (2nd ed. 1989)
Nadelmann	Conflict of Laws: International and Interstate (1972)
Niboyet	Traité de Droit International Privé Français (1944–1951)
North	Contract Conflicts (1982)
	Essays in Private International Law (1993)
Nussbaum	Principles of Private International Law (1943)
Nygh	Autonomy in International Contracts (1999)
	Conflict of Laws in Australia (5th ed. 1991)
O'Malley and Layton	European Civil Practice (1989)
Oppenheim	International Law (9th ed. Jennings and Watts, 1992)
Patchett	Recognition of Commercial Judgments and Awards in the Commonwealth (1984)
Phillimore	Commentaries on International Law (3rd ed. 1879–1889)
Piggott	Foreign Judgments (3rd ed. 1908)
Plender	European Contracts Convention (1991)
Rabel	Conflict of Laws: A Comparative Study (2nd ed. 1958–1964)
Read	Recognition and Enforcement of Foreign Judgments in the Common Law Units of the British Commonwealth (1938)
Reichert-Facilides and d'Oliveira	International Insurance Contract Law in the EC (1993)
Restatement	American Law Institute's Restatement of the Conflict of Laws Second (1971)
Robertson	Characterization in the Conflict of Laws (1940)
Sammartano and Morse	Public Policy in Transnational Relationships (1992)
Savigny	Conflict of Laws (Guthrie's Translation) (2nd ed. 1880)
Schlosser	Report on the Convention of 9 October 1978 on the Association of the Kingdom of Denmark, Ireland and the United Kingdom of Great Britain and Northern Ireland to the Covention on jurisdiction and the enforcement of judgments in civil and commercial matters and to the Protocol on its interpretation by the Court of Justice: Official Journal of the European Communities, 1979, C59, p. 71
Scoles and Hay	Conflict of Laws (2nd ed. 1992)
Smart	Cross-Border Insolvency (2nd ed. 1998)
Story	Conflict of Laws (8th ed. 1883)
Strömholm	Torts in the Conflict of Laws (1961)
Sykes and Pryles	Australian Private International Law (3rd ed. 1991)
Tizzano	Report on the Protocols on the interpretation by the Court of Justice of the Rome Convention of 19 June 1980 on the law applicable to contractual obligations: Official Journal of the European Communities, 1990, C219, p. 1
Van den Berg	The New York Convention of 1958 (1981)
Verhagen	Agency in Private International Law (1995)
Weintraub	Commentary on the Conflict of Laws (3rd ed. 1986)
Westlake	Private International Law (7th ed. 1925)
Wolff	Private International Law (2nd ed. 1950)
Zaphiriou	The Transfer of Chattels in Private International Law (1955)

PART ONE

PRELIMINARY MATTERS

PART ONE deals with matters which are preliminary to the principal topics **I–001** hereafter discussed in this book.

CHAPTER 1 discusses the general nature of the conflict of laws; the interpretation of statutes implementing international conventions; and the operation of statutes in the conflict of laws. It also defines certain geographical and technical terms constantly used in this book, and discusses the determination of the connecting factor.

CHAPTER 2 deals with two matters of great theoretical difficulty, namely, Characterisation and the Incidental Question.

CHAPTER 3 deals with the factor of time in the conflict of laws.

CHAPTER 4 deals with Renvoi or the meaning of the expression "law of a country".

CHAPTER 5 deals with the exclusion of a foreign rule of law on grounds of public policy and with the refusal of English courts to enforce foreign penal, revenue or other public laws or to entertain an action founded on an act of state.

CHAPTER 6 contains the common law rules (as modified by statute) for ascertaining the domicile and residence of a natural person. The domicile and residence of corporations are not dealt with in this chapter but in Chapter 30. Domicile for the purposes of the Civil Jurisdiction and Judgments Act 1982 is dealt with in Chapter 11.

CHAPTER 1

NATURE AND SCOPE OF THE CONFLICT OF LAWS[1]

Introduction. The branch of English law known as the conflict of laws is **1–001**
that part of the law of England which deals with cases having a foreign
element. By a "foreign element" is meant simply a contact with some system
of law other than English law. Such a contact may exist, for example, because
a contract was made or to be performed in a foreign country, or because a tort
was committed there, or because property was situated there, or because the
parties are not English.[2] In the conflict of laws, a foreign element and a foreign
country[3] mean a non-English element and a country other than England. From
the point of view of the conflict of laws, Scotland and Northern Ireland are for
most but not all purposes as much foreign countries as France or
Germany.[4]

If an action is brought in an English court for damages for breach of a **1–002**
contract made in England between two Englishmen and to be performed in
England, there is no foreign element, the case is not a case in the conflict of
laws, and the English court will naturally apply English internal or domestic
law. But if the contract had been made in Switzerland between two Swiss and
was to be performed in Switzerland, then the case would be (for an English
court, but not for a Swiss court) a case in the conflict of laws, and the English
court would apply Swiss law to most of the matters in dispute before it,[5] just
as a Swiss court would naturally apply Swiss law to all such matters. If we
change the facts once more and assume that the contract was made in
Switzerland between an Englishman and a Swiss but was to be performed in
England, then the case is a case in the conflict of laws not only for an English
court but also for a Swiss court and indeed for any court in the world in which
the contract is litigated and that court will have to decide whether and for what

---

[1] There is an enormous literature on the nature and scope of the subject: see especially Cavers,
The Choice of Law Process (1965); Cavers (1933) 47 Harv. L. Rev. 173, reprinted in *The
Choice of Law* (1985), Chap. 1; Cook, *Logical and Legal Bases of the Conflict of Laws* (1942),
Chaps. 1–3; Cheatham and Reese (1952) 52 Col. L. Rev. 959; Kahn-Freund (1974) *Recueil des
Cours*, III, Chaps. 1 and 2, reprinted as *General Problems in Private International Law*; Kegel
(1964) *Recueil des Cours*, II, 95; Kegel, *International Encyclopedia of Comparative Law*, Vol.
III, Chap. 3 (1986); Anton, Chap. 2; Scoles and Hay, Chap. 2.

[2] That is, English by domicile or by residence. There is no such thing as English nationality.

[3] For the meaning of "country," see *post*, paras. 1–060 *et seq.*

[4] The qualification has to be made because (1) England, Scotland and Northern Ireland share a
common court of last resort; (2) many statutes (especially those implementing an international
convention) apply to all three parts of the United Kingdom; (3) Scotland and Northern Ireland
are in a special position as regards (a) jurisdiction in actions *in personam* (*post*, Rules 27 and
28) and the reciprocal enforcement of judgments *in personam* (Rule 49); (b) the reciprocal
recognition of divorces (Rule 78), grants of probate (Rule 123) and receiving orders in
bankruptcy (Rule 165); (c) the reciprocal enforcement of maintenance orders (Rule 88(2));
(d) the effect of bankruptcy as an assignment of the debtor's property (Rule 166) and as a
discharge of his contracts (Rule 171).

[5] Not to all matters, because in an English court matters of procedure are governed by English
domestic law. See Rule 17.

purposes the Swiss or the English elements are the more significant, and apply Swiss or English law accordingly. It is cases of this last type, where the facts are distributed between two or more countries, which give rise to the problem of renvoi, discussed in Chapter 4.

1–003　　In contradistinction to public international law, which seeks primarily to regulate the relations between different sovereign States and is, at any rate in theory, the same everywhere, the rules of the conflict of laws (or private international law as it is sometimes called) are different from country to country. Even between England and Scotland there are some significant differences, notably in connection with the jurisdiction of courts in actions *in personam*, while between England and Australia, the common law provinces of Canada, New Zealand and the United States on the one hand, and civil law States like those of continental Europe and Latin America on the other, the differences are much more deep-seated.

1–004　　**Jurisdiction and choice of law.** The questions that arise in conflict of laws cases are of two main types: first, has the English court jurisdiction to determine this case? And secondly, if so, what law should it apply? There may sometimes be a third question, namely, will the English court recognise or enforce a foreign judgment purporting to determine the issue between the parties? Of course this third question arises only if there is a foreign judgment, and thus not in every case. But the first two questions arise in every case with foreign elements, though the answer to one of them may be so obvious that the court is in effect only concerned with the other. The law of every modern country has rules dealing with these questions, called conflict of laws—in contrast to its domestic or internal law.

1–005　　The English rules of the conflict of laws differ from those adopted in many continental European countries in one important respect. There are many situations in which, if the English court has jurisdiction, it will apply English domestic law. This is true, for example, of most issues in proceedings for divorce and separation,[6] for the guardianship, custody[7] and adoption[8] of minors, and for the maintenance of wives and children.[9] Conversely, there are many situations in which, if a foreign court has jurisdiction according to English rules of the conflict of laws, its judgment or decree will be recognised in England, regardless of the grounds on which it was based or the choice of law rule which it applied.[10] Thus, in the English conflict of laws, questions of jurisdiction frequently tend to overshadow questions of choice of law. Or, to put it differently, it frequently happens that if the question of jurisdiction (whether of the English or the foreign court) is answered satisfactorily, the question of choice of law does not arise.

1–006　　**Justification.** What justification is there for the existence of the conflict of laws? Why should we depart from the rules of our own law and apply those of another system? This is a vital matter on which it is necessary to be clear before we proceed any further. The main justification for the conflict of laws is that it implements the reasonable and legitimate expectations of the parties

---

[6] See Rule 77(1).
[7] See Rule 92(4).
[8] See *post*, para. 20–009.
[9] See Rule 86(5).
[10] See Rules 36, 41, 79, 81.

to a transaction or an occurrence.[11] This can best be seen by considering what would happen if the conflict of laws did not exist.

Theoretically, it would be possible for English courts to close their doors to all except English litigants.[12] But if they did so, grave injustice would be inflicted not only on foreigners but also on Englishmen. An Englishman who had made a contract with a Scotsman in Glasgow or with an American in New York would be unable to enforce it in England; and if the courts of other countries adopted the same principle, the contract could not be enforced in any country in the world.   **1–007**

Theoretically, it would be possible for English courts, while opening their doors to foreigners, to apply English domestic law in all cases. But if they did so, grave injustice would again be inflicted not only on foreigners but also on Englishmen. For instance, if two English people married in France in accordance with the formalities prescribed by French law, but not in accordance with the formalities prescribed by English law, the English court, if it applied English law to the validity of the marriage, would have to treat the parties as unmarried persons and their children as illegitimate.   **1–008**

Theoretically, it would be possible for English courts, while opening their doors to foreigners and while ready to apply foreign law in appropriate cases, to refuse to recognise or enforce a foreign judgment determining the issue between the parties. But if they did so, grave injustice and inconvenience would result. For instance, if a divorce was granted in a foreign country in which the parties were settled, and afterwards one of them remarried in England, he or she might be convicted of bigamy. Or if a plaintiff sued a defendant in a foreign country for damages for breach of contract or for tort, and eventually obtained a judgment in his favour, he might find that the defendant had surreptitiously removed his assets to England, and then would have to start all over again to enforce his rights.   **1–009**

Comity. It was at one time supposed that the doctrine of comity was a sufficient basis for the conflict of laws.[13] Comity is a term of very elastic content. Sometimes it connotes courtesy or the need for reciprocity; at other times it is used as a synonym for the rules of public international law.[14] Story used it to mean more than mere courtesy, but something rather less than equivalent to international law.[15] Dicey was highly critical of the use of comity to explain the conflict of laws ("a singular specimen of confusion of thought produced by laxity of language"[16]): English courts apply, *e.g.* French law in order to do justice between the parties, and not from any desire to show courtesy to the French Republic, nor even in the hope that if English courts apply French law in appropriate cases, French courts will be encouraged in   **1–010**

---

[11] See Anton, pp. 40–41; Rheinstein (1944) 19 Tulane L. Rev. 4, 17–24.

[12] Subject to treaty obligations (such as the 1968 Convention and the Lugano Convention, *infra*, Chap. 11) and to any question of "denial of justice" under the rules of public international law. See Brownlie, *Principles of Public International Law* (5th ed. 1998), pp. 531–533.

[13] Story (1st ed. 1834), pp. 33–35. See generally Yntema (1966) 65 Mich. L. Rev. 9; F.A. Mann, *Foreign Affairs in English Courts* (1986), pp. 134–137.

[14] Oppenheim, *International Law* (9th ed. Jennings and Watts 1992), Vol. 1, pp. 50–51.

[15] *Cf. Hilton v. Guyot*, 159 U.S. 113, 163–164 (1895) (" . . . neither a matter of absolute obligation, on the one hand, nor of mere courtesy and good will, upon the other"); *Soc. Nationale Industrielle Aérospatiale v. U.S. District Court*, 482 U.S. 522, 543 (1987) (" . . . the spirit of co-operation in which a domestic tribunal approaches the resolution of cases touching the laws and interests of other sovereign states").

[16] 1st ed. 1896, p. 10.

appropriate cases to apply English law. In the United States recognition of foreign judgments has been said to rest on considerations of comity and reciprocity,[17] but comity has been rejected as the basis for the recognition of foreign judgments in England.[18]

1–011   The concept of comity is increasingly used in common law countries, not as an explanation for the system of the conflict of laws, but as a tool for applying or re-shaping the rules of the conflict of laws. In particular, it is used in a sense which owes much to the rules of public international law, namely respect for the territorial jurisdiction of other states. The English courts have long emphasised that in the application of the rules for service out of the jurisdiction special care is needed to avoid conflict with international comity, *i.e.* with the jurisdiction of the state in which service is to be effected.[19] More recently, comity has been invoked to justify the caution which is required in the exercise of the power to grant injunctions to restrain proceedings in foreign courts. Comity requires that the English forum should have a sufficient interest in, or connection with, the matter in question to justify the indirect interference with the foreign court which such an injunction entails.[20] So also, in the exercise of the jurisdiction to grant extra-territorial provisional remedies such as *Mareva* injunctions, "it is becoming widely accepted that comity between the courts of different countries requires mutual respect for the territorial integrity of each other's jurisdiction".[21] Similarly, the Court of Appeal held that the Charities Act 1993 did not apply to a charity established under Indian law, because as a matter of comity the jurisdiction of the court to control charities could only be exercised in relation to English charities, and any attempt to control foreign charities would be akin to an encroachment upon the sovereignty of a foreign state.[22]

1–012   Comity is also invoked in those areas of the conflict of laws which touch on the foreign relations of the United Kingdom, to justify restraint in the application of English law or policy. When the Court of Appeal held that Soviet decrees confiscating property in Russia were to be recognised in England, Scrutton L.J. warned that it would be a serious breach of international comity to postulate that the legislation of a foreign sovereign state was contrary to essential principles of justice and morality.[23] Conversely, it has been said that it would be a breach of international comity for the English court to enforce a contract, even if otherwise valid under English law, designed to break the

---

[17] See Scoles and Hay, pp. 960–961. *Cf. Morguard Investments Ltd. v. De Savoye* [1990] 3 S.C.R. 1077, 1096–1097 (Sup. Ct. Can.).

[18] *Schibsby v. Westenholz* (1870) L.R. 6 Q.B. 155, 159; *Adams v. Cape Industries plc* [1990] Ch. 433, 513 (C.A.), *post*, para. 14–007. But comity requires, in the context of judicial assistance, co-operation with foreign courts to give effect to letters rogatory: *State of Minnesota v. Philip Morris Inc.* [1998] I.L.Pr. 170, 176 (C.A.); contrast *Settebello Ltd. v. Banco Totta and Acores* [1985] 1 W.L.R. 1050, 1057 (C.A.). See *post*, paras. 8–071; 8–076.

[19] *e.g. Field v. Bennett* (1886) 56 L.J.Q.B. 89, 91; *The Brabo* [1949] A.C. 326, 347, 357; *The Chaparral* [1968] 2 Lloyd's Rep. 158, 163 (C.A.).

[20] *Soc. Nationale Industrielle Aérospatiale v. Lee Kui Jak* [1987] A.C. 871, 895 (P.C.); *Airbus Industrie GIE v. Patel* [1999] 1 A.C. 119, 133. See also, *e.g. CSR Ltd. v. Cigna Insurance Australia Ltd.* (1997) 189 C.L.R. 345, 395–396. See, *post*, para. 12–062.

[21] *Crédit Suisse Fides Trust SA v. Cuoghi* [1998] Q.B. 818, 827 (C.A.), *per* Millett L.J.

[22] *Gaudiya Mission v. Brahmachary* [1998] Ch. 341 (C.A.). *Cf. Hartford Fire Insurance Co. v. State of California*, 509 U.S. 764, 817 (1993); *Amchem Products Inc. v. Workers' Compensation Board* [1993] 1 S.C.R. 897, 934 (Sup.Ct.Can.).

[23] *Luther v. Sagor* [1921] 3 K.B. 532, 558–559 (C.A.); *cf. Igra v. Igra* [1951] P. 404, 412. See also *Fayed v. Al-Tajir* [1988] Q.B. 712, 730 (C.A.).

laws of a friendly foreign country.[24] And more recently it has been re-affirmed that in the interests of comity the English court should refrain from sitting in judgment on the internal affairs of another state,[25] and from deciding whether a foreign state has been responsible for a breach of its treaty obligations.[26]

Sometimes, however, the application of foreign law by a municipal court is required by public international law. Thus the United Kingdom may be bound by treaty to provide that its courts will apply foreign law, *e.g.* under the EEC Convention on the Law Applicable to Contractual Obligations.[27] Or the application by a court of its own law, rather than foreign law, to a wholly foreign transaction may be regarded by other states as a breach of international law.[28]

1–013

Late development in England. Although the conflict of laws has been intensively studied by continental jurists since the thirteenth century, it is of comparatively recent origin in England.[29] A few rules of the English conflict of laws can be traced back to the late seventeenth century. But the subject first came into prominence in English courts towards the end of the eighteenth century, mainly because of conflicts between the laws of England and Scotland. In the nineteenth century its development was enormously accelerated by the rapid increase in commercial and social intercourse between England and the continent of Europe, and with the British territories overseas. In the twentieth century this development has been still further accelerated by the mass movement of populations, stimulated by wars and their aftermath and by technical advances in the means of transport and communications. It has not been easy for the conflict of laws to adapt itself to the changes in social and commercial life which the twentieth century has witnessed. Many of its rules were first laid down in the nineteenth century and seem better suited to nineteenth century conditions than to those of the twentieth century. Obvious examples are furnished by the law of torts[30] and (in spite of recent statutory change[31]) by the common law rules relating to domicile, particularly the rules making it so difficult to shake off a domicile of origin.[32] Remedies for this situation have been sought in the introduction of habitual residence as an alternative to domicile as a jurisdictional or connecting factor,[33] and in a gradual move away from the double actionability rule for foreign torts until its

1–014

---

[24] *Foster v. Driscoll* [1929] 1 K.B. 470, 510 (C.A.); *Regazzoni v. K. C. Sethia Ltd.* [1958] A.C. 301, 327. See Collins (1995–6) 6 King's Coll. L.J. 20, and *post*, paras. 5–009; 32–236.
[25] *A Ltd. v. B. Bank* [1997] F.S.R. 165, 172 (C.A.).
[26] *Westland Helicopters Ltd. v. Arab Organisation for Industrialisation* [1995] Q.B. 282. See Rule. 3.
[27] Chap. 32, *post*.
[28] *Cf. Midland Bank plc v. Laker Airways Ltd.* [1986] Q.B. 689 (C.A.). For literature on the relationship between private and public international law, see also para. 1–084, n. 5, *infra*.
[29] For the history of the conflict of laws, see Story, pp. 2–20; Westlake, pp. 7–22; Cheshire and North, Chap. 2; Wolff, Chap. 3; Lorenzen, Chap. 7; Anton, Chaps. 1 and 2; Beale, Vol. 3, pp. 1880–1975; Gutzwiller, *Geschichte des Internationalprivatrechts* (1977); Gutzwiller (1929) *Recueil des Cours*, IV, pp. 289–400; Meijers (1934) *Recueil des Cours*, III, pp. 547–686; Sack, in *Law, A Century of Progress* (1935), Vol. 3, pp. 342–454; (with special reference to the history in England); Llewelfryn Davies (1937) 18 B.Y.I.L. 49–78; De Nova (1966) *Recueil des Cours*, II, pp. 441–477; Lipstein (1972) *Recueil des Cours*, I, pp. 104–166.
[30] See *post*, Chap. 35.
[31] Domicile and Matrimonial Proceedings Act 1973, ss.1, 3, 4; see Rules 14–16.
[32] See *post*, Chap. 6, especially Rules 7, 10, 13(2).
[33] See *e.g.* Rules 23, 75, 76(2), 79(1)(a), 135(1). For the meaning of "connecting factor," see *post*, paras. 1–074 *et seq.*

eventual abolition by statute.[34] In the United States the reaction against nineteenth-century ideas has gone much further than it has in England. The "softening of concepts"[35] in the Second Restatement (1971) may be compared with the rigid dogmatism of the First Restatement (1934); and there is an influential school of writers who believe that traditional rules of the conflict of laws have served their purpose, and that they should be scrapped and a fresh start made.[36]

1–015   **Sources.** The three most important sources of the English conflict of laws are statutes, the decisions of the courts and the opinions of jurists. They are placed in this order because there can be no doubt that statutes have become potentially by far the most important source, and their importance seems likely to increase rather than to diminish in future. Until the middle of the twentieth century, Parliamentary intervention in the conflict of laws was haphazard, sporadic and (compared with the mass of case law) slight and unimportant. Statutes were occasionally passed to remedy some glaring anomaly or injustice,[37] to facilitate the reciprocal enforcement of judgments within the United Kingdom or the Commonwealth or with such foreign States as were prepared to offer reciprocal treatment,[38] or (on one occasion only) to codify a very small part of the subject.[39] But since the middle of the twentieth century there has been an increasing stream of statutes implementing international conventions,[40] and a few very important ones prepared by the Law Commission as part of a thorough-going and well-considered reform of the

---

[34] See *Boys v. Chaplin* [1971] A.C. 356; *Red Sea Insurance Co. Ltd. v. Bouygues S.A.* [1995] 1 A.C. 190 (P.C.); Private International Law (Miscellaneous Provisions) Act 1995, Pt. III, *post*, Chap. 35.

[35] This phrase is used by Kahn-Freund (1974) *Recueil des Cours*, III, pp. 406–413.

[36] See Currie, *Selected Essays on the Conflict of Laws* (1963); Cavers, *The Choice of Law Process* (1965); Ehrenzweig, especially pp. 307–326; Leflar, McDougal and Felix, Chap. 11; Scoles and Hay, Chap. 2.

[37] *e.g.* Wills Act 1861; Matrimonial Causes Act 1937, s.13; Law Reform (Miscellaneous Provisions) Act 1949, s.1; Family Allowances and National Insurance Act 1956, s.3 (all of which have since been repealed and replaced by more comprehensive enactments).

[38] *e.g.* Judgments Extension Act 1868; Maintenance Orders (Facilities for Enforcement) Act 1920; Administration of Justice Act 1920, Part II; Foreign Judgments (Reciprocal Enforcement) Act 1933; Maintenance Orders Act 1950.

[39] Bills of Exchange Act 1882, s.72. For recent codifications in civil law countries see Private International Law Revision Act, 1986, Federal Republic of Germany (translation in (1988) 27 *International Legal Materials* 1); Federal Law of Private International Law, 1987, Switzerland (on which see Karrer and Arnold. *Switzerland's Private International Law Statute 1987* (1989); Samuel (1988) 37 I.C.L.Q. 681); Private International Law Reform Act, 1995, Italy.

[40] *e.g.* Administration of Justice Act 1956, ss.3 and 4 (now Supreme Court Act 1981, ss.21 and 22); Carriage by Air Act 1961; Wills Act 1963; Diplomatic Privileges Act 1964; Carriage of Goods by Road Act 1965; Uniform Laws on International Sales Act 1967; Consular Relations Act 1968; International Organisations Act 1968; Adoption Act 1968; Carriage of Goods by Sea Act 1971; Recognition of Divorces and Legal Separations Act 1971 (now Family Law Act 1986, Pt. II); Maintenance Orders (Reciprocal Enforcement) Act 1972, Pt. II; Carriage by Railway Act 1972 (replaced by International Transport Conventions Act 1983); Carriage of Passengers by Road Act 1974; Arbitration Act 1975 (replaced by Arbitration Act 1996, ss.9 and 100–104); State Immunity Act 1978; Carriage by Air and Road Act 1979; Merchant Shipping Act 1979, ss.14–16 and Sched. 3, ss.17–19 and Sched. 4 (replaced by Merchant Shipping Act 1995, ss.183–185 and Scheds. 6 and 7); Civil Jurisdiction and Judgments Act 1982 (as amended by Civil Jurisdiction and Judgments Act 1991); Civil Aviation (Eurocontrol) Act 1983; Child Abduction and Custody Act 1985; Contracts (Applicable Law) Act 1990.

law.[41] The English rules of the conflict of laws have been radically affected by conventions negotiated under the auspices of the Hague Conference on Private International Law[42] and under the auspices of the European Communities, especially the 1968 Convention on jurisdiction and the enforcement of judgments in civil and commercial matters (and the parallel Lugano Convention) and the Rome Convention on the Law Applicable to Contractual Obligations.[43]

Of course this increasing activity of Parliament does not mean that the function of the courts is restricted to statutory interpretation. There remain large areas of conflict of laws where case law is still the most important source, and the courts still have a creative part to play. An important new source of case law is the jurisprudence of the European Court of Justice, which has given judgment in more than 100 references on the 1968 Convention on jurisdiction and the enforcement of judgments in civil and commercial matters.[44]   **1–016**

In the English conflict of laws the courts have been influenced by the opinions of jurists, both foreign and English, to a far greater extent than in most other subjects. The most influential foreign jurists have been Ulrich Huber (1636–1694), who was successively a professor of law and a judge in Friesland; Joseph Story (1779–1845), who was simultaneously a justice of the Supreme Court of the United States and a professor of law at the Harvard Law School; and the nineteenth century German jurist Friedrich Carl von Savigny.   **1–017**

Interpretation of statutes implementing international conventions.[45]   **1–018**
Statutes implementing international conventions have become such an important source of the English conflict of laws that a few words must be said about the English rules relating to their interpretation. In England, unlike some continental European countries and the United States, international treaties and conventions do not have the force of law merely by reason of having been ratified by the Government, at least in so far as the rights and duties of private

---

[41] Matrimonial Proceedings (Polygamous Marriages) Act 1972, now Matrimonial Causes Act 1973, s.47; Domicile and Matrimonial Proceedings Act 1973; Matrimonial and Family Proceedings Act 1984, Pt. III; Foreign Limitation Periods Act 1984; Family Law Act 1986, Pt. I; Family Law Reform Act 1987; Private International Law (Miscellaneous Provisions) Act 1995.

[42] See especially the Hague Conventions on the conflict of laws relating to the form of testamentary dispositions (Wills Act 1963); the recognition of divorces and legal separations (Family Law Act 1986); the taking of evidence abroad in civil or commercial matters (Evidence (Proceedings in Other Jurisdictions) Act 1975); civil aspects of international child abduction (Child Abduction and Custody Act 1985). On the Hague Conventions see North, *Essays in Private International Law* (1993), p. 225; Lipstein (1993) 42 I.C.L.Q. 553; TMC Asser Institute, *The Influence of the Hague Conference on Private International Law* (1993); McClean (1992) *Recueil des Cours*, II, p. 267; von Overbeck, *ibid.*, 9; Fassberg (1993) Israel L. Rev. 460; *The Hague Conference on Private International Law* (Carrington and Dyer, eds.) in (1994) 57 Law & Contemp. Prob., No. 3; McClean, in *E Pluribus Unum* (ed. Borrods 1996), p. 205.

[43] Civil Jurisdiction and Judgments Act 1982, Scheds. 1 and 3C; Contracts (Applicable Law) Act 1990, Sched. 1.

[44] *Post*, paras. 11–049 *et seq.*

[45] See F.A. Mann, *Studies in International Law* (1973), pp. 614–633; F.A. Mann, *Further Studies in International Law* (1990), pp. 270–301; F.A. Mann, *Foreign Affairs in English Courts* (1986), Chap. 5; Sinclair (1963) 12 I.C.L.Q. 508, esp. pp. 525–551; Higgins, in *The Effect of Treaties in Domestic Law*, ed. Jacobs and Roberts, 1987, p. 123; Gardiner (1995) 44 I.C.L.Q 620.

persons are concerned. In the United Kingdom, a treaty provision does not become law until it has been implemented by statute or statutory instrument.[46] There are several legislative techniques for giving the force of law to international conventions.[47] The statute may be based on the convention (the convention itself not being incorporated in the statute) and the statute may[48] or may not[49] indicate in the long title or the preamble that it is intended to give effect to the convention. The statute may incorporate the English text of the convention (or a translation of the French or other language text) in a schedule.[50] Or the statute may incorporate the English and French (or other language) text of the convention in different parts of the schedule, and may contain an express provision that in case of any inconsistency the French version shall prevail.[51] Different principles of interpretation may apply to each of these cases,[52] if only because each technique presents different problems to the courts.

1–019   The following principles of interpretation may be deduced from the decisions of the English courts.

1–020   (1) The purpose of an international convention is to harmonise the laws of all contracting states on the particular topic dealt with by the convention. It is therefore very important that the interpretation of the convention should be the same, so far as possible, in all contracting states.[53] This is to some extent a counsel of perfection, because not only are international conventions drafted in a style very different from that of United Kingdom Acts of Parliament, but also English rules for the interpretation of statutes are different from (and usually much stricter than) those applied by courts in continental European countries or even in the United States. English courts have therefore been

---

[46] *Att.-Gen. for Canada v. Att.-Gen. for Ontario* [1937] A.C. 326 (P.C.). For modern examples see *British Airways Board v. Laker Airways Ltd.* [1985] A.C. 58, 83; *J.H. Rayner (Mincing Lane) Ltd. v. Department of Trade and Industry* [1990] 2 A.C. 418, 477, 500; *Littrell v. Government of the United States (No. 2)* [1995] 1 W.L.R. 82 (C.A.); *Ex p. Amnesty International, The Times*, December 11, 1998.

[47] The European Commission has recommended that, when implementing the EEC Convention on the Law Applicable to Contractual Obligations (on which see *post*, Chap. 32), a Member State (in this case, Germany) should make full use of its constitution to ensure that its courts can resort directly to the wording of the Convention and to avoid changes in the content, formulation and order of the provisions of the Convention: *Official Journal of the European Communities* [1985] O.J. L44/42; [1985] 2 C.M.L.R. 49.

[48] *e.g.* Wills Act 1963; Adoption Act 1968; Maintenance Orders (Reciprocal Enforcement) Act 1972; Arbitration Act 1975 (replaced by Arbitration Act 1996); State Immunity Act 1978.

[49] *e.g.* Children Act 1975, s.24; Supreme Court Act 1981, ss.21 and 22; Family Law Act 1986, Pt. II (replacing Recognition of Divorces and Legal Separations Act 1971, which did refer to the convention). Although the Evidence (Proceedings in Other Jurisdictions) Act 1975 was passed in order, among other reasons, to enable the United Kingdom to ratify the Hague Evidence Convention of 1970, it was held that it is to be construed against the background of previous United Kingdom legislation and not solely by reference to the 1970 Convention: *Re State of Norway's Application (Nos. 1 and 2)* [1990] 1 A.C. 723, 796.

[50] *e.g.* Carriage of Goods by Sea Acts 1924 and 1971; Diplomatic Privileges Act 1964; Carriage of Goods by Road Act 1965; Uniform Laws on International Sales Act 1967; Consular Relations Act 1968; Carriage of Passengers by Road Act 1974; Civil Jurisdiction and Judgments Act 1982, Scheds. 1, 3C; Contracts (Applicable Law) Act 1990, Sched. 1; Merchant Shipping Act 1995, Scheds. 6 and 7.

[51] *e.g.* Carriage by Air Act 1961, s.1(2) and Sched. 1; Carriage by Air (Supplementary Provisions) Act 1962, s.1(2) and Sched.; Carriage by Air and Road Act 1979, s.1(1) and Sched. 1.

[52] *James Buchanan & Co. Ltd. v. Babco Forwarding and Shipping (U.K.) Ltd.* [1978] A.C. 141, 152.

[53] This passage was quoted with approval in *Sidhu v. British Airways plc* [1997] A.C. 430, 444.

compelled to relax some of their rules of interpretation when the statute gives effect to an international convention. They will, it has been said, interpret the implementing statute "in a normal manner appropriate for the interpretation of an international convention, unconstrained by technical rules of English law, or by English legal precedent, but on broad principles of general acceptation."[54] They will also listen to the citation of cases from the courts of other contracting states and will give effect to a prevailing current of foreign opinion on the true construction of the convention.[55] But these are only aids to interpretation, and the value of foreign court decisions will depend on the reputation and standing of the foreign court.[56] On the other hand, the House of Lords has emphatically rejected the notion that in interpreting such a statute the English courts should completely abandon traditional English methods of interpretation, and in particular the notion that, if there is a gap in the convention, English courts are entitled to fill it by judicial legislation.[57]

(2) If the text of the convention is not incorporated in the statute, is the court **1–021** entitled to look at the convention? It was at one time supposed that the court could only do so if the statute was ambiguous and if it referred expressly to the convention.[58] But it has become clear that this is not so and that the court can look at the convention, even though it is not expressly referred to in the statute, provided the statute is ambiguous and provided the court is satisfied by extrinsic evidence that the statute was intended to implement the convention. This is because there is a prima facie presumption that Parliament does not intend to act in breach of international law, including specific treaty obligations. But if the statute is unambiguous it must be given effect, whether it carries out the treaty obligations or not.[59] According to Lord Denning M.R., there is no requirement that the statute must be ambiguous[60] and Lord

---

[54] *Stag Line Ltd. v. Foscolo, Mango & Co. Ltd.* [1932] A.C. 328, 350; *James Buchanan & Co. Ltd. v. Babco Forwarding and Shipping (U.K.) Ltd., supra,* at pp. 152, 160, 161; *Ulster-Swift Ltd. v. Taunton Meat Haulage Ltd.* [1977] 1 W.L.R. 625, 628 (C.A.); *Fothergill v. Monarch Airlines Ltd.* [1981] A.C. 251, 282, 293; *The Hollandia* [1983] 1 A.C. 565, 572; *The Antares (No. 2)* [1986] 2 Lloyd's Rep. 633, 637, affd. [1987] 1 Lloyd's Rep. 424 (C.A.).

[55] See *e.g. Corocraft Ltd. v. Pan American Airways Inc.* [1969] 1 Q.B. 616 (C.A.); *Wilson, Smithett & Cope Ltd. v. Terruzzi* [1976] Q.B. 683 (C.A.); *James Buchanan & Co. Ltd. v. Babco Forwarding and Shipping (U.K.) Ltd., supra,* at pp. 153–154, 161; *Antwerp United Diamond B.V.B.A. v. Air Europe* [1996] Q.B. 317, 330–331 (C.A.); *Sidhu v. British Airways plc* [1997] A.C. 430, 451–453; *Herd v. Clyde Helicopters Ltd.* [1997] A.C. 534, 553–555. In *Ulster-Swift Ltd. v. Taunton Meat Haulage Ltd., supra,* at pp. 631–632, it appeared that no less than 12 different interpretations of the relevant articles of the convention had been adopted by 30 decisions of the courts of 6 continental European countries, and for that reason the Court of Appeal was not asked to examine them.

[56] *Fothergill v. Monarch Airlines Ltd.* [1981] A.C. 251, 284, 295. See also *The River Rima* [1988] 1 W.L.R. 758, 765 (H.L.); *ICI plc v. MAT Transport Ltd.* [1987] 1 Lloyd's Rep. 354, 359; *Gatewhite Ltd. v. Iberia Lineas Aereas* [1990] 1 Q.B. 326, 332–335.

[57] *James Buchanan & Co. Ltd. v. Babco Forwarding and Shipping (U.K.) Ltd., supra,* at pp. 153, 156, 160–161. This gap-filling method had been adopted by Lord Denning M.R. in the Court of Appeal: [1977] Q.B. 208, 213–214.

[58] See *e.g. Ellerman Lines Ltd. v. Murray* [1931] A.C. 126. In *James Buchanan & Co. Ltd. v. Babco Forwarding and Shipping (U.K.) Ltd., supra,* at p. 153. Lord Wilberforce said that this oft-cited case was untypical and should no longer be followed.

[59] *Salomon v. Commissioners of Customs and Excise* [1967] 2 Q.B. 116, 143–144 (C.A.); *Post Office v. Estuary Radio Ltd* [1968] 2 Q.B. 740, 757 (C.A.); *cf. I.R.C. v. Collco Dealings Ltd.* [1962] A.C.1.

[60] *Salomon v. Commissioners of Customs and Excise, supra,* at p. 141; *The Banco* [1971] P. 137, at p. 151; but contrast *R. v. Chief Immigration Officer, Heathrow Airport, ex p. Salamat Bibi* [1976] 1 W.L.R. 979, 984 (C.A.).

Wilberforce has said that the suggestion that resort to a foreign text is only permissible if the English text is ambiguous "states the rule too technically."[61] In other cases judicial statements of the principle have omitted the preliminary requirement of ambiguity.[62] The differing judicial approaches may be reconciled on the basis that it may only become apparent that the words of the statute are ambiguous (or "loose textured"[63]) after resort to the international convention.

1–022 (3) If the convention is expressed in two languages, *e.g.* English and French, each text being equally authentic, but only the English text is incorporated in the statute, is the court entitled to look at the French text as an aid to its construction? This is a question on which conflicting views have been expressed, but the better opinion would appear to be that the court is so entitled,[64] at any rate if the statute and the English text are ambiguous or "loose-textured". Where a Convention is concluded under the auspices of the European Communities, all language versions are equally authentic, and for that reason the Brussels and Lugano Conventions are scheduled to the Civil Jurisdiction and Judgments Act 1982 (as amended) for "convenience of reference"[65] and the Rome Convention is scheduled to the Contracts (Applicable Law) Act 1990 for "ease of reference".[66] There can be no doubt in such cases that the process of interpretation will inevitably involve a comparison between the different language versions.[67]

1–023 (4) If the court is required by statute,[68] or decides for itself, to look at the French text of the convention, how should it inform itself of the meaning of the French words? In *Fothergill v. Monarch Airlines Ltd.*[69] the House of Lords held that it was inappropriate to lay down precise rules, because, as Lord Wilberforce put it, the process of ascertaining the meaning of the foreign language must vary according to the subject matter: the court may use its own knowledge of the foreign language,[70] or it may have resort to such aids as

---

[61] *James Buchanan & Co. Ltd. v. Babco Forwarding and Shipping (U.K.) Ltd., supra*, at p. 152.

[62] *e.g. The Eschersheim* [1976] 1 W.L.R. 430, 436 (H.L.); *Garland v. British Rail Engineering Ltd.* [1983] 2 A.C. 751, 771, *per* Lord Diplock (but this may be because he regarded the requirement of ambiguity as implicit). For more orthodox statements see *Fothergill v. Monarch Airlines Ltd.* [1981] A.C. 251, 299 (Lord Roskill); *Government of Kuwait v. Sir Frederick Snow and Partners* [1984] A.C. 426, 435 (Lord Brandon); *J.H. Rayner (Mincing Lane) Ltd. v. Department of Trade and Industry* [1990] 2 A.C. 418, 500–502 (Lord Oliver).

[63] *Cf. Gatoil International Inc. v. Arkwright-Boston Manufacturers Mutual Insurance Co.* [1985] A.C. 255, 262, *per* Lord Wilberforce.

[64] See *Corocraft Ltd. v. Pan American Airways Inc.* [1969] 1 Q.B. 616 (C.A.); *Post Office v. Estuary Radio Ltd.* [1968] 2 Q.B. 740, 760 (C.A.); *Ulster-Swift Ltd. v. Taunton Meat Haulage Ltd.* [1977] 1 W.L.R. 625, 632 (C.A.); *James Buchanan & Co. Ltd. v. Babco Forwarding and Shipping (U.K.) Ltd.* [1978] A.C. 141, 152, 161, 166–167; *The Antonis P. Lemos* [1985] A.C. 711, 731; *Silber Ltd v. Islander Trucking Ltd.* [1985] 2 Lloyd's Rep. 243.

[65] ss.2(2), 3A(2).

[66] s.2(4).

[67] See, *e.g.* Case 150/80 *Elefanten Schuh GmbH v. Jacqmain* [1981] E.C.R. 1671, 1685. *Cf.* Collins, *European Community Law in the United Kingdom* (4th ed. 1990), pp. 133–134.

[68] *e.g.* Carriage by Air Act 1961, s.1(2); Carriage by Air (Supplementary Provisions) Act 1962, s.1(2).

[69] [1981] A.C. 251, 273–274, 286, 293–294, 299–300. See also *James Buchanan & Co. Ltd. v. Babco Forwarding and Shipping (U.K.) Ltd.* [1978] A.C. 141, 152–153; *Semco Salvage and Marine Pte Ltd. v. Lancer Navigation Co. Ltd.* [1997] A.C. 455, 471.

[70] *e.g. Corocraft Ltd. v. Pan American Airways Inc.* [1969] 1 Q.B. 616 (C.A.) (insertion of "and" in English text).

dictionaries, interpreters or expert witnesses,[71] depending on the degree and nature of the difficulty of interpretation.

(5) In construing a purely English statute, the court can have regard to **1–024** "*travaux préparatoires*" such as reports of Royal Commissions, the Law Commission, committees and the like in order to see what the "mischief" was with which the Act was intended to deal, although, prior to the decision of the House of Lords in *Pepper v. Hart*,[72] the court could not take into account direct statements of what the Act was intended or understood to mean nor could it look at the reports of Parliamentary debates in *Hansard*.[73] It has been established by two decisions of the House of Lords that cautious use of *travaux préparatoires* may be made as an aid to interpretation, provided that two conditions are fulfilled: first, that the material is public and accessible; second, that it clearly and indisputably points to a definite legislative intention. In the first case,[74] the House of Lords considered the minutes of the Hague Conference which led to the Hague Protocol to the Warsaw Convention, but was not able to derive much assistance from them. In the second case,[75] the House of Lords resorted to the published proceedings of the conference which led to the Brussels Convention relating to the arrest of seagoing ships to confirm its interpretation of the extent of the Scottish jurisdiction in admiralty.

As Kerr J. pointed out in *Fothergill v. Monarch Airlines Ltd.*[76] the modern **1–025** practice in international conventions is often to replace *travaux préparatoires* by an authoritative report or commentary from an official *rapporteur* to fill in gaps, comment on ambiguities, and generally to enlarge upon matters which cannot conveniently be compressed into the text of the convention. He suggested that it would be highly desirable that statutes implementing international conventions which are supplemented by such a report should expressly provide that the report may be referred to as an aid to interpretation. It was probably as a result of this suggestion that the Civil Jurisdiction and Judgments Act 1982 provided that the court may consider the official reports on the Brussels Convention on jurisdiction and the enforcement of judgments in civil and commercial matters of 1968 in interpreting the Convention and the intra-United Kingdom rules based on it.[77]

Most of the principles discussed above are well illustrated by two cases. In **1–026** *James Buchanan & Co. Ltd. v. Babco Forwarding and Shipping (U.K.) Ltd.*,[78] the defendants agreed to carry a quantity of whisky from the plaintiffs' bonded warehouse in Glasgow to Teheran. The contract was expressed to be subject to the Convention on the Carriage of Goods by Road scheduled to the

---

[71] *Cf. The Antonis P. Lemos* [1985] A.C. 711, 731.

[72] [1993] A.C. 593, where it was held that reference to clear ministerial statements would be permitted where legislation was ambiguous or obscure or otherwise led to absurdity.

[73] *Black-Clawson International Ltd. v. Papierwerke Waldhof-Aschaffenburg A.G.* [1975] A.C. 591; *Davis v. Johnson* [1979] A.C. 264.

[74] *Fothergill v. Monarch Airlines Ltd.* [1981] A.C. 251. See also *Sidhu v. British Airways plc* [1997] A.C. 430, 448–449; *Semco Salvage and Marine Pte. Ltd. v. Lancer Navigation Co. Ltd.* [1997] A.C. 455, 468–469; *Herd v. Clyde Helicopters Ltd.* [1997] A.C. 534, 552–553.

[75] *Gatoil International Inc. v. Arkwright-Boston Manufacturers Mutual Insurance Co.* [1985] A.C. 255. See also *Hiscox v. Outhwaite* [1992] 1 A.C. 562, 593.

[76] [1978] Q.B. 108, 119; see also [1981] A.C. 251, 295, *per* Lord Scarman.

[77] ss.3(3), 3B(2) (a similar provision in relation to the Lugano Convention, added by the Civil Jurisdiction and Judgments Act 1991), 16(3), *post*, para. 11–041. See also Contracts (Applicable Law) Act 1990, s.3(3), *post*, para. 32–014.

[78] [1977] Q.B. 208 (C.A.); [1978] A.C. 141.

Carriage of Goods by Road Act 1965. Owing to the negligence of the defendants' lorry driver in leaving the lorry containing the whisky unattended in a London suburb for three days, the whisky was stolen. The value of the whisky when it left the bonded warehouse was £7,000. But the plaintiffs, being unable to prove that the whisky had been exported, were obliged by law to pay and did pay £30,000 to the Customs and Excise by way of duty. They sought to recover £37,000 from the defendants, who admitted liability for £7,000 but denied that they were liable to pay more. Article 23 (1) and (2) of the Convention provided that the compensation payable by the carrier should be calculated by reference to the value of the goods at the place and time at which they were accepted for carriage. The Court of Appeal and the House of Lords were unanimous that the value of the whisky when it left the bonded warehouse was its value *ex* duty, *i.e.* £7,000. But Article 23 (4) provided that in addition, the carriage charges, customs duties and other charges incurred in respect of the carriage of the goods should be refunded in full. In the Court of Appeal Lord Denning M.R. held that there was a gap in Article 23 (4) which the court was entitled to fill by asking itself what would best give effect to the presumed purpose of the convention and lead to a just result. Roskill and Lawton L.JJ. held that they could look at the French text of the convention and that its provisions resolved the ambiguity in favour of the plaintiffs. But a bare majority of the House of Lords, rejecting both views that had found favour in the Court of Appeal and restoring the judgment of Master Jacob, held that, by applying English rules of interpretation appropriately to an international convention, the words "other charges incurred in respect of the carriage" in Article 23 (4) were wide enough to cover the duty, because they included the way in which the goods were carried, miscarried or lost.

1–027   In *Fothergill v. Monarch Airlines Ltd.*,[79] the plaintiff returned by air from a holiday in Italy, the carrier being the defendants. The carriage, being "international carriage," was subject to the Warsaw Convention as amended by the Hague Protocol scheduled to the Carriage by Air Act 1961. Some time after he got home he noticed that some of the contents of his suitcase were missing. The defendants rejected his claim for compensation for the loss on the ground that he had not notified them within seven days as, they alleged, he should have done under Article 26 (2) of the convention. This provides that "in the case of damage, the person entitled to delivery must complain to the carrier forthwith after the discovery of the damage, and at the latest within seven days from the date of receipt." Kerr J. held that according to its natural meaning "damage" in Article 26 (2) did not include loss and that, prima facie, the article did not bar the plaintiff's claim. He then turned to the French text, where the corresponding phrase is *En cas d'avarie*, and concluded with the aid of a dictionary that *avarie* means damage or injury; so there was no inconsistency between the English and French texts. He then looked at certain *travaux préparatoires*, consisting of the minutes of 34 meetings at The Hague in 1955 at which the Hague Protocol had been negotiated. These clearly showed that a proposal to amend Article 26 (2) had been withdrawn on the understanding that "damage" was to be understood as including "partial loss." But he declined to give effect to this on the ground that it would give

---

[79] [1978] Q.B. 108; [1980] Q.B. 23 (C.A.); [1981] A.C. 251. See also *Swiss Bank Corp. v. Brink's MAT Ltd.* [1986] Q.B. 853.

an artificial and unacceptable meaning to Article 26 (2) and would adversely affect the rights of ordinary air passengers, who could not be expected to know that such material existed.

Two years after Kerr J. gave judgment in this case, but before his judgment was affirmed by the Court of Appeal, it was prospectively reversed by section 2 of the Carriage by Air and Road Act 1979,[80] which provides that in Article 26 (2) of the Warsaw Convention the references to damage shall be construed as including loss of part of the baggage or cargo in question. Hence it is apparent that parliamentary intervention may be required if the construction of an international convention by English courts appears to be at variance with that adopted in other countries which are parties to the convention.   1–028

In the Court of Appeal Browne and Lane L.JJ. agreed with Kerr J. that the minutes of the meetings at The Hague in 1955 could not be allowed to resolve the ambiguity in Article 26 (2). Lord Denning M.R. (who supported the result on another ground) thought the court should give effect to the understanding in the minutes as to the meaning of Article 26 (2), in order that the Convention should be given the same meaning by the courts of all signatory countries. But in 1981 the House of Lords reversed the judgments of Kerr J. and the Court of Appeal and held that "damage" included partial damage, in the light of the purpose of Article 26 (2) and of textbooks and articles which supported that conclusion. It held that the English court may make cautious use of *travaux préparatoires*, provided that the material was public and accessible and pointed clearly towards a definite legislative intention; but in the circumstances of the case a majority held that it was not necessary to resort to that material to reach the result arrived at by the House.   1–029

Under what was Article 177, and is now Article 234, of the Treaty of Rome establishing the European Community, the European Court of Justice has the last word on the interpretation of that treaty, and any national court in any of the European Communities countries may, and if it is a court of last resort must, refer any such question of interpretation to the European Court for a ruling, if it considers that a decision on the question is necessary to enable it to give judgment.[81] There are also conventions concluded between the member States of the European Communities which contain a Protocol giving the European Court jurisdiction to give rulings on their interpretation. By far the most important of these conventions in practice is the Brussels Convention on jurisdiction and the enforcement of judgments in civil and commercial matters of 1968. In 1971 the original members of the EEC entered into a Protocol conferring jurisdiction on the European Court to give rulings on the interpretation of the 1968 Convention. The Protocol entered into force in 1975, and the European Court has delivered many important decisions on the meaning of the 1968 Convention. The effect of the Civil Jurisdiction and Judgments Act 1982 is that courts in the United Kingdom are entitled (and some are bound) to refer questions of interpretation of the 1968 Convention to the European Court for preliminary rulings.[82]   1–030

Similarly, it was envisaged that the European Court would have jurisdiction to give rulings on the implementation of the Rome Convention. Under the Protocols on the interpretation of that Convention, certain courts in the United   1–031

---

[80] Adding a new s.4A to the Carriage by Air Act 1961.

[81] See Collins, *European Community Law in the United Kingdom* (4th ed. 1990), Chap. 3.

[82] See *post*, paras. 11–044 *et seq.* See also para. 11–011 for proposals to replace the 1968 Convention by a Council Regulation, with the consequence that references would be made to the European Court under Art. 234 of the E.C. Treaty.

Kingdom would be entitled (but not bound) to refer questions of interpretation on the Convention to the European Court.[83]

1–032   **Statutes and the conflict of laws.**[84] From the point of view of the conflict of laws, statutory provisions may conveniently be divided into six classes: (1) those which lay down a rule of substantive or domestic law without any indication of its application in space; (2) those which lay down a particular or unilateral rule of the conflict of laws purporting to indicate when a rule of substantive or domestic law is applicable; (3) those which lay down a general or multilateral rule of the conflict of laws purporting to indicate what law governs a given question; (4) those containing a limitation in space or otherwise which restricts the scope of a rule of substantive or domestic law (self-limiting statutes); (5) those which apply in the circumstances mentioned in the statute, even though they would not be applicable under the normal rules of the conflict of laws (overriding statutes); and (6) those which do not apply in the circumstances mentioned in the statute, even though they would be applicable under the normal rules of the conflict of laws (self-denying statutes). These categories are by no means mutually exclusive: some statutes may fall within more than one category. Only statutes in categories (2) and (3) above deal *expressis verbis* with the conflict of laws; the rest do not.

1–033   (1) *Statutes with no indication of their application in space.* Statutes of this kind are of course by far the most common. They are frequently expressed in general terms without any limitations of space and purport to apply *e.g.* to "every will," "all contracts," or "any married woman." Obviously, they cannot be read literally, because the Parliament of the United Kingdom does not legislate for the whole world.

1–034   It has often been said that there is a presumption that Parliament does not design its statutes to operate beyond the territorial limits of the United Kingdom.[85] But if this presumption still exists, it is one which is easily rebutted. For instance, it has not prevented the application of the Fatal Accidents Acts to a collision on the high seas off the east coast of the United States between a Panamanian ship manned by a Spanish crew and a Russian

---

[83] Contracts (Applicable Law) Act 1990, s.3(1) and Sched. 3, *post*, Chap. 32. But it is likely that the Rome Convention will be replaced by a Council Regulation, and that references to the European Court will be made under Art. 234 of the E.C. Treaty. The Rome Convention Protocols are not likely, therefore, to come into force.

[84] There is a substantial literature on this subject, of which the following is only a selection: Morris (1946) 62 L.Q.R. 170; Unger (1967) 83 L.Q.R. 427; Kelly (1969) 18 I.C.L.Q. 249; F.A. Mann (1972–73) 46 B.Y.I.L. 117; Kelly, *Localising Rules in the Conflict of Laws* (1974), especially Chap. 5; Kahn-Freund (1974) *Recueil des Cours*, III, pp. 234–247; Lipstein (1977) 26 I.C.L.Q. 884; Thomson (1980) 43 M.L.R. 650, 662–668. The reader should be warned that there is no agreement among writers about terminology or even about the categories into which particular statutes fall.

[85] Bennion, *Statutory Interpretation* (3rd ed. 1997), pp. 252–254; *Tomalin v. S. Pearson & Son Ltd.* [1909] 2 K.B. 61, 64 (C.A.); *Yorke v. British and Continental Steamship Co. Ltd.* (1945) 78 Ll.L.R. 181, 182, 184 (C.A.); *C.E.B. Draper & Son Ltd. v. Edward Turner & Son Ltd.* [1965] 1 Q.B. 424, 432, 435 (C.A.), overruled by *Hardwick Game Farm v. Suffolk Agricultural Poultry Producers Association* [1969] 2 A.C. 31. "Extra-territorial" operation in connection with the law of contract sometimes means operation with regard to contracts governed by foreign law: a United Kingdom statute of the category under discussion does not normally apply unless the contract is governed by the law of some part of the United Kingdom. Contrast overriding and self-denying statutes, *post*, paras. 1–049 *et seq.*

trawler manned by Russian sailors, some of whom were drowned.[86] Nor did it prevent the application of the Theft Act 1968 to a theft of crayfish committed by Western Australian fishermen 22 miles off the coast of Western Australia.[87] In other contexts, such as taxation or bankruptcy, it is sometimes said that prima facie legislation is applicable only to British subjects or to foreigners who, whether for a long or short time, have made themselves during that time subject to English jurisdiction.[88] But that presumption can be displaced. Thus in *Re Paramount Airways Ltd.*[89] it was held that the expression "any person" under section 238 of the Insolvency Act 1986, which enables the administrator or liquidator to apply for an order reversing a transaction entered into by the company with any person at an undervalue, is not subject to any implied limitation as to extra-territorial effect; it applies to any person wherever resident, but the court will not exercise its discretion unless it is satisfied that the defendant has a sufficient connection with England for it to be just and proper to make an order despite the foreign element. So also in *Re Seagull Manufacturing Co. Ltd.*[90] it was held that section 133 of the Insolvency Act 1986 (which allows the public examination of "any person" in the course of a winding-up) applies to all relevant persons who concern themselves in the affairs of the company, irrespective of whether they were British subjects or within the jurisdiction of the court at the relevant time. This interpretation was justified on the basis that Parliament could not have intended that the section could be evaded by the person leaving the jurisdiction.

As a typical example of statutes of the first type, we select for discussion **1–035** section 2 of the Marriage Act 1949. This provides that "a marriage between persons either of whom is under the age of sixteen years shall be void." Obviously, this enactment cannot be read literally so as to apply to all marriages in the world. Obviously, it must be limited in some way, either personally, or territorially, or both. Does it apply to all marriages celebrated in England, or to all marriages between parties domiciled in England, or only to marriages celebrated in England between parties domiciled in England?[91]

A court, when confronted by a statute of its own law or of foreign law **1–036** which is expressed in general terms like this, could use one of two methods to determine its scope. The first is to interpret the statute in the light of its purpose and background so as to read into it the limitations which the legislature would have expressed if it had given thought to the matter. This is an artificial method, and perhaps a dangerous one, because *ex hypothesi* the legislature gave no thought to the matter—if it had done so it would have expressed the limitations.[92] The second method is to apply general principles derived from the conflict of laws—*i.e.* first characterise the question as

---

[86] *The Esso Malaysia* [1975] Q.B. 198; *cf. Davidsson v. Hill* [1901] 1 K.B. 606. See Collins (1974) 90 L.Q.R. 447. See *post*, para. 35–071.

[87] *Oteri v. The Queen* [1976] 1 W.L.R. 1272 (P.C.).

[88] See *Clark v. Oceanic Contractors Inc.* [1983] 2 A.C. 130.

[89] [1993] Ch. 223 (C.A.).

[90] [1993] Ch. 345 (C.A.). In *Re Seagull Manufacturing Co. Ltd. (No. 2)* [1994] Ch. 91 it was held that the power to make an order under Company Directors Disqualification Act 1986, s.6(1), against "a person" extended to any person, whether or not a British subject, irrespective of where the conduct rendering him unfit to be a director took place. See also *Arab Bank plc v. Merchantile Holdings Ltd.* [1994] Ch. 71; *Jyske Bank (Gibraltar) Ltd. v. Spjeldnaes, The Times*, November 6, 1998; *McIsaac and Wilson, Petrs*, 1995 S.L.T. 498; *Re Doyle* (1993) 112 A.L.R. 653. Contrast *Re Sherlock* (1991) 102 A.L.R. 156.

[91] For discussion of the possible scope of the statute and its predecessor, the Age of Marriage Act 1929, see Beckett (1934) 15 B.Y.I.L. 46, 64–65; Morris (1946) 62 L.Q.R. 170–171.

[92] See Unger (1952) 15 M.L.R. 88.

relating to capacity to marry,[93] and then apply the relevant conflict rule to the question so characterised.[94]

1–037   In *Pugh v. Pugh*,[95] the court adopted both of these methods, and reached the surprising conclusion that the section applies to all marriages between parties one at least of whom is domiciled in England, even if the party domiciled in England was over sixteen and the party under sixteen had capacity to marry under the law of her domicile.[96]

1–038   (2) *Statutes with a particular choice of law clause.* Conflict rules differ from rules of domestic law in that they do not lay down a substantive rule but merely indicate which system of domestic law is applicable. But conflict rules are of two kinds, particular or unilateral and general or multilateral. A statute containing a particular or unilateral conflict rule answers the question, When does the system of law of which the statute forms part apply? A statute containing a general or multilateral conflict rule answers the more general question, What law applies?

1–039   A good example of the former type is section 1 of the Marriage (Scotland) Act 1977, which provides in subsection (1) that "No person domiciled in Scotland may marry before he attains the age of 16," and in subsection (2) that "A marriage solemnised in Scotland between persons either of whom is under the age of 16 shall be void."[97] This section neatly avoids the strange result which the English court reached in *Pugh v. Pugh*.

1–040   What should a court do when confronted by a particular or unilateral rule in a foreign statute? A court which rejects renvoi[98] might refuse to apply the rule, simply because it is a conflict rule. But quite often the statute can be dissected into (a) a rule of domestic law and (b) a conflict rule indicating when the rule of domestic law is to apply. In such circumstances a court faced with such a foreign statute might justifiably apply (a) but, rejecting renvoi, not (b). But if it did so, it might distort the meaning of the statute and apply it where, under the terms of the statute itself, it is inapplicable. For instance, if an English court had to consider the validity of a marriage celebrated in Austria between a domiciled Scotsman and a domiciled Hungarian girl under the age of sixteen (the marriage being valid by Austrian and Hungarian law), it would, if it dissected section 1 of the Marriage (Scotland) Act 1977 in the manner suggested, presumably hold the marriage void. Yet it is certain that a Scottish court would hold the marriage valid, because the section is expressed to apply only (a) where the party domiciled in Scotland is under the age of sixteen, or (b) where the marriage is solemnised in Scotland. If the English court dissected the section into (a) a rule of Scots domestic law and (b) a particular or unilateral conflict rule indicating when Scots law is to apply, and applied (a) but not (b), it would create a "limping" marriage—that is, a marriage valid in Scotland (and in Austria and Hungary) but void in England. Thus it would

---

[93] For capacity to marry, see Rule 68 and Exceptions thereto.

[94] For characterisation, see Chap. 2, *post.*

[95] [1951] P. 482. A marriage was celebrated in Austria between a man domiciled in England and a girl of 15 domiciled in Hungary. The marriage was valid by Austrian and Hungarian law.

[96] A dictum at pp. 491–492 suggests that the section would also apply to marriages celebrated in England, regardless of the domicile of the parties. This is entirely in accordance with Exception 2 to Rule 68.

[97] A far less successful particular or unilateral choice of law clause is s.2(3) of the same statute, dealing with marriages within the prohibited degrees.

[98] For renvoi, see Chap. 4, *post.*

seem preferable for the English court to apply section 1 as it stands, and hold the marriage valid.

Other examples of particular or unilateral choice of law clauses in statutes are the Law Reform (Frustrated Contracts) Act 1943, s.1(1)[99]; the Marriage (Enabling) Act 1960, s.1(3)[1]; the Inheritance (Provision for Family and Dependants) Act 1975, s.1(1)[2]; and the Legitimacy Act 1976, s.1(2).[3]   **1–041**

The desirability of particular or unilateral choice of law clauses as a legislative technique is strongly criticised by some writers,[4] and equally strongly defended by others.[5]   **1–042**

(3) *Statutes with a general choice of law clause.* Statutes containing general or multilateral conflict rules are rare in English law, but examples can be found in section 72(1) and (2) of the Bills of Exchange Act 1882[6]; and the Wills Act 1963.[7] They both seek to answer the question "What law applies?"—in the first case to the formal and essential validity of bills of exchange, in the second case to the formal validity of wills. Another example can be constructed from sections 2 and 3 of the Legitimacy Act 1976. Section 2 provides that where the parents of an illegitimate person marry one another, the marriage shall, if the father is at the date of the marriage domiciled in England, render that person, if living, legitimate from the date of the marriage. Taken by itself, this would be a rule of English domestic law coupled with a particular or unilateral conflict rule, purporting to answer the question "When does English law apply?" But section 3 provides that where the parents of an illegitimate person marry one another and the father is not at the time of the marriage domiciled in England but is domiciled in a country by the law of which the illegitimate person became legitimated by virtue of such subsequent marriage, that person, if living, shall in England be recognised as having been so legitimated from the date of the marriage.[8] These two sections, added together, yield a general or multilateral conflict rule to the effect that the law of the father's domicile at the date of the marriage determines whether an illegitimate person is legitimated by the subsequent marriage of his parents.[9]   **1–043**

On the other hand, it is seldom possible for English courts to do what courts in continental European countries have often done, namely, to derive a general or multilateral conflict rule from a particular or unilateral one contained in a statute. This is because in England the common law is never displaced by a statute unless the statute expressly abolishes the rule of common law.[10] The common law is the rule and the statute is the exception which applies only to the extent expressed therein. Only if there is no common law authority would   **1–044**

---

[99] *Post*, para. 34–020.

[1] *Post*, para. 17–073.

[2] *Post*, para. 27–048.

[3] *Post*, para. 20–026.

[4] Morris (1946) 62 L.Q.R. 170, 172; Unger (1967) 83 L.Q.R. 427, 436–448.

[5] F. A. Mann (1964) 80 L.Q.R. 29, 31; (1972–73) 46 B.Y.I.L. 117, 134; Currie, p. 116.

[6] See Rule 193(1) and (2).

[7] See Rule 135.

[8] See Rule 101 and Comment thereto.

[9] See F. A. Mann (1972–73) 46 B.Y.I.L. 117, 118–119; Kahn-Freund (1974) *Recueil des Cours*, III, p. 236.

[10] For example, s.8(1) of the Legitimacy Act 1926 (the predecessor of s.3 of the Legitimacy Act 1976) was held not to have abolished the common law rule (Rule 100) whereby legitimation by subsequent marriage is governed by the law of the father's domicile at the time of the child's birth and at the time of the subsequent marriage: see *post*, para. 20–049.

it be permissible for an English court to derive a multilateral rule from a unilateral one contained in a statute.

1–045   (4) *Self-limiting statutes.* A statute may provide that some of its provisions apply only to British citizens, or to British ships, or to the capital city, or on Sundays, or during the close season for various classes of game birds, or to certain kinds of employees. Such "self-limiting provisions" as they have been called are clearly not rules of the conflict of laws whether multilateral or unilateral. They limit the application of the statute to certain persons, things, events, times or places connected in a specified way with the country whose legislature enacted the statute. If they are contained in a United Kingdom statute applying to England, they should apply only when it has first been decided that English domestic law applies, unless the statute provides otherwise. If they are contained in a foreign statute, the English court should apply the statute with its self-limiting provisions, otherwise it will distort the meaning of the statute and apply it where, under the terms of the statute itself, it is inapplicable.[11] If an English court finds that a foreign statute is inapplicable because of its self-limiting provisions, it should apply those statutory provisions or common law rules of the foreign law which, under that law, are applicable in that situation.

1–046   A statute from the field of labour law may be cited as an example of a self-limiting statute in English law. Section 196 of the Employment Rights Act 1996, re-enacting earlier legislation, provides that certain provisions of that Act do not apply where under his contract of employment the employee ordinarily works outside Great Britain.[12]

1–047   Although the distinction between them is plain enough in principle, it is not always easy to distinguish between unilateral conflict rules and self-limiting provisions; nor has any writer succeeded in formulating a satisfactory test for distinguishing between them. One writer suggests that if the statute uses terminology which is recognised in the conflict of laws, such as domicile or place of celebration of a marriage, then it enacts a unilateral conflict rule but if it uses terminology which is not so recognised, such as place of work, then it enacts a self-limiting provision.[13] But this is not entirely satisfactory, because the words used in the statute are surely less significant than the substance of the matter.

1–048   If a statute is expressed in general terms without any self-limiting provisions, courts are sometimes willing to read such provisions into it under the guise of interpreting the statute. This is true whether the statute forms part of the court's own law or of foreign law. This was one reason (not the only one) why the Privy Council, sitting on appeal from the New Zealand Court of Appeal, held that a New Zealand borrower could not take advantage of a

---

[11] *Adamastos Shipping Co. v. Anglo-Saxon Petroleum Co.* [1959] A.C. 133 is not contrary to this submission, because the foreign statute there in question had been incorporated in an English contract and therefore had to be interpreted as part of the contract and not applied as foreign law. The self-limiting provisions of the statute were held by a bare majority of the House of Lords to be inconsistent with the other terms of the contract and therefore had to be rejected in order to make sense of the whole. For the difference between the incorporation of a foreign statute and the application of foreign law, see *post*, paras. 32–086 *et seq.*

[12] For discussion of the predecessors of this enactment, see F. A. Mann (1966) 82 L.Q.R. 316; Hughes (1967) 83 L.Q.R. 180; Unger (1967) 83 L.Q.R. 427, 428–433; F. A. Mann (1972–73) 46 B.Y.I.L. 117, 136–137. See also *post*, Rule 182. For another example of a self-limiting provision, see the Unfair Contract Terms Act 1977, s.26.

[13] Unger (1967) 83 L.Q.R. 427, 429 n. 6.

Victorian statute which purported to reduce the rate of interest on certain mortgages.[14] It was one reason why an English court held that the general words in section 2 of the Marriage Act 1949 applied only to marriages between parties domiciled in England.[15] It was also one reason why the New York Court of Appeals held that an Ontario statute exonerating the driver of a car from liability for personal injuries to a gratuitous passenger did not apply to a motor accident in Ontario when the parties were New Yorkers: the statute, it was thought, was intended to protect Ontario drivers and their insurance companies, not New York ones.[16] This method of implying self-limiting provisions in statutes is very far from being new. From the thirteenth century to the middle of the nineteenth century, *i.e.* during the era of the statutists, it dominated the theory and practice of the conflict of laws. The meagreness of the results achieved by the statutists should be warning enough to show that it is a method to be used with caution.[17]

(5) *Overriding statutes.* Statutes of the fifth class are those which must be **1–049** applied regardless of the normal rules of the conflict of laws, because the statute says so. Since all the examples of overriding statutes to be discussed below are taken from the law of contract, it should be pointed out at the outset of the discussion that, according to standard doctrine in the conflict of laws, a statute does not normally apply to a contract unless it forms part of the governing law of the contract, or unless (being a statute in force in the forum) it is procedural. This was true at common law *e.g.* of Stamp Acts,[18] statutes affecting the validity of wagering contracts,[19] statutes reducing or otherwise regulating the rate of interest,[20] statutes providing for moratoria[21] or abrogating gold clauses.[22] It is also (subject to exceptions discussed in connection with Rule 177) the general rule under the EEC Convention on the Law Applicable to Contractual Obligations ("the Rome Convention"), which has been given effect in the United Kingdom by the Contracts (Applicable Law) Act 1990. Overriding statutes are an exception to the general rule that statutes only apply if they form part of the applicable law. One of the main reasons for the overriding character of such legislation is that otherwise the intention of

---

[14] *Mount Albert Borough Council v. Australasian etc., Life Assurance Society Ltd.* [1938] A.C. 224, 236–239, 243 (P.C.). *Cf. Wanganui-Rangitikei Electric Power Board v. Australian Mutual Provident Society* (1934) 50 C.L.R. 581.

[15] *Pugh v. Pugh* [1951] P. 482; see *ante*, para. 1–037.

[16] *Babcock v. Jackson*, 12 N.Y. 2d. 473, 191 N.E. 2d. 279, 284 (1963); see *post*, para. 35–004. This is perhaps the least convincing part of the judgment.

[17] One of the *quaestiones famosissimae* discussed by the statutists was the English rule of primogeniture. They eventually decided that if the English "statute" said that land descended to the eldest son, the statute was real, but if it said that the eldest son succeeded to the land, it was personal. See Beale, Vol. 3, pp. 1890–1891.

[18] *Royal Exchange Assurance v. Vega* [1902] 2 K.B. 384 (C.A.); *Norske Atlas Insurance Co. Ltd. v. London General Insurance Co. Ltd.* (1927) 28 Ll.L.R. 104; *Maritime Insurance Co. Ltd. v. Assekuranz Union von 1865* (1935) 52 Ll.L.R. 16.

[19] *Robinson v. Bland* (1760) 2 Burr. 1077; *Quarrier v. Colston* (1842) 1 Ph. 147; *Saxby v. Fulton* [1909] 2 K.B. 208 (C.A.); and see *Moulis v. Owen* [1907] 1 K.B. 746 (C.A.). See *post*, Rule 199.

[20] *Mount Albert Borough Council v. Australasian, etc., Life Assurance Society Ltd.* [1938] A.C. 224 (P.C.); *Barcelo v. Electrolytic Zinc Co. of Australasia Ltd.* (1932) 48 C.L.R. 391; *Wanganui-Rangitikei Electric Power Board v. Australian Mutual Provident Society* (1934) 50 C.L.R. 581.

[21] *Re Helbert Wagg & Co. Ltd.* [1956] Ch. 323.

[22] *R. v. International Trustee for the Protection of Bondholders A.G.* [1937] A.C. 500. See *post*, Rule 208.

the legislature to regulate certain contractual matters could be frustrated if it were open to the parties to choose some foreign law to govern their contract.[23]

1–050   Laws of this kind are referred to as "mandatory rules" or *lois de police* or *lois d'application immédiate*.[24] Where such legislation is part of the law of the forum it applies because it is interpreted as applying to all cases within its scope. Thus in contract cases, United Kingdom legislation will be applied to affect a contract governed by foreign law if on its true construction the legislation is intended to override the general principle that legislation relating to contracts is presumed to apply only to contracts governed by the law of a part of the United Kingdom. Article 7(2) of the Rome Convention provides that nothing in the Convention is to restrict the application of the rules of the law of the forum in a situation where they are mandatory irrespective of the law otherwise applicable to the contract.

1–051   Mandatory rules which are not part of the law of the forum or of the applicable law are not normally applied by the English court.[25] It has, however, been suggested in literature and case law on the continent that the forum may take account of foreign mandatory rules even if they do not form part of the applicable law.[26] This suggestion is reflected in Article 7(1) of the Rome Convention, which provides for the application of the mandatory rules of a country other than that of the forum or the *lex causae* if the situation has a close connection with that country. The United Kingdom exercised its right of reservation to Article 7(1) when it signed the Rome Convention, and accordingly this provision is not in force in the United Kingdom.[27]

1–052   A first example of an overriding statute is taken from the Defence Regulations 1939 made under section 3(1) of the Emergency Powers (Defence) Act 1939, which were considered in the leading case of *Boissevain v. Weil*.[28] These made it an offence for any British subject (except an authorised dealer) to borrow foreign currency without Treasury permission and consequently made a contract concluded in contravention of this prohibition illegal and void. The defendant, a British subject involuntarily resident in Monaco during the war, borrowed a sum of French francs from the plaintiff, a Dutchman also so resident, and promised to repay him in sterling as soon as the law of England would allow her to do so. In the Court of Appeal Denning L.J. held that the plaintiff could not recover, because the governing law of the contract was English law and therefore the statute applied and rendered it illegal. But the House of Lords held that the statute applied regardless of the governing law

---

[23] *Irish Shipping Ltd. v. Commercial Union Assurance Co. plc* [1991] 2 Q.B. 206, 220–221 (C.A.), discussing, but not deciding, the territorial scope of the Third Parties (Rights Against Insurers) Act 1930; see paras. 35–042 *et seq.*, *post*.

[24] Batiffol and Lagarde, Vol. 1, pp. 425–430, Vol. 2, pp. 280–281; Fawcett [1990] C.L.J. 44.

[25] *Cf. Kleinwort, Sons & Co. v. Ungarische Baumwolle Industrie A.G.* [1939] 2 K.B. 678 (C.A.), subject to a possible exception in the case of illegality under the law of the place of performance, on which see paras. 32–141 *et seq.*, *post*. See also Lipstein, in *Mélanges Zajtay* (1982), pp. 357–378.

[26] See Batiffol and Lagarde, Vol. 2, pp. 280–281.

[27] Contracts (Applicable Law) Act 1990, s.2(3). But there are other provisions of the Rome Convention which are in force and which require the application of mandatory foreign rules irrespective of the applicable law (see Art. 5(2) on the application, in consumer contracts, of the law of the habitual residence of the consumer) or irrespective of the chosen law (Art. 3(3), Art. 6(1)). See Rules 175, 181 and 182, *post*.

[28] [1949] 1 K.B. 482 (C.A.); [1950] A.C. 327.

of the contract.[29] Of course it was immaterial in this case that the illegality happened to be imposed by a statute. Similar results have been reached when the illegality is imposed by a rule of common law, *e.g.* the rule that champertous contracts,[30] contracts in restraint of trade[31] or contracts involving trading with the enemy[32] or breaking the laws of a friendly foreign country[33] are illegal.

Section 204(1) of the Employment Rights Act 1996 provides that "for the **1–053** purposes of this Act it is immaterial whether the law which (apart from this Act) governs any person's employment is the law of the United Kingdom, or of a part of the United Kingdom, or not."[34] Of course this does not mean that the Act applies to all contracts of employment in the world, regardless of their connection with the United Kingdom. (We have already seen that section 196 of the Act provides that certain of its provisions do not apply when the employee ordinarily works outside Great Britain[35]). But it does mean that the draftsman, instead of enacting (or leaving it to be assumed) that the Act applies only when the applicable law of the contract of employment is the law of some part of the United Kingdom, has cut across the normal rules of the conflict of laws and laid down his own rules for the application of the Act. His method has two advantages. It prevents the parties evading the Act by choosing foreign law as the governing law of the contract of employment. It also secures the benefits of the Act to employees who work here for foreign employers and whose contracts of employment might well be governed by foreign law.

Further examples of these overriding or peremptory provisions may be **1–054** taken from the law of consumer protection and from insurance law. The Unfair Contract Terms Act 1977[36] lays down, in the interests of consumers, certain mandatory rules. The parties to certain contracts cannot contract out of these rules[37] and to prevent them from doing so indirectly by agreeing that some foreign law should be the applicable law of their contract, section 27 (2) provides that the Act has effect notwithstanding any contract term purporting to apply the law of some country outside the United Kingdom, if either of two conditions laid down in the subsection is satisfied.[38] In *Akai Pty. Ltd. v. People's Insurance Co. Ltd.*[39] the New South Wales subsidiary of a Japanese multi-national took out with a Singaporean insurance company a policy covering credit risks in Australia. The policy was expressed to be governed

---

[29] Hence, conversely, if the defendant had not been a British subject, the Defence Regulations would not have applied even if English law had been the law of the contract: the overriding statute also carried its own self-limitation.

[30] *Grell v. Levy* (1864) 10 C.B. (N.S.) 73.

[31] *Rousillon v. Rousillon* (1880) 14 Ch.D. 351.

[32] *Dynamit A.G. v. Rio Tinto Co.* [1918] A.C. 260.

[33] *Regazzoni v. K. C. Sethia, Ltd.* [1958] A.C. 301.

[34] See the articles cited in n. 12, *supra*. And see *post*, Rule 182.

[35] *Ante*, para. 1–046.

[36] The Act repeals and re-enacts (with some modifications) s.55A of the Sale of Goods Act 1893, added by s.5(1) of the Supply of Goods (Implied Terms) Act 1973, but it is much wider in scope. On s.5(1) of the Act of 1973, see F. A. Mann (1974) 90 L.Q.R. 42; (1977) 26 I.C.L.Q. 903. On s.27 of the Act of 1977, see F. A. Mann (1978) 27 I.C.L.Q. 661.

[37] Unless the contract is an "international supply contract" as defined in s.26. That definition follows closely the definition in the Uniform Laws on International Sales Act 1967, on which see *post*, para. 33–101.

[38] These are (a) that the term appears to have been imposed wholly or mainly for the purpose of enabling the party imposing it to evade the application of the Act; or (b) that in the making of the contract one party dealt as consumer and was then habitually resident in the United Kingdom and the essential steps necessary for the making of the contract were taken there.

[39] (1996) 188 C.L.R. 418.

by English law and provided for the exclusive jurisdiction of the English courts. Australian insurance legislation invalidated defences which would otherwise be available to the insurers at common law or under the terms of the contract (and which were available under English law), and provided that it applied where the applicable law of the contract was the law of an Australian state: it also provided that where, but for any express choice of foreign law, the applicable law would have been the law of an Australian state, the applicable law was to be regarded as the law of that state. The High Court of Australia held that the effect of the legislation was to override the choice of English law and to invalidate the choice of English jurisdiction, and to enable the insured to sue in New South Wales so as to prevent the insurer relying on common law and contractual defences. But in subsequent English proceedings by the insurer for a declaration that it was not liable to the insured it was held that the English court's jurisdiction by virtue of the contractual submission was not affected by the decision of the High Court of Australia, and that there was no legal basis for the English court to give effect to the public policy of Australia reflected in its legislation.[40]

1–055   Other examples of overriding statutes are furnished by provisions invalidating contractual terms as a sanction for the contravention of statutory requirements, *e.g.* concerning the disclosure of facts or the adequate disclosure of contractual terms by one party to another. Thus, hire-purchase legislation has been applied in Scotland[41] when the contract was entered into in Scotland, though it was governed by the law of another country. The reason was that the statute was directed against the making of contracts in a form which did not sufficiently safeguard the interests of the economically weaker party. It has also been held in Scotland[42] that the provisions of the Truck Act[43] against deductions from wages applied if the deductions were made in Scotland, irrespective of the applicable law of the contract. Section 44 of the Patents Act 1977 renders void certain conditions or terms whereby a patentee abuses his monopoly power by, for example, requiring a customer or a licensee to acquire other products as a condition of the supply of the patented product or of a licence to work the invention. In *Chiron Corp. v. Organon Teknika Ltd. (No. 2)*[44] it was held that the section applies to contracts or licences relating to United Kingdom patents, irrespective of whether the contract or licence is governed by English law or foreign law: the object of the legislation is to prevent a person who obtains the privilege of monopoly protection under a United Kingdom patent from enforcing his patent rights if he has abused them. That being the object, it was wholly irrelevant what the applicable law of the contract was; it was the effect of the contract relative to the United Kingdom patent which was decisive.

1–056   All the examples of overriding statutes which have so far been discussed might be described as crystallised rules of public policy, because they lay down mandatory rules which the parties cannot contract out of, directly or indirectly. The remaining examples about to be discussed are taken from the

---

[40] *Akai Pty. Ltd. v. People's Insurance Co. Ltd.* [1998] 1 Lloyd's Rep. 90; Reynolds [1998] L.M.C.L.Q. 1.

[41] *English v. Donnelly*, 1958 S.C. 494 (not followed in *Hong Kong Shanghai (Shipping) Ltd. v. The Cavalry* [1987] H.K.L.R. 287); *cf. Kay's Leasing Corporation Pty. Ltd. v. Fletcher* (1964) 116 C.L.R. 124; *Att. Gen.'s Reference No. 1 of 1987* (1987) 47 S.A.S.R. 152.

[42] *Duncan v. Motherwell Bridge and Engineering Co. Ltd.*, 1952 S.C. 131.

[43] Truck Act 1831, ss.2, 3.

[44] [1993] F.S.R. 567 (C.A.).

law of international transport. They all express the public policy which is inherent in the unification of international transport law. The statutes have this in common with the other examples, namely, that they apply regardless of the applicable law of the contract. Section 1(1) of the Carriage by Air Act 1961, section 1 of the Carriage of Goods by Road Act 1965, section 1(2) of the Carriage of Goods by Sea Act 1971, section 1(1) of the Carriage of Passengers by Road 1974, and section 183(1) of the Merchant Shipping Act 1995 provide that the provisions of the international conventions set out in the Schedules to those Acts shall have the force of law in the United Kingdom.[45] The conventions all contain provisions which determine when they are applicable. These provisions make use of factors quite different from the applicable law of the contract of carriage. The applicable law of the contract is thus generally irrelevant in the law of international transport, where the matter is regulated by an international convention; and the statutory provisions mentioned above apply whether the applicable law of the contract is that of some part of the United Kingdom or of some foreign country.

Thus in *Corocraft Ltd. v. Pan American Airways Inc.*,[46] a contract was made **1–057** in New York between an American consignor and an American airline for the carriage of diamonds from New York to London. The diamonds were stolen at London airport by a servant of the carrier. When sued by the consignee for non-delivery, the carrier argued that the Warsaw Convention set out in the Carriage by Air Acts did not apply, because the governing law of the contract was that of New York. This argument was rejected on the ground that the Convention had been given the force of law in the United Kingdom by statute.[47] Similarly in *The Hollandia*[48] a machine was shipped from Scotland to the Dutch West Indies, on a Dutch vessel to the Netherlands, and on a Norwegian vessel for the remainder of the voyage. The machine was seriously damaged while being unloaded in the Dutch West Indies. The bill of lading provided for Dutch law and Dutch jurisdiction, and contained a limitation of liability, the effect of which was that the liability of the carriers would be limited to about £250. It was held that the Hague-Visby Rules (the effect of which was to limit the liability of the carriers to about £11,000), which are scheduled to the Carriage of Goods by Sea Act 1971 and which have "the force of law,"[49] applied in proceedings in England notwithstanding the choice of Dutch law as the governing law.[50] These statutes are therefore examples of overriding statutes, because they must be applied regardless of the normal rules of the conflict of laws.

(6) *Self-denying statutes.* Self-denying statutes are the opposite of over- **1–058** riding statutes: they do not apply in the circumstances where the statute says

---

[45] See Rules 189 and 190. See also International Transport Conventions Act 1983, s.1(1), which does not schedule the conventions, but whose effect is the same.

[46] [1969] 1 Q.B. 616.

[47] At pp. 630–631. The point was not argued in the C.A.

[48] [1982] Q.B. 872 (C.A.), affd. [1983] 1 A.C. 565, on which see F. A. Mann (1983) 99 L.Q.R. 376, (1984) 100 L.Q.R. 369; Jaffey (1984) 100 L.Q.R. 198. See also *The Antares (Nos. 1 and 2)* [1987] 1 Lloyd's Rep. 424 (C.A.), on which see F. A. Mann (1987) 103 L.Q.R. 523.

[49] s.1(3).

[50] In the House of Lords the principal question was the applicability of a clause conferring jurisdiction on the Dutch courts, and it seems to have been accepted that the Court of Appeal was right in holding that the 1971 Act overrode the choice of law: see [1983] 1 A.C. 565, 573. The actual decision would now probably be different: see *post*, para. 12–116.

they shall not apply, even though they would apply under the normal rules of the conflict of laws. The only example of such a statute in English law appears to be section 27(1) of the Unfair Contract Terms Act 1977, which is the converse of section 27(2). Section 27(2) provides, as we have seen,[51] that the Act has effect notwithstanding any contract term purporting to apply the law of some country outside the United Kingdom. Section 27(1)[52] provides that where the applicable law of a contract is the law of any part of the United Kingdom only by choice of the parties (and apart from that choice would be the law of some country outside the United Kingdom), certain provisions of the Act do not operate as part of the law applicable to the contract. Thus, if the applicable law of the contract would have been the law of some foreign country, because the transaction is most closely connected with that system of law, but the parties choose the law of some part of the United Kingdom as the applicable law, the mandatory rules of the Act do not apply to the contract.

1–059   The English and Scottish Law Commissioners explained why it was necessary to include section 27(1) in the Act.[53] They pointed out that the parties to contracts of which the applicable law would otherwise be the law of some country other than England or Scotland often choose English law or Scots law as the applicable law of their contracts, sometimes by an express term to the effect,[54] more often through the medium of an arbitration clause.[55] The effect of imposing the controls contained in the Act in relation to these contracts might well be to discourage foreign businessmen from agreeing to arbitrate their disputes in England or Scotland. The suggestion was that this would strike a heavy blow at the City of London as a centre for international arbitration.[56]

1–060   **Meaning of "country."** This word has from long usage become almost a term of art among English-speaking writers on the conflict of laws, and it is vitally important to appreciate exactly what it means. It was defined by Dicey as "the whole of a territory subject under one sovereign to one body of law." He suggested that a better expression might be "law district": but this phrase has never found much favour with English-speaking writers, who prefer the more familiar word "country." England, Scotland, Northern Ireland, the Isle of Man, Jersey, Guernsey, Alderney, Sark, each British colony, each of the Australian states and each of the Canadian provinces is a separate country in the sense of the conflict of laws, though not one of them is a State known to public international law. However, for some purposes larger units than these may constitute countries. Thus, the United Kingdom is one country for the purposes of the law of negotiable instruments,[57] Great Britain is one country for most purposes of the law of companies,[58] Australia is one country for the

---

[51] *Ante*, para. 1–054.
[52] As amended by Contracts (Applicable Law) Act 1990, s.5 and Sched. 4.
[53] *Second Report on Exemption Clauses*, Law Com. No. 69, para. 232.
[54] See Rule 173.
[55] See *post*, paras. 32–092 *et seq.*
[56] Dr. F. A. Mann criticised the provisions of s.27(1): (1977) 26 I.C.L.Q. 903, 907–909, 911; (1978) 27 I.C.L.Q. 661; but he did not cite the Law Commissions' explanation quoted in the text.
[57] Bills of Exchange Act 1882.
[58] Companies Act 1985.

purposes of the law of marriage[59] and matrimonial causes,[60] and Canada is one country for the purposes of the law of divorce.[61]

Nor is there any doubt that for most purposes of the conflict of laws each **1–061** State within the United States is a "country." Thus a contract will be governed by the law of New York or Arizona, but not by the law of the United States; and a judgment of the New York State court will be recognised as a New York judgment, and not as an American judgment. In *Adams v. Cape Industries plc*,[62] however, an issue arose as to whether, for the purposes of the enforcement in England of a judgment of a United States federal court sitting in Texas, the residence or presence of the judgment debtors in another State of the Union, Illinois, amounted to residence or presence also in the law district in which the federal court sat, namely Texas. The federal court (and not the State court in Texas) had jurisdiction because of the parties' "diversity of citizenship," but it exercised jurisdiction under the rules applicable in the State in which it sat, and (except as regards procedure) it did not apply federal law to the case, but State law. But the federal court was a court established by the United States, and not by the State of Texas. In these circumstances, Scott J. decided that the United States as a whole was the "country" for the purposes of the jurisdiction of the federal court. The Court of Appeal did not find it necessary to decide the question, but indicated that it inclined to the view that Scott J. was correct.[63]

On the other hand, Wales is not a country, because its system of law is **1–062** the same as that of England. Nor is it necessary that a country in the sense of the conflict of laws should have a separate legislature. For example, the Australian Capital Territory and the District of Columbia have no such legislature and yet they are countries: and Northern Ireland did not cease to be a country when its legislature was suspended in 1972.[64]

The reader should be warned that although, as mentioned above, "country" **1–063** has become almost a term of art among English-speaking writers on the conflict of laws, yet the practice of Parliamentary draftsmen is far from uniform. For Parliament, when enacting rules of the conflict of laws, refers sometimes to a "country,"[65] sometimes to a "territory"[66] and sometimes to a "place."[67] This usually causes no confusion, because the meaning is always the same. Where it is not the same, Parliament has endeavoured to distinguish the concepts.[68]

Meaning of "State." The word State has various meanings. Whatever **1–064** may be its meaning in public international law or constitutional law, in this book it means the whole of a territory subject to one sovereign power. Thus, to give some examples, the United Kingdom and Colonies, France, the United States, and each of the independent members of the Commonwealth, whether it does or does not form part of Her Majesty's dominions, is a State. But

---

[59] Marriage Act 1961 (Aus.).
[60] Family Law Act 1975, ss.39(3) and (4), 103 (Aus.).
[61] Divorce Act R.S.C. 1970, c.D–8, ss.5(1)(*a*), 14 (Can.).
[62] [1990] Ch. 433 (Scott J. and C.A.).
[63] *Ibid.* at pp. 484–492 (Scott J.), 550–557 (C.A.).
[64] Northern Ireland (Temporary Provisions) Act 1972.
[65] *e.g* Arbitration Act 1996, s.103(2); Legitimacy Act 1976, s.3; Unfair Contract Terms Act 1977, s.27.
[66] *e.g.* Wills Act 1963, s.1; Family Law Act 1986, s.49.
[67] *e.g.* Bills of Exchange Act 1882, s.72; British Nationality Act 1981, s.47(2).
[68] Family Law Act 1986, s.49; Rule 79, *post.*

England, Scotland, New York, Ontario, and New South Wales are not States nor is any British colony or dependent (or overseas) territory.

1–065   A State may or may not coincide with a country in the sense of the conflict of laws. Unitary States like Sweden, the Netherlands and New Zealand, where the law is the same throughout the State, are "countries" in this sense. But composite States like the United Kingdom, the United States, Australia and Canada are not.

1–066   **Meaning of "foreign."** Because of this distinction between "country" and "State," the word "foreign" as used in this book normally means simply "not English." It does not mean foreign in the political sense. Thus the expression "foreign country" means any country except England, and applies as much to Scotland or Northern Ireland as to France or Italy; and the expressions "foreign judgment" and "foreign arbitration award" mean judgments or awards given or made outside England.

1–067   **Geographical expressions.** A writer on the conflict of laws is constantly making use of certain geographical expressions which he assumes are familiar to his readers and which he endeavours always to use in the same sense. But since this assumption may not always be well founded, it seems desirable to supply some definitions.[69]

1–068   *England* includes Wales and the town of Berwick-on-Tweed,[70] and adjacent islands, such as the Isle of Wight or Anglesey or Lundy Island,[71] and the territorial waters adjacent thereto.[72]

1–069   *Great Britain* means England as above defined, and Scotland and its adjacent territorial waters. It includes the islands of Orkney and Shetland, the Hebrides and Rockall[73] which (in spite of their great distance from the mainland) are part of Scotland. The breadth of the territorial waters of the United Kingdom is now 12 miles.[74]

---

[69] See also Interpretation Act 1978, Sched. 1, "British Islands", "England", "United Kingdom". The use of the expression "British Isles", which means the same as "British Islands", is now virtually obsolete in statutes.

[70] Wales and Berwick Act 1746, s.3. However, s.4 of the Welsh Language Act 1967 provided that references to "England" in future Acts of Parliament should no longer include Wales: see now Interpretation Act 1978, Sched. 3, Pt. I. But it seems desirable to adhere to Dicey's definition for reasons of convenience and especially of brevity. It would be cumbersome to have to add "or Wales" after "England" and "or Welsh" after "English" every time those words were used.

[71] See *Harman v. Bolt* (1931) 47 T.L.R. 219, with reference to Lundy.

[72] See the Territorial Waters Jurisdiction Act 1878; the Continental Shelf Act 1964, s.1(7), as amended by the Oil and Gas Enterprise Act 1982, and S.I. 1964 No. 697; and other orders in *Halsbury's Statutory Instruments*, vol. 22 (1996), p. 275. The Orders affecting areas designated by the Continental Shelf Act 1964, s.1(7), no longer apply to those areas which are now within territorial waters as a result of the Territorial Sea Act 1987: S.I. 1987 No. 1265. The extent of British jurisdiction is a matter to be determined by the Crown, represented by the Secretary of State for Home Affairs, and is properly presented to the court by the Attorney-General: *The Fagernes* [1927] P. 311 (C.A.). See *R. v. Kent Justices, ex p. Lye* [1967] 2 Q.B. 153; *Post Office v. Estuary Radio Ltd.* [1968] 2 Q.B. 740 (C.A.) (Thames Estuary). On the legal status of the sea-bed see *Shetland Salmon Farmers Assn. v. Crown Estate Commissioners*, 1991 S.L.T. 166.

[73] Island of Rockall Act 1972, s.1.

[74] Territorial Sea Act 1987, s.1; Territorial Waters Order in Council 1964 (made under the royal prerogative), as amended. See also S.I. 1989 No. 482 (Straits of Dover and Isle of Man); S.I. 1997 No. 278 (Jersey). On the compatibility of the baselines with European Community law see Case C–146/89 *Commission v. United Kingdom* [1991] E.C.R. I–3533.

The United Kingdom means Great Britain and Northern Ireland and their **1–070** adjacent territorial waters.[75] It does not include the Republic of Ireland.[76] Nor for historical reasons does it include the Channel Islands or the Isle of Man.[77]

British Islands means the United Kingdom, the Channel Islands and the Isle **1–071** of Man and their adjacent territorial waters.

The Commonwealth is used in its widest sense to include all territories **1–072** which form part of the dominions of the Crown or which acknowledge the Queen as Head of the Commonwealth, and the territorial waters adjacent thereto.[78] It includes not only the older Dominions but also the Republics and other independent States which, for one reason or another, have ceased to be part of Her Majesty's dominions.[79] It also includes the remaining British Dependent territories.[80] But it does not include the Republic of Ireland.[81]

The United Kingdom is of course part of the Commonwealth as above **1–073** defined. But sometimes it is necessary to distinguish between the United Kingdom and the rest of the Commonwealth. This is done by referring either to "any part of the Commonwealth outside the United Kingdom" or to "the Commonwealth overseas." Either of these expressions as used in this book includes the dependencies of the United Kingdom (*i.e.* the Channel Islands and the Isle of Man) and the Colonies.

Connecting factors. Like any other legal subject, the conflict of laws has **1–074** its technical terms, some of which must now be explained.

The rules of the conflict of laws are, traditionally, expressed in terms of juridical concepts or categories and localising elements or connecting factors.[82] Typical rules of the conflict of laws state that succession to immovables is governed by the law of the *situs*; that the formal validity of a marriage is governed by the law of the place of celebration; and that capacity to marry is governed by the law of each party's antenuptial domicile. In these examples, succession to immovables, formal validity of marriage and capacity to marry are the categories, while *situs*, place of celebration and domicile are the connecting factors.

The *lex causae* is a convenient shorthand expression denoting the law **1–075** (usually but not necessarily foreign) which governs the question. It is used in contradistinction to the *lexi fori*, which always means the domestic law of the

---

[75] Royal and Parliamentary Titles Act 1927, s.2(1); Interpretation Act 1978, Sched. 1. References to Ireland or to the United Kingdom in pre–1922 statutes do not now usually include the Republic of Ireland: see the Irish Free State (Consequential Adaptation of Enactments) Order, S.R. & O. 1923, No. 405; and see the Ireland Act 1949. See also Roberts-Wray, *Commonwealth and Colonial Law* (1966), pp. 32–35. As to Northern Irish territorial waters, a resident magistrate held that they belong to the Republic of Ireland, but his decision was reversed by the C.A.: *D.P.P. for Northern Ireland v. McNeill* [1975] N.Ir. 177.

[76] Ireland Act 1949, s.1(3).

[77] On the status of the Channel Islands see *Rover International Ltd. v. Cannon Film Sales Ltd.* [1987] 1 W.L.R. 1597; *Chloride Industrial Batteries Ltd. v. F. & W. Freight Ltd.* [1989] 1 W.L.R. 823 (C.A.).

[78] See Roberts-Wray, *op. cit.*, pp. 1–29, 86–89. The definition there suggested (p. 14) seems too complicated for the purposes of this book.

[79] *Cf.* British Nationality Act 1981, Sched. 3.

[80] *Cf.* British Nationality Act 1981, Sched. 6.

[81] Ireland Act 1949, s.1(1). Pakistan and South Africa have re-joined the Commonwealth: Pakistan Act 1990; South Africa Act 1995.

[82] This expression (first suggested by Falconbridge) seems the best English equivalent of the French and German technical terms "point de rattachement" and "Anknüpfungspunkt."

forum, *i.e.* (if the forum is English) English law. The *lex causae* may be more specifically denoted by a variety of expressions, usually in Latin, such as the *lex domicilii* (law of the domicile),[83] *lex patriae* (law of the nationality), *lex loci contractus* (law of the country where a contract is made),[84] *lex loci solutionis* (law of the country where a contract is to be performed or where a debt is to be paid),[85] *lex loci delicti* (law of the country where a tort is committed),[86] *lex situs* (law of the country where a thing is situated),[87] *lex loci celebrationis* (law of the country where a marriage is celebrated),[88] *lex loci actus* (law of the country where a legal act takes place), *lex monetae* (law of the country in whose currency a debt or other legal obligation is expressed). The terms of *lex loci disgraziae* (law of the place where a bill of exchange is dishonoured) and *lex loci stabuli* (law of the place where a motor car is garaged) are used only in jest.

1–076   **Determination of the connecting factor.** A fundamental problem in the conflict of laws is whether the connecting factor should be determined by the *lex fori* or by the *lex causae*. Since the determination of the *lex causae* depends on the determination of the connecting factor, it is no longer controversial among learned writers that the connecting factor should be determined by the *lexi fori*.[89] Although the reported cases are all concerned with domicile, it may be assumed that English law has adopted this prevailing opinion, and that, for the purpose of an English conflict rule, the connecting factor will be determined by English law as the *lexi fori*.[90]

1–077   The proposition that the *lex fori* determines the connecting factor has two related but distinct aspects. The first is that the *lexi fori* defines what it means, *e.g.* by domicile at common law[91]; the second is that it also determines whether, so defined, the connecting factor links a given issue with one legal system or with another.[92]

1–078   For the purposes of an English conflict rule, English law defines what domicile means, and also whether a person is or was domiciled in England or in some foreign country. There is therefore nothing to prevent an English court from deciding that, for the purposes *e.g.* of succession to movables, a Frenchman domiciled in France has acquired an English domicile of choice, even though French law may consider that he has not lost his French domicile,[93] or that an Englishwoman domiciled in England has acquired a domicile of choice

---

[83] See Rules 4–16 with reference to the domicile of individuals, and Rule 152 with reference to the domicile of corporations.

[84] As to where a contract is made, see *post*, para. 11–155.

[85] As to where a contract is to be performed, see *post*, paras. 11–173 *et seq.*; 11–250 *et seq.*

[86] As to where a tort is committed, see *post*, paras. 35–085 *et seq.*

[87] As to the *situs* of things, see Rule 112.

[88] As to where a marriage is celebrated, see *post*, para. 17–013.

[89] Many of the writers who discuss the determination of the connecting factor do so in connection with their discussion of the problem of characterisation: see Robertson, pp. 104–117; Lorenzen, pp. 97–100, 123–127; Falconbridge, pp. 129–133. But the two questions are really quite distinct. What is significant for present purposes is that even writers who advocate characterisation in accordance with the *lex causae* admit that the *lex fori* should define the connecting factor: see *e.g.* Wolff, s.131.

[90] This passage was approved in *The T.S. Havprins* [1983] 2 Lloyd's Rep. 356.

[91] But whether a person is domiciled in a foreign country for the purposes of the Civil Jurisdiction and Judgments Act 1982 (as amended) may depend on the law of the foreign country: see *post*, para. 11–064.

[92] Kahn-Freund (1974) *Recueil des Cours*, III, pp.388–395.

[93] *Re Martin* [1900] P.211 (C.A.).

in France, even though French law may consider that she has not lost her English domicile.[94] Nor is there anything to prevent an English court from deciding that, for the purposes *e.g.* of divorce jurisdiction, a man is domiciled in England, even though a Scottish court has recently decided that, for the same purposes, he is domiciled in Scotland.[95]

There are three real exceptions, and one apparent exception, to the proposition that for the purposes of an English conflict rule the *lex fori* defines the connecting factor.   **1–079**

The first real exception is concerned with nationality. Nationality is an exception to the second of the two aspects of the proposition mentioned above, but not to the first. If the *lex fori* uses nationality as a connecting factor, it must define what it means by nationality, and say *e.g.* what is to happen when the person concerned has two or more nationalities or none, or is a national of a composite or "plurilegal" State like the United Kingdom, which comprises more than one country.[96] But the *lex fori* can never say whether a person is a national of a foreign State. That can only be done by the law of the State concerned.[97] This is not an exception that has much importance in the English conflict of laws, because there are very few English conflict rules that are expressed in terms of nationality.[98]   **1–080**

The second and third real exceptions are provided by statute. The Family Law Act 1986 provides that if either spouse was domiciled in a foreign country in the sense of that country's law, and it uses the concept of domicile as a ground of jurisdiction, a divorce or legal separation obtained in that country must be recognised in England.[99] The effect of the Civil Jurisdiction and Judgments Act 1982 (as amended) is that, where an individual is not domiciled (within the meaning of the Act) in the United Kingdom, in order to determine whether he is domiciled in another State which is a party to the 1968 Convention or the Lugano Convention, the English court must apply the law of that State.[1]   **1–081**

The apparent exception arises in connection with the doctrine of renvoi.[2] It can best be understood from an example. Suppose that a person dies intestate domiciled in France in the English sense, but in England in the French sense, leaving movables in England. In order to determine who is entitled to these movables, the English court will refer to French law as the law of the intestate's last domicile but, finding that French law would refer to English law because according to French law he was domiciled in England, it may   **1–082**

---

[94] *Re Annesley* [1926] Ch. 692; *contra, Re Johnson* [1903] 1 Ch. 821, but this case has been heavily criticised and is no longer law, see *post*, para. 4–013, n. 21. See also Rule 8, *post*.

[95] See *Wilson v. Wilson* (1872) 10 M. 573; *Wilson v. Wilson* (1872) L.R. 2 P. & D. 435.

[96] In *Re O'Keefe* [1940] Ch. 124 the English judge attempted to do this; he should have left it to the Italian expert witnesses to say what the *lex patriae* meant in the case of a British subject.

[97] *Stoeck v. Public Trustee* [1921] 2 Ch. 67, 78, 82; *Re Chamberlain's Settlement* [1921] 2 Ch. 533; *cf. Oppenheimer v. Cattermole* [1976] A.C. 249.

[98] For some rare examples, see Wills Act 1963, s.1, and Rule 135; Family Law Act 1986, s.46(1)(b)(iii), and Rule 79(1)(c). The latter is an example of nationality being used, not as a connecting factor, but as a jurisdictional factor; but the principle is the same.

[99] Family Law Act 1986, s.46(5). This again is an example of domicile being used, not as a connecting factor, but as a jurisdictional factor: but see *Lawrence v. Lawrence* [1985] Fam. 106, 133 (C.A.), *per* Purchas L.J. (a minority view). For recognition of foreign divorces and legal separations, see Rule 79.

[1] Civil Jurisdiction and Judgments Act 1982, Sched. 1, Art. 52; Sched. 3c, Art. 52. For corporations, *cf.* s.42(7). For domicile under the 1982 Act, see Rule 23, *post*.

[2] For renvoi, see Chap. 4, *post*.

then proceed to decide the case exactly as a French court would.[3] This is an apparent but not a real exception to the principle that, for the purposes of an English conflict rule, the *lex fori* must determine the connecting factor, because French law is being allowed to determine the question of domicile not for the purposes of an English conflict rule but for the purposes of a French conflict rule. The justification for allowing French law to do so is that it would be intolerable to accept a reference (renvoi) from French to English law if that reference was required by a French conflict rule expressed in terms *e.g.* of nationality, but not to do so if it was required by a French conflict rule expressed in terms of domicile in the French sense. To draw such a distinction would be to submit to the tyranny of labels.

1–083   **The name of the subject.** The branch of law whose nature we have been considering has been called by various names, of which the two most usual are the conflict of laws and private international law.

1–084   The term "conflict of laws" has won a great deal of authority by reason of its use by Huber, Story, Dicey, Beale and the American Law Institute's Restatements. It is not however completely satisfactory because it describes only that part of the subject which deals with the question of choice of law to the exclusion of the question of jurisdiction, which in England is an essential part of the subject. In civil law countries, the usual title for the subject is private international law, which has been preferred by a number of English writers, notably Westlake and Cheshire. Westlake's view was that the subject falls under international law, denoting "the department which treats of the selection to be made in each action between various national jurisdictions and laws."[4] One obvious objection to this use of the term "international" is that it is a very different employment of the word from its normal meaning in the phrase "international law" which denotes the law governing the relations between States.[5] Another objection is that questions can and do arise just as frequently between the laws of *e.g.* England and Scotland, Ontario and Quebec, New York and California or Victoria and New South Wales as they do between the laws of *e.g.* England and France or England and Germany and there is obviously nothing international about questions of the former kind. Wolff[6] observed, however, that since "both titles are used throughout the world and as nobody has found a better one, it hardly seems worth while to devote further thought to this merely terminological issue".

---

[3] *Re Annesley* [1926] Ch. 692. The evidence of French law in this case was that French law would refer to English law, not because the testatrix was domiciled in England in the French sense, but because she was a British subject; but this was erroneous, see *post*, para. 4–033, n. 95.

[4] Westlake, p. 5.

[5] For the relations between public and private international law, see Lipstein (1942) 27 Tr. Grot. Soc. 142; (1944) 29 *ib.* 51; Stevenson (1952) 52 Col.L.Rev. 561; Wortley (1954) *Recueil des Cours*, I. p. 245; Hambro (1962) *Recueil des Cours*, I, p. 1; Lipstein (1972) *Recueil des Cours*, I, pp. 167–194; Kahn-Freund (1974) *Recueil des Cours*, III, pp. 165–196; Collier, *Conflict of Laws* (2nd ed. 1994), pp. 387–396; McLachlan [1993] Hague Yb. Int. L. 125.

[6] p. 10.

CHAPTER 2

CHARACTERISATION AND THE INCIDENTAL QUESTION

A. CHARACTERISATION[1]

The problem of characterisation, also known as classification,[2] was "dis-   **2–001**
covered" independently and almost simultaneously by the German jurist
Kahn[3] and the French jurist Bartin[4] at the end of the nineteenth century, and
was introduced to American lawyers by Lorenzen in 1920[5] and to English
lawyers by Beckett in 1934.[6]

Nature of the problem. Characterisation is a fundamental problem in all   **2–002**
traditional systems of the conflict of laws, that is to say the systems applicable
in England and other European countries. It results from the fact that the rules
which have been evolved to deal with choice-of-law problems are expressed
in terms of juridical concepts or categories and localising elements or connecting factors.[7] This structure may be illustrated by considering some typical
rules of the English conflict of laws: "succession to immovables is governed
by the law of the *situs*"; "the formal validity of a marriage is governed by the
law of the place of celebration"; "capacity to marry is governed by the law of
the parties' domicile." In these examples, succession to immovables, formal
validity of marriage and capacity to marry are the categories, while *situs*,
place of celebration and domicile are the connecting factors.

    The problem of characterisation consists in determining which juridical   **2–003**
concept or category is appropriate in any given case. Assume, for example,
that it is claimed that a marriage is void because the parties did not have the

---

[1] Lorenzen, Chaps. 4 and 5; Beckett (1934) 15 B.Y.I.L. 46; Unger (1937) 19 Bell Yard 3;
Robertson, *Characterisation in the Conflict of Laws* (1940); Falconbridge, Chaps. 3–5; Cook,
Chap. 8; Cormack (1941) 14 So. Calif.L.Rev. 221–243; Lederman (1951) 29 Can. Bar Rev. 3,
168; Rabel, Vol. I, pp. 47–72; Bland (1957) 6 I.C.L.Q. 10; Inglis (1958) 74 L.Q.R. 493,
503–516; Ehrenzweig in Nadelmann, von Mehren and Hazard (eds.), *XXth Century Compar-
ative and Conflicts Law* (1961), pp. 395 *et seq.*; Turpin [1959] *Acta Juridica* 222; Kahn-Freund
(1974) *Recueil des Cours*, III, pp. 369–382; Dine [1983] Jur. Rev. 73; Forsyth (1998) 114
L.Q.R. 141. For the more extensive Continental literature, see Robertson, pp. xxv–xxix;
Lorenzen, Chap. 4; and particularly (in addition to citations elsewhere in this chapter) Neuner,
Der Sinn der Internationalprivatrechtlichen Norm (1932); Meriggi, "Saggio Critico sulle
Qualificazioni" (1932) 2 *Rivista Italiana di Diritto Internazionale Privato* 189, French transla-
tion in (1933) 28 *Revue de Droit International Privé* 201; Ago (1936) *Recueil des Cours*, IV,
p. 243; Niederer, *Die Frage der Qualifikation* (1940); Niederer, *Einführung in die allgemeinen
Lehren des Internationalen Privatrechts* (2nd ed. 1956), pp. 389–391; Wengler, *Festschrift für
Martin Wolff* (1952), pp. 337 *et seq.*; Rigaux, *La Théorie des Qualifications* (1956).
[2] "Qualification" is the term used by Continental writers.
[3] (1891) 30 Jhering's *Jahrbücher* 1, reprinted in *Abhandlungen* I (1928) 1–123.
[4] (1897) Clunet 225, 466, 720; *cf.* Bartin, *Principes de Droit International Privé* (1930), Vol. I,
pp. 221–239; Bartin (1930) *Recueil des Cours*, I, p. 565.
[5] (1920) 20 Col. L. Rev. 247; reprinted in Lorenzen, Chap. 4.
[6] (1934) 15 B.Y.I.L. 46.
[7] For the meaning of "connecting factors," see *ante*, paras. 1–074 *et seq.*

consent of their parents: should this be regarded as falling into the category "formal validity of a marriage" or should one take the view that it comes under "capacity to marry"? The answer could clearly determine the outcome of the case: this would be so if the law of the parties' domicile required them to obtain the consent of their parents, while the law of the place where the marriage was celebrated did not.

2–004   It might seem possible to solve the above problem simply on the basis of normal legal reasoning—though the untutored assumption of most lawyers that parental consent relates to capacity is not in fact the solution adopted by the English courts[8]—but the next problem may seem more difficult. Assume that a testator domiciled in England makes a will disposing of land in Utopia (such will not being made in contemplation of marriage) and subsequently marries. He dies shortly afterwards. Is the will revoked by the marriage? Under the law of England it will be, but we will assume that this is not the case under the law of Utopia. In such a situation, the answer to the question whether the will is revoked could depend on whether the issue is characterised as one relating to succession or to matrimonial law (proprietary consequences of marriage).[9]

2–005   It will be seen from the above examples that the problem of characterisation arises whenever a system of conflict of laws is based on categories and connecting factors. In such a system, it is always necessary to determine which is the appropriate category in any given case. Since the English rules of the conflict of laws are based on categories and connecting factors, there is no way of avoiding the problem, though it may be ameliorated by selecting narrower and more specific categories. Thus the problem set out in the previous paragraph would disappear if there were a category "revocation of a will by subsequent marriage."[10]

2–006   **Theories.** The problem of characterisation has given rise to a voluminous literature, much of it highly theoretical.[11] The consequence is that there are almost as many theories as writers and the theories are for the most part so abstract that, when applied to a given case, they can produce almost any result. They appear to have had almost no influence on the practice of the courts in England. For this reason, no attempt will be made to summarise them in detail, though the main features of the most important will be outlined.

2–007   Before doing this, however, we must consider a little more closely what a court does when confronted with a characterisation problem. What exactly is it that is characterised—an issue, a set of facts or a rule of law? Obviously, it can be any of these, depending on the way the court approaches the problem. For example, in one case members of the Court of Appeal referred to characterisation of "the issue",[12] "the question in this action",[13] "the relevant

---

[8] See *Ogden v. Ogden* [1908] P. 46 (C.A.), discussed at para. 17–019, *post*.

[9] It was in these terms that the Court of Appeal analysed the problem in the leading case on the subject, *Re Martin* [1900] P. 211. It concluded that it fell within the category "matrimonial law."

[10] The problem of characterisation can be entirely avoided only by adopting a system of conflict of laws, such as the American doctrine of interest analysis, which does not use categories.

[11] See n. 1, *ante*.

[12] *Macmillan Inc. v. Bishopsgate Investment Trust plc (No. 3)* [1996] 1 W.L.R. 387, 391 (C.A.) *per* Staughton L.J.

[13] *Ibid.*, at p. 393, *per* Staughton L.J.

rule of law"[14] and the "juridical concept or category".[15] In the example given above, the court could ask itself whether revocation of a will by subsequent marriage, as an abstract issue, is to be regarded as falling into the area of succession or matrimonial law; alternatively, it could consider how the facts of the case should be characterised. Both these approaches, it is suggested, amount to the same thing. But, as Auld L.J. observed in *Macmillan Inc. v. Bishopsgate Investment Trust plc (No. 3)*, the characterisation of the issue "requires a parallel exercise in classification of the relevant rule of law."[16] Once it is decided that the issue raised by the proceedings relates to matrimonial law rather than to succession, it logically follows that section 18 of the Wills Act 1837, the relevant provision of English law which deals with the revocation of a will by subsequent marriage, is characterised as a rule of matrimonial law.[17] Alternatively, the court could start by seeking to characterise section 18 of the Wills Act 1837. As will be shown below, this latter procedure can lead to difficulties which do not arise if the court characterises the issue.

The task which most of the writers have set themselves is that of determining which system of law should decide how legal rules and institutions should be characterised. Two main schools of thought have emerged: that favouring the *lex fori* and that favouring the *lex causae*. **2–008**

The great majority of Continental writers follow Kahn and Bartin in thinking that, with certain exceptions,[18] the process of characterisation should be performed in accordance with the domestic law of the forum.[19] If the forum has to characterise a rule or institution of foreign law, it should inquire how the corresponding or most closely analogous rule or institution of its own law is characterised, and apply that characterisation to the foreign institution or rule. The principal argument put forward in favour of this view is that if the foreign law is allowed to determine in what situations it is to be applied, the law of the forum would lose all control over the application of its own conflicts rules, and would no longer be master in its own home. Several arguments have been advanced against this view. In the first place, it is said that it may result in the forum refusing to apply a rule of foreign law in cases where it would be applicable if its nature were properly appreciated,[20] or in the forum applying a rule of foreign law in cases where according to that law it is not applicable, with the result that the foreign law is distorted, so that the law applied to the case is neither the law of the forum nor the foreign law nor the law of any country whatever. Secondly, this view is said to break down when there is no close analogy in the *lex fori* to an institution or rule of the foreign law.[21] Thus there is no close analogy in English domestic law to the **2–009**

---

[14] *Ibid.*, at p. 407, *per* Auld L.J.
[15] *Ibid.*, at p. 417, *per* Aldous L.J.
[16] [1996] 1 W.L.R. 387, 407.
[17] It ought also to follow that any foreign rule which addresses the same issue should be characterised in the same way. See para. 2–038.
[18] One of Bartin's exceptions was the characterisation of interests in property as interests in movables or immovables, which he said must be determined by the *lex situs*: (1897) Clunet 250–253.
[19] Beckett (1934) 15 B.Y.I.L. 46, 49–57; Lorenzen, Chap. 4, esp. pp. 91–93; Robertson, pp. 25–38. This theory was adopted in the South African case of *Laconian Marine Enterprises Ltd. v. Agromar Lineas Ltd.*, 1986 (3) S.A. 509, 517–524.
[20] *Ogden v. Ogden* [1908] P. 46 (C.A.) is sometimes said to be such a case: see *post*, para. 17–019.
[21] See *The Colorado* [1923] P.102 (C.A.). But see Mendelssohn-Bartholdy (1935) 16 B.Y.I.L. 38–39.

French system of community property, and no close analogy in French domestic law to the English trust. Yet the English and French conflict rules are framed in terms wide enough to accommodate the rights and duties arising from French community property[22] and the English trust[23] respectively.

2–010   Other Continental writers[24] think that the process of characterisation should be performed in accordance with the *lex causae*, that is, the appropriate foreign law. According to Wolff,[25] "every legal rule takes its classification from the legal system to which it belongs." The argument advanced in favour of this view is that to say that the foreign law is to govern, and then not apply its characterisation, is tantamount to not applying it at all. But this view bristles with difficulties, and few writers have adopted it. In the first place, it is arguing in a circle to say that the foreign law governs the process of characterisation before the process of characterisation has led to the selection of the appropriate legal system. Secondly, if there are two potential applicable foreign laws, why should the forum adopt the characterisation of one rather than that of the other?

2–011   The problem with these (and most of the other[26]) theories is that they assume that every legal system contains rules that unambiguously characterise every other rule in that system or, if one prefers, every legal issue. This is simply not true. In some cases, legal systems may give indications regarding the characterisation of rules they contain—for example, a rule may appear under one or another heading in the civil code of a Continental country—but this is certainly not always the case and, in any event, the place of the rule in that part of the code may be the result of accident. Because section 18 of the Wills Act 1837 appears in a statute entitled the "Wills Act," it does not necessarily follow that English law characterises it as relating to succession. Indeed, the Court of Appeal in *Re Martin*[27] did not so characterise it. Furthermore, the fact that a rule of law is characterised in one way for one purpose does not necessarily mean that it should be characterised in the same way for all other purposes.

2–012   It follows, therefore, that the characterisation of a rule of law for any purpose other than that of the conflict of laws cannot be relied upon for conflicts purposes. However, in the case of a foreign system of law, even such a characterisation will be of use only where the relevant categories in the foreign system of the conflict of laws are the same as those in that of the forum: this means not only that they should have the same name, but that they should mean the same thing. If this is not the case, one is not comparing like with like. As might be expected, this is almost impossible to determine. Moreover, cases in which particular rules of law (or issues) are characterised for the purposes of the conflict of laws are not common.

2–013   **Examples of characterisation in English law.** There are several English cases in which questions of characterisation have come before the courts.

---

[22] *De Nicols v. Curlier* [1900] A.C. 21.

[23] Robertson, p. 33.

[24] For example, Despagnet (1898) Clunet 253; Wolff, ss. 138–157. See, further, Becket *op. cit.* at p. 58; Lorenzen, Chap. 4, esp. pp. 94–95 and Robertson, pp. 27, 32.

[25] p. 154.

[26] Other theories include that of primary and secondary characterisation, according to which one characterises twice—first according to the *lex fori* and then according to the *lex causae*—and a *via media* put forward by Falconbridge. On the former, see Robertson, *passim*, and on the latter, see Falconbridge, Chap. 3, esp. pp. 58–62.

[27] [1900] P. 211.

Thus it has been held that the question whether interests in property are interests in movables or immovables must be determined in accordance with the *lex situs*[28]; that whether the defendant has a defence to a claim for restitution of shares on the basis of bona fide purchase relates to property rather than to restitution[29]; that the English rule that a personal representative can postpone the sale of assets relates to administration and not to succession[30]; that the English rule that a legacy to an attesting witness is void is a rule of essential validity and not of formality[31]; that the English rule as to the burden of proof of testamentary capacity is a rule of procedure and not of substance[32]; and that French rules prohibiting the marriage of minors without the consent of their parents,[33] and Argentine rules permitting marriages to be celebrated by proxy,[34] relate to the formalities of marriage and not to capacity to marry.[35] Unfortunately, however, most of these cases give little indication of the method used by the court to reach its conclusion. The cases which do give such an indication are relatively few in number. They will now be considered in detail.

Re Cohn. The first is *Re Cohn*.[36] This concerned two German women who were killed in an air raid in London in circumstances in which it could not be determined which of them died first. One of them, Mrs. Oppenheimer, was entitled to movable property under the will of the other, Mrs. Cohn, but only if she survived the latter. Since Mrs. Cohn was domiciled in Germany, succession to her estate was, as far as movable property was concerned, governed by the law of Germany. As the matter was before an English court, however, all questions of procedure, including questions of evidence, were governed by the law of England. The two relevant categories were, therefore, "succession to movable property" and "procedure and evidence." The connecting factor attached to the former was domicile (leading to German law) and that attached to the latter was the place of the action, England.   **2–014**

Under English law, it was laid down by section 184 of the Law of Property Act 1925 that where two persons die in circumstances rendering it uncertain which of them survived the other, such deaths will, for all purposes affecting the title to property, be presumed to have occurred in order of seniority, and accordingly the younger will be deemed to have survived the elder. If this rule were applicable, Mrs. Oppenheimer would be deemed to have survived Mrs. Cohn. Under German law, on the other hand, the presumption was that they died simultaneously. The result was that Mrs. Oppenheimer could take under the will only if the English presumption were applied.   **2–015**

---

[28] *Re Hoyles* [1911] 1 Ch. 179 (C.A.); *post*, Rule 111.
[29] *Macmillan Inc. v. Bishopsgate Investment Trust plc (No. 3)* [1996] 1 W.L.R. 387.
[30] *Re Wilks* [1935] Ch. 645; followed in *Re Kehr* [1952] Ch.26 (statutory power to appoint trustees of infant's share and statutory powers of maintenance and advancement); see *post*, para. 26–034.
[31] *Re Priest* [1944] Ch. 58. See now Wills Act 1968.
[32] *In the Estate of Fuld (No. 3)* [1968] P. 675, 696–697.
[33] *Simonin v. Mallac* (1860) 2 Sw. & Tr. 67; *Ogden v. Ogden* [1908] P. 46 (C.A.). See *post*, paras. 17–018 *et seq.*
[34] *Apt v. Apt* [1948] P. 83 (C.A.). See *post*, para. 17–011.
[35] For further examples, see Beckett (1934) 15 B.Y.I.L. 46, 66–81; Falconbridge, pp. 73–123; Robertson, pp. 164–188, 245–279.
[36] [1945] Ch. 5 (Uthwatt J.).

2–016   The court was thus faced with a problem of characterisation. How did it go about solving it? Interestingly, it did not characterise the concept of survivorship in the abstract. Instead, it looked first at the English provision and decided that it was inapplicable because it was not concerned with proof[37]:

> "The fact proved in this case is that it is impossible to say whether or not Mrs. Oppenheimer survived Mrs. Cohn. Proof stops there. Section 184 of the Law of Property Act 1925 does not come into the picture at all. It is not part of the law of evidence of the *lex fori*, for the section is not directed to helping in the ascertainment of any fact but contains a rule of substantive law directing a certain presumption to be made in all cases affecting the title to property."

2–017   Having thus characterised the English rule as being part of the law of succession rather than the law of evidence, the judge next turned his attention to the German rule. This was contained in legislation passed in 1939, which amended a provision of the German Civil Code. The latter provision was contained in Book I of the Code, which was entitled "General Principles," and was found under the heading "Natural Persons." His conclusion was that the German rule should also be characterised as falling within the category "succession" rather than "procedure and evidence." His reason was that its "terms and the place in which the repealed article dealing with the same general subject-matter was to be found" made it clear that this was the correct characterisation. The result was that the German rule was applicable and Mrs. Oppenheimer did not take under the will.

2–018   What are we to make of this method of solving the problem? The first point to make is that the judge was characterising rules of law, not the general issue. Secondly, there can be little doubt that each rule was characterised independently of the other: the mere fact that the English rule was characterised as relating to succession did not *necessarily* mean that the German rule had to be characterised in the same way. On the particular facts of the case this was what actually occurred, but on other facts the result could have been different.

2–019   This illustrates one of the great drawbacks of this approach. What would have happened if the German rule had been contained in a part of the German Civil Code headed "Evidence"? Presumably, the court would have regarded it as being part of the law of procedure and consequently inapplicable. The result would have been that *neither* rule would have applied—a rather awkward situation.[38] Alternatively, the court might have characterised the English rule as being part of the law of evidence. In this case, *both* rules might have been applicable.[39]

2–020   There have in fact been cases in which courts have reached absurd results through the application of this method of characterisation. The most notorious is probably a decision of the German Reichsgericht in 1882.[40] In this case, an action was brought in a German court on promissory notes issued in a foreign country and governed by the law of that country. The limitation period had

---

[37] [1945] Ch. 5, 7–8.
[38] In such a situation it would have been impossible to prove that Mrs. Oppenheimer survived Mrs. Cohn, nor would there have been any justification for distributing the latter's estate on the assumption that this was the case; consequently, Mrs. Oppenheimer would not have been entitled to take under the will.
[39] It could in fact be argued that in such a case the court would be obliged to find, *as a matter of fact*, that Mrs. Oppenheimer survived Mrs. Cohn. If this were so, the German rule could not come into play, since it applied only where it could not be proved who died first.
[40] *Entscheidungen des Reichsgerichts*, Vol. VII, p. 21.

expired under both the foreign law and under German law, so one might have thought that the action was bound to fail. The Reichsgericht, however, held that it could succeed. It reached this surprising conclusion by characterising, not the general question of limitation of actions, but the two rules contained in the foreign system of law and in German law. It concluded that the foreign rule was procedural and therefore inapplicable; the German rule, on the other hand, was characterised as substantive and therefore also inapplicable. The result was that neither applied.[41]

This brings us to our third point concerning *Re Cohn*. Given that the German rule was clearly of the same nature as the English (it also applied only where it could not be ascertained which person died first) why was it necessary for the English court to characterise it separately? The English court characterised the English rule as relating to succession on the entirely reasonable ground that it was not intended to help the court establish who in fact died first, but laid down a rule on the distribution of property to be followed in cases in which this could not be determined. The German rule did exactly the same. Surely, there could be no question of characterising it differently. If, through some accident of history, it had been set out in some part of the Code under the heading "Evidence," should this really have made the English court characterise it as procedural? Should it, moreover, have made any difference if it had been established that German courts characterised it as procedural for the purposes of their conflict rule?   **2–021**

If one defines a rule of survivorship as a rule which is applicable only in circumstances in which it cannot be ascertained who died first, can one not say that all rules of survivorship are part of the law of succession, rather than the law of evidence? The advantage of such a conclusion, if it had been reached by the court in *Re Cohn*, would have been that the problem would be solved for ever. As it is, however, lawyers in future cases must always, at least in theory, consult experts in the foreign system of law to discover how the foreign rule on survivorship is characterised by the foreign system.   **2–022**

Re Maldonado. The second case to consider is *Re Maldonado*,[42] which concerned a woman domiciled in Spain who died intestate and without living relatives. She left movable property in England, which was claimed by both the Spanish Government and the British Crown. This raised the question whether the applicable rule was that of Spanish law, which said that it went to the Spanish state, or English law, which said that it escheated to the Crown. This in turn depended on whether it came within the scope of the conflict rule which provides that succession to movables is governed by the law of the deceased's domicile (in which case the Spanish rule would apply) or whether it simply raised a question of ownerless property, *bona vacantia*, in which case it would be covered by the rule that title to property is governed by the law of the place where the property is situated. Since the property in question was in England, this would lead to the application of the English rule.   **2–023**

The Court of Appeal held that since, under Spanish law, the Spanish state succeeded to property in such a situation as the final heir (*ultimus heres*), it was entitled to the movables in England. The English rule never came into the picture because the property was never ownerless: on the death of the   **2–024**

---

[41] This decision has not been followed in later cases in Germany: see Wolff, p. 161, n. 1. For further discussion of the way in which statutes of limitation should be characterised, see *post*, paras. 7–040 *et seq.*
[42] [1954] P. 223 (C.A.).

deceased it passed to the Spanish state. If, on the other hand, the Spanish state had not claimed the property under the law of succession, but on some other basis—for example, as *bona vacantia*—the position would have been different: two earlier cases show that the claim of the British Crown would have been preferred.[43]

2–025   At first sight, this decision might seem an entirely logical application of the English conflict rule. The truth of the matter is, however, that the difference between the English and Spanish rules was merely verbal. Most legal systems have a rule that the state takes the property of anyone who dies intestate and without heirs. It has been shown by Lipstein[44] that, until the nineteenth century, this rule was regarded on the Continent (as in England) as a *jus regale*, a prerogative right under public law akin to eminent domain. Then certain German writers put forward the view that in Roman law the state took as heir. This new theory spread rapidly during the middle of the nineteenth century and was adopted in many Continental codes, including the Spanish Civil Code of 1889. The content of the rule was not, however, affected by the change in its theoretical foundation. Today some countries adopt the one theory and some the other, but this appears to have no practical consequences as regards the rules applied, both procedural and substantive.[45]

2–026   In view of this, one is entitled to question whether the approach adopted by the Court of Appeal—which again involved characterisation of a rule of law, rather than an issue, and which may be regarded as an application of the theory that characterisation must be determined according to the *lex causae*— was sound. Is it desirable that the right to property in England should depend on a verbal formulation with no real content?

2–027   Another difficulty is that this approach gives rise to the same problem as *Re Cohn*: in future cases involving countries other than Spain, lawyers in England will have to discover which theory is adopted by the *lex domicilii*. This may sometimes be hard to discover. Would it not have been better for the court to have recognised that there is a real functional difference between rules of law giving a relative of the intestate the right to succeed and those giving such a right to the state or some other public authority or institution? The former are intended to uphold the presumed wishes of the intestate, while the latter are an expression of governmental power. The English court could then define the English conflict rule with greater precision by ruling that the concept of "succession" as used in the rule does not include a claim of the latter kind.[46]

2–028   **Adams *v*. National Bank of Greece.** It might be thought from what was said above that English courts normally apply foreign law to characterise rules of law belonging to a foreign system. This is what they did in *Re Maldonado* and, less explicitly, in *Re Cohn*. However, these two cases are exceptional: normally English courts look to foreign law only to discover the nature and

---

[43] *Re Barnett's Trusts* [1902] 1 Ch. 847; *Re Musurus* [1936] 2 All E.R. 1666.
[44] [1954] C.L.J. 22.
[45] Lipstein, *op. cit.*, pp. 25–26.
[46] See *post*, paras. 27–012 *et seq*. The only American cases to have followed *Re Maldonado* appear to be two decisions of the New York Court of Appeals, *Re Utassi's Will*, 15 N.Y. 2d 436; 209 N.E. 2d 65 (1965) and *Khotim v. Mikheev*, 41 N.Y. 2d 845; 362 N.E. 2d 253 (1977), but the rule laid down in these cases was subsequently reversed by legislation: see the New York Estates, Powers and Trusts Law, para. 4–1.5.

scope of the foreign rule, not to determine how it (or the general issue) should be characterised.[47]

Adams v. National Bank of Greece[48] is a good illustration. In 1927, a Greek bank, the National Mortgage Bank of Greece, issued sterling-denominated mortgage bonds, which were repayable in 1957. The bonds contained a provision that they were governed by English law and they were guaranteed by another Greek bank, the National Bank of Greece. During the war, payment of interest on the bonds ceased and in 1949 Greek legislation provided for a moratorium on all further payments. The bondholders were unable to obtain redress because the Greek banks in question did no business in England and were not subject to the jurisdiction of the English courts. If the bondholders had sued in Greece, the Greek courts would have applied the moratorium legislation.

2–029

In 1953, however, a Greek law provided for the amalgamation of the National Bank of Greece and a third Greek bank, the Bank of Athens. The new bank was called the National Bank of Greece and Athens. The Greek law provided that the new bank was the universal successor to all the assets and liabilities of the old banks. This meant that the National Bank of Greece and Athens was liable on the bonds, though, of course, the moratorium legislation prevented any action being brought against it in Greece. However, the Bank of Athens had been carrying on business in England and the new amalgamated bank continued to do so. Consequently, it was subject to the jurisdiction of the English courts, and a bondholder, Metliss, brought action in England claiming that it was liable under the guarantee. In *National Bank of Greece and Athens v. Metliss*[49] the House of Lords held in favour of Metliss. The moratorium legislation was held to be inapplicable since it purported to alter obligations under a contract and was therefore to be characterised as contractual. Consequently, it could not affect a contract governed by English law.

2–030

Four days after the judgment at first instance was given, the Greek government passed a new law amending the law under which the banks were amalgamated. The new law provided that the amalgamated bank would be the universal successor to all the rights and obligations of the old banks, except obligations, whether as principal or guarantor, under bonds payable in foreign currency. The National Bank of Greece and Athens, which subsequently changed its name to the National Bank of Greece, immediately stopped making payments under the bonds. Another bondholder, Adams, brought new proceedings in the English courts. Did the new law relieve the National Bank of Greece from its liability under the bonds? This depended on how it was characterised. There can be no doubt that the new law was intended by those responsible for its enactment to be characterised as relating to the amalgamation of the banks. If this characterisation had been adopted by the English courts, they would have been obliged to hold that it was applicable in the case before them and that it gave a defence to the banks. The House of Lords, however, rejected this approach and gave judgment for Adams.

2–031

The whole point of the second Greek law was to force the English courts to apply the moratorium rule by re-enacting it as part of the amalgamation

2–032

---

[47] See, for example, *Huntington v. Attrill* [1893] A.C. 150 (P.C.) (especially at p. 155); *Ogden v. Ogden* [1908] P. 46 (C.A.); *Re Korvine's Trusts* [1921] 1 Ch. 343; *Re Craven's Estate* [1937] Ch. 423 (better reported in 53 T.L.R. 694); *Apt v. Apt* [1948] P. 83 (C.A.); *U.S. v. Inkley* [1989] Q.B. 255 (C.A.) (especially at p. 265).

[48] [1961] A.C. 255.

[49] [1958] A.C. 509.

legislation. The House of Lords, however, refused to be taken in by this: they took the view that if the effect of the law was to discharge or alter a contractual right, it had to be regarded as contractual, whatever label might be attached to it by its author.[50] The purpose of the Greek law was to relieve the new bank of liability under the bonds and this purpose was not affected by the attempt of the Greek legislator to disguise it as something else.[51]

2–033   This case shows the undesirability of characterising rules of foreign law according to the legal system to which they belong. Attempts by foreign legislatures to force English courts to apply particular rules of law will, of course, be rare. But even when there is no deliberate manipulation, there is no reason why the English court should allow foreign law to decide whether a particular rule should be applied in the case before it.

2–034   **Conclusions.** In essence, characterisation is a process of refining English conflict rules by expressing them with greater precision. If the relevant rule is, for example, "succession to movables is governed by the *lex domicilii* of the deceased," characterisation involves deciding precisely which issues should be governed by the *lex domicilii*. The term "succession" is simply a useful way of referring to the bundle of issues that are regarded as appropriate for determination by the *lex domicilii*. To believe that a term such as "succession" has an objectively defined meaning which exists independently of the purpose for which it is used is mere conceptualism. It is, therefore, pointless to search for the "true" meaning of the term. Moreover, since the purpose of the exercise is to reformulate rules of English law, it is contrary to principle to look to foreign law for the answer. This seems to have been recognised by the English courts. For example, in *Macmillan Inc. v. Bishopsgate Investment Trust plc (No. 3)*, the most recent English case in which the issue of characterisation received extended judicial discussion, Auld L.J. accepted that "the proper approach is to look beyond the formulation of the claim and to identify according to the *lex fori* the true issue or issues thrown up by the claim and the defence."[52]

2–035   The way the court should proceed is to consider the rationale of the English conflict rule and the purpose of the rule of substantive law to be characterised. On this basis, it can decide whether the conflict rule should be regarded as covering the rule of substantive law.[53] In some cases, the court might conclude that the rule of substantive law should not be regarded as falling within either of the two potentially applicable conflict rules. In this situation, a new conflict rule should be created.

2–036   Revocation of a will by the subsequent marriage of the testator will serve as an example to demonstrate this methodology. The English rule, which is found in section 18 of the Wills Act 1837, as substituted by section 18 of the Administration of Justice Act 1982, is subject to certain exceptions, one of which is that if it appears from the will that, at the time when it was made, the testator was expecting to be married to a particular person and that he intended

---

[50] [1961] A.C., at p.274, *per* Viscount Simonds.
[51] See also at p. 283, *per* Lord Reid: " . . . we must look at the substance and effect of a foreign law . . . "
[52] [1996] 1 W.L.R. 387, 407 (C.A.).
[53] This approach borrows from interest analysis, but it is used to develop and refine the traditional English rules of the conflict of laws, not to replace them.

that the will should not be revoked by the marriage, it will not be revoked by his marriage to that person.[54] This suggests that the purpose of the rule is to give expression to the presumed intention of the testator: except where the will is made in contemplation of marriage, one might assume that the change of circumstances brought about by the marriage will be such that the average testator would want to make a different disposition of his property. Scottish and French law take a different view. To which testators is it appropriate to apply the English rule? The best way of answering this question is to ask which testators would be most likely deliberately to have refrained from revoking their will because they thought it would be automatically revoked by reason of the English rule. The answer must be: those testators who, at the time of their marriage, thought that their affairs would be governed by English law. This suggests the law of the domicile at the time of marriage, both for movables and immovables.

This result cannot be attained by characterising the question as relating to **2–037** succession (essential validity of a will). In such a case, the governing law would be, in the case of movables, the law of the testator's domicile at death and, in the case of immovables, the *lex situs*. If the question is characterised as a matter of matrimonial law, as was done by the Court of Appeal in *Re Martin*,[55] the applicable law would traditionally have been that of the *husband's* domicile at the time of marriage. Where the will is that of a woman, this would be unacceptable today. In Chapter 28 it is suggested that, where the parties to a marriage are domiciled in different countries, the matrimonial property regime should today be determined by the law of the country with which the parties and the marriage have their closest connection.[56] If revocation by subsequent marriage is characterised as being an aspect of the matrimonial property regime, this is the law that would govern. There is, however, an important difference between the matrimonial property regime in general and revocation of a will: the former must be governed by the same system of law for both spouses; the latter need not be. Consequently, there is good reason for regarding it as a special aspect of matrimonial law, with its own choice-of-law rule, the law of the domicile of the testator or testatrix at the time of the marriage. Alternatively, it could be regarded as an independent conflict category in its own right (with the same choice-of-law rule). If the question had been free from authority, the latter would have been the better solution.[57]

Rules which are essentially of the same kind,[58] whether English or foreign, **2–038** should be characterised in the same way. Examples have already been given of the difficulties caused by the failure of the courts to do this. Statutes of limitation provide a further example, one which also illustrates the defects of

---

[54] s. 18(3).

[55] [1900] P. 211.

[56] See *post*, para. 28–009.

[57] See further *post*, paras. 27–086 *et seq.*

[58] In deciding whether rules are essentially the same, one should disregard verbal formulations and consider the function of the rules. For an example of rules which are superficially the same, but in fact different, see *post*, paras. 17–082 *et seq.* (prohibition against remarriage after divorce); for a case where the English courts have been criticised for adopting the same characterisation for essentially similar rules (when they should have been criticised for adopting an inappropriate characterisation in the first place), see *post*, paras. 17–018 *et seq.* (parental consent to marriage).

mechanical reasoning. The approach of the courts when faced with a question of limitation of actions has traditionally been to inquire whether the limitation rule in issue takes away both the right and the remedy or only the remedy. A limitation rule of the former kind will be applied if (and only if) it forms part of the law governing the substance of the matter (the *lex causae*), while a rule of the latter kind is regarded as being procedural and is applicable if (and only if) it is part of the law of the forum.[59] The reasoning behind this distinction is that a rule which extinguishes a right is just as much substantive as a rule which creates a right, while a rule which leaves the right intact can only be procedural.[60]

2–039   Once it is accepted that characterisation is concerned with the redefinition of the English conflict rule, however, this reasoning is seen as artificial. The difference between the two kinds of limitation rule is of little significance for most purposes. Except in a few special situations,[61] it makes no difference to the parties whether the rule is of the one kind or the other. Except in those special situations, a right without a remedy is the same as no right at all. Why should the determination of the governing law depend on such a distinction?

2–040   If we apply the methodology suggested above, it becomes apparent that there is no justification for regarding any limitation rule as procedural, even if it does not extinguish the substantive right.[62] The rationale of the English conflict rule that matters of procedure are governed by the law of the forum is one of practicality and convenience. This clearly applies to matters such as service of process or courtroom procedure. It does not apply to statutes of limitation: it is no more impractical or inconvenient to apply a foreign limitation rule that extinguishes only the remedy than it is to apply one that extinguishes the right as well.[63]

2–041   Besides being wrong in principle, the traditional approach produced unfortunate results. First, it required the practitioner to discover into which category the relevant rule fell. This could not always have been an easy task, especially in the case of a foreign rule. Secondly, in so far as it resulted in the application of the English rule, it could produce injustice, since a foreign debtor might have destroyed his receipts in reliance on the foreign limitation period. Thirdly, it could, as was pointed out above, lead to the absurd result of judgment being given for the plaintiff even though the claim was statute-barred under *both* relevant laws.[64]

2–042   Fortunately, the false turn taken by the English courts has been corrected by the Foreign Limitation Periods Act 1984 and the Contracts (Applicable Law) Act 1990,[65] the effect of which is that the foreign periods of limitation will be

---

[59] A number of English and foreign rules have been characterised as procedural for this purpose; see *British Linen Co. v. Drummond* (1830) 10 B. & C. 903; *Don v. Lippmann* (1837) 5 Cl. & F. 1 (a Scottish case); *Huber v. Steiner* (1835) 2 Bing.N.C. 202; *S.A. de Prayon v. Koppel* (1933) 77 S.J. 800.

[60] See *post*, paras. 7–040 *et seq.*

[61] For example, where set-off is pleaded.

[62] See the judgment of La Forest J. in *Tolofson v. Jensen* [1994] 3 S.C.R. 1022 (Sup.Ct.Can.).

[63] See the dissenting judgments of Mason C.J. and Deane J. in *McKain v. Miller & Co.* (1991) 174 C.L.R. 1 (High Ct. Australia). See, further, Beckett (1934) 15 B.Y.I.L. 46 at p. 66; Cook (1933) 42 Yale L.J. 333 at pp. 343–344. For a discussion of the general question, see *Classification of Limitation in Private International Law*, Law Com. No. 114 (1982).

[64] See *ante*, para. 2–020.

[65] Sched. 1, Art. 10(1)(d).

applied when the *lex causae* is the foreign law and the English periods when the *lex causae* is English law. It makes no difference whether the law extinguishes both the right and the remedy or the remedy alone.[66] However, characterisation rules based on the same superficial reasoning still exist in the case of other issues, for example section 4 of the Statute of Frauds.[67]

It is hoped that enough has been said to demonstrate how the problem **2–043** should be approached. Characterisation has been made needlessly difficult by writers (and judges) who have created a conflict problem within a conflict problem by insisting that characterisation itself involves a choice of law, that is to say that any court faced with a characterisation problem must first decide what law should be applied to decide the matter. Once this idea is rejected, the way lies open for the courts to seek commonsense solutions based on practical considerations.

B. THE INCIDENTAL OR PRELIMINARY QUESTION[68]

THE incidental[69] or preliminary question is a technical problem of consider-   **2–044** able difficulty which was first noticed by academic writers on the Continent.[70] It arises in this way. Suppose that an English court is called upon to decide a

---

[66] For a fuller discussion of this topic, see *post*, paras. 7–040 *et seq.* Two further examples of uniform characterisation rules are found in s.3 of the Wills Act 1963. The first concerns provisions requiring special formalities to be observed by testators answering a particular description (for example, those under a certain age) and the second concerns provisions that witnesses to the execution of a will must possess certain qualifications. The Wills Act lays down that both classes of provisions are to be characterised as formal requirements, irrespective of how they may be regarded by the legal system of which they are part. It is easy to see that these characterisation rules serve a purpose. The policy behind the Wills Act is to uphold the validity of wills by providing that a will is formally valid if it complies with the requirements of any one of a number of different legal systems (see Rule 135, *post*). By characterising as formalities the two kinds of provisions mentioned above, the Act brings those provisions under the same regime, thus making it less likely that they will operate to invalidate a will. For examples of the way s.3 applies, see *post*, para. 27–039, Illustrations 2 and 3.

[67] *Leroux v. Brown* (1852) 12 C.B. 801, discussed *post*, paras. 27–018 *et seq.* This decision was doubted by Willes J. in *Williams v. Wheeler* (1806) 8 C.B. (N.S.) 299, 316, and *Gibson v. Holland* (1865) L.R. 1 C.P. 1, 8 and condemned by nearly every writer who has discussed it: Cheshire and North, pp. 40, 68; Beckett (1934) 15 B.Y.I.L. 46, 69–71; Falconbridge, pp. 98–105; Robertson, pp. 254–255; Cook, pp. 229–231; Lorenzen, Chap. 11; and see *post*, para. 7–018. Many writers contrast the decision with that of the French Cour de Cassation in *Benton c. Horeau*, 1880 *Clunet* 480. See also the decision of the Supreme Court of California in *Bernkrant v. Fowler*, 55 Cal. 2d 588, 360 P. 2d 906 (1961), discussed *post*, para. 7–020.

[68] Wengler, "Die Vorfrage im Kollisionenrecht" (1934) 8 *Rabel's Zeitschrift*, 148–251; Wengler, *The Law Applicable to Preliminary (Incidental) Questions* in *International Encyclopedia of Comparative Law*, Vol. III, Chap. 7; Melchior, *Die Grundlagen des Deutschen Internationalen Privatrechts* (1932) pp. 245–265; Schuz, *Modern Approach to the Incidental Question* (1997); Raape (1934) *Recueil des Cours*, IV, p. 405 at pp. 485–495; Maury (1936) *Recueil des Cours*, III, p. 329 at pp. 558–563; De Nova (1966) *Recueil des Cours*, II, p. 434 at pp. 557–569; Schmidt (1992) *Recueil des Cours*, II, p. 305; Breslauer, *The Private International Law of Succession in England, America and Germany* (1937), Chap. 4, pp. 18–21; Robertson, Chap. 6, pp. 135–156; Wolff, ss. 196–200; Cormack (1941) 14 So. Calif. L. Rev. 243–249; Gotlieb (1955) 33 Can. Bar Rev. 523–555; Rigaux, *La Théorie des Qualifications* (1956), pp. 444–467; Louis-Lucas, 1957 *Rev. Crit.*, p. 153; Lagarde, 1960 *Rev. Crit.*, p. 459; Wengler, 1966 *Rev. Crit.*, pp. 165–215; Hartley (1967) 16 I.C.L.Q. 680–691; Gotlieb (1977) 26 I.C.L.Q. 734.

[69] This term is used by Wolff and is considered the most suitable English expression. The French and German terms are "question préalable" and "Vorfrage."

[70] The discovery of the problem is often attributed to the German jurists Melchior and Wengler in 1932–34, but it had in fact been discussed prior to this: see Gotlieb (1977) 26 I.C.L.Q. 734, 735, n. 5.

question which has foreign elements and, in order to do so, has to consider a subsidiary question which also has foreign elements. Suppose that by the relevant English rule of the conflict of laws the main question is governed by the law of a foreign country. Should the subsidiary question be governed by the English conflict rule appropriate to that question, or should it be governed by the appropriate conflict rule of the foreign system of law governing the main question? An illustration will make this clearer. Suppose[71] that a Greek national domiciled in Greece dies intestate leaving movables in England. By the English conflict of laws rule, succession to his movables is governed by Greek domestic law as the law of his domicile. Suppose that by Greek domestic law the wife of an intestate is entitled to a share of his movables. Such a share is claimed by W on the ground that she was the wife of the intestate. Suppose that the marriage between the intestate and W was celebrated in England and, though perfectly valid by English domestic law (which is the applicable law under the English conflict rule), was formally void by Greek domestic law (which is applicable under the Greek conflict rule) because no Greek priest was present at the ceremony. Will W's claim to a share in the intestate's movables be determined by the English or the Greek conflict rule?

2–045 It will be appreciated that this is a fundamental problem that can arise in any conflicts system (at least if it is of the traditional type). It will occur if, but only if, the following three conditions are satisfied. First, the main question must by the English conflict rule be governed by the law of some foreign country. Secondly, there must be a subsidiary question involving foreign elements which is capable of arising in its own right and which has a conflict rule of its own available for its determination. Thirdly, the English conflict rule for the determination of the subsidiary question must lead to a different result from the corresponding conflict rule adopted by the country whose law governs the main question.[72]

2–046 In the past, academic writers have tried to find a general solution, based on logic and theory, that would apply in every case, though they are sharply divided as to what it should be.[73] The main arguments may be illustrated by taking as an example the problem set out above of the Greek dying intestate. According to one view, W should not be permitted to share in the estate because otherwise full effect would not be given to the English conflict rule that succession to the movables is governed by Greek law; according to another view, however, W *should* be permitted to share in the estate because otherwise full effect would not be given to the English conflict rule that the validity of the marriage is governed by English law. Put another way, the first view strives to maintain international harmony (by adopting the same solution as a Greek court would[74]) while the second gives priority to internal harmony (since W would be regarded as the deceased's wife for other purposes).

2–047 Recently, however, the view has been gaining ground that it is neither possible nor desirable to find a solution which would apply in every case.

---

[71] Wolff, p. 206.

[72] *Cf.* Robertson, pp. 148–149. In order to simplify the discussion in the text, it is assumed that the English conflict rule refers the main question to the law of a foreign country directly and not by way of renvoi (transmission) from the law of another foreign country. Such a case of transmission would involve problems of greater complexity which are discussed by Gotlieb (1955) 33 Can. Bar Rev. 523, 526–528.

[73] See the references in n. 68, *supra.*

[74] To this extent, it has something in common with renvoi.

Rather, each situation should be looked at separately in order to find a solution that produces the best results in that situation. As one writer put it, "there is really no problem of the incidental question, but as many problems as there are cases in which incidental questions can arise."[75] Instead of trying to solve the problem on the basis of general theory, one should consider the practical consequences in each situation. Following this approach, we will now discuss some of the situations in which the problem most commonly occurs.

Bigamy. At first sight it might be thought that (where no question of polygamy arises) bigamy could not produce a problem in the conflict of laws, since all legal systems prohibit it. The difficulty, however, lies in the fact that, while all relevant systems of law may unite in rejecting bigamy, they may disagree as to whether or not a particular marriage is bigamous. This could occur where one of the parties to the marriage has entered into a previous marriage and, according to the conflict rules of one country, this marriage is valid and subsisting at the time of the second marriage while, according to the conflict rules of the other country, this is not the case. Such a situation could arise where the one regards the first marriage as valid, while the other regards it as void *ab initio*; or where a decree of nullity or divorce is not recognised by the one, but is recognised by the other. **2–048**

In this situation, the principal question is whether the second marriage is invalid for bigamy. This raises a question of capacity,[76] which is governed (in general[77]) by the law of the parties' domicile. (It will be assumed, for the sake of simplicity, that the parties are both domiciled in the same country.) That law will no doubt say that the second marriage is valid only if neither party to it is a party to an earlier, subsisting marriage. This latter question is the incidental question and the problem then becomes: should one decide the incidental question by the conflict rules of the domicile or by the English conflict rules? **2–049**

This problem can arise in two different situations: the first is where the prior marriage is valid and subsisting under the English conflict rules but not under the conflict rules of the domicile (for example, if a prior divorce is not recognised in England but is recognised in the country of the domicile); in the second, the position is reversed and the prior marriage is subsisting according to the conflict rules of the domicile but not according to the English conflict rules. These situations should be distinguished because the consequences of applying the conflict rules of the domicile differ markedly in the two cases: in the first, it will mean that, in English eyes, *both* marriages are valid and subsisting; while in the second, *neither* marriage will be valid and subsisting. **2–050**

The Canadian case of *Schwebel v. Ungar*[78] is an example of the first situation. Here the wife married her first husband in Hungary, where they were both domiciled, and this marriage was valid under all relevant systems of conflict of laws. Later the couple, who were both Jews, decided to emigrate to Israel. While *en route* to Israel, they were divorced by a Jewish ghet in Italy. This divorce was not recognised by the law of Hungary (where they were still domiciled), nor by the law of Italy, but was recognised by the law of Israel. **2–051**

---

[75] Gotlieb (1955) 33 Can. Bar Rev. 523, 555; for a survey of the various schools of thought, see Gotlieb (1977) 26 I.C.L.Q. 734, 751–760.

[76] See *post*, paras. 17–080 *et seq.*

[77] For the general rule, and the exceptions, see *post*, paras. 17R–054 *et seq.*

[78] (1964) 48 D.L.R. (2d) 644 (Sup.Ct.Can.), affirming (1963) 42 D.L.R. (2d) 622 (Ont. C.A.).

The parties then acquired a domicile of choice in Israel, where they were regarded as having the status of single persons. Some time later the wife came to Toronto and, while still domiciled in Israel, married her second husband. Beforehand, the parties consulted a rabbi, who told them that it was legal for them to marry. They lived together for a few years and a child was born. Later, however, differences arose between them and the husband brought proceedings for nullity on the ground that the marriage was bigamous. The Supreme Court of Canada, affirming the decision of the Ontario Court of Appeal, held that the marriage was valid. Unfortunately, it is not entirely clear on what ground this conclusion was reached. Under Ontario law, the general rule for the recognition of a foreign divorce was that the divorce must be granted, or recognised, by the courts of the country in which the couple were domiciled at the time of the divorce. Under this rule, the divorce was invalid. There are, however, passages in the judgments of both courts which suggest that they were prepared to lay down an exception to this general rule to allow the recognition of the divorce on the facts of the case. This exception would presumably be that a divorce will also be recognised in Ontario if it is recognised by the law of the country in which, at any subsequent time, the parties become domiciled.[79] If this was the ground of the decision, the problem of the incidental question did not arise. It is, however, possible that the correct interpretation of the judgment is that the Canadian courts were prepared to uphold the second marriage without recognising the divorce. If this was so, the case is an example of the incidental question.[80]

2–052   If the second view is correct, it means that the courts decided the incidental question (the validity of the divorce) by the conflict rules of Israel, the country whose law governed the main question (the wife's capacity to marry). If this is the correct interpretation of the case—and there are passages in the judgments which suggest that it is[81]—the results are strange. If, before the marriage, the wife had petitioned the Ontario courts for a declaration that the divorce was valid, they would have ruled that it was not.[82] Moreover, if, after the marriage, the first husband had come to Ontario and petitioned for a declaration of status, or a decree of nullity with reference to the first marriage, the courts would have ruled that he was still married. In other words, the wife would, in Ontario eyes, have been monogamously married to two different men at the same time. In spite of these conceptual difficulties, however, this may have been the fairest result on the facts of the case, since the parties had married in good faith and had lived together for some time.[83]

2–053   There is no English case in which the problem has arisen in the same way as in *Schwebel v. Ungar*, but there are a number of cases concerning the situation in which the first marriage is no longer subsisting according to English conflict rules but is subsisting according to the conflict rules of the

---

[79] See (1964) 48 D.L.R. (2d) 644, 649 and (1963) 42 D.L.R. (2d) 622, 634.

[80] This assumes that the question whether the marriage was invalid for bigamy was governed *solely* by the law of the wife's domicile immediately prior to the marriage. It could, however, be argued that the marriage would be valid only if it complied with the law of *both* Israel and Ontario. The latter could be relevant either as the law of the place of celebration (as to which see *post* paras. 17E–093 *et seq.*) or as the *lex domicilii* of the second husband (on the basis that he lacked capacity to marry a woman who was a party to a subsisting marriage, a view approved by Simon P. in *Padolecchia v. Padolecchia* [1968] P. 314, 336); see further *post*, para. 17–081.

[81] See (1964) 48 D.L.R. (2d) 644, 649 and (1963) 42 D.L.R. (2d) 622, 633.

[82] See Cheshire and North, pp. 48–49.

[83] The real contention between the parties was in fact a dispute regarding the wife's rights in the matrimonial home in Toronto.

domicile. The first of these is the old case of *Ingham v. Sachs*,[84] in which a man domiciled in Austria had divorced his first wife in Berlin and married his second wife in England. The court held[85] that the divorce would be recognised in England, but it was argued that, as it would not be recognised in Austria, he nevertheless lacked capacity to remarry under the law of his domicile. This argument was rejected by the court and the marriage held valid.[86] A similar argument was, however, accepted in the more modern case of *Padolecchia v. Padolecchia*.[87] Here a man domiciled in Italy divorced his first wife in Mexico and married his second wife in England. Sir Jocelyn Simon P. held that, as the divorce would not be recognised by the Italian rules of the conflict of laws, the second marriage was invalid. *Schwebel v. Ungar* was approved. However, as the divorce would also not have been recognised under the English conflict rules, the result would (as the court recognised) have been the same whichever approach had been applied.

A case in which the choice of approach *was* decisive was *R. v. Brentwood Marriage Registrar*.[88] Here the husband, an Italian national domiciled in Switzerland, divorced his first wife in Switzerland and then wanted to marry a Spanish national, also domiciled in Switzerland. He could not do this in Switzerland because the Swiss conflict rule on capacity to marry looked to the law of the nationality, and the divorce was not recognised under the Italian conflict rule. The couple came to England to get married but the registrar refused to marry them. An application for mandamus was rejected by the Divisional Court. In this case the problem was complicated by the introduction of renvoi, though the court did not analyse it in these terms. This is because the divorce was valid under both English and Swiss law; it was not recognised under Italian law and this law governed the main question (the husband's capacity) under the Swiss conflict rule. By virtue of the renvoi doctrine the English court was applying Italian law to decide the main question; it was also applying the Italian conflict rule to decide the incidental question. **2–054**

The results of this decision were in some ways unfortunate. As she was a Swiss national, the first wife was able to remarry in Switzerland and had done so. But the husband was barred from marriage as long as he retained his Italian nationality. In effect he was in a state of matrimonial limbo: his first marriage was no longer subsisting under either English or Swiss conflict rules but it nevertheless prevented him from remarrying. In spite of this, however, there were arguments in favour of the decision: the parties had no connection with England and came here simply to evade the law of the country in which they were domiciled and in which they intended to live. The case did not really concern England and if the order had been granted it could have been regarded as an interference in the affairs of Switzerland. For these reasons the court said that it would not have exercised its discretion to grant the order even if it had been established that there was no impediment to the marriage. **2–055**

---

[84] (1886) 56 L.T. 920.

[85] On grounds that would not be acceptable today.

[86] As the second wife was domiciled in England, the same result would have been reached on the basis of the rule in *Sottomayor v. De Barros (No. 2)* (1879) 5 P.D. 94 (discussed *post*, at paras. 17E–101 *et seq.*), in which case the problem of the incidental question would not have arisen.

[87] [1968] P. 314. See also *In the Marriage of Barriga* (1981) F.L.C. para. 91–088.

[88] [1968] 2 Q.B. 956. For a similar decision in Scotland, see *Rojas, Petr.*, 1967 S.L.T. (Sh.Ct.) 24.

2–056   The solution to the incidental question applied in the *Brentwood Marriage Registrar* case has, however, been overturned by Parliament. Under section 50 of the Family Law Act 1986, where a decree of divorce or nullity is granted by an English court, or is recognised in England, the fact that the decree would not be recognised elsewhere will not preclude either party to the marriage from remarrying in England, nor will it render the remarriage of either party invalid, irrespective of whether the remarriage takes place within or outside the United Kingdom.[89] This solves the problem in the situations covered by the Act[90]; it does not, however, mean that the same solution will apply in the reverse case, that is where the divorce or nullity decree is not recognised in England, but is recognised in the foreign country: it remains to be seen whether *Schwebel v. Ungar*[91] will be followed in England.[92]

2–057   **Legitimacy.** The incidental question can occur here if, as will often be the case, the legitimacy of the child depends on the validity of the parents' marriage. The problem then arises whether this latter question should be decided by English conflict rules or by the conflict rules of the country whose law governs the main question. The matter is often complicated by the fact that the question of legitimacy may itself be incidental to a question of succession. Where this is so, an incidental question of the second degree may arise. For the sake of simplicity, however, it will be assumed for the moment that the legitimacy of the child is the principal question; succession will be dealt with separately below.

2–058   Under Rule 97,[93] a child is legitimate in England (1) if he was born in lawful wedlock (*i.e.* if his parents' marriage was valid under English conflict rules) or (2) if he is legitimate by the law of the domicile of each of his parents at the date of his birth. The latter case includes the situation where he is legitimate under the law of the domicile by reason of the fact that, under the conflict rules of that country (or those countries), his parents' marriage was valid. This means that the child will be legitimate if the parents' marriage is valid either by English conflict rules or by the conflict rules of the parents' domicile. In other words, the incidental question is decided by whichever of the two systems of conflict of laws is more favourable to the child's legitimacy.

2–059   The second alternative may be made clearer if we take as an example a slightly modified version of the facts in *Re Bischoffsheim*.[94] H and W, while

---

[89] This replaces s.7 of the Recognition of Divorces and Legal Separations Act 1971, which was, however, more limited in scope: it applied only to remarriages in the United Kingdom after a foreign divorce. For cases (before the 1986 Act) applying the same solution to situations outside the scope of the 1971 Act, see *Perrini v. Perrini* [1979] Fam. 84 (remarriage following a foreign decree of nullity) and *Lawrence v. Lawrence* [1985] Fam. 106 (C.A.) (remarriage outside the United Kingdom). The decisions in both these cases would have been the same under the 1986 Act.

[90] One situation not covered by the Act to which the same solution should nevertheless be applied is where there is no decree of divorce or nullity, but the first marriage is void *ab initio* under the English rules of the conflict of laws, though it is valid under the foreign rules of the conflict of laws.

[91] *Supra.*

[92] See *Recognition of Foreign Nullity Decrees*, Law Com. No. 137 (1984), para. 6.60.

[93] See *post* paras. 20R–008 *et seq.*

[94] [1948] Ch. 79. This case has been subject to criticism (discussed at paras. 20–016 *et seq., post*) but most of this does not apply to the problem discussed here.

domiciled in England,[95] go through a ceremony of marriage in New York. Under English internal law, the marriage is invalid because the parties lack the capacity to marry each other. Under the English conflict rule, this question is decided by the law of the domicile and the marriage is therefore invalid in England. Under New York law, on the other hand, the marriage is valid. Let us assume that under the New York conflict rule the validity of the marriage is governed by the internal law of New York.[96] The marriage is therefore valid under the New York conflict rule. After the marriage, H and W acquire a domicile in New York and a child is born to them. Let us assume that the principal question before an English court is whether the child is legitimate.[97] If we refer that question to the law of the parents' domicile at the date of the child's birth (New York law), we find that it depends on the answer to an incidental question, the validity of the marriage. If we decide this incidental question by New York conflict rules, we find that the child is legitimate.[98] If, on the other hand, the marriage had been valid by the English conflict rule and invalid by the New York conflict rule, the first branch of the rule could have been applied and the child would still have been legitimate.

Succession. In general, questions of succession are governed, in the case 2–060 of movables, by the law of the domicile of the deceased at death and, in the case of immovables, by the *lex situs*.[99] Under this law, the right to share in the estate may depend on whether a person is the wife or child of the deceased (or of some other person). If the principal question is the right to share in the estate, what law should decide these incidental questions?

There is authority to suggest that, in some situations at least, the conflict 2–061 rules of the *lex successionis* should be applied. In the Australian case of *Haque v. Haque*,[1] the deceased, a Moslem who was at all times domiciled in India, married his first wife in India under Islamic law and had two daughters by her. He later went through an Islamic ceremony of marriage in Australia with his second wife. This was valid under Islamic law but did not comply with the formal requirements of Australian law and was consequently invalid under the Australian conflict rule. A son and daughter were born of this union. Subsequently, the second wife was divorced under Islamic law. The husband then died, after making a will leaving his estate to his brother. The High Court of Australia held that the law governing succession to his movables was the law of India, under which Islamic law was to be applied. This grants succession rights, in various shares, to a man's wives, sons and daughters. The High

---

[95] In *Re Bischoffsheim* it was uncertain whether the parties were domiciled in England or in New York, but Romer J. held that the child would be legitimate even if they were domiciled in England.

[96] In *Re Bischoffsheim* it was stated by Romer J. that the marriage was valid under New York law but it is unclear whether this meant only under New York internal law or also under the New York conflict rules. It is, however, quite likely that the marriage would have been valid under the New York conflict rules, either on the ground that capacity to marry is governed by the law of the place of celebration or on the ground that, under New York law, the parties were domiciled in New York at the date of the marriage.

[97] In *Re Bischoffsheim* the principal question was actually whether the child could take under an English will. The additional complications raised by this are discussed *post*, at paras. 20–034 *et seq.*

[98] In addition to *Re Bischoffsheim*, authority for this conclusion may be found in *Hashmi v. Hashmi* [1972] Fam. 36 and *Seedat's Executors v. The Master* 1917 A.D. 302 (South Africa).

[99] See paras. 27R–010 *et seq., post.*

[1] (1962) 108 C.L.R. 230.

Court held that in order to determine who was the "wife," "son," or "daughter" of the deceased for this purpose, the validity of the deceased's marriages had to be decided by Islamic law.[2] Under this, both marriages were valid and, though the second wife was excluded by reason of the divorce, her children could share in the estate together with the first wife and her two daughters.

2–062   This case raised special problems because a system of religious law was involved, but it is likely that the same approach would have been applied even if this had not been the case.[3] This does not, however, mean that the conflict rules of the *lex successionis* will necessarily be applied in all cases, particularly where this would lead to the exclusion of someone regarded by English conflict of laws as the wife or child of the deceased. Thus, for example, it is by no means certain that, in the problem given at the beginning of this discussion,[4] the wife's claim would be rejected, especially if she had lived with her husband in England up until his death.

2–063   **Conclusions.** Only three areas of the law have been discussed but it is hoped that enough has been said to show both the varied situations in which the problem can arise and the varied considerations that should be taken into account in order to find a solution. In particular, it is suggested that *a priori* reasoning should be avoided and a flexible approach adopted, taking into account policy considerations such as those of favouring legitimacy and upholding the validity of marriages.

---

[2] Unfortunately the court did not consider whether this was the law that would have been applicable under Indian conflict rules, but it is likely that it was. See also *per* Lord Greene M.R. in *Baindail v. Baindail* [1946] P. 122, 127 (C.A.).

[3] See *Re Johnson* [1903] 1 Ch. 821.

[4] See *ante*, para. 2–044.

CHAPTER 3

THE TIME FACTOR

THE conflict of laws deals primarily with the application of laws in space. Yet **3–001** as in other branches of law, so in the conflict of laws, problems of time cannot be altogether ignored. There is a considerable continental literature on the time factor in the conflict of laws, and a growing awareness of the problem by English writers,[1] though as might be expected the courts have dealt with it in a somewhat empirical fashion.

Three different types of problem have been primarily identified by writers. **3–002** The time factor may become significant if there is a change in the content of the conflict rule of the forum, or in the content of the connecting factor[2] (for example, where a person's domicile is changed), or in the content of the *lex causae*, that is, the foreign law to which the connecting factor refers. It so happens that the Wills Act 1963[3] furnishes a statutory solution to each type of problem in so far as it may arise in connection with the formal validity of wills. The Act laid down a new conflict rule (or rules) in substitution for earlier rules contained in the Wills Act 1861. In the first place, section 7(2) provides that the Act shall come into force on January 1, 1964; section 7(3) repeals the Wills Act 1861; and section 7(4) provides that the repeal of that Act shall not invalidate a will executed before January 1, 1964. Secondly, section 1 provides that a will shall be treated as properly executed if its execution conformed to the internal law in force in the country where, at the time of its execution or of the testator's death, he was domiciled or had his habitual residence, or in a State of which, at either of those times, he was a national.[4] The section thus indicates the time with reference to which the connecting factors of domicile, habitual residence and nationality must be ascertained. Thirdly, section 6(3) provides that regard shall be had to the formal requirements of a particular law at the time of execution, but that this shall not prevent account being taken of an alteration of law affecting wills executed at that time if the alteration enables the will to be treated as properly executed. Thus, retrospective alterations in the *lex causae* made after the

---

[1] Roubier, *Le Droit Transitoire* (2nd ed. 1960); Gavalda, *Les Conflits dans le temps en droit international privé* (1955); F. A. Mann (1954) 31 B.Y.I.L. 217 (with copious references to continental literature and case-law); Grodecki (1959) 35 B.Y.I.L. 58; Spiro (1960) 9 I.C.L.Q. 357; Rabel, Vol. 4, pp. 503–519; Batiffol and Lagarde, Vol. 1, pp. 512–524; Lewald (1939) *Recueil des Cours*, III, 5, 94–99; Wengler (1958) *Rabel's Zeitschrift* 535–572; Rigaux (1966) *Recueil des Cours*, I, 333; Kahn-Freund (1974) *Recueil des Cours*, III, 139, 398–403, 441–446; Grodecki, in Lipstein ed., *International Encyclopedia of Comparative Law*, Vol. III, Chap. 8 (1975); Pryles (1980) 6 Monash U.L.Rev. 225; Fassberg (1990) 39 I.C.L.Q. 856; (1979) 58 *Annuaire de l'Institut de Droit International*, Vol. I, pp. 1–96; *ibid.* Vol. II, pp. 179–190; (1981) 59 *Annuaire de l'Institut de Droit International*, Vol. I, pp. 285–293; *ibid.* Vol. II, pp. 52–115, 246–251.

[2] For the meaning of this expression, see *ante*, para. 1–074.

[3] See Rule 135 and Comment thereto.

[4] The Act also permits conformity with the law of the place of execution. But since this is a constant and not a variable connecting factor, it raises no problems as to time.

execution of the will are relevant if they validate but irrelevant if they invalidate the will.

3–003　**Changes in the conflict rule of the forum.**　A change in the conflict rule of the forum (which French writers call *le conflit transitoire*) probably does not differ from a change in any other rule of law and its effect must therefore be ascertained in accordance with the familiar English rules of statutory interpretation and of judicial precedent. It is unnecessary to discuss those rules in a work on the conflict of laws, but we must call attention briefly to the different ways in which such changes may occur and to some problems which are peculiar to the conflict of laws.

3–004　In English law such changes may occur in three ways: a statute may alter an earlier statutory rule; a statute may alter an earlier rule of judge-made law; or a judicial decision may reverse an earlier judicial rule, or declare a new one. The Wills Act 1963 (noted above) is an example of the first type, and section 72 of the Bills of Exchange Act 1882 is an example of the second.[5] In each of these cases there is usually no problem, because the statute usually contains precise language indicating when it comes into force and to what extent, if any, it is retrospective. If it does not do so, one is thrown back on the general principles of statutory construction, according to which there is a strong but rebuttable presumption that a statute is not intended to have retrospective effect unless it is procedural or declaratory.[6]

3–005　One curious example may be noted of a statutory provision which was evidently intended to lay down a new conflict rule in substitution for an earlier judge-made rule, but which, because it did not expressly abolish the earlier rule, was held by the courts to leave the old rule subsisting side by side with the new. This is section 8(1) of the Legitimacy Act 1926 (now repealed and replaced by section 3 of the Legitimacy Act 1976). At common law, the question whether an illegitimate child was legitimated by the subsequent marriage of his parents was held to depend on the law of the father's domicile at the date of the child's birth and at the date of the subsequent marriage.[7] Section 8(1) of the Legitimacy Act 1926 provided that where the parents of an illegitimate person marry or have married one another, whether before or after the commencement of the Act, and the father was or is, at the time of the marriage, domiciled in a foreign country by the law of which the illegitimate person became legitimated by virtue of such subsequent marriage, that person, if living, should be recognised as having been so legitimated from the commencement of the Act or from the date of the marriage, whichever last happened, notwithstanding that his father was not at the time of the birth of such person domiciled in a country in which legitimation by subsequent marriage was permitted by law.[8] One may surmise that the framers of this subsection intended to abolish the rule of common law and to make the father's domicile at the date of the child's birth irrelevant in future. But they did not use express language to this effect, and so the courts have held that the

---

[5] See Rules 192 and 193 and Comment thereto. In *Re Marseilles Extension Railway and Land Co.* (1885) 30 Ch.D. 598 the court in 1885 applied the pre-1882 rules of common law to a bill of exchange drawn, accepted and indorsed before the Act came into force.
[6] Bennion, *Statutory Interpretation* (3rd ed. 1997), pp. 235 *et seq.*
[7] See Rule 100.
[8] See Rule 101.

old rule of common law still exists and can still be resorted to by a litigant if it suits him to do so, as in some situations it does.[9]

3–006 Judge-made law is retrospective in operation, whereas statute law is usually prospective. Some very strange consequences sometimes follow from a retrospective alteration in a conflict rule of the forum by judicial or legislative action, especially in the field of family relations. Thus, the English conflict rule for the recognition of foreign divorces was radically altered by judicial action in 1953[10] and again in 1967,[11] and by legislative action in 1972[12] and again in 1986.[13] In *Hornett v. Hornett*,[14] a man domiciled in England married in 1919 a woman domiciled before her marriage in France. They lived together in France and England until 1924, when the wife obtained a divorce in France. The husband heard about this divorce in 1925. He then resumed cohabitation with his wife in England until 1936, when they parted. No children were born of this cohabitation. In 1969 the husband petitioned for a declaration that the divorce would be recognised in England. Although it could not have been recognised before 1967, the divorce was recognised under the new judge-made rule declared by the House of Lords in that year.[15]

3–007 If we alter the facts a little, the consequences of this retrospective alteration of the conflict rule are startling:

(a) If children had been born of the resumed cohabitation between the parties after the divorce, would they have been legitimate when born, but rendered illegitimate by the subsequent recognition of the decree?

(b) If the husband had gone through a ceremony of marriage with another woman in 1945, and his second marriage had been annulled for bigamy in 1950, and his second wife had then remarried, would the result of recognising the divorce in 1971 be to invalidate the nullity decree and also the second wife's second marriage?

(c) If the husband had died intestate in 1940, and a share in his property had been distributed to his French wife as his surviving spouse, would she have had to return it when the new conflict rule declared by the House of Lords in 1967 validated her French divorce?[16]

3–008 **Changes in the connecting factor.** From the temporal point of view the connecting factor in a rule of the conflict of laws may be either constant or variable. It may be of such a character that it necessarily refers to a particular moment of time and no other, or it may be liable to change so that further definition is required. For instance, a conflict rule which referred the question of an illegitimate child's legitimation to the law of his father's domicile would be meaningless unless it defined the moment of time at which the father's

---

[9] See *e.g. Re Askew* [1930] 2 Ch. 259; *Re Hurll* [1952] Ch. 722; see *post*, paras. 20R–071 *et seq.*

[10] *Travers v. Holley* [1953] P. 246 (C.A.); *post*, para. 18–062.

[11] *Indyka v. Indyka* [1969] 1 A.C. 33; *post*, para. 18–063.

[12] Recognition of Divorces and Legal Separations Act 1971, repealed and replaced by Family Law Act 1986, Part II. The provisions of the 1971 Act for recognising divorces obtained in foreign countries outside the British Isles were retrospective: s.10(4).

[13] Family Law Act 1986, Part II. These provisions are, in general, retrospective: see s.51(1), (2), (3). See *post*, para. 18–067, and Rule 81.

[14] [1971] P. 255. See also *Edward v. Edward Estate* [1987] 5 W.W.R. 289 (Sask. C.A.).

[15] *Indyka v. Indyka* [1969] 1 A.C. 33.

[16] See the powerful arguments adduced by Latey J. in the court of first instance and by Russell L.J. (dissenting) in the Court of Appeal in *Indyka v. Indyka* [1967] P. 233, 244–245, 262–263.

domicile was relevant. This is achieved by section 3 of the Legitimacy Act 1976, which defines this moment as the time of the father's marriage. Similarly, the simple rule that a person domiciled in a 1968 Convention Contracting State shall be sued in the courts of that State[17] needs to be given greater precision if the defendant's domicile is not constant. Does the court's jurisdiction depend upon the defendant being domiciled in the forum when process is issued or when it is served?[18]

3–009 Examples of constant connecting factors in the English conflict of laws include the *situs* of an immovable, the place where a marriage is celebrated, a will executed, or a tort committed. Examples of varying connecting factors include the *situs* of a movable, the flag of a ship, and the nationality, domicile or residence of an individual.

3–010 The question whether one should refer, *e.g.* to the law of the father's domicile at the date of the child's birth or at the date of the subsequent marriage in order to discover whether a child has been legitimated is simply a question of formulating the most convenient and just conflict rule, and the time factor, though it cannot be disregarded, is not the dominant consideration.[19] It does not seem to differ in principle from the question whether one should refer to the law of the father's or of the mother's domicile. The question is discussed elsewhere in this book as and when it arises, and here it is only necessary to give the reader a brief outline of the type of problem which requires solution. Should the law of the matrimonial domicile at the time of the marriage or at the time of each subsequent acquisition determine the rights of husband and wife to movable property acquired after the date of their marriage?[20] Is capacity to make a will[21] and is the construction of wills[22] governed by the law of the testator's domicile at the time of making the will or at the time of his death? Is revocation of wills governed by the law of the testator's domicile at the time of his death or at the time of the alleged act of revocation?[23] Is the monogamous or polygamous character of a marriage determined once and for all at its inception, or may it change by reason of subsequent events, *e.g.* a change in the parties' domicile?[24] If chattels are taken from one country to another by someone not the owner and disposed of there to a third party, does the first or the second *lex situs* determine whether the owner loses his title?[25] Since a decision on any of these questions has no relevance to any of the others, it is obviously impossible to formulate a general principle.

3–011 Once the time at which the connecting factor must exist has been ascertained, an additional problem of time may arise. Is the court, in ascertaining the existence of the connecting factor at the relevant time, confined to scrutinising facts and circumstances which exist at that time or can it take account of facts and circumstances which are subsequent thereto?[26] Again it

---

[17] Civil Jurisdiction and Judgments Act 1982, Sched. 1, Art. 2.

[18] See *Canada Trust Co. v. Stoltzenberg (No. 2)* [1998] 1 W.L.R. 547 (C.A.), *post*, para. 11–231.

[19] For this reason, it has been doubted whether it is appropriate to treat a change in the connecting factor (which French writers call *le conflit mobile*) as a problem of time in the conflict of laws. See Grodecki (1959) 35 B.Y.I.L. 58.

[20] See Rule 153.

[21] See Rule 134.

[22] See Rule 139.

[23] See Rule 142.

[24] See Rule 71.

[25] See Rule 117.

[26] See Pryles (1980) 6 Monash U.L. Rev. 225, 240–242.

would appear that it is not possible to formulate a general principle. The relevance or otherwise of subsequent facts and circumstances will vary in the light of the function of the choice of law rule of which the particular connecting factor forms part. Thus in ascertaining the law applicable to a contract, at common law, only facts and circumstances existing at the time the contract was made could be examined.[27] On the other hand when it was necessary to determine whether, at the time of the institution of proceedings for nullity in a foreign country, the petitioner had a real and substantial connection with that country with the result that the foreign nullity decree could be recognised in England, at common law it was possible that events subsequent to the institution of proceedings could be looked at.[28]

Changes in the lex causae. Changes in the *lex causae* present much the most important and difficult problems of time in the conflict of laws, especially when the change purports to have retrospective effect. The overwhelming weight of opinion among writers is that the forum should apply the *lex causae* in its entirety, including its transitional rules. This is certainly the prevailing practice of courts on the continent of Europe. It is probably the prevailing practice of the English courts, although there is one case, *Lynch v. Provisional Government of Paraguay*,[29] which is often cited for the contrary proposition. Much confusion has resulted from ambiguous formulations of the conflict rule, and these in turn have suffered from a failure to distinguish between constant and variable connecting factors. If, for example, the forum's conflict rule says that succession to immovables is governed by the *lex situs*, the connecting factor is constant, no further definition is required, and it is natural and proper for courts to apply the *lex situs* as it exists from time to time. But if the forum's conflict rule says that succession to movables is governed by the law of the deceased's domicile, the connecting factor is variable, further definition is required to make the rule more precise, and so the words "at the time of his death" are added in order to define the time at which his domicile is relevant. The effect is to exclude reference to any earlier domicile, but courts have sometimes assumed that the effect is also to exclude changes in the law of the domicile made after the death of the deceased. This assumption, it is submitted, is unnecessary and improper, for the two questions are really quite distinct. **3–012**

Although it must be emphasised that the problem is always basically the same, namely, should the forum apply or disregard subsequent changes in the *lex causae*, it will be convenient to deal with it under the following heads, arranged according to subject-matter: (a) succession to immovables; (b) succession to movables; (c) torts; (d) discharge of contracts; (e) legitimation; (f) matrimonial property; (g) validity of marriage. In conclusion, something will be said on (h) the extent to which public policy may occasionally induce the forum to refuse recognition to foreign retrospective laws, and on (i) the **3–013**

---

[27] *Whitworth Street Estates (Manchester) Ltd. v. James Miller and Partners Ltd.* [1970] A.C. 583. The position is probably otherwise under the Rome Convention on the Law Applicable to Contractual Obligations (Contracts (Applicable Law) Act 1990, Sched. 1), Art. 4: see Giuliano-Lagarde Report [1980] O.J. C282/20. See *post*, para. 32–038. The 1990 Act applies to contracts entered into after April 1, 1991. See *post*, para. 32–002.

[28] *Law v. Gustin* [1976] Fam. 155, 160. The law relating to the recognition of foreign annulments is now contained in the Family Law Act 1986, Part II. The Act does not adopt the test of real and substantial connection. See *post*, paras. 18–103 *et seq.*

[29] (1871) L.R. 2 P. & D. 268.

time problem in cases where it may be necessary to refer to a foreign law other than the *lex causae* as a *datum* which is relevant to deciding the case.

3–014   (a) *Succession to immovables.* In *Nelson v. Bridport*,[30] the King of the Two Sicilies granted land in Sicily to Admiral Nelson for himself and the heirs of his body, with power to appoint a successor. By his will the Admiral devised the land to trustees in trust for his brother W for life with remainders over. After the Admiral's death, and in the lifetime of W, a law was passed in Sicily abolishing entails and making the persons lawfully in possession of such estates the absolute owners thereof. Taking advantage of this law, W devised the land to his daughter, from whom it was claimed by the remainderman under the Admiral's will. In giving judgment for the defendant, Lord Langdale M.R. took it for granted that he had to apply the law of Sicily as it existed from time to time and not as it was at the time of the Admiral's death or at the time of the original grant.

3–015   (b) *Succession to movables.* However, an opposite result was reached in *Lynch v. Provisional Government of Paraguay*.[31] A testator who had been dictator of Paraguay died domiciled there having by his will left movable property in England to the plaintiff. Two months after his death, but before probate of the will had been granted in England, there was a revolution in Paraguay, and the new Government passed a decree declaring all the testator's property wherever situate to be the property of the State and depriving his will of any validity in England or elsewhere. This decree purported to relate back to the testator's death. The plaintiff applied for a grant of probate as universal legatee under the will. Her application was opposed by the new Government. The Government's opposition was bound to fail, because the decree was penal[32] and because property in England could not be confiscated by a foreign Government.[33] But Lord Penzance, in granting probate to the plaintiff, preferred to rest his judgment on the ground that English law adopts the law of the domicile "as it stands at the time of the death" and does not undertake to give effect to subsequent retrospective changes in that law. In support of this proposition he quoted Story's formulation that succession to movables is governed by the law of the domicile "at the time of the death," without appearing to realise that the last six words were intended to qualify "domicile" and not "law," and that Story was never considering the effect of subsequent retrospective changes in the law.

3–016   Lord Penzance's manifest inclination to uphold the will on the peculiar facts of the case is understandable, but his wide formulation has been much criticised by writers[34] on the ground that it failed to give effect to the transitional law of the *lex causae*, and appeared to do so irrespective of the content of that law. If, for example, the will had been defective in point of form, *e.g.* because the law of Paraguay required all wills to be witnessed by a notary public, and after the testator's death it was discovered that a witness, though practising as a notary, was not qualified to do so, and the will had been

---

[30] (1846) 8 Beav. 547.

[31] (1871) L.R. 2 P. & D. 268.

[32] *Cf. Banco de Vizcaya v. Don Alfonso de Borbon y Austria* [1935] 1 K.B. 140; see Rule 3.

[33] See Rule 120. See also *Adams v. National Bank of Greece and Athens S.A.* [1958] 2 Q.B. 59, 76 (affd. [1961] A.C. 255) and Wengler (1958) *Rabel's Zeitschrift* 563–564, esp. n. 22.

[34] See F. A. Mann (1954) 31 B.Y.I.L. 217, 234; Grodecki (1959) 35 B.Y.I.L. 58, 67–69, where various interpretations of the decision are discussed.

validated by retrospective legislation in Paraguay, it is hard to suppose that Lord Penzance would have thought it "inconvenient and unjust" to give effect to that legislation.

The decision was followed without much discussion in *Re Aganoor's* **3–017** *Trusts*.[35] In that case, a testatrix died in 1868 domiciled in Padua having by her will given a settled legacy to A for life and if he died without children to B for life and then to B's children living at B's death. This was valid by the Austrian law in force in Padua in 1868; but on September 1, 1871, the Italian Civil Code came into force and forbade trust substitutions, dividing the ownership between the persons in possession on that date and the first persons entitled in remainder who were born or conceived before then. B died in 1891 leaving children. A died in 1894 without children. It was held that the settled legacy was valid and that the change in the law in force in Padua made after the death of the testatrix would be ignored. This result is diametrically opposite to that which was reached in *Nelson v. Bridport*.[36]

If it is true that in succession to movables no account is to be taken of **3–018** subsequent changes in the *lex causae* made after the death of the testator, that proposition is subject to an important qualification so far as the formal validity of wills is concerned. For, as we have seen,[37] section 6(3) of the Wills Act 1963 provides that retrospective alterations in the *lex causae* made after the execution of the will are relevant in so far as they validate but irrelevant in so far as they invalidate the will. This enactment is not in terms confined to alterations in the law made before the death of the testator, and there seems no reason to read into it words which are not there.

(c) *Torts*. In *Phillips v. Eyre*,[38] an action for assault and false imprisonment **3–019** was brought in England against the ex-Governor of Jamaica. The acts complained of took place in Jamaica while the defendant was engaged in suppressing a rebellion which had broken out in the island. The acts were illegal by the law of Jamaica as it stood at the time of the tort; but the defendant pleaded that they had been subsequently legalised by an Act of Indemnity passed in Jamaica with retrospective effect. The Court of Exchequer Chamber gave effect to this defence. It follows from this decision that even in 1870 English law had no objection to foreign retrospective legislation as such and what was true in 1870 must be even more true today when retrospective legislation has become a more familiar phenomenon in English domestic law. It must be admitted, however, that the circumstances in *Phillips v. Eyre* were rather special, in that the *lex causae* was that of a British colony, there was no difference between the *lex fori* and the *lex causae* except in regard to the Act of Indemnity, and that Act was of a kind familiar to English domestic law. Still, it remains true that the Court of Exchequer Chamber adopted a wholly different approach from that of Lord Penzance in *Lynch's* case.[39]

(d) *Discharge of contracts*. At common law, the discharge of contracts **3–020** affected the substance of the obligation and therefore normally depended on

---

[35] (1895) 64 L.J.Ch. 521; criticised by F. A. Mann (1954) 31 B.Y.I.L. 217, 234; Grodecki (1959) 35 B.Y.I.L. 58, 69–70.

[36] (1846) 8 Beav. 547; *ante*, para. 3–014.

[37] *Ante*, para. 3–002.

[38] (1870) L.R. 6 Q.B. 1.

[39] (1871) L.R. 2 P. & D. 268.

the law which governed the contract.[40] The position is the same under the Rome Convention on the Law Applicable to Contractual Obligations, implemented in the United Kingdom by the Contracts (Applicable Law) Act 1990. According to that Convention the law found applicable to the contract by reference to the rules of the Convention governs both matters of "performance,"[41] and the "various ways of extinguishing obligations."[42] Numerous common law decisions clearly established that the content of the rules of the governing law was that which existed from time to time and that therefore legislation enacted in the country whose law governed the contract after the date of the contract may have the effect of discharging or modifying the contractual obligations of the parties.[43] Although the Rome Convention is silent on this question, there would appear to be no doubt that the position under the Convention is the same as at common law. A striking example of the problem at common law, which, it is submitted, would be resolved in the same way under the Convention is the case of *R. v. International Trustee for the Protection of Bondholders A.G.*[44] In February 1917 the British Government floated a 250 million dollar loan on the New York money market. The capital was repayable at holder's option either in New York in gold coin of the United States or in London in sterling at a specified rate of exchange. In 1933 a Joint Resolution of Congress provided that all gold coin and gold value clauses attached to obligations expressed in dollars were against public policy and that all dollar obligations whenever incurred could be discharged upon payment, dollar for dollar, in any coin or currency which was legal tender at the time of payment. The bondholders sought to enforce the gold clause according to its terms. But the House of Lords held that the law governing the contract was the law of New York and that therefore the gold clause had been abrogated by the Joint Resolution, with the result that the loan could be repaid in New York in depreciated paper dollars.

3–021   In *Adams v. National Bank of Greece and Athens S.A.*[45] the House of Lords refused to apply a Greek law which purported retrospectively to exonerate a Greek bank from liability under a contract of guarantee governed by English law. The House was not unanimous in its reasons for reaching this conclusion[46]; but the main reason seems to have been that since the law applicable to the contract was English, no Greek law could discharge one party's obligation thereunder.[47] The same solution would be reached under the provisions of the Rome Convention on the Law Applicable to Contractual Obligations. Since English law governed the contract, that law would determine

---

[40] See *post*, paras. 32–007, 32–201 *et seq.*

[41] Rome Convention, Art. 10(1)(*b*). See *post*, paras. 32–191—32–197.

[42] *Ibid.*, Art. 10(1)(*d*). See *post*, paras. 32–201 *et seq.*

[43] *Re Chesterman's Trusts* [1923] 2 Ch. 466, 478 (C.A.); *Perry v. Equitable Life Assurance Society* (1929) 45 T.L.R. 468; *Assicurazioni Generali v. Cotran* [1932] A.C. 268 (P.C.); *De Beéche v. South American Stores Ltd.* [1935] A.C. 148; *R. v. International Trustee for the Protection of Bondholders A.G.* [1937] A.C. 500; *Kornatzki v. Oppenheimer* [1937] 4 All E.R. 133; *Kahler v. Midland Bank Ltd.* [1950] A.C. 24; *Jabbour v. Custodian of Israeli Absentee Property* [1954] 1 W.L.R. 139, 157 (where there was a change of sovereignty in the *locus contractus*); *Re Helbert Wagg & Co. Ltd.* [1956] Ch. 323, 341–342.

[44] [1937] A.C. 500. *Cf. New Brunswick Ry. v. British and French Trust Corporation* [1939] A.C. 1.

[45] [1961] A.C. 255.

[46] See, for a detailed analysis of the judgments, Grodecki (1961) 24 M.L.R. 701, 706–714.

[47] See, in particular, the judgment of Lord Reid and that of Diplock J. in the court of first instance: [1958] 2 Q.B. 59.

whether the obligation of the bank was extinguished,[48] and Greek law could have no effect on the issue.[49] The case is noteworthy in the present context because all five members of the House went out of their way to approve the principle of *Lynch's* case.[50] But only Lord Tucker based his judgment squarely on that decision, and Lord Reid was not satisfied that it should be applied to a case like the one before him. It is submitted that this is the preferable view, and the view which should certainly be adopted in cases falling within the Rome Convention on the Law Applicable to Contractual Obligations.

(e) *Legitimation.* As we have seen,[51] section 3 of the Legitimacy Act 1976 **3–022** provides for the recognition in England of a foreign legitimation if the father of the illegitimate person was, at the date of the subsequent marriage, domiciled in a foreign country by whose law the illegitimate person became legitimate by virtue of such marriage.[52] The subsection is confined to legitimation by subsequent marriage and does not extend to other modes and the legitimation is recognised from the date of the marriage, and not from any earlier date. Hence even if the effect of the foreign *lex causae* is to legitimate the illegitimate person retrospectively from the date of his birth, he cannot be recognised as legitimate in England from that date under section 3 of the Act. But there seems no reason why he should not be recognised in England as having been retrospectively legitimated from the date of his birth under the common law rule,[53] provided his father was domiciled in the foreign country at the date of the illegitimate person's birth as well as at the date of the subsequent marriage, and provided the marriage had this retrospective effect under the foreign law. Scott L.J. in *Re Luck*[54] appeared to think that the effect of legitimation under the common law rule was always retrospective, even in the absence of any retrospective effect in the *lex causae*. But the cases cited by him do not seem to support this view, which appears to be contrary to principle. If the law of France says that an illegitimate person is legitimated as from the date of the marriage, there is no reason why English law should say that he was legitimated as from the date of his birth.

Section 2 of the Legitimacy Act 1976 provides for the legitimation of the **3–023** child if the father was domiciled in England at the time of the subsequent marriage. Statutes very similar to the English Act are in force in many other countries, including Northern Ireland. None of these statutes contains any provision for recognising a legitimation effected under any of the others except in so far as they refer to legitimation by subsequent marriage. If the father of an illegitimate person marries the mother while domiciled, *e.g.* in Northern Ireland after the coming into force of the Northern Irish Act, there is of course no difficulty about recognising the legitimation in England under section 3 of the Act of 1976. But if the marriage took place before the coming into force of the Northern Irish Act, and the father was dead, or no longer

---

[48] Rome Convention, Art. 10(1)(*d*). See *post*, paras. 32–201 *et seq.*
[49] Under the Convention, it would seem that the only way in which Greek law could impinge on the issue is through the operation of Art. 7(1). But Art. 7(1) does not have the force of law in the United Kingdom since the United Kingdom entered the permitted reservation to it: see Contracts (Applicable Law) Act 1990. s.2(2) and Sched. 1, Art. 22(1)(*a*). See *post*, paras. 32–045, 32–138 *et seq.*
[50] [1961] A.C. 255, 275–276, 282, 285, 287.
[51] *Ante*, para. 3–005.
[52] See Rule 101.
[53] See Rule 100 and *ante*, para. 3–005.
[54] [1940] Ch. 864, 898–899 (C.A.). See *post*, para. 20–059, n. 12.

domiciled in Northern Ireland, when the Northern Irish Act came into force, the child is undoubtedly legitimate in Northern Ireland. But he cannot be recognised as having been legitimated in England under section 3 of the English Act, because it is confined to cases where "the illegitimate person became legitimated by virtue of such subsequent marriage"; and he became legitimated by virtue of the Northern Irish Act, not by virtue of the subsequent marriage. Yet it seems anomalous that a person should be recognised in Northern Ireland but not in England as having been legitimated when the statute law of the two countries is couched in almost identical terms.[55] The solution seems to be to fall back on the English common law rule (which is probably not confined to legitimation by subsequent marriage[56]) and apply the law of the country in which the father was domiciled at the date of the child's birth and the date of the subsequent marriage, as that law stands at the time of the proceedings in England.[57] It is only by giving effect to subsequent changes in the *lex causae* that the anomalous situation referred to above can be avoided. It is noteworthy that, for purposes of British citizenship, a person is deemed to have been legitimated by the subsequent marriage of his parents if, by the law of the place where his father was domiciled at the time of the marriage, the marriage operated immediately *or subsequently* to legitimate him.[58]

3–024   (f) *Matrimonial property.* In *Sperling v. Sperling*,[59] a husband and wife, domiciled in East Germany, married there in 1954. The marriage was not subject to any community property régime. They emigrated to South Africa in 1957 and acquired a domicile in the Transvaal. In 1965 the East German law was altered with retrospective effect so as to provide for community of acquisitions after marriage. The Appellate Division of the Supreme Court of South Africa held that this retrospective law must receive effect in South Africa. The reference to East German law as the law of the matrimonial domicile meant the whole of its law, including its transitional law, and public policy did not forbid its application.

3–025   (g) *Validity of marriage.* In *Starkowski v. Att.-Gen.*,[60] H1 and W, both Roman Catholics domiciled in Poland, went through a ceremony of marriage in Austria in May 1945 in a Roman Catholic church. They lived together until 1947, when they separated, having acquired a domicile of choice in England. In 1950 W went through a ceremony of marriage in England with H2, a Pole domiciled in England. In May 1945 a purely religious marriage without civil ceremony was void by Austrian law. But in June 1945 a law was passed in

---

[55] If the marriage takes place before the commencement of the English Act of 1926 or the Northern Irish Act of 1928, neither Act requires the father to be living at the date of such commencement.

[56] See *post*, paras. 20–062 *et seq.*

[57] *Cf. Re Hagerbaum* [1933] I.R. 198. The Australian and New Zealand courts have laid down a much more stringent rule: see *post*, paras. 20–065 *et seq.* The decision in *Heron v. National Trustees Executors and Agency Co. of Australasia Ltd.* [1976] V.R. 733 is consistent with the suggestion in the text; but the case was decided under s.90 of the Australian Marriage Act 1961. The question has not yet arisen in England. See *post*, paras. 20–067 *et seq.*

[58] British Nationality Act 1981, s.47(2).

[59] 1975 (3) S.A. 707. To the same effect is *Topolski v. The Queen* (1978) 90 D.L.R. (3d) 66, a decision of the Federal Court of Canada. The question has often come before courts in continental Europe: see Grodecki, in Lipstein (ed.), *International Encyclopedia of Comparative Law*, Vol. III, Chap. 8, paras. 45–48.

[60] [1954] A.C. 155.

Austria retrospectively validating such marriages if they were duly registered. The marriage between H1 and W was registered in 1949, but without W's knowledge or consent, after she had acquired a domicile in England, and after she had separated from H1.[61] The House of Lords held that the Austrian ceremony was valid and the English ceremony was bigamous and void. Lord Reid stated the question to be decided as follows[62]: "Are we to take the law of that place (*sc.* the place of celebration) as it was when the marriage was celebrated, or are we to inquire what the law of that place now is with regard to the formal validity of that marriage?"—a question which he answered by saying "There is no compelling reason why the reference should not be to that law as it is when the problem arises for decision."[63] Lord Cohen distinguished *Lynch*[64] somewhat faintly on the ground that it involved a remotely different subject-matter.[65] Lord Tucker agreed with Barnard J. in the court of first instance[66] that *Lynch* would have been of more assistance if the second ceremony had preceded the registration of the first.[67] But these distinctions seem illusory because, as is shown by Lord Reid's formulation quoted above, the problem was basically the same. The House of Lords adopted a different approach from that of Lord Penzance and (it is submitted) a preferable one.

(h) *Public policy.* The prevailing practice of the English courts thus seems to be to apply the *lex causae* as it exists from time to time and to give effect if need be to retrospective changes therein. But the consequences of giving effect to retrospective changes in the law are sometimes so extraordinary that public policy must occasionally impose qualifications and exceptions. There is an almost complete lack of English authority on this question. The discussion that follows is therefore highly speculative. It will throw the problem into the clearest possible relief if we consider some variations on the facts of the *Starkowski* case and consider what decision an English court might be expected to reach.   **3–026**

(1) If the Austrian marriage had been originally valid but had later been retrospectively invalidated by Austrian legislation, it would seem that, on grounds of policy, the marriage should be held valid in England. There is, however, at least one decision of a French court to the opposite effect.[68]   **3–027**

(2) If either party had obtained an English nullity decree annulling the Austrian marriage for informality before it was registered, it would seem that foreign retrospective legislation should not be allowed to invalidate the English nullity decree.[69]

---

[61] Dr. F. A. Mann thought that the breakdown of the marriage before the registration of the Austrian ceremony should have led the House of Lords to an opposite conclusion: (1954) 31 B.Y.I.L. 217, 243–245. But this seems unacceptable for the reasons given by Grodecki (1959) 35 B.Y.I.L. 58, 75–76.

[62] [1954] A.C. 155, 170.

[63] [1954] A.C. 155, 172.

[64] (1871) L.R. 2 P. & D. 268.

[65] [1954] A.C. 155, 180.

[66] [1952] P. 135, 144.

[67] [1954] A.C. 155, 175.

[68] *Guerra c. Tissander*, Tribunal de Tulle, January 6, 1944, in 1947 *Rev. Crit.* 304. The decision is approved by Grodecki, in Lipstein (ed.), *International Encyclopedia of Comparative Law*, Vol. III, Chap. 8, para. 30; and see para. 34(3).

[69] *Cf. Starkowski v. Att.-Gen.* [1954] A.C. 155, 172, where Lord Reid, who alone adverted to this point, expressly refrained from deciding it. See also *Von Lorang v. Administrator of Austrian Property* [1927] A.C. 641, 651.

3–028   (3) What would the position have been if the English ceremony had preceded and not followed the registration of the Austrian ceremony? The majority of the House of Lords expressly left this question open in the *Starkowski* case.[70] It is submitted that the English ceremony should have been held valid. A similar point was decided by the British Columbia Court of Appeal in *Ambrose v. Ambrose*.[71] A wife obtained an interlocutory judgment for divorce from her first husband in California, where they were domiciled, on November 25, 1930. This judgment could become final, and so entitle either party to remarry, at the expiration of one year, either on the application of either party or on the court's own motion. It was not in fact made final until 1939. Meanwhile in 1935 the wife went through a ceremony of marriage in the State of Washington with her second husband, who was domiciled in British Columbia. They lived together in British Columbia until 1956, when they separated. The wife then took advantage of a Californian statute passed in 1955 and obtained an order from the Californian court in 1958 which retrospectively backdated the divorce to November 25, 1931, the earliest date on which final judgment could have been obtained. The second husband then petitioned for nullity in British Columbia on the ground that the second ceremony was bigamous. The court granted a decree. It distinguished *Starkowski v. Att.-Gen.* on two grounds. First, the defect in that case was formal and could be corrected by the *lex loci celebrationis*, which remained constant throughout whereas the defect in the instant case related to capacity, a matter which was governed by the law of the wife's antenuptial domicile: but she ceased to be domiciled in California in 1939, and was therefore domiciled in British Columbia, and not in California, when she obtained her order from the Californian court in 1958. Secondly, in *Starkowski v. Att.-Gen.* the retrospective validation of the Austrian ceremony preceded the English ceremony, whereas in the instant case the Washington ceremony preceded the retrospective validation of the Californian divorce.

3–029   (i) *Foreign law as datum.* Finally, attention must be drawn to a problem of time which may arise when, although a particular foreign law is not the *lex causae*, it may nevertheless be necessary to refer to it as a *datum* or fact which is relevant to deciding the case.[72] In this situation it appears that foreign law is applied as it exists at a particular time rather than as it exists from time to time.[73] For example, parties may in a contract incorporate provisions of foreign law as a "shorthand" method of stating contractual terms and conditions. Accordingly it may be necessary to look to that foreign law, not as the law governing the contract, but in order to identify the terms and conditions thus incorporated. In such circumstances the court will look to the content of the foreign law as at the time the contract was made.[74] Conversely the content of the governing law will, as we have seen, in general be determined as it exists from time to time.[75]

---

[70] [1954] A.C. 155, 168, 176, 182.

[71] (1961) 25 D.L.R. (2d) 1 (B.C.C.A); criticised by Castel (1961) 39 Can. Bar Rev. 604; Hartley (1967) 16 I.C.L.Q. 680, 699–703; Grodecki, *op. cit.*, para. 34(1).

[72] As to foreign law as datum see *post*, para. 35–015.

[73] See Pryles (1980) 6 Monash U.L. Rev. 225, 234–236 where examples are discussed.

[74] *Timm v. Northumbrian Shipping Co.* (1937) 58 Ll.L.R. 45; affd. [1939] A.C. 397; *Vita Food Products Inc. v. Unus Shipping Co. Ltd.* [1939] A.C. 277, 291 (P.C.) The position is the same under the Rome Convention on the Law Applicable to Contractual Obligations: see *post*, paras. 32–086 *et seq.* where the problem of incorporation by reference is discussed.

[75] *Ante*, para. 3–012.

CHAPTER 4

RENVOI[1]

RULE 1—In the Rules and Exceptions in this book the law of a country   4R–001
(*e.g.* the law of the country where a person is domiciled)
    (1) means, when applied to England, the domestic law of England;
    (2) means, when applied to any foreign country, usually the domestic
       law of that country, sometimes any domestic law which the courts
       of that country would apply to the decision of the case to which the
       Rule refers.

COMMENT

4–002

The term "law of country," *e.g.* the law of England or the law of Italy is
ambiguous. It means in its narrower and most usual sense the domestic law of
any country, *i.e.* the law applied by its courts in cases which contain no foreign
element. It means in its wider sense all the rules, including the rules of the
conflict of laws, which the courts of a country apply.

4–003

(1) **When "country" is England.** When any Rule, applied to the circumstances of a given case, directs that the case be determined in accordance with
the law of England, then the term "law of England" must mean the domestic
law of England. If the term were used in a more general sense and meant
whatever law or principle an English court would apply to the case, the Rule
would constitute an unmeaning truism; for we are dealing with cases decided
by an English court, and any case so decided must be determined in accordance with some law or principle which the English court applies to it. If by
the law of England were meant any principle which the English courts would
apply to the case, the Rule would afford no guidance whatever.

4–004

---

[1] The literature on this subject is immense. See Bate, *Notes on the Doctrine of Renvoi* (1904);
Bentwich, *The Law of Domicile in its Relation to Succession and the Doctrine of Renvoi*
(1911); Baty, *Polarized Law* (1914), pp. 116 *et seq.*; Mendelssohn-Bartholdy, *Renvoi in
Modern English Law* (1937); Abbott (1908) 24 L.Q.R. 137; Jethro Brown (1909) 25 L.Q.R.
149; Schreiber (1918) 31 Harv.L.R. 523; Morris (1937) 18 B.Y.I.L. 32; Griswold (1938) 51
Harv.L.R. 1165; Cowan (1938) 87 U. of Penn.L.Rev. 34; Griswold (1939) *ibid.* 257; Cormack
(1941) 14 So.Calif.L.Rev. 249–275; Raeburn (1948) 25 B.Y.I.L. 211; Inglis (1958) 74 L.Q.R.
493; Kahn-Freund (1974) *Recueil des Cours*, III, pp. 431–437; Briggs (1998) 47 I.C.L.Q. 877.
The fullest discussion in English is to be found in Falconbridge, Chaps. 6–10. For continental
literature, see Rabel, Vol. I, pp. 75–90; Lewald (1929) *Recueil des Cours*, IV, p. 519; Niboyet,
Traité, Vol. 3, pp. 435–487; Batiffol and Lagarde, Vol. 1, pp. 491–509; Melchior, *Die
Grundlagen des Deutschen Internationalen Privatrechts* (1932), pp. 192–245; Franceskakis, *La
Théorie du Renvoi* (1958). There are conflicting decisions on this matter in the New York
courts: see *Re Tallmadge*, 181 N.Y. Supp. 336 (1919); *Re Schneider's Estate*, 198 Misc. 1017,
96 N.Y.S. 2d 652 (1950) discussed by Morris (1951) 4 Int.L.Q. 268, where an attempt is made
to reconcile the two cases. These and other American cases are discussed by Falconbridge,
Chap. 10.

4–004   (2) **When "country" is a foreign country.** When any Rule applied to the circumstances of a given case directs that the case be determined in accordance with the law, *e.g.* of Italy, then the term "law of Italy" means usually the domestic law of Italy, but sometimes means any system of law which the Italian courts would hold applicable to the particular case. This ambiguity in the expression "law of Italy" gives rise to the difficult problem of renvoi.

4–005   **Nature of the problem.**   The problem of renvoi arises whenever a rule of the conflict of laws refers to the "law" of a foreign country, but the conflict rule of the foreign country would have referred the question to the "law" of the first country or to the "law" of some third country. The classic illustration is that of the British citizen who dies intestate domiciled in Italy, leaving movables in England. The English conflict rule refers to the law of the domicile (Italian law), but the Italian conflict rule refers to the national law, which may for the moment be assumed to be English law. Here we have a patent conflict of conflict rules involving a reference back (remission) to the forum. Had the intestate been a German instead of a British national we should have had a patent conflict of conflict rules involving a reference on (transmission) to German law. Had the intestate been domiciled in New York in the English sense but in England in the New York sense, and both the English and the New York conflict rules agreed that intestate succession to movables was governed by the law of the domicile, we should have had a latent conflict of conflict rules, arising from the fact that though the English and New York conflict rules were in apparent agreement, they differed in what constitutes domicile.[2]

4–006   In these situations, a court might conceivably resolve the ambiguity in three different ways.[3]

(a) The court might apply the domestic rule of the foreign country, that is, the law of the foreign country applicable to a purely domestic situation arising therein, without regard to the elements which render the situation a conflict of laws situation for the foreign law. Thus, in the case of a British citizen dying intestate domiciled in Italy, and leaving movables in England, the English court might (if it adopted this method of solution) apply the purely domestic rule of Italian law applicable to Italians, disregarding the fact that the intestate was a British citizen. This method requires proof of the domestic law of the foreign country, but does not require proof of its conflict rules. It has been recommended (*obiter*) by two English judges on the ground that it is "simple and rational,"[4] but rejected in another case after a comprehensive review of the authorities.[5]

4–007   (b) If the conflict rule of the foreign country refers back to the law of the forum or on to the law of a third country, the court might accept the reference and apply the domestic law of the forum or the domestic law of the third

---

[2] At least two important differences between English and New York rules as to domicile may be suggested: (1) in New York the abandonment of a domicile of choice does not involve the revival of the domicile of origin (contrast Rule 13(2)(ii)); (2) in New York a domicile of origin is more easily displaced by a domicile of choice than it is in England.

[3] Morris (1937) 18 B.Y.I.L. 32, 33; Falconbridge, pp. 173–174; First Report of the Private International Law Committee (1954) (Cmd. 9068), para. 23.

[4] *Re Annesley* [1926] Ch. 692, 708–709; *Re Askew* [1930] 2 Ch. 259, 278; *cf. Barcelo v. Electrolytic Zinc Co. of Australasia* (1932) 48 C.L.R. 391, 437.

[5] *Re Ross* [1930] 1 Ch. 377, 402. The review was so comprehensive that four months elapsed between the hearing and delivery of the judgment.

country. The former process is technically known as "accepting the renvoi."[6] Thus, in the case of a British citizen dying intestate domiciled in Italy, leaving movables in England, the English court might (if it adopted this method of solution) apply the domestic rule of English law, that is the rule laid down in the Administration of Estates Act 1925 (as amended), disregarding the fact that the intestate was domiciled in Italy. This method requires proof of the conflict rules of the foreign country relating to succession, but does not require proof of the foreign rules about renvoi. It has been adopted by some Continental courts in a number of celebrated cases,[7] and is sometimes enjoined by Continental legislatures,[8] but it is not the current doctrine of the English courts. It may conveniently be called the theory of "partial" or "single" renvoi.

(c) The court might decide the case in exactly the same way as it would be 4–008 decided by the foreign court. Thus, in the case of a British citizen dying intestate domiciled in Italy, leaving movables in England, the English court (if it adopted this method of solution) would decide the case as it would be decided by the Italian court. If the Italian court would refer to English "law" and would interpret that reference to mean English domestic law,[9] then the English court would apply English domestic law. If on the other hand the Italian court would refer to English "law" and interpret that reference to mean English conflict of laws, and would "accept the renvoi" from English law and apply Italian domestic law, then the English court would apply Italian domestic law. This method requires proof not only of the conflict rule of the foreign country relating to succession but also of the foreign rules about renvoi. In spite of its greater complexity, it seems to represent the present doctrine of the English courts, at least in certain contexts. It may conveniently be called the theory of "total" or "double" renvoi.

Origin and development. The doctrine of renvoi obtained a foothold in 4–009 English law through the medium of cases on the formal validity of wills. In that context, three factors favoured its recognition: first, the rigid rule of the English conflict of laws which at that time insisted on compliance with one form and one form only for wills, that of the testator's last domicile[10]; secondly, a more flexible rule in neighbouring European countries (where people of English origin were likely to settle), which allowed compliance with the forms prescribed by either the testator's personal law or the law of the place where the will was made; and thirdly, a judicial bias in favour of upholding wills which admittedly expressed the last wishes of the testator and were defective only in point of form. The fountain-head of authority is *Collier*

---

[6] This expression must be distinguished from accepting the doctrine of the renvoi, which the forum may do without necessarily accepting the first reference back. The former expression means stopping the game of ping-pong with the return of the service. The latter means continuing the game until the other player gets tired of it.

[7] OLG Lübeck, March 21, 1861, 14 Seuffert's Archiv, p. 164; *Bigwood v. Bigwood* (1881) Belgique Judiciaire, p. 758; *L'Affaire Forgo*, 1883 *Clunet* 64; *L'Affaire Soulié*, 1910 *Clunet* 888; Falconbridge, pp. 147–149.

[8] *e.g.* art. 27 of the Introductory Law of the German Civil Code (1900).

[9] This is in fact what the Italian court would do: see Introduction to the Italian Civil Code, art. 30.

[10] The law has since been amended, first by the Wills Act 1861, and now by the Wills Act 1963. See Rule 135.

v. Rivaz,[11] where the court had to consider the formal validity of a will and six codicils made by a British subject who died domiciled in Belgium in the English sense, but in England in the Belgian sense because he had not obtained the authorisation of the Belgian Government to establish his domicile in Belgium, as required by Article 13 of the Code Napoleon. The will and two of the codicils were made in local Belgian form and were admitted to probate in England without argument. Four of the codicils were opposed because they were not made in local Belgian form, though they were made in English form. Upon proof that by Belgian law the validity of wills made by foreigners not legally domiciled in Belgium was governed by "the laws of their own country," Sir H. Jenner admitted these codicils to probate, remarking that "the court sitting here to determine it, must consider itself sitting in Belgium under the peculiar circumstances of this case."[12] He did not consider the possibility that a Belgian court might have accepted the renvoi from English law and applied Belgian domestic law.

4–010   The fact that the will and the two codicils made in Belgian form were admitted to probate as well as the four codicils made in English form means that the English conflict rule for the formal validity of wills was interpreted as a rule of alternative reference either to the domestic rules or to the conflict rules of the law of the domicile. For this reason, *Collier v. Rivaz* cannot be regarded as an authority favouring the renvoi doctrine as a principle of general application, because according to the doctrine the initial reference is never to the domestic rules of the foreign law. Moreover, a rule of alternative reference, while practicable for the formal validity of wills, is impracticable for the essential (or intrinsic) validity of wills or for intestacy. In such cases the court must choose between the domestic rules and the conflict rules of the foreign law. It cannot apply both, for it must decide whether or not the testator had disposing power, whether or not he died intestate, and if he did, who are the next-of-kin.[13] It is one thing to uphold a will if it complies with the formalities prescribed by either the domestic rules or the conflict rules of the law of the domicile. It is quite another thing to allow the next-of-kin entitled under the domestic rules of the law of the domicile to share the property with the next-of-kin entitled under its conflict rules.

4–011   *Collier v. Rivaz* was disapproved in *Bremer v. Freeman*,[14] where on almost identical facts the Privy Council, on appeal from the Prerogative Court of Canterbury, refused to admit to probate the will of a British subject who died domiciled in France in the English sense, but in England in the French sense (because she had not complied with Article 13), on the ground that it was made in English but not in French form. Since *Bremer v. Freeman* is the only English decision on the renvoi doctrine of appellate authority,[15] it would be a very important case if the judgment were unequivocal; but unfortunately the

---

[11] (1841) 2 Curt. 855; stated *post*, para. 4–033, Illustration 1; discussed by Falconbridge, pp. 143–145, 151–152; Abbott (1908) 24 L.Q.R. 143; Schreiber (1918) 31 Harv.L.R. 539–541; Morris (1937) 18 B.Y.I.L. 43–44; Mendelssohn-Bartholdy, pp. 58–64. See also *Maltass v. Maltass* (1844) 1 Rob. 67, 72; *Frere v. Frere* (1847) 5 Notes of Cases 593; *Ross v. Ross* (1894) 25 S.C.R. 307.

[12] As to the possible origin of this famous formula, see Falconbridge, pp. 190–191.

[13] Falconbridge, p. 152.

[14] (1857) 10 Moo.P.C. 306, 374; followed in *Hamilton v. Dallas* (1875) 1 Ch.D. 257 (partial intestacy).

[15] By "English decision ... of appellate authority" is meant the decision of a court sitting in England on appeal from a court sitting in England. Decisions of the Privy Council on appeal from Commonwealth courts are purposely excluded.

reasoning is so intricate and so ambiguous that it has been claimed as an authority both for[16] and against[17] the doctrine, and few modern lawyers have the patience to unravel its intricacies. The condemnation of *Collier v. Rivaz* was, however, expressed in unambiguous terms.

The decision in *Bremer v. Freeman* led to the passing of Lord Kingsdown's 4–012 Act 1861 which in certain circumstances enabled testators who were British subjects and who were disposing of personal estate to choose between the forms prescribed by no fewer than four systems of law. This extreme indulgence might have been supposed to destroy the argument in favour of interpreting the reference to foreign law as an alternative reference either to its domestic rules or to its conflict rules and it seems likely that Parliament intended to refer only to the former. However, in *In bonis Lacroix*[18] a British subject made two wills in France, one in French form and one in English form, and both were admitted to probate, the latter on the ground that it was made in accordance with the conflict rules of the law of the place where it was made (*lex loci actus*). As in *Collier v. Rivaz*, it was necessary to refer to the domestic rules as well as the conflict rules of the foreign law in order to admit both wills to probate.

In *Re Johnson*,[19] the renvoi doctrine was applied in a case of partial 4–013 intestacy, and it led to the application of the law of the testatrix' domicile of origin (Malta). But the main ground of the decision was that since the law of the country in which she had established a domicile *animo et facto* (Baden) refused to recognise that she was domiciled there, she had not effectually lost her domicile of origin. This reasoning is inconsistent with the well-settled rule that for the purpose of an English conflict rule domicile means domicile in the English sense,[20] and *Re Johnson* has been subsequently disapproved.[21]

Down to 1926, the few decisions and dicta which recognised the renvoi 4–014 doctrine were all consistent with a theory of partial or single renvoi. That is to say, the English court first referred to the conflict rules of the relevant foreign law and, where there was a reference back to English law,[22] applied the domestic rules of English law, without considering the possibility that the law of the foreign country might accept the renvoi from English law and apply its own domestic law. In *Re Annesley*,[23] Russell J. introduced the doctrine of double or total renvoi (but without citing any authority or giving any reasons for doing so) and applied French domestic law as the law of the domicile on the ground that a French court would have done so by way of renvoi from

---

[16] Jethro Brown (1909) 25 L.Q.R. 149–150; *Re Ross* [1930] 1 Ch. 377, 393–395.

[17] Abbott (1908) 24 L.Q.R. 144; Bate, pp. 11–13, 110–111; Mendelssohn-Bartholdy, p. 69; Morris (1937) 18 B.Y.I.L. 44–45 *cf.* Falconbridge, pp. 152–153, 228.

[18] (1877) 2 P.D. 94.

[19] [1903] 1 Ch. 821; criticised by Dicey (1903) 19 L.Q.R. 244; Pollock (1920) 36 L.Q.R. 92; Bate, pp. 19, 115; Abbott (1908) 24 L.Q.R. 144–145; Jethro Brown (1909) 25 L.Q.R. 145; Lorenzen, pp. 44–47; Schreiber (1918) 31 Harv.L.R. 544–557; Falconbridge, pp. 212, 214; Morris (1937) 18 B.Y.I.L. 45–48.

[20] *Post*, Rule 8.

[21] *Casdagli v. Casdagli* [1918] P. 89, 119–120; *Re Annesley* [1926] Ch. 692, 705; *Re Askew* [1930] 2 Ch. 259, 272, where Maugham J. said: "I think the case of *Re Johnson* and the reasons given for that decision by Farwell J. are no longer of authority."

[22] *Re Trufort* (1887) 36 Ch.D. 600 was a case of transmission from the law of the domicile (French law) to the law of the nationality (Swiss law), but the case was complicated by the existence of a treaty between France and Switzerland and of a Swiss judgment in favour of the plaintiff.

[23] [1926] Ch. 692; stated *post*, para. 4–033, Illustration 2.

English law. He expressed[24] his personal preference for reaching this result by a more direct route, that is, by the application of French domestic law in the first instance without any renvoi at all; but this part of his judgment has not been followed.[25] This theory of double or total renvoi is of course quite different from the theory of single or partial renvoi because, by inquiring how the foreign court would decide the case, it envisages the possibility that the foreign court might "accept the renvoi" and apply its own domestic law, as happened in *Re Annesley* and *Re Askew*.[26]

4–015   Confusion between the two theories was, however, introduced by an *obiter dictum* of the Privy Council in *Kotia v. Nahas*,[27] where it was said: "In the English courts, phrases which refer to the national law of a *propositus* are to be construed, not as referring to the law which the courts of that country would apply in the case of its own national domiciled in its own country with regard (where the situation of the property is relevant) to property in its own country, but to the law which the courts of that country would apply to the particular case of the *propositus*, having regard to what in their view is his domicile (if they consider that to be relevant) and having regard to the situation of the property in question (if they consider that to be relevant)." This statement was, it is submitted, no more than a dictum, because the Privy Council was considering a clause in the Palestine Succession Ordinance which expressly provided for partial renvoi in the following terms: "Mulk land shall be distributed in accordance with the national law of the deceased .... Where the national law imports the law of ... the situation of an immovable, the law so imported shall be applied." The Privy Council was sitting on appeal from a Palestine court and was considering a rule of the Palestine conflict of laws which was expressed in statutory form and had no counterpart in the English conflict of laws, and therefore anything said about the English conflict of laws was necessarily *obiter*. But even as a dictum the statement cannot, it is submitted, be considered accurate, because it confuses two different theories, the theory of partial renvoi and the theory of total renvoi, which differ not only in their starting point but also in their result. They differ in their starting point because the former theory does not inquire how the foreign court would decide the case nor consider the possibility that the foreign court might "accept the renvoi" from the law of the forum. They differ in their result because, if the foreign law refers to the law of the forum, that law is invariably applied under the former theory but is not invariably applied under the latter.[28]

4–016   Nevertheless, the dictum of the Privy Council was the principal authority relied upon for the application of the renvoi doctrine in *Re Duke of Wellington*.[29] This case is not an impressive authority in favour of the doctrine, because neither the judge nor the reporter indicated any difference between

---

[24] [1926] Ch. 692, 708–709.

[25] *Re Ross* [1930] 1 Ch. 377, 402. See, however, *Re Askew* [1930] 2 Ch. 259, 278.

[26] [1930] 2 Ch. 259; stated *post*, para. 4–033, Illustration 4.

[27] [1941] A.C. 403, 413.

[28] It is clear that the Palestine Ordinance involved "accepting the renvoi" and not "deciding the case as the national law would decide it." *Cf.* the criticisms of Falconbridge, pp. 223–225.

[29] [1947] Ch. 506; affirmed on other grounds, [1948] Ch. 118 (C.A.); stated *post*, para. 4–035, Illustration 6; discussed (1948) 64 L.Q.R. 264, 321; (1948) 11 M.L.R. 232; Falconbridge, pp. 229–232.

the domestic rules of English law and the relevant foreign law, nor why it was necessary to choose between them. The testator, who was a British subject domiciled in England, made a Spanish will giving land and movables in Spain to the person who should fulfil two stated qualifications, and made an English will giving all the rest of his property on trust for the person who should fulfil one of the qualifications. At his death there was no person who fulfilled both qualifications, and questions arose as to the devolution of the property in Spain. It appeared that Spanish law, as the *lex situs* of the land, referred questions of succession to the national law of the testator and would not accept the renvoi back to Spanish law. Wynn-Parry J. therefore applied English domestic law and held that the gift in the Spanish will failed for uncertainty and that the Spanish property fell into the residue disposed of by the English will. However, it was nowhere stated that the construction of the Spanish will would have been different in Spanish domestic law and, indeed, if the construction of the Spanish will was the only point at issue, it would seem that English domestic law should have been applied without any reference to Spanish law, because the testator was domiciled in England.[30] One of the counsel engaged in the case furnished the information that by Spanish domestic law the testator could in the circumstances only dispose of half of his property and that the other half passed to his mother as heiress. It may be that this is the explanation of the decision; but it must be admitted that there is no trace of this to be found in the report. Whatever may have been the reason for referring to Spanish law, it is clear that the judge, although he relied mainly on a dictum enunciating a theory of single renvoi, was in fact adopting a theory of double renvoi. Otherwise, there would have been no occasion to inquire whether Spanish law would "accept the renvoi" from English law—an inquiry which occupied much space in the judgment.

Lord Kingsdown's Act 1861 was repealed and replaced by the Wills Act **4–017** 1963 which allows an even wider choice of law for the formal validity of wills. The Act refers throughout to the internal law of the legal systems which it authorises, thus excluding renvoi.[31] But it does not in terms abolish the old rule of common law that a will is formally valid if it complies with the formalities prescribed by the law of the testator's last domicile; and it may be that a renvoi from this law is still possible.[32]

General conclusion from the cases. The history of the renvoi doctrine in **4–018** English law is the history of a chapter of accidents. The doctrine originated as a device for mitigating the rigidity of the English conflict rule for the formal validity of wills. The passing of Lord Kingsdown's Act in 1861 rendered this mitigation no longer necessary, at any rate in cases where the testator was a British subject. But the doctrine was applied in cases falling within that Act, and was extended far beyond its original context to cases of intrinsic validity of wills and to cases of intestacy. In 1926 the theory underlying the doctrine underwent a significant change, but no authorities were cited nor reasons

---

[30] *Studd v. Cook* (1883) 8 App.Cas. 577; Rule 142; (1948) 11 M.L.R. 233–234.
[31] "Internal law" is defined in s.6(1) to mean, in relation to any territory or state, the law which would apply in a case where no question of the law in force in any other territory or state arose.
[32] *Post*, para. 27–035.

given for making the change.[33] Two of the cases which have been relied on as establishing the doctrine have been subsequently overruled or dissented from.[34] In three other cases, the decision would have been the same if the court had referred to the domestic rules of the foreign law in the first instance.[35] And in three cases,[36] none of the parties was concerned to argue that the foreign law meant foreign domestic law. Nevertheless, until the matter is reviewed by a higher court it must be taken that the theory of double or total renvoi is the doctrine of the English courts in the situations in which they are willing to refer to the conflict rules of the foreign law. Hence, if the foreign law refers to English law and rejects the renvoi doctrine altogether, the result is that English domestic law is applicable; while if the foreign law refers to English law and adopts the doctrine of single renvoi, the result is that the foreign domestic law is applicable.

4–019   **Scope of the doctrine.** The English renvoi doctrine has been applied to the formal[37] and intrinsic[38] validity of wills and to cases of intestate succession.[39] It has been applied when the reference has been to the law of the domicile,[40] the law of the place where a will was made (*lex loci actus*),[41] and the law of the place where an immovable was situated (*lex situs*).[42] Outside the field of succession, it seems to have been applied in England only to legitimation by subsequent marriage.[43] There are indications that it might be applied to the formal validity of marriage,[44] and to capacity to marry.[45] In Canada it has been held applicable to matrimonial property.[46] It no longer applies to the formal validity of wills, at any rate in cases falling within the Wills Act 1963. It does

---

[33] *Re Annesley* [1926] Ch. 692.

[34] *Collier v. Rivaz* (1841) 2 Curt. 855, in *Bremer v. Freeman* (1857) 10 Moo.P.C. 306, 374; *Re Johnson* [1903] 1 Ch. 821, in *Re Annesley* [1926] Ch. 692, 705, and *Re Askew* [1930] 2 Ch. 259, 272.

[35] *Re Annesley* [1926] Ch. 692; *Re Askew* [1930] 2 Ch. 259; *In the Estate of Fuld* (*No. 3*) [1968] P. 675.

[36] *Re Johnson* [1903] 1 Ch. 821; *Re O'Keefe* [1940] Ch. 124; *Re Duke of Wellington* [1947] Ch. 506. In *Re O'Keefe*, the originating summons did not even suggest the possibility that Italian domestic law was applicable. For a statutory recognition of renvoi in cases of capacity to make a will, see Mental Health Act 1983, s.97(4)(*b*) and Exception to Rule 108, *post*.

[37] *Collier v. Rivaz* (1841) 2 Curt. 855; *Frere v. Frere* (1847) 5 Notes of Cases 593; *In bonis Lacroix* (1877) 2 P.D. 94; *In the goods of Brown-Sequard* (1894) 70 L.T. 811; *In the Estate of Fuld* (*No. 3*) [1968] P. 675; *Ross v. Ross* (1894) 25 S.C.R. 307. But under the Wills Act 1963 (Rule 138, *post*) renvoi is throughout excluded, and the reference is always to the internal law of the foreign country.

[38] *Re Trufort* (1887) 36 Ch.D. 600; *Re Annesley* [1926] Ch. 692; *Re Ross* [1930] 1 Ch. 377; and (perhaps) *Re Duke of Wellington* [1947] Ch. 506.

[39] *Re Johnson* [1903] 1 Ch. 821; *Simmons v. Simmons* (1917) 17 S.R.N.S.W. 419, discussed by Morris (1951) 4 Int.L.Q. 244; *Re O'Keefe* [1940] Ch. 124. But see *Re Thom* (1987) 40 D.L.R. (4th) 563 (Man.) where, however, the court seems to have misunderstood renvoi.

[40] *Collier v. Rivaz, supra; Re Trufort, supra; Re Johnson, supra; Simmons v. Simmons, supra; Re Annesley, supra; Re Ross, supra; Re Askew, supra; Re O'Keefe, supra; In the Estate of Fuld* (*No. 3*), *supra*.

[41] *In bonis Lacroix, supra; Ross v. Ross, supra*.

[42] *Re Ross, supra; Re Duke of Wellington, supra*. Cf. *Re Bailey* [1985] 2 N.Z.L.R. 656, where it was held applicable to the Inheritance (Provision for Family and Dependants) Act 1975.

[43] *Re Askew, supra*.

[44] *Taczanowska v. Taczanowski* [1957] P. 301, 305, 318 (C.A.); *post*, paras. 17–026 *et seq.*

[45] *R. v. Brentwood Marriage Registrar* [1968] 2 Q.B. 956. The actual decision in this case would now be different because of s.50 of the Family Law Act 1986: see *ante*, paras. 2–054 *et seq.*

[46] *Vladi v. Vladi* (1987) 39 D.L.R. (4th) 563 (N.S.). See *post*, para. 4–026.

not apply in the field of contract[47] or in relation to torts.[48] It does not seem appropriate that the doctrine should be applied to the construction of wills, because that is governed by the law presumably intended by the testator, *i.e.* prima facie by the law of his domicile,[49] and it must be assumed that the testator would expect the domestic rules of that law to apply.[50]

Even in the sphere in which the doctrine has been most frequently applied, **4–020** namely, succession to movables and immovables, it must be stressed that for every case which supports the doctrine there are hundreds of cases in which the domestic rules of the foreign law have been applied without any reference to its conflict rules, though it must be admitted that most of these can be explained on the ground that no one was concerned to argue that the reference to foreign law included its rules of the conflict of laws.[51] There is therefore as yet no justification for generalising the few English cases on renvoi into a general rule that a reference to foreign "law" always means the conflict rules of the foreign country, and (it is submitted) no justification for the statement that "the English courts have generally, *if not invariably*, meant by 'the law of the country of domicile' the whole law of that country as administered by the courts of that country."[52]

Much of the discussion of the renvoi doctrine has proceeded on the basis **4–021** that the choice lies in all cases between its absolute acceptance and its absolute rejection. The truth would appear to be that in some situations the doctrine is convenient and promotes justice, and that in others it is inconvenient and ought to be rejected.[53] In some cases the doctrine may be a useful means of arriving at a result which is desired for its own sake. For instance, if the court wishes to sustain a marriage which is alleged to be formally invalid, or to promote uniformity of distribution in a case of succession to movables where the deceased left movables in two or more countries, or to avoid conflicts with the *lex situs* in a case of title to land or conflicts with the law of the domicile in a case involving personal status, then the doctrine of renvoi may sometimes afford a useful (though troublesome) device for achieving the desired result. On the other hand, in all but exceptional cases the

---

[47] Art. 15 of the Rome Convention on the Law Applicable to Contractual Obligations (Contracts (Applicable Law) Act 1990, Sched. 1). For matters outside the scope of the Convention, see *Amin Rasheed Shipping Corp. v. Kuwait Insurance Co.* [1984] A.C. 50, 61–62; *Re United Railways of Havana and Regla Warehouses Ltd.* [1960] Ch. 52, 96–97, 115; see also *Rosencrantz v. Union Contractors Ltd.* (1960) 23 D.L.R. (2d) 473 (B.C.). Dicta to the contrary in *Vita Food Products Inc. v. Unus Shipping Co.* [1939] A.C. 277, 292 (P.C.) and *Ocean Steamship Co. v. Queensland State Wheat Board* [1941] 1 K.B. 402 (C.A.) must be taken to have been overruled.

[48] Private International Law (Miscellaneous Provisions) Act 1995, s.9(5). As regards matters which fall outside the scope of the statutory provisions and continue to be governed by the common law, there is no direct English authority. There is Scottish and American authority that renvoi is inapplicable in tort cases: *M'Elroy v. M'Allister*, 1949 S.C. 110, 126; *Haumschild v. Continental Casualty Co.*, 7 Wis. 2d 130, 141–142, 95 N.W. 2d 814, 820 (1959); *Pfau v. Trent Aluminium Co.*, 55 N.J. 2d 511, 263 A. 2d 129, 136–137 (1970).

[49] Rule 139.

[50] See, however, *Re Gansloser* [1952] Ch. 30 (the order made in 1932); and (on one interpretation) *Re Duke of Wellington* [1947] Ch. 506, discussed *ante*, para. 4–016.

[51] For example, in *Macmillan Inc. v. Bishopsgate Investment Trust plc (No. 3)* [1996] 1 W.L.R. 387 (C.A.), a case involving competing claims to shares in a New York company, there was an argument for renvoi, "but mercifully (or sadly, as the case may be)" (at p. 405, *per* Staughton L.J.) it was abandoned.

[52] *Re Ross* [1930] 1 Ch. 377, 390 (italics added).

[53] *Cf.* Falconbridge, p. 141.

theoretical and practical difficulties involved in applying the doctrine[54] outweigh any supposed advantages it may possess. The doctrine should not therefore be invoked unless it is plain that the object of the English conflict rule in referring to a foreign law will on balance be better served by construing the reference to mean the conflict rules of that law.

4–022   From the above point of view, it is thought that the following situations present a relatively strong case for the application of the doctrine:

(a) *Title to land situated abroad.*[55] If the question before the English court is whether a person has acquired a proprietary interest in land situated abroad, the court (so far as it has jurisdiction to deal with the matter at all[56]) will apply the *lex situs*, the law of the place where the land is situated. One of the reasons for applying the *lex situs* is that any adjudication which was contrary to what the *lex situs* had decided or would decide would be in most cases a *brutum fulmen*, since in the last resort the land can only be dealt with in a manner permitted by the *lex situs*. This reason can only be implemented if the *lex situs* is interpreted to mean the law which the *lex situs* would apply. Suppose, for instance, that a British citizen domiciled in England dies intestate leaving land in Spain; and that by Spanish domestic law X is entitled to the land, but that the Spanish courts would apply English domestic law according to which Y is entitled. It would be manifestly useless for an English court to decide that X was entitled to the land, because he could never recover it from Y in Spain.[57] "The meaning of the term 'law of the *situs*' can be ascertained best from a consideration of the reasons underlying the existence of the rule. The primary reason for its existence lies in the fact that the law-making and law-enforcing agencies of the country in which land is situated have exclusive control over such land."[58] However, the Wills Act 1963 excludes renvoi even in the case of immovables so far as the formal validity of wills is concerned.

4–023   (b) *Title to movables situated abroad.*[59] A similar argument suggests that when the English court applies the *lex situs* to determine the title to movables situated abroad, it should interpret the *lex situs* broadly so as to include whatever the courts of the *situs* have decided or would decide.[60] The argument is much weaker than in the case of land, because the movables may be taken out of the jurisdiction of the foreign court.

4–024   (c) *Formal validity of marriage.* Factors similar to those which originally favoured the application of the renvoi doctrine as a device for sustaining the formal validity of wills[61] also favour its application as a device for sustaining the formal validity of a marriage celebrated abroad. These factors are, first, a rigid rule of the English conflict of laws which normally requires compliance

---

[54] *Post*, paras. 4–027—4–031.
[55] Falconbridge, pp. 141, 217–220; Cheshire and North, p. 66; Cook, pp. 264, 279–280; Lorenzen, p. 78.
[56] English courts do not normally try questions of title to foreign land: Rule 114.
[57] For this reason it is submitted that the decision in *Re Ross* [1930] 1 Ch. 377 was correct so far as the immovables were concerned, subject to what is said later (para. 4–030) about the difficulty arising from the reference by the foreign law to the national law of a British citizen.
[58] *Re Schneider's Estate*, 198 Misc. 1017, 96 N.Y.S. 2d 652, 656 (1950).
[59] Falconbridge, p. 142; Cheshire and North, p. 66; *post*, para. 24–007.
[60] *Cf. Winkworth v. Christie, Manson & Woods Ltd.* [1980] Ch. 496, 514.
[61] *Ante*, para. 4–009.

with the *lex loci celebrationis*[62]; secondly, a more flexible rule in neighbour-ing European countries (where English people are likely to get married) which allows compliance with either the *lex loci* or the personal law of the parties; and thirdly, a strong judicial bias in favour of the validity of marriage. There is, however, no English[63] case which actually sustains the validity of a marriage on the ground that it was formally valid by the law which the *lex loci celebrationis* would apply. But it is a legitimate inference from *Taczanowska v. Taczanowski*[64] that such a marriage would be upheld. This does not mean that a marriage would be held formally invalid for failure to comply with the formalities prescribed by whatever system of domestic law would have been referred to by the conflict rules of the *lex loci celebrationis*. It merely means that a marriage may be formally valid if the parties comply with the formal-ities prescribed by either the domestic rules of the *lex loci celebrationis* or whatever system of domestic law the *lex loci celebrationis* would apply. Thus, the reference to the *lex loci celebrationis* in the case of formalities of marriage is an alternative reference to either its conflict rules or its domestic rules. It is not a justification for elevating the renvoi doctrine into a rule of general application.

(d) *Certain cases of transmission.*[65] Where the foreign law referred to by   **4–025**
the English court would refer to a second foreign law, and the second foreign law would agree that it was applicable, the case for applying the second foreign law is strong. Thus, if a German national domiciled in Italy died leaving movables in England, and Italian and German law both agreed that German domestic law was applicable because the *propositus* was a German national, it seems that the English court should accept the situation and apply German domestic law. For the practical advantages of deciding the case the way the Italian and German courts would decide it (especially if the *proposi-tus* left movables in Italy and Germany as well as in England) seem to outweigh the theoretical disadvantages of this mild form of transmission. If, on the other hand, the second foreign law would not agree that it was applicable, then there seems no reason why it should be applied. Thus, if a Danish national domiciled in Italy died leaving movables in England, and Italian law would apply the law of the nationality, and Danish law would apply the law of the domicile, neither law recognising any renvoi from the other, it seems that the English court should apply Italian domestic law.[66]

The interplay of renvoi and public policy gave rise to an interesting   **4–026**
problem in a case on matrimonial property, decided in Nova Scotia, Canada.[67] The Nova Scotia conflict rule (laid down by statute[68]) provided that the governing law was that of the place where the spouses had their last common

---

[62] Rule 67.
[63] *Re Lando's Estate*, 112 Minn. 257, 127 N.W. 1125 (1910) is an American decision to this effect. See Lorenzen, pp. 55–56, 77–78.
[64] [1957] P. 301, 305, 318; see *post*, para. 4–036, Illustration 7; *cf. Hooper v. Hooper* [1959] 1 W.L.R. 1021.
[65] Griswold (1938) 51 Harv.L.R. 1190; Lorenzen, pp. 76–77; Bate, pp. 112–114; Ehrenzweig, pp. 338–340; *cf. Re Trufort* (1887) 36 Ch.D. 600; *R. v. Brentwood Marriage Registrar* [1968] 2 Q.B. 956; *Mason v. Rose*, 176 F. 2d 486 (2d Cir. 1949).
[66] Wolff, p. 203.
[67] *Vladi v. Vladi* (1987) 39 D.L.R. (4th) 563 (N.S.).
[68] Matrimonial Property Act, S.N.S. 1980, c. 9, s.22(1).

habitual residence.[69] On the facts of the case, this was Germany. The German conflict rule, however, referred to the law of Iran, the country of which the spouses were nationals. The Nova Scotia court was prepared in principle to apply renvoi and follow the transmission to Iranian law. However, it considered that the application of Iranian matrimonial property law would be contrary to substantial justice (public policy) because it was unfair to women. This raised the question whether it should apply the internal law of Germany or the *lex fori* (which is normally applicable when the relevant provision of foreign law is contrary to public policy). It chose the former on the ground that the rejection of Iranian law did not justify disregarding the original reference to German law.

4–027   **Difficulties in the application of the doctrine.** It remains to discuss certain difficulties in the application of the total renvoi doctrine, some of which perhaps have not been adequately considered by English courts. These are as follows.

4–028   (a) *Unpredictability of result.* The doctrine makes everything depend on "the doubtful and conflicting evidence of foreign experts."[70] Moreover, it is peculiar to this theory of renvoi that it requires proof, not only of the foreign choice-of-law rules, but of the foreign rules about renvoi—and there are few matters upon which it is more difficult to obtain reliable information.[71] In Continental countries, decided cases, at least of courts of first instance, are not binding as authorities to be followed, and doctrine changes from decade to decade. Consequently, as Wynn-Parry J. said in *Re Duke of Wellington*,[72] "it would be difficult to imagine a harder task than that which faces me, namely, of expounding for the first time either in this country or in Spain the relevant law of Spain as it would be expounded by the Supreme Court of Spain, which up to the present time has made no pronouncement on the subject, and having to base that exposition on evidence which satisfies me that on this subject there exists a profound cleavage of legal opinion in Spain and two conflicting decisions of courts of inferior jurisdiction." The difficulty is not confined to the judge: it also confronts the lawyer advising his client, for he has to investigate not only the relevant English conflict rule but also (1) the choice-of-law rules of the foreign law; (2) the prevailing theory of renvoi in the foreign country; and (3) the domestic rules of the foreign law. He cannot advise with confidence, because at any of these stages (and particularly the second) he cannot tell what evidence of foreign law may have been collected on the other side.

4–029   The English cases show that the effect of acquiring a domicile in a foreign country may sometimes be to make the foreign domestic law applicable,[73] sometimes English domestic law,[74] sometimes the law of the domicile of

---

[69] Unlike similar statutes in certain other Canadian provinces, the Nova Scotia Act referred simply to "the law" of the last common habitual residence, not "the internal law." The latter would have excluded the possibility of renvoi.

[70] *Re Askew* [1930] 2 Ch. 259, 278. *Cf.* Lorenzen, p. 127.

[71] See, *e.g. Tezcan v. Tezcan* (1992) 87 D.L.R. (4th) 503, 519–521 (B.C.C.A.), a case in which, although the foreign law's choice of law rules were proved, its rules on renvoi were not.

[72] [1947] Ch. 506, 515.

[73] *Re Annesley* [1926] Ch. 692; *Re Askew* [1930] 2 Ch. 259.

[74] *Re Ross* [1930] 1 Ch. 377.

origin,[75] and sometimes the law of yet a fourth country.[76] There is no certainty that different results will not be reached in any future case in which the same foreign laws are involved, because foreign law is a question of fact and has to be proved by evidence in each case.[77] Moreover, if the evidence of foreign law is misleading or inadequate, the English court may reach a result which is unreal and unjust to the point of absurdity. Thus, in *Re O'Keefe*[78] the intestate had lived in Italy for the last forty-seven years of her life and was clearly domiciled there. Yet the effect of the total renvoi doctrine was that her movables were distributed not in accordance with the Italian domestic law with which she might be expected to be most familiar, and in reliance on which she may have refrained from making a will, but in accordance with the domestic law of Eire, a political unit which only came into existence during her long sojourn in Italy, of which she was not a citizen, and which she had never visited in her life except for a "short tour" with her father sixty years before her death. The only possible justification for such a result is that it may have enabled the movables in England to devolve in the same way as the movables in Italy. But of course in many cases uniformity of distribution is unattainable so long as some systems of law refer to the national law and others to the law of the domicile. For instance, uniformity of distribution would be impossible on any theory if an Italian national died intestate domiciled in England, for the English and Italian courts would each distribute the movables subject to its control in accordance with its own domestic law.

(b) *The national law of a British citizen.*[79] The most frequent occasion for   **4–030**
applying the total renvoi doctrine has been the conflict between English law, which refers to the law of the domicile in succession to movables and in other cases, and the laws of some Continental countries, which refer to the law of the nationality. If the *propositus* is a British or American citizen, the foreign court's reference to his national law is meaningless, for there is no such thing as a "British" or "American" or even a "United Kingdom" law of succession, nor is there any such thing as "English" nationality. If the English court decides for itself how the foreign court might be expected to interpret its reference to the national law of a British citizen, as has been done in some cases, it is not necessarily deciding the case as the foreign court would decide it. Thus in *Re Johnson*[80] and *Re O'Keefe*[81] it was assumed, without any evidence of foreign law, that the national law of a British subject meant the law of his domicile of origin. If, on the other hand, the English court allows

---

[75] *Re Johnson* [1903] 1 Ch. 821; *Re O'Keefe* [1940] Ch. 124.

[76] *Re Trufort* (1887) 36 Ch.D. 600; *R. v. Brentwood Marriage Registrar* [1968] 2 Q.B. 956.

[77] *Post*, Rule 18 (but see the Civil Evidence Act 1972, s.4(2)). In *Simmons v. Simmons* (1917) 17 S.R.N.S.W. 419 the N.S.W. court concluded, on expert evidence, that French law does not accept the renvoi, but an opposite conclusion was reached on expert evidence in *Re Annesley* [1926] Ch. 692.

[78] [1940] Ch. 124; stated *post*, para. 4–034, Illustration 5. The short unreserved judgment has given rise to "a flood of writings in all corners of the world, but particularly in Italy": Nadelmann (1969) 17 Am.J.Comp.L. 418, 444. The case recalls the much-criticised decision of Farwell J. in *Re Johnson* [1903] 1 Ch. 821, as to which, see *ante*, para. 4–013, nn. 19 and 21.

[79] See the valuable discussion in Falconbridge, pp. 199–216. *Cf.* Cook, pp. 239–244.

[80] [1903] 1 Ch. 821, 826: "According to the law of Baden, the legal succession to the property of the deceased of which she has not disposed by will is governed solely by the law of the country of which the testatrix was a subject at the time of her death."

[81] [1940] Ch. 124, 129: "Italian lawyers cannot say what is the meaning of the law of the nationality when there is more than one system of law of the nationality."

the foreign expert witness to assume that the national law of a British citizen is English law, as has been done in other cases, it is basing its decision on a manifestly false premiss. Thus, in *Re Ross*[82] the evidence was that "the Italian courts would determine the case on the footing that the English law applicable is that part of the law which would be applicable to an English national (*sic*) domiciled in England." In *Re Askew*,[83] the expert witness stated: "I am informed and believe that John Bertram Askew was an Englishman (*sic*). Therefore English law would be applied by the German court." Of course it can be argued that if the English court seeks to discover what decision the foreign court would reach, the grounds on which the foreign court would arrive at its decision are irrelevant. But there is reason to believe that at least the Italian courts do not now interpret the national law of a British citizen to mean either English law or the law of his domicile of origin, but on the contrary interpret it to mean Italian law if he is domiciled in Italy.[84] If this is so, it means that, for this reason also, the cases of *Re Ross* and *Re O'Keefe* are no longer reliable guides.

4–031   (c) *Circulus inextricabilis.*   As we have seen, the effect of applying the doctrine of total renvoi is to make the decision turn on whether the foreign court rejects the renvoi doctrine or adopts a theory of single or partial renvoi. But if the foreign court also adopts the doctrine of total renvoi, then logically no solution is possible at all unless either the English or the foreign court abandons its theory, for otherwise a perpetual *circulus inextricabilis* would be constituted.[85] So far, this difficulty has not yet arisen, because English courts have not yet had occasion to apply their renvoi doctrine to the law of a country which adopts the same doctrine. It is perhaps unlikely that any foreign country will adopt different conflict rules from, but the same renvoi doctrine as, those prevailing in England. Consequently, this difficulty (unlike the first two which have been mentioned) is more academic than practical. Yet the possibility remains, and the *circulus inextricabilis* cannot (it is submitted) be dismissed as "a (perhaps amusing) quibble."[86] "With all respect to what Maugham J. said in *Re Askew*," said the Private International Law Committee,[87] "the English judges and the foreign judges would then continue to bow to each other like the officers at Fontenoy." It is hardly an argument for the doctrine of total renvoi that it is workable only if the other country rejects it.[88]

4–032   **Conclusion.**   As a purely practical matter it would seem that a court should not undertake the onerous task of trying to ascertain how a foreign court would decide the question, unless the situation is an exceptional one and the advantages of doing so clearly outweigh the disadvantages. In most situations,

---

[82] [1930] 1 Ch. 377, 404, stated *post*, para. 4–034, Illustration 3.

[83] [1930] 2 Ch. 259, 276.

[84] De Nova, *Il Richiamo di Ordinamenti Plurilegislativi: Studio di Diritto Interlocale ed Internazionale Privato* (1940); De Nova, *Il Caso In re O'Keefe e la Determinazione della Lex Patriae di un Cittadino Britannico domiciliato all' Estero*, in *Festschrift für Leo Raape* (Hamburg, 1948); De Nova, 1953 *Rev. Crit.* 143, 147–155; De Nova, 1955 *Rev. Crit.* 1, 15; De Nova (1966) *Recueil des Cours*, II, pp. 545–557 (in English); Falconbridge, pp. 207–210.

[85] Morris (1937) 18 B.Y.I.L. 37; Falconbridge, pp. 175, 179, 183; Lorenzen, p. 67. Even writers who approve of the total renvoi doctrine admit that it may produce a *circulus inextricabilis*: Wolff, p. 201; Griswold (1938) 51 Harv.L.R. 1192–1193.

[86] *Re Askew* [1930] 2 Ch. 259, 267.

[87] First Report (1954) Cmd. 9068, para. 23(3).

[88] *Cf.* Lorenzen, pp. 126–127.

the balance of convenience surely lies in interpreting the reference to foreign law to mean its domestic rules. Although the doctrine of renvoi was favoured by Westlake[89] and Dicey,[90] the great majority of writers, both English and foreign, are opposed to it. Lorenzen says[91]: "Notwithstanding the great authority of Westlake and Dicey, it may reasonably be hoped that, when the doctrine with all its consequences is squarely presented to the higher English courts, they will not hesitate to reject the decisions of the courts that have lent colour to renvoi in the English law." There is no case which prevents the Court of Appeal (still less the House of Lords) from reviewing the whole problem, and it is submitted that such a review is long overdue.[92]

ILLUSTRATIONS[93]

1. T, a British subject of Irish domicile of origin and subsequent English domicile of choice, **4–033** died domiciled in Belgium in the English sense, but not in the Belgian sense because he had not obtained the authorisation of the Belgian Government to establish his domicile in Belgium as required by Article 13 of the Code Napoleon (since repealed). He left a will and six codicils. The will and two of the codicils were executed in the form required by Belgian domestic law. Four of the codicils were executed in the form required by English domestic law but not in the form required by Belgian domestic law. Evidence was given that by Belgian law the succession to foreigners in T's situation was governed by "the laws of their own country." The will and all six codicils were admitted to probate.[94]

2. T, a British subject of English domicile of origin, died domiciled in France in the English sense, but not in the French sense because she had not obtained authority from the French Government to establish her domicile in France as required by Article 13 of the Code Napoleon (since repealed). She left a will which purported to dispose of all her property. By French law, T could only dispose of one-third of her property because she left two children surviving her. Evidence was given that a French court would refer to English law as T's national law and would accept the renvoi back to French law, French domestic law was applied and T's will was only effective to dispose of one-third of her property.[95]

3. T, a British subject of English domicile of origin, died domiciled in Italy leaving movables **4–034** in England and Italy and immovables in Italy. By her will T gave her property in England to her niece X and her property in Italy to her grand-nephew Y with usufruct to his mother X for life. T's only son A claimed that by Italian domestic law he was entitled to one-half of her property as his *legitima portio.* The validity of T's will was governed by Italian law as the law of her domicile in respect of movables and by Italian law as the lex situs in respect of immovables. Evidence was given that the Italian courts would refer to English law as the law of T's nationality in respect of both movables and immovables, and would not accept the renvoi back to Italian law. English domestic law applied and A's claim was rejected.[96]

---

[89] Chap. 2.
[90] 5th ed., Appendix 1.
[91] Lorenzen, p. 53.
[92] With the object of eliminating conflicts between the law of the domicile and the law of the nationality, a draft Convention was approved at The Hague in 1951 (text in Appendix B to the First Report of the Private International Law Committee (1954), Cmd. 9068). Since it is impossible for the United Kingdom to ratify the Convention unless domicile in English law is defined to mean habitual residence (and there is no prospect of that in the foreseeable future), it is unlikely that the United Kingdom will ratify the Convention. See the Seventh Report of the Private International Law Committee (1963), Cmnd. 1955, paras. 13–17. The Convention is not in force.
[93] All these Illustrations are of the second branch of clause (2) of this Rule, that is, they are all cases in which the law of a foreign country has been interpreted to mean "any domestic law which the courts of that country apply to the decision of the case." Illustrations of the first branch of clause (2) of the Rule, that is, cases in which the law of a foreign country has been interpreted to mean its domestic law, will be found elsewhere in this book.
[94] *Collier v. Rivaz* (1841) 2 Curt. 855; see now Wills Act 1963, s.1.
[95] *Re Annesley* [1926] Ch. 692. In fact, French law referred to English law because the testatrix was domiciled in England in the French sense. The evidence of French law was erroneous.
[96] *Re Ross* [1930] 1 Ch. 377.

4. A, a British subject of English domicile of origin, separated from his wife, acquired a domicile of choice in Germany, formed an association with a German woman, and had by her a daughter, D. While still domiciled in Germany, A obtained a divorce from his wife in the German court and subsequently married the mother of D. Under the settlement made on the occasion of his first marriage, the proper law of which was English, A had a special power of appointment among the children of any subsequent marriage. A purported to exercise the power in favour of D. By English domestic law, D was illegitimate,[97] but by German domestic law she was legitimated by the subsequent marriage of her parents. Evidence was given that the German courts would refer to English law as the law of A's nationality and would accept the renvoi back to German law. German domestic law applied and D was therefore legitimate and an object of the power.[98]

4–035
5. T, a British subject, who was born in India in 1860, acquired a domicile of choice in Italy in 1890, and lived there until her death intestate in 1937. She left two sisters of the whole blood and a brother and sister of the half blood. T's father was born in 1835 in County Clare and T's domicile of origin was consequently in that part of Ireland which in 1937 was called Eire and is now called the Republic of Ireland. Evidence was given that the Italian courts would refer the succession to T's movables to the law of the country to which she belonged at the time of her death. This was construed to mean the law of Eire, although T was not a citizen of Eire and had never been there in her life except for a short tour with her father in 1878. Hence the brother and sister of the half blood were entitled to share equally with the two sisters of the whole blood.[99]

6. T, a British subject domiciled in England, by his Spanish will gave land and movables in Spain to the person who on his death would become Duke of Wellington and Duke of Ciudad Rodrigo. On T's death there was no such person, because the two dukedoms became separated for the first time since 1814. By his English will T gave all the rest of his property to the person who on his death would become Duke of Wellington. For some unexplained reason it was necessary to refer to Spanish law in order to determine the devolution of the Spanish land. Evidence was given that the Spanish courts would refer to English law as the law of T's nationality and would not accept the renvoi back to Spanish law. English domestic law applied and the Spanish land and movables fell into the residue disposed of by the English will.[1]

4–036
7. H and W, both Polish nationals domiciled in Poland, marry in Italy in accordance with the form prescribed by Polish domestic law, but not in the form prescribed by Italian domestic law. Evidence is given that the Italian courts would recognise a marriage celebrated in Italy in accordance with the forms prescribed by the law of the parties' common nationality. The marriage of H and W is (*semble*) valid.[2]

8. T was domiciled at all material times in Germany. He resided in Ontario between 1940 and 1946, when he became a Canadian citizen and therefore a British subject. He died in 1962, before the Wills Act 1963 came into operation. He left a will and four codicils, two of which were executed in Germany in the form required by English and Ontario law but not in the form required by German law. Evidence was given that a German court would refer in the first instance to the law of Ontario as the national law of the testator and would accept the renvoi back to German law, and would refer in the second instance to German domestic law as the *lex loci actus*. German domestic law was applied and the two codicils were formally invalid.[3]

---

[97] See Legitimacy Act 1926, s.1(2) (since repealed).

[98] *Re Askew* [1930] 2 Ch. 259.

[99] *Re O'Keefe* [1940] Ch. 124. If Italian domestic law had been applied the half-brother and half-sister would each have been entitled to a half share: Italian Civil Code, Book II, Title ii, para. 570, s.2. Thus they would each have got half of what Irish law gave them. Under English domestic law they were entitled to nothing.

[1] *Re Duke of Wellington* [1947] Ch. 506: affirmed on grounds not involving any reference to the law of Spain [1948] Ch. 118 (C.A.); discussed *ante*, para. 4–016.

[2] See *Taczanowska v. Taczanowski* [1957] P. 301 (C.A.), where, however, the marriage was not valid by Polish domestic law and was held valid on another ground. See *post*, paras. 17–026 *et seq.*

[3] *In the Estate of Fuld (No. 3)* [1968] P. 675.

Chapter 5

THE EXCLUSION OF FOREIGN LAW

Rule 2—**English courts will not enforce or recognise a right, power, capacity, disability or legal relationship arising under the law of a foreign country, if the enforcement or recognition of such right, power, capacity, disability or legal relationship would be inconsistent with the fundamental public policy of English law.**[1]   5R–001

Comment

Rule 2 expresses in very general terms the principle[2] that a foreign law, which   **5–002** is otherwise applicable according to the English rules of the conflict of laws, will not be applied or enforced in England if the law, or the result of its application, is contrary to public policy. "There is abundant authority that an English court will decline to recognise or apply what would otherwise be the appropriate foreign rule of law when to do so would be against English public policy."[3]

In English domestic law it is now well settled that the doctrine of public   **5–003** policy "should only be invoked in clear cases in which the harm to the public is substantially incontestable, and does not depend upon the idiosyncratic inferences of a few judicial minds."[4] In the conflict of laws it is even more necessary that the doctrine should be kept within proper limits, otherwise the whole basis of the system is liable to be frustrated. "The courts are not free to refuse to enforce a foreign right at the pleasure of the judges, to suit the individual notion of expediency or fairness. They do not close their doors unless help would violate some fundamental principle of justice, some prevalent conception of good morals, some deep-rooted tradition of the common weal."[5] As a result the courts will be slower to invoke public policy in cases involving a foreign element than when a purely municipal legal issue is involved.[6]

---

[1] Kahn-Freund, *Selected Writings* (1978), Chap. 9; Lloyd, *Public Policy* (1953), Chap. 5; Sammartano and Morse, *Public Policy in Transnational Relationships* (1992); Paulsen and Sovern (1956) 56 Col. L.R. 969; Carter (1984) 55 B.Y.I.L. 111, (1993) 42 I.C.L.Q. 1; Bucher (1993) *Recueil des Cours*, II, p. 9; Leslie, 1995 Jur. Rev. 477; Enonchong (1996) 45 I.C.L.Q. 633.

[2] See *Guardianship Convention Case* (*Netherlands v. Sweden*) 1958 I.C.J. Rep. 53, at pp. 90–95, *per* Judge Lauterpacht, for a valuable discussion of the role of public policy, and for the conclusion that it is a general principle of law in the field of the conflict of laws.

[3] *Vervaeke v. Smith* [1983] 1 A.C. 145, 164, *per* Lord Simon of Glaisdale.

[4] *Fender v. St. John-Mildmay* [1938] A.C. 1, 12.

[5] *Loucks v. Standard Oil Co.*, 224 N.Y. 99, 111, 120 N.E. 198, 202 (1918).

[6] *Vervaeke v. Smith* [1983] 1 A.C. 145, 164.

5–004 The doctrine of public policy has assumed far less prominence in the English conflict of laws than have corresponding doctrines in the laws of foreign countries, *e.g.* France and Germany. One reason for this may be that the courts invariably apply English domestic law in proceedings for divorce[7] and separation,[8] for the guardianship, custody[9] and adoption of minors,[10] and for the maintenance of wives and children.[11] Thus, foreign law is inapplicable in many important departments of family law in which, in foreign countries, its exclusion on grounds of public policy is of frequent occurrence. The doctrine of renvoi,[12] too, sometimes results in the application of English domestic law instead of foreign law; and it should be borne in mind that all questions of procedure are governed by English domestic law as the *lex fori*,[13] though the reason for this is not policy but convenience.

5–005 A distinction should be drawn between the foreign law itself, on the one hand, and the effect of its application on the other.[14] There is, understandably, a reluctance to hold that a foreign law as such is contrary to public policy.[15] "An English court will refuse to apply a law which outrages its sense of justice or decency. But before it exercises such power it must consider the relevant foreign law as a whole."[16] In recent years, influenced by the impact of the European Convention on Human Rights, the House of Lords has on two occasions indicated that a foreign law should be disregarded if it represents a serious infringement of human rights. In *Oppenheimer v. Cattermole*[17] a majority expressed the view, *obiter*, that Nazi nationality decrees depriving absent German Jews of their nationality and confiscating their property fell within this category. As Lord Cross put it, "a law of this sort constitutes so grave an infringement of human rights that the courts of this country ought to refuse to recognise it as a law at all."[18] In *Williams & Humbert Ltd. v. W. & H. Trade Marks (Jersey) Ltd.*[19] it was accepted that in appropriate circumstances the court would disregard a foreign confiscatory decree which offended principles of human rights.

---

7 Rule 77(1).

8 *Ibid.*

9 Rule 92(4).

10 *Post*, para. 20–099.

11 Rule 86(7); paras. 18–194—18–195.

12 Rule 1.

13 Rule 17. Dicey regarded this rule also as an example of public policy (3rd ed., p. 37), but it too is better regarded as a fixed rule of law.

14 *Cf.* Contracts (Applicable) Law Act 1990, Sched. 1, Art. 16 (application of foreign law manifestly incompatible with public policy).

15 See, *e.g. Luther v. Sagor* [1921] 3 K.B. 532, 559 (C.A.); *Oppenheimer v. Cattermole* [1976] A.C. 249, 277–278; *The Playa Larga* [1983] 2 Lloyd's Rep. 171, 190 (C.A.).

16 *In the Estate of Fuld (No. 3)* [1968] P. 675, 698. See also *Winkworth v. Christie, Manson and Woods Ltd.* [1980] Ch. 496, 514. On foreign laws licensing prostitution or slavery see *Robinson v. Bland* (1760) 2 Burr. 1077, 1084; *Regazzoni v. K.C. Sethia, Ltd.* [1956] 2 Q.B. 490, 524 (C.A.); affd. [1958] A.C. 301. Contrast *Santos v. Illidge* (1860) 8 C.B. (N.S.) 861.

17 [1976] A.C. 249.

18 At p. 278. See also p. 283, *per* Lord Salmon. It is not likely that the suggestion in *Frankfurther v. W. L. Exner Ltd.* [1947] Ch. 629, 644, that Nazi decrees relating to property in Austria would be recognised, would be followed today.

19 [1986] A.C. 368, 428, *per* Lord Templeman. See also *The Playa Larga* [1983] 2 Lloyd's Rep. 171, 190 (C.A.); *Settebello Ltd. v. Banco Totta and Acores* [1985] 1 W.L.R. 1050, 1056 (C.A.).

What is usually in question, however, is not the foreign law in the abstract,   **5–006**
but the results of its enforcement or recognition in England in the concrete
case. Thus, the courts may well regard a foreign law which permits polygamy,
or the marriage of step-father and step-daughter, as unwise or even immoral.
But, if such a marriage has taken place under a foreign law according to which
it is valid, and especially if children have been born, it may be better to
recognise it than to disturb settled family relationships by holding the marriage invalid and the children illegitimate on grounds of public policy. Everything depends upon the nature of the question which arises. Thus, until 1972
no polygamously-married spouse could obtain a divorce from the courts[20]; but
the spouses would be treated as married persons and thus incapable of
contracting a valid marriage in England[21]; the children would be treated as
legitimate[22]; and the wife would be entitled to assert rights of succession and
other rights on the footing that she was a wife.[23] Again, to take an improbable
but striking example, if a foreign law permitted a bachelor aged fifty to adopt
a spinster aged seventeen, the courts might hesitate to award the custody of the
girl to her adoptive father: but that is no reason for not allowing her to succeed
to his property as his "child" on his death intestate.[24] Public policy in such
cases is not absolute but relative.

The doctrine of public policy may not only induce a court to refuse to   **5–007**
enforce or recognise, *e.g.* a contract or a marriage when it would be valid
under the applicable foreign law. It may also produce the opposite effect and
lead to the enforcement or recognition of, *e.g.* a contract or a marriage which
under the applicable foreign law would be invalid. Thus, foreign legislation
which invalidates a contract or a marriage may be disregarded if it is penal,[25]
or foreign exchange control legislation which affects a contract governed by
foreign law, but which is passed, not with the genuine object of protecting the
State's economy, but as an "instrument of oppression" may be disregarded on
the ground of public policy,[26] and a contract not enforceable under its applicable law may as a result be enforceable in England. On the other hand, the
effect of the doctrine of public policy always is to exclude the application of
foreign law which would otherwise be applicable. In one case,[27] the doctrine
was anomalously applied so as to invoke the application of a foreign law
which would otherwise have been inapplicable; but this case has been convincingly criticised and has not been followed.[28]

---

[20] *Hyde v. Hyde* (1866) L.R. 1 P. & D. 130; see now Matrimonial Causes Act 1973, s.47(1), and
Rule 75.
[21] *Baindail v. Baindail* [1946] P. 122 (C.A.); *post*, para. 17–185.
[22] *Bamgbose v. Daniel* [1955] A.C. 107 (P.C.); *post*, para. 17–187.
[23] *Coleman v. Shang* [1961] A.C. 481 (P.C.); *Shahnaz v. Rizwan* [1965] 1 Q.B. 390; *Re Sehota*
[1978] 1 W.L.R. 1506; *post*, paras. 17–191 *et seq.*
[24] See para. 20–123, *post*.
[25] See paras. 17–110; 32–233, *post*.
[26] *Re Helbert Wagg & Co. Ltd.* [1956] Ch. 323, 351. See also *The Playa Larga* [1983] 2 Lloyd's
Rep. 171, 190 (C.A.), and Carter (1983) 54 B.Y.I.L. 297.
[27] *Lorentzen v. Lydden & Co. Ltd.* [1942] 2 K.B. 202.
[28] *Bank voor Handel en Scheepvaart v. Slatford* [1953] 1 Q.B. 248, 263–264.

5–008   The reservation of public policy in conflict of laws cases is a necessary one, but "no attempt to define the limits of that reservation has ever succeeded."[29] All that can be done, therefore, is to enumerate the cases in which the recognition or enforcement of rights arising under foreign laws has been refused on this ground. It will be found that the doctrine has been principally invoked in two classes of case, namely (1) those involving foreign contracts, and (2) those involving a foreign status.

5–009   **(1) Contracts.**[30] The effect of Article 16 of the Rome Convention on the Law Applicable to Contractual Obligations[31] is that the application of a rule of law of any country may be refused if its application is manifestly incompatible with English public policy. At common law English courts refused to enforce champertous contracts,[32] contracts in restraint of trade,[33] contracts entered into under duress or coercion,[34] or contracts involving collusive and corrupt arrangements for a divorce,[35] or trading with the enemy,[36] or breaking the laws of a friendly country,[37] even though such contracts were valid under their applicable law. On the other hand, they have enforced contracts for the loan of money to be spent on gambling abroad,[38] and for foreign loans which contravened the English Moneylenders Acts.[39] In general, it is certainly untrue that contracts governed by a foreign law will not be enforced in England if they are contrary to some rule of the common law which the parties to an English contract cannot disregard. Thus, a foreign contract made without consideration will be enforced in England.[40]

---

[29] Westlake, p. 51.

[30] For detailed discussion, see Rule 180.

[31] Contracts (Applicable Law) Act 1990, Sched. 1.

[32] *Grell v. Levy* (1864) 10 C.B. (N.S.) 73. In this case the litigation was to take place in England. Cf. *Trendtex Trading Corp. v. Crédit Suisse* [1980] Q.B. 629, affd. [1982] A.C. 679. See also *Fraser v. Buckle* [1996] 2 I.L.R.M. 34. The principle would not apply to a champertous contract relating to litigation in France or the United States, where champerty is lawful: *Re Trepca Mines Ltd. (No. 2)* [1963] Ch. 199, 218 (C.A.). Cf. *National Surety Co. v. Larsen* [1929] 4 D.L.R. 918 (B.C.C.A.), where a contract to indemnify bail, valid by the law of Washington where the litigation was pending, was upheld in British Columbia, though such contracts were illegal by British Columbia law.

[33] *Rousillon v. Rousillon* (1880) 14 Ch.D. 351; but the case does not amount to a decision on the point. Contrast *Apple Corps. Ltd. v. Apple Computer Inc.* [1992] F.S.R. 431 (foreign law on restraint of trade not applicable if contract governed by English law).

[34] *Kaufman v. Gerson* [1904] 1 K.B. 591 (C.A.); but see *post*, para. 12–231.

[35] *Hope v. Hope* (1857) 8 De G.M. & G. 731. In this case the divorce was to take place in England. Would the principle apply to a contract to procure a divorce abroad? See *Addison v. Brown* [1954] 1 W.L.R. 779.

[36] *Dynamit A.G. v. Rio Tinto Co.* [1918] A.C. 260.

[37] *De Wütz v. Hendricks* (1824) 2 Bing. 314; *Foster v. Driscoll* [1929] 1 K.B. 470 (C.A.); *Regazzoni v. K. C. Sethia, Ltd.* [1958] A.C. 301. However, in these cases the contract was governed by English law. See also *Royal Boskalis Westminster N.V. v. Mountain* [1999] Q.B. 674, 692 (C.A.); *Soleimany v. Soleimany* [1999] Q.B. 785, 794 (C.A.).

[38] *Saxby v. Fulton* [1909] 2 K.B. 208 (C.A.).

[39] *Shrichand v. Lacon* (1906) 22 T.L.R. 245.

[40] *Re Bonacina* [1912] 2 Ch. 394 (C.A.). As to statutory rules, see *ante*, paras. 1–049 *et seq.*

(2) Status. Although those incidents of a foreign status which are rele-　5–010
vant[41] to an issue before a court are normally recognised, an incapacity
imposed for reasons which it would be contrary to public policy to enforce is
disregarded as a penal incapacity. The courts have thus said or held that
incapacities imposed on account of slavery,[42] religion or religious vocation,[43]
alien nationality,[44] race,[45] divorce[46] and (perhaps unjustifiably) physical
incompetence[47] and prodigality,[48] will be disregarded. Although incapacities
imposed for these reasons have traditionally been described as "penal"
incapacities, the description is somewhat misleading in that they are not
necessarily imposed for a breach of the criminal law, *i.e.* of a "penal law"
such as is referred to in Rule 3(1).[49] However if this is appreciated, and if it
is observed that the present context is one of recognition whilst that of Rule
3(1) is one of enforcement,[50] then no harm attends upon the use of the
traditional term.

Public policy may require that a capacity existing under a foreign law　5–011
should be disregarded in England[51]: but the circumstances would have to be
extreme before such a course becomes justifiable. Thus, the courts recognise

---

[41] That is to say, indicated as relevant by an English choice of law rule. Since those rules
alwaysrefer to a territorial system of law, rules existing under, *e.g.* a person's religious
discipline are immaterial unless they are incorporated into the appropriate territorial law: *Re De
Wilton* [1900] 2 Ch. 481; *Chetti v. Chetti* [1909] P. 67, 78; *R. v. Hammersmith Superintendent
Registrar of Marriages* [1917] 1 K.B. 634, 643; *Preger v. Preger* (1926) 42 T.L.R. 281;
Papadopoulos v. Papadopoulos [1930] P. 55, 64; *MacDougall v. Chitnavis*, 1937 S.C. 390, 398,
403, 407. Cf. *Re Alison's Trusts* (1874) 31 L.T. 638; *Har-Shefi v. Har-Shefi (No. 2)* [1953] P.
220; *Cheni v. Cheni* [1965] P. 85; *Qureshi v. Qureshi* [1972] Fam. 173.
[42] *Smith v. Browne & Cooper* (1701) Holt K.B. 495; *Shanley v. Harvey* (1762) 2 Eden. 126;
Sommersett's Case (1771) 20 St. Tr. 1; *Chamberline v. Harvey* (1796) 5 Mod. 182; *Forbes v.
Cochrane* (1824) 2 B. & C. 448. Cf. *The Slave Grace* (1827) 2 Hag.Adm. 94; *Stewart v.
Garnett* (1830) 3 Sim. 398; *Ex p. Rucker* (1834) 3 L.J. Bk. 104; *Santos v. Illidge* (1860) 8 C.B.
(N.S.) 861.
[43] *Re Metcalfe's Trusts* (1864) 2 De G.J. & S. 122; *Stuart v. Prentiss* (1861) 20 U.C.R. 513. Cf.
Von Lorang v. Administrator of Austrian Property [1927] A.C. 641, 653.
[44] *Wolff v. Oxholm* (1817) 6 M. & S. 92; *Re Fried. Krupp A.G.* [1917] 2 Ch. 188; *Re Askew* [1930]
2 Ch. 259, 275; *Re Helbert Wagg & Co. Ltd.* [1956] Ch. 323, 345–346.
[45] *Oppenheimer v. Cattermole* [1976] A.C. 249, 265, 276–278, 282–283. In *Oppenheimer v. Louis
Rosenthal & Co.* [1937] 1 All E.R. 23 (C.A.) and *Ellinger v. Guinness Mahon & Co.* [1939]
4 All E.R. 16, the incapacities of Jews in Nazi Germany were taken into account in ordering
service out of the jurisdiction under R.S.C. Ord. 11. See also *Frankfurther v. W. L. Exner Ltd.*
[1947] Ch. 629, 636–637; *Novello & Co. v. Hinrichsen Edition Ltd.* [1951] Ch. 595, 604, affd.
on other grounds [1951] Ch. 1026 (C.A.).
[46] *Scott v. Att.-Gen.* (1886) 11 P.D. 128; *Lundgren v. O'Brien (No. 2)* [1921] V.L.R. 361; *Pezet v.
Pezet* (1947) 47 S.R. (N.S.W.) 45, 74. Cf. *R. v. Brentwood Superintendent Registrar of
Marriages* [1968] 2 Q.B. 956, where an inability to remarry was recognised on the basis that
an unattractive difference from English law did not make the disability a penal incapacity. *A
fortiori* where the foreign prohibition is analogous to an English rule: *Warter v. Warter* (1890)
15 P.D. 152; *Le Mesurier v. Le Mesurier* (1930) 46 T.L.R. 203. See also *Miller v. Teale* (1954)
92 C.L.R. 406; *Hellens v. Densmore* (1957) 10 D.L.R. (2d) 561 (Sup. Ct. Can.). Distinguish
Buckle v. Buckle [1956] P.181, which was decided on different grounds. See *post*, paras.
17–082 *et seq.*; 18–126.
[47] *Re Langley's Settlement Trusts* [1962] Ch. 541, 556–557 (C.A.); criticised by Grodecki (1962)
11 I.C.L.Q. 578; Collier [1962] C.L.J. 36.
[48] *Worms v. De Valdor* (1880) 49 L.J. Ch. 261; *Re Selot's Trusts* [1902] 1 Ch. 488; criticised by
Westlake, p. 48, and Cheshire and North, p. 129. Compare the continental practice: Rabel, Vol.
1, p. 190.
[49] Infamy is normally a consequence of criminal conviction and there are several American cases
where foreign incapacities consequent upon infamy have not been recognised, see Beale, Vol.
2, p. 657.
[50] As to this distinction see *Re Helbert Wagg & Co. Ltd.* [1956] Ch. 323, 345.
[51] *Cheni v. Cheni* [1965] P. 85, 98.

the validity of marriages within the prohibited degrees of English law[52] (provided they are valid under the applicable foreign law), but they might refuse to recognise a marriage between persons so closely related that sexual intercourse between them was incestuous by English criminal law,[53] or a marriage with a child below the age of puberty.[54]

5–012   The mere fact that a foreign status or relationship is unknown to English domestic law is not a ground for refusing to recognise its incidents.[55] Thus, legitimation by subsequent marriage was recognised and given effect to in England long before it became part of English domestic law.[56] The recognition of polygamous marriages is another example.[57]

5–013   **Other cases.** Apart from these two groups of cases, examples of the exclusion of foreign law on the ground of public policy are rare. It has been said that it is a principle of public policy that the courts should give effect to clearly established rules of international law.[58] It is not however contrary to public policy to recognise a decree of a foreign state expropriating property within its territory merely because it is "confiscatory," *i.e.* does not provide for compensation.[59] But it may be otherwise if the decree is penal or is discriminatory in such a way as to offend against public policy, or otherwise offends against the principles safeguarding human rights.[60] The recognition of a foreign decree of divorce[61] or nullity of marriage[62] or the enforcement of a foreign judgment *in personam*[63] may be refused on grounds of public policy, but reported instances are rare. There is no general principle that the application of a foreign law is contrary to public policy merely because it operates retrospectively.[64]

5–014   **Express statutory provision.** There is an increasing tendency for statutes in the area of the conflict of laws to provide for the application of public policy. Most[65] deal with foreign judgments or awards and allow for the non-recognition or non-enforcement on the ground that they are contrary to public

---

[52] *Re Bozzelli's Settlement* [1902] 1 Ch. 751 (marriage in 1880 with deceased brother's widow); *Re Pozot's Settlement* [1952] 1 All E.R. 1107, 1109 (marriage with step-daughter); *Cheni v. Cheni* [1965] P. 85 (marriage between uncle and niece).

[53] See *Brook v. Brook* (1861) 9 H.L.C. 193, 227–228; *Cheni v. Cheni, supra*, at p. 97.

[54] In *Mohamed v. Knott* [1969] 1 Q.B. 1, a marriage with a girl of 13, valid by Nigerian law, was recognised as valid in England. See Karsten (1969) 32 M.L.R. 212.

[55] *Phrantzes v. Argenti* [1960] 2 Q.B. 19; *Shahnaz v. Rizwan* [1965] 1 Q.B. 390, 401.

[56] Rule 100.

[57] *Baindail v. Baindail* [1946] P. 122 (C.A.); Rule 74.

[58] *Re Helbert Wagg & Co. Ltd.* [1956] Ch. 323, 349; *Oppenheimer v. Cattermole* [1976] A.C. 249, 278.

[59] Cases at n. 58, *supra*, and *Luther v. Sagor* [1921] 3 K.B. 532, 559 (C.A.); *Princess Paley Olga v. Weisz* [1929] 1 K.B. 718 (C.A.); *cf. Williams & Humbert Ltd. v. W. & H. Trade Marks (Jersey) Ltd.* [1986] A.C. 368, 427–428.

[60] See especially *Re Helbert Wagg & Co. Ltd., supra; Oppenheimer v. Cattermole, supra; Williams & Humbert Ltd. v. W. & H. Trade Marks (Jersey) Ltd., supra; The Playa Larga* [1983] 2 Lloyd's Rep. 171, 189–190 (C.A.), and see *post*, para. 25–008.

[61] *Post*, paras. 18–120 *et seq.*

[62] *Ibid.*

[63] See Rule 44, *post*.

[64] See *ante*, para. 3–026.

[65] For exceptions see Foreign Limitation Periods Act 1984, s.2; Contracts (Applicable Law) Act 1990, Sched. 1, Art. 16.

policy,[66] or, in an expression derived from international conventions in the area, "manifestly contrary to public policy."[67]

"Residual discretion." In some decisions the judges have stated that the courts possess a "residual discretion" to refuse to recognise a foreign status[68] conferred or imposed upon a person by the law of his domicile, or a foreign decree of divorce or nullity of marriage[69] granted by a foreign court, if the recognition would be improper or unjust or unconscionable in the circumstances of the particular case. In the first of the cases in which these statements were made it is probable that the court intended to do no more than call attention to the distinction between the recognition of a status and the recognition of its incidents.[70] In the later cases it may be that the courts intended to do no more than refer to the doctrine of public policy and to the analogous doctrine that foreign decrees of divorce and nullity will not be recognised in England if recognition would be contrary to natural justice.[71] But if the courts intended to reduce the whole of the conflict of laws, or even that part of it which is concerned with status, to the level of judicial discretion, it is submitted that this is contrary both to principle and to authority. For, as has been well said, "to state the law in terms of judicial discretion . . . is to admit that no certainty or predictability is attainable in this matter."[72] And again: "the courts might just as well abandon any attempt to formulate and apply defined rules of law if these can be overridden by an undefinable discretion."[73] And, as Lord Hodson said in *Boys v. Chaplin*,[74] "rules of law should be defined and adhered to as closely as possible lest they lose themselves in a field of judicial discretion where no secure foothold is to be found by litigants or their advisers."

5–015

ILLUSTRATIONS[75]

1. H, domiciled in South Africa, obtains a divorce from the South African court on the ground of W's adultery, and thereafter remains single. By Roman-Dutch law a decree of divorce does not permit an adulteress to contract another marriage until the remarriage of her husband. W acquires an English domicile and marries H2 in England. The marriage is valid, for although W's marital

5–016

---

[66] Administration of Justice Act 1920, s.9(2)(*f*); Foreign Judgments (Reciprocal Enforcement) Act 1933, s.4(1)(*a*)(v); Arbitration Act 1950, s.37(1); Adoption Act 1976, s.53(2)(*a*); Arbitration Act 1996, s.103(3); Civil Jurisdiction and Judgments Act 1982, Sched. 1, Art. 27(1); Sched. 3C, Art. 27(1).

[67] Family Law Act 1986, s.51(3)(*c*); State Immunity Act 1978, s.19(1)(*a*); Civil Aviation Act 1982, s.74A; Contracts (Applicable Law) Act 1990, Sched. 1, Art. 16.

[68] *Re Langley's Settlement* [1962] Ch. 541, 555, 557–558 (C.A.); *Russ v. Russ* [1963] P. 87, 100; [1964] P. 315, 327–328, 334, 335 (C.A.); *Cheni v. Cheni* [1965] P. 85, 98; *Qureshi v. Qureshi* [1972] Fam. 173, 201.

[69] *Gray v. Formosa* [1963] P. 259, 269, 270, 271 (C.A.); *Lepre v. Lepre* [1965] P. 52, 63. As to divorce, see now Family Law Act 1986, s.51(3)(*c*); *Kendall v. Kendall* [1977] Fam. 208; *Chaudhury v. Chaudhury* [1983] Fam. 19 (Wood J. and C.A.), and *post*, para. 18–120.

[70] *Re Langley's Settlement* [1962] Ch. 541, 554–555 (C.A.). As to this distinction, see also *Baindail v. Baindail* [1946] P. 122, 128 (C.A.).

[71] *Post*, para. 18–120.

[72] Grodecki (1962) 11 I.C.L.Q. 578, 582.

[73] Nygh (1964) 13 I.C.L.Q. 39, 51. See also Cheshire and North, pp. 129–130.

[74] [1971] A.C. 356, 378.

[75] For Illustrations concerning contracts, see *post*, paras. 32–329 *et seq.*

capacity depends upon the South African decree (for that was the only measure affecting her status as a married woman), the South African provision was penal.[76]

2. A, a French citizen domiciled in France, is a person of full age, but being of extravagant habits is, by a French court of competent jurisdiction, adjudged to be a "prodigal," and is placed under the control of a conseil judiciaire (legal adviser). He is, as a prodigal, incapable of receiving or giving a receipt for his movable property without the consent of such adviser. He becomes entitled to a fund in court in England. The status of a prodigal is unknown to English law.[77] A has a right to receive the fund in court on his own receipt without the consent of his legal adviser because (*inter alia*) the incapacity is a penal one.[78]

3. A Roman Catholic priest is a citizen of, and domiciled in, a foreign country, under whose law he is, as a priest, incapable of marriage. He marries an English-woman in England. The marriage is valid, *i.e.* English law does not recognise the disability as it is a penal one.[79]

4. A, a German Jew, emigrated to England in 1939 in order to escape persecution by the Nazis. In 1941 a German decree deprived absent Jews of their German nationality and their property. This deprivation would not be recognised in England.[80]

5–017   5. In 1954 W, a Belgian national domiciled in Belgium, goes through a ceremony of marriage in England with H1. The purpose of the marriage is to enable W to avoid being deported as a prostitute or undesirable alien, and H1 is induced to take part in the ceremony in return for a bribe of £50 and a ticket to South Africa. In March 1970 W goes through another ceremony of marriage with H2, one of the principals in the organisation which has been managing the activities of W as a prostitute. At the wedding party H2 dies of a heart attack, leaving substantial property. Subsequently, W, anxious to establish that she is the widow of H2, petitions the English court for a declaration that her marriage to H1 was null and void on the false ground that she had not consented to it because she was ignorant of the true nature of the ceremony, and in 1971 the petition is dismissed on the ground that W knew the true nature of the ceremony. W goes back to Belgium and obtains a decree from the Belgian courts that the marriage to H1 is a nullity because it was a mock marriage. The Belgian courts decide that although W's plea of lack of consent is *res judicata* by virtue of the decision of the English court, the plea of mock marriage is not barred because it had not been argued in the English proceedings. In 1973 W petitions the English court for a declaration that the Belgian decree of nullity is entitled to recognition. The petition is dismissed because, among other reasons, the English rule that a marriage celebrated in order to acquire nationality is a valid marriage is a rule which reflects a public policy of giving effect to marriages conducted in accordance with the proper formalities whether or not the parties intend to live together; the Belgian judgment reflected a conflicting public policy to the same facts as were finally ascertained by the English court; in any event, public policy precluded recognition of the Belgian decree because it was obtained only after, and because, W's fraudulent petition had been dismissed by the English court.[81]

---

[76] *Scott v. Att.-Gen.* (1886) 11 P.D. 128, as explained in *Warter v. Warter* (1890) 15 P.D. 152, 155.

[77] *Cf.* Mental Health Act 1983, Pt. VII.

[78] *Re Selot's Trusts* [1902] 1 Ch. 488; also *Worms v. De Valdor* (1880) 49 L.J.Ch. 261. These cases are apparently based on the (untenable) ground that there had been no change of status ([1902] 1 Ch. 492; 49 L.J.Ch. 262), and the penal nature of the French incapacity is a minor ground of decision. In both cases the issue would seem to have been governed by English domestic law; in *Worms v. De Valdor* the question was as to the plaintiff's ability to bring an action, which is a question of procedure to be resolved by the *lex fori*; while in *Re Selot's Trusts* the question was capacity to take under the will of a testator who presumably died domiciled in England. In *Re Langley's Settlement Trusts* [1962] Ch. 541, 557, Lord Evershed M.R. declined "to express any final view upon whether all that was said in the two cases . . . was justified."

[79] The marriage would also be valid under the rule in *Sottomayor v. De Barros (No. 2)* (1879) 5 P.D. 94; see Rule 68, Exception 3, *post.*

[80] *Oppenheimer v. Cattermole* [1976] A.C. 249, 265, 276–278, 282–283. It is submitted that the suggestion in *Frankfurther v. W. L. Exner Ltd.* [1947] Ch. 629, 644, that such legislation would be recognised as effective with regard to property in the legislating State would not be followed today: see n. 18, *ante.*

[81] *Vervaeke v. Smith* [1983] 1 A.C. 145.

RULE 3[82]—**English courts have no jurisdiction to entertain an action:**   **5R–018**
(1) for the enforcement, either directly or indirectly, of a penal,[83]
   revenue[84] or other public law[85] of a foreign State; or
(2) founded upon an act of state.[86]

COMMENT

General. There is a well-established and almost universal principle that the   **5–019**
courts of one country will not enforce the penal and revenue laws of another
country.[87] Although the theoretical basis for the Rule is a matter of some
controversy,[88] the best explanation, it is submitted, is that suggested by Lord

---

[82] F. A. Mann, *Foreign Affairs in English Courts* (1986), Chaps. 9 and 10; Baade, in Lipstein (ed.), *International Encyclopedia of Comparative Law*, Vol. III. Chap. 12 (1990). See generally, Institut de droit international, *Resolution on the activities of national courts and the international relations of their State*, Ann. 1993, pp. 327 *et seq.*

[83] *Folliott v. Ogden* (1789) 1 H.Bl. 123, affd. *sub nom. Ogden v. Folliott* (1790) 3 T.R. 326; *Lynch v. Provisional Government of Paraguay* (1871) L.R. 2 P. & D. 268, 272; *Huntington v. Attrill* [1893] A.C. 150 (P.C.); *Att.-Gen. for Canada v. Schulze*, (1901) 9 S.L.T. 4; *Raulin v. Fischer* [1911] 2 K.B. 93; *Banco de Vizcaya v. Don Alfonso de Borbon y Austria* [1935] 1 K.B. 140; *Frankfurther v. W. L. Exner Ltd.* [1947] Ch. 629; *Novello v. Hinrichsen Edition Ltd.* [1951] Ch. 595, affd. on different grounds [1951] Ch. 1026 (C.A.); *Re Helbert Wagg & Co. Ltd.* [1956] Ch. 323, 345; *Schemmer v. Property Resources Ltd.* [1975] Ch. 273, 288; *Att.-Gen. of New Zealand v. Ortiz* [1984] A.C. 1, 32, 35 (C.A.), affd. by H.L. on different grounds; *Williams & Humbert Ltd. v. W. & H. Trade Marks (Jersey) Ltd.* [1986] A.C. 368, 428; *U.S. v. Inkley* [1989] Q.B. 255, 264; *Larkins v. N.U.M.* [1985] I.R. 671; *Bank of Ireland v. Meeneghan* [1994] 3 I.R. 111; Restatement, s.89; Leflar (1932) 46 Harv. L.R. 193.

[84] *Municipal Council of Sydney v. Bull* [1909] 1 K.B. 7; *Cotton v. R.* [1914] A.C. 176, 195; *Indian and General Investment Trust Ltd. v. Borax Consolidated Ltd.* [1920] 1 K.B. 539, 549; *King of the Hellenes v. Brostrom* (1923) 16 Ll.L.R. 167, 190; *Re Visser* [1928] Ch. 877; *Re Cohen* [1950] 2 All E.R. 36, 39 (C.A.); *Peter Buchanan Ltd. v. McVey* [1954] I.R. 89, [1955] A.C. 516 n.; *Government of India v. Taylor* [1955] A.C. 491; *Metal Industries (Salvage) Ltd. v. Owners of S.T. "Harle,"* 1962 S.L.T. 114; *Rossano v. Manufacturers' Life Insurance Co.* [1963] 2 Q.B. 352, 376–378; *Brokaw v. Seatrain U.K. Ltd.* [1971] 2 Q.B. 476 (C.A.); *Re Lord Cable* [1977] 1 W.L.R. 7, 13; *Re State of Norway's Application (Nos. 1 and 2)* [1990] 1 A.C. 723, 807–809; *U.S.A. v. Harden* (1963) 41 D.L.R. (2d) 721 (Sup. Ct. Can.); *Stringham v. Dubois* [1993] 3 W.W.R. 273 (Alta. C.A.); *Commissioner of Taxes v. McFarland*, 1965 (1) S.A. 470; *Priestley v. Clegg*, 1985 (3) S.A. 955; M. Mann (1954) 3 I.C.L.Q. 465, (1955) 4 I.C.L.Q. 564; Castel (1964) 42 Can. Bar Rev. 277; Smart (1986) 35 I.C.L.Q. 704.

[85] *Emperor of Austria v. Day* (1861) 3 De G.F. & J. 217, 232, 238, 251; *Huntington v. Attrill* [1893] A.C. 150, 156 (P.C.); *Government of India v. Taylor* [1955] A.C. 491, 511; *R. v. Governor of Pentonville Prison, ex p. Budlong* [1980] 1 W.L.R. 1110, 1125 (D.C.); *Att.-Gen. of New Zealand v. Ortiz* [1984] A.C. 1, 20–21 (C.A.), *per* Lord Denning M.R.; *U.S. v. Inkley* [1989] Q.B. 255, 264 (C.A.); *Camdex International Ltd. v. Bank of Zambia (No. 2)* [1997] C.L.C. 714, 723–724, 736 (C.A.); *Att.-Gen. (U.K.) v. Heinemann Publishers Australia Pty. Ltd.* (1988) 165 C.L.R. 30, 41–43; *cf. Gotha City v. Sotheby's, The Times*, October 8, 1998; contrast *U.S. v. Ivey* (1995) 130 D.L.R. (4th) 674, affd. (1996) 139 D.L.R. (4th) 570 (Ont. C.A.); F. A. Mann, *Studies in International Law* (1973), p. 492; (1962) 11 I.C.L.Q. 481; (1971) *Recueil des Cours*, I, p. 107, at pp. 178–180; *Further Studies in International Law* (1990), pp. 355 and 389; Carter [1989] C.L.J. 417; Collins, *Essays*, 118–129; Collins, in *Mélanges Lalive* (1993), pp. 221–230; Verhoeven, *ibid.*, pp. 359–373.

[86] Holdsworth, *History of English Law*, Vol. 14, pp. 33–52; Harrison Moore, *Act of State in English Law* (1906); E. C. S. Wade (1934) 15 B.Y.I.L. 98; Gilmour, 1967 Jur. Rev. 149, [1970] Public Law 120; Collier [1968] C.L.J. 102; F. A. Mann, *Studies in International Law* (1973), p. 420; (1971) *Recueil des Cours*, I, p. 107, at pp. 145–156; Singer (1981) 75 A.J.I.L. 283; Oppenheim, *International Law* (9th ed. Jennings and Watts, 1992), Vol. 1, pp. 365–376.

[87] *Williams & Humbert Ltd. v. W. & H. Trade Marks (Jersey) Ltd.* [1986] A.C. 368, 428, *per* Lord Templeman; *Derby & Co Ltd. v. Weldon (No. 6)* [1990] 1 W.L.R. 1139 (C.A.), at 1154, *per* Staughton L.J.

[88] See F. A. Mann, *Studies in International Law* (1973), pp. 495–499.

Keith of Avonholm in *Government of India v. Taylor*,[89] that enforcement of such claims is an extension of the sovereign power which imposed the taxes, and "an assertion of sovereign authority by one state within the territory of another, as distinct from a patrimonial claim by a foreign sovereign, is (treaty or convention apart) contrary to all concepts of independent sovereignties." Although it was not necessary to decide the precise theoretical basis for the rule, in *Re State of Norway's Application (Nos. 1 and 2)*[90] Lord Goff of Chieveley was inclined to agree with this view. Clause (1) of Rule 3 describes those laws which a foreign State may seek to enforce solely as an exercise of sovereignty, and which "by the law of nations are exclusively assigned to their domestic forum."[91] Whether a foreign law falls within the categories of those laws which the English court will not enforce is a matter for English law. Thus whether the foreign law regards the law in question as a penal law[92] or a revenue law[93] or a public law[94] is irrelevant.

5–020   Rule 3 is framed in terms of lack of jurisdiction, and it has frequently been cited by the courts,[95] but claims made within the scope of the Rule have usually been dismissed on the merits or been struck out.[96] This was so even in *Huntington v. Attrill*,[97] where the Privy Council used the terminology of jurisdiction, and which was the principal authority for Rule 3 when it was first formulated.[98] In the eleventh edition of this book it was suggested that it is the foreign State which has no international jurisdiction to enforce its law abroad, and the English court will not exercise its own jurisdiction in aid of an excess of jurisdiction by the foreign State. The substance of this view was adopted in *Re State of Norway's Application (Nos. 1 and 2)*,[99] but in view of its wide acceptance in judicial decisions, Rule 3 has been retained in its traditional form.

5–021   Direct enforcement occurs where a foreign State or its nominee seeks to obtain money or property, or other relief, in reliance on the foreign rule in question.[1] But indirect enforcement is also prohibited, for a foreign State cannot be allowed to do indirectly what it cannot do directly. Indirect enforcement is, however, easier to describe than to define. Rule 3(1) relates only to *enforcement*, but it does not prevent *recognition* of a foreign law of the type in question, and it is sometimes difficult to draw the line between an issue involving merely recognition of a foreign law and indirect enforcement of it.

---

[89] [1955] A.C. 491, 511. *Cf. Att.-Gen. of New Zealand v. Ortiz* [1984] A.C. 1 (C.A.), at pp. 20–21, *per* Lord Denning M.R., at p. 32, *per* Ackner L.J.

[90] [1990] 1 A.C. 723, 808. *Cf. Att.-Gen. (U.K.) v. Heinemann Publishers Australia Pty. Ltd.* (1988) 165 C.L.R. 30, 40–44.

[91] *Huntington v. Attrill* [1893] A.C. 150, 156 (P.C.).

[92] *Ibid.; Att.-Gen. of New Zealand v. Ortiz* [1984] A.C. 1, 32 (C.A.), affd. by H.L. on different grounds; *U.S. v. Inkley* [1989] Q.B. 255, 265 (C.A.).

[93] *Metal Industries (Salvage) Ltd. v. Owners of S.T. "Harle,"* 1962 S.L.T. 114, 116.

[94] *Att.-Gen. (U.K.) v. Heinemann Publishers Australia Pty. Ltd.* (1988) 165 C.L.R. 30, 46.

[95] See, *e.g. Re Visser* [1928] Ch. 877, 882; *Government of India v. Taylor* [1955] A.C. 491, 507; *Att.-Gen. of New Zealand v. Ortiz* [1984] A.C. 1, 20 (C.A.); *Williams & Humbert Ltd. v. W. & H. Trade Marks (Jersey) Ltd.* [1986] A.C. 368, 437.

[96] See, *e.g. Re Visser, supra; Att.-Gen. of New Zealand v. Ortiz, supra.*

[97] [1893] A.C. 150 (P.C.).

[98] At p. 155. See 1st ed., p. 220.

[99] [1990] 1 A.C. 723, 808.

[1] *Brokaw v. Seatrain U.K. Ltd.* [1971] 2 Q.B. 476, 483 (C.A.); *Att.-Gen. of New Zealand v. Ortiz* [1984] A.C. 1, 32 (C.A.), *per* Ackner L.J., affd. by H.L. on different grounds; *Williams & Humbert Ltd. v. W. & H. Trade Marks (Jersey) Ltd.* [1986] A.C. 368, 437.

Where direct or indirect enforcement does not arise, a foreign law of a type   **5–022**
falling within Rule 3(1) will be recognised if it is relevant to the issue,[2] and
provided it is not contrary to public policy.[3] For example, a contract invalid
according to a penal or revenue law of its applicable law, or performance of
which is prohibited by a penal law of the place of performance, may be held
to be invalid or unenforceable[4]; and the English court will refuse to restrain
trustees from acting in compliance with foreign fiscal legislation forming part
of the proper law of the trust.[5] Likewise trustees will be entitled to be
indemnified out of an estate in England in respect of such sums which they
have been personally compelled to pay abroad in satisfaction of a foreign
government's claim for estate duty upon that estate even though the claim
would have been unenforceable in this country.[6]

Indirect enforcement occurs where the foreign State (or its nominee) in   **5–023**
form seeks a remedy, not based on the foreign rule in question, but which in
substance is designed to give it extra-territorial effect; or where a private party
raises a defence based on the foreign law in order to vindicate or assert the
right of the foreign State. An example of the former is the case of a foreign
company in liquidation which seeks to recover from one of its directors assets
under his control which the liquidator (appointed by the court at the instance
of foreign revenue authorities) would use only for the purpose of satisfying
the foreign State's unsatisfied claim for taxes due from the company.[7] On the
other hand, in *Williams & Humbert Ltd. v. W. & H. Trade Marks (Jersey) Ltd.*[8]
the Spanish Government expropriated shares in various Spanish companies,
and appointed new directors to those companies and their English subsidiaries. The new directors commenced actions in England in the name of their
respective companies to recover assets in the hands of former shareholders
and alleged to belong to the plaintiff companies. The House of Lords held that
the action was not an indirect enforcement of the Spanish decree: it was
designed to vindicate the rights of the plaintiff companies, and not to satisfy
claims by the Spanish State. Nor, in *Re State of Norway's Application (Nos. 1
and 2)*,[9] was it an exercise of extra-territorial sovereignty for a foreign State
to seek the assistance of the English court to obtain evidence for the enforcement of its revenue laws in its own country.

Examples of cases where a private party raises a claim or defence in order   **5–024**
to vindicate or assert the rights of a foreign State include the case of a bank

---

[2] *Re Emery's Investment Trusts* [1959] Ch. 410; *Regazzoni v. K. C. Sethia, Ltd.* [1956] 2 Q.B.
490, 515 (C.A.), affd. [1958] A.C. 301, 322, 324, 328, 330; *Att.-Gen. of New Zealand v. Ortiz*
[1984] A.C. 1, 20 (C.A.), *per* Lord Denning M.R.

[3] *Re Helbert Wagg & Co. Ltd.* [1956] Ch. 323, 345–349.

[4] See, *e.g. Foster v. Driscoll* [1929] 1 K.B. 470 (C.A.); *Regazzoni v. K. C. Sethia, Ltd., supra.* See
also, *post,* paras. 32–141 *et seq.*; 32–236 *et seq.*

[5] *Re Lord Cable* [1977] 1 W.L.R. 7, 24–25. *Cf. Scottish National Orchestra Society Ltd. v.
Thomson's Executor,* 1969 S.L.T. 325; *Bath v. British and Malayan Trustees Ltd.* [1969] 2
N.S.W.R. 114; *Jones v. Borland,* 1969(4) S.A. 29.

[6] *Re Lord Cable* [1977] 1 W.L.R. 7, 15; *Re Reid* (1970) 17 D.L.R. (3d) 199 (B.C.C.A.) (not
followed in *Stringham v. Dubois* [1993] 3 W.W.R. 273 (Alta. C.A.)).

[7] *Peter Buchanan Ltd. v. McVey* [1954] I.R. 89, [1955] A.C. 516n. (as explained in *Williams &
Humbert Ltd. v. W. & H. Trade Marks (Jersey) Ltd.* [1986] A.C. 368), distinguished in *Ayres
v. Evans* (1981) 39 A.L.R. 129; *Priestley v. Clegg,* 1985(3) S.A. 955; *Re Tucker* [1988] L.R.C.
(Comm.) 995 (Isle of Man).

[8] [1986] A.C. 368 criticised by F. A. Mann, *Further Studies in International Law* (1990), p. 389.
Cf. Bank of Ethiopia v. National Bank of Egypt and Liguori [1937] 1 Ch. 513; *Banco de Bilbao
v. Sancha and Rey* [1938] 2 K.B. 176; *Brown, Gow, Wilson v. Beleggings-Societeit N.V.* (1961)
29 D.L.R. (2d) 673 (Ont.).

[9] [1990] 1 A.C. 723, 809.

which seeks delivery of securities owned by the former King of a foreign country and held by his agent in London in order to deliver them to the foreign State, which had declared all the ex-King's property forfeit on account of his alleged treason[10]; or the case of a debtor who seeks to defeat a claim against him by pleading that the debt has been attached through a garnishee order served by or on behalf of a foreign State in respect of tax liabilities[11]; or the case of a shipowner who refuses to hand over goods to their owner because it has received a notice of levy from a foreign government which under its own law has encumbered the goods with a lien in respect of unpaid tax.[12] Where, however, the foreign government has a patrimonial claim,[13] *e.g.* to the property of unsuccessful revolutionaries or former governments, or where it claims or reclaims property which it has reduced into its possession,[14] the case is not one of enforcement of title, but of recognition, and the claim will be enforced. The foreign State may sue to prevent injury to its property, and in this context it was held in the nineteenth century that the Emperor of Austria could sue to restrain the manufacture of counterfeit bank notes,[15] and most recently that the Kingdom of Spain had an arguable case (on a striking-out application) that it could sue to restrain the use of forged export licences.[16]

5–025   **Penal laws.** "The common law considers crimes as altogether local, and cognisable and punishable exclusively in the country where they are committed . . . Chief Justice Marshall, in delivering the opinion of the Supreme Court, said: 'The courts of no country execute the penal laws of another'."[17] In *Huntington v. Attrill*[18] the Privy Council defined penal to include not only crimes in the strict sense, but "all breaches of public law punishable by pecuniary mulct or otherwise, at the instance of the state government, or someone representing the public" and (adopting the test laid down by the United States Supreme Court[19]) "all suits in favour of the state for the recovery of pecuniary penalties for any violation of statutes for the protection

---

[10] *Banco de Vizcaya v. Don Alfonso de Borbon y Austria* [1935] 1 K.B. 140. Contrast *Kahler v. Midland Bank* [1950] A.C. 24, criticised by F. A. Mann, *Studies in International Law* (1973), pp. 506–508.

[11] *Rossano v. Manufacturers' Life Insurance Co.* [1963] 2 Q.B. 352. *Cf. Van de Mark v. Toronto-Dominion Bank* (1989) 68 O.R. (2d) 379.

[12] *Brokaw v. Seatrain U.K. Ltd.* [1971] 2 Q.B. 476 (C.A.), where on an interpleader the U.S. Government argued unsuccessfully that the effect of the notice of levy should be recognised on the basis that the rule as to non-enforcement of revenue claims applied only to direct actions in courts of law. *Cf. Bank of Ireland v. Menneghan* [1994] 3 I.R. 111.

[13] *Government of India v. Taylor* [1955] A.C. 491, 511, *per* Lord Keith of Avonholm.

[14] *e.g. King of Two Sicilies v. Willcox* (1851) 1 Sim.(N.S.) 301; *U.S.A. v. Prioleau* (1865) 2 H. & M. 559; *U.S.A. v. McRae* (1867) L.R. 3 Ch. App. 79; *U.S.S.R. v. Belaiew* (1925) 42 T.L.R. 21.

[15] *Emperor of Austria v. Day* (1861) 3 De G.F. and J. 217, 253–254.

[16] *Kingdom of Spain v. Christie, Manson & Woods Ltd.* [1986] 1 W.L.R. 1120 (discussed in *Associated Newspapers Group plc v. Insert Media Ltd.* [1988] 1 W.L.R. 509, 512–513). On the question whether a foreign State may seek to recover assets taken by former rulers or officials see Collins, in *Mélanges Lalive* (1993), pp. 221–230; and *cf. Republic of the Philippines v. Marcos*, 862 F. 2d 1355 (9th Cir.), cert. den. 490 U.S. 1035 (1988) (where such a claim was permitted) with *Duvalier v. Etat haïtien*, Cour de cassation, France, 1990, in 1991 *Clunet* 137 (where the claim was disallowed). The point was not taken in *Republic of Haiti v. Duvalier* [1990] 1 Q.B. 202 (C.A.).

[17] Story, ss.620–621, citing *The Antelope* (1825) 10 Wheat. 66, 123. See also *Folliott v. Ogden* (1789) 1 H.Bl. 123, 135, *per* Lord Loughborough; *Ogden v. Folliott* (1790) 3 T.R. 726, 733, *per* Buller, J.

[18] [1893] A.C. 150, 156 (P.C.).

[19] *Wisconsin v. Pelican Insurance Co.*, 127 U.S. 265, 292 (1888).

of its revenue or other municipal laws, and to all judgments for such penalties." Thus for this purpose a penal law is a law which punishes[20] or prevents[21] an offence. To come within this principle the law does not have to be part of the criminal code of the foreign country. Thus a law intended to protect the historic heritage of New Zealand by forfeiting historic articles illegally exported was held to be penal[22]; so also in Ireland it was held that the process of sequestration of assets of the National Union of Mineworkers after its civil contempt of court in England was penal in nature.[23] The penalty must normally be exigible by the State,[24] and therefore an action for punitive damages by a private person will not be regarded as penal.[25]

Since "the essential nature and real foundation of a cause of action are not **5–026** changed by recovering judgment upon it,"[26] the English court will not enforce a foreign criminal judgment.[27]

Revenue laws. " . . . [T]here is a well recognised rule, which has been **5–027** enforced for at least 200 years or thereabouts, under which these courts will not collect the taxes of foreign states for the benefit of the sovereigns of those foreign states".[28] This is because "tax gathering is not a matter of contract but of authority and administration as between the State and those within its jurisdiction."[29] Accordingly, the courts do not enforce foreign revenue laws, nor judgments based on foreign revenue claims.[30] In *Government of India v. Taylor*[31] Lord Keith of Avonholm accepted that this rule was subject to contrary agreement by treaty or convention, and it has been held that the State of Norway could seek the extradition of its national for offences of false accounting, forgery and theft which were connected with tax offences.[32]

The expression "revenue law" has not been defined, but certainly includes **5–028** a rule requiring a non-contractual payment of money or kind in favour of central or local government. Thus rules imposing an income tax,[33] a capital

---

[20] *Huntington v. Attrill* [1893] A.C. 150 (P.C.).
[21] *Schemmer v. Property Resources Ltd.* [1975] Ch. 273, 288.
[22] *Att.-Gen. of New Zealand v. Ortiz* [1984] A.C. 1, 34–35 (C.A.), *per* Ackner and O'Connor L.JJ., affd. by H.L. on different grounds.
[23] *Larkins v. N.U.M.* [1985] I.R. 671.
[24] *Huntington v. Attrill* [1893] A.C. 150, 157–158.
[25] *S.A. Consortium General Textiles v. Sun and Sand Agencies Ltd.* [1978] Q.B. 279, 299–300, 305–306 (C.A.). But an action for treble damages under U.S. anti-trust law may be an action for a penalty, since the right to treble damages is granted so that private parties may act as "private attornies-general" to vindicate the anti-trust law: see *post*, paras. 14–020; 14–244 *et seq.*
[26] *Wisconsin v. Pelican Insurance Co.*, 127 U.S. 265, 292 (1888).
[27] Rule 35, *post*.
[28] *Re Visser* [1928] Ch. 877, 884, *per* Tomlin J. See also *King of the Hellenes v. Brostrom* (1923) 16 Ll.L.R. 167, 190 at p. 193.
[29] *Government of India v. Taylor* [1955] A.C. 491, 514.
[30] On such judgments see, *post*, Rules 35(1) and 47; *Government of India v. Taylor* [1955] A.C. 491, 506; *U.S.A. v. Harden* (1963) 41 D.L.R. (2d) 721 (Sup. Ct. Can.); *Commissioner of Taxes v. MacFarland*, 1965 (1) S.A. 470. *Cf. Att.-Gen. for Canada v. Schulze* (1901) 9 S.L.T. 4 (foreign judgment for costs awarded in revenue case). See Stoel (1967) 16 I.C.L.Q. 663.
[31] [1955] A.C. 491, 511.
[32] *R. v. Chief Metropolitan Stipendiary Magistrate, ex p. Secretary of State for the Home Department* [1988] 1 W.L.R. 1204 (D.C.).
[33] *Indian and General Investment Trust Co. Ltd. v. Borax Consolidated Ltd.* [1920] 1 K.B. 539, 550; *U.S.A. v. Harden* (1963) 41 D.L.R. (2d) 721 (Sup. Ct. Can.).

gains tax,[34] a profits levy,[35] a succession duty,[36] a municipal contribution,[37] a compulsory state insurance scheme contribution,[38] and a customs duty[39] have been characterised as revenue laws; but rules under which a State can recover social security payments[40] or obtain legal aid contributions[41] have not been so characterised. The character to be given exchange control regulations is not clear. Although they may not be revenue laws,[42] it has been doubted (it is submitted, correctly) whether the courts would entertain proceedings under a foreign exchange control regulation for the repatriation of funds situate in England.[43]

5–029   Although it was once said that revenue laws are never recognised abroad,[44] this proposition had no justification and it is clear that a foreign revenue law which is part of the applicable law may be recognised.[45] Accordingly where no question of enforcement arises, foreign revenue laws are applied by the courts if they are relevant to an issue, although in individual cases such laws may (like any other foreign rule) have to be disregarded on grounds of public policy. Thus a contract which violates the customs regulations of the governing law will be treated as invalid in England.

5–030   **Public laws.** The expression "other public law" refers to all those rules (other than penal and revenue laws) which are enforced as an assertion of the authority of central or local government. The prohibition on enforcement of public law as such has not received the direct approval of the House of Lords

---

[34] *Government of India v. Taylor* [1955] A.C. 491.

[35] *Peter Buchanan Ltd. v. McVey* [1954] I.R. 89, [1955] A.C. 516n.

[36] *Cotton v. R.* [1914] A.C. 176, 195 (P.C.); *Re Visser* [1928] Ch. 877; *Re Lord Cable* [1977] 1 W.L.R. 7, 13; *Bath v. British and Malayan Trustees Ltd.* [1969] 2 N.S.W.R. 114; *Re Dwelle Estate* (1969) 69 W.W.R. 212 (Alta.); *Jones v. Borland,* 1969 (4) S.A. 29.

[37] *Municipal Council of Sydney v. Bull* [1909] 1 K.B. 7, 12.

[38] *Metal Industries (Salvage) Ltd. v. Owners of S.T. "Harle,"* 1962 S.L.T. 114. The point seems to have been overlooked in *The Acrux* [1965] P. 391.

[39] *Holman v. Johnson* (1775) 1 Cowp. 341, 343; *cf. Att.-Gen. for Canada v. Schulze,* (1901) 9 S.L.T. 4; *King of the Hellenes v. Brostrom* (1923) 16 Ll.L.R. 167, 190; *Regazzoni v. K. C. Sethia, Ltd.* [1958] A.C. 301, 330.

[40] *Weir v. Lohr* (1967) 65 D.L.R. (2d) 717 (Man.).

[41] *Connor v. Connor* [1974] 1 N.Z.L.R. 632. In this case, and in *Weir v. Lohr, supra,* proceedings by private plaintiffs were held to be maintainable notwithstanding that the fruits of their litigation would be claimed by a foreign State which had paid social security claims or legal aid contributions and of which it was entitled to reimbursement. A direct claim by a foreign State for reimbursement would not be maintainable, it seems, unless it had a contractual or quasi-contractual character: see F. A. Mann (1971) *Recueil des Cours,* I, p. 107, at pp. 173–175.

[42] *Frankman v. Prague Credit Bank* [1948] 1 K.B. 730, 746; *Kahler v. Midland Bank* [1950] A.C. 24, 46–47, 57. But export regulations designed to protect foreign exchange were treated as revenue laws in *King of the Hellenes v. Brostrom, supra.*

[43] *Re Lord Cable* [1977] 1 W.L.R. 7, 13. See also *Camdex International Ltd. v. Bank of Zambia (No. 2)* [1997] C.L.C. 714 (C.A.). *Cf. Banco do Brasil v. A. C. Israel Commodity Co.,* 12 N.Y. 2d 371, 190 N.E. 2d 235 (1963), cert. den. 376 U.S. 906 (1964); contrast *Banco Frances e Brasileiro v. Doe,* 36 N.Y. 2d 592, 331 N.E. 2d 502, cert. den. 423 U.S. 867 (1975).

[44] See, *e.g. Holman v. Johnson* (1775) 1 Cowp. 341, 342. Foreign rules requiring documents to be stamped as a prerequisite of validity have long been recognised: *Alves v. Hodgson* (1797) 7 T.R. 241, 243; *Clegg v. Levy* (1812) 3 Camp. 166; *Bristow v. Sequeville* (1850) 5 Exch. 275. Contrast *James v. Catherwood* (1823) 3 Dow. & Ry. (K.B.) 190.

[45] See *Re Visser* [1928] 1 Ch. 877; *Government of India v. Taylor* [1955] A.C. 491, 505, 513; *Regazzoni v. K. C. Sethia, Ltd.* [1956] 2 Q.B. 490, 515 (C.A.); affd. [1958] A.C. 301, 322, 324, 328, 330.

and has been the subject of conflicting dicta in lower courts. It is submitted[46] that the prohibitions on the enforcement of penal[47] and revenue laws are examples of a wider principle that a State cannot enforce its public law or its political or prerogative rights.[48] As Lord Keith of Avonholm put it in *Government of India v. Taylor*,[49] an assertion of sovereign authority by one State within the territory of another is contrary to all concepts of independent sovereign authorities.

There is, it is true, very little authority which deals directly with the general **5–031** principle. This is, at least partially, explained by the fact that States do not generally seek to enforce their public laws abroad and by the fact that it is difficult to see to what cause of action such claims could give rise. Thus in *Re Lord Cable*[50] the Indian Government sought to be joined in proceedings for the execution of a will trust, in order that it might argue (*inter alia*) that the will trustees should remit funds to India in accordance with Indian exchange control legislation. Joinder was refused because, among other grounds, Slade J. was not satisfied that the English court would ever entertain proceedings by a foreign State of which the sole purpose was directly to enforce its exchange control regulations. In that case, the Indian Government sought to be joined so that it could oppose an application by beneficiaries to restrain the trustees from remitting funds to India. But if it had commenced an action itself to require remittance of the funds to India in accordance with the exchange control regulations, it is clear that there would have been no cause of action appropriate to the claim. It is not necessary to assimilate exchange control regulations to revenue laws to arrive at that conclusion. There are no principles of the conflict of laws which deal with public rights of that kind.

In *Att.-Gen. of New Zealand v. Ortiz*[51] the New Zealand Government sought **5–032** to recover a valuable Maori carving which had been illegally exported from New Zealand. The carving had been bought by Ortiz and was in the possession of Sotheby's, the auctioneers, for sale on behalf of Ortiz. Under a New Zealand statute historic articles exported without permission were forfeited to the Crown. The defendants resisted the action on two principal grounds, (a) that under New Zealand law the forfeiture was not automatic and did not take effect unless the goods were seized by the authorities (which they had not been), and (b) that the New Zealand statute could not be enforced because it was a penal or public law. Staughton J. decided in favour of the New Zealand Government on the basis that (a) under New Zealand law forfeiture was automatic, and (b) the law was not penal and there was no general category of non-enforceability of foreign public law. In the Court of Appeal his decision was reversed, (a) unanimously on the basis that forfeiture was not automatic, and (b) *per* Lord Denning M.R. on the basis that the statute was a public law which would not be enforced, and *per* Ackner and O'Connor L.JJ. on the basis that it was a penal law. The decision of the Court of Appeal

---

[46] This submission was approved in *U.S. v. Inkley* [1989] Q.B. 255, 264 (C.A.).

[47] Which were defined in *Huntington v. Attril* [1893] A.C. 150, 156 (P.C.) to include all breaches of "public law" punishable by fine or otherwise.

[48] The expression used in *Emperor of Austria v. Day* (1861) 3 De G.F. and J. 217, 232, 238, 251.

[49] [1955] A.C. 491, 511, quoted above, para. 5–019.

[50] [1977] 1 W.L.R. 7.

[51] [1982] Q.B. 349, revd. [1984] A.C. 1 (C.A. and H.L.).

was affirmed by the House of Lords solely on the ground that the New Zealand statute did not provide for automatic forfeiture, and the House of Lords pointed out that the views of the Court of Appeal on the applicability of the principle of non-enforceability of penal or public laws were *obiter*, and that the House, having heard no argument on this aspect, would not express any conclusion on the correctness of the opinions of the Court of Appeal. The view of Staughton J. on the relevant aspect was that the authorities did not support a general principle that public laws should not be enforced, and that the better approach was to consider in each individual case whether there was a special ground of public policy which required the law in question not to be enforced. Lord Denning M.R., after a review of the authorities,[52] adopted the view expressed in this book that foreign public laws are not enforceable in this country, because they are acts done in the exercise of sovereign authority which will not be enforced outside the territory of the foreign State. Ackner L.J. did not reach a concluded view, but indicated some support for Staughton J.'s conclusion. In *Williams & Humbert Ltd. v. W. & H. Trade Marks (Jersey) Ltd.*,[53] the facts of which have been summarised above,[54] the defendants to claims by Spanish companies whose shares had been expropriated by the Spanish State sought to resist the claims on the ground (*inter alia*) that the proceedings were an attempt to enforce a foreign law which was penal or otherwise ought not to be enforced by the court, *i.e.* that the action was an attempted enforcement of a foreign public law and contrary to public policy. The House of Lords upheld the striking out of this defence on the basis that the action did not amount to enforcement, direct or indirect, of the Spanish decree. Accordingly, the decision is no authority on the question whether there is a residual category of foreign public laws which the English court will not enforce.

5–033   More recently, in *U.S. v. Inkley*[55] the United States Government sought to enforce in England a default judgment which it had obtained against the defendant in Florida. The defendant had been arrested on fraud charges and had given an appearance bond as a condition of his being released on bail. He absconded, and a default judgment was entered on the bond. The Court of Appeal refused to enforce the judgment. The primary basis of the decision appears to have been that the purpose of the proceedings was to enforce the criminal or penal law. But the Court of Appeal (Purchas L.J. and Heilbron J.) expressly accepted that there is a third residual category of foreign public law which the court will not enforce.[56] The authority of the judgment is weakened

---

[52] Those which are sometimes said to support the general rule include *Don Alonso v. Cornero* (1613) Hob. 212 (where it was held that the English court would not enforce a Spanish decree of forfeiture; but the decree was penal and the property concerned was forfeited when it was outside Spain); *King of Italy v. De Medici* (1918) 34 T.L.R. 623 (where the court refused to grant an interlocutory injunction at the instance of the Italian Government in respect of the Medici family papers said to have been illegally exported; but the grounds of the decision are not clear).

[53] [1986] A.C. 368. For criticism of this decision see F.A. Mann, *Further Studies in International Law* (1990), p. 389. For a decision in a related action in the United States see *Williams & Humbert Ltd. v. W. & H. Trade Marks (Jersey) Ltd.*, 840 F. 2d 73 (D.C. Cir. 1988).

[54] *Ante*, para. 5–023.

[55] [1989] Q.B. 255 (C.A.).

[56] At p. 264.

by the fact that, in reaching this view, the Court of Appeal relied on the judgment of Ackner L.J. in *Att.-Gen. of New Zealand v. Ortiz,* when it is plain that he inclined to the view of Staughton J. that there was no such residual category. In *Camdex International Ltd. v. Bank of Zambia (No. 2)*[57] judgment creditors of the Bank of Zambia sought a garnishee order against a Zambian company which operated all the main copper mines in Zambia, and which kept the proceeds of its metal sales on the London Metal Exchange in London. Under Zambian exchange control regulations the company was obliged to remit a proportion of its income to the judgment debtors, the Bank of Zambia, and the judgment creditors argued that this obligation constituted an attachable debt. The application was refused on the primary ground that the obligation on the garnishee to remit to the Bank of Zambia was not contractual and therefore did not amount to an attachable debt. But Simon Brown L.J., *obiter,* said that, even if there had been a contractual debt, it would not have been capable of attachment because the same objections which arose with regard to the enforcement of foreign revenue and penal laws applied equally to many other public laws, including particularly exchange control, the enforcement of which was no less political; and Phillips L.J. expressed the view that in the hypothetical situation that the Bank of Zambia sued in England to enforce a debt recoverable under exchange control laws, the current state of the authorities militated against the English court entertaining the claim, but indicated that he could not conclude with confidence that it would not do so.

　　The question of the enforceability of foreign public law did, however, arise for decision in Australia and New Zealand in the extensive litigation by the British Government in which it sought to restrain the publication of *Spycatcher,* a book written by Peter Wright, a former member of the British security services. The British Government claimed that the book had drawn on confidential knowledge obtained by Wright while he was an officer of the security services, and that consequently the proposed publication was a breach of fiduciary duty, or a breach of the equitable duty of confidence, or a breach of a contractual obligation of confidence. The High Court of Australia[58] accepted that there was a principle that the court should not enforce foreign public laws, in the sense that the court would not allow the enforcement outside the territory of the foreign sovereign of claims based on or related to the exercise of foreign governmental power. The High Court recognised that it was difficult to identify the foreign laws or rights which fell within the general principle, and suggested that, rather than refer to "public laws" it would be more apt to refer to "public interests" or "governmental interests" to signify that the rule applies to claims enforcing the interests of a foreign sovereign which arise from the exercise of certain powers peculiar to

5–034

---

[57] [1997] C.L.C. 714 (C.A.).
[58] *Att.-Gen. (U.K.) v. Heinemann Publishers Australia Pty. Ltd.* (1988) 165 C.L.R. 30, 42–43. Brennan J. agreed with the result, but would have based the decision simply on the basis that it was contrary to public policy to enforce an obligation of confidence in an action brought for the purpose of protecting the intelligence secrets and political information of a foreign government. In the N.S.W.C.A., Street C.J. and Kirby P. accepted that there was a third residual category, but Street C.J. dissented on the basis that such an action should be allowed if the local sovereign supported the claim of the foreign sovereign on the ground that disclosure would harm the public interest: (1987) 10 N.S.W.L.R. 86. For criticism see F.A. Mann (1988) 104 L.Q.R. 497; see also Collier [1989] C.L.J. 33.

government. Accordingly, the injunction was refused on the ground that the court would not enforce a claim arising out of acts of a foreign State in the exercise of such powers in the pursuit of its national security. The claim for relief arose out of, and was secured by, an exercise of the prerogative of the Crown, in the maintenance of national security, and the right or interest asserted was to be classified as a governmental interest, and not the vindication of private law obligations derived from the fiduciary and contractual relationship between Wright and the British Government. As a result, the action fell within the rule of international law which rendered the claim unenforceable. In New Zealand the Court of Appeal refused an injunction because the material in the book had already entered the public domain, and because it was in the New Zealand public interest that it should be published. Cooke P. seems to have accepted the residual category of "public laws," but considered that the secret service agent's duty of confidentiality should be enforced, at any rate if the local sovereign supported the claim.[59]

5–035   In Canada, however, the non-enforceability of "other public laws" has been said in *U.S. v. Ivey*[60] to rest on a shaky foundation. In that case the United States government was held entitled to enforce in Ontario default judgments obtained in a federal court in Michigan. The judgments were obtained under U.S. legislation which entitled the government to sue for reimbursment of the cost of remedial measures undertaken by the U.S. Environmental Protection Agency in relation to a waste disposal site operated by the defendants. At first instance it was held that even if the rule extended to "other public laws" it did not apply because (a) the claim was not an attempt by a foreign state to assert its sovereignty in Ontario; and (b) considerations of comity favoured enforcement of regulatory schemes aimed at environmental protection and control in North America. The Ontario Court of Appeal agreed, and held that the cost recovery action, although asserted by a public authority, was close to a common law claim for nuisance and was in substance of a commercial or private law nature.

5–036   The issue thus still remains open for decision in England whether the doctrine that penal and revenue laws will not be enforced extends to laws of a "political" or "public" character.[61] The weight of authority in England and abroad clearly indicates that there are limits on the extent to which a foreign State may seek to enforce its public law abroad, but that there is some difference of opinion as to the extent of those limits. The essential issue is whether the courts will refuse to enforce all public laws, as Lord Denning M.R. thought, or whether there should be a degree of flexibility based on special grounds of public policy which require the law in question not to be enforced, as Staughton J. thought.[62] The matter has been the subject of

---

[59] *Att.-Gen. (U.K.) v. Wellington Newspapers Ltd.* [1988] 1 N.Z.L.R. 129, 173–175. *Cf. Nanus Asia Inc. v. Standard Chartered Bank* [1990] 1 H.K.L.R. 396; contrast *Re Santa Fe Int. Corp.* (1984) 23 *Int. Leg. Mat.* 511.

[60] (1995) 130 D.L.R. (4th) 674, affd. (1996) 139 D.L.R. (4th) 570 (Ont. C.A.).

[61] *Regazzoni v. K. C. Sethia, Ltd.* [1958] A.C. 301, 318, *per* Lord Simonds. The question was also left open by the U.S. Supreme Court in *Banco Nacional de Cuba v. Sabbatino*, 376 U.S. 398, 414 (1964).

[62] See also the similar approach of Brennan J. in *Att.-Gen. (U.K.) v. Heinemann Publishers Australia Pty Ltd.* (1988) 165 C.L.R. 30, 50–52.

attention by the Institut de droit international and the International Law Association, each of which recommended a degree of flexibility in dealing with claims to enforce foreign public law.[63]

The public laws involved would include such topics as import and export **5–037** regulations,[64] trading with the enemy legislation,[65] price control regulations and anti-trust legislation. In practice probably the most important rules falling within the category are those which authorise governmental interference with private property, whether in the form of requisition, nationalisation or confiscation. The courts recognise the validity of a title acquired under such rules if the interference was valid and effective by the law of the country where the property was situate at the time when the transference of interest is alleged to have taken place.[66] If, after that date, the property is removed to England before it has been reduced into the possession of the foreign State, then it is submitted that the latter has a valid but unenforceable title: valid because the property was situate within its jurisdiction at the appropriate time, but unenforceable because the courts will not countenance a claim by the foreign State (or its nominee or agent[67]) based on an exercise of sovereign power.[68] If, however, the foreign State does reduce the property into its possession then there seems to be no objection to the protection of that possession in England, since protection of that possession would not involve enforcement of the rule of expropriation.[69] Where a foreign State by decree expropriates shares in a company subject to its jurisdiction, there is no objection to the management of that company appointed by the State procuring the company to recover assets owned by the company situated in England by an action in England. Such an

---

[63] The Institut de droit international (whose rapporteur was Professor Pierre Lalive) resolved in 1977 that claims based on the exercise of governmental power by foreign States should in principle be inadmissible, unless they were justified by reason of the subject matter of the claim, the needs of international co-operation or the interests of the States concerned: see Ann. 1975, pp. 157–183, 219–259; Ann. 1977, pp. 2–18, 328–331. This view was adopted by the French Cour de Cassation in *Guatemala v. SINCAFC*, 1990, in 1991 *Clunet* 137. The International Law Association (whose rapporteur was Mr P.B. Carter) resolved that foreign public laws should not be accorded special treatment, but that the forum may decline to enforce them on grounds of public policy: see Report of the 63rd Conference (1988), pp. 29–30; 719–757. See also *Basle Symposium on the Role of Public Law in Private International Law*, ed. Klein (1991); Lipstein in *United Kingdom Law in the 1980s*, ed. Banakas (1988), p. 38, at 53–58; Prott (1989) *Recueil des Cours*, V, p. 215, at pp. 291–297. For recovery of cultural property by Member States of the European Communities see, *post*, para. 24–008.
[64] Cf. *King of Italy v. De Medici, supra; King of the Hellenes v. Brostrom* (1923) 16 Ll.L.R. 167, 190 (decided on the basis that the law was a revenue law).
[65] Cf. *Lepage v. San Paulo Copper Estates Ltd.* [1917] W.N. 216; *Lorentzen v. Lydden & Co. Ltd.* [1942] 2 K.B. 202; and *Jabbour v. Custodian of Israeli Absentee Property* [1954] 1 W.L.R. 139. All of these decisions are inconsistent with the principle stated in the text, but the question discussed was not argued. *Lorentzen v. Lydden & Co. Ltd.* was not followed on other grounds in *Bank voor Handel en Scheepvaart N.V. v. Slatford* [1953] 1 Q.B. 248.
[66] *Bank voor Handel en Scheepvaart N.V. v. Slatford, supra; post*, Rule 120.
[67] Cf. *Banco de Vizcaya v. Don Alfonso de Borbon y Austria* [1935] 1 K.B. 140, 144.
[68] The question was reserved in *Carl Zeiss Stiftung v. Rayner and Keeler Ltd. (No. 2)* [1967] 1 A.C. 853, 924–925, 941, 962; see also [1964] R.P.C. 299, 335. See also Cheshire and North, p. 118, n. 6; F. A. Mann, *Studies in International Law* (1973), pp. 503–504; Wolff, ss.500–501.
[69] *Brokaw v. Seatrain U.K. Ltd.* [1971] 2 Q.B. 476, 482–483 (C.A.); *Att.-Gen. of New Zealand v. Ortiz* [1984] A.C. 1 (C.A.) at p. 24, *per* Lord Denning M.R. In the same sense *Banco Nacional de Cuba v. Sabbatino, supra*, n. 61.

action does not amount to direct or indirect enforcement of the expropriation decree.[70]

5–038　　**Act of State.**　The courts will not investigate the propriety of an act of the Crown performed in the course of its relations with a foreign State,[71] or enforce any right alleged to have been created by such an act unless that right has been incorporated into English domestic law.[72] Such acts are "acts of State," and "cannot be challenged, controlled or interfered with by municipal courts."[73] This proposition does not mean that an act of State is not recognised by the courts or that it cannot affect private rights existing prior to its commission.[74]

　　The expression "act of State" is also used to describe executive acts which are authorised or ratified by the Crown in the exercise of sovereign power.[75] The victim of such an act is in some circumstances denied any redress against the actor because the act, once it has been identified as an act of State, is one which the court has no jurisdiction to examine.[76] The defence can be raised in

---

[70] *Williams and Humbert: Ltd. v. W. & H. Trade Marks (Jersey) Ltd.* [1986] A.C. 368, a decision on a striking out application which did not involve examination of the general principle discussed in this section. See also *Bank of Ethiopia v. National Bank of Egypt and Liguori* [1937] 1 Ch. 513; *Banco de Bilbao v. Sancha and Rey* [1938] 2 K.B. 176; *Brown, Gow, Wilson v. Beleggings-Societeit N.V.* (1961) 29 D.L.R. (2d) 673, 709 (Ont.), on which see Ziegel and Dunlop (1962) 40 Can. Bar Rev. 490, 503; F. A. Mann (1962) 11 I.C.L.Q. 471, 490.

[71] *Secretary of State in Council of India v. Kamachee Boye Sahaba* (1859) 13 Moo.P.C. 22, 75; *Cook v. Sprigg* [1899] A.C. 572, 578 (P.C.); *Salaman v. Secretary of State for India* [1906] 1 K.B. 613 (C.A.); *Johnstone v. Pedlar* [1921] 2 A.C. 262, 290; *Secretary of State for India v. Sardar Rustam Khan* [1941] A.C. 356, 372 (P.C.). *Cf. R. v. Secretary of State for Foreign and Commonwealth Affairs, ex p. Pirbai, The Times,* October 17, 1985 (C.A.); *Ex p. Molyneux* [1986] 1 W.L.R. 331; *J.H. Rayner (Mincing Lane) Ltd. v. Department of Trade and Industry* [1990] 2 A.C. 418, 499; *R. v. Secretary of State for Home Affairs, ex p. Rees-Mogg* [1994] Q.B. 552.

[72] *Nabob of the Carnatic v. East India Co.* (1793) 2 Ves. 56, 60; *Cook v. Sprigg* [1899] A.C. 572, 578 (P.C.); *West Rand Central Gold Mining Co. Ltd. v. R.* [1905] 2 K.B. 391; *Vajesingji v. Secretary of State for India* (1924) L.R. 51 I.A. 357, 360 (P.C.); *Hoani Te Heuheu Tukino v. Aotea District Maori Land Board* [1941] A.C. 308 (P.C.). See also *Rustomjee v. R.* (1876) 2 Q.B.D. 69, 73; *Civilian War Claimants' Association v. R.* [1932] A.C. 14; *Republic of Italy v. Hambros Bank* [1950] Ch. 314; *Winfat Ltd. v. Att.-Gen. of Hong Kong* [1985] A.C. 733 (P.C.); *J.H. Rayner (Mincing Lane) Ltd. v. Department of Trade and Industry* [1990] 2 A.C. 418; *Re International Tin Council* [1989] Ch. 309 (C.A.); *Arab Monetary Fund v. Hashim (No. 3)* [1991] 2 A.C. 114; *Littrell v. Government of the United States (No. 2)* [1995] 1 W.L.R. 82 (C.A.); *Philipp Brothers v. Republic of Sierra Leone* [1995] 1 Lloyd's Rep. 289 (C.A.); *Lonrho Exports Ltd. v. Export Credits Guarantee Dept.* [1999] Ch. 158.

[73] *Salaman v. Secretary of State for India* [1906] 1 K.B. 613, 639 (C.A.).

[74] *Ibid.* at p. 640. For example, under the former practice relating to recognition of governments (see *post*, para. 25–004); acceptance by the court of recognition of a foreign régime which had changed the law of the foreign country could have involved an alteration in the court's attitude to private rights existing under the old law: *Luther v. Sagor* [1921] 3 K.B. 532 (C.A.). On the effect of executive statements see *Republic of Somalia v. Woodhouse Drake and Carey (Suisse) S.A.*; [1993] Q.B. 54; *Sierra Leone Telecommunications Co. Ltd. v. Barclays Bank plc* [1998] 2 All E.R. 821; *Kuwait Airways Corp. v. Iraqi Airways Co. (No. 2)* [1999] C.L.C. 31; Att.-Gen. for Fiji v. Robert Jones House Ltd. [1989] 2 N.Z.L.R. 69; and Warbrick (1986) 35 I.C.L.Q. 138; Wilmshurst (1986) 35 I.C.L.Q. 157; and on recognition of States see *Gur Corp. v. Trust Bank of Africa Ltd.* [1987] Q.B. 559 (C.A.). See generally Lauterpacht, *Recognition in International Law* (1947); Talmon, *Recognition of Governments in International Law* (1998).

[75] *Nissan v. Att.-Gen.* [1970] A.C. 179, 218, 238.

[76] *The Rolla* (1807) 6 C.Rob. 364, 366; *Buron v. Denman* (1848) 2 Exch. 167; *R. v. Crewe, ex p. Sekgome* [1910] 2 K.B. 576, 606, 624, 628 (C.A.); *Sobhuza II v. Miller* [1926] A.C. 518 (P.C.); *Nissan v. Att.-Gen.* [1970] A.C. 179, 216; *Buttes Gas and Oil Co. v. Hammer (Nos. 2 and 3)* [1982] A.C. 888, 930–931.

regard to an act performed outside the United Kingdom and its colonies against the person or property of an alien[77] and is also available in regard to the deportation[78] or internment[79] of an alien of enemy nationality. The defence is probably not available in regard to acts affecting the property in the United Kingdom of a non-resident alien.[80] It is an open question whether the defence can apply to acts performed outside the United Kingdom and its colonies against the person or property of a British citizen.[81] The defence is inapplicable to an act performed within the United Kingdom and its colonies against the person or property of a British citizen[82] or of a non-enemy alien present here.[83]

The expression "act of State" is also used in connection with the executive and legislative acts of foreign States. The expression is found in several contexts, and it may not be possible to extract a general principle which will apply to all of them. One line of authorities (concerning the rights of inhabitants of ceded territory) indicates that the English courts will not investigate the propriety of an act of a foreign government performed in the course of its relations with another State or to enforce any right alleged to have been created by such an act.[84] In *Buttes Gas and Oil Co. v. Hammer (Nos. 2 and 3)*[85] the House of Lords held that these cases are part of a "more general principle that the courts will not adjudicate on the transactions of foreign sovereign states." This principle, it was said, was not a variety of "act of State" but one of "judicial restraint or abstention" which was not one of discretion but was "inherent in the very nature of the judicial process." In that case the House of Lords stayed claims and counterclaims between two oil companies for defamation and conspiracy because the heart of the case concerned a question of title to a portion of continental shelf in the Middle East to which there were rival claims by the two rulers who had granted the

5–039

---

[77] *Buron v. Denman* (1848) 2 Exch. 167.

[78] *Netz v. Ede* [1946] Ch. 224. For the deportation of aliens of non-enemy nationality see Immigration Act 1971, s.3(5).

[79] *R. v. Bottrill, ex p. Kuechenmeister* [1947] K.B. 41 (C.A.).

[80] *Cf. Commercial and Estates Company of Egypt v. Board of Trade* [1925] 1 K.B. 271, 290 (C.A.); *Buttes Gas and Oil Co. v. Hammer* [1975] Q.B. 557, 573 (C.A.), revd. on other grounds [1982] A.C. 888.

[81] This point was left open by the majority of the House of Lords in *Nissan v. Att.-Gen.* [1970] A.C. 179, 221, 226–227, 236 and 240. Lord Reid (at p. 213) thought the defence could never apply in regard to a British subject "at least if he is also a citizen of the United Kingdom and Colonies." This category has now been replaced by British citizenship, British Dependent Territories citizenship and British Overseas citizenship (British Nationality Act 1981) and the status of British National Overseas (*ibid.* s.51(3)(a)(ii), as amended by S.I. 1986 No. 948). In *Buttes Gas and Oil Co. v. Hammer* [1975] Q.B. 557, 573 (revd. on other grounds [1982] A.C. 888) Lord Denning M.R. thought the defence is "probably not available" in the case of a "British subject", in current terminology a "Commonwealth citizen". See also Collier [1968] C.L.J. 102, 115–117; Polack (1963) 26 M.L.R. 138; Kato [1969] Public Law 219.

[82] *Walker v. Baird* [1892] A.C. 491 (P.C.).

[83] *Johnstone v. Pedlar* [1921] 2 A.C. 262.

[84] *Cook v. Sprigg* [1899] A.C. 572, 578 (P.C.); *Vajesingji v. Secretary of State for India* (1924) L.R. 51 I.A. 357, 360 (P.C.); *cf. Johnstone v. Pedlar* [1921] 2 A.C. 262, 290.

[85] [1982] A.C. 888. See also *Fayed v. Al Tajir* [1988] Q.B. 712, 725 (C.A.); *J.H. Rayner (Mincing Lane) Ltd. v. Department of Trade and Industry* [1990] 2 A.C. 418, 519; *Kuwait Airways Corp. v. Iraqi Airways, Financial Times*, July 17, 1992; *Arab Monetary Fund v. Hashim* [1993] 1 Lloyd's Rep. 543, 572, affd. on this aspect [1996] 1 Lloyd's Rep. 589, 596 (C.A.); *Kuwait Airways Corp. v. Iraqi Airways Co.* [1995] 1 W.L.R. 1147, 1167 (H.L.); *(No. 2)* [1999] C.L.C. 31; *Westland Helicopters Ltd. v. Arab Organisation for Industrialisation* [1995] Q.B. 282; *A Ltd. v. B Bank* [1997] I.L.Pr. 586 (C.A.); *cf. R. v. Secretary of State for Foreign and Commonwealth Affairs, ex p. Samuel, The Times*, August 17, 1989 (C.A.).

oil companies their respective concessions. It was held that there were no judicial or manageable standards by which the issues could be judged. Recently, however, it has been held that the decision of the House of Lords does not go so far as saying that the English court must automatically or invariably attribute to the conduct of a foreign State in its international relations a validity or legitimacy which it is obvious it does not bear, especially if the executive has expressed a clear attitude on the point.[86] Consequently it was held that a claim for wrongful interference with aircraft in the course of the Iraqi invasion of Kuwait was justiciable notwithstanding that it proceeded on the basis that the invasion was contrary to international law: the United Nations Security Council had declared the invasion illegal, called on all member States not to recognise the invasion, and demanded that Iraq rescind its actions purporting to annex Kuwait. It would be contrary to the international obligations of the United Kingdom were its courts to adopt an approach which was inconsistent with its duty under the United Nations Charter and under the relevant Security Council resolutions.

5–040   In the nineteenth century[87] it was held that the court could not enquire into a sovereign act done within the territory of the foreign State, and this principle was expressed by the United States Supreme Court[88] in a much quoted dictum which was in turn adopted by the Court of Appeal in England[89]:

> "Every sovereign State is bound to respect the independence of every other sovereign State, and the courts of one country will not sit in judgment on the acts of the government of another done within its own territory."

This principle is sometimes used as an alternative ground for a result which can also be reached by the application of the ordinary rules of the conflict of laws. Thus the executive seizure of property by a foreign sovereign within its territory will not give rise to an action in tort in England, either on the basis of this general principle, or because the act was lawful by the law of the place where it was committed and thus afforded a defence under the second rule in *Phillips v. Eyre*.[90] Nor can a former owner challenge title to property acquired from a foreign government which had been confiscated within its own territory, again either on the basis of the general principle or on the basis of the

---

[86] *Kuwait Airways Corp. v. Iraqi Airways Co. (No. 2)* [1999] C.L.C. 31.
[87] *Duke of Brunswick v. King of Hanover* (1844) 6 Beav. 1, 57–58; (1848) 2 H.L.C. 1, 17, 19, 21, 22, 24, 27. See also *Blad's Case* (1673) 3 Swan. 603 (P.C.), and *Blad v. Bamfield* (1674) 3 Swan. 604; *Carr v. Fracis Times & Co.* [1902] A.C. 176, 179–180; *Johnstone v. Pedlar* [1921] 2 A.C. 262, 290. See F. A. Mann, *Studies in International Law* (1973), p. 420; (1971) *Recueil des Cours*, I, p. 107, at pp. 148–149; Singer (1981) 75 A.J.I.L. 283; Staker (1987) 58 B.Y.I.L. 151, 234–250; Collins (1995–96) 6 King's Coll. L.J. 20.
[88] *Underhill v. Hernandez*, 168 U.S. 250, 252 (1897), affirming (1895) 65 F. 577; *Oetjen v. Central Leather Co.*, 246 U.S. 297, 304 (1918). See now *Banco Nacional de Cuba v. Sabbatino*, 376 U.S. 398 (1964); *First National City Bank v. Banco Nacional de Cuba*, 406 U.S. 759 (1972); *Alfred Dunhill of London Inc. v. Republic of Cuba*, 425 U.S. 682 (1976); Restatement Third, *Foreign Relations Law of the United States* (1987), s.443. In *Kirkpatrick & Co. Inc. v. Environmental Tectonics Corp. International*, 493 U.S. 400 (1990), noted by F. A. Mann (1990) 106 L.Q.R. 352, the U.S. Supreme Court held that the act of state doctrine was concerned only with questions involving the validity of acts of foreign sovereigns in their own territory. This decision was applied in *A Ltd v. B Bank* [1997] I.L.Pr. 586 (C.A.).
[89] *Luther v. Sagor* [1921] 3 K.B. 532, 548 (C.A.); *Princess Paley Olga v. Weisz* [1929] 1 K.B. 718, 724–725 (C.A.); *cf. Oppenheimer v. Cattermole* [1976] A.C. 249, 282; *Att.-Gen (U.K.) v. Heinemann Publishers Australia Pty. Ltd.* (1988) 165 C.L.R. 30, 40–41.
[90] *Carr v. Fracis Times & Co.*, *supra*. See *post*, para. 35–005.

rule that the validity of a confiscatory transfer of title depends on the *lex situs*.[91]

The general principle, however, is not an absolute one. In the first place, the **5–041** foreign legislative act may be disregarded if it is not applicable under the normal principles of the conflict of laws[92] or if it is contrary to public policy in England.[93] But although the English court may consider the expressed intention of the foreign legislation and the circumstances in which it was enacted, it will be slow to investigate the motives of the foreign legislator and to question its good faith.[94] Secondly, the extent to which foreign legislation which would otherwise be regarded as valid and applicable may be disregarded on the ground that it is contrary to public international law is a controversial question.[95] It has recently been held that Iraqi legislation, which would otherwise have been applicable as the *lex loci delicti*, could be disregarded on the ground that it arose out of the illegal occupation of Kuwait and was contrary to international law, including Iraq's obligations under resolutions of the United Nations Security Council.[96] Thirdly, there may be circumstances in which foreign legislation may be held by the English court to be unconstitutional under the foreign law. But the court will not entertain an action the object of which is to obtain a determination of the constitutionality of the foreign legislation.[97] Fourthly, the act of state doctrine has no application when it is clear that the relevant acts were done outside the foreign sovereign's territory.[98] Fifthly, it has no application in cases where a statute requires investigation of the propriety or the validity of foreign acts of state.[99]

ILLUSTRATIONS

(1) PENAL LAWS

1. X incurs a penalty of £100 for the infringement of the law of a foreign country prohibiting **5–042** the sale of spirits. The penalty is recoverable in the courts of the foreign country in an action for debt brought by an official of the foreign government. X is in England. The proper official brings an action in the High Court for the recovery of the £100. The claim cannot be maintained.[1]

2. Under the law of New York, the director of a trading corporation, who signs certain certificates with regard to the affairs of the corporation knowing such certificates to be false,

---

[91] *Luther v. Sagor; Princess Paley Olga v. Weisz, supra.* See Rule 120.

[92] *e.g.* as in *Bank voor Handel en Scheepvaart N.V. v. Slatford* [1953] 1 Q.B. 248.

[93] *Re Helbert Wagg & Co. Ltd.* [1956] Ch. 323; *Oppenheimer v. Cattermole* [1976] A.C. 249.

[94] This question has been touched upon in several cases, but has not been the subject of a considered decision: see *Frankfurther v. W. L. Exner Ltd.* [1947] Ch. 629; *Regazzoni v. K. C. Sethia, Ltd.* [1956] 2 Q.B. 490, 500, affd. [1958] A.C. 301, 326; *Re Helbert Wagg & Co. Ltd.* [1956] Ch. 323, 352; *The Playa Larga* [1983] 2 Lloyd's Rep. 171, 190 (C.A.); *Williams & Humbert Ltd. v. W. & H. Trade Marks (Jersey) Ltd.* [1986] A.C. 368, 436. In *Settebello v. Banco Totta and Acores* [1985] 1 W.L.R. 1050 (C.A.) it was held that the English court would not issue letters rogatory to a foreign court for the purpose of taking evidence on the motives of the Portuguese legislature because it would be contrary to "judicial comity."

[95] See *Kuwait Airways Corp. v. Iraqi Airways Co.* [1995] 1 W.L.R. 1147, 1166 (H.L.), and *post*, paras. 25–009 *et seq.*

[96] *Kuwait Airways Corp. v. Iraqi Airways Co. (No. 2)* [1997] C.L.C. 31, *ante*, para. 5–039.

[97] *Cf. A/S Tallinna Laevauhisus v. Estonian State S.S. Line* (1947) 80 Ll.L.R. 99 (C.A.); *Buck v. Att.-Gen.* [1965] Ch. 745 (C.A.); *Nuova Safim SpA v. Sakura Bank Ltd.* [1998] C.L.C. 306; *Hunt v. T & N plc* (1993) 109 D.L.R. (4th) 16 (Sup. Ct. Can.); and F. A. Mann, *Studies in International Law* (1973), p. 442; (1965) 14 I.C.L.Q. 985 (1971) *Recueil des Cours*, I, p. 107, at pp. 147–149; Kahn-Freund, in *Festschrift für F.A. Mann* (1977), p. 207. The statement in the text was approved in *Dubai Bank Ltd. v. Galadari (No. 5), The Times*, June 26, 1990.

[98] *The Playa Larga* [1983] 2 Lloyd's Rep. 171, 194 (C.A.).

[99] *R v. Bow Street Magistrate, ex p. Pinochet* [1998] 3 W.L.R. 1456, 1498 (H.L.). This decision was subsequently set aside: [1999] 2 W.L.R. 272 (H.L.).

[1] *Cf. Huntington v. Attrill* [1893] A.C. 150 (P.C.).

becomes personally liable for the debts of the corporation. Under this law X, a director of a New York company, becomes liable to A, a creditor, for a debt due from the company. X is in England. A brings an action against X for the debt. *Semble*, X may be made liable.[2]

3. The circumstances are the same as in Illustration 2, except that A has recovered judgment in the court of New York for the debt, and brings an action against X in England on the judgment. *Semble*, the judgment is enforceable.[3]

4. The King of Spain deposits securities with the Westminster Bank in London to the order of a Spanish bank as his agents. A decree by the Constituent Cortes of Spain declares the King to be guilty of treason, and all his assets are ordered to be seized for its own benefit by the Spanish State. The court will not order the delivery up of the securities deposited in England to a nominee of the Spanish Republic.[4]

5. X, a British subject, is charged with fraud in the United States, and is released on bail, on condition that he enters into an "appearance bond" in the sum of $48,000. He is allowed by the United States court to go back to England for a month, but he does not return to the United States, and the United States government obtains a civil judgment in the United States federal court in Florida on the bond. No action on the Florida judgment can be brought in England because the purpose of the bond was to ensure the presence of X for a criminal prosecution and to exact pecuniary penalties for non-attendance.[5]

(2) Revenue laws

5–043   6. Under an Act of Parliament of New South Wales the municipality of Sydney is authorised to carry out improvements in the city and to charge the cost to the owners of the property affected. X, an owner of property affected, is resident in England. The council of the municipality brings an action against X for the sum due from him under the New South Wales Act. The claim cannot be maintained.[6]

7. A company registered in England carries on business in India, where it becomes liable to capital gains tax on a sale of its undertaking. The company is wound up in England and the Indian Government lodges a claim in respect of the unpaid tax. The liquidator is justified in rejecting the proof because only liabilities which could have been enforced against the company in England are receivable, and the court would not have enforced the Indian Government's claim.[7]

8. X is the personal representative in England of a Dutch national domiciled at his death in Holland. Under Dutch law duties are payable in respect of his estate. An action is brought by the Queen of Holland against X to recover the sum due. The action fails.[8]

9. X & Co. is a Canadian insurance company with a branch in Egypt, which issues policies to A, under which money is due to A. X & Co. is served with a garnishee order by the Egyptian revenue authorities in respect of tax allegedly due by A to the Egyptian Government. The garnishee order does not afford X & Co. a defence in proceedings in England to recover the debt, since recognition of the order would constitute indirect enforcement of a foreign revenue law.[9]

10. T dies domiciled in South Africa leaving property in England and South Africa. A is his English executor. X is his South African executor. After payment of United Kingdom duties and debts there is a surplus of assets in A's hands. There are insufficient assets in South Africa to pay South African death duties. A seeks the direction of the court on how to dispose of the assets in his hands. Because the South African Government would be unable to enforce its claim for duties in England, it is A's duty to remit the surplus assets direct to the legatees and not to X.[10]

11. The circumstances are the same as in Illustration 10, except that some of the legatees reside in South Africa, and if these legatees are paid their legacies, they will be answerable to the South African Government to the extent of their legacies for duty on the whole estate. A's duty is to remit the surplus assets to X.[11]

12. X and Y, U.S. citizens, send some furniture by sea to Z, their son-in-law, who is living in London. The U.S. Government claim that X and Y owe the U.S. Treasury money for taxes, and while the ship is on the high seas the U.S. Treasury serves a notice of levy on the shipowners in

---

[2] *Cf. Huntington v. Attrill, supra.*

[3] *Huntington v. Attrill, supra.*

[4] *Banco de Vizcaya v. Don Alfonso de Borbon y Austria* [1935] 1 K.B. 140.

[5] *U.S. v. Inkley* [1989] Q.B. 255 (C.A.).

[6] *Municipal Council of Sydney v. Bull* [1909] 1 K.B. 7.

[7] *Government of India v. Taylor* [1955] A.C. 491. It is immaterial where the company is incorporated.

[8] *Re Visser* [1928] Ch. 877.

[9] *Rossano v. Manufacturers' Life Insurance Co.* [1963] 2 Q.B. 352.

[10] *Cf. Jones v. Borland*, 1969 (4) S.A. 29.

[11] *Cf. Scottish National Orchestra Society Ltd. v. Thomson's Executor*, 1969 S.L.T. 325.

respect of unpaid tax demanding surrender of all property belonging to X and Y. The property is not reduced into the possession of the U.S. Treasury, and Z is entitled to claim the furniture from the shipowners, because to give effect to the claim of the U.S. Government would be indirect enforcement of a revenue law.[12]

(3) OTHER PUBLIC LAWS

13. The government of a foreign State passes a decree expropriating certain jewellery belong- **5–044**
ing to X which is situate within that State at the time of the decree. X brings the jewellery to London, where it is claimed by the foreign government. *Semble*, the claim fails.[13]

14. In furtherance of their agreement for the establishment of an international monopoly, an English company is assigned certain American patents by an American corporation. The United States Government claims the cancellation of the assignment under the Sherman Anti-Trust Act. The claim fails.[14]

15. X bring manuscripts to England from Italy despite a decree of the Italian Government forbidding their export. The decree also grants the Italian State a first option to purchase the manuscripts. X seeks to dispose of them to Y in London, and the Italian Government claims an injunction to prevent such a disposal. *Semble*, the court will not grant an injunction.[15]

16. X brings an ancient Maori carving from New Zealand to England in contravention of a New Zealand statute which provides that historic articles illegally exported shall be forfeited to the Crown. The New Zealand Government brings an action in England against X for the return and delivery up of the carving. The action fails because the Crown has not acquired title under New Zealand law, but also, *per* Lord Denning M.R., because the New Zealand statute is a public law, or, *per* Ackner and O'Connor L.JJ., because it is a penal law.[16]

17. X is a German national resident in France. A state of war exists between Germany and France. The French custodian of enemy property duly appointed under French law, who is entitled thereunder to the control of all X's property, claims the payment to him of a dividend on shares held by X in an English company. *Semble*, the court will not order payment.[17]

18. X is a former member of the British security services, and Y is a publisher. X writes a book about his experiences, and proposes to publish it in (among other countries) Australia. The British Government seeks an injunction against X and Y in Australia to restrain publication. An injunction is refused because the purpose of the action by the British Government is to enforce a governmental interest, namely to protect the efficiency of its security service.[18]

19. A & Co. obtains a judgment in England against the Bank of Zambia. It seeks a garnishee order absolute in respect of funds held in London by X & Co., the biggest copper producer in Zambia. Under Zambian exchange control law, X & Co. is bound to transfer a proportion of the funds to the Bank of Zambia. The garnishee order nisi is set aside. Even if the obligation of X & Co. to the Bank of Zambia were a debt (which it is not) attachment of such a debt would be the enforcement of Zambian public law.[19]

(4) ACTS OF STATE

20. A obtains the right to work minerals in the territory of a foreign State from the government **5–045**
of that State. The territory of the foreign State is annexed by the Crown. A claims a declaration that the Crown must respect the concession. The court will not grant such a declaration.[20]

21. X, an officer of the Crown, duly authorised, destroys property of A, a Spanish subject, at a place outside the United Kingdom and Colonies. Spain and the United Kingdom are at peace, and X's act is tortious by the law of the place where it is committed. X's act is an act of State, and the court will not entertain an action by A against X.[21]

21. X is the bodyguard of Y, a foreign potentate, who is on a State visit to England. While attending a civic ceremony Y misunderstands the enthusiasm of the spectators and orders X to

---

[12] *Brokaw v. Seatrain U.K. Ltd.* [1971] 2 Q.B. 476 (C.A.).

[13] Suggested by *Don Alonso v. Cornero* (1613) Hob. 212; and *Princess Paley Olga v. Weisz* [1929] 1 K.B. 718 (C.A.).

[14] Suggested by *British Nylon Spinners Ltd. v. I.C.I. Ltd.* [1953] Ch. 19 (C.A.); [1955] Ch. 37.

[15] *Cf. King of Italy v. De Medici* (1918) 34 T.L.R. 623.

[16] *Att.-Gen. of New Zealand v. Ortiz* [1984] A.C. 1 (C.A. and H.L.).

[17] Based on the facts of *Lepage v. San Paulo Copper Estates Ltd.* [1917] W.N. 216, which, it is submitted, was wrongly decided.

[18] *Att.-Gen. (U.K.) v. Heinemann Publishers Australia Pty. Ltd.* (1988) 165 C.L.R. 30.

[19] *Cf. Camdex International Ltd. v. Bank of Zambia (No. 2)* [1997] C.L.C. 714 (C.A.).

[20] *Cook v. Sprigg* [1899] A.C. 592 (P.C.). See Crown Proceedings Act 1947, s.11(1).

[21] *Buron v. Denman* (1848) 2 Exch. 167. See Crown Proceedings Act 1947, ss.2(1) and 11(1).

shoot at them. X does so, and injures A, who is an innocent bystander. In an action by A, X may not plead act of State.

22. The Sheikh of Araby promulgates a decree which has the effect of depriving X of the right to exploit an oil-rich area and of giving that right to A. X says the decree was "cooked up" by A. A's action for slander is met by a defence of justification and a counterclaim for conspiracy. The claim and the counterclaim will be stayed because the pleadings involve the adjudication of the transactions of foreign States and the issues raised are non-justiciable.[22]

23. A & Co. seek to enforce a Swiss arbitration award against AOI, an international organisation formed in 1975 by a treaty between Egypt, Saudi Arabia, Qatar and the United Arab Emirates, with its headquarters and operations in Egypt. After the peace treaty between Egypt and Israel in 1979, the three Member States other than Egypt purport to suspend the operations of AOI and to set up a liquidation committee. Egypt passes legislation reconstituting the management of AOI. An issue arises as to whether the management appointed pursuant to the Egyptian legislation is properly authorised to represent the AOI. The constitution of AOI is governed by international law, and the authority of the management depended on whether the Egyptian legislation was a justifiable countermeasure in international law, which in turn depended on the issue whether the three States had acted in breach of the treaty setting up the AOI. That was a non-justiciable issue, because it was not open to the English court to determine whether a foreign sovereign State had broken or terminated a treaty.[23] Consequently, the Egyptian-appointed management is not able to adduce proof that it is properly authorised.

24. Iraq invades Kuwait in August 1990, and civil aircraft belonging to Kuwait Airways are seized and removed to Iraq. Iraqi legislation is enacted purporting to dissolve Kuwait Airways and to transfer its assets to Iraqi Airways, which then incorporates the aircraft in its fleet and makes use of them. In an action in England by Kuwait Airways against Iraqi Airways for wrongful interference, it is held that the Iraqi legislation is not capable of recognition in England, because it was exorbitant and contrary to international law.[24]

---

[22] *Buttes Gas and Oil Co. v. Hammer (Nos. 2 and 3)* [1982] A.C. 888.
[23] *Westland Helicopters Ltd. v. Arab Organisation for Industrialisation* [1995] Q.B. 282.
[24] *Kuwait Airways Corp. v. Iraqi Airways Co. (No. 2)* [1999] C.L.C. 31.

CHAPTER 6

DOMICILE AND RESIDENCE

1. GENERAL PRINCIPLES

**RULE 4—(1) A person[1] is, in general, domiciled in the country in which he   6R–001
is considered by English law to have his permanent home.**
**(2) A person may sometimes be domiciled in a country although he does
not have his permanent home in it.[2]**

COMMENT

Concepts of domicile. Rules 4 to 16 are concerned with the traditional   6–002
concept of domicile in English law. In most contexts within the English rules
of the conflict of laws, the word "domicile" refers to this concept; but,
unfortunately for the clarity of those rules, not in all such contexts. The
Brussels and Lugano Conventions on jurisdiction and the enforcement of
judgments in civil and commercial matters use the notion of domicile, without
defining it. The Civil Jurisdiction and Judgments Act 1982 which gives effect
to the Conventions in English law provides the necessary definitions, but the
resulting concept has little in common, save its name, with the traditional
concept.[3] It is to be noted that use of the concept introduced in the 1982 Act
is not strictly limited to cases falling within the Conventions.[4]

It is of course the case that in interpreting a contractual document, espe-   6–003
cially one not governed by English law, the court may attribute to the term
"domicile" a popular meaning differing from either of its technical meanings
in English law.[5]

Permanent home. The notion which lies at the root of the concept of   6–004
domicile is that of permanent home. "By domicile we mean home, the
permanent home; and if you do not understand your permanent home I am
afraid that no illustration drawn from foreign writers or foreign languages will

---

[1] As to domicile of corporations, see Rule 152.
[2] See Rules 5, 10 and 13 to 16.
[3] For the new concept, see Rule 23.
[4] *e.g.* Ord. 11, r.1(1)(*a*), (4) (in Civil Procedure Rules 1998, Sched. 1); see *post*, para.
11–135.
[5] *Cowley v. Heatley, The Times,* July 24, 1986 (interpretation of Commonwealth Games
Constitution).

very much help you to it."[6] A person may be said to have his home in a country if he resides in it without any intention of at present removing from it permanently or for an indefinite period. But a person does not cease to have his home in a country merely because he is temporarily resident elsewhere; and a person who has formed the intention of leaving a country does not cease to have his home in it until he acts according to that intention.

6–005 While the notion of permanent home can be explained largely in the light of commonsense principles, the same is certainly not true of domicile. Domicile is "an idea of law"[7] which diverges from the notion of permanent home in two principal respects. In the first place, the elements which are required for the acquisition of a domicile go beyond those required for the acquisition of a permanent home. In order to acquire a domicile of choice in a country a person must intend to reside in it permanently or indefinitely.[8] A person who intends to reside in a country for ten years and no more does not acquire a domicile in it, although he has his home there during the ten years. Again, a person cannot acquire a domicile of choice in a country in which he has never been physically present,[9] but he may well have his permanent home in it if he establishes his family there and intends shortly to join them. Secondly, domicile differs from permanent home in that the law in some cases says that a person is domiciled in a country whether or not he has his permanent home in it. Thus a person may in fact have no home, either because he is a permanent vagrant or because he has abandoned one home and has not yet acquired another; but the law nonetheless attributes a domicile to him.[10] Again, a person may in fact have a permanent home in one country but be domiciled in another because the law denies him or her the capacity of acquiring a domicile. Thus children under sixteen and mentally disordered persons may be domiciled in countries in which they do not have their permanent home.[11]

6–006 **Reform of the law of domicile.** The traditional concept of domicile has received repeated critical attention from law reform agencies in England and in other countries which have received the English common law.[12] Important reforms were made by Part I of the Domicile and Matrimonial Proceedings Act 1973[13] but they were limited to the special rules affecting the domicile of married women and children. Proposals for a new Code of Domicile made in 1954 by the Private International Law Committee[14] proved abortive, but after the enactment of reforming legislation in New Zealand[15] and Australia[16] the English and Scottish Law Commissions published in 1987 a report containing

---

[6] *Whicker v. Hume* (1858) 7 H.L.C. 124, 160; *cf. Re Craignish* [1892] 3 Ch. 180, 192; *Winans v. Att.-Gen.* [1904] A.C. 287, 288.

[7] *Bell v. Kennedy* (1868) L.R. 1 Sc. & Div. 307, 320; *cf. Bergner & Engel Brewing Co. v. Dreyfus*, 172 Mass. 154, 157, 51 N.E. 531, 532 (1898); *Garthwaite v. Garthwaite* [1964] P. 356, 378, 393 (C.A.).

[8] Rule 10.

[9] *Ibid.*

[10] Rule 5.

[11] Rules 15 and 16.

[12] See McClean, *Recognition of Family Judgments in the Commonwealth* (1983), Chap. 1.

[13] See paras. 6–084, 6E–098—6–104, *post*.

[14] Cmd. 9068 (1954). See Mann (1959) 8 I.C.L.Q. 457.

[15] Domicile Act 1976.

[16] A uniform Domicile Act enacted in the various Australian jurisdictions came into force on July 1, 1982: Victoria, 1978 (amended in 1982 to bring a variant s.8 into line with the text adopted

further proposals for the general reform of the law of domicile.[17] There is no prospect of these recommendations being implemented.

Area of domicile. The object of determining a person's domicile is to connect him for the purpose of a particular inquiry with some system or rule of law. To establish this connection it is sufficient to fix the person's domicile in a "country," that is, in a "territory subject under one sovereign to one body of law."[18] It is not necessary to show in what part of the country he had his permanent home.[19] It is also in general necessary to fix a person's domicile in a particular country, so that it is not sufficient to show that his permanent home is in a State[20] which contains several countries.[21] Thus a person who comes to the United Kingdom with the intention of settling in England or Scotland, or a person who goes to Australia with the intention of settling in Victoria or New South Wales, does not in the eyes of English law acquire a domicile in any of the "countries" in question until he effects his intention. But for some purposes a person may be domiciled in the United Kingdom, or in Canada or Australia, whether or not the United Kingdom or Canada or Australia are "countries" within the above definition.[22] This position is unsatisfactory and the English and Scottish Law Commissions have recommended the adoption in England of rules based on those in the modern Australian legislation, so that a person who is present in a federal or composite State with the intention to settle in that State for an indefinite period should, if he is not held under the general rules to be domiciled in any country within that State, be domiciled in the country therein with which he is for the time being most closely connected.[23] **6–007**

Difficulties sometimes arise when territories are divided or frontiers change.[24] After Ireland was divided in 1921 into Northern Ireland and what is now called the Republic of Ireland, it was held in Ireland that a man could be domiciled in Northern Ireland in 1907[25] or in the Republic in 1898,[26] in each case because he had his home in what subsequently became Northern Ireland and the Republic respectively. In neither of these cases did the court refer to an Order in Council made in pursuance of the Government of Ireland Act **6–008**

---

in the other jurisdictions); New South Wales and Northern Territory, 1979; South Australia and Tasmania, 1980; Queensland and Western Australia, 1981; the Commonwealth Parliament in respect of the law of the Commonwealth, the Australian Capital Territory and other Territories (with different numbering of principal sections), 1982.

[17] Law Com. No. 168; Scot. Law Cm. No. 107. The principal proposals are noted, *post*, in the context of the detailed examination of the relevant rule.

[18] *Ante*, paras. 1–060 *et seq.*

[19] *Re Craignish* [1892] 3 Ch. 180, 192; *Arnott v. Groom* (1846) 9 D. (Ct. of Sess.) 142.

[20] *Ante*, paras. 1–064—1–065.

[21] *Bell v. Kennedy* (1868) L.R. 1 Sc. & Div. 307; *Att.-Gen. for Alberta v. Cook* [1926] A.C. 444, 448–450 (P.C.); *Gatty v. Att.-Gen* [1951] P. 444; *Trottier v. Rajotte* [1940] 1 D.L.R. 433 (Sup. Ct. Can.); *Johnson v. Johnson* [1931] A.D. 391; *Smith v. Smith* 1970 (1) S.A. 146. And see Rule 6, *post*.

[22] *Post*, paras. 6–015—6–016; *e.g.* where, as in Canada and Australia, divorce is regulated by Federal law.

[23] *The Law of Domicile* (Law Com. No. 168), paras. 7.1–7.8. *Cf.* the uniform Domicile Act in the Australian jurisdictions, s.10.

[24] *Platt v. Att.-Gen. for New South Wales* (1878) 3 App.Cas. 336 (P.C.) (separation of Queensland from New South Wales); *Evans v. Evans* (1960) 2 W.I.R. 246 (separation of Dominica from the Leeward Islands). *Cf. Re O'Keefe* [1940] Ch. 124.

[25] *Re M.* [1937] N.Ir. 151. *Egan v. Egan* [1928] N.Ir. 159 must be regarded as turning on its special facts.

[26] *Re P.* [1945] Irish Jurist 17.

1920, which provides that "for the purpose of determining the domicile of any person, Northern Ireland shall be deemed always to have been a separate part of the United Kingdom."[27] "Separate" in this Order no doubt means "separate from the Republic."

6–009   Domicile is a connection with a locality and not with a group of persons.[28] Thus the House of Lords has rejected the argument that a person could not acquire a domicile in a country merely because he belonged to a group which, by treaty, enjoyed special privileges and some immunity from the jurisdiction of the local courts.[29] The nineteenth-century cases in which British residents in India were held to have acquired an "Anglo-Indian" domicile proceed in disregard of this principle and are now regarded as anomalous.[30]

ILLUSTRATIONS

6–010   1. D, who is domiciled in England, accepts employment in New Zealand under a contract of service by which he will be obliged to remain in New Zealand for ten years. He accordingly takes his family and belongings to New Zealand and sets up house there intending to return to England after the end of the ten years. Although his home is for the time being in New Zealand, he continues to be domiciled in England.

2. D, who is domiciled in England, intends to emigrate to New South Wales. He sends his family and belongings there, but himself stays behind in England, living in hotels, to wind up his affairs. During this period he continues to be domiciled in England although his home is in New South Wales.

3. D lives in England. He has no settled place of abode, but does not intend ever to leave England. Although he has no home, he is domiciled in England.

4. D, the descendant of a Scottish family, has a domicile of origin in Jamaica. In 1837 he leaves Jamaica "for good" and comes to Scotland. By 1838 he has not made up his mind whether to settle in Scotland, England or elsewhere. In 1838 he is domiciled in Jamaica although his home is not there.[31]

5. D was born in India in 1860. Her father at the time of her birth retained his Irish domicile of origin. The father's family lived, at his birth, in County Clare which is now in the Republic of Ireland. In 1940 a question arose as to D's domicile of origin. D's domicile of origin was assumed to be in the Republic of Ireland.[32]

6. D was born in 1890. His parents were married in 1907. D's father F was born and lived all his life in County Antrim which is now in Northern Ireland. F was domiciled in Northern Ireland in 1907 within the meaning of the Legitimacy Act (N.I.) 1928.[33]

6R–011   **RULE 5—No person can be without a domicile.**

COMMENT

6–012   It has been frequently laid down that no person can be without a domicile.[34] This Rule is based on the practical necessity of connecting every person with some system of law by which a number of his legal relationships may be regulated. Where a person is in fact homeless, the law nonetheless attributes

---

[27] S.R. & O. 1922 No. 77, art. 8.

[28] *Casdagli v. Casdagli* [1919] A.C. 145; *Grant v. Grant*, 1931 S.C. 238.

[29] *Casdagli v. Casdagli, supra.*

[30] *Casdagli v. Casdagli, supra.*

[31] *Bell v. Kennedy* (1868) L.R. 1 Sc. & Div. 307.

[32] *Re O'Keefe* [1940] Ch. 124.

[33] *Re M.* [1937] N.Ir. 151. *Cf. Re P.* [1945] Irish Jurist 17. Contrast *Egan v. Egan* [1928] N.Ir. 159, where on very special facts it was held that the *propositus* could elect to be domiciled in either Northern or Southern Ireland.

[34] *Udny v. Udny* (1869) L.R. 1 Sc. & Div. 441, 448, 453, 457; *Bell v. Kennedy* (1868) L.R. 1 Sc. & Div. 307, 320; *Re Craignish* [1892] 3 Ch. 180, 192.

a domicile to him in accordance with the Rules contained in this chapter. An independent person who has his permanent home in a country is domiciled in it. If he has no home but resides in a country with the intention of residing permanently in it, he is domiciled in that country.[35] If he has no home and no such intention, he is domiciled in the country of his domicile of origin.[36] If he has his home in the country of his domicile of origin, he continues to be domiciled there until he acquires a domicile of choice in another country.[37] Having acquired such a domicile of choice, he retains it until he abandons it: upon such abandonment, he may acquire a new domicile of choice; if he does not, his domicile of origin revives.[38] It will be seen that these Rules ensure that no person of full age and capacity can be without a domicile. Since the domicile of a dependent person is always either dependent on that of an ascertainable independent person or fixed by law,[39] it follows that no person can be without a domicile.

RULE 6—No person can at the same time for the same purpose have more than one domicile. 6R–013

COMMENT

Since the object of determining a person's domicile is to connect that person 6–014
with some system or rule of law, it is obvious that, for the purpose of any given inquiry, a person cannot have more than one domicile, and the Rule to this effect is now well established.[40] If a person has two homes in different countries, he is in the absence of a contrary intention domiciled in that country in which he has his principal home.[41]

It has, however, sometimes been suggested that a person may have different 6–015
domiciles for different purposes.[42] Such a possibility was the basis of one judgment in the Court of Appeal in *Lawrence v. Lawrence*,[43] where Purchas L.J.[44] argued that in certain circumstances, in the context of capacity to re-marry, a person could be treated for that limited purpose as having a domicile other than that which he would possess under the general rules. Less controversial illustrations are to be found in some federal or composite States. So, in Australia, the Family Law Act 1975 provides that divorce proceedings may be instituted if either party "is domiciled in Australia".[45] It was held in

---

[35] Rule 4.
[36] Rule 9.
[37] Rules 10 to 12.
[38] Rule 13.
[39] Rules 14 to 16.
[40] *Udny v. Udny* (1869) L.R. 1 Sc. & Div. 441, 448; *Saccharin Corporation Ltd. v. Chemische Fabrik von Heyden* [1911] 2 K.B. 516, 527 (C.A.); *Garthwaite v. Garthwaite* [1964] P. 356, 379 (C.A.); *Khan* (1965) 82 S.A.L.J. 147; for early statements of the view that a man could have two domiciles for certain purposes, see *Somerville v. Somerville* (1801) 5 Ves. 750, 786; *Re Capdevielle* (1864) 2 H. & C. 985, 1018. *Cf.* the New Zealand Domicile Act 1976, s.13: "A person domiciled in a country forming part of a union is also domiciled in that union."
[41] *Cf. Forbes v. Forbes* (1854) Kay 341, 367. Contrast *Huntley v. Gaskell* [1906] A.C. 56.
[42] *Att.-Gen. v. Rowe* (1862) 1 H. & C. 31, 45; *Yelverton v. Yelverton* (1859) 1 Sw. & Tr. 574, 585; *cf. Texas v. Florida*, 306 U.S. 398, 428–429 (1939); Cook, Chap. 7; Pollak (1933) 50 S.A.L.J. 449, 455–456; Reese (1955) 55 Col.L.Rev. 589; Fawcett (1985) Oxford J.L.S. 378.
[43] [1985] Fam. 106.
[44] At pp. 132–133.
[45] s.39(3)(*b*).

Lloyd v. Lloyd[46] that a similar provision in the Commonwealth Matrimonial Causes Act 1959[47] limiting access to the state courts which then exercised divorce jurisdiction to persons "domiciled in Australia" enabled a person who was domiciled in New South Wales to institute divorce proceedings in Victoria.[48] For the purpose of divorce jurisdiction the parties to the marriage were domiciled in "Australia" though for most other purposes they were domiciled in New South Wales. The expression "domiciled in the United Kingdom" similarly occurs in a number of Acts of the United Kingdom Parliament.[49] It would be possible for English courts to follow the reasoning of *Lloyd v. Lloyd* and so to hold that, for the purposes of such Acts, a person could be domiciled in the United Kingdom. This would be a welcome relaxation of the old idea that a person can only have one domicile for all purposes; but it would also raise many problems which are as yet unresolved.

6–016 In *Lloyd v. Lloyd* there was no doubt that the parties were domiciled in New South Wales. It is not clear what the position would have been had they been immigrants who had not yet decided in which of the Australian states they would settle. Is it necessary to establish a domicile in some law-district within Australia before one can be domiciled in Australia?[50] It is not necessary under the reformed law of domicile in force in Australia (and New Zealand)[51]; but that is not determinative for an English court which must apply the English law of domicile.[52] If an immigrant husband with an English domicile of origin were to die shortly after obtaining an Australian divorce and before he had decided in which Australian state to settle, there can be no doubt that the English court would hold that he died domiciled in England[53]; but there can equally be little doubt that the divorce would be recognised on the basis that he was domiciled in Australia. The Australian legislation would be taken into account by the English court not to determine the issue of domicile but simply to define the law district or "country" within which a person must be domiciled in the context of the divorce jurisdiction. To this extent, therefore, a person can be domiciled in two different countries for different purposes at the same time.

6R–017 **RULE 7—An existing domicile is presumed to continue until it is proved that a new domicile has been acquired.**

COMMENT

6–018 There is a presumption that a person continues to be domiciled in the country in which he is domiciled[54]; or, to put it differently, the burden of proving a

---

[46] [1962] V.R. 70; Cowen and Mendes da Costa (1962) 78 L.Q.R. 62.

[47] s.23(4); and see s.24(1).

[48] In *Lee v. Commissioner of Taxation* (1963) 6 F.L.R. 285 the court was inclined to accept the principle for tax purposes. *Cf. Re Benko* [1968] S.A.S.R. 243.

[49] *e.g.* Income and Corporation Taxes Act 1988, ss.65(4), 192(1), re-enacting earlier legislation; Inheritance Tax Act 1984, ss. 18, 48, 267. The last provision requires certain persons not domiciled in the United Kingdom to be treated as domiciled there for the purposes of the Act; but this falls short of establishing a separate domicile.

[50] *Cf. Att.-Gen. for Alberta v. Cook* [1926] A.C. 444, 449–450 (P.C.) and *Re Benko* [1968] S.A.S.R. 243.

[51] See the uniform Domicile Act of the Australian jurisdictions, s.10; Domicile Act 1976 (New Zealand), s.10.

[52] Rule 8.

[53] For the recommendation of the English and Scottish Law Commissions that would lead to a different conclusion, see *ante*, para. 6–007.

[54] *Att.-Gen. v. Rowe* (1862) 1 H. & C. 31, 42; *Bell v. Kennedy* (1868) L.R. 1 Sc. & Div. 307, 319; *Re Patience* (1885) 29 Ch.D. 976; *Re De Almeda* (1902) 18 T.L.R. 414 (C.A.).

change of domicile lies on those who assert it.[55] This presumption varies in strength according to the kind of domicile which is alleged to continue. It is weakest when that domicile is one of dependency[56] and strongest when the domicile is one of origin,[57] for "its character is more enduring, its hold stronger, and less easily shaken off."[58]

Conflicting views have been expressed as to the standard of proof required   **6–019**
to rebut the presumption. According to Scarman J., the standard is that adopted in civil proceedings, proof on a balance of probabilities, not that adopted in criminal proceedings, proof beyond reasonable doubt.[59] On the other hand, according to Sir Jocelyn Simon P., "the standard of proof goes beyond a mere balance of probabilities"[60]; and there is no doubt that the burden of proving that a domicile of origin has been lost is a very heavy one. Moreover, as Scarman J. himself added,[61] "two things are clear—first, that unless the judicial conscience is satisfied by evidence of change, the domicile of origin persists; and secondly, that the acquisition of a domicile of choice is a serious matter not to be lightly inferred from slight indications or casual words." Perhaps an Australian judge best summarised the result of the English authorities when he said that "the change of a domicile of origin must be proved beyond reasonable doubt, while the change of a domicile of choice may be proved on the balance of probabilities."[62]

In 1987 the English and Scottish Law Commissions recommended no   **6–020**
change in the rule that the burden of proving the acquisition of a new domicile falls on the person alleging it. They recommended that the normal civil standard of proof on a balance of probabilities should apply in all disputes about domicile and that no higher or different quality of intention should be required when the alleged change of domicile is from one acquired at birth than when it is from any other domicile.[63]

**RULE 8—For the purposes of an English rule of the conflict of laws, the   6R–021
question where a person is domiciled is determined according to English law.**

COMMENT

The principle that for the purposes of an English rule of the conflict of laws   **6–022**
domicile is determined according to English law is now well settled. Thus a person who is domiciled in England may acquire a domicile of choice in a foreign country without complying with the formalities required by the law of

---

[55] *Winans v. Att.-Gen.* [1904] A.C. 287; *Ramsay v. Liverpool Royal Infirmary* [1930] A.C. 588; *In the Estate of Fuld (No. 3)* [1968] P. 675, 685; *Fremlin v. Fremlin* (1913) 16 C.L.R. 212; *Holden v. Holden* [1968] N.Ir.7; *Terrassin v. Terrassin* [1968] 3 N.S.W.R. 600.

[56] *Post*, paras. 6–086—6–087.

[57] *Post*, para. 6–031.

[58] *Winans v. Att.-Gen., supra*, at p. 290; *cf. Henderson v. Henderson* [1967] P. 77, 80.

[59] *In the Estate of Fuld (No. 3)* [1968] P. 675, 685–686; *cf. Re Flynn (No. 1)* [1968] 1 W.L.R. 103, 115; *Re Edwards* (1969) 113 S.J. 108; *Buswell v. I.R.C.* [1974] 1 W.L.R. 1631, 1637 (C.A.).

[60] *Henderson v. Henderson* [1967] P. 77, 80; *Steadman v. Steadman* [1976] A.C. 536, 563.

[61] *In the Estate of Fuld (No. 3), supra*, at p. 686.

[62] *Re Cartier* [1952] S.A.S.R. 280, 291.

[63] *The Law of Domicile* (Law Com. No. 168), paras. 5.4, 5.6, 5.9. *Cf.* the uniform Australian Domicile Acts, s.12; New Zealand Domicile Act 1976, s.11.

that country for the acquisition of a domicile within it.[64] Again, in determining whether a person who was domiciled abroad has acquired a domicile of choice in England, the law of the country of the foreign domicile is disregarded.[65] It is of course perfectly possible for an English rule of the conflict of laws to make express use of the concept of domicile as understood in a foreign system of law. The Family Law Act 1986 provides an illustration: section 46 sets out the grounds for the recognition of overseas divorces, annulments and legal separations by reference (*inter alia*) to the domicile of one or both parties to the marriage, and provides that a party is to be treated as domiciled in the relevant foreign country if he is domiciled there either according to English law or according to the law of that country in family matters.[66]

6–023   It must be stressed that the principle that domicile is determined according to English law only applies "for the purposes of an English rule of the conflict of laws".[67] Under the *renvoi* doctrine[68] the court applies the conflict rule of a foreign country. If that rule is formulated in terms of "domicile," this will mean "domicile" in the sense of the foreign law. But these are exceptional situations and do not derogate from the principle that for the purpose of an English conflict rule domicile is determined according to English law.

Illustrations

6–024   1. D, a widow domiciled in England, goes to France and establishes her permanent home there. According to the French law, she does not thereby acquire a domicile in France, since she has not complied with the formalities then[69] required by French law for the acquisition of a domicile in France. For the purposes of English rules of the conflict of laws, D is domiciled in France.[70]

2. D, who is domiciled in New York, comes to England to perform a contract of service which will require his presence in England for ten years. He intends to make his home in England during those ten years, but thereafter to return to New York. By New York law he thereby acquires a domicile of choice in England; by English law he does not. For the purposes of English rules of the conflict of laws, D is not domiciled in England.[71]

3. D, whose domicile of origin is in Florida, acquires a domicile of choice in New York. Forty years later he resolves to leave New York and to settle in California. He sets out for California but dies on his way there in Illinois. By Florida, New York, Californian and Illinois law D died domiciled in New York; by English law he died domiciled in Florida. For the purposes of English rules of the conflict of laws, D died domiciled in Florida.

4. T dies domiciled in the English sense in an American State but in England according to the law of the State. His will is partially invalid by the law of the State because he failed to leave a "forced share" to W, his widow. There is evidence that the courts of the State would not apply its law to the validity of T's will. The English court will probably uphold T's will because the courts of T's domicile would uphold it as the will of a testator domiciled (in their sense) in England.[72] But the English court has no jurisdiction to make an order in favour of W under the Inheritance (Provision for Family and Dependants) Act 1975 because T died domiciled abroad in the English sense.[73]

---

[64] *Collier v. Rivaz* (1841) 2 Curt. 855; *Bremer v. Freeman* (1857) 10 Moo.P.C. 306; *Hamilton v. Dallas* (1975) 1 Ch.D. 257; *Re Annesley* [1926] Ch. 692; *Re Rowan* (1988) 8 I.L.R.M. 65. See *Gillespie v. Grant* [1992] 6 W.W.R. 599, 610 (Alta.).

[65] *Re Martin* [1900] P. 211 (C.A.). There was no division of opinion in the court on this point.

[66] See *post*, para. 18–074.

[67] *Cf.* the uniform Australian Domicile Acts, s.4(4), declaring that the Act "has effect to the exclusion of the application of the laws of any other country relating to any matter dealt with by" the Act.

[68] Rule 1.

[69] Article 13 of the French Civil Code. This article has since been repealed.

[70] *Re Annesley* [1926] Ch. 692.

[71] *Cf. Re Martin* [1900] P. 211, 227 (C.A.).

[72] See Rule 1 and *cf. Re Ross* [1930] 1 Ch. 377.

[73] See *post*, para. 27–048.

2. ASCERTAINMENT OF DOMICILE

A. *Domicile of origin*

RULE 9—(1) Every person receives at birth a domicile of origin: 6R–025

    (a) A legitimate child born during the lifetime of his father has his domicile of origin in the country in which his father was domiciled at the time of his birth[74];

    (b) A legitimate child not born during the lifetime of his father, or an illegitimate child, has his domicile of origin in the country in which his mother was domiciled at the time of his birth[75];

    (c) A foundling has his domicile of origin in the country in which he was found.[76]

(2) A domicile of origin may be changed as a result of adoption, but not otherwise.

COMMENT

The domicile of origin is a distinctive feature of the English concept of domicile. The English and Scottish Law Commissions, taking the view that the idea of the domicile of origin has "outlived its usefulness," have recommended that the domicile of origin, as a separate type of domicile determined according to a separate set of rules, should disappear from the laws of the United Kingdom. The domicile of a child would be determined in all cases by reference to the new rules recommended by the Law Commissions.[77] Until such time as these recommendations are acted upon, the domicile of origin remains of great importance.   6–026

A domicile of origin is attributed to every person at birth by operation of law.[78] This domicile does not depend on the place where the child is born, nor on the place where his mother or father reside, but on the domicile of the appropriate parent at the time of birth. As a result of this rule, a domicile of origin may be transmitted through several generations no member of which has ever resided for any length of time in the country of the domicile of origin.[79]   6–027

It is generally accepted that a legitimate child born during the lifetime of his father has his domicile of origin in the country in which his father was domiciled at the time of his birth. But it is, in fact, an open question whether this rule applies to a legitimate child born after the divorce of his parents. It is arguable that such a child should take his mother's domicile at birth. Where the parents are living apart at the time of the birth but are not divorced,   6–028

---

[74] *Udny v. Udny* (1869) L.R. 1 Sc. & Div. 441; *Somerville v. Somerville* (1801) 5 Ves. 750, 787; *Forbes v. Forbes* (1854) Kay 341.

[75] *Udny v. Udny* (1869) L.R. 1 Sc. & Div. 441, 457; *Re Grove* (1888) 40 Ch.D. 216 (C.A.); *cf. Urquhart v. Butterfield* (1887) 37 Ch.D. 357 (C.A.).

[76] *Cf. Re McKenzie* (1951) 51 S.R.N.S.W. 293. For a New Zealand statutory provision to this effect, see Domicile Act 1976, s.6(6).

[77] *The Law of Domicile* (Law Com. No. 168), paras. 4.21–4.24. For the recommendations as to the domicile of a child, see *post*, para. 6–096.

[78] *Udny v. Udny* (1869) L.R. 1 Sc. & Div. 441, 457.

[79] *Peal v. Peal* (1930) 46 T.L.R. 645 (also reported in [1931] P. 97, but not on this point); *Grant v. Grant*, 1931 S.C. 238; *cf. Re O'Keefe* [1940] Ch. 124.

different considerations apply. Although a child born of separated parents with different domiciles immediately acquires his mother's domicile as a domicile of dependence under section 4(1) and (2) of the Domicile and Matrimonial Proceedings Act 1973,[80] his domicile of origin will be that of his father. It might seem highly artificial to attribute to a child a domicile of origin which does not then become his effective domicile; but it is a domicile capable of revival throughout his lifetime[81] and its identification could be rendered unduly difficult if it depended upon proof, perhaps many years after the death of both parents, of the date upon which they began to live apart. It is generally assumed, although there is no authority on the point, that a posthumous child takes his mother's domicile at birth.

6–029   The rule as to the domicile of origin of a foundling is also generally accepted, although there is no direct English authority to support it. The rule also applies to a child who is not strictly speaking a foundling, but about the domicile of whose parents nothing is known.[82]

6–030   The domicile of a minor child may be changed as a result of adoption or legitimation, or of a change in his parents' domicile.[83] In the case of adoption, the child acquires a new domicile of origin for he is treated in law as born to the adopters in wedlock,[84] but in the other cases the new domicile which the child gets in this way is a domicile of dependency and not a domicile of origin.[85] Consequently, if the child in later life acquires a domicile of choice and then abandons it without acquiring another, the domicile which will revive[86] will be the domicile of origin, determined in accordance with the present Rule, and not the domicile of dependency imposed as a result of legitimation or of a change in his parents' domicile.

6–031   A domicile of origin is distinguishable from a domicile of choice in two respects. In the first place, a domicile of origin is more tenacious: in other words, it is more difficult to prove that a person has abandoned his domicile of origin than to prove that he has abandoned a domicile of choice.[87] Secondly, if a person leaves the country of his domicile of origin, intending never to return to it, he continues to be domiciled there until he acquires a domicile of choice in another country.[88] But if a person leaves the country of his domicile of choice, intending never to return to it, he forthwith ceases to be domiciled in that country; and unless and until he acquires a new domicile of choice his domicile of origin revives.[89]

---

[80] Rule 15, Exception.
[81] Rule 13.
[82] *Re McKenzie* (1951) 51 S.R.N.S.W. 293.
[83] Rule 15.
[84] Adoption Act 1976, s.39(1)(5), applying from the date of the adoption or from January 1, 1976, whichever is the later. See the uniform Domicile Act in the Australian jurisdictions, s.8(3).
[85] *Henderson v. Henderson* [1967] P. 77.
[86] Rule 13.
[87] *Jopp v. Wood* (1865) 4 D.J. & S. 616; *Douglas v. Douglas* (1871) L.R. 12 Eq. 617; *Re Wills-Sandford* (1897) 41 S.J. 366; *Winans v. Att.-Gen.* [1904] A.C. 287, distinguished in *Re Joyce* [1946] I.R. 277; *Huntly v. Gaskell* [1906] A.C. 56; *Re James* (1908) 98 L.T. 438; *Ramsay v. Liverpool Royal Infirmary* [1930] A.C. 588.
[88] *Somerville v. Somerville* (1801) 5 Ves. 750; *Re Capdevielle* (1864) 2 H. & C. 985; *Bell v. Kennedy* (1868) L.R. 1 Sc. & Div. 307; *Aikman v. Aikman* (1861) 3 Macq. 854; *Vincent v. Buchan* (1889) 16 R. 637; *Grant v. Grant*, 1931 S.C. 238; *Vien Estate v. Vien Estate* (1988) 49 D.L.R. (4th) 558 (Ont. C.A.).
[89] Rule 13.

ILLUSTRATIONS

1. In 1830 A, whose domicile of origin is English, goes to India. He there has a legitimate son,   **6–032**
B, who, while resident in India, has a legitimate son, C, who while resident in India, has a
legitimate son, D. A, B and C intend to retire to England at the age of sixty, but they all die in
India before reaching that age. D's domicile of origin is English.[90]

2. H and W are married and domiciled in Scotland. H dies and W immediately acquires a
domicile of choice in England. After she has done this, she gives birth to D, who is H's son. D's
domicile of origin is (*semble*) English.

3. D is the illegitimate son of A and B. A is a man domiciled in England; B is a woman
domiciled in France. Six months after D's birth, A marries B, thus legitimating D. D's domicile
of origin is French.

4. D is the illegitimate child of A and B, both of whom are domiciled in Scotland. D is
subsequently adopted in England by C and D, both of whom are domiciled in England. D's
domicile of origin is now deemed to be English.[91]

5. D, an illegitimate child, is born in a London hospital. Shortly after his birth his mother
disappears. Nothing is known about her domicile. His domicile of origin is English.[92]

6. D is born in England, the legitimate son of F who is domiciled in Scotland. Before D attains
the age of sixteen, F acquires a domicile of choice in England. D's domicile of origin is
Scottish.[93]

B. *Domicile of choice*

(1) ACQUISITION

RULE 10—Every independent person can acquire a domicile of choice by   6R–033
the combination of residence and intention of permanent or indefinite
residence, but not otherwise.

COMMENT

Residence.[94] For the purpose of this Rule "residence" means very little   **6–034**
more than physical presence. But it does mean something more: thus a person
is not resident in a country in which he is present "casually or as a traveller."[95]
"Residence in a country for the purposes of the law of domicile is physical
presence in that country as an inhabitant of it."[96] A person's state of mind may
be relevant to the issue whether he is present in a country as a traveller or as
an inhabitant; but, subject to this point, residence may be established without
any mental element. There is no requirement of *animus residendi*. The distinction between presence as a traveller and presence as an inhabitant helps to
reconcile the conflicting views which have been expressed on the question

---

[90] *Grant v. Grant*, 1931 S.C. 239; *cf. Peal v. Peal* (1930) 46 T.L.R. 645, 646 (also reported in
  [1931] P. 97, but not on this point).
[91] Adoption Act 1976, s.39(1)(5).
[92] *Cf. Re McKenzie* (1951) 51 S.R.N.S.W. 293.
[93] *Henderson v. Henderson* [1967] P. 77.
[94] See further *post*, paras. 6–114 *et seq.*
[95] *Manning v. Manning* (1871) L.R. 2 P. & D. 223, 226. The actual decision was not on a point
  of domicile. *Cf.* the New Zealand Domicile Act 1976, s.9(*c*): "he is in that country."
[96] *I.R.C. v. Duchess of Portland* [1982] Ch. 314, 318–9. *Cf. Re Newcomb*, 192 N.Y. 238, 84 N.E.
  950 (1908): "bodily presence as an inhabitant."

whether a soldier is resident in the barracks in which he is quartered.[97] It is submitted that the answer to this question depends on the facts of each case since the soldier's presence in barracks may approximate to that of a traveller or to that of an inhabitant, according to the circumstances of the case. Of course, a soldier may, and frequently will, lack the intention necessary for the acquisition of a domicile.[98]

6–035 It has been suggested[99] that the distinction between an inhabitant and a person casually present is of limited value in cases of dual or multiple residence, as a person who retains a residence in his domicile of origin can acquire a domicile of choice in a new country only if the residence established in that country was his "*chief* residence."[1] It is, however, submitted that questions as to the quality of residence are primarily relevant in considering whether the propositus has the *animus manendi*, the intention of permanent or indefinite residence.

6–036 It is not, as a matter of law, necessary that the residence should be long in point of time[2]: residence for a few days[3] or even for part of a day[4] is enough. Indeed, an immigrant can acquire a domicile immediately upon his arrival in the country in which he intends to settle.[5] The length of the residence is not important in itself: it is only important as evidence of *animus manendi*.[6] A person may be resident in a country although he lives in hotels there[7] or in the house of a friend,[8] and although he is staying there for some particular purpose such as conducting business[9] or taking part in legal proceedings.[10] On the other hand, a person spending short periods in a house he owns may be held not to be resident there; he may be there as a visitor and not as an inhabitant.[11]

6–037 It has been held that a domicile of choice cannot be acquired by illegal residence.[12] The reason for this rule is that a court cannot allow a person to acquire a domicile in defiance of the law which that court itself administers. But it is an open question whether the courts of one country would hold that a person could acquire a domicile of choice in some other country by residence there which was illegal under the law of the second country.[13] An

---

[97] See *Re E. R. Smith* (1896) 12 T.L.R. 223; *Sellars v. Sellars*, 1942 S.C. 206; *Willar v. Willar*, 1954 S.C. 144; *cf.* in another context *Atkinson v. Collard* (1885) 16 Q.B.D. 254.

[98] Rule 1.

[99] By Hoffmann J. in *Plummer v. I.R.C.* [1988] 1 W.L.R. 292.

[1] An expression used by Lord Westbury in *Udny v. Udny* (1869) L.R. 1 Sc. 6 Div. 441.

[2] *Bell v. Kennedy* (1868) L.R. 1 Sc. & Div. 307, 319; *Stone v. Stone* [1958] 1 W.L.R. 1287.

[3] *Fasbender v. Att.-Gen.* [1922] 2 Ch. 850, 857–858.

[4] *White v. Tennant*, 31 W.Va. 790, 8 S.E. 596 (1888); *cf. Miller v. Teale* (1954) 92 C.L.R. 406.

[5] *Bell v. Kennedy* (1868) L.R. 1 Sc. & Div. 307, 319.

[6] Rule 11.

[7] *Levene v. I.R.C.* [1928] A.C. 217; *Matalon v. Matalon* [1952] P. 233; *cf. Gordon v. Gordon* [1929] N.Z.L.R. 75.

[8] *Stone v. Stone* [1958] 1 W.L.R. 1287.

[9] *I.R.C. v. Lysaght* [1928] A.C. 234.

[10] *Matalon v. Matalon, supra.*

[11] *I.R.C. v. Duchess of Portland* [1982] Ch. 314.

[12] *Puttick v. Att.-Gen.* [1980] Fam. 1, 19; *Solomon v. Solomon* (1912) 29 W.N.(N.S.W.) 68; *Ex p. Parker* [1926] C.P.D. 255; *Ex p. MacLeod* [1946] C.P.D. 312; *Smith v. Smith*, 1962 (2) S.A. 930; *Lim v. Lim* [1973] V.R. 370, 372; *cf. Jablonowski v. Jablonowski* (1972) 28 D.L.R. (3d) 440 (Ont.) and also (on ordinary residence) *Re Abdul Manan* [1971] 1 W.L.R. 859 (C.A.) and *R. v. Governor of Pentonville Prison, ex p. Azam* [1974] A.C. 18. See generally Pilkington (1984) 33 I.C.L.Q. 885.

[13] Pollack (1934) 51 S.A.L.J. 11, 20.

English court clearly could hold that a domicile had been acquired by residence illegal under the foreign law.

The English and Scottish Law Commissions have recommended that in the **6–038** proposed statutory reformulation of the rules as to domicile the term "presence" should be used in place of "residence." They note in particular that a person arriving in a country with the requisite intention should acquire a domicile immediately on arrival.[14]

Intention.[15] The intention which is required for the acquisition of a **6–039** domicile is the intention to reside permanently or for an unlimited time in a country.[16] "It must be a residence fixed not for a limited period or particular purpose, but general and indefinite in its future contemplation."[17] This intention must be directed exclusively towards one country. Thus a person who leaves the country of his domicile with the intention of settling in one of several other countries does not acquire a domicile in any of those countries.[18] It is also sometimes said that there must be an intention of leaving the country of the previous domicile as well as an intention of residing in the country of the new domicile.[19] It is not necessary to prove an intention to acquire a domicile: indeed a layman is unlikely to form such a juristic intent.[20]

A person who determines to spend the rest of his life in a country clearly **6–040** has the necessary intention even though he does not consider his determination to be irrevocable.[21] It is, however, rare for the *animus manendi* to exist in this positive form: more frequently a person simply resides in a country without any intention of leaving it, and such a state of mind may suffice for the acquisition of a domicile of choice.[22] The fact that a person contemplates that he might move is not decisive[23]: thus a person who intends to reside in a country indefinitely may be domiciled there although he envisages the possibility of returning one day to his native country.[24] If he has in mind the

---

[14] *The Law of Domicile* (Law Com. No. 168), para. 5.7.

[15] See Fentiman [1991] C.L.J. 445.

[16] *Att.-Gen. v. Pottinger* (1861) 6 H. & N. 733, 747–748; *King v. Foxwell* (1876) 3 Ch.D. 518, 520; *Udny v. Udny* (1869) L.R. 1 Sc. & Div. 441, 458; *Doucet v. Geoghegan* (1878) 9 Ch.D. 441 (C.A.); *Waddington v. Waddington* (1920) 36 T.L.R. 359; *Gulbenkian v. Gulbenkian* [1937] 4 All E.R. 618, 626–627.

[17] *Udny v. Udny* (1869) L.R. 1 Sc. & Div. 441, 458; *Cramer v. Cramer* [1987] 1 F.L.R. 116 (C.A.). *Cf.* the New Zealand Domicile Act 1976, s.9(*d*): "he intends to live indefinitely in that country," and the Australian uniform Domicile Acts, s.9: "the intention to make his home indefinitely in that country."

[18] *Bell v. Kennedy* (1868) L.R. 1 Sc. & Div. 307; *Lee v. Commissioner of Taxation* (1963) 6 F.L.R. 285.

[19] *Lyall v. Paton* (1856) 25 L.J.Ch. 746, 749 (the actual decision would now go the other way under the doctrine of the revival of the domicile of origin); *cf. Moorhouse v. Lord* (1863) 10 H.L.C. 272; *Jopp v. Wood* (1865) 4 D.J. & S. 616.

[20] *Re Annesley* [1926] Ch. 692, 701; *Qureshi v. Qureshi* [1972] Fam. 173, 191; *I.R.C. v. Bullock* [1976] 1 W.L.R. 1178, 1183 (C.A.). For a different view, see Cook, pp. 203–207.

[21] *Stanley v. Bernes* (1830) 3 Hag.Ecc. 373, 437; *Gulbenkian v. Gulbenkian* [1937] 4 All E.R. 618; *I.R.C. v. Bullock* [1976] 1 W.L.R. 1178, 1185 (C.A.); *Commissioners of Inland Revenue v. Gordon's Executors* (1850) 12 D. (Ct.of Sess.) 657, 662.

[22] *e.g. Bell v. Bell* [1922] 2 I.R. 152; *cf. Att.-Gen. v. Kent* (1862) 1 H. & C. 12; contrast *Ramsay v. Liverpool Royal Infirmary* [1930] A.C. 588.

[23] *Re Steer* (1858) 3 H. & N. 594; *Att.-Gen. v. Pottinger* (1861) 6 H. & N. 733; *Att.-Gen. v. Kent* (1862) 1 H. & C. 12; *Drevon v. Drevon* (1864) 34 L.J.Ch. 129; *Doucet v. Geoghegan* (1878) 9 Ch.D. 441 (C.A.); *Davis v. Adair* [1895] 1 I.R. 379; *Ley v. Ley's Executors*, 1951 (3) S.A. 186, 194–195; *Gunn v. Gunn* (1956) 2 D.L.R. (2d) 351 (Sask. C.A.).

[24] *Stanley v. Bernes* (1830) 3 Hag. Ecc. 373, 438; *Henderson v. Henderson* [1967] P. 77, 80–81; *Hyland v. Hyland* (1971) 18 F.L.R. 461, 480.

possibility of such a return should a particular contingency occur, the possibility will be ignored if the contingency is vague and indefinite, for example making a fortune[25] or suffering some ill-defined deterioration in health[26]; but if it is a clearly foreseen and reasonably anticipated contingency, for example the termination of employment,[27] succession to entailed property,[28] a change in the relative levels of taxation as between two countries,[29] or the death of one's spouse,[30] it may prevent the acquisition of a domicile of choice. If a person intends to reside in a country for a fixed period only, he lacks the *animus manendi*, however long that period may be.[31] The same is true where a person intends to reside in a country for an indefinite time but clearly intends to leave the country at some time.[32]

6–041   In deciding whether a person has the intention to reside permanently or indefinitely in a country it is relevant to consider whether he became a naturalised citizen of that country,[33] but it is now[34] settled that this consideration is not decisive as a matter of law: indeed, it cannot well be where it is alleged that a person has acquired a domicile of choice in a country which, together with others, is included in the same State. Thus a person can acquire a domicile of choice in a country without naturalisation[35] and conversely a person does not necessarily acquire a domicile of choice in a country which has granted him naturalisation.[36] "It is not the law either that a change of domicile is a condition of naturalisation, or that naturalisation involves necessarily a change of domicile."[37]

6–042   **No other mode of acquisition.** "A new domicile is not acquired until there is not only a fixed intention of establishing a permanent residence in some other country, but until also this intention has been carried out by actual residence there."[38] Residence without intention is insufficient: this is shown by the many cases in which residence was clearly established and in which the

---

[25] *Doucet v. Geoghegan* (1878) 9 Ch.D. 441 (C.A.); *Henderson v. Henderson* [1967] P. 77, 80–81; *In the Estate of Fuld* (*No. 3*) [1968] P. 674, 685; *I.R.C. v. Bullock* [1976] 1 W.L.R. 1178, 1186 (C.A.).

[26] *Re Furse* [1980] 3 All E.R. 838.

[27] *In the Estate of Fuld* (*No. 3*) [1968] P. 674, 684.

[28] *Aikman v. Aikman* (1861) 4 L.T. 374, 376 (H.L.).

[29] *M.* (*C.*) *v. M.* (*T.*) (*No. 2*) [1990] 2 I.R. 52.

[30] *I.R.C. v. Bullock* [1976] 1 W.L.R. 1178 (C.A.); *cf. Anderson v. Laneuville* (1854) 9 Moo. P.C. 325 (death of mistress).

[31] *Cf. Att.-Gen. v. Rowe* (1862) 1 H. & C. 31, and the majority view in *Eilon v. Eilon*, 1965 (1) S.A. 703 (criticised by Kahn (1965) 82 S.A.L.J. 147). This view is not followed in America: Restatement, s.18.

[32] *Jopp v. Wood* (1865) 4 D.J. & S. 616; *Qureshi v. Qureshi* [1972] Fam. 173; *I.R.C. v. Bullock* [1976] 1 W.L.R. 1178 (C.A.); *O'Mant v. O'Mant*, 1947 (1) S.A. 26.

[33] See *D'Etchegoyen v. D'Etchegoyen* (1888) 13 P.D. 132, 134; *Qureshi v. Qureshi, supra*, at p. 190; *Sells v. Rhodes* (1905) 26 N.Z.L.R. 87.

[34] For the old view that there must be an intention "*exuere patriam,*" see *Moorhouse v. Lord* (1863) 10 H.L.C. 272, 283; *Jopp v. Wood* (1865) 4 D.J. & S. 616.

[35] *Brunel v. Brunel* (1871) L.R. 12 Eq. 298; *Doucet v. Geoghegan* (1878) 9 Ch.D. 441 (C.A.); *Re Grove* (1888) 40 Ch.D. 216 (C.A.); *Davis v. Adair* [1895] 1 I.R. 379; *Bell v. Bell* [1922] 2 I.R. 152; *cf. Winans v. Att.-Gen.* [1904] A.C. 287.

[36] *Wahl v. Att.-Gen.* (1932) 147 L.T. 382 (H.L.); *In the Estate of Fuld* (*No. 3*) [1968] P. 675; *Re Adams* [1967] I.R. 424; *Re Dix* [1951] N.Z.L.R. 642.

[37] *Wahl v. Att.-Gen., supra*, at p. 385.

[38] *Bell v. Kennedy* (1868) L.R. 1 Sc. & Div. 307, 319.

decisions turned solely on the question whether the *propositus* had the necessary intention.[39] Conversely, a domicile cannot be acquired by intention without residence.[40] It follows from this that a domicile cannot be acquired by merely setting out for the new country: actual arrival there is necessary.[41]

Reform. The English and Scottish Law Commissions have recommended   6–043
that the intention necessary for the acquisition of a new domicile by an adult should be an intention to settle in the country in question for an indefinite period.[42] Under the draft legislation prepared by the Law Commissions, the term "domicile of choice" would cease to be used; the proposed rules speak simply of the "domicile" possessed by an adult.

ILLUSTRATIONS

1. D, who is domiciled in England, decides to settle in Scotland. Without breaking up his   6–044
English home, he goes to Scotland to look for suitable accommodation. He does not thereby acquire a domicile in Scotland, since he is not resident there.

2. D, who is domiciled in England, determines to settle in Queensland. He sells his house in England, and, taking all his effects with him, embarks for Queensland. He acquires a domicile in Queensland immediately upon his arrival there.[43]

3. D, whose domicile of origin is Turkish, resides in England without any intention of residing anywhere else. He is domiciled in England.[44]

4. D, whose domicile of origin is French, resides in England. He intends to reside in England for an indefinite time but hopes when he has made his fortune to be able to return to France. He is domiciled in England.[45]

5. D, whose domicile of origin is Scottish, goes as a trader to India. He intends ultimately to return to Scotland. He retains his Scottish domicile.[46]

6. D's domicile of origin is in New Jersey. From 1850 to 1860 he works in Russia as a railway contractor. Between 1860 and 1893 he spends a substantial part of each year in England for the sake of his health. From 1893 until his death in 1897 he lives exclusively in England, in spite of his anti-British schemes and sentiments. He has not returned to the United States since his departure therefrom in 1850. He retains his domicile of origin in New Jersey.[47]

7. D's domicile of origin is English. For the last thirty years of his life he lives principally in Scotland, but retains two houses and business interests in England. He makes a Scottish will disposing of his land in Scotland and an English will disposing of the rest of his property. There is evidence that he did not wish to acquire a Scottish domicile as this would restrict his freedom of testation. He is domiciled in England at his death.[48]

8. D's domicile of origin is Scottish. After retiring from work, he lives with his family in Glasgow. When the family moves to Liverpool, he goes with them and lives in Liverpool for the

---

[39] See especially Rule 11.

[40] *Brown v. Smith* (1852) 15 Beav. 444; *Att.-Gen. v. Fitzgerald* (1856) 3 Drew. 610, 616; *In bonis Raffenel* (1863) 3 Sw. & Tr. 49; *Harrison v. Harrison* [1953] 1 W.L.R. 865. The rather doubtful case of *Att.-Gen. v. Dunn* (1840) 6 M. & W. 511 can perhaps be explained on the ground that the *propositus* was only present in the new country as a traveller. It was doubted in *Lyall v. Paton* (1856) 25 L.J.Ch. 746, as to which see para. 6–039, n. 19, *ante*.

[41] *Udny v. Udny* (1869) L.R. 1 Sc. & Div. 441, 449–450, 453–454, criticising a suggestion in *Munroe v. Douglas* (1820) 5 Madd. 379 that a domicile could be acquired *in itinere*.

[42] *The Law of Domicile* (Law Com. No. 168), paras. 5.8–5.22.

[43] *Cf. White v. Tennant*, 31 W. Va. 790, 8 S.E. 596 (1888); *Bell v. Kennedy* (1868) L.R. 1 Sc. & Div. 307, 319.

[44] *Gulbenkian v. Gulbenkian* [1937] 4 All E.R. 618.

[45] *Doucet v. Geoghegan* (1878) 9 Ch.D. 441 (C.A.).

[46] *Jopp v. Wood* (1865) 4 D.J. & S. 616; *cf. Browne v. Browne* (1917) 36 N.Z.L.R. 425.

[47] *Winans v. Att.-Gen.* [1904] A.C. 287.

[48] *Huntly v. Gaskell* [1906] A.C. 56.

last thirty-five years of his life, partly in lodgings and partly in a house together with other members of his family. He declares that he does not wish to return to Glasgow, but in his will (which is formally valid by Scots but not by English law) he describes himself as "a Glasgow man." He is domiciled in Scotland at his death.[49]

6–045   9. D, whose domicile of origin is in South Australia, comes to England in order to read for a law degree. He intends, on the completion of his course, to return to South Australia. He continues, while he is a student, to be domiciled in South Australia.

10. D, whose domicile of origin is Scottish, comes to England at the age of thirty to accept an appointment in England. The appointment is for an indefinite period, subject to a retiring age of sixty-five. D intends to reside in England until he reaches retiring age and then to return to Scotland. He retains his Scottish domicile.

11. D was born in Nova Scotia with a Nova Scotia domicile of origin in 1910. He came to live in England in 1932 and joined the Royal Air Force. He intended to return to Canada at the end of his service. In 1946 he married an Englishwoman. Although D had hoped to persuade her to make a home in Canada, she was unwilling to leave England. D resolved to live in England so long as his wife was alive, but to return to Nova Scotia on her death. D retained his domicile in Nova Scotia throughout.[50]

6R–046   **RULE 11—Any circumstance which is evidence of a person's residence, or of his intention to reside permanently or indefinitely in a country, must be considered in determining whether he has acquired a domicile of choice in that country.**

COMMENT

6–047   Of the two factors which must be shown in order to prove the acquisition of a domicile of choice, residence rarely causes much difficulty. Residence in a country is in itself some evidence of domicile, and may, in the rare case where no other evidence is available, be decisive.[51] It used to be said that residence gave rise to a presumption of domicile,[52] but it is doubtful whether this view would still be accepted[53]; and if such a presumption does exist it can easily be rebutted.[54] It is best to regard residence simply as some evidence of *animus manendi*. As such evidence, it increases in cogency with the length of the residence. But whatever the attitude of the law may once have been,[55] it is now settled that "mere length of residence by itself is insufficient evidence from which to infer the *animus*; but the quality of the residence may afford the necessary inference."[56]

6–048   Most disputes as to domicile turn on the question of whether the necessary intention accompanied the residence; and this question often involves very

---

[49] *Ramsay v. Liverpool Royal Infirmary* [1930] A.C. 588.

[50] *I.R.C. v. Bullock* [1976] 1 W.L.R. 1178 (C.A.); criticised by Carter (1976–1977) 48 B.Y.I.L. 362.

[51] *e.g. Re McKenzie* (1951) 51 S.R.N.S.W. 293.

[52] *Bruce v. Bruce* (1790) 2 Bos. & Pul. 229; *Bempde v. Johnstone* (1796) 3 Ves. 198; *Hodgson v. De Beauchesne* (1858) 12 Moo.P.C. 285; *Stanley v. Bernes* (1830) 3 Hagg.Ecc. 373; *King v. Foxwell* (1876) 3 Ch.D. 518; *Gillis v. Gillis* (1874) I.R. 8 Eq. 597; *Munster & Leinster Bank v. O'Connor* [1937] I.R. 462.

[53] *M'Lelland v. M'Lelland*, 1942 S.C. 502, 510; *Re Ah Hip* [1964] S.A.S.R. 232.

[54] See, for example, *Re Patience* (1885) 29 Ch.D. 976.

[55] In *Re Grove* (1888) 40 Ch.D. 216, 243, Lopes L.J. said that forty-five years' residence gave rise to an "almost irresistible" inference of domicile.

[56] *Ramsay v. Liverpool Royal Infirmary* [1930] A.C. 588, 595; *cf. Huntly v. Gaskell* [1906] A.C. 56.

complex and intricate issues of fact. This is because "there is no act, no circumstance in a man's life, however trivial it may be in itself, which ought to be left out of consideration in trying the question whether there was an intention to change the domicile. A trivial act might possibly be of more weight with regard to determining this question than an act which was of more importance to a man in his life-time."[57] There is, furthermore, no circumstance or group of circumstances which furnishes any definite criterion of the existence of the intention. A circumstance which is treated as decisive in one case may be disregarded in another, or even relied upon to support a different conclusion.[58]

Thus in some cases[59] long residence in a country has, while in others[60] it **6–049** has not, given rise to the inference of *animus manendi*; in some cases[61] the purchase of land or the taking of a lease or the building of a house has, while in others[62] it has not, given rise to necessary inference; in some cases[63] residence in furnished lodgings or hotels has led to a finding of *animus manendi*, while in others[64] this very mode of residence has been relied upon to negative the intent; in some cases[65] the fact that a person has married a native of the country of the alleged domicile has supported the inference of *animus manendi*, but this fact is clearly not decisive[66]; in some cases, great importance has been attached to the presence of a man's wife and children in

---

[57] *Drevon v. Drevon* (1864) 34 L.J.Ch. 129, 133.

[58] *Ibid.*

[59] *Att.-Gen. v. Fitzgerald* (1856) 3 Drew 610; *Cockrell v. Cockrell* (1856) 25 L.J.Ch. 730; *President of the United States v. Drummond* (1864) 33 Beav. 449; *Haldane v. Eckford* (1869) L.R. 8 Eq. 631; *Re Grove* (1888) 40 Ch.D. 216 (C.A.); *Re Eschmann* (1893) 9 T.L.R. 426; *Lord Advocate v. Brown's Trustees*, 1907 S.C. 333; *Moffett v. Moffett* [1920] 1 I.R. 57; *Munster & Leinster Bank v. O'Connor* [1937] I.R. 462; *Sells v. Rhodes* (1905) 26 N.Z.L.R. 87.

[60] *Douglas v. Douglas* (1871) L.R. 12 Eq. 617; *Winans v. Att.-Gen.* [1904] A.C. 287; *Ramsay v. Liverpool Royal Infirmary* [1930] A.C. 588; *Abraham v. Att.-Gen.* [1934] P. 17; *Aikman v. Aikman* (1861) 3 Macq. 854 (H.L.); *Steel v. Steel* (1888) 15 R. 896.

[61] *Curling v. Thornton* (1823) 2 Add. 6; *Anderson v. Laneuville* (1854) 9 Moo P.C. 325; *Forbes v. Forbes* (1854) Kay 341; *Aitchison v. Dixon* (1870) L.R. 10 Eq. 589; *Whicker v. Hume* (1858) 7 H.L.C. 124; *Doucet v. Geoghegan* (1878) 9 Ch.D. 441 (C.A.); *Re Craignish* [1892] 3 Ch. 180; *Re Wills-Sandford* (1897) 41 S.J. 366 (as to the land leased); *Fleming v. Horniman* (1928) 44 T.L.R. 315; *Boldrini v. Boldrini* [1932] P. 9 (C.A.); *In the Estate of Fuld (No. 3)* [1968] P. 675; *Re Flynn (No. 1)* [1968] 1 W.L.R. 103; *Sells v. Rhodes* (1905) 26 N.Z.L.R. 87; *cf. Re James* (1908) 98 L.T. 438 (retention of land).

[62] *De Bonneval v. De Bonneval* (1838) 1 Curt. 856; *Dalhousie v. M'Douall* (1840) 7 Cl. & F. 817; *Munro v. Munro* (1840) 7 Cl. & F. 842; *Re Wright's Trusts* (1856) 2 K. & J. 595; *Drevon v. Drevon* (1864) 34 L.J.Ch. 129; *The Lauderdale Peerage Case* (1885) 10 App.Cas. 692; *Wahl v. Att.-Gen.* (1932) 147 L.T. 382 (H.L.); *Re Wills-Sandford* (1897) 41 S.J. 366 (as to the land purchased); *Gillis v. Gillis* (1874) I.R. 8 Eq. 597; *cf. Wilson v. Wilson* (1872) L.R. 2 P. & D. 435 (retention of land).

[63] *Re Craignish* [1892] 3 Ch. 180; *Re Eschmann* (1893) 9 T.L.R. 426; *cf. In the goods of West* (1860) 6 Jur.(N.S.) 831 (retention of furnished room); contrast *Munster & Leinster Bank v. O'Connor* [1937] I.R. 462.

[64] *Cochrane v. Cochrane* (1847) 9 L.T.(O.S.) 167; *Douglas v. Douglas* (1871) L.R. 12 Eq. 617; *Winans v. Att.-Gen.* [1904] A.C. 287; *Arnott v. Groom* (1846) 9 D. 142.

[65] *In the goods of James Smith* (1850) 2 Rob.Ecc. 332; *Doucet v. Geoghegan* (1878) 9 Ch.D. 441 (C.A.); *Re Grove* (1888) 40 Ch.D. 216 (C.A.); *Re Eschmann* (1893) 9 T.L.R. 426; *In the Estate of Fuld (No. 3)* [1968] P. 675; *Clarke v. Newmarsh* (1836) 14 S. (Ct. of Sess.) 488; *Moffett v. Moffett* [1920] 1 I.R. 57; *Sells v. Rhodes* (1905) 26 N.Z.L.R. 87.

[66] *Douglas v. Douglas* (1871) L.R. 12 Eq. 617; *Moynihan v. Moynihan (No. 2)* [1997] 1 F.L.R. 59; *cf. Abraham v. Att.-Gen.* [1934] P. 17; *Re Bethell* (1888) 38 Ch.D. 220; *Cramer v. Cramer* [1987] 1 F.L.R. 116 (C.A.). Similar considerations apply to stable relationships outside marriage: *Spence v. Spence*, 1995 S.L.T. 335.

a country,[67] but this again is not decisive[68]; in some cases[69] the fact that a person has business interests in a country has been relied on to support a finding of *animus manendi*, while in others[70] the fact that a person went to a country in pursuance of business interests has negatived the intent; and the desire of a person to be buried in a country has in some cases[71] been treated as an important factor, but in others[72] discounted. Many other circumstances have been taken into account in order to determine whether a person has the necessary intention: for example, the place in which his papers and personal belongings are kept,[73] or in which the bulk of his property or investments are to be found,[74] the form and contents of a will,[75] the exercise of[76] or refusal to exercise[77] political rights such as voting or being registered as a voter or as a resident,[78] the fact of naturalisation,[79] decisions made as to the nationality of children,[80] the education of children,[81] the membership of clubs[82] or of

---

[67] *Forbes v. Forbes* (1854) Kay 341; *Platt v. Att.-Gen. for New South Wales* (1878) 3 App.Cas. 336 (P.C.); *D'Etchegoyen v. D'Etchegoyen* (1882) 13 P.D. 132; *Att.-Gen. v. Yule* (1931) 145 L.T. 9 (C.A.); *Re Ah Hip* [1964] S.A.S.R. 232.

[68] *Abraham v. Att.-Gen.* [1934] P. 17; *cf. Wahl v. Att.-Gen.* (1932) 147 L.T. 382 (H.L.); *I.R.C. v. Bullock* [1976] 1 W.L.R. 1178, 1185 (C.A.).

[69] *Cockrell v. Cockrell* (1856) 25 L.J.Ch. 730; *Re Eschmann* (1893) 9 T.L.R. 426; *Wahl v. Att.-Gen.* (1932) 147 L.T. 382 (H.L.); *Abraham v. Att.-Gen.* [1934] P. 17; *In the Estate of Fuld (No. 3)* [1968] P. 675; *Spurway v. Spurway* [1894] 1 I.R. 385; *Brooks v. Brooks' Trustees* (1902) 4 F. 1014; affd. *sub. nom. Huntly v. Gaskell* [1906] A.C. 56; *Healy v. Healy* [1936] R. & N. 278; *Hyland v. Hyland* (1971) 18 F.L.R. 461.

[70] *D'Etchegoyen v. D'Etchegoyen* (1882) 13 P.D. 132; *I.R.C. v. Cohen* (1937) 21 T.C. 301; *M'Lelland v. M'Lelland*, 1942 S.C. 502; *Haque v. Haque* (1962) 108 C.L.R. 230; but a person who goes to trade in a country will acquire a domicile in it if he retires there: *Re Sillar* [1956] I.R. 344.

[71] *Heath v. Samson* (1851) 14 Beav. 441; *Crookenden v. Fuller* (1859) 1 Sw. & Tr. 441; *Re de Almeda* (1902) 18 T.L.R. 414 (C.A.); *Munster & Leinster Bank v. O'Connor* [1937] I.R. 462; *Re Adams* [1967] I.R. 424, 449–450: *cf. Haldane v. Eckford* (1869) L.R. 8 Eq. 631 (reinterment of children); *Stevenson v. Masson* (1873) L.R. 17 Eq. 78 (sale of grave plot).

[72] *Att.-Gen. v. Wahlstatt* (1864) 3 H. & C. 374; *Platt v. Att.-Gen. for New South Wales* (1878) 3 App.Cas. 336 (P.C.); *Re Garden* (1895) 11 T.L.R. 167; *Huntly v. Gaskell* [1906] A.C. 56; *Bradfield v. Swanton* [1931] I.R. 446.

[73] *De Bonneval v. De Bonneval* (1838) 1 Curt. 856; *Whicker v. Hume* (1858) 7 H.L.C. 124; *Zanelli v. Zanelli* (1948) 64 T.L.R. 556 (C.A.); *cf. Att.-Gen. v. Wahlstatt* (1864) 3 H & C 374.

[74] *Firebrace v. Firebrace* (1878) 4 P.D. 63; *I.R.C. v. Bullock* [1976] 1 W.L.R. 1178 (C.A.); *Cramer v. Cramer* [1987] 1 F.L.R. 116 (C.A.).

[75] *Curling v. Thornton* (1823) 2 Add. 6; *Thornton v. Curling* (1824) 8 Sim. 310; *Lyall v. Paton* (1856) 25 L.J.Ch. 746 (as to which see para. 6–039, n. 19, *ante*); *Drevon v. Drevon* (1864) 34 L.J.Ch. 129; *Haldane v. Eckford* (1869) L.R. 8 Eq. 631; *Doucet v. Geoghegan* (1878) 9 Ch.D. 441 (C.A.); *Re Grove* (1888) 40 Ch.D. 216 (C.A.); *Re Garden* (1895) 11 T.L.R. 167; *In the Estate of Fuld (No. 3)* [1968] P. 675; *I.R.C. v. Bullock* [1976] 1 W.L.R. 1178 (C.A.); *Moffett v. Moffett* [1920] 1 I.R. 57; *Sells v. Rhodes* (1905) 26 N.Z.L.R. 87; contrast *Bremer v. Freeman* (1857) 10 Moo.P.C. 306; *Douglas v. Douglas* (1871) L.R. 12 Eq. 617.

[76] *Drevon v. Drevon* (1864) 34 L.J.Ch. 129; this factor was held to be of small importance in *De Bonneval v. De Bonneval* (1838) 1 Curt. 856.

[77] *I.R.C. v. Bullock* [1976] 1 W.L.R. 1178 (C.A.).

[78] *Spence v. Spence*, 1995 S.L.T. 335.

[79] *Ante*, para. 6–041.

[80] *Re Rowan* [1988] I.L.R.M. 65.

[81] *In the goods of West* (1860) 6 Jur.(N.S.) 831; *President of the United States v. Drummond* (1864) 33 Beav. 449; *Cramer v. Cramer* [1987] 1 F.L.R. 116 (C.A.); *cf. Re Grove* (1888) 40 Ch.D. 216 (C.A.) (baptism); *Stevenson v. Masson* (1873) L.R. 17 Eq. 78 (making an establishment for children).

[82] *Re Craignish* [1892] 3 Ch. 180 (C.A.); *Re Sillar* [1956] I.R. 344; *Re Adams* [1967] I.R. 424.

religious or charitable associations,[83] the relations between a man and his family,[84] the place where he was divorced[85] (especially where divorce or re-marriage is socially unacceptable in one of the relevant countries[86]), his character,[87] his social habits,[88] and even the way in which he spells his name[89] have all been treated as relevant to the issue of intention. It must be emphasised that this list is not exhaustive: a person's "tastes, habits, conduct, actions, ambitions, health, hopes and projects" are all regarded as "keys to his intention."[90] Thus it is frequently very difficult to determine a person's domicile, and the resulting uncertainty has given rise to criticism and to proposals for reform of the law.[91]

In determining whether a person has the necessary intention, the court takes into consideration not only the mode but also the place of residence. There is a presumption against the acquisition of a domicile of choice by a person in a country whose religion, manners and customs differ widely from those of his own country.[92] This applies not only to Englishmen or Scotsmen going to *e.g.* India or China, but also to *e.g.* Indians or Pakistanis coming to England.[93] But this presumption is rebuttable: there is no rule of law against the acquisition of a domicile of choice by such a person in such a country.[94] Where several countries are included in one State, it is probably easier to prove a change of domicile from one such country to another than from one such country to a politically foreign country.[95]

6–050

---

[83] *Re de Almeda* (1902) 18 T.L.R. 414 (C.A.); *Spence v. Spence*, 1995 S.L.T. 335 (membership of synagogue and Jewish burial society).

[84] *Att.-Gen. v. Wahlstatt* (1864) 3 H. & C. 374; *Fleming v. Horniman* (1928) 44 T.L.R. 315; *Ramsay v. Liverpool Royal Infirmary* [1930] A.C. 588; *cf. Anderson v. Laneuville* (1854) 9 Moo.P.C. 325.

[85] *In the Estate of Fuld (No. 3)* [1968] P. 675; *M.(C.) v. M.(T.) (No. 2)* [1990] 2 I.R. 52.

[86] *Re Fleming* [1987] I.L.R.M. 638.

[87] *Winans v. Att.-Gen.* [1904] A.C. 287; *Huntly v. Gaskell* [1906] A.C. 56; *Ramsay v. Liverpool Royal Infirmary* [1930] A.C. 588; contrast *Re Sillar* [1956] I.R. 344.

[88] *Re Craignish* [1892] 3 Ch. 180 (C.A.); *Re James* (1908) 98 L.T. 438; *Winans v. Att.-Gen.* [1904] A.C. 287; *Moynihan v. Moynihan (No. 2)* [1997] 1 F.L.R. 59 (living "in the nature of a king" in his place of residence); *Lord Advocate v. Brown's Trustees*, 1907 S.C. 333.

[89] *Drevon v. Drevon* (1864) 34 L.J.Ch. 129; *cf.* as to change of name *Sells v. Rhodes* (1905) 26 N.Z.L.R. 87.

[90] *Per* Lord Atkinson in *Casdagli v. Casdagli* [1919] A.C. 145, 178, commenting on *Winans v. Att.-Gen.* [1904] A.C. 287.

[91] *Post*, paras. 6–133 *et seq.*

[92] *Maltass v. Maltass* (1844) 1 Rob.Ecc. 67; *Casdagli v. Casdagli* [1919] A.C. 145; *Steel v. Steel* (1888) 15 R. 896 ("Nobody in his senses ever goes to Burmah *sine animo revertendi*," at p. 909); *cf. Doucet v. Geoghegan* (1878) 9 Ch.D. 441, 453 ("It is well known that everyone who goes to India does so for the express purpose of making money and returning to this country as soon as possible"); *Grant v. Grant*, 1931 S.C. 238; *cf. Re Tootal's Trusts* (1882) 23 Ch.D. 532 where it was admitted that an Englishman had not acquired a domicile in China. A similar assumption underlies *Re Bethell* (1888) 38 Ch.D. 220 and *Haque v. Haque* (1962) 108 C.L.R. 230.

[93] *Qureshi v. Qureshi* [1972] Fam. 173; *Re Ah Chong* (1913) 33 N.Z.L.R. 384 (Chinese in New Zealand).

[94] *Casdagli v. Casdagli* [1919] A.C. 145; *Ali v. Ali* [1968] P. 564; *Hyland v. Hyland* (1971) 18 F.L.R. 461; *Lim v. Lim* [1973] V.R. 370; *cf. Lord Advocate v. Brown's Trustees*, 1907 S.C. 333.

[95] *Curling v. Thornton* (1823) 2 Add. 6, 17; *Whicker v. Hume* (1858) 7 H.L.C. 124, 159; *Moorhouse v. Lord* (1863) 10 H.L.C. 272, 287; *Winans v. Att.-Gen.* [1904] A.C. 287, 291; *Vincent v. Buchan* (1889) 16 R. 637; *Fremlin v. Fremlin* (1913) 16 C.L.R. 212, 234; *Walton v. Walton* [1948] V.L.R. 487; *Gunn v. Gunn* (1956) 2 D.L.R. (2d) 351 (Sask. C.A.); *Young v. Young* (1959) 21 D.L.R. (2d) 616 (Man. C.A.).

6–051   Direct declarations of intention call for special comment. The person whose domicile is in question may himself testify as to his intention,[96] but the court will view the evidence of an interested party with suspicion.[97] Declarations of intention made out of court may be given in evidence by way of exception to the hearsay rule.[98] The weight of such evidence will vary from case to case. To say that declarations as to domicile are "the lowest species of evidence"[99] is probably an exaggeration. The present law has been stated as follows: "Declarations as to intention are rightly regarded in determining the question of a change of domicile, but they must be examined by considering the persons to whom, the purposes for which, and the circumstances in which they are made, and they must further be fortified and carried into effect by conduct and action consistent with the declared expressions."[1] Thus in some cases the courts have relied to some extent on declarations of intention in deciding issues as to domicile[2]; indeed, in one case the declaration was decisive.[3] But in other cases the courts have refused to give effect to the declarations on the ground that they were inconsistent with the conduct of the *propositus*[4]: a domicile cannot be acquired[5] or retained[6] by mere declaration. The courts are, in particular, reluctant to give effect to declarations which refer in terms to "domicile" since the declarant is unlikely to have understood the meaning of the word.[7] Declarations which are equivocal have little effect: thus a declaration of intention to reside permanently in the United Kingdom is no evidence of acquisition of a domicile of choice in any of the countries which are

---

[96] *e.g. Udny v. Udny* (1869) L.R. 1 Sc. & Div. 441, 444; *D'Etchegoyen v. D'Etchegoyen* (1882) 13 P.D. 132; *White v. White* [1950] 4 D.L.R. 474, affd. [1952] 1 D.L.R. 133 (Man. C.A.).

[97] *Bell v. Kennedy* (1868) L.R. 1 Sc. & Div. 307, 313, 322–323; *Re Craignish* [1892] 3 Ch. 180, 190 (C.A.); *Qureshi v. Qureshi* [1972] Fam. 173, 192; *Moncrieff v. Moncrieff* [1934] C.P.D. 208; *Young v. Young* (1959) 21 D.L.R. (2d) 616 (Man. C.A.).

[98] *Bryce v. Bryce* [1933] P. 83; *Scappaticci v. Att.-Gen.* [1955] P. 47; *Re Cartier* [1952] S.A.S.R. 280; Cross (1956) 72 L.Q.R. 91, 108; Civil Evidence Act 1995.

[99] *Crookenden v. Fuller* (1859) 1 Sw. & Tr. 441, 450; *cf. De Bonneval v. De Bonneval* (1838) 1 Curt. 856; *Anderson v. Laneuville* (1854) 9 Moo.P.C. 325.

[1] *Ross v. Ross* [1930] A.C. 1, 6–7. "Expression" seems to be a misprint for "intention."

[2] *Dalhousie v. M'Douall* (1840) 7 Cl. & F. 817; *Munro v. Munro* (1840) 7 Cl. & F. 842; *Att.-Gen. v. Fitzgerald* (1856) 3 Drew 610; *In the goods of West* (1860) 6 Jur. (N.S.) 831; *Briggs v. Briggs* (1880) 5 P.D. 163; *D'Etchegoyen v. D'Etchegoyen* (1882) 13 P.D. 132; *Goulder v. Goulder* [1892] P. 240; *Re Eschmann* (1893) 9 T.L.R. 426; *Waddington v. Waddington* (1920) 36 T.L.R. 359; *Abraham v. Att.-Gen.* [1934] P. 17; *Gillis v. Gillis* (1874) I.R. 8 Eq. 597; *Bell v. Bell* [1922] 2 I.R. 152; *Re de Hosson* [1937] I.R. 467; *P.L. v. An tArd Chlaraitheoir* [1995] 2 I.L.R.M. 241; *Vincent v. Buchan* (1889) 16 R. 637; *Hyland v. Hyland* (1971) 18 F.L.R. 461.

[3] *Wilson v. Wilson* (1872) L.R. 2 P. & D. 435. In *Wilson v. Wilson* (1872) 10 M. 573, the Court of Session reached an opposite conclusion on the same facts; but the husband's evidence though admissible in England was inadmissible in Scotland.

[4] *Att.-Gen. v. Pottinger* (1861) 6 H. & N. 733; *Doucet v. Geoghegan* (1878) 9 Ch.D. 441 (C.A.); *Chaudhary v. Chaudhary* [1985] Fam. 19 (no appeal was taken at this point); *Moffett v. Moffett* [1920] 1 I.R. 57; *Re Rowan* [1988] I.L.R.M. 65; *M.(C.) v. M.(T.) (No. 2)* [1990] 2 I.R. 456; *Robinson v. Robinson's Trustees,* 1934 S.L.T. 183; *Spence v. Spence,* 1995 S.L.T. 335; *Re Dix* [1951] N.Z.L.R. 642; as to conflicting declarations see *Fleming v. Horniman* (1928) 44 T.L.R. 315; *Terrassin v. Terrassin* [1968] 3 N.S.W.R. 600.

[5] *Brown v. Smith* (1852) 15 Beav. 444.

[6] *Re Steer* (1858) 3 H. & N. 594; *Doucet v. Geoghegan* (1878) 9 Ch.D. 441 (C.A.); *Re Liddell-Grainger's Will Trusts* (1936) 53 T.L.R. 12; *Moffett v. Moffett* [1920] 1 I.R. 57; *Robinson v. Robinson's Trustees,* 1934 S.L.T. 183.

[7] *Re Steer* (1858) 3 H. & N. 594; *Re Annesley* [1926] Ch. 692; *Att.-Gen. v. Yule* (1931) 145 L.T. 9 (C.A.); *Re Liddell-Grainger's Will Trusts* (1936) 53 T.L.R. 12; *Re Flynn (No. 1)* [1968] 1 W.L.R. 103, 111; *Re Adams* [1967] I.R. 424, 448; *cf. Re Sillar* [1956] I.R. 344, 355.

included in the United Kingdom[8]; although it might be evidence of the abandonment of a domicile elsewhere.

In order to determine where a person was domiciled at a particular time, the court may take into consideration his conduct after that time.[9] But of course such evidence is not decisive.[10]

6–052

Rule 12—Without prejudice to the generality of the foregoing Rule, in determining whether a person intends to reside permanently or indefinitely in a country the court may have regard to:
  (1)   the motive for which he has taken up residence there;
  (2)   the fact that the residence was not freely chosen;
  (3)   the fact that the residence was precarious.

6R–053

Comment

In order that a person may acquire a domicile of choice it has been said that there must be "a residence freely chosen, and not prescribed or dictated by any external necessity, such as the duties of office, the demands of creditors, or the relief from illness."[11] But this must not be understood to mean that only a person who is able to exercise the most perfect freedom of choice can acquire a domicile of choice: indeed, if this were so the acquisition of a domicile of choice would be a rare event. The statement that there must be "a residence freely chosen" is not, in truth, a rigid rule of law: it merely indicates that where the residence is not freely chosen the inference of *animus manendi*, which might otherwise be drawn from the fact of residence, ought not to be drawn from that fact alone.[12] If the necessary intention is proved by other means, it is clear that a domicile of choice can be acquired although the residence is not freely chosen. This may be illustrated by reference to two types of situation.

6–054

In the first type, a person is alleged to lack the *animus manendi* because he has some special motive for coming to, staying in, or leaving a country. One view is that the existence of such a motive negatives the necessary intention.[13] This is true if the existence of the special motive leads to the conclusion that the residence was intended to cease upon the accomplishment of the purpose for which it was taken up.[14] But, apart from such considerations, the predominant view is that the existence of a special motive does not negative, and may indeed help to establish,[15] the necessary intention. Thus a person who resides in a country in deference to his father's dying injunction,[16] or to his

6–055

---

[8] *Wahl v. Att.-Gen.* (1932) 147 L.T. 382 (H.L.); *Buswell v. I.R.C.* [1974] 1 W.L.R. 1631 (C.A.).

[9] *Bremer v. Freeman* (1857) 10 Moo.P.C. 306, 358–359; *Re Grove* (1888) 40 Ch.D. 216 (C.A.); *Moffett v. Moffett* [1920] 1 I.R. 57; *P.L. v. An tArd Chlaraitheoir* [1995] 2 I.L.R.M. 241; *Lee v. Commissioner of Taxation* (1963) 6 F.L.R. 285.

[10] See *Donaldson v. Donaldson* [1949] P. 363, where D was held to be domiciled in Florida at the time of his divorce although he soon afterwards left the United States.

[11] *Udny v. Udny* (1869) L.R. 1 Sc. & Div. 441, 458.

[12] *Bempde v. Johnstone* (1796) 3 Ves. 198, 201–202.

[13] *White v. White* [1950] 4 D.L.R. 474, affd. [1952] 1 D.L.R. 133 (Man. C.A.).

[14] *Re Furse* [1980] 3 All E.R. 838, 844 (residence in England to keep growing children apart from undesirable cousins).

[15] *Somerville v. Somerville* (1801) 5 Ves. 750; *De Greuchy v. Wills* (1879) 4 C.P.D. 362; *Spurway v. Spurway* [1894] 1 I.R. 385.

[16] *Somerville v. Somerville* (1801) 5 Ves. 750.

wife's wishes,[17] or in order to marry,[18] or to be with her putative husband,[19] or because the climate suits his troupe of performing chimpanzees,[20] may acquire a domicile there. It is immaterial that the motive is to enjoy a more favourable legal system. Thus a person who resides in a country to evade the rule against accumulations,[21] to achieve freedom of testation,[22] to secure a more favourable tax régime,[23] or to institute[24] or escape from[25] matrimonial proceedings, may acquire a domicile there.

6–056   In the second type of situation, a person is alleged to lack the *animus manendi* because his presence in the country is due to some physical or legal compulsion. Such compulsion may make it improbable that the necessary intent has in fact been formed.[26] But if it is proved that a person wants to be where he is forced to be, there is no rule of law to prevent his acquiring a domicile of choice there.[27]

6–057   Another type of situation, which is usually discussed together with the preceding one, is its converse: a person may lack the *animus manendi* because his residence in a country, though freely chosen, is precarious, that is, liable to be terminated against his will. This danger may well negative the necessary intent as a matter of fact, but it does not as a matter of law prevent the acquisition of a domicile of choice.[28]

6–058   The application of these principles may be illustrated with reference to the following classes of persons:

1. Prisoners;
2. Persons liable to deportation;
3. Refugees and fugitives;
4. Invalids;
5. Members of the armed forces;
6. Employees;
7. Diplomats.

6–059   **(1) Prisoners.** A prisoner normally retains during imprisonment the domicile which he had at its commencement. Such a person, even if he can be considered to reside where he is imprisoned,[29] is unlikely to intend to reside

---

[17] *Aitchison v. Dixon* (1870) L.R. 10 Eq. 589. *Cf. I.R.C. v. Bullock* [1976] 1 W.L.R. 1178 (C.A.), where the husband planned to return to his native country should his wife predecease him.

[18] See *Fasbender v. Att.-Gen.* [1922] 2 Ch. 850 (C.A.) and contrast *Arnott v. Groom* (1846) 9 D. 142. It is arguable that the intention to reside permanently is conditional on the celebration of the marriage and is nullified if that does not take place: *cf. Cramer v. Cramer* [1987] 1 F.L.R. 116 (C.A.).

[19] *Re Cooke's Trusts* (1887) 56 L.T. 737; *Von Lorang v. Administrator of Austrian Property* [1927] A.C. 641.

[20] *Wood v. Wood* [1957] P. 254 (C.A.).

[21] *Haldane v. Eckford* (1869) L.R. 8 Eq. 631.

[22] *Huntly v. Gaskell* [1906] A.C. 56; *cf. Crookenden v. Fuller* (1859) 1 Sw. & Tr. 441.

[23] *Spence v. Spence*, 1995 S.L.T. 335.

[24] *Drexel v. Drexel* [1916] 1 Ch. 251.

[25] *Firebrace v. Firebrace* (1878) 4 P.D. 63.

[26] *e.g. Re Duleep Singh* (1890) 6 T.L.R. 385 (C.A.).

[27] See especially the cases concerning members of the armed forces, *post*, paras. 6–063 *et seq.*

[28] See specially the cases concerning persons liable to be deported or whose residence permit is liable to be terminated, *infra*.

[29] Contrast *Dunston v. Paterson* (1858) 5 C.B.(N.S.) 267 with *Butler v. Dolben* (1756) 2 Lee 312.

there permanently or indefinitely.[30] If a prisoner does form such an intention, he acquires a domicile of choice there.[31]

(2) Persons liable to deportation. A person who resides in a country from 　**6–060** which he is liable to be deported may lack the *animus manendi* because his residence is precarious.[32] But if in fact he forms the necessary intention, he acquires a domicile of choice. This applies both where he is given permission to reside for an unlimited period but is liable to deportation[33] and also where he is given permission to reside for a limited period which can be extended at the discretion of the authorities of the country in question.[34] Once such a person has acquired a domicile of choice he does not lose it merely because a deportation order has been made against him[35]; he only loses it when he is actually deported.[36] It has even been held that a person who has acquired an English domicile of choice did not lose it by being deported, as he intended to return to this country and as his re-entry would not have been illegal.[37]

(3) Refugees and fugitives. A person who leaves a country as a political 　**6–061** refugee, as a fugitive from criminal justice, or in order to evade his creditors, has a special motive for leaving it, but he has no special motive for entering any other particular country, nor is his residence in another country in any sense enforced. The question which causes more difficulty in cases of this kind is whether the fugitive intends to abandon his domicile in the first country: if he does, the acquisition of a new domicile in the second country will readily be assumed. The question is one of fact in each case. If a political refugee intends to return to the country from which he fled as soon as the political situation changes, he retains his domicile there[38] unless the desired political change is so improbable that his intention is discounted and treated as merely an exile's longing for his native land[39]; but if his intention is not to return to that country even when the political situation has changed, he can acquire a domicile of choice in the country to which he has fled.[40] In the case of a fugitive from criminal justice, the intention to abandon his domicile in the country from which he has fled will readily be assumed, unless perhaps the punishment which he seeks to escape is trivial, or by the law of that country

---

[30] *Collier v. Rivaz* (1841) 2 Curt. 855; *In the goods of Napoleon Bonaparte* (1853) 2 Rob.Ecc. 606, 610; *Burton v. Fisher* (1828) Milward's Reps. 183, 191–192; *Moffat v. Moffat* (1866) 3 W.W. & A'B. 87; *Whitehouse v. Whitehouse* (1900) 21 N.S.W.L.R. Div. 16.

[31] *Stifel v. Hopkins*, 477 F. 2d 1116 (6th Cir. 1973); and see *Udny v. Udny* (1869) L.R. 1 Sc. & Div. 441, 458.

[32] But note that illegal residence may not be recognised as residence for the purpose of the acquisition of a domicile: *ante*, para. 6–037.

[33] *Boldrini v. Boldrini* [1932] P. 9 (C.A.); *Van Rensburg v. Ballinger*, 1950 (4) S.A. 427.

[34] *Zanelli v. Zanelli* (1948) 64 T.L.R. 556 (C.A.); *Szechter v. Szechter* [1971] P. 286; *cf. May v. May* [1943] 2 All E.R. 146 (residence permitted for a particular purpose); *Hyland v. Hyland* (1971) 18 F.L.R. 461; *Lim v. Lim* [1973] V.R. 370.

[35] *Cruh v. Cruh* [1945] 2 All E.R. 545; *cf. Jablonowski v. Jablonowski* (1972) 28 D.L.R. (3d) 440 (Ont.) (where the order was made after the institution of the proceedings in question).

[36] *Ex p. Donelly* [1915] W.L.D. 29; *Ex p. Gordon* [1937] W.L.D. 35.

[37] *Thiele v. Thiele* (1920) 150 L.T.J. 387; *cf. Ex p. Macleod* [1946] C.P.D. 312; and *Drakensbergpers Bpk. v. Sharpe*, 1963 (4) S.A. 615, where the re-entry would have been illegal. *Quaere*, whether an English court would take account of the fact that re-entry into a foreign country was illegal under the law of that country: *cf. ante*, para. 6–037.

[38] *De Bonneval v. De Bonneval* (1838) 1 Curt. 856; *Commissioners of Charitable Donations in Ireland v. Devereux* (1842) 13 Sim. 14; *Re Lloyd Evans* [1947] Ch. 695.

[39] *Cf. ante*, para. 6–040.

[40] *May v. May* [1943] 2 All E.R. 146; *In the Matter of Wu* (1994) F.L.C. 92–477.

a relatively short period of prescription bars liability to punishment.[41] Similarly, a person who leaves a country to evade his creditors may lose his domicile there[42]; but if he plans to return as soon as he has paid[43] or otherwise got rid of[44] his debts, there is no change of domicile.

6–062   **(4) Invalids.**   Conflicting views have been expressed on the question whether a person who resides in a country for the sake of his health acquires a domicile there. Some judges have thought that such a person could not,[45] while others have thought that he might,[46] by such residence acquire a domicile. The two objections to the acquisition of a domicile are that the residence has been taken up for some special motive, and that it may not be freely chosen. But these factors merely make it improbable in fact that a domicile has been acquired[47]: they do not make it impossible in law. A person who is temporarily detained in a country because he is for the time being too ill to be moved, or who goes to a country for the temporary purpose of undergoing a course of medical treatment, clearly does not acquire a domicile of choice there. On the other hand a person who determines to settle in a new country because he believes that he will enjoy better health there may well intend to live there permanently or indefinitely,[48] but of course he does not necessarily have this intention.[49] It has been suggested that a distinction ought to be drawn between persons whose move from one country to another is dictated by immediate danger and those who move simply in order to enjoy better health.[50] But this, too, appears to be a factual rather than a legal distinction. A person who goes to another country to overcome some immediate danger to his health may well intend to return after the danger has passed; and a person who is mortally ill may well move from one country to another to alleviate his last sufferings, without any intention of breaking up his old home.[51] But if a person is told that he will die in six months if he stays in the country of his present domicile, but will live for ten years if he goes to another country, it is perfectly possible, and indeed likely, that he will form the intention of residing permanently or indefinitely in the second country, and thus acquire a domicile there.

6–063   **(5) Members of the armed forces.**   It was at one time thought that a member of the armed forces could not, as a matter of law, acquire a domicile

---

[41] *Re Martin* [1900] P. 211 (C.A.).

[42] *Udny v. Udny* (1869) L.R. 1 Sc. & Div. 441; *De Greuchy v. Wills* (1879) 4 C.P.D. 362; *Re Robertson* (1885) 2 T.L.R. 178 (C.A.), but contrast the report of this case in [1885] W.N. 217; cf. *Spurway v. Spurway* [1894] 1 I.R. 385; *Briggs v. Briggs* (1880) 5 P.D. 163.

[43] *Re Wright's Trusts* (1856) 2 K. & J. 595.

[44] *Pitt v. Pitt* (1864) 4 Macq. 627 (H.L.).

[45] *Moorhouse v. Lord* (1863) 10 H.L.C. 272, 283; *Udny v. Udny* (1869) L.R. 1 Sc. & Div. 441, 458.

[46] *Hoskins v. Matthews* (1855) 8 De G.M. & G. 13, 28–29.

[47] See *Gillis v. Gillis* (1874) I.R. 8 Eq. 597.

[48] *Hoskins v. Matthews* (1855) 8 De G.M. & G. 13; *Aitchison v. Dixon* (1870) L.R. 10 Eq. 589; *Bradford v. Swanton* [1931] I.R. 446; *Re Adams* [1967] I.R. 424.

[49] *Att.-Gen. v. Fitzgerald* (1856) 3 Drew. 610; *Re James* (1908) 98 L.T. 438; *The Lauderdale Peerage Case* (1885) 10 App.Cas. 692, 740; and see *Winans v. Att.-Gen.* [1904] A.C. 287, where, however, this point was not much relied on.

[50] *Hoskins v. Matthews* (1855) 8 De G.M. & G. 13, 28.

[51] e.g. *Att.-Gen. v. Fitzgerald* (1856) 3 Drew. 610.

of choice during service[52]: he could not do so where he was stationed because his residence there was enforced, nor elsewhere because his residence in any place was necessarily precarious.[53] This view no longer prevails. It has long been settled that a person can acquire a domicile of choice in a country which he may have to leave on being recalled to active service.[54] It is also clear that a member of the armed forces can, during service, acquire a domicile of choice either in the country in which he is stationed[55] or elsewhere,[56] provided that he has established the necessary residence[57] and formed the necessary intention. Of course, in the great majority of cases a member of the armed forces does not intend to make his permanent home where he is stationed, and retains the domicile which he had on entering service.[58]

The law on this topic was at one time obscured by the theory, influenced by   **6–064** the now discredited cases on "Anglo-Indian" domicile, that anyone who entered the service of a foreign government thereby acquired a domicile in the foreign country. While a British subject joining the British armed forces would retain the domicile he had on joining, a foreign recruit would at once acquire a domicile in some part of the United Kingdom.[59] The theory rested on an assumption that to serve a foreign government necessarily implies a duty to reside in the foreign country (which is not necessarily the case in modern conditions) and on the notion that a man's intentions must be presumed to be consistent with his duty. It is submitted that none of this is good law. In all issues as to domicile the existence of the *animus manendi* is a question of fact. A supposed duty to have that intention is immaterial. It has even been suggested that the existence of a duty tends to negative, rather than to support, the inference of *animus manendi*.[60]

(6) Employees. A person who goes to a country in pursuance of a contract   **6–065** of employment is in a position similar to that of a member of the armed forces

---

[52] *Re E. R. Smith* (1896) 12 T.L.R. 223; *Ex p. Cunningham* (1884) 13 Q.B.D. 418, 425 (C.A.); *Re Macreight* (1885) 30 Ch.D. 165, 168.

[53] See *Craigie v. Lewin* (1843) 3 Curt. 435, where a lieutenant in the army of the East India Company was held not to have resumed his Scottish domicile of origin because he was liable to be recalled to India.

[54] *Cockrell v. Cockrell* (1856) 25 L.J.Ch. 730; *Att.-Gen. v. Pottinger* (1861) 6 H. & N. 733; *Commissioners of Inland Revenue v. Gordon's Executors* (1850) 12 D. 657.

[55] *Donaldson v. Donaldson* [1949] P. 363 (which set at rest doubts raised in *Hodgson v. De Beauchesne* (1858) 12 Moo.P.C. 285, as to whether a soldier in the British army can acquire a domicile in a politically foreign country); *Cruickshanks v. Cruickshanks* [1957] 1 W.L.R. 564, 568; *Clarke v. Newmarsh* (1836) 14 S. 488; *Willar v. Willar*, 1954 S.C. 144; *Nicol v. Nicol*, 1948 (2) S.A. 613, where the conflicting South African decisions on this question are exhaustively discussed; *Ex p. Glass*, 1948 (4) S.A. 379; *Hibbs v. Wynne*, 1949 (2) S.A. 10; *Schache v. Schache* (1931) 31 S.R.N.S.W. 633; *Cox v. Cox* [1945] V.L.R. 105; *Armstead v. Armstead* [1954] V.L.R. 733; *Auld v. Auld* [1952] V.L.R. 455; *Wilkinson v. Wilkinson* [1949] 1 W.W.R. 249 (Alta.); *Young v. Young* (1959) 21 D.L.R. (2d) 616 (Man. C.A.).

[56] *Baker v. Baker* [1945] A.D. 708; *Stone v. Stone* [1958] 1 W.L.R. 1287.

[57] *Ante*, para. 6–034.

[58] *Tovey v. Lindsay* (1813) 1 Dow. 117, 124; *Brown v. Smith* (1852) 15 Beav. 444; *Yelverton v. Yelverton* (1859) 1 Sw. & Tr. 574; *Firebrace v. Firebrace* (1878) 4 P.D. 63; *Re Macreight* (1885) 30 Ch.D. 165; *Att.-Gen. v. Napier* (1851) 6 Exch. 217, 218–219 (in argument); *The Lauderdale Peerage Case* (1885) 10 App.Cas. 692, 739–740; *Cruickshanks v. Cruickshanks* [1957] 1 W.L.R. 564; *Sellars v. Sellars*, 1942 S.C. 206; *Wilton v. Wilton* [1946] 2 D.L.R. 397 (Ont.); *McBeth v. McBeth* [1954] 1 D.L.R. 590 (B.C.); *Patterson v. Patterson* (1955) 3 D.L.R. (2d) 266 (N.S.); *Fitzgibbon-Lloyd v. Fitzgibbon-Lloyd* [1944] V.L.R. 29.

[59] *Forbes v. Forbes* (1854) Kay 341; *Ex p. Cunningham* (1884) 13 Q.B.D. 418 (C.A.); *cf. Urquhart v. Butterfield* (1887) 37 Ch.D. 357, 385–386 (C.A.) as to civil servants.

[60] *Allardice v. Onslow* (1864) 33. L.J.Ch. 434, 436.

in that his residence is in a sense enforced and may, if the contract provided for his possible removal to another country, be precarious. These factors are perhaps of less weight in the case of an employee than in the case of a soldier; an employee always undertakes the duties of his employment of his own free will and can almost always terminate his employment by giving appropriate notice. The question whether an employee who is sent to a country intends to reside there permanently or indefinitely remains in the last resort a question of fact. There is, for this purpose, no distinction between public servants and other employees. If such persons go to the country to which they are sent for the temporary purpose of performing the duties of their office or employment, they do not acquire a domicile of choice there.[61] But if they go to the country not merely to work, but also to settle in it, they do acquire a domicile of choice.[62]

6–066   **(7) Diplomats.** Diplomats are simply a special category of public servants and their domicile is governed by the same principles. The fiction of extra-territoriality of embassies does not apply for the purpose of ascertaining the domicile of a person of this class.[63] Nor is it material that he is to some extent immune from the jurisdiction of the local courts.[64] It is a question of fact whether he has formed the intention of residing permanently or indefinitely in the country to which he is sent. Generally, of course, he forms no such intention,[65] but occasionally he may do so and thus acquire a domicile of choice.[66] If a person has acquired a domicile of choice in a country, he does not lose it merely by reason of being appointed to a diplomatic post in that country by the country of his nationality.[67]

Illustrations

6–067   (1) Prisoners
    1. D, whose domicile of origin is Irish, is detained in Belgium as a prisoner of war from 1803 to 1814. He does not thereby acquire a Belgian domicile. He continues to reside in Belgium of his own free will from 1814 to 1829. He acquires a Belgian domicile.[68]

6–068   (2) Persons Liable to Deportation
    2. D, an Italian, resides in England. Under the Aliens Order 1920, he is liable, in certain circumstances, to be deported. He can acquire a domicile of choice in England.[69]

---

[61] *Att.-Gen. v. Rowe* (1862) 1 H. & C. 31; *Grant v. Grant*, 1931 S.C. 238; *Eilon v. Eilon*, 1965 (1) S.A. 703; *Terrassin v. Terrassin* [1968] 3 N.S.W.R. 600; *cf. Moncrieff v. Moncrieff* [1934] C.P.D. 208, the reasoning of which is, however, difficult to reconcile with the cases of persons liable to deportation: *ante*, para. 6–060.

[62] *In the goods of James Smith* (1850) 2 Rob.Ecc. 332; *Commissioners of Inland Revenue v. Gordon's Executors* (1850) 12 D. 657; *Gunn v. Gunn* (1956) 2 D.L.R. (2d) 351 (Sask. C.A.); *Waggoner v. Waggoner* (1956) 2 W.W.R. 74 (Alta.); *Russell v. Russell* [1935] S.A.S.R. 85.

[63] *Att.-Gen. v. Kent* (1862) 1 H. & C. 12, 28, 29. The fiction was rejected in another context in *Radwan v. Radwan (No. 1)* [1973] Fam. 24.

[64] *Cf. Casdagli v. Casdagli* [1919] A.C. 145.

[65] *e.g. Udny v. Udny* (1869) L.R. 1 Sc. & Div. 441 (as to Colonel Udny's domicile of origin); *Niboyet v. Niboyet* (1878) 4 P.D. 1 (C.A.).

[66] *Naville v. Naville*, 1957 (1) S.A. 280; *cf. Heath v. Samson* (1851) 14 Beav. 441, where, however, the domicile may have been acquired at a time when the *propositus* held no diplomatic appointment.

[67] *Att.-Gen. v. Kent* (1862) 1 H. & C. 12; *Sharpe v. Crispin* (1869) L.R. 1P. & D. 611.

[68] *Collier v. Rivaz* (1841) 2 Curt. 855.

[69] *Boldrini v. Boldrini* [1932] P. 9 (C.A.).

3. D, an Italian, comes to England and is given permission to reside here for six months. There is evidence that this permission would be readily extended. He can acquire a domicile of choice in England.[70]

4. D, a German, acquires a domicile of choice in England. In 1919 he is repatriated to Germany against his will. He intends to return to England shortly and there is no Home Office order prohibiting his return. He continues to be domiciled in England.[71]

(3) Refugees and Fugitives

6–069

5. D, whose domicile of origin is English, acquires a domicile of choice in Belgium. In 1940 he is forced by the German invasion to leave Belgium, and comes to England. He intends to return to Belgium after the end of the German occupation. He continues to be domiciled in Belgium.[72]

6. D, who is domiciled in Germany, comes to England in 1939 as a refugee from Nazi oppression. He does not intend to return to Germany even if the Nazis are overthrown. On forming the intention to reside permanently in England, he acquires an English domicile.[73]

7. D, who is domiciled in France, leaves that country to escape punishment for a crime, and comes to England. By French law, his liability to punishment is extinguished after twenty years. He can, and does, acquire a domicile of choice in England before the expiration of this period.[74]

8. D, who is domiciled in England, goes to France to evade his creditors. He loses his English domicile,[75] unless he intends to pay his debts if and when he can, and then to return to England.[76]

(4) Invalids

6–070

9. D, who is domiciled in England, establishes his home in Italy because he thinks that the warmer climate there will be good for his health. He acquires a domicile of choice in Italy.[77]

(5) Members of the Armed Forces

6–071

10. D, an officer on active service in the Royal Air Force, while stationed in Florida forms the intention of residing there permanently. He acquires a domicile of choice there.[78]

11. D, an American serviceman, determines to settle in England. At the relevant time he is not stationed in England, but he spends all his leave here. He is domiciled in England.[79]

12. D, whose domicile of origin is English, gets a domicile of dependency in Jersey. He joins the army and soon afterwards becomes an independent person; but he forms no intention of settling anywhere. Although he is stationed out of Jersey, he continues to be domiciled there.[80]

(6) Employees

6–072

13. D, whose domicile of origin is English, is appointed Chief Justice of Ceylon. He intends to hold this office until he has earned his pension and then to return to England. He retains his English domicile.[81]

14. D, whose domicile of origin is in Manitoba, enters into the service of a corporation which owns cinemas in various provinces of Canada. By way of promotion he is offered, and accepts, the office of manager of a cinema in Saskatchewan. He accordingly moves to Saskatchewan and resides there with the intention of residing there for an indefinite period. He acquires a domicile of choice in Saskatchewan.[82]

(7) Diplomats

6–073

15. D, who is domiciled in France, resides for several years in England as French consul. He does not thereby acquire an English domicile.[83]

---

[70] *Zanelli v. Zanelli* (1948) 64 T.L.R. 556 (C.A.).
[71] *Thiele v. Thiele* (1920) 150 L.T.J. 387.
[72] *Re Lloyd Evans* [1947] Ch. 695.
[73] *May v. May* [1943] 2 All E.R. 146.
[74] *Re Martin* [1900] P. 211 (C.A.).
[75] *Udny v. Udny* (1869) L.R. 1 Sc. & Div. 441.
[76] *Re Wright's Trusts* (1856) 2 K. & J. 595.
[77] *Hoskins v. Matthews* (1855) 8 De G.M. & G. 13.
[78] *Donaldson v. Donaldson* [1949] P. 363.
[79] *Stone v. Stone* [1958] 1 W.L.R. 1287; *cf. Baker v. Baker* [1945] A.D. 708.
[80] *Re Macreight* (1885) 30 Ch.D. 165.
[81] *Att.-Gen. v. Rowe* (1862) 1 H. & C. 31.
[82] *Gunn v. Gunn* (1956) 2 D.L.R. (2d) 351 (Sask. C.A.).
[83] *Niboyet v. Niboyet* (1878) 4 P.D. 1 (C.A.).

16. D, whose domicile of origin is Portuguese, in 1819 comes to England and acquires an English domicile of choice. In 1857 he is appointed attaché to the Portuguese embassy in England. He retains his English domicile.[84]

(2) Loss

6R–074 RULE 13—(1) A person abandons a domicile of choice in a country by ceasing to reside there and by ceasing to intend to reside there permanently or indefinitely, and not otherwise.
(2) When a domicile of choice is abandoned, either
(i) a new domicile of choice is acquired; or
(ii) the domicile of origin revives.

COMMENT

6–075 A domicile of choice is lost when both the residence and the intention which must exist for its acquisition are given up.[85] It is not lost merely by giving up the residence[86] nor merely by giving up the intention.[87] It is not necessary to prove a positive intention not to return: it is sufficient to prove merely the absence of an intention to continue to reside.[88] The intention is not considered to have been given up merely because the propositus is dissatisfied with the country of the domicile of choice.[89] In order to show that the intention has been given up, it may be desirable to prove the formation of an intention to reside in another country,[90] but such proof is not essential as a matter of law. Although it has been suggested that residence is given up by "leaving this country or, perhaps more accurately, arriving in another"[91] it is submitted that residence can simply be given up. The view that residence in one country can only be given up by arriving in another seems to be a relic of the discarded doctrine that a domicile of choice cannot be lost by mere abandonment.[92]

6–076 On abandoning a domicile of choice, a person may acquire a new domicile of choice, or he may return to and settle in the country of his domicile of origin. He may also simply abandon his domicile of choice without acquiring a home in another country. It was at one time thought that in such a case the previous domicile was retained until a new one was acquired.[93] But it is now

---

[84] *Att.-Gen. v. Kent* (1862) 1 H. & C. 12.

[85] *Udny v. Udny* (1869) L.R. 1 Sc. & Div. 441, 450; *e.g. Fleming v. Horniman* (1928) 44 T.L.R. 315; *Bradfield v. Swanton* [1931] I.R. 446.

[86] *Lyall v. Paton* (1856) 25 L.J.Ch. 746, as to which see para. 6–039, n. 19, *ante*; *Bradford v. Young* (1885) 29 Ch.D. 617 (C.A.); *Thiele v. Thiele* (1920) 150 L.T.J. 387; *Re Lloyd Evans* [1947] Ch. 695; *cf. Bell v. Bell* [1922] 2 I.R. 152, but it is difficult to say in that case that the *propositus* had not also given up the intention.

[87] *In the goods of Raffenel* (1863) 3 Sw. & Tr. 49; *Zanelli v. Zanelli* (1948) 64 T.L.R. 556 (C.A.); *I.R.C. v. Duchess of Portland* [1982] Ch. 314. *Cf. Plummer v. I.R.C.* [1988] 1 W.L.R. 292 where the Rule was criticised *obiter* on the theory that the *propositus* may lose a domicile of choice though continuing to be resident, if his "chief residence" is established elsewhere.

[88] *Re Flynn (No. 1)* [1968] 1 W.L.R. 103, 113–115, *per* Megarry J. (*obiter*), approving the wording of the Rule; *Qureshi v. Qureshi* [1972] Fam. 173, 191.

[89] *Re Marrett* (1887) 36 Ch.D. 400 (C.A.).

[90] See *Att.-Gen. v. Gasquet* (1877) 41 J.P. 487; 42 J.P. 346.

[91] *Zanelli v. Zanelli* (1948) 64 T.L.R. 556, 557 (C.A.).

[92] *Expressed in Munroe v. Douglas* (1820) 5 Madd. 379, 404. See now *Udny v. Udny* (1869) L.R. 1 Sc. & Div. 441.

[93] *Munroe v. Douglas, supra.* This is still the predominant American view: Restatement, s.19, Comment *b* and Illustration 5.

settled that where a person simply abandons a domicile of choice his domicile of origin revives by operation of law.[94] This rule has been much criticised since it may result in a person's being domiciled in a country with which his connection is stale or tenuous and which, indeed, he may never even have visited. It has been abolished in New Zealand and Australia, and replaced by a statutory rule that a domicile continues until a new domicile is acquired.[95] The English and Scottish Law Commissions have proposed similar legislation.[96]

ILLUSTRATIONS

1. D, a German, acquires a domicile of choice in England. In 1919 he is repatriated to Germany, but intends to return to England as soon as possible and to reside there permanently. He retains his English domicile.[97]   **6–077**

2. D, whose domicile of origin is English, acquires a domicile of choice in France on marrying a Frenchman. After her husband's death, she resolves to return to England. She never succeeds in leaving France. She retains her French domicile.[98]

3. D, whose domicile of origin is Scottish, acquires a domicile of choice in England. Later he abandons his English domicile and goes to France, but does not acquire a domicile of choice there. His Scottish domicile of origin revives.[99]

4. D's domicile of origin is English. He emigrates to the United States and in 1953 becomes a naturalised American citizen and acquires a domicile of choice in New York. In 1960 he moves to Germany, without at that time losing his domicile of choice. In 1967 he decides to make his permanent home in England, but does not return to live in England until 1972. His English domicile of origin revives in 1967.[1]

5. D's domicile of origin is English. At the age of twenty-five he emigrates to the United States, becomes a naturalised American citizen, and acquires a domicile of choice in New York. He never revisits England. At the age of sixty-five he decides to leave New York and settle in California. He sets out for California but dies on his way there in Illinois. He dies domiciled in England.[2]

C. *Domicile of dependency*

RULE 14—The domicile of a dependent person is, in general, the same as, and changes (if at all) with, the domicile of the person on whom he is, as regards his domicile, legally dependent.   6R–078

COMMENT

The general principle is that a dependent person has the domicile of the person on whom he is considered by law to be dependent. The class of dependent   **6–079**

---

[94] *Udny v. Udny* (1869) L.R. 1 Sc. & Div. 441; *King v. Foxwell* (1876) 3 Ch.D. 518; *Harrison v. Harrison* [1953] 1 W.L.R. 865; *Re Flynn (No. 1)* [1968] 1 W.L.R. 103, 108; *Tee v. Tee* [1974] 1 W.L.R. 213 (C.A.); *Holden v. Holden* (1914) 33 N.Z.L.R. 1032; *Ex p. Donelly* [1915] W.L.D. 29; *Ex p. Gordon* [1937] W.L.D. 35; *Strike v. Gleich* (1879) O.B. & F. 50.

[95] See, for New Zealand: Domicile Act 1976, s.11; for Australia, the uniform Domicile Acts of the Australian jurisdictions, s.6.

[96] *The Law of Domicile*, para. 5.25.

[97] *Thiele v. Thiele* (1920) 150 L.T.J. 387.

[98] *In the goods of Raffenel* (1863) 3 Sw. & Tr. 49 (where the French domicile was one of dependency).

[99] *Udny v. Udny* (1869) L.R. 1 Sc. & Div. 441.

[1] *Tee v. Tee* [1974] 1 W.L.R. 213 (C.A.).

[2] *Cf. Nelson v. Nelson* [1925] 3 D.L.R. 22 (Alta.), where the revival of an inappropriate domicile of origin was averted by the court's unprincipled use of the concept of nationality.

persons was greatly reduced in size by the Domicile and Matrimonial Proceedings Act 1973.[3] It now comprises children who are under sixteen and unmarried[4] and mentally disordered persons.[5] Previously the age of independence was the age of majority, eighteen years (or, before 1970, twenty-one[6]) and the class of dependents included all married women.[7] The English and Scottish Law Commissions have recommended new statutory rules for determining the domicile of individuals, including children and mentally disordered persons, under which there would be no place for a domicile of dependency as a distinct concept.[8]

6–080   It follows from the general principle that a dependent person cannot acquire a domicile of choice by his own act. Thus although a child under sixteen may have a home separate from that of his parents he cannot acquire an independent domicile unless he is married.

6–081   Where a person is not *sui juris*, but there is no person in existence on whom he is dependent, his domicile cannot for the time being be changed at all. Such is the position of a child without parents or guardians, and probably of a child without parents but with a guardian.[9] The same is also in certain circumstances true of a mentally disordered person.[10]

6–082   Our Rule applies to dependent persons, wherever they are domiciled and whatever is their power under the law of that domicile to acquire a new domicile by their own act. Although it has been suggested that a person's capacity to acquire a new domicile may be governed by the law of his previous domicile, or by the law of the intended new domicile,[11] it is submitted that such capacity is for the purposes of the Rules in this book governed by English law. Any other view is inconsistent with the rule that the question where a person is domiciled must be decided in accordance with English law.[12] Moreover, in dealing with the domicile of Scottish children, English courts have nearly always treated them as dependent persons and have not considered the possibility that by Scots law they might have capacity to acquire a domicile of their own.[13] And in cases on the former dependent domicile of a married woman, it was always assumed that if a woman domiciled in England married a man domiciled abroad,[14] or vice versa,[15] she took his domicile regardless of the foreign law.

---

[3] The Act came into force on January 1, 1974: s.17(5).

[4] Rule 15. A child under 16 can be validly married under some systems of law; see *post*, para. 17–078.

[5] Rule 16.

[6] See Family Law Reform Act 1969, s.1(1), which effected the reduction; it came into effect on January 1, 1970.

[7] See *post*, paras. 6–084 *et seq.*

[8] *The Law of Domicile* (Law Com. No. 168), paras. 4.4–4.8 and *post*, para. 6–096.

[9] Rule 15(4).

[10] Rule 16.

[11] See *Urquhart v. Butterfield* (1887) 37 Ch.D. 357, 380 (C.A.); *Haque v. Haque* (1962) 108 C.L.R. 230, 240—but there the law of the intended new domicile was also the *lex fori*; Graveson (1950) 3 Int.L.Q. 149; Clive, 1966 Jur.Rev. 1, 9–12.

[12] Rule 8.

[13] *Re Beaumont* [1893] 3 Ch. 490; *Att.-Gen. v. Yule* (1931) 145 L.T. 9, 15 (C.A.); *Henderson v. Henderson* [1967] P. 77. See however *Urquhart v. Butterfield* (1887) 37 Ch.D. 357 (C.A.).

[14] *e.g. In the goods of Raffenel* (1863) 3 Sw. & Tr. 49; *Re Cooke's Trusts* (1887) 56 L.T. 737; *Armitage v. Att.-Gen.* [1906] P. 135; *Ogden v. Ogden* [1908] P. 46 (C.A.); *Chapelle v. Chapelle* [1950] P. 134; *Lepre v. Lepre* [1965] P. 52; *cf. Garthwaite v. Garthwaite* [1964] P. 356 (C.A.).

[15] *Robinson-Scott v. Robinson-Scott* [1958] P. 71.

It has been suggested that a domicile of dependency is simply a domicile of   **6–083**
choice,[16] but the two kinds of domicile differ in three respects. In the first
place, a domicile of choice can, while a domicile of dependency cannot, be
abandoned. Secondly, a domicile of dependency is imposed, whereas a domicile of choice is always acquired. Thirdly, it is easier to prove that a formerly
dependent person has abandoned his last domicile of dependency than it is to
prove the abandonment of a domicile of choice.[17]

Married women. Until the coming into effect of the Domicile and   **6–084**
Matrimonial Proceedings Act 1973, a married woman was dependent for the
purposes of the law of domicile upon her husband. This was the case even if
she were a minor; her dependence on her husband prevailed over her dependence on her father. Thus, the domicile of a married woman was the same as,
and changed with, the domicile of her husband. That rule, which applied even
if the spouses had been living apart and in different countries for many
years,[18] reflected social conditions and attitudes of a past age; it was "the last
barbarous relic of a wife's servitude."[19] It also produced serious inconvenience in practice, notably in the context of jurisdiction in matrimonial causes,
alleviated by special legislative provisions.[20] The rule has been abolished for
purposes of divorce jurisdiction in Canada,[21] and for all purposes in New
Zealand,[22] Australia,[23] and in the Republic of Ireland.[24]

The domicile of a married woman is now ascertained by reference to the   **6–085**
same factors as in the case of any other individual capable of having an
independent domicile.[25] The fact of her marriage and the domicile, residence
and nationality of her husband will be relevant factors[26] but not determinative
of her domicile. Where the spouses are living together, there must be a strong
probability of their having the same domicile, but this is an observation of fact
and not a rule of law. In appropriate circumstances, such spouses may have
different domiciles.

Termination of dependency. On ceasing to be dependent, a person often   **6–086**
continues to be domiciled in the country of his last domicile of dependency.
A child reaching the age of sixteen will usually retain the domicile of the
appropriate parent as a domicile of choice.[27] But he now has the normal
capacity to change his domicile, and such a change may result from acts done

---

[16] *Udny v. Udny* (1869) L.R. 1 Sc. & Div. 441, 457; *Re Wallach* [1950] 1 All E.R. 199, 200.
[17] *Re Cooke's Trusts* (1887) 56 L.T. 737; *Harrison v. Harrison* [1953] 1 W.L.R. 865; *Re Scullard*
[1957] Ch. 107; *Henderson v. Henderson* [1967] P. 77, 82–83; *Arnott v. Groom* (1846) 9 D. 142;
Crumpton's Judicial Factor v. Finch-Noyes, 1918 S.C. 378; *Spurway v. Spurway* [1894] 1 I.R.
385; *Hyland v. Hyland* (1971) 18 F.L.R. 461; *cf. Miller v. Teale* (1954) 92 C.L.R. 406.
[18] See *e.g. Re Scullard* [1957] Ch. 107 (separation of 46 years; in different countries for about 30
of those years).
[19] *Gray v. Formosa* [1963] P. 259, 267 (C.A.).
[20] See paras. 18–002 *et seq, post.*
[21] Divorce Act 1968, s.6(1).
[22] Domicile Act 1976, s.5.
[23] See the uniform Domicile Acts of the Australian jurisdictions, s.5.
[24] Domicile and Recognition of Foreign Divorces Act 1986. In *M.(C.) v. M.(T.) (No. 2)* [1990] 2
I.R. 52, the dependent domicile of a married woman was held to have been unconstitutional as
offending against the principles of equality before the law and of equal rights in marriage (Arts.
41 and 42 of the Constitution of Ireland).
[25] Domicile and Matrimonial Proceedings Act 1973, s.1(1).
[26] *Cf.* para. 6–049, nn. 67–68, *ante,* for the corresponding case of the husband's domicile.
[27] *In the goods of Patten* (1860) 6 Jur.(N.S.) 151; *Re Macreight* (1885) 30 Ch.D. 165; *Gulbenkian
v. Gulbenkian* [1937] 4 All E.R. 618.

during dependency. Cases on the former dependent domicile of married women established that a married woman who settled in a country other than that of her husband's domicile could acquire a domicile there as soon as dependency ended, on the death of the husband or a decree absolute of divorce or of nullity of marriage. A widow did not, after becoming a widow, have to establish a new residence or form a new *animus manendi*; it was therefore no bar to the acquisition of a domicile of choice that she never knew of her husband's death.[28] The same result should follow even if the dependent person, having settled in a country, is temporarily absent from it at the time dependency ends.[29]

6–087   Where immediately before January 1, 1974, a woman was married and then had her husband's domicile by dependence, she is treated as retaining that domicile (as a domicile of choice, if it is not also her domicile of origin) unless and until it is changed by acquisition or revival of another domicile either on or after that date.[30] This means that any such married woman who had before 1974 settled in a country other than that of her husband's domicile would acquire a new domicile of choice on January 1, 1974 and without further action on her part.[31] In all other cases, however, the domicile of such a married woman will change only in accordance with the rules for the loss of a domicile of choice[32] or, where her continuing domicile is her domicile of origin, for the acquisition of a domicile of choice.[33] In these latter cases, the wife's history and circumstances before 1974 are treated as irrelevant, with the result that she may possess, at least for some time after January 1, 1974, what the English and Scottish Law Commissions describe as "a bogus or artificial domicile."[34]

6–088   The Commissions have proposed[35] the replacement of section 1(2) of the Domicile and Matrimonial Proceedings Act 1973 by fresh transitional provisions on the model of the uniform Domicile Acts in the Australian jurisdictions.[36] Under these provisions the proposed statutory rules as to domicile would apply to times before those rules came into force but only for the purpose of determining where, at a time after the rules came into force, a person was domiciled.

ILLUSTRATIONS

6–089   1. D, whose domicile of origin is English, at the age of seventeen travels to Dublin with the intention of making his permanent home there. By English law, D has capacity to acquire a domicile of choice; by Irish law he has not. D is domiciled in the Republic of Ireland.

2. D was born in England with an English domicile of origin in 1930. In 1948, his parents acquired a domicile of choice in South Australia. In 1950, D went to New Zealand with the intention of settling there. He continued to entertain this intention until he reached the then age

---

[28] *Re Scullard* [1957] Ch. 107; *cf. Re Cooke's Trusts* (1887) 56 L.T. 737.
[29] *Cf. Harrison v. Harrison* [1953] 1 W.L.R. 865, stated as Illustration 2, *post*.
[30] Domicile and Matrimonial Proceedings Act 1973, s.1(2).
[31] *I.R.C. v. Duchess of Portland* [1982] Ch. 314, 319.
[32] *i.e.* Rule 13, *ante; I.R.C. v. Duchess of Portland* [1982] Ch. 314, stated as Illustration 3, *post*.
[33] *i.e.* Rule 10, *ante*.
[34] Working Paper No. 88, *The Law of Domicile* (1985), para. 8.3.
[35] Report on *The Law of Domicile* (Law Com. No. 168), para. 8.7.
[36] s.4(1)(2). *Cf.* the virtually identical provisions in Domicile Act 1976 (New Zealand), ss.3, 4.

of majority in 1951, but before that time he returned to England for a temporary purpose. As soon as he reached twenty-one he lost his South Australian domicile of dependency.[37]

3. W, whose domicile of origin was in Quebec, married H, domiciled at all material times in England, in 1948. Each year, W spent some 10 or 12 weeks (and H some six weeks) in their house in Quebec; the remainder of the year they lived in their house in England. In 1975, H and W decided that when, at some future time, H retired, they would take up full-time residence in Quebec. On January 1, 1974, W's domicile of dependence in England was deemed to be a domicile of choice there. This domicile was not lost at the time of W's annual visits to Quebec in 1974 or subsequent years; for the purposes of domicile, she remained resident in England.[38]

RULE 15—Subject to the Exception hereinafter mentioned, the domicile of an unmarried child under sixteen is determined as follows: **6R–090**

(1) **the domicile of a legitimate child is, during the lifetime of his father, the same as, and changes with, the domicile of his father;**

(2) **the domicile of a legitimated child is, from the time at which the legitimation takes effect, during the lifetime of his father, the same as, and changes with, the domicile of his father;**

(3) **the domicile of an illegitimate child and of a child whose father is dead is, in general, the same as, and changes with, the domicile of his mother;**

(4) **the domicile of a legitimate or legitimated child without living parents, or of an illegitimate child without a living mother, probably cannot be changed;**

(5) **the domicile of an adopted child is determined as if he were the legitimate child of the adoptive parent or parents.**

COMMENT

(1) Legitimate children. The rule that the domicile of a legitimate child   **6–091** depends on that of his father is well established.[39] Although the rule has sometimes been criticised,[40] much of the force of those criticisms was removed by the Domicile and Matrimonial Proceedings Act 1973 which introduced important qualifications to the rule. It does not apply to a child aged sixteen or over,[41] or to one who is married under that age[42]; nor in some cases in which the parents of the *propositus* are living apart.[43] Parents living together may exceptionally have different domiciles,[44] and it is necessary to have a rule indicating which domicile should be attributed to the child. It is not

---

[37] *Harrison v. Harrison* [1953] 1 W.L.R. 865. But he did not acquire a domicile of choice in New Zealand on the ground that he had not resided there since coming of age (*sed quaere*).

[38] Domicile and Matrimonial Proceedings Act 1973, s.1(2); *I.R.C. v. Duchess of Portland* [1982] Ch. 314.

[39] *Re Duleep Singh* (1890) 6 T.L.R. 385 (C.A.); *Gulbenkian v. Gulbenkian* [1937] 4 All E.R. 618; *Henderson v. Henderson* [1967] P. 77; *Spurway v. Spurway* [1894] 1 I.R. 385.

[40] *Re P. (G.E.) (An Infant)* [1965] Ch. 568, 589 (C.A.), though Lord Denning M.R. may have had the rule as to revival of a domicile of origin as much in mind as the present rule; Blaikie, 1984 Jur.Rev. 1.

[41] Domicile and Matrimonial Proceedings Act 1973, s.3(1). This provision extends to England and Northern Ireland: s.3(2). In Scotland, a child can acquire a domicile of choice at the end of pupillarity, 14 in the case of a boy, 12 in that of a girl; see Anton, p. 133; Clive, 1966 Jur.Rev. 1; the Scottish Law Commission has recommended that the age be raised to 16, as in England: *The Law of Domicile*, para. 4.28.

[42] Domicile and Matrimonial Proceedings Act 1973, s.3(1). For New Zealand, see the Domicile Act 1976, s.6(2); for the Australian jurisdictions, the uniform Domicile Acts, s.7.

[43] See the Exception to this Rule, *post*.

[44] See para. 6–085, *ante*.

unreasonable that the child should be dependent upon the father for the purposes of domicile; in the majority of families such a rule reflects the child's economic dependence upon his father.

There is no English authority to support the view accepted in some American jurisdictions that a child may gain capacity to acquire a domicile by being emancipated or abandoned.[45]

6–092   **(2) Legitimated children.** Although there is no authority on the point, it is submitted that the domicile of a legitimated child is determined as follows: until the time when the legitimation takes effect, his domicile depends on his mother's in accordance with clause (3) of this Rule; when the legitimation takes effect, the child's domicile becomes dependent on his father's, at any rate if the legitimation is due to the marriage of the child's parents; if the parents begin to live apart, the Exception to this Rule will apply; after the father's death, the child's domicile depends once again on his mother's in accordance with clause (3) of this Rule.

6–093   **(3) Illegitimate and fatherless children.** The general rule is that the domicile of an illegitimate or fatherless child depends on that of his mother.[46] But in this case the rule is probably less general in scope than is the rule applying to a child whose domicile depends on that of his father. "The change in the domicile of an infant which . . . may follow from a change of domicile on the part of the mother, is not to be regarded as a necessary consequence of a change of the mother's domicile, but as the result of the exercise by her of a power vested in her for the welfare of the infants, which, in their interest, she may abstain from exercising, even when she changes her own domicile."[47] Thus it was held that the remarriage of a widow, which at that time led to her getting a new domicile of dependence, did not of itself affect the domicile of her children.[48] Similarly if the mother acquires a new domicile of choice (whether or not related to remarriage) but leaves the child behind in the country of the previous domicile she may be said to have abstained from exercising her power of changing the child's domicile.[49] It does not follow as a matter of law that the mother can only change the child's domicile by physically taking the child to the country of the new domicile. There is New Zealand authority for the proposition that the power vested in the mother extends to giving the child a domicile in a country other than that in which the mother is or has been domiciled,[50] but it is difficult to justify so extensive a power, unless it is also given to the father of a legitimate child.[51]

6–094   **(4) Children without living parents.** It is an open question whether the domicile of a child without living parents can be changed by his guardian.

---

[45] Restatement, s.22, comment *f.*

[46] *Potinger v. Wightman* (1817) 3 Mer. 67; *Johnstone v. Beattie* (1843) 10 Cl. & F. 42, 66, 138; *Arnott v. Groom* (1846) 9 D. 142; *Crumpton's Judicial Factor v. Finch-Noyes*, 1918 S.C. 378.

[47] *Re Beaumont* [1893] 3 Ch. 490, 496–497.

[48] *Re Beaumont, supra; Re G.* [1966] N.Z.L.R. 1028; *cf. Crumpton's Judicial Factor v. Finch-Noyes*, 1918, S.C. 378.

[49] *Re Beaumont, supra; cf. Johnstone v. Beattie* (1843) 10 Cl. & F. 42, 138. Although Lord Campbell dissented, he agreed with the majority on this point.

[50] *Re G.* [1966] N.Z.L.R. 1028.

[51] *Cf.* Blaikie, 1984 Jur.Rev. 1.

There is no English authority on this point.[52] It may be that a distinction can be drawn between "natural guardians" (*i.e.* grandparents), who have the power to change the child's domicile, and others, who do not.[53] Alternatively, it may be that a guardian has power to change the child's domicile to a country in which he is recognised as guardian, but not otherwise.[54] But these are speculative possibilities so far as English law is concerned, and the safest view appears to be that the domicile of a child without living parents cannot be changed. The same rule probably holds good for an illegitimate child whose mother is dead but whose father is alive.

(5) Adopted children. An adopted child is treated in law as the legitimate child of his adoptive parent or parents.[55] Accordingly his domicile will be determined in accordance with the appropriate clauses of this Rule and of the Exception thereto, as if he were such a legitimate child. 6–095

Reform. The English and Scottish Law Commissions have recommended[56] new statutory rules as to the domicile of children which would replace those stated in Rule 15 and the Exception thereto. Under the proposed rules the domicile of a child (*i.e.* any person under 16, whether married or unmarried, and whether or not that person was a parent) would be determined as follows. The child would be domiciled in the country with which he was for the time being most closely connected. Where the child's parents were domiciled in the same country and the child had his home with either or both of them, it would be presumed, unless the contrary were shown, that the child was most closely connected with that country. Where the child's parents were not domiciled in the same country and he had his home with one of them, but not with the other, it would similarly be presumed that the child was most closely connected with the country in which the parent with whom he had his home was domiciled. No presumption would apply in cases in which the parents were domiciled in separate countries and the child had a home with both of them; nor in cases where the child had a home with neither parent. For the purposes of these rules, "parent" includes parents who are not married to one another; there would no longer be separate rules applying to legitimate, illegitimate and legitimated children.[57] No change is proposed in the case of adopted children, whose adoptive parents will be the "parents" to whom the rules will refer. 6–096

---

[52] In *Potinger v. Wightman* (1817) 3 Mer. 67, the guardian was the child's mother. The case was explained on this ground in *Johnstone v. Beattie* (1843) 10 Cl. & F. 42, 66 (in argument).

[53] Restatement, s.22, comment *i*.

[54] This would avoid the difficulty "that a person may be guardian in one place and not in another"; *Douglas v. Douglas* (1871) L.R. 12 Eq. 617, 625.

[55] Adoption Act 1976, s.39(1)(5), applying from the date of the adoption or from January 1, 1976, whichever is the later. The words in Domicile and Matrimonial Proceedings Act 1973, s.4(5) referring to adopted children were repealed by Children Act 1975, s.108 and Sched. 4, Pt. I. Similar principles apply in Australia (see the uniform Domicile Acts, s.8(3)(5)(6)) and New Zealand (see Domicile Act 1976, s.6; Adoption Act 1955, s.16(2)(*f*) as amended by Domicile Act 1976, s.14(2)). For the United States, see Restatement, s.22, comment *g*.

[56] *The Law of Domicile* (Law Com. No. 168), Part IV.

[57] There would be no place for the power of election which seems to be enjoyed at common law by a parent in certain circumstances, *i.e.* under *Re Beaumont* [1893] 3 Ch. 490 (*ante*, para. 6–093).

Illustrations

6–097   1. D, a legitimate child whose father is domiciled in England, is sent, at the age of fourteen, to live with his uncle in France. D's father then acquires a domicile in Ireland. D thereupon gets an Irish domicile and cannot acquire a domicile of choice in France until he reaches the age of sixteen.[58]

2. D was born in 1950, the illegitimate son of A, a woman domiciled in France, and B, a man domiciled in Scotland. In 1955, A acquires a domicile of choice in England. In 1960 B marries A, thus legitimating D. In 1965, B acquires a domicile of choice in New Zealand. D is domiciled from 1950 to 1955 in France from 1955 to 1960 in England; from 1960 to 1965 in Scotland and from 1965 in New Zealand.

3. W and H1 are domiciled in Scotland; they have two legitimate children, D1 and D2. After H1's death, W marries H2; they acquire domiciles of choice in England. W takes D1 to reside with her and H2 in England, but leaves D2 to reside with her aunt in Scotland. D1 gets an English domicile, but D2 continues to be domiciled in Scotland.[59]

4. D is a child whose parents are dead and who is domiciled in Scotland. G, who is also domiciled in Scotland, is appointed D's guardian in Scotland. Subsequently, G acquires an English domicile of choice. *Semble*, D continues to be domiciled in Scotland whether or not he resides with G in England.

6E–098   *Exception*—**The domicile of a legitimate or legitimated unmarried child under sixteen whose parents are living apart, or were living apart at the death of the mother, is determined as follows:**

  (1)   if he has his home with his mother and has no home with his father, the domicile of the child is the same as, and changes with, the domicile of his mother;

  (2)   if the preceding clause has applied to him at any time and he has not since had a home with his father, the domicile of the child is the same as, and changes with, the domicile of his mother;

  (3)   if at the time of the death of his mother, his domicile was the same as that of his mother by virtue of clause (1) or (2), and he has not since had a home with his father, the domicile of the child is the domicile his mother last had before she died;

  (4)   in any other case, the domicile of the child is the same as, and changes with, the domicile of his father.

Comment

6–099   This Exception states the effect of section 4 of the Domicile and Matrimonial Proceedings Act 1973, which regulates the domicile of a dependent child as at any time after January 1, 1974, when his father and mother are alive but living apart, or were living apart at the date of the death of the mother.[60] The general object of the provision is to create a number of additional cases in which the domicile of dependency of a child will be that of its mother; previously existing rules of law to that effect[61] are expressly preserved.[62]

6–100   The Exception only applies if the parents are "living apart." That phrase is not defined in the Act, but it clearly connotes something more than the mere

---

[58] See *Spurway v. Spurway* [1894] 1 I.R. 385.
[59] See *Re Beaumont* [1893] 3 Ch. 490.
[60] For comparable provisions along similar lines, see Domicile Act 1976 (New Zealand), s.6 and the uniform Domicile Acts of the Australian jurisdictions, s.8. For the proposed replacement of the English provisions, see *ante*, para. 6–096.
[61] *e.g.* those stated in clause (3) of Rule 15.
[62] Domicile and Matrimonial Proceedings Act 1973, s.4(4).

absence of one spouse from the matrimonial home for a short period. Parents who share a matrimonial home may have different domiciles[63]; if the temporary absence of a father for hospital treatment or on business meant that such parents were "living apart," the domicile of their child would be governed by the Exception and, unless the child were held to retain a home with the absent father, the child's domicile might change with undesirable frequency. It is submitted that parents should not be taken to be "living apart" despite one parent's temporary absence if they continue to belong to the same household.

If the parents are living apart, the usual rule that the domicile of dependency **6–101** of their child under sixteen will be the domicile of the father applies in many cases. It applies when the child's home is with his father, and when the child's last home with either parent was with his father. It also applies if, since the parents began to live apart, the child has had no home with either parent, his home being, for example, with grand-parents, foster-parents, or in a residential institution. But if at any time the child has a home with the mother and has no home with the father, the usual rule is displaced, and the child's domicile of dependency becomes that of the mother.[64] Once the child becomes dependent on the mother for the purposes of domicile, he remains so dependent until he acquires a home with his father.[65] This applies even after the death of the mother, her last domicile continuing to be the child's domicile of dependence.[66]

Where the child's domicile follows that of the mother under these statutory **6–102** provisions, there is no room for the exercise by her of any discretion as to what the child's domicile should be, such as exists at common law in the case of illegitimate and fatherless children.[67] The statutory provisions cease to apply on the death of the father, for the parents are no longer "living apart," and the child's domicile continues to depend on that of the mother by virtue of the common law rules; but it would seem inappropriate in such circumstances for the fact of the father's death to give rise to a discretionary power vested in the mother which she did not enjoy under the statutory rules.

In determining whether a child has a home with a parent, it will be relevant **6–103** to consider not only the amount of time they live together but also the state of the relationships between the child and his parents, matters such as where a young child's toys and possessions are usually kept, and, especially in the case of an older child, the child's own view of the matter.[68] The question is whether the child has a home with a particular person, and not whether he has a home in a particular place. It is possible for a child to have two homes, one with each parent,[69] or one with a parent and one with some other person. Circumstances are so variable that it is dangerous to seek to formulate detailed rules. For example, if a child lives most of the year with his mother, spending time with his father only during the school holidays, it may well be that he will be regarded as having his home with his mother. But a child at boarding school,

---

[63] *e.g. I.R.C. v. Bullock* [1976] 1 W.L.R. 1178 (C.A.) where the matrimonial home was in England but the husband remained domiciled in his native country to which he planned to return if he survived his English wife.
[64] Domicile and Matrimonial Proceedings Act 1973, s.4(2)(*a*).
[65] *Ibid.* s.4(2)(*b*).
[66] *Ibid.* s.4(3).
[67] *Re Beaumont* [1893] 3 Ch. 490; see *ante*, para. 6–093.
[68] *Cf. Re P. (G. E.) (An Infant)* [1965] Ch. 568, 585 (C.A.), where a child's ordinary residence was defined in terms of his home.
[69] Domicile and Matrimonial Proceedings Act 1973, s.4(2)(*a*).

spending the school holidays with one parent will probably be treated as having his home with that parent.[70] A newly-born child remaining for a short period in a maternity hospital will have a home, unless both parents have repudiated him. The existence and terms of any custody or residence order are not determinative, but may be relevant evidence. The same applies to a court order placing the child in the care of the local authority, which does not preclude the possibility of the child having a home with a parent, as where the child is returned home on trial by the authority.

ILLUSTRATIONS

6–104   1. In 1973, H, domiciled in Scotland, marries W, domiciled in England. They live together in Scotland and have a child C, born in 1974. In 1975 they separate and W returns to England, intending to remain permanently, and taking C with her. In 1980 W dies, and C goes to live in Scotland, with G, his paternal grandmother. C has had no home with H since the separation between H and W. C is domiciled in Scotland until 1975 and in England from 1975 until 1990, when he attains the age of sixteen and becomes capable of having an independent domicile.[71]

     2. The circumstances are the same as in Illustration 1, except that G spends 1982 in Canada visiting another son, and during that period C has a home with H. C then becomes domiciled in Scotland, and retains H's domicile as his domicile of dependency until 1990.[72]

6R–105   **RULE 16—A mentally disordered person cannot acquire a domicile of choice and, subject to the Exception hereinafter mentioned, retains, while he remains mentally disordered, the domicile which he had when he began to be legally treated as insane.**

COMMENT

6–106   An independent person who becomes mentally disordered may lose the capacity of acquiring a domicile on the ground that he is "unable to exercise any will."[73] Since the abandonment, no less than the acquisition, of a domicile of choice involves the "exercise" of "will," such a person retains the domicile which he had when he began to be legally treated as insane.[74]

6–107   The English cases which support these statements are, with one exception,[75] concerned with persons who were "lunatics so found" by inquisition. This procedure, and the term "lunatic," are obsolete in English domestic law, which now recognises and makes provision for many kinds and degrees of

---

[70] See *Re P. (G. E.) (An Infant), supra; A, Petitioners*, 1953 S.L.T. (Sh.Ct.) 45 (continuous care and possession of child for purposes of adoption; test held to be whether the child had his home with petitioners; such a home established despite child's absence for training except at weekends and holiday periods).

[71] Domicile and Matrimonial Proceedings Act 1973, s.4(2)(*a*), (3).

[72] *Ibid.* s.4(3).

[73] *Urquhart v. Butterfield* (1887) 37 Ch.D. 357, 382 (C.A.); but Cotton L.J. added the qualification: "whatever his wish may have been." Cf. *Bempde v. Johnstone* (1796) 3 Ves. 198.

[74] *Hepburn v. Skirving* (1861) 9 W.R. 764; *Re Bariatinski* (1843) 13 L.J.Ch. 69, 71 (in argument); *Crumpton's Judicial Factor v. Finch-Noyes*, 1918 S.C. 378; *Rifkin v. Rifkin* [1936] W.L.D. 69; *Kertesz v. Kertesz* [1954] V.L.R. 195. For the ordinary residence of a mentally disordered person, see *R. v. London Borough of Waltham Forest, ex p. Vale, The Times*, February 25, 1985, *post*, para. 6–122.

[75] *Re Bariatinski, supra*; but the princess there in question was "admitted to be a decided lunatic" (p. 70). In *Re S. (Hospital Patient: Foreign Curator)* [1996] 1 F.L.R. 167, the enquiry as to the domicile of the patient was taken no further than the date upon which he became mentally disordered; but the relevance to his domicile of any later expressions of view (examined for other purposes in the judgment) seems not to have been the subject of argument.

mental disorder.[76] Most persons who suffer from such disorder are treated in the community or are admitted to hospital "informally"[77] (*i.e.* as voluntary patients); a few are subjected to guardianship[78]; others are detained or liable to be detained, compulsorily for observation and treatment[79]; and provision is also made for the administration by the court of the property of mentally disordered persons.[80] Not all those who suffer from one of the recognised types of mental disorder will be regarded as dependent persons within the Rule. Although there is no authority on the point, the question whether a mentally disordered person can change his domicile would appear to be a question of fact, as are other questions of capacity in English law: does the *propositus* have the ability to form the necessary intention?[81] It seems inappropriate to link the question of capacity for the purposes of the law of domicile to the use of compulsory detention or guardianship.[82] The use of these procedures depends, at least in part, on the practice of social workers and hospital staff which may be more closely related to the immediate circumstances and willingness to co-operate of the patient than to factors relevant to the law of domicile.

Where the rule that a mentally disordered person cannot change his dom-   **6–108** icile applies, it is quite general in scope. Thus it does not seem that such a person's domicile will be changed because he is moved from one country to another by the person in charge of him, or under the direction of the appropriate administrative authority.[83]

For the purposes of an English rule of the conflict of laws, the question   **6–109** where a person is domiciled is determined according to English law.[84] Accordingly, the fact that a person domiciled in a foreign country has been declared legally insane under the law of that country will not determine, in an English court, the issue of his capacity to acquire a domicile of choice elsewhere.

Reform. The effect of the law as stated in the Rule is to fix the domicile   **6–110** of the mentally disordered person at a certain date; it cannot be changed even if, as may happen in a few cases, he acquires a permanent home in another country. The English and Scottish Law Commissions have recommended[85] new statutory rules as to the domicile of mentally disordered persons, referred to as "adults under disability", which would replace those stated in this Rule and the Exception hereto. Under the proposed rules, an adult lacking the capacity to form the intention necessary for acquiring a domicile would be domiciled in the country with which he was for the time being most closely connected. When that capacity was restored to him, he would retain the domicile he had immediately before it was restored, but could of course then acquire a new domicile under the rules applying to adults generally.

---

[76] As defined in s.1(2) of the Mental Health Act (1983).
[77] See *ibid.* s.131 (as amended by Children Act 1989, Sched. 13, para. 48(5)).
[78] *Ibid.* ss.7–10.
[79] *Ibid.* ss.2–6.
[80] *Ibid.* Part VII.
[81] See *The Law of Domicile*, para. 6.9.
[82] A possibility canvassed in earlier editions of this book: *cf.* 10th ed., p. 140.
[83] *e.g.* under Part VI of the Mental Health Act 1983.
[84] Rule 8, *ante.*
[85] *The Law of Domicile* (Law Com. No. 168), Part VI.

ILLUSTRATIONS

6–111   1. D, who is domiciled in India, becomes insane and is sent to England. He retains his Indian domicile so long as he remains insane,[86] even although he resides in England as a lunatic for forty-eight years.[87]

2. D was born in 1859 with a domicile of origin in Barbados. His father died in 1870. Shortly afterwards his mother resumed her domicile of origin in Scotland, taking D with her. D continued to reside in Scotland till 1882, when he became insane and was placed in a Scottish institution. He died in 1916 without having recovered his sanity. From 1870 onwards D was domiciled in Scotland.[88]

3. The circumstances are the same as in Illustration 2, except that D is placed in an English institution from 1882 until his death. D dies domiciled in Scotland.

6E–112   *Exception*—**The domicile of a person who is born mentally disordered or becomes so disordered while he is a dependent child is determined, so long as he remains mentally disordered, as if he continued to be a dependent child.**[89]

ILLUSTRATIONS

6–113   1. D is the legitimate child of H, who is domiciled in Portugal. D becomes insane at the age of fifteen and remains insane. When D is twenty-five years old, H acquires a domicile in England. D gets an English domicile.[90]

2. D, a legitimate minor whose domicile of origin is in New Zealand, becomes insane. After her father's death she is at the age of thirteen sent by her mother to Scotland and placed in an institution there. When D is aged twenty-nine (and still insane) her mother marries a man domiciled in England and so gets an English domicile. There is no evidence of any intention on the mother's part to change D's domicile. D continues to be domiciled in New Zealand.[91]

3. RESIDENCE

6–114   Residence is an essential element in the concept of domicile, but residence, ordinary residence and habitual residence are increasingly used, both by the legislature and by the courts,[92] as connecting or jurisdictional factors in their own right.[93]

6–115   **Residence.**[94] The word "residence" has different meanings in different branches of the law. It is clear that it must be distinguished from mere presence, the state of being found in a country, but the nature of the distinction

---

[86] *Hepburn v. Skirving* (1861) 9 W.R. 764.
[87] *Cf. Bempde v. Johnstone* (1976) 3 Ves. 198; *cf. Re Mackenzie* (unrep.), referred to in *Re Mackenzie* [1941] Ch. 69, 71, 74.
[88] *Crumpton's Judicial Factor v. Finch-Noyes*, 1918 S.C. 378.
[89] *Sharpe v. Crispin* (1869) L.R. 1 P. & D. 611; *Re G.* [1966] N.Z.L.R. 1028. The former case is not decisive, as the court held that if D was capable of choosing a domicile he had, as a matter of fact, chosen that of his father. In America, the Exception only applies if the mentally disordered person continues to reside with his parent: Restatement, s.23, comment *c*.
[90] *Cf. Sharpe v. Crispin* (1869) L.R. 1 P. & D. 611, especially at p. 618.
[91] *Re G.* [1966] N.Z.L.R. 1028.
[92] *Re P. (G. E.) (An Infant)* [1965] Ch. 568 (C.A.) (ordinary residence).
[93] The term "normally resident" is used, though for different purposes, in the Customs and Excise Duties (Personal Reliefs for Goods Permanently Imported) Order 1992, S.I. 1992 No. 3193; see the detailed definition in Art. 3.
[94] See Farnsworth (1952) 38 Tr.Grot.Soc. 59; McClean (1962) 11 I.C.L.Q. 1153.

and the factors which should be taken into account will vary with the subject-matter.

It has been suggested that there is now "a rule of construction that prima facie at least residence involves some degree of permanence."[95] This view gains support from Viscount Cave L.C.'s reliance in a taxation context[96] upon the Oxford English Dictionary definition of "reside," "to dwell permanently or for a considerable time, to have one's settled or usual abode. . . . " This definition has been influential in those decisions emphasising, in a number of contexts, the need for some degree of permanence.[97] However, the actual case in which Viscount Cave L.C. was delivering his opinion involved a taxpayer who spent only a small part of each year in this country, and stayed in hotels on each visit, but was held to be resident for tax purposes.[98] Decisions in other contexts have recognised residence as having been established without any element of permanence.[99] Mere fleeting or casual presence will, however, not constitute residence.[1]

6–116

For tax purposes, it has been held that the question where a person is resident is one of fact.[2] But the question must nonetheless be "determined on proper legal principles"[3]; and for other legal purposes the question has been described as "a mixed question of law and fact."[4] All the circumstances must be taken into account, the weight to be given to the various aspects of the facts varying with the circumstances. So in a matrimonial causes context, the location of the matrimonial home, and the situation of spouse and children was significant[5]; for some purposes it is sufficient to describe a person as resident where he works, while for other purposes this is not sufficient[6]; in some contexts a man may be said to be resident where he sleeps, but this will not be an appropriate criterion in others.[7]

6–117

It is possible to be resident in a country despite a temporary absence[8]; and, at least in some contexts, to have two or more residences.[9]

---

[95] *Brokelmann v. Barr* [1971] 2 Q.B. 602, 611–612.

[96] *Levene v. I.R.C.* [1928] A.C. 217, 222.

[97] *Re Adoption Application No. 52 of 1951* [1952] Ch. 16 (adoption); *Fox v. Stirk* [1970] 2 Q.B. 463 (C.A.) (electoral registration qualifications); *Brokelmann v. Barr* [1971] 2 Q.B. 602 (exemptions from customs duty).

[98] *Levene v. I.R.C.* [1928] A.C. 217. See the companion case, *I.R.C. v. Lysaght* [1928] A.C. 234.

[99] *e.g. Matalon v. Matalon* [1952] P. 233 (judicial separation).

[1] *Manning v. Manning* (1871) L.R. 2 P. & D. 223; *Armytage v. Armytage* [1898] P. 178; *Sinclair v. Sinclair* [1968] P. 189 (C.A.). *Cf.* Resolution (72) 1 of the Committee of Ministers of the Council of Europe on the Standardisation of the Legal Concepts of "Domicile" and of "Residence," Annex, Rule 8: "A man has a residence in a country . . . if he dwells there for a certain period of time."

[2] *I.R.C. v. Lysaght* [1928] A.C. 234.

[3] *Pickles v. Foulsham* (1923) 9 Tax Cas. 261, 274 (the passage does not appear in the report at [1923] 2 K.B. 413).

[4] *Sinclair v. Sinclair* [1968] P. 189, 213 (C.A.).

[5] *Sinclair v. Sinclair, supra,* at p. 232.

[6] Contrast *Ablett v. Basham* (1856) 5 E. & B. 1019 (indorsement of writ of summons) with *Haslope v. Thorne* (1813) 1 M. & S. 103 (affidavit to hold bail).

[7] Contrast *R. v. Vice-Chancellor of Oxford University* (1872) L.R. 7 Q.B. 471 (membership of university body) with *Walcot v. Botfield* (1854) Kay 534 (condition of residence imposed in will); *cf. Re Brauch* [1978] Ch. 316 (C.A.) (bankruptcy; a case on ordinary residence).

[8] *Dasent v. Dasent* (1850) 1 Rob.Eccl. 800, 803; *Fox v. Stirk* [1970] 2 Q.B. 463, 475 (C.A.).

[9] *I.R.C. v. Lysaght* [1928] A.C. 234; *Sinclair v. Sinclair* [1968] P. 189, 232 (C.A.).

6–118   **Ordinary residence.** It has sometimes been said that "ordinary residence" means nothing more or less than "residence,"[10] but it is submitted that the better view is that the adjective does add something,[11] an element of continuity, order, or settled purpose.

6–119   So, in a tax context, it has been said that ordinary residence "connotes residence in a place with some degree of continuity and apart from accidental or temporary absences"[12] and that "if it has any definite meaning I should say it means according to the way in which a man's life is usually ordered."[13] In the context of entitlement to educational awards, it was held that ordinary residence refers to a person's abode in a particular place or country which he has adopted voluntarily and for settled purposes as part of the regular order of his life for the time being, whether of short or long duration.[14] It is not essential to ordinary residence that it should be for a commercial or any other specific purpose.[15]

6–120   It was held in the context of jurisdiction in matrimonial causes that a person who habitually lives in a country may continue to be ordinarily resident there while he is actually resident in another country, *e.g.* during a prolonged stay in the second country for business or professional purposes; and that a wife who accompanies her husband on such occasions may similarly retain her ordinary residence in the first country.[16] On the other hand, ordinary residence in the first country will cease when the original connection with it is completely severed, *e.g.* if the persons in question decide to emigrate to the second country and dispose of their home in the first.[17] The fact that a person keeps a home available for immediate occupation in a country is evidence of ordinary residence there[18]; but it is probably not a necessary condition of ordinary residence. Thus a person may be ordinarily resident in a country although he has no home in it at all but lives in hotels.[19] And it is submitted that a person who lets his house for a short period while he is away for business or professional purposes remains ordinarily resident where that house is.

---

[10] *Levene v. I.R.C.* [1928] A.C. 217, at p. 225 *per* Viscount Cave, L.C.; *Hopkins v. Hopkins* [1951] P. 116, 112 (matrimonial jurisdiction); *Lowry v. Lowry* [1952] P. 252, 255 (magistrates' matrimonial jurisdiction).

[11] *Re Erskine* (1893) 10 T.L.R. 32 (C.A.); *Re Bright* (1901) 18 T.L.R. 37 (C.A.) (bankruptcy cases); *Levene v. I.R.C.* [1928] A.C. 217, 232 *per* Lord Warrington; *I.R.C. v. Lysaght* [1928] A.C. 234, 243, 248 *per* Lords Sumner and Buckmaster (tax cases); *Stransky v. Stransky* [1954] P. 428, 437 (matrimonial jurisdiction); *R. v. Barnet London Borough Council, ex p. Nilish Shah* [1982] Q.B. 688 (C.A.) at pp. 722–723 *per* Eveleigh L.J., at pp. 729–30 *per* Templeman L.J. (entitlement to educational awards).

[12] *Levene v. I.R.C.* [1928] A.C. 217, 225. In the Income and Corporation Taxes Act 1988, s.334, ordinary residence is contrasted with occasional residence; see *Reed (Inspector of Taxes) v. Clark* [1986] Ch. 1, decided under identical provisions in earlier legislation.

[13] *Levene v. I.R.C., supra,* at p. 232. *Cf. Thomson v. Minister of National Revenue* [1946] 1 D.L.R. 689 (Sup. Ct. Can.); Farnsworth (1951) 67 L.Q.R. 32.

[14] *R. v. Barnett London Borough Council, ex p. Nilish Shah* [1983] 2 A.C. 309.

[15] *Re Brauch* [1978] Ch. 316 (C.A.).

[16] *Stransky v. Stransky* [1954] P. 428; *Lewis v. Lewis* [1956] 1 W.L.R. 200. *Cf. Casey v. Casey,* 1968 S.L.T. 56 (wife's visit to seek reconciliation with separated husband did not interrupt ordinary residence). Contrast *R. v. Lancashire C.C., ex p. Huddleston* [1986] 2 All E.R. 941 (C.A.) (ordinary residence broken by prolonged, albeit not permanent, residence abroad).

[17] *Hopkins v. Hopkins* [1951] P. 116; *cf. Macrae v. Macrae* [1949] P. 397 (C.A.) Contrast *Levene v. I.R.C.* [1928] A.C. 217.

[18] As in *Stransky v. Stransky* and *Lewis v. Lewis, supra.*

[19] As in the *Lysaght* and *Levene* cases, *supra.* See also *Re Bright* (1903) 19 T.L.R. 203 (C.A.); *Re Brauch* [1978] Ch. 316 (C.A.). *Cf. Re Norris* (1888) 4 T.L.R. 452 (C.A.) (hotel room taken on long-term basis for use as required).

Ordinary residence can be changed in a day.[20] For certain purposes at least **6–121** a person may be ordinarily resident in two or more countries.[21] It has been held in immigration cases that a person who is in a country illegally cannot be ordinarily resident there; section 50(5) of the British Nationality Act 1981 expressly provides that a person is not to be treated as ordinarily resident in the United Kingdom for the purposes of that Act at a time when he is there in breach of the immigration laws.[22]

It has been said[23] that a child of tender years "who cannot decide for **6–122** himself where to live" is ordinarily resident in his parents' matrimonial home[24]; and that this ordinary residence cannot be changed by one parent without the consent of the other. If the parents are living apart and the child is, by agreement between them, living with one of them, he is ordinarily resident in the home of that one and his ordinary residence is not changed merely because the other parent takes the child away from that home.[25] Similar considerations will apply in the case of a mentally handicapped person incapable of making an independent decision as to where to live and totally dependent upon a parent or guardian; he will be ordinarily resident with that person, though a second ordinary residence (for example during a stay in an institution) may also be acquired.[26]

Habitual residence.[27] Habitual residence has long been a favourite expres- **6–123** sion of the Hague Conference on Private International Law. It appears in many Hague Conventions and therefore in English statutes giving effect to them; but is increasingly used in statutes not based on international conventions. One of its first uses at The Hague was in the context of the custody of children,[28] largely because of the artificiality of the notion of domicile as applied to young children.[29] No definition of habitual residence has ever been included in a Hague Convention; this has been a matter of deliberate policy, the aim being to leave the notion free from technical rules which can produce rigidity and inconsistencies as between different legal systems. In those contexts, the expression is not to be treated as a term of art but according to the ordinary

---

[20] *Macrae v. Macrae* [1949] P. 397, 403 (C.A.).

[21] *Re Norris* (1888) 4 T.L.R. 452 (C.A.); *Cooper v. Cadwalader* (1904) 5 Tax Cas. 201; *Pittar v. Richardson* (1917) 87 L.J.K.B. 59, 61; *Britto v. Secretary of State for the Home Department* [1984] Imm. A.R. 93; *R. v. Nottinghamshire C.C., ex p. Jain* [1989] C.O.D. 442 (D.C.).

[22] *Re Abdul Manan* [1971] 1 W.L.R. 859 (C.A.); *R. v. Governor of Pentonville Prison, ex p. Azam* [1974] A.C. 18; *R. v. Secretary of State for the Home Department, ex p. Margueritte* [1983] Q.B. 180 (C.A.) (see *R. v. Barnet London Borough Council, ex p. Shah* [1983] 2 A.C. 309, 343); *Chelliah v. Immigration Appeal Tribunal, The Times,* October 15, 1985 (C.A.). *Cf. Trotter v. Trotter* (1992) 90 D.L.R. (4th) 554 (Ont.) (person on visitor's permit and lacking landed immigrant status could become habitually resident), applied in *Alexiou v. Alexiou* (1996) 41 Alta. L.R. (3d) 90 (in context of divorce jurisdiction).

[23] *Re P. (G. E.) (An Infant)* [1965] Ch. 568, 585–586 (C.A.).

[24] "Even if he is away at boarding school," which may be in another country.

[25] The domicile of the child may be changed: see Exception to Rule 15.

[26] *R. v. London Borough of Waltham Forest, ex p. Vale, The Times,* February 25, 1985.

[27] Cavers (1972) 21 Am.Univ.L.R. 475, reprinted in Cavers, *The Choice of Law* (1985), Chap. 13; Hall (1975) 24 I.C.L.Q. 1.

[28] Convention of June 12, 1902.

[29] See Cavers, *loc. cit.,* at p. 477; van Hoogstraten (1967) *Recueil des Cours,* III, 343, 359. In Manitoba, habitual residence and domicile are identical; Domicile and Habitual Residence Act 1983.

and natural meaning of the two words it contains.[30] The Court of Appeal has emphasised that habitual residence is primarily a question of fact to be decided by reference to the circumstances of each particular case.[31] A resolution of the Committee of Ministers of the Council of Europe declared that "in determining whether a residence is habitual, account is to be taken of the duration and the continuity of the residence as well as of other facts of a personal or professional nature which point to durable ties between a person and his residence."[32] However, the English and Scottish Law Commissions, in recommending that habitual residence should not replace domicile as a general connecting factor, noted the "allegedly undeveloped state" of habitual residence as a legal concept, citing in particular uncertainties as to the place of intention and as to the length of time required for residence to become habitual,[33] and there is a regrettable tendency of the courts, despite their insistence that they are not dealing with a term of art, to develop rules as to when habitual residence may and may not be established.

6–124   It is evident that "habitual residence" must be distinguishable from mere "residence" but the adjective "habitual" indicates a quality of residence rather than its length.[34] It is submitted that the duration of residence, past or prospective, is only one of a number of relevant factors. It has, however, been said that habitual residence means "a regular physical presence which must endure for some time,"[35] and that habitual residence cannot be acquired in a single day as "an appreciable period of time and a settled intention" are required.[36] Although the "settled intent" has been identified as one to take up long-term residence in the country concerned,[37] care must be taken not to allow habitual residence to be confused with domicile and it is submitted that a settled purpose to reside in a country does not necessarily involve any long-term plan.[38] In any event, the element of settled purpose is not necessarily determinative,[39] and the better view seems to be that evidence of intention may be important in particular cases (*e.g.* in establishing habituation when the actual period or periods of residence have been short) but is not essential.[40] If long-term residence is established in a new country, the habitual residence will be there even if the propositus lives in an exclusively expatriate group (as in

---

[30] *Re J. (A Minor) (Abduction)* [1990] 2 A.C. 562; *Re R. (Wardship: Child Abduction)* [1992] 2 F.L.R. 481 (C.A.); *Dickson v. Dickson*, 1990 S.C.L.R. 692; *F. v. S. (Wardship: Jurisdiction)* [1993] 2 F.L.R. 686 (C.A.) (burden of proof); *Findlay v. Findlay (No. 2)*, 1994 S.L.T. 709. See also *Pershadsingh v. Pershadsingh* (1987) 60 O.R. (2d) 437.

[31] *Re M. (Minors) (Residence Order: Jurisdiction)* [1993] 1 F.L.R. 495 (C.A.).

[32] Resolution (72) 1 of the Committee of Ministers of the Council of Europe on the Standardisation of the Legal Concepts of "Domicile" and "Residence", Annex, r. 9.

[33] *The Law of Domicile* (Law Com. 168), paras. 3.5–3.8.

[34] *Cruse v. Chittum* [1974] 2 All E.R. 940; *Hack v. Hack* (1976) 6 Fam. Law 177.

[35] *Cruse v. Chittum, supra*, at p. 942, *per* Lane J.

[36] *Re J. (A Minor) (Abduction)* [1990] 2 A.C. 562, *obiter* as the issue in the case was the loss rather than the acquisition of habitual residence; *M. v. M. (Abduction: England and Scotland)* [1997] 2 F.L.R. 263 (C.A.); *Re A. (Abduction: Habitual Residence)* [1998] 1 F.L.R. 497 (habitual residence contracted with holiday visits); *Dickson v. Dickson*, 1990 S.C.L.R. 692.

[37] *A. v. A. (Child Abduction: Habitual Residence)* [1993] 2 F.L.R. 225, 235.

[38] See *Re J. (A Minor) (Abduction)* [1990] 2 A.C. 562; *Moran v. Moran*, 1997 S.L.T. 541; *Watson v. Jamieson*, 1998 S.L.T. 180; *Commissioner, Western Australia Police v. Dormann* (1997) F.L.C. 92–766.

[39] *Hack v. Hack* (1976) 6 Fam. Law 177.

[40] *Cf.* Law Com. No. 48 (1972), para. 42 and n. 55.

a forces' base) which simulates ordinary life in his home country.[41] Habitual residence may continue during temporary absences,[42] but will be lost if a person leaves a country with a settled intention not to return to it.[43] In appropriate circumstances, it may be lost in a day.[44]

The element of settled intent cannot be required in all cases, for a young **6–125** child is treated as having an habitual residence for adoption purposes.[45] In many cases the habitual residence of a child will be that of whichever of his parents has sole custody.[46] There is a special provision in section 41 of the Family Law Act 1986 to the effect that the removal from or retention outside a part of the United Kingdom of a child without the consent of all those having the right to determine its place of residence does not change the child's habitual residence until the expiry of one year from the date of the removal or retention.[47] This has been held to apply only to cases in which the child is removed to, or retained in, another part of the United Kingdom,[48] but the courts have adopted a more general proposition that a child's habitual residence cannot be changed by the unilateral action of one parent and remains unchanged unless circumstances arise which quite independently point to a change in its habitual residence.[49] Where the parents are in agreement, they may change the habitual residence of a child without changing their own.[50] If parents separate and one of their children goes by agreement to live with one parent, it does not necessarily follow that the child's habitual residence is changed; all the circumstances must be considered, a change in habitual residence being more likely if the child is to live with the relevant parent permanently or for the indefinite future.[51]

In appropriate cases, it would seem that a person could be without any **6–126** habitual residence[52]; habitual residence in two or more places would also seem possible.[53] Different views have been expressed about the relationship between habitual residence and ordinary residence. It has sometimes been said

---

[41] *Re A. (Minors) (Abduction: Habitual Residence)* [1996] 1 All E.R. 24.
[42] *Oundjian v. Oundjian* (1979) 1 F.L.R. 198 (habitual residence throughout period of one year despite absences totalling 149 out of 365 days); *Rellis v. Hart*, 1993 S.L.T. 738; *Re M. (Minors) (Residence Order: Jurisdiction)* [1993] 1 F.L.R. 495, 501 (C.A.); *Re B.M. (A Minor) (Wardship: Jurisdiction)* [1993] 1 F.L.R. 979; *H. v. H. (Child Abduction: Stay of Domestic Proceedings)* [1994] 1 F.L.R. 530.
[43] *Re J. (A Minor) (Abduction)*, *supra*.
[44] *Re M. (Minors) (Residence Order: Jurisdiction)* [1993] 1 F.L.R. 495, 500 (C.A.).
[45] Adoption Act 1976, s.17(2).
[46] *Re J. (A Minor) (Abduction)*, *supra*; *Re M. (Minors) (Residence Order: Jurisdiction)* [1993] 1 F.L.R. 495, 500 (C.A.); *Re B. (Minors) (Abduction) (No. 2)* [1993] 1 F.L.R. 993; *Re O. (A Minor) (Abduction: Habitual Residence)* [1993] 2 F.L.R. 594.
[47] See *post*, para. 19–039.
[48] *Re M. (Minors) (Residence order: Jurisdiction)* [1993] 1 F.L.R. 495 (C.A.).
[49] *Re A. (A Minor) (Wardship: Jurisdiction)* [1995] 1 F.L.R. 767 (child taken to Pakistan); *Re O. (Child Abduction: Re-Abduction)* [1997] 2 F.L.R. 712; *Re M. (A Minor) (Habitual Residence)* [1996] 1 F.L.R. 887 (C.A.); *State Central Authority v. McCall* (1995) F.L.C. 92–552; *Artso v. Artso* (1995) F.L.C. 92–566.
[50] *Re A. (A Minor) (Wardship: Jurisdiction)* [1995] 1 F.L.R. 767 (sending a child to a boarding school abroad would not itself have this effect).
[51] *Findlay v. Findlay (No. 2)*, 1994 S.L.T. 709.
[52] *Hack v. Hack* (1976) 6 Fam. Law 177: "unless one led a nomadic life" one had to have a habitual residence somewhere; *Re J. (A Minor) (Abduction)*, *supra*.
[53] *Commissioner, Western Australia Police v. Dormann* (1997) F.L.C. 92–766. *Cf. Cameron v. Cameron*, 1996 S.C. 17 to the contrary, but that in the context of the Hague Convention on the Civil Aspects of International Child Abduction where the structure of the Convention so dictates.

that habitual residence is "something more than" ordinary residence,[54] but the "something more" is elusive. It has been held that there is no real distinction between the two concepts, and that it is proper to apply the test for ordinary residence, as referring to a person's abode in a particular place or country which he has adopted voluntarily[55]; and for settled purposes as part of the regular order of his life for the time being,[56] to interpret "habitually resident" in section 5(2) of the Domicile and Matrimonial Proceedings Act 1973.[57] It is submitted that both concepts can indeed be understood in this way, but that the courts should not apply to habitual residence the whole body of case law which has grown up around ordinary residence. It is greatly to be hoped that the courts will resist the temptation to develop detailed and restrictive rules as to habitual residence which might make it as technical a term of art as common law domicile.[58] The facts and circumstances of each case should continue to be assessed without resort to presumptions or presuppositions.

4. DOMICILE, RESIDENCE AND NATIONALITY

6–127   The concept of domicile remains of fundamental importance in the rules of the conflict of laws prevailing in common law countries. But its pre-eminence is less secure than was formerly the case. Despite reforms made by statute, or proposed by law reform agencies, in the law of domicile with the object of removing its less satisfactory features, the courts and, especially, the legislature, are making increasing use of various forms of residence[59] and of nationality[60] as connecting factors, a reflection in part of the growing influence of international conventions on the English rules of the conflict of laws.

6–128   **Domicile and nationality.**[61]   Until the beginning of the nineteenth century domicile was universally regarded as the personal law for purposes of the conflict of laws. The change from domicile to nationality on the continent of Europe started in France with the promulgation of the Code Napoleon in 1804. One of the principal objects of the codifiers was to substitute a uniform law throughout the whole of France for the different *coutumes* of the French

---

[54] *Cruse v. Chittum* [1974] 2 All E.R. 940, 943 (but *cf.* the dictum immediately following, that habitual residence is similar to the residence normally required as part of domicile, a view described by Hall, *loc. cit.* at p. 12, as "idiosyncratic and even misconceived"); *Oundjian v. Oundjian* (1979) 1 F.L.R. 198, 202–203.

[55] In *Cameron v. Cameron*, 1996 S.C. 17, the court expressed doubt as to whether in every case residence must be voluntarily adopted before there can be habitual residence, using as examples the mythical case of Robinson Crusoe and the real example of Nelson Mandela as a prisoner.

[56] *i.e.* the test adopted in *R. v. Barnet London Borough Council, ex p. Nilish Shah* [1983] 2 A.C. 309, 344 and applied in *Re M. (Minors) (Residence Order: Jurisdiction)* [1993] 1 F.L.R. 495 (C.A.).

[57] *Kapur v. Kapur* [1984] F.L.R. 920; *K. (C.) v. K.(C.)* [1994] 1 I.R. 250 (inconclusive discussion of the relationship between ordinary and habitual residence). *Cf. Levene v. I.R.C.* (1928) 13 Tax Cas. 486, 493 ("ordinary" said to mean "habitual"); Australian Family Law Act 1975, s.4(1) ("ordinary residence" includes "habitual residence" for purposes of Act); Law Com. No. 48 (1972), para. 42.

[58] *D. v. D. (Custody: Jurisdiction)* [1996] 1 F.L.R. 574.

[59] See para. 6–114.

[60] *e.g.* Wills Act 1963, s.1; Family Law Act 1986, s.46(1)(*b*)(iii).

[61] Nadelmann (1969) 17 Am.J. Comp. Law 418; de Winter (1969) *Recueil des Cours* III, p. 347; Law Com. No. 48, (1972) paras. 19–26.

provinces. In matters of personal status these *coutumes* applied to persons domiciled within the province, wherever they happened to be. It was natural that the new uniform law should apply to Frenchmen everywhere, and article 3(1) of the Civil Code provided that "the laws governing the status and capacity of persons govern Frenchmen even though they are residing in foreign countries." No provision was expressly made for the converse case of foreigners residing in France, but the French courts held that in matters of status and capacity they too were governed by their national law. The provisions of the French code were adopted in Belgium and Luxembourg, and similar provisions were contained in the Austrian code of 1811 and the Dutch code of 1829.

The change from domicile to nationality on the continent of Europe was **6–129** accelerated by Mancini's famous lecture delivered at the University of Turin in 1851. Under Mancini's influence, article 6 of the Italian Civil Code (1865) provided that "the status and capacity of persons and family relations are governed by the laws of the nation to which they belong." Mancini's ideas proved extremely influential outside Italy too, and in the second half of the nineteenth century the principle of nationality replaced that of domicile in code after code in continental Europe, although domicile was often retained in specific contexts. The result is that the nations of the world have become divided in their definition of the personal law; and it is this fact more than any other which impedes international agreement on uniform rules of the conflict of laws. What then are the arguments in favour of nationality and domicile as the personal law?

The advocates of nationality claim that it is more stable than domicile **6–130** because nationality cannot be changed without the formal consent of the State of new nationality. However, as has been well said,[62] "the principle of nationality achieves stability, but by the sacrifice of a man's personal freedom to adopt the legal system of his own choice. The fundamental objection to the concept of nationality is that it may require the application to a man, against his own wishes and desires, of the laws of a country to escape from which he has perhaps risked his life."

It is also claimed that nationality is easier to ascertain than domicile **6–131** because a change of nationality involves a formal act of naturalisation and does not depend on the subjective intentions of the *propositus*. This is undoubtedly true, though there may be difficult cases of double nationality or of statelessness. But it does not follow that the most easily ascertained law is the most appropriate law. Many immigrants who have no intention of returning to their country of origin do not trouble to apply for naturalisation.

The decisive consideration for countries like the United Kingdom, the **6–132** United States, Australia and Canada is that, save in a very few respects, there is no such thing as United Kingdom, American, Australian or Canadian law. Since the object of referring matters of status and capacity to the personal law is to connect a man with some one legal system for many legal purposes, nationality breaks down altogether if the State contains more than one country in the sense of the conflict of laws.[63] International conventions commonly contain provisions seeking to resolve this problem; they may leave it to the

---

[62] Anton, p. 123.
[63] See *Re O'Keefe* [1940] Ch. 124, and *ante*, para. 4–030.

law of the nationality to determine the territorial unit whose law is to govern, or rely on some other connecting factor to make that determination.[64]

6–133   **The replacement of domicile?** The growing importance of statute law, commonly based on international conventions, in the conflict of laws is raising the possibility that domicile may come to be replaced by some other connecting factor. As long ago as 1964 a learned commentator described domicile as "a superannuated concept."[65]

6–134   The notion of habitual residence appears to be emerging as a concept acceptable to lawyers from both common law and civil law traditions, as representing a compromise between domicile and nationality, or at least as a more acceptable connecting factor than domicile to be used as an alternative to nationality. The reform of the law of domicile in England is taking the concept closer to that of habitual residence, which is also not far removed from the understanding of domicile prevalent in United States jurisdictions.[66] The Irish Law Reform Commission, in a thinly-argued report published in 1983,[67] recommended the replacement of domicile by habitual residence; but the English and Scottish Law Commissions in a Report[68] published in 1987 made a firm recommendation that domicile should be reformed but not replaced by another general connecting factor in English law.

---

[64] *e.g.* the Hague Convention on Matrimonial Property Regimes, art. 16 (prepared in 1976).
[65] Kahn-Freund (1964) 27 M.L.R. 55, 57.
[66] See de Winter (1969) *Recueil des Cours*, III, p. 347, at pp. 419–493; Cavers (1972) 21 Am.Univ.L.R. 475.
[67] Report on Domicile and Habitual Residence as Connecting Factors in the Conflict of Laws, L.R.C. 7; *cf.* the earlier Working Paper No. 10 (1981).
[68] *The Law of Domicile*, paras. 3.4–3.16.

PART TWO

PROCEDURE

CHAPTER 7 deals with procedural questions, including the distinction **II–001** between matters of substance and matters of procedure, remedies and process, evidence, set-off and counterclaim, priorities, damages and statutes of limitation.

CHAPTER 8 deals with a number of significant procedural issues which arise in the conduct of international litigation: injunctions to restrain removal or dissipation of assets before judgment (*Mareva* injunctions or freezing injunctions), international judicial assistance in relation to service of process and the taking of evidence abroad, and the taking of security for costs.

CHAPTER 9 deals with the mode of proving foreign law.

CHAPTER 7

SUBSTANCE AND PROCEDURE

RULE 17—All matters of procedure are governed by the domestic law of the country to which the court wherein any legal proceedings are taken belongs (*lex fori*). 7R–001

COMMENT

The principle that procedure is governed by the *lex fori* is of general application and universally admitted.[1] In a body of Rules such as those contained in this book, which state the principles enforced by an English court, the maxim that procedure is governed by the *lex fori* means in effect that it is governed by the ordinary law of England without any reference to any foreign law whatever. Thus the English court will always apply its own rules of procedure, and will, moreover, refuse to apply any foreign rule which in its view is procedural.[2] In deciding whether a foreign rule is procedural, the court refers to the foreign law in order to determine whether the rule is of such a nature as to be procedural in the English sense.[3] 7–002

While procedure is governed by the *lex fori*, matters of substance are governed by the law to which the court is directed by its choice of law rule (*lex causae*).[4] Dicey wrote that English lawyers gave "the widest possible extension to the meaning of the term 'procedure.' "[5] As a matter of history, this is true[6]; and a court may, even today, be tempted to extend the meaning of "procedure" in order to evade an unsatisfactory choice of law rule.[7] But in general the attitude expressed by Dicey has fallen into disfavour precisely because it tends to frustrate the purposes of choice of law rules. Thus some questions which were at one time thought of wholly in terms of procedure are now considered to be procedural in some of their aspects only. The development of the law as to damages[8] illustrates this process. 7–003

The difficulty in applying this Rule lies in discriminating between rules of procedure and rules of substance. The distinction is by no means clear-cut. In 7–004

---

[1] Ailes (1941) 39 Mich.L.Rev. 392. The distinction between substance and procedure is often discussed in and illustrated by reference to cases involving limitation periods; the actual decisions in many of these cases would be different since the Foreign Limitation Periods Act 1984, considered *post*, paras. 7–043 *et seq.*

[2] *e.g. Hansen v. Dixon* (1906) 23 T.L.R. 56.

[3] *Huber v. Steiner* (1835) 2 Bing.N.C. 202; *cf. Société Anonyme Metallurgique de Prayon v. Koppel* (1933) 77 S.J. 800; Beckett (1934) 15 B.Y.I.L. 46, 75; Robertson, pp. 248–253; Cook, p. 224; *ante*, Chap. 2.

[4] *Huber v. Steiner* (1835) 2 Bing.N.C. 202, 210.

[5] 1st ed., p. 712.

[6] *Cf.* Lorenzen, pp. 339–340.

[7] *e.g. Grant v. McAuliffe*, 41 Cal. 2d 859, 246 P. 2d 944 (1953); *Kilberg v. Northeast Airlines Inc.*, 9 N.Y. 2d 34, 172 N.E. 2d 526 (1961); Currie, Chap. 3; see *post*, para. 35–041.

[8] *Post*, paras. 7–034 *et seq.*

drawing it, regard should be had in each case to the purpose for which the distinction is being used and to the consequences of the decision in the instant context.[9] The rule under examination must be considered as a whole, without giving undue weight to the verbal formula selected by previous judges or by the draftsman of a statute to introduce the rule. So, the words "where proceedings are taken in any court ... " have been held to introduce a rule of substance.[10] The mechanistic approach, sometimes found in English cases, of relying on the classification of the introductory verbal formula as used in a quite different statute,[11] or of accepting a classification as procedural or substantive made for some purpose quite unrelated to the conflict of laws,[12] is now discredited. The distinction may have to be drawn in one place for the purpose of this Rule but in another place for the purpose of the rule that statutes affecting procedure are, while statutes affecting substance are not, presumed to have retrospective effect. This is not to say that the distinction may not be drawn in the same place for many purposes: it is merely to deny that it must necessarily be drawn in the same place for all purposes. The primary object of this Rule is to obviate the inconvenience of conducting the trial of a case containing foreign elements in a manner with which the court is unfamiliar. If, therefore, it is possible to apply a foreign rule, or to refrain from applying an English rule, without causing any such inconvenience, those rules should not necessarily, for the purpose of this Rule, be classified as procedural.[13]

7–005   **Contracts (Applicable Law) Act 1990.** A number of matters dealt with in this chapter are affected by the Contracts (Applicable Law) Act 1990, which gives effect in English law to the Rome Convention on the Law Applicable to Contractual Obligations 1980. Its relevance here is that a number of its provisions extend the scope of the application of the *lex causae*, the law governing the contract, to cover some issues which under the common law position reflected in the Rule are matters of procedure governed by the *lex fori*. These provisions, noted at appropriate places in this chapter but more fully considered in Chapter 32, concern remedies for breach of contract, including assessment of damages,[14] and certain matters of evidence: proof of

---

[9] Falconbridge, p. 304; *Block Bros. Realty Ltd. v. Mollard* (1981) 122 D.L.R. (3d) 323 (B.C.C.A.).

[10] *Shrichand & Co. v. Lacon* (1906) 22 T.L.R. 245. Similarly, a rule which provides that a person "may not bring proceedings for the recovery of damages" unless certain conditions are satisfied has been construed as a rule of substance: *Sherwood v. Webb* (1992) 28 N.S.W.L.R. 251. See also *James Hardie & Co. Pty Ltd. v. Hall* (1998) 43 N.S.W.L.R. 554.

[11] *e.g. Moulis v. Owen* [1907] 1 K.B. 746, 753 (C.A.); *Hill v. William Hill (Park Lane) Ltd.* [1949] A.C. 530, 579, where decisions under the Gaming Acts 1845 and 1892 were influenced by the earlier classification of the same formula ("No action shall be brought ... ") in the Statute of Frauds 1677, s.4. *Cf. Toronto-Dominion Bank v. Martin* [1985] 4 W.W.R. 557 (Sask.); *Horseshoe Club Operating Co. v. Bath* [1998] 3 W.W.R. 128 (B.C.).

[12] *e.g. Leroux v. Brown* (1852) 12 C.B. 801, 827. *cf.* Cook, Chap. 6.

[13] *Bateman & Litman Real Estate Ltd. v. Big T Motel Ltd.* (1964) 44 D.L.R. (2d) 474, affd. 49 D.L.R. (2d) 480 (Sask. C.A.), citing the corresponding text in the 7th edition of this work. See also *Shaik Sahied bin Abdullah Bajerai v. Sockalingam Chettiar* [1933] A.C. 342, 346 (P.C.); *The Zollverein* (1856) Swab. 96, 98; *Nihalchand Navalchand v. McMullan* [1934] 1 K.B. 171 (C.A.) as explained in (1935) 16 B.Y.I.L. 210; *Merchants Bank of Canada v. Elliot* [1918] 1 W.W.R. 698 (an English case of which there is only a Canadian report); *Monterosso Shipping Co. Ltd. v. International Transport Workers Federation* [1982] I.C.R. 675, 681–682 (C.A.).

[14] Contracts (Applicable Law) Act 1990, s.2 and Sched. 1, Art. 10(1)(*c*); see *post*, paras. 32–198 *et seq.*

a contract[15] and provisions of the law of contract as to the burden of proof and presumptions of law.[16]

(1) Nature of remedy and method of enforcement. The nature of the **7–006** remedy is a matter of procedure to be determined by the *lex fori*.[17] Thus if the claimant is by the *lex causae* entitled only to damages but is by English law entitled to specific relief, the latter type of remedy is available in England.[18] Conversely, an English court will not grant specific relief where to do so is contrary to the principles of English law: thus no injunction can be obtained in England for breach of negative stipulations in a foreign contract of service if such an injunction would in effect amount to specific enforcement of the contract.[19] Again, a remedy which is discretionary according to English law cannot be demanded as of right in an English court merely because this is possible according to the *lex causae*.

Generally speaking the principle that the forum grants its own remedies in **7–007** respect of wrongs governed by a foreign law only applies if two conditions are satisfied. First, the *lex causae* must give the claimant some remedy against the defendant in respect of a wrong similar in character to that alleged in the English proceedings.[20] Secondly, the English remedy sought must "harmonise with the right according to its nature and extent as fixed by the foreign law."[21] Thus English remedies will be refused if they are so different from those provided by the *lex causae* as "to make the right sought to be enforced a different right."[22] Although an action in England will not fail merely because the claim is unknown to English law, it will fail if English law has no appropriate remedy for giving effect to the claimant's alleged foreign right.[23]

The method of enforcing a judgment is a matter of procedure.[24] The *lex fori* **7–008** determines what property of the defendant is available to satisfy the judgment, and in what order. Thus if the *lex causae* provides that mortgage debts are to be satisfied primarily out of the mortgaged property, this does not prevent the forum from ordering the satisfaction of such debts out of the debtor's property generally.[25] But if the *lex causae* provided that only the mortgaged property was liable for the debt, this would amount to a rule of substance to the effect that by the *lex causae* the "debtor" was under no personal liability. Such a rule would, therefore, be applied by the forum.[26] Conversely, a court would not

---

[15] *Ibid.*, Sched. 1, Art. 14(2); see *post*, para. 32–176.

[16] *Ibid.*, Sched. 1, Art. 14(1); see *post*, para. 32–054. See also Art. 10(1)(*d*) on limitation of actions, which makes no change in the position in English law.

[17] *Flack v. Holm* (1820) 1 J. & W. 405; *De la Vega v. Vianna* (1830) 1 B. & Ad. 284; *Liverpool Marine Credit Co. v. Hunter* (1868) L.R. 3 Ch.App. 479, 486.

[18] *Baschet v. London Illustrated Standard Co.* [1900] 1 Ch. 73; *Boys v. Chaplin* [1971] A.C. 356, 394.

[19] *Cf. Warner Brothers Pictures Incorporated v. Nelson* [1937] 1 K.B. 209; where, however, this point was not discussed.

[20] *McMillan v. Canadian Northern Ry. Co.* [1923] A.C. 120 (P.C.).

[21] *Phrantzes v. Argenti* [1960] 2 Q.B. 19, 35.

[22] At p. 36.

[23] *Ibid.*; *Khalij Commercial Bank Ltd. v. Woods* (1985) 17 D.L.R. (4th) 358 (Ont.).

[24] *Minister of Public Works of Kuwait v. Sir Frederick Snow and Partners* [1983] 1 W.L.R. 818, 829 (C.A.).

[25] *Cf. Northern Trusts Co. v. McLean* [1926] 3 D.L.R. 93 (Ont. C.A.); *243930 Alberta Ltd. v. Wickham* (1987) 61 O.R. (2d) 731.

[26] *Melan v. Fitzjames* (1797) 1 Bos. & P. 138 is perhaps distinguishable from *De la Vega v. Vianna* (1830) 1 B. & Ad. 284 along the lines suggested in the text.

apply a rule of its own domestic law protecting the debtor from personal liability where the *lex causae* imposed such liability upon him.[27]

7–009   In the case of a contract, the principle that the nature of the remedy is a matter for the *lex fori* is affected by the provisions of the Rome Convention on the Law Applicable to Contractual Obligations 1980, given effect in English law by the Contracts (Applicable Law) Act 1990. The law applicable to a contract by virtue of Articles 3 to 6 and 12 of the Convention governs, within the limits of the powers conferred on the court by its procedural law,[28] the consequences of breach, including the assessment of damages so far as it is governed by rules of law.[29]

7–010   **(2) Parties.** In determining who are the proper parties to proceedings, the first question is whether the claimant or defendant is the sort of person or body that can be made a party to litigation. This is a question for the *lex fori*.[30] Thus proceedings could not be commenced in England in the name of a dead man, even though this was possible by the *lex causae*.[31] The same applies, *mutatis mutandis*, and subject to statutory exceptions,[32] to actions by and against dissolved companies,[33] though the question whether a company has been dissolved must be decided by reference to the law of the place of incorporation.[34] Again, a foreign body which does not have legal personality and which does not carry on business in England cannot, as such, sue or be sued in England.[35] There is, however, no reason why a foreign entity which enjoys legal personality under the law of the country where it is established should not be able to participate in proceedings in England even though it has not been expressly incorporated. "The courts of one country give recognition, by a comity of nations, to a legal personality created by the law of another country."[36] In *Bumper Development Corporation v. Commissioner of Police for the Metropolis*[37] an Indian temple, which was recognised as having legal personality under Indian law, was permitted to sue in English proceedings,

---

[27] *Canadian Acceptance Corp. Ltd. v. Matte* (1957) 9 D.L.R. (2d) 304 (Sask. C.A.); *Sigurdson v. Farrow* (1981) 121 D.L.R. (3d) 183 (Alta.). *Cf. 243930 Alberta Ltd. v. Wickham* (1987) 61 O.R. (2d) 731 where provisions virtually identical to those classified as substantive in *Canadian Acceptance Corp. Ltd. v. Matte* (1957) 9 D.L.R. (2d) 304 (Sask. C.A.) and *Sigurdson v. Farrow* (1981) 121 D.L.R. (3d) 183 (Alta.) were held to be procedural.

[28] *i.e.* the forum court is not required to make an order unknown to its legal system.

[29] Contracts (Applicable Law) Act 1990, s.2 and Sched. 1, Art. 10(1)(*c*). See further, *post*, paras. 32–198 *et seq.*

[30] *Oxnard Financing S.A. v. Rahn* [1998] 1 W.L.R. 1465 (C.A.).

[31] *Banque Internationale de Commerce de Petrograd v. Goukassow* [1923] 2 K.B. 682, revd. on other grounds [1925] A.C. 150.

[32] See *Russian & English Bank v. Baring Brothers & Co. Ltd.* [1936] A.C. 405; *cf. post*, paras. 30–050 *et seq.*

[33] *Banque Internationale de Commerce de Petrograd v. Goukassow* [1923] 2 K.B. 682 (C.A.), revd. on other grounds: [1925] A.C. 150; *Deutsche Bank v. Banque des Marchands de Moscou* (1932) 158 L.T. 364 (C.A.).

[34] *Lazard Brothers & Co. v. Midland Bank Ltd.* [1933] A.C. 289; *cf.* paras. 30–010 *et seq.*, *post*.

[35] *Von Hellfeld v. Rechnitzer* [1914] 1 Ch. 748.

[36] *Chaff v. Hay Acquisition Committee v. J.A. Hemptill and Sons Pty. Ltd.* (1947) 74 C.L.R. 375, 390, *per* McTiernan J. (cited with approval by Lord Templeman in *Arab Monetary Fund v. Hashim (No. 3)* [1991] 2 A.C. 114, 162). See also *Skyline Associates v. Small* (1975) 56 D.L.R. (3d) 471 (B.C.C.A.); *International Association of Science and Technology for Development v. Hamza* (1995) 122 D.L.R. (4th) 92 (Alta.C.A.).

[37] [1991] 1 W.L.R. 1362 (C.A.).

notwithstanding the fact that the temple, which was "little more than a pile of stones",[38] lacked the basic characteristics of a legal person under English law. Similarly, in *Oxnard Financing S.A. v. Rahn*[39] it was decided that a partnership which, though not a corporation, had legal personality under Swiss law could be sued in England either by reference to the partnership name or by reference to the names of its members.

Assuming that a claimant is capable of suing in the above sense, the next **7–011** question is whether he is the proper claimant in the particular action before the court.[40] Clearly he is not if by the *lex causae* the right which he is seeking to enforce did not vest in him but in someone else.[41] If the right is vested in him, further problems may arise from rules of the *lex causae* or of the *lex fori* to the effect that the claimant may not sue in his own name or in his own name alone, but must sue in the name of some third party, or in the name of himself and of a third party jointly. The authorities are divided on the question whether rules requiring the assignee of a debt to sue in the name of, or together with, the assignor are substantive or procedural. The authorities which support the view that such rules are procedural[42] can all be explained on other grounds; and the authorities which treat the matter as substantive[43] can be supported on the ground that the application of foreign rules of this kind will not, in general, cause any procedural inconvenience to the court. The principal object of such rules appears to be to protect the debtor; and if the *lex causae* does not give him such protection it is hard to see why he should have it when he is sued in England.

In some cases, the claimant claims to be entitled to sue in England in a **7–012** representative capacity, relying on an appointment made under foreign law. As Parker J. observed in *Kamouh v. Associated Electrical Industries International Ltd.*,[44] two conflicting principles can be found, "first, that [the English] courts should as a matter of comity give effect to the curator's or tuteur's right under foreign law to sue in his own name; second, that municipal procedure should be applied." The first principle applies in the case of trustees in bankruptcy,[45]

---

[38] [1991] 1 W.L.R. 1362, 1371, *per* Purchas L.J.

[39] [1998] 1 W.L.R. 1465 (C.A.).

[40] The *obiter dictum* of Lord Diplock in *Bankers Trust International Ltd. v. Todd Shipyards Corporation* [1981] A.C. 221, 235 (P.C.) that "any question as to who is entitled to bring a particular kind of proceeding in an English court ... is a question of jurisdiction ... to be decided by English law as the *lex fori*" cannot be supported, and must be confined to the special context of maritime liens. See *post*, para. 7–032.

[41] *Ross v. Sinhjee* (1891) 19 R. 31; Hancock, p. 124; *Lucas v. Coupal* [1931] 1 D.L.R. 391 (Ont.); Falconbridge, pp. 120–123; *cf. Hartmann v. Konig* (1933) 50 T.L.R. 114 (H.L.).

[42] In *Wolff v. Oxholm* (1817) 6 M. & S. 92 English law was both the *lex fori* and the *lex causae*. In *Jeffery v. M'Taggart* (1817) 6 M. & S. 126 and *Barber v. Mexican Land Co.* (1899) 16 T.L.R. 127 the *leges causae* were not intended to have extraterritorial effect. In *Regas Ltd. v. Plotkins* (1961) 29 D.L.R. (2d) 282 (Sup. Ct. Can.) the *lex fori* was also the proper law of the debt; and it is arguable that the action succeeded on the ground that the assignee was also the original creditor and sued as such: see p. 287 and (1959) 22 D.L.R. (2d) 169, 174.

[43] *Innes v. Dunlop* (1800) 8 T.R. 595; *O'Callaghan v. Thomond* (1810) 3 Taunt. 82; *cf. Trimbey v. Vignier* (1834) 1 Bing.N.C. 151.

[44] [1980] Q.B. 199, 206.

[45] *Smith v. Buchanan* (1800) 1 East 6, 11; *O'Callaghan v. Thomond* (1810) 3 Taunt. 82; *Alivon v. Furnival* (1834) 1 Cr.M. & R. 277, 296; *Macaulay v. Guaranty Trust Co. of New York* (1927) 44 T.L.R. 99; *Obers v. Paton's Trustees* (1897) 24 R. 719; *Kamouh v. Associated Electrical Industries International Ltd.* [1980] Q.B. 199, 206. See Rule 167.

liquidators,[46] receivers,[47] administrators of alien enemy property,[48] and curators of mentally disordered persons (though in this last case the curator should join the mentally disordered person, suing by his next friend, as co-claimant).[49] But the second principle, precluding the claimant from relying on his foreign appointment, applies to administrators of deceased persons,[50] and to administrators of absentees' property.[51]

7–013   The final question is whether the person sued is the proper defendant to the action. In some foreign systems of law a defendant cannot be sued unless and until some other person has been sued first. For instance, in some foreign systems a creditor cannot sue an individual partner until he has first sued the firm and its assets have been exhausted, or cannot sue a surety until he has first sued the principal debtor. Such rules are in sharp contrast to the rule of English law that any partner may be sued alone for the whole of the partnership debts, or that a surety may be sued without joining the principal debtor. The question is whether such a rule of foreign law is substantive or procedural. If the *lex causae* regards the defendant as under no liability whatever unless other persons are sued first, the rule is substantive and must be applied in English proceedings.[52] If on the other hand the *lex causae* regards the defendant as liable, but makes his liability conditional on other persons being sued first, then the rule is procedural and is ignored in English proceedings.[53]

7–014   **(3) Evidence.** "The law of evidence," it has been said, "is the *lex fori* which governs the courts. Whether a witness is competent or not; whether a certain matter requires to be proved by writing or not; whether certain evidence proves a certain fact or not; that is to be determined by the law of the country where the question arises, where the remedy is sought to be enforced and where the court sits to enforce it."[54] On the other hand, "it is not everything that appears in a treatise on the law of evidence that is to be classified internationally as adjective law, but only provisions of a technical or procedural character—for instance rules as to the admissibility of hearsay

---

[46] *Bank of Ethiopia v. National Bank of Egypt and Liguori* [1937] Ch. 513, 524. *Cf. North Australian Territory Co. v. Goldsbrough Mort & Co.* (1889) 61 L.T. 716. See Rule 158.

[47] *Schemmer v. Property Resources Ltd.* [1975] Ch. 273, especially at p. 287; *Macaulay v. Guaranty Trust Co. of New York* (1927) 44 T.L.R. 99, which was, however, treated as a bankruptcy case; *Re Young* [1955] Qd.R. 254; *Kamouh v. Associated Electrical Industries International Ltd.* [1980] Q.B. 199, 206; *White v. Verkouille* [1990] 2 Qd.R. 191. *Cf. Perry v. Zissis* [1977] 1 Lloyd's Rep. 607, 615 (C.A.). See Rule 159.

[48] *Lepage v. San Paulo Copper Estates Ltd.* [1917] W.N. 216.

[49] *Didisheim v. London and Westminster Bank* [1900] 2 Ch. 15 (C.A.); *Pélégrin v. Coutts & Co.* [1915] 1 Ch. 696; *Kamouh v. Associated Electrical Industries International Ltd.* [1980] Q.B. 199, 206; *Re S.* [1951] N.Z.L.R. 122. See Rule 109.

[50] *Carter and Crost's Case* (1585) Godb. 33; *Tourton v. Flower* (1735) 3 P. Will. 369, 370; *New York Breweries Co. Ltd. v. Att.-Gen.* [1899] A.C. 62; *Finnegan v. Cementation Co. Ltd.* [1953] 1 Q.B. 688 (C.A.); *Kamouh v. Associated Electrical Industries International Ltd.* [1980] Q.B. 199, 206. See Rule 127.

[51] *Kamouh v. Associated Electrical Industries International Ltd.* [1980] Q.B. 199.

[52] *General Steam Navigation Co. v. Guillou* (1843) 11 M. & W. 877; *The Mary Moxham* (1876) 1 P.D. 107 (C.A.).

[53] *General Steam Navigation Co. v. Guillou* (1843) 11 M. & W. 877; *Bullock v. Caird* (1875) L.R. 10 Q.B. 276; *Re Doetsch* [1896] 2 Ch. 836; *Subbotovsky v. Waung* [1968] 3 N.S.W.R. 216, affd. on other grounds *sub nom. Waung v. Subbotovsky* [1968] 3 N.S.W.R. 499; (1969) 121 C.L.R. 337; *Johnson Matthey & Wallace Ltd. v. Alloush* (1984) 135 N.L.J. 1012 (C.A.). For criticism see Wolff, p. 240; Rabel, Vol. 2, pp. 118–119; Anton, p. 745.

[54] *Bain v. Whitehaven and Furness Junction Ry.* (1850) 3 H.L.C. 1, 19.

evidence or what matters may be noticed judicially."[55] Thus the *lex causae* generally determines what are the facts in issue[56]; and it may do so by providing that no evidence need, or may, be given as to certain matters, for instance as to compliance, or failure to comply with, certain formalities of a marriage ceremony. Such provisions are substantive.[57] On the other hand, as a general rule, the *lex fori* determines how the facts in issue must be proved.

Exceptions to this general rule may be provided by legislation.[58] A contract   **7–015** or an act intended to have legal effect may be proved by any mode of proof recognised in English law or by any of the laws referred to in Article 9 of the Rome Convention on the Law Applicable to Contractual Obligations 1980, given effect in English law by the Contracts (Applicable Law) Act 1990, under which that contract or act is formally valid, provided that a mode of proof recognised by a foreign law is only available in English proceedings if it can be administered by English law.[59]

The following problems in the law of evidence call for special consideration.

Admissibility. Questions as to the admissibility of evidence are decided in   **7–016** accordance with the *lex fori*.[60] Thus a document may be received as evidence by the English court although it is inadmissible by the *lex causae*.[61] Conversely, copies of foreign documents, though admissible by the *lex causae*, are inadmissible in England,[62] unless they comply with the English rules as to the admissibility of secondary evidence of documents.[63] The latter rule is now subject to a statutory exception. Under the Evidence (Foreign, Dominion and Colonial Documents) Act 1933,[64] the Crown has power to make Orders in Council providing, *inter alia*, that official and properly authenticated copies of foreign public registers shall be admissible in the United Kingdom to prove the contents of such registers.[65]

A distinction has been drawn between extrinsic evidence adduced to inter-   **7–017** pret a written document, *e.g.* a contract, and extrinsic evidence adduced to add to, vary or contradict its terms. The admissibility of the former is a question

---

[55] *Mahadervan v. Mahadervan* [1964] P. 233, 243.

[56] *The Gaetano and Maria* (1882) 7 P.D. 137 (C.A.).

[57] *Mahadervan v. Mahadervan, supra*, distinguished in *Dubai Bank Ltd. v. Galadari (No. 5), The Times*, June 26, 1990, where the text was cited with approval.

[58] See, *e.g. McAllister v. General Medical Council* [1993] A.C. 388 (P.C.) in which it was held that, by virtue of the Medical Act 1983 and the rules made under it, proceedings before the Professional Conduct Committee of the General Medical Council were governed by English law, even in a case where the Committee sat in Scotland.

[59] Contracts (Applicable Law) Act 1990, s.2 and Sched. 1, Art. 14(2). See *post*, para. 32–176.

[60] *Yates v. Thomson* (1835) 3 Cl. & F. 544; *Bain v. Whitehaven and Furness Junction Ry.* (1850) 3 H.L.C. 1.

[61] *Bristow v. Sequeville* (1850) 5 Exch. 275; contrast *Alves v. Hodgson* (1797) 7 T.R. 241 and *Clegg v. Levy* (1812) 3 Camp. 166, where the document was not merely inadmissible by the *lex causae* but an utter nullity.

[62] *Appleton v. Braybrook* (1817) 6 M. & S. 34; *Brown v. Thornton* (1837) 6 Ad. & E. 185; *Finlay v. Finlay* (1862) 31 L.J.P. 149.

[63] As in *Roe v. Roe* (1916) 115 L.T. 792; *Brown v. Brown* (1917) 116 L.T. 702; see also *Abbott v. Abbott* (1860) 4 Sw. & Tr. 254.

[64] As amended by s.5 of the Oaths and Evidence (Overseas Authorities and Countries) Act 1963, which abolished the requirement of reciprocity.

[65] For existing orders, see *The Supreme Court Practice 1999*, 38/10/5. See also *Motture v. Motture* [1955] 1 W.L.R. 1066.

of interpretation, governed in the case of a contract by its applicable law.[66] The admissibility of the latter is a question of evidence, governed, subject to the possible effect of the Rome Convention, by the *lex fori*.[67] Thus in *St. Pierre v. South American Stores Ltd.*[68] a question arose as to the meaning of the covenant to pay rent contained in a lease of land in Chile and governed by Chilean law. It was held that evidence of negotiations prior to the contract and of subsequent writings was admissible, although it was inadmissible by English law. On the other hand, in *Korner v. Witkowitzer*[69] the plaintiff sued to recover arrears of pension under a contract governed by Czech law. In order to obtain leave to serve notice of the writ out of the jurisdiction he had to prove that the contract was broken in England. It was held by Denning L.J. that evidence of an oral agreement whereby the plaintiff was to receive his pension in the country in which he might be living when it accrued was inadmissible, since this would be to vary the terms of the written agreement. Although matters of evidence and procedure are generally outside the scope of the Rome Convention, given effect in English law by the Contracts (Applicable Law) Act 1990, Article 14(2) provides that a contract or an act intended to have legal effect may be proved by any means of proof recognised by the law of the forum or by any of the laws which govern formal validity under the Convention, provided that the mode of proof can be administered in the forum. It is submitted, though with some hesitation, that this will in some cases render admissible evidence of the type declared inadmissible under English law in *Korner v. Witkowitzer*.

7–018   *Requirement of written evidence.*[70] Section 4 of the Statute of Frauds 1677 provided that "no action shall be brought" on a number of contracts unless the agreement, or a note or memorandum thereof, was in writing. Section 4 now applies only to contracts of guarantee. It was held in *Leroux v. Brown*[71] that section 4 contained a rule of procedure and therefore prevented the enforcement in England of an oral contract governed by French law which could have been sued upon in France. This decision has been severely criticised by writers[72] on the ground that no serious procedural inconvenience would be caused by admitting oral evidence of a contract within section 4: indeed the court is bound to admit such evidence if the contract is not set up for the purpose of enforcement but as a defence. To characterise the section as procedural merely because it says "no action shall be brought" is to regard the form of the section as more important than its substance. To characterise it as procedural for the purposes of the conflict of laws merely because it had

---

[66] Contracts (Applicable Law) Act 1990, Sched. 1, Art. 10(1)(*a*) (giving effect to the Rome Convention). The same position obtained at common law: *St. Pierre v. South American Stores Ltd.* [1937] 1 All E.R. 206, 209; affd. [1937] 3 All E.R. 349 (C.A.). *Cf. Re Barker* [1995] 2 V.R. 439 (in which it was held that whether a German will was intended to affect an earlier Australian will was to be determined by the *lex fori* rather than the *lex domicilii*).

[67] *Korner v. Witkowitzer* [1950] 2 K.B. 128, 162–163 (C.A.); affd. *sub nom. Vitkovice v. Korner* [1951] A.C. 869.

[68] *Supra.*

[69] *Supra.*

[70] Restatement, s.141.

[71] (1852) 12 C.B. 801; the same result was reached in *Acebal v. Levy* (1834) 10 Bing. 376, but it was not argued in that case that the contract was governed by foreign law.

[72] Falconbridge, pp. 98–102; Robertson, p. 255; Beckett (1934) 15 B.Y.I.L. 46, 69–71; Cook, pp. 229–231.

previously been characterised as procedural for some purposes of English domestic law is to lose sight of the purpose of the characterisation.

The decision has been judicially doubted[73] and the court once refused (on somewhat specious reasoning) to apply section 4 to a French contract relating to English land,[74] but it has twice been approved *obiter* in the House of Lords[75] and the Court of Appeal, having considered the earlier criticisms, has declared itself unwilling to disturb the decision.[76] Mustill L.J., with whom Woolf L.J. agreed, declared the reasoning in *Leroux v. Brown* to be "unassailable," and noted that Parliament had not taken the opportunity presented by two amendments to the Statute of Frauds to limit its effect to contracts governed by English law; only the House of Lords could overturn the decision. Purchas L.J. similarly declared himself unwilling to disturb it. The effect of *Leroux v. Brown* appears to have been greatly reduced by the Contracts (Applicable Law) Act 1990; Article 14(2) of the Rome Convention, to which the Act gives effect, allows the proof of a contract by reference to the law governing the issue of formal validity as an alternative to the law of the forum.[77]   **7–019**

Very different from the approach of the Court of Common Pleas in *Leroux v. Brown* was that of the Supreme Court of California in *Bernkrant v. Fowler*.[78] There the court refused to apply the Californian Statute of Frauds to an oral Nevada contract on the ground that, having regard to "the scope of the statute in the light of applicable principles of the conflict of laws," it did not apply to foreign contracts. The court stressed the "basic policy of upholding the expectations of the parties by enforcing contracts valid under the only law apparently applicable," and the lack of any "interest" which California might have in applying its statute to a foreign contract.   **7–020**

Section 53(1)(*b*) of the Law of Property Act 1925, re-enacting section 7 of the Statute of Frauds, provides that "a declaration of trust respecting any land ... must be manifested and proved by some writing." There is support for the view that this enactment contains a rule of procedure.[79] There is, as yet, no authority on the question whether requirements of written evidence imposed by other statutes are substantive or procedural.   **7–021**

Difficult problems may arise where both the *lex causae* and the *lex fori* contain provisions analogous to the Statute of Frauds which differ from each other in the stringency of their requirements. Questions of this kind have not yet arisen for decision in England. It is not impossible that the court might, in the circumstances of a particular case, decide that the rule of the *lex causae* is substantive, whereas the rule of the *lex fori* is procedural, in which case both rules would *prima facie* be applicable. Conversely, it might be decided that the   **7–022**

---

[73] *Williams v. Wheeler* (1860) 8 C.B.(N.S.) 299, 316; *Gibson v. Holland* (1865) L.R. 1 C.P. 1, 8; *Rawley v. Rawley* (1876) 1 Q.B.D. 460, 461.

[74] *Re De Nicols (No. 2)* [1900] 2 Ch. 410; see *post*, paras. 28–020 *et seq.*

[75] *Maddison v. Alderson* (1883) 8 App. Cas. 467, 474; *Morris v. Baron & Co.* [1918] A.C. 1, 15.

[76] *Irvani v. G. and H. Montage GmbH* [1990] 1 W.L.R. 667 (C.A.) where the Statute of Frauds was, however, ultimately held inapplicable on the facts.

[77] See further, *post*, para. 32–176.

[78] 55 Cal. 2d 588, 360 P. 2d 906 (1961); stated *post*, para. 7–054, Illustration 9. For comment see Cavers in *Perspectives of Law* (ed. Pound, Griswold and Sutherland), pp. 38–68. See also *Intercontinental Planning Ltd. v. Daystrom Inc.*, 300 N.Y.S. 2d 817, 248 N.E. 2d 576 (1969). Other jurisdictions in the United States adopt different approaches, *e.g.* that statutes of frauds should always be classed as substantive (*Muccilli v. Huff's Boys' Store Inc.*, 12 Ariz.App. 584, 473 P. 2d 786 (1970)).

[79] An *obiter dictum* in *Rochefoucauld v. Boustead* [1897] 1 Ch. 196, 207 (C.A.).

rule of the *lex causae* is procedural and the forum's rule substantive, in which case strict logic might suggest that neither should apply; and indeed a lower court in New York once reached this absurd result.[80] However, given that the purpose of classification is to determine the proper scope of the forum's conflict rules,[81] there should be no question of an English court seeking to classify the Statute of Frauds differently from analogous foreign rules; either the English rule and the analogous rule of the *lex causae* are both procedural, in which case the English rule is applicable, or they are both substantive and the *lex causae* governs.

7–023   Section 179 of the Trade Union and Labour Relations (Consolidation) Act 1992 provides that in certain cases a collective agreement "shall be conclusively presumed not to have been intended by the parties to be a legally enforceable contract" unless it is in writing and contains a provision declaring that the parties did intend to enter into a legally enforceable contract. The Court of Appeal held that the predecessor of section 179 contained a substantive and not merely a procedural rule.[82] May L.J. distinguished the cases on the Statutes of Frauds and the Limitation Acts, where the statutory language and context were different[83]; Lord Denning M.R. declared the reasoning in those cases to be unsatisfactory, the true distinction in the present context being between the existence of a contract (a question of substantive law) and remedies for breach (a procedural question).[84]

7–024   *Witnesses.* Whether a witness is competent[85] or compellable, or whether he can claim privilege,[86] all appear to be questions for the *lex fori*.[87] Of course, if, as is often the case, questions of competence, compellability or privilege depend on the matrimonial status of a witness, the question of status must be referred to the appropriate *lex causae* before the English rule of evidence can be applied.

7–025   *Functions of judge and jury.* Two questions arise in determining the functions of judge and jury: whether, in a given case, there should be trial by jury at all; and, if so, what are the respective functions of judge and jury. It is submitted that both these questions must be left exclusively to the *lex fori* since they involve issues of procedural convenience, and, it may be added, of public policy.[88]

7–026   *Burden of proof.* Although there is some authority for the proposition that, at common law, questions relating to the burden of proof are matters for the

---

[80] *Marie v. Garrison*, 13 Abb. N.C. 210 (1883); criticised by Lorenzen, p. 339, n. 59; *cf.* Cook, pp. 225–228.
[81] See Chap. 2.
[82] *Monterosso Shipping Co. Ltd. v. International Transport Workers' Federation* [1982] I.C.R. 675 (C.A.).
[83] At p. 685.
[84] At pp. 681–682.
[85] *Bain v. Whitehaven & Furness Junction Ry.* (1850) 3 H.L.C. 1, 19.
[86] For privilege claims under the Evidence (Proceedings in Other Jurisdictions) Act 1975, see *post*, para. 8–075.
[87] A dictum in *Re Atherton* [1912] 2 K.B. 251, 255–256 is contrary to the proposition in the text, but the actual decision turned on the interpretation of s.17(1) of the Bankruptcy Act 1883 (now repealed). *Cf. F. F. Seeley Nominees Pty. Ltd. v. El Ar Initiations (U.K.) Ltd.* (1990) 96 A.L.R. 468 (S. Austr.) (privilege against self-incrimination; offence under foreign law).
[88] See Hancock, pp. 148–153, who would leave the second question to the *lex causae*.

lex fori,[89] there is much to be said for treating them as substantive, for the outcome of a case can depend on where the burden of proof lies. As Lorenzen says,[90] "the statement that courts should enforce foreign substantive rights but not foreign procedural laws has no justifiable basis if the so-called procedural law would normally affect the outcome of the litigation." This is reflected in the Restatement proposition that where the primary purpose of the rule as to burden of proof in the *lex causae* is to affect decision of the issue rather than to regulate the conduct of the trial, it will be applied in preference to the rule in the *lex fori*.[91] This principle has been applied in many contexts, including some American cases on the burden of proving or disproving contributory negligence,[92] and the burden of proving that an insurer was given notice of an accident.[93]

In the case of a contract, the law governing the contract under the Rome **7–027** Convention on the Law Applicable to Contractual Obligations 1980, given effect in England by the Contracts (Applicable Law) Act 1990, applies to the extent that it contains, in the law of contract as opposed to the law of procedure, rules which determine the burden of proof.[94]

Presumptions. In order to determine whether presumptions are rules of **7–028** substance or rules of procedure, it is necessary to distinguish between three kinds of presumptions: presumptions of fact, and irrebuttable and rebuttable presumptions of law. Presumptions of fact arise when, on proof of certain basic facts, the trier of fact may, but need not, find the existence of a presumed fact. Presumptions of fact have, strictly speaking, no legal effect at all, and need not be considered here. So far as presumptions of law are concerned, there is a statutory rule that, in the case of a contract, the law governing the contract under the Rome Convention applies to the extent that it contains, in the law of contract as opposed to the law of procedure, rules which raise presumptions of law.[95] No distinction is drawn in this provision between presumptions of law which are rebuttable and those which are irrebuttable; it appears to apply to both categories. The distinction does, however, need to be observed in considering the position at common law. Irrebuttable presumptions of law arise when, on proof of the basic facts, the trier of fact must find the presumed fact in any event.[96] An example is the presumption of survivorship contained in section 184 of the Law of Property Act 1925. It is now generally agreed that, even for the purposes of domestic law, irrebuttable presumptions of law are rules of substance, and this is also true for the purpose of the conflict of laws.[97] Rebuttable presumptions of law arise when, on proof of the basic facts, the trier of fact must find the presumed fact unless the contrary is proved. For the purpose of the conflict of laws they must be further subdivided into those which apply only in certain contexts, and those which apply in all types of case. Examples of the first type are the presumptions of

---

[89] *The Roberta* (1937) 58 Ll.L.R. 159, 177; *In the Estate of Fuld (No. 3)* [1968] P. 675, 696–697. The law in Scotland is the same: Anton, p. 746, citing *Mackenzie v. Hall* (1854) 17 D. 164.
[90] Lorenzen, p. 134.
[91] s.133; and see Annot., 35 A.L.R. 3d 289.
[92] *Fitzpatrick v. International Ry.* 252 N.Y. 127, 169 N.E. 112 (1929). See Restatement, s.133, Illustrations 2–4.
[93] *Peterson v. Warren* 31 Wis. 2d 547, 143 N.W. 2d 560 (1966).
[94] Contracts (Applicable Law) Act 1990, s.2 and Sched. 1, Art. 14(1). See *post*, para. 32–054.
[95] Contracts (Applicable Law) Act 1990, s.2 and Sched. 1, Art. 14(1).
[96] *Cf. Cross and Tapper on Evidence* (8th ed. 1995), Chap. 3.
[97] *Re Cohn* [1945] Ch. 5.

resulting trust, advancement, satisfaction and ademption, and the presumptions contained in section 2 of the Perpetuities and Accumulations Act 1964 to the effect that a female under the age of twelve or over the age of fifty-five cannot have a child. All these are thought to be so closely connected with the existence of substantive rights that they ought to be characterised as rules of substance.[98]

7–029 Examples of the second type of presumptions are the presumptions of marriage,[99] legitimacy,[1] and death, which apply (although not always in precisely the same way) to all types of case. It is uncertain whether such presumptions are rules of substance or rules of procedure. In cases involving presumptions of marriage the courts have applied the *lex causae* whenever that law was proved[2]; and a dictum on the subject treats such a presumption as a rule of substance.[3] But where it is sought to base a presumption on cohabitation in a number of different countries, whose laws on the subject differ, the forum may have no option but to apply its own rule.[4] There is no direct authority on the question whether the common law presumptions of legitimacy and death are rules of substance or of procedure.

7–030 *Estoppel.* For the purposes of English domestic law, estoppel is sometimes said to be a rule of evidence.[5] Whether, for the purpose of this Rule, it should be regarded as a rule of substance or as a rule of procedure is an entirely open question, the answer to which may well vary with the type of estoppel under consideration. Thus the question whether a principal is estopped from denying his agent's authority to deal with a third party probably depends on the *lex causae*.[6] On the other hand, the question precisely when an estoppel by record arises probably depends on the *lex fori*,[7] although, of course that law may distinguish for this purpose between the effect of foreign and domestic judgments.[8]

7–031 **(4) Set-off and counterclaim.** Set-off is of two kinds. It may be a claim of a certain kind which the defendant has against the claimant and which can conveniently be tried together with the claim against the defendant. The

---

[98] Thus it was assumed in *Stevenson v. Masson* (1873) L.R. 17 Eq. 78 that the presumption of ademption was a rule of substance; *cf.* Wolff, s.221, who also explains *Re Cohn, supra,* on this ground.

[99] See *post,* paras. 17–045 *et seq.*

[1] Now much weakened by s.26 of the Family Law Reform Act 1969.

[2] *Hill v. Hibbit* (1870) 25 L.T. 183; *De Thoren v. Att.-Gen.* (1876) 1 App.Cas. 686. In *Re Shephard* [1904] 1 Ch. 456, *Re Taplin* [1937] 3 All E.R. 105 and *Mahadervan v. Mahadervan* [1964] P. 233 the court applied the English rule—but there was no evidence of a different rule of the *lex causae*. In *Leong Sow Nom v. Chin Yee You* [1934] 3 W.W.R. 686 (B.C.) (discussed by Falconbridge, pp. 314–315) the court refused to apply its own presumptions even though there was no evidence of the *lex causae*.

[3] *Mahadervan v. Mahadervan* [1964] P. 233, 242.

[4] *Cf. post,* paras. 17–046 *et seq.*

[5] *Low v. Bouverie* [1891] 3 Ch. 82, 105 (C.A.). See generally *Cross and Tapper on Evidence* (8th ed. 1995), pp. 107–108.

[6] *Post,* paras. 33–421 *et seq.* *Cf. Allen v. Hay* (1922) 69 D.L.R. 193 (Sup. Ct. Can.), suggesting that estoppel by conduct is a rule of substance for the present purpose. A dictum in *Cuthbertson v. Cuthbertson* [1952] 4 D.L.R. 814, 818 (Ont.) may perhaps suggest the contrary.

[7] *Vervaeke v. Smith* [1983] 1 A.C. 146, 162 (estoppel *per rem judicatam* based on an English judgment). The statement in *Carl Zeiss Stiftung v. Rayner & Keeler Ltd.* (*No.* 2) [1967] 1 A.C. 853, 919 that "estoppel is a matter for the *lex fori*" was made in this context and should, it is submitted, be restricted to it. See also Illustration 13, *post,* para. 7–054.

[8] Rules 35, 41 and especially paras. 14–112 *et seq., post.*

question whether a set-off of this kind can be raised in an action is one of procedure for the *lex fori*.[9] A set-off may, on the other hand, amount to an equity directly attaching to the claim[10] and operate in partial or total extinction thereof; an example is the *compensation de plein droit* of French law.[11] The question whether a set-off of this kind exists is one of substance for the *lex causae, i.e.* the law governing the claim which the defendant asserts has been discharged in whole or in part.[12] A counterclaim is a claim by the defendant which, though not operative by way of set-off, can conveniently be tried together with the claim against the defendant. The question whether a claim can be raised by way of counterclaim is one of procedure for the *lex fori*.[13]

(5) Priorities. The priorities as between claimants to a limited fund which   7–032 is being distributed by a court are governed by the *lex fori*.[14] The existence and quantification of each creditor's claim is of course a matter for the *lex causae* of the claim,[15] but once the claims are established the *lex fori* determines priorities, for the court "is primarily concerned in doing evenhanded justice between competing creditors whose respective claims to be a creditor may have arisen under a whole variety of different and, it may be, conflicting systems of national law."[16] The principle is well established[17]; a creditor can neither gain priority by virtue of a special rule in the foreign law governing his claim[18] nor lose priority by virtue of such a rule.[19] In order to assign a foreign claim to the appropriate class in the order of priorities under the *lex fori*, the court will examine the events on which the claim was founded and give the

---

[9] *Meyer v. Dresser* (1864) 16 C.B. (N.S.) 646. See also Case C–341/93 *Danvaern Production A/S v. Schuhfabriken Otterbeck GmbH & Co.* [1995] E.C.R. I–2053.

[10] See *Holmes v. Kidd* (1858) 3 H. & N. 891, and contrast *Re Overend, Gurney & Co.* (1868) L.R. 6 Eq. 344.

[11] See Rabel, Vol. 3 (2nd ed.), pp. 474–475; Wolff, pp. 233–234.

[12] See *MacFarlane v. Norris* (1862) 2 B. & S. 783, where, however, there does not appear to have been any conflict between the *lex fori* and the *lex causae; Meridien BIAO Bank GmbH v. Bank of New York* [1997] 1 Lloyd's Rep. 437 (C.A.); *cf. Allen v. Kemble* (1848) 6 Moo.P.C. 314, but in this case the *lex fori* was also the *lex causae; Rouquette v. Overmann* (1875) L.R. 10 Q.B. 525, 540–541. In *Maspons v. Mildred, Goyeneche & Co.* (1882) 9 Q.B.D. 530 (C.A.), affd. without reference to this point (1883) 8 App.Cas. 874, it is not clear whether English law was applied as *lex fori* or as *lex causae*: the contract sued upon was governed by English law. See Wood, *English and International Set-Off* (1989), Chap. 23.

[13] *South African Republic v. Compagnie Franco-Belge du Chemin de Fer du Nord* [1897] 2 Ch. 487 (C.A.).

[14] *Bankers Trust International Ltd. v. Todd Shipyards Corp.* (*The Halcyon Isle*) [1981] A.C. 221 (P.C.).

[15] *The Colorado* [1923] P. 102 (C.A.), as explained in *The Zigurds* [1932] P. 113 and *Bankers Trust International Ltd. v. Todd Shipyards Corp.* (*The Halcyon Isle*), *supra*.

[16] *Bankers Trust International Ltd. v. Todd Shipyards Corp.* (*The Halcyon Isle*) [1981] A.C. 221, 230–231 (P.C.).

[17] *The Milford* (1858) Swa. 362, approved in *The Tagus* [1903] P. 44; *The Jonathan Goodhue* (1859) Swa. 524; *The Union* (1860) Lush. 128; *Maspons v. Mildred, Goyeneche & Co.* (1882) 9 Q.B.D. 530 (C.A.), affd. without reference to this point (1883) 8 App.Cas. 874; *Re Kloebe* (1884) 28 Ch.D. 175; *Canada Deposit Insurance Corp. v. Canadian Commercial Bank* (1994) 121 D.L.R. (4th) 360 (Alta.). *Cf. Clark v. Bowring*, 1908 S.C. 1168; *Todd Shipyards Corp. v. Altema Compania Maritima S.A.* (*The Ioannis Daskalelis*) (1972) 32 D.L.R. (3d) 571 (Sup. Ct. Can.), disapproved in *Bankers Trust International Ltd. v. Todd Shipyards Corporation* (*The Halcyon Isle*) [1981] A.C. 221 (P.C.).

[18] *e.g. Pardo v. Bingham* (1868) L.R. 6 Eq. 485.

[19] *e.g. Ex p. Melbourn* (1870) L.R. 6 Ch.App. 64. Contrast *Cook v. Gregson* (1854) 2 Drew. 286 (foreign asset administered according to the priorities under the foreign law).

claim the priority to which it would be entitled under the *lex fori* if those events had occurred within the territorial jurisdiction of the court.[20]

7–033 The principle that priorities are governed by the *lex fori* is not, however, a universal one.[21] Thus it is probable that the priority of competing assignments of a debt is governed by the law applicable to the debt.[22] It is possible, also, that the priority of claims against foreign land is governed by the *lex situs*.[23]

7–034 **(6) Damages.** In the case of contracts, the assessment of damages is a matter for the *lex causae*. This is the effect of the Rome Convention, given effect in English law by the Contracts (Applicable Law) Act 1990: the law applicable to a contract by virtue of Articles 3 to 6 and 12 of the Convention governs, within the limits of the powers conferred on the court by its procedural law, the consequences of breach, including the assessment of damages so far as it is governed by rules of law.[24] In other cases, although there are dicta to the effect that damages depend on the *lex fori*,[25] it now seems clear that the law relating to damages is partly procedural and partly substantive.[26] A distinction must be drawn between remoteness and heads of damage, which are questions of substance governed by the *lex causae*, and measure or quantification of damages, which is a question of procedure governed by the *lex fori*.[27] The former include the question in respect of what items of loss the claimant can recover compensation. The latter includes the method to be used in assessing the monetary compensation which the defendant must pay in respect of those items of loss for which he is liable.

7–035 The distinction between remoteness of damage and measure of damages was drawn by Pilcher J. in *D'Almeida Araujo Lda. v. Sir Frederick Becker and Co. Ltd.*,[28] a case of contract decided before the enactment of the Contract (Applicable Law) Act 1990, where he applied the law governing the contract and not the *lex fori* to the former question.

7–036 The rule that questions of heads of damages are substantive applies to actions in tort as well as to actions in contract. Thus in *Boys v. Chaplin*[29] a

---

[20] *Bankers Trust International Ltd. v. Todd Shipyards Corp. (The Halcyon Isle)* [1981] A.C. 221 (P.C.); followed in *The Ship "Betty Ott" v. General Bills Ltd.* [1992] 1 N.Z.L.R. 655 (C.A.), which cited with approval the equivalent paragraph of text in the 11th ed.

[21] The statutory exception in Maritime Conventions Act 1911, s.7 (apportionment of salvage) was repealed by Merchant Shipping Act 1995, s.314, Sched. 12.

[22] Rule 118. Questions as to the priority of competing assignments must be distinguished from questions as to the validity of competing assignments: contrast *Kelly v. Selwyn* [1905] 2 Ch. 117, with *Republica de Guatemala v. Nunez* (1926) 42 T.L.R. 625; [1927] 1 K.B. 669 (C.A.).

[23] See *Norton v. Florence Land and Public Works Co.* (1877) 7 Ch.D. 332.

[24] Contracts (Applicable Law) Act 1990, s.2 and Sched. 1, Art. 10(1)(*c*). See *post*, paras. 32–198 *et seq.*

[25] *e.g. Kremezi v. Ridgway* [1949] 1 All E.R. 662, 664; *Kohnke v. Karger* [1951] 2 K.B. 670, 677.

[26] *Boys v. Chaplin* [1971] A.C. 356, 379.

[27] This distinction was recognised in *Boys v. Chaplin, supra*; *per* Lord Hodson at p. 379, *per* Lord Guest at pp. 381–382, *per* Lord Wilberforce at p. 393, *per* Lord Pearson at p. 395. See, to the same effect, *Breavington v. Godleman* (1988) 169 C.L.R. 41; *Waterhouse v. Australian Broadcasting Corp.* (1989) 86 A.C.T.R. 1, 19. *Cf.* Anton, p. 402.

[28] [1953] 2 Q.B. 329, following *Livesley v. Horst Co.* [1925] 1 D.L.R. 159 (Sup. Ct. Can.) and Cheshire, 4th ed., pp. 659–660. See further, for damages in contract, *post*, paras. 32–198 *et seq.*; for damages in tort, *post*, paras. 35–052 *et seq.*

[29] [1971] A.C. 356, *per* Lord Hodson at p. 379, *per* Lord Wilberforce at p. 393, *per* Lord Pearson at pp. 394–395. The dissentients were Lord Guest at p. 382 and Lord Donovan at p. 383.

majority of the House of Lords held that the question whether damages were recoverable for pain and suffering was a question of substance.

The proposition that remoteness or heads of damage are governed by the *lex*   **7–037** *causae* is supported by a number of cases in which it was held that the question whether a debt carries interest depends on the governing law of the debt.[30] It is further supported by a number of Scots cases in which it was held that no claim for *solatium* could be maintained in Scotland by the spouse or near relative of a person killed in a country by whose law no such claim was recognised.[31] The proposition that the quantification of damages is governed by the *lex fori* is illustrated by the fact that in an English court damages must be assessed once and for all except in cases where provisional damages are awarded in a personal injuries case.[32] An English court has no power to award periodical payments by way of damages, nor to increase an award of damages if the injuries become aggravated after a final judgment has been delivered. These rules would undoubtedly be applied even though different rules might exist in the *lex causae*.[33]

Statutory provisions limiting a defendant's liability are prima facie sub-   **7–038** stantive[34]; but the true construction of the statute may negative this view. The proper classification of rules which limit the amount of damages recoverable was considered by the High Court of Australia in *Stevens v. Head*,[35] a case involving an action arising out of a road accident in New South Wales brought by the plaintiff in Queensland. One of the questions facing the court was whether or not a provision in the Motor Accidents Act 1988 of New South Wales which limited the amount of damages which could be recovered in respect of non-economic loss was a substantive rule to be applied as part of the *lex causae*. Although a minority took the view that a rule which imposes a ceiling on damages is substantive—because it is not directed to governing or regulating the mode or conduct of court proceedings—the majority held that the statutory provision in question was procedural as it did not touch the heads of liability in respect of which damages might be awarded, but simply related to the quantification of damages. In *Caltex Singapore Pte Ltd. v. BP Shipping Ltd.*[36] Clarke J., while accepting that rules limiting liability are prima facie substantive, relied on *Stevens v. Head* and held that section 272 of the Singapore Merchant Shipping Act 1970 (and the equivalent English provision),[37] under which the defendant in a collision action has the right to limit liability, is not a substantive rule.

---

[30] See Rule 196; *cf.* Rule 195.
[31] *Kendrick v. Burnett* (1897) 25 R. 82; *Naftalin v. L.M.S.*, 1933 S.C. 259; *M'Elroy v. M'Allister*, 1949 S.C. 110; contrast *Kemp v. Piper* [1971] S.A.S.R. 25.
[32] Supreme Court Act 1981, s.32A (as inserted by Administration of Justice Act 1982, s.6).
[33] *Kohnke v. Karger* [1951] 2 K.B. 670; *Boys v. Chaplin* [1971] A.C. 356, 394.
[34] This is suggested by two dicta in *Cope v. Doherty* (1858) 4 K. & J. 367, 384–385, and (1858) 2 De G. & J. 614, 623. The actual decision has long been obsolete: see *The Amalia* (1863) 1 Moo.P.C.(N.S.). 471. Acts of indemnity are substantive: *cf. Phillips v. Eyre* (1870) L.R. 6 Q.B. 1 (Ex.Ch.). See *Allan J. Panozza & Co. Pty. Ltd. v. Allied Interstate (Qld.) Pty. Ltd.* [1976] 2 N.S.W.L.R. 192, especially at p. 198.
[35] (1993) 176 C.L.R. 433. For criticism of the decision see Opeskin (1993) 109 L.Q.R. 533. See also *Goryl v. Greyhound Australia Pty. Ltd.* (1994) 179 C.L.R. 463; *Rahim v. Crawther* (1997) 17 W.A.R. 559.
[36] [1996] 1 Lloyd's Rep. 286. This decision was overruled on other grounds in *The Herceg Novi* [1998] 4 All E.R. 238 (C.A.).
[37] Merchant Shipping Act 1894, s.503 (which was replaced by Merchant Shipping Act 1979, s.17). The 1979 Act has since been repealed and the current provision is Merchant Shipping Act 1995, s.185 (as amended by Merchant Shipping and Maritime Security Act 1997, s.15).

7–039   It may be questioned whether the approach adopted in these cases is either desirable in terms of policy or entirely consistent with the authorities. The primary purpose of classifying a rule as substantive or procedural is "to determine which rules will make the machinery of the forum court run smoothly as distinguished from those determinative of the rights of [the] parties."[38] From this perspective provisions or rules dealing with the measure of damages should not be seen as procedural in nature. Furthermore, a close reading of the leading authorities (in particular *Boys v. Chaplin*) suggests that the scope of the choice of law rule that the quantification of damages is governed by the *lex fori* should be restricted to rules relating to the method whereby damages are assessed (*e.g.* the English rule that damages are assessed once and for all) and should not encompass rules which fix or limit the extent of the defendant's liability.[39]

7–040   **(7) Statutes of limitations.** English law distinguishes two kinds of statutes of limitation: those which merely bar a remedy and those which extinguish a right[40]; this common law rule was well-established, although it was subjected to searching judicial criticism, doubting whether the distinction between "right" and "remedy" provided an acceptable basis on which to proceed.[41] Statutes of the former kind are procedural, while statutes of the latter kind are substantive. In general, the English law as to limitation of actions has been regarded as procedural,[42] but sections 3(2), 17 and 25(3) of the Limitation Act 1980 are probably substantive since they expressly extinguish the title of the former owner. Sometimes a statute creates an entirely new right of action unknown to the common law and at the same time imposes a shorter period of limitation than that applicable under the general law. An example is the Civil Liability (Contribution) Act 1978; where a person becomes entitled to a right to recover contribution under section 1 of that Act the limitation period is two years.[43] There is Scottish, Australian and American authority in favour of the view that such special periods of limitation are substantive[44] even though they are contained in a different statute from that creating the right.[45]

---

[38] *Tolofson v. Jensen* [1994] 3 S.C.R. 1022, 1072, *per* La Forest J.
[39] See the judgment of Mason C.J. in *Stevens v. Head* (1993) 176 C.L.R. 433, 448–451.
[40] *Phillips v. Eyre* (1870) L.R. 6 Q.B. 1, 29 (Exch. Ch.); *Black-Clawson Ltd. v. Papierwerke Waldhof-Aschaffenberg A.G.* [1975] A.C. 591, 630; *Higgins v. Ewing's Trustees*, 1925 S.C. 440, 449; *McKain v. R. W. Miller & Co. (South Australia) Pty. Ltd.* (1991) 174 C.L.R. 1 (High Ct. Australia). *Cf. Chase Securities Corp. v. Donaldson* (1945) 325 U.S. 304, 313.
[41] See the dissenting judgments in *McKain v. R. W. Miller & Co. (South Australia) Pty. Ltd.*, *supra*. See also *Tolofson v. Jensen*, *supra*, in which the Supreme Court of Canada, endorsing *Clark v. Naqvi* (1990) 63 D.L.R. (4th) 361 (N.B.C.A.), rejected the traditional common law classification of statutes of limitation and the distinction between right and remedy on which it is based and held that statutes of limitation are to be classified as substantive; *Michalski v. Olson* [1998] 3 W.W.R. 37 (Man.C.A.).
[42] *Williams v. Jones* (1811) 13 East 439; *Ruckmaboye v. Mottichund* (1851) 8 Moo.P.C. 4; *Commonwealth of Australia v. Dixon* (1988) 13 N.S.W.L.R. 601; *Byrnes v. Groote Eylandt Mining Co. Pty. Ltd.* (1990) 19 N.S.W.L.R. 13; *Clark v. Naqvi* (1990) 63 D.L.R. (4th) 361 (N.B. C.A.).
[43] Limitation Act 1980, s.10.
[44] *Goodman v. L.N.W. Ry.* (1877) 14 S.L.R. 449; *M'Elroy v. M'Allister*, 1949 S.C. 110, 125–128, 137; *Maxwell v. Murphy* (1957) 96 C.L.R. 261; *The Harrisburg*, 119 U.S. 199 (1886); *cf. Bournias v. Atlantic Maritime Co.*, 220 F.2d 152 (2d Cir. 1955); contrast *Kerr v. Palfrey* [1970] V.R. 825.
[45] *Davis v. Mills*, 194 U.S. 451 (1904). See Restatement, s.143, comment *c*.

Where proceedings in England concern a matter which is under English   **7–041**
choice of law rules to be governed by English law, *i.e.* English law is both the
lex fori and the *lex causae*, nothing turns upon the classification of the English
statute of limitations which is applicable in any event. Where the *lex causae*
is that of a foreign country difficult questions can arise. The English law on
this point has been greatly simplified by the Foreign Limitation Periods Act
1984, but an account of the position at common law will indicate the difficulties it sought to resolve.[46]

The position at common law. The *lex causae* and the *lex fori* may differ not   **7–042**
only in their periods of limitation but also in the nature of their limitation
provisions. In considering foreign rules as to limitation the English courts
applied their own classification based on the distinction between barring a
right and extinguishing a remedy. The position resulting from this approach,
which would still be adopted in countries following the English common law
rules, can be illustrated by reference to the different situations which can arise:
(i) if the statutes of limitation of the *lex causae* and of the *lex fori* are both
procedural, an action will fail if it is brought after the period of limitation of
the *lex fori* has expired although that of the *lex causae* has not yet expired[47];
but will succeed if the period of limitation of the *lex fori* has not yet expired
although that of the *lex causae* has expired.[48] The first limb of this rule may
still leave it open to the defeated claimant to seek his remedy in another
jurisdiction. But its second limb has been criticised in that it may in effect
enable a creditor to enlarge his rights by choosing a suitable forum; and that
it may cause injustice to a debtor who, in reliance of the *lex causae*, has
destroyed his receipts.[49] (ii) If the statute of limitation of the *lex causae* is
substantive but that of the *lex fori* is procedural, the *lex fori* will probably
apply if its period of limitation is shorter than that of the *lex causae* on the
ground that it is inconvenient for the *forum* to hear what it considers to be stale
claims.[50] But once a substantive period of limitation of the *lex causae* has
expired, no action can be maintained even though a procedural period of
limitation imposed by the *lex fori* has not yet expired: in such a case there is

---

[46] For the similar process of reform in Australia see the Law Reform Commission's Report No.
58 on choice of law and *Gardner v. Wallace* (1995) 184 C.L.R. 95, which examines the drafting
and effect of the uniform legislation which was enacted in response to the report.

[47] *Don v. Lippmann* (1837) 5 Cl. & F. 1, where it is, however, not clear whether Scots law was
applied as *lex fori* or as the law of the debtor's residence; *Dupleix v. De Roven* (1705) 2 Vern.
540 supports the proposition in the text but was not decided on the principles here discussed;
see also *Re Lorillard* [1922] 2 Ch. 638 (C.A.); *Allard v. Charbonneau* [1953] 2 D.L.R. 442
(Ont. C.A.).

[48] *Huber v. Steiner* (1835) 2 Bing.N.C. 202; *Harris v. Quine* (1869) L.R. 4 Q.B. 653, approved
in *Re Low* [1894] 1 Ch. 147, 162 (C.A.) and *Black-Clawson International Ltd. v. Papierwerke
Waldhof-Aschaffenburg A.G.* [1975] A.C. 591; *Alliance Bank of Simla v. Carey* (1880) 5 C.P.D.
429; *Finch v. Finch* (1876) 45 L.J.Ch. 816; *Société Anonyme Métallurgique de Prayon v.
Koppel* (1933) 77 S.J. 800; *Carvell v. Wallace* (1873) 9 N.S.R. 165; *Bondholders Securities
Corporation v. Manville* [1933] 4 D.L.R. 699 (Sask. C.A.); *Waung v. Subbotovsky* (1969) 121
C.L.R. 337; *Pederson v. Young* (1964) 110 C.L.R. 162; *Scotland v. Bargen* (1982) 39 A.L.R.
644; *McKain v. R. W. Miller & Co. (South Australia) Pty. Ltd.* (1991) 174 C.L.R. 1 (High Ct.
Australia).

[49] Wolff, s.219. See the dissenting judgments in *McKain v. R. W. Miller & Co. (South Australia)
Pty. Ltd., supra.*

[50] *British Linen Co. v. Drummond* (1830) 10 B. & C. 903 (see p. 909, n. (*c*) for the substantive
nature of the Scots rule there under discussion). This case was approved in *Fergusson v. Fyffe*
(1841) 8 Cl. & F. 121. See, to similar effect, *C.(D.H.) v. T.(D.H.)* (1987) 11 R.F.L. 147 (N.S.).
Cf. Lopez v. Burslem (1843) 4 Moo.P.C. 300.

simply no right left to be enforced.[51] (iii) If the statutes of limitation of the *lex causae* and of the *lex fori* are both substantive, it is probable that the same results would follow as in the case just considered.[52] (iv) If the statute of the *lex causae* is procedural and that of the *lex fori* substantive, strict logic might suggest that neither applies, so that the claim remains perpetually enforceable. A notorious decision of the German Supreme Court once actually reached this absurd result.[53] But writers have suggested various ways of escape from this dilemma,[54] and it seems probable that a court would apply one statute or the other.

7–043   *Under the Foreign Limitation Periods Act 1984.* The Act was based on the recommendations of the Law Commission.[55] It adopts the general principle, subject to an exception based on public policy, that the limitation rules of the *lex causae* are to be applied in actions in England,[56] even if those rules do not lay down any limitation period for the claim.[57] English limitation rules are not to be applied unless English law is the *lex causae* or one of two *leges causae* governing the matter.[58] The double actionability rule as to foreign torts, which applies to acts or omissions occurring before the entry into force of Part III of the Private International Law (Miscellaneous Provisions) Act 1995[59] and to defamation claims as defined by section 13 of the 1995 Act,[60] illustrates the case of two *leges causae*.[61] In such a case the limitation rules of the law both of England and of the relevant foreign country will apply and the expiry of either limitation period will bar the action. The applicable provisions of the foreign *lex causae* are defined to include both procedural and substantive rules with respect to a limitation period,[62] but any renvoi is excluded[63] and the English court must disregard any rule under which a limitation period is or may be extended or interrupted in respect of the absence of a party from any specified jurisdiction or country.[64] If the foreign *lex causae* confers a discretion, an English court must so far as is practicable exercise that discretion in the manner in which it is exercised in comparable cases by the courts of the foreign country.[65] English law as the *lex fori* does, however, determine

---

[51] Thus in *Harris v. Quine* (1869) L.R. 4 Q.B. 653, 658 it was said that the decision would have gone the other way had the Manx statute of limitations been substantive; *cf.* similar dicta in *Huber v. Steiner* (1835) 2 Bing.N.C. 202, 210. *Cf.* also *Black-Clawson International Ltd. v. Papierwerke Waldhof-Aschaffenburg A.G.* [1975] A.C. 591.

[52] *Cf. Kuhne & Nagel A.G. Zurich v. A.P.A. Distributors Pty. Ltd.*, 1981 (3) S.A. 536 (W.), applying the *lex causae* in preference to the *lex fori* in such a case.

[53] (1882) 7 R.G.Z. 21. More recent German decisions have refused to follow this precedent.

[54] Beckett (1934) 15 B.Y.I.L. 46, 76–77; Cook, pp. 220 *et seq.*; Falconbridge, pp. 292–295.

[55] *Classification of Limitation in Private International Law.* Law Com. No. 114 (1982). For commentaries on the Act, see Carter (1985) 101 L.Q.R. 68; Stone [1985] L.M.C.L.Q. 497.

[56] The same principle applies to arbitrations whose seat is in England: Arbitration Act 1996, s.13. See Hill (1997) 46 I.C.L.Q. 274, 297.

[57] *Dubai Bank Ltd. v. Abbas* [1998] I.L.Pr. 391.

[58] s.1(1)(2).

[59] Part III came into force on May 1, 1996: S.I. 1996 No. 995.

[60] See *post*, paras. 35–014 *et seq.*

[61] *Metall und Rohstoff A.G. v. Donaldson, Lufkin and Jenrette Inc.* [1990] Q.B. 391 (C.A.); *Re ERAS EIL Actions* [1992] 1 Lloyd's Rep. 570 (C.A.). For the application of s.1(2) in a different factual context see *Gotha City v. Sotheby's, The Times*, October 8, 1998.

[62] s.4.

[63] ss.1(5), 4(2).

[64] s.2(3); but rules relating to extensions, etc., for other reasons, *e.g.* infancy, are applicable: s.4(1)(*a*).

[65] s.1(4).

whether, and the time at which, proceedings have been commenced[66]; that is, the *terminus ad quem* of the limitation period prescribed by a foreign *lex causae* is to be determined by English law.[67]

To the general principle, there is one major exception. The principle is not **7–044** to be applied to the extent that it conflicts with English public policy.[68] Where there is such a conflict, section 1 of the Act does not apply.[69] The effect is that the issue is then governed by the common law principles, under which the limitation periods prescribed by English law as the *lex fori* will be applied. It is declared that there is a conflict with public policy to the extent that undue hardship would be caused to a person who is, or might be, a party.[70] A finding of "undue hardship" must depend on all the circumstances of the particular case; it was found present where defendants had agreed to an extension of time which turned out to be ineffectual under the foreign *lex causae*[71] and in a case involving a foreign limitation period of only 12 months, where the plaintiff had spent some time in hospital and had been led to believe that her claim would be met.[72] In a dispute involving competing claims to personal property, it has been held (*obiter*) that it would be contrary to public policy to allow a foreign limitation rule to be relied upon by a thief or by any transferee of stolen property other than a purchaser in good faith.[73] It has also been suggested that a foreign limitation period may be disapplied in a situation where the action has become time barred as a consequence of the defendant's deliberate concealment of relevant facts.[74] However, the mere fact that the foreign limitation period is shorter than the English period does not, without more, give rise to "undue hardship".[75] Similarly, it is not contrary to public policy to apply a foreign limitation period under section 1 simply on the ground that the foreign law does not have an equivalent of section 33 of the Limitation Act 1980 (under which the limitation period may be disapplied in certain circumstances).[76] If within the foreign limitation period the claimant acquires all the material required for bringing the action, it is not contrary to public policy to apply the foreign rule even if he is only a few days late in commencing proceedings.[77] The exception may also be relied upon in cases where the foreign *lex causae* does not lay down a limitation period at all or where the foreign limitation period is significantly longer than that under English law; in appropriate circumstances the English court might decline to apply the foreign rule, holding that the action must fail. In any case in which a claim is made for equitable relief, and the claim is not statute-barred, the English courts have a discretion to withhold relief, for example on the grounds of acquiescence or laches; the Act does not prevent the exercise of this

---

[66] s.1(3).
[67] Including Limitation Act 1980, s.35, in relation to claims by way of set-off, counterclaims, and to the addition or substitution of new claims or parties: s.1(3).
[68] s.2(1).
[69] *Ibid.*
[70] s.2(2). See Law Com. No. 114 (1982), paras. 4.44–4.48 for a discussion of possible cases of hardship.
[71] *The Komninos S* [1990] 1 Lloyd's Rep. 541 (revd. but not on this point, [1991] 1 Lloyd's Rep. 370 (C.A.)).
[72] *Jones v. Trollope Colls Cementation Overseas Ltd., The Times*, January 26, 1990 (C.A.).
[73] See *Gotha City v. Sotheby's, The Times*, October 8, 1998.
[74] *Ibid.*
[75] *Durham v. T & N Noble plc*, May 1, 1996 (unrep.).
[76] *Connelly v. RTZ Corporation plc (No. 2)*, December 2, 1998 (unrep.).
[77] *Arab Monetary Fund v. Hashim* [1996] 1 Lloyd's Rep. 589 (C.A.).

discretion but does require the court to have regard to the provisions of the foreign *lex causae*.[78]

7–045   The Act does not affect any action commenced in England before October 1, 1985, the date on which it was brought into force, nor any matter in respect of which the limitation period would, apart from the Act, have expired before that date.[79]

7–046   *Contracts (Applicable Law) Act 1990.*   The law applicable to a contract by virtue of Articles 3 to 6 and 12 of the Rome Convention, given effect by the Contracts (Applicable Law) Act 1990, governs prescription and the limitation of actions.[80] This application of the *lex causae* achieves the same result as the Foreign Limitation Periods Act 1984. The application of the governing law under the 1990 Act may be refused if its application would be manifestly contrary to English public policy,[81] whereas under the 1984 Act the relevant public policy is indicated by the "undue hardship" provision of the 1984 Act.[82]

7–047   *Other rules imposing time-limits.*   There are two questions raising issues similar to those arising in connection with statutes of limitations which can be considered here. They do not concern limitation periods and are not within the scope of the 1984 Act.

7–048   First, there are certain legal rights which must be exercised within a reasonable time, for example, the right to repudiate a marriage settlement made during minority or the right to rescind a contract for misrepresentation. The *lex fori* might differ from the *lex causae* in its method of calculating what was a reasonable time: thus under one system time might run from the making of the contract and under the other from the time when the party purporting to rescind discovered his rights. It seems that such matters should be determined by the *lex causae* since the relevant rules operate, if at all, so wholly to extinguish the right to rescind; and since the application of foreign rules will not cause any procedural inconvenience.[83] Where the case falls within the scope of the Rome Convention as given effect by the Contracts (Applicable Law) Act 1990, the matter is governed by the applicable law, which is declared to govern "the various ways of extinguishing obligations, and prescription and limitation of actions."[84] Secondly, a contract may itself provide a period of limitation shorter than that imposed by the general law. Such a provision, which is analogous to one limiting or agreeing damages,[85] will also be governed by the applicable law.[86]

---

[78] s.4(3).

[79] s.7(3). See *Jones v. Trollope Colls Cementation Overseas Ltd., The Times*, January 26, 1990 (C.A.): it is immaterial that the event giving rise to the action occurred before October 1985.

[80] Contracts (Applicable Law) Act 1990, Sched. 1, Art. 10(1)(*d*). See *post*, para. 32–206.

[81] *Ibid.*, Sched. 1, Art. 16.

[82] *i.e.*, s.2(2), considered above. See *post*, para. 32–206, for the view that Art. 16 does not impose a stricter test than the 1984 Act.

[83] See, to similar effect, Law Com. No. 114 (1982), paras. 4.52–4.53.

[84] Contracts (Applicable Law) Act 1990, Sched. 1, Art. 10(1)(*d*).

[85] *Cf. Godard v. Gray* (1870) L.R. 6 Q.B. 139, 147–148.

[86] *Cf. Allan J. Panozza & Co. Pty. Ltd. v. Allied Interstate (Qld.) Pty. Ltd.* [1976] 2 N.S.W.L.R. 192 (N.S.W.C.A.) (contractual term requiring notice of any loss to be given to carrier within five days was held to be procedural).

(8) Miscellaneous cases. It has been suggested that the question whether   7–049
a debtor is entitled to contribution from a co-debtor is governed by the *lex fori*
as it "depends not upon contract but upon equity."[87] But it is hard to see why
the forum should always apply its own views of "equity" to such a question.
The *lex causae* is applied in most circumstances as a result of the Contracts
(Applicable Law) Act 1990. The effect of Article 13(2) of the Rome Convention, given effect by the 1990 Act, appears to be that where several persons are
subject to the same contractual claim and one of them has satisfied the
creditor, the law which governs the claim also determines whether that person
may exercise the rights which the creditor had against the other debtor, and if
so whether he may do so in full or only to a limited extent. The precise scope
of Article 13 is unclear; its heading speaks of "subrogation," which may
suggest a more limited scope than appears from the text of the Article
itself.

The question whether a civil action can be brought in respect of acts
constituting a crime before criminal proceedings have been taken in the matter
is one of procedure.[88]

There is virtually no English authority[89] on the question whether the rules   7–050
which determine whether an action lies at the suit of, or against, the representatives of a deceased person are substantive or procedural. The predominant American view is that these rules are substantive.[90] The related
question whether the death of a human being gives rise to an action at the suit
of a third party who has suffered loss as a result of the death is also one of
substance.[91]

Opinion is divided on the question whether the rules which determine the   7–051
tortious liability of spouses towards one another are substantive or procedural.[92] In English domestic law, section 1(1) of the Law Reform (Husband
and Wife) Act 1962 provides that "the parties to a marriage shall have the like
right of action in tort against each other as if they were not married." Section
1(2) provides that the court may stay such an action if (a) no substantial
benefit would accrue to either party from its continuation; or (b) the case could
more conveniently be disposed of under section 17 of the Married Women's
Property Act 1882. Section 1(2) is procedural, for its objects are to protect the
courts from the task of having to try petty domestic disputes, to determine in
which courts disputes as to the title or possession of property are to be tried,
and to ensure that the availability of an action in tort does not oust the court's
jurisdiction under section 17 of the Act of 1882. Section 1(1) is harder to
classify, but for the present purpose it seems to be immaterial which classification is adopted. In the present context, three problems may arise where

---

[87] *American Surety Co. of New York v. Wrightson* (1910) 103 L.T. 663, 665.
[88] *Scott v. Seymour* (1862) 1 H. & C. 219.
[89] An *obiter dictum* in *Batthyany v. Walford* (1887) 36 Ch.D. 269, 278 may suggest that the
     question is one of procedure.
[90] Restatement, s.124, Illustration 2, and s.167; Currie, Chap. 3; and see *post*, paras.
     35–033—35–034, 35–041.
[91] *Kendrick v. Burnett* (1897) 25 R. 82, 89; *cf. Naftalin v. L.M.S.*, 1933 S.C. 259; *M'Elroy v.
     M'Allister*, 1949 S.C. 110. See *post*, para. 35–055.
[92] Wolff, s.222, and Hancock, pp. 235–236 regard these rules as substantive; but see also Hancock
     (1962) 29 U. of Chic.L.Rev. 237, commenting on *Haumschild v. Continental Casualty Co.*, 7
     Wis. 2d 130, 95 N.W. 2d 814 (1959), where the court found it unnecessary to determine
     whether such rules were substantive or procedural. Kahn-Freund (1952) 15 M.L.R. 133 shows
     that in English domestic law the rules are partly substantive and partly procedural. And see
     post, para. 35–040.

proceedings are brought in England by one spouse against the other on a tort governed by a foreign law. (1) If the *lex causae*[93] allowed the proceedings, they would succeed in England however section 1(1) was classified, but the court could stay them. (2) If the *lex causae* contained a substantive prohibition against such proceedings, they would fail in England, for, even if the English rules were procedural, they could not operate on a cause of action non-existent by its proper law. (3) The most difficult case is where the *lex causae* contains a prohibition against such proceedings which is purely procedural in the English sense: a rule of the *lex causae* prohibiting proceedings during marriage but permitting them after divorce might be classified in this way. Strict logic would suggest that the proceedings could be brought in England even during the continuance of the marriage, and it would again be immaterial whether section 1(1) of the 1962 Act was substantive or procedural.[94] But this result is open to the objection that it may lead to "forum shopping"; and it is no answer to say that the court can stay the proceedings, for the statutory grounds for taking this course may not exist. It might therefore be better to dismiss the proceedings even if the rule of the *lex causae* is procedural. This course would certainly not cause any procedural inconvenience in England.

Illustrations

(1) Nature of Remedy and Method of Enforcement

7–052   1. A, the owner of a French copyright, brings an action against X in England claiming various remedies for infringement. In France, A could not have obtained an injunction against X. He can obtain an injunction against X in England.[95]

2. A and X are domiciled in Greece, A is the daughter of X. A, who has just been married, claims that by Greek law X is under an obligation to provide her with a dowry. A's claim is dismissed, not because it is unknown to English law, but because by Greek law the amount of the dowry is within the discretion of the court and varies in accordance with X's wealth and social position and the number of his children, and with A's behaviour. English law therefore has no remedy for giving effect to Greek law.[96]

(2) Parties

7–053   3. A company which was incorporated in Russia is dissolved by a Russian decree. This decree is recognised in England, so that, according to English law, the company ceases to exist. The decree is not recognised in France so that, according to French law, the company continues to exist. An action cannot be maintained in England in the name of the company to recover a debt governed by French law.[97]

4. Y in Ireland obtains a judgment against X which he subsequently assigns to A. By an Irish statute such assignments are permitted and the assignees are entitled to sue in their own names. By English law, an assignee can only sue the debtor by joining the assignor as a party to the action. A can sue X in his own name in England.[98]

5. X's ship damages A's pier in Spain because of the negligence of the master and crew. By Spanish law, the master and crew are liable for the damage but X is not. By English law, the master and crew and X are all liable. X cannot be sued in England.[99]

---

[93] As to what is the *lex causae* see *post*, para. 35–040.

[94] This would only be material if s.1(1) *restricted* a right existing under a substantive provision of the *lex causae*, but it plainly cannot have this effect.

[95] *Baschet v. London Illustrated Standard* [1900] 1 Ch. 73.

[96] *Phrantzes v. Argenti* [1960] 2 Q.B. 19.

[97] *Banque Internationale de Commerce de Petrograd v. Goukassow* [1923] 2 K.B. 682 (C.A.); revd. on other grounds [1925] A.C. 150.

[98] *O'Callaghan v. Thomond* (1810) 3 Taunt. 82.

[99] *The Mary Moxham* (1876) 1 P.D. 107 (C.A.).

6. X, a member of a Scots partnership, is sued in England for a partnership debt. By Scots law, all the other members of the firm, or the firm itself, have to be joined in the action. By English law this is not necessary. X can be sued alone in England.[1]

7. K had a claim against A & Co. for £100,000. In November 1973 he left his residence in Paris and disappeared. In February 1974 a court in Lebanon appointed X as administrator of K's property, K being declared an absentee. In Lebanese law, X could pursue K's claim, suing in his own name. In English law, unless an absent claimant is presumed dead there is no way in which another can sue on his behalf. X's action in England is dismissed.[2]

(3) Evidence

8. A sues X in England to recover back £200 paid by A to X for shares in a projected foreign   **7–054**
company. To prove payment of the £200, A tenders unstamped receipts given in Prussia. By Prussian law, such receipts are inadmissible in evidence. By English law they are admissible. The receipts are admissible.[3]

9. T orally agrees to make a will in favour of A by forgiving him a debt. A is domiciled in Nevada; the contract is made there and the debt is secured by a mortgage on land in Nevada. T dies domiciled in California without having fulfilled his promise. X is his executor. The contract is valid by the law of Nevada. By a Californian statute, contracts to make a will are "invalid unless the same or some note or memorandum thereof is in writing subscribed by the party to be charged or his agent." A can recover damages from X in California, wherever T was domiciled at the date of the contract.[4]

10. A sues X in New York for personal injuries inflicted by X upon A in Ontario. By New York law, A can only succeed if he can prove that he was not guilty of contributory negligence. By Ontario law, X's liability is reduced if he can show that A was guilty of contributory negligence. The burden of proving contributory negligence is on X.[5]

11. M, domiciled in Germany, by will leaves movable property to her daughter D, also domiciled in Germany, if D survives M. M and D are killed in England in circumstances rendering it uncertain which of them survived the other. By English law, D is, for all purposes affecting the title to property, deemed to have survived M. By German law, M and D are presumed to have died simultaneously. Both these rules are rules of substance so that the German rule applies and D takes no interest under M's will.[6]

12. A wife domiciled in a foreign country there deposits a sum of money in a bank in the name of her husband. By the law of that country, this transaction gives rise to a presumption of advancement. By English law it does not. *Semble*, an English court will apply the foreign presumption and hold that the husband is beneficially entitled to the money.

13. W divorces H in England on the ground of his adultery with Q and subsequently publishes abroad the statement that H has committed adultery with Q. Under the law of the place of publication, H could, in a defamation action against W, give evidence in disproof of the alleged adultery with Q; in English domestic law an estoppel by record would prevent him from giving such evidence.[7] The estoppel by record would (*semble*) operate in an action in England on the alleged foreign tort.

(4) Set-Off and Counterclaim

14. X contracts with A in Prussia for the carriage of goods from Memel to London. Part of the   **7–055**
goods is not shipped, and X deducts £41, the value of that part, from the freight due under the contract. By Prussian law X in these circumstances has the right to set off the £41, but there is no partial extinction of the liability to pay freight. By English law, the £41 could not be set off. A sues X for freight in England. X is not entitled in the English proceedings to set off the £41 against the freight due to A.[8]

(5) Priorities

15. In an action *in rem* in England against an Argentine ship, claims are made by the master   **7–056**
and by a mortgagee. By Argentine law, the master has priority in respect of wages paid during the

---

[1] *Bullock v. Caird* (1875) L.R. 10 Q.B. 276; *cf. Re Doetsch* [1896] 2 Ch. 836.

[2] *Kamouh v. Associated Electrical Industries International Ltd.* [1980] Q.B. 199.

[3] *Bristow v. Sequeville* (1850) 5 Exch. 275.

[4] *Bernkrant v. Fowler*, 55 Cal. 2d 588, 360 P. 2d 906 (1961).

[5] *Fitzpatrick v. International Ry.* 252 N.Y. 127, 169 N.E. 112 (1929); *cf. Central Vermont Ry. v. White*, 238 U.S. 507 (1914).

[6] *Re Cohn* [1945] Ch. 5.

[7] *Cross and Tapper on Evidence* (8th ed. 1995), pp. 80 *et seq.*

[8] *Meyer v. Dresser* (1864) 12 C.B. (N.S.) 646.

last voyage only. By English law he has priority in respect of all wages. The master is entitled to priority in respect of all wages.[9]

16. In an action *in rem* in England against a French ship, claims are made by A, the holder of a French *hypothèque*, and by B, an English necessaries man. By French law, necessaries men have priority over holders of *hypothèques*. By English law, necessaries men are postponed to mortgagees of a ship. A has priority over B. French law governs the existence and scope of A's claim, but English law determines priorities, and the proper classification for those purposes, of the *hypothèque*.[10]

17. In an action *in rem* in England against a foreign ship, claims are made by A, a New York necessaries man, and by B, a mortgagee of the ship. By English law necessaries men are postponed to mortgagees. By the law of the United States, necessaries men have a maritime lien and enjoy priority over mortgagees. The court will not recognise A's claim to a maritime lien, for had the repairs carried out by A been executed in England no maritime lien would have been created. Accordingly B has priority.[11]

18. H and W were domiciled in Java and married there. H by ante-nuptial marriage contract settled a sum of money on W for her separate use. By the law of Java, claims arising out of such a contract were postponed to the claims of all third parties unless the contract was registered. H subsequently came to England where he was made bankrupt. In the English bankruptcy proceedings, W was entitled to prove against H's estate in respect of the debt created by the marriage contract in competition with H's other creditors although the contract was not registered.[12]

(6) Damages

7–057   19. A is injured in a road accident in Malta as a result of X's negligence. A and X are British servicemen ordinarily resident in England and temporarily stationed in Malta. By Maltese law A could only recover damages for financial loss directly suffered, expenses, and loss of wages—in this case, £53. By English law, he could also recover damages for pain and suffering—in this case, a further £2,250. English law applies and A can recover £2,303—but not because the question of "heads of damage" is procedural.[13]

(7) Limitation of Actions

7–058   20. X is indebted to A under a contract governed by Scots law. By that law, A's right is extinguished after 40 years. By English law, A's remedy is barred after six years. After 10 years, A sues X in England. The action fails[14]; but after the coming into effect of the Foreign Limitation Periods Act 1984 the action may proceed.[15]

21. The facts are as in Illustration 20, except that A commences his action after 25 years, having given X to understand many years before that no action would be brought. The additional facts were immaterial before the coming into effect of the Foreign Limitation Periods Act 1984. Thereafter, the English court may decline on grounds of public policy to apply the Scots limitation rule because of the hardship to X; the English rule will then apply, and the action will fail.[16] After the coming into force of the Contracts (Applicable Law) Act 1990, the Scottish limitation rule will apply unless its application would be manifestly contrary to public policy.[17]

22. A is defamed in a foreign country by X. A sues X in England. The claim is statute-barred by English law but not by the *lex loci delicti*. The action fails.[18]

23. A is injured in a road accident in Pakistan caused by the negligence of an employee of X & Co. Immediately after the accident A is flown to Germany where she spends seven months in

---

[9] *The Tagus* [1903] P. 44.
[10] *The Colorado* [1923] P. 102 (C.A.) as interpreted in *Bankers Trust International Ltd. v. Todd Shipyards Corporation* (*The Halcyon Isle*) [1981] A.C. 221 (P.C.).
[11] *Bankers Trust International Ltd. v. Todd Shipyards Corporation* (*The Halcyon Isle*) [1981] A.C. 221 (P.C.). *Cf. Todd Shipyards Corporation v. Altema Compania Maritima S.A.* (*The Ioannis Daskalelis*) (1972) 32 D.L.R. (3d) 571 (Sup.Ct.Can.).
[12] *Ex p. Melbourn* (1870) L.R. 6 Ch.App. 64.
[13] *Boys v. Chaplin* [1971] A.C. 356; discussed *post*, paras. 35–006 *et seq.*
[14] *British Linen Co. v. Drummond* (1830) 10 B. & C. 903.
[15] Foreign Limitation Periods Act 1984, s.1. Contracts (Applicable Law) Act 1990, Sched. 1, Art. 10(1)(c) achieves the same result.
[16] Foreign Limitation Periods Act 1984, ss.1, 2.
[17] Contracts (Applicable Law) Act 1990, Sched. 1, Art. 16; see para. 5–009, *ante*.
[18] *Cf. M'Elroy v. M'Allister* 1949 S.C. 110; Foreign Limitation Periods Act 1984, s.1(1)(2).

hospital. In correspondence with A, a representative of X & Co suggests that A's claim will be settled. A starts proceedings in England within the three-year limitation period laid down by English law, but after the expiry of the one-year limitation period under Pakistani law. The rule of Pakistani law, according to which A's claim is time-barred, is disapplied on the ground that, in the circumstances, its application would cause undue hardship.[19]

---

[19] *Jones v. Trollope Colls Cementation Overseas Ltd.*, *The Times*, January 26, 1990 (C.A.).

CHAPTER 8

INTERNATIONAL LITIGATION: PROTECTIVE MEASURES AND JUDICIAL ASSISTANCE

8–001   Recent years have seen a large growth in cross-border litigation, and this Chapter is concerned with a number of significant procedural issues in the conduct of international litigation. The topics examined in this chapter are (1) injunctions to restrain removal or dissipation of assets before judgment (*Mareva* injunctions or freezing injunctions); (2) judicial assistance and service of process; (3) judicial assistance and the taking of evidence abroad; and (4) the taking of security for costs.

8–002   **(1) Injunctions to restrain removal or dissipation of assets before judgment: the *Mareva* or freezing injunction.** Relaxation of exchange controls and the development of electronic banking have made the international transfer of funds easy and almost instantaneous. These developments have led to a much greater attention to the need for interim protection to ensure the enforceability of judgments and to prevent defendants from frustrating their effectiveness by moving funds from one country to another.[1] Provisional and protective measures have two main objects: the first is to ensure that, reading final determination of a dispute, the status quo will be maintained; a second, and related, object is to secure the ultimate judgment of the court by preventing the defendant from disposing of assets pending final determination of the proceedings. The first object is achieved in English law by the interlocutory injunction, and by similar orders in other systems of law; the second object is achieved in England by a special form of interim injunction known as the *Mareva* injunction,[2] and in countries not following the English system by judicial attachments of assets.

8–003   Before 1975 there was no effective procedure available in England whereby a claimant could seize the assets of a defendant before obtaining judgment. Until the nineteenth century the process of "foreign attachment" was available as part of the custom of London, but it fell into disuse after it was decided by the House of Lords that it was not available where the garnishee was (as it frequently would be) a corporation.[3] Nor was it thought possible for a

---

[1] See generally on protective measures in international cases Collins (1992) *Recueil des Cours*, III, p. 9, reprinted in Collins, *Essays*, p. 1; Fallon (1993) 7 Rev. dr. Univ. Libre Bruxelles 43; Vareilles-Sommières, 1996 *Rev. Crit.* 397; Bermann (1997) 35 Col. J. Tr. L. 553. See also International Law Association, Committee on International Civil and Commercial Litigation, *Provisional and Protective Measures in International Litigation*, Second Interim Report, 1996.

[2] Described as a "freezing injunction" in CPR 25.1(1)(f).

[3] *Mayor and Aldermen of the City of London v. London Joint Stock Bank* (1881) 6 App.Cas. 393. See *Rasu Maritima S.A. v. Pertamina* [1978] Q.B. 644, 657–658 (C.A.). For the history of foreign attachment in the United States see *Ownbey v. Morgan*, 256 U.S. 94 (1921), and the severe limitations imposed by *Shaffer v. Heitner*, 433 U.S. 186 (1977). In Case C–398/92 *Mund & Fester v. Hatrex Internationaal Transport* [1994] E.C.R. I–467 it was held that the rule in the

creditor to obtain an injunction to restrain the alleged debtor from parting with his property.[4]

Since 1975, however, the English courts have developed a practice whereby **8–004** the court may grant an interlocutory injunction to restrain a defendant from disposing of or dealing with his assets.[5] In two cases[6] in that year the Court of Appeal, in each case with Lord Denning M.R. presiding, decided that such an injunction could be granted to restrain a foreign defendant from removing its assets from the jurisdiction. The injunction, as subsequently developed and extended, became known as the *Mareva* injunction, after the second of the cases. The practice has since been followed in Canada,[7] Australia[8] and New Zealand.[9]

In 1981 the practice was given statutory authority by section 37(3) of the **8–005** Supreme Court Act 1981,[10] which confirmed that the power of the court to grant an interlocutory injunction restraining a party to any proceedings from removing from the jurisdiction, or otherwise dealing with assets located within the jurisdiction, is exercisable whether or not that party is domiciled, resident or present within the jurisdiction. Section 37(3) did not turn the *Mareva* injunction into a statutory remedy; it assumed that the remedy existed, and tacitly endorsed its validity.[11] Consequently, section 37(3) does not inhibit the extension of the *Mareva* jurisdiction by the court.[12]

The description of an injunction as a *Mareva* injunction is a convenient **8–006** label to describe an injunction restraining the removal or dissipation of assets in which the claimant claims no proprietary interest, and strictly it should be distinguished from cases in which the claimant seeks to trace assets.[13] Thus, if the claim relates to a particular fund or to a particular piece of property, the

---

German Code of Civil Procedure that an attachment could be granted automatically in cases where a judgment was to be enforced abroad (whereas in other cases it could only be granted where enforcement would be impossible or substantially more difficult) was discriminatory, and therefore contrary to what is now Article 12 of the E.C. Treaty.

[4] *Lister & Co. v. Stubbs* (1890) 45 Ch.D. 1, 14 (C.A.) and other cases discussed in *Rasu Maritima S.A. v. Pertamina, supra,* at 659–660, *per* Lord Denning M.R.; *The Siskina v. Distos Compania Naviera S.A.* [1979] A.C. 210, 260, *per* Lord Hailsham; *Derby & Co. Ltd. v. Weldon (Nos. 3 & 4)* [1990] Ch. 65, 88–89, *per* Neill L.J. See also Report of the Committee on the Enforcement of Judgment Debts, 1969, Cmnd. 3909.

[5] For a full and excellent account see Gee, *Mareva Injunctions and Anton Piller Relief* (4th ed. 1998).

[6] *Nippon Yusen Kaisha v. Karageorgis* [1975] 1 W.L.R. 1093 (C.A.); *Mareva Compania Naviera S.A. v. International Bulkcarriers S.A.* [1975] 2 Lloyd's Rep. 509 (C.A.). The *Mareva* injunction extends not only to the removal of assets, but also to their dissipation: *Rahman (Prince Abdul) bin Turki al Sudairy v. Abu-Taha* [1980] 1 W.L.R. 1268 (C.A.); CPR 25.1(1)(f)(ii).

[7] *Chitel v. Rothbart* (1982) 141 D.L.R. (3d) 268 (Ont. C.A.); and other cases referred to by Rogers and Hately (1982) 60 Can.B.Rev. 1, 33–35. For the special problems of the practice in a federal system see *Aetna Financial Services Ltd. v. Feigelmann* [1985] 1 S.C.R. 2.

[8] See, *e.g. Riley McKay Pty. Ltd. v. McKay* [1982] 1 N.S.W.L.R. 264; *Hiero Pty. Ltd. v. Somers* (1983) 47 A.L.R. 605; *Devlin v. Collins* (1984) 37 S.A.S.R. 98; *Perth Mint v. Mickelberg (No. 2)* [1985] W.A.R. 117; *Pearce v. Waterhouse* [1986] V.R. 603; *Jackson v. Sterling Industries Ltd.* (1987) 162 C.L.R. 612.

[9] *Hunt v. B.P. Exploration (Libya) Ltd.* [1980] 1 N.Z.L.R. 104.

[10] This removed doubts which had been expressed in some of the early cases. See also *Bekhor & Co. Ltd. v. Bilton* [1981] Q.B. 923, 936 (C.A.); *The Siskina v. Distos Compania Naviera S.A.* [1979] A.C. 210, 261.

[11] *Mercedes Benz A.G. v. Leiduck* [1996] A.C. 284, 299 (P.C.).

[12] See *Babanaft International Co. S.A. v. Bassatne* [1990] Ch. 13, 26 (C.A.).

[13] See *A v. C* [1981] Q.B. 956n; *P.C.W. (Underwriting Agencies) Ltd. v. Dixon* [1983] 2 All E.R. 158; *Aetna Financial Services Ltd. v. Feigelmann* [1985] 1 S.C.R. 2, 13; *cf. Bankers Trust Co. v. Shapira* [1980] 1 W.L.R. 1274 (C.A.); *Republic of Haiti v. Duvalier* [1990] 1 Q.B. 202, 214 (C.A.); *Mercedes Benz v. Leiduck* [1996] A.C. 284, 300 (P.C.).

injunction might relate only to that fund or property. So also, an injunction in relation to a claim to a particular fund would not be subject to the normal proviso in a *Mareva* injunction allowing the use of the money for normal business purposes or for legal fees.[14]

8–007   In order to obtain a *Mareva* injunction the claimant must show that he has at least a good arguable case on the merits,[15] and that there is a real risk that a judgment would be unsatisfied if the injunction were not granted.[16] The fundamental principle underlying the jurisdiction is that, within the limits of its powers, no court should permit a defendant to take action designed to ensure that subsequent orders of the court are rendered less effective than would otherwise be the case.[17]

8–008   Although Lord Denning M.R. expressed the view that a *Mareva* injunction operated *in rem*,[18] it does not operate as an attachment on property as such, but is relief *in personam*, restraining the owner of the assets from dealing with them. Accordingly, it does not achieve priority over the security interests of third parties,[19] nor does it give the claimant security rights in priority to other creditors.[20] Consequently, a defendant will normally be allowed to make payments to his creditors in the normal course of business.[21] The injunction must not be used so as to amount to an instrument of oppression which would bring about the cessation of ordinary trading and the court must look at all the circumstances of the case in deciding whether, and to what extent, the injunction should be varied in order to allow the defendant to make payments.[22] The injunction will not be granted unless the claimant gives the usual cross-undertaking in damages.[23]

It has been held by the Court of Appeal that it will not be granted in relation to a cause of action which will accrue, but has not yet accrued.[24] In *Mercedes*

---

[14] *Polly Peck International plc v. Nadir* [1992] 2 Lloyd's Rep. 238 (C.A.).

[15] *Rasu Maritima S.A. v. Pertamina* [1978] Q.B. 644 (C.A.); *Ninemia Corp. v. Trave GmbH* [1983] 1 W.L.R. 1412 (C.A.); *Derby & Co. Ltd. v. Weldon* [1990] Ch. 48, 57–58 (C.A.). Since the application is made without notice (*ex parte*), full and frank disclosure of relevant matters must be made. For the effect of failure to disclose related proceedings in other jurisdictions see *Behbehani v. Salem* [1989] 1 W.L.R. 723 (C.A.).

[16] *Third Chandris Shipping Corp. v. Unimarine S.A.* [1979] Q.B. 654 (C.A.); *Ninemia Corp. v. Trave GmbH* [1983] 1 W.L.R. 1412 (C.A.); *Patterson v. BTR Engineering (Aust.) Ltd.* (1989) 18 N.S.W.L.R. 319.

[17] *Derby & Co. Ltd. v. Weldon (Nos. 3 & 4)* [1990] Ch. 65, 76, *per* Lord Donaldson M.R.; *The Coral Rose (No. 1)* [1991] 1 Lloyd's Rep. 563, 568 (C.A.); *Atlas Maritime Co. S.A. v. Avalon Maritime Ltd. (No. 3)* [1991] 1 W.L.R. 917, 920–921 (C.A.).

[18] *Z Ltd. v. A-Z* [1982] Q.B. 558, 573 (C.A.), said to have been *per incuriam* in *Att.-Gen. v. Times Newspapers Ltd.* [1992] 1 A.C. 191, 215, *per* Lord Ackner.

[19] *Cretanor Maritime Co. Ltd. v. Irish Marine Management Ltd.* [1978] 1 W.L.R. 966 (C.A.).

[20] *Iraqi Ministry of Defence v. Arcepey Shipping Co. S.A. (The Angel Bell)* [1981] Q.B. 65; *Bekhor & Co. Ltd. v. Bilton* [1981] Q.B. 923, 942 (C.A.); *Derby & Co. Ltd. v. Weldon* [1990] Ch. 65, 76 (C.A.); *Mercedes Benz v. Leiduck* [1996] A.C. 284, 300 (P.C.); *Aetna Financial Services Ltd. v. Feigelmann* [1985] 1 S.C.R. 2, 26; *Jackson v. Sterling Industries Ltd.* (1987) 162 C.L.R. 612, 618, 621.

[21] The "*Angel Bell* variation", established in *Iraqi Ministry of Defence v. Arcepey Shipping Co. S.A.* [1981] Q.B. 65. See also *Admiral Shipping v. Portlink Ferries Ltd.* [1984] 2 Lloyd's Rep. 166 (C.A.); *Avant Petroleum Inc. v. Gatoil Overseas Inc.* [1986] 2 Lloyd's Rep. 236 (C.A.).

[22] *The Coral Rose* [1991] 1 Lloyd's Rep. 563 (C.A.); *Atlas Maritime Co. S.A. v. Avalon Maritime Ltd. (No. 3)* [1991] 1 W.L.R. 917 (C.A.).

[23] *Third Chandris Shipping Corp. v. Unimarine S.A.* [1979] Q.B. 654, 668 (C.A.).

[24] *The Veracruz I* [1992] 1 Lloyd's Rep. 353 (C.A.), criticised by Collins (1992) 108 L.Q.R. 175; *The P* [1992] 1 Lloyd's Rep. 470; *Zucker v. Tyndall Holdings plc* [1992] 1 W.L.R. 1127 (C.A.).

Benz A.G. v. Leiduck,[25] however, Lord Nicholls of Birkenhead, in a dissenting opinion on an aspect not dealt with by the majority, doubted the correctness of the principal authorities to this effect. He considered that in such a case there was no reason in principle why an anticipatory injunction could not be granted, and preferred the Australian authority in that sense.[26]

There are two important ways in which the jurisdiction is made effective. **8–009** First, the court may make ancillary orders in aid of *Mareva* relief to enable the claimant to obtain disclosure of documents or information from a defendant concerning his assets,[27] and even an ancillary order restraining a defendant from leaving the jurisdiction and requiring him to deliver up his passport.[28] Secondly, a third party, such as a bank with which the defendant has an account, is guilty of contempt of court if it knowingly assists in a breach of the order, *i.e.* if knowing the terms of the injunction it wilfully assists the defendant to disobey.[29] This is so whether or not the defendant has been served with or knows of the order, because the third party would be guilty of conduct which knowingly interferes with the administration of justice by causing the order of the court to be disobeyed.[30]

Worldwide *Mareva* injunctions.[31] The *Mareva* injunction was developed **8–010** in order to prevent the removal of assets from the jurisdiction, and it was assumed by Parliament[32] and held by the Court of Appeal[33] that the exercise of the *Mareva* jurisdiction was limited to assets within the jurisdiction. In

---

[25] [1996] A.C. 284, 312 (P.C.). See Collins (1996) 112 L.Q.R. 28.

[26] *Patterson v. B.T.R. Engineering (Australia) Ltd.* (1989) 18 N.S.W.L.R. 319 (N.S.W.C.A.).

[27] See, *e.g. A v. C* [1981] Q.B. 956; *Bekhor & Co. Ltd. v. Bilton* [1981] Q.B. 923 (C.A.); *House of Spring Gardens Ltd. v. Waite* [1985] F.S.R. 173 (C.A.); *Bank of Crete S.A. v. Koskotas* [1991] 2 Lloyd's Rep. 587 (C.A.); *(No. 2)* [1992] 1 W.L.R. 919. As to privilege against self-incrimination in such cases see *Sociedade Nacional de Combustiveis de Angola U.E.E. v. Lundqvist* [1991] 2 Q.B. 310 (C.A.); *cf. Den Norske Bank A.S.A. v. Antonatos* [1999] Q.B. 271 (C.A.).

[28] *Bayer A.G. v. Winter* [1986] 1 W.L.R. 497 (C.A.), applied in *Re Oriental Credit* [1988] Ch. 204. For the remedy of an order for the issue of a writ prohibiting a debtor from leaving the realm (*ne exeat regno*), where his absence will materially prejudice the claimant in the prosecution of the action see *Felton v. Callis* [1969] 1 Q.B. 200; *Lipkin Gorman v. Cass, The Times,* May 29, 1985. It has been held that this writ may issue in aid of a *Mareva* injunction (*Al Nakhel for Contracting & Trading Ltd. v. Lowe* [1986] Q.B. 235; *cf. Thaya v. Thaya* [1987] 2 F.L.R. 142) but the better view is that it may not be issued solely for the purpose of enforcing a *Mareva* injunction, and that in such a case the appropriate remedy is an injunction to restrain the defendant from leaving the jurisdiction: *Allied Arab Bank v. Hajjar* [1988] Q.B. 787. See also *Morris v. Murjani* [1996] 1 W.L.R. 848 (C.A.) (court has power under Insolvency Act 1986, s.333, to issue injunction to prevent bankrupt from leaving country). See Gee, *op cit. supra,* n. 5, pp. 341–342; Harpum [1986] C.L.J. 189; Anderson (1987) 103 L.Q.R. 246; Andrews [1988] C.L.J. 364.

[29] *Z Ltd. v. A-Z* [1982] Q.B. 558 (C.A.). See also CPR PD25, Annex.

[30] *Ibid.* at 578, *per* Eveleigh L.J., approved in *Att.-Gen. v. Times Newspapers Ltd.* [1992] 1 A.C. 191.

[31] See Collins (1989) 105 L.Q.R. 262, reprinted in Collins, *Essays,* p. 189; Andrews [1989] C.L.J. 199; Hogan (1989) 17 Eur. L. Rev. 191; Malek and Lewis [1990] L.M.C.L.Q. 88; Kaye (1990) 9 Civ.J.Q. 12; Capper (1991) 54 M.L.R. 329; Rogers [1991] L.M.C.L.Q. 231. For earlier discussion see Collins (1981) 1 Yb. Eur. L. 249; McLachlan (1987) 36 I.C.L.Q. 669, 674–676.

[32] Supreme Court Act 1981. s.37(3), para. 8–005, *ante.*

[33] *Ashtiani v. Kashi* [1987] Q.B. 888 (C.A.). See also *The Bhoja Trader* [1981] 2 Lloyd's Rep. 256 (C.A.); *cf. Allied Arab Bank v. Hajjar* [1988] Q.B. 787, 796; *Reilly v. Fryer* [1988] 2 F.T.L.R. 69 (C.A.). Contrast *Re A Company* [1985] B.C.L.C. 333 (C.A.); *Bayer A.G. v. Winter* [1986] 2 F.T.L.R. 111, 112.

several Commonwealth jurisdictions, however, this limitation on the scope of *Mareva* injunctions was not accepted.[34]

8–011   In a series of decisions of the Court of Appeal in 1988 it was held, reversing previous practice, that *Mareva* injunctions and ancillary disclosure orders could be granted in relation to assets abroad. First, in *Babanaft International Co. S.A. v. Bassatne*[35] an injunction was granted, after judgment in a fraud action, restraining the judgment debtors from disposing of any of their assets worldwide. Secondly, in *Republic of Haiti v. Duvalier*[36] an injunction was granted (in aid of proceedings pending in France[37]) restraining the defendants from dealing with their assets wherever situated and requiring the defendants to disclose information relating to their assets worldwide. Thirdly, in two decisions in *Derby & Co. Ltd. v. Weldon*[38] it was held that a pre-judgment *Mareva* injunction and ancillary disclosure could be granted in relation to assets worldwide in the course of litigation pending in England, irrespective of whether the defendant had assets in England.[39]

8–012   It was subsequently held in *Derby & Co. Ltd. v. Weldon (No. 6)*[40] that the jurisdiction could be exercised to order the transfer of assets from one foreign jurisdiction to another, or to restrain the transfer of assets from one foreign jurisdiction to another, or to order the return to England of assets from a foreign jurisdiction. But it was emphasised that these were highly exceptional orders, and in that decision the order was limited to restraining the return to Switzerland (where, according to the evidence, the English order might not be recognised) of deposits made outside Switzerland by Swiss banks acting on the instructions of the defendants.

8–013   The basis for the development of the worldwide *Mareva* injunction was the recognition that the *Mareva* injunction operates *in personam*, and that where the defendant is personally subject to the jurisdiction of the court, an injunction may be granted in appropriate circumstances to control his activities abroad.[41] Although exceptional or special circumstances must be present to justify a worldwide *Mareva*, that does not mean more than that the court

---

[34] *Ballabil Holdings Pty. Ltd. v. Hospital Products Ltd.* (1985) 1 N.S.W.L.R. 155; *Coombs & Barei Construction Pty. Ltd. v. Dynasty Pty. Ltd.* (1986) 42 S.A.S.R. 413; *Yandil Holdings Pty. Ltd. v. Insurance Co. of North America* (1987) 7 N.S.W.L.R. 571; *National Australia Bank v. Dessau* [1988] V.R. 521; *Banco Ambrosiano Holdings S.A. v. Dunkeld Ranching Ltd.* (1987) 85 Alta. R. 278 (C.A.) (but contrast *Zellers Inc. v. Doobay* [1989] 3 W.W.R. 497 (B.C.)); *Mooney v. Orr* [1995] 1 W.W.R. 517 (B.C.); *Asean Resources Ltd. v. Ka Wah International Merchant Finance Ltd.* [1987] L.R.C. (Comm.) 835. See also *Deutsche Bank AG v. Murtagh* [1995] 1 I.L.R.M. 381.

[35] [1990] Ch. 13 (C.A.), stated *post*, para. 8–091, Illustration 3.

[36] [1990] 1 Q.B. 202 (C.A.), stated *post*, Illustration 4.

[37] See Civil Jurisdiction and Judgments Act 1982, s.25(1), and Sched. 1, Art. 24.

[38] [1990] Ch. 48 (C.A.); (*Nos. 3 & 4*) [1990] Ch. 65 (C.A.), *post*, Illustration 5. See also *Ghoth v. Ghoth* [1992] 2 All E.R. 920 (C.A.).

[39] Before these cases it was often said that a plaintiff who sought *Mareva* relief must give grounds for a belief that the defendant had assets within the jurisdiction. That this was the normal case did not mean that it was a necessary pre-condition: [1990] Ch. at 77–80.

[40] [1990] 1 W.L.R. 1139.

[41] *Babanaft International Co. S.A. v. Bassatne* [1990] Ch. 13, at 38, 41 (C.A.); *Derby & Co. Ltd. v. Weldon (No. 6)* [1990] 1 W.L.R. 1139, 1149 (C.A.); *Crédit Suisse Fides Trust S.A. v. Cuoghi* [1998] Q.B. 818, 826 (C.A.). See Kerr, *Injunctions* (6th ed. Paterson, 1927), p. 11, and (among many other examples) *Acrow (Automation) Ltd. v. Rex Chainbelt Inc.* [1971] 1 W.L.R. 1676 (C.A.); *Att.-Gen. v. Barker* [1990] 3 All E.R. 257 (C.A.). For the territorial scope of *Anton Piller* orders (the "search and seizure" orders sanctioned by *Anton Piller K.G. v. Manufacturing Processes Ltd.* [1976] Ch. 55 (C.A.)) *cf. Cook Industries v. Galliher* [1979] Ch. 439; and contrast *Protector Alarms Ltd. v. Maxim Alarms Ltd.* [1978] F.S.R. 442; *Altertext Inc. v. Advanced Data Communications Ltd.* [1985] 1 W.L.R. 457. The *Anton Piller* jurisdiction is

should go no further than necessity dictates, and that in the first instance it should look to assets within the jurisdiction.[42] The jurisdiction will be exercised more readily after final judgment has been obtained against the defendant, or if the claim is a proprietary claim.[43] It may be appropriate to make an order even if it will not be recognised by the courts of the country where the assets are situated, since the English court may still make its order effective by striking out the defence if the defendant disobeys the order.[44] It has been held that the English court will not normally grant a worldwide injunction in connection with proceedings in England to enforce a foreign judgment or foreign arbitration award.[45] But this view has been doubted,[46] and it is submitted that there is no reason in principle why in appropriate circumstances (for example, where the judgment or award debtors are present in England) such an order should not be made.

Worldwide *Mareva* injunctions almost invariably provide for disclosure of assets outside the jurisdiction. In those cases where an effective order can be made, it is likely to be the disclosure order which will be the most useful in practical terms. If proper disclosure is made of assets abroad, the claimant will be in a position to make an application in the relevant foreign court for an attachment. The practical consequence is that in such cases it is really the *Mareva* injunction which is ancillary to the disclosure order, rather than the traditional relationship in which it was the disclosure order which was ancillary to the *Mareva* injunction. For the disclosure order will be the main remedy in England, and the *Mareva* injunction will, in the words of Nicholls L.J.[47] be a "holding" injunction, to give the claimant time to apply to the relevant foreign court for appropriate orders of attachment or the like.[48] **8–014**

The practice in relation to worldwide *Mareva* injunctions is subject to two important limitations. First, in order to prevent harassment of the defendant and unnecessary multiplicity of actions, the claimant must normally undertake not to make use of information disclosed under the order in foreign proceedings without the permission of the court.[49] Secondly, what has become known as "the *Babanaft* proviso" has been inserted in such orders in order to make it clear that the English court is not purporting to make third parties abroad **8–015**

---

given statutory authority by Civil Procedure Act 1997, s.7, which is limited to premises within the jurisdiction: s.7(3); but, by analogy with Supreme Court Act 1981, s.37(3), it is not likely to preclude the extension of the jurisdiction by the court: *ante*, para. 8–005. Orders under Civil Procedure Act 1997, s.7, are now called "search orders": CPR 25.1(1)(h).

[42] *Derby & Co. Ltd. v. Weldon (Nos. 3 & 4)* [1990] Ch. 65, 79 (C.A.).

[43] See, *e.g. Republic of Haiti v. Duvalier* [1990] 1 Q.B. 202, at 213–214, *per* Staughton, L.J. (C.A.). After judgment, a disclosure order relating to assets worldwide may be made under Ord. 48 (in CPR, Sched. 1): *Interpool Ltd. v. Galani* [1988] Q.B. 738 (C.A.); *cf. Maclaine Watson & Co. Ltd. v. International Tin Council (No. 2)* [1989] Ch. 286 (C.A.); *Gidrxslme Shipping Co. Ltd. v. Tantomar Transportes Maritimos Ltd.* [1995] 1 W.L.R. 295; *Yandil Holdings Pty. Ltd. v. Insurance Co. of North America* (1987) 7 N.S.W.L.R. 571.

[44] *Derby & Co. Ltd. v. Weldon (Nos. 3 & 4)* [1990] Ch. at 81.

[45] *Rosseel N.V. v. Oriental Commercial Shipping (U.K.) Ltd.* [1990] 1 W.L.R. 1387 (C.A.).

[46] *Crédit Suisse Fides Trust S.A. v. Cuoghi* [1998] Q.B. 818, 829 (C.A.).

[47] *Babanaft International Co. S.A. v. Bassatne* [1990] Ch. at 41.

[48] See Collins (1989) 105 L.Q.R. 262, 297 (and in Collins, *Essays*, at p. 223), on which see *Grupo Torras S.A. v. Sheikh Fahad Mohammed Al-Sabah*, unrep., February 16, 1994 (C.A.), *per* Steyn L.J. See also *Crédit Suisse Fides Trust S.A. v. Cuoghi* [1998] Q.B. 818, 827–828 (C.A.).

[49] *Babanaft International Co. S.A. v. Bassatne* [1990] Ch. at 41, 47; *Republic of Haiti v. Duvalier* [1990] 1 Q.B. at 217; *Derby & Co. Ltd. v. Weldon* [1990] Ch. at 55–56, 60; *Tate Access Floors Inc. v. Boswell* [1991] Ch. 512, 525; *Re Bank of Credit and Commerce International S.A.* [1994] 1 W.L.R. 708 (C.A.).

subject to the contempt powers of the English court. It has already been seen[50] that a third party who, knowing of a *Mareva* injunction, assists in the breach of the order (*e.g.* a bank allowing payments to be made by the defendant) is guilty of that type of contempt of court which consists in the interference with the administration of justice. But if the third party is wholly outside the jurisdiction of the court, the third party is either not to be regarded as being in contempt or it would involve an excess of jurisdiction to seek to punish the third party for that contempt.[51]

8–016   The current form of the *Babanaft* proviso, as elaborated in subsequent cases (particularly *Derby & Co. Ltd. v. Weldon (Nos. 3 & 4)*[52]) is: "The terms of this order do not affect or concern anyone outside the jurisdiction of this court until it is declared enforceable by or is enforced by a court in the relevant country and then they are to affect him only to the extent they have been declared enforceable or have been enforced unless the person is: (a) a person to whom this order is addressed or an officer or an agent appointed by power of attorney of that person; or (b) a person who is subject to the jurisdiction of this court and (i) has been given written notice of this order at his residence or place of business within the jurisdiction of this court and (ii) is able to prevent acts or omissions outside the jurisdiction of this court which constitute or assist in a breach of the terms of this order."[53]

8–017   The effect of this proviso is that if the defendant has an account with a foreign branch of an English bank, the bank (being a bank resident in England) will, after service of the order, be required not to allow withdrawals.[54] If the defendant has an account with the head office of, or another foreign branch or subsidiary of, a foreign bank which has a branch in England, the position is more controversial.[55] It seems to have been accepted in one case[56] that a French bank with a branch in London might be in contempt if its New Caledonia subsidiary allowed the defendant to withdraw money from an account there: in that case a proviso was inserted in the order[57] to protect the bank if it complied with what it reasonably believed to be its obligations, contractual or otherwise, under the law of the place where the assets were situate or under the applicable law of the account in question, and a similar proviso is now part of the Commercial Court practice.[58]

8–018   **Relationship between jurisdiction to determine the merits and jurisdiction to order interim protection.** Where the English court has jurisdiction over the substance of a case, it also plainly has jurisdiction to grant interim

---

[50] See para. 8–009, *ante.*
[51] *Derby & Co. Ltd. v. Weldon (Nos. 3 & 4)* [1990] Ch. 65, at 82, *per* Lord Donaldson M.R. See Collins (1989) 105 L.Q.R. at 281–286, or Collins, *Essays*, pp. 208–212.
[52] [1990] Ch. at 84. See also *Ghoth v. Ghoth* [1992] 2 All E.R. 920 (C.A.).
[53] CPR PD25, Annex.
[54] *Securities and Investments Board v. Pantell S.A.* [1990] Ch. 426, 433.
[55] See Collins (1989) 105 L.Q.R. 262, 284–286 (reprinted in Collins, *Essays*, pp. 211–212); Malek and Lewis [1990] L.M.C.L.Q. 88, 92–97.
[56] *Baltic Shipping Co. v. Transatlantic Shipping Ltd.* [1995] 1 Lloyd's Rep. 673.
[57] Following suggestions by Saville J., then the judge in charge of the Commercial Court, in his 1993 end of year statement: see Gee, *op. cit. supra*, n. 5, pp. 291–292.
[58] *Commercial Court Guide* (1999), para. F 19.10.

measures to preserve the position pending adjudication of the merits.[59] If proceedings are pending, or are contemplated, in a foreign country, the claimant may wish to preserve its position by seeking interim relief in England. For example, it may be only in England that there are assets available to satisfy a judgment granted in the foreign country to whose jurisdiction the defendant is amenable, and the claimant may be advised to seek a *Mareva* injunction to prevent the defendant from making itself judgment-proof.

Until section 25(1) of the Civil Jurisdiction and Judgments Act 1982 came **8–019** fully into force in 1997, there was a serious gap in English law. In *The Siskina*[60] plaintiff cargo-owners had a claim against a one-ship Panamanian company for damages for wrongful detention of their cargo in Cyprus. After discharge of the cargo the defendants' only asset, their ship, sank and their underwriters in London were due to pay the insurance proceeds there. The bills of lading provided that the courts of Genoa, Italy, would have exclusive jurisdiction over cargo claims. The plaintiffs sought to assert jurisdiction in England on the basis that their claim for a *Mareva* injunction was an injunction "sought ordering the defendant to do or refrain from doing anything within the jurisdiction" (*i.e.* not to remove or dispose of the insurance proceeds pending the outcome of the Genoese proceedings) within the meaning of what is now Order 11, r. 1(1)(*b*), Rule 27, clause (2).[61] The House of Lords held that the English court had no jurisdiction to grant such an injunction against foreign defendants otherwise than in support of a cause of action in respect of which the defendant was amenable to the jurisdiction. More recently, in *Mercedes Benz A.G. v. Leiduck*,[62] the Privy Council held that the Hong Kong court had no power under Order 11 to restrain a foreign defendant from disposing of shares in a Hong Kong company pending a civil fraud action against him in Monaco. In that case the Privy Council drew a distinction between two questions. The first was one of jurisdiction: whether, even if the court had power to grant *Mareva* relief in aid of foreign proceedings, Order 11, r. 1(1) authorised service of proceedings on a foreign defendant. The second issue was whether, questions of service apart, the court had power to grant a free-standing injunction to restrain the disposition of the defendants' assets pending adjudication of the substance of the claim in a foreign court. The Privy Council held, by a majority, that the purpose of Order 11 was to give jurisdiction to the court to adjudicate on a claim advanced in an action or matter, and an application for a *Mareva* injunction alone was not an action or matter which would decide and give effect to rights. There was therefore no mechanism to allow service out of the jurisdiction on the defendant. Accordingly, it was not necessary to decide the second question. But Lord Nicholls of Birkenhead delivered a powerful dissenting opinion: he thought that *The Siskina*, to the extent that it held that the right to obtain an interlocutory

---

[59] This obvious point is expressly confirmed in Case C–391/95 *Van Uden Maritime B.V. v. Firma Deco-Line* [1998] E.C.R. I–7091; [1999] 2 W.L.R. 1181, 1208 and in Case C–99/96 *Mietz v. Intership Yachting Sneek B.V.* [1999] I.L.Pr 541, 568.

[60] [1979] A.C. 210 (reversing the majority decision of the Court of Appeal: Lord Denning M.R. described it as the most disappointing reversal of his career: *Due Process of Law* (1980), p. 141). See also *Perry v. Zissis* [1977] 1 Lloyd's Rep. 607, 616 (C.A.); *Caudron v. Air Zaire* [1986] I.L.R.M. 10. See Collins, *Essays*, pp. 30–34.

[61] CPR, Sched. 1.

[62] [1996] A.C. 284 (P.C.), criticised Collins (1996) 112 L.Q.R. 28.

injunction was dependant on there being an existing cause of action justiciable in England, was no longer good law.[63]

8–020   The effect of these decisions has been reversed by section 25 of the Civil Jurisdiction and Judgments Act 1982 and Order 11, r. 8A. Section 25(1) was enacted in order to give effect to Article 24 of the 1968 Brussels Convention on jurisdiction and the enforcement of judgments in civil and commercial matters,[64] but it has since 1987 applied to proceedings commenced or to be commenced in a State which is party to the 1968 Convention (and the parallel Lugano Convention) and also (since 1997) to proceedings in countries which are party to neither Convention. Article 24 of the 1968 Convention (and of the Lugano Convention) provides that application may be made to the courts of a Contracting State for such provisional, including protective, measures as may be available under the law of that State even if, under the Convention, the courts of another Contracting State have jurisdiction as to the substance of the matter. In *Republic of Haiti v. Duvalier*[65] it was suggested that Article 24 *requires* each Contracting State to make available, in aid of the courts of another Contracting State, such provisional or protective measures as its own domestic law would afford if its courts were trying the substantive action. It is not likely that Article 24 imposes any such requirement. It is suggested that Article 24 is merely permissive, but the point is of little significance since section 25 of the 1982 Act gives the necessary powers.

8–021   **Section 25 of the 1982 Act.** Section 25(1) provides that the English court has power to grant interim relief where (a) proceedings have been or are to be commenced in a 1968 Convention or Lugano Convention Contracting State (or in another part of the United Kingdom) and (b) the subject matter of the proceedings is within the scope of the Conventions.[66] Provision was made in section 25(3) for the power to be extended by Order in Council so as to be exercisable in relation to proceedings commenced or to be commenced otherwise than in a 1968 or Lugano Convention Contracting State, and to proceedings whose subject matter was not within the scope of the Conventions. The power was so extended in 1997.[67]

8–022   An application under section 25(1) is now made by the application procedure under the Civil Procedure Rules 1998, Part 23. For service outside the jurisdiction, application may be made for permission under Order 11, r. 8A, which requires the party seeking an order for permission to serve outside the

---

[63] In Jersey (a major centre for off-shore funds) the Court of Appeal applied the reasoning of Lord Nicholls of Birkenhead on the second issue and held that where the Jersey court had *in personam* jurisdiction over the defendant (by virtue of its submission to the jurisdiction) it could grant a *Mareva* injunction in aid of foreign proceedings: *Solvalub Ltd. v. Match Investments Ltd.* [1998] I.L.Pr. 419.

[64] See generally Chap. 11, *post*.

[65] [1990] 1 Q.B. 202, 212 (C.A.). See also *Alltrans Inc. v. Interdom Holdings Ltd.* [1991] 4 All E.R. 458, 468 (C.A.); *Crédit Suisse Fides Trust S.A. v. Cuoghi* [1998] Q.B. 818, 827 (C.A.). *Cf. X v. Y* [1990] 1 Q.B. 220, 228.

[66] As determined by Art. 1, on which see *post*, paras. 11–013 *et seq.* s.24 gives the court power to grant interim relief where the jurisdiction of the English court over the substance of the action is merely doubtful. Accordingly the court may grant an injunction even where an issue remains to be decided about the jurisdiction of the court over the substance of the matter. In practice, therefore, a *Mareva* injunction may be granted without notice against a defendant who is to be served out of the jurisdiction under Ord. 11, r 1.(1) or (2): see Gee, *supra*, n. 5, p. 62.

[67] S.I. 1997 No. 302.

jurisdiction to depose that the claimant has a good claim to an interim remedy.[68]

For the purposes of section 25 "interim relief" means interim relief of any **8–023** kind which the court has power to grant in proceedings relating to matters within its jurisdiction other than (a) a warrant for the arrest of property, or (b) provision for obtaining evidence.[69] Consequently, the arrest of ships in admiralty proceedings *in rem* is outside the scope of the section; obtaining evidence is excluded because provision is made for obtaining evidence for foreign courts by the Evidence (Proceedings in Other Jurisdictions) Act 1975 (giving effect to the Hague Convention on the Taking of Evidence Abroad in Civil or Commercial Matters)[70]; but section 25 can be used to preserve evidence (as in an *Anton Piller* order[71]) or to obtain information about the location of assets.[72]

The European Court has held[73] that the expression "provisional, including **8–024** protective, measures" in Article 24 is to be given an autonomous Convention interpretation, and means measures which are intended to maintain the status quo in order to protect rights pending their final adjudication. In *Van Uden Maritime B.V. v. Firma Deco-Line*[74] the European Court considered the controversial question[75] whether an interim order requiring payment on account of a claim (in that case a contractual claim) is to be classified as a provisional measure within the meaning of Article 24. It accepted that an interim payment may be necessary to ensure the efficacy of the decision on the substance. But it recognised that such an order may pre-empt the decision on the substance, and that if the plaintiff could obtain it at the court of his domicile (as has happened in France) the jurisdictional rules of the 1968 Convention could be circumvented. Accordingly, an interim payment of a contractual consideration did not constitute a provisional measure within the meaning of Article 24 unless, first, repayment to the defendant of the sum awarded was guaranteed if the plaintiff was ultimately unsuccessful on the substance, and, second, the measure sought related only to specific assets of the defendant located or to be located within the territorial jurisdiction of the court to which the application for provisional measures was made.

On an application for interim relief under section 25, the court may refuse **8–025** to grant the relief if, in the opinion of the court, the fact that the court has no independent jurisdiction in relation to the subject-matter of the proceedings makes it inexpedient for the court to grant it. In *Crédit Suisse Fides Trust S.A. v. Cuoghi*[76] substantive proceedings for civil fraud were pending in Switzerland (a party to the Lugano Convention) against a defendant who was resident and domiciled in England. The plaintiffs applied to the English court under

---

[68] See *post*, para. 11–141.

[69] s. 25(7).

[70] See *post*, paras. 8–053 *et seq*.

[71] Now called a "search order": CPR 25.1(1)(h).

[72] See Gee, *op. cit. supra*, n. 5, p. 85, referring to an unreported decision in the *Republic of Haiti v. Duvalier* litigation.

[73] Case C–261/90 *Reichert v. Dresdner Bank (No. 2)* [1992] E.C.R. I–2149.

[74] Case C–391/95 [1998] E.C.R. I–7091; [1999] 2 W.L.R. 1181; and see also Case C–99/96 *Mietz v. Intership Yachting Sneek B.V.* [1999] I.L.Pr 541.

[75] See Collins, *Essays*, pp. 37–39.

[76] [1998] Q.B. 818 (C.A.), not following *S & T Bautrading v. Nordling* [1997] 3 All E.R. 718 (C.A.). Cf. *Republic of Haiti v. Duvalier* [1990] 1 Q.B. 202, 216–217 (C.A.).

section 25(1)[77] for a worldwide *Mareva* injunction and an ancillary disclosure order relating to assets worldwide, in aid of the Swiss proceedings. Refusing an application to confine the injunction and disclosure order to assets in England, the Court of Appeal held that it was not "inexpedient" to grant the relief in the light of the facts that the defendant was domiciled in England, the Swiss court had no jurisdiction (under Swiss law) to make such an order against a non-resident, and there was no reason to believe that the Swiss court would not welcome assistance from the courts of the country where the defendant was resident. Millett L.J. said[78] that where a similar order had been applied for and has been refused by the foreign court, it would generally be wrong for the English court to interfere; and Lord Bingham of Cornhill C.J. said[79] that it might weigh against the grant of relief by the English court that the foreign court could have granted such relief and had not done so, particularly if it had been asked to grant such relief and had declined.

8–026   In *Refco Inc. v. Eastern Trading Co.*[80] the proceedings on the substance of the claim were in a federal court in Illinois, and the plaintiffs sought *Mareva* relief in England. The judge at first instance, Rix J., granted interim relief pending an application which he required the plaintiffs to make in Illinois for relief similar to that sought in England. The plaintiffs did not make the application because the principles in Illinois for the grant of interim relief were so different from those in English law that the plaintiffs would have been bound to fail, and accordingly the *Mareva* relief in England lapsed. An appeal to the Court of Appeal by the plaintiffs failed on the ground that security which they had obtained elsewhere made *Mareva* relief unnecessary, but the Court of Appeal also considered the effect of the non-availability of similar relief in Illinois on the ancillary jurisdiction in England. Morritt L.J. and (it seems) Potter L.J. took the view that the principle was the same where, as in the *Crédit Suisse* case, the foreign court had no jurisdiction to grant interim relief, and where, as in the *Refco* case, the foreign court had jurisdiction, but would in principle not exercise it; and, provided that it did not hamper case management in the foreign court, there was no reason why the English court should not be able to grant ancillary relief in such a case if it were otherwise appropriate. But Millett L.J. thought that the English court should be very slow to grant relief where the foreign court would not have granted it even against persons present within its own jurisdiction and having assets there.

8–027   In *Republic of Haiti v. Duvalier*[81] and *Crédit Suisse Fides Trust S.A. v. Cuoghi*[82] the court granted worldwide *Mareva* relief in support of proceedings in, respectively, France and Switzerland. In the former case the relief was effective because the defendants had solicitors in England who held assets for them abroad, and in the latter case the defendant was domiciled in England. In each case therefore the fact that the court had no jurisdiction apart from section 25 (in the former case because the substance of the case had no relevant connection with England, and in the latter case because there were already proceedings in Switzerland) did not make it "inexpedient for the court

---

[77] Although the defendant was domiciled in England, the effect of Art. 21 of the Lugano Convention was that the prior Swiss proceedings deprived the English court of jurisdiction over the substance of the claim: *post*, Rule 31(4).
[78] At 829.
[79] At 831.
[80] [1999] 1 Lloyd's Rep. 159 (C.A.).
[81] [1990] 1 Q.B. 202 (C.A.).
[82] [1998] Q.B. 818 (C.A.).

to grant" the relief within the meaning of section 25(2). Subsequently the European Court has ruled[83] that the grant of provisional or protective measures on the basis of Article 24 is conditional on, among other conditions, the existence of a real connecting link between the subject-matter of the measures sought and the territorial jurisdiction of the Contracting State before whose court the measures are sought. There is no reason to suppose that the decisions of the Court of Appeal would require reconsideration in the light of this ruling. In each case, notwithstanding the worldwide nature of the relief, there was a real connecting link with England, which was the only place where an effective order could be made.[84]

Interim relief where proceedings stayed. A claimant may commence an   **8–028** action *in personam* or *in rem* in England in a case where (apart from the 1968 or the Lugano Convention) the defendant may be entitled to a stay of the proceedings, either as a matter of discretion (*e.g.* on the ground that some other court is the appropriate forum, or that there is a jurisdiction clause providing for the exclusive jurisdiction of the courts of another country) or as a matter of right, such as where the defendant is entitled to a mandatory stay under the Arbitration Act 1996.

Where the stay is discretionary, the court may allow a *Mareva* injunction to   **8–029** remain in force as a condition of the stay.[85] The position with regard to cases where there is a mandatory stay because there is an arbitration agreement between the parties has been substantially altered by the Arbitration Act 1996. The position prior to the 1996 Act was that the court had express power under section 12(6) of the Arbitration Act 1950 "for the purpose of and in relation to a reference" to make orders in respect of (*inter alia*) interim injunctions as it had in relation to actions. This power entitled the court to continue a *Mareva* injunction notwithstanding that the defendant was entitled to a stay of proceedings. But section 12(6) did not apply to arbitration in a foreign country. If the place of arbitration was abroad, but the defendant was subject to the *in personam* jurisdiction of the English court, it was held by the House of Lords in *Channel Tunnel Group Ltd. v. Balfour Beatty Ltd.*[86] (a case involving an application for an interim injunction to restrain the defendants from suspending work on the Channel tunnel) that the court could grant interim relief because it had jurisdiction over the substantive cause of action (and consequently the decision in *The Siskina*[87] was not a bar to relief); but the onus was on the applicant to prove that it was appropriate for the English court to grant relief rather than leaving to the court at the seat of the arbitration; and the discretion to grant such relief should not be exercised if that would be to preempt the decision of the arbitral tribunal.

The position under the Arbitration Act 1996 is as follows. Unless otherwise   **8–030** agreed by the parties, the court has wide power to grant interim relief,

---

[83] Case C–391/95 *Van Uden Maritime B.V. v. Firma Deco-Line* [1999] 2 W.L.R. 1181, 1210.
[84] *Cf.* [1998] Q.B. 818, 829.
[85] *Cf. Spiliada Maritime Corp. v. Cansulex Ltd.* [1987] A.C. 460, 483; *The Rena K* [1979] Q.B. 377, 407. In *Phonogram Ltd. v. Def American Inc., The Times,* October 7, 1994, it was held that the court had power to grant an interim injunction in English proceedings which had been stayed because of parallel proceedings in California, but the power would only be exercised in an unusual case because otherwise it might pre-empt the ruling of the foreign court. See also *Law v. Garrett* (1878) 8 Ch.D. 26, 38 (C.A.).
[86] [1993] A.C. 334.
[87] [1979] A.C. 210.

including the grant of an interim injunction.[88] If the case is one of urgency the court may, on the application of a party or proposed party to the arbitral proceedings, make such orders as it thinks necessary for the purpose of preserving evidence or assets.[89] But if the case is not one of urgency, the court is to act only on the application of a party to the arbitral proceedings made with the permission of the arbitral tribunal or the agreement in writing of the other parties.[90] In any case the court may act only if or to the extent that the arbitral tribunal (or relevant arbitral institution) has no power or is unable for the time being to act effectively.[91] By contrast with the position under the Arbitration Act 1950, these powers are not limited to English arbitrations. They are exercisable even if the seat of the arbitration is outside England, or if no seat has been designated or determined, but the court may refuse to exercise its powers to grant interim relief if, in the opinion of the court, the fact that the seat of the arbitration is outside England, or that when designated or determined it is likely to be outside England, makes it inappropriate to do.[92]

8–031   **The relationship between security in Admiralty proceedings *in rem* and proceedings in other tribunals.** The *Mareva* injunction is a remedy *in personam* designed to ensure the effectiveness of the final judgment which the claimant seeks. In Admiralty procedings *in rem* the *res* may be arrested by the court and kept in the custody of the Admiralty Marshal until it is released. Where a claim *in rem* is brought against a ship or other property and the property is arrested or other security is given to prevent arrest or obtain release from arrest, the question arises whether the arrested property or other security may be retained even if the proceedings are stayed on the ground that the dispute ought to be decided by another tribunal, *e.g.* under the inherent jurisdiction of the court[93] or under Articles 17 or 21 to 22 of the 1968 Convention or the Lugano Convention,[94] or under section 9 of the Arbitration Act 1996.[95] The position is now regulated[96] by section 26 of the Civil Jurisdiction and Judgments Act 1982 and section 11 of the Arbitration Act 1996. Their combined effect is that where the court stays or dismisses Admiralty proceedings on the ground that the dispute should be submitted to the determination of the courts of another part of the United Kingdom or of an overseas country, or stays the proceedings on the ground that the dispute should be submitted to arbitration, the court may order that property arrested be retained as security for the satisfaction of any judgment or award, or order

---

[88] s. 44(1),(2)(*e*). In Case C–391/95 *Van Uden Maritime B.V. v. Firma Deco-Line* [1998] E.C.R. I–7091; [1999] 2 W.L.R. 1181, at paras. 24–25, it seems to be suggested that if the respondent to the arbitration is domiciled in a 1968 Convention Contracting State, this power is ultimately exercised on the basis of Art. 24 of the 1968 Convention: *sed quaere*.

[89] s.44(3).

[90] s.44(4).

[91] s.44(5).

[92] s.2(3).

[93] Rule 31(1).

[94] Rules 31(4) and 32(3).

[95] Rule 58.

[96] Before section 26 of the 1982 Act came into force in 1984, the question had been raised in a number of cases involving arbitration clauses, in which somewhat artificial distinctions had been drawn between security for the action *in rem*, and security for the arbitration: see *The Golden Trader* [1975] Q.B. 348; *The Rena K* [1979] Q.B. 377; *The Andria* [1984] Q.B. 477 (C.A.); *The Tuyuti* [1984] Q.B. 838 (C.A.); *cf. The Bazias 3* [1993] Q.B. 673, 680–681 (C.A.); and see Mustill and Boyd, *Commercial Arbitration* (2nd ed. 1989), pp. 339–341.

that the stay or dismissal of the proceedings be conditional on the provision of equivalent security.

These provisions are similar to (but not identical with) Article 7 of the Brussels Arrest Convention of 1952, which provides that if the court within whose jurisdiction a ship has been arrested does not have jurisdiction to decide upon the merits, the bail or other security given to procure its release shall provide that it is given as security for the satisfaction of any judgment which may eventually be pronounced by a court having jurisdiction to decide upon the merits. It was held in *The Nordglimt*[97] that section 26 of the 1982 Act should be construed so as to conform to the provisions of the Brussels Arrest Convention. Consequently it was said (*obiter*) that section 26 applied even if proceedings were struck out for want of jurisdiction, rather than stayed or dismissed. It was also held that section 26 applied where the foreign proceedings or arbitration proceedings had already been commenced at the time of the institution of the proceedings in England.[98]

8–032

Both section 26 of the 1982 Act and section 11 of the Arbitration Act 1996 contemplate that where Admiralty proceedings are stayed or dismissed on the ground that the dispute should be submitted to the determination of the courts of a foreign country or to arbitration, the court may order either (a) that the ship be retained as security for the satisfaction of any ultimate judgment, or by the foreign court award by the arbitral tribunal or (b) that the stay or dismissal be conditional on the provision of equivalent security for the satisfaction of the judgment or award.

8–033

The question has arisen whether it is possible for the court to make the second form of order in cases where the court is obliged to order a stay or decline jurisdiction. The court is obliged to order a stay or decline jurisdiction where the parties have agreed to submit their disputes to arbitration[99] or where they have agreed to the jurisdiction of the courts of a Contracting State to the 1968 Convention or the Lugano Convention, or where proceedings have first been commenced in such a country.[1] In *The World Star*[2] it was held that, where the court is required to make an order staying the proceedings under what is now section 9 of the Arbitration Act 1996, the court cannot make the second form of order, *i.e.* to attach conditions to the grant of a stay. The reason is that the essence of such a condition is that if it is not complied with the stay is removed and the proceedings continue. But where a stay is mandatory, the court has no power to remove the stay[3]; and the same would apply if the court is under a duty to decline jurisdiction under the 1968 Convention or the

8–034

---

[97] [1988] Q.B. 183, overruled on other grounds in *Republic of India* v. *India Steamship Co. Ltd.* (*No. 2*) [1998] A.C. 878. See also *Clipper Shipping Co. Ltd. v. San Vincente Partners*, 1989 S.L.T. 204. For the practice see *The Emre II* [1989] 2 Lloyd's Rep. 182; *The Sylt* [1991] 1 Lloyd's Rep. 240; *The Bazias 3* [1993] Q.B. 673 (C.A.).

[98] See also *The Jalamatsya* [1987] 2 Lloyd's Rep. 164, followed in *Allonah Pty. Ltd. v. The Amanda N* (1989) 90 A.L.R. 391. In *The Silver Athens (No. 2)* [1986] 2 Lloyd's Rep. 583 it was held that where proceedings had already been stayed before an arrest was effected, an application could be made for the stay to be lifted in order to arrest the vessel and to apply for an order that the security be retained.

[99] Arbitration Act 1996, s.9, which is not limited (as was Arbitration Act 1975, s.1) to international cases: Rule 58.

[1] Rules 32(3) and 31(4).

[2] [1986] 2 Lloyd's Rep. 274, decided on 1982 Act, s.26, before it was amended by the Arbitration Act 1996 to remove arbitration from its scope. For the position prior to the 1982 Act, see *The Rena K* [1979] Q.B. 377, 400; *cf. The Tuyuti* [1984] Q.B. 838, 849 (C.A.).

[3] Mustill and Boyd, p.341.

Lugano Convention.[4] It is not, however, necessary to resolve the apparent inconsistency between the provisions of section 26 of the 1982 Act and section 11 of the Arbitration Act 1996 and the mandatory provisions of the 1968 and Lugano Conventions and the New York Convention. The same practical result is reached by the first form of order, namely to retain the vessel as security. This is through the use of the discretion of the court to release the vessel from arrest.[5] That power is normally exercised only if security is provided by guarantee or otherwise for the claim, interest and costs.[6] Neither the retention of the vessel nor the exercise of the discretion to release it upon provision of equivalent security involves the imposition of a condition,[7] and if the owner of the vessel which has been arrested wishes to secure its release, it will in practice have no alternative but to provide equivalent security.

8–035   **(2) Judicial assistance: service of process.** Service of process and the gathering of evidence were seen in the common law tradition as matters for the claimant or his agents.[8] So far as the service of documents is concerned, there are obvious practical advantages in the service of documents through the court service and in England Part 6 of the Civil Procedure Rules 1998 now makes provision for this, while allowing the party concerned to notify the court that he wishes to serve the document himself.[9] In sharp contrast is the principle of the classical civil law tradition, under which these matters are official acts, to be carried out on behalf of the State as an exercise of its judicial sovereignty. It follows that, as between countries in that civil law tradition, the service of process or the taking of evidence abroad will necessarily involve the co-operation of the official authorities in each country. The claimant in an English action may similarly have to resort to official channels in order to serve process or obtain evidence abroad. Although simple procedures such as service by post are increasingly recognised and used in international practice, they are still objected to by a number of countries as infringing their sovereignty or as inconsistent with the approach of their national law in treating service of process as necessarily a formal and official act.

8–036   The term "international judicial (or, legal) assistance" is used to describe the procedures for international co-operation in these matters, procedures which have been developed and simplified in more recent years to cope with the ever-increasing volume of business.[10]

8–037   **Service of process.** A number of modes of effecting the service of process have become established in international practice. The use of consular channels is well-established and is recognised in the Vienna Convention on Consular Relations 1963. Article 5 of that Convention, given the force of law in the United Kingdom by the Consular Relations Act 1968,[11] recognises as a consular function that of transmitting judicial and extra-judicial documents or executing letters rogatory or commissions to take evidence for the courts of

---

[4] See Hartley (1989) 105 L.Q.R. 640, 656–660.
[5] CPR PD49F, para. 6.6(1), replacing R.S.C. Ord. 75, r.13.
[6] *The Bazias 3* [1993] Q.B. 673 (C.A.).
[7] *Cf. The Tuyuti* [1984] Q.B. 838, 849 (C.A.).
[8] See, *e.g. South Carolina Insurance Co. v. Assurantie Maatschappij "De Zeven Provincien" N.V.* [1987] A.C. 24, 41–42, *per* Lord Brandon.
[9] CPR 6.3(1)(b).
[10] See McClean, *International Judicial Assistance* (1992).
[11] s.1(1).

the sending State in accordance with international agreements in force or, in the absence of such international agreements, in any other manner compatible with the laws and regulations of the receiving State.[12] A distinction is sometimes drawn between the direct consular channel in which the consular officer effects service of the document, and the indirect consular channel in which he transmits the document to an appropriate authority in the receiving State with a view to service being effected by that authority. In some States, these modes of service are permitted only where the addressee is a national of the State represented by the consular officer.

In a number of European countries in the civil law tradition there exists an **8–038** office of huissier, or official process server. International practice in these countries recognises the use of huissiers for the service of documents originating outside the jurisdiction and received directly from a party concerned or indirectly through official channels or through a huissier in the State of origin.

The United Kingdom is party to a number of bilateral Civil Procedure **8–039** Conventions which commonly provide for service through the consular channel or through the judicial authorities (including huissiers) of the receiving State.[13]

The Hague Convention on the service abroad of judicial and extra-judicial **8–040** documents in civil or commercial matters, 1965,[14] to which the United Kingdom is also party, is the most important multilateral convention in this field and has influenced the form of a number of regional conventions.[15] Although the Hague Convention preserves the possibility of using the traditional modes of service to the extent that they are compatible with the law of the requested State,[16] it introduces a new and preferred mode in which documents are sent to a designated Central Authority in the State in which service is required, to be served by the formal methods prescribed in the law of that State, or by informal delivery, or by any particular method specified in the request for service which is compatible with the local law.[17]

There has been much debate as to whether the Hague Convention is **8–041** mandatory, excluding forms of service abroad not permitted by its provisions; by its own terms it applies "in all cases, in civil and commercial matters, where there is occasion to transmit a judicial or extra-judicial document for service abroad."[18] In *Volkswagenwerk A.G. v. Schlunk*,[19] the United States Supreme Court held that the provisions of the Hague Service Convention were mandatory, and that whenever there was occasion to transmit a document for service abroad only those methods of service permitted by the Convention could be used. The Court, however, also held that it was for the *lex fori* to

---

[12] Art. 5(j).

[13] See Ord. 11, r. 6(2) (Civil Procedure Rules 1998, Sched. 1) and *The Supreme Court Practice 1999*, para. 11/6/3.

[14] For text see Cmnd. 3986. See also the Practical Handbook on the operation of the Convention prepared by the Permanent Bureau of The Hague Conference.

[15] *e.g.* the Inter-American Convention on Letters Rogatory, 1975 especially as amended by the Protocol of 1979; see McClean, *op. cit.*, 16–51.

[16] Arts. 8 and 9 (consular and diplomatic channels), Art. 10 (postal channels, judicial authorities and huissiers). Where the foreign country objects to a mode of service (*e.g.* the use of the post), service by that mode will be bad: see Ord. 11, r. 5(2), and *cf. Re an English Judgment* [1993] I.L.Pr. 653 (OLG Hamm, 1992).

[17] Arts. 2, 5.

[18] Art 1, and see the Explanatory Report of Mr Taborda Ferreira, *Actes et Documents* of the 10th Session, vol. 3, p. 367.

[19] 486 U.S. 694 (1988).

determine when such service abroad was required and that the Convention did not prohibit reliance on provisions of the *lex fori* allowing service on a defendant resident abroad to be effected, for example, by service on a wholly-owned subsidiary within the forum country. The Supreme Court would subject State laws allowing such service only to the Due Process Clause of the United States Constitution, requiring only that any form of substituted service be reasonably calculated to apprise interested parties of the pendency of the action and afford them an opportunity to present their objections.[20] Although this decision has been criticised as one reading United States principles into an international text, the Netherlands Supreme Court has taken a similar view.[21]

8–042   The mandatory quality of the Hague Convention does not stand in the way of the traditional service of English process by an agent in another common law country. Given that the country concerned would raise no objection, the service can be treated as falling within the convention provision[22] allowing "any person interested in a judicial proceeding" to effect service through a "competent person" in the State of destination; the latter phrase has always been treated as including solicitors.

8–043   *European Union Convention.* A Convention (which is not yet in force) on the service in Member States of the European Union of judicial and extra-judicial documents in civil and commercial matters was signed in 1997.[23] It builds on the experience gained under the Hague Convention and provides for a system of communication between decentralised agencies communicating directly one to the other.

8–044   The Convention applies in civil and commercial matters where a judicial or extrajudicial document has to be transmitted from one Member State to another for service there.[24] Each Member State must designate "transmitting agencies" and "receiving agencies", competent for the transmission and receipt of documents.[25] These are intended to be local agencies, though it is possible for a Member State to designate an agency to act over the whole of its territory, and indeed to act as both transmitting and receiving agency.[26] In addition each Member State must designate a "central body" responsible for (a) supplying information to the transmitting agencies; (b) seeking solutions to any difficulties which may arise during transmission of documents for service; and (c) forwarding, in exceptional cases, at the request of a transmitting agency, a request for service to the competent receiving agency.[27] The Explanatory Report emphasises that use of the central bodies to handle documents is truly exceptional; examples given are those of a general strike or natural disaster bringing a region's public services to a standstill.

---

[20] Three Justices joined in a concurring opinion which would approve of the mode of service adopted in the particular case as being permitted by the Convention which was designed to ensure that documents should be brought to the attention of the addressee in sufficient time (Convention, preamble).

[21] *Segers and Rufa B.V. v. Mabanaft GmbH* N.J. 1986, 764. See McClean, *op. cit*, pp. 34–41.

[22] Art. 10(*c*).

[23] For text see [1997] O.J. C261. For commentary see the official explanatory report (*ibid.* C261/26) and Kennett (1998) 17 C.J.Q. 284. A Protocol to the Convention provides for its interpretation by the European Court.

[24] Art. 1(1).

[25] Art. 2(1)(2).

[26] See Explanatory Report, pp. 28–29.

[27] Art. 3.

In principle, judicial documents are to be transmitted directly and as soon **8–045** as possible between the relevant transmitting and receiving agencies. Any method of transmission may be used, provided that the content of the document received is true and faithful to that of the document forwarded and that all information in it is easily legible.[28] This means that electronic means may be used, provided they are available in both countries concerned. The Convention prescribes a standard form of request for service which must accompany the document and be completed in a language which the Member State addressed has indicated it can accept.[29] The document itself need not be translated, but the addressee may refuse to accept the document if it is in a language other than the official language of the Member State (or part of that State) where service is to be effected or a language of the Member State of transmission which the addressee understands.[30] A transmitting agency is required to warn the applicant for service of this risk.[31]

A receiving agency is required to acknowledge receipt of a document, **8–046** within seven days of its receipt, using a standard form prescribed in the Annex to the Convention.[32] It must itself serve the document or have it served, either in accordance with the law of the Member State addressed or by a particular form requested by the transmitting agency, unless such a method is incompatible with the law of that Member State. Service must be effected as soon as possible.[33] A certificate of service must be provided by the receiving agency using a prescribed form.[34] If it has not been possible to effect service within one month of receipt, the receiving agency must inform the transmitting agency using another prescribed form.[35] In general, the service of judicial documents attracts no charge or claim for reimbursement of taxes or costs, but the applicant must pay or reimburse the costs occasioned by the employment of a judicial officer or of a person competent under the law of the Member State addressed, or the use of a particular method of service.[36]

The Convention permits the use of other modes of service: the use of **8–047** consular or diplomatic channels "in exceptional circumstances"[37]; service directly through its diplomatic or consular agents on persons residing in another Member State, without application of any compulsion (though a Member State may prohibit this mode of service where the addressee is not a national of the State of origin)[38]; service by post (though a Member State may impose conditions on the use of this mode)[39]; and, unless this is objected to by the State of service, direct service by any person interested in a judicial proceeding through the judicial officers, officials or other competent persons of the Member State addressed.[40] Extrajudicial documents may be transmitted

---

[28] Art. 4(1)(2).
[29] Art. 4(3).
[30] Art. 8(1).
[31] Art. 5.
[32] Art. 6(1).
[33] Art. 7.
[34] Art. 10.
[35] Art. 7.
[36] Art. 11.
[37] Art. 12.
[38] Art. 13.
[39] Art. 14.
[40] Art. 15.

for service in another Member State in accordance with the same provisions.[41]

8–048   Article 19 of the Convention applies Articles 15 and 16 of the Hague Convention, prohibiting judgment in default of appearance unless either (a) there is proof of service or delivery of the document in sufficient time to enable the defendant to defend; or (b) the Member State in which judgment is sought had declared that its courts could give judgment if the document was transmitted by one of the methods provided for in this Convention, a period of time of not less than six months, considered adequate by the judge in the particular case, had elapsed since the date of the transmission of the document, and no certificate of any kind had been received, even though every reasonable effort had been made to obtain it through the competent authorities of the State addressed.[42]

8–049   *Service abroad of process originating in England.* Order 11 (re-enacted in the Civil Procedure Rules 1998, Schedule 1) allows service by the claimant or his agent, either by personal service or by a mode of service in accordance with the law of the country in which service is effected[43]; service through the judicial authorities of, or British consular officers in, States with which a bilateral Civil Procedure Convention exists, subject to the terms of the relevant Convention[44]; service in accordance with the Hague Convention through the relevant Central Authority or through judicial authorities or the consular channel[45]; and, in non-convention countries, through the government of the relevant country or the consular channel so far as the local law permits.[46] Service abroad by post is only permitted under an order for service by an alternative method, or substituted service as it was formerly called. Nothing in the relevant rule[47] or in any order or direction of the court made by virtue of it can authorise or require the doing of anything in a country in which service is effected which is contrary to the law of that country.[48] It will take a very strong case, for example express representation by the defendant that the method of service was lawful, to persuade the court to allow to stand service which was contrary to the law of the country in which it was effected.[49]

8–050   Additionally, the parties to a contract in respect of which an action is brought in the High Court may agree upon the use of any mode of service, whether within or out of the jurisdiction, and service in accordance with such an agreement is good.[50]

8–051   Where service is to be effected in accordance with the Hague Convention by a method prescribed by the internal law of the State in which service is required, that State may require that the document to be served be accompanied by a translation into its official language. A declaration indicating that this requirement would be insisted on has been made by most of the States

---

[41] Art. 16.
[42] See also Art. 19(2) allowing judgments by default to be set aside in certain circumstances.
[43] Ord. 11, r. 5(2)(3).
[44] Ord. 11, r. 6(2).
[45] Ord. 11, r. 6(2A).
[46] Ord. 11, r. 6(3).
[47] Ord. 11, r. 5.
[48] Ord. 11, r. 5(2).
[49] *The Sky One* [1988] 1 Lloyd's Rep. 238 (C.A.).
[50] CPR 6.15. Leave may be required under Ord. 11, r. 1(1): see post, para. 11–112.

party to the Convention.[51] The method of informal delivery under the Convention does not require a translation, but is only available when the addressee is prepared to accept service voluntarily. The supply of a translation in cases not under the Hague Convention may be required by the law of the State addressed or under a bilateral Civil Procedure Convention. In all cases the provision of a translation reduces the scope for an argument by the addressee that he had insufficient knowledge of the document to enable him to make a prompt defence.[52]

Service in England of process originating abroad. There is no objection in   **8–052** English law to the use of the consular channel, nor to service by post. Foreign parties are also free to effect service through the agency of an English solicitor. Where the document to be served originates in a Contracting State to the Hague Convention, the Central Authority[53] will act, and these official channels will also respond to requests under bilateral Civil Procedure Conventions or, in practice, in other cases from foreign judicial, consular or diplomatic sources.[54]

(3) Judicial assistance: obtaining evidence abroad. In countries in the   **8–053** common law tradition the preparation of a case for trial is the private responsibility of the parties. The taking of evidence by a foreign consul or commissioner for the purposes of foreign court proceedings will in such countries meet with no legal objection and require few if any preliminary formalities. Many civil law countries view the obtaining of evidence as part of the judicial function, and the actions of agents of a foreign court may be seen as offending the sovereignty of the State in its judicial aspect. If evidence is to be obtained in such countries official intervention will normally be required, though bilateral and multilateral civil procedure conventions may exist to regulate and simplify the procedures.

Obtaining evidence abroad for use in English proceedings. English law   **8–054** makes ample provision enabling parties to English proceedings to obtain evidence abroad. The powers given are exercised with the greatest discretion,[55] partly because of the sensitivities of other countries but also to avoid unnecessary expense, delay and inconvenience. For these reasons the English courts are reluctant to grant applications by a claimant (who has chosen to sue in England) for evidence, especially his own evidence, to be taken abroad.[56] In appropriate circumstances, however, the court will exercise its powers. For example, in *News International plc v. Clinger*,[57] an order was made on the plaintiff's application for cross-examination of a defendant before an examiner (the judge himself) in Israel in support of a *Mareva* injunction. The taking

---

[51] See Convention, Art. 5(3).

[52] See Hague Convention, Art. 15(1)(2), 16(1) for the relevance of such an argument under that Convention.

[53] The Foreign Office. There are additional authorities ("other authorities" under Art. 18(1)) in the various parts of the United Kingdom; in England this is the Senior Master of the Supreme Court.

[54] See the Practical Handbook cited in n. 14, *supra*, for statements by the United Kingdom government as to English practice.

[55] *Settebello Ltd. v. Banco Totta & Acores* [1985] 1 W.L.R. 1050 (C.A.).

[56] *e.g. Berdan v. Greenwood* (1880) 20 Ch.D. 764n. (C.A.), stated as Illustration 8, para. 8–092, *post*.

[57] unreported, August 16, 1996, Ch.D.

of evidence before an examiner was allowed by the terms of the relevant bilateral civil procedure convention, and it was held that this included evidence on an interlocutory issue.[58]

8–055 The same reluctance will not be applied on a defendant's application. There may be circumstances in which, while England is an appropriate forum, the practical realities are such that unless the defendant can give evidence abroad he will be unable to defend the action. To avoid such oppression and unfairness, the court will exercise its powers to enable the evidence to be taken abroad.[59]

8–056 The court will require to be satisfied that the witness cannot attend for examination in England, as a result of proven ill-health[60] or, in some cases, the disproportionate cost of travel,[61] and that the witness has material evidence to give.[62] Where the credibility of the witness is especially important, and particularly where there is an issue as to his identity,[63] the court will not make an order depriving the claimant of the opportunity to test the evidence by cross-examination in open court.[64]

8–057 The court acts under its general power to order depositions to be taken before an examiner, with appropriate disclosure of documents before the examination takes place.[65] A number of different procedures are available when the person to be examined is out of the jurisdiction. That most generally available involves the issue of a Letter of Request to the judicial authorities of the foreign country asking the foreign court to take or cause to be taken the required evidence. The Letter may be accompanied by interrogatories and may request that cross-examination be permitted. A second procedure entails the appointment of a special examiner to take the evidence abroad; this is only available if the government of the foreign country allows such examinations,[66] and only a few States will make available the assistance of their courts to grant measures of compulsion should the witness be unwilling to appear before the examiner. Finally, a British consul may be appointed to act as a special examiner, either in accordance with a Civil Procedure Convention with the relevant foreign country or with the consent of the Foreign Secretary.[67] Where a person is to have his evidence taken outside the jurisdiction, he may be examined on oath or affirmation or otherwise in accordance with the procedure of the country where the examination is to take place.[68] Although the court normally acts under what was Order 39 of the Rules of the Supreme

---

[58] The defendant's attendance would be voluntary, despite the fact that his failure to attend would mean that his affidavit evidence would not be used in evidence under CPR 32.7.

[59] *Ross v. Woodford* [1894] 1 Ch. 38, stated as Illustration 9, para. 8–092, *post*.

[60] *Berdan v. Greenwood, supra; Haynes v. Haynes* (1962) 35 D.L.R. (2d) 602 (B.C.).

[61] *Wong Doo v. Kana Bhana* [1973] N.Z.L.R. 1455 (C.A.).

[62] *Hardie Rubber Co. Pty. Ltd. v. General Tire and Rubber Co.* (1973) 129 C.L.R. 521; *Lucas Industries Ltd. v. Chloride Batteries Australia Ltd.* (1978) 45 F.L.R. 160. *Cf. Ehrmann v. Ehrmann* (1896) 2 Ch.D. 611 (C.A.) (insufficient that evidence would "bolster" other evidence).

[63] *Nadin v. Bassett* (1884) 25 Ch.D. 21 (C.A.).

[64] *Hardie Rubber Co. Pty. Ltd. v. General Tire and Rubber Co.* (1973) 129 C.L.R. 521 (difficulties of conducting cross-examination in Japan). *Cf. The Adolf Leonhardt* [1973] 2 Lloyd's Rep. 318, where Brandon J. appointed himself a special examiner to sit for part of the trial in the Netherlands. See McClean, *op. cit.*, pp. 75–80.

[65] CPR 34.8.

[66] CPR 34.13(4).

[67] CPR PD34, para. 5.8.

[68] CPR 34.13(5).

Court,[69] and is now Rule 34.13 of the Civil Procedure Rules 1998, the power to issue a Letter of Request derives from the inherent jurisdiction. So, for example, even if no order could be made to require a company to produce documents (because any such order must be part of one for the examination of a witness and a company cannot attend to give oral evidence), the court had power to make whatever *request* of a foreign court (which did not involve the making of an *order*) was desirable in the interests of justice and to which the foreign court would be likely to be receptive (*e.g.* because the request came within the broad terms of the Hague Convention, in which "evidence" is not defined).

It is only in very exceptional circumstances that the English court will make an order against someone who is not a party to the English proceedings to produce documents situated in a foreign jurisdiction or to allow such documents to be inspected or copied.[70] The use of a witness summons[71] or the making of an order for the inspection of books under section 7 of the Bankers' Books Evidence Act 1879 in respect of such documents is an infringement of the sovereignty of the foreign State; such an infringement can only be justified by exceptional grounds of urgent necessity.[72] The same principles apply where the English court is asked to make an order for disclosure of documents against someone who is joined as a defendant solely for that purpose[73]; although in form this involves disclosure by a party, in substance it is an order against a third party.[74] An order under section 236 of the Insolvency Act 1986 may be made in respect of documents located abroad. Insofar as that involves an assertion of sovereignty, it is one authorised by the Parliament and where the section is applicable the courts will not require proof of exceptional circumstances or urgency.[75]   **8–058**

Where evidence is to be obtained from another part of the United Kingdom, the same procedures are available as in the case of a politically foreign country. The sensitivities surrounding the issue of state sovereignty are, of course, absent but the English court will nonetheless exercise care before approving an order. So, when a Letter of Request is to be addressed to a court in another part of the United Kingdom, the English court as the requesting court will itself examine the proposed request to see if it is one which meets the requirements of the requested court[76] such as those laid down by the   **8–059**

---

[69] *Panayiotou v. Sony Music Entertainment (U.K.) Ltd.* [1994] Ch. 142.

[70] *MacKinnon v. Donaldson, Lufkin and Jenrette Securities Corp.* [1986] Ch. 482; *Re Mid East Trading Ltd.* [1998] 1 All E.R. 577 (C.A.).

[71] Replacing the former subpoena *duces tecum*: CPR 34.2(1)(b).

[72] *Ibid.; London and Counties Securities Ltd. v. Caplan* (May 26, 1978; unreported); *R. v. Grossman* (1981) 73 Cr.App.R. 302 (C.A.).

[73] *i.e.* under the principle in *Norwich Pharmacal Co. v. Customs and Excise Commissioners* [1974] A.C. 133 and *Bankers Trust Co. v. Shapira* [1980] 1 W.L.R. 1274 (C.A.), the person concerned having become "mixed up in the tortious acts of others." See *Mercantile Group (Europe) A.G. v. Aiyela* [1994] Q.B. 366 (C.A.) (in context of *Mareva* injunction against third party once a defendant but against whom original action discontinued); *Omar v. Omar* [1995] 1 W.L.R. 1426 (documents discovered used as basis for amended action); *Jade Engineering (Coventry) Ltd. v. Antiference Window Systems Ltd.* [1996] F.S.R. 461, where the principle in *Norwich Pharmacal Co. v. Customs and Excise Commissioners* was applied where the wrong-doer was abroad.

[74] *MacKinnon v. Donaldson, Lufkin and Jenrette Securities Corp.* [1986] Ch. 482. *Cf. Fusco v. O'Dea* [1994] 2 I.L.R.M. 389 (Sup. Ct.).

[75] *Re Mid East Trading Ltd.* [1998] 1 All E.R. 577 (C.A.).

[76] *Stewart v. Callaghan*, 1996 S.L.T. (Sh.Ct.) 12.

House of Lords in *Re Westinghouse Uranium Contract Litigation M.D.L. Docket No. 235.*[77]

8–060   A growing number of countries, including the United Kingdom, are parties to the Hague Convention on the Taking of Evidence Abroad in Civil and Commercial Matters 1970,[78] which establishes clear procedures and improves the flow of information between Contracting States. Chapter I of the Convention is concerned with the Letters of Request procedure and applies to Letters issued by the judicial authorities of a Contracting State in civil or commercial matters to obtain evidence intended for use in judicial proceedings, commenced or contemplated.[79] The request can cover a variety of forms of evidence, including oral testimony and the inspection of documents or other property,[80] and is sent to a Central Authority designated for the purposes of the Convention in the country in which the evidence is to be taken.[81] The Convention does not exclude the use of other methods of obtaining evidence provided for under the national law of the State in which the evidence is sought.[82]

8–061   In *Société Nationale Industrielle Aérospatiale v. U.S. District Court for the Southern District of Iowa*[83] the United States Supreme Court held that the Hague Convention does not provide an exclusive or mandatory set of procedures, nor even a preferred set of procedures to which first resort must always be had. The court did, however, recognise the need for considerations of comity to be addressed before orders were made which would be regarded by the foreign State concerned as an infringement of its sovereignty.[84] The English court has taken a similar approach, confirming an order for discovery against a French company despite an argument that first resort should have been had either to the Hague Convention or to the bilateral Civil Procedure Convention between the United Kingdom and France.[85]

8–062   Under Article 23 of the Convention, inserted at the proposal of the United Kingdom, a reservation is permitted. A Contracting State may declare "that it will not execute Letters of Request issued for the purpose of obtaining pretrial discovery of documents as known in Common Law countries." It is now recognised amongst delegates at the Hague Conference that this Article was poorly drafted. It also seems that the authors of the Convention failed to address important questions as to the relationship between a reservation under Article 23 and the primary provisions of the Convention which is concerned with "evidence" and "other judicial acts," concepts which few of the signatory States would regard as including the more extensive forms of discovery

---

[77] [1978] A.C. 547 (see *post*, para. 8–076).
[78] For text see Cmnd. 3991. See the Practical Handbook on the operation of the Convention prepared by the Permanent Bureau of The Hague Conference, and McClean, *op. cit.*, Chap. 3.
[79] Art. 1.
[80] See Art. 3(1)(*f*)(*g*). The appointment of a technical expert to assist the court is not within the scope of the Hague Convention: *Sté Luxguard v. Sté S.N. Sitaco* [1996] I.L.Pr. 5 (Cr d'app., Versailles, 1993) (exploring relationship between that Convention and Brussels Convention of 1968).
[81] In the United Kingdom, as in most countries, the Central Authority and other relevant authorities are the same as those acting in respect of the Hague Convention on the Service of Process; see para. 8–040, *supra*.
[82] Art. 27(*c*).
[83] 482 U.S. 522 (1987).
[84] See Slomanson (1988) 37 I.C.L.Q. 391; Born and Hoing (1990) 24 Int.L. 393; McClean, *op. cit.*, pp. 107–118.
[85] *The Heidberg* [1993] 2 Lloyd's Rep. 324.

procedures. The phrase "pre-trial discovery of documents as known in Common Law countries" obscures significant differences between the procedures available in countries following the practice contained in what was R.S.C. Order 24 and is now Part 31 of the Civil Procedure Rules 1998 and the much more extensive procedures available in many jurisdictions in the United States which can include wide-ranging requests for non-parties to the action to make oral depositions or to produce documents[86] which may not necessarily be relevant to the issues but could possibly assist the plaintiff to formulate allegations against the defendant. The United Kingdom's reservation under Article 23 contains a statement of its intended scope, which is reflected in the Evidence (Proceedings in Other Jurisdictions) Act 1975.[87] A number of other Contracting States have revised their own reservations to incorporate this statement.[88]

Chapter II of the Convention is concerned with the Taking of Evidence by Diplomatic Officers, Consular Agents and Commissioners. Diplomatic agents and consular officers may take the evidence of nationals of the State they represent without seeking prior permission from the authorities of the State in which they serve; a Contracting State may however declare that prior permission is required in these cases.[89] Where diplomats or consuls wish to take the evidence of other persons, or where a commissioner is appointed to take any evidence, prior permission is required (and may be given subject to conditions) unless the Contracting State concerned has made a declaration waiving this requirement.[90] A Contracting State may declare its willingness to make available appropriate assistance to obtain the evidence by compulsion in any of these cases.[91]   **8–063**

It is a principle of English civil procedure that a party obtains by his own means the evidence he needs to support his case. The means used may include the taking in foreign countries of any steps which may lawfully be taken there, such as the making of a direct application to a foreign court for a procedural remedy available under the law of that court, for example an extensive order for discovery which a United States court may make under its own procedural rules even if the evidence is intended for use in English proceedings.[92] United States courts may assist litigants in cases before foreign tribunals by ordering discovery under a federal statutory provision[93] which enables a district court to order a person living within its district to give his testimony or statement or to produce a document or other thing for use in a proceeding in a foreign or international tribunal. The order may be made not only in response to a request made by such a tribunal but also on the application of any interested person. Some Circuit Court of Appeals have held that this power may be exercised even where the material sought is not discoverable under the law of   **8–064**

---

[86] And, indeed, other forms of information; Art. 23 refers only to the discovery *of documents*.

[87] s.2(4): see *post*, para. 8–074.

[88] See Collins (1986) 35 I.C.L.Q. 765 (reprinted in Collins, *Essays*, p. 289) and the Report of the Special Commission of the Hague Conference on the operation of the Convention, *Actes et Documents* of the Fourteenth Session, 420–1.

[89] Art. 15.

[90] Arts. 16, 17.

[91] Art. 18.

[92] *South Carolina Insurance Co. Assurantie Maatshappij "De Zeven Provincien" N.V.* [1987] A.C. 24.

[93] 28 U.S.C., s.178.

the foreign jurisdiction,[94] though other courts do impose a "discoverability" requirement,[95] especially where the applicant is a private individual as opposed to a foreign court.[96] No prior application to the foreign court is required,[97] but the court will guard against applications which would cause offence to the foreign court[98] or are vehicles for harassment.[99] This power is not intended to provide discovery of documents maintained within the foreign forum.[1] It does not apply to arbitration proceedings.[2] The English court will not restrain a party from taking such steps in a foreign country unless they amount to unconscionable conduct interfering with the due process of the English court or invade the legal or equitable rights of another party.[3]

8–065   As between the different parts of the United Kingdom, the same principles no doubt obtain, but the requested court might well give closer attention to the question whether a similar remedy were available in the part in which the principal action was to be heard. So, in ordering disclosure of documents in Scotland to assist a party to an English patent action, the Inner House of the Court of Session noted that it might not serve the ends of justice to do what would not be done by the court in which the main proceedings were in train.[4]

8–066   **Obtaining evidence in England for use in another jurisdiction.** In many cases it is possible for evidence to be taken in England for use in foreign proceedings. This may occur with or without the involvement of the authorities of this country.

8–067   *Taking evidence without the assistance of the English court.* There is no objection in English law to the taking of evidence required for use in foreign proceedings without the intervention or permission of an English court or official agency. Such intervention will be required if measures of compulsion are required against an unwilling witness. However, the oath may only be administered in England with lawful authority. A person appointed by a court or other judicial authority of a foreign country does have power to administer oaths in the United Kingdom for the purpose of taking evidence in civil proceedings carried on under the law of that foreign country,[5] and a foreign diplomatic agent or consular officer has a general power to administer oaths in accordance with the law of the country he represents.[6]

---

[94] *Re Application of Gianola Aldunate*, 3 F. 3d 53 (2d Cir. 1993); *Metallgesellschaft A.G. v. Hodapp*, 121 F. 3d 77 (2d Cir. 1998); *Re Application of Bayer A.G.*, 146 F. 3d 188 (3d Cir. 1998).
[95] *Lo Ka Chun v. Lo To*, 858 F. 2d 1564 (11th Cir. 1988); *Re Application of Asta Medica S.A.*, 981 F. 2d 1 (1st Cir. 1992).
[96] *Re Letters Rogatory from First Court, Caracas*, 42 F. 3d 308 (5th Cir. 1995).
[97] *Re Application of Malev Hungarian Airlines*, 964 F. 2d 97 (2d Cir. 1992), cert. den. *sub nom. United Technologies International v. Malev Hungarian Airlines*, 113 S.Ct. 179 (1992).
[98] *Re Application of Bayer A.G.*, 146 F. 3d 188 (3d Cir. 1998).
[99] *Re Request for Assistance from Ministry of Legal Affairs of Trinidad and Tobago*, 848 F. 2d 1151 (11th Cir. 1988).
[1] *Re Application of Sarrio S.A. for Assistance before Foreign Tribunal* [1996] I.L.Pr. 564 (S.D.N.Y. 1995) (but point reserved on appeal: 119 F. 3d 143 (2d Cir. 1997)).
[2] *National Broadcasting Co. v. Bear Stearns & Co.*, 165 F. 3d 184 (2d Cir. 1999). See Smit (1997) 8 Am. Rev. Int. Arb. 153.
[3] *Ibid.*
[4] *Union Carbide Corp. v. BP Chemicals Ltd.*, 1995 S.L.T. 972.
[5] Oaths and Evidence (Overseas Authorities and Countries) Act 1963, s.1.
[6] Consular Relations Act 1968, s.10(1).

Taking evidence by order of the High Court. The High Court may order the **8–068** taking of evidence in England at the request of a foreign court or tribunal under the Evidence (Proceedings in Other Jurisdictions) Act 1975 and R.S.C. Order 70 (re-enacted in the Civil Procedure Rules 1998, Schedule 1) which "must be read closely with the provisions of" the Act.[7] The Court of Appeal has held that there is no inherent jurisdiction to act in aid of a foreign court; put more narrowly, the only powers available to the courts in this context are those set out in the Act.[8] Although the Act was passed to enable the United Kingdom to ratify the Hague Convention on the Taking of Evidence Abroad in Civil or Commercial Matters 1970, it does not reproduce the provisions of the Convention. The Act contains additional material, notably in relation to criminal proceedings,[9] and is drafted so as to apply to all requests for assistance whether or not made under the Convention.

The requirements of the Act in cases concerning foreign civil proceedings **8–069** are as follows. When an application is made to the High Court under the Act,[10] the court must be satisfied that the application is made in pursuance of a request issued by or on behalf of a court or tribunal exercising jurisdiction in another part of the United Kingdom or in a country or territory outside the United Kingdom,[11] or by the European Court.[12] The court must be satisfied that the evidence is to be obtained for the purposes of civil proceedings[13] which have either been instituted before the requesting court or whose institution before that court is contemplated.[14] The request will be refused where the foreign proceedings have been settled or discontinued.[15] The court may not order any steps to be taken unless they are steps which could be required to be taken by way of obtaining evidence for the purposes of civil proceedings in the English court.[16]

In this context "civil proceedings" means "proceedings in any civil or **8–070** commercial matter."[17] Given that there is in this context no internationally acceptable definition of a "civil or commercial matter," the English court must satisfy itself that the proceedings concern a civil or commercial matter under the laws of both the requesting and requested countries.[18] For the purposes of English law, "proceedings in any civil matter" includes all proceedings other than criminal proceedings, and "proceedings in any commercial matter" fall within "proceedings in any civil matter." So far as the

---

[7] *R. v. Rathbone, ex p. Dikko* [1985] Q.B. 630, 644. Corresponding powers are given to the Court of Session and the High Court of Justice in Northern Ireland. The jurisdiction is wholly statutory: *Boeing Co. v. P.P.G. Industries Inc.* [1988] 3 All E.R. 839 (C.A.).

[8] *Re Pan American Airways Inc.'s Application* [1992] Q.B. 854 (C.A.).

[9] Now repealed and replaced by the provisions of the Criminal Justice (International Co-operation) Act 1990.

[10] Either by an agent of a party or by the Treasury Solicitor: Ord. 70, r. 3; see also CPR PD34, para. 6.

[11] s.1(*a*).

[12] Evidence (European Court) Order 1976 (S.I. 1976 No. 428) made under s.6 of the Act.

[13] Including the pre-trial stages of such proceedings: *Re Westinghouse Uranium Contract Litigation M.D.L. Docket No. 235* [1978] A.C. 547, 633–4. In the absence of evidence to the contrary, the High Court will accept the statement of the requesting court as to the nature of the proceedings: *ibid.* at p. 634.

[14] s.1(*b*).

[15] *Re International Power Industries Inc., The Times*, July 25, 1984; [1985] B.C.L.C. 128.

[16] s.2(3).

[17] s.9(1).

[18] *Re State of Norway's Application (Nos. 1 and 2)* [1990] 1 A.C. 723, where the history of United Kingdom legislation since the Foreign Tribunals Evidence Act 1856 is examined. See F. A. Mann (1989) 105 L.Q.R. 341.

law of a requesting country is concerned, reference is to be made to the law and practice of that country, having regard to the manner in which classification is ordinarily made in that country.[19] This approach may be contrasted with that taken by a Special Commission of the Hague Conference in April 1989, that it was desirable that the words "civil and commercial" should be interpreted in an autonomous manner, without reference exclusively either to the law of the requesting country or to the law of the requested country, or to both laws cumulatively. The Commission recognised that there existed in international practice a "grey area" between private and public law. Developments in practice had led bankruptcy, insurance and employment to be treated as within "civil and commercial matters" but most countries excluded tax matters.[20] In English law, fiscal matters are properly within the category of "civil and commercial," and a request by a foreign country for assistance in obtaining evidence to be used in the enforcement of revenue law of that country in proceedings before the courts of that country does not constitute direct or indirect enforcement of the revenue law of a foreign State.[21]

8–071   The Act is concerned with the process by which "evidence" is to be obtained. It has already been noted that few of the authors of the Hague Convention would regard the term "evidence" as including all the material capable of being gathered in the extensive forms of pre-trial discovery found in United States jurisdictions.[22] A Letter of Request seeking such material may be seeking both evidence, which would be admissible at trial, and other material which though relevant to issues in the case would be inadmissible as evidence. This distinction is related to that drawn in cases under earlier legislation[23] between "direct" evidence and "indirect" material sought by way of discovery. The English court can only order the taking of evidence, and must decline to assist a foreign court if its Letter of Request is solely seeking material of the "indirect" variety.[24] The English courts are, however, anxious to assist foreign courts wherever possible, and in *State of Minnesota v. Philip Morris Inc.*,[25] Lord Woolf M.R. indicated that the benefit of any doubt should be given to the applicant; in that case the breadth of the proposed questioning made the Letter of Request irremediable. The judge at first instance had made an order with a limitation that the scope of the questioning was to be limited "only to elicit evidence admissible at trial", and Scottish courts have followed a similar practice where this would enable the request to be accepted.[26] This practice was fully examined by the Court of Appeal in

---

[19] *Ibid.*

[20] See the Report of the Work of the Commission, pp. 26–27, noted F. A. Mann (1990) 106 L.Q.R. 354 (but *quaere* whether Mann is justified in describing the opinion of the 1989 Special Commission as an "authentic interpretation"). *Cf.* Szladits, "Structure and the Divisions of the Law," *Int.Encyc.Comp. L.*, Vol. II, Chap. 2, discussed in *Re State of Norway's Application (Nos. 1 and 2), supra,* and Lipstein (1990) 39 I.C.L.Q. 120.

[21] *Re State of Norway's Application (Nos. 1 and 2)* [1990] 1 A.C. 723; *cf.* Rule 3(1).

[22] *Ante,* para. 8–062.

[23] *i.e.* the Foreign Tribunals Evidence Act 1856 (which remains in force in some Commonwealth jurisdictions): *Burchard v. Macfarlane* [1891] 2 Q.B. 241 (C.A.); *Radio Corp. of America v. Rauland Corp.* [1956] 1 Q.B. 618; *Re Scholnick and Bank of Nova Scotia* (1987) 59 O.R. (2d) 538.

[24] *Re Westinghouse Uranium Contract Litigation M.D.L. Docket No. 235* [1978] A.C. 547 at p. 610; *Lord Advocate, Ptr.*, 1998 S.C. 87.

[25] [1998] I.L.Pr. 170 (C.A.). See also *First American Corp. v. Zayed* [1999] 1 W.L.R. 1154 (C.A.).

[26] *Lord Advocate, Ptr.*, 1993 S.C. 638 where the court also specified the presence of a legal representative of the witness who could object to unacceptable questions.

Golden Eagle Refinery Co. Inc. v. Associated International Insurance Co.,[27] where the Letter of Request was found to have a dual or hybrid purpose: to seek testimony for use at trial and also to make enquiries as to discovery which were unknown in English procedure. The Court of Appeal rejected an argument that the mere presence of the second purpose deprived the English court of jurisdiction to make any order under the 1975 Act. It approved an order limited to obtaining and recording testimony appropriate to be given at trial, with certain additional safeguards.

The distinction between the legitimate gathering of evidence and mere   **8–072** "fishing", important in the case of requests for the production of documents,[28] is less easy to apply in the case of oral testimony. As the Court of Appeal has observed, if oral evidence is being sought for the purpose of use at trial and if there is good reason to believe that the intended witness has knowledge of matters in issue so as to be likely to be able to give relevant evidence, the application cannot be regarded as mere "fishing".[29] The English court will, however, bear in mind the need to protect intended witnesses from an oppressive request.[30]

The High Court has wide powers in giving effect to the application for   **8–073** assistance. It may make such provision for obtaining evidence in England as appears appropriate for giving effect to the request in pursuance of which the application is made.[31] It may, in particular, make provision for the examination of witnesses, either orally or in writing[32]; for the production of documents; for the inspection, photographing, preservation, custody or detention of any property; for the taking of samples of any property and the carrying out of any experiments on or with any property; for the medical examination of any person; and for the taking and testing of samples of blood from any person.[33] A request made by a foreign court as to the manner of taking evidence should be allowed unless what is proposed is so contrary to established English procedures that it ought not to be permitted.[34] The High Court will not seek to determine in advance whether the evidence sought is relevant to the issues likely to arise in the foreign proceedings, this being a matter for the requesting court.[35] The High Court may not, however, require any particular steps to be taken unless they are steps which can be required to be taken by way of obtaining evidence for the purposes of civil proceedings (of any description) in the High Court; but unsworn testimony may be received if the foreign court so requests.[36] Thus interrogatories cannot be administered under

---

[27] C.A., unreported, February 19, 1998.

[28] See *post*, para. 8–074.

[29] *First American Corp. v. Zayed* [1999] 1 W.L.R. 1154 (C.A.), referring to the test used if a subpoena is challenged.

[30] *Ibid.*

[31] s.2(1). See *Lord Advocate v. Sheriffs*, 1978 S.C. 56, 61.

[32] See Ord. 70, r. 4 as to the appointment of an examiner (applying CPR 34.9, 34.10 and 34.14); *R. v. Rathbone, ex p. Dikko* [1985] Q.B. 630.

[33] s.2(2).

[34] *J. Barber and Sons v. Lloyd's Underwriters* [1987] Q.B. 103 (videotaping the making of depositions); *Harris v. Baker* (1986) 42 S.A.S.R. 316 (request that evidence be taken before court reporter).

[35] *Re Westinghouse Uranium Contract Litigation M.D.L. Docket No. 235* [1978] A.C. 547 at p. 654; *Re Asbestos Insurance Coverage Cases* [1985] 1 W.L.R. 331 at p. 339 (H.L.); *Re Friction Division Products, Inc. and E. I. du Pont de Nemours & Co., Inc. (No. 2)* (1986) 32 D.L.R. (4th) 105, 116 (Ont.).

[36] s.2(3), which applies to both oral and documentary evidence: *Re Westinghouse Uranium Contract Litigation M.D.L. Docket No. 235, supra* at p. 634.

the Act in England to a corporation as such, even though this is possible by the *lex causae* or by the domestic law of the requesting court.[37] An order requiring a corporation to produce documents must similarly be made in the English form, *i.e.* that the corporation should "by its proper officer" attend and produce the documents.[38] Conversely, the court cannot make an order for the taking of evidence for use in foreign proceedings except in accordance with the Act, even if the particular evidence sought could have been obtained under the rules relating to corresponding proceedings in the English courts.[39] The court may not make an order under the Act binding on the Crown or on any person in his capacity as an officer or servant of the Crown.[40]

8–074　　Under the Act, the court may not require a person to state what documents relevant to the foreign proceedings are in his possession, custody or power, or to produce any documents other than particular documents specified in the court's order as being documents appearing to the court to be, or to be likely to be, in his possession, custody or power.[41] "Fishing" arises where what is sought is not evidence as such, but information which may lead to a line of enquiry which would disclose evidence; it is a search, a roving enquiry, for material in the hope of being able to raise allegations of fact.[42] For this reason, the statutory reference to "particular documents specified in the order" is to be given a strict construction. It is not sufficient to refer to a class of documents (*e.g.* "all bank statements for 1984"); the order must refer to individual documents or a specific group of documents (*e.g.* "monthly state-ments for 1984 relating to the current account at X & Co.'s Bank").[43] There must be evidence that the documents actually exist and are likely to be in the respondent's possession; mere conjecture is not enough.[44] If a request for assistance is framed too widely, it may be possible for the English court to order partial compliance with the request, striking out the impermissible material; but the English court will not undertake the task of redrafting the request.[45]

8–075　　It is however possible under the Act to order the production of documents by a third party even though this is not ancillary to the oral examination of that party as a witness.[46] A witness whose evidence is to be taken by virtue of an order under the Act may claim any privilege existing in English law[47] or in the

---

[37] *Penn-Texas Corp. v. Murat Anstalt* [1964] 1 Q.B. 40 (C.A.) (decided under an earlier statute).

[38] *Penn-Taxas Corp. v. Murat Anstalt (No. 2)* [1964] 2 Q.B. 647 (C.A.).

[39] *Re Westinghouse Uranium Contract Litigation M.D.L. Docket No. 235, supra*, at p. 610.

[40] s.9(4); *Re Pan American Airways Inc.'s Application* [1992] Q.B. 854 (C.A.).

[41] s.2(4).

[42] *Re State of Norway's Application (No. 1)* [1990] 1 A.C. 723 (C.A.); affd. on other grounds (H.L.).

[43] The examples are given by Lord Fraser in *Re Asbestos Insurance Coverage Cases* [1985] 1 W.L.R. 331 at pp. 337–338 (H.L). See also *Boeing Co. v. P.P.G. Industries Inc.* [1988] 3 All E.R. 839 (C.A.).

[44] *Re Asbestos Insurance Coverage Cases* [1985] 1 W.L.R. 331, 338 (H.L.).

[45] *cf. Re Westinghouse Uranium Contract Litigation M.D.L. Docket No. 235, supra* and *Re State of Norway's Application, supra.*

[46] *Re Westinghouse Uranium Contract Litigation M.D.L. Docket No. 235, supra*, at p. 654; *cf.* the position under the Foreign Tribunals Evidence Act 1856; *Burchard v. Macfarlane* [1891] 2 Q.B. 241 (C.A.).

[47] s.3(1)(*a*). See *e.g. Re Sarah Getty Trust* [1985] Q.B. 956; *Re Mulroney and Coates* (1986) 27 D.L.R. (4th) 118 (Ont.) (Crown privilege).

law of the foreign country from which the request emanated.[48] Assistance will therefore be refused where a duty of confidentiality placed upon a party to a particular relationship, for example a banker or financial adviser in his relationship with a customer, is regarded, under English law or the law of the foreign country, as outweighing the duty to give all relevant information to the court.[49] A party to the foreign proceedings in which the foreign court issued the letters rogatory which are being executed under the Act has standing to apply to set aside an *ex parte* order giving effect to the letters rogatory, even if he is not a person to whom the order is addressed.[50]

The court's powers under the Act are discretionary.[51] In the interests of comity, it will wish to assist by giving effect to the foreign court's request[52] "unless it is driven to the clear conclusion that it cannot properly do so."[53] In the *Westinghouse* case, the English court received a request seeking pretrial discovery in connection with anti-trust proceedings in the United States. The House of Lords took note of the view of the United Kingdom Government that the wide investigatory procedures under United States anti-trust legislation against persons outside the United States who were not United States citizens constituted an infringement on the proper jurisdiction and sovereignty of the United Kingdom. It was held that possible prejudice to the sovereignty of the United Kingdom could be taken into account by the English court in exercising its discretion.[54] The Protection of Trading Interests Act 1980[55] which was enacted primarily in the context of hostility to the United States' anti-trust jurisdiction provides that the English court must refuse to make an order in response to a foreign court's request if it is shown that the request infringes the jurisdiction of the United Kingdom or is otherwise prejudicial to the sovereignty of the United Kingdom. A certificate signed by or on behalf of the Secretary of State to the effect that the request is such an infringement or is so prejudicial is conclusive,[56] but such a certificate is not an essential prerequisite.[57] **8–076**

The Secretary of State may also give directions for prohibiting compliance with certain orders of foreign courts or authorities requiring any person in the United Kingdom to produce any commercial document not within the territorial jurisdiction of the foreign country, or to provide commercial information **8–077**

---

[48] s.3(1)(*b*): *e.g.* the privilege under the Fifth Amendment to the United States Constitution; *Re Westinghouse Uranium Contract Litigation M.D.L. Docket No. 235, supra. Cf. Appeal Enterprises Ltd. v. First National Bank of Chicago* (1984) 46 O.R. (2d) 590 (privilege under foreign law only available to local residents did not avail resident of requested country, assistance not depending on "precise reciprocity").

[49] *Re State of Norway's Application (No. 1)* [1990] 1 A.C. 723 (C.A.); affd. on other grounds (H.L.).

[50] *Boeing Co. v. P.P.G. Industries Inc.* [1988] 3 All E.R. 839 (C.A.).

[51] For the exercise of the discretion in the case of expert witnesses, see *Seyfang v. G. D. Searle & Co.* [1973] Q.B. 148 (under the Foreign Tribunals Evidence Act 1856).

[52] *Re Westinghouse Uranium Contract Litigation M.D.L. Docket No. 235, supra* at p. 560 (C.A.) and at p. 618.

[53] *Re State of Norway's Application (No. 1), supra.*

[54] *Cf.* Art. 12(*b*) of Hague Convention on the Taking of Evidence Abroad 1970. See *Fullmer v. Cape York Cattle Co.* [1987] 1 Qd.R. 6 (issue raised, but not resolved, whether a court might properly refuse to assist a foreign court in connection with litigation concerning title to land in the country of the requested court).

[55] Extending powers conferred in carriage by sea cases in Shipping Contracts and Commercial Documents Act 1964 (repealed).

[56] Protection of Trading Interests Act 1980, s.4.

[57] *Re State of Norway's Application (No. 1), supra.*

compiled from such documents, or to publish any such document or information.[58] A direction may be given if it appears to the Secretary of State that a requirement infringes the jurisdiction of the United Kingdom or is otherwise prejudicial to the sovereignty of the United Kingdom, or if compliance with it would be prejudicial to the security or foreign relations of the United Kingdom.[59] Except in cases where the requirement is concerned only with the publication of documents or information, a direction may also be given if the requirement is not for the purposes of actual or contemplated civil proceedings or actual criminal proceedings in the foreign country, or if it is wholly or mainly for the purposes of obtaining pre-trial discovery of documents.[60] It is an offence knowingly to contravene any such direction.[61]

8–078   *Assistance to overseas regulatory authorities.* The Secretary of State for Trade and Industry has wide powers to obtain information under section 447 of the Companies Act 1985. The Companies Act 1989 enables this information to be disclosed to an overseas regulatory authority[62] to assist it in the exercise of its regulatory functions.[63] The 1989 Act also gave new powers to examine persons on oath and to require the production of documents and the giving of other assistance; these powers may be exercised whenever the Secretary of State considers that there is good reason for their exercise in response to a request for assistance from an overseas authority.[64] There are exemptions on the ground of legal professional privilege,[65] and restrictions on the disclosure of the information obtained under these powers.[66] These powers complement the growing international network of Memoranda of Understanding between regulatory bodies.[67]

8–079   *Legalisation.* The practice of legalisation, which involves the official attestation of the origins of a document, can be an unnecessary source of delay in international litigation and other transactions. The Hague Convention Abolishing the Requirement of Legalisation for Foreign Public Documents 1961, to which the United Kingdom and many other countries are party, applies to public documents[68] which have been executed in the territory of one Contracting State and which have to be produced in the territory of another Contracting State. Any requirement that a diplomatic or consular agent should certify the authenticity of the signature, the capacity in which the signatory acted, or the identity of any stamp or seal on a document is abolished.[69] Instead a simple certificate, or "apostille," in a prescribed form issued by the

---

[58] Protection of Trading Interests Act 1980, s.2(1). The direction may be given in anticipation of the imposition of a requirement by a foreign court or authority. See the orders considered in *British Airways Board v. Laker Airways Ltd.* [1985] A.C. 58. "Document" includes data storage devices; s.2(6).

[59] Protection of Trading Interests Act 1980, s.2(2).

[60] *Ibid.* s.2(3).

[61] *Ibid.* s.3(1).

[62] Defined in Companies Act 1989, s.82(2).

[63] Companies Act 1985, s.449(1)(*c*), (*m*), inserted by Companies Act 1989, s.65(2).

[64] Companies Act 1989, ss.82, 83.

[65] *Ibid.* s.83(5).

[66] *Ibid.* ss.86, 87 as amended by S.I. 1997 No. 2781.

[67] See McClean, *op. cit.*, Chap. 11.

[68] Defined in Art. 1(2) as including court and administrative documents, notarial acts and official certificates placed on documents signed by a person in his private capacity.

[69] Arts. 1, 2.

competent authority of the State from which the document originates (in the United Kingdom, the Foreign and Commonwealth Office) suffices.[70]

(4) Security for costs. The Civil Procedure Rules 1998 provide[71] that **8–080** where, on the application of the defendant, it appears to the court that the claimant is ordinarily resident out of the jurisdiction,[72] then if, having regard to all the circumstances of the case, the court thinks it just to do so, it may order the claimant to give such security for the defendant's costs as it thinks just. For this purpose, a corporation is ordinarily resident where its central management and control is exercised.[73] This power of the High Court is in origin inherent and dates back to the middle of the eighteenth century.[74] Its justification is that "if a verdict is given against the plaintiff he is not within reach of our law so as to have process served upon him for costs."[75] By ordering security for costs the court will ensure that a successful defendant will have a fund available within the jurisdiction against which he can enforce a judgment for costs.[76] It is clear from the language of the rule, which in its present form dates from 1962, that this power of the High Court is to be exercised only when the circumstances make its use appropriate; what was once an inflexible rule requiring every plaintiff ordinarily resident abroad to give security is now a matter of discretion.[77] In particular, if a judgment for costs can be readily enforced in the country in which the claimant has such a fund, use of the power to order security will normally be inappropriate.

Principles governing the exercise of the power. The discretion of the court **8–081** extends to ordering security as against a claimant resident abroad even where there is a co-claimant resident in England,[78] though this power was formerly thought not to exist.[79] It may be relevant in considering the exercise of this discretion that the English claimant is a wholly-owned subsidiary of the foreign claimant; the distinct legal entity enjoyed by the subsidiary may be outweighed by the commercial realities. Where there are co-claimants in England and abroad, and there is a reasonable prospect of unsuccessful claimants each being ordered to bear an *aliquot* share of the costs, it may be appropriate to order the claimants resident abroad to provide security only for a proportion of the costs, but each case must be considered on its own facts.[80] If an English claimant has been made a party unnecessarily or improperly, perhaps in the hope of evading an order for security for costs, the court will

---

[70] See Art. 4 and the annexed Model Certificate.

[71] Ord. 23, r. 1(1), in CPR, Sched. 1.

[72] This is the most important of the four cases specified in the rule, and the only one which concerns the conflict of laws. See *Appah v. Monseu* [1967] 1 W.L.R. 893.

[73] *Re Little Olympian Each Ways Ltd. (No. 2)* [1995] 1 W.L.R. 560 (applying *De Beers Consolidated Mines Ltd. v. Howe* [1906] A.C. 455, 458 and *Unit Construction Co. Ltd. v. Bullock* [1960] A.C. 351, 363, 365).

[74] The earliest reported case appears to be *Meliorucchy v. Meliorucchy* (1750) 2 Ves. Sen. 24, a decision of Lord Hardwicke.

[75] *Pray v. Edie* (1786) 1 T.R. 267.

[76] *Porzelack K.G. v. Porzelack (U.K.) Ltd.* [1987] 1 W.L.R. 420, 422.

[77] *Aeronave S.p.A. v. Westland Charters Ltd.* [1971] 1 W.L.R. 1445 (C.A.).

[78] *Slazengers Ltd. v. Seaspeed Ferries International Ltd.* [1988] 1 W.L.R. 221 (C.A.); *The Alpha* [1991] 2 Lloyd's Rep. 52 (C.A.).

[79] *Winthrop v. Royal Exchange Assurance Co.* (1755) Dick. 282; *D'Hormusgee v. Grey* (1882) 10 Q.B.D. 13.

[80] *Slazengers Ltd. v. Seaspeed Ferries International Ltd.* [1988] 1 W.L.R. 221 (C.A.); *The Alpha* [1991] 2 Lloyd's Rep. 52 (C.A.).

order that he cease to be a party[81] and security for costs may then be required.[82] No order will be made if the claimant shows that he has substantial property within the jurisdiction which could be made available to satisfy any order as to costs.[83] It has been held that an order will not be made against a Crown servant resident abroad in order to carry out his official duties,[84] but these cases are best understood as illustrations of the court's discretion. An order can be made against a foreign sovereign.[85] An order can be made if the claimant goes to live abroad after the issue of process, and can include past as well as future costs.[86]

8–082   The fact that the claimant is compelled to take proceedings in England, *e.g.* because of an English jurisdiction clause[87] in a contract, is not a sufficient reason for not ordering him to give security.

If the defendant admits liability, the claimant will not be ordered to give security for costs,[88] even if the defendant counterclaims.[89]

8–083   It is a cardinal principle that a defendant resident abroad is never ordered to give security for costs, not even if the claimant is also resident abroad.[90] But it is not always easy to determine whether a person is in substance in the position of a plaintiff or a defendant. Order 23, rule 1(3) provides that references in the rule to a claimant and a defendant shall be construed as references to the person (howsoever described on the record) who is in the position of claimant or defendant, as the case may be, in the proceeding in question, including a proceeding on a counterclaim. The courts look at the substance of the matter and not merely at the form, and regard any person who assumes the position of an actor in the proceeding in question as a claimant,[91] and any person who is really defending himself against attack as a defendant.[92] If the defendant brings a counterclaim which arises out of an independent cause of action and is really in the nature of a cross-action, or which is pursued after the claim has been determined, he may be ordered to give

---

[81] CPR 19.3.
[82] *Jones v. Gurney* [1913] W.N. 72.
[83] *Hamburger v. Poetting* (1882) 47 L.T. 249; *Re Apollinaris Co.'s Trade Marks* [1891] 1 Ch. 1 (C.A.); *Kevorkian v. Burney (No. 2)* [1937] 4 All E.R. 468 (C.A.). Contrast *Ebrard v. Gassier* (1884) 28 Ch.D. 232 (C.A.); *Clarke v. Barber* (1890) 6 T.L.R. 256, where the property was not considered sufficiently substantial.
[84] *Colebrook v. Jones* (1751) Dick. 154 (consul); *Evelyn v. Chippendale* (1839) 9 Sim. 497 (colonial harbourmaster).
[85] *Republic of Costa Rica v. Erlanger* (1876) 3 Ch.D. 62 (C.A.); *The Newbattle* (1885) 10 P.D. 33 (C.A.); *Duff Development Co. v. Government of Kelantan* (1925) 41 T.L.R. 375; *Ministère de la Culture et de la Communication de France v. Lieb, The Times*, December 24, 1981.
[86] *Massey v. Allen* (1879) 12 Ch.D. 807; *Caldwell v. Sumpters* [1972] Ch. 478, revd. on other grounds *ibid.* (C.A.).
[87] *Aeronave S.P.A. v. Westland Charters Ltd.* [1971] 1 W.L.R. 1445 (C.A.).
[88] *De St. Martin v. Davis & Co.* [1884] W.N. 86.
[89] *Winterfield v. Bradnum* (1878) 3 Q.B.D. 324 (C.A.).
[90] *Naamlooze Vennootschap v. Bank of England* [1948] 1 All E.R. 465 (C.A.).
[91] See, *e.g. Apollinaris Co. v. Wilson* (1886) 31 Ch.D. 632 (C.A.); *Re Pretoria Pietersburg Ry.* [1904] 2 Ch. 359 (claimant in a winding up); *Duff Development Co. v. Government of Kelantan* (1925) 41 T.L.R. 375 (party to an arbitration asking that an arbitrator be ordered to state a special case).
[92] See, *e.g. Re Percy and Kelly Nickel etc. Co.* (1876) 2 Ch.D. 531 (shareholder opposing creditor's winding up petition); *Re Miller's Patent* (1894) 70 L.T. 270 (owner of patent resisting petition for revocation); *Re La Société Anonyme des Verreries de l'Etoile* [1893] W.N. 119 (same for trade mark); *Re B (Infants)* [1965] 1 W.L.R. 946 (motion by husband to vary custody order in favour of wife); *Visco v. Minter* [1969] P. 82.

security[93]; but if the counterclaim arises out of the same transaction and is in substance in the nature of a defence to the proceedings, security will not be ordered.[94] But the matter is one for the discretion of the court and each case must depend on its own merits.[95] "The principle seems to be that where a defendant counter-attacks on the same front on which he is being attacked by the plaintiff, it will be regarded as a defensive manoeuvre. But if he opens a counter-attack on a different front, even to relieve pressure on the front attacked by the plaintiff, he is in danger of an order for security for costs."[96] So a defendant in interpleader proceedings, or proceedings analogous thereto, can be ordered to give security for costs if he is in substance a claimant.[97] But if both claimants to the thing in dispute are resident abroad, the court is reluctant to make an order against one and not against the other.[98] A third party is not a defendant for the purposes of Order 23, rule 1; that is concerned with those who are claimants and defendants in the proceedings as a whole.[99]

Enforceability of judgments for costs. The use made of the power to order **8–084** security for costs is limited by a consideration already referred to, the ease with which judgments for costs can be enforced in the country in which the claimant has assets. Within the United Kingdom, the effect of the Civil Jurisdiction and Judgments Act 1982 is that such judgments given by an English court can very easily be enforced in other parts of the United Kingdom. Security will only be ordered against claimants ordinarily resident in other such parts if there are special circumstances such as the insolvency of the claimant company.[1] Similar principles were applied at one time where the plaintiff was ordinarily resident in a Contracting State to the 1968 Convention or the Lugano Convention, for in such countries enforcement is similarly readily available.[2] Where a judgment for costs would be in a country to which Part II of the Administration of Justice Act 1920 or Part I of the Foreign Judgments (Reciprocal Enforcement) Act 1933 has been extended by Order-in-Council,[3] the position is rather different: the procedure for enforcement in such cases is not automatic, and may involve a contest in the foreign country, and the court will weigh the circumstances before deciding whether to order security for costs. If it appears that the judgment can be enforced almost as

---

[93] *Sykes v. Sacerdoti* (1885) 15 Q.B.D. 423 (C.A.); *Lake v. Haseltine* (1885) 55 L.J.Q.B. 205; *cf. The Julia Fisher* (1877) 2 P.D. 115.

[94] *Mapleson v. Masini* (1879) 5 Q.B.D. 144; *Neck v. Taylor* [1893] 1 Q.B. 560 (C.A.).

[95] *New Fenix Compagnie etc. v. General Accident etc. Corporation* [1911] 2 K.B. 619 (C.A.).

[96] *Visco v. Minter* [1969] P. 82, 85.

[97] *Tomlinson v. Land and Finance Corporation Ltd.* (1884) 14 Q.B.D. 539 (C.A.); *Tudor Furnishers Ltd. v. Montague & Co.* [1950] Ch. 113.

[98] *Belmonte v. Aynard* (1879) 4 C.P.D. 221, 352 (C.A.); *Maatschappij voor Fondsenbezit v. Shell Transport and Trading Co.* [1923] 2 K.B. 166 (C.A.); *cf. Tudor Furnishers Ltd. v. Montague & Co., supra.*

[99] *Taly N.D.C. International N.V. v. Terra Nova Insurance Co. Ltd.* [1986] 1 All E.R. 69 (C.A.).

[1] *D.S.Q. Property Co. Ltd. v. Lotus Cars Ltd.* [1987] 1 W.L.R. 127 (Northern Ireland company); *Silvera v. Al-Rashidi* [1994] I.L.Pr. 332 (C.A.); *Dynaspan (U.K.) v. H. Katzenberger Baukonstruktionen G.m.b.H. & Co. K.G.* [1995] 1 B.C.L.C. 536. See also *Flender Werft A.G. v. Aegean Maritime Ltd.* [1990] 2 Lloyd's Rep. 27 (Isle of Man company).

[2] *De Bry v. Fitzgerald* [1990] 1 W.L.R. 552 (C.A.); *Porzelack K.G. v. Porzelack (U.K.) Ltd.* [1987] 1 W.L.R. 420. For the effect of the Treaty of Rome on such cases, see *infra.*

[3] See Rules 46 and 47.

easily as in England, no security will be ordered,[4] but it will be otherwise if there may be difficulty and delay.[5]

8–085   *European law.* The use of the power to order security is further restricted by the Treaty of Rome, Article 12[6] of which prohibits, within the scope of the Treaty, any discrimination on grounds of nationality. In *Berkeley Administration Inc. v. McClelland*[7] the Court of Appeal held that as Order 23 was based on residence and not nationality it did not discriminate, even covertly, on the ground of nationality and so did not offend against the Treaty provision. Subsequent decisions of the European Court have established the contrary position. In 1994, the European Court held, in *Mund & Fester v. Hatrex Internationaal Transport*,[8] that a German law, under which the fact that the judgment would have to be enforced abroad was sufficient justification for the seizure of a defendant's assets in order to obtain security for the enforcement of the judgment, involved covert discrimination contrary the Treaty unless it could be justified by objective circumstances. Where enforcement would be sought in a Contracting State to the 1968 Convention, there could be no presumption that the need for enforcement amounted to such circumstances. This judgment had clear implications for the practice of ordering security for costs, and in a later case,[9] the European Court held that the Treaty precluded such an order against a legal person established in a foreign State (where no such order would be made against a legal person from the forum State) where the action was connected with the exercise of fundamental freedoms guaranteed by Community law.

8–086   In the light of the *Mund & Fester* decision, the Court of Appeal held that the English practice as to security for costs, although based on the ordinary residence of the plaintiff, must be regarded as covertly discriminatory on grounds of nationality and so contrary to what is now Article 12 of the Treaty.[10] Although Sir Thomas Bingham M.R. tentatively suggested in *Fitzgerald v. Williams*[11] that an order for security for costs against a plaintiff who was a national of another European Community country might be objectively justified if there were very cogent evidence of substantial difficulty in enforcing an English judgment in that country, it is difficult to reconcile this suggestion with the approach of the European Court. That Court observed in the *Mund & Fester* case that the Contracting States to the 1968 Convention are to be regarded as constituting a single entity, and that would seem to preclude any objective justification in cases falling within the material scope of the Convention.

8–087   The discretion to order security for costs under Order 23 against a foreign claimant still exists, but it must be exercised in a manner not inconsistent with

---

[4] *Thune v. London Properties* [1990] 1 W.L.R. 562 (C.A.) (enforceability in Norway).

[5] *Lonkar v. J. O. Simms* (not yet reported, January 28, 1998) (C.A.) (India).

[6] Originally Art. 7, and later Art. 6.

[7] [1990] 2 Q.B. 407 (C.A.).

[8] Case C–398/92 [1994] E.C.R. I–467.

[9] Case C–43/95 *Data Delecta Akt. v. M.S.L. Dynamics Ltd.* [1996] E.C.R. I–4661, followed in Case C–323/95 *Hayes v. Kronenberger* [1997] E.C.R. I–1711 and (in respect of an order made before the forum country acceded to the Treaty of Rome) Case C–122/96 *S. A. Saldanha v. Hiross Holding A.G.* [1997] E.C.R. I–5325.

[10] *Fitzgerald v. Williams* [1996] Q.B. 657 (C.A.). For Irish authorities to the same effect, see *Maher v. Phelan* [1996] 1 I.L.R.M. 359; *Proetta v. Neil* [1996] 1 I.L.R.M. 457; *Pitt v. Bolger* [1996] 1 I.R. 108 (following *Fitzgerald v. Williams*).

[11] [1996] Q.B. 657 at 675.

Community law.[12] An order may, for example, be made against a company ordinarily resident in a Contracting State on grounds of impecuniosity which would have justified an order against an English company under section 726 of the Companies Act 1985.[13]

International conventions. Insofar as international conventions make it **8–088** easier to enforce a judgment for costs in another country, they reduce the need for ordering security. Many conventions have a more direct effect in excluding the power to order security for costs. For example Chapter III of the Hague Convention on Civil Procedure of 1954 and its successor Chapter II of the Convention on International Access to Justice of 1980[14] prohibit any requirement of security, by reason only of their foreign nationality or residence, from persons (including legal persons) habitually resident in a Contracting State who are plaintiffs or parties intervening before the courts of another Contracting State. The United Kingdom is not a party to either convention but comparable provisions are found in a number of bilateral conventions on civil procedure.[15] Another type of provision, found in conventions dealing with a particular subject-matter, prohibits any requirement of security in cases falling within the scope of the convention. This type of provision is found in a number of conventions to which the United Kingdom is party: the Geneva Convention on the Contract for the International Carriage of Goods by Road,[16] the Geneva Convention on the Contract for the International Carriage of Passengers and Luggage,[17] the Convention concerning International Carriage by Rail,[18] and the Hague Convention on the Civil Aspects of International Child Abduction.[19] The Paris, Brussels and Vienna Conventions on Third Party Liability in the Field of Nuclear Energy each contain a general provision that "this Convention shall be applied without any discrimination based on nationality, domicile or residence".[20] Yet other conventions contain more limited provisions, prohibiting the requirement of security for costs on certain specified grounds. Article 45 of the 1968 and Lugano Conventions prohibits the requirement of security on the ground of foreign nationality, domicile or residence of a party who in one Contracting State applies for the enforcement of a judgment in another Contracting State; the developing case-law of the European Court on the interpretation of what is now Article 12 of the Treaty of Rome[21] renders this provision almost otiose.

Security for costs in arbitrations. Unless the parties have agreed otherwise, **8–089** an arbitral tribunal has the power to order a claimant to provide security for the costs of the arbitration.[22] However, this power cannot be exercised on the

---

[12] *Chequepoint S.A.R.L. v. McClelland* [1997] Q.B. 51 (C.A.).

[13] *Ibid.* (order against French company made upheld).

[14] Art. 17 of the 1954 Convention, based solely on nationality; Art. 14 of the 1980 Convention, adding considerations of residence.

[15] *e.g.* Convention on Security for Costs and Judicial Assistance of April 15, 1936 between the United Kingdom and France, art. 3.

[16] The "CMR Convention", Art. 31(5); see Carriage of Goods by Road Act 1965.

[17] The "CVR Convention", Art. 21(5); see Carriage of Passengers by Road Act 1974.

[18] The "COTIF Convention", Art. 18(4); see International Transport Conventions Act 1983.

[19] Art. 22; see Child Abduction and Custody Act 1985.

[20] Paris Convention 1960, Art. 14(*a*); Brussels Convention 1962, Art. 12(3); Vienna Convention 1963, Art. 13. See *post*, para. 15–040.

[21] See *ante*, para. 8–085.

[22] Arbitration Act 1996, s.38(2)(3).

ground that the claimant is an individual ordinarily resident outside the United Kingdom or a corporation or association incorporated or formed under the law of a country outside the United Kingdom or whose central management and control is exercised outside the United Kingdom.[23] This express provision means that the arbitrator may not exercise a power equivalent to that of the court and just examined. It was formerly the case that the court itself could intervene to order security for costs in an arbitration but this power was removed by the Arbitration Act 1996.[24]

8–090   *Effect of human rights law.* The English practice, and that based upon it in other common-law countries, has been the subject of complaint on human rights or constitutional grounds. The European Commission of Human Rights has rejected as manifestly ill-founded an application in which it was argued that the dismissal by the Court of Appeal of an appeal on the failure of the appellants, who were resident abroad, to lodge security for costs amounted to a denial of access to court, contrary to Article 6(1) of the European Convention on Human Rights.[25] In Canada, provisions as to security for costs by non-resident plaintiffs have been attacked as contravening the principle of equality before the law in section 15(1) of the Canadian Charter of Rights and Freedoms. Although successful in one case,[26] the balance of authority is clearly against this argument.[27] The Irish High Court has held that a requirement that a plaintiff give security for costs did not fetter any of his rights under the Irish Constitution.[28]

ILLUSTRATIONS

(1) INJUNCTIONS TO RESTRAIN REMOVAL OF ASSETS FROM THE JURISDICTION

8–091   1. A & Co., Japanese shipowners, let three ships on charter to X and Y, who fail to pay the hire and cannot be traced. They have funds in bank accounts in London. The court will issue an injunction, on the application of A & Co., restraining X and Y from removing any of their assets from the jurisdiction.[29]

2. X & Co., a Panamanian company, own a vessel, which they let on charter. On the failure of the charterers to pay the charter freight in full, X & Co. cause the vessel to be arrested in Cyprus by order of the courts of Cyprus and the cargo is unloaded. Subsequently the vessel sinks and becomes a total loss. X & Co. claim against their insurers, London underwriters. The bills of lading contain a clause conferring exclusive jurisdiction on the Italian courts. The cargo-owners commence an action in the High Court against X & Co., alleging breach of duty or of contract. The court may issue an injunction restraining X & Co. from removing the insurance moneys from the jurisdiction if the cargo-owners have commenced, or are to commence, proceedings in Italy.[30]

---

[23] *Ibid.* s.38(3). See the Department of Trade and Industry's Advisory Committee on International Commercial Arbitration Law's Report on the Arbitration Bill (February 1996), esp. pp. 44–45 and 76–77.

[24] Repealing Arbitration Act 1950, s.12(6)(*a*) and reversing the effect of *S.A. Coppée Lavalin N.V. v. Ken-Ren Chemicals and Fertilizers Ltd.* [1995] 1 A.C. 38.

[25] *Application No. 14551/89 v. United Kingdom.*

[26] *Kask v. Shimizu* (1986) 28 D.L.R. (4th) 64 (Alta.) (where reliance was also placed on the mobility rights in section 6 of the Charter).

[27] *Isabelle v. Campbellton Regional Hospital* (1987) 38 D.L.R. (4th) 638 (N.B.); *Crothers v. Simpson Sears Ltd.* (1988) 51 D.L.R. (4th) 529 (Alta. C.A.): *Lapierre v. Barrette* (1988) 59 D.L.R. 4th 200 (Que. C.A.).

[28] *Salih v. General Accident Fire and Life Assurance Corp. Ltd.* [1987] I.R. 628.

[29] *Nippon Yusen Kaisha v. Karageorgis* [1975] 1 W.L.R. 1093 (C.A.).

[30] These are the facts of *The Siskina v. Distos Compania Naviera S.A.* [1979] A.C. 210, the effect of which is reversed by Civil Jurisdiction and Judgments Act 1982, s.25(1).

3. A, a Panamanian company, obtains a judgment in England for $15 million against X and Y Lebanese nationals, one of whom lives mainly in Switzerland and the other mainly in Greece. They carry on business through a network of companies incorporated in such places as Panama, Liberia and the Dutch Antilles. The court grants a *Mareva* injunction extending to assets outside the jurisdiction.[31]

4. The Republic of Haiti commences proceedings in France to recover more than $20 million alleged embezzled by former President "Baby Doc" Duvalier. English solicitors for Duvalier hold assets on his behalf in various countries. The court grants a worldwide *Mareva* injunction in aid of the French proceedings, and the English solicitors are ordered to disclose the nature, location and value of Duvalier's assets known to them.[32]

5. A brings an action in England against X and Y, individuals, and Z, a Luxembourg corporation, for conspiracy and fraudulent breach of fiduciary duty. The court grants a *Mareva* injunction over X and Y's foreign assets and appoints a receiver of the assets of Z.[33]

6. A & Co. sues X (who is resident and domiciled in Switzerland), alleging that X had participated in the fraudulent misappropriation of A & Co.'s funds by Y, a former employee of A & Co. A & Co. applies in England for a worldwide *Mareva* injunction, and an associated disclosure order, in aid of the Swiss proceedings. Although similar relief is not available under Swiss procedure, the English court may grant it because the relief available in England in aid of foreign proceedings is not limited to remedies which could be granted by the court which will try the substantive dispute.[34]

(2) JUDICIAL ASSISTANCE: SERVICE OF PROCESS

7. A obtained the leave of the court to serve process out of the jurisdiction on X at a stated **8–092** address in Lugano or elsewhere in Switzerland. X applied for service to be set aside on the grounds that personal service by the agent of a foreign plaintiff without the leave of the Swiss authorities was a criminal offence under the Swiss Penal Code. The court set the service aside. In the circumstances, and despite the expiry of both the writ and the relevant limitation period, the court renewed the validity of the writ for four months to allow other modes of service to be used.[35]

(3) JUDICIAL ASSISTANCE: OBTAINING EVIDENCE ABROAD

8. A brings an action in England against B, claiming commission due under a contract **8–093** concerning the supply of rifles to the Russian Government. A is resident at Bucharest and applies for an order that his evidence be taken there. He suffers from heart disease and claims that the cross-Channel sea crossing could endanger his life had he to attend in London. A's evidence will be crucial and cross-examination will be important to B's case. The application is refused.[36]

9. A brings an action in England against B on an alleged contract to transfer shares in a South African company. The contract is made while B was temporarily resident in England; he is still so resident when the writ was issued. B subsequently returns to his permanent home in Johannesburg. He wishes to defend the action but cannot afford another journey to England. B applies for an order enabling his evidence to be taken in South Africa. It is granted.[37]

10. Letters of request from a court in Virginia seek production of a series of specified documents and of any memoranda, correspondence or other documents relating thereto. An order will be made in respect of the specified documents only.[38]

11. Letters of request from a Californian court seek the production of written instructions from the plaintiff or his agents to obtain specified insurance policies. There is no evidence that written instructions existed. No order for the production of the documents will be made.[39]

12. Letters of request from a court in Virginia seek an order that A should give evidence and that B & Co. should produce specified documents. A claims privilege against self-incrimination under section 14(1) of the Civil Evidence Act 1968. B & Co. claim privilege against self-

---

[31] *Babanaft International Co. S.A. v. Bassatne* [1990] Ch. 13 (C.A.).

[32] *Republic of Haiti v. Duvalier* [1990] 1 Q.B. 202 (C.A.). The action in France was subsequently dismissed: 1991 *Clunet* 137.

[33] *Derby & Co. Ltd. v. Weldon* (*Nos. 3 & 4*) [1990] Ch. 65 (C.A.).

[34] *Crédit Suisse Fides Trust S.A. v. Cuoghi* [1998] Q.B. 818 (C.A.).

[35] *The Sky One* [1988] 1 Lloyd's Rep. 238 (C.A.).

[36] *Berdan v. Greenwood* (1880) 20 Ch.D. 764n. (C.A.).

[37] *Ross v. Woodford* [1894] 1 Ch. 38.

[38] Evidence (Proceedings in Other Jurisdictions) Act 1975, s.2(4)(*b*); *Re Westinghouse Uranium Contract Litigation M.D.L. Docket No. 235* [1978] A.C. 547.

[39] *Re Asbestos Insurance Coverage Cases* [1985] 1 W.L.R. 331 (H.L.).

incrimination under the Fifth Amendment to the United States Constitution. Both claims will be upheld and no order made.[40]

13. Letters of request from a court in Norway issued, with the concurrence of both parties, in proceedings brought to challenge a tax assessment sought an order that A and B, English bankers, should give evidence. No order was made owing to the unacceptable width of the questions sought to be asked, and, in the circumstances, to respect the bankers' duty of confidentiality. Second, more narrowly drawn, letters of request were received. An order was made, the proceedings being civil proceedings under both English and Norwegian law; the request did not amount to an attempt to enforce the revenue law of Norway.[41]

(4) SECURITY FOR COSTS

8–094

14. P, a Northern Ireland company in receivership and liquidation, brings an action in England alleging conspiracy to defraud. D seeks an order for security for costs under Order 23, r. 1(1). Although such an order will generally not be made against a claimant ordinarily resident in the United Kingdom, the financial circumstances of the claimant justify the making of an order on these facts.[42]

15. P, ordinarily resident in Norway, is trustee of the insolvent estate of a deceased person. He commences an action in England seeking to recover property held by D and said to belong to the estate. D seeks an order for security for costs. English judgments are enforceable in Norway under the Foreign Judgments (Reciprocal Enforcement) Act 1933, but enforcement will not be automatic. The court has a discretion to make an order for security.[43]

16. P, ordinarily resident in the Irish Republic, commences proceedings in England against D claiming damages for fraudulent misrepresentation in connection with investments in works of art. D seeks an order for security for costs. To make such an order would amount to covert discrimination on grounds of nationality contrary to what is now Article 12 of the Treaty of Rome, unless it could be justified by objective circumstances relating to difficulties in obtaining enforcement of any judgment as to costs. As Ireland is a Contracting State to the 1968 Convention, enforcement there presents no difficulty and no order will be made.[44]

17. P, a French company ordinarily resident in France, brings an action for defamation against D. D seeks an order for security for costs, alleging the impecuniosity of P. The circumstances alleged are such that were P. an English company, an order for security would be made under section 726(1) of the Companies Act 1985. To make a similar order against a French company would involve no discrimination and so would not offend against the Treaty of Rome. An order will be made.[45]

---

[40] Evidence (Proceedings in Other Jurisdictions) Act 1975, s.3; *Re Westinghouse Uranium Contract Litigation M.D.L. Docket No. 235, supra.*
[41] *Re State of Norway's Application (Nos. 1 and 2)* [1990] 1 A.C. 723.
[42] *D.S.Q. Property Co. v. Lotus Cars* [1987] 1 W.L.R. 127.
[43] *Thune v. London Properties Ltd.* [1990] 1 W.L.R. 562 (C.A.).
[44] *Fitzgerald v. Williams* [1996] Q.B. 657 (C.A.) following Case C–398/92 *Mund & Fester v. Hatrex Internationaal Transport* [1994] E.C.R. I–467.
[45] *Chequepoint SARL v. McClelland* [1997] Q.B. 51 (C.A.), distinguishing *Fitzgerald v. Williams* [1996] Q.B. 657 (C.A.).

CHAPTER 9

PROOF OF FOREIGN LAW[1]

RULE 18—(1) In any case to which foreign law applies, that law must be pleaded and proved as a fact to the satisfaction of the judge by expert evidence or sometimes by certain other means.
(2) In the absence of satisfactory evidence of foreign law, the court will apply English law to such a case.[2]

9–001

COMMENT

(1) Foreign law a fact. The principle that, in an English[3] court, foreign law is a matter of fact has long been well established.[4] It has two important practical consequences.

9–002

(i) *Foreign law must be pleaded.* The general rule is that if a party wishes to rely on a foreign law he must plead it in the same way as any other fact.[5] Unless this is done, the court will decide a case containing foreign elements as though it were a purely domestic English case.[6] There is, however, a statutory exception to this principle. If a case is governed by the law of some Commonwealth country, the court may order that law to be ascertained under the British Law Ascertainment Act 1859[7] if it regards such ascertainment as "necessary or expedient for the proper disposal of" the action. Orders for the ascertainment of a foreign law under this Act have been made at the court's own motion although the foreign law was not pleaded.[8]

9–003

---

[1] Fentiman, *Foreign Law in English Courts* (1998).
[2] This Rule was explicitly approved in *Bumper Development Corp. v. Commissioner of Police of the Metropolis* [1991] 1 W.L.R. 1362, 1369 (C.A.). For approval in New Zealand see *Mount Cook (Northland) Ltd. v. Swedish Motors Ltd.* [1986] 1 N.Z.L.R. 720.
[3] In certain foreign jurisdictions, the principle that *curia novit ius* requires the court to discover and apply a foreign law which its rules of the conflict of laws make applicable. This may create substantial difficulty in practice. See, *e.g. Re Claim Against Croatian Branch of Slovenian Bank* [1998] I.L.Pr. 269 (German Fed. Sup. Ct., 1996).
[4] *Fremoult v. Dedire* (1718) 1 P. Wms. 429; *Mostyn v. Fabrigas* (1774) 1 Cowp. 161, 174; *Nelson v. Bridport* (1845) 8 Beav. 527; *Bankers and Shippers Insurance Co. of New York v. Liverpool Marine and General Insurance Co. Ltd.* (1926) 24 Ll.L.R. 85, 93 (H.L.); *Ottoman Bank of Nicosia v. Chakarian (No. 2)* [1938] A.C. 260, 279 (P.C.); *A/S Tallinna Laevauhisus v. Estonian State Steamship Line* (1947) 80 Ll.L.R. 99, 107, 113 (C.A.).
[5] *King of Spain v. Machado* (1827) 4 Russ. 225, 239; *Ascherberg, Hopwood & Crew Ltd. v. Casa Musicale Sonzogno* [1971] 1 W.L.R. 173, 1128 (C.A.).
[6] *Post*, para. 9–025. In *Male v. Roberts* (1800) 3 Esp. 163, Lord Eldon seems to have required proof of Scots law although it was not pleaded; but the case would not now be followed on this point.
[7] *Post*, para. 9–023.
[8] *Topham v. Duke of Portland* (1863) 1 De G.J. & S. 517, varied, but without reference to this point *sub nom. Duke of Portland v. Topham* (1864) 11 H.L.C. 32; *Eglinton v. Lamb* (1867) 15 L.T. 657.

9–004   (ii) *Foreign law must be proved.* English courts take judicial notice of the law of England and of notorious facts, but not of foreign law.[9] Consequently, foreign law must be proved[10] in each case: it cannot be deduced from previous English decisions in which the same rule of foreign law has been before the court,[11] although such decisions may be admissible in evidence for the purpose of proving foreign law.[12] Indeed, it is perfectly possible for the English court to reach different conclusions in different cases as to the effect of a given rule of foreign law.[13]

9–005   In the following exceptional cases, foreign law need not be proved:

(a) Foreign law need not be proved where a statute expressly provides that it shall be judicially noticed.[14]

(b) Foreign law may sometimes be judicially noticed as a notorious fact: thus judicial notice has been taken of the fact that roulette is not unlawful in Monte Carlo.[15] On the other hand, it has been held that judicial notice could not on this ground be taken of the fact that continental lawyers adopt a more liberal attitude than English lawyers towards the construction of documents, since this fact is not notorious.[16]

9–006   (c) The court may take judicial notice of a foreign law if its content is, at least in part, determined by a rule of English law, and if, according to English law, the foreign law is the same as, or substantially similar to, English law. Thus it was and is, though of little contemporary relevance, a rule of English law that settlers from the United Kingdom carry with them to a new colony, which before their arrival had no civilised system of law, the common law of England and English statutory law, in so far as it is applicable to the conditions prevailing in the colony.[17] The court can take judicial notice of the common law of such a colony,[18] and can decide, as a matter of law, whether a given

---

[9] *Fremoult v. Dedire* (1718) 1 P.Wms. 429; *Nelson v. Bridport* (1845) 8 Beav. 527; *Lloyd v. Guibert* (1865) L.R. 1 Q.B. 115, 129.

[10] *Ganer v. Lanesborough* (1790) Peake 25; *Brenan and Galen's Case* (1847) 10 Q.B. 492, 498; *Bumper Development Corp. v. Commissioner of Police of the Metropolis* [1991] 1 W.L.R. 1362, 1368 (C.A.); *Macnamara v. Hatteras* (*Owners*) [1931] I.R. 73, 337; [1933] I.R. 675. Where a foreign law confers a discretion on the foreign court administering it, evidence may be given as to the manner in which that foreign court exercises that discretion: *National Mutual Holdings Pty. Ltd. v. Sentry Corp.* (1989) 87 A.L.R. 539, 556.

[11] *M'Cormick v. Garnett* (1854) 5 D.M. & G. 278; *Re Marseilles Extension Railway and Land Co.* (1885) 30 Ch.D. 598, 602; *Lazard Brothers & Co. v. Midland Bank Ltd.* [1933] A.C. 289, 297–298; *Schnaider v. Jaffe* (1916) 7 C.P.D. 696. This principle was lost sight of in *Simons v. Simons* [1939] 1 K.B. 490, 495, and in *Re Sebba* [1959] Ch. 166.

[12] Civil Evidence Act 1972, s.4(2), *post*, para. 9–021.

[13] *Lazard Brothers & Co. v. Midland Bank Ltd.* [1933] A.C. 289; *Ottoman Bank of Nicosia v. Chakarian* [1938] A.C. 260 (P.C.). This possibility is recognised in Civil Evidence Act 1972, s.4(2) proviso.

[14] See Maintenance Orders Act 1950, s.22(2); *cf. Knight v. Knight* [1925] 2 D.L.R. 467, 469 (Man.); and Civil Evidence Act 1972, s.4(2), *post*, para. 9–021.

[15] *Saxby v. Fulton* [1909] 2 K.B. 208, 211; *cf. Harold Meyers Travel Service Ltd. v. Magid* (1975) 60 D.L.R. (3d) 42, 44, affd. on other grounds (1977) 77 D.L.R. (3d) 32 (Ont. C.A.); *Re Turner* [1906] W.N. 27, where judicial notice was taken of the fact that the laws of the different States of the German Empire varied considerably.

[16] *Hartmann v. Konig* (1933) 50 T.L.R. 114, 117 (H.L.).

[17] *Cooper v. Stuart* (1889) 14 App.Cas. 286, 291–292 (P.C.); *Terrell v. Secretary of State for the Colonies* [1953] 2 Q.B. 482, 492; Halsbury, *Laws of England* (4th ed., reissue), Vol. 6, paras. 1101–1103; Roberts-Wray, *Commonwealth and Colonial Law* (1966), pp. 539–557.

[18] *Limerick v. Limerick* (1863) 4 Sw. & Tr. 252, 253. *Cf. Re Nesbitt* (1844) 14 L.J.M.C. 30, 32, where judicial notice was taken of the fact that the common law of England prevailed in Ireland.

English statute applies to the colony.[19] Of course, this principle does not enable the court to take judicial notice of laws passed by the legislature of the colony.[20]

(d) An appellate court which has jurisdiction to determine appeals from the courts of several countries takes judicial notice of the laws of any of those countries when it hears an appeal from a court in any one of them. Thus the House of Lords, when hearing an English or Northern Irish appeal, takes judicial notice of Scots law[21]; and conversely, when hearing a Scottish appeal, the House takes judicial notice of English or Northern Irish law.[22] Similarly, the Supreme Court of Canada takes judicial notice of the laws of all the Provinces when it hears an appeal from any one of them.[23] It seems that the same principle applies to the Judicial Committee of the Privy Council.[24] In these cases, the foreign law, which was a matter of fact in the courts below, becomes a matter of law on appeal.   **9–007**

(e) Foreign law need not be proved if it is admitted.[25] Such admission may be express but may also occur where a party, by his pleading (now called statement of case), is deemed by the applicable procedural rules to admit the foreign law upon which his opponent has relied.[26]   **9–008**

(f) The court may decide a question of foreign law without proof if it is requested to do so by both parties. But except in cases concerning the interpretation of foreign statutes, the courts are reluctant to take this course.[27]

(g) In a few cases, the courts have determined questions of foreign law although, so far as one can see from the reports, no evidence of the foreign law was given. Thus in *Re Cohn*[28] the court construed and applied a section of the German Civil Code which was not proved, and as to the effect of which no evidence was given. Again, the courts have in a number of cases applied colonial laws without proof.[29]   **9–009**

---

[19] *e.g. Terrell v. Secretary of State for the Colonies* [1953] 2 Q.B. 482.

[20] For proof of Colonial statutes, see para. 9–022, *post*.

[21] *De Thoren v. Att.-Gen.* (1876) 1 App.Cas. 686; *Elliot v. Joicey* [1935] A.C. 209, 236; *MacShannon v. Rockware Glass Ltd.* [1978] A.C. 795, 815, 821.

[22] *Douglas v. Brown* (1831) 2 Dow. & Cl. 171 (H.L.); *Cooper v. Cooper* (1888) 13 App.Cas. 88.

[23] *Logan v. Lee* (1907) 39 S.C.R. 311; *Canadian Pacific Ry. v. Parent* [1917] A.C. 195, 201 (P.C.); *Pettkus v. Becker* (1980) 117 D.L.R. (3d) 257, 278 (Sup.Ct.Can.).

[24] *Cf.* British Law Ascertainment Act 1859, s.4; *post*, para. 9–023.

[25] *e.g.* in *Moulis v. Owen* [1907] 1 K.B. 746 (C.A.) it was admitted that a wagering contract was lawful by French law; *cf. The Torni* [1932] P. 27 and 78 (C.A.) where the text of a Palestine Ordinance was admitted.

[26] *Prowse v. European and American Steam Shipping Co.* (1860) 13 Moo. P.C. 484 (plea in confession and avoidance); *cf.* CPR 16.5(3) and 16.7.

[27] *Beatty v. Beatty* [1924] 1 K.B. 807 (C.A.) where the court was helped by a deposition made by a foreign lawyer for the purposes of the case but not used at the trial; as to the interpretation of foreign statutes, see *F. & K. Jabbour v. Custodian of Israeli Absentee Property* [1954] 1 W.L.R. 139, 147–148; *Re Marshall* [1957] Ch. 507 (C.A.); *cf. Re Sebba* [1959] Ch. 166; *Wilson, Smithett & Cope Ltd. v. Terruzzi* [1976] Q.B. 683, 692; *post*, paras. 9–018 *et seq.*

[28] [1945] Ch. 5.

[29] *e.g. Re Baker's Trusts* (1871) L.R. 13 Eq. 168; *Re Barlow's Will* (1887) 36 Ch.D. 287 (C.A.); *Roe v. Roe* (1916) 115 L.T. 792; *L. (orse. B.) v. L.* (1919) 36 T.L.R. 148; *Bonhote v. Bonhote* [1920] W.N. 142. The colonial laws in these cases might have been proved under the Colonial Laws Validity Act 1865, s.6 or under the Evidence (Colonial Statutes) Act 1907 (para. 9–022, *post*) but these Acts are not mentioned in the reports.

9–010   Although foreign law is a question of fact, it is "a question of fact of a peculiar kind." Thus in *Parkasho v. Singh*[30] a Divisional Court reversed a manifestly erroneous decision by magistrates on a question of foreign law, while recognising that appellate courts are slow to interfere with trial courts on a question of fact.

9–011   The treatment of foreign law as a question of fact to be pleaded and proved by either or both of the parties means that the question of the applicability of foreign law in a case involving the conflict of laws may ultimately depend, in England, on the rules of procedure and evidence since it is to that legal category that the question belongs once this approach is accepted.[31] The consequences may be illustrated by an example. According to the Rome Convention on the Law Applicable to Contractual Obligations, implemented in the United Kingdom in the Contracts (Applicable Law) Act 1990,[32] a "contract shall be governed by the law chosen by the parties."[33] A contract which becomes the subject of English litigation may contain an express choice of foreign law. Although the language of the Rome Convention may suggest that the court is bound to apply the foreign law chosen, the rules of the Convention are expressed, subject to a limited exception,[34] not to apply to matters of evidence and procedure[35]: and it is apparently the case that whether a particular rule belongs to this category is a matter for the law of the forum.[36] If neither party relies on the chosen foreign law, the case will be decided exclusively by reference to English law since the procedural or evidential nature of the English rule concerning pleading and proof of foreign law is untouched by the Rome Convention.[37] The same result ensued in cases involving contracts governed by foreign law at common law which were also decided exclusively by reference to English law since neither party saw fit to plead or prove a foreign law which was of undoubted relevance according to normal rules of the conflict of laws.[38]

9–012   **(2) To be proved to the satisfaction of the judge.** Formerly, questions of foreign law had to be submitted to the jury. This rule was altered by statute,

---

[30] [1968] P. 233, 250; approved in *Dalmia Dairy Industries Ltd. v. National Bank of Pakistan* [1978] 2 Lloyd's Rep. 223, 286 (C.A.); *The Amazonia* [1990] 1 Lloyd's Rep. 236 (C.A.); *Bumper Development Corp. v. Commissioner of Police of the Metropolis* [1991] 1 W.L.R. 1362, 1370 (C.A.); *James Hardie & Co Ltd. v. Putt* (1998) 43 N.S.W.L.R. 554, 573–574 (C.A.).

[31] For the practical reasons why parties might not plead and prove foreign law, see Fentiman, *ante*, n. 1, Chap. 5. See also *Muduroglu Ltd. v. T.C. Ziraat Bankasi* [1986] 1 Q.B. 1225, 1246 (C.A.).

[32] See *post*, para. 32–002.

[33] Rome Convention, Art. 3(1). See *post*, Rule 173.

[34] See Art. 14.

[35] Art. 1(2)(*h*).

[36] Giuliano-Lagarde Report, [1980] O.J. C282, pp. 35–36.

[37] Art. 3(2) of the Rome Convention (*post*, para. 32–082) enables the parties to change the law originally chosen to apply to the contract. According to Giuliano-Lagarde, p. 18, if "the choice of law is made or changed in the course of proceedings the question arises as to the limits within which the choice or change can be effective. However, the question falls within the ambit of the national law of procedure, and can be settled only in accordance with that law." This observation reinforces the view of the English approach expressed in the text. For analysis of the role of Rule 18 in the context of the Rome Convention, see Fentiman, *ante*, n. 1, pp. 80–97.

[38] *e.g. Aluminium Industrie Vaassen B.V. v. Romalpa Aluminium Ltd.* [1976] 1 W.L.R. 676 (C.A.). See *post*, paras. 33–111 *et seq.*

so that now questions of foreign law are decided by the judge alone.[39] This rule applies to criminal trials.[40]

(3) Mode of proof[41]

(i) *Expert evidence.* It is now well settled that foreign law must, in general, be proved by expert evidence.[42] Foreign law cannot be proved merely by putting the text of a foreign enactment before the court, nor merely by citing foreign decisions or books of authority.[43] Such materials can only be brought before the court as part of the evidence of an expert witness,[44] since without his assistance the court cannot evaluate or interpret them.

　　9–013

No precise or comprehensive answer can be given to the question who, for this purpose, is a competent expert.[45] A judge or legal practitioner[46] from the foreign country is always competent. But in civil proceedings there is no longer any rule of law (if indeed there ever was) that the expert witness must have practised, or at least be entitled to practise, in the foreign country. For section 4(1) of the Civil Evidence Act 1972[47] provides that "it is hereby declared that in civil proceedings a person who is suitably qualified to do so on account of his knowledge or experience is competent to give expert evidence as to [foreign law[48]] irrespective of whether he has acted or is entitled to act as a legal practitioner [in the foreign country]."[49] Under these principles, which are probably declaratory of the law,[50] a former practitioner

　　9–014

---

[39] Originally Administration of Justice Act 1920, s.15. For the High Court see Supreme Court Act 1981, s.69(5); for county courts see County Courts Act 1984, s.68; for all other courts, including the Crown Court, the original provision presumably remains in force.

[40] *R. v. Hammer* [1923] 2 K.B. 786.

[41] See generally *MCC Proceeds Inc. v. Bishopsgate Investment Trust plc (No. 4)* [1999] C.L.C. 418 (C.A.). For analysis of the method of proof, and consideration of alternative approaches, see Fentiman, *ante,* n. 1, pp. 173–264.

[42] *Baron de Bode's Case* (1845) 8 Q.B. 208, 246–267; *Nelson v. Bridport* (1845) 8 Beav. 527, 536; *The Earldom of Perth* (1846) 2 H.L.C. 865, 873; *Castrique v. Imrie* (1870) L.R. 4 H.L. 414, 430; *Sussex Peerage Case* (1844) 11 Cl. & F. 85, 115; *Bumper Development Corp. v. Commissioner of Police of the Metropolis* [1991] 1 W.L.R. 1362, 1368 (C.A.) ("trite law"); *O'Callaghan v. O'Sullivan* [1925] 1 I.R. 90, 119. The earlier view, that expert evidence was not sufficient to prove foreign written laws (last expressed by Lord Campbell in the *Sussex Peerage Case (supra)* at pp. 114–115) has now clearly been abandoned.

[43] *Nelson v. Bridport* (1845) 8 Beav. 527, 542; *Buerger v. New York Life Assurance Co.* (1927) 96 L.J.K.B. 930, 940, 942 (C.A.); *Bumper Development Corp. v. Commissioner of Police of the Metropolis* [1991] 1 W.L.R. 1362, 1371 (C.A.); *cf. Callwood v. Callwood* [1960] A.C. 659 (P.C.).

[44] *Bumper Development Corp. v. Commissioner of Police of the Metropolis, ibid.*

[45] Falconbridge, Chap. 47: as to probate matters, see Non-Contentious Probate Rules 1987 (S.I. 1987 No. 2024), r. 19.

[46] This would presumably include a person such as a notary public: *cf. In the Goods of Whitelegg* [1899] P. 267.

[47] This gives effect to the Seventeenth Report of the Law Reform Committee, Cmnd. 4489 (1970).

[48] Including Scots and Northern Irish law.

[49] See *Associated Shipping Services Ltd. v. Department of Private Affairs of H.H. Sheikh Zayed Bin Sultan Al-Nahayan, Financial Times,* July 31, 1990 (C.A.). In *Bristow v. Sequeville* (1850) 5 Exch. 275, 277, it was held that a person who had studied the law of a foreign country but who had never practised there was not competent. This case was followed in *In the Goods of Bonelli* (1875) 1 P.D. 69 and *Re Turner* [1906] W.N. 27 but is rendered obsolete by s.4(1). In any event that ruling had been relaxed in subsequent cases: see, *e.g.* the cases cited in nn. 52–56, *infra,* and Seventeenth Report of the Law Reform Committee, Cmnd. 4489 (1970), para. 19.

[50] *Clyne v. Federal Commissioner of Taxation (No. 2)* (1981) 57 F.L.R. 198, 203.

in the foreign country may be competent,[51] as may be a person who is entitled to practise in the foreign country but who has not done so,[52] a person who although he has neither practised nor been entitled to practise in the foreign country, has practised in a second foreign country whose law is the same as that of the first,[53] and a person who although having no knowledge or experience of the foreign law based on study or practice has nevertheless become conversant with a point of foreign law through work involving contact with that foreign law.[54] There can be no doubt also, that an academic lawyer who has specialised in the law of the foreign country is competent[55] and it is common for such persons to supply expert evidence.[56] In principle, a witness may be competent although he is not a lawyer of any kind providing that, by virtue of his profession or calling, he has acquired a practical knowledge of a foreign law,[57] though such persons will, of course, only be regarded as experts in that part of the foreign law with which they are bound, by virtue of their profession or calling, to be familiar. In practice, however,

---

[51] *Re Duke of Wellington* [1947] Ch. 506, 514–515; *Re Banque des Marchands de Moscou* [1958] Ch. 182; *Rossano v. Manufacturers' Life Insurance Co.* [1963] 2 Q.B. 352, 373; *Kertesz v. Kertesz* [1954] V.L.R. 195; *Etler v. Kertesz* (1960) 26 D.L.R. (2d) 209 (Ont. C.A.). Tsarist lawyers who practised law before the 1917 Revolution were often allowed to give evidence of Soviet law although they had no practical experience of it. See, *e.g. Russian Commercial and Industrial Bank v. Comptoir d'Escompte de Mulhouse* [1925] A.C. 112; *Employers Liability Co. v. Sedgwick, Collins & Co.* [1927] A.C. 95; *Buerger v. New York Life Assurance Co.* (1927) 96 L.J.K.B. 930 (C.A.). But the evidence of Soviet lawyers was preferred if available: *Lazard Brothers & Co. v. Midland Bank Ltd.* [1933] A.C. 289, 299.

[52] *Barford v. Barford* [1918] P. 140; *Perlak Petroleum Maatschappij v. Deen* [1924] 1 K.B. 111 (C.A.). *Cf. Etler v. Kertesz* (1960) 26 D.L.R. (2d) 209 (Ont. C.A.), where the witness had only practised in the foreign country for a brief period but had for many years been entitled to do so.

[53] *Reinblatt v. Gold* (1928) Que.R. 45 K.B. 136; affd. [1929] S.C.R. 74; also reported on another point [1929] 1 D.L.R. 959 (Sup.Ct.Can.). The authorities conflict as to whether an English barrister who has acquired a knowledge of foreign law through practice before the Privy Council is competent: see *Wilson v. Wilson* [1903] P. 157 (competent); *Cartwright v. Cartwright* (1878) 26 W.R. 684 (not competent).

[54] *Associated Shipping Services Ltd. v. Department of Private Affairs of H.H. Sheikh Zayed Bin Sultan Al-Nahayan, Financial Times*, July 31, 1990 (C.A.) (lawyer employed as legal adviser to defendant competent expert on question whether defendant an independent juridical entity).

[55] *Brailey v. Rhodesia Consolidated Ltd.* [1910] 2 Ch. 95 (Reader in Roman-Dutch law to the Council of Legal Education); *cf. Dalrymple v. Dalrymple* (1811) 2 Hagg. Con. 54, 81 ("learned professors"). An English solicitor who had never practised in Chile but who had considerable experience of its laws was held competent in *In the Goods of Whitelegg* [1899] P. 267.

[56] *e.g. Bodley Head v. Flegon* [1972] 1 W.L.R. 680; *R. v. Registrar-General of Births, Deaths and Marriages, ex. p. Minhas* [1977] Q.B. 1; *X A.G. v. A Bank* [1983] 2 All E.R. 464.

[57] *e.g.* Governor of a Colony (*Cooper-King v. Cooper-King* [1900] P. 65); ambassador (*In the Goods of Oldenburg* (1884) 9 P.D. 234); embassy official (*In the Goods of Dost Aly Khan* (1880) 6 P.D. 6); vice-consul (*Lacon v. Higgins* (1822) Dow & Ry. N.P. 38); bishop (*Sussex Peerage Case* (1844) 11 Cl. & F. 85; *R. v. Naoum* (1911) 24 O.L.R. 306 (C.A.)); parish priests (*R. v. Savage* (1876) 13 Cox C.C. 178 (not competent); *R. v. Ilich* [1935] N.Z.L.R. 90; *Saari v. Nykanen* [1944] 4 D.L.R. 619 (Ont.) (competent)); merchant (*Vander Donckt v. Thellusson* (1849) 8 C.B. 812, though it has been said that the court may refuse to admit the evidence of such a witness where that of a qualified lawyer is readily available: *Direct Winters Transport v. Duplate Canada Ltd.* (1962) 32 D.L.R. (2d) 278 (Ont.), disapproved in *Clyne v. Federal Commissioner of Taxation (No. 2)* (1981) 57 F.L.R. 198, 202–203); bank manager (*De Beéche v. South American Stores Ltd.* [1935] A.C. 148; *Ajami v. Comptroller of Customs* [1954] 1 W.L.R. 1405 (P.C.), followed in *Associated Shipping Services Ltd. v. Department of Private Affairs of H.H. Sheikh Zayed Bin Sultan Al-Nahayan, Financial Times*, July 31, 1990 (C.A.) where, however, the witness was a lawyer not an expert in the foreign law by virtue of study or qualification, but as a result of experience through work: see *ante*, text at n. 54); police officer (*Guerin v. Proulx* (1982) 37 O.R. (2d) 558).

there will be few cases in the modern law where it will be necessary to rely on the expert evidence of such persons[58]: for it is safe to assume that, almost invariably, such evidence will be obtained from a legal practitioner or an academic lawyer with the relevant expertise. It is, of course, a truism that a person who has no special knowledge of foreign law is not competent.[59]

(ii) *Use of foreign sources.* An English court will not conduct its own   **9–015** researches into foreign law.[60] But if an expert witness refers to foreign statutes, decisions or books, the court is entitled to look at them as part of his evidence.[61] But the court is not entitled to go beyond this: thus if a witness cites a passage from a foreign law-book he does not put the whole book in evidence since he does not necessarily regard the whole book as accurate.[62] Similarly, if the witness cites a section from a foreign code or a passage from a foreign decision the court will not look at other sections of the code or at other parts of the decision without the aid of the witness, since they may have been abrogated by subsequent legislation.

If the evidence of the expert witness as to the effect of the sources quoted   **9–016** by him is uncontradicted, "it has been repeatedly said that the court should be reluctant to reject it,"[63] and it has been held that where each party's expert witness agrees on the meaning and effect of the foreign law, the court is not entitled to reject such agreed evidence, at least on the basis of its own research into foreign law.[64] But while the court will normally accept such evidence it will not do so if it is "obviously false,"[65] "obscure,"[66] "extravagant,"[67] or "patently absurd,"[68] or if "he never applied his mind to the real point of law",[69] or if "the matters stated by [the expert] did not support his conclusion according to any stated or implied process of reasoning"[70]; or if the relevant

---

[58] For examples see *Guerin v. Proulx, supra; Associated Shipping Services Ltd. v. Department of Private Affairs of H. H. Sheikh Zayed Bin Sultan Al-Nahayan, supra.*

[59] *e.g. R. v. Povey* (1852) Dears. 32; *R. v. Naguib* [1917] 1 K.B. 359; *Perlak Petroleum Maatschappij v. Deen* [1924] 1 K.B. 111 (C.A.); *Clyne v. Federal Commissioner of Taxation (No. 2)* 57 F.L.R. 198.

[60] *Di Sora v. Phillipps* (1863) 10 H.L.C. 624, 640; *Bumper Development Corp. v. Commissioner of Police of the Metropolis* [1991] 1 W.L.R. 1362, 1369 (C.A.), approving the proposition in the text.

[61] *Nelson v. Bridport* (1845) 8 Beav. 527, 541; *Concha v. Murietta* (1889) 40 Ch.D. 543 (C.A.); *Lazard Brothers & Co. v. Midland Bank Ltd.* [1933] A.C. 289, 298; *Bumper Development Corp. v. Commissioner of Police of the Metropolis, supra.*

[62] *Nelson v. Bridport* (1845) 8 Beav. 527, 542; *Waung v. Subbotovsky* [1968] 3 N.S.W.R. 261, 499.

[63] *Sharif v. Azad* [1967] 1 Q.B. 605, 616 (C.A.). See *Buerger v. New York Life Assurance Co.* (1927) 96 L.J.K.B. 930, 941 (C.A.); *Koechlin & Cie. v. Kestenbaum* [1927] 1 K.B. 616, 622, revd. on appeal but not on this point: [1927] 1 K.B. 889, 895 (C.A.); *Re Banque des Marchands de Moscou* [1958] Ch. 192; *Rossano v. Manufacturers' Life Insurance Co.* [1963] 2 Q.B. 352; *O'Callaghan v. O'Sullivan* [1925] 1 I.R. 90, 119; *Macnamara v. Hatteras (Owners)* [1933] I.R. 675, 695, 699; *Etler v. Kertesz* (1960) 26 D.L.R. (2d) 209 (Ont. C.A.).

[64] *Bumper Development Corp. v. Commissioner of Police of the Metropolis* [1991] 1 W.L.R. 1362 (C.A.).

[65] *O'Callaghan v. O'Sullivan* [1925] 1 I.R. 90, 119.

[66] *Allen v. Hay* (1922) 69 D.L.R. 193, 195–196 (Sup.Ct.Can.).

[67] *Buerger v. New York Life Assurance Co.* (1927) 96 L.J.K.B. 930, 941 (C.A.).

[68] *A/S Tallinna Laevauhisus v. Estonian State Steamship Line* (1947) 80 Ll.L.R. 99, 108 (C.A.).

[69] *Re Valentine's Settlement* [1965] Ch. 831, 855 (C.A.), *per* Salmon L.J., dissenting; *cf. Callwood v. Callwood* [1960] A.C. 659 (P.C.).

[70] *Associated Shipping Services Ltd. v. Department of Private Affairs of H.H. Sheikh Zayed Bin Sultan Al-Nahayan, Financial Times,* July 31, 1990 (C.A.).

foreign court would not employ the reasoning of the expert even if it agreed with the conclusion.[71] In such cases the court may reject the evidence and examine the foreign sources to form its own conclusion as to their effect. Similarly, the court may reject an expert's opinion as to the meaning of a foreign statute if it is inconsistent with the text or the English translation and is not justified by reference to any special rule of construction of the foreign law.[72] It should, however, be noted in this connection that quite simple words may well be terms of art in a foreign statute.[73]

9–017   If the evidence of several expert witnesses conflicts as to the effect of foreign sources, the court is entitled, and indeed bound, to look at those sources in order itself to decide between the conflicting testimony.[74] Similarly, where the evidence of expert witnesses as to the constitutionality or *vires* of foreign legislation conflicts, it seems that the court can determine the question,[75] provided at any rate that it is one which, according to the foreign law, is determinable by ordinary judicial proceedings.[76] In addition the territory of what was once a single country may be divided, for instance in times of revolution or civil war, or as a result of enemy occupation; and the question may then arise which of two legislatures or systems of courts has the right to determine the law of any given part of that territory. In this situation, the problem to be resolved is not one of proof of foreign law but rather that of identifying the appropriate law-maker. The evidence of expert witnesses is irrelevant on the latter issue which is discussed elsewhere in this work.[77] Once, of course, the appropriate law-maker has been identified, the question of proving what the content of the law handed down by that law-maker actually is will have to be determined by reference to the evidence of an appropriately qualified expert.

---

[71] *Macmillan Inc. v. Bishopsgate Investment Trust plc (No. 3)* [1995] 1 W.L.R. 978, 1009; the decision to reject the expert evidence was approved in *MCC Proceeds Inc. v. Bishopsgate Investment Trust plc (No. 4)* [1999] C.L.C. 418 (C.A.).

[72] *A/S Tallinna Laevauhisus v. Estonian State Steamship Line, supra.*

[73] *e.g.* "kindred" and "incidental" in *Camille and Henry Dreyfus Foundation Inc. v. I.R.C.* [1954] Ch. 672, 692 (C.A.); affd. [1956] A.C. 39.

[74] *Dalrymple v. Dalrymple* (1811) 2 Hagg.Con. 54; *Trimbey v. Vignier* (1834) 1 Bing.N.C. 151; *Devaux v. Steele* (1840) 6 Bing.N.C. 360; *Nelson v. Bridport* (1845) 8 Beav. 527, 537; *Bremer v. Freeman* (1857) 10 Moo.P.C. 306; *Concha v. Murietta* (1889) 40 Ch.D. 543 (C.A.); *Guaranty Trust Corporation of New York v. Hannay* [1918] 2 K.B. 623 (C.A.); *Russian Commercial and Industrial Bank v. Comptoir d'Escompte de Mulhouse* [1923] 2 K.B. 630, reversed [1925] A.C. 112 on the ground that the Court of Appeal had misinterpreted the foreign law; *Princess Paley Olga v. Weisz* [1929] 1 K.B. 718 (C.A.); *Re Duke of Wellington* [1947] Ch. 506; *In the Estate of Fuld (No. 3)* [1968] P. 675, 700–703; *Dubai Bank Ltd. v. Galadari (No. 5), The Times,* June 26, 1990; *Bumper Development Corp. v. Commissioner of Police of the Metropolis* [1991] 1 W.L.R. 1362, 1369–1370 (C.A.), expressly approving the proposition in the text; *MCC Proceeds Inc. v. Bishopsgate Investment Trust plc (No. 4)* [1999] C.L.C. 418 (C.A.); *Kolbin and Sons v. Kinnear,* 1930 S.C. 724; *Macnamara v. Hatteras (Owners)* [1933] I.R. 675, 699–700.

[75] *King of the Hellenes v. Brostrom* (1923) 16 Ll.L.R. 167, 190, 192; *Re Amand* [1941] 2 K.B. 239; *Re Amand (No. 2)* [1942] 1 K.B. 445; *A/S Tallinna Laevauhisus v. Estonian State Steamship Line* (1947) 80 Ll.L.R. 99, 114 (C.A.); *Dubai Bank Ltd. v. Galadari (No. 5), The Times,* June 26, 1990; F. A. Mann, *Studies in International Law* (1973), pp. 444–449.

[76] Lipstein (1967) 42 B.Y.I.L. 265. It is doubtful whether the court can determine such a question if in the foreign country it cannot be decided by a court at all (as in Switzerland) or only by a special constitutional court (as in Germany). See Kahn-Freund, *Festschrift für F.A. Mann* (1977), pp. 207–225.

[77] See *post,* para. 25–004. For special provisions relating to corporations, see Foreign Corporations Act 1991, discussed *post,* para. 30–015.

Since the effect of foreign sources is primarily a matter for the expert **9–018** witness, it is desirable, when proving a foreign statute, also to obtain evidence as to its interpretation.[78] It may happen, however, that the text of a foreign statute is admitted, or that it is proved without expert evidence under the Evidence (Colonial Statutes) Act 1907,[79] or that the expert fails to give any evidence as to its interpretation. In such cases, the court can put its own construction on the foreign statute.[80] The court may also undertake this task at the express request of the parties.[81] In all these cases the court acts on the assumption that the foreign rules of construction are the same as those of English law.[82]

The function of the expert witness in relation to the interpretation of foreign **9–019** statutes must be contrasted with his function in relation to the construction of foreign documents. In the former case, the expert tells the court what the statute means, explaining his opinion, if necessary, by reference to foreign rules of construction. In the latter case, the expert merely proves the foreign rules of construction, and the court itself, in the light of these rules, determines the meaning of the documents.[83] Where a document which is to be construed by English law incorporates the words of a foreign statute as part of its terms, the court construes the document without reference to foreign rules of construction,[84] unless the parties to the document intend it to be construed in accordance with such foreign rules.[85]

Considerable weight is usually given to the decisions of foreign courts as **9–020** evidence of foreign law,[86] though such decisions can only, it seems, be referred to if referred to in the evidence of an expert witness[87] and, further, must be interpreted in the light on the meaning attributed to the decisions by the expert rather than according to the court's independent research involving material not referred to by the expert.[88] But the court is not bound to apply a foreign decision if it is satisfied, as a result of all the evidence, that the decision does not accurately represent the foreign law.[89] Where foreign decisions conflict, the court may be asked to decide between them, even

---

[78] *Baron de Bode's Case* (1845) 8 Q.B. 208, 251, 265–266; *Castrique v. Imrie* (1870) L.R. 4 H.L. 414, 430; *Higgins v. Ewing's Trustees*, 1925 S.C. 440; *Allen v. Standard Trusts Co.* (1919) 49 D.L.R. 399 (Man.).

[79] *Post*, para. 9–022.

[80] *e.g. Prowse v. European and American Steam Shipping Co.* (1860) 13 Moo.P.C. 484; *Papadopoulos v. Papadopoulos* [1930] P. 55; *The Torni* [1932] P. 78 (C.A.); *Jasiewicz v. Jasiewicz* [1962] 1 W.L.R. 1426; *Mahadervan v. Mahadervan* [1964] P. 233.

[81] *Ante*, para. 9–008, n. 27.

[82] *F. & K. Jabbour v. Custodian of Israeli Absentee Property* [1954] 1 W.L.R. 139, 147–148.

[83] *Trotter v. Trotter* (1828) 4 Bli.(N.S.) 502; *King of Spain v. Machado* (1827) 4 Russ. 225, 239–240; *Rouyer Guillet & Cie v. Rouyer Guillet & Co. Ltd.* [1949] 1 All E.R. 244 (C.A.); *Mount Cook (Northland) Ltd. v. Swedish Motors Ltd.* [1986] 1 N.Z.L.R. 720, 727.

[84] *Dobell v. Steamship Rossmore Co.* [1895] 2 Q.B. 408 (C.A.); *cf.*, paras. 32–086 *et seq.*, *post*.

[85] See *Stafford Allen and Sons Ltd. v. Pacific Steam Navigation Co.* [1956] 1 W.L.R. 629 (C.A.).

[86] *Beatty v. Beatty* [1924] 1 K.B. 807 (C.A.); *Re Annesley* [1926] Ch. 692; *Bankers and Shippers Insurance Co. of New York v. Liverpool Marine and General Insurance Co. Ltd.* (1926) 24 Ll.L.R. 85 (H.L.); *In the Estate of Fuld (No. 3)* [1968] P. 675, 701–702; *Walpole v. Ewer* (1789) Ridg.temp.H. 276n. perhaps goes too far.

[87] *Bumper Development Corp. v. Commissioner of Police of the Metropolis* [1991] 1 W.L.R. 1362, 1370–1371 (C.A.).

[88] *Ibid.*

[89] *Guaranty Trust Corporation of New York v. Hannay* [1918] 2 K.B. 623 (C.A.); *Callwood v. Callwood* [1960] A.C. 659 (P.C.).

though in the foreign country the question still remains to be authoritatively settled.[90]

9–021   (iii) *Other modes of proof.* Under certain statutes, proof of foreign law may sometimes be dispensed with.

By the Civil Evidence Act 1972, section 4(2),[91] where, whether before or after the passing of that act, any question of foreign law[92] has been determined in civil or criminal proceedings at first instance in the High Court, the Crown Court, a court of quarter sessions[93] or the county palatine Courts of Chancery of Lancaster or Durham,[94] or in any appeal therefrom, or in the Privy Council on appeal from any court outside the United Kingdom,[95] then any finding made or decision given on that question is admissible in evidence in any civil proceedings, and the foreign law shall be taken to be in accordance with that finding or decision unless the contrary is proved. The finding or decision as to foreign law must be reported or recorded in citable form, which means that it must be reported or recorded in writing in a report, transcript or other document which could be cited as an authority in legal proceedings in England if the question had been one of English law.[96] Except with the permission of the court, a party may not adduce any such finding or decision as evidence of foreign law unless he has in accordance with rules of court notified every other party of his intention to do so.[97] The subsection does not apply if the subsequent proceedings are before a court which can take judicial notice of the foreign law. Thus a determination of a point of Scots law by the High Court or the Court of Appeal is not even prima facie evidence of that point in subsequent proceedings before the House of Lords. Nor is the determination prima facie binding if there are conflicting findings or decisions on the same question.[98]

9–022   By the Evidence (Colonial Statutes) Act 1907,[99] copies of laws made by the legislature of any "British possession,"[1] if purporting to be printed by the government printer of the "British possession," can be received in evidence in the United Kingdom without proof that the copies were so printed. Under this Act, the text of such laws can be proved without expert evidence[2]; but the court may require expert evidence to show that the alleged law is still in force.[3] The Act continues to apply to the legislation of many Commonwealth

---

[90] *Re Duke of Wellington* [1947] Ch. 506; *Breen v. Breen* [1964] P. 144.

[91] This gives effect to the Seventeenth Report of the Law Reform Committee, Cmnd. 4489 (1970), para. 64; *cf. Phoenix Marine Inc. v. China Ocean Shipping Co.* [1999] 1 Lloyd's Rep. 682.

[92] Including Scots or Northern Irish law.

[93] Courts of quarter sessions were abolished by the Courts Act 1971, s.3.

[94] These courts were abolished on their merger with the High Court: *ibid.* ss.41, 57(3)(*b*).

[95] Civil Evidence Act 1972, s.4(4).

[96] s.4(5).

[97] s.4(3).

[98] s.4(2), proviso.

[99] For a similar, but less general, provision, see Colonial Laws Validity Act 1865, s.6. See also Isle of Man Act 1979, s.12(1).

[1] *i.e.* "any part of [Her] Majesty's dominions exclusive of the United Kingdom ... ": s.1(3).

[2] *Taylor v. Taylor* [1923] W.N. 65; *Waterfield v. Waterfield* (1929) 73 S.J. 300; *Papadopoulos v. Papadopoulos* [1930] P. 55. See also the cases cited *ante*, para. 9–009.

[3] *Brown v. Brown* (1917) 116 L.T. 702; *R. v. Governor of Brixton Prison, ex p. Shuter* [1960] 2 Q.B. 89; *Jasiewicz v. Jasiewicz* [1962] 1 W.L.R. 1426.

countries which are no longer part of Her Majesty's dominions, *e.g.* because they have become republics.[4]

By the British Law Ascertainment Act 1859, a court in any part of Her **9–023** Majesty's dominions may, if it thinks necessary or expedient for the proper disposal of an action, state a case for the opinion of a court in any other part of Her Majesty's dominions in order to ascertain the view of that court as to the law applicable to the facts of the case stated.[5] The Act continues to apply to many Commonwealth countries which are no longer part of Her Majesty's dominions.[6] The court may take advantage of the provisions of the Act of its own motion[7] and may, on the other hand, refuse to state a case on request if it is satisfied that it already has enough evidence of the foreign law.[8] The court has a complete discretion whether or not to state a case.[9] There are very few reported cases in which it has done so, because the procedure is expensive and involves delay. The opinion of the foreign court is binding on the English court now that the power of submitting such opinion to the jury as evidence of the foreign law[10] has become obsolete.[11] But the opinion is not binding on the House of Lords if it was given by a court over which the House exercises appellate jurisdiction; and similarly the opinion of a court over which the Privy Council exercises appellate jurisdiction does not bind the Privy Council.[12]

Although statutory provision was made for the application of similar **9–024** procedures to the ascertainment of the law of foreign countries outside the Commonwealth, no international conventions to this end were ever concluded.[13] However, a multilateral convention serving the same purposes was signed in London in 1968. The European Convention on Information on Foreign Law[14] came into effect in the following year; the great majority of Member States of the Council of Europe, including the United Kingdom, have ratified the Convention. Where proceedings have actually been instituted, a judicial authority in any Contracting State may make a request for information under the Convention.[15] The request must state the nature of the case, the questions on which information concerning the law of the requested State is desired, and the facts necessary both for the proper understanding of the request and for the formulation of an exact and precise reply.[16] The request must be for information as to law and procedure in civil and commercial fields, or as to judicial organisation, but other matters may be raised if they are incidental to primary questions falling within that area.[17] The request is

---

[4] This is the effect of provisions in Acts of the United Kingdom Parliament for the continuation of existing laws in relation to such countries when they cease to form part of Her Majesty's dominions: *Jasiewicz v. Jasiewicz* [1962] 1 W.L.R. 1426.

[5] s.1. See *The Supreme Court Practice 1999*, para. 39/3/14 for the form in which a case should be stated.

[6] For the reason given in n. 4, *supra*.

[7] *Ante*, para. 9–003.

[8] *MacDougall v. Chitnavis*, 1937 S.C. 390, 407–408.

[9] *Lord v. Colvin* (1860) 1 Dr. & Sm. 24.

[10] s.3.

[11] *Ante*, para. 9–012; *MacDougall v. Chitnavis*, 1937 S.C. 390, 400.

[12] s.4; *De Thoren v. Att.-Gen.* (1876) 1 App.Cas. 686.

[13] See Foreign Law Ascertainment Act 1861, repealed in 1973.

[14] For text, see Treaty Series No. 117 (1969) (Cmnd. 4229); Rodger & Van Doorn (1997) 46 I.C.L.Q. 151.

[15] Art. 3(1).

[16] Art. 4(1)(2).

[17] Arts. 1(1), 4(3).

transmitted through designated national liaison organs,[18] and a reply may be prepared by the liaison organ of the requested State, or by an official or private body or an individual qualified lawyer on its behalf.[19] The information given in the reply does not bind the judicial authority from which the request emanated.[20] No provision has been made in English rules of court as to the practice under this Convention.[21]

9–025   **(4) Burden of proof.** The burden of proving foreign law lies on the party who bases his claim or defence on it.[22] If that party adduces no evidence, or insufficient evidence, of the foreign law, the court applies English law.[23] This principle is sometimes expressed in the form that foreign law is presumed to be the same as English law until the contrary is proved.[24] But this mode of expression has given rise to uneasiness in certain cases. Thus in one case the court refused to apply the presumption of similarity where the foreign law was not based on the common law,[25] and in others it has been doubted whether the court was entitled to presume that the foreign law was the same as the statute law of the forum.[26] In view of these difficulties it is better to abandon the terminology of presumption, and simply to say that where foreign law is not proved, the court applies English law.[27] There is one exception to this rule. In a trial for bigamy, the validity of the first marriage may depend on a rule of foreign law. In such a case, the prosecution must prove that the marriage is valid according to that law. If no evidence of foreign law is given, the court will not apply English law but will direct an acquittal.[28]

---

[18] The United Kingdom has designated the Legal and Executive Branch of the Foreign and Commonwealth Office.

[19] Art. 6(1)(2).

[20] Art. 8.

[21] See O'Malley and Layton, p. 239, for the suggestion that an English court may take advantage of the provisions of this Convention under its powers to issue letters of request for the taking of evidence abroad (as to which see *ante*, paras. 8–064 *et seq.*) or under the court's inherent jurisdiction. See also Fentiman, *ante*, n. 1, pp. 239–244; *cf. Panayiotou v. Sony Music Entertainment (U.K.) Ltd.* [1994] Ch. 142, 149–150.

[22] *Brown v. Gracey* (1821) Dow. & Ry.N.P. 41n.; *Dynamit A.G. v. Rio Tinto Co.* [1918] A.C. 260, 295, 301; *Guaranty Trust Co. of New York v. Hannay* [1918] 2 K.B. 623, 655 (C.A.); *Schapiro v. Schapiro* [1904] T.S. 673; *Rodden v. Whatlings Ltd.*, 1961 S.C. 132; *Furlong v. Burns & Co. Ltd.* (1964) 43 D.L.R. (2d) 689 (Ont.); *Morgardshammar v. Radomski & Co. Ltd.* (1983) 145 D.L.R. (3d) 111 (Ont.), appeal dismissed (1984) 5 D.L.R. (4th) 576 (Ont. C.A.). For the burden of proving the law applicable to the tort, if it is a foreign law, in actions on foreign torts, see Fentiman, *ante*, n. 1, pp. 97–106; see also *post*, para. 35–060.

[23] *Lloyd v. Guibert* (1865) L.R. 1 Q.B. 115, 129; *Nouvelle Banque de l'Union v. Ayton* (1891) 7 T.L.R. 377; *Hartmann v. Konig* (1933) 50 T.L.R. 114, 117 (H.L.); *Re Tank of Oslo* [1940] 1 All E.R. 40, 42 (C.A.); *Re Parana Plantations Ltd.* [1946] 2 All E.R. 214, 217–218; *Szechter v. Szechter* [1971] P. 286, 296; *cf. Pickering v. Stephenson* (1872) L.R. 14 Eq. 322. *Ward v. Dey* (1849) 1 Rob.Ecc. 759 appears to be based on this principle.

[24] *e.g. Dynamit A.G. v. Rio Tinto Co.* [1918] A.C. 260, 295; *The Parchim* [1918] A.C. 157, 161 (P.C.); *The Colorado* [1923] P. 102, 111 (C.A.); *Casey v. Casey* [1949] P. 420, 430 (C.A.); *University of Glasgow v. The Economist, The Times*, July 13, 1990.

[25] *Guépratte v. Young* (1851) 4 De G. & Sm. 217.

[26] *Purdom v. Pavey* (1896) 26 S.C.R. 412, 417; *Schnaider v. Jaffe* (1916) 7 C.P.D. 696; *cf. The Ship "Mercury Bell" v. Amosin* (1986) 27 D.L.R. (4th) 641 (F.C.A.).

[27] See Fentiman, *ante*, n. 1, pp. 147–148.

[28] *Cf. R. v. Naguib* [1917] 1 K.B. 359 where a marriage under foreign law was relied on by the defence. As to proof of foreign marriage, see Fentiman, *ante*, n. 1, pp. 226–230, and *post*, paras. 17–037 *et seq.*

PART THREE

JURISDICTION AND FOREIGN JUDGMENTS

PART THREE deals with the jurisdiction of the High Court in claims *in personam* and in claims *in rem*, the enforcement of foreign judgments, and with arbitration and the enforcement of foreign awards.

CHAPTER 10 deals with the jurisdictional immunities of foreign States, foreign diplomats and consuls and members of international organisations.

CHAPTER 11 deals with the jurisdiction of the High Court in claims *in personam* under the common law, under the Civil Procedure Rules (including Order 11) and under the 1968 and Lugano Conventions on jurisdiction and the enforcement of judgments in civil and commercial matters.

CHAPTER 12 deals with the jurisdiction of the High Court to stay proceedings when it is necessary to prevent injustice, with *lis alibi pendens* under the 1968 and Lugano Conventions, with injunctions to restrain foreign proceedings (anti-suit injunctions), and the effect in England of a contractual provision that all disputes between the parties are to be referred to the jurisdiction of the courts of a specified country.

CHAPTER 13 deals with the jurisdiction of the High Court in Admiralty claims *in rem*.

CHAPTER 14 deals with the enforcement and recognition in England of foreign judgments *in personam* and *in rem*, and in particular with the jurisdiction of foreign courts to give such judgments, and with the defences that may be raised in England against their enforcement or recognition. It states the rules contained in the common law, in the Administration of Justice Act 1920 (which deals with the reciprocal enforcement of judgments between the United Kingdom and certain countries of the Commonwealth overseas), in the Foreign Judgments (Reciprocal Enforcement) Act 1933 (which deals with the reciprocal enforcement of judgments between the United Kingdom and certain other countries) and in the Civil Jurisdiction and Judgments Act 1982 (Part I of which deals with the reciprocal enforcement of judgments between the United Kingdom and the other States which are party to the 1968 and Lugano Conventions; and Part II of which deals with the reciprocal enforcement of judgments within the United Kingdom).

CHAPTER 15 deals with the jurisdiction of English courts and the enforcement and recognition of foreign judgments in certain cases arising out of multilateral conventions, to which special rules apply.

CHAPTER 16 deals with the law governing arbitration agreements and arbitration procedure; with the duty of the court to stay proceedings brought in England by a party to a submission to arbitration; the enforcement in England of foreign arbitration awards at common law, under the Arbitration Act 1950, under the Arbitration Act 1996, under the Administration of Justice Act 1920 and the Foreign Judgments (Reciprocal Enforcement) Act 1933 and under the Arbitration (International Investment Disputes) Act 1966.

III–001

III–002

III–003

III–004   The jurisdiction of English and foreign courts in matrimonial causes[1]; guardianship, custody and maintenance of minors[2]; legitimacy, legitimation and adoption[3]; mentally disordered persons[4]; the administration of estates of deceased persons[5]; succession[6]; the winding up of companies[7]; and bankruptcy,[8] are not dealt with in this Part but in the Chapters respectively dealing with these subjects.

---

[1] See Chap. 18, *post.*
[2] See Chap. 19, *post.*
[3] See Chap. 20, *post.*
[4] See Chap. 21, *post.*
[5] See Chap. 26, *post.*
[6] See Chap. 27, *post.*
[7] See Chap. 30, *post.*
[8] See Chap. 31, *post.*

CHAPTER 10

JURISDICTIONAL IMMUNITIES

RULE 19[1]—Subject to the Exceptions hereinafter mentioned, a foreign   10R–001
State is immune from the jurisdiction of the English courts.

COMMENT

Introductory. The basic principle, confirmed by section 1(1) of the State   10–002
Immunity Act 1978, and now subject to far-reaching statutory exceptions, is
that a foreign State is immune from the jurisdiction of the courts of the United
Kingdom. In the words of Lord Atkin (described by Lord Denning M.R. as a
"classic restatement"[2]) "the courts of a country will not implead a foreign
sovereign, that is, they will not by their process make him against his will a
party to legal proceedings, whether the proceedings involve process against
his person or seek to recover from him specific property or damages."[3] The
immunity is derived ultimately from the rules of public international law, and
from the maxim of that law, *par in parem non habet imperium*. The relevant
rules became part of the English common law,[4] and are now reflected in the
State Immunity Act 1978.

In the nineteenth century and for much of the twentieth century the "abso-   10–003
lute" rule of immunity prevailed, whereby foreign States and sovereigns were
accorded immunity for all activities, whether governmental or commercial.
But the increase in state trading in the twentieth century led a number of
countries to develop a distinction, generally called the "restrictive" theory,
between acts of government, *acta jure imperii*, and acts of a commercial
nature, *acta jure gestionis*.[5] Under the restrictive theory, States were immune
in respect of acts of government but not in respect of commercial acts. An
early attempt to exclude immunity in the case of ships and cargoes owned or
operated by States for commercial purposes, the Brussels Convention of 1926,
achieved only limited support, and was not ratified by the United Kingdom
until 1979. The enormous increase in state trading after the Second World War

---

[1] There is a very considerable literature on the subject of State immunity: see, in particular,
Schreuer, *State Immunity: Some Recent Developments* (1988), with extensive bibliography at
pp. 177–189; Brownlie, *Principles of Public International Law* (5th ed. 1998), Chap. XVI;
Oppenheim, *International Law* (9th ed. Jennings and Watts, 1992), pp. 341–363; Brownlie,
Ann. de l'Institut de droit international, Vol. 62–I, p. 13 (1987), *ibid.* Vol. 63–I, p. 13 (1989);
Lauterpacht (1951) 28 B.Y.I.L. 220; Sinclair (1980) *Recueil des Cours*, II, p. 113; Trooboff
(1986) *Recueil des Cours*, V, p. 235; Greig (1989) 38 I.C.L.Q. 243 and 560. For the recognition
and enforcement in England of foreign judgments against foreign States, see *post*, Rule 38.
[2] *Trendtex Trading Corporation v. Central Bank of Nigeria* [1977] Q.B. 529, 555 (C.A.).
[3] *The Cristina* [1938] A.C. 485, 490. *Cf. The Parlement Belge* (1880) 5 P.D. 197, 207, 214–215
(C.A.). See on immunity from taxation *R. v. I.R.C., ex p. Camacq Corp.* [1990] 1 W.L.R. 191
(C.A.).
[4] *The Cristina* [1938] A.C. 485, 490; *Trendtex Trading Corporation v. Central Bank of Nigeria*
[1977] Q.B. 529, 553–554, 567–569, 578–579 (C.A.).
[5] See Lauterpacht (1951) 28 B.Y.I.L. 220, 222–226.

led the United States Department of State to announce, in 1952, its adherence to the restrictive theory,[6] and the distinction between governmental and commercial acts was applied by the United States courts[7] and was in 1976 enacted in federal legislation.[8] In 1972 a European Convention on State Immunity, severely restricting the scope of immunity, was concluded under the auspices of the Council of Europe, and came into force in 1976.[9]

10–004   In the United Kingdom the courts applied the absolute theory[10] both in relation to actions *in rem* against trading ships[11] and actions *in personam* involving trading activities,[12] but in 1975 the Privy Council held that a foreign government was not entitled to claim immunity in an action *in rem* against a vessel used for trading purposes,[13] and in 1977 the Court of Appeal held, by a majority, that a State was not entitled to immunity in respect of commercial transactions.[14] In 1981, after the law had been altered by statute, the House of Lords confirmed that the restrictive theory of immunity applied at common law.[15]

10–005   **State Immunity Act 1978.**[16] The law of sovereign immunity in the United Kingdom is now regulated by the State Immunity Act 1978, which introduced or confirmed a number of major exceptions to the basic rule of immunity, and was designed in part to implement the European Convention on State Immunity.[17] The principal provisions of the Act do not apply to proceedings in

---

[6] In the "Tate letter," quoted in Whiteman, *Digest of International Law*, Vol. 6, pp. 569–571.

[7] See, *e.g. Victory Transport Inc. v. Comisaria General de Abastesimientos y Transportes*, 336 F.2d 354 (2d Cir. 1964), cert.den. 381 U.S. 934 (1965).

[8] Foreign Sovereign Immunities Act 1976, text in (1976) 15 *International Legal Materials* 1388, with amendments *ibid.* (1989), Vol. 28, p. 396.

[9] For text see Cmnd. 7742. See Sinclair (1973) 22 I.C.L.Q. 254. The Convention came into force for the United Kingdom on October 4, 1979.

[10] Subject to certain possible exceptions, such as actions relating to trust funds and immovable property: see 9th ed. at pp. 143–144.

[11] *The Porto Alexandre* [1920] P. 30 (C.A.). *Cf. The Cristina* [1938] A.C. 485, 490 (*per* Lord Atkin), 512 (*per* Lord Wright).

[12] *Compania Mercantil Argentina v. U.S. Shipping Board* (1924) 40 T.L.R. 601 (C.A.); *Kahan v. Pakistan Federation* [1951] 2 K.B. 1003 (C.A.); *Baccus S.R.L. v. Servicio Nacional del Trigo* [1957] 1 Q.B. 438 (C.A.).

[13] *The Philippine Admiral* [1977] A.C. 373, approving dicta of Lord Maugham in *The Cristina* [1938] A.C. 485, 519–520.

[14] *Trendtex Trading Corporation v. Central Bank of Nigeria* [1977] Q.B. 529 (C.A.); *Hispano Americana Mercantile S.A. v. Central Bank of Nigeria* [1979] 2 Lloyd's Rep. 277 (C.A.). For earlier formulations of Lord Denning see *Rahimtoola v. Nizam of Hyderabad* [1958] A.C. 379, 422–423 and *Thai-Europe Tapioca Service Ltd. v. Government of Pakistan* [1975] 1 W.L.R. 1485, 1491–1492 (C.A.). For similar developments in Ireland, Canada, New Zealand and South Africa see *Government of Canada v. Employment Appeals Tribunal* [1992] I.L.R.M. 325 (Sup.Ct.); *McElhinney v. Williams* [1996] 1 I.L.R.M. 276 (Sup.Ct.); *Zodiac International Products Inc. v. Polish People's Republic* (1977) 81 D.L.R. (3d) 656 (Qu. C.A.); *The Ship "Atra" v. Lorac Transport Ltd.* (1986) 28 D.L.R. (4th) 309 (Fed. C.A.); *Reid v. Republic of Nauru* [1993] 1 V.R. 251; *Reef Shipping Co. Ltd. v. The Ship "Fua Kavenga"* [1987] 1 N.Z.L.R. 550; *Governor of Pitcairn v. Sutton* [1995] 1 N.Z.L.R. 426 (C.A.); *Controller and Auditor-General v. Davison* [1996] 2 N.Z.L.R. 278 (C.A.); *Inter-Science Research and Development Services Pty. Ltd. v. Republica de Moçambique*, 1980 (2) S.A. 111.

[15] *The I Congreso del Partido* [1983] 1 A.C. 244. See also *Alcom Ltd. v. Republic of Colombia* [1984] A.C. 580; *Planmount v. Republic of Zaire* [1981] 1 All E.R. 1110.

[16] See F. A. Mann, *Further Studies in International Law* (1990), p. 302; Delaume (1979) 73 A.J.I.L. 185. Similar legislation has been enacted in South Africa (Foreign States Immunities Act 1981) and in Canada (State Immunity Act 1982), and in Australia (Foreign State Immunities Act 1985; see Law Reform Commission, Report No. 24, 1984).

[17] See *supra*, n. 9.

respect of matters that occurred before it came into force in 1978.[18] The Act is to be construed against the background of generally recognised principles of public international law.[19] It has, however, been held that, where a State is immune under the 1978 Act, it remains immune even if the acts complained of are alleged to be contrary to international law, and accordingly the Government of Kuwait was immune from a civil claim in respect of alleged torture.[20]

It is important to note that the 1978 Act lays down a number of *exceptions*   **10–006**
to the immunity of a foreign State. It does not *confer* jurisdiction on the English courts which they would otherwise not have, and the Act expressly provides that the method of service on foreign States laid down by the Act does not affect any rules of court whereby leave is required for the service of process outside the jurisdiction.[21] Thus the exception relating to commercial transactions does not relieve the claimant of the necessity of bringing an appropriate case within the provisions of Order 11, r. 1(1), of the Rules of the Supreme Court (now in the Civil Procedure Rules 1998, Schedule 1) or of the 1968 and Lugano Conventions (discussed in Chapter 11), unless (for example) the defendant is a foreign State which has submitted to the jurisdiction or is a separate entity with a branch in England. In this respect the 1978 Act[22] differs from its United States counterpart, the Foreign Sovereign Immunities Act 1976, which enacts rules of personal jurisdiction over foreign States.

Meaning of State. The immunity from suit applies to any foreign or   **10–007**
Commonwealth State other than the United Kingdom, and it applies not only to the State itself but also to the sovereign of the State in his public capacity,[23] to the government of the State, and any department of its government.[24] The Court of Appeal has held that for this purpose the Commissioner of the Australian Federal Police is to be regarded as part of the State or government of Australia: the protection afforded by the 1978 Act to States would be undermined if employees or officers could be sued as individuals for matters of state conduct in respect of which the State they were serving had immunity. Section 14(1) of the 1978 Act had to be read as affording to individual

---

[18] See *Sengupta v. Republic of India* [1983] I.C.R. 221 (E.A.T.).

[19] *Alcom v. Republic of Colombia* [1984] A.C. 580, 597.

[20] *Al-Adsani v. Government of Kuwait, The Times*, March 29, 1996; 107 Int. L. R. 536 (C.A.), applying *Argentine Republic v. Amerada Hess Shipping Corp.*, 488 U.S. 428 (1989) and *Siderman de Blake v. Republic of Argentina*, 965 F.2d 699 (9th Cir. 1992). But in *R. v. Bow Street Magistrate, ex p. Pinochet (No.3)* [1999] 2 W.L.R. 827 (H.L.) it was held that there is no immunity from criminal jurisdiction in respect of acts of torture for which a former head of state is alleged to be responsible.

[21] s.12(7).

[22] The European Convention on State Immunity laid down jurisdictional links, but they were not enacted in the 1978 Act.

[23] The sovereign in his personal capacity is assimilated to the head of a diplomatic mission, with certain modifications (in particular, immunities and privileges are not to be subject to restrictions by reference to nationality or residence): State Immunity Act 1978, s.20. See also *Bank of Credit and Commerce International (Overseas) Ltd. v. Price Waterhouse* [1997] 4 All E.R. 108 (third party notice against Ruler of Abu Dhabi, who was also President of the United Arab Emirates; held he was entitled to immunities of head of diplomatic mission, and not to State immunity: although he was acting in his public capacity *vis-à-vis* Abu Dhabi (which is a constituent territory of the United Arab Emirates), he was not acting in a public capacity on behalf of the United Arab Emirates). On the position of former heads of state see *R. v. Bow Street Magistrate, ex p. Pinochet (No.3)* [1999] 2 W.L.R. 827 (H.L.). See generally Watts (1994) *Recueil des Cours*, III, 9.

[24] State Immunity Act 1978, s.14(1).

employees or officers of a foreign State protection under the same cloak as protected the State itself.[25]

10–008   An entity (referred to in the Act as a "separate entity") which is distinct from the executive organs of the government of the State and is capable of suing or being sued is entitled to immunity only if (a) the proceedings relate to anything done by it in the exercise of sovereign authority and (b) the circumstances are such that a State would have been immune.[26] There is no express requirement that such a separate entity be owned or controlled by the foreign State, but it would be a considerable extension of the doctrine of immunity to apply the notion of separate entity to *any* agent of the foreign State, and it is therefore suggested that a separate entity not owned or controlled by the State is not capable of acting in the exercise of sovereign authority.[27] For a separate entity to be immune, there are two requirements. The first is that the proceedings must relate to something "done by it in the exercise of sovereign authority."[28] This requirement is by its terms additional to the second requirement, namely that the circumstances must be such that a State would have been immune. In *Kuwait Airways Corp. v. Iraqi Airways Co.*[29] it was held that acts "done by it in the exercise of sovereign authority" meant *acta jure imperii* in the sense in which that expression had been adopted by English law from public international law, *i.e.* governmental acts, as opposed to acts which any private citizen could perform. In the case of acts done by a separate entity, they are not *acta jure imperii* simply because they are done on the directions of the State or because their purpose is to serve the interests of the State, since they may not possess the character of a governmental act.[30]

10–009   Even where a State is not immune because one of the exceptions applies, its property (except that used for commercial purposes) is immune from process of execution,[31] but the property (of whatever kind) of a separate entity (other than a central bank) would be subject in such circumstances to execution if the proceedings did not relate to something done by it in the exercise of sovereign

---

[25] *Propend Finance Pty Ltd. v. Sing*, *The Times*, May 2, 1997; 111 Int. L.R. 611 (C.A.). *Cf. Re P (Diplomatic Immunity: Jurisdiction)* [1998] 1 F.L.R. 1026, 1034 (affd. on other grounds at 1035, C.A.). See also *Schmidt v. Home Secretary* [1995] 1 I.L.R.M. 301 (Metropolitan Police to be treated as officers of the Crown); *Jaffe v. Miller* (1993) 13 O.R. (3d) 745 (Ont. C.A.); *University of Calgary v. Colorado School of Mines* [1996] 2 W.W.R. 596 (Alta.).

[26] State Immunity Act 1978, s.14(1)–(2). Separate entity includes a State's central bank or other monetary authority, to whose property special rules apply: see *post*, para. 10–013.

[27] In *Kuwait Airways Corp. v. Iraqi Airways Co.* [1995] 1 W.L.R. 1147, 1158 (H.L.) it was said (*obiter*) that it was probable that the expressions "any entity" and "separate entity" were intended to refer to an entity or separate entity of a State. In Canada it has been held that for the purposes of the Canadian State Immunity Act 1985 (" 'agency of a foreign state' means any legal entity that is an organ of the foreign state but that is separate from the foreign state") a bank which assisted a United States undercover agent to entrap an arms dealer was "an organ of the foreign State": *Walker v. Bank of New York* (1994) 111 D.L.R. (4th) 186 (Ont. C.A.); *sed quaere.*

[28] This additional requirement derives from Art. 27(2) of the European Convention, where it appears as "acts performed by the entity in the exercise of sovereign authority (*acta jure imperii*)." See *Kuwait Airways Corp. v. Iraqi Airways*, *Financial Times*, July 17, 1992.

[29] [1995] 1 W.L.R. 1147, 1156 (H.L.) *post*, para. 10–030.

[30] Lord Goff of Chieveley gave as an example *Arango v. Guzman Travel Advisers Corp.*, 621 F. 2d 137 (5th Cir. 1980), in which Dominicana (the national airline of the Dominican Republic) was held entitled to plead sovereign immunity under the United States Foreign Sovereign Immunities Act 1976, on the ground that it was impressed into service by Dominican immigration officials, acting pursuant to the country's laws, to perform the functions which led to the plaintiff being re-routed.

[31] See *post*, paras. 10–011 *et seq.*

authority. Further, a number of the exceptions laid down in the Act are narrowly defined, and the additional requirement that the proceedings relate to something done in the exercise of sovereign authority may widen some of the exceptions in relation to a separate entity. Thus, a State is not immune as respects proceedings relating to a contract of employment, but this exception is subject to a number of qualifications.[32] If the defendant were a separate entity, it would not be immune even if the qualifications would have applied to a defendant State, because in normal circumstances such proceedings would not relate to something done in the exercise of sovereign authority.

The immunities granted to States may be extended by Order in Council to any constituent territory of a federal State, and in the absence of such an Order a constituent territory is treated as a separate entity.[33]

A certificate by or on behalf of the Secretary of State is conclusive evidence on any question whether any country is a State, whether any territory is a constituent territory of a federal State or as to the person or persons to be regarded as the head or government of a State.[34]

Property. The immunity protects a foreign State not only in direct pro- **10–010** ceedings against it *in personam* but also in indirect proceedings against property which is in its possession or control or in which it claims an interest.[35] Thus if a foreign State has an interest in property situated within the jurisdiction, whether proprietary, possessory or of some lesser nature, a claim which affects its interest will be stayed, even though it is not brought against it personally, but is, *e.g.* a claim *in rem* against a ship[36] or a claim *in personam* against its bailee[37] or agent.[38] The rule is not limited to ownership, and applies to lesser interests which may not merely be not proprietary but not even possessory, so that it applies to property under the control of the foreign State,[39] and perhaps also to property in respect of which it has no beneficial interest but only the legal title.[40] The 1978 Act provides that the court may entertain proceedings against a person other than a State notwithstanding that the proceedings relate to property in its possession or control, or in which it claims an interest, if the State would not have been immune had the proceedings been brought against it, or, in the case where the State merely claims an interest, if the claim is neither admitted nor supported by prima facie evidence.[41]

---

[32] See *post*, para. 10–035.

[33] s.14(5)–(6). See S.I. 1979 No. 457 (Austria); S.I. 1993 No. 2809 (Germany).

[34] s.21(*a*). The certificate is not susceptible to judicial review: *R. v. Secretary of State for Foreign Affairs, ex p. Trawnik, The Times*, February 21, 1986 (C.A.).

[35] This was the rule at common law (see, *e.g. The Cristina* [1938] A.C. 485, 490, 507) and is implicit in the 1978 Act: see ss.2(4)(*b*), 6 and 10. "Property" includes a credit balance on a bank account: *Alcom v. Republic of Colombia* [1984] A.C. 580, 602.

[36] *The Parlement Belge* (1880) 5 P.D. 197 (C.A.); *The Jupiter* [1924] P. 236 (C.A.); *The Cristina* [1938] A.C. 485; *The Arantzazu Mendi* [1939] A.C. 256.

[37] *U.S.A. and Republic of France v. Dollfus Mieg et cie. and Bank of England* [1952] A.C. 582.

[38] *Rahimtoola v. Nizam of Hyderabad* [1958] A.C. 379.

[39] *The Cristina* [1938] A.C. 485; *The Arantzazu Mendi* [1939] A.C. 256.

[40] *Rahimtoola v. Nizam of Hyderabad* [1958] A.C. 379, 403, *per* Lord Reid.

[41] s.6(4). Cf. *Juan Ysmael & Co. Inc. v. Indonesian Government* [1955] A.C. 72, 89–90 (P.C.); *Rahimtoola v. Nizam of Hyderabad* [1958] A.C. 379, 410; *Shearson Lehman Brothers Inc. v. Maclaine Watson & Co. Ltd.* [1988] 1 W.L.R. 16, 29–31 (H.L.); *Australian Federation of Islamic Councils Inc. v. Westpac Banking Corp.* (1989) 17 N.S.W.L.R. 623.

10–011   **Execution.** A foreign State is also immune from the processes of execution.[42] The 1978 Act provides that relief shall not be given against a State by way of injunction[43] or order for specific performance or for the recovery of land or other property, and that the property of a State shall not be subject to any process for the enforcement of a judgment[44] or arbitration award or, in an action *in rem*, for its arrest, detention or sale.[45] In Scotland it has been held that the immunity did not prevent the assumption of jurisdiction *in personam* over a foreign State, where the jurisdiction was based on the presence of immovable property owned by the State, even if the property itself (the United States Consulate-General in Edinburgh) was not subject to process of execution.[46] *In personam* jurisdiction based on the possession of immovable property in Scotland does not (by contrast with arrestment of movables) involve any taking of possession, or interference with the right to dispose, of the property. If any such taking were involved, the result could not be justified.

10–012   The immunity from injunctive relief and execution is subject to two important exceptions. First, such relief may be given or process may be issued with the written consent (which may be contained in a prior agreement) of the State.[47] It has been held that a waiver of immunity in relation to property will allow a *Mareva* injunction to be granted against a foreign State, but that a contractual waiver of immunity from execution will not be regarded as extending to diplomatic premises.[48] Secondly, the immunity from process does not prevent the issue of any process in respect of property which is for the time being in use or intended for use for commercial purposes.[49] "Commercial purposes" means[50] the purposes of those transactions which are defined as "commercial transactions" in section 3(3) and which are discussed below in connection with Exception 2 to this Rule. Thus execution cannot issue against a credit balance on a bank account kept by a foreign State for the purpose of meeting the ordinary expenditure of its embassy; but it may issue where the account was earmarked for the discharge of liabilities incurred in commercial transactions.[51]

---

[42] See Crawford (1981) 75 A.J.I.L. 820; Fox (1985) 34 I.C.L.Q. 114; Byers (1995) 44 I.C.L.Q. 882.

[43] See *Soleh Boneh International Ltd. v. Government of Uganda* [1993] 2 Lloyd's Rep. 208 (C.A.) (order for provision of security for arbitral award not an injunction for this purpose).

[44] Provision is made for a master or district judge to inform the Foreign and Commonwealth Office before execution can issue against a foreign or Commonwealth state: *Supreme Court Practice* (1999), para. 46/2/15.

[45] s.13(2). This immunity applies to a State's central bank or other monetary authority even if it is a "separate entity": s.14(4).

[46] *Forth Tugs Ltd. v. Wilmington Trust Co.*, 1987 S.L.T. 153.

[47] s.13(3). A submission merely to the jurisdiction is not to be regarded as a consent to execution: *ibid. Cf. Arab Banking Comp. v. International Tin Council* (1986) 77 Int.L.R. 1.

[48] *A Co. Ltd. v. Republic of X* [1990] 2 Lloyd's Rep. 520 (criticised on the latter point by F. A. Mann (1991) 107 L.Q.R. 362).

[49] s.13(4). But this exception does not apply, otherwise than in actions *in rem*, to States which are parties to the European Convention on State Immunity unless the process is for enforcing a judgment which is not subject to appeal or (if a default judgment) liable to be set aside, and the State has made a declaration under Article 24 of the Convention (which provides that a contracting State may declare that its courts shall be entitled to entertain proceedings against contracting States to the extent that its courts are entitled to entertain proceedings against non-contracting States), or the process is for enforcing an arbitral award: *ibid.* The certificate of the Secretary of State as to whether a State is a party to the European Convention or has made a declaration under Article 24 is conclusive: s.21(*c*).

[50] s.17(1).

[51] *Alcom v. Republic of Colombia* [1984] A.C. 580, 604.

A central bank or other monetary authority is accorded special treatment **10–013** under the Act.[52] If it is not distinct from the executive organs of the State and not capable of suing or being sued, it will be on precisely the same footing as a State, but if (as is more likely to be the case) it is a separate entity within the meaning of the Act, it will differ from other separate entities in the following respects: first, even if it is not entitled to immunity from suit, its property will normally be immune from execution because the property of a central bank or other monetary authority, irrespective of whether it is a separate entity, is not regarded as in use or intended for use for commercial purposes[53]; secondly, it is specifically provided that where a central bank or other monetary authority is a separate entity it is entitled to immunity from injunctive relief and execution as if it were a State.[54] In practice, therefore, the property of a State's central bank will only be liable to process of execution if it has waived, in writing, its immunity from execution.[55]

The head of a State's diplomatic mission in the United Kingdom (or the **10–014** person for the time being performing his functions) is deemed to have authority to give, on behalf of the State, consent to execution,[56] and the certificate of any such person to the effect that any property is not in use or intended for use by or on behalf of the State for commercial purposes shall be accepted as sufficient evidence of that fact unless the contrary is proved.[57]

Procedure. When a question of immunity is raised, then the question **10–015** whether a State is or is not immune under the 1978 Act must be decided as a preliminary issue before the substantive action can proceed.[58]

The Act of 1978 deals with a number of matters which may conveniently **10–016** be dealt with under the heading of procedure. First, it provides that a court is to give effect to the immunity conferred by the Act even though the State does not appear in the proceedings in question.[59] Secondly, the Act provides for a method of service on a State by transmission through the Foreign and Commonwealth Office to the Ministry of Foreign Affairs of the State.[60] As indicated above[61] the claimant is not thereby relieved of the need to bring the case within one of the heads of R.S.C., Order 11 in cases in which they

---

[52] See Blair [1998] C.L.J. 374.

[53] s.14(4).

[54] *Ibid.* It is also entitled to immunity from penalty in respect of failure to disclose or produce documents or information, as to which see text at n. 69, *infra*.

[55] s.13(3).

[56] s.13(5). But any other duly authorised representative would also have authority.

[57] s.13(5).

[58] *J. H. Rayner (Mincing Lane) Ltd. v. Department of Trade and Industry* [1989] Ch. 72, 194–195, 252 (C.A.), affd. without reference to this point [1990] 2 A.C. 418; *A Co. Ltd. v. Republic of X* [1990] 2 Lloyd's Rep. 520, 525. *Cf. Advisory Opinion on the Difference Relating to Immunity from Legal Process of a Special Rapporteur of the Commission on Human Rights*, International Court of Justice, April 29, 1999, para. 63 (questions of immunity must be expeditiously decided *in limine litis*).

[59] s.1(2). See *United Arab Emirates v. Abdelghafar* [1995] I.C.R. 65 (E.A.T.).

[60] s.12(1). See *Kuwait Airways Corp. v. Iraqi Airways Co.* [1995] 1 W.L.R. 1147 (H.L.): service by the Foreign and Commonwealth Office on the Iraqi embassy was insufficient. See also *Westminster City Council v. Iran* [1986] 1 W.L.R. 979. Service is deemed to be effected on receipt at the Ministry. When service is effected in this way, the time for acknowledgment of service is two months: s.12(2). See also Ord. 11, r. 7 (in CPR, Sched.1).

[61] *Ante*, para. 10–006.

apply.[62] A State which appears in proceedings cannot thereafter object that service was not properly effected upon it.[63] Service by transmission through the Foreign and Commonwealth Office is not necessary if the State has agreed to a different method of service,[64] and in such a case permission to serve out of the jurisdiction is required only if the defendant State is not a party to the 1968 Convention or the Lugano Convention on jurisdiction and the enforcement of judgments in civil and commercial matters[65] and the place designated for service by the agreement is outside the jurisdiction.[66]

10–017 Thirdly, no judgment in default may be given against a State unless it is proved that service has been properly effected and the time for acknowledgment of service has expired.[67] A copy of a default judgment is to be transmitted through the Foreign and Commonwealth Office to the Ministry of Foreign Affairs of the State, and the time for applying to have the judgment set aside begins to run two months after receipt of the copy judgment.[68]

10–018 Fourthly, as regards disclosure of documents, the Act provides that no penalty by way of committal or fine is to be imposed in respect of any failure or refusal by a State to disclose or provide any document or other information in proceedings to which it is a party.[69]

10–019 **Miscellaneous.** Provision may be made, by Order in Council, to restrict or extend the immunities of a State under the Act if (as the case may be) they exceed those accorded by the law of that State to the United Kingdom, or are less than those required by any international agreement to which that State and the United Kingdom are parties.[70]

10–020 The 1978 Act does not affect immunities under the Diplomatic Privileges Act 1964 or the Consular Relations Act 1968.[71] It does not apply to proceedings relating to anything done by or relating to the armed forces of a State while present in the United Kingdom, and has effect subject to the Visiting

---

[62] s.12(7).

[63] s.12(3).

[64] s.12(6).

[65] See *post*, paras. 11–005 *et seq.*

[66] See R.S.C., Ord. 11, r. 1(1)(*d*)(iv); *post*, paras. 11–164; 12–111—12–112.

[67] s.12(4); CPR PD12, para. 4.4.

[68] s.12(5). See also CPR 40.10 and Ord. 46, r. 6(4)(*a*)(iii). See *Crescent Oil and Shipping Services Ltd. v. Importang UEE* [1998] 1 W.L.R. 919 (no alternative contractual method can be agreed).

[69] s.13(1). No doubt the court could draw appropriate inferences from the failure to give discovery, or even strike out its defence: *cf.* CPR PD31, para. 5.4. See also Art. 18 of the European Convention.

[70] s.15(1). There are no such orders in force. An order was made in relation to the U.S.S.R., which was replaced by an order which required notice to a consular officer of applications for warrants of arrest in an action *in rem* against a ship owned by Russia, the Ukraine and Georgia or cargo aboard it, and prevented execution against ships or cargo owned by them. It had been held, after the break-up of the Soviet Union, that the order relating to the U.S.S.R. did not apply to the Russian Federation, even though the United Kingdom Government regards it as continuing the legal personality of the former Soviet Union (*Coreck Maritime GmbH v. Sevrybokholodflot*, 1994 S.L.T. 983) nor to the Republic of the Ukraine, even though the United Kingdom Government regards it (and the other former Soviet Republics) as successor States to the U.S.S.R. (*The Giuseppe di Vittorio* [1998] 1 Lloyd's Rep. 136 (C.A.)). The order was repealed by S.I. 1999 No. 668.

[71] s.16(1). See *Alcom Ltd. v. Republic of Colombia* [1984] A.C. 580; *A Co. Ltd. v. Republic of X* [1990] 2 Lloyd's Rep. 520.

Forces Act 1952.[72] Nor does it apply to proceedings to which section 17(6) of the Nuclear Installations Act 1965 applies,[73] or to criminal proceedings.[74]

ILLUSTRATIONS

1. A, an English company, is granted a concession by the Government of Ruritania to work mines in Ruritania. The Government repudiates the contract, and A brings an action for damages in England. The court has no jurisdiction.[75]   **10–021**

2. A's assets in Ruritania are confiscated by the Government of Ruritania. A brings an action in England for damages. The court has no jurisdiction.[76]

3. A claims damages for a libel published in England in the official newspaper of the Government of Ruritania, which owns and runs the newspaper. The court has no jurisdiction.[77]

4. The circumstances are the same as in Illustration 3, except that the newspaper is published by a department which is separate from the executive organs of the Government and is capable of suing and being sued. The court has jurisdiction.[78]

5. A, an English bank, lends money under a loan agreement to the State of Ruritania, with a guarantee by the Central Bank of Ruritania, which is a separate entity distinct from the State. The contract contains an express submission to the jurisdiction of the English courts. The State defaults on the loan. The court has jurisdiction over the State under Exception 1 below and over the Central Bank because it is a separate entity and the proceedings do not relate to something done by it in the exercise of sovereign authority in circumstances in which the State would be immune.[79] The court gives judgment for A against both defendants. The State has a stock of grain in London in the name of its Ministry of Agriculture, which is in the process of selling the stock. The Central Bank has sterling deposits with the Bank of England. A may levy execution against the grain, because it is intended for use for commercial purposes,[80] but not against the sterling deposits,[81] unless there has been written consent in the loan agreement or otherwise to execution against the property of the State.[82]

6. In August 1990 Iraq invaded Kuwait. On the orders of the Iraqi government civil aircraft belonging to Kuwait Airways were flown by Iraqi Airways to Iraq, and then incorporated into the Iraqi Airways fleet and used for its own flights. Iraqi Airways is a separate entity. It is immune from suit in respect of the taking of the aircraft and their removal from Kuwait to Iraq because that conduct constituted an exercise of governmental power by the State of Iraq. But it is not immune in respect of the subsequent retention and use of the aircraft because they were not acts done in the exercise of sovereign authority, but were acts done by Iraqi Airways in consequence of the vesting in it of the aircraft by Iraqi legislative decree.[83]   **10–022**

7. A, a French company, is the owner of sixty-four gold bars deposited in a French bank at Limoges. In 1944 the bars are looted by German troops and taken to Germany, but recovered in the following year by allied troops. They are then deposited in the Bank of England on behalf of the Governments of the United Kingdom, France and the United States. A sues the bank claiming delivery of the bars and damages for their detention. The bank moves to stay the proceedings on the ground that they implead two foreign sovereign States which decline to submit to the jurisdiction. It is then discovered that the bank had sold thirteen of the bars by mistake. The action

---

[72] s.16(2).

[73] s.16(3). See *post*, para. 15–040.

[74] s.16(4).

[75] State Immunity Act 1978, s.1(1).

[76] *Ibid.* s.1(1).

[77] *Ibid.* s.1(1).

[78] *Ibid.* s.14(2). Contrast *Krajina v. Tass Agency* [1949] 2 All E.R. 274 (C.A.), decided at common law.

[79] State Immunity Act 1978, s.14(2). *Cf. Trendtex Trading Corp. v. Central Bank of Nigeria* [1977] Q.B. 529 (C.A.), decided at common law.

[80] *Ibid.* s.13(4).

[81] *Ibid.* s.14(4).

[82] *Ibid.* s.13(3).

[83] *Kuwait Airways Corp. v. Iraqi Airways Co.* [1995] 1 W.L.R. 1147 (H.L.).

is allowed to proceed in respect of the thirteen bars because the bank by its own act had determined the bailment, but is stayed as regards the fifty-one bars.[84]

8. A, the Nizam of Hyderabad, has funds on deposit with a London bank. X, the Finance Minister of Hyderabad, is one of the persons entitled to operate the account. When Indian troops are invading Hyderabad, X, acting in the supposed interests of A, but without actual authority from A to do so, transfers the account into the name of Y, the High Commissioner of Pakistan in the United Kingdom. Y receives the account as agent for Pakistan and on the instructions of the Foreign Minister thereof. A sues X, Y (who has ceased to be High Commissioner but who has not yet accounted to Pakistan) and the bank, claiming the money. Y asks for a stay on the ground that the action impleads the State of Pakistan, although that State claims no beneficial interest in the money. The court has no jurisdiction, because the fund is in the legal control of the State of Pakistan.[85]

9. A, a Philippines company, charters a ship to the Indonesian Government for the carriage of troops, legal possession of the ship remaining with A. A's agent, who has (as the Indonesian Government knows) no authority from A to do so, purports to sell the ship to the Government. A brings an action *in rem* against the ship claiming possession as owner. The court has jurisdiction because the Indonesian Government's title to the ship is manifestly defective.[86]

10–023   10. A's ship is run down and damaged on the high seas by a ship owned and operated by the Government of Ruritania as a troop-carrier. A brings an action *in rem* in England against the ship for damages. The court has no jurisdiction, because the ship is not in use or intended for use for commercial purposes.[87]

11. A obtains a default judgment against the Republic of Colombia for goods sold and delivered. The embassy of the Republic maintains a current account with a bank in London in the name of the Republic. The account is used for the normal expenses of the embassy. A obtains a garnishee order nisi attaching the bank account. The garnishee order is set aside because the debt represented by the credit balance on the account is not property which is "in use or intended for use for commercial purposes."[88]

12. The Government of Ruritania enters into a barter agreement, whereby it buys a quantity of rice from A, an English company, and agrees to supply cocoa and coffee in return, and to make up the difference by paying additional sums. The agreement contains a term that the Government waives whatever defence it may have of sovereign immunity for itself and its property. When the Government fails to make up the difference, A obtains leave to issue and serve a writ outside the jurisdiction, and is granted an *ex parte Mareva* injunction, which is confirmed *inter partes*. The waiver amounts to an agreement that the property of the State can be made the subject of a *Mareva* injunction, but it is discharged to the extent that it affects diplomatic premises.[89]

13. A enters into a contract to supply machinery to the Government of Iraq. When the Government repudiates the contract, A sues in England. Meanwhile, the British embassy in Baghdad has been closed down, and Iraq has broken off diplomatic relations with the United Kingdom; but the Iraqi embassy in London continues to function and is recognised as a diplomatic mission. A purports to serve the writ on the Iraqi embassy, and it is received by an accredited diplomat. The court has jurisdiction under Exception 2 below, but the service is ineffective.[90]

10E–024   *Exception* **1—A State is not immune as respects proceedings in respect of which it has submitted to the jurisdiction of the courts of the United Kingdom.**[91]

---

[84] These are the facts of *U.S.A. and Republic of France v. Dollfus Mieg et cie. and Bank of England* [1952] A.C. 582, which, it seems, would be decided in the same way under the 1978 Act.

[85] These are the facts of *Rahimtoola v. Nizam of Hyderabad* [1958] A.C. 379, which, it seems, would be decided in the same way today.

[86] These are the facts of *Juan Ysmael & Co. Inc. v. Indonesian Government* [1955] A.C. 72 (P.C.), which would be decided in the same way today: s.6(4) of the 1978 Act. Contrast Illustration to Exception 10, para. 10–054, *post*.

[87] State Immunity Act 1978, s.10(2).

[88] State Immunity Act 1978, s.13(2)(*b*), (4); *Alcom v. Republic of Colombia* [1984] A.C. 580.

[89] *A Co. Ltd. v. Republic of X* [1990] 2 Lloyd's Rep. 520.

[90] *Ibid.* s.12(1). *Cf. Kuwait Airways Corp. v. Iraqi Airways Co.* [1995] 1 W.L.R. 1147 (H.L.).

[91] s.2(1). For other specific statutory provisions for waiver see paras. 15–011; 15–017, *post*.

COMMENT

At common law, sovereign immunity could be waived by or on behalf of the **10–025** foreign State,[92] but waiver had to have taken place at the time the court was asked to exercise jurisdiction[93] and could not be constituted by, or inferred from, a prior contract to submit to the jurisdiction of the court or to arbitration.[94] The Act, however, has made a far-reaching and beneficial change by providing expressly that a State may submit (a) after the dispute giving rise to the proceedings has arisen or (b) by a prior written agreement.[95] In addition, a State will be deemed to have submitted if it has instituted the proceedings[96]; or if it has intervened or taken any steps in the proceedings, unless the intervention has been made or the steps taken (a) for the purpose only of claiming immunity or asserting an interest in property in circumstances such that the State would have been entitled to immunity if the proceedings had been brought against it, or (b) in ignorance of facts entitling it to immunity (if those facts could not reasonably have been ascertained) and immunity is claimed as soon as reasonably practicable.[97] Whether any other steps taken in the proceedings will amount to a submission will depend on general principles discussed in Chapter 11.[98]

Once a foreign State has waived its immunity, it will be treated just like any **10–026** other litigant in such matters as security for costs[99] and disclosure of documents,[1] but the Act provides that no penalty by way of committal or fine shall be imposed in respect of any failure or refusal by or on behalf of a State to disclose or produce any document or other information for the purpose of proceedings to which it is a party.[2]

---

[92] See Cohn (1958) 34 B.Y.I.L. 260.

[93] *Mighell v. Sultan of Johore* [1894] 1 Q.B. 149 (C.A.); *Duff Development Co. v. Government of Kelantan* [1924] A.C. 797; *Kahan v. Pakistan Federation* [1951] 2 K.B. 1003 (C.A.); *A Co. Ltd. v. Republic of X* [1990] 2 Lloyd's Rep. 520 (criticised by F. A. Mann (1991) 107 L.Q.R. 362).

[94] *Duff Development Co. v. Government of Kelantan, supra*; *Kahan v. Pakistan Federation, supra*; *Baccus S.R.L. v. Servicio Nacional del Trigo* [1957] 1 Q.B. 438 (C.A.); *Compania Mercantil Argentina v. United States Shipping Board* (1924) 93 L.J.K.B. 816 (C.A.). Contrast *Standard Chartered Bank v. International Tin Council* [1987] 1 W.L.R. 641; but see *A Co. Ltd. v. Republic of X* [1990] 2 Lloyd's Rep. 520.

[95] s.2(2), on which see *Ahmed v. Saudi Arabia* [1996] I.C.R. 25 (C.A.). But a provision in an agreement that it is to be governed by the law of the United Kingdom is not of itself a submission: *ibid*. The agreement need not necessarily be between the parties to the litigation, since the submission may be constituted by an international agreement: s.17(2).

[96] s.2(3)(*a*).

[97] ss.2(3)(*b*), 2(4) and 2(5). See also *Propend Finance Pty Ltd. v. Sing, The Times*, May 2, 1997; 111 Int. L.R. 611 (C.A.). For cases of alleged mistake see *The Jassy* [1906] P. 270; *Baccus S.R.L. v. Servicio Nacional del Trigo* [1957] 1 Q.B. 438 (C.A.).

[98] *post*, Rule 25. See *Kuwait Airways Corp. v. Iraqi Airways Co.* [1995] 1 Lloyd's Rep. 25 (C.A.) (revd. in part on other grounds: see [1995] 1 W.L.R. 1147, 1164 (H.L.)); *cf. Jaffe v. Miller* (1993) 13 O.R. (3d) 745 (Ont. C.A.); *Robinson v. Kuwait Liaison Office* (1997) 145 A.L.R. 68. See also *London Branch of the Nigerian Universities Commission v. Bastians* [1995] I.C.R. 358 (E.A.T.).

[99] *Republic of Costa Rica v. Erlanger* (1876) 3 Ch.D. 62 (C.A.); *The Newbattle* (1885) 10 P.D. 33 (C.A.); *Ministère de la Culture v. Lieb, The Times*, December 24, 1981. But *cf.* Art. 17 of the European Convention.

[1] *United States of America v. Wagner* (1867) L.R. 2 Ch.App. 582; *South African Republic v. Compagnie Franco-Belge du Chemin de Fer du Nord* [1898] 1 Ch. 190, 195.

[2] s.13(1). See n. 69, *ante*.

10–027   A submission in respect of any proceedings extends to any appeal, but not to a counterclaim unless it arises out of the same legal relationship or facts as the claim.[3]

A submission to jurisdiction is not a submission to execution, but process of execution may be issued with the written consent of the State.[4]

10–028   The head of State's diplomatic mission in the United Kingdom, or the person for the time being performing his functions, is deemed to have authority to submit to proceedings on behalf of the State; and any person who has entered into a contract on behalf and with the authority of a State is deemed to have authority to submit on its behalf in respect of proceedings arising out of the contract.[5]

10E–029   ***Exception 2—A State is not immune as respects proceedings relating to (a) a commercial transaction entered into by the State; or (b) an obligation of the State which by virtue of a contract (whether a commercial transaction or not) falls to be performed wholly or partly in the United Kingdom.***[6]

Comment

10–030   This extremely important Exception applies to two quite separate classes of transaction. The first is the commercial transaction, which is defined as (a) any contract for the supply of goods or services; (b) any loan or other transaction for the provision of finance (and any guarantee or indemnity in respect thereof or of any other financial obligation); and (c) any other transaction or activity (whether of a commercial, industrial, financial, professional or other similar character) into which a State enters or in which it engages otherwise than in the exercise of sovereign authority. Thus, for example, contracts for the purchase or sale of goods required for public purposes, such as arms, are within the Exception. Contracts for the supply of goods and services, and financial transactions, are likely to comprise the vast majority of commercial transactions, and it is not therefore likely that it will frequently be necessary to consider what other transactions a State may enter into "otherwise than in the exercise of sovereign authority." The expression "in the exercise of sovereign authority" refers to the concept of *acta jure imperii* in public international law, and in *Kuwait Airways Corp. v. Iraqi Airways Co.*[7] it was said that the ultimate test of what constitutes an act *jure imperii* is whether the

---

[3] s.2(6). *Cf. Sultan of Johore v. Bendahar* [1952] A.C. 318 (P.C.) (appeal); *South African Republic v. Compagnie Franco-Belge du Chemin de Fer du Nord* [1897] 2 Ch. 487 (C.A.); [1898] 1 Ch. 190 (counterclaim); *U.S.S.R. v. Belaiew* (1925) 42 T.L.R. 21 (counterclaim).

[4] s.13(3), *ante*, para. 10–012, n. 47.

[5] s.2(7). See *Malaysian Industrial Development Authority v. Jeyasingham* [1998] I.C.R. 307 (E.A.T.).

[6] s.3(1).

[7] [1995] 1 W.L.R. 1147, 1156 (H.L.), *per* Lord Goff of Chieveley, applying *The I Congreso del Partido* [1983] 1 A.C. 244 and *Alcom v. Republic of Colombia* [1984] A.C. 580.

act in question is of its own character a governmental act, as opposed to an act which any private citizen can perform.[8]

The second category is proceedings relating to an obligation of the State **10–031** which falls to be performed wholly or partly in the United Kingdom.[9] This Exception applies whether or not the transaction is a commercial one, and whether or not the contract was made in the United Kingdom,[10] but it does not apply if each of the three following conditions is met: the contract is not a commercial transaction (as defined above), the contract was made in the territory of the State concerned, and the obligation in question is governed by its administrative law.[11] The notion of the contract being governed by administrative law is derived from Article 4(2)(c) of the European Convention on State Immunity, and is a notion which is foreign to the common law, although it is widespread in civil law countries, where it comprises a large variety of contracts concluded by the State, including concessions and state loans. Whether a contract is governed by its administrative law would (*semble*) fall to be determined by that country's law, at any rate if the contract is not governed by English law.

It must be emphasised that neither of these categories *confers* jurisdiction **10–032** on the English court. If the State does not submit to the jurisdiction, then even if the transaction is a commercial one, or the obligation in question falls to be performed in the United Kingdom, the requirements of Order 11, r. 1(1), or of the 1968 Convention, or of the Lugano Convention must be satisfied before the English court will have jurisdiction.[12]

This Exception does not apply (i) if the parties to the dispute are States or have otherwise agreed in writing,[13] or (ii) if the proceedings relate to a contract of employment.[14]

---

[8] For the position at common law see *Littrell v. Government of the United States (No. 2)* [1995] 1 W.L.R. 82 (C.A.), where it was held, in an action based on allegedly negligent treatment of a member of the U.S. airforce at a United States military hospital in England, that the activity of providing medical treatment to members of the armed forces at a base was an activity *jure imperii*; *Holland v. Lampen-Wolfe* [1999] 1 W.L.R. 188 (C.A.), where, in an action for libel by an American civilian employed to teach courses at U.S. bases in Europe, it was held that an unfavourable report by an educational services officer on the plaintiff's teaching was part of the activity of the provision of education for the purpose of maintaining U.S. forces in a foreign country and therefore *jure imperii*. These were cases at common law, since the 1978 Act does not apply to proceedings in relation to the armed forces of a foreign State in the United Kingdom: s.16(2). See also *Arab Republic of Egypt v. Gamal Eldin* [1996] I.C.R. 13 (E.A.T.); *McElhinney v. Williams* [1996] 1 I.L.R.M. 276 (Sup. Ct.) (immunity for acts of member of British forces on checkpoint duty in Northern Ireland). *Cf. United States v. Public Service Alliance of Canada* [1992] 2 S.C.R. 50 ("commercial activity"); *Saudi Arabia v. Nelson*, 507 U.S. 349 (1993), ("based upon a commercial activity carried on in the United States by the foreign state": action for personal injuries sustained in Saudi Arabia by plaintiff who had been recruited in the United States not so based); *Republic of Argentina v. Weltover, Inc.*, 504 U.S. 607 (1992) ("action ... based upon an act outside the territory of the United States in connection with a commercial activity of the foreign state elsewhere and that act causes a direct effect in the United States": state subject to U.S. jurisdiction for breach of contract claim on failure to pay bonds payable in New York).

[9] *Cf.* the position under the Civil Jurisdiction and Judgments Act 1982, Scheds. 1 and 3C, Art. 5(1), *post*, paras. 11–250 *et seq.*

[10] It is not necessary that the State be a party to the contract, if it has some secondary liability: *J. H. Rayner (Mincing Lane) Ltd. v. Department of Trade and Industry* [1989] Ch. 72, 194–195, 222, 252 (C.A.), affd. on other grounds [1990] 2 A.C. 418 (H.L.).

[11] s.3(2).

[12] *Ante*, para. 10–006.

[13] s.3(2).

[14] s.3(3).

ILLUSTRATION

10–033   A, an English company, enters into a contract, governed by English law, to supply arms to the Government of Ruritania. When the Government repudiates the contract, A sues in England. The court has jurisdiction because the contract is one for the supply of goods.[15]

10E–034   *Exception 3—A State is not immune as respects proceedings relating to a contract of employment between the State and an individual where (a) the contract was made in the United Kingdom or (b) the work is to be wholly or partly performed in the United Kingdom.*[16]

COMMENT

10–035   This Exception does not apply if either (a) at the time the proceedings are brought, the employee is a national of the State concerned, or (b) if at the time the contract was made the employee was neither a national of, nor habitually resident in, the United Kingdom[17]; but in each of those cases the Exception *does* apply where the work is for an office, agency or establishment maintained in the United Kingdom for commercial purposes[18] unless, at the time the contract was made, the employee was habitually resident in the State concerned. Nor does the Exception apply if the parties to the contract have agreed in writing that the courts of the United Kingdom shall not have jurisdiction[19]; but the parties cannot effectively agree that the courts shall not have jurisdiction where the law of the United Kingdom requires the proceedings to be brought before a court of the United Kingdom.[20] This Exception does not apply to proceedings concerning the employment of members of a diplomatic mission or of a consular post.[21]

ILLUSTRATIONS

10–036   1. A, a British citizen, is employed by the Government of Ruritania on a five-year contract, made in England, to manage its tourist office in London. He is dismissed after one year and sues the Government for damages. The court has jurisdiction.[22]

2. The facts are the same as in Illustration 1, except that A is a national of Ruritania who is resident in England. The court has jurisdiction because the work is for an establishment maintained for commercial purposes.[23]

3. The facts are the same as in Illustration 2, except that when the contract is executed A is habitually resident in Ruritania. The court has no jurisdiction.[24]

---

[15] s.3(3)(*a*).

[16] s.4(1). See Fox (1995) 66 B.Y.I.L. 97; Garnett (1997) 64 I.C.L.Q. 81. "Proceedings relating to a contract of employment" include proceedings in relation to statutory rights and duties arising out of the contract of employment: s.4(6). For the common law position see *Sengupta v. Republic of India* [1983] I.C.R. 221 (E.A.T.); *Reid v. Republic of Nauru* [1993] 1 V.R. 251; *Governor of Pitcairn v. Sutton* [1995] 1 N.Z.L.R. 426.

[17] s.4(2)(*a*)–(*b*). For meaning of national of the United Kingdom see s.4(5), as amended by British Nationality Act 1981, s.52(6) and Sched. 7.

[18] See s.17(1) for meaning of this expression.

[19] s.4(2)(*c*).

[20] s.4(4). See Employment Rights Act 1996, s.203. *Cf.* Civil Jurisdiction and Judgments Act 1982, Sched. 1, Art. 17(6) and Sched. 3C, Art. 17(5), *post*, para. 12–095.

[21] s.16(1)(*a*).

[22] s.4(1).

[23] ss.4(2)(*a*) and 4(3).

[24] ss.4(2)(*a*) and 4(3).

***Exception* 4—A State is not immune as respects proceedings in respect of (a) death or personal injury or (b) damage to or loss of tangible property, in each case where it was caused by an act or omission in the United Kingdom.**[25]

10E–037

ILLUSTRATION

A's tug, whilst at anchor in a fog off Dover, is run down and damaged by the Ostend-Dover packet which carries mail as well as passengers and cargo and is owned by the King of the Belgians and operated by his servants. A brings an action for damages against the Kingdom of Belgium. The court has jurisdiction.[26]

10–038

***Exception* 5—A State is not immune as respects proceedings relating to any interest of the State in, or its possession or use of, immovable property in the United Kingdom, or any obligation of the State arising therefrom.**[27]

10E–039

COMMENT

This Exception does not apply to proceedings concerning title to, or possession of, property used for the purposes of the State's diplomatic mission.[28] Proceedings for breach of covenant in a lease are not proceedings concerning title or possession.[29]

10–040

ILLUSTRATIONS

1. A leases premises in Oxford Street, London, to the Government of Ruritania. The premises are to be used as a tourist office. The Government falls into arrears with its payment of rent. A sues for arrears of rent and for possession. The court has jurisdiction.[30]

10–041

2. A leases a flat in Kensington to the French Government for use as a private residence for a member of the French embassy and his family. In breach of a covenant in the lease A is denied access to the flat when A seeks to enter to carry out repairs necessitated by dry rot in the premises. After the flat has been vacated, A claims damages against the French Government for the loss caused as a result of the refusal to permit entry. The court has jurisdiction. The action does not concern title or possession, and the premises were not used "for the purposes of a diplomatic mission" because they were used primarily as a private residence.[31]

***Exception* 6—A State is not immune as respects proceedings relating to an interest arising by way of succession, gift or *bona vacantia* in movable or immovable property, nor does any interest of a State in property prevent exercise of any jurisdiction relating to the estates of the deceased persons**

10E–042

---

[25] s.5.

[26] s.5. Contrast *The Parlement Belge* (1880) 5 P.D. 197 (C.A.), an action *in rem* decided at common law.

[27] s.6(1). *Cf. The Charkieh* (1873) L.R. 4 Adm. & Ecc. 59, 97; *Sultan of Johore v. Bendahar* [1952] A.C. 318 (P.C.); *Thai-Europe Tapioca Service Ltd. v. Government of Pakistan* [1975] 1 W.L.R. 1485, 1490–1491 (C.A.).

[28] s.16(1)(*b*).

[29] *Intpro Properties (U.K.) Ltd. v. Sauvel* [1983] Q.B. 1019 (C.A.).

[30] s.6(1).

[31] *Intpro Properties (U.K.) Ltd. v. Sauvel, supra.*

or persons of unsound mind or to insolvency, the winding up of companies or the administration of trusts.[32]

COMMENT

10–043   Prior to the Act it was recognised that the Chancery Division had jurisdiction to distribute a trust fund among the beneficiaries, notwithstanding the entitlement of a foreign sovereign to an interest therein,[33] and that the Companies Court had jurisdiction to wind up a company, even though a foreign sovereign might be interested in any surplus assets.[34] The effect of Exception 6 is that a foreign State which is a creditor of an insolvent company cannot claim its debts in priority to other creditors, since a winding up order does not of itself affect the property of the State, *i.e.* the chose in action represented by a bank deposit.[35]

10–044   Although the Act provides that a State's interest in property will not prevent the exercise of jurisdiction relating to the administration of trusts, it seems that a foreign State cannot be made liable as a trustee, unless one of the other Exceptions is applicable.[36]

10E–045   *Exception* **7—A State is not immune as respects proceedings relating to:**
   (a) any patent, trade-mark, design or plant breeders' rights belonging to the State, and registered or protected in the United Kingdom or for which the State has applied in the United Kingdom;
   (b) an alleged infringement by the State in the United Kingdom of any patent, trade mark, design, plant breeders' rights or copyright; or
   (c) the right to use a trade or business name in the United Kingdom.[37]

10E–046   *Exception* **8—A State is not immune as respects proceedings relating to its membership of a body corporate, an unincorporated body or a partnership which (a) has members other than States, and (b) is incorporated or constituted under the law of the United Kingdom or is controlled from or has its principal place of business in the United Kingdom, being proceedings arising between the State and the body or its other members or, as the case may be, between the State and the other partners, unless provision to the contrary has been made by agreement in writing or by the instrument establishing the body or partnership.**[38]

---

[32] s.6(2)–(3).

[33] See *Rahimtoola v. Nizam of Hyderabad* [1958] A.C. 379, 397, 398, 401, 408, 420.

[34] *Re Russian Bank for Foreign Trade* [1933] Ch. 745, 769–770.

[35] *Re Rafidain Bank, The Times*, July 22, 1991; [1992] B.C.L.C. 301.

[36] *Rahimtoola v. Nizam of Hyderabad* [1958] A.C. 379, 401, 408. But see *Duke of Brunswick v. King of Hanover* (1848) 2 H.L.C. 1, 25 and *cf. Gladstone v. Musurus Bey* (1862) 1 H. & M. 495, 503.

[37] s.7.

[38] s.8. On the application of this provision to very unusual circumstances see *Maclaine Watson & Co. Ltd. v. International Tin Council* [1989] Ch. 253, 282–283 (C.A.), affd. on other grounds [1990] 2 A.C. 418.

Exception 9—**Where a State has agreed in writing to submit a dispute** 10E–047
which has arisen, or may arise, to arbitration, it is not immune as respects
proceedings in the courts of the United Kingdom which relate to the
arbitration, except (a) where contrary provision is made or (b) where the
arbitration agreement is between States.[39]

COMMENT

This Exception applies to proceedings relating to the arbitration, including 10–048
proceedings to enforce the arbitration agreement or for review of an award.
The Bill which resulted in the 1978 Act expressly provided that this Exception
did not apply to proceedings for the enforcement of the award.[40] Although the
question is not free from doubt, it is suggested that the Exception does not
apply to enforcement of an award.[41]

Exception 10—**In admiralty proceedings (or proceedings on any claim** 10E–049
which could be made the subject of admiralty proceedings) a State is not
immune as respects:
  (a) **an action *in rem* against a ship belonging to that State, or an action**
       ***in personam* for enforcing a claim in connection with such a ship,**
       if, at the time when the cause of action arose, the ship was in use
       or intended for use for commercial purposes[42]**; or**
  (b) **an action *in rem* against a cargo belonging to that State if both the**
       cargo and the ship carrying it were, at the time when the cause of
       action arose, in use or intended for use for commercial purposes;
       or an action *in personam* for enforcing a claim in connection with
       such a cargo if the ship carrying it was then in use or intended for
       use for commercial purposes.[43]

COMMENT

At common law there was a division of judicial opinion on the question 10–050
whether a ship owned by a foreign sovereign but used for ordinary commercial purposes was immune from the jurisdiction,[44] but the modern authorities
were against such an immunity.[45] Section 10 of the Act of 1978 enacts,
broadly, the principle that ships or cargoes owned[46] by a foreign State in use,
or intended for use, for commercial purposes[47] are not immune.

---

[39] s.9.
[40] s.13(2)(*b*) provides that the property of a State is not to be subject to any process for the enforcement of an award.
[41] See Fox (1988) 37 I.C.L.Q. 1, 14–16; contrast F. A. Mann, *Further Studies in International Law* (1990), at p. 319.
[42] s.10(2).
[43] s.10(4).
[44] See *The Porto Alexandre* [1920] P. 30 (C.A.); *The Cristina* [1938] A.C. 485; *Zarine v. Owners of S.S. Ramava* [1924] I.R. 148; *Flota Maritima Browning de Cuba S.A. v. Republic of Cuba* [1962] S.C.R. 598.
[45] In *The Philippine Admiral* [1977] A.C. 373 (approved in *The I Congreso del Partido* [1983] 1 A.C. 244) the Privy Council followed the views expressed by the majority in *The Cristina* [1938] A.C. 485 that no immunity could be claimed for vessels used only for commercial purposes. See also *Thai-Europe Tapioca Service Ltd. v. Government of Pakistan* [1975] 1 W.L.R. 1485, 1491 (C.A.).
[46] Or in its possession or control or in which it claims an interest: s.10(5).
[47] For meaning of commercial purposes see s.17(1).

10–051　　Where proceedings *in rem* are brought against a sister ship to enforce a claim in connection with another ship,[48] the Exception does not apply as regards the sister ship unless, at the time when the cause of action relating to that other ship arose, both ships were in use or intended for use for commercial purposes.[49]

10–052　　If the proceedings are *in personam* to enforce a claim in connection with a cargo carried on a ship in use for commercial purposes, it seems that Exception (b) above applies whether or not the cargo is in use or intended for use for commercial purposes.

10–053　　If the State in question is a party to the Brussels Convention for the Unification of Certain Rules Concerning the Immunity of State-owned Ships of 1926, and the claim relates to the operation of, or the carriage of cargo or passengers on, a ship owned or operated by that State, or the carriage of cargo owned by that State on any other ship, Exceptions 2 to 4 above do not apply.[50]

ILLUSTRATION

10–054　　The Government of the Philippines sells a ship, the *Philippine Admiral*, to X by a contract whereby X has possession and control but the Government retains title until the price is paid in full. Before the price is paid in full, X, which operates the ship for commercial purposes, charters the ship to A. At the time of the charterparty and immediately thereafter the ship is under repair. X falls into arrears with the instalments under the sale contract and cancels the charterparty. A, the charterer, and B, ship repairers, bring an action *in rem* against the ship for breach of charterparty and for repair charges respectively. The Government continues to own the ship. The court has jurisdiction because the ship was in commercial use.[51]

10E–055　　***Exception* 11—A State is not immune as respects proceedings relating to its liability for value added tax, customs duty, agricultural levy, or rates in respects of premises occupied by it for commercial purposes.**[52]

10R–056　　**RULE 20—Subject to certain qualifications, English courts have no jurisdiction to entertain an action or other proceeding against any person entitled to immunity under the Diplomatic Privileges Act 1964 or the Consular Relations Act 1968.**[53]

COMMENT

10–057　　In its judgments in the *Diplomatic and Consular Staff* (*United States v. Iran*) cases the International Court of Justice re-affirmed that the principles of

---

[48] Under the Supreme Court Act 1981, s.21(4), as to which see *post*, paras. 13–013 *et seq.*

[49] s.10(3).

[50] s.10(6).

[51] *Ibid.* s.10(2). These are the facts of *The Philippine Admiral* [1977] A.C. 373 (P.C.), decided at common law. Contrast Illustration 10 to Rule 19, *ante*.

[52] s.11. This list is exhaustive of the taxes in respect of which there is no immunity: s.16(5).

[53] Brownlie, *Principles of Public International Law* (5th ed. 1998), Chap. XVII; Oppenheim, *International Law* (9th ed. Jennings and Watts, 1992), pp. 1090–1105, 1142–1149; Denza, *Diplomatic Law* (2nd ed. 1998); Brown (1988) 37 I.C.L.Q. 53. See also Diplomatic Relations and Immunities Act 1967 (Rep. of Ireland); Diplomatic Privileges and Immunities Act 1967 and Consular Privileges and Immunities Act 1972 (Aus.); Foreign Missions and International Organizations Act 1991 (Can.); Diplomatic Privileges and Immunities Act 1968, ss.3–7, 13–18 (N.Z.). For the immunities of a Head of State, his family and servants see State Immunity Act 1978, s.20 and *ante*, para. 10–006. n. 23.

diplomatic and consular immunity were deep-rooted in international law; the institution of diplomacy, with its concomitant privileges and immunities, had withheld the test of centuries, and the unimpeded conduct of consular relations had been established since ancient times; every State which maintained diplomatic or consular relations was under an obligation to recognise the imperative obligations, now codified in the Vienna Convention on Diplomatic Relations of 1961 and the Vienna Convention on Consular Relations of 1963.[54] The privileges and immunities conferred by international law have been recognised at common law for centuries.[55]

Diplomats. Subject to a number of qualifications, which will be discussed below, no ambassador, High Commissioner or other head of a diplomatic mission duly accredited by another State to the Court of St. James, and no member of his staff, can be sued or impleaded in an English court, nor can his property be seized. This immunity from suit was formerly secured by the Diplomatic Privileges Act 1708, which has always been treated as declaratory of the common law.[56] It was repealed and replaced by the Diplomatic Privileges Act 1964, which gives effect to the Vienna Convention on Diplomatic Relations (1961).[57] Section 1 of the Act provides that the following provisions of the Act shall have effect in substitution for any previous enactment or rule of law; and section 2 enacts those articles of the Convention[58] which are set out in Schedule 1 as part of the law of the United Kingdom. Hence, much of the old case law is now only of historical interest. The articles of the Convention will no doubt be interpreted so as to secure the greatest possible measure of conformity with the law of other parties to the Convention.[59]   **10–058**

The Act authorises the withdrawal of immunity from the diplomatic mission of a State which fails to accord proper immunity to Her Majesty's mission in that State.[60] Conversely, the United Kingdom has reciprocal arrangements with certain States whereby their diplomatic missions are granted more extensive immunities than those provided by the Convention. The Act makes provision for continuing these arrangements.[61]   **10–059**

The most important single change effected by the Convention in the law of the United Kingdom is that it abolishes the principle of absolute immunity: diplomatic immunity, even that of the head of mission himself, is now only qualified. The Convention divides persons entitled to diplomatic immunity into three categories[62]: (1) "diplomatic agents," namely, the head of the mission and members of his diplomatic staff; (2) "members of the administrative and technical staff," *e.g.* persons employed in secretarial, clerical and communications duties, such as typists, translators and coding clerks; and (3) "members of the service staff," namely, members of the staff of the mission in its domestic service, such as cooks, cleaners, porters and chauffeurs.   **10–060**

---

[54] 1979 I.C.J. Rep. 7, at 19–20; 1980 I.C.J. Rep. 3, at 42.
[55] See, *e.g. Engelke v. Musmann* [1928] A.C. 433, 459 *per* Lord Phillimore.
[56] For the circumstances in which it was passed, see *Taylor v. Best* (1854) C.B. 487, 491–493.
[57] For a commentary on the Act and the Convention, see Buckley (1965–1966) 41 B.Y.I.L. 321. See also Hardy, *Modern Diplomatic Law* (1968), pp. 52–68; Denza, *Diplomatic Law* (2nd ed. 1998); Satow, *Guide to Diplomatic Practice* (5th ed. 1979).
[58] Cmnd. 2565.
[59] See *ante*, para. 1–020.
[60] s.3(1).
[61] s.7(1). See *London Gazette*, October 2, 1964, March 2, 1965, and September 2, 1966.
[62] Sched. 1, Art. 1.

10–061   (1) Provided that they are not nationals of nor permanently resident in the receiving State, diplomatic agents enjoy complete immunity from criminal jurisdiction, and immunity from civil and administrative jurisdiction and from execution except in three cases:

(a) a real action relating to private immovable property situated in the United Kingdom (unless it is held on behalf of the sending State for the purposes of the mission)[63];

(b) an action relating to succession in which the diplomatic agent is involved as executor, administrator or beneficiary as a private person;

(c) an action relating to any professional or commercial activity exercised by the diplomatic agent in the United Kingdom outside his official functions.[64]

10–062   A like immunity is conferred on the members of the family of a diplomatic agent forming part of his household, unless they are nationals of the receiving State,[65] *i.e.* British citizens, British Dependent Territories citizens, British Overseas citizens and British Nationals Overseas.[66]

10–063   (2) The members of the administrative and technical staff of the mission, together with the members of their families forming part of their respective households, provided they are not nationals of nor permanently resident in the receiving State, enjoy a like immunity, but with the important qualification that immunity from civil and administrative jurisdiction does not extend to acts performed outside the course of their duties.[67]

10–064   (3) The members of the service staff of the mission, provided they are not nationals of nor permanently resident in the receiving State, only enjoy immunity from jurisdiction in respect of acts performed in the course of their duties.[68]

10–065   Thus, the difference between the immunity of (1) diplomatic agents and that of (2) administrative and technical staff is that the latter is confined to acts performed in the course of their official duties so far as civil (but not criminal) jurisdiction is concerned. The differences between the immunity of (2) administrative and technical staff and that of (3) service staff are that the latter does not extend to members of their families, nor, as regards criminal jurisdiction, to acts performed outside the course of their duties.

10–066   Private servants of members of the mission (who are not employees of the sending State) enjoy immunity only to the extent admitted by the receiving State.[69] Diplomatic agents who are nationals of or permanently resident in the receiving State only enjoy immunity from jurisdiction in respect of official acts performed in the exercise of their functions, except in so far as additional

---

[63] "Real action," a term taken from the civil law, signifies "an action where ownership or possession of immovable property is claimed" (Satow, *Guide to Diplomatic Practice* (5th ed. 1979), p. 125); *Intpro Properties (U.K.) Ltd. v. Sauvel* [1983] Q.B. 1019 (C.A.); see also Szaszy, *International Civil Procedure* (1967), p. 408; Denza, *Diplomatic Law* (2nd ed. 1998), pp. 238–240. On immunity of property used for diplomatic purposes see also *Alcom Ltd. v. Republic of Colombia* [1984] A.C. 580; *Westminster City Council v. Iran* [1986] 1 W.L.R. 979; *A Co. Ltd. v. Republic of X* [1990] 2 Lloyd's Rep. 520. See also Diplomatic and Consular Premises Act 1987; *R. v. Secretary of State of Foreign and Commonwealth Affairs, ex p. Samuel, The Times,* August 17, 1989; (1989) 83 Int.L.R. 232 (C.A.).

[64] Diplomatic Privileges Act 1964, Sched. 1, Art. 31.

[65] *Ibid.* Art. 37(1). See *Re C.* [1959] Ch. 363; *R. v. Guildhall Magistrates' Court, ex p. Jarrett-Thorpe, The Times,* October 6, 1977; O'Keefe (1976) 25 I.C.L.Q. 329.

[66] s.2(2) of the Act; British Nationality Act 1981, s.51(3). Dependent Territories are now known as Overseas Territories.

[67] Sched. 1, Art. 37(2). See Whomersley (1992) 41 I.C.L.Q. 848.

[68] *Ibid.* Art. 37(3).

[69] Diplomatic Privileges Act 1964, Sched. 1, Art. 37(4), Art. 1(*h*).

immunities may be granted by the receiving State.[70] Other members of the staff of the mission and private servants who are nationals of or permanently resident in the receiving State enjoy immunities only to the extent admitted by the United Kingdom as receiving State; but the receiving State must exercise its jurisdiction over those persons in such a manner as not to interfere unduly with the performance of the functions of the mission.[71] The "extent admitted by the receiving State" and the "additional immunities" here referred to mean such as may be specified by Order in Council.[72] Orders in Council provide that a person who is a member of the mission of specified independent countries of the Commonwealth, or the Republic of Ireland, or who is a private servant of such a member, and is a citizen of that country and also a British citizen,[73] shall be entitled to the same privileges and immunities as he would have been entitled to if he were not a British citizen, etc.[74]

Every person entitled to immunity from jurisdiction enjoys it from the moment he enters the territory of the receiving State to take up his post or, if he is already there, from the moment when his appointment is notified to the appropriate Ministry of the receiving State.[75] In the former case it is not also necessary that his appointment be notified to, or accepted by, the department of the Secretary of State concerned.[76] He enjoys the immunity even if he only became entitled to it after the commencement of the proceedings.[77] When his functions come to an end, his immunity normally ceases at the moment when he leaves the country, or on the expiry of a reasonable period in which to do so; except in the case of acts performed in the exercise of his functions, when it continues to subsist.[78] But if the proceedings are commenced before his immunity ceases, and have not been struck out, the proceedings may continue after his immunity ceases.[79] If he dies, the members of his family continue to enjoy any immunity to which they were entitled until the expiry of a reasonable period in which to leave the country.[80] The running of the Statute of Limitations is suspended during such time as the defendant enjoys diplomatic immunity.[81]   **10–067**

The Convention deals with immunity from the jurisdiction "of the receiving State." It does not deal with immunity from the jurisdiction of any other   **10–068**

---

[70] *Ibid.* Art. 38(1).

[71] *Ibid.* Art. 38(2).

[72] s.2(6) of the Act.

[73] Or a British Dependent Territories citizen or a British Overseas citizen or a British National (Overseas).

[74] S.I. 1999 No. 670.

[75] Sched. 1, Art. 39(1) and s.2(2) of the Act.

[76] *R. v. Home Secretary, ex p. Bagga* [1991] 1 Q.B. 485 (C.A.), doubting *R. v. Governor of Pentonville Prison, ex p. Teja* [1971] 2 Q.B. 274; *R. v. Lambeth Justices, ex p. Yusufu* [1985] Crim.L.R. 510; *R. v. Governor of Pentonville Prison, ex p. Osman (No. 2), The Times*, January 5, 1989. These were immigration or extradition cases. See also Brown (1988) 37 I.C.L.Q. 53, 54–59.

[77] *Ghosh v. D'Rozario* [1963] 1 Q.B. 106 (C.A.).

[78] Diplomatic Privileges Act 1964, Sched. 1, Art. 39(2). *Cf. Musurus Bey v. Gadban* [1894] 2 Q.B. 352 (C.A.); *Zoernsch v. Waldock* [1964] 1 W.L.R. 675; *Re Regina & Palacios* (1984) 45 O.R. (2d) 269. *Cf. Re P (Children Act: Diplomatic Immunity)* [1998] 1 F.L.R. 624 and *Re P (Diplomatic Immunity: Jurisdiction), ibid.* 1026. See also *R v. Bow Street Magistrate, ex p. Pinochet (No. 3)* [1999] 2 W.L.R. 827, 893–895, 906 (H.L.).

[79] *Shaw v. Shaw* [1979] Fam. 62 (divorce petition).

[80] Diplomatic Privileges Act 1964, Sched. 1, Art. 39(3).

[81] *Musurus Bey v. Gadban* [1894] 2 Q.B. 352 (C.A.).

State.[82] There is only one reported English case[83] in which such immunity has been discussed. In that case the plaintiff sought leave to serve notice of the writ out of the jurisdiction on the Venezuelan Ambassador to France. His application was refused on the ground that the case did not fall within the terms of Order 11, rule 1, of the Rules of the Supreme Court; and conflicting views were expressed on the question whether the proposed defendant was entitled to diplomatic immunity.

10–069   **Foreign consuls.** Foreign consuls and members of their staffs are not within the terms of the Vienna Convention on Diplomatic Relations. It appears to be accepted that they were entitled to immunity from suit at common law in respect of their official acts, but not in respect of their private acts.[84] This is confirmed by the Consular Relations Act 1968, which enacts as part of the law of the United Kingdom those articles of the Vienna Convention on Consular Relations (1963) which are set out in the Schedule.[85] Under that Convention, consular officers and consular employees[86] are not amenable to jurisdiction in respect of acts performed in the exercise of consular functions, except in civil actions (a) arising out of a contract made by the consular officer or consular employee in which he did not contract expressly or impliedly as an agent of the sending State, or (b) by a third party for damage arising from an accident in the United Kingdom caused by a vehicle, vessel or aircraft.[87] A third exception is contained in the Consular Conventions Act 1949, which makes provision for the grant of probate or letters of administration to foreign consular officers in respect of foreign nationals dying possessed of property in the United Kingdom,[88] and deprives them of any immunity in respect of any act done in connection with any such grant.[89]

10–070   The Consular Relations Act 1968[90] also empowers the Crown by Order in Council[91] to confer consular immunities on (a) persons in the service of countries of the Commonwealth or of the Republic of Ireland, holding offices involving the performance of duties substantially corresponding to those which, in the case of a foreign sovereign power, would be performed by a consular officer; and (b) any person recognised by the United Kingdom Government as the chief representative in the United Kingdom of a state or province of a country within the Commonwealth.

---

[82] Except in the one case of a diplomatic agent passing through the territory of one State in order to take up or return to a post in another State or to return to his own country: Art. 40. It has been held, in a criminal case, that Art. 40 is not limited to cases of mere transit: *R. v. Guildhall Magistrates' Court, ex p. Jarrett-Thorpe, The Times,* October 6, 1977. But *cf. R. v. Governor of Pentonville Prison, ex p. Teja* [1971] 2 Q.B. 274. See Brown (1988) 37 I.C.L.Q. 53, 59–63.

[83] *New Chile Gold Mining Co. v. Blanco* (1888) 4 T.L.R. 346. *Cf. Rush v. Rush* [1920] P. 242 (C.A.), where the point was not argued.

[84] See *Engelke v. Musmann* [1928] A.C. 433, 437–438; *S. v. Penrose,* 1966 (1) S.A. 5; noted in (1966) 83 S.A.L.J. 126; *Cf. R. v. Jiminez-Paez* (1993) 98 Cr. App. R. 239 (C.A.). See also Beckett (1944) 21 B.Y.I.L. 34; Lee, *Consular Law and Practice* (2nd ed. 1991), Chap. 29; Parry, *British Digest of International Law* (1965), Vol. 8, pp. 141–166.

[85] s.1(1). For the full text see Cmnd. 5219.

[86] For definitions, see Sched. 1, Art. 1(*d*) and (*e*).

[87] *Ibid.* Art. 43; see also Arts. 53, 57, 58, 71.

[88] See *post,* para. 26–015.

[89] s.3, which applies to States specified by Order in Council under s.6(1).

[90] s.12, as substituted by the Diplomatic and other Privileges Act 1971, Sched.

[91] See S.I. 1985 No. 1983.

Waiver. Diplomatic and consular immunity may be waived by the sending   **10–071**
State[92] and a waiver by the head or acting head of the mission is deemed to
be a waiver by that State.[93] Waiver must always be express, except that the
initiation of proceedings precludes the claimant from invoking immunity from
jurisdiction in respect of any counterclaims directly connected with the principal claim.[94] Thus the court has no jurisdiction to entertain a counterclaim for
damages for libel or slander in an action by a head of mission for breach of
contract.[95] Waiver of immunity from jurisdiction in civil or administrative
proceedings does not imply waiver of immunity in respect of the execution of
the judgment, for which a separate waiver is required.[96] Waiver is not defined,
but in both Acts the expression is derived from international conventions, and
it should not therefore be given the narrow scope it had at common law.[97]

Evidence. If in any proceedings any question arises whether or not any   **10–072**
person is entitled to diplomatic or consular immunity, a certificate issued by
or under the authority of the Secretary of State stating any fact relating to that
question is conclusive evidence of that fact.[98] The Foreign and Commonwealth Office is notified of the appointments, arrivals and departure of the
staff of diplomatic missions and consular posts.[99] The notification will normally indicate the category and the nationality and residence of the person
concerned.

ILLUSTRATIONS

1. X, a member of the diplomatic staff of a foreign embassy, is the tenant of a private house   **10–073**
in Hampstead. X can be sued by the landlord for possession on the expiry of the lease.[1]
2. T dies intestate and letters of administration to his estate are granted to X. X is subsequently
appointed ambassador of a foreign State accredited to the Court of St. James. A, claiming to be

---

[92] Diplomatic Privileges Act 1964, Sched. 1, Art. 32(1); Consular Relations Act 1968, Sched. 1,
Art. 45(1). See generally *Propend Finance Pty Ltd. v. Sing, The Times*, May 2, 1997; 111 Int.
L.R. 611 (C.A.).

[93] Diplomatic Privileges Act 1964, s.2(3); Consular Relations Act 1968, s.1(5). At common law
it was doubtful whether the head of the mission could waive his own immunity without the
authority of the sending State (on which see *Re Republic of Bolivia Exploration Syndicate, Ltd.*
[1914] 1 Ch. 139; *Re Suarez* [1918] 1 Ch. 176, 191; Parry, *Digest of International Law* (1965),
Vol. 7, pp. 872–875) but s.2(3) of the Diplomatic Privileges Act 1964 appears to render
unnecessary an investigation whether a waiver by the head of the mission has the sanction of
the sending State.

[94] Diplomatic Privileges Act 1964, Sched. 1, Art. 32(2) and (3); Consular Relations Act 1968,
Sched. 1, Art. 45(2) and (3).

[95] *Cf. High Commissioner for India v. Ghosh* [1960] 1 Q.B. 134 (C.A.), decided at common law.
See Simmonds (1960) 9 I.C.L.Q. 334.

[96] Diplomatic Privileges Act 1964, Sched. 1, Art. 32(4); Consular Relations Act 1968, Sched. 1,
Art. 45(4). *Cf. Re Suarez* [1917] 2 Ch. 131, decided at common law.

[97] In *A Co. Ltd. v. Republic of X* [1990] 2 Lloyd's Rep. 520 (criticised by F. A. Mann (1991) 107
L.Q.R. 362) it was held (applying the obsolete rule on State immunity: para. 10–025, text at
n. 94, *ante*) that immunity from execution over diplomatic property could not be waived by
contract, but only by an undertaking or consent given to the court when the court was asked
to exercise jurisdiction. But this condition is not required by the Vienna Convention nor by the
1964 Act and the authorities to this effect were convincingly criticised by Cohn (1958) 34
B.Y.I.L. 260. *Cf. Standard Chartered Bank v. International Tin Council* [1987] 1 W.L.R.
641.

[98] Diplomatic Privileges Act 1964, s.4; Consular Relations Act 1968, s.11.

[99] See Vienna Convention on Diplomatic Relations, Art. 10 and Vienna Convention on Consular
Relations, Art. 24 (neither Article is scheduled to the relevant Act). But notification is not a
condition of immunity: *ante*, para. 10–067, n. 76.

[1] Diplomatic Privileges Act 1964, Sched. 1, Art. 31(1)(*a*). Contrast *Engelke v. Musmann* [1928]
A.C. 433, decided at common law.

one of T's next-of-kin, begins an administration action against X, asking for an account and that T's estate may be administered by the court. The court has jurisdiction.[2]

3. X, the ambassador of a foreign State, is a partner in a London publishing firm. He can be sued for partnership debts.[3]

4. W brings an action *in rem* against a yacht registered in the name of her husband H, claiming that it had been bought with money belonging to her. The yacht is laid up in an English yacht yard, and is in the possession and control of H. H is on the diplomatic staff of a foreign embassy. H appears under protest and moves to have the writ set aside. The court will set it aside, for W's action does not fall within any of the exceptions to H's diplomatic immunity.[4]

10–074

5. A is injured in a motor accident caused by the negligence of X, the chauffeur to a foreign ambassador, and a member of the service staff of the mission, who was driving the ambassador's car. X is not a British citizen. If X was at the time of the accident on an official journey, he is not liable to pay damages to A; but if he was on a frolic of his own, he is so liable.[5] In neither case is the ambassador vicariously liable.[6]

6. X, the Ruritanian consul in Manchester, refuses a visa to A, and subsequently without justification describes A to newspaper reporters as a disreputable person. The court has jurisdiction to entertain an action by A against X for defamation, but not in respect of the refusal of the visa, which is an act performed in the exercise of consular functions.[7]

7. A, the High Commissioner for India, brings an action against X claiming damages for breach of contract. X counterclaims for damages for slander. The court has no jurisdiction to hear X's counterclaim, which is ordered to be struck out.[8]

8. X, a member of the administrative and technical staff of the Indian High Commission, is prosecuted for obtaining a railway ticket by false pretences. At the committal proceedings X's solicitor purports to waive his immunity. Nothing is said about it at the trial, and X is convicted. Three months later, the High Commissioner for India writes a letter to the Commonwealth Relations Office waiving X's immunity. X appeals against his conviction, which is quashed. The alleged waiver by his solicitor is inoperative because it was made without authority. The alleged waiver by the High Commissioner is inoperative because it did not purport to be retrospective.[9]

10R–075   **RULE 21—Subject to certain qualifications, English courts have no juris- diction to entertain an action or other proceeding against an international organisation or its officials specially protected by or under statute.[10]**

COMMENT

10–076   There has been a proliferation of international organisations established by States under public international law, particularly since the Second World War.[11] In 1949 the International Court of Justice, in its famous advisory

---

[2] Diplomatic Privileges Act 1964, Sched. 1, Art. 31(1)(*b*). Contrast *Re Suarez* [1917] 2 Ch. 131; [1918] 1 Ch. 176 (C.A.), decided at common law.

[3] Diplomatic Privileges Act 1964, Sched. 1, Art. 31(1)(*c*). Contrast *Magdalena Steam Navigation Co. v. Martin* (1859) 2 E. & E. 94, decided at common law.

[4] *Cf. The Amazone* [1940] P. 40 (C.A.).

[5] Diplomatic Privileges Act 1964, Sched. 1, Art. 37(3).

[6] *Ibid.* Art. 31(1). As to the liability of the insurance company, see *Dickinson v. Del Solar* [1930] 1 K.B. 376.

[7] Consular Relations Act 1968, Sched. 1, Art. 43. *Cf. Princess Zizianoff v. Bigelow* (Cour de Cassation, France) (1927–1928) 4 Int.L.R. 384.

[8] *High Commissioner for India v. Ghosh* [1960] 1 Q.B. 134 (C.A.).

[9] *R. v. Madan* [1961] 2 Q.B. 1 (C.C.A.). Even if the High Commissioner's letter did purport to be retrospective, it is difficult to see how the court could have had jurisdiction to try X.

[10] International Organisations Acts 1968 and 1981; Commonwealth Secretariat Act 1966; Arbitra- tion (International Investment Disputes) Act 1966; International Monetary Fund Act 1979; Overseas Development and Co-operation Act 1980; Multilateral Investment Guarantee Agency Act 1988. See also Diplomatic Relations and Immunities Act 1967, ss.7–49 (Rep. of Ireland); International Organisations (Privileges and Immunities) Act 1963 (Aus.); Foreign Missions and International Organizations Act 1991 (Can.); Diplomatic Privileges and Immunities Act, 1968, ss.8–12 (N.Z.).

[11] See generally Bowett, *Law of International Institutions* (5th ed. Sands and Klein, 1999); Seidl- Hohenveldern, *Corporations in and under International Law* (1987), Pt. II.

opinion in the *Reparation for Injuries* case, declared that the United Nations was an international person, *i.e.* a subject of international law and capable of possessing international rights and duties.[12] But the International Court also accepted that not all its rights and duties must be on the international plane, any more than all the rights and duties of a State must be. Accordingly, many international organisations enter into private law transactions, but generally their constitutive instruments provide for immunities and privileges.[13] Since 1944 there has been provision in United Kingdom legislation for the conferment of immunities and privileges, and of the legal capacities of a body corporate, on international organisations.[14]

Following the financial collapse of the International Tin Council in 1985   **10–077** there were several years of extensive litigation in proceedings by creditors against the International Tin Council and its members. The International Tin Council was an organisation established in 1954, whose members in 1985 included 23 States (including the United Kingdom) and the EEC, and whose headquarters were in London. The main action against the Member States and the EEC failed on the ground that it was the International Tin Council, and not its members, which had contracted with the plaintiffs, and that, since it had been established in English law as a separate legal person, only it was liable on the contracts, and its members were not so liable. The question whether the International Tin Council's constitutive instrument (the Sixth International Tin Agreement) constituted it the agent for its members as undisclosed principals was not justiciable, but even if it were justiciable, the International Tin Council was not acting as agent. It was also held that a receiver should not be appointed to enforce in its name any rights it might have for contribution from its members, because such a claim would be a claim under the Sixth International Tin Agreement and would not be justiciable.[15]

In the course of this litigation it was held that apart from legislation an   **10–078** international organisation has no immunity at common law analogous to that of a State.[16] Kerr L.J. referred to an argument made on behalf of the International Tin Council in the course of proceedings in New York that it was entitled to sovereign immunity as "astonishing,"[17] and a similar claim to immunity made by the EEC was described by him as "ill-judged and untenable."[18]

The International Organisations Act 1968, which repealed and replaced the   **10–079** International Organisations (Immunities and Privileges) Act 1950, empowers

---

[12] 1949 I.C.J. Rep. 174, at 179.

[13] See Jenks, *International Immunities* (1961).

[14] For the history see *J. H. Rayner (Mincing Lane) Ltd. v. Department of Trade and Industry* [1989] Ch. 72, 143–146 (C.A.); [1990] 2 A.C. 418, 483–484, 494–495; Marston (1991) 40 I.C.L.Q. 403.

[15] *J. H. Rayner (Mincing Lane) Ltd. v. Department of Trade and Industry* [1990] 2 A.C. 418.

[16] *Standard Chartered Bank v. International Tin Council* [1987] 1 W.L.R. 641, 647–648; *Maclaine Watson & Co. Ltd. v. International Tin Council (No. 3), The Times,* June 27, 1988.

[17] [1989] Ch. at 172.

[18] *Ibid.* at 203; and see 252–253 *per* Ralph Gibson L.J. But in *Arab Monetary Fund v. Hashim* [1993] 1 Lloyd's Rep. 543, 573–574, revd. in part on other grounds [1996] 1 Lloyd's Rep. 589 (C.A.), it was held that the director-general of an international organisation (of which the United Kingdom was not a member) was entitled to immunity from suit at common law (incorporating customary international law) in respect of his official acts, but the defendant was not entitled to immunity in a fraud action by the organisation because the alleged acts of fraud could not be regarded as official acts, and the bringing of suit by the organisation necessarily involved a waiver of immunity.

the Crown by Order in Council to confer immunity from suit and legal process in the United Kingdom upon any international organisation[19] of which the United Kingdom is a member[20]; to confer the like immunity from suit and legal process as is accorded to the head of a diplomatic mission upon representatives to the organisation or representatives on, or members of, any of its organs, committees or other subordinate bodies, upon specified high officers of the organisation and persons employed by or serving as experts or as persons engaged on missions for the organisation[21]; and to confer a limited immunity from suit, extending only to things done or omitted to be done in the course of the performance of official duties, upon specified subordinate officers and servants of the organisation.[22] No such immunity may be conferred upon any person as the representative of Her Majesty's Government in the United Kingdom or as a member of his staff.[23]

10–080   The Act further provides for the conferring of immunity from suit on the judges, registrars and other officers of any international tribunal, or parties to any proceedings before any such tribunal, and their advocates and witnesses[24]; and on representatives of foreign and Commonwealth States and their official staffs attending conferences in the United Kingdom.[25]

10–081   If in any proceedings a question arises whether any person is or is not entitled to any immunity, a certificate issued by or under the authority of the Secretary of State stating any fact relating to that question is conclusive evidence of that fact.[26]

10–082   Orders in Council made under the International Organisations (Immunities and Privileges) Act 1950 continue in force notwithstanding the repeal of that

---

[19] Including organisations composed of Commonwealth States: International Organisations Act 1968, s.1(1), as amended by International Organisations Act 1981, s.1.

[20] s.1(1), (2)(b) and Sched. 1, Part I, para. 1. See s.4 for conferment of legal capacity on international organisations of which the United Kingdom is not a member and which maintain establishments in the United Kingdom pursuant to an agreement with the United Kingdom. No provision is made for immunity of such organisations or of other international organisations of which the United Kingdom is not a member, except that s.4A (added by the International Organisations Act 1981, s.2) enables immunities to be conferred on international commodity organisations of which the United Kingdom is not a member. *Cf.* International Sugar Organisation Act 1973. In *Arab Monetary Fund v. Hashim (No. 3)* [1991] 2 A.C. 114 (on which see F. A. Mann (1991) 107 L.Q.R. 357; Marston [1991] C.L.J. 218) it was held that an international organisation, of which the United Kingdom was not a member, and which had its headquarters in the United Arab Emirates under whose law it was given legal personality, had capacity to sue in England even though legal capacity had not been conferred upon it in English law: the conferment of legal personality by the UAE created a corporate body which the English court recognised. See also F. A. Mann (1967) 42 B.Y.I.L. 145, 171–174 (also in *Studies in International Law* (1973), pp. 586–589); Jenks, *International Immunities* (1961), pp. 32–34.

[21] s.1(2)(c) and Sched. 1, Part II, para. 9. This immunity extends to the members of the official staff of such representatives, provided they are recognised as holding a rank equivalent to that of diplomatic agent (s.1(4) and Sched. 1, Part IV, para. 20); and to the members of the family forming part of the household of such representatives, high officers, and members of their official staffs holding diplomatic rank (*ibid.* para. 23(1), (2) and (3)).

[22] s.1(2)(d) and Sched. 1, Part III, para. 14. This immunity extends to members of the technical and administrative staff of such representatives (s.1(4) and Sched. 1, Part IV, para. 21) and to members of their families forming part of their households (*ibid.* para. 23(4)).

[23] s.1(6)(b).

[24] s.5(1), (2).

[25] s.6, as amended by International Organisations Act 1981, s.1(3). S.5A (added by International Organisations Act 1981, s.3) enables immunities to be conferred on representatives (whether of governments or not) attending conferences convened in the United Kingdom by international organisations.

[26] International Organisations Act 1968, s.8. See also *Zoernsch v. Waldock* [1964] 1 W.L.R. 675.

Act.[27] Orders in Council have been made applying the 1968 Act and its predecessor to many international organisations, from the United Nations and its specialised agencies to a number of organisations dealing with limited and highly technical matters.[28]

In the *International Tin Council* litigation it was held that immunity from **10–083** "suit and legal process" (a phrase occurring in Schedule 1 to the 1968 Act as well as in the Order in Council relating to the International Tin Council) embraced all forms of adjudicative and enforcement jurisdiction, and clearly included proceedings to wind up the organisation. Nor were winding-up proceedings within the exception to immunity in the Order in Council relating to the enforcement of an arbitration award, but were rather an alternative method of recovering the debt. Accordingly, for this reason (among others) there was no jurisdiction to wind up the organisation.[29]

The privileges and immunities of the European Communities and their **10–084** officials are provided for by what is now Article 291 of the E.C. Treaty and by the Protocol of April 8, 1965 on the privileges and immunities of the European Communities, which is annexed to the 1965 Treaty Establishing a Single Council, and a Single Commission of the European Communities (the Merger Treaty).[30] These take effect under the European Communities Act 1972.[31] But subject to special provisions for members of the European Parliament (and for judges of the European Court of Justice in the Protocols on the Statute of the Court of Justice) Article 291 does not provide for immunity from suit. It was held that the European Economic Community (now the European Community) was not entitled to any immunity from legal process analogous to that of a foreign State, even though it exercises powers which are analogous to those of sovereign States, such as the right to receive and send diplomatic missions and the power to enter into treaties. There is no basis for such immunity from suit in the European Communities treaties, or in the law of the United Kingdom, or in customary international law.[32]

---

[27] International Organisations Act 1968, s.12(5).

[28] For the organisations on which immunities have been conferred see Halsbury, *Laws of England*, 4th ed., Vol. 18, para. 1598.

[29] *Re International Tin Council* [1987] Ch. 419, 452–456; affd. [1989] Ch. 309, 331–334 (C.A.). See also *Shearson Lehman Brothers Inc. v. Maclaine Watson & Co. Ltd. (No. 2)* [1988] 1 W.L.R. 16 (H.L.) and *Maclaine Watson & Co. Ltd. v. International Tin Council (No. 2)* [1989] Ch. 286 (C.A.) (inviolability of archives: the International Tin Council sought, unsuccessfully, to prevent production by third parties of documents emanating from it, and to resist an order for production in proceedings in respect of the enforcement of an arbitral award); *Amalgamated Metal Trading Ltd. v. Department of Trade and Industry, The Times*, March 21, 1989 (misrepresentation claim against Member States and EEC); Case C–241/87 *Maclaine Watson & Co. Ltd. v. Council and Commission* [1990] E.C.R. 1797 (claims for damages in European Court: opinion of Darmon A.-G. on admissibility); *Standard Chartered Bank v. International Tin Council* [1987] 1 W.L.R. 641 (contractual waiver of immunity from suit effective); *Arab Banking Corp v. International Tin Council* (1986) 77 Int.L.R. 1 (waiver of immunity from suit not a waiver of immunity from *Mareva* injunction); *International Tin Council v. Amalgamet Inc.*, 524 N.Y.S. 2d 971, affd. 529 N.Y.S. 2d 983 (App.Div. 1988). See also *Mukoro v. European Bank for Reconstruction and Development* [1994] I.C.R. 897 (E.A.T.) for immunity from proceedings in industrial tribunal under Race Relations Act 1976.

[30] Art. 28.

[31] s.2(1).

[32] *J. H. Rayner (Mincing Lane) Ltd. v. Department of Trade and Industry* [1989] Ch. 72, 196–203, 252–253 (C.A.), affd. on other grounds [1990] 2 A.C. 418.

10–085   The International Monetary Fund Act 1979[33] and the Overseas Development and Co-operation Act 1980[34] empower the Crown by Order in Council to make provision for the carrying into effect of the agreements relating to the immunities of international financial organisations (the International Monetary Fund, the World Bank, the International Finance Corporation and the International Development Association) and their officers and employees.

10–086   The Commonwealth Secretariat Act 1966 provides that the Commonwealth Secretariat shall have immunity from suit and legal process except in respect of a civil action for damage caused by a motor-vehicle belonging to or operated on behalf of the Secretariat or in respect of a motor traffic offence involving such a motor-vehicle; and in respect of arbitration proceedings relating to any written contract entered into by or on behalf of the Secretariat. It also provides that any senior officer of the Secretariat who is recognised as such by the Secretary of State and who is a citizen of an independent country of the Commonwealth, and any member of his family forming part of his household, other than a member who is a British citizen[35] only, shall, if permanently resident outside the United Kingdom, have the like privileges and immunities as are accorded by law to a diplomatic agent and the members of his family; and that every other officer and servant of the Secretariat shall have immunity from suit and legal process in respect of acts or omissions of his in the course of the performance of official duties, except in respect of a civil action for damage caused by a motor-vehicle belonging to or driven by him, or in respect of a motor traffic offence involving such a vehicle.[36]

10–087   The Arbitration (International Investment Disputes) Act 1966 provides that the International Centre for the Settlement of Investment Disputes shall enjoy immunity from all legal process; and that the chairman and members of its Administrative Council, conciliators, arbitrators, officers and employees of its Secretariat, and parties to conciliation and arbitration proceedings and their advocates and witnesses shall enjoy immunity from legal process with respect to acts performed by them in the exercise of their functions.[37]

10–088   The possibility of waiver of the immunities thereby conferred is specifically provided for by the Orders in Council[38] made under the International Organisations Act 1968 and earlier legislation, by the Commonwealth Secretariat Act 1966[39] and by the Arbitration (International Investment Disputes) Act 1966.[40]

---

[33] s.5(1).

[34] s.9. See also Multilateral Investment Guarantee Agency Act 1988, s.3.

[35] Or British Dependent Territories citizen, or British Overseas citizen, or British National (Overseas).

[36] s.1(2) and Sched., paras. 1, 5, 6 and 10(1).

[37] s.4(1) and Sched., Arts. 20, 21(*a*) and 22.

[38] See *ante*, para. 10–082, n. 28. See *Standard Chartered Bank v. International Tin Council* [1987] 1 W.L.R. 641.

[39] s.1(2) and Sched., para. 8.

[40] Sched. 1, Arts. 20 and 21(*a*).

CHAPTER 11

JURISDICTION IN CLAIMS IN PERSONAM

1. GENERAL PRINCIPLE

RULE 22[1]—(1) The High Court has jurisdiction to entertain a claim *in* personam if, and, only if, the defendant is served with process in England or abroad in the circumstances authorised by, and in the manner prescribed by, statute or statutory order.   11R–001

(2) Where a claim relates to a civil or commercial matter within the meaning of the Brussels and the Lugano Conventions on jurisdiction and the enforcement of judgments in civil and commercial matters (respectively "the 1968 Convention" and "the Lugano Convention," and together "the Conventions") the High Court has jurisdiction to entertain a claim *in personam* solely in accordance with the provisions of the Conventions.

COMMENT

Claim in personam. A claim *in personam* may be defined positively as a   11–002
claim brought against a person to compel him to do a particular thing, *e.g.* the
payment of a debt or of damages for a breach of contract or for tort, or the
specific performance of a contract; or to compel him not to do something, *e.g.*
when an injunction is sought. A claim *in personam* may be negatively
described as any claim which is not an Admiralty claim *in rem*, a probate
claim, or an administration claim. It may be well, though hardly necessary, to
add that a claim *in personam* does not include a proceeding for divorce or
judicial separation, or for a declaration of nullity of marriage or of legitimacy,
or a proceeding in bankruptcy or regarding the custody of minors, or an
application to set aside an arbitral award.

Service of process. Clause (1) of this Rule expresses the general principle   11–003
that in England service of process is the foundation of the court's jurisdiction

---

[1] The Rules in this Chapter must be read subject to the Rules in Chap. 10. As to the power of
the court to stay proceedings, see *post*, Chap. 12. On jurisdiction in the United States see Scoles
and Hay, Chaps. 5 to 11; Restatement, ss.26–52.

to entertain a claim *in personam*. Every claim in the High Court commences with the issue of what was previously a writ or originating summons and is now called a "claim form".[2] When process cannot legally be served upon a defendant, the court can exercise no jurisdiction over him. In proceedings *in personam* the converse of this statement holds good, and whenever a defendant can be legally served with process, then the court, on service being effected, has jurisdiction to entertain a claim against him. Hence in proceedings *in personam* the rules as to service define the limits of the court's jurisdiction. The methods of service are laid down by the Civil Procedure Rules 1998 ("CPR"), and provision is made for substituted service (now called "service by an alternative method") on individual defendants where personal service cannot be effected.[3]

11–004   **The 1968 Convention and the Lugano Convention.**[4] Prior to the Civil Jurisdiction and Judgments Act 1982 ("the 1982 Act") coming into full force on January 1, 1987 the position in England, broadly, was that the High Court had jurisdiction over (a) persons who were present in England at the time of service of process, and (b) in certain specified cases over persons who were outside England. In the latter case it was generally (except for certain cases mainly arising under international conventions) necessary for the permission of the court to be obtained for issue of process and its service outside the jurisdiction. In each case the exercise of the court's jurisdiction was subject to a discretion: in the former case it was subject to the discretion to stay the proceedings under Rule 31; in the latter case the issue and service of process out of the jurisdiction was subject to the discretion of the court.

The position following the incorporation of the 1968 Convention and the Lugano Convention by the 1982 Act (as amended[5] by the Civil Jurisdiction and Judgments Act 1991, "the 1991 Act") is substantially different. The mere presence of the defendant in England is no longer a sufficient basis of jurisdiction if he is domiciled in another part of the United Kingdom or in another Contracting State, and where the Conventions confer jurisdiction on the English court its discretion not to exercise it is severely curtailed.[6]

11–005   The origin of the 1968 Convention lay in the notion that the ideals of the European Economic Community would be furthered by the greater facilitation of the enforcement of judgments between the Member States. Negotiations for the Convention began in 1959. It was signed in 1968 and entered into force for the original Contracting States (Belgium, Federal Republic of Germany, France, Italy, Luxembourg, Netherlands) in 1973. In 1971 they entered into a Protocol conferring jurisdiction on the European Court to interpret the 1968 Convention, and the Protocol entered into force in 1975. In 1978 the United Kingdom, the Republic of Ireland and Denmark entered into an Accession

---

[2] See CPR, Pt. 7.
[3] CPR, Pt. 6.
[4] On the Conventions see generally Collins, *Civil Jurisdiction and Judgments Act 1982* (1983); Hartley, *Civil Jurisdiction and Judgments* (1984); Anton, *Civil Jurisdiction in Scotland* (1984); Kaye, *Civil Jurisdiction and Enforcement of Foreign Judgments* (1987); O'Malley and Layton, *European Civil Practice* (1989); Briggs and Rees, *Civil Jurisdiction and Judgments* (2nd ed. 1997); Gaudemet-Tallon, *Les Conventions de Bruxelles et de Lugano* (2nd ed. 1996); Weser, *Convention communautaire sur la compétence judiciaire et l'exécution des décisions* (1975).
[5] References in this Chapter to the 1982 Act are references to it as amended by the 1991 Act.
[6] See *post*, paras. 11–225; 12–013 *et seq.*

Convention with the original Contracting States ("the 1978 Accession Convention"). The 1978 Accession Convention contained some important modifications of the 1968 Convention.

Conventions were signed in 1982 for the accession of Greece ("the 1982 Accession Convention")[7] and in 1989 for the accession of Spain and Portugal ("the 1989 Accession Convention").[8] The 1982 Accession Convention amended the 1968 Convention (as amended by the 1978 Accession Convention) only to the extent necessary to adjust it to accommodate the accession of Greece. But the 1989 Accession Convention (also known as the San Sebastian Convention) made a number of substantive changes.[9] The 1968 Convention as amended by the 1978, 1982 and 1989 Accession Conventions is now in force between the United Kingdom and all the Contracting States. A Convention for the accession of Austria, Finland and Sweden was signed in 1996, but has not yet been ratified by the United Kingdom.[10] **11–006**

The Lugano Convention was opened for signature in 1988. It was adopted by the 12 Member States of the European Communities and by the six Member States of the European Free Trade Association (EFTA) (Austria, Finland, Iceland, Norway, Sweden and Switzerland).[11] The purpose of the Lugano Convention was to strengthen the economic co-operation between these two groupings of European States. Negotiations proceeded from 1985 between these groupings on the drafting of what was then called a parallel Convention to the Brussels Convention. The United Kingdom ratified the Lugano Convention in 1991, and it came into force for the United Kingdom in 1992.[12] The Lugano Convention is substantially[13] the same as the 1968 Convention as amended by the 1978 Accession Convention and the 1989 Accession Convention. An important distinction between the 1968 Convention and the Lugano Convention is that the European Court has no jurisdiction to give preliminary rulings on the interpretation of the Lugano Convention: the EFTA Member States would not have accepted that the European Court, **11–007**

---

[7] The text of the 1982 Accession Convention is in Collins, p. 251; Anton, *Civil Jurisdiction*, p. 281; O'Malley and Layton, p. 1854; and in *Official Journal of the European Communities* [1982] O.J. L388, with Report by Evrigenis and Kerameus at [1986] O.J. C298/1.

[8] [1989] O.J. L285, with report by de Almeida Cruz, Desantes Real and Jenard [1990] O.J. C189/35.

[9] The Lugano Convention was negotiated before the 1989 Accession Convention and the variations from the 1968 Convention are substantially derived from the Lugano Convention: see especially Arts. 5(1), 6(4), 16(1), 17 and 21 and the deletion of Art. 52(3).

[10] [1997] O.J. C15/2. An unofficial consolidated version of the 1968 Convention as amended by the 1978, 1982, 1989 and 1996 Accession Conventions is at [1998] O.J. C27/1. On the transitional provisions of the 1968 and Lugano Conventions see Case C–163/95 *Von Horn v. Cinnamond* [1997] E.C.R. I–5451; [1998] Q.B. 214; *Davy International Ltd. v. Voest Alpine Industrieanlagenbau GmbH* [1999] 1 All E.R. 103 (C.A.) (both cases involving the application of Art. 21: see, *post*, para. 12–040).

[11] Text in 1982 Act, Sched. 3C.

[12] Austria, Finland and Sweden have since joined the European Union, but the Lugano Convention remains in force as between the present and former EFTA countries, and all the other European Community countries, until the 1996 Accession Convention comes into force as between the relevant States. The 1996 Accession Convention is not yet in force for the United Kingdom. Negotiations are in progress at the Hague Conference on Private International Law for a worldwide convention on jurisdiction and the enforcement of judgments, the successive drafts of which have been much influenced by the 1968 and Lugano Conventions. A preliminary draft Convention was adopted by the Special Commission in June 1999.

[13] But not quite identical (see especially Arts. 5(1), 16(1), 17(5)) and there are special provisions on the relationship between the Lugano Convention and the 1968 Convention: Art. 54B.

an institution of the European Communities, should have jurisdiction to rule on the Lugano Convention. Instead, the Second Protocol to the Lugano Convention and two accompanying Declarations made by the signatory States contain special provisions designed to lead to uniformity of interpretation both as between national courts and between the two Convention systems.[14]

11–008   Both the 1968 Convention and the 1978 Accession Convention were the subject of substantial reports which were sent to the governments concerned at the same time as the draft Conventions. The reports were, respectively, by M. Jenard (the rapporteur of the working party for the 1968 Convention) and Professor Schlosser (the rapporteur of the working party for the 1978 Accession Convention). The Lugano Convention was the subject of a report by M. Jenard and Mr. Möller (a Finnish judge) which was submitted to the Member States of the European Communities and of EFTA before the diplomatic conference at Lugano in 1988. Each of these reports (and the reports on the 1982 and 1989 Accession Conventions) has a special status in relation to the interpretation of the Conventions.[15]

11–009   The original purpose of the 1968 Convention was to facilitate the enforcement of judgments between the Contracting States, but both the 1968 Convention and the Lugano Convention also provide a detailed set of rules dealing with the circumstances in which courts in the Contracting States may exercise jurisdiction in matters within the scope of the Conventions. The approach of the Conventions is quite different from that of the United Kingdom bilateral conventions governing the recognition and enforcement of foreign judgments. Those conventions, which take effect in the United Kingdom through the Foreign Judgments (Reciprocal Enforcement) Act 1933,[16] do not regulate the circumstances in which the court which is originally seised may exercise jurisdiction: they merely tell the enforcing court in which circumstances the jurisdiction of the original court must be recognised, and they allow the enforcing court to investigate whether the original court had international jurisdiction. This is frequently called a system of "indirect" rules of jurisdiction, which do not affect the courts of the State in which the action is originally brought, and only become relevant at the stage of enforcement.

11–010   By contrast, the 1968 Convention and the Lugano Convention lay down a very elaborate system of jurisdictional rules, to which the court in which the action is originally brought must adhere—this is a system of "direct" rules of jurisdiction. The primary basis of jurisdiction under the Conventions over those "domiciled" in a Contracting State is the "domicile" of the defendant. The Conventions do not define domicile, and leave its determination to national law; corporations are to be treated as domiciled where they have their seat, but the determination of the seat is also left to national law.[17] In addition

---

[14] *Post*, paras. 11–052 *et seq.*

[15] The Jenard reports on the 1968 Convention and the 1971 Protocol and the Schlosser report on the 1978 Accession Convention are at [1979] O.J. C59 and are hereinafter cited as "Jenard" and "Schlosser." They are also in O'Malley and Layton, pp. 1553 and 1658; and in Butterworths, *International Litigation Handbook* (ed. McBain *et al.* 1999), ss.5001 and 5002. The Jenard-Möller report on the Lugano Convention is at [1990] O.J. C189/57 and in Butterworths, *ante*, s.5041. The Scottish Committee on Jurisdiction and Enforcement under the Chairmanship of Lord Maxwell published a report ("the Maxwell Report") in 1980 on (*inter alia*) the practical aspects of the implementation of the 1968 Convention. On the history of the 1968 Convention see Jenard, p. 3; Schlosser, paras. 1–3; Maxwell Report, paras. 1.9–1.15.

[16] See *post*, Rule 47.

[17] See 1982 Act, ss.41 to 46, *post*, Rule 23.

to the courts of the domicile of the defendant, there are other special bases of jurisdiction, such as the place of performance of a contractual obligation and the place of a tort, and there are certain areas of exclusive jurisdiction which displace the domicile. Provision is also made for submission to jurisdiction by contract or by appearance, and for certain other procedural matters, including *lis alibi pendens* and jurisdiction to order provisional measures.

There have been negotiations for revision of the 1968 and Lugano Conventions. It is anticipated that the 1968 Convention will be replaced by a Council Regulation. One practical effect of the rules being enacted in a Council regulation is that references to the European Court will no longer be under a separate Protocol, but will be under the new Article 234 of the Treaty establishing the European Community, which supersedes Article 177: references to the European Court under such a regulation can only be made by a court or tribunal of a Member State against whose decisions there is no judicial remedy under national law.[18]   **11–011**

Forum conveniens. In *Effer SpA v. Kantner*[19] the European Court emphasised that the rules on jurisdiction in the 1968 Convention were designed in part to confer jurisdiction on the national court which was best qualified to determine a dispute. The application, however, of the rules may lead to a claim being subject to the jurisdiction of a court which does not have the closest connection with the dispute.[20] Nevertheless, it is generally accepted that the jurisdictional rules of the 1968 Convention and the Lugano Convention are not subject to a discretion in the national court to stay an action on the basis that the courts of some other Contracting State are the more appropriate forum.[21] This question is dealt with more fully in connection with Rule 31, together with the related, but not identical, question of whether the court may stay proceedings brought in England under the Convention rules on the ground that the courts of a non-Contracting State are more appropriate.[22]   **11–012**

Sphere of application of the Conventions. Civil and commercial matters. Article 1 of each Convention provides that it is to apply in civil and commercial matters whatever the nature of the court or tribunal and that it is not to extend, in particular, to revenue, customs or administrative matters. In addition it is specifically provided that it is not to apply to the status or legal capacity of natural persons; rights in property arising out of a matrimonial relationship; wills and succession; bankruptcy, proceedings relating to the winding-up of insolvent companies or other legal persons, judicial arrangements, compositions and analogous proceedings, social security; or arbitration. In civil law countries "civil" law (which includes commercial law) is generally contrasted with "public" law. The term "civil and commercial" is not a term of art in the United Kingdom, although it appears as early as the Foreign Tribunals Evidence Act 1856, and the United Kingdom is party to   **11–013**

---

[18] See Arts. 65 and 68.
[19] Case 38/81 [1982] E.C.R. 825, 834.
[20] Case C–282/92 *Custom Made Commercial Ltd. v. Stawa Metallbau GmbH* [1994] E.C.R. I–2913.
[21] See *post*, paras. 11–225, 12–013 *et seq.*; *Aiglon Ltd. v. Gau Shan Co. Ltd.* [1993] 1 Lloyd's Rep. 164; and Schlosser, paras. 76–81; O'Malley and Layton, p. 368; Kaye, pp. 269, 1244.
[22] See *Re Harrods (Buenos Aires) Ltd.* [1992] Ch. 72 (C.A.), in which a reference by the House of Lords to the European Court was withdrawn when the case was settled.

several bilateral treaties with some of the original 1968 Convention Contracting States for the recognition and enforcement of judgments in "civil and commercial matters"[23] and to Hague Conventions which are similarly limited.[24] In the original Contracting States there is a well-developed separate corpus of law dealing with the activities of public bodies acting in the exercise of public functions. It is claims by and against these authorities in relation to those functions which are effectively excluded by the general words of Article 1. But the precise boundaries of civil and public law differ even in the civil law countries and therefore the question arose at an early stage in the life of the 1968 Convention as to what system of law was to be applied to solve any difficulties of classification.

11–014   In a consistent series of decisions of the European Court, commencing in 1976 in the *Eurocontrol* case,[25] the Court held that the concept must be given an independent Convention meaning in the light of "the objectives and scheme of the Convention" and "the general principles which stem from the corpus of the national legal systems."[26] This case concerned a claim for route charges levied on aircraft owners by Eurocontrol, an international organisation set up by treaty. The Court held that judgments in favour of such a body might be within the scope of the 1968 Convention, but not where the public authority was acting in the exercise of its powers. Thus in *Netherlands State v. Rüffer*[27] the European Court held that an action for the recovery of the costs involved in the removal of a wreck in a public waterway, administered by the State pursuant to an international obligation and in its capacity as a public authority in the administration of that waterway, was not a civil or commercial matter. More recently, in *Sonntag v. Waidmann*[28] the European Court held that, even if it were joined to criminal proceedings, a civil action for compensation for injury following a criminal act was civil in nature; and that the activity of a school teacher in a state school while supervising pupils during a school trip did not constitute an exercise of public authority.

11–015   The second sentence of Article 1, para. 1, of each Convention provides expressly that it "shall not extend, in particular, to revenue, customs or administrative matters." This provision was added by the 1978 Accession Convention following the request of the United Kingdom in the accession negotiations. The exclusion of revenue and customs matters reflects the general principle found in most countries that foreign tax laws will not be

---

[23] With Belgium (S.R. & O. 1936 No. 1169); France (S.R. & O. 1936 No. 609); Germany (S.I. 1961 No. 1199); Italy (S.I. 1973 No. 1894). There are treaties with two of the Lugano Convention signatories: Austria (S.I. 1962 No. 1339) ("civil and commercial matters"); Norway (S.I. 1962 No. 636) ("civil matters"). The European Court has held that the meaning of the expression may be different in a bilateral convention from its meaning in the 1968 Convention: Joined Cases 9 and 10/77 *Bavaria and Germanair v. Eurocontrol* [1977] E.C.R. 1517.

[24] Service Abroad of Judicial and Extrajudicial Documents in Civil or Commercial Matters (1965); Taking of Evidence Abroad in Civil or Commercial Matters (1970), on which see *Re State of Norway's Application* (*Nos. 1 & 2*) [1990] 1 A.C. 723, criticised by F. A. Mann (1989) 105 L.Q.R. 341. *Cf. Irish Aerospace (Belgium) N.V. v. European Organisation for the Safety of Air Navigation* [1992] 1 Lloyd's Rep. 383 ("commercial" in Art. 86, EEC Treaty; now Art. 82, EC Treaty).

[25] Case 29/76 *LTU GmbH v. Eurocontrol* [1976] E.C.R. 1541.

[26] [1976] E.C.R. at p. 1552. See also Joined Cases 9 and 10/77 *Bavaria and Germanair v. Eurocontrol* [1977] E.C.R. 1517; Case 133/78 *Gourdain v. Nadler* [1979] E.C.R. 733; Case 814/79 *Netherlands State v. Rüffer* [1980] E.C.R. 3807; Case C–172/91 *Sonntag v. Waidmann* [1993] E.C.R. I–1963.

[27] Case 814/79 [1980] E.C.R. 3807.

[28] Case C–172/91 [1993] E.C.R. I–1963.

enforced.[29] In most of the original 1968 Convention Contracting States and in the EFTA countries claims relating to the exercise of powers by public authorities are usually within the jurisdiction of special administrative courts. But the exclusion of "administrative matters" from the Conventions does not relate to the tribunal in which the claim is brought or by which the judgment is given; it relates to the nature of the legal relationship between the parties or the subject-matter of the action.[30]

It is settled that maintenance claims are covered by the Conventions. They **11–016** are within the concept of "civil matters," they are not excluded by Article 1, para. 2, and Article 5(2) makes specific provision for such claims.[31] It is likely that claims for damages caused by restrictive practices or unfair competition, which often have public law elements, come within the scope of the Conventions. Finally, the Conventions apply to labour or employment law claims (which in some countries are not regarded as part of the civil law), at least to the extent that they are not claims by or against public authorities in some capacity other than as employer.[32]

Matters expressly excluded from the scope of the Conventions. Article **11–017** 1, para. 2, excludes, as has been seen, four general categories from the scope of the Convention: (1) status; (2) bankruptcy; (3) social security; and (4) arbitration. These categories are excluded for two main reasons: first, to exclude one category which fell within the borderland of civil and public law, namely social security; secondly, to exclude those cases where there was a great disparity between the Contracting States in relation both to substantive law and private international law, particularly where there were other conventions in force or in draft; it was thought that to bring these areas within the scope of the 1968 Convention might interfere with the unification process being pursued in the European Communities.[33]

Status or legal capacity of natural persons.[34] The most important area **11–018** excluded by this provision is divorce, but it also excludes judgments relating to voidability and nullity of marriage, judicial separation, death, status and legal capacity of minors, legal representation of mental patients, nationality or domicile of individuals, custody and adoption of children, guardianship. But they are only excluded if the proceedings deal directly with these questions. If they arise only in an incidental fashion the case will not be excluded from the scope of the Conventions. The fact that a proceeding or judgment deals with matters which fall outside the scope of the Conventions will not prevent

---

[29] See *ante*, paras. 5–027 *et seq.*

[30] *LTU GmbH v. Eurocontrol, ante; Netherlands State v. Rüffer, ante. Cf. Re Senator Hanseatische Verwaltungsgesellschaft mbH* [1997] 1 W.L.R. 515 (C.A.); *Bank of Scotland v. IMRO*, 1989 S.L.T. 432; *Short v. British Nuclear Fuels plc* [1997] 1 I.L.R.M. 161 (Sup. Ct.).

[31] See Case 120/79 *De Cavel v. De Cavel (No. 2)* [1980] E.C.R. 731; Case C–220/95 *Van den Boogaard v. Laumen* [1997] E.C.R. I–1147; [1997] Q.B. 759.

[32] Case 25/79 *Sanicentral v. Collin* [1979] E.C.R. 3423, 3429; Case 133/81 *Ivenel v. Schwab* [1982] E.C.R. 1891. See now also Arts. 5(1) and 17(5) (with minor differences between the Conventions).

[33] See Jenard, p. 10.

[34] In 1998 the members of the European Union concluded a Convention (which is not yet in force) on jurisdiction and the recognition and enforcement of judgments in matrimonial matters: [1998] O.J. C221/1, *post*, para. 18–083.

orders which do fall within it from being enforced.[35] Maintenance orders, in relation both to spouses and to children, are within the Conventions.[36]

11–019 *Rights in property arising out of a matrimonial relationship ("régimes matrimoniaux").* This exception is considered in a later chapter.[37]

11–020 *Wills and succession.* Matters relating to wills and succession were excluded because it was thought that the divergence in laws, especially in the relevant rules of private international law, among the original 1968 Convention Contracting States was so great that it would be premature to include them before the rules of private international law had been unified.[38] The expression "wills and succession" covers all claims to testate or intestate succession, including disputes as to validity or interpretation of wills setting up trusts; but disputes concerning the relations of the trustee with persons other than beneficiaries may come within the scope of the Conventions.[39]

11–021 *Bankruptcy, etc.* This exclusion extends to bankruptcy, proceedings relating to the winding-up of insolvent companies or other legal persons, judicial arrangements, compositions and analogous proceedings. Bankruptcy was excluded because of the great disparities in national practice between the original 1968 Convention Contracting States, because of its proximity to public law, and because a draft Bankruptcy Convention was being considered by the Community.[40] In *Gourdain v. Nadler*[41] the European Court held that for proceedings to be excluded on the basis that they concerned bankruptcy, etc., it was necessary that they must derive directly from the bankruptcy or winding-up and be closely connected with the bankruptcy proceedings. Thus a claim by an English liquidator against the directors of a company for fraudulent trading under section 630 of the Companies Act 1985 would be outside the scope of the Conventions. But an action by a liquidator to recover debts due to an insolvent company would not be excluded, since the claim in no sense relates to bankruptcy.[42] Nor would a claim against directors for breach of duty be excluded, even if the company is subject to insolvency proceedings in another Contracting State.[43]

11–022 *Social security.* This was excluded because in some countries it was a matter of public law and in others it fell within the borderline area between

---

[35] See Case 120/79 *De Cavel v. De Cavel (No. 2)* [1980] E.C.R. 731.
[36] *Post*, Rules 84, 88, 95.
[37] *Post*, para. 18–190.
[38] See Jenard, p. 11.
[39] Under Art. 5(6), *post* Rule 28, clause (6); see Schlosser, para. 52. See also Case 25/81 *CHW v. GJH* [1982] E.C.R. 1189, where a question was raised (but not decided) as to whether an application for the return of a "codicil" was excluded from the scope of the 1968 Convention as relating to wills and succession. See also *Re Hayward* [1997] Ch. 45.
[40] For the subsequent history see Fletcher, *Insolvency in Private International Law* (1999), Chap. 6.
[41] Case 133/78 [1979] E.C.R. 733, 744.
[42] This passage was approved in *Re Hayward* [1997] Ch. 45, 54.
[43] *Grupo Torras S.A. v. Sheikh Fahad Mohammed Al-Sabah* [1995] 1 Lloyd's Rep. 374, 400, affd. on other grounds [1996] 1 Lloyd's Rep. 7 (C.A.). Contrast *Firswood Ltd. v. Petra Bank* [1996] C.L.C. 608 (C.A.).

private law and public law; in some countries it was within the jurisdiction of the ordinary courts, and in others within the jurisdiction of administrative tribunals, and sometimes both.[44]

Arbitration. The final area excluded in Article 1 is "arbitration." Arbitra-   **11–023** tion was excluded from the 1968 Convention because of the other international instruments in force or in contemplation dealing with the subject.[45]

The Jenard Report indicated that the 1968 Convention did not apply to the   **11–024** recognition and enforcement of arbitral awards; nor did it determine the jurisdiction of courts in respect of litigation relating to arbitration, for example, proceedings to set aside an arbitral award, or deal with the recognition of judgments given in such proceedings.[46] But the Report gave no further elucidation. In the course of the negotiations which led to the 1978 Accession Convention, the United Kingdom took the view that the exclusion covered all disputes which the parties had agreed should be settled by arbitration, including any secondary disputes connected with the arbitration. The original Contracting States, on the other hand, thought that it had a narrower purpose, namely to exclude proceedings in national courts which related to arbitration proceedings which were contemplated, or were in progress, or had concluded. It was agreed that no amendment should be made to the original text, and that the new Contracting States could deal with the problem in their implementing legislation.[47] It is clear from the Schlosser Report that most of the discussion concerned the question whether the exclusion of arbitration from the scope of the 1968 Convention meant that Contracting States could refuse to enforce judgments given by foreign courts in proceedings brought in breach of arbitration agreements.[48] But the Schlosser Report also suggested that the 1968 Convention did not apply to court proceedings which were ancillary to arbitration proceedings, such as the appointment or dismissal of arbitrators, the fixing of the place of arbitration, or the extension of time limits; nor to a judgment determining whether an arbitration agreement was valid or not.

In *Marc Rich & Co. A.G. v. Società Italiana Impianti P.A. (The Atlantic*   **11–025** *Emperor)*[49] Italian sellers sold a cargo of crude oil to Swiss buyers. The contract was made by an exchange of telexes, one of which (from the buyers) contained a provision for English law and London arbitration. But the Italian sellers did not reply to the telex. Following delivery the buyers alleged that the oil had been contaminated with water. The Italian sellers sued the Swiss buyers in the Italian courts claiming a declaration that they were not liable to the buyers and denying that they were bound by the arbitration clause contained in the telex. The Swiss buyers commenced an arbitration, claiming damages, and sought in English proceedings the appointment of an arbitrator, and the Italian sellers argued that under Article 21 of the 1968 Convention they were entitled to a stay because the Italian proceedings had priority.

---

[44] Jenard, p. 12.
[45] *Ibid.* p. 13.
[46] p. 13. See also Schlosser, para. 65.
[47] Schlosser, para. 61. It is not clear how this would have been possible. But the 1982 Act did not deal with this issue.
[48] See para. 62, and *post*, paras. 14–187 *et seq.*
[49] [1989] 1 Lloyd's Rep. 548 (Hirst J. and C.A.).

11–026   In the first reference from a United Kingdom court on the 1968 Convention, the European Court held[50] that, by excluding arbitration from the scope of the 1968 Convention on the ground that it was already covered by international Conventions, the Contracting States intended to exclude arbitration "in its entirety", including proceedings brought before national courts. The appointment by a court of an arbitrator was covered by the exclusion because it was a measure adopted by the State as part of the process of setting arbitration proceedings in motion. This conclusion was corroborated by the Schlosser Report,[51] according to which the 1968 Convention did not apply to court proceedings which were ancillary to arbitration proceedings, such as the appointment or dismissal of arbitrators. This was so even if the judicial proceedings necessarily involved the question of the existence or validity of an arbitration agreement. The test for determining whether the proceedings were outside the scope of the exclusion was the nature of the subject-matter of the proceedings. If the subject-matter of the proceedings was the appointment of an arbitrator, the fact that the court had to resolve a preliminary issue did not justify the application of the Convention; and it would be contrary to the principle of legal certainty for the applicability of the Convention to vary according to whether there was a preliminary issue.

11–027   The actual ruling in that case was the narrow one that the exclusion of arbitration in Article 1(4) extends to proceedings before a national court concerning the appointment of an arbitrator, even if the existence or validity of an arbitration agreement is a preliminary issue in that litigation.[52] In a second case before the European Court, *Van Uden Maritime B.V. v. Deco-Line*,[53] one of the questions was whether the jurisdiction of a national court to order provisional measures in support of arbitration was within the scope of the 1968 Convention, or excluded because of Article 1(4). The Court held that proceedings to obtain provisional measures in aid of arbitration were not excluded. After referring to the views of the Schlosser Report,[54] the Court said that the critical question was the nature of the rights which the proceedings sought to protect. Where the subject-matter of the application for provisional measures related to a question which fell within the scope *ratione materiae* of the 1968 Convention, the Convention was applicable even if arbitration proceedings had been, or were to be, commenced on the substance of the case. The Court also said that where the parties had validly excluded the jurisdiction of the courts in disputes arising under a contract and had referred the dispute to arbitration, there were no courts which had jurisdiction under the Convention as to the substance of the case.

11–028   Consequently both cases emphasise that the exclusion of arbitration from the scope of the 1968 Convention depends on the subject-matter of the proceedings. In the period between these cases, the arbitration exclusion was

---

[50] Case C–190/89 [1991] E.C.R. I–3855. The Swiss buyers contested the jurisdiction of the Italian courts, but after their objection was dismissed they defended the case on the merits, and were refused an injunction in England to restrain the Italian proceedings because they had submitted to the Italian jurisdiction: *The Atlantic Emperor* (*No. 2*) [1992] 1 Lloyd's Rep. 624 (C.A.).

[51] Para. 64. Professor Schlosser changed his views and submitted (as did M. Jenard) an opinion on behalf of the Italian sellers: published at (1991) 7 Arb.Int. 227 and 243. The Court also relied on the Evrigenis-Kerameus Report on the 1982 Accession Convention, [1986] O.J. C298/1, 10.

[52] See generally Hascher (1996) 12 Arb.Int. 233, (1997) 13 Arb.Int. 33; Van Houtte (1997) 13 Arb.Int. 85.

[53] Case C–391/95 [1998] E.C.R. I–7091, [1999] 2 W.L.R. 1181.

[54] Text following n. 48, *ante*.

considered in several English cases, not all of which are easy to reconcile. It has been held that proceedings for a declaration that salvage services were provided pursuant to a valid and binding agreement were excluded from the operation of the Convention, because their object was to establish the validity of the appointment of an arbitrator under the agreement[55]; and that a French judgment making a French award enforceable was not entitled to enforcement under the 1968 Convention because the enforcement of arbitration awards was outside its scope.[56]

There are a number of controversial questions which are not yet finally   **11–029**
settled. One of them is whether the English court may enjoin proceedings in the courts of another Contracting State on the ground that the foreign proceedings are in breach of an arbitration clause. This question is dealt with in Chapter 12, where it is suggested that nothing in the Conventions prevents the English court from granting such an injunction.[57] Another important question is whether a decision of a court in another Contracting State that there is no valid arbitration agreement, or giving judgment in disregard of what English law would regard as a valid arbitration agreement, is entitled to recognition or enforcement under the Conventions. This is dealt with in Chapter 14, where it is suggested that (unless the defendant in the foreign proceedings has submitted to the jurisdiction of the foreign court to determine the merits): (a) a determination by the court of another Contracting State on the existence or validity of an arbitration agreement is not entitled to recognition under the Conventions; (b) a final judgment by the court of another Contracting State in disregard of an arbitration agreement falls within the scope of the Conventions, but may be refused recognition on public policy grounds.[58]

Ancillary claims and provisional measures. It is clear that applications   **11–030**
for provisional measures, such as preservation of property or interim injunctions, are within the scope of the Conventions[59] and it is equally clear that provisional orders for interim payments, *e.g.* in respect of damages or of maintenance, are also within them.[60] The European Court has recognised that procedures authorising provisional and protective measures are found in the legal systems of the Contracting States; but the grant of these measures requires special care on the part of the national court and detailed knowledge of the actual circumstances in which the measures are to take effect; the courts of the Contracting State where the assets subject to the measures sought are located are those best able to assess the need for the measures and the

---

[55] *The Lake Avery* [1997] 1 Lloyd's Rep. 540. Contrast *The Xing Su Hai* [1995] 2 Lloyd's Rep. 15; *Lexmar Corp. v. Nordisk Skibsrederforening* [1997] 1 Lloyd's Rep. 289.

[56] *ABCI v. Banque Franco-Tunisienne* [1996] 1 Lloyd's Rep. 495, affd. on other aspects [1997] 1 Lloyd's Rep. 531 (C.A.). See Hascher (1996) 12 Arb.Int. 233, 239–240, for criticism of the reasoning. *Cf. Allied Vision Ltd. v. VPS Film Entertainment GmbH* [1991] 1 Lloyd's Rep. 392, 399.

[57] *Post*, paras. 12–128 *et seq.*, and see *Toepfer International GmbH v. Soc. Cargill France* [1997] 2 Lloyd's Rep. 98 (Colman, J.: the Court of Appeal made a reference to the European Court on this issue, but the case was settled: [1998] 1 Lloyd's Rep. 379). Contrast *Toepfer International GmbH v. Molino Boschi Srl* [1996] 1 Lloyd's Rep. 510, 512–513.

[58] *Post*, paras. 14–187 *et seq.* See *Phillip Alexander Securities and Futures Ltd. v. Bamberger* [1997] I.L.Pr. 73, 94–102, affd. on other grounds, *ibid.* 104 (C.A.). *Cf. The Atlantic Emperor (No. 2)* [1992] 1 Lloyd's Rep. 624, 632 (C.A.). Contrast *The Heidberg* [1994] 2 Lloyd's Rep. 287.

[59] See Art. 24, *ante*, paras. 8–021 *et seq.*; Case 143/78 *De Cavel v. De Cavel (No. 1)* [1979] E.C.R. 1055; *Babanaft International Co. S.A. v. Bassatne* [1990] Ch. 13, 29–32 (C.A.).

[60] Case 120/79 *De Cavel v. De Cavel (No. 2)* [1980] E.C.R. 731.

conditions on which they are to be granted; it was for this reason that Article 24 of the 1968 Convention allowed applications for provisional and protective measures to be made to the courts of a Contracting State even if, under the Convention, the courts of another Contracting State had jurisdiction as to the substance of the matter.[61] Where a case involves some aspects which are within the Conventions and others which are not, those aspects which are within the Conventions are severable. But if the ancillary claims are concerned essentially with a matter which is excluded from the scope of the Conventions, the ancillary claims themselves are outside their scope.[62]

11–031   **Relationship with other conventions.** Title VII of each of the 1968 Convention and the Lugano Convention deals with its relationship with other conventions. First, Article 54B of the Lugano Convention provides that it (and not the 1968 Convention) is to be applied: (a) in matters of jurisdiction, where the defendant is domiciled in the territory of a Contracting State which is not a member of the European Communities,[63] or where Article 16 or 17 of the Lugano Convention confers jurisdiction on the courts of such a Contracting State; (b) in relation to *lis pendens* or to related actions as provided for in Articles 21 and 22[64] of the Lugano Convention, when proceedings are instituted in a Contracting State which is not a member of the European Communities and in a Contracting State which is a member of the European Communities; (c) in matters of recognition and enforcement, where either the State in which the judgment was rendered or the State in which recognition or enforcement is sought is not a member of the European Communities.

11–032   These provisions are of concern to the courts of the 1968 Convention Contracting States, including the United Kingdom, when they have to decide how the two Conventions inter-relate. The 1968 Convention continues to apply to relations between the Contracting Parties to it. It also applies where a person domiciled outside the territory of a Member State of the European Communities and outside the territory of any other State party to the Lugano Convention, *e.g.* a person domiciled in the United States, is sued in a 1968 Convention Contracting State.[65] But where a defendant is domiciled or deemed to be domiciled in a State which is a party to the Lugano Convention, Article 54B of the Lugano Convention must be applied. Thus if a defendant domiciled in Switzerland is sued in England, jurisdiction will only exist in cases provided for by the Lugano Convention, and Article 4 of the 1968 Convention (jurisdiction over defendants not domiciled in a 1968 Convention Contracting State)[66] will not apply. The Lugano Convention will apply if the Swiss courts possess exclusive jurisdiction under Articles 16 or 17[67]; or if recognition or enforcement of a judgment rendered in Switzerland is sought in England; or if the same or similar causes of action are being pursued in Switzerland and England.[68]

---

[61] Case 125/79 *Denilauler v. SNC Couchet Frères* [1980] E.C.R. 1553, 1570.
[62] Case 143/78 *De Cavel v. De Cavel (No. 1)* [1979] E.C.R. 1055; Case 25/81 *CHW v. GJH* [1982] E.C.R. 1189; Case 120/79 *De Cavel v. De Cavel (No. 2)* [1980] E.C.R. 731.
[63] The Lugano Convention continues to apply to Austria, Finland and Sweden: those countries are members of the European Communities, but are not yet parties to the 1968 Convention.
[64] *Post*, Rule 31(4).
[65] Jenard-Möller, p. 67.
[66] *Post*, para. 11–078.
[67] *Post*, Rule 29.
[68] Jenard-Möller, pp. 67–68.

Secondly, Article 55 of each of the Conventions provides that the existing **11–033** treaties on the recognition and enforcement of judgments (all bilateral, except for the Benelux Treaty 1961 and two Scandinavian Conventions of 1932 and 1977) are to be superseded, including those in force between the United Kingdom and other Contracting States, to the extent that the Conventions apply to the subject-matter of the specific conventions.[69]

Article 57(1) deals with other treaties governing jurisdiction or the recogni- **11–034** tion and enforcement of judgments, and provides: "This Convention shall not affect any conventions to which the Contracting States are or will be parties and which, in relation to particular matters, govern jurisdiction or the recognition or enforcement of judgments." What is now Article 57(2)[70] of the 1968 Convention provides that with a view to its uniform interpretation Article 57(1) shall be interpreted so that (as regards the assumption of jurisdiction) (a) the 1968 Convention is not to prevent a court of a Contracting State which is a party to a convention on a particular matter from assuming jurisdiction in accordance with it, even if the defendant is domiciled in another Contracting State which is not a party; (b) but where the defendant is domiciled in another Contracting State and does not enter an appearance, the court must examine whether it has jurisdiction and whether the defendant has had an opportunity to arrange for his defence.[71] Subject to some drafting differences, Article 57(2) of the Lugano Convention is to the same effect.[72]

The United Kingdom is a party to several such conventions, which are **11–035** discussed in Chapters 13 (jurisdiction *in rem*) and 15 (international conventions). Some of the conventions lay down direct rules of jurisdiction which are different from those of the 1968 Convention and the Lugano Convention, including such bases as diverse as that of the court of the place of destination under the Warsaw Convention on international carriage by air or the arrest of a ship under the Brussels Convention (1952) on arrest of seagoing ships. Section 9(1) of the 1982 Act (as amended by the 1991 Act) provides that the relevant provisions of Article 57 of the Conventions shall have effect in relation to any statutory provision implementing any such other convention in the United Kingdom, and in relation to any rule of law so far as it has the effect of so implementing any such other convention.

The effect of these provisions is that, notwithstanding the normal jurisdic- **11–036** tional rules of the Conventions, the English court may exercise jurisdiction in accordance with the provisions of international Conventions to which the United Kingdom is a party, such as the Brussels Arrest Convention and the Brussels Collision Convention of 1952.[73] The effect of Article 57(2) is that in these cases the court which is entitled to exercise jurisdiction under the treaty may do so and its judgment will be enforced in another Contracting State under the 1968 Convention even if the defendant is domiciled in that other

---

[69] See Joined Cases 9 and 10/77 *Bavaria and Germanair v. Eurocontrol* [1977] E.C.R. 1517; Art. 56.

[70] Previously 1978 Accession Convention, Art. 25(2).

[71] Under Art. 20, *post*, paras. 11–057 *et seq.*

[72] See also 1968 Convention, Art. 57(3), and Lugano Convention, Protocol No. 3, para. 1, which assimilate relevant provisions in acts of the European Communities (or, in the case of the 1968 Convention, national laws harmonised thereunder) to conventions within the scope of Art. 57(1).

[73] *The Deichland* [1990] 1 Q.B. 361 (C.A.); *The Po* [1991] 2 Lloyd's Rep. 206 (C.A.); *The Nordglimt* [1988] Q.B. 183; *The Anna H* [1995] 1 Lloyd's Rep. 11 (C.A.) and see also *The Netty* [1981] 2 Lloyd's Rep. 57; *Clipper Shipping Co. Ltd. v. San Vincente Partners*, 1989 S.L.T. 204.

State and that other State is not a party to the relevant international convention. Article 57(4) of the Lugano Convention allows the Contracting State in which recognition or enforcement of a judgment is sought to refuse recognition or enforcement if that State is not a party to the convention in question and the person against whom recognition or enforcement is sought is domiciled in that State.[74]

11–037   It does not follow that, where a specialised convention is applicable, the 1968 and Lugano Conventions are entirely superseded. Thus the Brussels Arrest Convention contains rules on jurisdiction, but no rules on *lis alibi pendens*. Accordingly, the *lis pendens*[75] provisions of the 1968 and Lugano Conventions apply, because their rules are excluded "solely in relation to questions governed by a specialised convention."[76] But a provision in bills of lading for the exclusive jurisdiction of German courts has been held not to deprive the English court of jurisdiction under the Brussels Arrest Convention, even though the Arrest Convention had no provision equivalent to Article 17 of the 1968 Convention giving effect to jurisdiction clauses.[77] That was because to deprive the English court of jurisdiction would involve a conflict between the jurisdictional provisions of the Arrest Convention and the 1968 Convention; in such cases the specialised convention prevailed.[78]

11–038   **Civil Jurisdiction and Judgments Act 1982.** The 1982 Act brought into effect for the United Kingdom the rules of jurisdiction provided for by the 1968 Convention, as amended by the Accession Convention of 1978, and applied similar (but not identical) rules for allocating jurisdiction as between the constituent parts of the United Kingdom.[79] It also provided for the recognition and enforcement of judgments emanating from other Contracting States, and introduced a revised system for the enforcement of judgments given by courts of one part of the United Kingdom in other parts. Amendments to the 1982 Act and its schedules came into force in 1989 to take account of the 1982 Accession Convention (Greece) and in 1991 to take account of the 1989 Accession Convention. The Civil Jurisdiction and Judgments Act 1991 was enacted to amend the 1982 Act in order to give effect to the Lugano Convention. One consequence of the introduction of the Convention system in the United Kingdom is that there will be three sets of basic rules of jurisdiction in the United Kingdom: one set for cases within the Conventions (mainly, but not only, where the defendant is domiciled in another Contracting State); a second set, similar but not identical to the first, where the defendant is domiciled in another part of the United Kingdom; and a third set, substantially different from the first two, where the defendant is not domiciled in a Contracting State.

11–039   The 1982 Act and the 1968 and Lugano Conventions supersede any inconsistent prior legislation. This may have some unexpected results going beyond

---

[74] For other provisions in relation to recognition and enforcement of judgments see *post*, Rule 48.

[75] Rule 31(4).

[76] Case C–406/92 *The Tatry* [1994] E.C.R. I–5439, 5471; [1999] Q.B. 515, 533. The same conclusion had been reached in *The Nordglimt* [1988] Q.B. 183 and *The Linda* [1988] 1 Lloyd's Rep. 175. Contrast *Deaville v. Aeroflot Russian International Airlines* [1997] 2 Lloyd's Rep. 67 (Warsaw Convention); *Pearce v. Ove Arup Partnership Ltd.* [1999] 1 All E.R. 769, 801–802 (C.A.) (European Patent Convention). See also *post*, paras. 13–033 *et seq.*

[77] *Post*, Rule 32.

[78] *The Bergen* [1997] 1 Lloyd's Rep. 380. A stay of proceedings was subsequently granted: *The Bergen (No.2)* [1997] 2 Lloyd's Rep. 710.

[79] For the special position of Gibraltar see S.I. 1997 No. 2602, and *post*, Rule 49(3).

amendment of the existing general rules relating to jurisdiction and judgments. Thus the effect of Article 17 is that where parties, one of whom is domiciled in a Contracting State, agree that a court in a Contracting State is to have jurisdiction, that court shall have exclusive jurisdiction. This provision will be discussed in detail below[80] but for present purposes it is sufficient to point out that where it applies the jurisdiction of the courts of the defendant's domicile will be wholly ousted, if another court has been chosen. The law of the United Kingdom contains provisions which prevent parties from contracting out of the jurisdiction of United Kingdom courts. Thus section 203 of the Employment Rights Act 1996 is intended to prevent an English employee of a German company from effectively agreeing that any claims brought by the employee should be brought in a German court. There are similar laws in other countries.

But the effect of the decision of the European Court in *Sanicentral GmbH*   **11–040**
v. Collin[81] was that an agreement under Article 17 to oust the jurisdiction of the local court in favour of the courts of another Contracting State had to be given effect notwithstanding the mandatory nature of the employment legislation of the local law. The European Court held that employment disputes came within the 1968 Convention, and that a jurisdiction clause in a contract between a French worker and a German employer conferring jurisdiction on a German court deprived the French courts of jurisdiction, notwithstanding that the jurisdiction clause was void by French law when it was entered into (before the Convention came into force in 1973). The effect of the decision is far-reaching. The Court disclaimed any intention on the part of the Convention to affect rules of substantive law, but held that "in matters of civil jurisdiction, the national procedural laws applicable to the cases concerned are set aside in the matters governed by the Convention in favour of the provisions thereof."[82]

Interpretation of the Conventions. The 1982 Act[83] provides that the 1968   **11–041**
Convention (and the Accession Conventions) and the Lugano Convention shall have "the force of law in the United Kingdom," and that judicial notice shall be taken of them. The English texts of the 1968 Convention (as amended by the Accession Conventions), the 1971 Protocol (as amended), the transitional and final provisions of the Accession Conventions, and the Lugano Convention are scheduled to the 1982 Act (as amended) for "convenience of reference." The United Kingdom court may consider the reports on the Conventions in ascertaining the meaning or effect of any provision of the Conventions (and also the equivalent provisions in the intra-United Kingdom rules) and give them such weight as is appropriate in the circumstances.[84]

---

[80] *Post*, Rule 32.
[81] Case 25/79 [1979] E.C.R. 3423.
[82] At p. 3429; *cf.* Case 150/80 *Elefanten Schuh GmbH v. Jacqmain* [1981] E.C.R. 1671. The Conventions now contain special provisions for jurisdiction clauses in employment contracts: *post*, para. 12–095.
[83] s.2(2).
[84] ss.3(3), 3B(2), 16(3)(*b*). There have been many decisions of national courts in the original Contracting States which are usefully collected in Court of Justice of the European Communities, *Digest of Case-law relating to the European Communities*, D Series; Pocar, *Codice delle Convenzioni sulla Giurisdizione e l'Esecuzione delle Sentenze Straniere nella CEE* (1980). See also Kaye (ed.), *European Case Law on the Judgments Convention* (1998). *Cf. Fothergill v. Monarch Airlines* [1981] A.C. 251, 284, *per* Lord Diplock, on the value of foreign precedents.

11–042   The effect is that many problems which have arisen in the United Kingdom with regard to the interpretation of international conventions will not arise in the case of the Conventions incorporated by the 1982 Act.[85] The court will be able to consider the foreign language texts of the Conventions and the official reports may be resorted to for the purpose of interpretation. In the case of the 1982 Act, it is "the Conventions" which are given the force of law and it is only "for convenience of reference" that the English texts are set out in the Schedules. The United Kingdom court is entitled, and bound, to look at the texts in other languages where a problem of interpretation arises. There is therefore no room for a rule in this context that the other language versions may be resorted to only in the case of ambiguity in the English text. All language texts of the Conventions are equally authentic.[86] The effect is that the English version of the Conventions in Schedules 1 to 3C to the 1982 Act is only one of the authentic versions, and resort may be had to the others for the purposes of interpretation. A striking example of this occurred when the European Court held, basing itself on the French text of Article 18 of the 1968 Convention, that an appearance to contest the jurisdiction was not to be regarded as a submission even if at the same time the defendant pleaded to the merits in the alternative. The other language texts required the protest to be solely to contest the jurisdiction if it was to escape being a voluntary submission, but the Court preferred the French text as being more in keeping with the objectives and spirit of the 1968 Convention.[87]

11–043   **The 1968 Convention and references to the European Court.** The effect of section 3(1) to (2) of the 1982 Act is that any question as to the meaning or effect of any provision of the 1968 Convention shall, if not referred to the European Court, be determined in accordance with the principles laid down by, and any relevant decision of, the European Court; and that judicial notice is to be taken of any decision of, or expression of opinion by, the European Court on any such question.

11–044   The United Kingdom court may, and, in some circumstances, must refer questions of interpretation to the European Court under the 1971 Protocol. For the purposes of proceedings in the United Kingdom the 1971 Protocol must be read together with section 6 of the 1982 Act, which identifies the appellate courts in the United Kingdom in proceedings relating to the recognition and enforcement of judgments of other Contracting States. The combined effect of the 1971 Protocol and section 6 is that jurisdiction is conferred on the European Court to give rulings on the interpretation of the 1968 Convention, the 1971 Protocol and the Accession Conventions.

11–045   Where a question of interpretation of the Conventions is raised in a case before one of certain specified courts "that court shall, if it considers that a decision on the question is necessary to enable it to give judgment" request the European Court to give a ruling. If such a question is raised before any of the other courts entitled to make references the court may, if it considers that a decision on the question is necessary to enable it to give judgment, request

---

[85] *Ante*, paras. 1–018 *et seq.*
[86] Art. 68, 1968 Convention; Art. 14, 1971 Protocol; Arts. 37(2) and 41, 1978 Accession Convention; Art. 13(2), 1982 Accession Convention; Art. 30(2), 1989 Accession Convention; Art. 18, 1996 Accession Convention; Art. 68, Lugano Convention.
[87] Case 150/80 *Elefanten Schuh GmbH v. Jacqmain* [1981] E.C.R. 1671, 1685. See also Case 38/81 *Effer SpA v. Kantner* [1982] E.C.R. 825, 834; Case C–305/88 *Isabelle Lancray S.A. v. Peters und Sickert K.G.* [1990] E.C.R. I–2725.

the European Court to give a ruling thereon. The English courts which must make a request in appropriate cases for a preliminary ruling are: (1) the House of Lords; (2) the Court of Appeal on appeal from a decision of the High Court on an appeal against an order registering or refusing to register a judgment; (3) the High Court in relation to recognition of enforcement of a maintenance order by way of case stated. The English courts which may make a request are: (1) the High Court when hearing an appeal against registration of a judgment; (2) the magistrates' court when hearing an application to set aside registration of a maintenance order; (3) any other court sitting in an appellate capacity.[88]

Provision is also made for "the competent authority"[89] of a Contracting State to request a ruling from the European Court if judgments given by courts of that State conflict with the interpretation given either by the European Court or in a judgment of an appellate court in another Contracting State. The judgment of the European Court in such cases will have a purely advisory effect.   **11–046**

The mere fact that one of the parties contends that the dispute gives rise to a question of interpretation does not mean that the English court is bound to consider that a true question of interpretation arises. If the English court considers that there is no room for reasonable doubt as to the interpretation and that the matter would be equally obvious in the courts of the other States it need not make a reference; but the court must bear in mind that the different language versions are equally authenic and that interpretation involves a comparison of the different language versions; in a clear case, however, the English court may refrain from making a reference.[90]   **11–047**

It should also be noted that in relation to intra-United Kingdom jurisdiction and Scottish rules of jurisdiction, the 1982 Act provides[91] that, in determining any question as to the meaning or effect of any provision in Schedule 4 and of any provision in Schedule 8 derived to any extent from the 1968 Convention, regard is to be had to any relevant principles laid down by, and any relevant decision of, the European Court and to the reports on the 1968 Convention and the Accession Conventions. In *Kleinwort Benson Ltd. v. City of Glasgow District Council*[92] the European Court held that it had no jurisdiction to interpret provisions in Schedule 4 to the 1982 Act. Schedule 4 took the 1968 Convention as a model only, and did not wholly reproduce its terms. The Court also referred to the fact that Schedule 4 could be modified (pursuant to section 47 of the 1982 Act) to produce divergence from the corresponding provision of the 1968 Convention as interpreted by the European Court; in cases under the 1968 Convention, section 3 of the 1982 Act required the United Kingdom court to determine them in accordance with the principles laid down by, and any relevant decision of, the European Court; by contrast, in cases under Schedule 4, section 16(3)(*a*) merely provided that "regard" should be had to such principles and decisions. Accordingly, any replies given   **11–048**

---

[88] Which means sitting in any case involving a challenge before a higher jurisdiction: Schlosser, para. 255. See Case 80/83 *Habourdin International S.A. v. SpA Italocremona* [1983] E.C.R. 3639; Case 56/84 *Von Gallera v. Maître* [1984] E.C.R. 1769. For the procedure see Ord. 114 (in Civil Procedure Rules 1998, Sched. 1).

[89] In the United Kingdom the competent authority will be the Law Officers.

[90] See, *e.g. Jordan Grand Prix Ltd. v. Baltic Insurance Group* [1999] 2 W.L.R. 134, 140 (H.L.) (*acte clair*) and *cf.* on the exercise of discretion, *The Nile Rhapsody* [1994] 1 W.L.R. 382 (C.A.); *Jarrett v. Barclays Bank plc* [1999] Q.B. 1 (C.A.).

[91] ss.16(3), 20(5). See also S.I. 1997 No. 2602 (Gibraltar).

[92] Case C–346/93 [1995] E.C.R. I–615; [1996] Q.B. 57.

by the European Court to the English court would be purely advisory, since the interpretation would not be binding on the English court.[93] To give such replies would be to alter the function of the Court under the 1971 Protocol, namely that of a court whose judgments were binding.

11–049   The European Court has given judgment in more than 100 cases on the 1968 Convention. The Court has emphasised that the 1968 Convention must be interpreted by reference to its principles and objectives in the light of its preamble and Article 220 of the EC Treaty (now Article 293); thus the Court takes into account the purposes of the simplification of formalities regarding the reciprocal recognition and enforcement of judgments and of strengthening the legal protection of persons within the European Communities.[94] The Court has encouraged uniformity in the Contracting States by interpreting most provisions of the 1968 Convention which have come before it according to a Convention interpretation, rather than by a purely national interpretation.

11–050   A common problem has been whether terms in the Convention are to be interpreted according to national law (usually that of the *lex fori*) or according to an independent Convention concept. In a few cases the Convention itself supplies the answer by referring to national law, or by supplying a Convention definition. But more commonly the Convention is silent, and the strong tendency of the Court has been to interpret terms in the Convention in accordance with an independent concept: *e.g.* "civil and commercial matters" in Article 1[95]; "contract" in Article 5(1)[96]; "matters relating to tort, delict or quasi-delict" in Article 5(3)[97]; "place where the harmful event occurred" in Article 5(3)[98]; "consumer" and "instalment credit terms" in Article 13[99]; "rights *in rem* in immovable property"[1] and "tenancies of immovable property"[2] in Article 16(1); "proceedings concerned with registration or validity of patents" in Article 16(4)[3]; "proceedings concerned with the enforcement of

---

[93] In *Kleinwort Benson Ltd. v. Glasgow City Council* [1999] 1 A.C. 153 Lord Goff of Chieveley and Lord Clyde adverted to, but did not decide, the question whether in a Sched. 4 case it might not be possible to adopt a broader concept of contractual obligation under Art. 5(1) (on which see paras. 11–243 *et seq., post*) than existed in European law.

[94] Among many others see Case 33/78 *Somafer S.A. v. Saar-Ferngas A.G.* [1978] E.C.R. 2183; Case 144/86 *Gubisch Maschinenfabrik A.G. v. Palumbo* [1987] E.C.R. 4861; Case C–351/89 *Overseas Union Insurance Ltd. v. New Hampshire Insurance Co.* [1991] E.C.R. I–3317; [1992] Q.B. 434. On the principle of "legal certainty" see, *e.g.* Case 38/81 *Effer SpA v. Kantner* [1982] E.C.R. 825, 834; Case C–190/89 *Marc Rich & Co. A.G. v. Soc. Italiana Impianti P.A.* [1991] E.C.R. I–3855.

[95] Case 29/76 *LTU GmbH v. Eurocontrol* [1976] E.C.R. 1541; Joined Cases 9 and 10/77 *Bavaria and Germanair v. Eurocontrol* [1977] E.C.R. 1517; Case 133/78 *Gourdain v. Nadler* [1979] E.C.R. 733; Case 814/79 *Netherlands State v. Rüffer* [1980] E.C.R. 3807; Case C–172/91 *Sonntag v. Waidmann* [1993] E.C.R. I–1963.

[96] Case 34/82 *Peters v. ZNAV* [1983] E.C.R. 787; Case 9/87 *Arcado v. Haviland S.A.* [1988] E.C.R. 1539; Case C–26/91 *Soc. Jakob Handte et cie GmbH v. TMCS* [1993] E.C.R. I–3967; Case C–51/97 *Réunion européenne S.A. v. Spliethoff's Bevrachtingskantoor B.V.* [1998] E.C.R. I–6511. Contrast Case 12/76 *Industrie Tessili Italiana Como v. Dunlop A.G.* [1976] E.C.R. 1473 ("place of performance").

[97] Case 189/87 *Kalfelis v. Schröder* [1988] E.C.R. 5565; Case C–261/90 *Reichert v. Dresdner Bank (No. 2)* [1992] E.C.R. I–2149.

[98] Case 21/76 *Bier v. Mines de Potasse d'Alsace S.A.* [1976] E.C.R. 1735, [1978] Q.B. 708.

[99] Case C–89/91 *Shearson Lehman Hutton Inc. v. TVB* [1993] E.C.R. I–139; Case 150/77 *Société Bertrand v. Paul Ott K.G.* [1978] E.C.R. 1431; Case C–99/96 *Mietz v. Intership Yachting Sneek B.V.* [1999] I.L.Pr. 541.

[1] Case 115/88 *Reichert v. Dresdner Bank* [1990] E.C.R. I–27.

[2] Case 73/77 *Sanders v. Van der Putte* [1977] E.C.R. 2383.

[3] Case 288/82 *Duijnstee v. Goderbauer* [1983] E.C.R. 3663.

judgments" in Article 16(5)[4]; whether there has been an agreement on jurisdiction under Article 17[5]; "provisional, including protective measures" in Article 24[6]; "ordinary appeal" in Articles 30 and 38[7]; and "an offence which was not intentionally committed" in Article II of the Protocol.[8] But where the reference is to procedural concepts the tendency towards an autonomous interpretation is less marked.[9]

The object of interpreting the terms of the Convention autonomously is to 11–051 ensure that the Convention is fully effective, and to ensure uniform application of the Convention, so as to avoid as far as possible multiplication of the bases of jurisdiction in relation to the same legal relationship and to reinforce legal protection by allowing the plaintiff easily to identify the court before which he may bring an action and the defendant reasonably to foresee the court before which he may be sued.[10] These objects have been used to justify an avoidance of an excessively liberal interpretation of the expression "harmful event" in Article 5(3)[11] and have justified a Convention, rather than a national, interpretation of Article 5(5) on the meaning of "branch, agency or other establishment."[12] The Court has held that the exceptions to Article 2, which gives primacy to the court of the domicile, which is the basic jurisdictional rule of the Conventions, are to be construed strictly,[13] particularly those rules (Article 16 on exclusive jurisdiction, and Article 17 on prorogation) which altogether exclude the jurisdiction of the court of the domicile.[14] Those provisions which safeguard the procedural rights of the defendant are to be interpreted liberally.[15]

The Lugano Convention: special provisions. It was necessary to make 11–052 special provision for interpretation of the Lugano Convention, because the

---

[4] Case C–261/90 *Reichert v. Dresdner Bank (No. 2), supra.*

[5] Many of the cases on Art. 17 from Case 24/76 *Salotti v. RÜWA* [1976] E.C.R. 1831 to (especially) Case 214/89 *Powell Duffryn plc v. Petereit* [1992] E.C.R. I–1745.

[6] Case C–261/90 *Reichert v. Dresdner Bank (No. 2), supra.*

[7] Case 43/77 *Industrial Diamond Supplies v. Riva* [1977] E.C.R. 2175.

[8] Case 157/80 *Rinkau* [1981] E.C.R. 1391.

[9] See Case 365/88 *Kongress Agentur Hagen GmbH v. Zeehaghe B.V.* [1990] E.C.R. I–1845; Case 56/79 *Zelger v. Salinitri* [1980] E.C.R. 89; Case 148/84 *Deutsche Genossenschaftsbank v. Brasserie du Pêcheur S.A.* [1985] E.C.R. 1981; Case 145/86 *Hoffmann v. Krieg* [1988] E.C.R. 645. But contrast Case 144/86 *Gubisch Maschinenfabrik A.G. v. Palumbo* [1987] E.C.R. 4861.

[10] Case C–125/92 *Mulox IBC Ltd. v. Geels* [1993] E.C.R. I–4075; Case C–383/95 *Rutten v. Cross Medical Ltd.* [1997] E.C.R. I–1000; [1997] I.C.R. 715; Case C–295/95 *Farrell v. Long* [1997] E.C.R. I–1683; [1997] Q.B. 842.

[11] Case 220/88 *Dumez France S.A. v. Hessische Landesbank* [1990] E.C.R. I–49.

[12] Case 33/78 *Somafer S.A. v. Saar-Ferngas A.G.* [1978] E.C.R. 2183.

[13] See, *e.g.* Case 189/87 *Kalfelis v. Schröder* [1988] E.C.R. 5565; Case 32/88 *Six Constructions Ltd. v. Humbert* [1989] E.C.R. 341; Case 220/88 *Dumez France S.A. v. Hessische Landesbank* [1990] E.C.R. I–49; Case C–89/91 *Shearson Lehman Hutton Inc. v. TVB* [1993] E.C.R. I–139; Case C–269/95 *Benincasa v. Dentalkit Srl* [1997] E.C.R. I–3767; [1998] All E.R. (E.C.) 135; Case C–51/97 *Réunion européenne S.A. v. Spliethoff's Bevrachtingskantoor B.V.* [1998] E.C.R. I–6511.

[14] Case 24/76 *Salotti v. RUWA* [1976] E.C.R. 1831; Case 25/76 *Galeries Segoura Sprl v. Bonakdarian* [1976] E.C.R. 1851; Case 73/77 *Sanders v. Van der Putte* [1977] E.C.R. 2383; Case 115/88 *Reichert v. Dresdner Bank* [1990] E.C.R. I–27; Case C–292/93 *Lieber v. Göbel* [1994] E.C.R. I–2535.

[15] Case 150/80 *Elefanten Schuh GmbH v. Jacqmain* [1981] E.C.R. 1671; Case 166/80 *Klomps v. Michel* [1981] E.C.R. 1593. *Cf.* Case 125/79 *Denilauler v. SNC Couchet Frères* [1980] E.C.R. 1553.

European Court has no jurisdiction to interpret the Lugano Convention[16] and because the EFTA Member States would not have accepted a new régime under which an institution of the Communities on which they were not represented would rule, as a court of last resort, on the Lugano Convention. Nor was it desirable to create a new court for that purpose, since that would have created the possibility of conflicting rulings.[17]

11–053   Instead, in order to achieve uniformity, Protocol 2 on the Uniform Interpretation of the Lugano Convention, which is reproduced in Schedule 3C to the 1982 Act, provides that the courts of each Contracting State shall, when applying and interpreting the provisions of the Convention, pay due account to the principles laid down by any relevant decision delivered by courts of other Contracting States concerning provisions of the Lugano Convention. Section 3B(1) of the 1982 Act gives effect to that provision; and section 3B(2) provides that the Jenard-Möller report may be considered in ascertaining the meaning or effect of any provisions of the Lugano Convention and shall be given such weight as is appropriate in the circumstances. Protocol 2 also sets up a system of exchange of information and consultation between the Contracting States, the object of which is to collate information (at the European Court) on decisions of national courts (and the European Court) which have been delivered pursuant to the 1968 and Lugano Conventions, and to exchange views on the functioning of the Lugano Convention, particularly with regard to the case law collated and the application of Article 57 (relationship with other Conventions).

11–054   Two Declarations[18] signed, respectively, by the Member States of the European Communities and the EFTA Member States should also be noted: the Member States of the European Communities declared that they considered it appropriate that the European Court should, when interpreting the 1968 Convention, pay due account to the rulings (of national courts) on the Lugano Convention. Conversely, EFTA Member States declared that they considered it appropriate that their courts, when interpreting the Lugano Convention, should pay due account to the rulings contained in the case law of the European Court and of the courts of the Member States of the European Communities in respect of provisions of the 1968 Convention which were substantially reproduced in the Lugano Convention.

11–055   **Method of challenge to jurisdiction.** A defendant who has been served with process and wishes to challenge the jurisdiction of the English court should file an acknowledgment of service and apply, within the period for filing a defence, for service to be set aside or other appropriate relief.[19] Where the defendant does not challenge the *existence* of jurisdiction but wishes to persuade the court not to exercise it, *e.g.* because, in a non-Convention case, England is not the *forum conveniens* or there is an agreement between the

---

[16] It is not possible to obtain a ruling on the Lugano Convention by the use of what is now Art. 234 (previously Art. 177) of the E.C. Treaty: *Agnew v. Lansförsakringsbolagens A.B.* [1997] 4 All E.R. 937 (C.A.).

[17] Jenard-Möller, para. 110.

[18] [1988] O.J. L319/37, 40; Cm. 1362, pp. 31, 32.

[19] CPR, Pt 11, replacing R.S.C., Ord. 12, r. 8. It is not necessary that service of the application be made within the period: *Carmel Exporters (Sales) Ltd. v. Sealand Services Ltd.* [1981] 1 W.L.R. 1068; *Broken Hill Pty. Co. Ltd. v. Xenakis* [1982] 2 Lloyd's Rep. 304. The court has power to order disclosure of documents on the application, but the power will be exercised rarely: *Canada Trust Co. v. Stolzenberg* [1995] 1 W.L.R. 1582 (C.A.); *Rome v. Punjab National Bank (No. 1)* [1989] 2 Lloyd's Rep. 424. See *post*, para. 11–110, for the effect of this procedure.

parties conferring jurisdiction on the courts of another country,[20] he should apply under Part 11 of the Civil Procedure Rules for a stay of the English proceedings and not for process to be set aside,[21] as an application to stay proceedings is not a challenge to the jurisdiction of the court.[22]

The new Civil Procedure Rules provide that, upon the failure of an applica- **11–056** tion for a declaration that the court has no jurisdiction or that its jurisdiction should not be exercised, the acknowledgment of service will cease to have effect and the defendant has a further period in which to file a further acknowledgment of service; and if the further acknowledgment of service is filed the defendant is treated as having accepted that the court has jurisdiction to try the claim.[23]

Examination by the court of its jurisdiction. Normally an English court **11–057** is not required of its own motion to consider whether it has jurisdiction, although where a plaintiff seeks permission to serve a defendant out of the jurisdiction under Rule 27, *i.e.* Order 11, r. 1(1), he has to satisfy the court that the case is a proper one for service out of the jurisdiction.[24] But there are some cases where the court itself must, as a result of express provisions of the Conventions, declare of *its own motion* that it has no jurisdiction. The effect of Articles 19 and 20[25] is that the English court must do so in the following two cases: first, where the claim is principally concerned with a matter over which the courts of another Contracting State have exclusive jurisdiction by virtue of Article 16; secondly, where the defendant is domiciled in another Contracting State and does not enter an appearance, and the English court does not have jurisdiction under the Conventions.

If the defendant fails to give notice of intention to defend, a default **11–058** judgment may not be entered unless it is shown that the defendant was properly served.[26] The Civil Procedure Rules 1998 give effect to these requirements by: (a) requiring a claim form which is to be served out of the jurisdiction to be endorsed with a statement that the court has power under the 1982 Act to deal with the claim, and that no proceedings based on the same cause of action are pending between the parties in another Convention terri- tory or in another part of the United Kingdom[27]; (b) requiring, before judg- ment in default of notice of filing of acknowledgment of service is entered on a claim form served out of the jurisdiction without permission under the 1982 Act or served within the jurisdiction on a defendant domiciled in another Contracting State or in another part of the United Kingdom, an application supported by evidence that the claim is one which the court has power to hear and decide, that no other court has exclusive jurisdiction under the 1982 Act,

---

[20] See Rules 31 and 32.

[21] See *The Fehmarn* [1958] 1 W.L.R. 159, 161 (C.A.); *The Eleftheria* [1970] P. 94, 98.

[22] *Bankers Trust Co. v. Galadari* [1986] 2 Lloyd's Rep. 446, 449 (C.A.). But see *The Sydney Express* [1988] 2 Lloyd's Rep. 257.

[23] CPR 11(7). But even if the defendant does not file the further acknowledgment of service and takes no further part, any resulting default judgment will be enforceable in other Contracting States: *post*, paras. 14–202; 14–208.

[24] Ord. 11, r. 4.

[25] These provisions apply, in modified form, in intra-United Kingdom cases. On Art. 19 see Case 288/82 *Duijnstee v. Goderbauer* [1983] E.C.R. 3663; *Coin Controls Ltd. v. Suzo International (U.K.) Ltd.* [1999] Ch. 33.

[26] See Art. 20(2), (3); Art. IV, Protocol to 1968 Convention and Protocol No. 1 to Lugano Convention; *Noirhomme v. Walklate* [1992] 1 Lloyd's Rep. 427.

[27] CPR PD7, para. 3.5.

and that the claim has been properly served in accordance with Article 20 of Schedule 1, 3C or 4 of the 1982 Act.[28]

2. DOMICILE

11R–059 **RULE 23—(1) For the purposes of Rules 27 to 30 the domicile of an individual shall be determined as follows:**

    (a) an individual is domiciled in the United Kingdom (or a particular part of the United Kingdom) if he is resident in, and the nature and circumstances of his residence indicate that he has a substantial connection with, the United Kingdom (or that part)[29];

    (b) an individual is domiciled in a particular place in the United Kingdom if he is domiciled in the part of the United Kingdom in which that place is situated and is resident in that place[30];

    (c) an individual who is not domiciled in the United Kingdom in accordance with paragraph (a) of this clause is domiciled in another Contracting State[31] if by the law of that State he is domiciled in that State[32];

    (d) an individual is domiciled in a State other than a Contracting State if he is resident in, and the nature and circumstances of his residence indicate that he has a substantial connection with, that State.[33]

(2) For the purposes of Rules 27 to 30[34] a corporation or association is domiciled at its seat,[35] which for those purposes[36] shall be determined as follows:

    (a) a corporation or association has its seat in the United Kingdom if either (i) it was incorporated under the law of a part of the United Kingdom or (ii) its central management and control is exercised in the United Kingdom[37];

    (b) a corporation or association has its seat in a particular part of the United Kingdom (or in a particular place in the United Kingdom) if it has its seat in the United Kingdom and (i) it has its registered office or other official address in that part (or that place), or (ii) its central management and control is exercised in that part (or that place), or (iii) it has a place of business in that part (or that place)[38];

    (c) a corporation or association has its seat in a State other than the United Kingdom if (i) it was incorporated under the law of that

---

[28] CPR 12.10(b)(i), (ii), PD12, para 3.

[29] 1982 Act, s.41(2), (3).

[30] s.41(4).

[31] For Contracting States see *ante*, paras. 11–006 *et seq.*

[32] Art. 52(2), in 1982 Act, Scheds 1 and 3C.

[33] s.41(7).

[34] For the special rules (in connection with insurance and consumer contracts) relating to branches of persons who would otherwise be regarded as domiciled outside the United Kingdom see s.44 and *post*, paras. 11–303; 11–324.

[35] s.42(1).

[36] For the seat of a corporation for the purposes of Art. 16(2) (exclusive jurisdiction) see s.43 and *post*, para. 11–333.

[37] s.42(3).

[38] s.42(4), (5).

State and has its registered office or other official address there or (ii) its central management and control is exercised in that State, provided that it shall not be regarded as having its seat in a Contracting State if by the law of that State it does not have its seat there.[39]

COMMENT

The concept of domicile under the Conventions and the 1982 Act is relevant in several contexts, to determine whether a person is domiciled in one of the Contracting States[40] or in a particular Contracting State[41]; whether a person is domiciled outside the Contracting States[42]; whether a person is domiciled outside a particular Contracting State[43]; whether a person is domiciled in a particular place[44]; whether a person is domiciled in a part of the United Kingdom, and, if so, which part.[45] "Domicile" was not defined in the 1968 Convention. This was so because among other reasons it was thought that a new uniform definition of domicile properly belonged in a convention on uniform law rather than in a jurisdiction and judgments convention.[46] In the original Contracting States the domicile of an individual was close to the notion of habitual residence, although its meaning differed somewhat as between the States.[47] In the case of corporations, the 1968 Convention assimilated domicile to the "seat", but the original Contracting States had differing approaches to the determination of the seat, some preferring the "siège réel" or effective seat, and others the "siège statutaire" or law of incorporation. Consequently the 1968 Convention limited itself to providing, in Articles 52 and 53, rules regulating what law would determine the domicile of an individual or corporation for the purposes of the Convention, and the Lugano Convention contains identical provisions.   **11–060**

Clause (1) of the Rule. Individuals. Article 52 provides that in order to determine whether a party is domiciled in the Contracting State whose courts are seised of the matter, the court is to apply its internal law. If a party is not domiciled in the State whose courts are seised of the matter, then, in order to determine whether the party is domiciled in another Contracting State, the court is to apply the law of that other State.   **11–061**

The application of Article 52 to the common law of domicile[48] in the United Kingdom as it stood prior to the 1982 Act would have produced a serious imbalance, because the traditional concept of domicile with its emphasis on permanent home would have excluded many persons settled, but not domiciled, in the United Kingdom from the provisions of the 1968 Convention, and included many persons settled outside, but domiciled within, the United   **11–062**

---

[39] s.42(6), (7).
[40] Arts. 2(1); 3; 4(2); 5; 6; 8(1); 11; 12(3); 13(1)(3); 14; 15; 17; 20; 36.
[41] 1968 Convention Protocol, Art. I, Lugano Convention Protocol No. 1, Art. I.
[42] Arts. 4(1); 8(2); 12(4); 13(2); 17.
[43] Arts. 32; 45.
[44] Arts. 5(2); 6(1); 8(1)(2); 32(2).
[45] 1982 Act, Sched. 4. See, *e.g. Davenport v. Corinthian Motor Policies at Lloyd's*, 1991 S.L.T. 774.
[46] Jenard, pp. 15–16.
[47] Schlosser, para. 73. The Convention concept of domicile is adopted for non-Convention cases under Ord. 11, r. 1: see Ord. 11, r. 1(4).
[48] See *ante*, Chap. 6.

Kingdom. Accordingly, it was agreed in the negotiations for accession to the 1968 Convention that the United Kingdom (and the Republic of Ireland) would include in their legislation for the purposes of the Convention a definition of domicile which would reflect more the concept of domicile as understood in the original Contracting States. This was effected in the 1982 Act by a definition of domicile of individuals based on a combination of residence in, and substantial connection with, the United Kingdom. The main differences between the concept of domicile in the 1982 Act and at common law are that there is no question of the need for a "permanent home" under the 1982 Act; the concept of domicile of origin has no role under the 1982 Act; under the 1982 Act it will be possible for a person to have more than one domicile, whereas at common law only one domicile is possible. At common law the question where a person is domiciled depends on English law as the *lex fori*, whereas under the Convention scheme the United Kingdom court must apply the law of another Contracting State to determine whether a party is domiciled in that State.

11–063   The first principle in Article 52 is that in order to determine whether an individual is domiciled in the Contracting State whose courts are seised of the matter, the court is to apply its internal law.[49] When a court in the United Kingdom is the court seised, the relevant internal law is to be found in section 41 of the 1982 Act, which provides that an individual is domiciled in the United Kingdom if and only if he is resident in the United Kingdom and the nature and circumstances of his residence indicate that he has a substantial connection with the United Kingdom.[50] In the case of an individual who is resident in the United Kingdom and has been so for the last three months or more, the requirement of substantial connection is presumed to be fulfilled unless the contrary is proved.[51] "Residence" is not defined in the 1982 Act but it indicates some degree of permanence or continuity.[52]

11–064   If a party is not domiciled in the State whose courts are seised of the matter, then, in order to determine whether the party is domiciled in another Contracting State, the court is to apply the law of that other State.[53] This provision did not require specific treatment in the 1982 Act because under the Convention rules (which have the force of law) the United Kingdom court will apply the law of the relevant Contracting State. The Conventions lay down no rules for determining the domicile of a person who is not domiciled in a Contracting State, and section 41(7) of the 1982 Act provides that an individual is domiciled in a State other than a Contracting State if and only if he is resident in that State and the nature and circumstances of his residence indicate that he has a substantial connection with that State.[54]

11–065   It is frequently necessary to determine the "place" of an individual's domicile, or the part of the United Kingdom in which he is domiciled. An

---

[49] Art. 52(1).

[50] 1982 Act, s.41(2).

[51] s.41(6). The critical date for determination of domicile is the date the proceedings are issued, and the claimant must establish a good arguable case that the defendant is domiciled in the jurisdiction: *Canada Trust Co. v. Stolzenberg (No. 2)* [1998] 1 W.L.R. 547 (C.A.); *cf. Petrotrade Inc. v. Smith* [1998] 2 All E.R. 346 (enforced presence as a result of bail conditions on arrest not residence).

[52] *Bank of Dubai Ltd. v. Abbas* [1997] I.L.Pr. 308 (C.A.).

[53] Art. 52(2).

[54] The presumption based on three months' residence does not apply to this case.

individual is domiciled in a particular place in the United Kingdom if, and only if, he is (a) domiciled in the part of the United Kingdom in which that place is situated; and (b) resident in that place.[55] He is domiciled in a particular part of the United Kingdom if, and only if, (a) he is resident in that part; and (b) the nature and circumstances of his residence indicate that he has a substantial connection with that part,[56] but if he is domiciled in the United Kingdom and has no substantial connection with any particular part, he is to be treated as domiciled in the part of the United Kingdom in which he is resident.[57] The latter provision deals with the case where a person has ties with the United Kingdom but does not stay long at any place.

It will be apparent from the above that a person may be domiciled in more than one Contracting State. Section 41 seeks to answer the questions (a) whether an individual is domiciled in the United Kingdom and (b) whether an individual is domiciled in a State other than a Contracting State. It does not answer the question whether he is domiciled in another Contracting State, since that question depends, by Article 52(2), on the law of that other State. This may be illustrated by the case of a person, who is from New York by origin, and who lives both in Paris and London. He is on a visit to New York. May he be sued in a contract dispute in England (a) on the basis of service on him out of the jurisdiction under Rule 27, clause (4), *i.e.* Order 11, r. 1(1)(*d*), on the theory that the contract is governed by English law,[58] or (b) on the basis of the 1968 Convention rules by virtue of his domicile in the United Kingdom?[59] If he is domiciled in a Contracting State, the provisions of Order 11, r. 1(1)(*d*) cannot be applied under the Convention.[60] The English court will have first to decide whether he is domiciled in the United Kingdom; this will turn on whether he is resident in the United Kingdom and whether the nature and circumstances of his residence indicate that he has a substantial connection with the United Kingdom and, in particular, with England (which will be presumed in each case from three months' residence). If he is so domiciled, then he may be sued in England on the basis of the Convention and intra-United Kingdom rules. If he is not so domiciled, then he may object to the jurisdiction on the basis that he is domiciled in France and must be sued there: in that case the court will apply French law to determine his domicile. If he is not domiciled in the United Kingdom or France, then the English court may exercise jurisdiction. But if he is domiciled in the United Kingdom under the 1982 Act, it will be no answer for him to say that he is also domiciled in France under French law, because the English court will be able to exercise jurisdiction unless a French court is first seised.[61]

11–066

Clause (2) of the Rule. Corporations and associations. Article 53(1) provides that for the purposes of the Conventions, the seat of a company or other legal person or association of natural or legal persons shall be treated as its domicile. In order to determine that seat, the court is to apply its rules of private international law. Thus although the Conventions refer to the "seat" of

11–067

---

[55] 1982 Act, s.41(4).
[56] s.41(3).
[57] s.41(5).
[58] *Post*, para. 11–161.
[59] *Post*, para. 11–230.
[60] Subject to the transitional provisions of what is now Art. 54(3).
[61] 1968 Convention, Arts. 21 and 22: *post*, Rule 31(4).

a corporation as its domicile, they do not define seat, but instead provide a choice of law rule for its determination. The concept of "seat" of a corporation has no precise equivalent in the law of the United Kingdom (where the domicile of a corporation is the place of its incorporation)[62] and it was necessary to provide expressly in the 1982 Act for the determination of the domicile of corporations and associations. This has been effected in section 42, which provides that a corporation or association has its seat in the United Kingdom if and only if (a) it was incorporated or formed under the law of a part of the United Kingdom and has its registered office or some other official address in the United Kingdom or (b) its central management and control is exercised in the United Kingdom.[63]

11–068 A corporation or association which does not have its seat in the United Kingdom has its seat in a State other than the United Kingdom if and only if (a) it was incorporated or formed under the law of that State and has its registered office or some other official address there or (b) its central management or control is exercised in that State.[64] It follows that for the purposes of the Conventions a corporation can have its seat (and therefore its domicile) in more than one State. Thus a Panamanian company with its central management and control in Germany will have its seat for the purposes of the 1982 Act both in Panama and in Germany.[65]

11–069 But a corporation is not to be regarded as having its seat in a Contracting State if the courts of that State would not regard it as having its seat there.[66] Thus if the question arises whether a Bermuda company with Dutch directors and which holds board meetings in Amsterdam and Paris can be treated as not being domiciled in a 1968 Convention Contracting State, the English court will first find that it was not formed under the law of, and does not have its central management and control in, the United Kingdom; it will then consider whether its central management and control is in the Netherlands or France; if it finds that its central management and control is in the Netherlands and not in France, the English court will only be able to treat it as not being domiciled in a Contracting State if by the law of the Netherlands the seat of a company depends, not on its place of management, but on its registered office; in that event, as a result of the rules in the 1982 Act the company will not be domiciled in a Contracting State and the Convention rules on jurisdiction will not normally apply.

11–070 A foreign company with a branch in Great Britain must file with the Registrar of Companies the name and address of a person authorised to accept process on its behalf in respect of the business of the branch.[67] Under the new Civil Procedure Rules 1998, however, service may in addition be effected at any place of business of the company within the jurisdiction[68]; and in such a case (it seems) the process need not be in respect of the business of the

---

[62] See *post*, Rule 152.
[63] 1982 Act, s.42(2). On the meaning of "central management and control" see *post*, para. 30–006.
[64] s.42(6).
[65] *The Deichland* [1990] 1 Q.B. 361 (C.A.), *per* Neill and Stuart-Smith L.JJ., Sir Denys Buckley *dubitante*. See also *The Rewia* [1991] 2 Lloyd's Rep. 325 (C.A.), where a Liberian company had its central management and control in Germany.
[66] s.42(7).
[67] Companies Act 1985, s.690A, *post*, para. 11–096.
[68] CPR 6.5(6).

company within the jurisdiction. But under the Convention scheme, as implemented by the 1982 Act, such a company is not domiciled in the United Kingdom unless its central management and control is conducted there. Thus for a French company to be capable of being sued in England or Scotland one of the other heads of jurisdiction will have to be applicable, *e.g.* Article 5(5) which confers jurisdiction, in relation to disputes arising out of the operations of a branch, on the courts of the place of the branch. But if a corporation has its seat in the United Kingdom, then it will be regarded as having a seat in each part of the United Kingdom in which it has a place of business.[69]

Where it is necessary to determine the "place" of domicile of a corporation **11–071** or association, it has its seat in a particular place in the United Kingdom if and only if it has its seat in the part of the United Kingdom in which that place is situated and has its registered office or some other official address in that place or its central management and control is exercised in that place.[70] For the purposes of allocation of jurisdiction within the United Kingdom, a corporation or association has its seat in a particular part of the United Kingdom if it has its seat in the United Kingdom and it has its registered office or some other official address in that part, or its central management and control is exercised in that part, or it has a place of business in that part.[71]

The Conventions do not indicate what corporate bodies are included within **11–072** the expression "or other legal person or association of natural or legal persons" in Article 53(1). Schlosser[72] suggests that the similar expression in Article 16(2) applies to partnerships established under United Kingdom law, but although section 50 of the 1982 Act defines corporation to include Scottish partnerships, there must be room for doubt as regards English partnerships, since in English law the expression "unincorporated association" normally connotes such bodies as clubs and charitable and social organisations, and section 50 of the 1982 Act defines "association" as an unincorporated body of persons. But other language versions of the Conventions use expressions which are apt to include partnerships. Whether the expression must be given a national or a uniform interpretation has not been decided,[73] but it is very likely that it would be given a uniform interpretation. In Scotland it was assumed that a Lloyd's syndicate was an association for this purpose.[74]

Articles 8(2) and 13(2) provide that, in the case of insurance and consumer **11–073** contracts, a person who is not domiciled in a Contracting State is deemed to be domiciled in a Contracting State in which it has a branch in connection with disputes arising out of the operations of that branch. Although this applies both to individuals and companies it is likely to be of practical relevance mainly in relation to corporate defendants. Section 44 of the 1982 Act confirms that for the purposes of proceedings arising out of the operations of a branch, agency or other establishment in the United Kingdom, a person who is deemed for the purposes of the Conventions to be domiciled in the

---

[69] 1982 Act, s.42(4)(*c*).

[70] s.42(5).

[71] s.42(4). "Place" of business connotes some degree of permanence; *cf. The Theodohos* [1977] 2 Lloyd's Rep. 428; *South India Shipping Corp. Ltd. v. Export-Import Bank of Korea* [1985] 1 W.L.R. 858 (C.A.).

[72] Para. 162.

[73] See Collins, p. 42; Anton, *Civil Jurisdiction*, p. 107; Kaye, p. 338.

[74] *Davenport v. Corinthian Motor Policies at Lloyd's*, 1991 S.L.T. 774. A Lloyd's syndicate is, in law, a body of persons each of whom accepts personal liability to the extent of his "line" but who is not responsible for any other members of the syndicate.

United Kingdom by virtue of Article 8(2) and Article 13(2) shall, for the purposes of those proceedings, be treated for the purposes of the 1982 Act as so domiciled, and as domiciled in the part of the United Kingdom in which the branch, agency or establishment in question is situated.

11–074 **Trusts.** Article 53(2), which was added to the 1968 Convention by the 1978 Accession Convention, provides that in order to determine whether a trust is domiciled in the Contracting State whose courts are seised of the matter[75] the court shall apply its rules of private international law. The relevant rule of private international law in the United Kingdom is enacted by section 45 of the 1982 Act, which provides that a trust is domiciled in the United Kingdom if and only if it is domiciled in a part of the United Kingdom. It is domiciled in a part of the United Kingdom if and only if the system of law of that part is the system of law with which the trust has its closest and most real connection.[76]

ILLUSTRATIONS

11–075   1. X, an individual, has lived at all material times in London. For the purposes of the Conventions and the 1982 Act the Contracting State in which he is domiciled is the United Kingdom and the part of the United Kingdom in which he is domiciled is England.[77]
     2. X, an individual, is staying in London but his home and his work are in Edinburgh. For the purposes of the Conventions and the 1982 Act the Contracting State in which he is domiciled is the United Kingdom and the part of the United Kingdom in which he is domiciled is Scotland.[78]
     3. X, an individual, has residences both in New York and Geneva. He has a substantial connection with New York, and by Swiss law he is domiciled in Switzerland. X is domiciled both in New York and in Switzerland.[79]
     4. X Ltd., a company incorporated under the Companies Act 1985, has its registered office in London, and its central management and control is exercised in Bermuda. Its seat (and therefore its domicile) is in the United Kingdom (and the part of the United Kingdom in which it has its seat and domicile is England) and also in Bermuda.[80]
     5. X Ltd., a company incorporated under the Companies Act 1985, has its registered office in Edinburgh and has branches in London and Belfast. Its seat (and domicile) is in the United Kingdom, and also in Scotland, England and Northern Ireland.[81]
     6. X N.V., a Dutch company, has its official address in Rotterdam, and its central management and control is exercised in London. Its seat (and domicile) is in the Netherlands and also in the United Kingdom (and the part of the United Kingdom in which it has its seat and domicile is England).[82]
     7. X Ltd., a Panamanian company, has German directors and its central management and control is exercised in Germany. It has its seat (and domicile) in Panama, and also in Germany.[83]
     8. X Inc., a New York insurance company, has a branch in London, but its central management and control is exercised in New York. It has its seat (and its domicile) in New York,[84] except that

---

[75] See Art. 5(6), *post*, para. 11–276.
[76] 1982 Act, s.45(3).
[77] s.41(2), (3).
[78] *Ibid.*
[79] s.41(7); Art. 52(2).
[80] s.42(3), (4), (6).
[81] ss.42(3)(*a*); 43(4)(*a*), (*c*).
[82] s.42(3), (4), (6).
[83] s.42(7); *The Deichland* [1990] 1 Q.B. 361 (C.A.). It would have had a seat (and domicile) solely in Panama if by German law the seat of a company had depended on its place of incorporation.
[84] s.42(6).

for the purposes of the insurance provisions of the Conventions it is deemed to be domiciled in the United Kingdom (and in England).[85]

3. RULES RELATING TO JURISDICTION

A. *Where the 1968 Convention and the Lugano Convention do not apply or where the defendant is not domiciled in the United Kingdom or any part thereof or in any other State which is party to the 1968 Convention or the Lugano Convention*

RULE 24—The High Court has jurisdiction, subject to Rules 29 and 30 (exclusive jurisdiction under the Conventions) and Rules 53 and 54 (international conventions) to entertain a claim *in personam* against a defendant (other than a person domiciled or deemed to be domiciled in another State party to the Conventions[86] or in Scotland or Northern Ireland) who is present in England[87] and duly served there with process.　　　**11R–076**

COMMENT

As has been seen above, the foundation of jurisdiction *in personam* is service of process. Until the 1982 Act came into force the English court, subject to certain exceptions deriving from rules contained in international conventions which are referred to in Rule 53 below, had jurisdiction over any person who could be served with process in England even if he was only temporarily present in England. Since the 1982 Act the position is significantly different, and this head of jurisdiction is branded as an "exorbitant jurisdiction."[88] Article 3(2) provides that the rule of English law which enables jurisdiction to be founded on service on the defendant during his temporary presence may not be applied as against any person domiciled in a Contracting State other than the United Kingdom. The effect of the provisions relating to jurisdiction within the United Kingdom in Schedule 4 to the 1982 Act is that, in general, jurisdiction based on mere presence cannot be applied as regards defendants domiciled in Scotland and Northern Ireland.　　　**11–077**

It should be noted, however, that where a case falls outside the scope of the Conventions[89] this Rule will apply even if the defendant is domiciled in a Contracting State or in another part of the United Kingdom. But as regards cases within the scope of the Conventions it will apply only to defendants not domiciled in any of the Contracting States. Article 4[90] provides that where the defendant is not domiciled in a Contracting State, the jurisdiction of the courts of each Contracting State shall be determined by the law of that State. This includes its "exorbitant" rules of jurisdiction.　　　**11–078**

---

[85] s.44(2), *post*, para. 11–303.

[86] For Contracting States see *ante*, paras. 11–006 *et seq.*

[87] For this purpose a person on board a ship of the Royal Navy, wherever situate, is considered as being in England, and Ord. 11, r. 1(1), *i.e.* Rule 27, is inapplicable to him: *Seagrove v. Parks* [1891] 1 Q.B. 551.

[88] See Schlosser, para. 86.

[89] As to which see *ante*, paras. 11–012 *et seq.*

[90] On which see *Re Harrods (Buenos Aires) Ltd.* [1992] Ch. 72, 100 (C.A.); *Balkanbank v. Taher (No.2)* [1995] 1 W.L.R. 1067, 1074 (C.A.); *Haji-Ioannou v. Frangos* [1999] 2 Lloyd's Rep. 337 (C.A.).

11–079   But Article 4 is expressly subject to Article 16 which provides that in five circumstances the courts of specified Contracting States shall have exclusive jurisdiction "regardless of domicile". These cases are discussed in connection with Rules 29[91] and 114[92] and it is sufficient at this point to indicate that the English court will not have jurisdiction, even as regards a non-domiciliary of any Contracting State,[93] in the following cases: (1) in proceedings which have as their object rights *in rem* in, or tenancies of, immovable property, where the property is situated in another Contracting State; (2) in proceedings which have as their object the validity of the constitution, the nullity or the dissolution of companies or other legal persons or associations of natural or legal persons, or the decision of their organs, where the company, legal person or association has its seat in another Contracting State; (3) in proceedings which have as their object the validity of entries in public registers, where the register is kept in another Contracting State; (4) in proceedings concerned with the registration or validity of patents, trade marks, designs or other similar rights required to be deposited, where the deposit or registration has been applied for or taken place (or deemed to have taken place) in another Contracting State; (5) in proceedings concerned with the enforcement of judgments, where the judgment has been or is to be enforced in another Contracting State.

11–080   Article 17 contains rules relating to clauses conferring jurisdiction on the courts of a Contracting State, which are discussed in detail below.[94] Where they apply the chosen court or courts will have exclusive jurisdiction. If one at least of the parties is domiciled in a Contracting State, the English court will not have jurisdiction under this Rule if the parties have validly conferred exclusive jurisdiction on the courts of another Contracting State. If neither of the parties is domiciled in a Contracting State and the parties have conferred jurisdiction on the courts of a Contracting State other than the United Kingdom the English court may not exercise jurisdiction unless the chosen court has declined jurisdiction.[95]

Rule 24 is also subject to Rules 53 and 54, which deal with jurisdiction under international conventions incorporated by statute. Under these conventions presence is not a sufficient basis of jurisdiction.

11–081   The jurisdiction under this Rule remains operative even if the defendant leaves the country, so far as the original claim is concerned, but the claimant cannot amend by adding a new claim unless permission to serve the amended claim form out of the jurisdiction is obtainable.[96]

The application of this Rule differs according as to whether the defendant is an individual, a partnership firm, or a corporation.

11–082   *Individuals.* Any individual who is present in England is liable to be served with process in proceedings *in personam*, however short may be the period for which he is present in England. Thus an American who has flown from New York to London and intends to leave on the same day is liable to be served with process in proceedings brought to recover a debt due to the claimant

---

[91] *Post*, para. 11–153.
[92] *Post*, para. 23R–021.
[93] Even if he purports to submit to the jurisdiction: Art. 18.
[94] *Post*, Rule 32.
[95] In such a case it may be that the English court would initially assume jurisdiction under this Rule, subject to an application for a stay under Rule 31.
[96] *Cf.* cases at para. 11–129, n. 38, *post*; Restatement, s.26.

incurred by the American and payable in New York. No doubt in some cases the exercise of such a jurisdiction may be exorbitant,[97] and it has been contended that process cannot rightly be served on a foreigner who is not strictly speaking resident in England.[98] But temporary presence as a basis of jurisdiction was emphatically affirmed by the Court of Appeal[99] and has the support of weighty dicta by Lord Russell of Killowen.[1] The history of English procedure bears out this view; the right of an English court to entertain an action depended originally upon a defendant being served in England with the King's writ, and this again was only part of the general doctrine that any person whilst in England owed at least temporary allegiance to the King. But the court has a discretion to refuse to entertain proceedings if to do so might work injustice, where, for example, the claim is contested and the case has no connection with England.[2]

As will be seen below, a foreign corporation or partnership firm which **11–083** carries on business in England is amenable to the jurisdiction of the court. The question therefore arises whether the court has jurisdiction to entertain proceedings *in personam* against an individual who is not in England, but who carries on business in England. The effect of R.S.C. Order 81, r. 9 (reproduced in the Civil Procedure Rules 1998, Sched. 1) is that an individual foreigner trading within the jurisdiction but resident outside the jurisdiction may be served with process at his place of business within the jurisdiction. It had been held under the wording as it was prior to amendment as from 1987, that the rules relating to service on a partnership (which allow service at the principal place of business within the jurisdiction) did not apply to an individual trading as a firm who resided out of the jurisdiction but who carried on business within the jurisdiction through a branch.[3] This anomalous distinction between foreign individual traders and foreign partnerships has been removed. But it would seem that if the foreigner carries on business in his own name this jurisdiction cannot be exercised.[4] This is not likely to be of practical importance since it is not easy to envisage a cause of action arising out of the operation of the business which would not come within one of the heads of jurisdiction under Order 11, r. 1(1), *i.e.* Rule 27.

---

[97] The United States Supreme Court has held that the transient jurisdiction rule, as it is called in the United States, is not contrary to the due process clause of the Constitution: *Burnham v. Superior Court of California*, 495 U.S. 604 (1990) (an inter-State, and not an international, case) on which see Collins (1991) 107 L.Q.R. 10; Hay, 1990 U.Ill.L.Rev. 593.

[98] See also Ehrenzweig, 65 Yale L.J. 289 (1956).

[99] *Colt Industries Inc. v. Sarlie* [1966] 1 W.L.R. 440 (C.A.); *Maharanee of Baroda v. Wildenstein* [1972] 2 Q.B. 283 (C.A.). Art. 3(2) assumes that the rule is part of English law, and it was accepted as such in *Adams v. Cape Industries plc* [1990] Ch. 433, 518 (C.A.).

[1] See *Carrick v. Hancock* (1895) 12 T.L.R. 59, 60. See also *Forbes v. Simmons* (1914) 20 D.L.R. 100 (Alta.); *Laurie v. Carroll* (1958) 98 C.L.R. 310, 323. Where a man has been brought by force of law from one Canadian province to another, or from one Australian state to another, service of process on him in the second province or state has been held to be good: *Doyle v. Doyle* (1974) 52 D.L.R. (3d) 143 (Newf.); *John Sanderson Ltd. v. Giddings* [1976] V.R. 421; *Baldry v. Jackson* [1976] 1 N.S.W.L.R. 19, affd. on different grounds [1976] 2 N.S.W.L.R. 415. Should, however, a foreigner be fraudulently enticed within the jurisdiction, that may be a good reason for setting aside service; see *Stein v. Valkenhuysen* (1858) E.B. & E. 65; *Watkins v. North American Lands, etc. Co.* (1904) 20 T.L.R. 534 (H.L.); *Perrett v. Robinson* [1985] 1 Qd.R. 83.

[2] See Rule 31, *post.*

[3] *St. Gobain, etc. v. Hoyermann's Agency* [1893] 2 Q.B. 96 (C.A.).

[4] Cases cited [1893] 2 Q.B. at p. 103.

11–084   The Civil Procedure Rules 1998 provide for a number of alternative methods of service within the jurisdiction.[5] The methods include: personal service, *i.e.* leaving the document with the person to be served; service by first class post to the usual or last known residence of the person to be served; service through a document exchange or by fax. It is not necessary that the defendant be in England when the process is issued, but he must be in England when it is served.[6]

11–085   Where it appears to the court that there is a good reason to authorise service by a method not permitted by the rules, the court may order service to be effected by an alternative method,[7] or, as it was previously known, by a method of substituted service. In 1915, Lord Reading summed up the law on when substituted service will be allowed in the following three propositions[8]: (1) "The general rule is that an order for substituted service of writ of summons within the jurisdiction cannot be made in any case in which, at the time of the issue of the writ, there could not be at law a good personal service of the writ because the defendant is not within the jurisdiction." (2) "This general rule is not applied where the court is satisfied that the defendant went outside the jurisdiction before the issue of the writ in order to evade the service of the writ within it." (3) "If the defendant went out of the jurisdiction after the issue of the writ, although not for the purpose of evading service, substituted service may be allowed if the court is satisfied that the issue of the writ came to his knowledge before he went outside the jurisdiction and special circumstances show that such substituted service would be just." Thus, in this last exceptional situation, the court in effect exercises jurisdiction over a defendant who is in England at the time of the *issue* of process as though he were in England at the time for the *service* of process.[9]

11–086   Lord Reading's second proposition was rejected by the High Court of Australia[10] after a comprehensive and detailed review of the English authorities. The court set aside an order for substituted service which had been made because the defendant had left the jurisdiction the day before the writ was issued in order to evade service. The court pointed out that Lord Reading's second proposition was not supported by the cases which he cited; and that he could hardly have meant that a complete stranger to the jurisdiction who comes in for the most temporary purpose remains liable to its exercise by substituted service if, but only if, his motive in leaving was to avoid personal service.[11] The court also observed that Lord Reading's view was "open to the objection, first, that it departs altogether from the principles upon which the exercise of English jurisdiction in actions *in personam* rests; secondly, that it cannot be reconciled with the doctrine, that where the writ may not be served personally, an order for substituted service may not be made; thirdly, that it

---

[5] CPR, Pt. 6 and Practice Direction.

[6] Where process is served by post, it is deemed to be served the second day after it was posted: CPR 6.7. For the position when the defendant is abroad when the process is received, but subsequently returns to England see *Barclays Bank of Swaziland Ltd. v. Hahn* [1989] 1 W.L.R. 506 (H.L.); *India Videogram Ltd. v. Patel* [1991] 1 W.L.R. 173.

[7] CPR 6.8.

[8] *Porter v. Freudenberg* [1915] 1 K.B. 857, 887–888 (C.A.).

[9] *Jay v. Budd* [1898] 1 Q.B. 12 (C.A.); *Trent Cycle Co. v. Beattie* (1899) 15 T.L.R. 176 (C.A.).

[10] *Laurie v. Carroll* (1958) 98 C.L.R. 310, applied in *Mondial Trading Pty. Ltd. v. Interocean Marine Transport Inc.* (1985) 65 A.L.R. 155.

[11] At pp. 325–327, 329–332.

ignores the implications of Order 11, r. 1(1) [*i.e.* Rule 27]; fourthly, that it does not involve a matter of procedure but an extension of jurisdiction."[12]

In *Myerson v. Martin*[13] the Court of Appeal refused to allow substituted service of a writ issued for service within the jurisdiction where the defendant was outside the jurisdiction at the date of the issue of the writ. Lord Denning M.R. rested his decision on the ground that substituted service was not possible in the circumstances; Waller and Eveleigh L.JJ. thought that the court had a jurisdiction to order substituted service, but that it should not be exercised in the circumstances. It is submitted that the view of the High Court of Australia and of Lord Denning M.R. is the preferable one, and that there is no jurisdiction to order service by an alternative method of process for service within the jurisdiction[14] on a defendant who was outside the jurisdiction at the time of issue.   **11–087**

Partnerships.[15] Process can be served as of right on any individual who is in England at the time of service; and the fact that the defendant is a member of a partnership firm is no exception to this rule. But, before 1891, process could not be served as of right on any partnership firm which carried on business in England if the partners were not in England at the time for the service of the process and did not submit to the jurisdiction.[16] To meet the inconvenience arising out of this situation, the Rules of the Supreme Court were changed in that year, and the relevant rule now provides as follows[17]: " . . . any two or more persons claiming to be entitled, or alleged to be liable, as partners in respect of a cause of action and carrying on business [in England] may sue, or be sued, in the name of the firm (if any) of which they were partners at the time when the cause of action accrued."   **11–088**

This rule appears at first sight to do little more than allow and regulate "claims by and against firms" and not to touch the extent of the court's jurisdiction. But it had in reality a wider effect than this, at any rate as regards proceedings *against* partnerships, and in such proceedings may extend the jurisdiction of the court over defendants who are absent from England. For the Civil Procedure Rules[18] provide, in claims against a firm carrying on business in England in a firm name, a mode of serving process at the firm's principal or last known place of business in England which is applicable whether the partners are in England or not. Hence, under the rule, the court has jurisdiction to entertain proceedings against persons who are not in England.   **11–089**

The following points deserve notice.

(1) The rule applies only to partners carrying on business in England, and carrying it on under a firm name.[19] Otherwise it is necessary to sue each   **11–090**

---

[12] At p. 332.

[13] [1979] 1 W.L.R. 1390 (C.A.).

[14] For service by an alternative method of process for service out of the jurisdiction, see *post*, para. 11–121, n. 14.

[15] On the question whether a foreign entity is a corporation or a partnership, see *Von Hellfeld v. Rechnitzer* [1914] 1 Ch. 748 (C.A.); *Oxnard Financing S.A. v. Rahn* [1998] 1 W.L.R. 1496 (C.A.).

[16] *Russell v. Cambefort* (1889) 23 Q.B.D. 526 (C.A.), *Western National Bank v. Perez* [1891] 1 O.B. 304 (C.A.).

[17] Ord. 81, r. 1 (in CPR, Sched. 1).

[18] CPR 6.4(5), 6.5(6), and PD6, para. 4.

[19] *Von Hellfeld v. Rechnitzer* [1914] 1 Ch. 748 (C.A.); *Nova v. Grove* (1982) 140 D.L.R. (3d) 527 (Alta. C.A.). As to when business is carried on in England see *Grant v. Anderson* [1892] 1 Q.B. 108 (C.A.); *Singleton v. Roberts & Co.* (1894) 70 L.T. 687; and *post*, paras. 11–100 *et seq.*

partner, naming them separately in the claim form, which must be served in the ordinary way in England or by permission of the court under Order 11 (*i.e.* Rule 27) elsewhere.

11–091   (2) It extends to a firm, all or any of whose members are foreigners. "If the firm carries on business [in England], then whether it is an English or a foreign firm, and whether it also carries on business in a colony or abroad or not, a writ may be issued against the partners in the firm name without leave . . . "[20]

11–092   (3) The effect of the Civil Procedure Rules is that process may be served at the principal place of business of the partnership on any person who, at the time of service, has the control or management of the partnership business there, or by post or by fax to that place. In such cases, process is duly served on the firm, whether or not any member of the firm is outside England. Thus, process cannot be served on the firm abroad[21] unless permission is given under Order 11, *i.e.* Rule 27.[22] If the firm is duly served in England, permission may be given to serve a partner outside England under Order 11, r. 1(1)(*c*), *i.e.* Rule 27(3), on the ground that he is a necessary or proper party to the claim.[23]

11–093   (4) In proceedings against a firm in the firm name, execution can as a rule issue only against the property of the partnership which is in England or against the property in England of partners who are served in England or who submit to the jurisdiction of the court by acknowledging service as partners or who are served abroad by permission of the court under Order 11, *i.e.* Rule 27.[24] Thus the private property in England of a partner outside England is protected from execution, unless he acknowledges service or service out of the jurisdiction is allowed under Order 11.[25]

11–094   *Corporations.*[26]   In this case also presence in England at the time of service is enough to give the court jurisdiction. This principle applies easily enough where the defendant is an individual, since the question whether a man is at a given moment in England is easily answered; but when the defendant is a corporate body, some difficulty may arise in determining whether the corporation can be treated as being present in England, since the presence of a corporation is to some extent a fiction.

11–095   In the case of a company registered in England under the Companies Act 1985, or any other Act, no difficulty arises. Even if the company is formed to carry on business abroad, nevertheless it is present in England by virtue of its incorporation here, and service of process can always be effected by leaving it at, or sending it by post to, the registered office of the company in England.[27] If a company registered in Scotland carries on business in England, process of any court in England may be served[28] on it by leaving it at or

---

[20] *Worcester, etc., Banking Co. v. Firbank* [1894] 1 Q.B. 784, 788 (C.A.).

[21] *Von Hellfeld v. Rechnitzer* [1914] 1 Ch. 748 (C.A.).

[22] *Hobbs v. Australian Press Association* [1933] 1 K.B. 1 (C.A.). Contrast *Dobson v. Festi, Rasini & Co.* [1891] 2 Q.B. 92 (C.A.), decided before the rules were altered in June 1891.

[23] *West of England Steamship Owners' Association v. John Holman & Sons* [1957] 3 All E.R. 421n. Alternatively, the claimant may sue all the partners individually "trading as. . . . " (the firm name), *ibid.*

[24] Ord. 81, r. 5.

[25] See *Lindsay v. Crawford and Lindsays* (1911) 45 Ir.L.T. 52. So as regards charging orders: *Brown, Janson & Co. v. Hutchinson & Co.* [1895] 1 Q.B. 737.

[26] See generally Fawcett (1988) 37 I.C.L.Q. 645.

[27] s.725(1). See *Addis Ltd. v. Berkeley Supplies Ltd.* [1964] 1 W.L.R. 943.

[28] But *jurisdiction*, as distinct from service, will depend on the modified version of the 1968 Convention in 1982 Act, Sched. 4.

sending it by post to the principal place of business of the company in England, addressed to the manager or head officer there,[29] and a copy of the process must be sent to the registered office in Scotland.[30] In addition, under the Civil Procedure Rules 1998, a company registered in England may be served at its principal office, or at any place of business within the jurisdiction which has a real connection with the claim.[31]

The position with regard to foreign companies is more complex. A com-   **11–096**
pany incorporated outside the United Kingdom and Gibraltar which has a branch in England must file with the Registrar of Companies a return containing particulars (*inter alia*) of the names and addresses of all persons resident in Great Britain authorised to accept on the company's behalf service of process in respect of the business of the branch.[32] Accordingly, process may be served on such person[33] in respect of the carrying on of the business of the branch.[34]

Where the foreign company has a place of business which is not a branch,[35]   **11–097**
the position is as follows. A company incorporated outside Great Britain which establishes a place of business in Great Britain must file with the Registrar of Companies the name and address of a person resident in Great Britain authorised to accept service of process on behalf of the company.[36] Process is sufficiently served if it is addressed to the person whose name appears on the file.[37] If a company to which these provisions apply defaults in the obligation to register the names of persons authorised to accept service, or if the person named dies or ceases to reside in Great Britain or refuses to accept service on behalf of the company or for any reason cannot be served,[38] the process may be served by leaving it at or sending it by post to any place of business established by the company in Great Britain.[39] If the company has ceased to carry on business in England, process cannot be served by leaving it at a former place of business.[40] But it may be served on a person authorised to accept service, even if he is no longer present or resident in England, by being addressed to him and left at the address last notified.[41]

---

[29] s.725(2).

[30] s.725(3).

[31] CPR 6.2(2)(a), 6.5(6).

[32] Companies Act 1985, s.690A and Sched. 21A, para. 3(e), which were added in 1992 to implement the 11th Company Law Directive 89/666/89.

[33] Where process is addressed to the company itself, rather than to the person named as authorised to accept service, the service is irregular, but may be cured under what is now CPR 3.10: *Boocock v. Hilton International Co.* [1993] 1 W.L.R. 1065 (C.A.).

[34] s.694A(2). In *Saab v. Saudi American Bank* [1998] 1 W.L.R. 937 it was held that the requirement that the process be "in respect of the carrying on of the business of the branch" required it to involve the business of the branch, but not exclusively.

[35] See *post*, para. 11–100 for the meaning of place of business. There is no definition of branch for the purpose of these provisions: *cf.* ss.698(2)(*b*), 699A(3).

[36] s.695(1)(*b*)(ii). This obligation applies to Northern Ireland companies which establish a branch or place of business in Great Britain, since s.690A does not apply to Northern Ireland companies.

[37] s.695(1).

[38] There is no procedure by which a name can be withdrawn from the file without the substitution of a fresh one: Buckley, *Companies Acts*, 14th ed., p. 859. But it appears from *South India Shipping Corp. Ltd. v. Export-Import Bank of Korea* [1985] 1 W.L.R. 585 (C.A.) that a foreign company persuaded the Registrar of Companies to remove its file on the ground that it had registered in error.

[39] ss.694A(3), 695(2).

[40] *Deverall v. Grant Advertising Inc.* [1955] Ch. 111 (C.A.).

[41] *Rome v. Punjab National Bank (No.2)* [1989] 1 W.L.R. 1211 (C.A.).

11–098   The Civil Procedure Rules 1998 provide that in addition to the methods of service for foreign companies under sections 694A and 695 of the Companies Act 1985, service may be effected at any place of business of the company within the jurisdiction.[42] This provides, it seems, not only an additional mode of service on companies which have complied with the registration requirements of the Companies Act 1985, but also to those foreign companies which carry on business in England without complying with the requirements as to registration of a person authorised to accept service.

11–099   These provisions are exclusively concerned with *service*. If the foreign company is domiciled in a Contracting State which is a party to the 1968 Convention or the Lugano Convention, *jurisdiction* will depend on the provisions of the relevant Convention. In cases outside the Conventions, the cause of action need not be in respect of a transaction effected through the corporation's place of business in England.[43] It may be quite independent,[44] but the lack of connection of the claim with the place of business in England may be a ground for a stay under Rule 31.[45]

11–100   The expression "place of business" is not defined in the Companies Act 1985 or in the Civil Procedure Rules 1998, but it includes a share transfer or share registration office[46] and therefore has a wide meaning. It is clear that, as at common law, the "place" of business must be a fixed and definite one[47]; the activity must have been carried on for a sufficient time for it to be characterised as a business, but nine days were held sufficient in one case at common law.[48] It is not necessary that the activity within the jurisdiction should constitute a substantial part of, or be incidental to, the main objects of the foreign company. In *South India Shipping Corp. Ltd. v. Export-Import Bank of Korea*[49] a foreign bank was held to have been duly served at a place in England where it conducted external relations with other banks and carried

---

[42] CPR 6.2(2)(b), (c); 6.5(6). A "corporation" may also be served at any place within the jurisdiction where it carries on its activities. In relation to service on companies registered in England and Wales, the Rules draw a distinction between companies and other corporations, but no such distinction is made expressly in relation to foreign entities. It is therefore possible that a foreign company may be served at a place (other than a place of business) where it carries on its activities. This is not likely to make any practical difference. Personal service is effected by leaving process with "a person holding a senior position", as enumerated in CPR PD6, para. 6.2.

[43] Except where service is effected under s.690A and Sched. 21A, para. 3(e) (foreign companies with branch in England).

[44] See *South India Shipping Corp. Ltd. v. Export-Import Bank of Korea* [1985] 1 W.L.R. 585 (C.A.), and older authorities, including *Haggin v. Comptoir d'Escompte de Paris* (1889) 23 Q.B.D. 519 (C.A.); *La Bourgogne* [1899] A.C. 431; *Logan v. Bank of Scotland (No. 1)* [1904] 2 K.B. 495 (C.A.); *A/S Dampskib Hercules v. Grand Trunk Pacific Ry. of Canada* [1912] 1 K.B. 222 (C.A.).

[45] *Logan v. Bank of Scotland (No. 2)* [1906] 1 K.B. 152–153; *First National Bank of Boston v. Union Bank of Switzerland* [1990] 1 Lloyd's Rep. 32 (C.A.); contrast *European Asian Bank v. Punjab Bank* [1982] 2 Lloyd's Rep. 356 (C.A.).

[46] s.698; *The Madrid* [1937] P. 40; cf. *A/S Dampskib Hercules v. Grand Trunk Pacific Ry. of Canada* [1912] 1 K.B. 222 (C.A.); and contrast *Badcock v. Cumberland Gap Co.* [1893] 1 Ch. 362, decided at common law.

[47] *The Theodohos* [1977] 2 Lloyd's Rep. 428; *Saccharin Corporation Ltd. v. Chemische Fabrik A.G.* [1911] 2 K.B. 516 (C.A.); *Okura & Co. Ltd v. Forsbacka Jernverks A/B* [1914] 1 K.B. 715 (C.A.).

[48] See *Dunlop Pneumatic Tyre Co. Ltd. v. A.G. Cudell & Co.* [1902] 1 K.B. 342 (C.A.), where the place of business was a stand at an exhibition.

[49] [1985] 1 W.L.R. 585 (C.A.), stated *post*, para. 11–105, Illustration 13. Contrast *National Commercial Bank v. Wimborne* (1979) 11 N.S.W.L.R. 156 (local correspondent bank not place of business of foreign bank).

out preliminary work in relation to granting or obtaining loans, but where it did not conclude any banking transactions.

The business must be that of the corporation. The normal case will be a branch of a foreign corporation, where there will be no doubt that the place of business is that of the corporation.[50] In the overwhelming majority of cases, the corporation will comply with the filing requirements of the Companies Act 1985, and service can be effected in accordance with the provisions of the Act. Accordingly in practice a real problem will normally only arise where the corporation's business is alleged to be carried on by a representative or agent, who is not an officer or employee of the corporation, and who may act as a representative or agent for other corporations in addition. Service may be effected on the representative or agent if the business is that of the corporation, and not solely the business of the representative or agent who acts for it in England. Where the representative or agent has power to make contracts on behalf of the foreign corporation and displays its name on his premises, there will be little difficulty in establishing that the place of business is that of the corporation.[51]   **11–101**

In *Adams v. Cape Industries plc*[52] the Court of Appeal, in a case involving the presence or residence of a corporation in a foreign country for the purpose of the enforcement of a foreign judgment, undertook an exhaustive examination of the old authorities on the presence of a corporation at common law. It concluded that, although the power to contract was of great importance, it was not the only factor, and that the question whether the representative had been carrying on the foreign corporation's business or had been doing no more than carry on his own business would necessitate an investigation of the functions he had been performing and all aspects of the relationship between him and the corporation, including the following: (a) whether or not the fixed place of business from which the representative operated was originally acquired for the purpose of enabling him to act on behalf of the corporation; (b) whether the corporation had directly reimbursed him for (i) the cost of his accommodation at the fixed place of business; (ii) the cost of his staff; (c) what other contribution, if any, the overseas corporation made to the financing of the business carried on by the representative; (d) whether the representative was remunerated by reference to transactions, *e.g.* by commission, or by fixed regular payments or in some other way; (e) what degree of control the corporation exercised over the running of the business conducted by the representative; (f) whether the representative reserved part of his accommodation or part of his staff for conducting business related to the corporation; (g) whether the representative displayed the corporation's name at his premises or on his stationery, and if so, whether he did so in such a way as to indicate that he was a representative of the corporation; (h) what business, if any, the representative transacted as principal exclusively on his own behalf; (i) whether the representative made contracts with customers or other third parties in the name of the corporation, or otherwise in such manner as to bind it; (j) if so, whether the representative required specific authority in advance before binding the corporation to contractual obligations. But the presence of   **11–102**

---

[50] *e.g. South India Shipping Corp. Ltd. v. Export-Import Bank of Korea* [1985] 1 W.L.R. 585 (C.A.); *cf. Newby v. Van Oppen Co.* (1872) L.R. 7 Q.B. 293; *Haggin v. Comptoir d'Escompte de Paris* (1889) 23 Q.B.D. 519 (C.A.).

[51] *Saccharin Corporation Ltd. v. Chemische Fabrik A.G.* [1911] 2 K.B. 516 (C.A.); contrast *Okura & Co. Ltd. v. Forsbacka Jernverks A/B* [1914] 1 K.B. 715 (C.A.).

[52] [1990] Ch. 433, 523–531 (C.A.).

a power to contract on behalf of the foreign corporation was not an exclusive or necessary condition, although it was of great importance and was the principal test.[53]

Illustrations

(1) Individuals

11–103   1. A, an American company, brings proceedings against X, an American, in respect of a debt incurred in New York and serves process on X while X is staying for a few days in a London hotel. The court has jurisdiction.[54]

2. A, an English theatrical agent, brings proceedings against X, an American theatrical agent, claiming damages for breach of contract and other relief. X is domiciled and resident in New York, but he was temporarily present in England for a week until the day before the proceedings were commenced, when he returned to the United States in order to evade service. A obtains an order for service by an alternative method on X's London solicitors. X through his solicitors moves to have the order and the claim form set aside. The court sets them aside.[55]

3. A and X are solicitors practising in Jersey. A comes to England, intending to stay indefinitely, and brings proceedings against X and others claiming damages for conspiracy. At that time, X is in Jersey, but he often comes to England on business. He is in England for a week shortly after the proceedings are commenced, but manages to evade service. A obtains an order for service by an alternative method. The court sets it aside.[56]

(2) Partnerships

11–104   4. Y and Z are residing in Natal. They carry on business under the firm name of X & Co. both in Natal and England. A sues X & Co. upon a promissory note made by Y and Z in Cape Town and payable at their London office, and A brings proceedings against them in the name of X & Co. The court has jurisdiction.[57]

5. A brings proceedings against X & Co., a New York firm carrying on business in New York and having no place of business in England. The three partners of X & Co. are all in the United States. The court has no jurisdiction.[58]

(3) Corporations

11–105   6. X & Co. is a Saudi bank. It establishes a branch in England and registers N, who is resident in England, as the person authorised to accept service. A has a claim against X & Co. which arises (in part) out of the business of the branch. A commences proceedings against X & Co., and serves process on N. The court has jurisdiction.[59]

7. The facts are as in Illustration 6, except that the claim has no connection with the branch, and the claim form is served by leaving it at the branch. The court has jurisdiction.[60]

8. The facts are as in Illustration 7, except that X & Co. is a French bank. Service is valid, but the court has no jurisdiction unless the case falls within one of the clauses of Rule 28.

9. X & Co. is a Panamanian ship-owning company, which has no place of business in England. N, its president, resides in London. A brings proceedings against X & Co. for damage to cargo and serves process on N. The court has no jurisdiction.[61]

10. X & Co. is a Japanese corporation which manufactures goods in Japan. It employs N as sole agent in England. N rents an office in London and is paid by commission. He has authority to make contracts for the sale of X & Co.'s goods. He delivers the goods out of stocks in his office or under his control at public wharves in London. He also acts as agent for another foreign corporation. A brings proceedings against X & Co. claiming damages for breach of contract and serves process on X & Co. by leaving a copy at N's office. The court has jurisdiction.[62]

---

[53] [1990] Ch. 433, 531.
[54] *Colt Industries Inc. v. Sarlie* [1966] 1 W.L.R. 440 (C.A.).
[55] *Cf. Laurie v. Carroll* (1958) 98 C.L.R. 310.
[56] *Myerson v. Martin* [1979] 1 W.L.R. 1390 (C.A.).
[57] *Worcester, etc., Banking Co. v. Firbank* [1894] 1 Q.B. 784 (C.A.); R.S.C., Ord. 81, r. 1.
[58] *Cf. Von Hellfeld v. Rechnitzer* [1914] 1 Ch. 748 (C.A.).
[59] Companies Act 1985, s.690A and Sched. 21A, para. 3(e); *Saab v. Saudi American Bank* [1998] 1 W.L.R. 937.
[60] CPR 6.2(2), 6.5(6). But the defendant may apply for a stay of proceedings: see Rule 31.
[61] *The Theodohos* [1977] 2 Lloyd's Rep. 428.
[62] Companies Act 1985, s.695(2). In this and the succeeding Illustrations it is assumed that X & Co. is not registered as an oversea company under Part XXIII of the Companies Act 1985. *Cf. Saccharin Corporation Ltd. v. Chemische Fabrik A.G.* [1911] 2 K.B. 516 (C.A.).

11. X & Co. is a Polish corporation which manufactures steel in Poland. It employs N & Co. as its sole agents in the United Kingdom. N & Co. also act as agents for other corporations and carry on business as merchants on their own account. They have no general authority to make contracts on behalf of X & Co. but obtain orders and submit them to X & Co. for approval. X & Co. ships the steel direct to purchasers in England. N & Co. receive payment from the purchasers and remit the amount to X & Co. less their agreed commission. A brings proceedings against X & Co. claiming damages for breach of contract and serves X & Co. at N & Co.'s office. The court has no jurisdiction.[63]

12. X & Co. is a Japanese shipping company. It employs N as agent in London for the booking of freight and issue of passenger tickets. N is paid by commission and has no concern with the management of X & Co. The only name appearing on the door of his office is his own name, but on the window of the ground floor his name is exhibited as agent for X & Co. and other shipping companies. A brings proceedings against X & Co. claiming damages in respect of a collision in which one of X & Co.'s ships was involved. The court has no jurisdiction.[64]

13. X & Co., a Korean bank with its main business in Korea, gives a guarantee to A & Co., an Indian corporation, whereby X & Co. guarantees the repayment to A & Co. of advance payments made by A & Co. to N & Co., a Korean company, in connection with shipbuilding contracts entered into between A & Co. and N & Co. The transaction has no connection with England. When N & Co. defaults, A & Co. commences proceedings in 1984 in England against X & Co. and serves process on the London office of X & Co. The representative office had been registered under Part X of the Companies Act 1948 (now Part XXIII of the Companies Act 1985) but the registration was deleted in 1983. The representative office does not conclude any banking transactions in London, but it has premises and staff, it conducts external relations with other banks and financial institutions, and carries out preliminary work in relation to granting or obtaining loans. Process is validly served because these activities make the representative office a place of business within what is now s.695 of the Companies Act 1985.[65]

RULE 25—Subject to Rule 29, the High Court has jurisdiction to entertain a claim *in personam* against a person who submits to the jurisdiction of the court.   11R–106

COMMENT

A person who would not otherwise be subject to the jurisdiction of the court may preclude himself by his own conduct from objecting to the jurisdiction, and thus give the court an authority over him which, but for his submission, it would not possess. This principle is also expressed in Article 18 of the Conventions.[66]   11–107

A person who begins proceedings in general gives the court jurisdiction to entertain a counterclaim against him which may extend to cases in which, if separate proceedings were to be brought, permission to serve process under Order 11, r. 1(1), *i.e.* Rule 27, might not be obtainable.[67] Although it is   11–108

---

[63] *Okura & Co. Ltd. v. Forsbacka Jernverks A/B* [1914] 1 K.B. 715 (C.A.).

[64] Cf. *The Lalandia* [1933] P. 56.

[65] *South India Shipping Corp. Ltd. v. Export-Import Bank of Korea* [1985] 1 W.L.R. 585 (C.A.).

[66] *Post*, para. 11–346.

[67] *Republic of Liberia v. Gulf Oceanic Inc.* [1985] 1 Lloyd's Rep. 539, 544, 547 (C.A.); *Metal Scrap Trade Corp. Ltd. v. Kate Shipping Co. Ltd.* [1990] 1 W.L.R. 115, 130 (H.L.); *Balkanbank v. Taher (No. 2)* [1995] 1 W.L.R. 1067 (C.A.) (application for worldwide *Mareva* injunction under 1982 Act, s.25 an "action" for purposes of defendant's counterclaim). See also *Derby & Co. Ltd. v. Larsson* [1976] 1 W.L.R. 202, 205 (H.L.). It has been held that a defendant added on the application, not of the plaintiff, but of other defendants, was entitled to counterclaim against a foreign plaintiff notwithstanding that it would not have been possible to obtain leave to serve the plaintiff under Order 11, r. 1(1), *i.e.* Rule 27, if the plaintiff had been sued in a separate action: *Union Bank of the Middle East v. Clapham* (1981) 125 S.J. 862 (C.A.); *sed quaere. Cf. Soc. Commerciale de Réassurance v. Eras International Ltd. (No.2)* [1995] 2 All E.R. 78 (foreign plaintiff may be subject to claim by third party). Mere appearance as claimant in interpleader proceedings is not submission to the jurisdiction: see *Eschger & Co. v. Morrison, Kekewich & Co.* (1890) 6 T.L.R. 145 (C.A.).

sometimes said that it is not necessary that the counterclaim be related to the claim,[68] the true principle is that a counterclaim is allowed so that justice can be done as between the parties.[69] In English law this principle is given effect by the rule that the court may require a counterclaim to be disposed of separately.[70]

11–109 A person who appears voluntarily after service on him submits to the jurisdiction, even though he is out of England at the time of issue and service of the process. He may, for instance, instruct his solicitor to accept service on his behalf; and the Civil Procedure Rules 1998 provide that where a solicitor is authorised to accept service on behalf of a party, in principle process must be served on the solicitor.[71] But the solicitor may accept service of proceedings on the basis that the defendant remains free to contest the jurisdiction in the same way as if the claimant had obtained permission to serve abroad and had effected service abroad.[72] If the defendant instructs his solicitor to accept service and the solicitor communicates those instructions to the claimant, the defendant will be regarded as having submitted, even if the instructions are withdrawn.[73]

11–110 A defendant who wishes to dispute the jurisdiction of the court to try the claim, or to argue that the court should not exercise its jurisdiction, must file an acknowledgment of service and apply to the court for an order declaring that it has no jurisdiction or should not exercise any jurisdiction which it may have. The application must be made within the period for filing a defence.[74] It is provided that a defendant who acknowledges service does not, by doing so, lose any right to dispute the court's jurisdiction, unless he fails to make an application within the period for filing a defence.[75] If the court does not make a declaration that it has no jurisdiction or will not exercise its jurisdiction, the acknowledgment of service ceases to have effect and the defendant has a further period in which to file a further acknowledgment of service; if the defendant then files a further acknowledgment of service, he is to be treated

---

[68] See, *e.g.* Restatement, s.34.

[69] *Griendtoveen v. Hamlyn & Co.* (1892) 8 T.L.R. 231; *Factories Insurance Co. Ltd. v. Anglo-Scottish General Commercial Insurance Co. Ltd.* (1913) 29 T.L.R. 312. See also *South African Republic v. Compagnie Franco-Belge du Chemin de Fer du Nord* [1897] 2 Ch. 487, 492 (C.A.), [1898] 1 Ch. 190; *High Commissioner for India v. Ghosh* [1960] 1 Q.B. 134, 141 (C.A.) (state immunity cases, now governed by State Immunity Act 1978, s.2(6), which expressly provides that the counterclaim must arise out of the same legal relationship or facts as the claim); *National Commercial Bank v. Wimborne* (1979) 11 N.S.W.L.R. 156, 169–176, approved in *Marlborough Harbour Board v. Charter Travel Co.* (1989) 18 N.S.W.L.R. 223, 232. See now Art. 6(3), 1968 Convention and Lugano Convention.

[70] CPR 3.1(2)(e), 20.9. *Cf. Republic of Liberia v. Gulf Oceanic Inc.* [1985] 1 Lloyd's Rep. 539 (C.A.); *Metal Scrap Trade Corp. v. Kate Shipping Co. Ltd.* [1990] 1 W.L.R. 115 (H.L.).

[71] CPR 6.4(2). An agreement to accept service is not *per se* a waiver in advance of any irregularity (such as failure to serve in time): *Caribbean Gold Ltd. v. Alga Shipping Ltd.* [1993] 1 W.L.R. 1100. On acceptance of service induced by misrepresentation, see *Beecham Group plc v. Norton Healthcare Ltd.* [1997] F.S.R. 81, 88.

[72] *Sphere Drake Insurance plc v. Gunes Sikorta* [1988] 1 Lloyd's Rep. 139 (C.A.).

[73] *Manta Line v. Sofianites* [1984] 1 Lloyd's Rep. 14 (C.A.). *Cf. Carmel Exporters (Sales) Ltd. v. Sea-Land Services Inc.* [1981] 1 W.L.R. 1068, 1077–1078; *Broken Hill Pty. Co. Ltd. v. Xenakis* [1982] 2 Lloyd's Rep. 304.

[74] CPR 11(1), (4).

[75] CPR 11(3), (5). *Cf. The Messiniaki Tolmi* [1984] 1 Lloyd's Rep. 266 (C.A.). A request for an extension of time to file a defence does not prevent an application under CPR 11(1): *ISC Technologies Ltd. v. Guerin*, 1990, unreported, cited in *Kurz v. Stella Musical GmbH* [1992] Ch. 196.

as having accepted that the court has jurisdiction to try the claim.[76] These rules give expression to the general principle that a person who appears merely to contest the jurisdiction of the court does not thereby submit.[77] In order to establish that the defendant has, by his conduct in the proceedings, submitted or waived his objection to the jurisdiction, it must be shown that he has taken some step which is only necessary or only useful if the objection has been waived or never been entertained at all.[78]

Submission has been inferred when the defendant applied to strike out part **11–111** of the claim endorsed on a writ.[79] It has also been inferred when the defendant filed affidavits and appeared through counsel to argue the merits[80] on the plaintiff's application for an injunction; or when the defendant consented *inter partes* to the continuance of a *Mareva* injunction without reserving his right to contest the jurisdiction[81]; when he moved to set aside a default judgment and at the same time applied for an order that the plaintiff deliver a statement of claim[82]; and when he applied for an order for security for costs.[83] The clear trend of the modern authorities is that the defendant will not be regarded as having submitted by making an application in the proceedings, provided that he has specifically reserved his objection to the jurisdiction.[84]

Submission may also be inferred from the terms of a contract. At common **11–112** law, the mere agreement of the parties that the High Court was to have jurisdiction to determine disputes arising out of a contract between them was insufficient by itself to give the court jurisdiction, because the defendant could not be legally served with process if he was out of England.[85] But if one party to the contract nominated an agent resident in England to accept service of process on his behalf, he was deemed to submit to the jurisdiction, and service

---

[76] CPR 11(7), (8). R.S.C., Ord. 12, r. 8, which is replaced by CPR 11, did not apply to applications for a stay of proceedings (as distinct from applications to set aside service), and it was held that an application for a stay of proceedings was not to be regarded as a submission if it were made as an alternative to an application for the proceedings to be set aside on the basis that the court had no jurisdiction: *Williams & Glyn's Bank v. Astro Dinamico* [1984] 1 W.L.R. 438 (H.L.). It has also been held that an application for a stay under what is now Arbitration Act 1996, s.9, *post*, Rule 58, is not a submission: *Finnish Marine Co. Ltd. v. Protective National Insurance Co.* [1990] 1 Q.B. 1078.

[77] *Re Dulles' Settlement (No. 2)* [1951] Ch. 842 (C.A.).

[78] *Rein v. Stein* (1892) 66 L.T. 469, 471, *per* Cave J., affd. [1892] 1 Q.B. 753, approved in *Williams & Glyn's Bank v. Astro Dinamico* [1984] 1 W.L.R. 438, 444 (H.L.); *Air Nauru v. Niue Airlines Ltd.* [1993] 2 N.Z.L.R. 632; *cf. Laurie v. Carroll* (1958) 98 C.L.R. 310, 335–336.

[79] *The Messiniaki Tolmi* [1984] 1 Lloyd's Rep. 266 (C.A.).

[80] *Boyle v. Sacker* (1888) 39 Ch.D. 249 (C.A.). But not merely where the purpose was to seek to have a *Mareva* injunction discharged: *Obikoga v. Silvernorth Ltd., The Times*, July 6, 1983.

[81] *Esal Ltd. v. Pujara* [1989] 2 Lloyd's Rep. 479 (C.A.), distinguishing *Obikoga v. Silvernorth Ltd., The Times*, July 6, 1983. *Cf. The Xing Su Hai* [1995] 2 Lloyd's Rep. 15 (compliance with disclosure order not a submission when made subject to reservation as to jurisdiction).

[82] *Fry v. Moore* (1889) 23 Q.B.D. 395 (C.A.). *Cf. Ngcobo v. Thor Chemical Holdings Ltd., The Times*, November 10, 1995 (C.A.) (service of defence after leave to appeal given from judge's refusal to stay: appeal struck out); *Williams v. Society of Lloyd's* [1994] 1 V.R. 274 (request for particulars not a submission).

[83] *Lhoneux Limon & Co. v. Hong Kong Banking Corporation* (1886) 33 Ch.D. 446. But the position will be different if he makes it clear that the application is without prejudice to the objection to the jurisdiction and if the application is limited to the costs of the challenge to the jurisdiction: see *Hewden Stuart Heavy Cranes Ltd. v. Leo Gottwald*, unrep., 1992 (C.A.) (a case on Art. 18, 1968 Convention, *post*, paras. 11–094 *et seq.*); *cf. Catalyst Research Corp. v. Medtronic Inc.* (1982) 131 D.L.R. (3d) 767 (Fed. C.A.).

[84] *Williams & Glyn's Bank v. Astro Dinamico, supra; Esal Ltd. v. Pujara, supra; Catalyst Research Corp. v. Medtronic Inc., supra.*

[85] See *British Wagon Co. v. Gray* [1896] 1 Q.B. 35 (C.A.). The actual decision would now be different because of Ord. 11, r. 1(1)(*d*)(iv): see Rule 32(1).

could be effected on the agent in accordance with the contract.[86] This rule of the common law is confirmed by CPR 6.15,[87] which gives effect to the principle that the parties to a contract may agree that the High Court shall have jurisdiction to determine any dispute between them, and also provides machinery for serving the process in the manner laid down in the contract.[88] But there is an important distinction between the case where the mode of serving the process specified in the contract involves service in England, and the case where it involves service abroad. In the former case, service may be effected as of right without special leave. But in the latter case permission must be obtained for the service of process out of England, unless of course the defendant submits to the jurisdiction in some other way; but permission will normally be granted under Order 11, r. 1(1)(*d*)(iv), *i.e.* Rule 27(4), and under any other clause of Rule 27 which may be applicable.[89]

11–113   In *Employers' Liability Assurance Corporation v. Sedgwick, Collins & Co.*,[90] three of their Lordships suggested that an overseas company which files the name and address of a person authorised to accept service[91] thereby submits to the jurisdiction of the English courts. But to say that a corporation which, under the threat of a heavy fine, files with the Registrar of Companies the name of a person authorised to accept service of process on its behalf thereby submits to the jurisdiction seems even more artificial than saying that a corporation which establishes a place of business in England is deemed to be present in England. For this reason the jurisdiction of the court over foreign corporations is discussed in connection with Rule 24[92] and not in connection with Rule 25. There is perhaps more justification for saying that a foreign partnership firm which carries on business in England thereby submits to the jurisdiction[93] since in this case no question of a penalty arises. But for reasons of convenience this case also is discussed in connection with Rule 24[94] in order that all the cases on carrying on business in England may be considered together.

11–114   The principle of submission can give the court jurisdiction only to the extent of removing objections thereto which are purely personal to the party submitting, as, for example, that he has not been duly served with process.[95] Submission cannot give the court jurisdiction to entertain proceedings which in itself lies beyond the competence or authority of the court. Thus, even as regards defendants who are not domiciled in a State which is party to the 1968 Convention or the Lugano Convention, submission cannot confer jurisdiction

---

[86] *Tharsis Sulphur Co. v. Société des Métaux* (1889) 58 L.J.Q.B. 435; *Montgomery Jones & Co. v. Liebenthal & Co.* [1898] 1 Q.B. 487 (C.A.); *Reversionary Interest Society Ltd. v. Locking* [1928] W.N. 227.

[87] Previously R.S.C., Ord. 10, r. 3.

[88] An *ad hoc* agreement, not expressly contemplated by CPR 6.15, will also be effective: *Kenneth Allison Ltd. v. Limehouse & Co.* [1992] 2 A.C. 105.

[89] See *post*, Rule 32(1) and, *e.g. The Chaparral* [1968] 2 Lloyd's Rep. 158 (C.A.); *The Vikfrost* [1980] 1 Lloyd's Rep. 560 (C.A.).

[90] [1927] A.C. 95, 104, 107, 114–115.

[91] *Ante*, para. 11–096.

[92] *Ante*, paras. 11–094 *et seq.*

[93] *Hobbs v. Australian Press Association* [1933] 1 K.B. 1, 18 (C.A.).

[94] *Ante*, paras. 11–088 *et seq*

[95] For the purposes of amendment statements of case to add new claims, a foreign defendant who submits should be treated as a party who only came into the proceedings by virtue of service out of the jurisdiction. Accordingly, a new claim can only be added if it is such that, independently of the original claim, permission would be granted to serve out of the jurisdiction: *Beecham Group Ltd. v. Norton Healthcare Ltd.* [1997] F.S.R. 81.

on the English court where the courts of another Contracting State have exclusive jurisdiction under Article 16.[96] The principle of submission does not apply to a suit for divorce[97] or nullity; nor (*semble*) does it apply to proceedings relating to foreign land which the court has no jurisdiction to try[98]; nor to proceedings in magistrates' courts which derive their jurisdiction from statute.[99]

ILLUSTRATIONS

1. A, an English bank, sues X & Co. and Y & Co., Panamanian companies with their **11–115** management in New York. X & Co. and Y & Co. apply for a declaration that the English court has no jurisdiction, and at the same time apply for a stay on the ground that England is not the appropriate forum. The application for a stay is not a submission to the jurisdiction or a waiver of the objection to the jurisdiction because the application for a stay is not inconsistent with the protest to the jurisdiction.[1]

2. A, a U.S. company, sues X & Co., a Panamanian company, in England. X & Co. applies for a declaration that the court has no jurisdiction, and makes a separate application for security for its costs of its jurisdictional application. The application for security for costs is not a submission.[2]

3. X & Co. is a Delaware corporation carrying on business in Pennsylvania and having no place of business in England. A is a company with a registered office in Glasgow, carrying on business in England. There is a contract between A and X & Co. which provides that the parties submit to the jurisdiction of the High Court and that N of London should be the agent of X & Co. to accept service of process on its behalf. A brings an action against X & Co. for breach of contract. Process is served upon N. The court has jurisdiction.[3]

RULE 26—The High Court has jurisdiction to entertain proceedings *in* **11R–116** *personam* **if each claim made therein is one which by virtue of an enactment (other than those mentioned in Rule 27(15), (17), (18), (19)) the court has power to hear and determine notwithstanding that the person against whom the claim is made is not in England or that the wrongful act, neglect or default giving rise to the claim did not take place in England.**[4]

COMMENT[5]

This Rule is based on Order 11, r. 1(2)(*b*). Before the 1982 Act it was the only **11–117** case in which a writ could be served without leave on a defendant out of England in an action *in personam* (as opposed, *e.g.* to a petition in a matrimonial cause[6]). It was originally directed to what is now section 74(6) of and Schedule 4 to the Civil Aviation Act 1982 which was, in its original form, passed in order to implement the Brussels Convention of December 13, 1960, on co-operation for the safety of air navigation.[7] In addition, it applies to

---

[96] *Post*, Rule 29. But the jurisdiction agreement provisions of Art. 17, which also apply in certain circumstances where a defendant is not domiciled in a Contracting State, are subject to the principle of submission: Case 150/80 *Elefanten Schuh GmbH v. Jacqmain* [1981] E.C.R. 1671.

[97] Domicile and Matrimonial Proceedings Act 1973, s.5(2)(3).

[98] Rule 113.

[99] *Forsyth v. Forsyth* [1948] P. 125, 136 (C.A.).

[1] *Cf. Williams & Glyn's Bank v. Astro Dinamico* [1984] 1 W.L.R. 438 (H.L.).

[2] *Cf. Hewden Stuart Heavy Cranes Ltd. v. Leo Gottwald*, unrep., 1992 (C.A.) (a case on Art. 18, 1968 Convention).

[3] *Cf. Tharsis Sulphur Co. v. Société des Métaux* (1889) 58 L.J.Q.B. 435.

[4] Ord. 11, r. 1(2)(*b*).

[5] In CPR, Sched. 1.

[6] *Post*, para. 18–017.

[7] Text in Cmnd. 1373.

actions brought under other legislation implementing international conventions, which are discussed in Chapter 15. It also applies to claims brought under the Protection of Trading Interests Act 1980 to "clawback" awards of multiple damages made by foreign courts.[8] Rule 26 applies to these cases even if the defendant is domiciled in a State party to the 1968 Convention or the Lugano Convention. In the case of the statutes implementing international conventions this is because Article 57 of those Conventions[9] allows United Kingdom courts to assume jurisdiction in accordance with multilateral conventions governing jurisdiction in particular matters notwithstanding that the defendant is domiciled in a Contracting State, whether or not it is a party to the multilateral convention. Proceedings under the Protection of Trading Interests Act 1980 are probably outside the scope of the Conventions since it is doubtful whether claims of the type contemplated by the 1980 Act can be classified as civil or commercial matters.

11–118   Order 11, r. 1(2)(*b*) does not apply to proceedings brought under certain statutes which are already included in Order 11, r. 1(1).[10] Hence the permission of the court must be obtained for service of process out of the jurisdiction in any proceedings falling within those statutes. This is why the words in brackets have been added to the Rule for the sake of clarity, although they do not appear in Order 11, r. 1(2)(*b*).

11–119   Under this Rule, as under Rules 24 and 25, the court exercises jurisdiction *ex debito justitiae* and not, as it does under Rule 27, a discretionary jurisdiction. Where service may be made out of the jurisdiction under this Rule, it is not open to the claimant to rely on Rule 27 if for some reason the jurisdictional requirements under this Rule cannot be met.[11]

11R–120   **RULE 27—The High Court has jurisdiction to entertain a claim *in personam* against a defendant (other than a person domiciled or deemed to be domiciled in another State party to the 1968 Convention or the Lugano Convention[12] or in Scotland or Northern Ireland) who is not in England at the time for the service of process whenever it assumes jurisdiction in any of the cases mentioned in this Rule.[13]**

COMMENT

11–121   If the defendant is not in England and served there with process and does not submit to the jurisdiction, the court has no jurisdiction at common law to entertain a claim *in personam* against him. But this common law principle was modified, first by sections 18 and 19 of the Common Law Procedure Act 1852, and later by the Rules of the Supreme Court, Order 11. Under Order 11 (which is reproduced in Schedule 1 to the Civil Procedure Rules 1998 and supplemented by a Practice Direction) the court has jurisdiction in a number of cases, corresponding to the 21 clauses of this Rule, a discretionary power

---

[8] *Post*, Rule 52.
[9] *Ante*, para. 11–034.
[10] Nuclear Installations Act 1965; Social Security Act 1975 (replaced by Social Security Contributions and Benefits Act 1992); Drug Trafficking Offences Act 1986; Banking Act 1987; Criminal Justice Act 1988; Immigration (Carriers' Liability) Act 1987.
[11] *Cf. Arctic Electronics Co. (U.K.) Ltd. v. McGregor Sea & Air Services Ltd.* [1985] 2 Lloyd's Rep. 510.
[12] For Contracting States see *ante*, paras. 11–006 *et seq.*
[13] R.S.C., Ord. 11, r. 1 (in CPR, Sched. 1); Collins, *Essays*, p. 226. On service of orders made in proceedings see Ord. 11, r. 9(4) and *Union Bank of Finland v. Lelakis* [1997] 1 W.L.R. 590 (C.A.).

to permit service of process[14] on a defendant irrespective of nationality who is out of England. Before these various cases are stated and discussed, the following general points should be noted.

(1) There is an essential difference between the jurisdiction exercised by the court when the defendant is in England (Rule 24) or when he submits to the jurisdiction (Rule 25) and its jurisdiction when the action comes under any of the clauses of Rule 27. Under Rules 24 and 25, the jurisdiction of the court is not discretionary[15]; the claimant has a right to demand that it shall be exercised, though the court has a discretion to stay the action to prevent injustice.[16] But under Rule 27, the jurisdiction of the court is essentially discretionary, for the court may, if it sees fit, decline to allow the service of process, and thus decline to exercise its jurisdiction.

    11–122

(2) Four cardinal points have been emphasised in the decided cases.[17] First, the court ought to be exceedingly careful before it allows process to be served on a foreigner out of England. This has frequently been said to be because service out of the jurisdiction is an interference with the sovereignty of other countries,[18] although today all countries exercise a degree of jurisdiction over

    11–123

---

[14] Substituted service (now called service by an alternative method) may be allowed at the discretion of the court either within or without England: Ord. 11, r. 5(1); see *Ford v. Shepherd* (1885) 34 W.R. 63; *Western, etc., Building Society v. Rucklidge* [1905] 2 Ch. 472. In *The Vrontados* [1982] 2 Lloyd's Rep. 241 (C.A.) it was held by a majority (Lord Denning M.R. dissenting) that service could be effected on directors of a company who were present in England, without an order for substituted service, of a writ for service out of the jurisdiction if the law of the foreign country provided that service on a company was effective if its directors were served: *sed quaere*. See also *The Handgate* [1987] 1 Lloyd's Rep. 142 (C.A.); *The Sky One* [1988] 1 Lloyd's Rep. 238. The mode of service is regulated by Ord. 11, rr. 5–8; there are numerous conventions, of which the most important is the Hague Convention of 1964, Cmnd. 2613. See *The Supreme Court Practice 1999*, notes to Ord. 11, r. 5 and r. 6. For the European Union Convention see *ante*, paras. 8–043 *et seq*. Service must be effected exactly where authorised; thus service in Hong Kong in lieu of Japan is a nullity; *Bonnell v. Preston* (1908) 24 T.L.R. 756 (C.A.). Process may not be served abroad in a manner which is contrary to the law of the foreign country: Ord. 11, r. 5(2), but the court retains a discretion under CPR 3.10 to waive the irregularity: *The Sky One* [1988] 1 Lloyd's Rep. 238; *The Anna* [1994] 2 Lloyd's Rep. 379; *National Commercial Bank v. Haque* [1994] C.L.C. 230 (C.A.); contrast *The Goldean Mariner* [1989] 2 Lloyd's Rep. 390, 398, affd. [1990] 2 Lloyd's Rep. 215 (C.A.); *The Oinoussin Pride* [1991] 1 Lloyd's Rep. 126. On the effect of failure to obtain permission in an appropriate case see *Leal v. Dunlop Bio-Processes Ltd.* [1984] 1 W.L.R. 874 (C.A.); *Atco Industries (Aust.) Pty. Ltd. v. Ancla Maritima S.A.* (1984) 35 S.A.S.R. 408.

[15] But it is discretionary in cases to which CPR 6.15, applies: see *ante*, para. 11–112.

[16] See Rule 31. Although a stay of proceedings is the normal remedy, the court has power to strike out or dismiss the action in appropriate circumstances: *Haji-Ioannou v. Frangos* [1999] 2 Lloyd's Rep. 337 (C.A.).

[17] See, especially for the first three points, *Société Générale de Paris v. Dreyfus Bros.* (1885) 29 Ch.D. 239, 242–243; (1887) 37 Ch.D. 215, 224, 225 (C.A.); *The Hagen* [1908] P. 189, 201 (C.A.); *Re Schintz* [1926] Ch. 710, 716–717 (C.A.).

[18] See, *e.g. George Monro Ltd. v. American Cyanamid Corporation* [1944] K.B. 432, 437 (C.A.); *The Brabo* [1949] A.C. 326, 357; *Mackender v. Feldia* [1967] 2 Q.B. 590, 599 (C.A.); *Derby & Co. Ltd. v. Larsson* [1976] 1 W.L.R. 202, 204 (H.L.); *The Sky One* [1988] 1 Lloyd's Rep. 238, 241 (C.A.). Lord Diplock expressed the view that the jurisdiction under Ord. 11 was an exorbitant one, which ran counter to comity since it was a wider jurisdiction than was recognised in English law as being possessed by courts of foreign countries: *The Siskina v. Distos Compania Naviera S.A.* [1979] A.C. 210, 254; *Amin Rasheed Shipping Corp. v. Kuwait Insurance Co. Ltd.* [1984] A.C. 50, 65; and see also *The Alexandros P.* [1986] Q.B. 464, 478; *Insurance Co. of Ireland v. Strombus International Insurance* [1985] 2 Lloyd's Rep. 138, 146 (C.A.); *Spiliada Maritime Corp. v. Cansulex Ltd.* [1987] A.C. 460, 481. But it is suggested that the jurisdiction exercised under Ord. 11 is not exorbitant, since it is similar to the jurisdiction exercised by many countries, and is also in many respects similar to the rules in the 1968 and Lugano Conventions: see Collins (1991) 107 L.Q.R. 10, 13–14.

persons abroad. Secondly, if there is any doubt in the construction of any of
the heads of Order 11, r. 1(1), that doubt ought to be resolved in favour of the
defendant. Thirdly, since the application for permission is made without
notice to the defendant, a full and fair disclosure of all relevant facts ought to
be made.[19] Fourthly, the court will refuse permission if the case is within the
letter but outside the spirit of the Rule.[20]

11–124   (3) In exercising its jurisdiction under Rule 27 the court will consider, *inter
alia*, whether England is the *forum conveniens*. This principle has been
established since the nineteenth century,[21] and finds its modern expression in
the speeches of Lord Wilberforce in *Amin Rasheed Shipping Corp. v. Kuwait
Insurance Co.*[22] and of Lord Goff of Chieveley in *Spiliada Maritime Corp. v.
Cansulex Ltd.*[23] The claimant must show good reasons why service on a
foreign defendant should be permitted, and in considering this question the
court must take into account the nature of the dispute, the legal and practical
issues involved, such questions as local knowledge, availability of witnesses
and their evidence, and expense. The fundamental question (as it is in cases
of staying of actions on *forum non conveniens* grounds[24]) is to identify the
forum in which the case can suitably be tried for the interests of all the parties
and for the ends of justice. To justify the exercise of the discretion, the
claimant has to show that England is clearly the appropriate forum for the trial
of the action.[25]

11–125   Where the defendant is present in a country which has the civil law system
it is wrong for the English court to compare the relative efficiency of the civil
law and common law procedures for the determination of disputed facts, or to
compare the reputation and standing of the foreign court with the English
court.[26] But the court may take into account that the claimant will be deprived

---

[19] See also *Ellinger v. Guinness Mahon & Co.* [1939] 4 All E.R. 16; *Macaulay (Tweeds) Ltd. v.
Independent Harris Tweed Producers Ltd.* [1961] R.P.C. 184, 193–196; *The Nimrod* [1973] 2
Lloyd's Rep. 91, 95; *G.A.F. Corporation v. Amchem Products Inc.* [1975] 1 Lloyd's Rep. 601,
607–608; *The Hida Maru* [1981] 2 Lloyd's Rep. 510 (C.A.); *Electric Furnace Co. v. Selas
Corp. of America* [1987] R.P.C. 23 (C.A.); *The Volvox Hollandia* [1988] 2 Lloyd's Rep. 361,
372, (C.A.); *Trafalgar Tours Ltd. v. Henry* [1990] 2 Lloyd's Rep. 298 (C.A.); *Newtherapeutics
Ltd. v. Katz* [1991] Ch. 226; *The Olib* [1991] 2 Lloyd's Rep. 108; *ABCI v. Banque Franco-
Tunisienne* [1996] 1 Lloyd's Rep. 485, affd. [1997] 1 Lloyd's Rep. 531 (C.A.); *ANCAP v.
Ridgley Shipping Inc.* [1996] 1 Lloyd's Rep. 570.
[20] *Johnson v. Taylor Bros.* [1920] A.C. 144, 153; *Rosler v. Hilbery* [1925] Ch. 250, 259–260
(C.A.); *George Monro Ltd. v. American Cyanamid Corporation* [1944] K.B. 432, 437, 442
(C.A.); *Beck v. Value Capital Ltd. (No. 2)* [1975] 1 W.L.R. 6, affd. [1976] 1 W.L.R. 572n.
(C.A.).
[21] See *post*, Rule 31(3).
[22] [1984] A.C. 50.
[23] [1987] A.C. 460.
[24] See Rule 31(1), (2), *post*.
[25] [1987] A.C. at 480–482. See also *The Handgate* [1987] 1 Lloyd's Rep. 142 (C.A.); *Islamic
Arab Insurance Co. v. Saudi Egyptian American Reinsurance Co.* [1987] 1 Lloyd's Rep. 315
(C.A.); *E.I. du Pont de Nemours v. Agnew* [1987] 2 Lloyd's Rep. 585, 588–589 (C.A.);
Roneleigh Ltd. v. MII Exports Inc. [1989] 1 W.L.R. 619 (C.A.); *Metall und Rohstoff A.G. v.
Donaldson Lufkin & Jenrette Inc.* [1990] 1 Q.B. 391, 482–489 (C.A.); *The Goldean Mariner*
[1989] 2 Lloyd's Rep. 390, affd. [1990] 2 Lloyd's Rep. 25 (C.A.); *The Oinoussin Pride* [1991]
1 Lloyd's Rep. 126; *Bank of Baroda v. Vysya Bank Ltd.* [1994] 2 Lloyd's Rep. 87; *McConnell
Dowell Constructors Ltd. v. Lloyd's Syndicate 396* [1988] 2 N.Z.L.R. 257. In jurisdictions, such
as New Zealand and Canada, where service outside the jurisdiction is allowed without leave in
specified circumstances, the court retains its discretion to set aside service on the application
of the defendant: see *Kuwait Asia Bank E.C. v. National Mutual Life Nominees Ltd.* [1991] 1
A.C. 187, 217 (P.C.); and other cases cited *post*, para. 12–038, n. 58.
[26] *Amin Rasheed Shipping Corp. v. Kuwait Insurance Co.* [1984] A.C. 50, 65.

of a fair trial in the foreign country, especially for political or racial reasons.[27] Where the claimant has acted reasonably in commencing proceedings in England, and has not acted unreasonably in failing to commence proceedings in the foreign jurisdiction, and would be met by a time bar in the foreign jurisdiction if permission to serve outside the jurisdiction were to be set aside, the court may make it a condition of setting aside permission that the defendant should waive the time bar in the foreign proceedings.[28] If the parties have agreed that the dispute between them shall be referred to the exclusive jurisdiction of a foreign court[29] or to arbitration,[30] permission will normally be refused.

(4) Order 11, r. 4(2), provides that permission to serve out of the jurisdiction **11–126** shall not be granted unless it shall be made "sufficiently to appear" to the court that the case is a proper one for such service. This provision imposes on the claimant the burden of showing good reason why service should in the circumstances be permitted on a foreign defendant.[31]

The claimant must show that he has a cause of action against the defendant **11–127** and that the case falls within one of the heads of jurisdiction in Order 11, r. 1(1). In *Seaconsar Far East Ltd. v. Bank Markazi Iran*[32] the House of Lords, resolving earlier inconsistent authorities, considered the question of the standard of proof which the claimant had to discharge on these questions, and the relationship of the strength of the claimant's case to the issue of *forum conveniens*. It was held that the standard of proof in respect of the cause of action was whether, on the affidavit evidence, there was a serious question to be tried, *i.e.* a substantial question of fact or law, or both, which the claimant *bona fide* desired to have tried. The standard to be applied in considering whether the jurisdiction of the court had been sufficiently established under one or more of the heads of Order 11, r. 1(1) was that of the good arguable case, *i.e.* a strong case for argument.[33] But if the applicability of Order 11, r. 1(1) depends on a question of law or construction, there is no room for the

---

[27] *Oppenheimer v. Louis Rosenthal & Co.* [1937] 1 All E.R. 23 (C.A.); *Ellinger v. Guinness Mahon & Co.* [1939] 4 All E.R. 16. Contrast *Jeyaretnam v. Mahmood, The Times,* May 21, 1992.

[28] *Spiliada Maritime Corp. v. Cansulex Ltd.* [1987] A.C. at 483–484.

[29] *Re Schintz* [1926] Ch. 710 (C.A.); *Mackender v. Feldia* [1967] 2 Q.B. 590 (C.A.). Contrast *Ellinger v. Guinness Mahon & Co.* [1939] 4 All E.R. 16; *Evans Marshall & Co. Ltd. v. Bertola S.A.* [1973] 1 W.L.R. 349 (C.A.); *Re Jogia (A Bankrupt)* [1988] 1 W.L.R. 484. See Rule 32(2), *post.*

[30] *A. & B. v. C. & D.* [1982] 1 Lloyd's Rep. 166, affd. *sub nom. Qatar Petroleum v. Shell International Petroleum* [1983] 2 Lloyd's Rep. 35 (C.A.).

[31] *Amin Rasheed Shipping Corp. v. Kuwait Insurance Co.* [1984] A.C. 50, 72; see also *G.A.F. Corporation v. Amchem Products Inc.* [1975] 1 Lloyd's Rep. 601, 609 (C.A.).

[32] [1994] 1 A.C. 438. In the light of this decision, it is submitted that little assistance can now be derived from the many earlier authorities mentioned in the previous edition of this work, p. 319.

[33] See *Vitkovice Horni a Hutni Tezirstvo v. Korner* [1951] A.C. 869. In *Attock Cement Co. Ltd. v. Romanian Bank for Foreign Trade* [1989] 1 W.L.R. 1147 (C.A.) it was held that, where there is a disputed question of fact which is essential to the applicability of Ord. 11, r. 1(1), the court had to reach a provisional or tentative conclusion that the plaintiff was probably right. It has been held that this test cannot stand with the decision in the *Seaconsar* case: *Agrafax Public Relations Ltd. v. United Scottish Society Inc.* [1995] I.L.Pr. 753 (C.A.); *Canada Trust Co. v. Stolzenberg (No. 2)* [1998] 1 W.L.R. 547 (C.A.). As regards the relevant date for the existence of the factual circumstances to be taken into account see *I.S.C. Technologies Inc. v. Guerin* [1992] 2 Lloyd's Rep. 430 and *B.M.G. Trading Ltd. v. McKay* [1998] I.L.Pr. 691 (C.A.).

application of the test of good arguable case: the court must decide the question on the application to set aside.[34]

11–128   In *Seaconsar Far East Ltd. v. Bank Markazi Iran* the House of Lords also considered the relationship between the standard of proof on the existence of the cause of action and the principle of *forum conveniens*. It disapproved the view that they were inter-related in the sense that the more conspicuous the presence of one element the less consistent with the demands of justice that the other should also be conspicuous.[35] A case particularly strong on the merits could not compensate for a weak case on *forum conveniens*; and a very strong connection with the English forum could not justify a weak case on the merits, if a stronger case on the merits would otherwise be required. The two elements are separate and distinct. The invocation of the principle of *forum conveniens* springs from the often expressed anxiety that great care should be taken in bringing before the English court a foreigner who owes no allegiance here. But if jurisdiction is established under Order 11, r. 1(1), and it is also established that England is the *forum conveniens*, there is no good reason why any particular degree of cogency should be required in relation to the merits of the claimant's case.[36]

11–129   (5) Proceedings may fall at the same time within more than one of the clauses of Rule 27.[37] Thus a claim for the breach of a contract made in England falls within clause (4), but if the contract be a contract affecting land in England, the action falls also within clause (8). But if proceedings fall within one or more of the clauses it is not permissible to litigate any other cause of action which does not fall within one of the clauses.[38] Where permission to serve out of the jurisdiction is based on one cause of action it cannot be treated as permission based on some other cause of action.[39] Nor, if a claim has been put forward on one legal basis, can the claimant subsequently justify leave on another legal basis, unless, perhaps, that other legal basis has been referred to in the evidence in support of the application.[40]

11–130   (6) A defendant who wishes to contest the jurisdiction of the court, either on the ground that the case is not within Order 11, or that the case is not a proper one for the exercise of the discretion, should acknowledge service of

---

[34] *E. F. Hutton & Co. (London) Ltd. v. Mofarrij* [1989] 1 W.L.R. 488 (C.A.); *cf. The Brabo* [1949] A.C. 326; *B.P. Exploration Co. (Libya) Ltd. v. Hunt* [1976] 1 W.L.R. 786; *The Delfini* [1990] 1 Lloyd's Rep. 252 (C.A.); *Kuwait Asia Bank E.C. v. National Mutual Life Nominees Ltd.* [1991] 1 A.C. 187 (P.C.). Contrast *Unilever plc v. Gillette (U.K.) Ltd.* [1989] R.P.C. 583, 602 (C.A.).

[35] *Soc. Commerciale de Réassurance v. Eras International Ltd.* [1992] 1 Lloyd's Rep. 570, 588 (C.A.), *per* Mustill L.J.

[36] [1994] 1 A.C. at 456.

[37] *Tassell v. Hallen* [1892] 1 Q.B. 321, 323–325.

[38] *Holland v. Leslie* [1894] 2 Q.B. 450 (C.A.); *Waterhouse v. Reid* [1938] 1 K.B. 743 (C.A.); *The Siskina v. Distos Compania Naviera S.A.* [1979] A.C. 210, 255. *Cf. Beck v. Value Capital Ltd. (No. 2)* [1975] 1 W.L.R. 6, affd. [1976] 1 W.L.R. 572n. (C.A.); *Tricon Industries Pty. Ltd. v. Abel Lemon & Co. Pty. Ltd.* [1988] 2 Qd.R. 464; *Australian Iron & Steel Pty. v. Jumbo (Curacao) N.V.* (1988) 14 N.S.W.L.R. 507; *David Syme & Co. Ltd. v. Grey* (1992) 38 F.C.R. 303.

[39] *Parker v. Schuller* (1901) 17 T.L.R. 299 (C.A.); *Soc. Commerciale Réassurance v. Eras International Ltd.* [1992] 1 Lloyd's Rep. 570, 613 (C.A.).

[40] *Metall und Rohstoff A.G. v. Donaldson Lufkin & Jenrette Inc.* [1990] 1 Q.B. 391, 436 (C.A.). See also *Excess Insurance Co. Ltd. v. Astra S.A. Insurance and Reinsurance Co.* [1997] C.L.C. 160 (C.A.)

the proceedings, and, within the period for filing a defence, apply to the court for an order declaring that it has no jurisdiction.[41]

1968 Convention and Lugano Convention and intra-United Kingdom jurisdiction. As indicated above,[42] there are a number of cases in which exclusive jurisdiction may be vested in the courts of other Contracting States even though the defendant is not domiciled in a Contracting State. In such a case the English court would not be able to exercise jurisdiction under Order 11, r. 1(1). This will be a rare case since it is not easy to envisage any but the most unlikely circumstances which would both give exclusive jurisdiction to the courts of another Contracting State under Article 16 and also found jurisdiction in England under Order 11, r. 1(1). Cases in which exclusive jurisdiction is given to the courts of another Contracting State under Article 17 and which also come within Order 11, r. 1(1) are easier to imagine. In such cases the English court would not be entitled to assume jurisdiction under, for example, Order 11, r. 1(1)(*d*)(iii), clause (4), on the basis that the contract is governed by English law. But even apart from the Conventions the English court would be reluctant to assume jurisdiction in such a case.[43] Similar considerations apply where the defendant is domiciled in Scotland or Northern Ireland. But the cases of overlap are likely to be even rarer because the cases of exclusive jurisdiction under Article 16 in Schedule 4 to the 1982 Act are narrower than the corresponding Article 16 in the Conventions, and Article 17 in Schedule 4 does not attribute conclusive effect to jurisdiction clauses.[44]   **11–131**

Conversely there will be a number of rare cases in which a defendant domiciled in another Contracting State or in Scotland or Northern Ireland may be sued under Order 11, r. 1(1). These will include cases outside the scope of the Conventions because they are not civil or commercial matters or are otherwise excluded by Article 1 of the Conventions. Examples would be claims to enforce arbitral awards and revenue claims. Both are excluded by Article 1 of the Conventions from their scope, and both may found jurisdiction under Order 11, r. 1(1)[45] over persons not present in England and who are domiciled in another Contracting State or in Scotland or Northern Ireland.   **11–132**

In the rare cases in which Order 11, r. 1(1) will apply to defendants domiciled in Scotland or Northern Ireland, Order 11, r. 4(3) provides that if it appears to the court that there may be a concurrent remedy in Scotland or Northern Ireland, the court, in deciding whether to grant permission, shall have regard to the comparative cost and convenience of proceeding there or in England, and (where that is relevant) to the powers and jurisdiction of the Sheriff Court in Scotland or the county court or courts of summary jurisdiction in Northern Ireland. The object of this rule is to protect persons living in Scotland or Northern Ireland from the inconvenience of an action which, though it might be brought in England, would cause them unnecessary cost.   **11–133**

---

[41] CPR 11(1), (2). See *ante*, para. 11–055.
[42] *Ante*, para. 11–079.
[43] *Ante*, para. 11–125, n. 29.
[44] *Post*, para. 12–109.
[45] Clauses (13) and (14), *post*.

It is not an additional ground for giving permission to serve out of the jurisdiction, but an additional obstacle that the claimant has to surmount.[46]

11R–134   **(1) The court may assume jurisdiction if a remedy is sought against a person domiciled in England.**[47]

COMMENT

11–135   In this clause, which before its amendment in 1983 applied to persons domiciled or ordinarily resident in England, the expression "domiciled" is to be interpreted in accordance with the provisions of sections 41 to 46 of the 1982 Act.[48] The clause applies not only to individuals but also to partnerships and bodies corporate.[49] The term "remedy" in this clause is apparently used in the widest sense and includes the recovery of a debt, or of damages in an action for breach of contract or tort,[50] or an injunction requiring an act abroad.[51] Hence domicile in England is of itself a ground of jurisdiction against a defendant who might otherwise, on account of his absence from England, be exempt from the jurisdiction of the court. If he is domiciled in England he would be put in the same position as a person who is in this country.[52]

11–136   This head of Order 11, r. 1(1) is likely to be of little practical significance, since permission to serve process outside the jurisdiction on a defendant domiciled in England is required only in cases falling outside the scope of the 1968 and Lugano Conventions. If the case falls within either of those Conventions (or within the intra-United Kingdom provisions of Schedule 4 to the 1982 Act) permission to serve out of the jurisdiction is not required.[53]

11R–137   **(2) The court may assume jurisdiction if an injunction is sought ordering the defendant to do or refrain from doing anything in England (whether or not damages are also claimed in respect of a failure to do or the doing of that thing).**[54]

COMMENT

11–138   The injunction need not be the only relief sought, but it must be the substantial relief sought: permission will be refused if the claim for an injunction is not made bona fide, but merely to bring the case within the clause.[55] Permission

---

[46] See *Tottenham v. Barry* (1879) 12 Ch.D. 797; *Kinahan v. Kinahan* (1890) 45 Ch.D. 78; *Washburn, etc., Co. v. Cunard Co.* (1889) 5 T.L.R. 592; *Re De Penny* [1891] 2 Ch. 63; *Williams v. Cartwright* [1895] 1 Q.B. 142 (C.A.); *Macaulay (Tweeds) Ltd. v. Independent Harris Tweed Producers Ltd.* [1961] R.P.C. 184, 192–193.

[47] Ord. 11, r. 1(1)(*a*).

[48] Ord. 11, r. 1(4). See *ante*, Rule 23.

[49] See Interpretation Act 1978, Sched. 1.

[50] See *Hadad v. Bruce* (1892) 8 T.L.R. 409.

[51] *Re Liddell's Settlement* [1936] Ch. 365 (C.A.).

[52] *Ibid.* at p. 374.

[53] See Rule 28, clause (1).

[54] Ord. 11, r. 1(1)(*b*).

[55] Compare *Watson v. Daily Record* [1907] 1 K.B. 853 (C.A.); *De Bernales v. New York Herald* (1893) 68 L.T. 658; [1893] 2 Q.B. 97n. (C.A.); *Alexander & Co. v. Valentine & Sons* (1908) 25 T.L.R. 29 (C.A.); *G.A.F. Corporation v. Amchem Products Inc.* [1975] 1 Lloyd's Rep. 601, 605–606; *Joynt v. McCrum* [1899] 1 I.R. 217.

will also be refused if a foreign court can more conveniently deal with the question,[56] or if there is no real ground to anticipate repetition of the action complained of,[57] or if the injunction cannot be made effective in England.[58] To come within this clause the injunction sought in the action has to be part of the substantive relief to which the claimant's cause of action entitles him, *e.g.* an injunction to restrain a threatened breach of contract.[59]

In *The Siskina*[60] the House of Lords held that this clause cannot be used to found an action, or obtain interim relief, when the only claimed basis of jurisdiction is an interlocutory injunction to restrain a defendant from removing his assets out of the jurisdiction.[61] The same result was reached by the Privy Council in *Mercedes Benz A.G. v. Leiduck*,[62] on the basis that clause (2) applied only to claims advanced in an action and for relief founded on a right asserted by the claimant in that action, to be enforced ultimately through the medium of a judgment given by the court in that action. A *Mareva* injunction in support of proceedings in a foreign court was not such a claim, and therefore service of process claiming a *Mareva* injunction only did not fall within clause (2).   **11–139**

Under the 1968 Convention and the Lugano Convention the courts of a Contracting State may exercise jurisdiction to grant interim relief of this kind even though the courts of another Contracting State have jurisdiction over the substance of the matter,[63] and section 25(1) of the 1982 Act gives the English court power to grant interim relief in such cases within the scope of the 1968 Convention and the Lugano Convention and in intra-United Kingdom cases. This power has been extended under section 25(3) to give the court power to grant interim relief so as to make it exercisable in relation (*inter alia*) to proceedings commenced or to be commenced in non-Contracting States or to proceedings outside the scope of the Conventions. Consequently, the effect of the decisions in *The Siskina* and *Mercedes Benz A.G. v. Leiduck* has been reversed.   **11–140**

A claim form for an interim remedy under section 25 may be served out of the jurisdiction with the permission of the court under Order 11, r. 8A.[64] An application for the grant of permission must be supported (*inter alia*) by evidence of a belief that the applicant has a good claim to an interim remedy. On an application for interim relief under section 25 of the 1982 Act, the court may refuse to grant the relief if, in the opinion of the court, the fact that the   **11–141**

---

[56] *Société Générale de Paris v. Dreyfus* (1885) 29 Ch.D. 239; (1887) 37 Ch.D. 215 (C.A.); *Kinahan v. Kinahan* (1890) 45 Ch.D. 78; *Re De Penny* [1891] 2 Ch. 63; *Rosler v. Hilbery* [1925] Ch. 250 (C.A.).

[57] *De Bernales v. New York Herald* (1893) 68 L.T. 658; [1893] 2 Q.B. 97n. (C.A.). Compare *Watson v. Daily Record Ltd.* [1907] 1 K.B. 853 (C.A.), and contrast *Alexander & Co. v. Valentine & Sons* (1908) 25 T.L.R. 29.

[58] See *Marshall v. Marshall* (1888) 38 Ch.D. 330 (C.A.).

[59] *James North & Sons Ltd. v. North Cape Textiles Ltd.* [1984] 1 W.L.R. 1428 (C.A.).

[60] *The Siskina v. Distos Compania Naviera* [1979] A.C. 210; followed in *Caudron v. Air Zaire* [1986] I.L.R.M. 10; *Suncorp Realty Inc. v. PLN Investments, Inc.* (1985) 23 D.L.R. (4th) 83 (Man.); *cf. Perry v. Zissis* [1977] 1 Lloyd's Rep. 607 (C.A.). See *ante*, para. 8–019; and Collins, *Essays*, pp. 30–34.

[61] A *Mareva* injunction (after *Mareva Naviera S.A. v. International Bulkcarriers S.A.* [1975] 2 Lloyd's Rep. 509 (C.A.)), as to which see *ante*, paras. 8–004 *et seq.*

[62] [1996] A.C. 284 (P.C.).

[63] Art. 24, *post*, Rule 28, clause (22).

[64] This provision resolved doubts expressed in *Mercedes Benz A.G. v. Leiduck* [1996] A.C. 284, 304 (P.C.) on the correctness of the decisions in *Republic of Haiti v. Duvalier* [1990] Q.B. 202 (C.A.) and *X v. Y* [1990] 1 Q.B. 220 as to the applicability of R.S.C., Ord. 11, r. 1(2) (*post*, para. 11–225) and r. 1(1)(*b*) (clause (2)) in Convention cases.

court has no independent jurisdiction in relation to the subject-matter of the proceedings makes it inexpedient for the court to grant it.[65]

Illustrations

11–142   1. X, who is resident in New York, sends cards to A in London, through the post-office and otherwise, containing libellous and defamatory matter. A brings proceedings claiming an injunction to restrain X from sending such post-cards, and also claiming damages. The court may assume jurisdiction.[66]

2. X & Co. carry on business in South Africa. X & Co. at Manchester infringe A's trade mark. A brings proceedings to restrain infringement. The court may assume jurisdiction.[67]

3. X resides in New York, and there contracts with A & Co., an English company, to perform certain services in South Africa at a salary. He goes to South Africa, but returns thence before he has fully performed his contract. A & Co. refuse to pay X part of the salary which he claims. X threatens a petition for the winding-up of A & Co. A & Co. bring proceedings against X, claiming (1) rescission of contract, (2) return of moneys paid, (3) injunction to restrain X from presenting the petition. The court may assume jurisdiction.[68]

4. N, a trader in England, orders goods from X, a manufacturer in Illinois. X addresses the goods to N in England and delivers them to the Chicago post office by which they are forwarded to England. The goods are manufactured by X according to an invention protected by an English patent. Proceedings are brought by A, the patentee, against X, claiming an injunction against infringement of patent. The court has no jurisdiction, because the sale and delivery of the goods by X was complete when he delivered them to the post office in Chicago.[69]

5. X & Co., a Panamanian company, own a vessel, which they let on charter. On the failure of the charterers to pay the freight in full, X & Co. cause the vessel to be arrested in Cyprus by order of the courts of Cyprus and the cargo is unloaded. Subsequently the vessel sinks and becomes a total loss. X & Co. claim against their insurers, London underwriters. The cargo-owners commence proceedings in the High Court against X & Co., alleging breach of duty or of contract. The court may issue an injunction restraining X & Co. from removing the insurance moneys from the jurisdiction.[70]

11R–143   **(3) The court may assume jurisdiction against a person out of England if he is a necessary or proper party to a claim brought against a person duly served (whether within or out of England).[71]**

Comment

11–144   It may be necessary or proper that a claimant, A, should make not only one person, X, but also some other person, Y, defendant in the proceedings. This is so, for example, where X and Y are joint debtors,[72] or where A has a claim,

---

[65] s.25(2), on which see *Crédit Suisse Fides Trust S.A. v. Cuoghi* [1998] Q.B. 818 (C.A.), *ante*, para. 8–025.

[66] *Cf. Tozier v. Hawkins* (1885) 15 Q.B.D. 650, 680 (C.A.); *Dunlop Rubber Co. v. Dunlop* [1921] 1 A.C. 367. See also *Alexander & Co. v. Valentine & Sons* (1908) 25 T.L.R. 29.

[67] *Cf. Re Burland's Trade Mark* (1889) 41 Ch.D. 542. Contrast *Marshall v. Marshall* (1888) 38 Ch.D. 330 (C.A.).

[68] *Cf. Lisbon Berlyn Gold Fields v. Heddle* (1885) 52 L.T. 796.

[69] *Cf. Badische Anilin und Soda Fabrik v. Basle Chemical Works, Bindschedler* [1898] A.C. 200.

[70] Ord. 11, r. 8A, reversing the effect of *The Siskina v. Distos Compania Naviera S.A.* [1979] A.C. 210.

[71] Ord. 11, r. 1(1)(c).

[72] If one joint debtor is outside the jurisdiction he need not be joined in proceedings against the other or others: *Wilson, Sons & Co. v. Balcarres Brook S.S. Co.* [1893] 1 Q.B. 422 (C.A.).

alternatively, either against X or Y, or where otherwise the claims can be conveniently disposed of in the same proceedings.[73] This clause originally required X to be served within the jurisdiction but is not now so limited. It allows Y to be joined in the proceedings even though Y could not be served under any of the other clauses of this Rule if he had been sued alone, *e.g.* proceedings for a tort committed abroad.[74] But because the cause of action may have no connection with England, especial care is required before permission to serve out of the jurisdiction will be allowed.[75] In particular, the court should not grant permission under this clause as a matter of course merely because not to do so would mean that more than one set of proceedings would be required.[76]

In order that the court may have jurisdiction within clause (3) the following conditions must be fulfilled: **11–145**

(1) X must have been duly served. Service may be in England as of right,   **11–146** or abroad with permission under Order 11, r. 1(1) or as of right under Order 11, r. 1(2)(*b*). Clause (3) does not apply where X has not been served at the time when the application is made to serve Y,[77] but it has been held that in such a case the court has power to validate the permission to serve retrospectively.[78] Service on X includes service of a counterclaim in an action by X, so that where X brings proceedings in England and A serves a counterclaim on X's solicitor, A can join Y as an additional defendant to the counterclaim.[79] Where X is outside the jurisdiction and instructs solicitors to accept service on his behalf within the jurisdiction, A may join Y under this clause.[80]

(2) A must satisfy the court by written evidence that there is between A and   **11–147** X a real issue which A may reasonably ask the court to try. This requirement is imposed by Order 11, r. 1(4)(*d*).[81] In cases decided under the former version of this clause (which required also that the action be "properly brought" against X) it was said that Y could not be served under this clause if the sole

---

[73] CPR 7.3. This clause also applies, by CPR 20.3(1), to a third-party proceeding by X against Y (now called a "Part 20 claim"), on which see *Soc. Commerciale Réassurance v. Eras International Ltd.* [1992] 1 Lloyd's Rep. 570, 591–593 (C.A.); *cf. International Commercial Bank plc v. Insurance Corp. of Ireland plc* [1989] I.R. 453.

[74] *Williams v. Cartwright* [1895] 1 Q.B. 142, 145, 148 (C.A.); *The Duc d'Aumale* [1903] P. 18 (C.A.).

[75] *The Brabo* [1949] A.C. 326, 328; *Multinational Gas Co. v. Multinational Gas Services Ltd.* [1983] Ch. 258, 271 (C.A.); *Arab Monetary Fund v. Hashim (No. 4)* [1992] 1 W.L.R. 553, 557, affd. [1992] 1 W.L.R. 1176 (C.A.).

[76] *The Goldean Mariner* [1990] 2 Lloyd's Rep. 215 (C.A.).

[77] This follows from the wording of Ord. 11, r. 1(4)(*d*). See also *Yorkshire Tannery Ltd. v. Eglington Co.* (1884) 54 L.J.Ch. 81; *Collins v. North British, etc. Insurance Co.* [1894] 3 Ch. 228; *Tassell v. Hallen* [1892] 1 Q.B. 321; *Camera Care Ltd. v. Victor Hasselblad AB* [1986] 1 F.T.L.R. 348, 352–353 (C.A.); *Buttigeig v. Universal Terminal & Stevedoring Corp.* [1972] V.R. 626.

[78] *Kuwait Oil Tanker Co. S.A.K. v. Al Bader* [1997] 1 W.L.R. 1410 (C.A.) stated *post*, para. 11–151, Illustration 7. *Cf. The Cienvik* [1996] 2 Lloyd's Rep. 395, 403.

[79] *Derby & Co. Ltd. v. Larsson* [1976] 1 W.L.R. 202 (H.L.).

[80] *The Benarty (No. 1)* [1983] 1 Lloyd's Rep. 361 (C.A.), distinguishing *John Russell & Co. Ltd. v. Cayzer, Irvine & Co. Ltd.* [1916] 2 A.C. 298; followed, with some misgivings, in *Amanuel v. Alexandros Shipping Co.* [1986] Q.B. 464. A mere submission by X, without service of process on him, may not be sufficient to allow service on Y.

[81] Derived from *Ellinger v. Guinness, Mahon & Co.* [1939] 4 All E.R. 16, 22. See also *Soc. Commerciale Réassurance v. Eras International Ltd.* [1992] 1 Lloyd's Rep. 570 (C.A.); *The Ines* [1993] 2 Lloyd's Rep. 492; *The Xing Su Hai* [1995] 2 Lloyd's Rep. 15.

purpose of the action against X was to found jurisdiction against Y,[82] and this was reaffirmed by a majority of the Court of Appeal.[83] There is much to be said, however, for the minority view of May L.J. that these cases establish no more than that the claim against X must be a plausible one and not brought mala fide. This is probably also the position under the present version of the clause. Thus permission will not be granted if X has a complete answer to the claim by A,[84] or if Y has a complete answer.[85] But permission may be granted if the causes of action are alternative, so that the claim against one of them will ultimately fail.[86]

11–148   (3) Y, who is out of England, must be either a necessary or proper party to the proceedings. If Y is a proper party it is not also a requirement that he be a necessary party; but if adding Y is likely in practice to achieve no potential advantage for the claimant, it would not ordinarily be a proper case for service out of the jurisdiction.[87] The question whether Y is a proper party to proceedings against X depends on this: supposing both X and Y had been in England, would they both have been proper parties to the proceedings? If they would, and only one of them, X, is in this country, then Y is a proper party and permission may be given to serve him out of the jurisdiction.[88] It is not necessary that the alleged liability of Y be joint or several with that of X.[89]

11–149   In the rare cases falling outside the intra-United Kingdom provisions of the 1982 Act, clause (3) applies to a defendant domiciled or ordinarily resident in Scotland or Northern Ireland[90]; and Order 11, r. 4(3), which requires the court to have regard to the comparative cost and convenience of proceeding there or in England, applies to such a case.[91]

---

[82] See, *e.g. Witted v. Galbraith* [1893] 1 Q.B. 577; *Flower v. Rose & Co.* (1891) 7 T.L.R. 280; *Bloomfield v. Serenyi* [1945] 2 All E.R. 646 (C.A.); *Sharples v. Eason & Son* [1911] 2 I.R. 436 (C.A.); *Ross v. Eason & Son* [1911] 2 I.R. 459 (C.A.), distinguished in *Cooney v. Wilson and Henderson* [1913] 2 I.R. 402 (C.A.). That this is the purpose may be inferred from the fact that X is a subordinate or secondary defendant: *Yorkshire Tannery v. Eglington Co.* (1884) 54 L.J.Ch. 81; *Rosler v. Hilbery* [1925] Ch. 250.

[83] *Multinational Gas Co. v. Multinational Gas Services Ltd.* [1983] Ch. 258 (C.A.). See also *Goldenglow Nut Food Co. Ltd. v. Commodin (Produce) Ltd.* [1987] 2 Lloyd's Rep. 569, 578 (C.A.).

[84] *The Brabo* [1949] A.C. 326; *Witted v. Galbraith* [1893] 1 Q.B. 577 (C.A.); *Flower v. Rose & Co.* (1891) 7 T.L.R. 280.

[85] *Multinational Gas Co. v. Multinational Gas Services Ltd.* [1983] Ch. 258 (C.A.); *Kuwait Asia Bank E.C. v. National Mutual Life Nominees Ltd.* [1991] 1 A.C. 187 (P.C.); *DSQ Property Co. Ltd. v. Lotus Cars Ltd., The Times,* June 28, 1990 (C.A.) (in which both X and Y had a complete answer); *Barings plc v. Coopers & Lybrand* [1997] I.L.Pr. 12 (C.A.).

[86] *Massey v. Heynes* (1888) 21 Q.B.D. 330 (C.A.).

[87] *Electric Furnace Co. v. Selas Corp. of America* [1987] R.P.C. 23, 32–33 (C.A.).

[88] *Massey v. Heynes* (1888) 21 Q.B.D. 330, 338 (C.A.); *Lightowler v. Lightowler* [1884] W.N. 8; *The Elton* [1891] P. 265; *The Duc d'Aumale* [1903] P. 18 (C.A.); *Oesterreichische Export, etc. Co. v. British Indemnity Co. Ltd.* [1914] 2 K.B. 747 (C.A.); *Macaulay (Tweeds) Ltd. v. Independent Harris Tweed Producers Ltd.* [1961] R.P.C. 184; *Qatar Petroleum v. Shell International Petroleum* [1983] 2 Lloyd's Rep. 35 (C.A.); *The Goldean Mariner* [1989] 2 Lloyd's Rep. 390, 395 (approving the statement in the text), affd. [1990] 2 Lloyd's Rep. 215 (C.A.). See also *Aiglon Ltd. v. Gau Shan & Co. Ltd.* [1993] 1 Lloyd's Rep. 164.

[89] See, *e.g. Oesterreichische Export, etc., Co. v. British Indemnity Co. Ltd.* [1914] 2 K.B. 747 (C.A.); *Bank of N.S.W. v. Commonwealth Steel Co. Ltd.* [1983] 1 N.S.W.L.R. 69.

[90] See *Washburn, etc., Co. v. Cunard Co. & Parkes* (1889) 5 T.L.R. 592; *Croft v. King* [1893] 1 Q.B. 419; *Williams v. Cartwright* [1895] 1 Q.B. 142 (C.A.); *Oesterreichische Export, etc., Co. v. British Indemnity Co. Ltd.* [1914] 2 K.B. 747 (C.A.).

[91] *Washburn, etc., Co. v. Cunard Co. & Parkes* (1889) 5 T.L.R. 592; *Williams v. Cartwright* [1895] 1 Q.B. 142 (C.A.); *Macaulay (Tweeds) Ltd. v. Independent Harris Tweed Producers Ltd.* [1961] R.P.C. 184, 192–193.

Clause (3) applies where the defendant duly served in England or the   **11–150**
defendant sought to be served abroad is a partnership: the Interpretation Act
1978 provides that a "person" includes any body of persons corporate or
unincorporate.[92]

ILLUSTRATIONS

1. X, on instructions from Y, enters, as agent for Y, into a contract with A. Y repudiates the   **11–151**
contract. A brings proceedings against X, who is in England, for breach of warranty that X was
authorised to contract for Y, who is in New York, and has an alternative claim against Y if X was
authorised to contract for him. The court may assume jurisdiction to entertain an action against
Y as co-defendant with X.[93]

2. A & Co., an American company, own a patent for barbed wire. Y, carrying on business in
Japan, buys from N, in America, wire which is an infringement of A & Co.'s patent. X & Co.,
an English shipping company, carry the wire for Y and land it at Liverpool for transhipment to
Y in Japan. A & Co. bring proceedings against X & Co. to obtain an injunction against their
dealing with the wire. A & Co. apply for permission to add Y and serve Y in Japan. The court
may assume jurisdiction.[94]

3. A brings proceedings for deceit against X and Y in respect of a fraud jointly committed by
them in London. X is in England. Y is domiciled in New York. X has been served with process,
and Y is a necessary and proper party to the proceedings. The court may assume
jurisdiction.[95]

4. A brings proceedings against X, residing in England, who supplied him with defective
goods, and applies for permission to serve Y, residing in the United States, who designed the
goods. The court may assume jurisdiction.[96]

5. A brings proceedings against X, residing in the United States, who supplied him with
defective goods, and obtains permission to serve him abroad. X is served and defends the
proceedings. X applies for permission to serve a Part 20 claim (previously called third party
proceedings) against Y, who supplied him with the goods. The court may assume jurisdiction.

6. A & Co., a Liberian corporation, through its liquidator sues, alleging negligence and breach
of duty, X & Co., an English company, Y and others (directors of A & Co.), all resident abroad,
and Z & Co. and others, foreign companies who own the shares in A & Co. X & Co. and Y and
the other directors are not in a position to satisfy the substantial claim, and the predominant (but
not the sole) purpose of suing X & Co. is to enable A & Co. to join the parties outside the
jurisdiction. But as a matter of English company law Y and the other directors and Z & Co. and
the other shareholders are not liable to A & Co. Although the proceedings are "properly brought"
against X & Co., notwithstanding the predominant purpose of joining the foreign defendants, Y
and the other directors and Z & Co. and the other shareholders are not "proper parties" because
the proceedings against them is bound to fail.[97]

7. A brings proceedings against X and Y. X is resident in England, and Y is in Australia. Before
X has been served, A obtains an order for service on Y in Australia on the basis that Y is a
necessary or proper party. X is then served. Because it is a condition of the grant of permission
under clause (3) that X has already been served (which he had not), the permission to serve Y is
invalid; but the court may exercise its power to cure the irregularity by validating the grant of
permission retrospectively.[98]

(4) The court may assume jurisdiction if the claim is brought to   **11R–152**
enforce, rescind, dissolve, annul or otherwise affect a contract, or to
recover damages or obtain other relief in respect of the breach of a
contract, being (in either case) a contract which

---

[92] Sched. 1. See also *West of England Steamship Owners' Association v. John Holman & Sons*
[1957] 3 All E.R. 421n.

[93] *Massey v. Heynes* (1888) 21 Q.B.D. 330 (C.A.).

[94] *Cf. Washburn, etc., Co. v. Cunard Co. & Parkes* (1889) 5 T.L.R. 592.

[95] *Cf. Williams v. Cartwright* [1895] 1 Q.B. 142 (C.A.).

[96] *The Manchester Courage* [1973] 1 Lloyd's Rep. 386; see also *Adastra Aviation Ltd. v. Airparts
(N.Z.) Ltd.* [1964] N.Z.L.R. 393; *Pratt v. Rural Aviation Ltd.* [1969] N.Z.L.R. 46.

[97] *Multinational Gas Co. v. Multinational Gas Services Ltd.* [1983] Ch. 258 (C.A.).

[98] *Kuwait Oil Tanker Co. S.A.K. v. Al Bader* [1997] 1 W.L.R. 1410 (C.A.).

(i) **was made in England, or**
(ii) **was made by or through an agent trading or residing in England on behalf of a principal trading or residing out of England, or**
(iii) **is by its terms or by implication governed by English law, or**
(iv) **contains a term to the effect that the court shall have jurisdiction to hear and determine any action in respect of the contract.**[99]

COMMENT

11–153   This clause applies to four cases: (i) where a contract is made in England; (ii) where a contract is made by or through an agent trading or residing in England on behalf of a principal trading or residing abroad; (iii) where a contract is by its terms or by implication governed by English law; (iv) where a contract contains a submission to the jurisdiction of the English court. These cases are, of course, to be read disjunctively, *i.e.* it is sufficient if the claimant can bring his case within any one of them.[1] The claimant must have a good arguable case that the conditions of clause (4) are fulfilled, namely that there was a contract and that, *e.g.* it was made in England, and must also show that there is a serious issue to be tried on the merits of the claim.[2]

11–154   A "contract" in the clause has been held to include a quasi-contract,[3] and a covenant in a declaration of trust,[4] but not the mere holding of an office of director without a contract of employment.[5] A claim for a declaration that an indemnity is valid has been held to be a claim to "enforce" the contract[6]; and a claim for an injunction to restrain foreign proceedings in breach of an English arbitration clause is a claim to enforce the arbitration agreement.[7] It has also been held[8] that an action on a cheque governed by Greek law had a sufficiently direct link with a commodity contract (made between the same parties) governed by English law as to "otherwise affect" the commodity contract, but this seems to be an unjustifiable extension of clause (4). It includes an alleged contract, provided the claimant shows an arguable case that one existed.[9] A claim for a declaration that a contract has been frustrated

---

[99] Ord. 11, r. 1(1)(*d*).

[1] *Wansborough Paper Co. Ltd. v. Laughland* [1920] W.N. 344 (C.A.).

[2] *Seaconsar Far East Ltd. v. Bank Markazi Iran* [1994] 1 A.C. 438, 454–455. See *e.g. Maritrop Trading Corp. v. Guangzhou Ocean Shipping Co.* [1998] C.L.C. 224.

[3] *Bowling v. Cox* [1926] A.C. 751 (P.C.); *Rousou's Trustee v. Rousou* [1955] 1 W.L.R. 545; *Re Jogia (A Bankrupt)* [1988] 1 W.L.R. 484; *The Kurnia Dewi* [1997] 1 Lloyd's Rep. 552; *Durra v. Bank of N.S.W.* [1940] V.L.R. 170; *Earthworks Ltd. v. F. T. Eastment & Sons Ltd.* [1966] V.R. 24. A claim under statute for harbour dues is not a contractual or quasi-contractual claim for the purposes of clause (4): *Carlingford Harbour Commissioners v. Everard & Sons Ltd.* [1985] I.R. 50, following *Shipsey v. British and South American Steam Navigation Co. Ltd.* [1936] I.R. 65.

[4] *Official Solicitor v. Stype Investments Ltd.* [1983] 1 W.L.R. 214.

[5] *Newtherapeutics Ltd. v. Katz* [1991] Ch. 226.

[6] *Gulf Bank K.S.C. v. Mitsubishi Heavy Industries Ltd.* [1994] 1 Lloyd's Rep. 323.

[7] *Schiffartgesellschaft Detlev von Appen GmbH v. Voest Alpine Intertrading GmbH* [1997] 2 Lloyd's Rep. 279 (C.A.).

[8] *E. F. Hutton & Co. (London) Ltd. v. Mofarrij* [1989] 1 W.L.R. 488 (C.A.). But a claim for damages for breach of non-contractual bailment is not brought to enforce or otherwise affect the contracts evidenced by the bills of lading: *The Agia Skepi* [1992] 2 Lloyd's Rep. 467.

[9] *Hemelryck v. William Lyall Shipbuilding Co. Ltd.* [1921] 1 A.C. 698 (P.C.); *Cromie v. Moore* [1936] 2 All E.R. 177 (C.A.); *Vitkovice Horni A Hutni Tezirstvo v. Korner* [1951] A.C. 869; *Britannia Steamship Insurance Assn. v. Ausonia Assicuranzi SpA* [1984] 2 Lloyd's Rep. 98 (C.A.); *The Parouth* [1982] 2 Lloyd's Rep. 351 (C.A.); *Egon Oldendorff v. Libera Corp.* [1995] 2 Lloyd's Rep. 64; see *ante*, para. 11–127.

is a claim which "otherwise affects" a contract within the meaning of this clause.[10] But if, on the claimant's own showing, no such contract as he alleges was made with the defendant, permission will not be granted.[11]

(i) Where a contract is made in England. If the parties enter into negotiations by correspondence from different countries, the contract is made where the letter of acceptance is posted.[12] But in commercial transactions today communication by telephone, telex, fax and electronic mail is much more common than by post. It is now well established, following the decision of the Court of Appeal in *Entores v. Miles Far East Corporation*[13] (which has been approved by the House of Lords[14]) that if the parties use "instantaneous" means of communication such as telephone, fax or electronic mail,[15] the contract is made where the acceptance is communicated to the offeror. 11–155

It has been held that if a contract made in England contains a submission to arbitration in a foreign country, an action in England at common law to enforce the foreign arbitration award is within this part of the clause.[16]

The contract must actually be made in England as that phrase is understood in English law. It is not sufficient if it merely says that it shall be deemed to be so made, though this may be sufficient to make it one which "by its terms or by implication" is to be governed by English law.[17] A contract may be made in England within the meaning of this clause although it was preceded by a less formal agreement made abroad.[18] 11–156

(ii) Where a contract is made by or through an agent trading or residing in England on behalf of a principal trading or residing out of England. It will be observed that the clause says "by or through" an agent, not "by" an agent. Hence the case is within the clause, although the agent has 11–157

---

[10] *B.P. Exploration Co. (Libya) Ltd. v. Hunt* [1976] 1 W.L.R. 788; *Gulf Bank K.S.C. v. Mitsubishi Heavy Industries Ltd.* [1994] 1 Lloyd's Rep. 323, 327. *Cf. Insurance Corp. of Ireland v. Strombus International Insurance Co.* [1985] 2 Lloyd's Rep. 138 (C.A.) (rescission for non-disclosure); *The Olib* [1991] 2 Lloyd's Rep. 108 (claim for declaration that contract void for duress). *Cf. D.R. Insurance Co. v. Central National Insurance Co.* [1996] 1 Lloyd's Rep. 74.

[11] This statement was approved in *Finnish Marine Insurance Co. Ltd. v. Protective National Insurance Co.* [1990] 1 Q.B. 1078. In Australia it has been held that the words "otherwise affect" include a claim for inducement of breach of contract: *South A delaide Football Club v. Fitzroy Football Club* (1988) 92 F.L.R. 117. This is very doubtful: *cf. E. F. Hutton & Co. (London) Ltd. v. Mofarrij* [1989] 1 W.L.R. 488, 494 (C.A.).

[12] *Wansborough Paper Co. Ltd. v. Laughland* [1920] W.N. 344 (C.A.); *Benaim v. Debono* [1924] A.C. 514, 520 (P.C.); *Clarke v. Harper and Robinson* [1938] N.Ir. 162; *Williams v. Society of Lloyd's* [1994] 1 V.R. 274. See also *Cowan v. O'Connor* (1888) 20 Q.B.D. 640; *Lewis Construction Co. Ltd. v. M. Tichauer S.A.* [1966] V.R. 341.

[13] [1955] 2 Q.B. 327 (C.A.); *Gill & Duffus Landauer v. London Export Corp.* [1982] 2 Lloyd's Rep. 627; *Kelly v. Cruise Catering Ltd.* [1994] 2 I.L.R.M. 394; *Hampstead Meats Pty. Ltd. v. Emerson and Yates Pty. Ltd.* [1967] S.A.S.R. 109; *Express Airways v. Port Augusta Air Services* [1980] Qd. 543; *Mendelson-Zeller Co. Inc. v. T. & C. Providores Pty. Ltd.* [1981] 1 N.S.W.L.R. 366; *Re Modern Fashions Ltd.* (1969) 8 D.L.R. (3d) 590 (Man.); *McDonald & Sons Ltd. v. Export Packers Co. Ltd.* (1979) 95 D.L.R. (3d) 174 (B.C.).

[14] *Brinkibon Ltd. v. Stahag Stahl* [1983] 2 A.C. 34. *Cf. Bank of Baroda v. Vysya Bank Ltd.* [1994] 2 Lloyd's Rep. 87.

[15] But the place of receipt of electronic mail is a concept by no means free from difficulty.

[16] *Bremer Oeltransport v. Drewry* [1933] 1 K.B. 753 (C.A.). See *post*, para. 16–064. But see now Ord. 11, r. 1(1)(*m*), clause (13), *post*.

[17] See Rule 174 and *cf. British Controlled Oilfields Ltd. v. Stagg* [1921] W.N. 319.

[18] *Gibbon v. Commerz und Creditbank A.G.* [1958] 2 Lloyd's Rep. 113.

no authority to make contracts on behalf of his foreign principal, but only has authority to obtain orders and transmit them to his principal for acceptance or rejection.[19] This part of the clause is designed to bring within Rule 27 foreigners who transact business in England by or through agents, and consequently it does not apply where the agent's principal is the claimant. Hence a claimant cannot invoke clause (4)(ii) where the contract was made by or through his agent.[20]

11–158   If proceedings are brought by consignees of a cargo against foreign shipowners under the bills of lading, the case is not within this part of the clause if the charterparty (but not the bills of lading) was made by or through agents of the shipowners in England, even though it refers to the bills of lading and was made by charterers acting on behalf of the consignees.[21] It may be otherwise, however, if the charterers are identical with the consignees.

11–159   Rule 6.16 of the Civil Procedure Rules provides an alternative method of service if the conditions laid down in clause (4)(ii) of Rule 27 are satisfied together with two other conditions, namely, that the contract was made in England, and that the agent's authority has not been terminated or he is still in business relations with his principal. This method is to issue proceedings against the principal, and serve process with permission of the court on the agent in England.

11–160   When an order under CPR 6.16 has been obtained, a copy of the order and of the claim form must be sent to the defendant. The procedure is essentially discretionary, not normally to be resorted to when there is no difficulty in proceeding under Order 11, *i.e.* Rule 27. It is more appropriate in a case where the foreign principal has a general agent doing large business for him in England than where the foreign principal makes a single contract through a broker.[22]

11–161   **(iii) Where a contract by its terms or by implication is governed by English law.** The rules for ascertaining the governing law of a contract are considered in Rules 172 to 174.[23] When this provision first became part of Order 11 in 1920 the governing law of a contract was the law by which the parties intended, or might fairly be presumed to have intended, the contract to be governed. Only later did the courts draw a distinction between cases in which, in the absence of express choice, an intention to choose a system of law should be inferred, and those in which such an intention could not be inferred; in the latter case, the contract would be governed by the law with which the contract had its closest and most real connection. A similar distinction is drawn in the Rome Convention on the Law Applicable to Contractual Obligations, to which effect is given by the Contracts (Applicable Law) Act 1990. Article 1 of the Rome Convention applies its rules to "any situation involving a choice between the laws of different countries". The rules of the

---

[19] *National Mortgage and Agency Co. of N.Z. Ltd. v. Gosselin* (1922) 38 T.L.R. 832 (C.A.); *cf. BHP Petroleum Pty. Ltd. v. Oil Basins Ltd.* [1985] V.R. 725, affd. [1985] V.R. 756.

[20] *Union International Insurance Co. Ltd. v. Jubilee Insurance Co. Ltd.* [1991] 1 W.L.R. 415.

[21] *The Metamorphosis* [1953] 1 W.L.R. 543.

[22] See the Practice Memorandum quoted in *The Supreme Court Practice 1999*, 10/2/3. This has not yet been reproduced in the CPR Practice Directions.

[23] Several important cases on the common law rules as to the ascertainment of the governing law were decided under clause (4) of Rule 27, the most important modern example of which was *Amin Rasheed Shipping Corp. v. Kuwait Insurance Co.* [1984] A.C. 50.

Convention, as incorporated by the 1990 Act, have been applied[24] to determine whether a contract by its terms or by implication is governed by English law for the purposes of this clause. Order 11, r. 1(1)(d)(iii) still refers to a contract which "by its terms or by implication" is governed by English law, but it applies to all cases in which a contract is governed by English law.[25] It applied when the contract was governed by English law as the law with which the contract had its closest connection,[26] and it applies equally when English law is the governing law under Rule 174 because the contract is most closely connected with England.

Although the fact that a contract is governed by English law is an important **11–162** factor in the exercise of the discretion under this head in favour of the English forum,[27] it is not conclusive. This head of jurisdiction was described as exorbitant in *Amin Rasheed Shipping Corp. v. Kuwait Insurance Co.*,[28] where the House of Lords held that in the circumstances it was not appropriate for the English court to determine a dispute involving a marine insurance policy governed by English law when the Kuwaiti courts were the *forum conveniens*. Until that decision it was generally thought that the fact that a contract was governed by English law was in itself sufficient to justify leave. But now the claimant has a heavier burden. In *Amin Rasheed* Lord Diplock suggested[29] that, in order to justify leave under this head, the plaintiff had to show that justice could not be obtained by him in the foreign court, or could only be obtained at excessive cost, delay or inconvenience. But it was subsequently held that Lord Diplock was merely giving examples, and was not providing an exhaustive list, of the relevant factors.[30] The court has to consider all factors, and the fact that English law is the applicable law may be of great importance, or it may be of little consequence as seen in the context of the whole case.[31] Thus if there is likely to be no dispute on matters of law or construction, or if the law of the foreign forum is substantially the same as English law, the fact that English law is the applicable law will be of little weight. But where an issue of English public policy arises in relation to a contract which is (or may be) governed by English law, it is desirable that it should be decided by the English court[32]; conversely, where the foreign court may apply its own public policy to defeat a claim based on a contract governed by English law, that too is a reason for the English court taking jurisdiction.[33] If the claimant

---

[24] *Bank of Baroda v. Vysya Bank Ltd.* [1994] 2 Lloyd's Rep. 87; *Egon Oldendorff v. Libera Corp.* [1995] 2 Lloyd's Rep. 64, stated *post*, para. 11–167, Illustration 10.

[25] See [1984] A.C. at 69.

[26] *e.g. Mauroux v. Pereira* [1972] 1 W.L.R. 962; *Coast Lines Ltd. v. Hudig & Veder Chartering N.V.* [1972] 2 Q.B. 34 (C.A.); *Armadora Occidental S.A. v. Horace Mann Insurance Co.* [1977] 1 W.L.R. 1098 (C.A.).

[27] *B.P. Exploration Co. (Libya) v. Hunt* [1976] 3 All E.R. 879, 893, as explained in *The Elli 2* [1985] 1 Lloyd's Rep. 107, 118 (C.A.).

[28] [1984] A.C. 50, 65, Illustration 7, *post*. It is regarded as exorbitant in civil law countries; see Schlosser, para. 87.

[29] [1984] A.C. at 68.

[30] *Spiliada Maritime Corp. v. Cansulex Ltd.* [1987] A.C. 460, 480, approving *The Elli 2* [1985] 1 Lloyd's Rep. 107 (C.A.).

[31] [1987] A.C. at 481, 486. *Cf. New Hampshire Insurance Co. v. Strabag Bau AG* [1992] 1 Lloyd's Rep. 361, 370 (C.A.); *Trade Indemnity plc v. Forsakringsaktiebolaget Njord* [1995] 1 All E.R. 796; *Macsteel Commercial Holdings (Pty) Ltd. v. Thermasteel* [1996] C.L.C. 1403.

[32] *E. I. du Pont de Nemours v. Agnew* [1987] 2 Lloyd's Rep. 585 (C.A.); *Mitsubishi Corp. v. Alafouzos* [1988] 1 Lloyd's Rep. 191.

[33] *The Magnum* [1989] 1 Lloyd's Rep. 47 (C.A.).

has alternative remedies in contract and tort upon the same facts, he can choose his remedy.[34]

11–163   Although the 1968 Convention and the Lugano Convention supersede this clause as regards defendants domiciled in other Contracting States, it should be noted that there are transitional provisions which deal with cases where the parties to a dispute concerning a contract had agreed in writing that the contract was to be governed by English law. In such cases the English court may retain the right to exercise jurisdiction in the dispute over a domiciliary of another Contracting State. In the case of the 1968 Convention, the exception applies if the parties to the dispute had agreed in writing before January 1, 1987, that the contract was to be governed by the law of a part of the United Kingdom[35]; this is the relevant date not only in relation to domiciliaries of those States for which the Convention was then in force, but also for those States which acceded after 1987, namely Ireland, Greece, Spain and Portugal. In the case of the Lugano Convention, the critical date is the date of "the entry into force of this Convention."[36] It would seem that this means May 1, 1992, when the Lugano Convention first entered into force generally and also for the United Kingdom, and not any later date on which it came into force as between the United Kingdom and the Contracting State of which the proposed defendant is a domiciliary. The exceptions only apply if there is an express choice of English law in writing, and do not apply if the contract is governed by English law merely because a choice of English law can be implied or because the contract is most closely connected with England.[37]

11–164   **(iv) Where a contract contains a term to the effect that the court shall have jurisdiction to hear and determine any claim in respect of the contract.** This clause had its origin in 1920,[38] when it was introduced to allow service out of the jurisdiction in cases where there was a contractual submission but where no other head of Order 11, r. 1(1) was applicable. It is dealt with more fully in connection with Rule 32(1) on jurisdiction clauses which confer jurisdiction on English courts.[39]

ILLUSTRATIONS

(1) CONTRACT MADE IN ENGLAND

11–165   1. X, by letter posted in New York, orders goods from A in England. A accepts the order by letter posted in England. The contract is made in England and the court may assume jurisdiction.[40]

2. A in London sends an offer to buy goods to X in Tokyo. The offer is sent by the telex system of communication, whereby a message can be typed on a teleprinter in one country and instantaneously recorded in another. X accepts the offer in a similar manner. The contract is made in England and the court may assume jurisdiction.[41]

3. X in Delhi sends by telex an offer to sell goods to A in London. A accepts the offer by sending a telex to Delhi. The contract is made in Delhi and the court has no jurisdiction.[42]

---

[34] *Matthews v. Kuwait Bechtel Corporation* [1959] 2 Q.B. 57 (C.A.), stated *post*, para. 11–167, Illustration 6.

[35] 1968 Convention, Art. 54(3) (formerly 1978 Accession Convention, Art. 35).

[36] Lugano Convention, Art. 54(3).

[37] See *New Hampshire Insurance Co. v. Strabag Bau AG* [1992] 1 Lloyd's Rep. 361 (C.A.).

[38] To reverse the decision in *British Wagon Co. v. Gray* [1896] 1 Q.B. 35 (C.A.).

[39] See *post*, paras. 12–111 *et seq*.

[40] *Cf. Wansborough Paper Co. Ltd. v. Laughland* [1920] W.N. 344 (C.A.).

[41] *Cf. Entores Ltd. v. Miles Far East Corporation* [1955] 2 Q.B. 327 (C.A.).

[42] *Cf. Brinkibon Ltd. v. Stahag Stahl* [1983] 2 A.C. 34.

4. A charterparty made in London between A, a Swedish firm of shipowners, and X, who resides in Spain, contains a clause providing for the submission of disputes to arbitration in Stockholm. Under an arbitration conducted in Stockholm in pursuance of this clause, an award is made against X of £20,000, payable in English currency. A brings proceedings against X to enforce the award. The court may assume jurisdiction because the contract containing the submission to arbitration was made in England.[43]

(2) Contract made by or through an Agent Trading or Residing in England

11–166

5. X, who resides and carries on business in Canada, employs N, who resides and carries on business in England, as his agent to obtain orders for goods and submit them to X in Canada for acceptance or rejection. N has no authority to make contracts on X's behalf. N obtains an order from A and submits it to X, who accepts it. A brings proceedings against X for breach of warranty. The court may assume jurisdiction.[44]

(3) Contract by its Terms or by Implication to be Governed by English Law

11–167

6. A is employed by X & Co. in Kuwait under a contract governed by English law. He sustains personal injuries in Kuwait in the course of his employment there. He brings proceedings against X & Co. in England for breach of an implied term in the contract of service. The court may assume jurisdiction.[45]

7. X & Co., a Kuwaiti insurance company, issues a policy insuring a vessel owned by A & Co., a Liberian corporation. The policy is based on the form scheduled to the Marine Insurance Act 1906. The vessel is seized by the Saudi Arabian authorities and A & Co. claims under the policy for constructive total loss. X & Co. claims that the vessel was engaged in smuggling and that accordingly the exclusion in the policy relating to infringement of customs regulations applies. The court has jurisdiction because the policy is governed by English law. But the court will not exercise its jurisdiction because the Kuwaiti courts are the *forum conveniens* in the circumstances of the case.[46]

8. A & Co., Liberian shipowners, chartered a ship to Y & Co., an Indian company, for the carriage of a cargo of sulphur from Vancouver, Canada, to Indian ports. X & Co., a Canadian company, sold the sulphur to Y & Co., and bills of lading, expressed to be governed by English law, were issued to and accepted by X & Co. A & Co. allege that the cargo of sulphur was wet and caused severe corrosion of the ship, and claim under the contract of carriage contained in, or evidenced by, the bills of lading. The court assumes jurisdiction (even though much of the factual dispute relates to events in British Columbia), particularly because there has been extensive litigation in England arising out of a similar shipment on another ship owned by different shipowners, which had been settled, but in the course of which an enormous amount of factual and scientific evidence had been collected; the owners' insurers and solicitors are the same in both sets of litigation; and there is a dispute as to the effect under English law of the bill of lading contract and as to the nature of the obligations under the contract in respect of dangerous cargo.[47]

9. A & Co., a Japanese company, agrees to build a bulk carrier for Y & Co., a Greek company, which is owned by X, a Greek shipowner. The shipbuilding contract is governed by English law, and provides for arbitration in London. X signs a performance guarantee, which contains no express choice of law. X alleges that the guarantee is illegal and contrary to English public policy because it was drafted in such a way as to mislead the Japanese authorities about the price in order to obtain an export licence. The guarantee is governed by English law, and the court will exercise its jurisdiction against X because it is highly desirable that the issue of English public policy should be decided by the English court.[48]

10. A & Co., a German partnership, agrees with X & Co., a Japanese company, that X & Co. will charter to A & Co. two bulk carriers to be built for X & Co. in Japan. The charter contains a London arbitration clause. The court has jurisdiction because the charter is governed by English law under Rule 174.[49]

---

[43] *Cf. Bremer Oeltransport GmbH v. Drewry* [1933] 1 K.B. 753 (C.A.). The Conventions do not apply to the enforcement of arbitral awards: *ante*, paras. 11–024 *et seq.* See now clause (13), *post*.

[44] *Cf. National Mortgage and Agency Co. of N.Z. Ltd. v. Gosselin* (1922) 38 T.L.R. 832 (C.A.).

[45] *Matthews v. Kuwait Bechtel Corporation* [1959] 2 Q.B. 57 (C.A.).

[46] *Amin Rasheed Shipping Corp. v. Kuwait Insurance Co.* [1984] A.C. 50.

[47] *Spiliada Maritime Corp. v. Cansulex Ltd.* [1987] A.C. 460.

[48] *Mitsubishi Corp. v. Alafouzos* [1988] 1 Lloyd's Rep. 191 (a pre-1968 Convention case).

[49] *Egon Oldendorff v. Libera Corp.* [1995] 2 Lloyd's Rep. 64.

(4) Contract Contains a Term to the Effect that the Court shall have Jurisdiction

11–168   11. A contract is made abroad (and governed by foreign law) between A & Co., a Japanese company, and X & Co., an American company, whereby A & Co. agree to tow X & Co.'s oil rig from Venice, Louisiana, to Ravenna, Italy. The contract provides that "any dispute arising must be treated before the London court of justice." The tug and tow are forced to take refuge in Tampa, Florida, each alleging that this was the other's fault. X & Co. bring proceedings against A & Co. in Florida, and A & Co. bring an action against X & Co. in England. The court may assume jurisdiction.[50]

11R–169   **(5) The court may assume jurisdiction if the claim is brought in respect of a breach committed in England of a contract made in or out of England,[51] and irrespective of the fact, if such be the case, that the breach was preceded or accompanied by a breach committed out of England that rendered impossible the performance of so much of the contract as ought to have been performed in England.[52]**

COMMENT

11–170   A contract may be broken in one of three ways, namely, by express repudiation, implied repudiation or failure to perform.

Breach by express repudiation occurs when one party informs the other that he no longer intends to perform the contract. If X who is abroad writes a letter of repudiation to A in England, the breach is not committed in England.[53] On the other hand, if X who is abroad sends his agent to England, or writes to his agent who is in England, instructing him to repudiate the contract, and the agent does so, *e.g.* by letter posted in England to A in England, then the breach is committed in England.[54]

11–171   Breach by implied repudiation occurs when one party does an act which is inconsistent with his performance of the contract, for instance, when X promises to sell a house to A but sells it to B instead. Although there is no authority on the point, the breach in such a case presumably occurs where the inconsistent act is done. This principle would appear to apply wherever the contractual obligation consists in an omission rather than an act, *e.g.* an obligation not to sell certain goods in England. The clause would apply if the goods were sold there.

11–172   If a contract is broken in England by express or implied repudiation, it would seem to be immaterial, for the purposes of Order 11, r. 1(1)(*e*), whether or not the contract was to be performed in England. Formerly the rule referred to a contract which "according to the terms thereof ought to be performed in England"; but there are no such words in the operative part of the present rule.

---

[50] *Cf. The Chaparral* [1968] 2 Lloyd's Rep. 158 (C.A.). For the sequel in the American courts, see *M/S Bremen v. Zapata Offshore Co.*, 407 U.S. 1 (1972), [1972] 2 Lloyd's Rep. 315; Collins, *Essays*, p. 253; Kahn-Freund (1977) 26 I.C.L.Q. 825, 845–848.

[51] The remainder of this clause renders *Johnson v. Taylor Bros.* [1920] A.C. 144 obsolete.

[52] Ord. 11, r. 1(1)(*e*). It has been held that for the purposes of this clause, contract includes quasi-contract: *McFee Engineering Pty. Ltd. v. C.B.S. Construction Pty. Ltd.* (1980) 28 A.L.R. 339.

[53] *Cherry v. Thompson* (1872) L.R. 7 Q.B. 573, 579; *Holland v. Bennett* [1902] 1 K.B. 867 (C.A.), both approved in *Martin v. Stout* [1925] A.C. 359, 368–369 (P.C.); *Atlantic Underwriting Agencies Ltd. v. Compagnia di Assicurazione di Milano* [1979] 2 Lloyd's Rep. 240; *Safran v. Chani* [1970] 1 N.S.W.L.R. 70; *Stanley Kerr Holdings Pty. Ltd. v. Gibor Textile Enterprises Ltd.* [1978] 2 N.S.W.L.R. 372.

[54] *Mutzenbecher v. La Aseguradora Espanola* [1906] 1 K.B. 254 (C.A.); *Oppenheimer v. Louis Rosenthal & Co. A.G.* [1937] 1 All E.R. 23 (C.A.).

The normal form of breach is the failure of one party to perform one or **11–173** more of his obligations under the contract. In such a case it is not necessary that the whole contract was to be performed in England by both the parties thereto, but it is necessary that some part of it was to be performed in England and that there has been a breach of that part.[55] It is not sufficient if the contract or part of it might be performed either in England or abroad; it is necessary that the contract or part of it was to be performed in England and not elsewhere.[56] The contract need not contain an express term providing for performance in England.[57] It is enough if the court can gather that this was the intention of the parties by construing the contract in the light of the surrounding circumstances, including the course of dealing between the parties.[58] In most of the reported cases, the breach complained of was the failure to pay money, a matter in which it is especially difficult to determine the place of performance in the absence of an express term in the contract.[59] "The general rule is that where no place of payment is specified, either expressly or by implication, the debtor must seek out his creditor."[60] But this is only a general rule[61] and, as stated, it only applies where no place of payment is expressed *or implied* in the contract. It certainly does not mean that a creditor can confer jurisdiction on the English court merely by taking up his residence in England after the making of the contract.[62]

If the contract is for the sale of goods by a seller in England to a buyer **11–174** abroad, it will, in the absence of a contractual term to the contrary, be easy to infer that the buyer's obligation was to pay for the goods in England.[63] The same is the case if a principal in England sends goods to an agent abroad to be sold by him on commission.[64] But it is otherwise if, on the true construction of the contract, the only duty of the foreign agent is to sell the goods and remit the proceeds to England from abroad in a specified manner, because it will be inferred that his duty is at an end when he makes the remittance.[65] If a foreign principal appoints an agent in England to sell his goods on commission, it is

---

[55] *Rein v. Stein* [1892] 1 Q.B. 753 (C.A.).

[56] *Bell & Co. v. Antwerp London and Brazil Line* [1891] 1 Q.B. 103 (C.A.); *The Eider* [1893] P. 119 (C.A.); *Comber v. Leyland* [1898] A.C. 524; *Cuban Atlantic Sugar Sales Corporation v. Compania de Vapores San Elefterio Lda.* [1960] 1 Q.B. 187. *Cf. BHP Petroleum Pty. Ltd. v. Oil Basins Ltd.* [1985] V.R. 725, affd. [1985] V.R. 756.

[57] *Reynolds v. Coleman* (1887) 36 Ch.D. 453 (C.A.), decided at a time when the rule referred to a contract which "according to the terms thereof" ought to be performed in England.

[58] The course of dealing was stressed in the following cases: *Rein v. Stein* [1892] 1 Q.B. 753 (C.A.); *Fry & Co. v. Raggio* (1891) 40 W.R. 120; *Charles Duval & Co. Ltd. v. Gans* [1904] 2 K.B. 685 (C.A.); *O'Mara Ltd. v. Dodd* [1912] 2 I.R. 55; *Shallay Holdings Pty. Ltd. v. Griffith Co-operative Society Ltd.* [1983] 1 V.R. 760.

[59] See also Law Commission, *Report on Council of Europe Convention on Place of Payment of Money Liabilities (1972)*, Law Com. No. 109 (1981), p. 28.

[60] *The Eider* [1893] P. 119, 136–137 (C.A.). See also *Bank of Scotland v. Seitz*, 1990 S.L.T. 584 (a case on the 1968 Convention).

[61] See *Earthworks Ltd. v. F. T. Eastment & Sons Ltd.* [1966] V.R. 24; *B.P. Australia Ltd. v. Wales* [1982] Qd.R. 386.

[62] *Malik v. Narodni Banka Ceskoslovenska* [1946] 2 All E.R. 663 (C.A.); *cf. Fessard v. Mugnier* (1865) 18 C.B.(N.S.) 286.

[63] *Robey & Co. v. Snaefell Mining Co. Ltd.* (1887) 20 Q.B.D. 152; *Hassall v. Lawrence* (1887) 4 T.L.R. 23; *Fry & Co. v. Raggio* (1891) 40 W.R. 120; *O'Mara Ltd. v. Dodd* [1912] 2 I.R. 55.

[64] *Rein v. Stein* [1892] 1 Q.B. 753 (C.A.); *Charles Duval & Co. Ltd. v. Gans* [1904] 2 K.B. 685 (C.A.).

[65] *Comber v. Leyland* [1898] A.C. 524, a case "of a somewhat special character," *per* Stirling L.J. in *Charles Duval & Co. Ltd. v. Gans* [1904] 2 K.B. 685, 691 (C.A.).

usually inferred that the commission is payable in England.[66] In such a case, the fact that the agent claims an account of sales does not take the case out of the clause.[67]

11–175   The duties of the seller of goods under a c.i.f. contract are to ship the goods and deliver the shipping documents to the buyer. It is not his duty to deliver the goods to the buyer.[68] Consequently, if the foreign seller ships goods which are found to be defective upon their arrival in England,[69] or if he fails to ship them at all, the breach is not committed in England within the meaning of the clause. In *Johnson v. Taylor*,[70] the English buyer sought to bring the foreign seller within the clause by alleging a failure to deliver the shipping documents in respect of goods which the seller had failed to ship. The House of Lords refused leave to serve notice of the writ out of the jurisdiction, because the substantial part of the breach complained of was the failure to ship the goods, and this had occurred abroad. But this decision appears to be overruled by the concluding words of Order 11, r. 1(1)(*e*), which were added in the following year.

11–176   In a contract of service, wages or salary would normally be payable where the service is to be performed, in the absence of an express or implied term in the contract.[71] But if the servant is employed in only a nominal or consultative capacity, and is free to reside where he likes, his salary may be payable in England, if that is where he decides to live.[72] In a contract for services, it may be possible to infer that the fee or commission is payable at the contractor's usual place of business, even if the work is to be performed abroad.[73]

11–177   The fact that the contract provides for payment to be made in English currency has sometimes been held to yield the inference that payment was to be made in England,[74] but this is by no means a decisive consideration.[75] Conversely, the fact that payment is to be made in foreign currency does not necessarily mean that England was not to be the place of payment.[76] No inference as to the place of payment can properly be drawn from the fact that the contract contains a gold clause.[77]

11–178   If money is due under a compromise of a disputed claim, it is usually inferred that the money is payable where litigation is pending or would probably have taken place.[78]

An implied warranty of authority has been held to have been broken where the warranty was relied on.[79]

---

[66] *Hoerter v. Hanover, etc., Works* (1893) 10 T.L.R. 103 (C.A.); *International Corporation Ltd. v. Besser Manufacturing Co.* [1950] 1 K.B. 488 (C.A.).

[67] *Ibid.*

[68] See *Clemens Horst Co. v. Biddell* [1912] A.C. 18, approving the dissenting judgment of Kennedy L.J. in the C.A. [1911] 1 K.B. 214.

[69] *Crozier Stephens & Co. v. Auerbach* [1908] 2 K.B. 161 (C.A.); *Cordova Land Co. Ltd. v. Victor Bros. Inc.* [1966] 1 W.L.R. 793.

[70] [1920] A.C. 144.

[71] See *Malik v. Narodni Banka Ceskoslovenska* [1946] 2 All E.R. 663 (C.A.).

[72] *Vitkovice Horni A Hutni Tezirstvo v. Korner* [1951] A.C. 869.

[73] *Thompson v. Palmer* [1893] 2 Q.B. 80 (C.A.); *International Power and Engineering Consultants Ltd. v. Clark* (1964) 43 D.L.R. (2d) 394 (B.C.C.A.). Contrast *Auckland Receivers Ltd. v. Diners Club* [1985] 2 N.S.W.L.R. 652.

[74] *Fry & Co. v. Raggio* (1891) 40 W.R. 120.

[75] *Bremer Oeltransport GmbH v. Drewry* [1933] 1 K.B. 753 (C.A.).

[76] *Rein v. Stein* [1892] 1 Q.B. 753 (C.A.); *Drexel v. Drexel* [1916] 1 Ch. 251; *Vitkovice Horni A Hutni Tezirstvo v. Korner* [1951] A.C. 869.

[77] *Vitkovice Horni A Hutni Tezirstvo v. Korner, supra.*

[78] *Golden v. Darlow* (1891) 8 T.L.R. 57 (C.A.); *Anger v. Vasnier* (1902) 18 T.L.R. 596 (C.A.).

[79] *The Piraeus* [1974] 2 Lloyd's Rep. 266 (C.A.).

If the contract is governed by a foreign applicable law, the applicable law of the contract will determine where money due thereunder is payable.[80]

ILLUSTRATIONS

1. X, who resides in Toronto, is the owner of a New York newspaper. He employs A to act as London correspondent for the newspaper's European edition. He writes a letter from Naples to A in England, wrongfully dismissing him. The court has no jurisdiction by reason of the letter of repudiation.[81] But it would have jurisdiction if the letter was followed by non-payment of salary, because of the concluding words of the clause. **11–179**

2. By a contract made in the Canary Islands X & Co., a Brazilian insurance company, appoint A, a London insurance agent, to act as their exclusive agent for five years for insurance business in the United Kingdom, and her overseas Colonies and Dominions, in continental Europe (except Spain, Portugal and Turkey) and in the United States. After one year X & Co. send their agent-general to England with instructions to terminate A's appointment. The agent-general does so by letter posted in London to A in England. A brings proceedings against X & Co. for breach of contract. The court may assume jurisdiction.[82]

3. A, an American citizen resident in England, and X, an American citizen resident in the United States, agree that if A will transfer certain patents to X, X will transfer to A 500 shares in an English company. A transfers the patents but X refuses to transfer the shares. The court may assume jurisdiction.[83]

4. X & Co., a Panamanian company, charter a ship from A & Co., English shipowners, to load a cargo in London and proceed therewith to Rio de Janeiro and Santos. The charterparty provides that the freight shall be paid as to part at the ports of discharge and as to the balance in London, and that all lighterage at ports of discharge shall be at charterers' risk and expense. A & Co., having paid the lighterage at the ports of discharge, bring proceedings against X & Co. for reimbursement. The court has no jurisdiction.[84] **11–180**

5. A ship belonging to X & Co., Liberian shipowners, while on passage from New York to Bremen is stranded on the Wolf Rock, *i.e.* outside English territorial waters. A contract is made between the master and the agents of A & Co. and B & Co., Swedish and German salvage companies, whereby the salvage companies agree to salve the ship and tow it to Falmouth for repairs in return for 50 per cent. of its value when salved. The contract provides for payment of the salvage money to B & Co., the German company, no place of payment being specified. It is orally agreed between the agents of the two salvage companies that A & Co. will receive half the salvage money. Disputes arise as to the value of the ship when salved, and A & Co. bring proceedings against X & Co. for their share. The court has no jurisdiction.[85]

6. X & Co., a Manx company, order a boiler and machinery to be supplied by A & Co. in England and delivered to X & Co.'s mine in the Isle of Man for £585. A & Co. accept and execute the order. In proceedings by A & Co. for non-payment of the price, the court may assume jurisdiction.[86]

7. A sends goods from England to X, his agent in Brazil. X contracts with A to sell the goods and remit the proceeds to England by first-class bank bills. X sells the goods but keeps the **11–181**

---

[80] *Cf. Malik v. Narodni Banka Ceskoslovenska* [1946] 2 All E.R. 663 (C.A.); *Vitkovice Horni A Hutni Tezirstvo v. Korner* [1951] A.C. 869; and see *ibid. sub nom. Korner v. Witkowitzer* [1950] 2 K.B. 128, esp. at pp. 159–161. See now Contracts (Applicable Law) Act 1990, Sched. 1, Art. 10(1)(b).

[81] *Cf. Holland v. Bennett* [1902] 1 K.B. 867 (C.A.), following *Cherry v. Thompson* (1872) L.R. 7 Q.B. 573, 579 (promise in Germany to marry in Germany, repudiated by letter sent from Germany to England: held, broken in Germany). Contrast *Cooper v. Knight* (1901) 17 T.L.R. 299 (C.A.) (promise in England to marry in England, repudiated by letter sent from Belgium to England: held, broken in England).

[82] *Cf. Mutzenbecher v. La Aseguradora Espanola* [1906] 1 K.B. 254 (C.A.); *cf. Oppenheimer v. Louis Rosenthal & Co. A.G.* [1937] 1 All E.R. 23 (C.A.).

[83] *Reynolds v. Coleman* (1887) 36 Ch.D. 453 (C.A.).

[84] *Cf. Bell & Co. v. Antwerp London and Brazil Line* [1891] 1 Q.B. 103 (C.A.).

[85] *Cf. The Eider* [1893] P. 119 (C.A.), where the stranding occurred and the contract was made in English territorial waters. At that date the fact that a contract was made in England did not bring a case within clause (4), *ante*, para. 11–155.

[86] *Robey & Co. v. Snaefell Mining Co. Ltd.* (1887) 20 Q.B.D. 152.

proceeds. The court has no jurisdiction, because X can perform his part of the contract by posting the bills from Brazil.[87]

8. By a contract made in New York, A & Co., wine shippers in London, appoint X, a firm of New York wine merchants, their sole agents for the sale of champagne in the United States, Canada and Cuba. The contract does not state where the champagne is to be paid for, but the course of dealing between the parties is for X to pay by drafts on a London bank. The court may assume jurisdiction.[88]

9. By a contract made in the United States X & Co., an American company, appoint A & Co., an English company, their sole agents for the sale of X & Co.'s products in England and the countries of continental Europe, and agree to pay A & Co. a commission of 15 per cent. on all products sold. A & Co. bring proceedings against X & Co. claiming an account of all sales effected by them and payment of commission on such sales. The court may assume jurisdiction.[89]

11–182 10. A, a Czech, is employed by X & Co., a Czech bank, as manager of the bank's foreign exchange department. His contract of employment provides for salary to be paid in Czech crowns. In August 1939 A goes to Switzerland, partly on leave and partly to safeguard the bank's deposit of gold there in the event of war. A then proceeds to England. In proceedings by A for non-payment of salary, the court has no jurisdiction.[90]

11. By a contract made in Czechoslovakia in 1929 X & Co., a Czech company, agrees to pay a pension to A, a Czech, one of the directors of X & Co., on his retirement. The contract provides for payment in Czech crowns. It is agreed between the parties that A shall be entitled to live where he likes and to be paid his pension in the place where he resides. A retires in 1938, and by another contract X & Co. agrees to retain his services in a consultative capacity in Switzerland, France or England at A's option, and to pay him a salary of £2,000 a year in addition to his pension. A retires to England. In proceedings by A for non-payment of his pension and salary, the court may assume jurisdiction.[91]

12. A, a Newcastle mining engineer, is engaged by X to design and superintend the construction of docks which X is to build in Poland for the Polish Government. A brings proceedings against X for non-payment of his commission and travelling expenses to Poland. The court may assume jurisdiction.[92]

13. A bill of exchange is drawn by A in London on X and accepted by X in London, "payable at the C.M. Bank, Kandy." In proceedings by A for non-payment the court may assume jurisdiction, because under section 19 of the Bills of Exchange Act 1882 an acceptance payable at a particular place is a general acceptance unless it expressly states that the bill is to be paid there only and not elsewhere.[93]

11R–183 **(6) The court may assume jurisdiction if the claim is founded on a tort and the damage was sustained, or resulted from an act committed, within the jurisdiction.[94]**

Comment

11–184 The question where a tort is committed for the purposes of choice of law is fully considered elsewhere in this book.[95] Until the amendment of Order 11, r. 1(1) in 1987 jurisdiction could be assumed under this clause only if the action was "founded on a tort committed within the jurisdiction." As both the

---

[87] *Comber v. Leyland* [1898] A.C. 254.
[88] *Charles Duval & Co. Ltd. v. Gans* [1904] 2 K.B. 685 (C.A.).
[89] *International Corporation Ltd. v. Besser Manufacturing Co.* [1950] 1 K.B. 488 (C.A.).
[90] *Malik v. Narodni Banka Ceskoslovenska* [1946] 2 All E.R. 663 (C.A.).
[91] *Vitkovice Horni A Hutni Tezirstvo v. Korner* [1951] A.C. 869.
[92] *Cf. Thompson v. Palmer* [1893] 2 Q.B. 80 (C.A.). *Cf. International Power and Engineering Consultants Ltd. v. Clark* (1964) 43 D.L.R. (2d) 394 (B.C.C.A.).
[93] *Ex p. Hayward* (1887) 3 T.L.R. 687.
[94] Ord. 11, r. 1(1)(*f*). See generally *Transnational Tort Litigation: Jurisdictional Principles*, ed. McLachlan and Nygh (1996).
[95] *Post*, paras. 35–081 *et seq.*

Privy Council[96] and the Supreme Court of Canada[97] have pointed out, the competing theories for the determination of the place of a tort have been that (i) all ingredients of the cause of action must have occurred within the jurisdiction, or (ii) the last ingredient, the event which completes a cause of action, must have occurred within the jurisdiction, or (iii) the act which the defendant committed must have occurred within the jurisdiction.

In *Distillers Co. Ltd. v. Thompson*[98] the Privy Council adopted the test of the place where in substance the act or omission occurred which gave the plaintiff his cause of action. So that where the essence of the complaint was failure to warn the consumer of the dangers of a product (rather than the faulty manufacture of the product) the cause of action was held to have arisen at the place where the failure to warn occurred[99]; and the torts of negligent and fraudulent misrepresentation, where the negligent or fraudulent statement was communicated from one country to another, were held to have been committed where the statement was received and acted upon.[1] Prior to the adoption of that test, but consistently with it, it had been held that the tort of defamation was committed where the defamatory statements were published and not where they were posted or uttered.[2]   **11–185**

The current version of this clause was adopted in order to bring the tort provision of Order 11, r. 1(1) into line with the 1968 Convention and intra-United Kingdom provisions.[3] These provisions (and those of the Lugano Convention) grant jurisdiction to the courts of "the place where the harmful   **11–186**

---

[96] *Distillers Co. Ltd. v. Thompson* [1971] A.C. 458.

[97] *Moran v. Pyle National (Canada) Ltd.* (1973) 43 D.L.R. (3d) 239. In this case, discussed by Collins (1975) 24 I.C.L.Q. 325, the court held, in a product liability case where the plaintiff had suffered injury in one province from a product negligently made in another province, that the province where the harm had occurred could exercise jurisdiction. It was extended to purely economic loss in *Skyrotors v. Carrière Technical Industries* (1979) 102 D.L.R. (3d) 323 (Ont.); see also *Ichi Canada Ltd. v. Yamauchi Rubber Industry Co.* (1983) 144 D.L.R. (3d) 533 (B.C.C.A.).

[98] [1971] A.C. 458 (P.C.). This decision related to a differently formulated rule in N.S.W., but it was applied to the former English rule in *Diamond v. Bank of London and Montreal Ltd.* [1979] Q.B. 333 (C.A.); *Castree v. Squibb & Sons Ltd.* [1980] 1 W.L.R. 1248 (C.A.); *Multinational Gas Co. v. Multinational Gas Services Ltd.* [1983] Ch. 258 (C.A.); *cf. Russell v. Woolworth & Co.*, 1982 S.C. 20; *Kirkcaldy D.C. v. Household Manufacturing Ltd.*, 1987 S.L.T. 617; *Scott Lithgow Ltd. v. GEC Electrical Projects Ltd.*, 1992 S.L.T. 244 (cases on Scots law prior to the 1982 Act). The Supreme Court of Ireland has held that there is jurisdiction (for the purposes of the unamended clause (6)) if "*any* significant element" has occurred within the jurisdiction: *Grehan v. Medical Inc.* [1986] I.R. 528, 541–542.

[99] *Distillers Co. Ltd. v. Thompson, supra,* discussed by Bissett-Johnson (1970) 48 Can. Bar Rev. 548; Collins, *Essays,* pp. 234–237; *Castree v. Squibb & Sons Ltd., supra; Buttigeig v. Universal Terminal and Stevedoring Corp.* [1972] V.R. 626; *My v. Toyota Motor Co. Ltd.* [1977] 2 N.Z.L.R. 113.

[1] *Multinational Gas Co. v. Multinational Gas Services Ltd.* [1983] Ch. 258 (C.A.); *The Albaforth* [1984] 2 Lloyd's Rep. 91 (C.A.); *Original Blouse Co. Ltd. v. Bruck Mills Ltd.* (1963) 42 D.L.R. (2d) 174 (B.C.); *Petersen v. A/B Bahco* (1980) 107 D.L.R. (3d) 49 (B.C.); *Canadian Commercial Bank v. Carpenter* (1990) 62 D.L.R. (4th) 734 (B.C.C.A.); *National Bank of Canada v. Clifford Chance* (1996) 30 O.R. (3d) 746; *Pei v. Bank Bumiputra Malaysia Berhad* (1998) 41 O.R. (3d) 39. Contrast *Cordova Land Co. Ltd. v. Victor Bros Inc.* [1966] 1 W.L.R. 793 (C.A.). *Cf. Minster Investments Ltd. v. Hyundai Precision and Industry Co. Ltd.* [1998] 2 Lloyd's Rep. 621; but see *Domicrest Ltd. v. Swiss Bank Corp.* [1999] Q.B. 547, *post,* para. 11–264.

[2] *Bata v. Bata* [1948] W.N. 366 (C.A.); *Jenner v. Sun Oil Co.* [1952] 2 D.L.R. 526 (Ont.); *Pindling v. N.B.C.* (1984) 14 D.L.R. (4th) 391 (Ont.); *cf. Bree v. Marescaux* (1881) 7 Q.B.D. 434.

[3] See *post,* paras. 11–261 *et seq.*

event occurred" and this expression was interpreted by the European Court in 1976[4] to grant alternative jurisdiction to the courts of the places, if different, (a) where the damage occurred, and (b) where the event which gave rise to the damage occurred. Clause (6) accordingly applies where the claim is founded on a tort, and (a) the damage was sustained within the jurisdiction, or (b) the damage resulted from an act committed within the jurisdiction.

11–187   In *Metall und Rohstoff A.G. v. Donaldson Lufkin & Jenrette Inc.*[5] the Court of Appeal posed the question of what law is to be applied in resolving whether the claim is "founded on a tort", and answered it in part by citing a statement in the eleventh edition of this work that the question concerned the interpretation of a connecting factor, which would always be answered in accordance with English law.[6] Accordingly, relying exclusively on principles of English law, the Court of Appeal decided that claims based on constructive trust, or procuring a breach of trust, were not claims based on tort.[7]

11–188   Damage sustained within the jurisdiction must refer to recoverable damage, including recoverable economic loss. In Canada and Australia, similar wording has been held to apply to consequential pecuniary damage sustained in the forum flowing from physical injury caused outside the forum.[8] The fact that the centre of the claimant's business is within the jurisdiction does not necessarily mean that the economic damage is suffered there.[9] In the second part of the formula, "an act committed within the jurisdiction" also extends to negligent omissions such as a failure to give adequate warning about the dangers of a product. In the *Metall und Rohstoff* case it was held that, for the purposes of each part of the formula, it is not necessary that all of the damage be sustained within the jurisdiction, or that all of the acts be committed within the jurisdiction. Some significant damage must have occurred in England; or the damage (wherever suffered) must result from substantial and efficacious acts committed within the jurisdiction, irrespective of whether or not other substantial and efficacious acts have been committed elsewhere.[10]

11–189   By contrast, however, with Article 5(3) of the Conventions, the exercise of jurisdiction under clause (6) is discretionary, and the court must consider what is the *forum conveniens*. In principle the jurisdiction where the tort is committed is *prima facie* the natural forum for the determination of the dispute: "If the substance of an alleged tort is committed within a certain jurisdiction, it is not easy to imagine what other facts could displace the conclusion that the

---

[4] Case 21/76 *Bier v. Mines de Potasse d'Alsace S.A.* [1976] E.C.R. 1735, [1978] Q.B. 708. The European Court has tended to apply Art. 5(3) in a more restrictive way than the decisions under Ord. 11, r.1(1)(l).

[5] [1990] 1 Q.B. 391 (C.A.), overruled in *Lonrho plc v. Fayed* [1992] 1 A.C. 448 on other aspects.

[6] At pp. 437, 441.

[7] At pp. 473–474, 480–481. *Cf. Suncorp. Realty Inc. v. PLN Investments Inc.* (1985) 23 D.L.R. (4th) 83 (Man.) (action to set aside fraudulent conveyance not an action in tort).

[8] *Skyrotors Ltd. v. Carrière Technical Industries* (1979) 102 D.L.R. (3d) 323 (Ont.); *Vile v. von Wendt* (1979) 103 D.L.R. (3d) 356 (Ont.); *Poirier v. Williston* (1980) 113 D.L.R. (3d) 252, app. dismissed (1981) 118 D.L.R. (3d) 576 (Ont. C.A.); *Challenor v. Douglas* [1983] 2 N.S.W.L.R. 405; *Girgis v. Flaherty* [1984] 1 N.S.W.L.R. 56, affd. *sub nom. Flaherty v. Girgis* (1985) 4 N.S.W.L.R. 248.

[9] *Soc. Commerciale Réassurance v. Eras International Ltd.* [1992] 1 Lloyd's Rep. 570 (C.A.); *Bastone & Firminger Ltd. v. Nasima Enterprises (Nigeria) Ltd.* [1996] C.L.C. 1902. Contrast *Skyrotors Ltd. v. Carrière Technical Industries Ltd.* (1979) 102 D.L.R. (3d) 323 (Ont.).

[10] [1990] 1 Q.B. 391, 437 (C.A.).

courts of that jurisdiction are the natural forum."[11] But where the acts or omissions occur, and the damage is sustained, in different countries, the *forum conveniens* may depend on the extent to which the issues are likely to relate to liability or to damage, and the relative importance of the place of acting and the place of damage from the point of view of the convenience of the parties and of witnesses and the other factors which the court takes into account in the exercise of the discretion under Order 11.[12]

If the claimant has a cause of action in both contract and tort he can elect to sue in either and may apply for permission under clause (4), (5) or (6), at his option.[13]

ILLUSTRATIONS

1. A brings proceedings against X & Co., an American company, for a libel contained in X & Co.'s French and Belgian newspapers, of which only a few copies have been sold in England. A has no connection whatsoever with England, and has only taken up residence here for the purposes of the libel claim. His real complaint is the publication of the libel in France and Belgium. The court will not exercise jurisdiction.[14] **11–190**

2. Under a contract made in New York and governed by its law, X & Co., an American company, sell rat poison to A & Co., an English company. It is agreed that the property shall pass in New York. X & Co. omit to warn A & Co. that the poison is dangerous unless certain precautions are taken. An English farmer who purchases the rat poison from A & Co. in England suffers losses to his livestock in consequence of using it, and A & Co. are compelled to compensate him. A & Co. bring proceedings in tort for negligence against X & Co. The court has jurisdiction because the damage was sustained in England.[15]

3. X & Co., a Canadian company, manufactures and sells in Canada to Y & Co., its English wholly owned subsidiary, a drug the principal ingredient of which is obtained in bulk from German manufacturers. The drug is intended for resale in England. X & Co. does not warn either Y & Co. or potential purchasers, in the printed matter supplied with the drug, of the harmful effect on a foetus if the drug is taken by a pregnant mother. A, whose mother has purchased the drug in England, is born with defective eyesight and without arms. A brings proceedings for negligence against X & Co. for failure to warn his mother of the dangers of taking the drug while pregnant. The court may assume jurisdiction under this clause because the damage was sustained in England and it resulted from an act (negligent failure to warn) within the jurisdiction.[16]

4. Circular letters containing a libel on A are posted by X in New York to addressees in England. The court may assume jurisdiction.[17] **11–191**

5. A brings an action for libel in England against X & Co., the owner of an American broadcasting station. The alleged libel was contained in a broadcast transmitted by satellite from the station and heard in England. *Semble* the court may assume jurisdiction.[18]

6. A, a London commodity broker, wishes to purchase a consignment of sugar from U.S. brokers acting for undisclosed principals. In fact the sugar does not exist and the transaction is not completed. A alleges that an employee of X Ltd., a Nassau bank, had confirmed to him in London

---

[11] *The Albaforth* [1984] 2 Lloyd's Rep. 91, 96 (C.A.), *per* Robert Goff L.J., applied in *Metall und Rohstoff A.G. v. Donaldson Lufkin & Jenrette Inc.* [1990] 1 Q.B. 391, 484 (C.A.). See also *Electric Furnace Co. v. Selas Corp. of America* [1987] R.P.C. 23, 35 (C.A.); *ISC Technologies Ltd. v. Guerin* [1992] 2 Lloyd's Rep. 430; *Schapira v. Ahronson* [1998] I.L.Pr. 587 (C.A.); *Berezovsky v. Forbes Inc., The Times*, November 27, 1998 (C.A.).

[12] See *ante*, para. 11–124.

[13] *Matthews v. Kuwait Bechtel Corporation* [1959] 2 Q.B. 57 (C.A.).

[14] *Cf. Kroch v. Rossell et Cie* [1937] 1 All E.R. 725 (C.A.); contrast *Buttes Gas and Oil Co. v. Hammer* [1971] 3 All E.R. 1025 (C.A.). See also *Pillai v. Sarkar, The Times*, July 21, 1994. For the different position under the 1968 and Lugano Conventions, see *post*, paras. 11–263 *et seq.*

[15] *Cf. George Monro Ltd. v. American Cyanamid and Chemical Corporation* [1944] K.B. 432 (C.A.), decided under the previous version of clause (6), where it was held that even if the tort had been committed in England, the discretion would be exercised against the plaintiff.

[16] *Cf. Distillers Co. Ltd. v. Thompson* [1971] A.C. 458 (P.C.). The court would also have jurisdiction over X Ltd. under clause (3) in an action against Y Ltd.

[17] *Cf. Bata v. Bata* [1948] W.N. 366 (C.A.).

[18] *Cf.* see *Jenner v. Sun Oil Co.* [1952] 2 D.L.R. 526 (Ont.).

by telephone and telex that the sugar was available and the U.S. brokers were able to undertake the sale. In A's proceedings for negligent and fraudulent misrepresentation, the court has jurisdiction but will not exercise it because A does not have a good arguable case on the merits.[19]

11–192   7. A & Co., a Swiss company, trades on the London Metal Exchange with X & Co., an English company carrying on business as metal brokers, whose immediate parent company is Y & Co., an American company, and whose ultimate holding company is Z & Co., another American company. A & Co.'s chief aluminium trader, with the assistance of X & Co.'s employees, trades fraudulently. The fraud is discovered by X & Co., Y & Co., and Z & Co. and X & Co. (in breach of its contract with A & Co., and on the instruction of Y & Co. and Z & Co.) closes out A & Co.'s accounts and seizes metal warrants belonging to A & Co. which X & Co. had held as security for advances. A & Co. are awarded substantial damages against X & Co., but recover only a small proportion because X & Co. is insolvent. The court has jurisdiction in proceedings against Y & Co. and Z & Co. for inducement of breach of contract. Although the acts alleged against Y & Co. and Z & Co. of inducing or procuring a breach of contract had in the main taken place in New York, it was the breaches of contract by X & Co. which had caused A & Co. substantial damage in England and in substance the tort was committed in England.[20]

11R–193   **(7) The court may assume jurisdiction if the whole subject-matter of the proceedings is land situate in England (with or without rents or profits), or the perpetuation of testimony relating to land so situate.[21]**

11R–194   **(8) The court may assume jurisdiction if the claim is brought to construe, rectify, set aside or enforce an act, deed, will,[22] contract, obligation or liability affecting land situate in England.[23]**

COMMENT

11–195   Clauses (7) and (8) deal with two classes of jurisdiction relating to land situate in England, and are discussed in Chapter 23.[24]

11R–196   **(9) The court may assume jurisdiction if the claim is made for a debt secured on immovable property or is made to assert, declare or determine proprietary or possessory rights, or rights of security, in or over movable property, or to obtain authority to dispose of movable property, situate in England.[25]**

COMMENT

11–197   The version of this clause introduced in 1983 is considerably more extensive than its predecessor, which applied principally to actions relating to security over movable property. It applies to the following claims: (a) a claim for a debt secured on immovable property situate in England; (b) a claim to assert, declare or determine proprietary or possessory rights, or rights of security, in or over movable property situate within England; and (c) a claim to obtain

---

[19] *Cf. Diamond v. Bank of London & Montreal Ltd.* [1979] Q.B. 333 (C.A.).
[20] *Metall und Rohstoff A.G. v. Donaldson Lufkin and Jenrette Inc.* [1990] 1 Q.B. 391 (C.A.). The decision was overruled in *Lonrho plc v. Fayed* [1992] 1 A.C. 448 on other aspects. On inducement of breach of contract see also *Elguindy v. Core Laboratories Canada Ltd.* (1987) 60 O.R. (2d) 151 and *ante*, para. 11–154, n. 10.
[21] Ord. 11, r. 1(1)(*g*).
[22] This apparently refers to an administration action. Compare clause (11), *post.*
[23] Ord. 11, r. 1(1)(*h*).
[24] Rule 113.
[25] Ord. 11, r. 1(1)(*i*).

authority to dispose of movable property situate within the jurisdiction. The origin of this clause lies in a former defect arising from the fact that proceedings, *e.g.* for foreclosure or redemption, in respect of a mortgage of movable property, are not regarded by English law as founded on a breach of contract, whether or not the mortgage deed provides expressly for the payment of interest and the repayment of principal. This view, of course, rests on the fact that the mortgagee has, strictly speaking, a legal estate in or charge on the property, the subject of the mortgage, and proceedings for foreclosure are founded on his ownership, not on a breach of contract, though such a breach is the occasion for the claim to assert the right of ownership. There is obviously no good ground for refusing to exercise jurisdiction in the case of proceedings of this kind, and the *casus omissus* is now made good. The jurisdiction, it will be observed, is essentially directed *in rem*, and does not extend to personal jurisdiction over persons outside England beyond dealing with property in England. This distinguishes the jurisdiction wholly from the Scottish practice of arresting property as a means of founding jurisdiction in matters quite unconnected with the property.

ILLUSTRATIONS

1. X, as beneficial owner, conveyed to A by way of mortgage his interest in movables under **11–198** an English marriage settlement, in order to secure a loan and the interest payable on it. Both X and A were then resident in England, but X is now residing in Australia. A issues proceedings against X claiming an account of the sum due under the mortgage deed and enforcement of payment of that sum by foreclosure or sale, and applies to the court for leave to serve the summons on X in Australia. The court may allow service.[26]

2. A & Co., bankers, carrying on business in England, claim as against X, residing in Panama, a declaration that they are entitled to a charge on certain policies of life insurance deposited with them, and that the charge may be enforced by foreclosure. The court may assume jurisdiction.[27]

3. A, having obtained judgment against X for £2,000, obtains an order charging the judgment debt with interest on X's shares in a public company in England. X is resident in America. In order to enforce the charge A institutes proceedings asking for the sale of the shares. The court may assume jurisdiction.[28]

(10) The court may assume jurisdiction if the claim is brought to **11R–199** **execute the trusts of a written instrument, being trusts that ought to be executed according to English law and of which the person to be served with the claim form is a trustee or for any remedy which might be obtained in any such action.**[29]

COMMENT

This clause confers jurisdiction in proceedings against trustees to execute a **11–200** written trust governed by English law. Before its amendment in 1983 this clause related to the execution of trusts "as to property situate within the

---

[26] Contrast *Hughes v. Oxenham* [1913] 1 Ch. 254 (C.A.), which was decided in the opposite sense under what is now Ord. 11, r. 1(1)(*e*), *i.e.* clause (5), *ante*, and in which an alteration to the rules to cover such cases was suggested.

[27] Contrast *Deutsche National Bank v. Paul* [1898] 1 Ch. 283, decided under the old rules.

[28] Contrast *Kolchmann v. Meurice* [1903] 1 K.B. 534.

[29] Ord. 11, r. 1(1)(*j*).

jurisdiction" and it had been held[30] that the clause did not apply when a trustee of stock sold it in breach of trust before leaving England, so that where at the time of leave being given to serve him there was no property in England subject to the trust, service was set aside. This decision was criticised on the ground that the relevant date for determining the situation of the property was the date of accrual of the cause of action,[31] but the decision is now obsolete.

Illustration

11–201   X is sole trustee of an English settlement. Under the trusts of the settlement, A is beneficially entitled to stock. X sells the stock and leaves England, and has not returned there. There is no other property in England which is subject to the trusts of the settlement. The court has jurisdiction to entertain proceedings by A for execution of the trusts of the settlement.[32]

11R–202   **(11) The court may assume jurisdiction if the claim is made for the administration of the estate of a person who died domiciled[33] in England, or for any relief or remedy which might be obtained in any such action.[34]**

11R–203   **(12) The court may assume jurisdiction if the claim is brought in a probate action.[35]**

11R–204   **(13) The court may assume jurisdiction if the claim is brought to enforce any judgment or arbitral award.[36]**

Comment

11–205   This clause was introduced in 1983 to fill a gap which had been revealed in cases where judgment creditors sought to enforce at common law judgments emanating from countries whose judgments were not capable of registration in England. Where enforcement by registration is possible,[37] the *in personam* jurisdiction of the English court over the defendant is irrelevant.[38] But where it was not possible (*e.g.* in the case of a judgment of a United States court) the remedy open to a judgment creditor who wished to proceed against assets in England was an action *in personam* at common law against the judgment debtor. Where the judgment debtor was in England at the date of service of the writ, the English court had jurisdiction.[39] But where the judgment debtor was outside England, and was not domiciled[40] there, he could not be served with

---

[30] *Winter v. Winter* [1894] 1 Ch. 421.
[31] *Official Solicitor v. Stype Investments Ltd.* [1983] 1 W.L.R. 214.
[32] Contrast *Winter v. Winter* [1894] 1 Ch. 421, decided under the former version of this clause.
[33] Within the meaning of the 1982 Act, s.41: Ord. 11, r. 1(4).
[34] Ord. 11, r. 1(1)(*k*).
[35] Ord. 11, r. 1(1)(*l*).
[36] Ord. 11, r. 1(1)(*m*).
[37] Under the Administration of Justice Act 1920, Foreign Judgments (Reciprocal Enforcement) Act 1933, and the Civil Jurisdiction and Judgments Act 1982, Pts I and II. See *post*, Chap. 14.
[38] *Cf. Hunt v. B.P. Exploration Co. (Libya) Ltd.* (1980) 144 C.L.R. 565; *Hunt v. B.P. Exploration Co. (Libya) Ltd.* [1980] 1 N.Z.L.R. 104.
[39] As in *Colt Industries Inc. v. Sarlie (No. 1)* [1966] 1 W.L.R. 440 (C.A.).
[40] Or, under the previous version of Ord. 11, ordinarily resident there.

the writ and no head of Order 11 applied to the claim even though he had assets in England which could be attached to satisfy the judgment.[41] Clause (13) remedies this defect and allows service abroad on the judgment debtor in proceedings at common law to enforce a foreign judgment or award.[42] But it does not justify service out of the jurisdiction of process designed to enforce a judgment which has not yet been obtained but which may be obtained in the future.[43]

Illustration

A, an Englishman, obtains a judgment in California against X, a resident of California, who never **11–206** comes to England, but who owns property in England. The court may assume jurisdiction by A in proceedings against X to enforce the judgment at common law.[44]

(14) The court may assume jurisdiction if the claim is brought against **11R–207** **a defendant not domiciled[45] in Scotland or Northern Ireland in respect of a claim by the Commissioners of Inland Revenue for or in relation to any of the duties or taxes which have been, or are for the time being, placed under their care and management.[46]**

(15) The court may assume jurisdiction if in the action begun by the **11R–208** **writ the claim is brought under the Nuclear Installations Act 1965 or the Social Security Contributions and Benefits Act 1992.[47]**

Comment

The Nuclear Installations Act 1965 gives effect to various international **11–209** conventions on civil liability for nuclear occurrences to which the United Kingdom is a party. The jurisdiction of the United Kingdom courts under this Act is discussed in Chapter 15. There are circumstances under the conventions in which the jurisdiction of the court depends on international agreement at ministerial level, and this is why the rules of the conventions as to jurisdiction are not set out in a Schedule to the Act. The Social Security Contributions and Benefits Act 1992 provides for the payment of contributions to the Secretary of State by earners and employers. The inclusion of the Act in this clause allows proceedings to recover these contributions to be served abroad.

(16) The court may assume jurisdiction if the claim is made for a sum **11R–210** **to which the Directive of the European Communities dated March 15,**

---

[41] *Perry v. Zissis* [1977] 1 Lloyd's Rep. 607 (C.A.). In *Nominal Defendant v. Motor Vehicle Insurance Trust of W. Australia* (1983) 81 F.L.R. 29 it was held that a foreign judgment could be enforced under clause (5): *sed quaere*. The court followed, but doubted the correctness of, the dictum in *Grant v. Easton* (1883) 13 Q.B.D. 302, 303 that liability on a foreign judgment arises upon an implied contract to pay the amount of the judgment. But *Grant v. Easton* was not a case on service out of the jurisdiction.

[42] See, *e.g. Midland International Trade Services Ltd. v. Sudairy, Financial Times*, May 2, 1990.

[43] *Mercedes Benz A.G. v. Leiduck* [1996] A.C. 284 (P.C.).

[44] Contrast *Perry v. Zissis, supra*, decided before clause (13) was introduced.

[45] Within the meaning of the 1982 Act, ss.41–42: Ord. 11, r. 1(4).

[46] Ord. 11, r. 1(1)(*n*). See *I.R.C. v. Stype Investments Ltd.* [1982] Ch. 456.

[47] Ord. 11, r. 1(1)(*o*).

1976,[48] applies and service is to be effected in a country which is a Member State of the European Economic Community.[49]

COMMENT

11–211   This clause relates to claims by H.M. Customs and Excise for sums due under the European Agricultural Guidance and Guarantee Fund and for agricultural levies and customs duties.

11R–212   **(17) The court may assume jurisdiction if the claim is made under the Drug Trafficking Offences Act 1986.[50]**

COMMENT

11–213   This clause relates to claims in connection with the proceeds of drug trafficking.

11R–214   **(18) The court may assume jurisdiction if the claim is made under the Financial Services Act 1986 or the Banking Act 1987.[51]**

COMMENT

11–215   This clause relates to such claims as proceedings for damages for breach of conduct of business rules under the 1986 Act or claims for repayment of unauthorised deposits under the 1987 Act.

11R–216   **(19) The court may assume jurisdiction if the claim is made under Part VI of the Criminal Justice Act 1988.[52]**

COMMENT

11–217   This clause relates to claims in connection with the confiscation of the proceeds of crime.

11R–218   **(20) The court may assume jurisdiction if the claim is brought for money had and received or for an account or other remedy against the defendant as constructive trustee, and the defendant's alleged liability arises out of acts committed, whether by him or otherwise, within the jurisdiction.[53]**

COMMENT

11–219   A claim in constructive trust normally arises in one of three situations. The first is where a person receives for his benefit trust property transferred to him in breach of trust; he is liable as a constructive trustee if he received it with notice, actual or constructive, that it was trust property and that the transfer to

---

[48] No. 76/308/EEC, text in [1976] O.J. L73/18.
[49] Ord. 11, r. 1(1)(*p*). The EEC is now called the EC.
[50] Ord. 11, r. 1(1)(*q*).
[51] Ord. 11, r. 1(1)(*r*).
[52] Ord. 11, r. 1(1)(*s*).
[53] Ord. 11, r. 1(1)(*t*).

him was a breach of trust, or subsequently discovered the facts. The second is where a person receives trust property lawfully and then misappropriates it or otherwise deals with it in a manner inconsistent with the trust. The third is where a person knowingly assists in the furtherance of a fraudulent and dishonest breach of trust.[54] The first and second categories were often referred to as "knowing receipt" cases, and the third as "knowing assistance", and are referred to today as "recipient liability" and "accessory liability".[55] Clause (20) was added in 1990 after it had been held that a claim based on constructive trust (in each of the three categories) was not founded on a tort for the purposes of clause (6).[56]

There has been a division of judicial opinion as to the extent to which the relevant acts necessary to establish liability must occur in England in order to bring the case within clause (20). Millett J. held that the clause only applies if all the acts necessary to impose liability are committed in England; and that clause (20) therefore applies to knowing participation by acts in a fraudulent breach of trust committed in England, but not knowing receipt abroad of the proceeds of such fraud.[57] In subsequent proceedings in the same litigation, Hoffmann J. suggested, *obiter*, that this was too narrow a view and that clause (20) was primarily designed for a foreign entity which had not participated in the fraud but had been used as a receptacle for the proceeds.[58] The latter view was followed by Knox J. in *Polly Peck International plc v. Nadir.*[59] He held that a construction of clause (20) which required all the acts constituting the alleged constructive trust to have been committed in England would empty it of nearly all its practical utility. It was sufficient if some, at least, of the acts which gave rise to the claim (but not necessarily the acquisition of knowledge) had occurred in England.

(21) The court may assume jurisdiction if the claim is made under the Immigration (Carriers' Liability) Act 1987.[60]

COMMENT

The 1987 Act imposes liability (in a prescribed amount in relation to each passenger) on the owners or agents of a ship or aircraft in which a person has arrived in the United Kingdom and where that person has failed to produce a valid passport and (if applicable) a valid visa.

B. *Where the Defendant is Domiciled in a 1968 Convention or Lugano Convention Contracting State*[61] *or in Scotland or Northern Ireland*

RULE 28—Subject to Rules 29 and 30 (exclusive jurisdiction under the 1968 Convention and the Lugano Convention), 53 and 54 (international

11–220

11R–221

11–222

11R–223

---

[54] See, *e.g. Agip (Africa) Ltd. v. Jackson* [1990] Ch. 265, 291–293, affd. [1991] Ch. 547 (C.A.). See also *Ghana Commercial Bank v. C, The Times,* March 3, 1997.

[55] See *Royal Brunei Airlines Sdn. Bhd. v. Tan* [1995] 2 A.C. 378 (P.C.).

[56] *Metall und Rohstoff A.G. v. Donaldson Lufkin & Jenrette Inc.* [1990] 1 Q.B. 391, 473–474 (C.A.). See also *DSQ Property Co. Ltd. v. Lotus Car Sales Ltd., The Times,* June 28, 1990 (C.A.).

[57] *ISC Technologies Ltd. v. Guerin,* 1990, unreported (Millett J.).

[58] *ISC Technologies Ltd. v. Guerin* [1992] 2 Lloyd's Rep. 430.

[59] *The Independent,* September 2, 1992. See also *Nycal (U.K.) Ltd. v. Lacey* [1994] C.L.C. 12.

[60] Ord. 11, r.1(1)(*u*).

[61] For Contracting States, see *ante,* paras. 11–006 *et seq.*

conventions) and 31(3) (*lis alibi pendens*) the High Court has jurisdiction to entertain a claim *in personam* in a civil or commercial matter falling within the scope of the 1968 Convention or the Lugano Convention in the cases mentioned in this Rule.

COMMENT

11–224 This Rule deals with the heads of *in personam* jurisdiction under the 1968 Convention and the Lugano Convention, and the similar, but not identical, counterpart in Schedule 4 to the 1982 Act, which allocates jurisdiction within the United Kingdom in relation to matters within the scope of the Conventions. Although the heading of this section refers to the domicile of the defendant, several qualifications have to be made to it. First, even if the defendant is domiciled in a Contracting State the jurisdictional rules discussed here do not apply if the case is outside the scope of the Conventions.[62] Matters which are outside the scope of the Conventions or excluded from Schedule 4 will be governed by Rules 24 to 27. Secondly, the provisions of Article 16[63] (and the corresponding provisions of Schedule 4) are not confined to cases where the defendant is domiciled in a Contracting State (or in a particular part of the United Kingdom). Thirdly, Article 17[64] of the Conventions confers jurisdiction on the court chosen by a jurisdiction agreement where one of the parties is domiciled in a Contracting State, and that party may not necessarily be the defendant. Fourthly, powers under Article 24 of the Convention (given effect by section 25 of the 1982 Act) to grant interim remedies may be exercised where proceedings on the substance of the matter are proceeding in another Contracting State, irrespective of the domicile of the defendant.

11–225 It is important to note that the jurisdiction under this Rule is not subject to the discretion of the court even as regards defendants to be served outside England. By Order 11, r. 1(2)(*a*) service of process out of the jurisdiction is permissible without the permission of the court if the claim is one to which the 1968 Convention or the Lugano Convention or the intra-United Kingdom rules apply.[65] There is no room for the application of *forum conveniens* principles as between the Contracting States.[66] A defendant who wishes to dispute the jurisdiction of the court may apply for an order declaring that it has no jurisdiction, and also for an order setting aside service.[67] The European Court has held that it is for the national court to determine the standard of proof required to establish that the conditions for the establishment of jurisdiction under the 1968 Convention are satisfied, provided that they do not impair

---

[62] *Ante*, paras. 11–013 *et seq.*

[63] *Post*, Rule 29.

[64] *Post*, Rule 32(3). Where neither party is domiciled in a Contracting State, and the parties have by agreement provided for the jurisdiction of the courts of a Contracting State, the effect of Art. 17 is to deprive the courts of other Contracting States of jurisdiction unless the chosen courts have declined jurisdiction.

[65] The only exception is Ord. 11, r. 8A, which requires permission for the service of a claim form for an interim remedy under section 25(1) of the 1982 Act: see *ante*, para. 8–022.

[66] See para. 11–012, *ante*, and paras. 12–015 *et seq.*, *post*.

[67] CPR 11(1), (6). If the defendant is to be served out of the jurisdiction the claim form (and the particulars of claim, if contained in a separate document) must be endorsed with a statement that the court has power under the 1982 Act to deal with the claim and that no proceedings based on the same claim are pending between the parties in another part of the United Kingdom or another Convention territory: CPR PD7, para. 3.5. See also Practice Direction supplementing Ord. 11, para. 1.

the effectiveness of the Convention.[68] In England it has been held that the standard to be applied in considering whether the jurisdiction of the court has been established for the purposes of the Conventions is the same as that under Order, 11, r. 1(1), *i.e.* a good arguable case.[69]

Allocation of jurisdiction within the United Kingdom. The primary rule of jurisdiction in the 1968 Convention (and in the Lugano Convention) is that a defendant domiciled in a Contracting State is to be sued in the courts of that State. Because the United Kingdom is not a unitary State for the purposes of civil jurisdiction it was necessary to allocate jurisdiction as between its constituent parts. But instead of confining itself to determining in which part of the United Kingdom a party is domiciled, the 1982 Act goes much further in laying down rules for determining jurisdiction in cases where the parties are domiciled in different parts of the United Kingdom. These rules (which are set out in Schedule 4 to the Act) were closely modelled on those in the 1968 Convention but are not identical with them.[70] They apply where (a) the subject-matter of the proceedings is within the scope of the 1968 Convention as determined by Article 1 (whether or not the Convention or any other Convention has effect in relation to the proceedings) and (b) the defendant is domiciled in the United Kingdom or the proceedings are of a kind mentioned in Article 16 (exclusive jurisdiction).[71] Where, in a Convention case, the courts of the United Kingdom have jurisdiction as the Contracting State in which the defendant is domiciled, Schedule 4 determines in which part of the United Kingdom the defendant must be sued. Similarly, the reference in Article 16 is to the courts of "the Contracting State" in which the property is situate, the company has its seat, the register is kept, etc. In these cases too it is necessary to allocate the resulting jurisdiction. Where the defendant is not domiciled in the United Kingdom and Article 16 does not apply, the problem of intra-United Kingdom jurisdiction rarely arises in the Convention provisions set out in Schedules 1 and 3C. Allocation is irrelevant in those provisions[72] which give jurisdiction to a "place" and it will be that part of the United Kingdom in which that place is situated which will be the relevant part of the United Kingdom for the purposes of jurisdiction. Where the Conventions refer to a "court"[73] in which proceedings are pending it will be the law district in which the relevant court is situated which will be the court with jurisdiction.

11–226

There are two further cases which require allocation. First, Article 5(6) gives jurisdiction in actions against settlors, trustees or beneficiaries to the courts of the Contracting State in which the trust is domiciled, and the 1982 Act provides that any proceedings which by virtue of Article 5(6) are brought in the United Kingdom shall be brought in the courts of the part of the United

11–227

---

[68] Case C–68/93 *Shevill v. Presse Alliance* [1995] E.C.R. I–415, [1995] 2 A.C. 18.

[69] See *Canada Trust Co. v. Stolzenberg (No. 2)* [1998] 1 W.L.R. 547 (C.A.) applying *Tesam Distribution Ltd. v. Schuh Mode Team GmbH* [1990] I.L.Pr. 149 (C.A.) and *Mölnlycke AB v. Procter & Gamble Ltd.* [1992] 1 W.L.R. 1112 (C.A.), in the light of *Seaconsar Far East Ltd v. Bank Markazi Iran* [1994] 1 A.C. 438.

[70] The European Court has no jurisdiction to give preliminary rulings on the interpretation of Sched. 4 to the 1982 Act: Case C–346/93 *Kleinwort Benson Ltd. v. City of Glasgow District Council* [1995] E.C.R. I–615; [1996] Q.B. 57, *ante*, para. 11–048.

[71] 1982 Act, s.16(1).

[72] Arts. 5(1), (2), (3), (5) and 6(1).

[73] Arts. 5(4), (7), 6(2), (3) and 6A.

Kingdom in which the trust is domiciled.[74] Secondly, Article 14(1) allows a consumer to bring proceedings in the courts of the State in which he is domiciled, and the 1982 Act provides that any proceedings which, by virtue of Article 14(1) are brought in the United Kingdom by a consumer on the ground that he is himself domiciled there, shall be brought in the court for the part of the United Kingdom in which he is domiciled.[75]

11–228   The primary rule of jurisdiction in Schedule 4 is, like that in the 1968 Convention, the domicile of the defendant, but there are differences between Schedule 4 and its 1968 Convention equivalent in the other heads of jurisdiction. Certain types of proceeding are excluded from the operation of Schedule 4.[76] Most of these are cases which would fall outside the Convention scheme, but there are others, such as (a) winding-up of solvent companies or (b) proceedings concerned with registration of patents, etc., which are within the 1968 Convention but outside Schedule 4. The former is excluded because it was not appropriate to apply the standard tests for seats of companies in the intra-United Kingdom context, where place of incorporation is the only appropriate test for the winding-up of domestic companies. Proceedings relating to registration of patents, etc., are excluded because the principle of Article 16(4) cannot be applied to allocate jurisdiction between courts in the United Kingdom since the registers of patents, trade marks and designs are all situated in London. A new Article 5(8) confers jurisdiction on the courts of the part of the United Kingdom in which property is situated in proceedings (a) concerning a debt secured on immovable property or (b) which are brought in connection with proprietary or possessory rights, or security rights, in relation to movable property.[77] The provisions of Articles 7 to 12A relating to jurisdiction in matters relating to insurance are entirely deleted. It would follow from this that, in proceedings between an insurer and an insured, they must be brought in the court which has jurisdiction under the general Convention rules. A number of other differences of detail are noted at the appropriate points when the corresponding provisions of the 1968 Convention are discussed.[78]

ILLUSTRATIONS

11–229   1. A resides in London. While on a visit to France he is injured as a result of the negligence of X, who is domiciled in France. The court has no jurisdiction in proceedings by A against X.

2. A resides in London. While X, who is domiciled in France, is on a visit to England he negligently injures A. The court has jurisdiction in proceedings by A against X.[79]

3. A resides in London. While A and X, who is domiciled in England, are on a trip to France, A is injured as a result of the negligence of X. The court has jurisdiction in proceedings by A against X.[80]

---

[74] 1982 Act, s.10(2), *post*, para. 11–278.
[75] 1982 Act, s.10(3), *post*, clause (14). See also s.44(2) for the allocation of domicile in the case of insurers domiciled outside the Contracting States, but with a branch in a Contracting State, and in the equivalent case for consumer contracts.
[76] See Sched. 5.
[77] *Post*, clause (7).
[78] See especially Art. 5(3) (applies expressly in Sched. 4 to threatened wrongs), *post*, para. 11–265; Art. 5A and Art. 16(2) (decisions of organs of companies), *post*, para. 11–331; Art. 17 (removal of formal requirement; subject to mandatory legislation) *post*, para. 12–109.
[79] 1968 Convention, Art. 5(3).
[80] *Ibid.*, Art. 2.

4. The facts are as in Illustration 3, except that X is domiciled in Scotland. The court has no jurisdiction.[81]

5. A resides in London. While A and X, who is domiciled in Scotland, are driving in England A is injured as a result of the negligence of X. The court has jurisdiction.[82]

(1) The court has jurisdiction if the claim is made against a person   **11R–230**
domiciled in England.[83]

COMMENT

The basic principle of the Convention scheme (which is also reflected in the   **11–231**
intra-United Kingdom provisions of Schedule 4) is that persons domiciled in a Contracting State may be sued there, and may be sued in another Contracting State only by virtue of the special rules of jurisdiction in the Conventions. The primary rule of domicile as the basis of jurisdiction is set out in Article 2 which provides that "persons domiciled in a Contracting State shall, whatever their nationality, be sued in the courts of that State." In *Canada Trust Co. v. Stolzenberg (No. 2)*[84] it was held (by a majority) that the critical date for testing whether the defendant was domiciled in England for the purposes of Article 2 was the date of the *issue* of proceedings rather than the date of service.

Article 2 is expressly subject to the other provisions of the Conventions; but   **11–232**
the overriding importance of the principal rule of domicile has been the starting point of the European Court's interpretation of the scope of the special jurisdictions under the 1968 Convention, because the basis of the system of jurisdiction under Title II of the Convention "is the general conferment of jurisdiction on the court of the defendant's domicile"[85] and "it is in accord with the objective of the Convention to avoid a wide and multifarious interpretation of the exceptions to the general rule of jurisdiction contained in Article 2."[86]

It is the domicile of the defendant which is crucial for the purposes of   **11–233**
jurisdiction. Only rarely is the domicile of the claimant relevant.[87] If the defendant is not domiciled in a Contracting State, normally[88] Rules 24 to 27 apply. Article 3(1) provides that persons domiciled in a Contracting State may be sued in the courts of another Contracting State only by virtue of the rules set out in Articles 5 to 18. Article 3(2) contains a (non-exhaustive) catalogue of jurisdictional rules in various Contracting States which may not be invoked against domiciliaries of Contracting States. Strictly, this provision is not necessary and is merely declaratory, because Article 3(1) makes it clear that domiciliaries may only be sued in the circumstances set out in the relevant Convention. The rule in English law which is in effect branded as exorbitant is the rule allowing the exercise of jurisdiction over an individual by virtue of

---

[81] Sched. 4, Art. 2.

[82] *Ibid.*, Art. 5(3).

[83] 1968 Convention, Art. 2 and Lugano Convention, Art. 2, in 1982 Act, Scheds 1 and 3C; 1982 Act, Sched. 4, Art. 2.

[84] [1998] 1 W.L.R. 547 (C.A.).

[85] Case 12/76 *Industrie Tessili Italiana Como v. Dunlop A.G.* [1976] E.C.R. 1473, 1485.

[86] Case 33/78 *Somafer S.A. v. Saar-Ferngas A.G.* [1978] E.C.R. 2183, 2191.

[87] See Art. 5(2) (domicile of maintenance creditor); Art. 8(1)(2) (domicile of policyholder); Art. 13(1) (domicile of consumer).

[88] For exceptions see Arts. 8(2), 13(2), 16 and 17.

his mere presence at the time of the service of process.[89] But in practice the operation of this much-criticised rule does not today work inconvenience or injustice, since, in the case of a genuinely contested claim, the courts have come to accept that a stay of the proceedings will be granted if they have no real connection with England.[90]

11–234   Even if the defendant is domiciled in England, the court will not be able to assume jurisdiction in the following cases: (a) where the courts of another Contracting State have exclusive jurisdiction pursuant to Article 16[91]; (b) where the courts of Scotland or Northern Ireland have exclusive jurisdiction pursuant to Article 16 of Schedule 4[92]; (c) where the parties have agreed that the courts of another Contracting State or of Scotland or Northern Ireland shall have jurisdiction pursuant to the terms of Article 17 of the Conventions or Schedule 4[93]; (d) where proceedings involving the same cause of action have already been commenced in the courts of another Contracting State. In the latter case the court has no discretion (as it has if the proceedings are pending in Scotland or Northern Ireland) to assume jurisdiction.[94]

ILLUSTRATIONS

11–235   1. X, who resides in and is domiciled in France, is an art dealer. A is an Indian princess. X in France sells a picture to A for cash and represents that it was painted by the French artist Boucher. A is later advised that the picture was not painted by Boucher and issues a writ claiming rescission and damages. X is served at Ascot races during his temporary visit to England. Service will be set aside.[95]

2. A & Co., an American company, brings an action against X, who is domiciled in Switzerland, in respect of a debt incurred in New York, and serves X while X is staying for a few days at a London hotel. Service will be set aside.[96]

3. The facts are as in Illustration 2, except that X is domiciled in New York. The court has jurisdiction.[97]

4. The facts are as in Illustration 2, except that X is domiciled in Scotland. Service will be set aside.[98]

11R–236   **(2) The court has jurisdiction, subject to clauses (13) and (14) of this Rule, in matters relating to a contract, if England is the place of performance of the obligation in question.[99]**

COMMENT

11–237   This clause applies equally to defendants domiciled in another Contracting State or in Scotland or Northern Ireland. But it does not apply, as regards defendants domiciled (or deemed to be domiciled) in other Contracting States,

---

[89] Rule 24, *ante*.
[90] Rule 31, *post*.
[91] Rules 29 and 114, *post*.
[92] *Ibid.*
[93] *Post*, Rule 32(3).
[94] Rule 31, *post*.
[95] 1968 Convention, Art. 3. Contrast *Maharanee of Baroda v. Wildenstein* [1972] 2 Q.B. 283 (C.A.).
[96] Lugano Convention, Art. 3. Contrast *Colt Industries v. Sarlie* [1966] 1 W.L.R. 440 (C.A.).
[97] 1968 Convention, Art. 4.
[98] 1982 Act, Sched. 4, Art. 3.
[99] 1968 Convention, Art. 5(1) and Lugano Convention, Art. 5(1), in 1982 Act, Scheds. 1 and 3C; 1982 Act, Sched. 4, Art. 5(1). See Hertz, *Jurisdiction in Contract and Tort under the Brussels Convention* (1998); Hill (1995) 44 I.C.L.Q. 591; Kennett (1995) 15 Yb. Eur. L 193.

to disputes relating to contracts of insurance, for which special provision is made[1]; and it does not apply to disputes relating to consumer contracts as defined in the Conventions when the defendant is domiciled (or deemed to be domiciled) in another Contracting State or in Scotland or Northern Ireland.[2]

Article 5(1) confers jurisdiction "in matters relating to a contract, in the   **11–238** courts for the place of performance of the obligation in question." This provision relates to contractual claims ("en matière contractuelle"). In England, jurisdiction over persons not present, domiciled or resident within England may be exercised in non-Convention cases in contractual matters (a) where the contract was made within the jurisdiction, or (b) where the contract was made by or through an agent trading or residing within the jurisdiction, or (c) where the contract is by its terms, or by implication, governed by English law or (d) for a breach of contract committed within the jurisdiction; and (e) where there is a contractual choice of English jurisdiction.[3] The Convention rules are significantly different. There is no provision corresponding to (a), (b) or (c). Although (d) has some superficial similarity to the Convention rule, it differs from it in at least one important respect. Under the English rule it is possible to envisage a breach in England of a contractual obligation to be performed elsewhere, *e.g.* by express or implied repudiation.[4] Under the Conventions, however, jurisdiction is conferred on the place of performance of the obligation in question and not on the place of the breach.

Article 5(1) must be read subject to four other matters. First, Article 54(3)   **11–239** provides that if the parties to a dispute concerning a contract had agreed in writing before January 1, 1987[5] (in the case of the 1968 Convention) or before (in the case of the Lugano Convention) its entry into force,[6] that it was to be governed by the law of a part of the United Kingdom, the courts of the United Kingdom are to retain the right to exercise jurisdiction in the dispute. This means that, in addition to the place of performance jurisdiction under Article 5(1), the English court will retain the right to exercise jurisdiction under clause (4) of Rule 27.[7] It should be noted that: (a) this jurisdiction will remain discretionary; (b) it will apply only if there is an express choice of law in writing[8]; and (c) it will apply only if the choice of law is made before the relevant date. This jurisdiction will also apply (for agreements made before January 1, 1987) in relation to defendants domiciled in Scotland and Northern Ireland,[9] even though what is now Order 11, r. 1(1)(*d*)(iii), Rule 27, clause (4), did not formerly apply to defendants resident in Scotland.

Secondly, Article I of the 1968 Protocol and of Protocol No. 1[10] to the   **11–240** Lugano Convention provides that a person domiciled in Luxembourg who is sued in a court of another Contracting State pursuant to Article 5(1) may refuse to submit to the jurisdiction of the court; if the defendant does not enter

---

[1] *Post*, clause (13). But it does apply to reinsurance: see *post*, para. 11–302.

[2] *Post*, clause (14).

[3] *Ante*, Rule 27(4), (5).

[4] *Ante*, para. 11–172.

[5] The relevant date in relation to the Republic of Ireland is June 1, 1988.

[6] May 1, 1992.

[7] *Ante*, para. 11R–152.

[8] *New Hampshire Insurance Co. v. Strabag Bau* [1992] 1 Lloyd's Rep. 361 (C.A.).

[9] 1982 Act, Sched. 13, Pt II, para. 1(2).

[10] See also Art. 1a, for special provisions on enforcement in Switzerland of judgments based on Art. 5(1).

an appearance, the court shall declare of its own motion that it has no jurisdiction. This provision was originally designed to protect Luxembourg domiciliaries from the jurisdiction of Belgian courts and it is not easy to understand its continued justification.

11–241   Thirdly, it should be noted that under Article VB of the 1968 Protocol, inserted by the 1978 Accession Convention and amended by the 1989 Accession Convention, there are special provisions relating to disputes involving the terms of service of crews of ships registered in Denmark, Greece, Ireland and Portugal; the corresponding provision in Article 5B of Protocol No. 1 to the Lugano Convention adds Norway and Sweden.

11–242   Fourthly, there are special provisions for contractual claims (especially debts secured on immovable property) connected with actions in matters relating to rights *in rem* in immovable property, and for claims connected with tenancies.[11]

11–243   **Contract.** Whether a matter relates to a contract will not usually give rise to difficulty. There is a sufficiently common core on the meaning of contract to result in the term being given a Community interpretation. In four decisions[12] the European Court has confirmed that the concept of "matters relating to a contract" is to be regarded as an independent concept, and is not to be tested simply by reference to national law. In *Arcado Sprl v. Haviland*[13] a Belgian court asked the European Court whether proceedings relating to the repudiation of a commercial agency agreement and the payment of commission under it were proceedings in matters relating to a contract within Article 5(1). Under Belgian law (as under English law) it was clear that such proceedings were for breach of contract and for sums due under contract, but a doubt appears to have arisen because in France there have been suggestions that a claim for breach of contract in bad faith may be delictual in nature.[14] The European Court answered that there is no doubt that a claim for commission is contractual because it finds its basis in the agreement; and similarly a claim for compensation is contractual in nature because its basis is the failure to comply with a contractual obligation. The latter conclusion was supported by the fact that the EEC directives on commercial agents recognised the contractual nature of compensation in lieu of notice; and by the fact that the Rome Convention on the Law Applicable to Contractual Obligations[15] provided that the law applicable to a contract governed the consequences of failure to comply.

11–244   In *Soc. Handte et Cie GmbH v. TMCS*,[16] the plaintiffs were a French company which had bought metal-polishing machines from a Swiss company.

---

[11] Arts. 6(4) and 16(1), *post*, clauses (12) and (15).
[12] Case 34/82 *Peters v. ZNAV* [1983] E.C.R. 987; Case 9/87 *Arcado Sprl v. Haviland S.A.* [1988] E.C.R. 1539; Case C–26/91 *Soc. Jacob Handte et Cie GmbH v. TMCS* [1992] E.C.R. I–3967; Case C–51/97 *Réunion européenne S.A. v. Spliethoff's Bevrachtingskantoor B.V.* [1998] E.C.R. I–6511. See also, in relation to 1982 Act, Sched. 4, Art. 5(1), *Bank of Scotland v. IMRO*, 1989 S.L.T. 432, criticised by Mennie, 1990 S.L.T. (News) 1 (doubted whether obligations arising under bank's membership of self-regulating scheme were contractual in nature); *Engdiv Ltd. v. G. Percy Trentham Ltd.*, 1990 S.L.T. 617 (claim for contribution by architects against main contractors held a matter relating to a contract between main contractors and owners).
[13] *Supra.*
[14] See Allwood (1988) 16 Eur.L.Rev. 366.
[15] Contracts (Applicable Law) Act 1990, Sched. 1, Art. 10, *post*, Rule 178.
[16] *Supra.*

It fitted to the machines a suction system sold and installed by a French company. That system had been manufactured by a German company. Under French law the plaintiffs' claim against the German manufacturer that the equipment was unfit for its purpose was contractual in nature, even though there was no contract directly between the plaintiffs and the German company. The theory in French law is that the intermediate buyer transmits to the sub-buyer his contractual rights against the manufacturer. The European Court held that such a claim was not contractual for the purpose of Article 5(1). Article 5(1) only applies to cases in which there is an agreement freely entered into between the parties, and in most of the Contracting States such a claim would not be regarded as contractual. Similarly, it was held that although a claim by a consignee (or its insurer) against the carrier who has issued a bill of lading may be contractual, a claim against a carrier who is not in contractual relationship with the consignee is not within Article 5(1).[17]

The question has arisen in England whether an action to avoid an insurance **11–245** or re-insurance contract on the ground of misrepresentation or non-disclosure is a matter "relating to a contract" for the purposes of Article 5(1), and whether the duty of good faith can be the "obligation in question". These questions arise because the proceedings are based on breach of the duty of good faith owed to the insurer or re-insurer, and it is controversial as a matter of English law whether the duty of good faith is properly to be regarded as a contractual obligation or as an equitable obligation under the general law. It was held by the Court of Appeal in *Agnew v. Lansförsakringsbolagens AB*[18] that, even if the duty was not a contractual duty, nevertheless the action was a matter relating to the contract of re-insurance because it could not sensibly be regarded as being outside the scope of the contract: the duty of good faith had equitable origins, and it did not arise under the terms of the contract, but it was meaningless to talk of the duty except by reference to a contract. So also it was not necessary that the "obligation in question", the duty of good faith, should be classified as a contractual obligation.[19] Judgment in this case was given after the argument, but before the decision, in *Kleinwort Benson Ltd. v. Glasgow City Council*,[20] in which Lord Goff of Chieveley said in terms that Article 5(1) applied only where a claim was based on a particular contractual obligation.[21]

In *Kleinwort Benson Ltd. v. Glasgow City Council*[22] the House of Lords **11–246** held by a majority (Lords Nicholls and Mustill dissenting) that a claim for restitution of money paid under a purported contract which was void did not fall within Article 5(1),[23] as it was not a matter "relating to a contract".[24] A claim fell within Article 5(1) if it could properly be said to be based upon a particular contractual obligation, the place of performance of which was

---

[17] Case C–51/97 *Réunion européenne S.A. v. Spliethoff's Bevrachtingskantoor B.V.* [1998] E.C.R. I–6511.

[18] [1997] 4 All E.R. 937 (C.A.). An appeal to the House of Lords is pending. See also *Atlas Shipping Agency (UK) Ltd. v. Suisse Atlantique Société d'Armement Maritime S.A.* [1995] 2 Lloyd's Rep. 188.

[19] Disapproving *Trade Indemnity plc v. Forsakringsaktiebolaget Njord* [1995] 1 All E.R. 796.

[20] [1999] 1 A.C. 153.

[21] At p.167.

[22] *Supra.* See also *Strathaird Farms Ltd. v. G.A. Chattaway & Co.*, 1993 S.L.T. (Sh. Ct) 36.

[23] Sched. 4, in the same terms as the 1968 and Lugano Conventions. The European Court refused to give a ruling in the proceedings: see *ante*, para. 11–048.

[24] Nor was it a matter "relating to a tort or delict" within Article 5(3): see *post*, para. 11–260.

within the jurisdiction of the court. Where the claim was for the recovery of money paid under a supposed contract which in law never existed, it was impossible to say that the claim for the recovery of the money was based upon a particular contractual obligation. A claim to restitution based upon the principle of unjust enrichment did not *per se* fall within Article 5(1). It was not necessary to hold that a claim to restitution could never fall within Article 5(1). Very exceptionally, there might be particular circumstances in which it could properly be said that the claim in question, although a claim to restitution, was nevertheless based on a contractual obligation and fell within Article 5(1). Lord Goff left open the question whether Article 5(1) applied to a claim for the recovery of money paid under a valid contract on the ground of failure of consideration following the defendant's breach.

11–247 The jurisdiction under Article 5(1) may be invoked even if the existence of the contract is denied by the defendant. In *Effer SpA v. Kantner*[25] the dispositive holding was that the plaintiff may invoke this jurisdiction "even when the existence of the contract on which the claim is based is in dispute between the parties." It has been held that this is so even where it is the claimant who denies the existence of the contractual relationship and seeks a negative declaration that he is not bound by any obligation, and it is the defendant who asserts there is a contractual obligation,[26] but this must be regarded as doubtful.[27] The mere allegation of a contract is not enough to found jurisdiction: service may be set aside if there is no basis for the existence of a contract, *i.e.* no serious question which calls for a trial.[28]

11–248 **The obligation in question.** "The obligation in question" whose place of performance must be in England is the obligation which is the basis of the action. In *De Bloos Sprl v. Bouyer S.A.*[29] the European Court held that the "obligation" in Article 5(1) was the contractual obligation which formed the basis of the legal proceedings[30]; where the plaintiff seeks damages for faulty performance or non-performance of a contractual obligation, it is the latter obligation which is the relevant obligation for the purposes of Article 5(1). But as regards compensation for termination, it was for the national court to decide whether the obligation to pay it was a separate independent contractual obligation or whether it merely replaced the unperformed contractual

---

[25] Case 38/81 [1982] E.C.R. 825. See also Case 73/77 *Sanders v. Van der Putte* [1977] E.C.R. 2383 (jurisdiction under Art. 16(1) in dispute over existence of lease). *Cf.* Case C–269/95 *Benincasa v. Dentalkit Srl* [1997] E.C.R. I–3767 (jurisdiction clause effective under Art. 17 where party resisting its application claims contract is void).

[26] *Boss Group Ltd. v. Boss France S.A.* [1997] 1 W.L.R. 351 (C.A.). *Cf. Fisher v. Unione Italiana de Riassicurazione SpA* [1998] C.L.C. 682; also Batiffol and Lagarde, Vol. 2, pp. 475–476; *Soc. I.S.I. v. Soc. C.P.A.V.*, Cour de cassation, France, in 1983 *Rev. Crit.* 516, note Gaudemet-Tallon. See also the position under Ord. 11, r.1(1)(*d*), *ante*, para. 11–154.

[27] The decision was, however, mentioned with apparent approval by Lord Clyde in *Kleinwort Benson Ltd. v. Glasgow City Council* [1999] 1 A.C. 153, 182. See Briggs (1997) 58 B.Y.I.L. 331, 335.

[28] *Tesam Distribution Ltd. v. Shuh Mode Team GmbH* [1990] I.L.Pr. 149 (C.A.), applied in *Rank Film Distributors Ltd. v. Lanterna Editrice Srl* [1992] I.L.Pr. 58; *New England Reinsurance Corp. v. Messoghios Insurance Co. S.A.* [1992] 2 Lloyd's Rep. 251 (C.A.).

[29] Case 14/76 [1976] E.C.R. 1497.

[30] This is so even if it leads to a claim being subject to the jurisdiction of a court which does not have the closest connection with the dispute: Case C–282/92 *Custom Made Commercial Ltd. v. Stawa Metallbau GmbH* [1994] E.C.R. I–2913; *Boss Group Ltd. v. Boss France S.A.* [1997] 1 W.L.R. 351 (C.A.).

obligation.[31] This decision gave rise to considerable practical problems in cases of exclusive agency or distribution contracts where the defendant had repudiated a contract containing obligations to be performed in more than one country. In *Ivenel v. Schwab*[32] (a case concerned with a claim by a commission agent employed under a contract of employment) the European Court modified its approach to deal with a case involving mutual obligations to be performed in different countries. It held that in such a case the relevant obligation was the obligation which was characteristic of the contract. This is a concept borrowed from the Rome Convention on the Law Applicable to Contractual Obligations.[33] But in *Shenavai v. Kreischer*[34] the Court held that the decision in *Ivenel v. Schwab* was limited to contracts of employment.[35] In other cases it is not necessary or appropriate to identify the obligation which characterises the contract. Accordingly, in such cases regard should be had solely to the contractual obligations whose performance was sought.

Where a dispute is concerned with a number of obligations arising under **11–249** the contract, the court before which the matter is brought must be guided by the maxim *accessorium sequitur principale, i.e.* where various obligations are at issue, it will be the principal obligation which will determine jurisdiction. Thus in *Medway Packaging Ltd. v. Meurer Maschinen GmbH*[36] the English distributor of German machinery could sue in England for the German manufacturer's repudiation because the principal obligation which was the basis of the proceedings was the obligation to give reasonable notice of termination, which was performable in England at the distributor's place of business. Similarly, in *Union Transport plc v. Continental Lines S.A.*[37] English charterers could sue Belgian shipowners in London in a claim arising out of the shipowners' failure to ship a cargo of telegraph poles from Florida to Bangladesh. The relevant obligation was the obligation to nominate a vessel for the voyage charter, and the place of performance of that obligation was in London. In *Source Ltd. v. T.U.V. Rheinland Holding A.G.*[38] the plaintiffs, an English company, engaged a German company to conduct quality control inspections in the Far East of goods which the plaintiffs were proposing to import into England from suppliers in Hong Kong and Taiwan. When the plaintiffs received complaints about the quality of the goods, they instituted proceedings in England against the German company. It was held that the principal obligation of the contract was the inspection of the goods in the Far

---

[31] In England it is the latter: *cf. Photo Production Ltd. v. Securicor Transport Ltd.* [1980] A.C. 827, 849, *per* Lord Diplock, whose dicta, it is suggested, do not affect this conclusion. See *Medway Packaging Ltd. v. Meurer Maschinen GmbH* [1990] 1 Lloyd's Rep. 383, 389, affd. [1990] 2 Lloyd's Rep. 112 (C.A.).

[32] Case 133/81 [1982] E.C.R. 1891.

[33] See *post*, Rule 174.

[34] Case 266/85 [1987] E.C.R. 239.

[35] For which special provision is now made: see, *post*, paras. 11–253 *et seq*. See also *Mercury Publicity Ltd. v. Wolfgang Loerke GmbH* [1993] I.L.Pr 142 (C.A.).

[36] [1990] 2 Lloyd's Rep. 112 (C.A.). See also *Carl Stuart Ltd. v. Biotrace* [1993] I.L.R.M. 633. On distribution agreements in the context of Art. 5(1) see Hertz, *Jurisdiction in Contract and Tort under the Brussels Convention* (1998), pp. 132–138.

[37] [1992] 1 W.L.R 15 (H.L.).

[38] [1998] Q.B. 54 (C.A.), stated *post*, Illustration 5. See also *A.I.G. Group (U.K.) Ltd. v. The Ethniki* [1998] 4 All E.R. 301; *W.H. Martin Ltd. v. Feldbinder GmbH* [1998] I.L.Pr. 794. The principal obligation may be an implied term: *Raiffeisen Zentralbank Osterreich A.G. v. National Bank of Greece S.A.* [1999] 1 Lloyd's Rep. 408.

East and not the delivery of reports in England, and accordingly the English court did not have jurisdiction under Article 5(1).

11–250   **Place of performance.** Once the relevant contractual obligation has been determined, the next problem is what law determines where it is to be performed.[39] Article 5(1) is silent on this question. In *Industrie Tessili Italiana Como v. Dunlop A.G.*[40] the European Court held that it is for the court before which the matter is brought to establish whether the place of performance is situate within its territorial jurisdiction, and that it must for that purpose determine in accordance with its own rules of the conflict of laws what is the law applicable to the legal relationship in question, and define, in accordance with that law, the place of performance of the contractual obligation in question. This ruling was re-affirmed in 1994 in *Custom Made Commercial Ltd. v. Stawa Metallbau GmbH*,[41] where the European Court also held that the same principle applied where the conflict of laws rules of the court seised referred to a uniform law, such as Article 59(1) of the Uniform Law on the International Sale of Goods Act 1964, which provides that the buyer must pay the price to the seller at the seller's place of business, or, if he does not have a place of business, at his habitual residence (subject to agreement to the contrary).[42] Consequently, the German court had jurisdiction in an action for the price payable by an English buyer for goods supplied by a German seller. The reference had been made by the German Federal Supreme Court because the apparent effect of the combination of Article 5(1) of the 1968 Convention and Article 59(1) of the Uniform Law was to confer jurisdiction on the courts of the plaintiff's domicile, which was contrary to the general scheme of the 1968 Convention.

11–251   Thus, in sale of goods cases (subject to the special provisions relating to consumer contracts)[43] English courts will have jurisdiction over a French seller for damages for breach of warranty of quality if under the law applicable to the contract delivery was to be made in England.[44] Where the claim is for payment of the price it will be necessary to determine the due place of payment, a matter of some difficulty in the absence of agreement. Where there

---

[39] On place of performance see also *Ocarina Marine Ltd. v. Marcard Stein & Co.* [1994] 2 Lloyd's Rep. 524; *Sameon Co. S.A. v. N.V. Petrofina S.A.*, *The Times*, April 18, 1996; *Olympia Products Ltd. v. Mackintosh* [1992] I.L.R.M. 204; *Handbridge Services Ltd. v. Aerospace Communications Ltd.* [1993] 3 I.R. 342 (Sup.Ct.); *Ferndale Films Ltd. v. Granada Television Ltd.* [1993] 3 I.R. 363 (Sup.Ct.). Where the place of performance is in dispute, the claimant must show a good arguable case that England is the place of performance: *Mercury Publicity Ltd. v. Wolfgang Loerke GmbH* [1993] I.L.Pr. 142 (C.A.).

[40] Case 12/76 [1976] E.C.R. 1473, applied in *Domicrest Ltd. v. Swiss Bank Corp.* [1999] Q.B. 548. See also Case 133/81 *Ivenel v. Schwab, supra.*

[41] Case C–288/92 [1994] E.C.R. I–2913. The French Cour de Cassation has asked the European Court to reconsider the question whether the place of performance should be defined by the law governing the obligation or whether it should be determined autonomously in the light of the relationship creating the obligation and the circumstances of the case, and Ruiz-Jarabo Colomer A.-G. has recommended to the European Court that it should now adopt the latter approach: Case C–440/97 *GIE Groupe Concorde v. The Master of the Vessel "Suhadiwarno Panjan"* (pending). For the French proceedings see [1999] I.L.Pr. 141.

[42] Contrast *San Carlo Gruppo Alimentare SpA v. Vico* [1996] I.L.Pr. 493, (French Cour de Cassation, 1996) (Hague Convention on International Sale of Goods 1955, jurisdiction at domicile of buyer).

[43] As to which see *post*, clause (14).

[44] See generally Hertz, *op. cit., supra*, n. 36, pp. 114–124.

is no agreement, the normal English rule is that, in the absence of contrary indications, the debtor must seek out his creditor.[45] In practice, therefore, English courts will normally have jurisdiction in claims by the seller where the seller is English, and will normally have jurisdiction in claims by the buyer where the goods were to be delivered in England. The result will be different if the applicable law is foreign, and if the foreign law has a different rule.

The European Court has considered in two cases the question whether the parties may confer jurisdiction on the courts of a Contracting State by specifying that the performance of the obligation is deemed to be due there. The result of the cases is that a choice of the place of performance is effective for the purposes of Article 5(1), but it must be a place where the obligation is capable of being performed. In *Zelger v. Salinitri (No. 1)*[46] the European Court held that if the parties to the contract are permitted by the law applicable to the contract, subject to any conditions imposed by that law, to specify the place of performance of an obligation without satisfying any special condition of form, an agreement (even an oral agreement) on the place of performance of the obligation is sufficient to found jurisdiction in that place under Article 5(1). In the *MSG* case[47] the European Court acknowledged that the parties are free to agree on a place of performance for contractual obligations which differs from that which would be determined under the law applicable to the contract. But it held that they are nevertheless not entitled, with the sole aim of specifying the courts having jurisdiction, to designate a place of performance having no real connection with the reality of the contract at which the obligations arising under the contract could not be performed in accordance with the terms of the contract. **11–252**

Contracts of employment. In all countries certain aspects of labour or employment law claims are regulated by public law, but in *Sanicentral v. Collin*[48] the European Court confirmed that employment law came within the field of application of the 1968 Convention, and that litigation arising out of contracts of employment was subject to the Convention. It has already been seen that in *Ivenel v. Schwab*[49] the European Court held that, where claims were based on different obligations arising under a contract of employment, the obligation to be taken into account for the purposes of the application of Article 5(1) was the obligation which characterised the contact, which was normally the obligation to carry out the work. **11–253**

Article 5(1) of the Lugano Convention, and Article 5(1) of the 1968 Convention as amended by the 1989 Accession Convention, now contain special provision for employment contracts, but not in quite the same terms. Each of them confirms the decision in *Ivenel v. Schwab* by providing that in **11–254**

---

[45] *Ante*, para. 11–173. See *Gamlestaden plc v. Casa de Suecia S.A.* [1994] 1 Lloyd's Rep. 433; *Bank of Scotland v. Seitz*, 1990 S.L.T. 584; *Unidare plc v. James Scott Ltd.* [1991] 2 I.R. 88. Contrast *Royal Bank of Scotland v. Cassa di Risparmio delle Provincie Lombardi* [1992] I.L.Pr. 411 (C.A.).

[46] Case 56/79 [1980] E.C.R. 89.

[47] Case C–106/95 *Mainschiffahrts-Genossenschaft v. Les Gravières Rhénanes Sarl* [1997] E.C.R. I–911, [1997] Q.B. 731. See *post*, para. 12–104, on the relationship between the decisions in these cases and the requirements of Art. 17.

[48] Case 25/79 [1979] E.C.R. 3423; Jenard, p. 24.

[49] Case 133/81 [1982] E.C.R. 1891. See also Case 266/85 *Shenavai v. Kreischer* [1987] E.C.R. 239, 255–256, for the special characteristics of employment contracts.

individual contracts of employment[50] the place of performance of the obligation is that where the employee habitually carries out his work. If the employee does not carry out his work in any one country, the Lugano Convention provides that "this place shall be the place of business through which he was engaged"; whereas the 1968 Convention, as amended,[51] provides that in such a case "the employer may also be sued in the courts for the place where the business which engaged the employee was or is now situated."[52] In *Rutten v. Cross Medical Ltd.*[53] it was held that where an employee carried out his work in several Contracting States, the place where he habitually carried out his work was the place where he had established the effective centre of his working activities. The European Court emphasised that the purpose of these provisions is to afford protection to the employee, as the weaker party to the contract; that protection is best assured if disputes relating to a contract of employment fall within the jurisdiction of the courts of the place where the employee discharged his obligations towards his employer; that is the place where it is least expensive for the employee to engage in court proceedings.

11–255   The Rome Convention on the Law Applicable to Contractual Obligations[54] provides that, in the absence of express choice of law or unless it appears from the circumstances as a whole that the contract is more closely connected with another country, a contract of employment is governed by the law of the country in which the employee habitually carries out his work in performance of the contract, even if he is temporarily employed in another country; or if the employee does not habitually carry out his work in any one place, by the law of the country in which the place of business through which he was engaged is situated. The effect of the employment contract provisions in Article 5(1) of the 1968 Convention and the Lugano Convention is that in many countries the State which has jurisdiction will also be the State whose law governs.[55]

11–256   There is an important distinction between the versions of Article 5(1) in the Lugano Convention and in the amended 1968 Convention. Each gives jurisdiction to the courts of the place of business through which the employee was engaged in cases in which the employee does not habitually carry out his work in any one country. But the Lugano Convention does not expressly limit this jurisdiction to actions by the employee against the employer, whereas the amended 1968 Convention limits the basis of jurisdiction to cases in which the employer is being sued.[56] It is likely (but not certain) that the Lugano Convention would be interpreted in the same sense.[57] The expression "place

---

[50] It does not apply to collective agreements between employers and workers' representatives: Jenard-Möller, p. 73.

[51] 1982 Act, Sched. 4, Art. 5(1) (as amended) is identical.

[52] In relation to the unamended version of Art. 5(1), the European Court had held that where a French employee of a Belgian company worked in a number of non-Contracting States, Art. 5(1) was not applicable (Case 32/88 *Six Constructions Ltd. v. Humbert* [1989] E.C.R. 341), but that where the employee carried out his activities in more than one Contracting State, the place where the obligation characterising the contract had been or had to be performed was the place where or from which the employee mainly performed his obligations *vis-à-vis* his employer (Case C-125/92 *Mulox IBC Ltd. v. Geels* [1993] E.C.R. I-4075). For special provision in Art. 17 in relation to jurisdiction clauses in employment contracts, see *post*, para. 12–095.

[53] Case C–383/95 [1997] E.C.R. I–57, [1997] I.C.R. 715.

[54] Contracts (Applicable Law) Act 1990, Sched. 1, Art. 6(2), *post*, Rule 182(2).

[55] Jenard-Möller, p. 73.

[56] Almeida Cruz-Desantes Real-Jenard, p. 45.

[57] *Cf.* Jenard-Möller, p. 73, para. 44.

of business" is to be understood in a broad sense, and includes a branch or agency.[58]

An EC Directive,[59] which must be implemented by December 16, 1999, gives a right to an employee of an undertaking established in a Member State, who is "posted" to another Member State, to the benefit of the laws of the latter state with respect to (*inter alia*) health and safety at work. Article 6 of the Directive provides that the employee may sue the employer in the state to which the employee is posted, without prejudice to his right to sue elsewhere under, *e.g.* the 1968 and Lugano Conventions.

Proposals for reform. The operation of Article 5(1), as interpreted by the   **11–257** European Court, has given rise to criticism,[60] in particular because (especially where the obligation sued on is a payment obligation) it tends to give jurisdiction to the courts of the claimant's domicile, and does not fulfil the original expectation that it would give jurisdiction to the courts of the country with the closest connection with the dispute. There is a proposal for revision of the Conventions[61] to provide that, unless otherwise agreed, the place of the obligation in question shall, in the case of sale of goods, be the place where the goods were delivered or should have been delivered, and, in the case of the provision of services, be the place where the services were provided or should have been provided.

ILLUSTRATIONS

1. A in England sells goods to X in France. By English law the due place of payment of the   **11–258** price is England, and (in the circumstances of the case) by French law the due place of payment is France. The contract of sale is governed by English law. In proceedings by A against X for the price, the court has jurisdiction.[62]

2. The facts are as in Illustration 1, except that the contract of sale is governed by French law. The court has no jurisdiction.[63]

3. X & Co., a German company, appoints A to be the exclusive distributor of its machines in England. X & Co. repudiates the agreement and, in breach of the agreement, sells its machinery to Y & Co. The court has jurisdiction in proceedings by A against X & Co. for damages.[64]

4. A & Co., an English company, buys the business of L Ltd. from its receiver. L Ltd. had previously appointed X & Co., a French company, as the distributor of L Ltd.'s products in France. After A & Co. buys the business of L Ltd., A & Co., appoints a new French distributor. X & Co. complains that this is a breach of its distribution agreement. A & Co. brings proceedings in England for a declaration that it was not in a contractual relationship with X & Co. The court has jurisdiction, even though A & Co. claims there is no contract, because if there were a contract, it was to be performed in England by delivery of the products to X & Co. in England, and the negative obligations not to supply others extended to England as well as France.[64a]

5. A & Co. agrees to buy promotional goods from suppliers in Hong Kong and Taiwan for importation and resale in England. A & Co. engages X & Co., a German company, to conduct quality control inspections of the goods in the Far East prior to payment by A & Co. for the goods. X & Co. sends reports on the goods to A & Co. in England, and supplies certificates of quality to the sellers to enable them to obtain payment from A & Co. When A & Co. receives complaints

---

[58] de Almeida Cruz-Desantes Real-Jenard, p. 45.
[59] 96/71/EC, [1997] O.J. L18/1. See *post*, para. 33–072.
[60] See, *e.g.* Hill (1995) 44 I.C.L.Q. 591.
[61] See *ante*, para. 11–011.
[62] Case 12/76 *Industrie Tessili Italiana Como v. Dunlop A.G.* [1976] E.C.R. 1473.
[63] *Ibid.*
[64] *Medway Packaging Ltd. v. Meurer Maschinen GmbH* [1990] 2 Lloyd's Rep. 112 (C.A.).
[64a] *Boss Group Ltd. v. Boss France S.A.* [1997] 1 W.L.R. 351 (C.A.).

about the quality of the goods, it brings proceedings in England against X & Co. The court has no jurisdiction because the principal contractual obligation of X & Co. was the inspection of goods in the Far East rather than the supply of reports to A & Co. in England.[65]

6. A & Co., an English company, concludes with X & Co., a Belgian company, a voyage charter of a vessel to be nominated by X & Co. for the carriage of a cargo of telegraph poles from Florida to Bangladesh. A dispute arises, as a result of which X & Co. informs A & Co. that it is no longer interested in lifting the cargo. A & Co. sues for breach of charterparty. The court has jurisdiction, because the obligation in question is the obligation to nominate a vessel, and the place of performance of that obligation is England.[66]

7. A, who is domiciled in France, is employed by X & Co., a German company, to work for a year in England. After six months A is wrongfully dismissed. A sues X & Co. in England. The court has jurisdiction.[67]

8. A, who is domiciled in England, is employed through a recruitment office in London of X & Co., a French company, to work as a sales agent in Germany, France and Italy. A is wrongfully dismissed, and sues X & Co. in England. The court has jurisdiction.[68]

11R–259   **(3) The court has jurisdiction, in matters relating to tort, if England is the place where the harmful event occurred,[69] *i.e.* if England is the place where the damage occurred or where the event which gave rise to the damage occurred.[70]**

Comment

11–260   By Article 5(3)[71] jurisdiction is conferred in matters "relating to tort, delict or quasi-delict on the courts of the place where "the harmful event occurred." In *Kalfelis v. Schröder*[72] the European Court held that the expression "matters relating to tort, delict or quasi-delict" should not be interpreted solely by reference to national law, but should be regarded as an autonomous concept which "covers all actions which seek to establish the liability of a defendant and which are not related to a 'contract' within the meaning of Article 5(1)."[73] It was also held that where a national court had jurisdiction over an action in so far as it was based on tort or delict it did not for that reason alone have jurisdiction in relation to other types of claim. It has been decided that in those cases in English law where a claim may be based alternatively in contract and

---

[65] *Source Ltd. v. T.U.V. Rheinland Holding A.G.* [1998] Q.B. 54 (C.A.).
[66] *Union Transport plc v. Continental Lines S.A.* [1992] 1 W.L.R. 15 (H.L.).
[67] Art. 5(1), 1968 Convention.
[68] *Ibid.*
[69] 1968 Convention, Art. 5(3) and Lugano Convention, Art. 5(3), in 1982 Act, Scheds 1 and 3C; 1982 Act, Sched. 4, Art. 5(3).
[70] Case 21/76 *Bier v. Mines de Potasse d'Alsace S.A.* [1976] E.C.R. 1735, [1976] Q.B. 708.
[71] See generally *Transnational Tort Litigation: Jurisdictional Principles*, eds. McLachlan and Nygh (1996).
[72] Case 189/87 [1988] E.C.R. 5565. See also Case C–51/97 [1993] *Réunion européenne S.A. v. Spliethoff's Bevrachtingskantoor B.V.* [1998] E.C.R. I–6511.
[73] At p. 5585. This must be read in context, and does not include a claim for restitution: *Kleinwort Benson Ltd. v. Glasgow City Council* [1999] 1 A.C. 153, 167. See also Case C–261/90 *Reichert v. Dresdner Bank (No. 2)* [1992] E.C.R. I–2149 (action to set aside transaction in fraud of creditor not within Art. 5(3)); Case 814/79 *Netherlands State v. Rüffer* [1980] E.C.R. 3807, 3832–3835, *per* Warner A.G.; *Molnlycke AB v. Procter & Gamble Ltd. (No. 4)* [1992] R.P.C. 21 (C.A.) (patent infringement). In *Davenport v. Corinthian Motor Policies at Lloyd's*, 1991 S.L.T. 774, it was held that for the purposes of 1982 Act, Sched. 4, Art. 5(3), a statutory claim against an insurer for payment of a judgment by the insured is not based on tort or delict. *Cf. Kitechnology B.V. v. Unicor GmbH Plastmaschinen* [1995] F.S.R. 765 (C.A.) (breach of confidence: not decided whether within Art. 5(3)).

in tort,[74] the claim will be regarded for the purposes of the Conventions as being contractual in nature, and that Clause (3) will not be available as a head of jurisdiction.[75]

Most of the original Contracting States had a form of jurisdiction in tort **11–261** matters equivalent to Article 5(3); the draftsmen of the 1968 Convention deliberately left open the question whether the relevant "place" was the place where the wrongful act occurred or the place where the damage was suffered, if they were different places. The tendency of the English case law on the equivalent provision in Order 11 had been to look to the place where in substance the act or omission occurred which gave rise to the cause of action.[76] The point arose for decision under Article 5(3) in the European Court in *Bier v. Mines de Potasse d'Alsace*.[77] The European Court held that the "place" was to be determined, not by the diverging solutions of national law, but by a Convention rule and that the meaning of the expression "place where the harmful event occurred" in Article 5(3) must be interpreted so that the plaintiff has an option to commence proceedings either at the place where the damage occurred or at the place of the event giving rise to it.

The place of damage connotes the place where the physical damage is done **11–262** or the recoverable economic loss is actually suffered. Even though in one sense a claimant may suffer economic loss at the place of its business, that is not of itself sufficient to confer jurisdiction on that place, for otherwise the place of business of the claimant would almost automatically become another basis of jurisdiction.[78] In particular, a claimant cannot confer jurisdiction on the court of his domicile by alleging that, by suffering economic loss there, he was the victim of a harmful act committed abroad. Thus French companies, whose German subsidiaries had been made insolvent as a result of the alleged negligence of German banks in relation to a property development in Germany, could not sue the German banks in France. The fact that the French companies had experienced financial repercussions in France and had ascertained their loss there did not give the the the French court jurisdiction.[79] So also an Italian who claimed that the wrongful conduct of employees of Lloyds Bank in England had led to his arrest in England and seizure of promissory notes could not sue in Italy for the exchange value of the promissory notes and for damage to his reputation. The jurisdiction could not be interpreted so extensively as to encompass any place where the adverse consequences of an event which had already caused actual damage elsewhere could be felt.[80] A consignee of goods who complains that the goods were delivered in a damaged state may sue in the country where the damage occurred or where the

---

[74] See, *e.g. Matthews v. Kuwait Bechtel* [1959] 2 Q.B. 57 (C.A.).

[75] See *Source Ltd. v. T.U.V. Rheinland Holding A.G.* [1998] Q.B. 54 (C.A.). Contrast *Domicrest Ltd. v. Swiss Bank Corp.* [1999] Q.B. 548; *William Grant & Sons International Ltd. v. Marie-Brizard & Roger International S.A.*, 1998 S.C. 536. This will not normally make much practical difference, as the place of the tort will usually be the same as the place of performance of the obligation.

[76] *Ante*, para. 11–185. Ord. 11, r. 1(1)(*f*), Rule 27, clause (6), adopts the same solution as the Conventions.

[77] Case 21/76 [1976] E.C.R. 1735; [1978] Q.B. 708.

[78] *Cf.* Warner A.-G. in Case 814/79 *Netherlands State v. Rüffer* [1980] E.C.R. 3807, 3836.

[79] Case C–220/88 *Dumez France v. Hessische Landesbank* [1990] E.C.R. I–49.

[80] Case C–364/93 *Marinari v. Lloyds Bank plc* [1995] E.C.R. I–2719; [1996] Q.B. 217. *Cf. Kitechnology B.V. v. Unicor GmbH Plastmaschinen* [1995] F.S.R. 765 (C.A.); *Modus Vivendi Ltd. v. British Products Sanmex Co. Ltd.* [1996] F.S.R. 790.

event occurred which gave rise to the damage. But the place of damage is not the place of final delivery or the place where the damage was ascertained. To allow the consignee to sue in those places would in effect attribute jurisdiction to the place of the plaintiff's domicile. The place where the damage arose is the place where the carrier was to deliver the goods.[81]

11–263   The concept of "the place of the event giving rise" to the damage has received little elucidation from the European Court. In *Shevill v. Press Alliance*[82] the Court considered the question of the appropriate jurisdiction in the case of an action in England by plaintiffs established respectively in England, France and Belgium in respect of an alleged libel published in a French newspaper with a small circulation in England. The European Court held that the victim of a libel by a newspaper article distributed in several Contracting States may bring an action for damages against the publisher either before the courts of the Contracting State of the place where the publisher of the defamatory publication is established, which will have jurisdiction to award damages for all the harm caused by the defamation; or before the courts of each Contracting State in which the publication was distributed and where the victim claims to have suffered injury to his reputation, which will have jurisdiction to rule solely in respect of the harm caused in the State of the court seised. It also held that the criteria for assessing whether the event in question is harmful and the evidence required of the existence and extent of the harm alleged by the victim of the defamation are not governed by the 1968 Convention but by the substantive law determined by the national conflict of laws rules of the court seised, provided that the effectiveness of the 1968 Convention is not thereby impaired. Subsequently the House of Lords, applying this ruling, held that, where English law presumes that the publication of a defamatory statement is harmful to the person defamed without specific proof of damage, that is sufficient for the application of Article 5(3).[83]

11–264   In that case the place of the event giving rise to the damage was said to be the place where the publisher was established, since that was the place where the harmful event originated and from which the libel was issued and put into circulation. In *Domicrest Ltd. v. Swiss Bank Corp.*[84] it was held that, for the purposes of Article 5(3), in an action for negligent misstatement the place where the harmful event giving rise to the damage occurs is, by analogy with defamation, the place where the misstatement originated and that the place where the misstatement is received and relied upon is likely to be the place where the damage is suffered.

11–265   An important question which has not been settled is whether Article 5(3) justifies the assumption of jurisdiction to grant injunctions against threatened torts which have not been committed, *e.g.* defamation, passing off, or patent infringement. Where the tort has been committed within the jurisdiction, there is no doubt that the national court may grant an injunction restraining future

---

[81] Case C–51/97 *Réunion européenne S.A. v. Spliethoff's Bevrachtingskantoor B.V.* [1998] E.C.R. I–6511.

[82] Case C–68/93 [1995] E.C.R. I–415; [1995] 2 A.C. 18. See also *Mecklermedia Corp. v. D.C. Congress GmbH* [1998] Ch. 40; *Murray v. Times Newspapers Ltd.* [1995] 3 I.R. 244; *Ewins v. Carlton U.K. Television Ltd.* [1997] 2 I.L.R.M. 223.

[83] [1996] A.C. 959.

[84] [1999] Q.B. 548, not following *Minster Investments Ltd. v. Hyundai Precision and Industry Ltd.* [1988] 2 Lloyd's Rep. 621. See also *Source Ltd. v. T.U.V. Rheinland Holding Ltd.* [1998] Q.B. 54; *Waterford Wedgwood Ltd. v. David Nagli Ltd.*, *The Times*, May 13, 1998.

commission. Schlosser[85] gives hesitant support to the view that Article 5(3) would also provide a basis of jurisdiction in proceedings where the main object was to prevent the imminent commission of a tort. This might require a somewhat strained interpretation to be given to the word "occurred" but would clearly arrive at a practical and sensible result. The other view would require provisional measures to be taken in England under section 25 of the 1982 Act if England is the place where the threatened wrong might occur, and for the merits of the case to be fought at the place of the defendant's domicile. But as regards defendants domiciled in Scotland and Northern Ireland the version of Article 5(3) in Schedule 4 puts the matter beyond doubt in the sense that jurisdiction may be assumed on the basis of a threatened wrong.[86]

ILLUSTRATIONS

1. A brings proceedings against X & Co., a French company with its seat in France, for libel **11–266** contained in X & Co.'s French newspaper, of which only a few copies have been sold in England. The court has jurisdiction, but only in respect of damage to A's reputation in England.[87]

2. X & Co., a German company, manufacture in Germany a motor car with faulty brakes. The motor car fails in England, injuring A, the driver, who cannot work at his business in London for several months. A brings proceedings for negligence against X & Co. The court has jurisdiction.

3. The facts are as in Illustration 2, except that the accident occurs in Germany. The fact that A suffers economic loss to his business in England does not give the court jurisdiction.

4. X & Co., an English company, manufacture in England a motor car with faulty brakes. A, a Frenchman, buys it in France and is injured in an accident when the brakes fail. A brings proceedings against X & Co. The court has jurisdiction.[88]

5. A & Co. is an English company which supplies electronic goods. In a telephone conversation, an officer of X & Co., a Swiss bank, assures the agent of A & Co. in England that it would be safe to release goods to a buyer on receipt of payment orders from the bank. In reliance on the assurance, A & Co. releases goods to the buyer, who is unable to pay, and X & Co. refuses to honour the payment orders because it does not have funds from the buyer. In proceedings by A & Co. against X & Co. for negligent misrepresentation, it is held that the court has no jurisdiction because the place where the harmful event giving rise to damage occurred was the place where the misstatement occurred, in Switzerland, and not the place (England) where it was received and acted upon.[89]

6. A & Co. carry on business in England under the name "Harrods." X & Co., a French company, threaten to open a shop in London called "Harrods." (*Semble*) the court has jurisdiction under this clause in an action by A & Co. to restrain the passing-off and trade-mark infringement.

7. The facts are as in Illustration 5, except that X & Co. is a company registered in Scotland. The court has jurisdiction.[90]

(4) A criminal court has jurisdiction to make an order for damages or **11R–267** **restitution in criminal proceedings against a defendant domiciled in another Contracting State or in Scotland or Northern Ireland.**

---

[85] Para. 134. This view has been followed in German courts: see Kaye (ed.), *European Case Law on the Judgments Convention* (1998), p. 483. There is a proposal for revision of the Conventions (*ante*, para. 11–011) which will make it clear that Art. 5(3) applies to threatened torts.

[86] *Cf. WAC Ltd. v. Whillock*, 1990 S.L.T. 213.

[87] Case C–68/93 *Shevill v. Presse Alliance S.A.* [1995] E.C.R. I–415; [1995] 2 A.C. 18. *Cf. Kroch v. Rossell et Cie* [1937] 1 All E.R. 725 (C.A.), where the court did not exercise jurisdiction because A's real complaint related to the damage to his reputation in France and Belgium.

[88] 1968 Convention, Art. 2.

[89] *Domicrest Ltd. v. Swiss Bank Corporation* [1999] Q.B. 548.

[90] Sched. 4, Art. 5(3).

COMMENT

11–268   This clause, which is based on Article 5(4) of the Conventions, is included here for the sake of completeness since claims for restitution in criminal proceedings are outside the scope of this work.[91]

11R–269   **(5) The court has jurisdiction to determine a dispute arising out of the operations of a branch, agency or other establishment, if the branch, agency or other establishment is situated in England.**[92]

COMMENT

11–270   Article 5(5) confers jurisdiction in relation to a "dispute arising out of the operations of a branch, agency or other establishment" on the courts of the place where the branch, agency or other establishment is situated.[93] It relates only to defendants domiciled in a Contracting State, *i.e.* companies or firms with their seat in another Contracting State or in Scotland or Northern Ireland and a branch in England. Companies with their seats outside the Contracting States but with a branch in England fall within Rule 24.[94] By Article 8(2), however, an insurer not domiciled in a Contracting State but which has a branch, agency or other establishment in a Contracting State is, in disputes arising out of the operations of the branch, agency or establishment, deemed to be domiciled in that State; by Article 13(2) similar provision is made in relation to suppliers of goods and services in consumer contracts.[95]

11–271   Two main questions arise. First, what is a "branch, agency or other establishment"? Secondly, what disputes arise out of its operations? On the first question, it is clear that the concept must be interpreted by Convention standards and not by purely national notions.[96] The obvious case of a branch bearing the same business name and staffed by the employees of the main undertaking needs no comment. In two cases the European Court has declined to extend the concept of a branch to distributors or sales agents for goods of foreign companies. In *De Bloos Sprl v. Bouyer S.A.*[97] the Court held that one of the essential characteristics of the concept of branch or agency was the fact of being subject to the direction and control of the parent body; that the concept of "establishment" should be interpreted in a similar way, and that an exclusive distributor was therefore not a "branch," etc., of the manufacturer.

---

[91] Art. 5(4) is based on the idea, reflected in the legal systems of the original Contracting States, that the right to obtain compensation for damage suffered following behaviour contrary to criminal law is generally recognised as being civil in nature: Case C–172/91 *Sonntag v. Waidmann* [1993] E.C.R. I–1963. See also *Haji-Ioannou v. Frangos* [1999] 2 Lloyd's Rep. 337 (C.A.).

[92] 1968 Convention, Art. 5(5) and Lugano Convention, Art. 5(5), in 1982 Act, Scheds 1 and 3C; 1982 Act, Sched. 4, Art. 5(5). See Fawcett (1984) 9 Eur.L.Rev. 326.

[93] Art. 5(5) concerns the branch, etc., operations of the defendant. A claimant cannot confer jurisdiction on the court by relying on the presence of the *claimant's* branch: *New Hampshire Insurance Co. v. Strabag Bau* [1990] 2 Lloyd's Rep. 61, 68, affd. on other grounds [1992] 1 Lloyd's Rep. 361 (C.A.).

[94] *Ante*, paras. 11–094 *et seq.*

[95] See *post*, paras. 11–303 and 11–324, and 1982 Act, s.44.

[96] See Case 33/78 *Somafer S.A. v. Saar-Ferngas A.G.* [1978] E.C.R. 2183, 2190.

[97] Case 14/76 [1976] E.C.R. 1497.

In *Blanckaert and Willems P.V.B.A. v. Trost*[98] the Court held that an independent commercial agent who merely negotiates business, who is free to arrange his own work and decide what proportion of his time to devote to the interests of the undertaking which he agrees to represent, who may represent at the same time several firms competing in the same manufacturing marketing sector, and who merely transmits orders to the parent undertaking without being involved in either their terms or their execution does not have the character of a branch, agency, or other establishment within the meaning of Article 5(5).

In addition to the element of direction and control the Court has required the element of the "appearance of permanency." In *Somafer S.A. v. Saar-Ferngas A.G.*[99] the European Court held that the concept of branch, agency or other establishment implies a place of business which has the appearance of permanency, such as the extension of a parent body, so that third parties do not have to deal directly with such parent body but may transact business at the place of business constituting the extension. An important point which was raised but not decided in the *Somafer* case was whether the defendants were estopped from denying that they had an establishment in Germany by virtue of their letterhead which indicated that they had an office there. Advocate General Mayras thought that, having regard to the special nature of the jurisdiction under Article 5(5), appearances should be disregarded and the realities considered; it was for third parties who wished to rely on Article 5(5) to adduce evidence that the entity which they wished to bring before the national court was in fact subject to the control and direction of the parent company. But in *SAR Schotte GmbH v. Parfums Rothschild SARL*[1] the European Court held that, where the letterhead of a German company appeared to indicate that it was acting as a place of business of a French company, a third party which did business with it was entitled to rely on the appearance thus created. Accordingly the German court had jurisdiction over the French company because the dispute arose out of the operations of the establishment in Germany. This was so even though the French company maintained no dependent branch, agency or other establishment. What established jurisdiction in Germany was that the French company pursued its activities there through a German company (which, in the unusual circumstances of the case, was its parent company) with the same name and identical management which negotiated and conducted business in the name of the French subsidiary and which was used by the French subsidiary as an extension of itself. **11–272**

The second question will be whether the claim arises out of the operations of the branch, agency or other establishment. In *Somafer S.A. v. Saar-Ferngas A.G.* the European Court explained that the concept of operations included matters relating to the rights and contractual and non-contractual obligations concerning the actual management of the branch, agency, or other establishment itself, such as those relating to the situation of its building or the local engagement of staff to work there. It also included those relating to undertakings which had been entered into at the place of business in the name of the parent body and which had to be performed in the Contracting State where the place of business was established and also actions concerning torts arising from the activities in which it had engaged. **11–273**

---

[98] Case 139/80 [1981] E.C.R. 819, applied in *New Hampshire Insurance Co. v. Strabag Bau* [1990] 2 Lloyd's Rep. 61, 69, affd. on other grounds [1992] 1 Lloyd's Rep. 361 (C.A.).
[99] Case 33/78 [1978] E.C.R. 2183.
[1] Case 218/86 [1987] E.C.R. 4905.

11–274   The wording of Article 5(5) suggests that it grants jurisdiction to the courts of the place of the branch in relation to any contract entered into by it. In *Somafer S.A. v. Saar-Ferngas A.G.* the European Court seemed to limit the jurisdiction to cases where performance is to take place in the same Contracting State as the branch. That would have meant that Article 5(5) adds little to Article 5(1) in matters relating to contract. But in *Lloyd's Register of Shipping v. Soc. Campenon Bernard*[2] the Court held that it is not a pre-condition of jurisdiction under Article 5(5) that the obligations entered into by the branch in the name of its parent body were to be performed in the Contracting State in which the branch is situated.

It may be that an essential element of this jurisdiction is that it is designed for the benefit of third parties, and not for intra-company or intra-firm disputes.[3]

ILLUSTRATIONS

11–275   1. X & Co. is a French bank with a branch in London. Through the London branch it employs A to act as its manager in London. X & Co. repudiates the contract, and A brings proceedings in London against X & Co. The court has jurisdiction.

2. X & Co. is a German manufacturing company. It appoints Y, who is domiciled in England and has an office in London, as its non-exclusive agent for England. Y does not have authority to bind X & Co. Y agrees with A, who is domiciled in England, that X & Co. will sell a quantity of its products to A for delivery in France. X & Co. repudiates the agreement purportedly made by Y. The court does not have jurisdiction, since Y's office is not a branch of X & Co.[4]

11R–276   **(6) The court has jurisdiction if the claim is made against a settlor, trustee or beneficiary of a trust created by the operation of a statute, or by a written instrument, or created orally and evidenced in writing, if the trust is domiciled in England,[5] or, in the case of a trust instrument and where relations between settlor, trustee or beneficiary or their rights under the trust are involved, if the trust instrument confers jurisdiction on the English court.[6]**

COMMENT

11–277   Article 5(6) of each of the Conventions was first introduced by the 1978 Accession Convention to provide for jurisdiction over a settlor, trustee or beneficiary of a trust created by the operation of a statute, or by a written instrument, or created orally and evidenced in writing, in the courts of the Contracting State in which the trust is domiciled.[7] The phrase "created by the operation of a statute, or by a written instrument, or created orally and evidenced in writing" is intended to indicate that the rules apply only to cases in which a trust has been expressly constituted or for which provision is made

---

[2] Case C–439/93 [1995] E.C.R. I–961. See also *Re A Counterclaim under Italian law* [1995] I.L.Pr. 133 (German Fed.Sup.Ct., 1993).

[3] *Cf.* Reischl A.-G. in Case 14/76 *De Bloos Sprl v. Bouyer S.A.* [1976] E.C.R. 1497, 1519 and in Case 139/80 *Blanckaert and Willems P.V.B.A. v. Trost* [1981] E.C.R. 819, 838.

[4] Cases at para. 11–272, *supra.*

[5] 1968 Convention, Art. 5(6) and Lugano Convention, Art. 5(6), in 1982 Act, Scheds 1 and 3C; 1982 Act, Sched. 4, Art. 5(6).

[6] *Ibid.*, Art. 17(2).

[7] It is wider than clause (10) of Rule 27, *i.e.* Ord. 11, r. 1(1)(*j*), *ante.*

by statute—it does not include "constructive" or implied trusts.[8] Nor will it apply to testamentary trusts or to trustees in bankruptcy.[9] Article 5(6) is intended only to deal with disputes relating to the internal relationships of the trust, *e.g.* disputes between beneficiaries and trustees, and not to its external relations, *e.g.* the enforcement by third parties of contracts made by a trustee.[10]

By Article 53(2), whether a trust is domiciled in the Contracting State   **11–278** whose courts are seised, depends on its rules of private international law. The 1982 Act provides that a trust is domiciled in the United Kingdom if the trust has its closest and most real connection with a system of law of one of the constituent parts of the United Kingdom and that any proceedings which are brought in the United Kingdom by virtue of Article 5(6) shall be brought in the part of the United Kingdom in which the trust is domiciled.[11]

Article 17 of the Conventions and of Schedule 4 deal with jurisdiction   **11–279** provisions in trust instruments. Their effect is that, subject to other provisions of the Conventions for exclusive jurisdiction,[12] the English court will have exclusive jurisdiction in an action concerning relations between settlor, trustee or beneficiary or their rights or obligations under a trust instrument if the trust instrument confers jurisdiction on the English courts.

ILLUSTRATIONS

1. A, who is domiciled in England, is a beneficiary under a trust expressed to be governed by   **11–280** English law. X, who is domiciled in France, is a trustee. A brings proceedings against X. The court has jurisdiction.[13]

2. The facts are as Illustration 1, except that the trust is governed by Bermuda law. The court has no jurisdiction.

3. A trust deed governed by Bermuda law provides that all disputes arising out of it shall be submitted to the jurisdiction of the English court. A dispute arises concerning the right of X, a trustee domiciled in France, to charge for his professional services. The court has jurisdiction.[14]

(7) The court has jurisdiction over a defendant domiciled in Scotland   **11R–281** **or Northern Ireland in proceedings (a) concerning a debt secured on immovable property, or (b) which are brought to assert, declare or determine proprietary or possessory rights, or rights of security, in or over movable property, or to obtain authority to dispose of movable property, if the property is situated in England.**[15]

COMMENT

This is a head of jurisdiction conferred by Article 5(8) of Schedule 4 to the   **11–282** 1982 Act and has no directly corresponding provision in the jurisdictional

---

[8] Schlosser, para. 117.

[9] Art. 1, exclusion of wills and succession, bankruptcy. On trust deeds for creditors and marriage contract trusts see Maxwell Report, para. 5.63.

[10] Schlosser, para. 120.

[11] 1982 Act, ss.10(2) and 45.

[12] This may arise especially if settled land is involved.

[13] 1968 Convention, Art. 5(6); 1982 Act, ss.10(2), 45(2).

[14] Art. 17(2).

[15] 1982 Act, Sched. 4, Art. 5(8).

rules of the 1968 Convention or the Lugano Convention.[16] It applies to defendants domiciled in Scotland or Northern Ireland the head of jurisdiction conferred by Rule 27, clause (9), *i.e.* Order 11, r. 1(1)(*i*).[17]

ILLUSTRATION

11–283   X, who is domiciled in Scotland, borrows money from A, who is domiciled in Scotland, under an agreement which charges (*inter alia*) shares in a public company in England. A institutes proceedings in England to enforce the charge. The court has jurisdiction.

11R–284   **(8) The court, in cases where it has jurisdiction in an action relating to liability from the use or operation of a ship, has jurisdiction over claims for limitation of such liability.**[18]

COMMENT

11–285   A claim for limitation of liability allows a shipowner and others who incur liability in connection with a ship to limit their liability to a specific amount based on the tonnage of the ship. In England a claim for limitation of liability is brought against a potential claimant, or by way of counterclaim. The purpose of Article 6A, which originally was added by the 1978 Accession Convention, and applies also in intra-United Kingdom cases, is to allow limitation claims to be brought in the court of the domicile of the shipowner, or, *e.g.* in the court of the place where the harmful event occurred[19] or where the ship (or sister ship) has been arrested. But if the claimants have already brought proceedings in another Contracting State, the claim for limitation would have to be made by way of counterclaim abroad.[20]

11R–286   **(9) The court has jurisdiction, where a defendant is domiciled in England, over a co-defendant who is domiciled in another Contracting State or in another part of the United Kingdom.**[21]

COMMENT

11–287   Article 6(1) provides that a person domiciled in a Contracting State may also be sued, where he is one of a number of defendants, in the courts for the place where one of them is domiciled.[22] Article 6(1) refers to the "courts for the place" of the principal defendant's domicile, and not to the court of the State of the domicile. The High Court's jurisdiction[23] is not local and it will have

---

[16] But *cf.* Art.6(4).

[17] *Ante*, para. 11R–196.

[18] 1968 Convention, Art. 6A and Lugano Convention, Art. 6A, in 1982 Act, Scheds 1 and 3C; 1982 Act, Sched. 4, Art. 6A.

[19] See *The Falstria* [1988] 1 Lloyd's Rep. 495. *Cf. The Volvox Hollandia* [1988] 2 Lloyd's Rep. 361 (C.A.).

[20] See also CPR, PD49F, para. 3.

[21] 1968 Convention, Art. 6(1), and Lugano Convention, Art. 6(1), in 1982 Act, Scheds 1 and 3C; 1982 Act, Sched. 4, Art. 6(1).

[22] This has been held to mean domiciled at the date of issue of the proceedings, and not at the time when it is sought to join additional defendants: *Canada Trust Co. v. Stolzenberg (No.2)* [1998] 1 W.L.R. 547 (C.A.); *Petrotrade Inc. v. Smith* [1999] 1 W.L.R. 457.

[23] The jurisdiction of county courts is local.

jurisdiction under this clause whenever the principal defendant is domiciled in England. Although this head of jurisdiction fulfils a function similar to the "necessary or proper party" provisions of Order 11, r. 1(1)(*c*), *i.e.* Rule 27, clause (3),[24] it is narrower in scope than the latter. It was adopted in order to prevent the handing down in the Contracting States of judgments which are irreconcilable with one another.[25]

In *Kalfelis v. Schröder*[26] the European Court confirmed the view of the Jenard Report that Article 6(1) must be interpreted so as to avoid it being abused to oust the jurisdiction of the courts of the Contracting State in which a defendant is domiciled. There must therefore be a connection between the claims made against each of the defendants, and the nature of that connection is to be given a uniform interpretation: Article 6(1) applies where the proceedings brought against the various defendants are related when the proceedings are instituted, *i.e.* where it is expedient to hear and determine them together in order to avoid the risk of irreconcilable judgments resulting from separate proceedings. The most obvious case of such a risk is where there are joint debtors, but it is not limited to such a case.[27]

Under English law the claimant has to show that there is a real issue that the   **11–288**
court may reasonably be asked to try as to the liability of the additional defendant domiciled in England.[28] The court of the domicile must be validly seised of the claim. Thus if X is domiciled in England, but has agreed with A that the courts of France are to have exclusive jurisdiction over disputes between them, A cannot use Article 6(1) to justify bringing an action in England against X and adding Y and Z, domiciled in Germany, as additional defendants. If the additional defendant has a contract with the claimant providing for the exclusive jurisdiction of another court, then the provisions of Article 17 would supersede those of Article 6(1) and the chosen court would continue to have exclusive jurisdiction.[29]

ILLUSTRATIONS

1. A enters into a contract with X, who is domiciled in England and Y, who is domiciled in   **11–289**
France, whereby A is to perform services for X and Y in the Republic of Ireland. X and Y repudiate the contract. A brings proceedings against X in England, and seeks to join Y. The court has jurisdiction over Y.

2. A & Co. sues X & Co., domiciled in England, and Y & Co., its U.S. parent company, alleging that X & Co. and Y & Co. have infringed A & Co.'s patent for disposable nappies. A & Co. seek to join Z GmbH, a German subsidiary of Y & Co. Its primary purpose in joining Z

---

[24] *Ante*, para. 11R–143. It is not necessary, as it is under Ord. 11, r.1(1)(*c*), for the defendant domiciled in England to have been served before the joinder of the other defendants under Art. 6(1): *Canada Trust Co. v. Stolzenberg (No.2), ante.*

[25] Jenard, p. 26.

[26] Case 189/87 [1988] E.C.R. 5565. See *Aiglon Ltd. v. Gau Shan Co. Ltd.* [1993] 1 Lloyd's Rep. 164; *Gascoine v. Pyrah* [1994] I.L.Pr. 82 (C.A.); *Fort Dodge Animal Health Ltd. v. Akzo Nobel N.V.* [1998] F.S.R. 222 (C.A.); *Société Commerciale de Réassurance v. Eras International Ltd. (No.2)* [1995] 2 All E.R. 278; *Gannon v. B & I Steampacket Co.* [1993] 2 I.R. 359 (Sup.Ct.).

[27] *Cf.* Darmon A.-G. [1988] E.C.R. at 5575.

[28] *The Rewia* [1991] 2 Lloyd's Rep. 325, 329 (C.A.); *The Xing Su Hai* [1995] 2 Lloyd's Rep. 15; *Gannon v. B & I Steampacket Co. Ltd.* [1993] 2 I.R. 359 (Sup.Ct.)

[29] See *Hough v. P & O Containers Ltd.* [1998] 3 W.L.R. 851 (a case on Art. 6(2), *infra*). See also Droz, para. 92. *Cf. Soc. Berlit Staudt v. Cie d'assurances l'Alsacienne,* Cour de cassation, France, 1989, in 1991 *Clunet* 155.

GmbH is to obtain discovery of documents in its possession. Jurisdiction may be taken under Article 5(3), *i.e.* clause (3), but not (*semble*) under Article 6(1) where the predominant purpose is to obtain discovery.[30]

11R–290   **(10) The court has jurisdiction, where a defendant is sued in proceedings in England, to determine a third party claim[31] by the defendant against a person domiciled in another Contracting State or in another part of the United Kingdom, unless the proceedings were instituted in order to deprive the third party of the jurisdiction of the courts of the country which would otherwise be competent to determine the claim against him.[32]**

COMMENT

11–291   The English text of Article 6(2) provides for jurisdiction in proceedings on a warranty or guarantee or other third party proceedings[33] in the court seised of the original proceedings unless they were instituted solely with the object of removing the third party from the jurisdiction of the court which would otherwise be competent. The "demande en garantie" is equivalent to a claim for indemnity, and this provision deals with what in England is regulated by what was previously known as third party procedure and is now called Part 20 claims.[34] A third party may be sued in England, even if England has little connection with the claim against the third party, *e.g.* if the jurisdiction of the court is derived from a contract between the claimant and defendant. An attempt is made to prevent abuse of this head of jurisdiction by providing that it is not to apply if the original proceedings were brought solely with the object of removing the third party from the jurisdiction which would otherwise have been competent. If the third party has an agreement with the defendant providing for the jurisdiction of the courts of another Contracting State, the agreement will be given effect under Article 17[35] in priority to Article 6(2).[36]

11–292   In *Kongress Agentur Hagen GmbH v. Zeehaghe B.V.*[37] the European Court confirmed that Article 6(2) applied if the national court had jurisdiction under

---

[30] *Mölnlycke AB v. Procter & Gamble Ltd.* [1992] 1 W.L.R. 1112 (C.A.), *per* Dillon L.J. (Woolf and Leggatt L.JJ. expressed no view).

[31] A third party claim is now described as a "Part 20" claim (CPR 20.2) and a third party is now described as a Part 20 defendant (CPR PD20, para. 7).

[32] 1968 Convention, Art. 6(2), and Lugano Convention, Art. 6(2), in 1982 Act, Scheds. 1 and 3C; 1982 Act, Sched. 4, Art. 6(2).

[33] "une demande en garantie ou ... une demande en intervention."

[34] CPR, Pt. 20. See *e.g. Kinnear v. Falcon Films N.V.* [1996] 1 W.L.R. 920; *Waterford Wedgwood plc v. David Nagli Ltd., The Times*, May 13, 1998. Foreign third parties may now be joined as necessary or proper parties to an English proceeding under Ord. 11, r. 1(1)(c), Rule 27, clause (3), *ante*.

[35] *Post*, Rule 32(3).

[36] *Hough v. P & O Containers Ltd.* [1999] Q.B. 834. *Cf. Soc. de Groot Nijkerk v. Soc. Rhenania*, 1993 *Clunet* 151 (French Cour de cassation, 1992).

[37] Case C–365/88 [1990] E.C.R. I–1845. It would seem to follow that jurisdiction under Art. 6(2) is available even if the defendant in the original claim is domiciled outside the Contracting States and is sued on an "exorbitant" ground (such as mere presence) under Art. 4: *cf.* Kaye, p. 648; *Veenbrink v. Banque Internationale pour l'Afrique Occidentale*, French Cour de cassation, 1992, in 1993 *Clunet* 151, note Huet.

the 1968 Convention over the defendant in the plaintiff's original claim, irrespective of the domicile of the original defendant. In that case jurisdiction over the defendant had been taken on the basis of Article 5(1). It was also held that Article 6(2) does not *require* the national court to exercise jurisdiction against the third party, and it may apply its own procedural rules in order to determine whether the action is admissible, provided that the effectiveness of the Convention is not impaired, and, in particular, that leave to bring the claim on the guarantee is not refused on the ground that the third party resides or is domiciled in a Contracting State other than that of the court seised of the original proceedings.

In England the court has a wide discretion under the Civil Procedure Rules   **11–293**
1998 to dismiss or strike out third party (Part 20) claims. But the effect of the decision of the European Court is that the third party proceedings cannot be set aside solely on the ground of the delay which would be caused by the fact that the third party is domiciled in another Contracting State.[38]

ILLUSTRATIONS

1. A buys a French machine for delivery in England from X, who is domiciled in France and   **11–294**
who bought it from Y, who is also domiciled in France. The machine is faulty and A brings proceedings in England against X. X may join Y.[39]

2. The facts are as in Illustration 1, except that the machinery was bought and delivered in France. When A brings proceedings in England against X, X (who would not otherwise be subject to the jurisdiction) submits to the jurisdiction. *Semble*, X may join Y.

3. The facts are as Illustration 2, except that X submits to the jurisdiction as part of a collusive plan between A and X to procure that X may join Y in the English proceedings. The court has no jurisdiction.

4. The facts are as in Illustration 1, except that X's claim against Y is time-barred under French law. The court may set aside the claim against Y.

5. A film actor was injured in an accident while making a film in Spain, and subsequently died in hospital in Madrid. His administrators sued the film company, and the producer and director of the film. The defendants were able to join the Spanish orthopaedic surgeon and the Spanish hospital as third parties claiming contribution under the Civil Liability (Contribution) Act 1978 and damages for breach of contract allegedly concluded between the defendants and the hospital for treatment of the actor.[40]

6. A was injured while working for X & Co., an English company, as an electrician on board one of its ships while it was undergoing repairs in a German shipyard. A sued X & Co. in England for negligence and breach of statutory duty. The repairs were being done by Y & Co. pursuant to a contract which was governed by German law and provided for the jurisdiction of the Hamburg courts. The English court had no jurisdiction over X & Co.'s third party claim against Y & Co. because the jurisdiction agreement provisions of Article 17[41] took priority over the third party jurisdiction under Article 6(2).[42]

**(11) The court has jurisdiction, where a claimant domiciled in another   11R–295
Contracting State or in Scotland or Northern Ireland sues in England, to
determine a counterclaim arising from the same contract or facts on
which the original claim was based.**[43]

---

[38] See Lenz A.-G. [1990] E.C.R. I–1845, 1858.
[39] Case C–365/88 *Kongress Agentur Hagen GmbH v. Zeehaghe B.V.* [1990] E.C.R. I–1845.
[40] *Kinnear v. Falcon Films N.V.* [1996] 1 W.L.R. 920.
[41] *Post*, para. 12–108.
[42] *Hough v. P & O Containers Ltd.* [1999] Q.B. 834.
[43] 1968 Convention, Art. 6(3), and Lugano Convention, Art. 6(3), in 1982 Act, Scheds 1 and 3C;
   1982 Act, Sched. 4, Art. 6(3).

Comment

11–296 Article 6(3) provides that a person domiciled in a Contracting State may be sued on a counterclaim,[44] arising from the same contract or facts on which the original claim was based, in the court in which the original claim is pending. This is similar to the English rule of jurisdiction that a claimant submits to counterclaims.[45] In Article 6(3) the requirement that the claims be related is expressed in the following way: the counterclaim must (a) "arise" (b) from the same contract or (c) from the same facts (d) on which the original claim was "based." These requirements are stricter than a requirement that the matters merely be "related."

Illustration

11–297 A & Co., a company with its seat in Germany, buys a paper-making machine from X, who is domiciled in England, the price to be payable in Germany. When the machine fails A & Co., refuses to pay and sues X in England for damages. X counterclaims for the unpaid price. The court has jurisdiction.

11R–298   **(12) The court has jurisdiction in matters relating to a contract, if the action may be combined with an action against the same defendant in matters relating to rights *in rem* in immovable property situated in England.**

Comment

11–299 This clause is based on Article 6(4) of the 1968 Convention (which was added by the 1989 Accession Convention), and of the Lugano Convention. It is primarily concerned with actions to recover secured debts and to enforce the security, and is considered below in connection with clause (15).[46]

11R–300   **(13) In matters relating to insurance (but not as regards defendants domiciled in Scotland or Northern Ireland[47])**
     (1) the court has jurisdiction in an action against an insurer:
        (i) if the insurer is domiciled in England[48]; or

---

[44] "une demande reconventionnelle"—which is not quite the same as a counterclaim since it does not have to be brought in the same action: see Anton, *Civil Jurisdiction*, p. 88 on the Scots procedure of reconvention. Art. 6(3) does not regulate the circumstances when a set-off (as distinct from a counterclaim) may be raised. That is a matter for national law: Case C–341/93 *Danvaern Productions A/S v. Schuhfabriken Otterbeck GmbH & Co.* [1995] E.C.R. I–2053. Nor does it allow an additional party to be joined by counterclaim: *cf. Jordan Grand Prix Ltd. v. Baltic Insurance Group* [1999] 2 A.C. 127 (a case on Art. 11).

[45] *Ante*, para. 11–108. On the special problems raised by set-off or counterclaim when the parties have entered into an agreement providing for the exclusive jurisdiction of the courts of Contracting States see Case 23/78 *Meeth v. Glacetal Sàrl* [1978] E.C.R. 2133; Case 48/84 *Spitzley v. Sommer Exploitation S.A.* [1985] E.C.R. 787. See also *Hough v. P & O Containers Ltd.* [1999] Q.B. 834 (on Art. 6(2), *ante*), *Cf. Aectra Refining & Marketing Inc. v. Exmar N.V.* [1994] 1 W.L.R. 1634, 1649–1651 (C.A.) (arbitration).

[46] *Cf.* clause (7), *ante*.

[47] There is no equivalent in Sched. 4 of the provisions relating to insurance in the 1968 Convention. Proceedings relating to insurance contracts will therefore fall within the other provisions of Sched. 4, especially Art. 5(1). See *post*, para. 11–316.

[48] 1968 Convention, Art. 8(1)(1), Lugano Convention, Art. 8(1)(1), in 1982 Act, Scheds. 1 and 3C.

    (ii) **in disputes arising out of the operations of its branch, agency or other establishment, if the branch, agency or other establishment is in England[49]; or**

    (iii) **if the policyholder is domiciled in England[50]; or**

    (iv) **if the insurer is a co-insurer, and proceedings are brought in England against the leading insurer[51]; or**

    (v) **in the case of liability insurance or insurance of immovable property, if the harmful event occurred in England[52]; or**

    (vi) **in a third party claim by the insured in the case of liability insurance, where the insured has been sued in England[53]; or**

    (vii) **in the case of a counterclaim against the insurer, if the insurer has commenced proceedings in England arising from the same contract or facts[54]; or**

    (viii) **if the insurer has entered into an agreement conferring jurisdiction on the English court[55];**

(2) the court has jurisdiction over a policyholder, insured or beneficiary:

    (i) **if he is domiciled in England[56]; or**

    (ii) **in the case of a counterclaim, if he has commenced proceedings in England arising from the same contract or facts[57]; or**

    (iii) **in the case of the policyholder or insured, where a direct action has been brought against the insurer in England and the law governing direct actions permits the policyholder or insured to be joined[58]; or**

    (iv) **if the parties have conferred jurisdiction on the English court by agreement,**

        (a) **where the agreement was entered into after the dispute arose[59]; or**

        (b) **where the policyholder and insurer were both domiciled or habitually resident in England when the agreement was entered into[60]; or**

        (c) **where the agreement relates to insurance relating to loss of or damage to ships, aircraft or cargoes.[61]**

COMMENT

The draftsmen of the 1968 Convention made special provision for insurance   **11–301**
in order to protect policyholders.[62] In the negotiations for accession, the

---

[49] Arts. 7, 5(5).
[50] Art. 8(1)(2).
[51] Art. 8(1)(3).
[52] Art. 9.
[53] Art. 10(1).
[54] Arts. 11(2), 6(3).
[55] Art. 12(2).
[56] Art. 11(1).
[57] Art. 11(2).
[58] Art. 10(3).
[59] Art. 12(1).
[60] Art. 12(3).
[61] Art. 12(5).
[62] See Case 201/82 *Gerling v. Treasury Administration* [1983] E.C.R. 2503, 2516.

United Kingdom sought to adapt the Convention to meet the needs of the London insurance market; in particular, the United Kingdom stressed that the nature of the London market was such that a large proportion of its business was with policyholders outside the Community; and that a large proportion was insurance of "large risks" with substantial industrial and commercial concerns; neither of these groups needed the special protection of the Convention rules. The special position of the United Kingdom did result in some changes to the Convention, but these were not of a very far-reaching character, and did not much mitigate the problems of forum-shopping to which the insurance provisions give rise.[63]

11–302   The provisions discussed here apply "in matters relating to insurance." The expression is not defined, but the 1978 Accession Convention was negotiated on the basis that it did not apply to reinsurance, and the Schlosser Report said that reinsurance contracts could not be equated with insurance contracts, and that accordingly these provisions did not apply to reinsurance contracts.[64] The Court of Appeal has held that this view should be accepted.[65] Where there is doubt whether a contract is one of insurance, the national court (and ultimately the European Court) will have to apply a Convention, rather than a national, interpretation. In *New Hampshire Insurance Co. v. Strabag Bau AG*[66] the Court of Appeal rejected an argument[67] that what was on its face an insurance contract should not be so regarded for the purposes of these provisions because it was made between commercial concerns. It was held that the expression "matters relating to insurance" meant what it said and was not restricted to insurance for domestic or private purposes.

11–303   The complex effect of these provisions is summarised in clause (13). In addition to the heads of jurisdiction set out there, the defendant can also confer jurisdiction on the English court by submission under Article 18. The provisions apply only where the defendant is domiciled in a Contracting State, and where the defendant is not domiciled in a Contracting State Rules 24 to 25 and 27 will apply. This is subject to one important qualification. Article 8(2) provides that an insurer who is not domiciled in a Contracting State but has a branch, agency or other establishment in one of the Contracting States shall, in disputes arising out of the operations of the branch, etc., be deemed to be domiciled in that State. By virtue of section 44 of the 1982 Act, a person who is deemed to be domiciled in the United Kingdom as a result of Article 8(2) is to be treated as domiciled in the part of the United Kingdom in which the branch, etc., is situate. Thus for the purposes of the provisions of the Conventions on insurance a United States insurance company with branches in

---

[63] See Kerr (1978) Law Soc.Gaz. 1190; Collins, p. 68.

[64] Schlosser, para. 151; *Citadel Insurance Co. v. Atlantic Union Insurance Co. S.A.* [1982] 2 Lloyd's Rep. 543, 549 (C.A.). Whether it applies to reinsurance was raised, but not decided, in Case C–351/89 *Overseas Union Insurance Ltd. v. New Hampshire Insurance Co.* [1991] E.C.R. I–3317; [1992] Q.B. 434. The question has been referred to the European Court in Case C–412/98 *Group Josi Reinsurance Co. v. UGIC* (pending). See also *New Hampshire Insurance Co. v. Strabag Bau A.G.* [1992] 1 Lloyd's Rep. 361, 368–369 (C.A.); *Arkwright Mutual Insurance Co. v. Bryanston Insurance Co. Ltd.* [1990] 2 Q.B. 649, 655. See also *post*, Rule 187.

[65] *Agnew v. Lansförsäkringsbolagens* [1997] 4 All E.R. 937 (C.A.), approving *Trade Indemnity plc v. Försäkringsaktiebolaget Njord* [1995] 1 All E.R. 796.

[66] [1992] 1 Lloyd's Rep. 361 (C.A.).

[67] Based by analogy on Case 150/77 *Société Bertrand v. Paul Ott K.G.* [1978] E.C.R. 1431, *post*, para. 11–321.

London, Paris and Geneva will be deemed to be domiciled in England, France and Switzerland.

Policyholder, insured and beneficiary. The insurance provisions of the Conventions distinguish between policyholder, insured and beneficiary. The purpose of these expressions is to distinguish between the original party to the contract of insurance ("preneur d'assurance") who may not necessarily be the same person as the insured or beneficiary. The practical effect of these distinctions is considerable, particularly when the benefit of the policy is assigned or transmitted with goods, or when the beneficiary is different from the person who takes out the policy.   **11–304**

General scope. In insurance matters jurisdiction is determined by Articles 8 to 12A without prejudice to Article 4 (non-Contracting State domiciliaries) and Article 5(5) (disputes arising out of the operations of a branch, etc.).   **11–305**

Article 8 provides that an insurer domiciled in a Contracting State may be sued: (1) in the courts of the State where he is domiciled, or (2) in the Contracting State in which the policyholder is domiciled, or (3) if he is a co-insurer, in the courts of a Contracting State in which proceedings are brought against the leading insurer. The jurisdiction in favour of the policyholder's domicile will allow proceedings in that place by the policyholder but not also by the insured and the beneficiary if they are different from the policyholder. Article 8(1)(3) does not define leading insurer, and it does not impose an obligation for proceedings to be concentrated in one court. There is nothing to prevent a policyholder from suing the various co-insurers in different courts.[68] The effect of Articles 7 and 8(2) is that an insurer may normally be sued at any place where it has a branch if the dispute arises from an insurance contract entered into at that branch, whether or not the insurer is domiciled in a Contracting State.   **11–306**

Articles 9 and 10 create additional bases of jurisdiction against insurers. In the case of liability insurance (*i.e.* insurance against legal liability to third parties), jurisdiction is conferred on the courts of the State where the harmful event occurred.[69] The relevant harmful event is the event which gives rise to the cause of action against the insured party, and the English court will have jurisdiction if the damage occurred in England or the event which gave rise to the damage occurred in England.[70]   **11–307**

The court may also exercise jurisdiction in a third party claim by the insured against an insurer domiciled in another Contracting State if it is seised of an action by the injured party against the insured.[71] This would be so even if the parties to the original proceedings were both domiciled in England, but not if the insurer and insured are bound by a jurisdiction clause validly conferring jurisdiction on the courts of another Contracting State.   **11–308**

In the case of insurance of immovable property, the court may exercise jurisdiction if England is the place where the harmful event occurred,[72] which will in practice be the place where the immovable property is situated.   **11–309**

---

[68] Schlosser, para. 149.
[69] Art. 9.
[70] Case 21/76 *Bier v. Mines de Potasse d'Alsace S.A.* [1976] E.C.R. 1735; [1978] Q.B. 708.
[71] Art. 10(1); Jenard, p. 32.
[72] Art. 9.

11–310   Article 10(2)–(3) deals with direct proceedings against insurers, which are found, at least to a limited extent, in most of the Contracting States.[73] The effect of Article 10(2) is that these proceedings may only be brought in those places where the policyholder could have brought proceedings pursuant to Articles 7, 8 and 9. Jurisdiction is not therefore extended to the places where the injured party is domiciled unless, for example, that is also the place where the policyholder is domiciled.[74] Article 10(2) applies only "where such direct actions are permitted" under the *lex fori*, including its rules of private international law. The policyholder or insured may be joined "if the law governing such direct actions" provides for such joinder. The governing law in this context means, it seems, the law to which the private international law rules of the *lex fori* point. In England there is no clear answer as to the applicable law. Although the question of direct liability depends on the law governing the contract of insurance rather than on the rules applicable to torts,[75] the question what law governs the joinder of the policyholder or insured to such proceedings may be a question purely of procedure for the *lex fori*.[76] Where there is a jurisdiction agreement valid under Article 12, Article 10 (as between the parties to the agreement) is superseded by the agreement.[77]

11–311   Article 11[78] provides that, without prejudice to the right granted by Article 10(3) to join the policyholder or insured in a direct action, an insurer may bring proceedings only in the courts of the Contracting State in which the defendant is domiciled, irrespective of whether the defendant is the policyholder, the insured or a beneficiary, without prejudice to the right to bring a counterclaim in the court in which the original claim against the insurer is pending. This provision does not apply where the defendant is domiciled outside the Contracting States. In *Jordan Grand Prix Ltd. v. Baltic Insurance Group*[79] the House of Lords held that Article 11 applies to any insurer, whether or not domiciled in a Contracting State; and that for the purposes of Article 11 the reference to a counterclaim in the court in which the original claim against the insurer is pending meant a counterclaim against the original plaintiff. Consequently an insured who was sued in England could not add Irish domiciliaries as defendants to counterclaim.

11–312   **Jurisdiction clauses.**   Clauses attributing jurisdiction to courts receive special treatment in Articles 12 and 12A in the case of insurance contracts, and the general provisions of Article 17 do not apply, although the formal requirements of Article 17 are applicable.[80] The position with regard to insurance contracts may be summarised as follows: (1) if there is an arbitration agreement between the parties the case will be outside the scope of the Conventions[81]; (2) if there is a jurisdiction clause conferring jurisdiction on

---

[73] See, *e.g.* Third Parties (Rights Against Insurers) Act 1930.
[74] Jenard, p. 32.
[75] *Post*, paras. 35–042 *et seq.*
[76] It is not easy to envisage circumstances in which the policyholder or insured would be joined in proceedings under the Third Parties (Rights Against Insurers) Act 1930 and ss.151–152 of the Road Traffic Act 1988. The former transfers the rights of a bankrupt insured against his insurer to the third party. The latter makes an insurer of compulsory third party risk liable to the third party on an unsatisfied judgment against the insured.
[77] Schlosser, para. 148.
[78] See *New Hampshire Insurance Co. v. Strabag Bau* [1992] 1 Lloyd's Rep. 361 (C.A.).
[79] [1999] 2 A.C. 127.
[80] *Cf.* Case 201/82 *Gerling v. Treasury Administration* [1983] E.C.R. 2503.
[81] Art. 1(2)(4).

the courts of a particular State (perhaps even a non-Contracting State) then it will be given effect (a) in favour of a policyholder, insured or beneficiary generally[82]; (b) in favour of the insurer only if (i) it is entered into after the dispute has arisen,[83] or (ii) the agreement is between a policyholder and an insurer both domiciled[84] or habitually resident in the same Contracting State and confers jurisdiction on the courts of that State,[85] or (iii) the agreement was concluded with a policyholder not domiciled in a Contracting State, unless the insurance is compulsory or relates to immovable property in a Contracting State,[86] or (iv) it relates to one of the risks in Article 12A.[87] In *Charman v. WOC Offshore B.V.*[88] Staughton L.J. expressed the view (*obiter*, and differing from Hirst J. at first instance) that for a jurisdiction agreement to be effective under Article 12(5) it was necessary for it to relate to one of the risks in Article 12A, and no other: if it related to other risks, it was wholly ineffective and not merely to the extent it related to other risks.

The following points are worthy of note: first, it is not likely that express **11–313** agreements on choice of court after a dispute has arisen will in practice be common; secondly, the effect of Article 12(2) is that an exclusive jurisdiction clause will always be effective for the benefit of a policyholder, insured or beneficiary; thirdly, the relevant time for testing the domicile or habitual residence of the insurer and the policyholder under Article 12(3) is the date of the contract, and not (as under the previous version) the date of commencement of the proceedings; fourthly, Article 12(4) applies where the policyholder is not domiciled in a Contracting State, but there are proceedings by or against an insured or beneficiary in a Contracting State on a policy containing a jurisdiction clause. The conferment of jurisdiction is to be effective unless one of two exceptions is applicable: the first is where the insurance is compulsory, in which case no departure from the provisions of Article 8 to 11 is permitted, even if the policyholder is domiciled outside the Contracting States.[89] The second exception is for insurance relating to immovable property, where the other applicable provisions (especially Article 9) will continue to apply even if the national law of the State in which the immovable property is situated allows jurisdiction agreements.[90]

The risks set out in Article 12A are (1) any loss of damage to (a) ships, **11–314** offshore installations or aircraft, arising from perils relating to their use for commercial purposes or (b) goods in transit, other than passengers' baggage, where the transit consists of or includes carriage by ships or aircraft; (2) any liability, other than for bodily injury to passengers or loss of or damage to their baggage (a) arising out of the use or operation of ships, etc., (b) for loss or damage caused by goods in transit as above; (3) any financial loss connected[91] with the use or operation of ships, etc., in particular loss of freight or charter

---

[82] Art. 12(2).
[83] Art. 12(1).
[84] This may include an insurer not domiciled in a Contracting State but with a branch in a Contracting State in relation to a policy issued through that branch: Art. 8(2).
[85] Art. 12(3).
[86] Art. 12(4).
[87] Art. 12(5).
[88] [1993] 2 Lloyd's Rep. 551, 557–558 (C.A.).
[89] See Schlosser, para. 138; *e.g.* aviation and motor vehicle insurance.
[90] Schlosser, para. 139; *sed quaere*.
[91] See *Charman v. WOC Offshore B.V.* [1993] 2 Lloyd's Rep. 551 (C.A.) (jurisdiction agreement valid even if insurance covered land-based equipment, such as crawling crane, because sufficiently connected with sea-going vessels covered by insurance).

hire; (4) any risk or interest connected with any of those referred to in (1) to (3) above.

11–315   The practical effect of Article 12 is that an insurer in London can effectively confer exclusive jurisdiction on the English court by the original insurance contract only in the following cases: (1) where the policyholder is domiciled in the United Kingdom at the time the insurance contract is entered into, or (2) where the policyholder is not domiciled in any of the Contracting States at the time the insurance contract is entered into; or (3) the insurance relates to one of the major risks set out in Article 12A.

11–316   These provisions find no counterpart in the intra-United Kingdom scheme in Schedule 4 to the 1982 Act. This means that where the Conventions confer jurisdiction on the courts of the United Kingdom, a Scottish defendant will only be subject to the English jurisdiction in insurance matters where one of the general provisions in Schedule 4 applies. In practice the most likely cases are where the Scottish defendant is domiciled in England or where he is sued on an obligation in an insurance contract to be performed in England.

ILLUSTRATIONS

11–317   1. X & Co. and Y & Co. are German companies and are participants in a joint venture for the construction of an airport in Iraq. They take out a policy of insurance through London brokers in the London market indemnifying them against certain risks in connection with the project. The leading underwriter is A & Co., an American company, but the bulk of the risk is placed with English insurers, and the contract of insurance is impliedly governed by English law. The members of the joint venture claim on the policy for corrosion damage amounting to up to £60 million. A & Co. and the other insurers seek to avoid the policy for non-disclosure and commence proceedings in England against (*inter alios*) X & Co. and Y & Co. for a declaration that they have validly avoided the policy and are under no liability. The court has no jurisdiction.[92]

2. A, domiciled in England, takes out a policy of insurance covering his stamp collection with X & Co., a German insurance company. When the stamp collection is stolen X & Co. dispute liability under the policy. A sues X & Co. in England. The court has jurisdiction.[93]

3. The facts are as in Illustration 2, except that the insurance policy contains a clause providing that the German courts are to have exclusive jurisdiction over any disputes. The court has jurisdiction because the clause is ineffective.[94]

4. X, a resident of Palermo and domiciled in Italy, insures his valuable collection of antiques through a Lloyd's broker with A, a Lloyd's syndicate in London. The insurance policy provides for the exclusive jurisdiction of the English court. The antiques are stolen and A pays a substantial sum under the policy. A subsequently alleges that as a result of material non-disclosure it is entitled to avoid the policy and to have the compensation returned. A brings proceedings against X in London. The court has no jurisdiction.[95]

5. X, a Greek shipowner, insures his fleet with A, a Lloyd's syndicate. The policy provides for the exclusive jurisdiction of the English courts. A brings proceedings for rescission of the contract. The court has jurisdiction.[96]

11R–318   **(14) In proceedings concerning consumer contracts,**

    (1) the court has jurisdiction in an action against a supplier of goods, or lender, or supplier of services:

        (i) if the defendant is domiciled in England[97];

---

[92] 1968 Convention, Art. 11; *New Hampshire Insurance Co. v. Strabag Bau A.G.* [1992] 1 Lloyd's Rep. 361 (C.A.).

[93] 1968 Convention, Art. 8(1)(2).

[94] 1968 Convention, Art. 12.

[95] But a London arbitration clause in the policy would have been effective.

[96] 1968 Convention, Arts. 12(5), 12A.

[97] 1968 Convention, Art. 14(1), and Lugano Convention, Art. 14(1), in 1982 Act, Scheds. 1 and 3C.

    (ii) **if the consumer is domiciled in England**[98]**;**

   (iii) **if the defendant has a branch, agency or establishment in England and the dispute arises out of its operations**[99]**;**

   (iv) **in the case of a counterclaim against the supplier, etc., where he has commenced proceedings in England arising from the same contract or facts**[1]**;**

   (v) **if the supplier etc. has entered into an agreement conferring jurisdiction on the English court**[2]**;**

 (2) **the court has jurisdiction in an action against the consumer:**

    (i) **if the consumer is domiciled in England**[3]**;**

   (ii) **in the case of a counterclaim against the consumer, where the consumer has commenced proceedings in England arising from the same contract or facts**[4]**;**

   (iii) **if the parties conferred jurisdiction on the English court by agreement and either (a) the agreement was entered into after the dispute arose**[5]**; or (b) the supplier, etc., and the consumer were both domiciled or habitually resident in England.**[6]

In this clause a consumer contract means a contract concluded by a person for a purpose outside his trade or profession and which is

 (1) **a contract for the sale of goods on instalment credit terms; or**

 (2) **a contract for a loan repayable by instalments, or for any other form of credit, made to finance the sale of goods; or**

 (3) **any other contract for the supply of goods or a contract for the supply of services, where in the State of the consumer's domicile**[7] **(a) the conclusion of the contract was preceded by a specific invitation addressed to him or by advertising,**[8] **and (b) the consumer took the steps necessary for the conclusion of the contract.**[9]

COMMENT

The objectives of the consumer contract provisions of the 1968 Convention   **11–319** (reproduced in the Lugano Convention) were inspired by a desire to protect consumers; national laws, by contrast, were designed partly to protect the "weaker" party, but also to serve economic, monetary and savings policy.[10] The main change introduced by the 1978 Accession Convention was to make it clear that the provisions applied only to consumer contracts, and not to all

---

[98] Art. 14(1); 1982 Act, s.10(3).

[99] Arts. 13(1), 5(5); 1982 Act, s.44(2).

[1] Art. 14(3).

[2] Art. 15.

[3] Art. 14(2).

[4] Arts. 14(3), 6(5).

[5] Art. 15(1).

[6] Art. 15(3).

[7] Or, if the consumer is domiciled in the United Kingdom, in the part of the United Kingdom in which he is domiciled.

[8] This requirement is omitted for U.K. domiciliaries in Art. 13, Sched. 4.

[9] Art. 13.

[10] Case 150/77 *Société Bertrand v. Paul Ott K.G.* [1978] E.C.R. 1431. See generally Mennie, 1987 S.L.T. (News) 181.

instalment sales and financing contracts irrespective of whether the buyer was a businessman or a private consumer. In *Société Bertrand v. Paul Ott K.G.*[11] the European Court held, on the original wording of these provisions, that they applied only to private final consumers and not to those who were engaged, while buying the product, in trade or professional activities. This is confirmed by the new wording of Article 13, influenced by the drafts of the Rome Convention on the Law Applicable to Contractual Obligations, which makes special provision for choice of law in consumer contracts.[12]

11–320   The consumer contract provisions in clause (14) apply only where the defendant is domiciled, or deemed to be domiciled, in a Contracting State. Where the defendant is not so domiciled, then jurisdiction depends, under Article 4 (to which Article 13 is expressly subject), on the law of the Contracting State where the action is brought.[13] These provisions relate to proceedings concerning a contract concluded by a person for a purpose which can be regarded as being outside his trade or profession, "the consumer."[14] They apply to (1) contracts for the sale of goods on instalment credit terms; or (2) contracts for a loan repayable by instalments, or for any other form of credit, made to finance the sale of goods; or (3) any other contract for the supply of goods or a contract for the supply of services and where, in the State of the consumer's domicile, the conclusion of the contract was preceded by a specific invitation addressed to him or by advertising and the consumer took in that State the steps necessary for the conclusion of the contract.[15]

11–321   The meaning of sale of goods on "instalment credit terms" was considered in *Société Bertrand v. Paul Ott K.G.*[16] where the European Court held that it was necessary to give the expression a Convention interpretation, and that it meant a transaction in which the price is discharged by way of several payments or which is linked to a financing contract. In *Mietz v. Intership Yachting Sneek B.V.*[17] the European Court held that taking payment by instalments from the purchaser, but where the purchase price is paid in full by the time the purchaser takes possession, is not a sale on instalment credit terms.

11–322   The provisions are not limited to instalment sales and instalment loans to finance them, and apply also to contracts for the supply of goods or services where there has been an invitation to purchase (either specific or by advertising) and the consumer has taken the steps necessary to conclude the contract in the State of his domicile. The steps necessary to conclude the contract would seem to include buying by mail order (although in English law it is probable that it is the consumer who makes the offer and the seller who accepts) since Article 13(1)(3) was intended to cover mail order and door-step selling, but may have much wider effects, *e.g.* where a French company places

---

[11] *Supra.*
[12] See Contracts (Applicable Law) Act 1990, Sched. 1, and *post*, Rule 181.
[13] Case C–318/93 *Brenner v. Dean Witter Reynolds Inc.* [1994] E.C.R. I–4275.
[14] They do not apply to a contract which an individual has concluded with a view to pursuing a trade in the future: Case C–269/95 *Benincasa v. Dentalkit Srl* [1997] E.C.R. I–3767 (franchise agreement to sell dental hygiene products not within Art. 13). Nor do they apply to a claim by an assignee of a consumer, where the assignee is acting in pursuance of its trade or professional activity: Case C–89/91 *Shearson Lehman Hutton Inc. v. TVB* [1993] E.C.R. I–139.
[15] Art. 13(1).
[16] *Supra.*
[17] Case C–99/96 [1999] I.L.Pr. 541.

an advertisement in a United States publication which circulates in the United Kingdom. Where the provisions of the Conventions apply they supersede national law, *e.g.* the Consumer Credit Act 1974, section 141.[18]

The effect of Article 14 is that a consumer may bring proceedings in England if the supplier is domiciled in England or if the consumer is domiciled in England. The consumer may only be sued in England if he is domiciled in England; but a foreign consumer may be subject to a counterclaim if he sues in England, and, it seems, he may submit to the jurisdiction by voluntary appearance. **11–323**

Article 13(2) provides that where a consumer enters into a contract with a party who is not domiciled in a Contracting State but has a branch, agency or other establishment in one of the Contracting States, that party shall, in disputes arising out of the operations of the branch, etc., be deemed to be domiciled in that State; and section 44(2) of the 1982 Act provides that the defendant is deemed to be domiciled for this purpose in the part of the United Kingdom in which the branch is situate. **11–324**

Jurisdiction agreements. The consumer contract provisions of the Conventions may be departed from only by an agreement (1) which is entered into after the dispute has arisen or (2) which allows the consumer to bring proceedings in courts other than those indicated in the provisions, or (3) which is entered into when the consumer and the other party are both domiciled or habitually resident in the same Contracting State and which confers jurisdiction on the courts of that State, provided that such an agreement is not contrary to the law of that State.[19] The relevant date for testing domicile is that of the commencement of proceedings, subject to two points: first, if the provisions apply because of Article 13(1)(3) (advertising in the State of the consumer's domicile) then it will also be necessary to determine the consumer's domicile at the time of the conclusion of the contract; secondly, if there is a jurisdiction agreement which is to be upheld under Article 15(3) it will be necessary to consider the party's domicile at the date of the conclusion of the contract. In practice, therefore, standard form consumer contracts will only be effective to confer exclusive jurisdiction on the English court if both the consumer and the supplier are domiciled, or deemed to be domiciled, in England. **11–325**

These provisions apply as between the constituent parts of the United Kingdom[20] with certain modifications. First, their application is without prejudice to the jurisdiction of the court under Article 5(8)(*b*) of Schedule 4 in proceedings to enforce possessory or security rights in movable property. Thus a supplier may claim possession in the English court of goods held in England to the order of a consumer domiciled in Scotland. Secondly, the definition of the residual category of consumer contract is amended so as to omit the requirement that there be an invitation or advertising addressed to the consumer in the place of his domicile. Because the insurance provisions of the Conventions have been omitted from the intra-United Kingdom provisions of Schedule 4, Article 13 of Schedule 4 makes it clear that they are not caught by the consumer contract provisions. **11–326**

---

[18] *Cf.* Case 25/79 *Sanicentral v. Collin* [1979] E.C.R. 3423.
[19] Art. 15.
[20] See *Waverley Asset Management Ltd. v. Saha*, 1989 S.L.T. (Sh.Ct.) 87 (provisions do not apply to sale of unit trusts).

Illustrations

11–327   1. A & Co., an English company, sells an expensive piece of household equipment to X, an individual domiciled in France. The price is payable in England by instalments. When X defaults A & Co. commences proceedings in England. The court has no jurisdiction.

2. A, an individual domiciled in England, buys a washing machine from X & Co., a French company, while he is on a visit to France. The price is payable in France by instalments. A alleges that the machine is faulty and commences proceedings in England for the return of the instalments already paid. The court has jurisdiction.

3. The facts are as in Illustration 2, except that the contract provides for the exclusive jurisdiction of the French courts. The court has jurisdiction, because the clause is ineffective.

4. A, an individual domiciled in France, buys a washing machine on instalment credit terms from X & Co., a French company. The contract provides for the exclusive jurisdiction of the French courts. A moves to England and becomes domiciled there. When the machine proves to be faulty, A commences proceedings in England against X & Co. The court has no jurisdiction.

11R–328   **(15) The court has jurisdiction in proceedings which have as their object rights *in rem* in, or tenancies of, immovable property, if the property is situated in England.**[21]

Comment

11–329   This clause is based on Article 16(1)(a) of the Conventions, which provides that in proceedings which have as their object rights *in rem* in, or tenancies of, immovable property, the courts of the Contracting State in which the property is situated have exclusive[22] jurisdiction. The basic principle of Article 16(1) is found in the law of most countries.[23] The *lex situs* is paramount both from the point of view of convenience of evidence and because its law will apply.[24] Where the court has jurisdiction under this clause, it will also be able to deal with contractual claims connected with rights *in rem*, particularly debts secured on immovable property.[25] This clause is dealt with more fully in connection with the Rule relating to jurisdiction over immovable property.[26]

11R–330   **(16) The court has jurisdiction in proceedings which have as their object the validity of the constitution, the nullity or the dissolution of companies or other legal persons or associations of natural or legal persons, or the decisions of their organs, if the company, legal person or association has its seat in England.**[27]

---

[21] 1968 Convention, Art. 16(1)(a), and Lugano Convention Art. 16(1)(a), in 1982 Act, Scheds 1 and 3C; 1982 Act, Sched. 4, Art. 16(1).

[22] The courts of the domicile of the defendant also have jurisdiction if the proceedings have as their object tenancies of immovable property included for temporary private use for a maximum period of six consecutive months, and (under the 1968 Convention, Art. 16(1)(b), added by the 1989 Accession Convention) the landlord and tenant are natural persons and are domiciled in the same Contracting State, or (under the Lugano Convention, Art. 16(1)(b)) the tenant is a natural person and neither party is domiciled in the United Kingdom. See also 1982 Act, Sched. 4, Art. 16.

[23] See *post*, para. 23–003.

[24] Case 73/77 *Sanders v. Van Der Putte* [1977] E.C.R. 2383, 2390–2391. See White [1983] Conv. 180, 306.

[25] See clause (12), and *post*, para. 23–016.

[26] Rule 114.

[27] 1968 Convention, Art. 16(2), and Lugano Convention, Art. 16(2), in 1982 Act, Scheds 1 and 3C; 1982 Act, Sched. 4, Arts. 5A and 16(1).

COMMENT

This clause is based on Article 16(2) of the Conventions, which applies also   **11–331**
in intra-United Kingdom cases in a modified form. Article 16(2) provides that
in proceedings which have as their object the validity of the constitution, the
nullity or the dissolution of companies or other legal persons or associations
of natural or legal persons, or the decisions of their organs, the courts of the
Contracting State in which the company, legal person or association has its
seat shall have exclusive jurisdiction. The purpose of Article 16(2) is to avoid
conflicting judgments being given as regards the existence of a company or
with regard to the validity of the decisions of its organs, by providing that all
proceedings should take place in the courts of the State in which the company
has its seat, where information about the company will have been notified and
made public.[28] Schlosser[29] suggests that it applies to partnerships established
under United Kingdom law, but there is room for doubt as regards English
partnerships. It has been held, by reference to the French and German texts as
well as the English text, that the phrase "the validity of" governs not only the
constitution of the company, but also the decisions of its organs.[30]

The scope of the operation of Article 16(2) has been considered in two   **11–332**
decisions in England. In *Newtherapeutics Ltd. v. Katz*[31] an English company
sued two of its directors, one of whom was domiciled in the United States, and
the other of whom was domiciled in France, claiming that they had acted in
breach of duty, and without board authority, in signing contracts which
reduced amounts payable to a French company for which the English company was performing pharmaceutical trials. Knox J. held that the English
court had exclusive jurisdiction under Article 16(2) in relation to the claim
that the directors had acted without the authority of the board; but not in
relation to the claim that the directors were in breach of duty because they had
committed the company to a transaction which was so detrimental to the
interests of the company that no reasonable board could properly have
assented to it. The Court of Appeal, in *Grupo Torras S.A. v. Sheikh Fahad
Mohammed Al-Sabah*,[32] agreed with Knox J. on the first aspect, but left open
the question whether he was right on the second aspect. In the *Grupo Torras*
case the allegations against the directors were of a fraudulent conspiracy to
misappropriate a Spanish company's funds. It was held that Article 16(2) did
not apply so as to deprive the English court of jurisdiction: the subject matter
of the action was the fraud which it was alleged that the defendants had
practised on the company.

Article 16(2) does not itself indicate how the seat is to be determined, but   **11–333**
Article 53[33] provides that in order to determine the seat of a company, the
court seised shall apply its rules of private international law. In the United
Kingdom this is effected by section 43 of the 1982 Act, which provides for the
purposes of Article 16(2) that a corporation or association has its seat in the

---

[28] Jenard, p. 35.
[29] Para. 162.
[30] *Newtherapeutics Ltd. v. Katz* [1991] Ch. 226. This question was raised, but not decided, in
Grupo Torras S.A. v. Sheikh Fahad Mohammed Al-Sabah [1996] 1 Lloyd's Rep. 7 (C.A.).
There is a proposal for revision of the Conventions (*ante*, para. 11–011), which will make it
clear that the word "validity" does relate to the decisions of the various entities.
[31] [1991] Ch. 226; stated, *post*, Illustration 2. See Kaye (1991) 10 C.J.Q. 220.
[32] [1996] 1 Lloyd's Rep. 7 (C.A.). See also *Papanicolaou v. Thielen* [1997] I.L.Pr. 37.
[33] Which primarily concerns the seat of a company for the purposes of its domicile, but applies
also to the determination of a seat for the purposes of the Conventions, Art. 16(2).

United Kingdom if, and only if, (a) it was incorporated or formed under the law of a part of the United Kingdom or (b) its central management and control is exercised in the United Kingdom.[34] Thus under the 1982 Act a company incorporated under the Companies Act 1985 with its registered office in England, but with its central management and control in France, will be regarded in the United Kingdom as having its seat exclusively in England[35]; a company incorporated in the Netherlands with its central management and control in England will be regarded as having its seat in England, and also in the Netherlands if by Netherlands law its seat is in the Netherlands.[36]

11–334   Under the Conventions jurisdiction is vested *exclusively* in the courts of the Contracting State of the seat of the entity concerned, but the combined effect of Articles 5A and 16(1) of Schedule 4 is that although the English court will always have jurisdiction where the seat of the entity is in England, the jurisdiction will be non-exclusive as regards domiciliaries of Scotland and Northern Ireland where the proceedings have as their object a decision of an organ of the entity concerned.

Illustrations

11–335   1. Z Ltd. is a Netherlands company with its place of central management and control in England and most of its assets in England. X, Y and Z are directors and each of them is domiciled in the Netherlands. At a board meeting they resolve to transfer the assets of the company to Bermuda. A Ltd., which owns the share capital of Z Ltd., brings proceedings seeking a declaration that the board resolution is void and outside the powers of X, Y and Z. The court has jurisdiction.

2. A & Co., an English company, has a contract with a French company for the development of medicines for the treatment of AIDS. X, who is domiciled in France, is a director of A & Co. Shortly before he resigns as a director he executes (together with Y, another director, domiciled in the United States) a document varying the terms of A & Co.'s contract with the French company in a manner which A & Co. claims is substantially to its disadvantage. A & Co. claims (*inter alia*) that X and Y were in breach of duty by executing the variation documents in the absence of a board meeting and that it was beyond their powers as directors to sign them. The court has jurisdiction over X, but the writ is set aside since the action is bound to fail because A & Co. had waived all its claims against X.[37]

3. A & Co., a Spanish company, and its English subsidiary, B & Co., sue X, Y and Z, former directors of A & Co., claiming damages for breaches of directors' duties relating to a number of transactions entered into by them on behalf of A & Co. The English court has jurisdiction because the subject matter of the action is not the decision of the organs of A & Co., but the misappropriation of A & Co.'s money.[38]

11R–336   **(17) The court has jurisdiction in proceedings which have as their object the validity of entries in public registers, if the register is kept in England.[39]**

---

[34] s.43(2). Provision is made for allocation within the United Kingdom of jurisdiction in s.43(3)–(5). Association means an unincorporated body of persons, and corporation means a body corporate, and includes a partnership subsisting under Scots law: s.50. s.43(6)–(7) contains the rules for determining whether the corporation or association has its seat in another Contracting State, in which case the English court will have no jurisdiction unless (as is possible) the corporation or association also has its seat in England. See also *ante*, paras. 11–067 *et seq.*

[35] s.43(2), (3), (7).

[36] s.43(2), (3), (6), (7). *Cf. The Deichland* [1990] 1 Q.B. 361 (C.A.).

[37] *Newtherapeutics Ltd. v. Katz* [1991] Ch. 226.

[38] *Grupo Torras S.A. v. Sheikh Fahad Mohammed Al-Sabah* [1996] 1 Lloyd's Rep. 7 (C.A.).

[39] 1968 Convention, Art. 16(3), and Lugano Convention, Art. 16(3), in 1982 Act, Scheds 1 and 3C; 1982 Act, Sched. 4, Art. 16(3).

COMMENT

Article 16(3) deals with proceedings which have as their object the validity of   11–337
entries in public[40] registers, and assigns exclusive jurisdiction to the courts of
the Contracting State in which the register is kept.[41] It corresponds to the
provisions which appear in the internal laws of the original Contracting States
and covers entries in land registers, land charges registers and commercial
registers. In England it is not likely to be of practical significance except in
connection with problems relating to registered land, which would in any
event come within the provisions of Article 16(1).[42]

(18) The court has jurisdiction in proceedings concerned with the   11R–338
registration or validity of patents, trade marks, designs or other similar
rights required to be deposited or registered, if the deposit or registration
has been applied for or has taken place (or is deemed to have taken place)
in England.[43]

COMMENT

Article 16(4) assigns exclusive jurisdiction in proceedings concerned with   11–339
registration or validity of patents, trademarks, designs or other similar rights
required to be deposited or registered, to the courts of the Contracting State in
which the deposit or registration has been applied for, has taken place or is
under the terms of an international convention deemed to have taken place.
Article Vd of Protocol to the 1968 Convention (which was added by the
Accession Convention) and of the Protocol No. 1 to the Lugano Convention
provide, broadly, that the courts of each Contracting State are to have jurisdiction in proceedings concerned with the registration or validity of any European patent granted for that State, provided it is not a "Community patent"
which, if instituted, will be valid for the whole Community.[44]

The term "proceedings concerned with the registration or validity of pat-   11–340
ents" must be interpreted by reference to a uniform Convention concept, and
not by national law.[45] It includes proceedings connected with the place of the
grant of the right, such as proceedings[46] relating to the validity, existence or
lapse of the right, or an alleged right of priority by reason of an earlier
registration.[47] It does not apply to disputes relating to ownership.[48] Nor does

---

[40] See *Re Fagin's Bookshop plc* [1992] B.C.L.C. 188 (register of members of company held to be
public register: *sed quaere*).
[41] Or in the particular part of the United Kingdom in which the register is kept: Sched. 4, Art.
16(3).
[42] *Cf. Re Hayward* [1997] Ch. 45.
[43] 1968 Convention, Art. 16(4) and Lugano Convention, Art. 16(4), in 1982 Act, Scheds 1 and
3C.
[44] For the system of European Patents and Community Patents see Paterson, *The European Patent
System* (1992); *Kakkar v. Szelke* [1989] F.S.R. 225 (C.A.). There is no equivalent of Art. 16(4)
in the intra-United Kingdom provisions of Sched. 4 to the 1982 Act. Actions for infringement
could be brought at the domicile of the defendant or the place of infringement in accordance
with the normal rules. See also the jurisdiction provisions in the Protocol on Litigation to the
Agreement Relating to Community Patents of December 15, 1989 which will, when it comes
into force, take precedence over the 1968 Convention: [1989] O.J. L401/1.
[45] Case 288/82 *Duijnstee v. Goderbauer* [1983] E.C.R. 3663.
[46] See, *e.g. Napp Laboratories v. Pfizer Inc.* [1993] F.S.R. 150 (revocation petition).
[47] *Ibid.*
[48] *Ibid.*

Article 16(4) apply in principle to proceedings for infringement.[49] But in England an action for infringement of a patent may be defended on the basis that the patent is invalid. In *Coin Controls Ltd. v. Suzo International (U.K.) Ltd.*[50] it was held by Laddie J. that an action for infringement could be within Article 16(4) if the infringement proceedings were "principally concerned"[51] in a broad sense with validity, *i.e.* validity was a major feature of the litigation. This view was approved by the Court of Appeal in *Fort Dodge Animal Health Ltd. v. Akzo Nobel N.V.*,[52] but because it did not regard the question as free from doubt, the Court of Appeal made a reference to the European Court, which was withdrawn when the case was settled.

ILLUSTRATIONS

11–341   1. A petitions the High Court for revocation of a patent granted to X, the respondent, who is domiciled in Italy. The court has jurisdiction.[53]

2. A is the owner of a trade mark registered in the United Kingdom. X, domiciled in the Republic of Ireland (where the mark is not registered) uses the same mark in connection with his business in Dublin. A commences proceedings in England for an account of the profits X has made as a result of the passing-off and trade mark infringement. The court has no jurisdiction.[54]

3. A & Co., an English company, brings proceedings against X & Co., an English company, Y & Co., a Dutch company, and Z & Co., a German company, for infringement of UK, German and Spanish patents for a coin-dispensing machine. The defendants challenge the validity of the patents. The court has no jurisdiction over the claims for infringement of the German and Spanish patents because the proceedings became principally concerned with the validity of the patents.[55]

11R–342   **(19) The court has jurisdiction in proceedings concerned with the enforcement of judgments, if the judgment has been or is to be enforced in England.[56]**

COMMENT

11–343   This clause is based on Article 16(5) of the Conventions, and is included here only for the sake of completeness.[57]

---

[49] *Mölnlycke AB v. Procter & Gamble Ltd.* [1992] 1 W.L.R. 1112 (C.A.)

[50] [1999] Chap. 33; *post*, Illustration 3. These decisions are criticised by Fawcett and Torremans, *Intellectual Property and Private International Law* (1998), pp. 204–207, who prefer the contrary view expressed in the previous edition of this work, p. 386.

[51] See Art. 19, *ante*, para. 11–057.

[52] [1998] F.S.R. 222 (C.A.).

[53] See Patents Act 1977, s.72; *Encyclopedia of United Kingdom and European Patent Law* (ed. Vitoria & others), paras. 10-201–203.

[54] This Illustration was approved in *L.A. Gear Inc. v. Gerald Whelan & Sons Inc. Ltd.* [1991] F.S.R. 670.

[55] *Coin Controls Ltd. v. Suzo International (U.K.) Ltd.* [1999] Ch. 33.

[56] 1968 Convention, Art. 16(5), and Lugano Convention, Art. 16(5), in 1982 Act, Scheds 1 and 3C; 1982 Act, Sched. 4, Art. 16(5).

[57] See Collins, p. 83, for a fuller discussion. See also Case 220/84 *AS-Autoteile Service GmbH v. Malhe* [1985] E.C.R. 2267, where it was held that a court in which enforcement is sought cannot take jurisdiction (by dealing with an alleged set-off against the judgment debt) over a dispute which falls within the jurisdiction of another Contracting State. In Case C–261/90 *Reichert v. Dresdner Bank (No. 2)* [1992] E.C.R. I–2149 it was held that Art. 16(5) relates to measures taken to ensure the practical implementation of judgments, and did not apply to an action to set aside a transaction in fraud of creditors. *Cf. The Filiatra Legacy* [1994] 1 Lloyd's Rep. 513n.

(20) The court has jurisdiction over a dispute which the parties have   **11R–344**
agreed to submit to the English court if the agreement is in writing, or
evidenced in writing, or, in a form which accords with practices which the
parties have established between themselves, or in international trade or
commerce, in a form which accords with a usage of which the parties are
or ought to have been aware and which in such trade or commerce is
widely known to, and regularly observed by, parties to contracts of that
type involved in the particular trade or commerce concerned.[58]

COMMENT

This clause is based on Article 17 of the 1968 Convention (as amended by the   **11–345**
1978 and 1989 Accession Conventions)[59] and Article 17 of the Lugano
Convention. They contain (in somewhat different terms) special provisions
limiting the effect of jurisdiction agreements in contracts of employment.
Similar provisions (with some modifications) apply in the intra-United Kingdom cases under Article 17 of Schedule 4 to the 1982 Act. These Articles are
dealt with in connection with Rule 32.[60]

(21) The court has jurisdiction over a defendant who submits to its   **11R–346**
jurisdiction by appearance, except (a) where appearance was entered
solely to contest the jurisdiction, or (b) the courts of another Contracting
State have exclusive jurisdiction pursuant to the terms of the 1968 Con-
vention or the Lugano Convention.[61]

COMMENT

Article 18 of each of the Conventions provides that, in addition to jurisdiction   **11–347**
derived from other provisions, a court of a Contracting State before whom a
defendant enters an appearance shall have jurisdiction. It applies only to cases
within the scope of the Conventions, but if the case is within the scope of the
Conventions appearance will confer jurisdiction even though without appearance jurisdiction could not have been taken. Article 18 does not apply in a
case which is covered by the exclusive jurisdiction provisions of Article 16.[62]
But it does apply where the parties have agreed to submit their disputes to the
jurisdiction of the courts of a Contracting State under Article 17. In such a
case appearance by the defendant (including a defendant to a counterclaim[63])
in the courts of another State will confer jurisdiction on the courts of the
latter.[64]

The most difficult question which arises on Article 18 is the scope and   **11–348**
effect of the provision that appearance is not to confer jurisdiction if it "was
entered solely to contest the jurisdiction." In *Elefanten Schuh GmbH v.*

---

[58] 1968 Convention, Art. 17, and Lugano Convention, Art. 17, in 1982 Act, Scheds 1 and 3C;
1982 Act, Sched. 4, Art. 17.
[59] For parties see *ante*, paras. 11–006 *et seq.*
[60] On jurisdiction provisions in trust instruments, see *ante*, clause (6).
[61] 1968 Convention, Art. 18, and Lugano Convention, Art. 18, in 1982 Act, Scheds 1 and 3C;
1982 Act, Sched. 4, Art. 17.
[62] It does however apply, it seems, in insurance and consumer contract cases.
[63] Case 48/84 *Spitzley v. Sommer Exploitation S.A.* [1985] E.C.R. 787.
[64] Case 150/80 *Elefanten Schuh GmbH v. Jacqmain* [1981] E.C.R. 1671; Case 48/84 *Spitzley v.
Sommer Exploitation S.A.* [1985] E.C.R. 787.

Jacqmain[65] the European Court drew attention to the fact that the French text (unlike the English, German, Italian and Dutch texts) did not have any requirement that *only* jurisdiction must be contested[66] and held that a defendant did not submit by pleading to the merits as well as contesting the jurisdiction, but "only if the plaintiff and the court seised of the matter are able to ascertain from the time of the defendant's first defence that it is intended to contest the jurisdiction."[67] If the challenge to jurisdiction was not a preliminary matter[68] then, to avoid pleading to the merits being regarded as a submission, the challenge must not occur after the making of submissions which under national procedural law are considered to be the first defence put to the court.

11–349   In England, since 1979 (when conditional appearances were abolished) a defendant who wishes to contest the jurisdiction of the English court can do so without risk of submitting. Under the Civil Procedure Rules 1998 a defendant who wishes to dispute the jurisdiction of the court, or argue that the court should not exercise its jurisdiction, must file an acknowledgment of service and apply for an order declaring that it has no jurisdiction, or should not exercise any jurisdiction which it may have. A defendant who follows this course is not treated as having submitted to the jurisdiction, and does not thereby lose any right he may have to dispute the jurisdiction of the court. If the challenge to the jurisdiction or its exercise fails, the acknowledgment of service ceases to have effect. The defendant may then file a further acknowledgment of service, in which case he is treated as having accepted that the court has jurisdiction to try the claim.[69]

ILLUSTRATIONS

11–350   1. A, who is domiciled in England, enters into a contract with X, who is domiciled in France. The contract is to be performed wholly in France. In proceedings by A against X, X instructs English solicitors to accept service and serve a defence. The court has jurisdiction by virtue of X's submission.

2. A, who is domiciled in England, commences proceedings against X, who is domiciled in France, in connection with a tort committed in France, and seeks a *Mareva* injunction restraining X from removing his English assets. X files evidence resisting the injunction, in which (*inter alia*) he denies that he has committed any tort and indicates that he does not accept that the English court has jurisdiction. X's conduct does not amount to a submission.[70]

---

[65] *Supra*, n. 64; see also Case 27/81 *Rohr v. Ossberger* [1981] E.C.R. 2431; Case 25/81 *CHW v. GJH* [1982] E.C.R. 1189; Case 201/82 *Gerling v. Treasury Administration* [1983] E.C.R. 2503; *Kurz v. Stella Musical GmbH* [1992] Ch. 196. See also *The Xing Su Hai* [1995] 2 Lloyd's Rep. 15; *Clydesdale Bank plc v. Ions*, 1993 S.C.L.R. 964; *Campbell International Trading House Ltd. v. Van Aart* [1992] 2 I.R. 305; *Devrajan v. District Judge Ballagh* [1993] 3 I.R. 377. *Cf. The Atlantic Emperor (No. 2)* [1992] 1 Lloyd's Rep. 624 (C.A.); *Toepfer International GmbH v. Molino Boschi Srl* [1996] 1 Lloyd's Rep. 510 (cases on submission to jurisdiction of foreign court).

[66] "si la comparution a pour objet de contester la competence." The proposed revisions to the Conventions, *ante*, para. 11–011, remove the word "solely".

[67] At p. 1685.

[68] As it is under English law.

[69] CPR 11(1), (2), (3), (5), (7). An application for security for costs up to and including the hearing of the application to challenge jurisdiction is not an appearance for the purposes of Art. 18: *Hewden Stuart Heavy Cranes Ltd. v. Leo Gottwald*, unrep., 1992 (C.A.).

[70] *Cf. Obikoga v. Silvernorth Ltd., The Times*, July 6, 1983, distinguished in *Esal Ltd. v. Pujara* [1989] 2 Lloyd's Rep. 479 (C.A.), *ante*, para. 11–111.

(22) The court has jurisdiction to grant interim relief where proceed-   11R–351
ings have been or are to be commenced in another Contracting State or
in another part of the United Kingdom.[71]

COMMENT

Article 24 of each of the Conventions provides that application may be made   11–352
to the courts of a Contracting State for such provisional measures, including
protective measures, as may be available under the law of that State, even if,
under the Convention, the courts of another Contracting State have jurisdiction as to the substance of the matter. The Conventions apply to provisional
measures.[72] Section 25 of the 1982 Act gives the English court the powers
necessary to give effect to Article 24. In this case, by contrast with the other
bases of jurisdiction under the Convention, permission is required to serve
process claiming interim relief under section 25 abroad.[73] The jurisdiction to
grant interim measures is discussed in Chapter 8.

RULE 29—The court has no jurisdiction when the courts of another   11R–353
Contracting State[74] **or of Scotland or Northern Ireland have exclusive**
jurisdiction in the cases mentioned in this Rule.

COMMENT

The cases in this Rule are based on Article 16 of the Conventions, and their   11–354
counterparts in Schedule 4 for the purposes of intra-United Kingdom jurisdiction. Article 16 has been discussed in connection with the jurisdiction of the
English court, *i.e.* where England is the place of exclusive jurisdiction for the
purposes of Article 16. Detailed comment is not therefore necessary in
connection with this Rule. It is important to note that the exclusive jurisdiction
provisions of Article 16 are not subject to submission or contrary agreement
(unlike those of Article 17[75]), and apply irrespective of the domicile of the
defendant.

(1) The court has no jurisdiction in proceedings which have as their   11R–355
object rights *in rem* in, or tenancies of, immovable property situated in
another Contracting State or in Scotland or Northern Ireland,[76] **unless in**
the case of tenancies concluded for temporary private use for a maximum
period of six consecutive months (i) the defendant is domiciled in Eng-
land, and (ii) in the case of the 1968 Convention, the landlord and the
tenant are natural persons and are both domiciled in the United King-
dom,[77] **or, in the case of the Lugano Convention, the tenant is a natural**

---

[71] 1982 Act, s.25; 1968 Convention, Art. 24, and Lugano Convention, Art. 24, in 1982 Act,
Scheds. 1 and 3C; 1982 Act, Sched. 4, Art. 24.
[72] Case 143/78 *De Cavel v. De Cavel (No. 1)* [1979] E.C.R. 1055; Case 120/79 *De Cavel v. De Cavel (No. 2)* [1980] E.C.R. 731.
[73] Ord. 11, r. 8A.
[74] For Contracting States see *ante*, paras. 11–006 *et seq.*
[75] See Rules 30 and 32.
[76] 1968 Convention, Art. 16(1), and Lugano Convention, Art. 16(1), in 1982 Act, Scheds 1 and
3C; 1982 Act, Sched. 4, Art. 16(1).
[77] Or are both domiciled in England, if the property is situated in Scotland or Northern Ireland:
1982 Act, Sched. 4, Art. 16(1)(b).

person and neither party is domiciled in the Contracting State in which the property is situate.

COMMENT

11–356   This case is dealt with in connection with the Rule relating to jurisdiction over foreign land.[78]

11R–357   **(2) The court has no jurisdiction in proceedings which have as their object the validity of the constitution, the nullity or the dissolution of companies or other legal persons or associations of natural or legal persons or the decision of their organs if the company in question (or other legal person or association) (a) does not have its seat in England and (b) has its seat in another Contracting State or (except as regards proceedings relating to decisions of organs) in Scotland or Northern Ireland.[79]**

COMMENT

11–358   This clause, based on Article 16(2) of the Conventions, has been discussed above.[80] Three points should be noted. First, the version of Article 16(2) in Schedule 4 differs from that in the 1968 Convention. Under the Schedule 4 scheme the head of jurisdiction relating to decisions of organs of companies is not exclusive.[81] Secondly, Schedule 4 does not apply to winding up.[82] Thirdly, it is possible under the Convention scheme for more than one court to have exclusive jurisdiction.[83] This arises because Article 53 leaves it to the law of each Contracting State to determine the seat of a company in accordance with its rules of private international law. The United Kingdom rules in section 43 of the 1982 Act use the alternative tests of place of incorporation and place of central management and control. Thus, as has been seen,[84] by United Kingdom law a Dutch company with its place of central management and control in England may have its seat in both England and the Netherlands. This problem will not arise frequently in intra-United Kingdom cases because the effect of section 43(5) of the 1982 Act is that companies incorporated under the Companies Act 1985 and its predecessors will be regarded as having their seat in the part of Great Britain (England or Scotland) in which they have their registered office even if their place of central management and control is in another part.

11R–359   **(3) The court has no jurisdiction in proceedings which have as their object the validity of entries in public registers if the register is kept in another Contracting State or in Scotland or Northern Ireland.[85]**

---

[78] Rule 114.
[79] Art. 16(2), 1982 Act, Scheds 1 and 3C; 1982 Act, Sched. 4, Art. 16(2).
[80] Rule 28(16), *ante.*
[81] See Sched. 4, Art. 5A.
[82] Sched. 5, para. 1.
[83] Where actions come within the exclusive jurisdiction of more than one court, any court other than the court first seised must decline jurisdiction in favour of the court first seised: Art. 23, *post*, Rule 31(4).
[84] *Ante*, para. 11–069.
[85] Art. 16(3), 1982 Act, Scheds 1 and 3C; 1982 Act, Sched. 4, Art. 16(3).

(4) The court has no jurisdiction in proceedings concerned with the   11R–360
registration or validity of patents, trade marks, designs, or other similar
rights required to be deposited or registered, if the deposit or registration
in question has been applied for, has taken place or is under the terms of
an international convention deemed to have taken place in another Con-
tracting State.[86]

COMMENT

Article 16(4) has been discussed above.[87]   **11–361**

(5) The court has no jurisdiction in proceedings concerned with the   11R–362
enforcement of judgments if the judgment has been or is to be enforced
in another Contracting State.[88]

COMMENT

This clause is based on Article 16(5) of the 1968 Convention and the Lugano   **11–363**
Convention. It does not prevent the English court from making a disclosure
order relating to foreign assets situate in a Contracting State where the
judgment is to be enforced[89]: the reason is that the use of Order 48[90] (which
allows examination of a judgment debtor) in order to discover the *existence* of
foreign assets, does not confer jurisdiction on the English court in relation to
enforcement proceedings in any other country in which those assets may be
situate.[91] Nor does it prevent the grant of a *Mareva* injunction relating to
assets situate in another Contracting State where the claimant intends to
enforce a judgment.[92]

RULE 30—Unless the defendant submits to the jurisdiction, the court has   11R–364
no jurisdiction to determine a dispute which has arisen or may arise in
connection with a particular legal relationship in the following
circumstances:
    (1) if one or more of the parties is domiciled in a Contracting State
        and the parties have agreed in accordance with Article 17 of the
        1968 Convention or the Lugano Convention that the courts of
        another Contracting State are to have jurisdiction to settle any
        such dispute;
    (2) if none of the parties is domiciled in a Contracting State and the
        parties have agreed in accordance with Article 17 of the 1968
        Convention or the Lugano Convention that the courts of another

---

[86] Art. 16(4).
[87] *Ante*, paras. 11–338 *et seq.*
[88] Art. 16(5), 1982 Act, Scheds 1 and 3C; 1982 Act, Sched. 4, Art. 16(5). On Art. 16(5) see Case
    220/84 *AS-Autoteile Service GmbH v. Malhe* [1985] E.C.R. 2267; *The Filiatra Legacy* [1994]
    1 Lloyd's Rep. 513n.
[89] Collins, p. 83.
[90] Civil Procedure Rules 1998, Sched. 1.
[91] *Interpool Ltd. v. Galani* [1988] Q.B. 738 (C.A.).
[92] *Babanaft International Co. S.A. v. Bassatne* [1990] Ch. 13, 34–35 (C.A.) (where it was said that
    in such a case the English court would have jurisdiction under Art. 24, to grant the
    injunction).

Contracting State are to have jurisdiction to settle any such dispute and the courts chosen have not declined jurisdiction;

(3) if proceedings are brought against a settlor, trustee or beneficiary, which involve relations between them or their rights or obligations under a trust, and the trust instrument confers jurisdiction on the courts of another Contracting State.[93]

COMMENT

11–365 This rule is based on Article 17 of the Conventions, which is discussed below in connection with Rule 32.[94] Article 17 applies in two situations where the defendant is not domiciled in a Contracting State. First, it applies where either of the parties is domiciled in a Contracting State, so that where the claimant is domiciled in a Contracting State the chosen court will have jurisdiction irrespective of the domicile of the defendant. Secondly, if neither of the parties is domiciled in a Contracting State, no court other than the chosen court has jurisdiction unless the chosen court declines jurisdiction. By contrast with Article 16, Article 17 is subject to the principle of submission, so that a defendant may waive the jurisdiction agreement.[95]

ILLUSTRATIONS

11–366   1. A, who is domiciled in New York, enters into a contract with X, who is domiciled in England. The contract provides that the courts of France are to have exclusive jurisdiction. When a dispute arises A commences proceedings against X in England. The court has no jurisdiction.

2. The facts are as in Illustration 1, except that X instructs a solicitor to give notice of intention to defend and put in a defence on his behalf. The court has jurisdiction.

---

[93] Art. 17, 1982 Act. Scheds 1 and 3C. The corresponding provisions of Sched. 4 (as amended) do not provide for *exclusive* jurisdiction. Their effect is that a court which would have jurisdiction but for the jurisdiction clause will have a discretion not to give the clause effect: see Rule 34(3), *post*. For Contracting States see *ante*, paras. 11–006 *et seq.*

[94] *Post*, para. 12R–074.

[95] Case 150/80 *Elefanten Schuh GmbH v. Jacqmain* [1981] E.C.R. 1671.

CHAPTER 12

FORUM NON CONVENIENS, LIS ALIBI PENDENS, ANTI-SUIT INJUNCTIONS AND JURISDICTION AGREEMENTS

1. FORUM NON CONVENIENS, ANTI-SUIT INJUNCTIONS AND LIS ALIBI PENDENS

RULE 31—(1) English courts have jurisdiction, whenever it is necessary to prevent injustice, to stay or strike out proceedings in England.[1]   12R–001

(2) Subject to the provisions of the Brussels Convention and the Lugano Convention on jurisdiction and the enforcement of judgments in civil and commercial matters ("the 1968 Convention" and "the Lugano Convention" respectively), an English court has power to order a stay of proceedings on the basis that England is an inappropriate forum (*forum non conveniens*) if:

    (a) the defendant shows there to be another court with competent jurisdiction which is clearly and distinctly more appropriate than England for the trial of the action, and

    (b) it is not unjust that the claimant be deprived of the right to trial in England.[2]

(3) In considering whether to assume jurisdiction in any of the cases mentioned in Rule 27 (service out of the jurisdiction with the permission of the court) the court will generally require the claimant to show England to be the most appropriate forum for the trial of the claim.[3]

(4) Where the jurisdiction of the English court is derived from the 1968 Convention or the Lugano Convention (that is, from Rules 28 to 30, or 32(3)):

    (a) if proceedings involving the same cause of action and between the same parties have been brought in England and in another Contracting State, and the courts of that other Contracting State were

---

[1] The leading authorities are *Spiliada Maritime Corp. v. Cansulex Ltd.* [1987] A.C. 460 and *Connelly v. R.T.Z. Corp. plc* [1998] A.C. 854. See generally Briggs & Rees, *Civil Jurisdiction and Judgments* (2nd ed. 1997); Fawcett (ed.), *Declining Jurisdiction in Private International Law* (1995); Briggs (1983) 3 Leg. Studies 74, [1984] L.M.C.L.Q. 227, [1985] L.M.C.L.Q. 360; Schuz (1986) 35 I.C.L.Q. 374; Robertson (1987) 103 L.Q.R. 398; Slater (1988) 104 L.Q.R. 544; Juenger (1994) 16 Sydney L. Rev. 5, 28; Opeskin, *ibid.* 14; Bell (1995) 69 Aust. L.J. 124; Kennett [1995] C.L.J. 552.

[2] *Spiliada Maritime Corp. v. Cansulex Ltd.* [1987] A.C. 460, 475–478; *Connelly v. R.T.Z. Corp. plc* [1998] A.C. 854, 871–873.

[3] *Amin Rasheed Shipping Corp. v. Kuwait Insurance Co.* [1984] A.C. 50, 72, and *Spiliada Maritime Corp. v. Cansulex Ltd.* [1987] A.C. 460, 478–482. As the principles are closely related to those governing stays on the ground of *forum non conveniens*, see also the cases referred to under clauses (1) and (2) of this Rule.

seised first, the court must stay the English proceedings until such time as the jurisdiction of the court first seised is established; and where the jurisdiction of the court first seised is established, the court must decline jurisdiction[4];

(b) if related actions are brought in England and in another Contracting State, and the courts of that other Contracting State were seised first, the court may, while the actions are pending at first instance, stay its proceedings, or may decline jurisdiction if the court first seised has jurisdiction over both actions and its law permits the consolidation of related actions[5];

(c) if actions fall within the exclusive jurisdiction of the English court and of the courts of another Contracting State, any court other than the court first seised shall decline jurisdiction in favour of that court.[6]

(5) An English court may restrain a party over whom it has personal jurisdiction from the institution or continuance of proceedings in a foreign court[7], or the enforcement of foreign judgments[8], where it is necessary in the interests of justice for it to do so.

COMMENT

12–002   **Introduction.** The principal subject matter examined under this Rule may be described as the circumstances in which an English court has a discretion to exercise,[9] or to not exercise, or to adjudicate upon a foreign court's exercise[10] of, jurisdiction. It does not consider the cases where the answers to these questions will derive from a contractual agreement which designates the country or countries whose courts are to have jurisdiction to determine disputes: jurisdiction agreements conferring jurisdiction on English and foreign courts are examined under Rule 32. As a discretionary evaluation provides the principal mechanism by which the common law regulates and seeks to prevent clashes of jurisdiction which arise when proceedings take place in more than one court, it is necessary to examine it in conjunction with the very different mechanism by which the 1968 Convention and the Lugano Convention resolve this problem.

---

[4] Art. 21 of the 1968 Convention and the Lugano Convention: Civil Jurisdiction and Judgments Act 1982, Scheds. 1 and 3C. For the meaning of "Contracting States", see *ante*, paras. 11–006—11–008.

[5] Art. 22 of the 1968 and Lugano Conventions.

[6] Art. 23.

[7] The leading authorities are *British Airways Board v. Laker Airways Ltd.* [1985] A.C. 58; *Soc. Nat. Ind. Aérospatiale v. Lee Kui Jak* [1987] A.C. 871 (P.C.) and *Airbus Industrie G.I.E. v. Patel* [1999] 1 A.C. 119. The cases from which the principles were derived, and those which illustrate and apply these principles, are referred to in the Comment to clause (5) of this Rule. On injunctions granted in aid of a jurisdiction agreement, see clause (4) of Rule 32, *post*, para. 12–123. On injunctions to restrain proceedings brought in breach of an arbitration agreement, see *post*, para. 12–128.

[8] *Ellerman Lines Ltd. v. Read* [1928] 2 K.B. 144 (C.A.); *E.D. & F. Man (Sugar) Ltd. v. Haryanto (No. 2)* [1991] 1 Lloyd's Rep. 429 (C.A.).

[9] By staying proceedings instituted by right, under clause (2); by denying (or setting aside) permission to serve process out of the jurisdiction, under clause (3).

[10] By injunction to restrain the proceedings, under clause (5).

Though the common law material treated under this Rule covers a wide **12–003** range of legal situations, the thread which links them is that, because of the wide jurisdiction exercisable by the English court, recourse to the concept of the "natural forum" for the litigation represents a principled and even-handed means of deciding whether jurisdiction should be exercised.[11] If the English court has been seised with jurisdiction by the service of process on the defendant, in a case involving a foreign element a defendant who wishes to have the dispute resolved in another forum may apply for a stay of proceedings: the success of the application will depend in large measure upon the defendant showing that a foreign court is more appropriate than England for the trial of the proceedings. If the claimant requires the permission of the court to serve process on the defendant out of the jurisdiction in order to institute the proceedings, the question whether permission will be given, or will be set aside upon application by the defendant,[12] will depend in part upon the claimant showing England to be the most appropriate forum for the trial. If proceedings are being brought in a foreign court but the defendant in that action applies to the English court for an injunction to restrain his opponent[13] from continuation of that action, it will normally be a necessary, though not sufficient, condition for the grant of an injunction that England be the most appropriate forum for the trial.

Matters stand on a different footing when the jurisdiction of the English **12–004** court, or the jurisdiction of a foreign court, has been contractually agreed between the parties. The fundamental presumption is that an English court will uphold the agreement of the parties, and will generally grant such relief as will secure the performance of the jurisdictional agreement contained in the contract. The various issues which arise in this context are examined under Rule 32.

Spiliada Maritime Corp. v. Cansulex Ltd.,[14] the leading case in which the **12–005** common law rules were defined, referred to the English court as being "clearly or distinctly more appropriate"[15] than the competing foreign forum, or to another forum "which *prima facie* is clearly more appropriate for the trial of the action".[16] The test as laid down directed attention to whether one court was clearly more appropriate than another, and not to a search for "the natural forum" as such. But it must be acknowledged that the terminology of the "natural forum" has become irresistible, and that this convenient shorthand is now routinely used by the courts in comparing the relative strengths of connection between a court and a dispute. In the Comment to this Rule, therefore, the term "natural forum" is used as shorthand for the court identified by reference to the criteria laid down in *Spiliada Maritime Corp. v. Cansulex Ltd.*[17]

---

[11] *Cf. Airbus Industrie G.I.E. v. Patel* [1999] 1 A.C. 119, 131–133 (a case on injunctions to restrain foreign proceedings).

[12] See CPR, Part 11.

[13] The court must have jurisdiction *in personam* over the respondent to the application: *post*, para. 12–058.

[14] [1987] A.C. 460.

[15] At p. 477.

[16] At p. 478.

[17] [1987] A.C. 460.

12–006   **Clause (1) of the Rule.** English courts have an inherent jurisdiction, reinforced by statute,[18] to stay or strike out proceedings, whenever it is necessary to prevent injustice.[19] The jurisdiction may be exercised in cases which have nothing to do with the conflict of laws, or with the fact that a cause of action or ground of defence arises in a foreign country. But the cases in which a party to proceedings applies to have them stayed under this jurisdiction are very often, in some way or another, connected with transactions taking place in a foreign country or with litigation being conducted abroad. In such cases, according to English notions of the conflict of laws, an English court and a court in some foreign country may both be recognised as having jurisdiction to entertain proceedings, and the English court has a discretion to determine in which forum the dispute will be resolved, by using its power to grant or refuse a stay of the proceedings by the claimant[20] in the English court, or by exercising or refusing to exercise its power to authorise service out of the jurisdiction, or by using its power to enjoin a party who is (or who is threatening to become) a plaintiff in the foreign court from commencing or continuing proceedings in that court.[21] This topic has become of increasing modern importance as a result of a variety of factors including the greater ease of communication and travel; the tendency of courts in many countries to extend their jurisdiction over events and persons outside their territory; and a greater awareness of foreign laws and procedures, which in turn may lead to "forum-shopping".[22]

---

[18] Supreme Court Act 1981, s.49(3); Civil Jurisdiction and Judgments Act 1982, s.49; *cf.* CPR 3.1(2)(f). An application for a stay under clause (2) of this Rule is now made under CPR 11 and must in principle be made within the period for serving a defence: this is a departure from the previous practice under which a stay, unlike a challenge to the jurisdiction of the court, was not required to be sought at this stage: R.S.C. Ord. 12, r.8. If a stay is granted, the proceedings are still pending, so that what is now called a Part 20 claim (previously a contribution notice) may still be made against a defendant in relation to whom there is a stay (*Lister & Co. Ltd. v. E.G. Thomson (Shipping) Ltd. (No. 2)* [1987] 1 W.L.R. 1614) or a defendant may be added (*Rofa Sport Management A.G. v. DHL International (U.K.) Ltd.* [1989] 1 W.L.R. 902). For the power of the court to dismiss, rather than stay, proceedings, under clause (2) of the Rule, see *Haji-Ioannou v. Frangos* [1999] 2 Lloyd's Rep. 337, 348 (C.A.).

[19] In certain cases jurisdiction may be conferred on an English court by an international convention dealing with particular matters: see generally paras. 11–037, 13–033, and 15–008. The question whether an English court may stay proceedings on the ground of *forum non conveniens* in such a case depends upon whether the operation of the common law doctrine is expressly or impliedly permitted by the particular convention: *Milor Srl v. British Airways plc* [1996] Q.B. 702 (C.A.); *Deaville v. Aeroflot Russian International Airlines* [1997] 2 Lloyd's Rep. 67 (Warsaw Convention 1929).

[20] In exceptional cases, such as where the proceedings have been instituted to prevent time from running for limitation purposes, the stay may be granted on the application of the claimant: *Att. Gen. v. Arthur Andersen & Co.* [1989] E.C.C. 224 (C.A.); *cf. The Sylt* [1991] 1 Lloyd's Rep. 240; *cf. Centro Internationale Handelsbank A.G. v. Morgan Grenfell* [1997] C.L.C. 870. Contrast *Australian Commercial Research and Development Ltd. v. ANZ McCaughan Merchant Bank Ltd.* [1989] 3 All E.R. 65, affd. February 23, 1990 (C.A., unrep.); *Doe v. Armour Pharmaceutical Co. Inc.* [1994] 3 I.R. 78 (Sup. Ct.); *Manufacturers Life Ins. Co. v. Guarantee Co. of North America* (1987) 62 O.R. (2d) 147; *Dal Ponte v. Northern Manitoba Native Lodges Inc.* [1990] 4 W.W.R. 60, affd. [1990] 6 W.W.R. 273 (Man. C.A.). See Smart [1990] L.M.C.L.Q. 326.

[21] *British Airways Board v. Laker Airways Ltd.* [1985] A.C. 58, 80; see Comment to clause (5).

[22] This sentence was quoted with approval in *Amchem Products Inc. v. Workers' Compensation Board* [1993] 1 S.C.R. 897, 904 (Sup. Ct. Can.).

Forum non conveniens. The doctrine of *forum non conveniens, i.e.* that   **12–007**
some other forum is more "appropriate"[23] in the sense of more suitable for the
ends of justice, was developed by the Scottish courts in the nineteenth century,
and was adopted (with some modifications) in the United States.[24] The Scots
rule is that the court may decline to exercise jurisdiction, after giving consideration to the interests of the parties and the requirements of justice, on the
ground that the case cannot be suitably tried in the Scottish court nor full
justice be done there, but only in another court.[25] In England, *forum conveniens* has always been a relevant factor in the exercise of the discretion to
grant permission to serve out of the jurisdiction under Order 11, r. 1(1), *i.e.*
Rule 27, but until 1984 the English courts refused to accept that the jurisdiction to stay actions commenced against defendants who were sued in England
as of right could be based on *forum non conveniens* grounds.

Until the decision of the House of Lords in *The Atlantic Star*[26] a defendant   **12–008**
who sought a stay of English proceedings had a very heavy burden. In *St.
Pierre v. South American Stores (Gath and Chaves) Ltd.*[27] Scott L.J. restated
the principles on which the court acted, the effect of which was that a stay
would only be granted if the continuance of the action would work an injustice
in the sense that it would be "vexatious or oppressive", and if the stay would
not cause an injustice to the claimant. In *The Atlantic Star* a majority of the
House of Lords held that, although a plaintiff should not lightly be denied the
right to sue in an English court, the words "oppressive or vexatious" should,
in future, be interpreted more liberally: in considering whether a stay should
be granted, the court should take into account the advantage to the plaintiff
and any disadvantage to the defendant. In *MacShannon v. Rockware Glass
Ltd.*[28] a differently constituted House of Lords went considerably further
when all, except Lord Keith, were in favour of discontinuing the use of the
words "oppressive or vexatious" altogether. In this decision Lord Diplock
restated the governing principle as being that, in order to justify a stay, two
conditions had to be satisfied, one positive and the other negative: (a) the
defendant had to satisfy the court that there was another forum to whose
jurisdiction he was amenable in which justice could be done between the
parties at substantially less inconvenience or expense, and (b) the stay was not
to deprive the plaintiff of a legitimate personal or juridical advantage which
would be available to him if he invoked the jurisdiction of the English
court.[29]

---

[23] *Conveniens* does not mean "convenient": see *The Atlantic Star* [1974] A.C. 436, 475; *G.A.F.
Corp. v. Amchem Products Inc.* [1975] 1 Lloyd's Rep. 601, 607; *Spiliada Maritime Corp. v.
Cansulex Ltd.* [1987] A.C. 460, 474–475.
[24] *Gulf Oil Corp. v. Gilbert,* 330 U.S. 501 (1947); *Piper Aircraft v. Reyno,* 454 U.S. 235 (1981);
Scoles and Hay, pp. 373–382.
[25] *Société du Gaz de Paris v. La Société Anonyme de Navigation "Les Armateurs Français,"* 1926
S.C. (H.L.) 13, (1925) 23 Ll.L.R. 209; Anton, pp. 212–218.
[26] [1974] A.C. 436. Many cases decided before *The Atlantic Star, supra,* would be decided
differently today. The more important decisions are *McHenry v. Lewis* (1882) 22 Ch. D. 397
(C.A.); *Peruvian Guano Co. v. Bockwoldt* (1883) 23 Ch. D. 225; *The Christiansborg* (1885) 10
P.D. 141 (C.A.); *Logan v. Bank of Scotland (No. 2)* [1906] 1 K.B. 141; *Egbert v. Short* [1907]
2 Ch. 205; *Jopson v. James* (1908) 77 L.J. Ch. 824 (C.A.); *St. Pierre v. South American Stores
Ltd.* [1936] K.B. 382 (C.A.).
[27] [1936] 1 K.B. 382, 398 (C.A.).
[28] [1978] A.C. 795.
[29] [1978] A.C. 795, 812.

12–009   In *The Atlantic Star* and *MacShannon v. Rockware Glass Ltd.*[30] the House
of Lords declined to adopt the doctrine of *forum non conveniens* as part of
English law. In the latter decision, however, it was recognised that the
reformulation in these decisions of the principles on which the English court
acted was not far removed in practice from the doctrine of *forum non
conveniens.*[31] But by 1984, when *The Abidin Daver*[32] was decided, Lord
Diplock was able to say that, as a result of the successive decisions of the
House of Lords commencing with *The Atlantic Star*, "judicial chauvinism has
been replaced by judicial comity to an extent which I think the time is now
right to acknowledge frankly is, in the field of law with which this appeal is
concerned, indistinguishable from the Scottish legal doctrine of *forum non
conveniens.*"[33]

12–010   Finally, in *Spiliada Maritime Corp. v. Cansulex Ltd.*[34] the House of Lords
decided that Lord Diplock's formulation had given too great a prominence to
the "legitimate personal or juridical advantage" to the plaintiff in the continuance of the proceedings: "The basic principle is that a stay will only be
granted on the ground of *forum non conveniens* where the court is satisfied that
there is some other available forum, having competent jurisdiction, which is the
appropriate forum for the trial of the action, *i.e.* in which the case may be tried
more suitably for the interests of all the parties and the ends of justice."[35]

12–011   **Acceptance of the principle of *forum non conveniens* in other jurisdictions.** It follows from what has been said that the intellectual debt to the
Scottish doctrine of *forum non conveniens* is substantial; though it was also in
use in the United States for many years before its adoption in England, the role
there of *forum non conveniens* is slightly different[36] and the American authorities have not directly contributed to the development of the English doctrine.
Moreover, the doctrine has, to a greater or lesser extent, been adopted in
several common law jurisdictions,[37] most notably in Canada (where it governs

---

[30] For cases decided under the principles established in *The Atlantic Star* and *MacShannon v.
Rockware Glass Ltd.*, which remain of relevance, see *Camilla Cotton Oil Co. v. Granadex S.A.*
[1976] 2 Lloyd's Rep. 10 (H.L.); *The Wladyslaw Lokietek* [1978] 2 Lloyd's Rep. 520; *The
Wellamo* [1980] 2 Lloyd's Rep. 229; *Trendtex Trading Corp. v. Crédit Suisse* [1980] 3 All E.R.
721, 734, affd. [1982] A.C. 679; *The Netty* [1981] 2 Lloyd's Rep. 57; *European Asian Bank v.
Punjab Bank* [1982] 2 Lloyd's Rep. 356 (C.A.); *The Jalakrishna* [1983] 2 Lloyd's Rep. 628;
The Messiniaki Tolmi [1983] 1 Lloyd's Rep. 666, affd. [1984] 1 Lloyd's Rep. 267 (C.A.); *The
Abidin Daver* [1984] A.C. 398; *The Forum Craftsman* [1985] 1 Lloyd's Rep. 291 (C.A.); *The
Traugutt* [1985] 1 Lloyd's Rep. 76; *Muduroglu Ltd. v. T.C. Ziraat Bankasi* [1986] Q.B. 1225
(C.A.); *The Efthimis* [1986] 1 Lloyd's Rep. 244 (C.A.); *The Coral Isis* [1986] 1 Lloyd's Rep.
413; *The Evia Luck* [1986] 2 Lloyd's Rep. 165; *The Sidi Bishr* [1987] 1 Lloyd's Rep. 42.
[31] See [1978] A.C. 795, at pp. 812 (Lord Diplock), 822 (Lord Fraser) and *Hesperides Hotels Ltd.
v. Aegean Turkish Holidays Ltd.* [1979] A.C. 508 at pp. 537 (Lord Wilberforce) and 544 (Lord
Fraser). For an earlier (if premature) recognition of the same point *cf. Logan v. Bank of
Scotland (No. 2)* [1906] 1 K.B. 141.
[32] [1984] A.C. 398.
[33] At p. 411.
[34] [1987] A.C. 460.
[35] At p. 476.
[36] It was described as a "parallel development" in *Bank of Tokyo Ltd. v. Karoon* [1987] 1 A.C.
45n, 61 (C.A.). Its role owes much to the constitutional guarantee of due process under the Fifth
and Fourteenth Amendments to the Constitution of the United States: as this was interpreted in an
increasingly liberal manner, so allowing a plaintiff a greater freedom in deciding where to sue
(*International Shoe Co. v. Washington*, 326 U.S. 310 (1945)), the principle of *forum non
conveniens* developed as an antidote to allow courts to decline to exercise jurisdiction: *cf. Gulf
Oil Corp. v. Gilbert*, 330 U.S. 501 (1947); *Piper Aircraft Co. v. Reyno*, 454 U.S. 235 (1981).
[37] *Airbus Industrie G.I.E. v. Patel* [1999] 1 A.C. 119.

the staying of proceedings and the grant of injunctions against proceedings in foreign courts[38]), New Zealand,[39] Hong Kong,[40] Singapore,[41] and India.[42] In Australia, the High Court has adopted the doctrine in a form which continues to invoke the notions of vexation and oppression: a stay should be granted if the local court is a clearly inappropriate forum, which will be the case if continuation of the proceedings in that court would be oppressive in the sense of seriously and unfairly burdensome, prejudicial or damaging, or vexatious in the sense of productive of serious and unjustified trouble and harassment.[43]

Abuse of the process. Most cases involving a foreign element will be cases of competing jurisdictions in which a stay will normally be granted only if the foreign court is the natural or appropriate forum. There will be a residual category of cases in which English proceedings will be stayed even though England is the natural forum. Such cases will no doubt be rare and the onus on the defendant to prove injustice will be a heavy one,[44] but it is clear that an abuse of the process in the traditional sense, that is, resort to litigation for improper motives, such as harassment of the defendant, will justify a stay.[45]   12–012

Impact of the 1968 Convention and the Lugano Convention. As will be seen in connection with the discussion of clause (4) of the Rule below,[46] the 1968 Convention and the Lugano Convention contain specific rules in Articles 21 to 23 which deal with the problems of actions pending in different Contracting States. It has already been seen[47] that the effect of the 1968 Convention and the Lugano Convention, incorporated into English law by the Civil Jurisdiction and Judgments Act 1982 (as amended), is to confer jurisdiction on English courts and the courts of other Contracting States in certain specified circumstances. May an English court which has jurisdiction under either Convention[48] and in which proceedings have been commenced stay those proceedings on the ground that a court in another country is more appropriate for the resolution of the dispute? Section 49 of the 1982 Act   12–013

---

[38] *Amchem Products Inc. v. British Columbia (Workers' Compensation Board)* [1993] 1 S.C.R. 897, 920–921 (Sup. Ct. Can.). See also *Frymer v. Brettschneider* (1994) 115 D.L.R. (4th) 744 (Ont. C.A.), and the numerous cases cited in Castel, *Canadian Conflict of Laws* (4th ed. 1998), pp. 248–251.

[39] *McConnell Dowell Constructors Ltd. v. Lloyd's Syndicate 396* [1988] 2 N.Z.L.R. 257; *Club Méditerranée N.Z. v. Wendell* [1989] 1 N.Z.L.R. 216 (C.A.).

[40] *The Adhigina Meranti* [1988] 1 Lloyd's Rep 384 (H.K.C.A.).

[41] *Brinkerhoff Maritime Drilling Corp. v. P.T. Airfast Indonesia* [1992] 2 Sing. L.R. 776 (C.A.); *Oriental Insurance Co. Ltd. v. Bhavani Stores Pte. Ltd.* [1998] 1 Sing. L.R. 253 (C.A.).

[42] Cf. *Airbus Industrie G.I.E. v. Patel, supra*, at p. 132.

[43] *Voth v. Manildra Flour Mills Pty Ltd.* (1991) 171 C.L.R. 538; see also *Sentry Corp. v. Peat Marwick, Mitchell & Co.* (1990) 95 A.L.R. 11 (Fed. Ct.); *Henry v. Henry* (1996) 185 C.L.R. 571, 587 (High Ct.). See Pryles (1991) 65 A.L.J. 442; Brereton (1991) 40 I.C.L.Q. 895; Garnett (1999) 23 Melb. Univ. L.R. 30.

[44] *MacShannon v. Rockware Glass Ltd.* [1978] A.C. 795, 820, 826. Contrast *Spiliada Maritime Corp. v. Cansulex Ltd.* [1987] A.C. 460, 478.

[45] See, *e.g., The Christiansborg* (1885) 10 P.D. 141 (C.A.); *Egbert v. Short* [1907] 2 Ch. 205; *Re Norton's Settlement* [1908] 1 Ch. 471 (C.A.).

[46] Paras. 12–039 *et seq., post.*

[47] Chap. 11, *ante.*

[48] That is, in a civil or commercial matter in proceedings within the scope of the Conventions (*ante*, paras. 11–012 *et seq.*). If the court has jurisdiction in a matter outside the scope of the Conventions *ratione materiae* or *ratione temporis*, the Conventions have no application to the regulation of jurisdiction.

provides that nothing in the Act is to prevent any court in the United Kingdom from staying any proceedings on the ground of *forum non conveniens* or otherwise "where to do so is not inconsistent with the 1968 Convention or, as the case may be, the Lugano Convention."

12–014   First, there is no doubt that the English court may stay proceedings on the ground that a court in Scotland or Northern Ireland is the *forum conveniens*: in cases where the Conventions confer international jurisdiction on the courts of the United Kingdom, it is certainly not inconsistent with the Conventions for a court in one part of a Contracting State to stay proceedings in favour of a court in another part of the same Contracting State. Articles 21 to 23 have no counterpart in the provisions of Schedule 4 to the 1982 Act, which regulate jurisdiction as between the constituent parts of the United Kingdom. It follows that the English court may stay its proceedings in favour of a court in another part of the United Kingdom (or grant an injunction in an appropriate case) in accordance with the principles in clauses (1) and (2) of the Rule.[49]

12–015   Secondly, the predominant view[50] is that where the Conventions confer jurisdiction on the courts of the United Kingdom, there is no question of a discretion to stay the proceedings in favour of the courts of another Contracting State (or to enjoin proceedings commenced in another Contracting State) except in accordance with the specific rules relating to pending actions in Articles 21 to 23 of each Convention. Moreover, the European Court has made it clear that there is no room for considerations of *forum conveniens* to be interpolated into the jurisdictional provisions of the 1968 Convention: special jurisdiction under Article 5(1), for example, may not be renounced on the ground that the court identified has in fact no substantial connection with the dispute.[51] There is, however, it is suggested, a residual power in the English court to grant a stay of proceedings (and perhaps even an injunction to restrain the foreign proceedings) to prevent injustice, *e.g.* where there is evidence that the claimant is improperly using the proceedings to oppress the defendant, or is guilty of unconscionable conduct.[52] The European Court has held, in a different but related context, that a national court may apply its own procedural rules to determine whether an action is admissible, provided it does not reject an action on the ground that the defendant is resident or domiciled in another Contracting State.[53]

12–016   Thirdly, where proceedings are brought against a domiciliary of a non-Contracting State in accordance with Article 4 of the Convention, a stay may be granted in favour of the courts of another Contracting State. The Court of

---

[49] *Cumming v. Scottish Daily Record and Sunday Mail Ltd., The Times*, June 8, 1995 (see Collins (1995) 111 L.Q.R. 541) approving the view set out in the text, and not following *Foxen v. Scotsman (Publications) Ltd., The Times*, February 17, 1994 (a decision of the same judge; criticised Collins and Davenport (1994) 110 L.Q.R. 325) (libel actions in England; application for stay on *forum non conveniens* ground in favour of Scotland).

[50] Schlosser, pp. 97–99; Collins, p. 45; Anton, *Civil Jurisdiction*, p. 180; Mathers (1983) 3 Yb. Eur. L. 49, 61–62; Mennie, 1989 Jur. Rev. 150; Kaye pp. 269, 1244; O'Malley & Layton, p. 368. See also *Aiglon Ltd. v. Gau Shan Co. Ltd.* [1993] 1 Lloyd's Rep. 164; *Soc. Schimmel Pianofortefabrik GmbH v. Bion* [1992] I.L.Pr. 199 (French Cour de cassation, 1991).

[51] Case C–288/92 *Custom Made Commercial Ltd. v. Stawa Metallbau GmbH* [1994] E.C.R. I–2913; *cf.* Case C–354/93 *Marinari v. Lloyds Bank plc* [1995] E.C.R. I–2719, 2738–2739; *Boss Group Ltd. v. Boss France S.A.* [1997] 1 W.L.R. 315, 358 (C.A.).

[52] This has now been confirmed by *Turner v. Grovit* [1999] 3 All E.R. 616 (C.A.).

[53] Case C–365/88 *Kongress Agentur Hagen GmbH v. Zeehaghe B.V.* [1990] E.C.R. I–1845 (Art. 6(2), 1968 Convention); *Kinnear v. Falconfilms N.V.* [1996] 1 W.L.R. 920 (*forum conveniens* relevant to application for leave to issue third party notice).

Appeal[54] has explained that the power to stay proceedings over which the court had jurisdiction by reason of Article 4 did not subvert the scheme of the Convention; and it can be convincingly argued that if it were held that a stay could not be granted in such circumstances, this would have the unintended effect of widening the traditional rules of jurisdiction.[55] To avoid the objection that as an English court remained seised of proceedings which it stayed,[56] a court in another Contracting State would be prevented by Article 21[57] from accepting jurisdiction over a case still technically pending before the English court, in *Haji-Ioannou v. Frangos*[58] the Court of Appeal suggested that if the English proceedings were dismissed rather than stayed there would be no obstacle to the assumption of jurisdiction by the foreign court.[59]

Fourthly, a more controversial question arises where a defendant domiciled in England (or in another Contracting State) seeks a stay on the ground that a court in a non-Contracting State is the appropriate forum. In *Re Harrods (Buenos Aires) Ltd.*[60] the Court of Appeal decided (disapproving two first instance decisions to the contrary[61]) that the English court could stay an action against a defendant domiciled in England on the ground that the courts of a non-Contracting State (Argentina) were the appropriate forum. It was held that section 49 of the 1982 Act preserved the power of the court to stay or dismiss proceedings where to do so was not inconsistent with the 1968 Convention[62]; the Convention was intended to regulate jurisdiction as between the Contracting States, and it was not inconsistent with the letter or spirit of the Convention to stay proceedings on the ground of *forum non conveniens* in a case involving a conflict of jurisdiction between the English court and the courts of a non-Contracting State.

12–017

The decision is a controversial one. It has been suggested (and this suggestion was accepted by Bingham L.J. in the Court of Appeal) that the power to

12–018

---

[54] *Sarrio S.A. v. Kuwait Investment Authority* [1997] 1 Lloyd's Rep. 113, 124, 128–129 (C.A.); revd. on other grounds [1999] 1 A.C. 32; *Haji-Ioannou v. Frangos* [1999] 2 Lloyd's Rep. 337 (C.A.). See also *The Xin Yang* [1996] 2 Lloyd's Rep. 217.

[55] The principal argument to the contrary, namely that the power to stay proceedings duly commenced in favour of the courts of another Contracting State makes it unacceptably difficult for a claimant to ascertain whether a court within the Contracting States has jurisdiction (*cf.* Schlosser, para. 78), was rejected.

[56] *Ante*, para. 12–006, n. 18.

[57] See Clause (4)(a) of this Rule, *post*, para. 12–039.

[58] [1999] 2 Lloyd's Rep. 337. (C.A.).

[59] *Cf. Internationale Nederlanden Aviation Lease B.V. v. Civil Aviation Authority* [1997] 1 Lloyd's Rep. 80.

[60] [1992] Ch. 72 (C.A.) (on which see Briggs (1991) 107 L.Q.R. 180; Gaudemet-Tallon, 1991 *Rev. Crit.* 491); *The Po* [1991] 2 Lloyd's Rep. 206 (C.A.) (where it was accepted without argument that the decision in *Re Harrods (Buenos Aires) Ltd.* applied where the defendant was domiciled in another Contracting State, namely Italy); *Re Polly Peck International plc (No. 2)* [1998] 3 All E.R. 812, 830 (C.A.). See also *Société Commerciale de Réassurance v. Eras International Ltd. (No. 2)* [1995] 2 All E.R. 278, 298–299; and see Tebbens, in *Law and Reality: Essays in Honour of C. Voskuil* (1992) p. 47; North, in *Nouveaux itinéraires en droit: Hommage à François Rigaux* (1993), p. 373; Kennett [1995] C.L.J. 552, 561–562 (with references to foreign literature).

[61] *S. & W. Berisford plc v. New Hampshire Insurance Co.* [1990] 2 Q.B. 631 and *Arkwright Mutual Insurance Co. v. Bryanston Insurance Co. Ltd.* [1990] 2 Q.B. 649, criticised by Collins (1990) 106 L.Q.R. 535. See also Briggs [1991] L.M.C.L.Q. 10.

[62] At the time of the institution of the proceedings (see Art. 54, Lugano Convention) the Lugano Convention was not in force.

stay in favour of the courts of non-Contracting States remains in place because the 1968 Convention was intended to regulate jurisdiction as between Contracting States, which had no interest in requiring a Contracting State to exercise jurisdiction where the competing jurisdiction was in a non-Contracting State.[63] But it has also been said that the decision is wrong because the Convention is *not* simply concerned with jurisdiction as between Contracting States, and the use of a discretion to stay will prevent uniformity of jurisdictional rules in the European Community.[64] Moreover, if the court remains seised of the action after it has been stayed, the order serves to preclude the courts of another Contracting State being seised; the order accordingly does have an impact on other Contracting States.[65] Leave was given to appeal to the House of Lords, which made a reference to the European Court, in which it asked the European Court to rule on (*inter alia*) whether the 1968 Convention applies to the jurisdiction of the courts of a Contracting State in circumstances in which there is no conflict of jurisdiction with the courts of any other Contracting State; and whether it was inconsistent with the 1968 Convention for a court in a Contracting State to exercise a discretionary power to decline to hear proceedings brought against a person domiciled in that State if the jurisdiction of no other Contracting State is involved. But the reference was withdrawn when the case was settled.

12–019   Fifthly, a distinct question may arise when the court has jurisdiction over the defendant, for example, by reason of his domicile, but the action has a factual connection with a non-Contracting State which, were it with a Contracting State, would deprive the court of its jurisdiction under the Conventions. For example, the action may have as its object rights *in rem* in land in a non-Contracting State,[66] or be concerned the validity of a patent granted under a foreign law,[67] or be subject to an agreement conferring jurisdiction on the courts of a non-Contracting State[68]; or there may be a *lis alibi pendens* in a non-Contracting State.[69] It has been proposed by certain commentators[70] that in such a case the court may properly decline to accept jurisdiction by ascribing a "reflexive effect" to Articles 16, 17 and 21 of the Convention. It is reasoned that though the Conventions cannot impose jurisdiction on a non-Contracting State in such a case, there is nothing in them to preclude a national court deriving a rule by analogy from those provisions which would, in a case internal to the Contracting States, have overridden the basis upon

---

[63] Collins (1990) 106 L.Q.R. 536.
[64] Cheshire and North, p. 264. If a stay of proceedings will deprive the claimant of the right to obtain a judgment which may be enforced under the Conventions it may be unjust to order a stay: *International Credit and Investment Co. (Overseas) Ltd. v. Adham* [1999] I.L.Pr. 302 (C.A.).
[65] But it was suggested in *Haji-Ioannou v. Frangos* [1999] 2 Lloyd's Rep. 337 (C.A.) that the English action could be dismissed rather than stayed; if that were done the objection would not arise: *ante*, para. 12–016.
[66] *Cf.* Art. 16(1). A claim for the determination of title to foreign land was, as a matter of common law, one which the court had no jurisdiction to determine: Rule 114(3), *post*, para. 23–034. *Cf. Re Polly Peck International plc (No. 2)* [1998] 3 All E.R. 812 (C.A.), *post*, para. 23–027.
[67] *Cf.* Art. 16(4), *ante*, paras. 11–339 *et seq.*
[68] *Cf.* Art. 17, considered *post*, para. 12–087.
[69] *Cf.* Art. 21, considered *post*, clause (4) of the Rule.
[70] Droz, *La compétence judiciaire et l'effet des jugements dans la CEE* (1972), para. 164; Gaudemet-Tallon, *Les Conventions de Bruxelles et de Lugano* (2nd ed. 1996), paras. 75, 84, 93, 111.

which jurisdiction has been asserted.[71] If this is so, it would furnish a more limited basis for an English court to order a stay of proceedings in favour of the courts of a non-Contracting State, which is distinct from the proposition, accepted in *Re Harrods (Buenos Aires) Ltd.*, that the Conventions do not preclude the operation of the common law doctrine of *forum non conveniens* when the alternative forum lies in a non-Contracting State.

Clause (2) of the Rule. *Spiliada Maritime Corp. v. Cansulex Ltd.*[72] was a case involving the discretion to grant permission to serve out of the jurisdiction under Order 11, r. 1(1), *i.e.* Rule 27, but the opportunity was taken in that case to lay down common principles applicable in both Order 11 and stay cases. The fundamental principle enunciated by Lord Goff of Chieveley[73] is stated in clause (2) and is based on what he described as the classic statement in the leading Scottish case.[74]   **12–020**

The following propositions may be derived from the speech of Lord Goff of Chieveley, which has been applied in many subsequent cases.[75] First, in general the legal burden of proof rests on the defendant to persuade the court to exercise its discretion to grant a stay, although the evidential burden will rest on a party who seeks to establish the existence of matters which will assist him in persuading the court to exercise its discretion in his favour. Secondly, if the court is satisfied that there is another available forum which is *prima facie* the appropriate forum for the trial of the action,[76] the burden will shift to the claimant to show that there are special circumstances by reason of which justice requires that the trial should nevertheless take place in England. Thirdly, the burden on the defendant is not just to show that England is not the natural or appropriate forum, but to establish that there is another forum which is clearly or distinctly more appropriate than the English forum; accordingly, where (as in some commercial disputes) there is no particular forum which can be described as the natural forum, there may be no reason to grant a stay.[77]   **12–021**

---

[71] For a view which appears contrary to this analysis, and which appears to propose that the court has jurisdiction and may not decline to exercise it as the literal text of the Convention rules is inapplicable to the case, see de Almeida Cruz, etc. [1989] O.J. C189/35, at p. 47; also Jenard-Möller [1989] O.J. C189/57, at p. 76.

[72] [1987] A.C. 460.

[73] As Stephenson L.J. said of Robert Goff J. in *European Asian Bank AG v. Punjab Bank* [1982] 2 Lloyd's Rep. 356, 363: " . . . no Judge on the bench has had to study and state the principles on which proceedings in this country are stayed more often or more carefully than this learned Judge". Mr. Robert Goff Q.C. was counsel in *The Atlantic Star* [1974] A.C. 436; Robert Goff J. was the judge at first instance in *MacShannon v. Rockware Glass Ltd.* [1978] A.C. 795, and in *Trendtex Trading Corp. v. Crédit Suisse* [1980] 3 All E.R. 721, affd. [1982] A.C. 679; and Lord Goff of Chieveley was the author of the leading speeches or opinions in *Spiliada Maritime Corp. v. Cansulex Ltd.* [1987] A.C. 460; *de Dampierre v. de Dampierre* [1988] A.C. 92; *Soc. Nat. Ind. Aérospatiale v. Lee Kui Jak* [1987] A.C. 871; *Connelly v. R.T.Z. Corp. plc* [1998] A.C. 854; *Airbus Industrie G.I.E. v. Patel* [1999] 1 A.C. 119. See also *Bank of Tokyo v. Karoon* [1987] A.C. 45n. (C.A.).

[74] *Sim v. Robinow* (1892) 19 R. 665, 668.

[75] For stays in matrimonial proceedings under Matrimonial Causes Act 1973, Sched.1, para. 9(1) the approach is similar but not identical: *de Dampierre v. de Dampierre* [1988] A.C. 92; *Butler v. Butler* [1998] 1 W.L.R. 1208 (C.A.); see further *post*, para. 18–228.

[76] If the defendant has no defence to an application for summary judgment, so that no trial of the action is called for, the court should refuse a stay: *Bank of Credit and Commerce Hong Kong Ltd. v. Sonali Bank* [1995] 1 Lloyd's Rep. 227; *Standard Chartered Bank v. Pakistan National Shipping Corp.* [1995] 2 Lloyds Rep. 365.

[77] Citing *European Asian Bank A.G. v. Punjab and Sind Bank* [1982] 2 Lloyd's Rep. 356 (C.A.). See also *The Vishva Abha* [1990] 2 Lloyd's Rep. 312.

Fourthly, the court will look to see what factors[78] there are which point in the direction of another forum as being the "natural forum", *i.e.* that with which the action has the most real and substantial connection.[79] These will include factors affecting convenience or expense (such as availability of witnesses) and such other factors as the law governing the transaction and the places where the parties reside or carry on business. Fifthly, if the court concludes at that stage that there is no other available forum which is clearly more appropriate for the trial of the action, the court will ordinarily refuse a stay.[80] Sixthly, if, however, the court concludes that there is some other available forum which prima facie is clearly more appropriate,[81] it will ordinarily grant a stay unless there are circumstances by reason of which justice requires that a stay should not be granted. In that enquiry, the court will consider all the circumstances of the case, including circumstances which go beyond those taken into account when considering connecting factors with other jurisdictions.[82] Seventhly, a stay will not be refused simply because the claimant will thereby be deprived of "a legitimate personal or juridical advantage", provided that the court is satisfied that substantial justice will be done in the available appropriate forum.[83]

12–022   Most cases in which stay applications are made are in the Commercial Court.[84] In *Spiliada*, Lord Templeman (with whom Lord Griffiths and Lord Mackay expressly agreed) observed that the factors which the court is entitled to take account in considering whether one forum is more appropriate than another are legion; the resolution of disputes about the relative merits of trial in England and abroad was pre-eminently a matter for the judge at first instance; and he expressed the hope that the judge would be referred only to the speech of Lord Goff and not to other decisions on other facts; and that submissions would be measured in hours and not days.[85] It is nevertheless helpful to consider how the discretion is exercised in practice and what principles have emerged in relation to matters which did not arise directly for decision in *Spiliada* itself.

12–023   **Availability of the foreign forum.** The first limb of the *Spiliada* test requires it to be shown that the foreign forum is "available" as well as being more appropriate for the trial of the action. There are three aspects of availability to consider. First, it has been held that the foreign court is not

---

[78] The court has to consider with what forum the *issues* have the closest connection, and not simply weigh factors without reference to the likely issues: *E.I. du Pont de Nemours v. Agnew* [1987] 2 Lloyd's Rep. 585 (C.A.); *cf. Re Harrods (Buenos Aires) Ltd.* [1992] Ch. 72 (C.A.).

[79] Citing *The Abidin Daver* [1984] A.C. 398, 415.

[80] Citing *European Asian Bank A.G. v. Punjab and Sind Bank* [1982] 2 Lloyd's Rep. 356 (C.A.).

[81] If there are two such *fora*, both more appropriate than England, a stay may be granted: there is no requirement that one be more appropriate than the other.

[82] One of which can be the fact that the claimant will not obtain justice in the foreign jurisdiction: at p. 478, citing *The Abidin Daver* [1984] A.C. 398, 411. See *post*, para. 12–025.

[83] For Canadian authority which holds that loss of a juridical advantage is not a separate and distinct condition, but that it is part of the overall assessment of which is the appropriate forum, see *Amchem Products Inc. v. British Columbia (Workers' Compensation Board)* [1993] 1 S.C.R. 897, 933 (Sup.Ct.Can.) (an injunction case); *Frymer v. Brettschneider* (1994) 115 D.L.R. (4th) 744 (Ont. C.A.).

[84] As are most applications to set aside orders permitting service outside the jurisdiction.

[85] [1987] A.C. at 465. See also, *e.g.*, *The Nile Rhapsody* [1994] 1 Lloyd's Rep. 383, 388 (C.A.); *Haji-Ioannou v. Frangos* [1999] 2 Lloyd's Rep. 337, 356 (C.A.); *Askin v. Absa Bank* [1999] I.L.Pr. 471, 473 (C.A.).

"available" to a claimant unless, at the time of the application for a stay,[86] it was open to him to institute proceedings against the defendant as of right before that court. If, by contrast, the jurisdiction of that court would be open to him only if the defendant undertook to submit, and did later submit, to its jurisdiction, or if in due course the court granted leave to the claimant to commence the proceedings, the court is not available in the material sense. It follows that an undertaking by the defendant to submit to the jurisdiction of a foreign court cannot make the foreign court available if it would not have been so without his undertaking.[87] Secondly, and despite authority which had held that the foreign court must be one in which the claimant is in practice able to bring his claim,[88] it is now irrelevant to the availability of the foreign forum under this head that the claimant will be unable to fund his action[89]: the practical difficulties which he would encounter will have their impact, if any, under the second limb of the test where the question is whether it would be unjust to deprive him of the right to a trial in England. The same is true of evidence which tends to show that it would be difficult for the claimant to manage or supervise the process of litigation, or that he would not obtain a fair trial.[90] Thirdly, the claimant may seek to contend that the foreign court is not available to him on the ground that the claim which he makes in the English proceedings, or the remedy he seeks,[91] would be unavailable to him in the foreign court, or that because of the foreign court's choice of law rules, he would lose in the foreign court.[92] It is submitted that these matters are irrelevant to the issue of whether the foreign court is available, but that they may be taken into account under the second limb of the test. So also the impact, if any, of a time-bar which might be applied by the foreign court to preclude the claimant's proceedings is addressed under the second limb of the test.[93]

Identification of the natural forum. It has been seen that in *Spiliada* Lord   **12–024**
Goff of Chieveley indicated that the English court should look for the forum with which the dispute had the most real and substantial connection, and he referred in particular to factors affecting convenience or expense (such as availability of witnesses) and other factors including the law governing the

---

[86] *Lubbe v. Cape plc* [1999] I.L.Pr. 113 (C.A.). United States courts adopt a different approach. A foreign forum may be an available alternative forum if the defendant consents to submit to its jurisdiction as a condition of dismissal on *forum non conveniens* grounds: this was so in *Piper Aircraft Co. v. Reyno*, 454 U.S. 235 (1981) (see 479 F. Supp. 727, 731 (M.D. Penn. 1979)). For examples see *Re Union Carbide Gas Plant Disaster*, 809 F. 2d 195 (2d Cir. 1987); *Contact Lumber Co. v. P.T. Moges Shipping Co.*, 918 F. 2d 1446 (9th Cir. 1990); *P.T. United Can Co. v. Crown Cork & Seal Co.*, 138 F. 3d 65 (2d Cir. 1998).

[87] The position is otherwise where the undertaking to submit is made in the form of a jurisdiction agreement; *post*, Rule 32.

[88] *Mohammed v. Bank of Kuwait and the Middle East KSC* [1996] 1 W.L.R. 1483 (C.A.).

[89] *Connelly v. R.T.Z. Corp.* [1998] A.C. 854.

[90] *Cf. Mohammed v. Bank of Kuwait and the Middle East KSC, supra*, which is to be doubted on this point after *Connelly v. R.T.Z. Corp. plc, supra*; *Askin v. Absa Bank Ltd.* [1999] I.L.Pr. 471 (C.A.) (fugitive from justice not permitted to rely on unavailability of court to him).

[91] *Cf. Re Harrods (Buenos Aires) Ltd.* [1992] Ch 72 (C.A.: Argentine court unable to order majority shareholder to buy the shareholding of the petitioner).

[92] *post*, para. 12–027.

[93] See *post*, paras. 12–026 and 12–118.

relevant transaction.[94] If the legal issues are straightforward, or if the competing fora have domestic laws which are substantially similar, the governing law will be a factor of little significance. But if the legal issues are complex, or the legal systems very different, the general principle that a court applies its own law more reliably than does a foreign court[95] will point to the more appropriate forum, whether English or foreign.[96] If the foreign court would be unable or unwilling to apply the law which, in the opinion of an English court, should govern the claim, this will tend to suggest that the foreign court is not the most appropriate forum.[97] If a court has acquired a special expertise in the resolution of a particularly complex species of dispute, so that it would be in the interests of justice to allow it to resolve the present case also, this may, in exceptional cases, affect the identification of the natural forum.[98]

12–025   **Overcoming the prima facie case for a stay.** In a number of cases the English court, in deciding whether to grant a stay, took into account differences between English law and the procedural law prevailing in the competing forum, such as the more extensive discovery available to litigants in the United States and the less extensive discovery available in civil law jurisdictions. But it is clear from the decision of the House of Lords in *The Abidin Daver*[99] that in exercising the discretion it is not normally appropriate for the court to compare the quality of justice obtainable in a foreign forum which adopts a different procedural system (such as that of the civil law) with that obtainable in a similar case conducted in an English court. In *Spiliada*, Lord Goff of Chieveley said that injustice could not be said to be done if a party were in effect compelled to accept one of the well-recognised systems of procedural law in the appropriate foreign forum.[1] There may be cases where there is a risk that justice will not be obtained in a foreign court for ideological or political reasons, or because of the inexperience or inefficiency of the judiciary or excessive delay[2] in the conduct of the business of the courts, or the unavailability of appropriate remedies. But a would-be claimant in the English court who wishes to resist a stay of English proceedings on such a

---

[94] [1987] A.C. at 478.

[95] *The Eleftheria* [1970] P. 94, 105 ("a matter of common sense").

[96] *Charm Maritime Inc. v. Kyriakou* [1987] 1 Lloyd's Rep. 433 (C.A.); *Muduroglu Ltd. v. T.C. Ziraat Bankasi* [1986] Q.B. 1225, 1246 (C.A.); *E.I. Du Pont de Nemours v. Agnew* [1987] 2 Lloyd's Rep. 585 (C.A.); *Standard Steamship Owners' Protection and Indemnity Association (Bermuda) Ltd. v. Gann* [1992] 2 Lloyd's Rep. 528; *The Nile Rhapsody* [1994] 1 Lloyd's Rep. 382 (C.A.); *The Varna (No. 2)* [1994] 2 Lloyd's Rep. 41; *The Rothnie* [1996] 2 Lloyd's Rep. 206.

[97] *Banco Atlantico S.A. v. British Bank of the Middle East* [1990] 2 Lloyd's Rep. 504 (refusal by foreign court to apply proper law of the contract); *Midland Bank plc v. Laker Airways Ltd.* [1986] Q.B. 689 (C.A.) (application of U.S. anti-trust law to commercial activity in England).

[98] *Spiliada*, at pp. 484–486, where it is referred to as the "*Cambridgeshire* factor", after the ship which gave its name to the earlier litigation.

[99] [1984] A.C. 398, approving the approach in *Amin Rasheed Shipping Corp. v. Kuwait Insurance Co.* [1984] A.C. 50 (an Ord. 11 case) and in *The El Amria* [1981] 2 Lloyd's Rep. 119 (C.A.) (an exclusive jurisdiction clause case). See also *The Traugutt* [1985] 1 Lloyd's Rep. 76, 79.

[1] [1987] A.C. at 482–483, citing *Trendtex Trading Corp. v. Crédit Suisse* [1982] A.C. 679 (stay granted in favour of Swiss forum, where plaintiffs in fraud claim would not have benefit of extensive discovery available in England); see also *Re Harrods (Buenos Aires) Ltd.* [1992] Ch. 72, 126 (C.A.).

[2] *Cf. The Jalakrishna* [1983] 2 Lloyd's Rep. 628; *The Vishva Ajay* [1989] 2 Lloyd's Rep. 558.

ground must assert it candidly and support the allegation with positive and cogent evidence.[3]

If, however, the effect of a stay would be to deprive the claimant of the right to obtain a hearing[4] of his claim, the interests of justice may be served by refusing to stay the proceedings. Thus if the claimant is able to obtain financial support for proceedings if they are brought in England, but will be unable to obtain it if the claim must be brought in the foreign court and will as a result be unable to sue at all, it may be unjust to grant a stay of the proceedings.[5] Likewise, if the proceedings in the foreign court would be time-barred, it may be unjust to order a stay, unless the defendant undertakes to waive the time bar.[6]   **12–026**

Differences between the measure of recovery (or other remedies[7]) available in England and in the foreign court will not generally overcome the *prima facie* case for a stay of proceedings,[8] whether this follows from different judicial approaches to the assessment of damages or from statutory limitations upon the measure of recovery.[9] Similarly, if the claimant argues that he will win if permitted to sue in England, but will lose if compelled to sue in the foreign court, there is no presumption that a claimant is entitled to win or that a defendant must be liable. But it has been held that a claimant may overcome the case for a stay if he will lose by reason of the foreign court applying choice of law rules which are markedly at variance from those which are regarded by an English court as generally applicable as a matter of the conflict of laws,[10] or if the foreign court's approach to the awarding of costs consume the fruits of recovery and render any victory largely pyrrhic.[11] The case for a stay may also be overcome if to grant it would adversely affect the efficient conduct of   **12–027**

---

[3] *The Abidin Daver* [1984] A.C. 398, 411. See also *Muduroglu Ltd. v. T.C. Ziraat Bankasi* [1986] Q.B. 1225, 1247–1249 (C.A.); and *cf. Purcell v. Khayat, The Times*, November 23, 1987 (C.A.); *Jayaretnam v. Mahmood, The Times*, May 21, 1992. *Cf.* cases on Rule 27, para. 11–125, n. 27, *ante.*

[4] Including a case where the predictable delay in the foreign court is equivalent to his not obtaining a hearing at all: *The Vishva Ajay* [1989] 2 Lloyd's Rep. 558; *Pall Corp. v. Commercial Hydraulics (Bedford) Ltd.* [1989] R.P.C. 703 (C.A.); *The Al Battani* [1993] 2 Lloyd's Rep. 219, 223–224; *cf. The Nile Rhapsody* [1992] 2 Lloyd's Rep. 399, 413–414, affd. [1994] 1 Lloyd's Rep. 382 (C.A.).

[5] *Connelly v. R.T.Z. Corp. plc* [1998] A.C. 854; *Carlson v. Rio Tinto plc* [1999] C.L.C. 551.

[6] *Spiliada Maritime Corp. v. Cansulex Ltd., supra*, at p. 483–484; see *post*, para. 12–118.

[7] *Re Harrods (Buenos Aires) Ltd.* [1992] Ch. 72 (C.A.); *cf. The Falstria* [1988] 1 Lloyd's Rep. 495; *Intermetal Group Ltd v. Worslade Trading Ltd* [1998] I.L.Pr. 765 (Irish Sup. Ct.).

[8] *Spiliada Maritime Corp. v. Cansulex Ltd, supra*, at 482.

[9] *The Herceg Novi* [1998] 4 All E.R. 238 (C.A.) (not unjust to stay proceedings in favour of Singapore where Hague Rules would limit recovery to a lower figure than available in England under the Convention on Limitation for Maritime Claims 1976); approving *The Kapitan Shevtsov* [1998] 1 Lloyd's Rep. 199 (Hong Kong). *Cf. Baghlaf Al Safer Factory Co. Br. for Industry Ltd. v. Pakistan National Shipping Corp.* [1998] 2 Lloyd's Rep. 229 (C.A.) (reasonable for plaintiff to disregard jurisdiction agreement and sue in England where foreign court would limit liability to a fraction of the claim). But if it would be much more difficult to enforce internationally a judgment of the foreign court, it may be unjust to confine the claimant to the foreign court: *International Credit and Investment Co. (Overseas) Ltd. v. Adham* [1999] I.L.Pr. 302 (C.A.).

[10] *Britannia Steamship Insurance Association v. Ausonia Assicurazioni S.p.A.* [1984] 2 Lloyd's Rep. 95 (C.A.); *Banco Atlantico S.A. v. British Bank of the Middle East* [1990] 2 Lloyd's Rep. 504 (C.A.). *Cf. Irish Shipping Ltd. v. Commercial Union Assurance Co. plc* [1991] 2 Q.B. 206, 229–230 (C.A.) (preference for the conflict of laws rules of the forum).

[11] *Roneleigh Ltd. v. MII Exports Inc.* [1989] 1 W.L.R. 619 (C.A.); *Agrafax Public Relations Ltd. v. United Scottish Society Inc.* [1995] I.L.Pr. 753 (C.A.); *cf. The Vishva Ajay* [1989] 2 Lloyd's Rep. 558, *The Oinoussian Pride* [1991] 1 Lloyd's Rep 126; *The Al Battani* [1993] 2 Lloyd's Rep. 219.

litigation: in a case with multiple defendants, if the result of one defendant's obtaining a stay would be to force the claimant to bring his claim in two separate sets of proceedings, with the possible further consequence of inconsistent conclusions being reached by the two courts, it will not generally serve the interests of justice to order a stay.[12]

12–028   In determining whether, even though a foreign forum is the appropriate one, justice requires that a stay should not be granted, the court may take account of the fact that if the stay is granted the claimant will be deprived of security, and may make the stay conditional on retention of security.[13]

12–029   **Lis alibi pendens.** There are special rules in the 1968 Convention and the Lugano Convention for simultaneous actions which are pending in different Contracting States between the same parties and involving the same cause of action or related causes of action.[14] Where the case is not covered by the 1968 Convention or the Lugano Convention, it frequently happens that, in cases in which the English court is asked to stay English proceedings or restrain foreign proceedings, there are simultaneous actions pending in England and in a foreign country between the same parties and involving the same or similar issues.

12–030   Although it was once thought that there were special factors in cases of *lis alibi pendens*, it is now clear that the existence of simultaneous proceedings is simply an additional factor relevant to the determination of the appropriate forum. In *The Abidin Daver*[15] Lord Diplock said that, where proceedings were pending in a foreign court between the parties, and the defendant in the foreign proceedings commenced proceedings as plaintiff in England, then the additional inconvenience or expense which must result from allowing two sets of legal proceedings to be pursued concurrently in two different jurisdictions, where the same facts would be in issue and the testimony of the same witnesses required, could only be justified if the would-be plaintiff in England could establish objectively by cogent evidence that there was some personal or juridical advantage that would be available to him only in the English action and which was of such importance that it would cause injustice to deprive him of it. This was an application of his formula in *MacShannon v. Rockware Glass Ltd.*[16] to cases of *lis alibi pendens*. It has now been confirmed[17] that the principles enunciated in *Spiliada Maritime Corp. v. Cansulex*

---

[12] *Insurance Corp. of Ireland v. Strombus* [1985] 2 Lloyd's Rep. 138 (C.A.); *A.–G. v. Arthur Andersen & Co.* [1989] E.C.C. 224, 229; *Charm Maritime Inc. v. Kyriakou* [1987] 1 Lloyd's Rep. 433 (C.A.); *E.I. Du Pont de Nemours & Co. v. Agnew* [1987] 2 Lloyd's Rep. 585 (C.A.); *The Goldean Mariner* [1989] 2 Lloyd's Rep. 390, revd. on different grounds [1990] 2 Lloyd's Rep. 215 (C.A.); *First National Bank of Boston v. Union Bank of Switzerland* [1990] 1 Lloyd's Rep. 32 (C.A.); *New Hampshire Insurance Co. v. Strabag Bau A.G.* [1992] 1 Lloyd's Rep. 361 (C.A.); *The Abidin Daver* [1984] A.C. 398, 423; *Bouygues Offshore S.A. v. Caspian Shipping Co.* (Nos 1, 3, 4, 5) [1998] 2 Lloyd's Rep. 461 (C.A.); and *The El Amria* [1981] 2 Lloyd's Rep. 119 (C.A.); *The M.C. Pearl* [1997] 1 Lloyd's Rep. 556; *Citi-March Ltd. v. Neptune Orient Lines Ltd.* [1996] 1 W.L.R. 1367 (the latter three cases on jurisdiction agreements); *McConnell Dowell Constructors Ltd. v. Lloyd's Syndicate 396* [1988] 2 N.Z.L.R. 257, 41 (C.A.); *cf. Soc. Nat. Ind. Aérospatiale v. Lee Kui Jak* [1987] A.C. 871, 901 (P.C.) (a case on injunctions).
[13] *Spiliada Maritime Corp. v. Cansulex Ltd.* [1987] A.C. 460, 483; Civil Jurisdiction and Judgments Act 1982, s.26; *ante*, paras. 8–031 *et seq.*
[14] See clause (4) of the Rule discussed below, paras. 12–039 *et seq.*
[15] [1984] A.C. 398, 411–412.
[16] [1978] A.C. 795.
[17] *de Dampierre v. de Dampierre* [1988] A.C. 92, 108.

Ltd.[18] apply whether or not there are other proceedings already pending in the alternative forum: the foreign proceedings may be of no relevance at all, for example, if one party has commenced them for the purpose of demonstrating the existence of a competing jurisdiction,[19] or if the proceedings have not passed beyond the stage of initiating process. But if genuine proceedings have been started and have had some impact on the dispute between the parties,[20] especially if it is likely to have a continuing effect, then this may be a relevant (but not necessarily decisive[21]) factor when considering whether the foreign jurisdiction provides the appropriate forum.[22]

In *Australian Commercial Research and Development Ltd. v. ANZ McCaughan Merchant Bank Ltd.*[23] Sir Nicolas Browne-Wilkinson V.-C. approved the statement in the eleventh edition of this work that where the same plaintiff sues the same defendant in England and abroad it is not likely that the court would allow, except in very unusual circumstances,[24] the continuation of proceedings in two different jurisdictions. The court would put the plaintiff to his election. In that case the Vice-Chancellor said that if the plaintiff opted to continue the foreign proceedings the English proceedings could not merely be stayed; the plaintiff would have to discontinue them. But there may be cases (*e.g.* where one of the actions is brought to obtain security by way of an attachment of assets) where a stay rather than an order for discontinuance of English proceedings, or an injunction requiring foreign proceedings to be discontinued, would be appropriate. By contrast, where it is not open to the claimant to bring the whole of his claim before one court (*e.g.* where the proceedings may be founded on an attachment of assets in each of two jurisdictions, and both sets of assets are claimed by the claimant, or where the rules on enforcement of judgments mean that in practice two sets of proceedings represent the only way of obtaining relief), it may be regarded as reasonable to bring both sets of proceedings, and the claimant should not be required to elect.   **12–031**

Timing of application for a stay. Until the coming into force of the Civil Procedure Rules 1998 it was generally accepted that an application for a stay of proceedings was not a challenge to the jurisdiction of the court; and it followed that an application for a stay of proceedings was not required to be sought within the procedure, and within the time limited, for challenging the jurisdiction under R.S.C. Order 12, rule 8.[25] But CPR 11 requires that an application for a stay should be made within the period for filing a defence, and it follows that the previous sharp distinction between a challenge to the jurisdiction and an application for a stay has been eliminated. While, however, CPR 11 provides that a failure to apply under CPR 11 constitutes a waiver of   **12–032**

---

[18] [1987] A.C. 460.
[19] As in the cases of actions for negative declarations discussed *infra*, para. 12–033.
[20] See, *e.g., Cleveland Museum of Art v. Capricorn International S.A.* [1990] 2 Lloyd's Rep. 166; *cf. Meridien Biao Bank GmbH v. Bank of New York* [1997] 1 Lloyd's Rep. 437 (C.A.)
[21] See *Meadows Indemnity Co. Ltd. v. Insurance Corp. of Ireland plc* [1989] 2 Lloyd's Rep. 298 (C.A.).
[22] And see the cases cited in n. 12, *ante.*
[23] [1989] 3 All E.R. 65, affd. February 23, 1990 (C.A., unrep.)
[24] Such as where the proceedings were instituted purely to preserve the limitation position: *cf. ante*, para. 12–026.
[25] *The Messiniaki Tolmi* [1984] 1 Lloyd's Rep. 266, 270 (C.A.); *cf. Ngcobo v. Thor Chemicals (Holdings) Ltd., The Times*, November 10, 1995 (C.A.).

any objection to the jurisdiction,[26] no equivalent provision is made in relation a stay of proceedings. It is suggested that a court may, in an appropriate case, use its power under CPR 3.1(2)(a) to extend the time for making an application for a stay.

12–033   **Claims for negative declarations.**[27] A claim for a negative declaration is for a declaration by the court that the defendant has no valid claim or right against the claimant.[28] It used to be said that in England such a declaration will rarely be made, and that in most cases the person who seeks it will be left to set up his defence in the action when it is brought.[29] Sometimes a negative declaration has been sought in England in order to support a claim for an injunction to restrain foreign proceedings[30]; but it is clear that it is not a necessary pre-condition of the jurisdiction to grant an injunction to restrain foreign proceedings that there be a claim in the English proceedings apart from the claim that the claimant has an equitable right to restrain foreign proceedings.[31]

12–034   It frequently happens that a party seeks a negative declaration in the English court, or in the foreign court, in order to support a contention that the English court, or the foreign court (as the case may be), is the appropriate forum. Indeed, it has been said that claims for declarations, and in particular negative declarations, must be viewed with great caution in all situations involving possible conflicts of jurisdiction, since they lend themselves to improper attempts at forum shopping.[32] Accordingly, the English court will stay English proceedings for a negative declaration against defendants subject to the jurisdiction of the English court where a foreign court is the *forum conveniens*[33]; and the English court will not be disposed to authorise service out of the jurisdiction under Order 11, r. 1(1), *i.e.* Rule 27, in a claim for a negative declaration, unless England is the appropriate forum.[34] Nor will a claim in a foreign court for a negative declaration be of much weight in determining whether the foreign court is the appropriate forum for the purpose of staying English proceedings, or in determining whether the English court is the appropriate forum for the purposes of service out of the jurisdiction.[35]

---

[26] CPR 11(5).

[27] See Collins, *Essays*, p. 274; Bell (1995) 111 L.Q.R. 674.

[28] See Zamir & Woolf, *The Declaratory Judgment* (2nd ed. 1993), paras. 4.142–4.192.

[29] *Guaranty Trust Co. v. Hannay* [1915] 2 K.B. 536, 564–565 (C.A.). See also *Midland Bank plc v. Laker Airways Ltd.* [1986] Q.B. 689 (C.A.).

[30] *e.g. Smith Kline and French Laboratories Ltd. v. Bloch* [1983] 1 W.L.R. 730 (C.A.); *British Airways Board v. Laker Airways Ltd.* [1985] A.C. 58. *Cf. The Rama* [1996] 2 Lloyd's Rep. 281.

[31] *Guaranty Trust Co. of New York v. Hannay* [1915] 2 K.B. 536, 556 (C.A.); *cf. Midland Bank plc v. Laker Airways Ltd.* [1986] Q.B. 689 (C.A.).

[32] *The Volvox Hollandia* [1988] 2 Lloyd's Rep. 361, 371 (C.A.).

[33] *Camilla Cotton Oil Co. v. Granadex S.A.* [1976] 2 Lloyd's Rep. 10 (H.L.); *First National Bank of Boston v. Union Bank of Switzerland* [1990] 1 Lloyd's Rep. 32 (C.A.); *New Hampshire Insurance Co. v. Aerospace Finance Ltd.* [1998] 2 Lloyd's Rep. 539.

[34] *Insurance Co. of Ireland v. Strombus International Insurance Co.* [1985] 2 Lloyd's Rep. 138 (C.A.); *The Volvox Hollandia* [1988] 2 Lloyd's Rep. 361 (C.A.); *Charman v. WOC Offshore B.V.* [1993] 1 Lloyd's Rep. 378. *Cf. Finnish Marine Insurance Co. Ltd. v. Protective National Insurance Co.* [1990] 1 Q.B. 1078. Contrast *Gulf Bank K.S.C. v. Mitsubishi Heavy Industries Ltd.* [1994] 1 Lloyd's Rep. 323.

[35] *E.I. du Pont de Nemours v. Agnew* [1987] 2 Lloyd's Rep. 585 (C.A.); *Arkwright Mutual Insurance Co. v. Bryanston Insurance Co. Ltd.* [1990] 2 Q.B. 649 (overruled on other grounds: *Re Harrods (Buenos Aires) Ltd.* [1992] Ch. 72 (C.A.)); *Kawasaki Steel Corp. v. Owners of "Daeyang Honey"* (1993) 120 A.L.R. 109 (Fed. Ct.).

Indeed, the foreign proceedings for a negative declaration may be so artificial as to justify the grant of an injunction by the English court to restrain them.[36]

In many cases, however, there is a legitimate role for a bona fide claim for a negative declaration.[37] In modern commercial litigation, notably in the field of insurance, a party may have a legitimate commercial need to obtain an early determination upon his liability to another who may seek to claim against him: an insurer who wishes to know whether he should conduct the defence of a threatened claim against his insured[38]; a supplier who needs to know whether he is obliged to continue to supply a distributor or may, instead, deal elsewhere.[39] Where a stay of proceedings for a negative declaration is sought (or there is an application to set aside service out of the jurisdiction) the court will have to consider both the question whether there is justification for seeking that form of relief and the question whether England is the appropriate forum.[40] If, by contrast, such a declaration would be ignored in foreign legal proceedings between the parties and would therefore serve only to increase the risk of conflicting judgments, or if the proceedings are premature in the sense that the claimant has no reasonable apprehension of being sued by the defendant,[41] the claimant may be regarded as abusing the process of the court.[42] The court is therefore likely to exercise its discretion to strike out the application[43] or refuse to make the order, or to stay the proceedings, or to refuse to give permission to serve process out of the jurisdiction, as the case may be.[44]

The 1968 and Lugano Conventions and negative declarations. Where   12–036
the case is governed by the 1968 Convention or the Lugano Convention, the ordinary jurisdictional rules of the Convention, and special rules for *lis alibi pendens* in Articles 21 to 23, apply to actions for negative declarations and make no distinction to reflect the fact that one set of proceedings is in the form of an action for declaratory relief. In *Gubisch Maschinenfabrik KG v. Palumbo*[45] it was held that Article 21 (which gives priority to the court first seised) applies where, in relation to the same contract, one party applies to a court in a Contracting State for a declaration that a contract is inoperative, whilst the other institutes proceedings before the courts of another Contracting

12–035

---

[36] *Sohio Supply Co. v. Gatoil (USA) Inc.* [1989] 1 Lloyd's Rep. 588 (C.A.). Contrast *E.I. du Pont de Nemours v. Agnew (No. 2)* [1988] 2 Lloyd's Rep. 240 (C.A.).
[37] See *The Rama* [1996] 2 Lloyd's Rep. 281, 291; *Akai Pty Ltd. v. People's Insurance Co. Ltd.* [1998] 1 Lloyd's Rep. 90, 106; *New Hampshire Insurance Co. v. Aerospace Finance Ltd.* [1998] 2 Lloyd's Rep. 539, 543.
[38] *Cf. Booker v. Bell* [1989] 1 Lloyd's Rep. 516; *HIB Ltd. v. Guardian Insurance Co. Inc.* [1997] 1 Lloyd's Rep. 412; *Gan Insurance Co. Ltd. v. Tai Ping Insurance Co. Ltd.* [1998] C.L.C. 1072.
[39] *Boss Group Ltd. v. Boss France S.A.* [1997] 1 W.L.R. 351 (C.A.); *Smyth v. Behbehani* [1999] I.L.Pr. 599 (C.A.).
[40] The points are separate and distinct: *New Hampshire Insurance Co. v. Phillips Electronics* [1998] I.L.Pr. 256 (C.A.).
[41] *Gulf Bank K.S.C. v. Mitsubishi Heavy Industries Ltd.* [1994] 1 Lloyd's Rep. 323, at 329–330.
[42] *Boss Group Ltd. v. Boss France S.A., supra.*
[43] CPR 3.4.
[44] *New Hampshire Insurance Co. v. Aerospace Finance Ltd.* [1998] 2 Lloyd's Rep. 539.
[45] Case 144/86 [1987] E.C.R. 4861. *Cf.* Case C–351/89 *Overseas Union Insurance Ltd. v. New Hampshire Insurance Co.* [1991] E.C.R. I–3317, [1992] Q.B. 434; Case C–406/92 *The Tatry* [1994] E.C.R. I–5439; [1999] Q.B. 575; *Kloeckner & Co. A.G. v. Gatoil Overseas Inc.* [1990] 2 Lloyd's Rep. 177.

State for its enforcement. Likewise, in *The Tatry*,[46] where proceedings were brought in the Netherlands for a declaration that the carrier had no liability for alleged cargo damage, and subsequently an action was brought in England by the cargo owner in respect of damage to the cargo, it was held that Articles 21 and 22 (as the case may be)[47] were capable of applying to the proceedings in the English court: Articles 21 and 22 apply without regard to the nature or procedural nature of the claim and it is irrelevant, even if true, that they were instituted for the purpose of forum shopping.[48] Indeed, Tesauro A.-G. went so far as to characterise proceedings for a declaration of non-liability as being "generally allowed under the various national procedural laws and [as] entirely legitimate in every respect".[49] A further but direct consequence of this approach to the provisions on *lis alibi pendens* is that the jurisdictional provisions of the Convention also apply equally to claims for negative declarations, and may not be manipulated or distorted to prevent the bringing of such claims.[50]

12–037   **Clause (3) of the Rule.** The role of *forum conveniens* in the exercise of the discretion to grant permission for service out of the jurisdiction under Order 11, r. 1(1) has already been mentioned in connection with Rule 27. The first version of Order 11 in 1875 required, in cases of contract, the court to take into account "the comparative cost and convenience of proceeding in England or in the place of the defendant's residence"; from the 1883 revision of Order 11 this condition applied only to defendants in Scotland and Ireland (later Northern Ireland).[51] But it was also established from the earliest years of the application of Order 11 that, in cases falling outside the express provision, *forum conveniens* was a relevant factor.[52] Thus Scott L.J., who had in the previous year confirmed that *forum conveniens* was not a factor in the discretion to stay actions,[53] said that in Order 11 cases "if the reality of the cause of action is one which belongs to a foreign country, and not to this country, and above all, where it is a question which probably would be better tried ... in the foreign country, leave ought not to be granted."[54]

---

[46] Case C–406/92 [1994] E.C.R. I–5439; [1999] Q.B. 515.

[47] See clause (4) of this Rule; *post*, paras. 12–039 *et seq.*

[48] But it seems that there is no reason why an English court, seised with a claim for such relief, may not apply its substantive law to strike out the claim on non-jurisdictional grounds: *Boss Group Ltd. v. Boss France S.A.* [1997] 1 W.L.R. 351 (C.A.); *cf.* the view of Tesauro A.-G. in *The Tatry*, *supra*, at p. 5454, that it is "incumbent upon the court seised to ensure that any abuse is thwarted".

[49] At p. 5455.

[50] *Boss Group Ltd. v. Boss France S.A.* [1997] 1 W.L.R. 351 (C.A.). *Cf. Fisher v. Unione Italiana de Riassicurazione SpA* [1998] C.L.C. 682.

[51] See now Ord. 11, r. 4(3) (in Civil Procedure Rules 1998, Sched. 1) (which will now rarely apply: Civil Jurisdiction and Judgments Act 1982, Sched. 4).

[52] See *Strauss & Co. v. Goldsmid* (1892) 8 T.L.R. 512 (C.A.); *Rosler v. Hilbery* [1925] Ch. 250 (C.A.); *Maharanee of Baroda v. Wildenstein* [1972] 2 Q.B. 283, 294 (C.A.). See Piggott, Vol. 3, pp. 192–194; Collins (1972) 21 I.C.L.Q. 656. This line of authority was overlooked in *Oceanic Sun Line Special Shipping Co. Inc. v. Fay* (1988) 165 C.L.R. 197 (criticised by Collins (1989) 105 L.Q.R. 364). The High Court of Australia subsequently ruled that in cases of service out of the jurisdiction, the plaintiff had to show that the action would not ultimately be stayed on the ground that the forum was clearly inappropriate: *Voth v. Manildra Flour Mills Pty. Ltd.* (1990) 171 C.L.R. 538 (on which see Collins (1991) 107 L.Q.R. 182; Pryles (1991) 65 Aust. L.J. 442); *cf. Sydbank Soenderjylland A/S v. Bannerton Holdings Pty Ltd.* (1997) 149 A.L.R. 134 (Fed. Ct.).

[53] *St. Pierre v. South American Stores Ltd.* [1936] 1 K.B. 382 (C.A.).

[54] *Kroch v. Rossell et Cie* [1937] 1 All E.R. 725, 731 (C.A.).

The modern law on the role of *forum conveniens* in Order 11 cases is to be   **12–038**
found in the speeches of Lord Wilberforce in *Amin Rasheed Shipping Corp.*
v. Kuwait Insurance Co.[55] and of Lord Goff of Chieveley in *Spiliada Maritime*
Corp. v. Cansulex Ltd.[56] The effect of the latter decision was to endorse Lord
Wilberforce's statement of principle that in cases governed by Rule 27 the
claimant must show good reason why service of process on a foreign defendant should be permitted, and in considering this question the court must take
into account the nature of the dispute, the legal and practical issues involved,
such questions as local knowledge, availability of witnesses and their evidence, and expense. Lord Goff of Chieveley added that the fundamental
question (as it was in cases of staying of actions on *forum non conveniens*
grounds) was to identify the forum in which the case could suitably be tried
for the interests of all the parties and for the ends of justice.[57] To justify the
exercise of the discretion, the claimant has to show that England is clearly the
appropriate forum for the trial of the action.[58] But where the parties have
contractually agreed on England as a neutral forum, the court will normally
assume jurisdiction.[59]

Clause (4) of the Rule. Articles 21 to 23 of the 1968 Convention and of   **12–039**
the Lugano Convention contain specific rules under the heading "Lis
Pendens—Related Actions" to deal with the relationship between actions
pending in different Contracting States where, first, the proceedings involve
"the same cause of action" and, second, where the cause of action is not the
same, but the actions are related. The Conventions adopt a somewhat crude
solution[60] to the problem of *lis alibi pendens* by requiring, in the first class of
case, that any court other than the court first seised shall not exercise jurisdiction; in the second class of case they provide that any court, other than the
court first seised, *may*, while the actions are pending at first instance, stay its
proceedings or dismiss them for consolidation with the proceedings in the
court first seised. And in the uncommon case where actions fall within the
exclusive jurisdiction of two courts, Article 23 provides that the court seised
second must decline jurisdiction in favour of the court seised first.[61]

---

[55] [1984] A.C. 50, 72.
[56] [1987] A.C. 460, 478–482.
[57] *Cf. Lopez v. Chavarri* [1901] W.N. 115, 116 ("whether the true interests of justice would be
best served by trying the question here, or leaving it to the foreign tribunal").
[58] [1987] A.C. at 480–482. In jurisdictions, such as New Zealand or the Canadian provinces,
where service outside the jurisdiction is allowed without leave in specified circumstances, the
court retains its discretion to set aside service on *forum conveniens* grounds: *Kuwait Asia Bank*
E.C. v. National Mutual Life Nominees Ltd. [1991] A.C. 187, 217 (P.C.); *Singh v. Howden*
Petroleum Ltd. (1979) 100 D.L.R. (3d) 121 (Ont. C.A.); *Petersen v. A/B Bahco Ventilation*
(1979) 107 D.L.R. (3d) 49 (B.C.); *Canadian Commercial Bank v. Carpenter* (1990) 62 D.L.R.
(4th) 734 (B.C.C.A.). *Cf. Pendal Nominees Pty. Ltd. v. M. & A. Investments* (1989) 18
N.S.W.L.R. 383.
[59] See *infra*, Rule 32. But the fact that England is a *neutral* forum does not satisfy the general
requirement under this clause that England be the *natural* forum; and the choice of English *law*
as a neutral law is not an indication of England as a suitable forum for the solution of disputes:
Macsteel Commercial Holdings (Pty.) Ltd. v. Thermasteel (Canada) Ltd. [1996] C.L.C. 1403
(C.A.).
[60] A "tie-break rule": *Dresser U.K. Ltd. v. Falcongate Freight Management Ltd.* [1992] Q.B. 502,
514 (C.A.).
[61] Exclusive jurisdiction in this context plainly refers to Article 16; there is no authority to support
its being extended to other Articles in Title II of the Convention.

12–040   **Scope of application.** For Articles 21 to 23 to apply, the proceedings must be within the scope of the Convention *ratione materiae*.[62] Therefore parallel actions in different Contracting States to enforce a judgment from a non-Contracting State are not subject to Article 21, even if the same issues on the enforceability of the judgment arise in both sets of proceedings.[63] The same is true if the proceedings in the court seised second are generally or expressly excluded from the scope of the Conventions, such as where they have arbitration as their subject matter.[64] In principle the same analysis applies where the proceedings may be outside the Convention *ratione temporis*. But in *Von Horn v. Cinnamond*[65] the European Court interpreted Article 54 of the 1968 Convention[66] as meaning that where the proceedings in the court seised first were commenced on a date when the Convention was not in force, but those in the court seised second were instituted after[67] the coming into force of the Convention as between the two Contracting States, Article 21 would apply if it appeared to the court seised second that a judgment from the court first seised would be required to be recognised under the second paragraph of Article 54.[68] This was justified on the footing that Article 21 was to be interpreted to forestall the non-recognition of judgments on the ground of irreconcilability with a judgment of the local court.

12–041   Article 21 of each of the 1968 Convention (as amended by the 1989 Accession Convention)[69] and of the Lugano Convention[70] provides that where proceedings involving the same cause of action and between the same parties are brought in the courts of different Contracting States, any court other than the court first seised shall of its own motion stay its proceedings until such time as the jurisdiction of the court first seised is established; where the jurisdiction of the court first seised is established, any court other than the

---

[62] *Ante*, para. 11–012. Where the court has jurisdiction according to the provisions of an international convention on a particular matter, the application of Arts. 21 and 22 of the 1968 Convention or the Lugano Convention depends upon whether the particular convention contains its own provision for dealing with *lis alibi pendens*. If it does, its provisions exclude the application of Arts. 21 and 22; if it does not, Arts. 21 and 22 may be applied: Case C–406/92 *The Tatry* [1994] E.C.R. I–5439; [1999] Q.B. 515, and generally paras. 11–037, 13–033, and 15–008. Contrast *The Bergen* [1997] 1 Lloyd's Rep. 380, *post*, para. 12–089.

[63] Case C–129/92 *Owens Bank Ltd. v. Bracco* [1994] E.C.R. I–117; [1994] Q.B. 509; *Dubai Bank Ltd. v. Abbas* [1998] I.L.Pr 391.

[64] Case C–190/89 *Marc Rich and Co. A.G. v. Soc. Italiana Impianti P.A.* [1991] E.C.R. I–3855.

[65] [1997] E.C.R. I–5451; [1998] Q.B. 214.

[66] As amended by Art. 29 of the 1989 Accession Convention.

[67] Where the proceedings in the court seised second were also instituted before the coming into force of the Convention, *Von Horn* is inapplicable and Art. 21 will not apply: *Davy International Ltd. v. Voest Alpine Industrieanlagenbau GmbH* [1999] 1 All E.R. 103 (C.A.).

[68] That is, by reason of a bilateral treaty, or because the jurisdiction of the court seised first accorded with Title II of the Convention: Art. 54(2). Where the court seised second is uncertain whether this criterion would be satisfied, it should stay its proceedings until the court seised first has ruled on its jurisdiction.

[69] The purpose of the amendment was to ensure that the court which was not first seised did not have to decline jurisdiction until the jurisdiction of the other court was established: otherwise the plaintiff might be left (because, *e.g.*, of a time bar) without a remedy in either court: see de Almeida Cruz, etc. p. 48; Jenard-Möller, p. 78. Jurisdiction is not established if the question is under appeal in the foreign court: *William Grant and Sons International Ltd. v. Marie-Brizard Espana S.A.*, 1998 S.C. 536. See also *Sarrio S.A. v. Kuwait Investment Authority* [1997] 1 Lloyd's Rep. 113, 123, 128–129 (C.A.) revd. on different grounds: [1999] 1 A.C. 32; *Gamlestaden plc v. Casa de Suecia S.A.* [1994] 1 Lloyd's Rep. 433.

[70] See also Art. 54B(2)(b) on the relationship between the 1968 Convention and the Lugano Convention for the purposes of Arts. 21 and 22.

court first seised shall decline jurisdiction in favour of that court. The purpose of Article 21 is to prevent the courts of two Contracting States from giving inconsistent judgments, and to preclude so far as possible the non-recognition of a judgment under Article 27(3)[71] on the ground that it is irreconcilable with a judgment given by the courts of another Contracting State.[72]

Article 21 applies irrespective of whether the defendant is domiciled in a **12–042** Contracting State. Not only does Article 21 not contain any such express requirement, but its aim is to limit the risk of irreconcilable judgments, and it should therefore be interpreted broadly to cover, in principle, all situations of *lis pendens* before courts in Contracting States, irrespective of the parties' domicile. Accordingly, the English court was bound to decline jurisdiction over an American company which had, prior to the English proceedings, commenced proceedings in France in relation to the same subject-matter.[73] But Article 21 does not apply to proceedings commenced in non-Contracting States. Consequently if there are proceedings in a non-Contracting State involving the same parties, the English court has a discretion to stay the English proceedings, irrespective of which proceedings were commenced first, and whether or not the defendant in the English proceedings is domiciled in a Contracting State.[74]

Accordingly, where Article 21 applies the English court must decline **12–043** jurisdiction if it is not the court first seised and the jurisdiction of the other court is not challenged, or is established after it is challenged. But the court which is seised second must not itself normally investigate the jurisdiction of the court first seised. In *Overseas Union Insurance Ltd. v. New Hampshire Insurance Co.*[75] it was held that in such a case the court could only stay its proceedings until the court first seised had ruled on its own jurisdiction. But the European Court left open the question whether the answer was the same if the court seised second had exclusive jurisdiction "in particular under Article 16".[76] As a result, the scope of this possible exception to the application of Article 21 remains uncertain. There are three points to be made. First, Article 21 should be inapplicable when the court seised second has exclusive jurisdiction under Article 16,[77] for a judgment given by the court seised first in violation of Article 16 will be refused recognition in all Contracting States,[78] and there is no sensible purpose in deferring to a court whose judgment will be a nullity in England. Secondly, though the European Court has reiterated that the court seised second has no general right to review the jurisdiction of the court seised first,[79] this reasoning would justify extending the exception to those cases in which jurisdictional error by the court seised

---

[71] See para. 14–214, *post*.
[72] Case 42/76 *De Wolf v. Cox B.V.* [1976] E.C.R. 1759, 1767; Case 144/86 *Gubisch Maschinenfabrik KG v. Palumbo* [1987] E.C.R. 4861, 4874; Case C–351/89 *Overseas Union Insurance Ltd. v. New Hampshire Insurance Co.* [1991] E.C.R. I–3317; [1992] Q.B. 434, 457.
[73] Case C–351/89 *Overseas Union Insurance Ltd. v. New Hampshire Insurance Co.* [1991] E.C.R. I–3317; [1992] Q.B. 434.
[74] *Re Harrods (Buenos Aires) Ltd.* [1992] Ch. 72, 97–98 (C.A.), disapproving *Arkwright Mutual Insurance Co. v. Bryanston Insurance Co.* [1990] 2 Q.B. 649; *ante*, para. 12–017.
[75] Case C–351/89 [1991] E.C.R. I–3317; [1992] Q.B. 434; see also Case C–163/95 *Von Horn v. Cinnamond* [1997] E.C.R. I–5451; [1998] Q.B. 214.
[76] [1991] E.C.R. I–3317, 3351–3352; [1992] Q.B. at p. 459, where the reply given by the Court was stated to be "without prejudice" to this case.
[77] That is, under Section 5 of Title II of the Conventions; see *ante*, para. 11–328 *et seq*.
[78] Art. 28, first paragraph: *post*, para. 14–201.
[79] Case C–163/95 *Von Horn v. Cinnamond* [1997] E.C.R. I–5451; [1998] Q.B. 214.

first means that its judgment will not be recognised.[80] Thirdly, it has been held by the Court of Appeal[81] that, even if seised second, the English court may assume jurisdiction and may enjoin proceedings commenced in the court seised first, if the parties have conferred exclusive jurisdiction on the English court by agreement. The English court is in the best position to give effect to the agreement of the parties, but the compatibility with the 1968 and Lugano Conventions of an injunction to pre-empt the decision of the foreign court as to whether it will give effect to the English jurisdiction clause is controversial.[82]

Although Articles 21 to 23 distinguish between the concepts of declining jurisdiction, on the one hand, and staying proceedings on the other,[83] it is suggested that where the English court is required to decline jurisdiction it may do so by imposing an unconditional stay, which would enable measures of interim relief to remain in force without the need for a separate application under Article 24.[84]

12–044   **The same parties.** For the purposes of Article 21 the actions in the different Contracting States must be "between the same parties". It was held by the European Court in *The Tatry*[85] that in litigation involving multiple parties Article 21 applies as between pairs of plaintiff and defendant. Each *lis* between a plaintiff and a defendant has to be considered individually to determine which court was seised of it first in time, and Article 21 applied accordingly.[86] It was recognised by the Court that this may lead to an inconvenient fragmentation of litigation and it suggested that Article 22,[87] which allows, but does not require, a court seised second to stay or to dismiss its proceedings, may ameliorate the consequential difficulty.

12–045   The European Court also considered the application of Article 21, and the requirement that the proceedings be between the same parties, in relation to English admiralty actions *in rem*. In *The Tatry* proceedings had been brought in the Netherlands between a shipowner against cargo owners for a declaration that the shipowner owed no liability for damage allegedly done to the cargo; subsequently an admiralty action *in rem* was commenced by the cargo owners' arrest of the ship. Though as a matter of English procedural law (as it was then understood) the English action was against the ship as defendant, and not against any individual, and though once the owner entered an appearance the

---

[80] Sections 3 (insurance contracts) and 4 (consumer contracts) of Title II: see Art. 28, first paragraph.

[81] *Continental Bank N.A. v. Aeakos Compania Naviera S.A.* [1994] 1 W.L.R. 588 (C.A.), approved *obiter*: *The Angelic Grace* [1995] 1 Lloyd's Rep. 87 (C.A.). For the same conclusion at first instance, see also *Kloeckner & Co. Ltd. v. Gatoil Overseas Inc.* [1990] 1 Lloyd's Rep. 177; *Denby v. Hellenic Mediterranean Lines Co. Ltd.* [1994] 1 Lloyd's Rep. 320; *Toepfer International GmbH v. Molino Boschi S.r.l.* [1996] 1 Lloyd's Rep. 510; *Bank of Scotland v. Banque Nationale de Paris*, 1996 S.L.T. 103. But see *Toepfer International GmbH v. Soc. Cargill France S.A.* [1998] 1 Lloyd's Rep. 379, 388 (C.A.).

[82] In particular, the exclusive jurisdiction conferred by Art. 17 does not (by contrast with exclusive jurisdiction under Art. 16) justify non-recognition of a judgment given in conflict with it: Art. 28(1).

[83] Case C–351/89 *Overseas Union Insurance Ltd. v. New Hampshire Insurance Co.*, *supra*.

[84] See para. 11–352, *ante*.

[85] Case C–406/92 [1994] E.C.R. I–5439; [1999] Q.B. 515. For the reference from the Court of Appeal, see *The Maciej Rataj* [1992] 2 Lloyd's Rep. 552 (C.A.).

[86] For the operation of this principle in relation to amendment by joinder of defendants or by addition of new claims, see the discussion of the date of seisin, *post*, para. 12–053.

[87] *Post*, para. 12–055.

action became one *in personam* as well, it was ruled that this procedural difference between the English and Dutch actions could not of itself preclude the operation of Article 21. In *Republic of India v. India Steamship Co. Ltd. (No. 2)*[88] the House of Lords adopted the reasoning of the European Court in *The Tatry* in support of its conclusion that, as a matter of English law, an admiralty action *in rem* is to be regarded as brought against the shipowner as defendant as soon as the process in the action was served[89] or was acknowledged prior to service.

Proceedings may also be regarded as being between the same parties on the ground that there is identity of interest between two parties who are, at first sight, distinct. For example, when an insurer invokes its right of subrogation to defend proceedings in the name of its insured, the insurer and the insured may be regarded as the same party for the purpose of Article 21.[90] By contrast, claims brought (i) by the insurer of the hull of a vessel against the insurer of the cargo for a contribution to general average, and (ii) by the insurer of the cargo against the owner and charterer of the vessel for a declaration that they were not liable to contribute to the general average are not between the same parties unless it is established that, with regard to the subject matter of the disputes, the interests of the insurer of the hull of the vessel are identical to and indissociable from those of its insured, the owner and the charterer of that vessel.[91] The test of identity and indissociability of interest is for the national court to apply. It follows that a licensee and a licensor of intellectual property rights are not to be regarded as the same party if sued in separate proceedings by a single claimant,[92] but it has been held that a wholly-owned subsidiary may be regarded as the same party as its parent.[93]

12–046

The same cause of action. In *Gubisch Maschinenfabrik KG v. Palumbo*[94] it was held that the concept of the "same cause of action" had to be given an independent Convention interpretation and did not depend on the procedural law of the courts concerned. In that case a German seller was suing an Italian buyer in the German court for the price; the Italian subsequently sued the German seller in the Italian court for a declaration that he was not liable on the contract, or for its rescission. The expression "the same cause of action" is a translation of what appears in the French version as "le même objet et la même cause", and the European Court held that where the same parties were suing each other in two legal proceedings in different Contracting States which were based on the same contractual relationship, the "same cause of action" was involved, and it was not necessary for the two claims to be identical for them to involve the same subject matter. Accordingly, Article 21 applied even if one set of proceedings was for the price, and the other was a claim for a negative declaration or rescission.[95]

12–047

---

[88] [1998] A.C. 878; see *post*, para. 14–035.
[89] Approving *The Deichland* [1990] 1 Q.B. 361 (C.A.), and overruling *The Nordglimt* [1988] Q.B. 183.
[90] Case C–351/96 *Drouot Assurances S.A. v. Consolidated Metallurgical Industries* [1998] E.C.R. I–3075; [1999] Q.B. 497.
[91] *Ibid.*
[92] *Mecklermedia Corp. v. DC Congress GmbH* [1998] Ch. 40.
[93] *Berkeley Administration Inc. v. McClelland* [1995] I.L.Pr. 201 (C.A.).
[94] Case 144/86 [1987] E.C.R. 4861.
[95] See also Case C–351/89 *Overseas Union Insurance Ltd. v. New Hampshire Insurance Co.* [1991] E.C.R. I–3317, [1992] Q.B. 434.

12–048   In *The Tatry*,[96] it was held that actions have "le même objet" when the ends they have in view are the same, and "la même cause" when the facts and the rule of law relied on as the basis of the actions are the same. Consequently an action for a declaration that the owner of the vessel was under no liability to the cargo owner for damage to the cargo, and an action by the cargo owner against the owner of the vessel for damages in respect of damage done to the cargo, were in respect of the same cause of action for the purposes of Article 21.[97] But, as with the question whether an action is between the same parties, national procedural law will not be permitted to obscure the fact that, for the purposes of the Convention, two sets of proceedings involve the same cause of action. For example, there is no doubt that, as a matter of English law, proceedings against a shipowner to establish liability, and a limitation claim brought by that shipowner, would not be regarded as involving the same cause of action. But it does not follow that two such actions could not be regarded as involving the same cause of action for the purposes of Article 21.[98] If the criteria established in *The Tatry* are interpreted strictly, the causes of action are not the same. If, however, the predominant concern is to interpret Article 21 to avoid the possibility of courts in two Contracting States rendering judgments which are irreconcilable with each other, it may be correct to see such coincident[99] actions as falling within Article 21.

12–049   In any event, since the object of Article 21 is to prevent irreconcilable judgments, an application for provisional measures brought in one Contracting State under Article 24 will not preclude a later action on the substance in another Contracting State.[1]

12–050   **Date of seisin.** The next question is the determination of the time the relevant court is seised. In some countries (*e.g.* France, Germany, Italy, Luxembourg and the Netherlands) an action is considered pending only from the date of service of proceedings. In others (such as England and Belgium) an action is, for some purposes at least, regarded as pending once proceedings are issued.[2] The Conventions are silent as to the method of determining at

---

[96] Case C–406/92 [1994] E.C.R. I–5439; [1999] Q.B. 515.

[97] It appears to follow that where an action is brought in one Contracting State for substantive relief, and an action is brought in England for an anti-suit injunction to restrain the continuance of the first action, the causes of action are different as (at least) the end the actions have in view are different, and hence the criterion that they have "le même objet" is not satisfied: see *post*, para. 12–058. The actions may be connected, but will not usually be "related actions" for the purposes of Art. 22, as it will rarely be expedient for the application for an injunction to be consolidated with, or to be stayed pending the determination of, proceedings in the other court: *Toepfer International GmbH v. Molino Boschi S.r.l.* [1996] 1 Lloyd's Rep. 510; *Charterers Mutual Assurance Assn. Ltd. v. British and Foreign* [1998] I.L.Pr. 838. See also *Toepfer International GmbH v. Soc. Cargill France S.A.* [1997] 2 Lloyd's Rep. 98 (the reference to the European Court by the Court of Appeal [1998] 1 Lloyd's Rep. 379 was withdrawn).

[98] *The Happy Fellow* [1998] 1 Lloyd's Rep. 13 (C.A.); *cf. Mecklermedia Corp. v. DC Congress GmbH* [1998] Ch. 40 (passing off in England not the same cause of action as trademark infringement in Germany).

[99] *William Grant and Sons International Ltd. v. Marie-Brizard Espana S.A.*, 1998 S.C. 536.

[1] *Cf. Rank Film Distributors Ltd. v. Lanterna Editrice Srl* [1992] I.L.Pr. 58, 68–69; *Boss Group Ltd. v. Boss France S.A.* [1997] 1 W.L.R. 351, 356 (C.A.). Contrast *Virgin Aviation Services Ltd. v. CAD Aviation Services* [1991] I.L.Pr. 79, 85–86.

[2] But in the case of Belgium service is in general required before filing of the proceedings with the court.

which point in time a court is seised. The European Court held in *Zelger v. Salinitri (No. 2)*[3] that a common concept of *lis pendens* cannot be derived from national practice. Instead a court which has to consider whether to order a stay of its proceedings must resolve the question according to the rules of the national law of each country whose courts are alleged to be seised. The court "first seised" is the one before which the requirements for proceedings to become definitively pending are first fulfilled, and those requirements are to be determined in accordance with the national law of each of the courts concerned.[4]

The effect of the decision in *Zelger v. Salinitri (No. 2)* was thought to be **12–051** that, where English proceedings were issued after German proceedings were issued (but before they were served), the English proceedings were first in time.[5] This odd result might have required reconsideration by the European Court of its decision, but for the fact that in *Dresser U.K. Ltd. v. Falcongate Freight Management Ltd.*[6] the Court of Appeal decided that, although in England proceedings were commenced by the issue of an originating process, they became "definitively pending" (the expression used by the European Court) when they were served: definitively pending meant decisively, conclusively, finally or definitely pending, and it would be "artificial, far-fetched and wrong" to hold that proceedings were pending in that sense upon the mere issue of the proceedings: at that stage the involvement of the court was purely ministerial, the plaintiff was under no obligation to pursue or serve the proceedings, and the defendant was usually unaware of the proceedings and was not obliged to respond in any way.[7] The Court of Appeal stressed that it was in the "ordinary, straightforward case" that the court became seised at the time of service but that an exception to this might be made where an actual exercise of jurisdiction (*e.g.* the grant of a *Mareva* injunction or the making of an *Anton Piller* order) preceded service, and in such a case the court was seised when the interlocutory order was made; further exceptions and qualifications might arise in practice.

But in *The Sargasso*,[8] a differently constituted Court of Appeal disapproved **12–052** the proposition that there were exceptions to the rule that, for the purposes of Article 21, an English court was seised on service of the writ. The date of service rule was described as a single and practical rule which would readily be understood in England and in other jurisdictions which have to grapple

---

[3] Case 129/83 [1984] E.C.R. 2397. See also Case 144/86 *Gubisch Maschinenfabrik KG v. Palumbo* [1987] E.C.R. 4861, 4875. See also *Grupo Torras S.A. v. Sheikh Fahad Mohammed al-Sabah* [1996] 1 Lloyd's Rep. 7 (C.A.). For the unusual case of proceedings commenced in different Contracting States on the same day see OLG Koblenz, 1990, in [1991] I.L.Pr. 588.
[4] There is a proposal for revision of the Conventions (*ante*, para. 11–011) to provide that a court is deemed to be seised at the time when the document instituting the proceedings is lodged with the court, or if (under the applicable procedural law) it has to be served before it is issued by the court, when the document is received by the authority responsible for service.
[5] See *Kloeckner & Co. A.G. v. Gatoil Overseas Inc.* [1990] 1 Lloyd's Rep. 177 (relying on previous editions of this work and on Cheshire and North; see also Schlosser, para. 182).
[6] [1992] Q.B. 502 (C.A.) (a case on related actions under Art. 22).
[7] At p. 523, *per* Bingham L.J., applied in *A.G.F. v. Chiyoda Fire and Marine Co. (UK) Ltd.* [1992] 1 Lloyd's Rep. 325. See also *The Freccia del Nord* [1989] 1 Lloyd's Rep. 388 (Admiralty court seised of action *in rem* from the earlier of the time of service of writ or of arrest of ship, and not from time of issue).
[8] *Neste Chemicals S.A. v. D.K. Line S.A.* [1994] 3 All E.R. 180 (C.A.).

with the question when an English court is seised of proceedings.[9] In particular, as the Conventions treat proceedings brought to obtain provisional or protective measures as being independent of the jurisdictional scheme of the Conventions for proceedings on the merits,[10] a court which is seised with an application for such provisional measures ought not be regarded as being seised with the dispute itself. A court which exercised jurisdiction for the purpose of granting provisional measures could not be said to be definitively seised of the mertis of a dispute. Similarly, a court which exercised a jurisdiction merely to order service out of the jurisdiction was not by virtue of that limited exercise of jurisdiction definitively seised of the merits of the dispute. Accordingly, where the court had acted only in the sense that it had made an order granting permission to serve the writ out of the jurisdiction, it was not seised until service had been made.

12–053   In a case brought against multiple defendants, a court is not seised of the claim against a particular defendant unless and until he is served with process.[11] In relation to the addition of parties or claims by amendment of a claim form, although the doctrine of relation back may mean that, for some purposes, a court is seised of the claim raised by the amendment as from the date of the original claim form, the claim is not definitively pending before the court until the amendment is allowed[12] and for the purpose of Article 21, the court is seised of the claim only from the actual date on which the amendment is made.[13]

12–054   Article 21 requires that the action be still pending in the court first seised when the proceedings are commenced in the court second seised. So if the proceedings in the first court have terminated by judgment and are no longer pending,[14] or if they have been discontinued,[15] or if they have been struck out on *forum non conveniens* grounds,[16] on the relevant date, Article 21 will be inapplicable.

12–055   **Related actions and Article 22.** Where the actions fall outside Article 21, they may still fall within the scope of Article 22. Article 22 provides where related actions are brought in the courts of different Contracting States, any court other than the court first seised has the power (but not the duty), while the actions are pending at first instance, to stay its proceedings. Actions are "related" for the purposes of Article 22 if they are so closely connected that it is expedient to hear and determine them together to avoid the risk of

---

[9] It has been held that a court which is uncertain whether it was seised first or second may stay its proceedings in order to wait for the other court to rule upon the date upon which it was seised: *Polly Peck International Ltd. v. Citibank N.A.* [1994] I.L.Pr. 71.

[10] Art. 24: it follows that, notwithstanding Art. 21, applications for such relief may be made simultaneously in different Contracting States, *ante*, paras. 8–024 and 12–049.

[11] *Grupo Torras S.A. v. Sheikh Fahad Mohammed al-Sabah* [1996] 1 Lloyd's Rep. 7, 18, 21–22 (C.A.); *cf. Fox v. Taher* [1997] I.L.Pr. 441 (C.A.).

[12] If an order granting permission to amend is required, it appears that the claim is not pending until the amendment is actually made.

[13] *Grupo Torras S.A. v. Sheikh Fahad Mohammed al-Sabah* [1996] 1 Lloyd's Rep. 7, 24–25 (C.A.); *cf. Kinnear v. Falconfilms N.V.* [1996] 1 W.L.R. 920 (plaintiff needed to apply for leave to amend, giving the intended defendant an opportunity to commence proceedings of his own).

[14] *Berkeley Administration Inc. v. McClelland* [1995] I.L.Pr. 201 (C.A.): Title III of the Conventions may then require recognition of the judgment of the court seised first.

[15] *Internationale Nederlanden Aviation Lease B.V. v. Civil Aviation Authority* [1997] 1 Lloyd's Rep. 80, 93–94; *cf. Gamlestaden plc. v. Casa de Suecia S.A.* [1994] 1 Lloyd's Rep. 433.

[16] *Haji-Ioannou v. Frangos* [1999] 2 Lloyd's Rep. 337 (C.A.).

irreconcilable judgments resulting from separate proceedings.[17] The European Court has ruled[18] that the "risk of irreconcilable judgments" referred to in Article 22 is a more flexible concept than that described by similar[19] words in Article 27(3), and covers cases where the judgments may contain conflicting decisions without necessarily giving rise to mutually exclusive legal consequences. The House of Lords in *Sarrio S.A. v. Kuwait Investment Authority*[20] interpreted this condition as being satisfied if common issues of fact may arise and be decided in the two sets of proceedings, rejecting the narrower interpretation that the test of potential irreconcilability had to be assessed by reference to those issues which the courts would be *required* to determine in order to give judgment.

The relief which may be granted under Article 22 is either a stay of **12–056** proceedings, or the dismissal of the proceedings in order that they be consolidated in the proceedings pending at first instance in the court seised first. Though Jenard observes[21] that the power to stay proceedings is the primary duty of the court in a case to which Article 22 applies, the approach of the House of Lords in *Sarrio S.A. v. Kuwait Investment Authority* may mean that the more appropriate remedy would be for the court to decline jurisdiction in order that the proceedings be consolidated in the court seised first. If the court orders a stay of proceedings, it will presumably be in the situation where the action in the court first seised appears in the eyes of the court seised second to be likely to render *res judicata* issues raised for determination in the action in the court seised second, and therefore should be imposed until the court seised first gives judgment.[22] Where the English court proposes to decline jurisdiction for consolidation in the court in which the related action is pending at first instance, it is necessary that the court seised first have jurisdiction over the second action,[23] and that its[24] law permit the consolidation of the two actions. This method of dealing with a related action will be

---

[17] Art. 22, third paragraph.

[18] Case C–406/92 *The Tatry* [1994] E.C.R. I–5439; [1999] Q.B. 515; see also *Toepfer International GmbH v. Molino Boschi Srl* [1996] 1 Lloyd's Rep. 510; *De Pina v. MS Birka ICG* [1996] 1 Lloyd's Rep. 31; *Charterers Mutual Assurance Association Ltd. v. British & Foreign* [1998] I.L.Pr. 838; *The Turquoise Bleu* [1996] 1 I.L.R.M. 406.

[19] Not all language versions (see, for example the Italian language version, referred to in *The Tatry* at p. 5479) use terminology which suggests that Arts. 22 and 27(3) should share a common meaning.

[20] [1999] 1 A.C. 32. See *The Happy Fellow* [1998] 1 Lloyd's Rep. 13 (C.A.) (limitation action related to action claiming damages for collision damage done by a ship); *cf. Mecklermedia Corp. v. DC Congress GmbH* [1998] Ch. 40 (passing off action in England not related to trademark infringement action against licensees in Germany).

[21] At p. 41; applied in *Virgin Aviation Services Ltd. v. CAD Aviation Services* [1991] I.L.Pr. 79. *Cf. Centro Internationale Handelsbank A.G. v. Morgan Grenfell* [1997] C.L.C. 870.

[22] *Cf.* Droz, *op. cit. supra*, para. 12–019, n. 70, paras. 315–328; Gaudemet-Tallon, *ibid.*, paras. 299–301.

[23] Art. 22 does not confer jurisdiction over a related action as such, but allows a court which has jurisdiction over it to consolidate with a pending action.

[24] On this point see Collins, p. 98; Anton, *Civil Jurisdiction*, p. 124; Schockweiler, in Tebbens, Kennedy & Kohler, *Civil Jurisdiction and Judgments in Europe* (1992), at p. 160; it was assumed without discussion that it was the law of the court first seised which must permit consolidation in *Sarrio S.A. v. Kuwait Investment Authority* [1999] 1 A.C. 32; *William Grant and Sons International Ltd. v. Marie-Brizard Espana S.A.*, 1998 S.C. 536. The Evrigenis-Kerameus Report ([1986] O.J. C–298/1 at p. 19) states that it is the law of the court *not* first seised which is required to permit the consolidation of actions. The proposed revisions to the Conventions (*ante*, para. 11–011) resolve the point in favour of the law of the court first seised.

particularly appropriate in a case where the parties to the two sets of proceedings are not identical, and it is in the interests of justice that there be a single resolution of issues by which all parties are directly bound.

Articles 21 to 23 have no application to *lis alibi pendens* cases where the proceedings are pending in different parts of the United Kingdom.[25]

12–057   **Clause (5) of the Rule.** English courts have long exercised a jurisdiction to restrain a party from instituting or prosecuting proceedings in a foreign court.[26] As long ago as 1834 it was said that this jurisdiction is grounded "not upon any pretension to the exercise of judicial . . . rights abroad" but upon the fact that the party to whom the order is directed is subject to the *in personam* jurisdiction of the English court.[27] But although the injunction operates only *in personam* against the party to the foreign litigation, the remedy is an indirect interference with the process of the foreign court,[28] and

---

[25] But the doctrine of *forum non conveniens* will be applicable: *ante*, para. 12–015.
[26] The more significant older authorities include *Bushby v. Munday* (1821) 5 Madd. 297; *Portarlington v. Soulby* (1834) 3 My. & K. 104; *Carron Iron Co. v. Maclaren* (1855) 5 H.L.C. 416; *Hyman v. Helm* (1883) 24 Ch. D. 531 (C.A.); *Armstrong v. Armstrong* [1892] P. 98; *Vardopulo v. Vardopulo* (1909) 25 T.L.R. 518 (C.A.); *Cohen v. Rothfield* [1919] 1 K.B. 410 (C.A.); *Orr-Lewis v. Orr-Lewis* [1949] P. 347; *The Hartlepool* (1950) 84 Ll. L. Rep. 145; *The Soya Margareta* [1961] 1 W.L.R. 709; *The Tropaioforos (No. 2)* [1962] 1 Lloyd's Rep. 410; *Settlement Corporation v. Hochschild* [1966] Ch. 10. For modification of these principles in the light of the developing law of *forum conveniens*, see *Castanho v. Brown and Root (U.K.) Ltd.* [1981] A.C. 557; *British Airways Board v. Laker Airways Ltd.* [1985] A.C. 58; *South Carolina Insurance Co. v. Assurantie Maatschappij "de Zeven Provincien" N.V.* [1987] A.C. 24; also *The Lisboa* [1980] 2 Lloyd's Rep. 546 (C.A.); *Smith Kline & French Laboratories Ltd. v. Bloch (No. 1)* [1983] 1 W.L.R. 730 (C.A.); *Metall und Rohstoff A.G. v. ACLI Metals Ltd.* [1984] 1 Lloyd's Rep. 598 (C.A.); *Midland Bank plc v. Laker Airways Ltd.* [1986] Q.B. 689 (C.A.); *Bank of Tokyo Ltd. v. Karoon* [1987] A.C. 45n. The modern re-statement of the principles is to be found in *Soc. Nat. Ind. Aérospatiale v. Lee Kui Jak* [1987] A.C. 871 (P.C.) and in *Airbus Industrie G.I.E. v. Patel* [1999] 1 A.C. 119. For Scotland see *FMC Corp. v. Russell*, 1999 S.L.T. 99. For development of the principles in Canada, see *Amchem Products Inc.* v. *British Columbia (Workers' Compensation Board)* [1993] 1 S.C.R. 897 (Sup.Ct.Can.); *General Canada Investments Inc. v. Lehndorff United Properties (Canada)* [1996] 1 W.W.R. 154 (Alta.). For Australia, see *CSR Ltd. v. Cigna Insurance Australia Ltd.* (1997) 189 C.L.R. 345; also *In the Marriage of Takach* (1980) 47 F.L.R. 141; *Beecham (Australia) Pty. Ltd. v. Roque Pty. Ltd.* (1987) 11 N.S.W.L.R. 1; *National Mutual Holdings Pty Ltd. v. Sentry Corp.* (1989) 87 A.L.R. 539; *Re Siromath Pty. Ltd. (No. 3)* (1991) 25 N.S.W.L.R. 25; *Allstate Life Insurance v. ANZ Banking Group Ltd.* (1997) 142 A.L.R. 412 (Fed. Ct.). On the somewhat different practice in the United States, see *Airbus Industrie G.I.E. v. Patel* [1999] 1 A.C. 119, 136; and *Laker Airways Ltd. v. Sabena, Belgian World Airlines*, 731 F. 2d. 909 (D.C. Cir. 1984); Born, *International Civil Litigation in the United States* (3rd ed. 1996), pp. 475–490.
[27] *Portarlington v. Soulby* (1834) 3 My. & K. 104, 108, *per* Lord Brougham L.C. See, *e.g.*, *Castanho v. Brown & Root (U.K.) Ltd.* [1981] A.C. 557, 574; *E.D. & F. Man (Sugar) Ltd. v. Haryanto (No. 2)* [1991] 1 Lloyd's Rep. 429 (C.A.).
[28] See, *e.g.* *British Airways Board v. Laker Airways Ltd.* [1985] A.C. 58, 95; *South Carolina Insurance Co. v. Assurantie Maatschappij "de Zeven Provincien" N.V.* [1987] A.C. 24, 40. That the foreign court may regard the English injunction as a serious interference is shown by the reaction to the injunctions granted by the Court of Appeal in *British Airways Board v. Laker Airways Ltd.* [1984] Q.B. 142 (C.A.) (discharged [1985] A.C. 58); see *Laker Airways Ltd. v. Pan American World Airways*, 559 F. Supp. 1124, 1128 ("a direct interference") (D.D.C. 1983), affd. *sub. nom Laker Airways Ltd. v. Sabena, Belgian World Airways*, 731 F. 2d 909 (D.C. Cir. 1984); see also 577 F. Supp. 348, 354 ("intrusive") (D.D.C. 1983). And see, in the context of the 1968 Convention, the reaction of the Düsseldorf Court of Appeal to the interlocutory injunctions granted in *Phillip Alexander Securities and Futures Ltd. v. Bamberger* [1997] I.L.Pr. 73, affd. *ibid.* p. 104 (C.A.): *Re the Enforcement of an English anti-suit injunction* [1997] I.L.Pr. 320.

the jurisdiction must be exercised with caution,[29] particularly if the foreign plaintiff is suing in his own court.[30] Though the terminology may not be altogether accurate or elegant, such orders are now routinely referred to as "anti-suit injunctions"[31]; they may be granted on an interlocutory[32] or final basis.

Jurisdiction to grant the injunction. As the jurisdiction is exercised *in personam*, the court must have personal jurisdiction over the defendant under Rules 24 to 30. In other words, it must be possible to serve process upon the party against whom the order is sought.[33] Two specific points should be noted. First, if it is necessary to serve the defendant out of the jurisdiction in accordance with Rule 27 with the permission of the court, there is no head of Order 11, rule 1 which applies in terms to applications for an anti-suit injunction, although for those which are sought in connection with a contractual right not to be sued,[34] there will be no difficulty in principle. Secondly, where jurisdiction over the defendant is governed by the 1968 or the Lugano Conventions, the court must have jurisdiction under the relevant Convention.[35] If the proceedings to be restrained were commenced in the courts of the other Contracting State before the English court was seised, Article 21 of the Conventions requires the English court to declare that it has no jurisdiction if two proceedings have the same cause of action. In the light of the decision in *The Tatry*,[36] it is improbable that this condition applies where the English court is seised with only a claim for a final anti-suit injunction and no other relief on the merits of the dispute, for the two causes of action are not the same.[37] But where the injunction is sought within the context of proceedings for substantive relief, the application of Article 21 may be inescapable.

12–058

---

[29] *Settlement Corp. v. Hochschild* [1966] Ch. 10, 15; *Castanho v. Brown & Root (U.K.) Ltd.* [1981] A.C. 557, 573; *British Airways Board v. Laker Airways Ltd.* [1985] A.C. 58; *Soc. Nat. Ind. Aérospatiale v. Lee Kui Jak* [1987] A.C. 871, 892 (P.C.); *Airbus Industrie G.I.E. v. Patel* [1999] 1 A.C. 119.

[30] *Metall und Rohstoff A.G. v. ACLI Metals Ltd.* [1984] 1 Lloyd's Rep. 598, 613 (C.A.).

[31] *Cf. Airbus Industrie G.I.E. v. Patel* [1999] 1 A.C. 119, 127.

[32] An interlocutory anti-suit injunction may require greater caution before it is granted than would otherwise be demanded by the principles of *American Cyanamid Co. v. Ethicon Ltd.* [1975] A.C. 396: see *Apple Corps Ltd. v. Apple Computer Inc.* [1992] R.P.C. 70, 76; *Banque Cantonale Vaudoise v. Waterlily Maritime Inc.* [1997] 2 Lloyd's Rep. 347. It is "vastly different from other forms of interlocutory relief": *CSR Ltd. v. Cigna Insurance Australia Ltd.* (1997) 189 C.L.R. 345, 397. For an "anti-anti-anti-suit" injunction (interlocutory injunctions to restrain respondent from seeking order from foreign court which would purport to restrain his application for an anti-suit injunction) such as was granted by a Philadelphia court in relation to the litigation in *Smith Kline & French Laboratories Ltd. v. Bloch* [1983] 1 W.L.R. 730 (C.A.), see *Shell U.K. Exploration and Production Ltd. v. Innes*, 1995 S.L.T. 807.

[33] On whether an attempt to discontinue English proceedings may annul the jurisdiction of the English court over the respondent, see *Castanho v. Brown & Root (U.K.) Ltd.* [1981] A.C. 557; *Fakih Bros. v. A.P. Moller (Copenhagen) Ltd.* [1994] 1 Lloyd's Rep. 103.

[34] See Clause (4) of Rule 32.

[35] That is, under Rule 28. On whether the Convention context affects the exercise of the court's discretion to grant the injunction, see *post*, para. 12–066. For the specific jurisdictional argument in the context of an agreement for the jurisdiction of the English courts, see Comment to Clause (4) of Rule 32, *post*.

[36] Case C–406/92; [1994] E.C.R. I–5439; [1999] Q.B. 515, which requires the two sets of proceedings to have the same object and the same cause.

[37] *Cf. Continental Bank N.A. v. Aeakos Compania Naviera S.A.* [1994] 1 W.L.R. 588, 595–597 (C.A.) and cases on injunctions to restrain foreign proceedings in breach of arbitration agreements: *post*, para. 12–128.

12–059   **The exercise of the discretion.** The underlying principle is that the jurisdiction is exercised "where it is appropriate to avoid injustice",[38] or, as it was once put, where the foreign proceedings are "contrary to equity and good conscience".[39] Although it is possible to identify certain categories of cases in which the jurisdiction has been exercised "the width and flexibility of equity are not to be undermined by categorisation".[40] It was at one stage said[41] that, as with any injunction, an anti-suit injunction could be granted only to give effect to a legal or an equitable right not to be sued in the foreign court, with the consequence that all applications for an anti-suit injunction would be required to be founded on such a right.[42] But later authority acknowledged that this formulation could not be accepted without qualification[43]; and in the most recent authoritative formulation of the principles[44] there is no indication that the exercise of the discretion is limited by the need to demonstrate a legal or equitable right not to be sued.

12–060   The English court may restrain proceedings brought abroad in breach of a contract not to sue, or in breach of a contract to be bound by the result of English proceedings, to sue only in England,[45] or to submit disputes to arbitration.[46] The court will also restrain proceedings which interfere with "the due process of the court".[47] Thus the court will enjoin proceedings taken abroad to recover foreign assets, whereby the party taking them will obtain an unfair advantage over other claimants in an English administration, or bankruptcy or winding up.[48]

12–061   It is also clear that the court may restrain foreign proceedings which are "oppressive or vexatious" in the traditional sense.[49] For some years it was not clear what was the effect of the modern development of *forum non conveniens* principles in the staying of *English* actions on the exercise of the jurisdiction to enjoin *foreign* proceedings. In *Castanho v. Brown & Root (U.K.) Ltd.*[50] Lord Scarman (with whom all other members of the House concurred) said that it was no longer necessary to consider case law earlier than the developments in England since *The Atlantic Star*[51] and *MacShannon v. Rockware Glass Ltd.*[52] It was held that an injunction could be granted to restrain foreign proceedings in the circumstances in which a stay of English proceedings

---

[38] *Castanho v. Brown & Root (U.K.) Ltd.* [1981] A.C. 557, 573. For injunctions founded on contractual agreements as to choice of forum, see clause (4) of Rule 32.

[39] *Carron Iron Co. v. Maclaren* (1855) 5 H.L.C. 416, 439.

[40] *Castanho v. Brown & Root (U.K.) Ltd.* [1981] A.C. 557, 573. *Cf. Soc. Nat. Ind. Aérospatiale v. Lee Kui Jak* [1987] A.C. 871, 892 (P.C.).

[41] *British Airways Board v. Laker Airways Ltd.* [1985] A.C. 58, 81, applying *The Siskina* [1979] A.C. 210, 256.

[42] On the question whether choice of law principles would need to be developed to ascertain the existence of an equitable right not to be sued, see Briggs [1997] L.M.C.L.Q. 90.

[43] *South Carolina Insurance Co. v. Assurantie Maatschappij "De Zeven Provincien" N.V.* [1987] A.C. 24, 40.

[44] *Airbus Industrie G.I.E. v. Patel* [1999] 1 A.C. 119.

[45] Clause (4) of Rule 32.

[46] *Post*, para. 12–128.

[47] *South Carolina* case [1987] A.C. 24, 41; *National Mutual Holdings Pty Ltd. v. Sentry Corp.* (1989) 87 A.L.R. 539, 563; *CSR Ltd. v. Cigna Insurance Australia Ltd.* (1997) 189 C.L.R. 345.

[48] See *Soc. Nat. Ind. Aérospatiale v. Lee Kui Jak* [1987] A.C. 871, 893–894; paras. 26–032; 30–073; 31–034, *post; cf. Barclays Bank plc v. Homan* [1992] B.C.C. 757 (C.A.).

[49] *South Carolina* case [1987] A.C. 24, 41; *Aérospatiale* case [1987] A.C. 871, 893.

[50] [1981] A.C. 557.

[51] [1974] A.C. 436.

[52] [1978] A.C. 795.

would be ordered: as the law then stood, that would mean that an injunction would be granted if the English court was an available forum in which justice could be done at substantially less inconvenience and expense, and the injunction would not deprive the plaintiff in the foreign proceedings of a legitimate personal or juridical advantage which would be available in the foreign jurisdiction.[53]

In the *Aérospatiale* case, however, the Privy Council (speaking through Lord Goff of Chieveley) held that it was not right to treat the principles applicable in injunction cases as equivalent to those in *forum non conveniens* cases, as developed in *Spiliada Maritime Corp. v. Cansulex Ltd.*[54] If the principles were the same, it would mean a party could be restrained from proceeding in a foreign court on the sole ground that England was the natural forum. That could not be right, because it would lead to the conclusion that, in a case where there was simply a difference of view between the English court and the foreign court as to which was the natural forum, the English court could arrogate to itself, by the grant of an injunction, the power to resolve the dispute: such a conclusion would "be inconsistent with comity" and "disregard the fundamental requirement that an injunction will only be granted where the ends of justice so require."[55] The Privy Council held that where a remedy was available both in England and in the foreign court, the English court would in general only restrain the plaintiff from pursuing proceedings in the foreign court if the pursuit would be vexatious or oppressive. The English court must be the natural forum for the action, and it must take account of the injustice to the defendant if the plaintiff is allowed to pursue the foreign proceedings, and also the injustice to the plaintiff if he is not allowed to do so. The Supreme Court of Canada has broadly accepted the same principles while preferring to utilise the terminology of what is required for "the ends of justice".[56] The High Court of Australia, by contrast, has adopted a rather narrower definition, namely that "foreign proceedings are to be regarded as vexatious or oppressive only if there is nothing which can be gained by them over and above what may be gained in local proceedings",[57] but it also characterised as oppressive proceedings which were instituted in one court after an action had been begun in another court and which appeared to be brought for the dominant purpose of preventing the first action from continuing. **12–062**

In the result, an injunction may be granted if the proceedings in the foreign court are vexatious or oppressive. English courts have refrained from giving a comprehensive definition of these expressions; indeed, they have deliberately refrained[58] from marking the outer limits of their power to act to restrain **12–063**

---

[53] [1981] A.C. 557, 575. See also *British Airways Board v. Laker Airways Ltd.* [1985] A.C. 58, 80; *South Carolina* case [1987] A.C. 24, 40.

[54] [1987] A.C. 460.

[55] [1987] A.C. at 495. See also *E.I. du Pont de Nemours v. Agnew* (*No. 2*) [1988] 2 Lloyd's Rep. 240, 244–245 (C.A.).

[56] *Amchem Products Ltd. v. British Columbia* (*Workers' Compensation Board*) [1993] 1 S.C.R. 897. See also *Bank of America National Trust & Savings Ass. v. Widjaya* [1994] 2 Sing. L.R. 816 (C.A.); *Koh Kay Yew v. Inn Pacific Holdings Ltd.* [1997] 3 Sing. L.R. 121 (C.A.).

[57] *CSR Ltd. v. Cigna Insurance Australia Ltd.* (1997) 189 C.L.R. 345, 393; approving *Bank of Tokyo Ltd. v. Karoon* [1987] A.C. 45n. (C.A.). It follows from this decision that objection may not be taken to the form of the foreign proceedings, nor to the nature of the relief available from that court.

[58] *McHenry v. Lewis* (1882) 22 Ch.D. 397, 407–408 (C.A.); *Re Connelly Bros. Ltd.* [1911] 1 Ch. 731, 746 (C.A.); *Aérospatiale*, at p. 896.

conduct which may give rise to injustice or, if the need for caution is given its due weight, serious injustice. It has been held that vexation or oppression may be indicated by the following: subjecting the other party to oppressive procedures in the foreign court,[59] especially a party with no substantial connection with that jurisdiction[60]; bad faith in the institution of the proceedings,[61] or the institution of proceedings which are bound to fail[62]; extreme inconvenience caused by the foreign proceedings[63]; multiplicity of actions, especially where the foreign action might spawn further consequential litigation which might not be reconcilable with the foreign decision[64]; bringing proceedings which interfere with or undermine the control of the English court of its own process[65]; bringing proceedings which could and should have formed part of an English action brought earlier.[66]

12–064   If a prima facie case of oppression or vexation has been made out by the applicant the respondent will be entitled to show why it would nevertheless be unjust for an injunction to be granted: the interests of both parties must be borne in mind.[67] The respondent may point to substantive or procedural advantages, available to him in the foreign court, which will be lost if the injunction is granted. But if these advantages are available to him only in a forum which is not the natural forum, they will be given little weight, and may even be themselves seen as evidence of oppression.[68]

12–065   It was also indicated in *Aérospatiale* that before the English court was justified in granting an injunction to restrain vexatious or oppressive conduct,

---

[59] *A/S D/S Svendborg v. Wansa* [1996] 2 Lloyd's Rep. 559, affd. [1997] 2 Lloyd's Rep. 183 (C.A.) (threats of personal violence and power to manipulate the judges in the foreign forum); *cf. South Carolina Insurance Co. v. Assurantie Maatschappij "De Zeven Provincien" N.V.* [1987] A.C. 24 (application for discovery under U.S.C., s.1782: not oppressive or an interference with the due process of the court); contrast *Bankers Trust International plc v. PT Dharmala Sakti Sejahtera* [1996] C.L.C. 252 (application for discovery under U.S.C., s.1782 restrained).

[60] *Cf. British Airways Board v. Laker Airways Ltd.* [1985] A.C. 58 with *Midland Bank plc v. Laker Airways Ltd.* [1986] 1 Q.B. 689 (C.A.) (U.S. anti-trust pre-trial procedure). See also *Simon Engineering plc v. Butte Mining plc (No. 2)* [1996] 1 Lloyd's Rep. 91; *cf. Simon Engineering plc v. Butte Mining plc* [1996] 1 Lloyd's Rep 104n. (claim for treble damages under RICO (the U.S. Racketeer Influenced and Corrupt Organisations Act) may not be legitimate advantages in light of Protection of Trading Interests Act 1980).

[61] *McHenry v. Lewis* (1882) 22 Ch.D. 397, 414 (C.A.); *Re Connolly Bros. Ltd.* [1911] 1 Ch. 731 (C.A.); *Midland Bank plc v. Laker Airways Ltd* [1986] 1 Q.B. 689 (C.A.).

[62] *Smith Kline & French Laboratories v. Bloch* [1983] 1 W.L.R. 730 (C.A.), as explained in *British Airways Board v. Laker Airways Ltd.* [1985] A.C. 58, 86.

[63] *Logan v. Bank of Scotland (No. 2)* [1906] 1 K.B. 141 (C.A.).

[64] *Australian Commercial Research & Development Ltd. v. ANZ McCaughan Merchant Bank Ltd.* [1989] 3 All E.R. 65, affd. February 23, 1990 (C.A., unrep.); *Soc. Nat. Ind. Aérospatiale v. Lee Kui Jak* [1987] A.C. 871 (consequential action for contribution would not necessarily accept the foreign court's assessment of liability as *res judicata*); *Tracomin S.A. v. Sudan Oil Seeds Co. Ltd. (No. 2)* [1983] 1 W.L.R. 1026 (C.A.); *Sohio Supply Co. v. Gatoil (USA) Inc.* [1989] 1 Lloyd's Rep. 588 (C.A.) (jurisdiction clause case).

[65] *South Carolina Insurance Co. v. Assurantie Maatschappij "De Zeven Provincien" N.V.* [1987] A.C. 24 41, 44–45; *Bank of Tokyo Ltd. v. Karoon* [1987] A.C. 45n. (C.A.); *Bankers Trust International plc v. PT Dharmala Sakti Sejahtera* [1996] C.L.C. 252;

[66] By extension of the principle in *Henderson v. Henderson* (1843) 3 Hare 100: *Zeeland Navigation Co. Ltd. v. Banque Worms, The Times,* December 26, 1995 (*obiter*; injunction refused).

[67] *Soc. Nat. Ind. Aérospatiale v. Lee Kui Jak* [1987] A.C. 871 (P.C.).

[68] *Smith Kline and French Laboratories v. Bloch* [1983] 1 W.L.R. 730 (C.A.); *Simon Engineering plc v. Butte Mining plc* [1996] 1 Lloyd's Rep. 104n.; *(No. 2)* [1996] 1 Lloyd's Rep. 91. It is open to a respondent to undertake not to rely on or invoke such procedures in the foreign court, and thereby defeat the allegation of oppression: *Soc. Nat. Ind. Aérospatiale v. Lee Kui Jak* [1987] A.C. 871 (P.C.).

it was generally required that the court conclude that it provides the natural forum for the action.[69] This was reiterated in *Airbus Industrie G.I.E. v. Patel*[70] where it was said that this requirement—which was elevated to the status of a general rule requiring to be satisfied before the court may act—was necessary in order to respect the limits placed by comity upon the power of an English court to grant orders in relation to proceedings in foreign courts.[71] In the absence of such a connection with England it will be a very rare case in which the English court would be justified in granting an injunction against a defendant whose conduct was oppressive or vexatious. In that case French aircraft manufacturers were refused an injunction restraining English defendants from pursuing proceedings in Texas arising out of an aircraft accident in India. Although the English court had *in personam* jurisdiction over the defendants, it was contrary to comity to restrain the Texas proceedings because the English forum did not have a sufficient interest in, or connection with, the matter.

Where the court in which the proceedings are brought is that of a Contracting State to the 1968 Convention or the Lugano Convention, some cases[72] have recognised that the general scheme of the Conventions require additional restraint in the exercise of the discretion to grant an injunction. The European Court has held that a court in one Contracting State has no right to adjudicate upon the jurisdiction of a court in another Contracting State[73]; if the claim for an anti-suit injunction is in substance founded on the bare argument that the other court should have concluded that it had no jurisdiction under the Convention, it may be incompatible with the Convention for an injunction to be ordered. Moreover, an injunction may be refused recognition[74] by the court at which it is directed on the ground that it is contrary to public policy to allow a foreign court to rule upon the right of access[74] to a court; and it is appropriate to weigh this factor in the exercise of discretion to grant the injunction. By contrast, where the injunction is in substance directed at unconscionable conduct of the defendant, as distinct from an alleged jurisdictional error by the foreign court, there is no reason why an English court should not have recourse to its procedural law by granting an injunction to restrain such behaviour.[75] Moreover, where an injunction is sought on the footing that the plaintiff in the foreign proceedings has acted in breach of a jurisdiction agreement by suing in the foreign court, it has been held that the English court may grant an injunction in relation to proceedings in the courts

12–066

---

[69] [1987] A.C. 871, 896. For the case where the action may be brought only in the foreign forum, a so-called "single forum" case, *post*, para. 12–068.

[70] [1999] 1 A.C. 119; Males [1998] L.M.C.L.Q. 543.

[71] At 134–140. For the case where the application for an injunction is founded on breach of a jurisdiction agreement, and to which the rule laid down in *Airbus* (see p. 138) was not directed, see Clause (4) of Rule 32.

[72] *Phillip Alexander Securities & Futures Ltd. v. Bamberger* [1997] I.L.Pr 73, affd. *ibid.*, p. 104, 117 (C.A.); *Toepfer International GmbH v. Soc. Cargill France* [1998] 1 Lloyd's Rep. 379, 387–388 (C.A.).

[73] Case C–351/89 *Overseas Union Insurance Ltd. v. New Hampshire Insurance Co.* [1991] E.C.R. I–3317, 3350–3351; [1992] Q.B. 434, 458–459; Case C–163/95 *Von Horn v. Cinnamond* [1997] E.C.R. I–5451, 5476–5477; [1998] Q.B. 214, 241.

[74] *Phillip Alexander Securities & Futures v. Bamberger, supra.*

[75] Especially where this is a right guaranteed by the constitution: *Phillip Alexander Securities & Futures Ltd. v. Bamberger, supra.*

[76] Cf. Case C–365/88 *Kongress Agentur Hagen GmbH v. Zeehaghe B.V.* [1990] E.C.R. I–1845 (1968 Convention regulates jurisdiction, not procedure).

of another Contracting State.[77] As the English court will be applying the same jurisdictional rules as those which apply in the foreign court, and is, in particular, reinforcing a jurisdiction agreement by which both courts are bound, it may be most efficient for the English court to enforce the agreement itself.

12–067   It is not necessary for a claimant who seeks an injunction to restrain foreign proceedings to seek any relief in England on the substance of the dispute. Sometimes the claimant in the English proceedings has sought a negative declaration (*i.e.* a declaration that he is not liable to the defendant),[78] but this is not a pre-condition of the right to seek an injunction, although it may be appropriate if the claimant in England has some reason to establish his defence to the claim by the plaintiff in the foreign proceedings.[79] As early as 1915 it was said that a defendant could be restrained from instituting or continuing proceedings in a foreign court if a proper case of injustice were made out without any declaration of right.[80] This is because injunctions of this kind can be sought by defendants who are not seeking to assert any independent cause of action but simply a right not to be sued in a foreign court.[81] Thus when Midland Bank was granted an injunction restraining the liquidator of Laker Airways Ltd. from joining the bank in the United States anti-trust proceedings, the bank was refused a declaration that it was not liable to Laker Airways under English law.[82]

12–068   **"Single forum" cases.** The principles upon which the court exercises its discretion are modified in relation to cases where, if the foreign proceedings are discontinued in obedience to an injunction, the plaintiff in the foreign proceedings will not be able to bring his claim elsewhere. This situation arises when the cause of action relied on in the foreign court cannot be advanced in England,[83] and there is no cause of action available (as a matter of English domestic or private international law) to the claimant in England.[84] The House of Lords, in *British Airways Board v. Laker Airways Ltd.*[85] and the Court of Appeal, in *Midland Bank plc v. Laker Airways Ltd.*,[86] have considered those cases where an injunction may be granted to restrain foreign proceedings even where the would-be plaintiff in the foreign proceedings has no remedy in England. Both cases arose from the anti-trust proceedings brought, or threatened, in the United States against (among other defendants) certain British

---

[77] *Continental Bank N.A. v. Aeakos Compania Naviera S.A.* [1994] 1 W.L.R. 588 (C.A.) (a case involving a jurisdiction clause, said to represent a "paradigm case" for an injunction: p. 598); *The Angelic Grace* [1995] 1 Lloyd's Rep. 87 (C.A.) (a case involving an arbitration agreement). See *post*, paras. 12–123 *et seq.*

[78] As in *Smith Kline and French Laboratories v. Bloch* [1983] 1 W.L.R. 370 (C.A.); and in *British Airways Board v. Laker Airways Ltd.* [1985] A.C. 58.

[79] See [1985] A.C. at 81.

[80] *Guaranty Trust Co. of New York v. Hannay & Co.* [1915] 2 K.B. 536, 556 (C.A.).

[81] *Associated Newspapers Ltd. v. Insert Media Ltd.* [1988] 1 W.L.R. 509, 514.

[82] *Midland Bank plc v. Laker Airways Ltd.* [1986] Q.B. 689 (C.A.).

[83] The most usual reason being that it arises under a foreign statute which is territorial in its operation or which creates a cause of action which is excluded from application in England by English choice of law rules.

[84] *Cf. Simon Engineering plc v. Butte Mining plc (No. 2)* [1996] 1 Lloyd's Rep. 91, 95 (RICO affords a remedy, as distinct from providing a cause of action; therefore not a single forum case); *cf. Société Commerciale de Réassurance v. Eras International Ltd.* [1995] 2 All E.R. 278, 308–312.

[85] [1985] A.C. 58.

[86] [1986] Q.B. 689 (C.A.).

airlines and banks by the English liquidator of Laker Airways Ltd. in connection with an alleged conspiracy to drive Laker Airways Ltd. out of business. In *British Airways Board v. Laker Airways Ltd.* the House of Lords held that an injunction might be granted to restrain foreign proceedings even if the plaintiff in those proceedings had no remedy in England, but only if the bringing of the action in the foreign court were in the circumstances so unconscionable that it could be regarded as an infringement of an equitable right.[87] In the circumstances the British airlines were not entitled to an injunction, since by carrying on their business in the United States they had accepted that they were subject to United States law, including United States anti-trust law.[88] In the subsequent case of *Midland Bank plc v. Laker Airways Ltd.* the Court of Appeal held that two British banks were entitled to an injunction restraining the liquidator from joining them in the United States proceedings. They had been the bankers to Laker Airways Ltd., and it was alleged that they had joined in a conspiracy to deprive Laker Airways Ltd. of the benefits of a financial rescue package. It was held that for an English plaintiff to sue them in the United States on the basis of the extra-territorial application of United States anti-trust law to activities in England, intended to be governed by English law, was unconscionable and unjust.[89]

The timing of the application. In principle, the sooner the application for an injunction is made the better its chances of success, for the amount of wasted time and money will increase the longer the application is delayed,[90] and may be defeated if there has been submission to the foreign court.[91] There is some authority for the view that an application is premature if it has not been preceded by an application for jurisdictional relief in the foreign court[92]: as an anti-suit injunction will interfere with the procedures of the foreign court, it may be preferable that the foreign court be asked not to exercise jurisdiction. It would follow that the practice of applying to the foreign court first is appropriate, at least in cases where the foreign proceedings are not themselves vexatious. This has been described as the "normal" procedure,[93] and it has been said that there must be some good reason why the application

12–069

---

[87] [1985] A.C. 58, 81, 95.

[88] See also *Smith Kline & French Laboratories Ltd. v. Bloch (No. 2)*, *The Times*, November 13, 1984 (C.A.).

[89] [1986] Q.B. 689 (C.A.), distinguished in *Barclays Bank plc v. Homan* [1992] B.C.C. 757 (C.A.).

[90] *Toepfer International GmbH v. Molino Boschi srl* [1996] 1 Lloyd's Rep. 510; *A/S D/S Svendborg v. Wansa* [1996] 2 Lloyd's Rep. 559, 571–572, 573, affd. [1997] 2 Lloyd's Rep. 183 (C.A.).

[91] *Schiffahrtsgesellschaft Detlev von Appen GmbH v. Voest Alpine Intertrading GmbH* [1997] 2 Lloyd's Rep. 279, 288 (C.A.); see also *Tracomin S.A. v. Sudan Oil Seeds Co. Ltd. (No. 2)* [1983] 1 W.L.R. 1026 (C.A.); *Sohio Supply Co. v. Gatoil (USA) Inc.* [1989] 1 Lloyd's Rep. 588 (C.A.).

[92] *Pan American World Airways Inc. v. Andrews*, 1992 S.L.T. 268.

[93] *Barclays Bank plc v. Homan* [1992] B.C.C. 757, 762 (Hoffmann J.), affd. *ibid.* 777 (C.A.); *Shell U.K. Exploration and Production Ltd. v. Innes*, 1995 S.L.T. 807, 825 (Ct. of Sess.); *Deaville v. Aeroflot Russian International Airlines* [1997] 2 Lloyd's Rep. 67; *Charterers Mutual Assurance Association Ltd. v. British & Foreign* [1998] I.L.Pr. 838. It also appears to be the view of the Supreme Court of Canada: *Amchem Products Inc. v. British Columbia (Workers' Compensation Board)* [1993] 1 S.C.R. 897, 930–931, distinguished (in relation to interlocutory injunctions) in *CSR v. Cigna Insurance Australia Ltd* (1997) 189 C.L.R. 345, 395–397.

is made in England first.[94] But this approach was not specifically approved in *Airbus Industrie*,[95] and was specifically disapproved in *The Angelic Grace*,[96] and it is submitted that there is no general requirement that an application be first made to the foreign court. Certainly, the demands of comity must be respected before the English court may make such an order, but that if the court ascertains that England is clearly the natural forum for the resolution of the dispute, comity will have been respected,[97] and is not offended by the English court proceeding to grant an injunction.

ILLUSTRATIONS

12–070   1. A, a Scotsman living in Scotland, is injured in an accident while employed by X, an English company, at its Scottish factory. A is medically treated in Scotland, and all witnesses of fact live and work in Scotland. Medical and other expert witnesses are available in Scotland. A's action in England against X for negligence is stayed.[98]

2. A Turkish ship, owned by X, a Turkish state corporation, and a Cuban ship, owned by A, a Cuban state corporation, collide in Turkish territorial waters. Both ships are damaged in the collision. X sues A in the Turkish courts. Subsequently A arrests in England another ship owned by X and commences an action *in rem* against X in England. The Turkish court is the natural and appropriate forum, and A is unable to establish that there is some personal or juridical advantage which would be available only in England and which is of such importance that it would cause injustice to deprive A of it. The action in England is stayed.[99]

3. A & Co., a Liberian company, insure their cargo vessel with X & Co., a Kuwaiti insurance company, against war and marine risks under a Lloyd's standard form of marine insurance, which excludes loss caused by infringement of customs regulations. The vessel is detained by Saudi Arabian officials on the ground that it is engaged in smuggling oil. A & Co. sue in England, claiming that the vessel is a constructive total loss. The court has jurisdiction to grant leave under Ord. 11, r. 1(1) because the applicable law of the contract is English law, but the court will not exercise its jurisdiction because England is not the *forum conveniens*: the central issue is one of fact, whether the vessel was engaged in smuggling in the Gulf, and there is an available forum in Kuwait.[1]

12–071   4. A & Co., Liberian ship-owners, charter a carrier, *The Spiliada*, to Y & Co., an Indian company, for the carriage of sulphur from Vancouver, British Columbia, to Indian ports. X & Co., a Canadian company engaged in the export of sulphur, ship a cargo of sulphur on *The Spiliada* from Vancouver under bills of lading whose applicable law is English law. A & Co. sue X and Co. in England claiming that the sulphur was wet when loaded and caused severe corrosion. There is already a substantial trial proceeding in England arising out of similar allegations against X & Co. by a different shipowner concerning a cargo loaded at Vancouver for carriage to South Africa and Mozambique: there is, therefore, an accumulated expertise of the lawyers and experts in the other case, many of whom are also involved in the case of *The Spiliada*. The court has jurisdiction to grant permission to serve process under Order 11, r. 1(1) because the applicable law of the contract is English law, and will exercise its jurisdiction because England is the *forum conveniens*.[2]

5. A, a Portuguese citizen residing in Portugal, is employed by X, a Panamanian company, on one of its ships. While the ship is in an English port A is injured by what he alleges is the negligence of X and of Y, an English company, which provided shore services for the ship. Both

---

[94] *Arab Monetary Fund v. Hashim (No. 6)*, *The Times*, July 24, 1992. See also *Metall und Rohstoff A.G. v. ACLI (Metals) London Ltd.* [1984] 1 Lloyd's Rep. 598 (C.A.); *Bank of Tokyo Ltd. v. Karoon* [1987] A.C. 45n (C.A.).

[95] [1999] 1 A.C. 119: an anti-suit injunction had already been obtained in India, and dismissal in Texas on *forum conveniens* grounds was at that time unobtainable: p. 128.

[96] [1995] 1 Lloyd's Rep. 87, 95, 96 (C.A.) where it was pointed out that to order an injunction after the foreign court has specifically confirmed its jurisdiction may constitute a rather greater affront to comity.

[97] And may for this reason not have been respected by the foreign court.

[98] *MacShannon v. Rockware Glass Ltd.* [1978] A.C. 795.

[99] *The Abidin Daver* [1984] A.C. 398.

[1] *Amin Rasheed Shipping Corp. v. Kuwait Insurance Co.* [1984] A.C. 50.

[2] *Spiliada Maritime Corp. v. Cansulex Ltd.* [1987] A.C. 460.

X and Y are subsidiaries of Z, a Texan company. A brings an action in England against X and Y and by consent an interim payment of damages is made, and subsequently X admits liability. A is approached by an American firm of lawyers who persuade him to enforce his claim in the United States against X, Y and Z with legal fees to be on a contingency basis. A gives notice to discontinue the proceedings in England, and X and Y apply in England for an injunction to restrain A from pursuing the U.S. proceedings. The injunction is refused because the prospect of higher damages is a legitimate personal or juridical advantage and the Texas court was no less natural or appropriate a forum than England.[3]

6. X, an airline incorporated in Jersey, and in liquidation with an English liquidator, commences an action in the United States against A and B, two British airlines, and various other airlines and aircraft manufacturers. X claims in the U.S. action treble damages for breach of the U.S. anti-trust laws, arising out of (*inter alia*) allegedly anti-competitive fares fixed by the airline defendants. A and B commence an action in England against X claiming a declaration that they are not liable to X and an injunction restraining X from continuing with the U.S. proceedings. The injunction is refused because, although the court has jurisdiction to grant an injunction to restrain foreign proceedings in the circumstances, X has no remedy in England for the alleged wrong, and A and B do not show that A's conduct in bringing the U.S. proceedings is unconscionable.[4]

7. A is a passenger in a helicopter manufactured by X & Co., a French company, and operated   **12–072**
by Y & Co., an English company. A is killed in a crash in England. His widow and administrators sue X and Co. and Y & Co. both in England and in Texas. The Texas court has jurisdiction because X and Co. carries on business there, but the case otherwise has no connection with Texas. Under Texas law X and Co. cannot claim contribution from Y and Co. The court grants an injunction restraining the Texas proceedings.[5]

8. After a fatal accident at an Indian airport, X, who is resident in England, institutes proceedings in India against A, the French corporation which manufactured the aircraft. The proceedings make slow progress. X later commences proceedings against A in the courts of Texas. An Indian court orders X to discontinue the Texas proceedings on the ground of *forum conveniens*, but X is not within its personal jurisdiction and ignores the order. A seeks an injunction from the English courts to restrain X from continuing the Texas proceedings. The court refuses the injunction as England is not the natural forum for the litigation and to interfere with proceedings pending in Texas in such a case would be incompatible with the requirements of comity.[6]

9. X, a British citizen, enters into an English contract with A. He breaks it and by fraud obtains a foreign judgment against A. The court grants an injunction restraining X from enforcing the foreign judgment.[7]

10. A & Co., an English company, sell furniture to X and Co., an Italian company. The price is payable in England; delivery is to take place in Italy. After the goods are delivered, X & Co. sue A & Co. for damages in Italy, claiming that the furniture is not in conformity with the contract. Subsequently A & Co. sue X & Co. in England for the price. The court must decline jurisdiction.[8]

11. A & Co., an American insurance company with a place of business in England, reinsure   **12–073**
with X & Co., a Singapore insurance company, and Y & Co. and Z and Co., English insurance companies. The reinsurance is of insurance placed with A & Co. in connection with five warranties on products sold by a French company. A & Co. sue X & Co., Y & Co. and Z & Co. in France, claiming monies due under the reinsurance policies. The defendants challenge the jurisdiction of the French court. Subsequently, X & Co., Y & Co. and Z & Co. bring proceedings against A & Co. in England for a declaration that they have lawfully avoided the policies for non-disclosure. The English court must stay its proceedings until the French court has decided whether it has jurisdiction.[9]

---

[3] *Castanho v. Brown & Root (U.K.) Ltd.* [1981] A.C. 557.

[4] *British Airways Board v. Laker Airways Ltd.* [1985] A.C. 58. Contrast *Midland Bank plc v. Laker Airways Ltd.* [1986] Q.B. 689 (C.A.).

[5] *Cf. Soc. Nat. Ind. Aérospatiale v. Lee Kui Jak* [1987] A.C. 871.

[6] *Airbus Industrie G.I.E.* v. *Patel* [1999] 1 A.C. 119.

[7] *Ellerman Lines Ltd. v. Read* [1928] K.B. 144 (C.A.).

[8] Art. 21, 1968 Convention; Case 144/86 *Gubisch Maschinenfabrik KG v. Palumbo* [1987] E.C.R. 4861.

[9] Art. 21, 1968 Convention; *cf.* Case C–351/89 *Overseas Union Insurance Co. v. New Hampshire Insurance Co.* [1991] E.C.R. I–3317; [1992] Q.B. 434 (a case on the unamended Art. 21).

12. A & Co. issue proceedings in France against X & Co. on May 5, and they are served on X & Co. on May 21. X & Co. issue proceedings in England on May 7 and serve them on A & Co. on May 19. The English court is the court first seised.[10]

13. The facts are as in Illustration 11, except that the English proceedings are issued on April 27, and are served on May 25. The French court is the court first seised.

2. JURISDICTION AGREEMENTS

12R–074   **Rule 32—(1) Where a contract provides that all disputes between the parties are to be referred to the jurisdiction of the English courts, the court normally has jurisdiction to hear and determine proceedings in respect thereof.[11]**

(2) Subject to clause (3) of this Rule, where a contract provides that all disputes between the parties are to be referred to the exclusive jurisdiction of a foreign tribunal, the English court will stay proceedings instituted in England in breach of such agreement[12] (or, as the case may be, refuse to give permission to serve process out of the jurisdiction[13]) unless

---

[10] *Cf.* Case 129/83 *Zelger v. Salinitri (No. 2)* [1984] E.C.R. 2397; *Dresser U.K. Ltd. v. Falcongate Freight Management Ltd.* [1992] Q.B. 502 (C.A.).

[11] CPR 6.15; Ord. 11, r. 1(1)(*d*)(iv); 1968 Convention, Art. 17; Lugano Convention, Art. 17, in 1982 Act, Scheds. 1 and 3C; 1982 Act, Sched. 4, Art. 17 (a modified version). See, *e.g. The Chaparral* [1968] 2 Lloyd's Rep. 158 (C.A.); *Attock Cement Co. Ltd. v. Romanian Bank for Foreign Trade* [1989] 1 W.L.R. 1147, 1161 (C.A.); *Standard Steamship Owners' Protection and Indemnity Assn. (Bermuda) Ltd. v. Gann* [1992] 2 Lloyd's Rep. 528; *Akai Pty Ltd. v. People's Insurance Co.* [1998] 1 Lloyd's Rep. 90.

[12] *Gienar v. Meyer* (1796) 2 H.Bl. 603; *Law v. Garrett* (1878) 8 Ch.D. 26 (C.A.); *Austrian Lloyd S.S. Co. v. Gresham Life Assurance Society Ltd.* [1903] 1 K.B. 249 (C.A.); *Kirchner & Co. v. Gruban* [1909] 1 Ch. 413; *The Cap Blanco* [1913] P. 130 (C.A.); *The Media* (1931) 41 Ll.L.Rep. 80; *The Eleftheria* [1970] P. 94; *The Sindh* [1975] 1 Lloyd's Rep. 372 (C.A.); *The Makefjell* [1976] 2 Lloyd's Rep. 29 (C.A.); *The Kislovodsk* [1980] 1 Lloyd's Rep. 183; *The Star of Luxor* [1981] 1 Lloyd's Rep. 139; *Trendtex Trading Corp. v. Crédit Suisse* [1980] 3 All E.R. 721, affd. [1982] A.C. 679; *The Biskra* [1983] 2 Lloyd's Rep. 59; *The Sennar (No. 2)* [1985] 1 W.L.R. 490 (H.L.); *The Benarty (No. 2)* [1985] Q.B. 325 (C.A.); *The Iran Vojdan* [1984] 2 Lloyd's Rep. 380; *The Indian Fortune* [1985] 1 Lloyd's Rep. 344; *The Ruben Martinez Villena (No. 2)* [1988] 1 Lloyd's Rep. 435; *The Pioneer Container* [1994] 2 A.C. 324 (P.C.); *The Mahkutai* [1996] A.C. 650 (P.C.); *The Nile Rhapsody* [1994] 1 Lloyd's Rep. 382 (C.A.); *The Havhelt* [1993] 1 Lloyd's Rep. 523; *G. & E. Autobrokers v. Toyota Canada* (1980) 117 D.L.R. (3d) 707 (B.C.); *Volkswagen Canada Inc. v. Auto Haus Frohlich* [1986] 1 W.W.R. 380 (Alta. C.A.); *Oulton Agencies Inc. v. Knolloffice Inc.* (1988) 48 D.L.R. (4th) 545 (P.E.I.); *Fairfield v. Low* (1990) 71 O.R. (2d) 599; *Mithras Management Ltd. v. New Visions Entertainment Corp.* (1992) 90 D.L.R. (4th) 726 (Ont.); *Blackman & Co. v. Oliver Davey Glass Co.* [1966] V.R. 570; *Leigh & Mardon Pty. Ltd. v. PRC Inc.* (1993) 44 F.C.R. 88 (Fed. Ct.); *Williams v. Society of Lloyd's* [1994] 1 V.R. 274; *Francis Travel Marketing Pty. Ltd. v. Virgin Atlantic Airways* (1994) A.T.P.R. 41–332; *FAI General Insurance Co Ltd. v. Ocean Marine Mutual Protection and Indemnity Association* (1996) 41 N.S.W.L.R. 117. See Graupner (1943) 59 L.Q.R. 227; Cowen and Mendes da Costa (1965) 43 Can.Bar.Rev. 453; Bissett-Johnson (1970) 19 I.C.L.Q. 541; Pryles (1976) 24 I.C.L.Q. 543; Kahn-Freund (1977) 26 I.C.L.Q. 825; Robertson (1982) 20 Alta L. Rev. 296; Briggs, [1984] L.M.C.L.Q. 227, 241–9; Morse (1989) 1 African J. Int. Comp. L. 551; Sing [1995] L.M.C.L.Q. 182; Peel [1998] L.M.C.L.Q. 182; Bell (1996) 10 J. Contract. Law 53, 97; Hartley, in *Current Issues in European and International Law* (ed. White and Smythe, 1990), p. 156. For the United States see *M/S Bremen v. Zapata Offshore Co.*, 407 U.S. 1 (1972), [1972] 2 Lloyd's Rep. 315; *Carnival Cruise Lines, Inc. v. Shute*, 499 U.S. 585 (1991); Scoles and Hay, pp. 279–285. See generally Gaudemet-Tallon, *La prorogation volontaire de juridiction en droit international privé* (1965); Kaufmann-Kohler, *La clause d'élection de for dans les contrats internationaux* (1979). See also Hague Convention on the Choice of Court, 1965, which is not in force.

[13] See para. 12–114, n. 24, *post.*

the claimant proves that it is just and proper to allow them to continue.[14]

(3) Where the case falls within the scope of the 1968 Convention or the Lugano Convention, unless the defendant submits to the jurisdiction, the court has no jurisdiction to determine a dispute

   (a) if one or more of the parties is domiciled in a Contracting State and the parties have agreed in accordance with Article 17 that the courts of a Contracting State other than the United Kingdom are to have jurisdiction to settle any such dispute; or

   (b) if none of the parties is domiciled in a Contracting State and the parties have agreed in accordance with Article 17 that the courts of a Contracting State other than the United Kingdom are to have jurisdiction to settle any such dispute and the courts chosen have not declined jurisdiction.[15]

(4) An English court may restrain a party over whom it has personal jurisdiction from the institution or continuance of proceedings in a foreign court in breach of a contract to refer disputes to an English (or, *semble*, another foreign) court.[16]

COMMENT

Introductory. Rule 32 deals with the common case where parties[17] to a contract in international trade or commerce[18] agree in advance on the forum which is to have jurisdiction to determine disputes which may arise between them.[19] Three issues may arise in connection with such clauses. First, the contract may purport to confer jurisdiction on the English courts, and the

12–075

---

[14] *The Athenee* (1922) 11 Ll.L.Rep. 6 (C.A.); *The Vestris* (1932) 43 Ll.L.Rep. 86; *The Fehmarn* [1957] 1 W.L.R. 815; [1958] 1 W.L.R. 159 (C.A.); *The Adolf Warski* [1976] 2 Lloyd's Rep. 241 (C.A.); *Carvalho v. Hull, Blyth (Angola) Ltd.* [1979] 1 W.L.R. 1228 (C.A.) (where owing to a revolution in the foreign country the foreign court was a different court from that contemplated in the contract); *The Vishva Prabha* [1979] 2 Lloyd's Rep. 286; *The Panseptos* [1981] 1 Lloyd's Rep. 152; *The El Amria* [1981] 2 Lloyd's Rep. 119 (C.A.); *The Atlantic Song* [1983] 2 Lloyd's Rep. 394; *The Pia Vesta* [1984] 1 Lloyd's Rep. 169; *Standard Chartered Bank v. Pakistan National Shipping Corp.* [1995] 2 Lloyd's Rep. 365; *Citi-March Ltd. v. Neptune Orient Lines Ltd* [1996] 2 All E.R. 545; *The M.C. Pearl* [1997] 1 Lloyd's Rep. 566; *Bouygues Offshore S.A. v. Caspian Shipping Co. (Nos. 1, 3, 4 and 5)* [1998] 2 Lloyd's Rep. 461 (C.A.); *May (A.S.) & Co. Ltd. v. Robert Redford Co. Ltd.* (1969) 6 D.L.R. (3d) 288 (Ont.); *Maritime Telegraph & Telephone Co. v. Pre Print Inc.* (1996) 131 D.L.R. (4th) 171 (N.S.C.A.); *Hopkins v. Difrex S.A.* [1966] 1 N.S.W.R. 797; *Akai Pty. Ltd. v. People's Insurance Co.* (1997) 188 C.L.R. 418; *Apple Computer Inc. v. Apple Corps S.A.* [1990] 2 N.Z.L.R. 598; *Air Nauru v. Niue Airlines Ltd.* [1993] 2 N.Z.L.R. 632.

[15] 1968 Convention, Art. 17; Lugano Convention, Art. 17, in 1982 Act, Scheds. 1 and 3C. For Contracting States see *ante*, paras. 11–005 *et seq.*

[16] For injunctions to restrain foreign proceedings brought in breach of an agreement to arbitrate, see *post*, para. 12–128.

[17] For the position of third parties who may be bound by an agreement entered into between others, see *The Pioneer Container* [1994] 2 A.C. 324 (P.C.) (jurisdiction agreement between bailee and sub-bailee binding on bailor who had consented to the bailee sub-contracting the carriage "on any terms"); *cf. The Mahkutai* [1996] A.C. 650 (P.C.) (sub-contractor not entitled to rely on agreement between owner and principal contractor as jurisdiction agreement not within scope of "Himalaya" clause). For the same issue in the context of Art. 17 of the 1968 and Lugano Conventions, see *post*, para. 12–087. See generally Sing [1995] L.M.C.L.Q. 183. And for incorporation of a jurisdiction agreement from one contract to another, see *AIG Group (U.K.) Ltd. v. The Ethniki* [1998] 4 All ER 301.

[18] For a very early example see *Gienar v. Meyer* (1796) 2 Hy.Bl. 603.

[19] For jurisdiction clauses in trust instruments see *ante*, para. 11–279.

claimant may seek to invoke that jurisdiction. Whether (and if so, how) he may do so will be determined in part by whether the 1968 Convention or the Lugano Convention applies to the agreement: if they apply, the Conventions regulate the form, and to some extent the content, of the agreement; and the question whether permission is required to serve process out of the jurisdiction will be determined by whether the agreement is one to which the Conventions apply. The entitlement of an English court to exercise jurisdiction on the basis of such an agreement for the English courts is examined in clause (1) of the Rule. Second, the contract may purport to confer jurisdiction upon the courts of another country, and yet a claimant may commence,[20] or seek to commence,[21] proceedings in England. Whether the court will permit the action to proceed as a matter of common law, is examined in clause (2) of the Rule; whether it is obliged by the Conventions to dismiss the action is examined in clause (3) of the Rule. Thirdly, proceedings may be brought in a foreign court in breach of an agreement that they be brought in an English or in another foreign court. The principles which govern when such proceedings may be restrained by injunction are examined in clause (4) of the Rule. The parties may choose arbitration, which is dealt with in Chapter 16, or they may submit themselves to the jurisdiction of a court.

12–076   The chosen court may be a court in the country of one or both of the parties, or it may be a neutral forum.[22] The jurisdiction clause may provide for a submission to the courts of a particular country,[23] or to a court identified by a formula in a printed standard form,[24] such as a bill of lading referring disputes to the courts of the carrier's principal place of business.[25] Some jurisdiction clauses provide for the courts of a particular country to have *exclusive* jurisdiction; others provide for the courts of one or more countries to have non-exclusive jurisdiction, *i.e.* they confer jurisdiction on the courts of one or more countries without prejudice to the right of the parties to sue in any other court which may have jurisdiction.

12–077   A jurisdiction agreement is almost invariably part of a wider contract. The rules governing choice of law in contract are now contained in the Contracts (Applicable Law) Act 1990, which gives effect to the Rome Convention on the Law Applicable to Contractual Obligations and is dealt with fully in Chapters 32 and 33. Article 1(2)(*d*) of the Rome Convention provides that the rules of the Convention are not to apply to "agreements on the choice of court".[26] Consequently, the English court is not required by the Rome Convention to apply its rules to jurisdiction agreements. But as a matter of common law, normally a jurisdiction agreement (like arbitration agreements, which are also excluded by Article 1(2)(*d*) from the application of the Rome Convention) is governed by the law applicable to the contract of which it

---

[20] By service of process without the permission of the court.

[21] By service of process with the permission of the court.

[22] As in *The Chaparral* [1968] 2 Lloyd's Rep. 158, 163–164 (C.A.); see also *Attock Cement Co. Ltd. v. Romanian Bank for Foreign Trade* [1989] 1 W.L.R. 1147, 1161 (C.A.).

[23] On the effect of a change in the identity of the foreign country see *Carvalho v. Hull, Blyth (Angola) Ltd.* [1979] 1 W.L.R. 1228 (C.A.). *Cf. The Panseptos* [1981] 1 Lloyd's Rep. 152.

[24] Whether the agreement is standard form, or has been individually negotiated, may be relevant to the weight to be accorded to it: *The Bergen (No. 2)* [1997] 2 Lloyd's Rep. 710, 715.

[25] As in *The Eleftheria* [1970] P. 94; *The El Amria* [1981] 2 Lloyd's Rep. 119 (C.A.); *The Ruben Martinez Villena (No. 2)* [1988] 1 Lloyd's Rep. 435; *The Sylt* [1991] 1 Lloyd's Rep. 240; *The Rewia* [1991] 2 Lloyd's Rep. 325 (C.A.).

[26] For the reasons for the exclusion see Giuliano-Lagarde Report [1980] O.J. C282, at pp. 11–12.

forms a part. Accordingly, and as a matter of the common law principles of the conflict of laws, the law which governs the contract will also generally govern the agreement on choice of court. This means, as will be seen below, that this law governs the construction and interpretation of the agreement; it will also, in principle at least, govern the original validity of the agreement.[27]

It is a question of interpretation, governed by the law applicable to the **12–078** contract, or more accurately, the law governing the jurisdiction agreement,[28] whether a jurisdiction clause is exclusive or non-exclusive, *i.e.* whether it requires proceedings to be brought in a particular forum, or simply confers jurisdiction on the courts of a particular country without requiring proceedings to be brought there.[29] Some authorities suggest that the clause must provide in terms that the jurisdiction of the chosen court be exclusive,[30] but the true question is whether on its proper construction the clause *obliges* the parties to resort to the relevant jurisdiction, irrespective of whether the word "exclusive" is used.[31] Where the agreement is governed by English law, and in the absence of explanation to the contrary, the court may conclude that if the nominated court would have had jurisdiction by right in the absence of the agreement, the agreement would be idle unless it conferred *exclusive* jurisdiction on the nominated court.[32]

Where the court finds that the agreement is for the non-exclusive jurisdic-   **12–079** tion of the designated court (whether England or a foreign court), it cannot be argued that the institution of proceedings is a breach of contract; and any application for a stay of proceedings in favour of that foreign court will be determined on the basis of *Spiliada Maritime Corp. v. Cansulex Ltd.*[33] But the fact that a court was contractually chosen by the parties will be taken as clear evidence that it is an available forum, and that, in principle at least, it is not open to either party to object to the exercise of its jurisdiction at least on

---

[27] For the effect of an agreement on choice of court when it is alleged that the contract is void or voidable, or when the action is bought to have the contract declared unenforceable or a nullity, see *post*, para. 12–084.

[28] *Cf. Mackender v. Feldia A.G.* [1967] 2 Q.B. 590, 598, *per* Lord Denning M.R., and the cases on arbitration clauses, *post*, paras. 16–011 *et seq.*

[29] See *Evans Marshall & Co. Ltd. v. Bertola S.A.* [1973] 1 W.L.R. 349, 361–362. *Cf. Commercial Bank of the Near East plc v. A* [1989] 2 Lloyd's Rep. 319; *Green v. Australian Industrial Investment Ltd.* (1989) 90 A.L.R. 500. See also Kahn-Freund (1977) 26 I.C.L.Q. 825, 828–829. On these clauses under the 1968 Convention and the Lugano Convention see *Kurz v. Stella Musical GmbH* [1992] Ch. 196 and, *infra*, para. 12–107.

[30] *Hoerter v. Hanover, etc. Works* (1893) 10 T.L.R. 103 (C.A.); *Westcott v. Alsco Products of Canada Ltd.* (1960) 26 D.L.R. 281 (Nfld. C.A.); *Harrington v. Industrial Sales Ltd.* [1973] 2 W.W.R. 330, affd. [1973] 5 W.W.R. 577 (Sask. C.A.); *Khalij Commercial Bank Ltd. v. Woods* (1985) 17 D.L.R. (4th) 358 (Ont.); *Contractors Ltd. v. M.T.E. Control Gear Ltd.* [1964] S.A.S.R. 47. *Cf. Compagnie Commerciale André S.A. v. Artibell Shipping Co. Ltd.*, 1999 S.C.L.R. 349.

[31] This sentence was treated as correctly stating the law in *Sohio Supply Co. v. Gatoil (USA) Inc.* [1989] 1 Lloyd's Rep. 588, 591 (C.A.); *British Aerospace plc. v. Dee Howard Co.* [1993] 1 Lloyd's Rep. 368; *Continental Bank N.A. v. Aeakos Compania Naviera S.A.* [1994] 1 W.L.R. 588 (C.A.). See also *Ocarina Marine v. Macard Stein & Co.* [1994] 2 Lloyd's Rep. 524; *FAI General Insurance Co. Ltd. v. Marine Mutual Protection and Indemnity Assn.* (1996) 41 N.S.W.L.R. 117.

[32] *Sohio Supply Co. v. Gatoil USA Inc.*, *supra*; *A/S D/S Svendborg v. Wansa* [1997] 2 Lloyd's Rep. 368, 373 (C.A.); *British Aerospace plc v. Dee Howard Corp.* [1993] 1 Lloyd's Rep. 368; *FAI General Insurance Co. Ltd. v. Ocean Marine Mutual Protection and Indemnity Assn.*, *supra*.

[33] [1987] A.C. 460; see clause (2) of Rule 31, *ante*.

grounds which should have been foreseeable when the agreement was made.[34]

12–080   It is also a question of interpretation whether the claim which is the subject matter of the proceedings falls within its terms.[35] Where the jurisdiction agreement is governed by English law, the court may presume the agreement was intended to apply to all disputes arising between the parties and which are connected with the contract in which the agreement was contained.[36] Accordingly, if the claimant seeks to frame his claim in tort, or in equity,[37] and contends that the jurisdiction agreement does not extend to non-contractual claims, he will need to persuade the court that the parties intended to permit the claimant to frame a claim to fall outside the jurisdiction agreement: in the absence of a sensible commercial justification for such an intention (which would pave the way for the possibility of inconsistent judgments), the court is likely to interpret the dispute as one falling within the scope of the agreement.[38]

12–081   As a general rule, but subject to important exceptions, English courts (in common with the courts of other countries) will give effect to a choice of jurisdiction. If the English court is the chosen forum, the jurisdiction clause will be effective to confer jurisdiction on the English court; in certain circumstances, the court will have a discretion not to exercise it. If a foreign court is the chosen forum, then the English court will give effect to the choice by staying proceedings brought in breach of the jurisdiction clause or by refusing to give permission to serve process outside the jurisdiction; but (except in cases within the scope of Article 17 of the Conventions) the English court has a discretion to override the choice of jurisdiction.

12–082   The effectiveness of jurisdiction agreements is, in most countries, limited to a lesser or greater degree. In general, though English law accords to the parties a high degree of autonomy to choose the forum, it may override the parties' expressed choice, and the courts are not obliged to uphold and enforce the parties' choice to confer jurisdiction on an English or a foreign court[39]. But where the 1968 or the Lugano Convention governs the case, the position is different.[40] So, for example, an employee cannot contract out of the jurisdiction of an employment tribunal by agreeing in a contract of employment that

---

[34] *S & W Berisford plc v. New Hampshire Insurance Co.* [1990] 2 Q.B. 321 (disapproved on other grounds in *Re Harrods (Buenos Aires) Ltd.* [1992] Ch. 72 (C.A.)); *Standard Steamship Owners Protection and Indemnity Association (Bermuda) Ltd. v. Gann* [1992] 2 Lloyd's Rep. 528; *British Aerospace plc v. Dee Howard Co.* [1993] 1 Lloyd's Rep. 368; *The Rothnie* [1996] 2 Lloyd's Rep. 206.

[35] *The Sindh* [1975] 1 Lloyd's Rep. 372, 374 (C.A.); *The Sennar (No. 2)* [1984] 2 Lloyd's Rep 142, 148 (C.A.), affd. [1985] 1 W.L.R. 490 (H.L.); *Sarabia v. The Ocean Mindoro* [1997] 2 W.W.R. 116 (B.C.C.A.); *Francis Travel Marketing Pty. Ltd. v. Virgin Atlantic Airways* [1994] A.T.P.R. 41–332; *cf.* Case C–214/89 *Powell Duffryn plc v. Petereit* [1992] E.C.R. I–1745.

[36] *The Playa Larga* [1983] 2 Lloyd's Rep. 171; *Continental Bank N.A. v. Aeakos Compania Naviera S.A.* [1994] 1 W.L.R. 588 (C.A.); *The Pioneer Container* [1994] 2 A.C. 324 (P.C.); *Sarabia v. The Ocean Mindoro, supra.*

[37] *Kitechnology B.V. v. Unicor GmbH Plastmaschinen* [1995] F.S.R. 765 (C.A.).

[38] *Cf. Re the Import of Italian Sports Cars* [1992] I.L.Pr. 188 (OLG, Stuttgart, 1990); *Re-Missing Share Certificates* [1991] I.L.Pr. 298 (OLG, Münich, 1989); *Perfetto v. Parlapiano* [1993] I.L.Pr. 190 (Cour d'Appel, Liège, 1990).

[39] *Bouygues Offshore S.A. v. Caspian Shipping Co. (Nos 1, 3, 4, 5)* [1998] 2 Lloyd's Rep. 461 (C.A.).

[40] *Hough v. P & O Containers Ltd.* [1999] Q.B. 834.

all claims by him must be brought in a foreign tribunal,[41] but where the agreement is one to which the Conventions apply and which conforms to the requirements imposed by it, the agreement may not be invalidated on such grounds derived from national law.[42] The 1968 Convention and the Lugano Convention contain severe limitations on the effectiveness of jurisdiction agreements in insurance contracts, consumer contracts, and employment contracts.[43]

At common law, the validity of a jurisdiction agreement normally depends   **12–083** on its applicable law,[44] which for the reasons already given will normally be the law applicable to the contract of which it forms a part; and a jurisdiction agreement which is void or ineffective under that law will not be given effect in England. Nor will effect be given to a jurisdiction agreement which, although valid by the applicable law, offends against a mandatory rule of English law.[45] Where one of the parties challenges the effectiveness of the jurisdiction agreement on the ground that there was no consensus between the parties, or on the ground that the contract of which it forms a part is void or voidable, or has been terminated by frustration, questions of some difficulty arise.

Several solutions are possible: these issues may depend on the *lex fori*, or   **12–084** on the law of the chosen court, or on the applicable law governing the jurisdiction agreement, or on the law which would govern it if it were valid (putative applicable law) or on the applicable law or putative applicable law of the contract of which it forms a part. In *Mackender v. Feldia A.G.*[46] an insurance policy issued in England provided that it was to be governed by Belgian law and that any disputes arising under it were to be subject to the exclusive jurisdiction of the Belgian courts. Notwithstanding the jurisdiction clause, the underwriters sought leave to issue English proceedings and serve them on the insured abroad, claiming a declaration that the contract was void as contrary to public policy (because, allegedly, the jewellery insured under the policy was to be smuggled into Italy) or that it was voidable because the insured had failed to disclose that the jewellery was to be smuggled. The Court of Appeal held that service out of the jurisdiction should not be authorised because the parties had agreed that the dispute should be decided in Belgium. The decision on the foreign jurisdiction clause was that the allegation that the contract was tainted with illegality amounted to no more than that the contract was unenforceable on the ground of public policy: it did not follow that the jurisdiction clause was invalid. Nor did it follow from the allegation that the contract could be avoided for non-disclosure that the contract was void *ab initio*. Whether it was voidable depended on Belgian law

---

[41] Employment Rights Act 1996, s.203(1); see also, *e.g.*, Consumer Credit Act 1974, s.141(1); Carriage of Goods by Sea Act 1971, Sched. 1, Art. III.8; in Australia, Carriage of Goods by Sea Act 1991 (Cth.), s.11(2)(b); Insurance Contracts Act 1984 (Cth.) (applied in *Akai Pty. Ltd. v. People's Insurance Co.* (1997) 188 C.L.R. 418).

[42] Case 25/79 *Sanicentral GmbH v. Collin* [1979] E.C.R. 3423.

[43] See *ante*, paras. 11–312 (insurance), 11–325 (consumer contracts), and *post*, para. 12–095 (employment).

[44] *Mackender v. Feldia A.G.* [1967] 2 Q.B. 590, 602; *The Iran Vojdan* [1984] 2 Lloyd's Rep. 380; *The Frank Pais* [1986] 1 Lloyd's Rep. 529; Kahn-Freund (1977) 26 I.C.L.Q. 825, 827–833; Hartley, in *Current Issues in European and International Law* (ed. White and Smythe, 1990), p. 156.

[45] *The Hollandia* [1983] 1 A.C. 565, *infra*, para. 12–116.

[46] [1967] 2 Q.B. 590 (C.A.), on which see Collins, *Essays*, pp. 268–270. See also *Trendtex Trading Corp. v. Crédit Suisse* [1980] Q.B. 629, 675–676 (C.A.), approved [1982] A.C. 679, 704.

and should be decided by the Belgian court. Lord Denning M.R. and Diplock L.J. accepted that a jurisdiction clause might not be applicable if the issue was whether there ever had been any contract, *e.g.* if there were a plea of *non est factum* or some other issue relating to the existence of a *consensus ad idem*. Diplock L.J. thought that these questions would depend on English law, perhaps as the law which would have governed the contract (apart from the jurisdiction clause) had there been a contract.

12–085   In general the question whether a contract (or any term thereof) has come into existence depends on the law by which the contract would be governed if the contract (or term) were valid.[47] But for the English court to decide the question whether there was a contract between the parties at the jurisdictional stage would be, in effect, in all but the clearest cases, to try the merits. A practical solution would be for the English court to treat the jurisdiction clause as effective if a good arguable case is made out that the contract (and hence the clause) is valid under the law which would apply to it.[48] In deciding these questions, the court would apply English rules of the conflict of laws. But in cases where the contract does not appear to meet this standard of validity, it need not follow that the jurisdiction clause must be taken to be ineffective. It is an established principle of the law of arbitration that an arbitration agreement is severable from the contract there in which it is contained, and may survive the failure of the underlying contract.[49] As has been seen, there is authority for the proposition that a jurisdiction agreement may be regarded as severable from the contract in which it is contained, and that it may remain valid and binding, despite the avoidance of the contract, or the rescission of the voidable contract, or the discharge of the frustrated or broken contract, in which it is contained.[50] An Australian court has applied this principle to a jurisdiction clause.[51] It is submitted that there are good reasons of policy to support such an approach, for the parties, when they nominated a court with jurisdiction to settle their disputes, may well have expected this court to retain jurisdiction if the dispute were to concern the very validity of the contract. Moreover, in a case to which Article 17 of the 1968 Convention applies, the European Court has held that a jurisdiction agreement remains binding even though the action is brought for a declaration that the contract in which it was contained is ineffective.[52]

---

[47] *Post*, Rule 176. In *Oceanic Sun Line Special Shipping Co. Inc. v. Fay* (1988) 65 C.L.R. 197 it was held that the question whether a foreign jurisdiction clause had become part of the contract depended on the *lex fori*: see Briggs [1989] L.M.C.L.Q. 216, 218–221. *Cf. Harvey v. Ventilator-enfabrik Oelde GmbH* [1989] Trading L.R. 138 (C.A.); *The Heidberg* [1994] 2 Lloyd's Rep. 287.

[48] *Cf.* the approach in Ord. 11 cases, *ante*, para. 11–126.

[49] *Harbour Assurance Co. (U.K.) Ltd. v. Kansa General International Insurance Co. Ltd.* [1993] Q.B. 701 (C.A.); see also Arbitration Act 1996, s.7; *Ferris v. Plaister* (1994) 34 N.S.W.L.R. 474 (N.S.W.C.A.).

[50] *Mackender v. Feldia A.G.* [1967] 2 Q.B. 590 (C.A.), where it was indicated that it may be different in a case where the allegation is that the contract was void *ab initio* and was never the source of legal obligations, or when, *e.g.* duress is alleged to vitiate the jurisdiction agreement as well as the remainder of the contract: see *Credit Suisse First Boston (Europe) Ltd. v. Seagate Trading Co. Ltd.* [1999] 1 Lloyd's Rep 784.

[51] *FAI General Insurance Co. Ltd. v. Ocean Marine Mutual Protection and Indemnity Assn.* [1998] Lloyd's Rep I.R. 24; (1997) 41 N.S.W.L.R. 559 (N.S.W.S.C.); see also *Ash v. Corporation of Lloyd's* (1991) 87 D.L.R. (4th) 65, revd. on other grounds (1992) 94 D.L.R. (4th) 378 (Ont.C.A.).

[52] Case C–269/95 *Benincasa v. Dentalkit S.r.l.* [1997] E.C.R. I–3767.

In relation to jurisdiction agreements within the scope of Article 17 of the   **12–086**
Conventions it had been suggested[53] that questions of consensus should be
decided, not by the rules of the conflict of laws of the *lex fori*, but by the
internal law of the chosen forum. But this solution would not give an answer
in the case where the parties exchange conflicting printed contractual conditions, providing for the jurisdiction of different courts.[54] Nor would it be
appropriate to apply the law of the chosen court in all cases where one of the
parties disputes the allegation that it is a party to the choice, *e.g.* because of
alleged mistake, fraud or duress. The only solution capable of supplying a
general answer is that questions of validity should be determined by the law
of the court which is seised of the problem of validity, including its rules of
the conflict of laws.

Article 17 of the 1968 Convention and of the Lugano Convention.   **12–087**
Article 17, to which effect is given by the 1982 Act as amended, provides that
where parties, one or more of whom is domiciled in a Contracting State, have
agreed[55] that a court or the courts of a Contracting State are to have jurisdiction to settle any disputes which have arisen or which may arise in connection
with a particular legal relationship, that court or those courts shall have
exclusive jurisdiction. The European Court has emphasised that the formal
requirements[56] of Article 17 are to be strictly construed[57] because their
purpose is to ensure that parties have indeed consented to a jurisdiction
agreement derogating from the ordinary jurisdictional rules and that their
consent is clearly and precisely demonstrated.[58]

There is a question, not yet resolved by the European Court, as to the time   **12–088**
at which the requirement that one of the parties be domiciled in a Contracting
State must be fulfilled. It is generally accepted that Article 17 applies if at the
time of the conclusion of the jurisdiction agreement one of the parties is
domiciled in a Contracting State, even if by the time proceedings are commenced neither party is so domiciled.[59] But there is more controversy about
the converse situation, where neither is so domiciled at the time of the
conclusion of the contract, but at least one has become so domiciled by the
time proceedings are commenced. It is suggested that Article 17 should apply
to that case also. Article 17 also provides that, where none of the parties is

---

[53] Case 150/80 *Elefanten Schuh GmbH v. Jacqmain* [1980] E.C.R. 1671, at 1697–1699, *per* Slynn
   A.-G. See also Collins pp. 88–89; Hartley (1980) 5 Eur.L.Rev. 73.
[54] *Cf. O.T.M. Ltd. v. Hydranautics* [1981] 2 Lloyd's Rep. 211 (conflicting conditions with
   different choice of law and arbitration clauses).
[55] An assignee from one of the contracting parties clearly falls within Art. 17: Case 71/83 *The
   Tilly Russ* [1984] E.C.R. 2417, [1985] Q.B. 931; Case C–159/97 *Soc. Trasporti Castelletti
   Spedizioni Internazionali SpA v. Hugo Trumpy SpA* [1999] I.L.Pr. 492. But it has been held that
   the relationship between an owner of goods and a sub-bailee is not to be regarded as an
   agreement to a jurisdiction agreement contained in the contract between the owner and the
   bailee for the purposes of Art. 17, for Art. 17 requires the agreement to be contained in a
   contract, and between owner and sub-bailee there is none: *Dresser (U.K.) Ltd. v. Falcongate
   Freight Management Ltd.* [1992] Q.B. 502 (C.A.).
[56] *Post* para. 12–098.
[57] *Cf. I.P. Metal Ltd. v. Ruote O.Z.SpA* [1993] 2 Lloyd's Rep. 60.
[58] Case 26/76 *Salotti v. RÜWA* [1976] E.C.R. 1831; Case 25/76 *Galeries Segoura Sprl v.
   Bonakdarian* [1976] E.C.R. 1851; Case 71/83 *The Tilly Russ* [1984] E.C.R. 2417, [1985] Q.B.
   931; Case 221/84 *Berghoefer GmbH v. ASA S.A.* [1985] E.C.R. 2699; Case 313/85 *Iveco Fiat
   SpA v. Van Hool* [1986] E.C.R. 3337; *Mainschiffahrts-Genossenschaft eG. v. Les Gravières
   Rhénanes SARL* [1997] E.C.R. I–911; [1997] Q.B. 731; Case C–159/97 *Soc. Trasporti Castelletti Spedizioni Interazionali S.A. v. Hugo Trumpy SpA*, [1999] I.L.Pr. 492.
[59] See literature in O'Malley and Layton, pp. 570–571.

domiciled in a Contracting State, the courts of other Contracting States are to have no jurisdiction over the dispute unless the chosen court or courts have declined jurisdiction.

12–089   It is sometimes said that Article 17 only applies in cases with an international character.[60] Parties who are domiciled in one Contracting State may seek to confer jurisdiction on the courts of another State, *e.g.*, two Frenchmen may agree that the English courts shall have exclusive jurisdiction for their disputes. It is likely that Article 17 applies to such a case,[61] although where one Italian party sold shares in a German company to another Italian party, the Italian Corte di cassazione held that a clause providing for jurisdiction of the German courts was ineffective.[62] Where the court has jurisdiction by virtue of an international convention, whose precedence over the 1968 or the Lugano Convention is provided for by Article 57 of the Convention,[63] the question whether proceedings should be stayed or jurisdiction must be exercised is a matter governed by the particular convention and (if permitted by the particular convention) by national law. Accordingly where the English court has jurisdiction under Article 7 of the Arrest Convention,[64] and it is contended that an agreement conferring jurisdiction on the courts of Germany requires the court to stay its proceedings, the applicable principles are those of the common law, not Article 17 of the 1968 Convention.[65]

12–090   Article 17 refers only to the choice of a forum in the Contracting States. Where the parties have agreed to a forum outside the Contracting States, it is suggested that the English court may stay English proceedings against a defendant domiciled in the United Kingdom or in another Contracting State.[66]

---

[60] Jenard, pp. 37–38.

[61] *Ibid.* p. 38.

[62] *Finanziaria commerciale & Co. v. Sago Srl*, 1985, in *Digest* I–17.1.1–B22; contrast the decision to the opposite effect on the same facts in parallel German litigation: OLG Munich, 1985, in *Digest* I–21–B10. In *Re Leyland DAF Ltd. (No. 2)* [1994] 2 B.C.L.C. 106 (C.A.) the action was between two English companies, but the contractual arrangements were beneath the umbrella of a larger contractual relationship involving English and Dutch companies. For discussion of a related question whether Art. 17 applies to the case where two persons domiciled in the same Contracting State choose the courts of that State as the forum for their disputes see Jenard, pp. 37–38, and literature cited in Collins, p. 84.

[63] *Ante*, paras. 11–034 *et seq.*

[64] International Convention for Unification of Certain Rules relating to the Arrest of Sea-going Ships, 1952.

[65] *The Bergen* [1997] 1 Lloyd's Rep. 380; *The Bergen (No. 2)* [1997] 2 Lloyd's Rep. 710; *cf. Milor Srl v. British Airways plc* [1996] Q.B. 702 (C.A.); *Deaville v. Aeroflot Russian International Airlines* [1997] 2 Lloyd's Rep. 67 (Warsaw Convention; see *post*, para. 15–006).

[66] See *Arkwright Mutual Insurance Co. v. Bryanston Insurance Co. Ltd.* [1990] 2 Q.B. 649, 664 (overruled on other grounds: *Re Harrods (Buenos Aires) Ltd.* [1992] Ch. 72 (C.A.)); *The Nile Rhapsody* [1994] 1 Lloyd's Rep. 382 (C.A.). See also Schlosser, para. 176, and literature cited there. But in France it has been held that if the defendant is domiciled in a Contracting State a jurisdiction clause conferring jurisdiction on the courts of a non-Contracting State is ineffective: *Bruno v. Soc. Citibank*, Ct. App. Versailles, 1991, in 1992 *Rev. Crit.* 333, note Gaudemet-Tallon. If the parties have agreed to the exclusive jurisdiction of the English court, and the defendant (but not the claimant) is domiciled outside the Contracting States, the court has approached the matter as if it retained a discretion to exercise jurisdiction: *British Aerospace plc v. Dee Howard Co.* [1993] 1 Lloyd's Rep. 368. This can only be right if the combined effect of Arts. 4 and 17 in such a case is to limit the effect of Art. 17 to jurisdiction as between the Contracting States; but the point was not argued, and has little practical significance since it will be a very rare case in which an English court will not give effect to a valid English jurisdiction clause.

In *Powell Duffryn plc v. Petereit*[67] the European Court held that the concept   **12–091**
of an "agreement conferring jurisdiction" under Article 17 should be regarded
as an independent concept. The question arose in the context of whether the
administrator of a German company could sue an English shareholder for the
return of dividends which, it was alleged, had been wrongly paid. The statutes
of the company provided, in effect, that the German court would have
exclusive jurisdiction in relation to all disputes between shareholders and the
company. The English company argued that the jurisdiction clause in the
statutes did not amount to an "agreement" because the statutes were regulations which the shareholder could not dispute. A comparative survey of the
legal systems of the Contracting States showed that in some legal systems the
relationship between a company and its shareholders was regarded as contractual, and in others it was classified as institutional, regulatory or *sui
generis*. The European Court held that an autonomous interpretation of the
expression "agreement conferring jurisdiction" led to the conclusion that the
ties between the shareholders and a company were comparable to those
between the parties to a contract, and that the statutes of the company must be
regarded as a contract governing relationships between the shareholders *inter
se* and between the shareholders and the company. By becoming and remaining a shareholder the member submits to all the provisions of the statutes and
to company resolutions, irrespective of whether he agrees with them or even
knows of them.

Whether a particular dispute falls within the scope of a jurisdiction agree-   **12–092**
ment is a question of interpretation to be decided by the national court seised
of the question.[68]

The broad effect of Article 17, where clause (1) of Rule 32 applies, is to   **12–093**
confer jurisdiction on the English court if the parties have agreed to give it
jurisdiction notwithstanding that the defendant is domiciled in another Contracting State or, where neither party is domiciled in a Contracting State,
notwithstanding that the courts of another Contracting State may have, under
its law, jurisdiction over the dispute.[69] Where clause (3) of Rule 32 applies, its
effect is to deny jurisdiction to the English court if the parties have chosen to
submit their disputes to the jurisdiction of the courts of another Contracting
State. Article 17[70] also provides that if the jurisdiction agreement has been
concluded for the benefit of only one of the parties, that party retains the right
to sue in any other court which has jurisdiction under the Conventions. In
Anterist v. Crédit Lyonnais[71] the European Court held that this provision
applies only where it is clear from the wording of the jurisdiction clause, or
from evidence therein, or from the surrounding circumstances, that there was
a common intention to confer an advantage on one of the parties only. Clauses
which expressly stated the name of the party for whose benefit they were

---

[67] Case C–214/89 [1992] E.C.R. I–1745; see also *Re Jurisdiction in Internal Company Matters*
[1995] I.L.Pr. 424 (German Fed.Sup.Ct., 1993). *Cf. Copin v. Adamson* (1875) 1 Ex. D. 17; *Re
Schintz* [1926] Ch. 710 (C.A.).
[68] Case C–214/89 *Powell Duffryn plc v. Petereit* [1992] E.C.R. I–1745; Case C–269/95 *Benincasa
v. Dentalkit Srl* [1997] E.C.R. I–3767 (effective even though plaintiff seeks declaration of
nullity of contract).
[69] But *cf. British Aerospace plc v. Dee Howard Co.* [1993] 1 Lloyd's Rep. 368; *ante*, para.
12–090.
[70] 1968 Convention, Art. 17, penult. para.; Lugano Convention, Art. 17(4).
[71] Case 22/85 [1986] E.C.R. 1951; *cf. Ocarina Marine Ltd. v. Macard Stein & Co* [1994] 2
Lloyd's Rep. 524; *Soc Edmond Coignet S.A. v. Banca Commerciale Italiana* [1992] I.L.Pr. 450
(French Cour de cassation, 1990).

concluded and those which, while specifying the courts in which either party might sue the other, gave one of them a wider choice of courts must be regarded as clauses which were agreed for the exclusive benefit of one of the parties. An agreement conferring jurisdiction would not be regarded as having been concluded for the benefit of only one of the parties where all that was established was that the parties had agreed that the courts of the State in which that party was domiciled were to have jurisdiction. So that if a contract between X, domiciled in England, and A, domiciled in France, provides that all claims by X against A shall be brought in France, A may sue X in England under the general rules.[72]

12–094   The European Court has held that the provisions of Article 17 cannot be supplemented or overridden by national law. Thus, as has been seen, the law of the United Kingdom, in common with the law of other countries, prevents employees working in England for foreign employers from contracting out of the jurisdiction of employment tribunals.[73] But the European Court held in *Sanicentral GmbH v. Collin*[74] that a jurisdiction clause in an employment contract providing for the jurisdiction of the German courts had to be given effect in France, notwithstanding French legislation of a type similar to that in the United Kingdom.

12–095   The principle in that decision remains valid, but as regards contracts of employment it has been superseded by special (but not identical) provisions included in the 1968 Convention (as amended by the 1989 Accession Convention) and in the Lugano Convention. Article 17(5) of the Lugano Convention provides that in matters relating to individual contracts of employment an agreement conferring jurisdiction shall have legal force only if it is entered into after the dispute has arisen. The purpose of the provision was to ensure that the protection given to employees by the revised version of Article 5(1)[75] would not be taken away by the effect of jurisdiction clauses.[76] But when the 1989 Accession Convention was under negotiation it was thought that the provision in the Lugano Convention went too far, in that, read literally, it would mean that even the employee could not rely on a jurisdiction agreement entered into before the dispute arose.[77] Accordingly, the equivalent provision in the 1968 Convention, as amended, provides that the jurisdiction agreement is to have legal force only if it is entered into after the dispute has arisen, *or* if the employee invokes it to seise courts other than those which would already have jurisdiction, *i.e.* the courts for the defendant's domicile or those specified in Article 5(1).[78]

12–096   The principle that national laws may not supplement or override the provisions of Article 17 was applied in the context of national laws which

---

[72] On the possible application of this provision in the context of non-exclusive jurisdiction agreements, see *post*. para. 12–107.

[73] *Ante*, para. 12–082.

[74] Case 25/79 [1979] E.C.R. 3423. *Cf.*, on the formal requirements, Case 150/80 *Elefanten Schuh GmbH v. Jacqmain* [1981] E.C.R. 1671.

[75] See paras. 11–253 *et seq. ante*.

[76] Jenard-Möller, p. 77.

[77] de Almeida Cruz, etc., p. 47. It is by no means certain that this interpretation is correct. The European Court has no jurisdiction in relation to the Lugano Convention, but Art. 17(5) of the Lugano Convention could be interpreted as being solely for the benefit of the employee.

[78] The courts for the place where the employee carries out his work, or if he does not carry out his work in any one country, the courts for the place where the business which engaged the employee was or is situated: para. 11–254, *ante*; *cf.* Case C–125/92 *Mulox I.B.C. v. Geels* [1993] E.C.R. I–4075.

purported to override an actual or admitted agreement. A distinct issue arises where one party contends that he did not consent to the jurisdiction agreement. For example, if it is alleged that apparent consent was procured by misrepresentation or duress, or was entered into under mistake, the agreement on jurisdiction may fully comply with the requirements of form, yet if the national court is not entitled to examine the essential validity of the agreement, the fundamental purpose of Article 17 may be frustrated.[79] Whether any such examination should be founded on national law, or derived from an autonomous interpretation of the concept of agreement, is not clear. In *Benincasa v. Dentalkit Srl*[80] the European Court ruled out any role for the *lex causae* in assessing the validity of a jurisdiction agreement, and stated that the formal requirements of Article 17 were sufficient to ensure that there was a consensus; the same view, rejecting the argument that the validity of the clause may be tested by reference to any law other than Article 17 itself, was expressed in *Soc. Trasporti Castelletti Spedizioni Internazionali SpA v. Hugo Trumpy SpA*.[81] But recourse only to Article 17 may be an inadequate remedy against the use of fraud or duress. It is submitted that it should be held to be contrary to the requirements of good faith for one party to seek to invoke a jurisdiction agreement procured by such means,[82] whether formally compliant with Article 17 or not. An alternative approach, which is particularly appropriate when there is an allegation that the jurisdiction agreement was never accepted by one of the parties and so did not constitute an *agreement*, would be to consider that whether there has been a sufficient consensus which could satisfy Article 17 is a predominantly a question of fact for the court seised, and that it is to be answered without specific recourse to rules of national law.[83]

A jurisdiction agreement in an insurance contract or consumer contract is only effective to the extent allowed by Articles 12 and 15. The result is to limit severely the effectiveness of clauses conferring jurisdiction on English courts where the defendant is an insured (or policyholder or beneficiary), or a consumer, domiciled in another Contracting State; conversely, where the insured or consumer is domiciled in the United Kingdom, the effectiveness of a choice of a foreign court would be correspondingly limited.[84] Nor is a jurisdiction agreement effective if it purports to exclude the jurisdiction of a court which has exclusive jurisdiction under Article 16.[85] **12–097**

Formal requirements. A jurisdiction agreement, to be within the scope of Article 17 of the 1968 Convention (as amended) and of the Lugano Convention must be **12–098**

> "(a) in writing or evidenced in writing, or (b) in a form which accords with practices which the parties have established between themselves, or (c) in international trade or commerce, in a form which accords with a usage of which the parties are or ought to have been aware and which

---

[79] Which is to give effect to the intentions of the parties: Case 22/85 *Anterist v. Credit Lyonnais* [1986] E.C.R. 1951.

[80] Case C–269/95 [1997] E.C.R. I–3767. See also the Opinion of Lenz A-G in Case C–288/92 *Custom Made Commercial Ltd. v. Stawa Metallbau GmbH* [1994] E.C.R. I–2913.

[81] Case C–159/97 [1999] I.L.Pr 492.

[82] *Cf.* Case 221/84 *Berghöfer v. ASA S.A.* [1985] E.C.R. 2699.

[83] *Cf. I.P.Metal Ltd. v. Ruote O.Z. SpA* [1993] 2 Lloyd's Rep. 60; affd. [1994] 2 Lloyd's Rep. 560 (C.A.).

[84] See *ante*, paras. 11–312 *et seq.*, 11–325 *et seq.*

[85] See *ante*, para. 11–354.

in such trade or commerce is widely known to, and regularly observed by, parties to contracts of the type involved in the particular trade or commerce concerned."

12–099   The formal requirement in the original version of the 1968 Convention was that the jurisdiction agreement be "in writing or evidenced in writing". But this requirement, especially as it was very strictly interpreted by the European Court,[86] did not fit easily with the needs of international commerce, where the use of printed standard conditions, and communication by telex and fax are common. As a result, the 1978 Accession Convention added that the agreement could be in a form which accorded with practices in international trade or commerce of which the parties were or ought to have been aware.[87] This amendment was elaborated into its present form in the course of the negotiations for the Lugano Convention, and in turn the equivalent provision in the 1968 Convention was brought into line by the 1989 Accession Convention.[88] Thus there are now three ways in which a jurisdiction clause may be effective. First, it may be in writing or evidenced in writing. The effect of the decisions on the unamended 1968 Convention was that this requirement would not normally be fulfilled by the sending of standard printed conditions unless the recipient signed a document which expressly referred to the conditions.[89] In *Iveco Fiat SpA v. Van Hool N.V.*[90] the European Court considered the effect of a jurisdiction clause in a written agreement, which expressly provided that it could be renewed only in writing. The agreement expired, but continued in effect for another twenty years without any written extension. The European Court held that if the applicable law (*i.e.* the law governing the original contract) allowed the contract to be renewed without complying with the express provision that the renewal had to be in writing, then the conditions of Article 17 would be fulfilled: there would be a jurisdiction clause in writing or evidenced in writing. But if the applicable law did require the express provision to be complied with, the formal requirements of Article 17 would be complied with if one of the parties had confirmed in writing either the jurisdiction clause or the contractual terms which had been tacitly renewed (of which the jurisdiction clause formed a part) without any objection from the other party: in those circumstances the written confirmation would evidence the jurisdiction agreement.

---

[86] See Case 24/76 *Salotti v. RÜWA* [1976] E.C.R. 1831; Case 25/76 *Galeries Segoura Sprl v. Bonakdarian* [1976] E.C.R. 1851. Some measure of liberalisation could be seen in Case 71/83 *The Tilly Russ* [1984] E.C.R. 2417, [1985] Q.B. 931 (on which see North [1985] L.M.C.L.Q. 177), decided under the original wording. See also *Credit Suisse Financial Products v. Soc. Gen. d'Entreprises* [1997] I.L.Pr. 165 (C.A.) (signature on document referring to printed conditions containing jurisdiction agreement). The highest courts in the original Contracting States have applied Art. 17 restrictively: see, *e.g. Itier v. Soc. Genovesi*, French Cour de cassation, 1985, Digest I– 17.1.2.–B32; *Lejeune v. Soc. F.I.A.S.*, French Cour de cassation, 1989, in 1990 *Rev. Crit.* 358, note Gaudemet-Tallon, and 1991 *Clunet* 158, note Huet; *Luz v. Bertram*, Italian Corte di cassazione, 1991, in [1992] I.L.Pr. 202. See also *Jeumont-Schneider S.A. v. Gruppo Industriale Ercole Marelli SpA* [1994] I.L.Pr. 12 (Italian Corte di cassazione, 1990); *Re a Purchase of Yarn* [1995] I.L.Pr. 479 (German Fed.Sup.Ct., 1994); *cf. Fulgurit v. Cie d'Assurances PFA* [1996] I.L.Pr. 495 (French Cour de cassation, 1996); *Richard S.A. v. Pavan* [1998] I.L.Pr. 193 (illegible writing) (French Cour de cassation, 1996).

[87] Schlosser, para. 179.

[88] Jenard-Möller, p. 76; de Almeida Cruz, etc., p. 47. The amendments are based on the Vienna Convention on International Contracts for the Sale of Goods, 1980, Art. 9(2).

[89] Cases at n. 86, *supra*.

[90] Case 313/85 [1986] E.C.R. 3337. See also *I.P. Metal Ltd. v. Ruote O.Z. SpA* [1993] 2 Lloyd's Rep. 60, affd. [1994] 2 Lloyd's Rep. 560.

Where the requirement of written evidence is applicable, it is not necessary **12–100** that the party alleged to be bound by the jurisdiction clause be the party who has executed the written document. In *The Tilly Russ*[91] the European Court held that a jurisdiction clause in a bill of lading would be effective if the agreement of both the shipper and the carrier to the conditions had been expressed in writing; or if the jurisdiction clause had been the subject of an oral agreement between the shipper and the carrier, and the carrier had signed the bill of lading; or the bill of lading came within the framework of a continuing business relationship between the parties. As regards bills of lading, which are typical of the instruments to which the new wording of Article 17 was intended to apply, this decision is superseded, but it remains of assistance on the nature of the requirement of writing. That decision, and the subsequent decision in *Berghoefer GmbH v. ASA S.A.*,[92] show that where it is alleged that there is an oral agreement said to be evidenced in writing, it is not necessary that the writing be by the person alleged to be bound by the jurisdiction clause. Even as between the original parties to the agreement, it may be the party relying on Article 17 who alone has signed the document said to evidence the agreement. Thus in the latter case the European Court held that the formal requirements of Article 17 would be satisfied if there were an express oral agreement on jurisdiction between A and X, and if A wrote to X confirming the agreement and X raised no objection within a reasonable time of receipt of the letter. In these circumstances X would be bound by the jurisdiction agreement even though the only written document was signed by A.[93]

It has already been seen that in *Powell Duffryn plc v. Petereit*[94] the **12–101** European Court held that a jurisdiction clause in the statutes of a company was binding on its shareholders. It was also held that the requirement of writing was satisfied by the fact that the statutes were invariably in writing, irrespective of how the shares were acquired, provided that the statutes were lodged at a place which was accessible to shareholders (such as the company's registered office) or were kept in a public register.

The second way in which a jurisdiction clause may be effective is if it is in **12–102** a form which accords with practices which the parties have established between themselves.[95] This third way is, in international trade or commerce, in a form which accords with a usage of which the parties are or ought to be aware; in addition, this usage must be widely known to, and regularly observed by, parties to contracts of the type involved in the particular trade or commerce concerned. The European Court gave general guidance in *Mainschiffahrts-Genossenschaft eG v. Les Gravières Rhénanes SARL*.[96] As a result of that decision, and adapting the ruling in the light of the amended text of

---

[91] Case 71/83 [1984] E.C.R. 2417, [1985] Q.B. 931.
[92] Case 221/84 [1985] E.C.R. 2699. See also *Ocarina Marine Ltd. v. Macard Stein & Co.* [1994] 2 Lloyd's Rep. 524; *Firswood Ltd. v. Petra Bank* [1996] C.L.C. 608 (C.A.).
[93] *Cf.* Case C–106/95 *Mainschiffahrts-Genossenschaft eG v. Les Gravières Rhénanes SARL* [1997] ECR I–911; [1997] Q.B. 731.
[94] Case C–214/89 *Powell Duffryn plc v. Petereit* [1992] E.C.R. I–1745; *ante*, para. 12–091.
[95] *Cf.* Case 25/76 *Galeries Segoura Sprl v. Bonakdarian* [1976] E.C.R. 1851.
[96] Case C–106/95 [1997] E.C.R. I–911; [1997] Q.B. 731: the decision was based on the 1978 version of Art. 17, which merely required the agreement to be "in a form which accords with practices in that trade or commerce of which the parties are or ought to have been aware". The decision was applied in Case C–159/97 *Soc. Trasporti Castelletti Spedizioni Internazionali SpA v. Hugo Trumpy SpA* [1999] I.L.Pr. 492, also dealing with the 1978 version of Article 17. *cf.* Case C–282/92 *Custom Made Commercial Ltd. v. Stawa Metallbau GmbH* [1994] E.C.R. I–2913, 2934, *per* Lenz A.-G.

Article 17, the third category of formal validity will be satisfied if the conduct is consistent with a usage in force in the field of international trade or commerce in which the parties in question operate and the latter are aware or ought to be aware of the usage in question. It will be for the national court to determine whether such a usage exists and whether the parties to the contract were aware of it. A usage will exist in a branch of international trade or commerce in particular where a particular course of conduct is generally followed by contracting parties operating in that branch when they conclude contracts of a particular type. The fact that the contracting parties were aware of that usage will be made out in particular where they had previously had trade or commercial relations between themselves or with other parties operating in the branch of trade or commerce in question or where, in that branch, a particular course of conduct is generally and regularly followed when concluding a certain type of contract.

12–103   A third party beneficiary may take advantage of a jurisdiction clause between the actual parties to the contract and an assignee of a contract may be bound by a jurisdiction clause contained in it. Thus the European Court has held that a beneficiary of an insurance policy may rely, as against the insurer, on a jurisdiction clause in the insurance policy taken out by the insured[97]; and that a third party who has acquired a bill of lading may be bound by (and be entitled to rely upon) a jurisdiction clause in it if, under the relevant national law, the third party has succeeded to the rights and obligations of the shipper.[98]

12–104   The parties may, by agreeing orally the place of performance, achieve an object very similar to that of a choice of court under Article 17 but only if the place agreed on is genuine and is not solely chosen to establish a court as having jurisdiction. In *Zelger v. Salinitri (No. 1)*[99] the plaintiff was a Munich merchant and the defendant was a merchant in Sicily. The plaintiff alleged an express oral agreement that Munich was to be the place of performance for repayment, and the German Federal Supreme Court asked the European Court whether the informal agreement was sufficient to found jurisdiction under Article 5(1)[1] or whether the form in Article 17 was necessary. It was held that an informal agreement was sufficient; the jurisdiction of the court for the place of performance and that of the selected court were two distinct concepts and only agreements selecting a court were subject to the requirements of form prescribed by Article 17. By contrast, in *Mainschiffahrts-Genossenschaft eG v. Les Gravières Rhénanes SARL,*[2] the designated place of performance was described by the national court as being "abstract": it was a place at which contractual performance was impossible in fact, and which had been nominated with the sole aim of specifying a court with jurisdiction over the defendant. The European Court ruled that in such a case Article 5(1) was inapplicable, and that to be effective the clause was required to comply with the formalities of Article 17.

---

[97] Case 201/82 *Gerling v. Treasury Administration* [1983] E.C.R. 2503.

[98] Case 71/83 *The Tilly Russ* [1984] E.C.R. 2417, [1985] Q.B. 931; Case C–159/97 *Soc. Trasporti Castelletti Spedizioni Internazionali SpA v. Hugo Trumpy SpA* [1999] I.L.Pr. 492. *Cf. The Rewia* [1991] 2 Lloyd's Rep. 325, 336 (C.A.): contract contained in bill of lading issued for goods on a chartered ship is normally with the owner.

[99] Case 56/79 [1980] E.C.R. 89.

[1] *Ante,* Rule 28(2).

[2] Case C–106/95 [1997] E.C.R. I–911; *cf. Sarl Noge v. Götz GmbH* [1998] I.L.Pr. 189 (French Cour de Cassation, 1996).

In relation to Luxembourg domiciliaries there is a special provision which **12–105** is more restrictive than Article 17. Article I of the Protocol annexed to the 1968 Convention[3] provides that an agreement conferring jurisdiction, within the meaning of Article 17, shall be valid with respect to a person domiciled in Luxembourg "only if that person has expressly and specifically so agreed." In *Porta-Leasing GmbH v. Prestige International SA*[4] the European Court held that the aim of the Protocol could only be achieved if the clause had been accepted both expressly and specifically, and it therefore must be contained in a provision which is specially and exclusively devoted to jurisdiction, and the clause itself must be signed by the defendant Luxembourgeois.

Contents of the agreement. Although Article 17 speaks of submission to **12–106** "a court or courts of a Contracting State" it also applies if the courts of more than one Contracting State are contemplated by the contract as each having exclusive jurisdiction. In *Meeth v. Glacetal Sarl*[5] a contract provided that if a German buyer were to sue a French seller, the French courts alone would have jurisdiction, and if the French seller were to sue the German buyer the German courts alone would have jurisdiction. The French seller sued the German buyer in Germany, in accordance with the jurisdiction clause, for failure to pay for deliveries. The European Court held that, although Article 17 referred to a court in the singular, it could not be interpreted as intended to exclude the right to agree on two or more courts in a form which was based on widespread commercial practice.

The reasoning of *Meeth v. Glacetal Sarl* would require to be extended for **12–107** it to apply to a case in which two courts were given concurrent jurisdiction (as distinct from two courts each having exclusive jurisdiction over a particular type of action), but as their meaning is plain, there is no good reason why Article 17 should deny their validity and effectiveness according to their terms. Such an agreement may be regarded as "non-exclusive", in that it does not exclude the jurisdiction of all bar the designated court, but it does purport to exclude the jurisdiction of courts other than those designated, and therefore fits within the framework of Article 17. Similar reasoning may be used to support the validity under Article 17 of clauses in the form "the parties submit to the non-exclusive jurisdiction of the English court". Although it is not easy to fit "non-exclusive" jurisdiction clauses into the terms of Article 17, which contemplates that the chosen court will have exclusive jurisdiction, commonsense suggests that they should be given effect. In *Kurz v. Stella Musical GmbH*[6] it was argued that a non-exclusive submission by an English plaintiff and a German defendant to the jurisdiction of the English courts was not

---

[3] There is an identical provision for Luxembourg domiciliaries in Article I of Protocol No. 1 to the Lugano Convention.

[4] Case 784/79 [1980] E.C.R. 1517.

[5] Case 23/78 [1978] E.C.R. 2133.

[6] [1992] Ch. 196. Followed in *Gamlestaden v. Casa de Suecia S.A.* [1994] 1 Lloyd's Rep. 433; *cf. Barrett International Resorts Ltd. v. Martin*, 1994 S.L.T. 434 (non-exclusive jurisdiction of Scottish courts). And see *I.P. Metal Ltd. v. Ruote O.Z. SpA* [1993] 2 Lloyd's Rep. 60, 67, affd. [1994] 2 Lloyd's Rep. 560 (C.A.); *Hantarex SpA v. S.A. Digital Research* [1993] I.L.Pr. 501 (Ct. App. Paris, 1991) (non-exclusive jurisdiction of Paris court held valid); *cf. The Kherson* [1992] 2 Lloyd's Rep. 261, 264 (submission to Netherlands not exclusive jurisdiction). And *cf.* also *Belle Vue Mauricia Ltd. v. Canmaga Trade Corp.* [1991] I.L.Pr. 455 (Ct. App. Paris, 1990) (clause providing for jurisdiction of courts of Vaduz or Paris at plaintiff's option: held valid) with *Soc. Lyle et Scott v. Soc. Lisa Frey*, Ct. App. Paris, 1989, in 1990 *Clunet* 151, note Huet (vendor may designate jurisdiction of any court, in England or elsewhere: held ineffective).

sufficient to confer jurisdiction on the English court over the German defendant, because Article 17 contemplated only exclusive jurisdiction clauses. Hoffmann J. rejected this unmeritorious argument, and held that the non-exclusive choice was valid. The provision in Article 17 that the chosen jurisdiction was to be "exclusive" meant that the choice took effect to the exclusion of jurisdiction which would otherwise be available under the Convention: but the choice could be of more than one jurisdiction, expressly or impliedly. There the choice of English jurisdiction was valid, and it follows from this judgment that the defendant could also have been sued in Germany.[7]

12–108   Where a jurisdiction agreement is within the scope of Article 17, the chosen court will have jurisdiction (both as regards claims and counterclaims).[8] The defendant may waive the benefit of a jurisdiction clause and voluntarily submit to the jurisdiction of another court,[9] and if the defendant voluntarily enters a plea to the merits in the foreign court, he will be taken to have submitted to its jurisdiction.[10] But Article 17 prevails over the special jurisdiction conferred by Article 6 (which is permissive rather than exclusive). Accordingly, if A brings proceedings against B, and B wishes to make a third party claim against C, C is entitled to rely on a jurisdiction agreement between him and B, and (if this is the true construction of the agreement) to insist that any claim against him be brought in the designated court.[11]

12–109   **Intra-United Kingdom cases.**   The modified version of Article 17 in Schedule 4 to the 1982 Act deals with jurisdiction agreements which confer jurisdiction on the courts of a particular part of the United Kingdom. It is designed for cases in which the defendant is domiciled in another part of the United Kingdom. It differs in three important respects from Article 17 of the 1968 Convention, on which it is based. First, there are no formal requirements; secondly, it is subject to any national rules of law limiting the effectiveness of jurisdiction agreements, such as employment[12] and consumer credit legislation; thirdly, the clause confers jurisdiction, as opposed to exclusive jurisdiction, on the chosen court and consequently the chosen court may decline jurisdiction, and a court other than the chosen court may, if it otherwise has jurisdiction, override the clause in accordance with clause (2) of Rule 32.[13]

---

[7] Proposed revisions to the Conventions (*ante*, para. 11–011) will make it clear that non-exclusive jurisdiction clauses will be fully effective under Art. 17.

[8] On set-off and counterclaim see Case 23/78 *Meeth v. Glacetal Sarl* [1978] E.C.R. 2133 (where an unusual clause was involved: see Collins, pp. 89–90); Case 48/84 *Spitzley v. Sommer Exploitation S.A.* [1985] E.C.R. 787.

[9] Case 150/80 *Elefanten Schuh GmbH v. Jacqmain* [1981] E.C.R. 1671.

[10] *The Atlantic Emperor (No. 2)* [1992] 1 Lloyd's Rep. 624, 633 (C.A.); *Toepfer International GmbH v. Molino Boschi Srl* [1996] 1 Lloyd's Rep. 510, 515; and see Art. 18, *ante*, para. 11–346.

[11] *Hough v. P & O Containers Ltd.* [1999] Q.B. 834.

[12] It has been amended to include a special provision for employment contracts identical to that in the amended 1968 Convention, Art. 17(5), *ante*, para. 12–095: S.I. 1993 No. 603.

[13] *Cf. British Steel Corp. v. Allivane International Ltd.*, 1989 S.L.T. (Sh. Ct.) 57 (Scots court may override English jurisdiction clause if no real dispute). This decision was misunderstood in *Jenic Properties Ltd. v. Andy Thornton Architectural Antiques*, 1992 S.L.T. (Sh. Ct.) 5. See also *McCarthy v. Abowall (Trading) Ltd.*, 1993 S.L.T. (Sh. Ct.) 65; *Morrison v. Panic Link Ltd.*, 1993 S.C. 631 (English jurisdiction clause held non-exclusive).

Discretion. Where Article 17 applies, the chosen court has no discretion to **12–110** decline jurisdiction, and other courts have no power to override the jurisdiction agreement. But where it does not apply, the exercise of jurisdiction under clause (1) of Rule 32 is in theory subject to the discretion of the court, although (as will be seen) it is not likely in practice that the court would refuse to exercise it by staying an action or refusing leave to serve out of the jurisdiction. The court has a discretion under clause (2) of Rule 32 to override the choice of a foreign court.

Clause (1) of the Rule. At common law the mere agreement of the parties **12–111** that the High Court would have jurisdiction to determine disputes arising out of a contract between them was insufficient by itself to give the court jurisdiction, because the defendant could not effectively be served with a writ if he were outside England.[14] But if one party nominated an agent resident in England to accept service of process on his behalf, he was deemed to submit to the jurisdiction, and service could be effected on the agent in accordance with the contract.[15] Part 6 of the Civil Procedure Rules[16] provides that where a contract contains a term providing that, in the event of a claim being issued in relation[17] to the contract the claim form may be served by a method specified in the contract, the claim form is deemed to be served on the defendant if it is served by a method specified in the contract. If the place of service specified is within the jurisdiction, permission of the court for issue and service of process is not necessary. But (except where the case comes within Article 17 of the Conventions or of Schedule 4 to the 1982 Act[18]) if the contract provides for service outside the jurisdiction, or contains no provision for service and the defendant is outside the jurisdiction, permission to serve outside the jurisdiction is required. Permission can be obtained under what is now Order 11, r. 1(1)(*d*)(iv), the effect of which is that service outside the jurisdiction is permissible where the claim is brought in respect of a contract which contains a term to the effect that the High Court shall have jurisdiction to hear and determine any action in respect of the contract.

Order 11, r. 1(1)(*d*)(iv) had its origin in 1920,[19] when it was introduced to **12–112** allow service out of the jurisdiction in cases where there was a contractual submission but where no other head of Order 11, r. 1(1) was applicable. The point was formerly of greater importance than it is today, because prior to the regime under the 1982 Act, Rule 27(4)(i)–(iii) did not apply if the defendant was domiciled or ordinarily resident in Scotland, and Rule 27(5) did not apply if the defendant was domiciled or ordinarily resident in Scotland or Northern Ireland. Today cases will be rare in which Order 11, r. 1(1)(*d*)(iv) would be the only available head of jurisdiction, especially since, in the absence of an

---

[14] See *British Wagon Co. v. Gray* [1896] 1 Q.B. 35 (C.A.).
[15] *Tharsis Sulphur Co. v. Société des Métaux* (1889) 58 L.J.Q.B. 435; *Montgomery, Jones & Co. v. Liebenthal & Co.* [1898] 1 Q.B. 487 (C.A.); *Reversionary Interest Society Ltd. v. Locking* [1928] W.N. 227.
[16] CPR 6.15, replacing R.S.C., Ord. 10, r.3.
[17] CPR 6.16, and Ord. 11, r. 1(1)(d)(iv) apply only to actions "in respect of a contract" and there is no jurisdiction to allow service out of the jurisdiction where the parties have agreed to submit in respect of a tort: *The Anna L* [1994] 2 Lloyd's Rep. 379, 382.
[18] In which event service is permitted without permission under Ord. 11, r. 1(2).
[19] Ord. 11, r. 2a, added to reverse the decision in *British Wagon Co. v. Gray, supra.*

express choice of some other law, it will normally be inferred from the jurisdiction clause that English law is the governing law of the contract.[20] Very commonly the choice of English jurisdiction is accompanied by an express choice of English law.[21] Although permission to serve outside the jurisdiction may be required in cases outside the scope of Article 17, where the parties have agreed to an English forum it would require strong grounds for one of the parties to resist the exercise of jurisdiction by the English court.[22]

12–113   Where there is an agreement within the scope of Article 17 of the Conventions or of Schedule 4 to the 1982 Act conferring jurisdiction on the English court, permission to serve process out of the jurisdiction is not necessary, and, in the case of an agreement under Article 17, no question of the exercise of a discretion arises.

12–114   **Clause (2) of the Rule.** "Where plaintiffs sue in England in breach of an agreement to refer disputes to a foreign court, and the defendants apply for a stay, the English court, assuming the claim to be otherwise within its jurisdiction, is not bound to grant a stay but has a discretion whether to do so or not."[23] The court will exercise its discretion to grant a stay unless the claimant shows a strong case, more than that England is the *forum conveniens*, why the English proceedings should not be stayed. This is because the underlying principle is that the court makes people abide by their contracts. There is an even heavier burden on a claimant who applies to serve a foreign defendant out of the jurisdiction than on a claimant who institutes proceedings in England against a defendant present in England.[24] Where the defendant is present in England, or a ship is arrested in England in an action *in rem*, and the action is brought in breach of a jurisdiction agreement, the application by the defendant is to stay proceedings, and not to have them set aside.[25] It used to be said that the parties' submission to the jurisdiction of a foreign court was

---

[20] See *post*, para. 32–092.

[21] As in *The Vikfrost* [1980] 1 Lloyd's Rep. 560 (C.A.); *The Hida Maru* [1981] 2 Lloyd's Rep. 510 (C.A.); *The T.S. Havprins* [1983] 2 Lloyd's Rep. 356; *The Volvox Hollandia* [1988] 2 Lloyd's Rep. 361 (C.A.).

[22] *The Chaparral* [1968] 2 Lloyd's Rep. 158, 163–164 (C.A.); *Attock Cement Co. Ltd. v. Romanian Bank for Foreign Trade* [1989] 1 W.L.R. 1147, 1161 (C.A.); *Gulf Bank K.S.C. v. Mitsubishi Heavy Industries Ltd.* [1994] 1 Lloyd's Rep. 323; *Egon Oldendorff v. Libera Corp.* [1995] 2 Lloyd's Rep. 64; *cf. Kutchera v. Buckingham International Holdings Ltd.* [1988] I.R. 61. On the power of the court to restrain foreign proceedings brought in breach of a jurisdiction agreement see clause (4) of the Rule, *post*, para. 12–123.

[23] *The El Amria* [1981] 2 Lloyd's Rep. 119, 123 (C.A.) approving *The Eleftheria* [1970] P. 94, 99; applied in *The Pioneer Container* [1994] 2 A.C. 324, 347 (P.C.).

[24] *Evans Marshall & Co. Ltd. v. Bertola S.A.* [1973] 1 W.L.R. 349, 362. For other cases of service under Ord. 11 involving foreign jurisdiction clauses see *Hoerter v. Hanover, etc. Works* (1893) 10 T.L.R. 103 (C.A.); *Re Schintz* [1926] Ch. 710 (C.A.); *Ellinger v. Guinness Mahon & Co.* [1939] 4 All E.R. 16; *Mackender v. Feldia* [1967] 2 Q.B. 590 (C.A.); *Y.T.C. Universal Ltd. v. Trans Europa S.A.* [1973] 1 Lloyd's Rep. 480n. (C.A.); *Standard Steamship Owners' Protection and Indemnity Assn. (Bermuda) Ltd. v. Gann* [1992] 2 Lloyd's Rep. 528; *Citi-March Ltd. v. Neptune Orient Lines* [1996] 1 W.L.R. 1367; *Northern Sales Co. Ltd. v. Government Trading Corp. of Iran* (1991) 81 D.L.R. (4th) 316 (B.C.C.A.); *Ash v. Corporation of Lloyd's* (1992) 94 D.L.R. (4th) 378 (Ont. C.A.); *Contractors Ltd. v. M.T.E. Control Gear Ltd.* [1964] S.A.S.R. 47; *Lewis Construction Co. Ltd. v. M. Tichauer S.A.* [1966] V.R. 341.

[25] *The Fehmarn* [1958] 1 W.L.R. 159 (C.A.); *The Eleftheria* [1970] P. 94; *The Pia Vesta* [1984] 1 Lloyd's Rep. 169.

tantamount to a submission to arbitration within the meaning of the Arbitration Acts,[26] but is now settled that the court's jurisdiction to grant a stay is inherent rather than statutory.[27]

Clause (2) of Rule 32 is subject to the effect of Article 17 of the Conventions under clause (3). But Article 17 of Schedule 4 to the 1982 Act, which deals with jurisdiction agreements in intra-United Kingdom cases, does not give conclusive effect to an exclusive jurisdiction clause and therefore falls within the general principle of clause (2). **12–115**

English law as the *lex fori* determines the effect of the jurisdiction clause, and, in particular, the circumstances in which the court has a discretion to override it.[28] A stay will be refused if the choice of jurisdiction is contrary to a statutory rule against ousting the jurisdiction of the court[29] or against referring a dispute to the courts and law of a foreign country. Thus in *The Hollandia*[30] it was held that the effect of the Hague-Visby Rules scheduled to the Carriage of Goods by Sea Act 1971 was to prohibit the submission of a dispute to the courts of a foreign country which would give effect to a limitation of the liability of the carrier under the original Hague Rules. **12–116**

In exercising its discretion whether or not to grant a stay, the court considers all the circumstances of the case, and the following formulation[31] of the particular factors to be taken into account has been much relied upon: (1) in which country the evidence is available, and the effect of that on the relative convenience and expense of a trial in England or abroad; (2) whether the contract is governed by the law of the foreign country in question, and if so, whether it differs from English law in any material respect; (3) with what country either party is connected, and how closely; (4) whether the defendants genuinely desire trial in a foreign country, or are only seeking procedural advantages; (5) whether the plaintiffs would be prejudiced by having to sue in the foreign court because they would be deprived of security for their claim,[32] or be unable to enforce the judgment in their favour, or be faced with a time-bar not applicable in England, or for political, racial, religious or other reasons be unlikely to get a fair trial.[33] The fact that a stay will result in concurrent **12–117**

---

[26] See cases cited by Kahn-Freund (1977) 26 I.C.L.Q. 825, 833.

[27] *Racehorse Betting Control Board v. Secretary for Air* [1944] Ch. 114, 126 (C.A.); *The Fehmarn* [1958] 1 W.L.R. 159, 163 (C.A.); Mustill & Boyd, *Commercial Arbitration*, 2nd ed. 1989, pp. 461–462. For the duty of an English court to stay proceedings commenced in breach of an agreement to arbitrate, see Arbitration Act 1996, s.9; and see *post*, para. 16–037.

[28] See Kahn-Freund (1977) 26 I.C.L.Q. 825, 833–836.

[29] See, *e.g.* Consumer Credit Act 1974, s.141(1); Employment Rights Act 1996, s.203(1).

[30] [1983] 1 A.C. 565, distinguished in *The Benarty (No. 2)* [1985] Q.B. 325 (C.A.). The actual decision would now be different under Art. 17, because the Conventions which enact the Hague and Hague-Visby Rules are not within Art. 57, *ante*, para. 11–034. See also *Messageries Maritimes v. Wilson* (1954) 94 C.L.R. 577; *Kim Meller Imports Pty. Ltd. v. Eurolevant SpA* (1986) 7 N.S.W.L.R. 269; *Akai Pty. Ltd. v. People's Insurance Co. Ltd.* (1997) 188 C.L.R. 418; *Chowdhury v. Mitsui O.S.K. Lines Ltd.* [1970] 2 Lloyd's Rep. 272 (Pakistan).

[31] *The Eleftheria* [1970] P. 94, 100, *per* Brandon J., approved in the *The El Amria* [1981] 2 Lloyd's Rep. 119, 123–124, *per* Brandon L.J. (C.A.); *The Sennar (No. 2)* [1985] 1 W.L.R. 490, 500, *per* Lord Brandon (H.L.).

[32] Where the claimant would be entitled to security in England, but not in the foreign court, the stay may be made conditional on the claimant retaining the security: *The Eleftheria, supra*; Civil Jurisdiction and Judgments Act 1982, s.26. *Cf. The Sylt* [1991] 1 Lloyd's Rep. 240; *ante*, para. 8–031.

[33] On the effect of delay in the chosen forum see *Evans Marshall & Co. Ltd. v. Bertola* [1973] 1 W.L.R. 349 (C.A.); *The Vishva Prabha* [1979] 2 Lloyd's Rep. 286; *The El Amria, supra*; *The Nile Rhapsody* [1992] 2 Lloyd's Rep. 399; affd. [1994] 1 Lloyd's Rep. 382 (C.A.).

proceedings with different parties, but similar issues, may militate against a stay.[34]

12–118   *Effect of time bar.* Where a claimant sues in England in breach of a foreign jurisdiction clause it frequently happens that, by the time the defendant's application for a stay comes before the court, any action in the chosen forum is time-barred. If the existence of a time bar is taken into account in favour of the claimant in refusing a stay, it would deprive the defendant of an accrued defence in the chosen forum; if it is taken into account in favour of the defendant, the claimant would be left with no remedy at all.

12–119   In *Spiliada Maritime Corp. v. Cansulex Ltd.*[35] Lord Goff of Chieveley, approving the approach of Sheen J. in *The Blue Wave*,[36] said that if the plaintiff acted reasonably in commencing proceedings in England (and did not act unreasonably in failing to commence proceedings in the other forum, *e.g.* by issuing a protective writ) it would not be just to deprive the plaintiff of the benefit of having started proceedings in England within the applicable limitation period.[37] The court may make it a condition of the stay, or of the exercise of discretion against giving leave to serve out of the jurisdiction, that the defendant should waive the time bar in the foreign jurisdiction.

12–120   But, as in the *forum non conveniens* cases, the court will not take into account in favour of a claimant who seeks to avoid a foreign jurisdiction clause that the procedure in the foreign court is less favourable or less efficient than English procedure. Where the foreign court follows the civil law system and adopts the inquisitorial method without full discovery or cross-examination, it is not appropriate (otherwise than in wholly exceptional cases) for the English court to make a general comparison between the merits and demerits of the two systems.[38] Where the parties have agreed to submit their dispute to the jurisdiction of a court whose procedure does not allow full discovery, the parties have chosen that procedure, and the fact that a procedure which is generally applicable in the chosen jurisdiction is not helpful to a claimant is not a reason for refusing to give effect to the contractual choice of forum.[39]

---

[34] *The El Amria, supra*; *Evans Marshall & Co. Ltd. v. Bertola, supra*; *Citi-March Ltd. v. Neptune Orient Lines Ltd.* [1996] 1 W.L.R. 1367; *The M.C. Pearl* [1997] 1 Lloyd's Rep. 566; *Soc. Nat. Ind. Aérospatiale v. Lee Kui Jak* [1987] A.C. 871 (P.C.) (a case on anti-suit injunctions).

[35] [1987] A.C. 460, 483–484; see also *The Pioneer Container* [1994] 2 A.C. 324, 347–349 (P.C.).

[36] [1982] 1 Lloyd's Rep. 151; see *The Pioneer Container* [1994] 2 A.C. 324 (P.C.); *Citi-March Ltd. v. Neptune Orient Lines* [1996] 1 W.L.R. 1367; *The M C Pearl* [1997] 1 Lloyd's Rep. 566; *The Bergen (No. 2)* [1997] 2 Lloyd's Rep. 710, 719; *Baghlaf al Safer Factory Co. Br for Industry v. Pakistan National Shipping Corp.* [1998] 2 Lloyd's Rep. 229 (C.A.); *BMG Trading Ltd. v. McKay* [1998] I.L.Pr. 691, (C.A.). See also *The Adolf Warski* [1976] 1 Lloyd's Rep. 107, 113–114, affd. on different grounds [1976] 2 Lloyd's Rep. 241 (C.A.); *cf. The Vishva Prabha* [1979] 2 Lloyd's Rep. 286; *The Sennar (No. 2)* [1984] 2 Lloyd's Rep. 142, 155, 160 (C.A.), affd. [1985] 1 W.L.R. 490, 501 (H.L.); *The Indian Fortune* [1985] 1 Lloyd's Rep. 344. But see *The Media* (1931) 41 Ll.L.R. 80.

[37] The effect of the Foreign Limitation Periods Act 1984 may, of course, make the law of the chosen forum applicable (*ante*, para. 7–043), but if the claimant has commenced proceedings only in England, he may still be faced with a time-bar in the foreign court. Where Art. 17 applies, the effect of suing in the wrong forum may be that the claimant is faced with a time-bar in the chosen forum, with the result that the remedy is lost irrevocably: *The Rewia* [1991] 2 Lloyd's Rep. 325, 335 (C.A.).

[38] *The El Amria* [1981] 2 Lloyd's Rep. 119, 127 (C.A.), approved in *Amin Rasheed Shipping Corp. v. Kuwait Insurance Co.* [1984] A.C. 50 (an Ord. 11 case).

[39] *Trendtex Trading Corp. v. Crédit Suisse* [1980] 3 All E.R. 721, 736–737, affd. [1982] A.C. 679.

Clause (3) of the Rule. The effect of the 1968 Convention and the Lugano Convention. The Convention rules relating to jurisdiction clauses have been discussed above in detail.[40] Where they apply the court will not have a discretion to override the jurisdiction clause, so that it will normally have to set aside or stay its proceedings where a claimant sues in England in breach of a jurisdiction clause which conforms with the requirements of the Conventions. It should be noted that the English court may make an order for interim relief notwithstanding that the substance of the matter has been referred to the courts of another Contracting State.[41] The English court may disregard a foreign jurisdiction clause if it does not comply with the relevant Convention or is otherwise ineffective, but it may not do so, and must decline jurisdiction, if the chosen foreign court has first been seised of the proceedings between the parties; if the jurisdiction of the court first seised is being contested by the defendant, then the English court may stay its proceedings pending the outcome of the contest over jurisdiction in the foreign court.[42]

12–121

It may happen that the English court is the chosen court, but one of the parties first commences proceedings in another Contracting State in alleged breach of the jurisdiction clause. Must the English court stay its proceedings until the court first seised has ruled on the applicability of the English jurisdiction clause? It has been held that if the English court has exclusive jurisdiction under Article 17 pursuant to a jurisdiction agreement, then the proceedings will not be stayed under Article 21 even if a court in another Contracting State has been seised first.[43] The European Court has left open the question whether a court which has exclusive jurisdiction under the 1968 Convention ("in particular under Article 16") is entitled to allow its proceedings to continue even if a court in another Contracting State has been seised first.[44] But it also indicated that a possible basis for the exclusion of proceedings covered by Article 16 from the application of Article 21 was that the court second seised may refuse to recognise a judgment given in a case in which jurisdiction is taken in contravention of Article 16.[45] As a judgment given in a case where jurisdiction has been taken notwithstanding that the parties have conferred jurisdiction on the courts of another Contracting State cannot be refused recognition on that ground alone, it is unlikely that the European Court intended to authorise a court to give jurisdiction under Article 17 priority over the provisions for preventing a *lis alibi pendens* in Article 21.

12–122

Clause (4) of the Rule. The general principles upon which an English court may order a party who is subject to its personal jurisdiction not to institute, or to discontinue, proceedings in a foreign court have been examined above.[46]

12–123

---

[40] *Ante*, paras. 12–087 *et seq.*
[41] 1968 Convention, Art. 24; Lugano Convention, Art. 24; 1982 Act, s.25(1).
[42] Art. 21, *ante*, paras. 12–039 *et seq.*
[43] *Kloeckner & Co. A.G. v. Gatoil Overseas Inc.* [1990] 1 Lloyd's Rep. 177; *Denby v. Hellenic Mediterranean Lines Co. Ltd.* [1994] 1 Lloyd's Rep. 320; *Continental Bank N.A. v. Aeakos Compania Naviera S.A.* [1994] 1 W.L.R. 588 (C.A.); *Bankers Trust International plc v. RCS Editori SpA* [1996] C.L.C. 899; *Bank of Scotland v. Banque Nationale de Paris*, 1996 S.L.T. 103. On whether an English court may order an injunction to restrain the proceedings in the court seised first, see clause (4) of the Rule, *post*, para. 12–127.
[44] Case C–351/89 *Overseas Union Insurance Co. v. New Hampshire Insurance Co.* [1991] E.C.R. I–3317, [1992] Q.B. 434 (where the reference was to exclusive jurisdiction under Art. 16).
[45] See Art. 28(1).
[46] Clause (5) of Rule 31, *ante*, para. 12–057.

But where the basis for the exercise of the court's discretion is that the defendant has bound himself by contract not to bring the proceedings which he threatens to bring, or has brought, in the foreign court, the principles which guide the exercise of the discretion of the court are distinct from those which were examined under clause (5) of Rule 31. In summary, (i) the English court must have personal jurisdiction over the defendant, but this will almost always be available under Article 17 of the Conventions, through personal presence, or under Order 11, rule 1(1)(*d*)(iv); (ii) there is no need to show that there is oppression or vexation, nor that England is the natural forum for the claim; (iii) there is no obligation upon the applicant to seek relief from the foreign court first; and (iv) it has been held that the power may be exercised even if the proceedings are in another Contracting State to the 1968 or Lugano Conventions.

12–124   The requirement that the party to be restrained be subject to the personal jurisdiction of the court is unaffected by whether the claim is based on a contractual right not to be sued in the foreign court. Where the claim is within the scope of the 1968 Convention or the Lugano Convention, the jurisdiction of the English court will be established in accordance with Rule 28.[47] It has been seen above that the English courts have held that where Article 17 of the Convention confers jurisdiction on the English courts, the fact that the courts of another Contracting State were seised first with the proceedings on the same cause of action is no obstacle to the exercise of jurisdiction.[48] Where there is an agreement conferring jurisdiction on the English court but which is not within the Convention,[49] permission to serve process out of the jurisdiction may be sought under Order 11, rule (1)(1)(*d*)(iv).[50] If the claim for an injunction is founded upon a legal right not to be sued in the foreign court, but the basis of the right is something other than a contractual right to be sued in the English courts,[51] permission to serve out, if this is required, will have to sought upon another ground.

12–125   The manner in which the court will exercise its discretion to grant the injunction where the claimant in England has a legal right not to be sued in the foreign court reflects the legal character of the right which is sought to be enforced. Dealing with the substance of the discretion, Lord Diplock in *British Airways Board v. Laker Airways Ltd.*[52] spoke of cases in which the claimant had a legal right not to be sued in the foreign court[53] which may be enforced by an injunction. Those cases in which the courts have refined the criteria of

---

[47] *Ante*, para. 11R–223.
[48] *Ante*, para. 12–043. If the proceedings in the English courts are for only an anti-suit injunction it is arguable that the cause of action is not the same as in a claim for substantive relief in the foreign court. But the claim for an injunction may still be considered to be inconsistent with the overall scheme of the Convention: see *ante*, para. 12–066.
[49] Where neither party is domiciled in a Contracting State.
[50] *Ante*, para. 11–112.
[51] Such as a contractual right to be sued in the courts of a third country, or to submit differences to arbitration, or to bring no proceedings in respect of a dispute which has been settled. For an injunction to enforce a contractual right to have the dispute governed by English law, see *Shell International Petroleum Co. Ltd. v. Coral Oil Co. Ltd.* [1999] 1 Lloyd's Rep. 72.
[52] [1985] A.C. 58, 81.
[53] See also *Pena Copper Mines v. Rio Tinto Co.* (1912) 105 L.T. 846; *Ellerman Lines Ltd. v. Read* [1928] 2 K.B. 144 (C.A.); *Tracomin S.A. v. Sudan Oil Seeds Co. Ltd. (No. 2)* [1983] 1 W.L.R. 1026 (C.A.); *South Carolina Insurance Co. v. Assurantie Maatschappij "de Zeven Provincien" N.V.* [1987] A.C. 24, 40; *Schiffahrtsgesellschaft Detlev von Appen GmbH v. Voest Alpine Intertrading GmbH* [1997] 2 Lloyd's Rep. 279, 286 (C.A.); *Charterers Mutual Assurance Assn. Ltd. v. British & Foreign* [1998] I.L.Pr. 838.

vexation and oppression as the basis for an injunction,[54] and in which it has been stated that an English court should only act if it would be the natural forum for the trial of the action,[55] or that an equivalent interest in the forum must be shown to exist in order that the principles of comity are respected,[56] do not extend the requirement to cases where the court is asked to enforce a legal right not to be sued.[57]

If the applicant demonstrates that the plaintiff in the foreign proceedings is   **12–126** acting in breach of the applicant's legal right not to be sued, the court will be likely to order an injunction: it has been said that there must be shown to be a good reason why in such a case an injunction should not be ordered.[58] It will be very rare for an action for damages to be an appropriate response to a defendant who has instituted proceedings in a foreign court in breach of a contractual promise not to do so.[59] If the application is promptly brought and the injunction granted, it may mean that the foreign court has no need to investigate the propriety of proceedings brought before it[60]; there is no reason to suppose that application must first be made to the foreign court.[61]

If the foreign proceedings are brought in a Contracting State to the 1968 or   **12–127** Lugano Conventions the question arises whether it is consistent with the overall scheme of the Conventions for an English court to grant an injunction by way of enforcement of a jurisdiction agreement, but which relates to proceedings pending in the courts of another Contracting State. It has been seen that European Court has held that a court in one Contracting State does not have the right to make its own assessment of the jurisdiction of the court of another Contracting State over a pending action.[62] It has been held that the English court, even if seised after proceedings have been commenced in another Contracting State, may order an injunction by way of enforcement of an English jurisdiction or arbitration agreement.[63] The Court of Appeal held

---

[54] *Ante*, para. 12–063.
[55] *Soc. Nat. Ind. Aérospatiale v. Lee Kui Jak* [1987] A.C. 871 (P.C.).
[56] *Airbus Industrie G.I.E. v. Patel* [1999] 1 A.C. 119.
[57] *Ibid.* p. 138.
[58] *Standard Chartered Bank v. Pakistan National Shipping Corp.* [1995] 2 Lloyd's Rep. 365; *Akai Pty. Ltd. v. Peoples' Insurance Co. Ltd.* [1998] 1 Lloyd's Rep. 90.
[59] *Castanho v. Brown & Root (U.K.) Ltd.* [1980] 1 W.L.R. 833, 865–866 (C.A.), affd. [1981] A.C. 557; *Continental Bank N.A. v. Aeakos Compania Naviera S.A.* [1994] 1 W.L.R. 588, 598 (C.A.). On the availability and effectiveness of a claim for damages for breach of a jurisdiction or arbitration agreement see *The Lisboa* [1980] 2 Lloyd's Rep. 546 (C.A.); *Mantovani v. Carapelli S.p.A.* [1980] 1 Lloyd's Rep. 375 (C.A.); *Tracomin S.A. v. Sudan Oil Seeds Co. Ltd. (No. 2)* [1983] 1 W.L.R. 1026 (C.A.); *The Eastern Trader* [1996] 2 Lloyd's Rep. 585; *The Angelic Grace* [1995] 1 Lloyd's Rep. 87 (C.A.); *Compagnie des Messageries Maritimes v. Wilson* (1954) 94 C.L.R. 577, 587; *Anderson v. G.H. Mitchell & Sons Ltd.* (1941) 65 C.L.R. 543, 548; *Adelaide Steamship Industries Pty. Ltd. v. Commonwealth* (1974) 8 S.A.S.R. 425, 437.
[60] *The Angelic Grace* [1994] 1 Lloyd's Rep. 168, affd. [1995] 1 Lloyd's Rep. 87 (C.A.).
[61] *Cf. ante,* para. 12–069. But for a more cautious view, see *Credit Suisse First Boston (Europe) Ltd. v. MLC (Bermuda) Ltd.* [1999] 1 Lloyd's Rep. 767.
[62] See Case 351/89 *Overseas Union Insurance Ltd. v. New Hampshire Insurance Co.* [1991] E.C.R. I–3317; [1992] Q.B. 434; *ante,* para. 12–066.
[63] *Continental Bank N.A. v. Compania Aeakos Naviera S.A.* [1994] 1 W.L.R. 588 (C.A.); *Bankers Trust plc v. RCS Editori SpA* [1996] C.L.C. 899; *cf.* (for a more cautious view) *Phillip Alexander Securities and Futures Ltd. v. Bamberger* [1997] I.L.Pr. 73, affd. *ibid.* 104 (C.A.); *Toepfer International GmbH v. Soc. Cargill France* [1998] 1 Lloyd's Rep. 379, 387–388 (C.A.).

that Article 17 had mandatory effect, and even if proceedings had been commenced first in another Contracting State, Article 17 took priority over Articles 21 and 22, and the English court was not bound to decline jurisdiction or consider whether to grant a stay under the latter provisions; the principle of the autonomy of the parties, enshrined in Article 17, could not countenance the conclusion that a party would be able to override an exclusive jurisdiction agreement by pre-emptively suing in the courts of another Contracting State. The commercial utility of such summary and effective enforcement of agreements is obvious; nor will there be any risk of irreconcilable judgments if the relief is granted and the order obeyed. On the footing that the English court is simply acting to enforce the contractual agreement, there may be no direct conflict with the ruling in *Overseas Union Insurance*.[64] If it is not the jurisdiction of the foreign court, but the breach of agreement by the plaintiff in the foreign proceedings in seeking to invoke it, which justifies the relief, the granting of an injunction does not contradict the ruling of the European Court, which is concerned only to prevent one court reviewing another court's jurisdiction. But if the proceedings are threatened but have not been instituted, with the result that the English court is the only court seised when the application is made, there can be no objection to an injunction.

12–128   **Injunctions to restrain foreign proceedings in breach of arbitration agreement.** The English court has, since at least 1911,[65] exercised a jurisdiction *in personam*[66] to restrain by injunction foreign proceedings brought in breach of an agreement to refer disputes to arbitration. The injunction is granted on the theory that without it the claimant will be deprived of its contractual rights (the right to have disputes settled by arbitration) in a situation in which damages are manifestly an inadequate remedy.[67] In 1994, in *The Angelic Grace*,[68] Millett L.J. (with whom Neill L.J. expressly agreed) said that the time had come to lay aside the ritual incantation that this was a jurisdiction which should be exercised only sparingly and with great caution, and that there was no reason for diffidence in granting an injunction to restrain foreign proceedings, on the clear and simple ground that the defendant had promised not to bring them.

12–129   In that case an injunction was granted to restrain proceedings in Italy. Although Millett L.J. referred to the fact that Italy was a party to the 1968 Convention, no point appears to have been taken that it might be inconsistent with the 1968 Convention for the English court effectively to pre-empt the

---

[64] *Supra*, n. 62.

[65] *Pena Copper Mines Ltd. v. Rio Tinto Co. Ltd.* (1911) 105 L.T. 846 (C.A.). See also *The Maria Gorthon* [1976] 2 Lloyd's Rep. 720; *Marazura Navegacion S.A. v. Oceanus Mutual Underwriting Assn.* [1977] 1 Lloyd's Rep. 283; *Tracomin S.A. v. Sudan Oil Seeds Co. Ltd. (No.2)* [1983] 1. W.L.R. 1026 (C.A.); *The Golden Anne* [1984] 2 Lloyd's Rep. 489; *Marc Rich & Co. A.G. v. Soc. Italiana Impianti P.A. (No. 2)* [1992] 1 Lloyd's Rep. 624 (C.A.); *Sokana Industries Inc. v. Freyre & Co. Inc.* [1994] 2 Lloyd's Rep. 57; and cases cited in the following notes. See also *Canadian Home Insurance v. Cooper* (1986) 29 D.L.R. (4th) 419 (N.S.).

[66] Which can be exercised, even if the defendant is not in England, where among other cases, the arbitration agreement is governed by English law.

[67] *The Angelic Grace* [1995] 1 Lloyd's Rep. 87, 96, *per* Millett L.J.

[68] *Supra*. See also *Schiffahrtsgesellschaft Detlev von Appen v. Voest Alpine Intertrading GmbH* [1997] 2 Lloyd's Rep. 279, 285 (C.A.).

decision by the Italian court as to whether the latter had jurisdiction. But the point has arisen subsequently. In *Toepfer International GmbH v. Molino Boschi Srl*[69] an injunction restraining Italian proceedings was refused on the ground of the plaintiff's delay in seeking an injunction. It had also been argued that because the Italian proceedings had been commenced first, the English court had the duty (under Article 21 of the 1968 Convention) or the power (under Article 22) to decline jurisdiction or stay its own proceedings.[70] Mance J., *obiter*, expressed the view that the English proceedings were within the scope of the 1968 Convention; the exclusion of arbitration in Article 1(4)[71] did not extend to a declaration that the defendant was bound to arbitrate a particular dispute and to an injunction in support, because the declaration was not integral to the arbitration process. But the court would not have the obligation to decline jurisdiction under Article 21 because the claim for injunctive relief did not have the same object or cause of action as the claim in Italy The actions were related for the purposes of Article 22,[72] so that the English court had a discretion to stay its proceedings.

In *Toepfer International GmbH v. Cargill France S.A.*[73] Colman J. granted   **12–130**
an injunction to restrain French proceedings brought in breach of an arbitration agreement. His view was that, because the subject matter of the proceedings was the issue whether the dispute should be determined by the French court or by arbitration in England, the dispute was excluded from the operation of the 1968 Convention by Article 1(4); but he agreed with Mance J. that Article 21 was in any event inapplicable. On appeal the defendants (plaintiffs in the French proceedings) conceded that Article 21 did not apply as between the claims for relief in England and the underlying claim in France, but contended that it applied because the plaintiff in the English proceedings had first seised the French court of an objection to its jurisdiction. The Court of Appeal referred to the European Court the questions (a) whether the declaration that the French proceedings were in breach of the arbitration agreement and the injunction sought in support were excluded from the operation of the 1968 Convention by Article 1(4); and (b) whether the English proceedings constituted the same cause of action as the challenge to the jurisdiction of the French court for the purposes of Article 21.[74] The Court of Appeal expressed doubt as to whether a dispute as to jurisdiction could be a "cause of action" at all for the purposes of Article 21, but added that it seemed to be in fundamental conflict with the scheme of the 1968 Convention that the defendant in the French proceedings should, without entering a challenge to jurisdiction in that court, be able to commence proceedings in the English court in order to challenge the jurisdiction of the court first seised.

The case was settled, and the reference was withdrawn. It is submitted,   **12–131**
however, that Colman J. was correct in deciding that the English proceedings were outside the scope of the 1968 Convention, and that, in any event, Article

---

[69] [1996] 1 Lloyd's Rep. 510.
[70] *Ante*, Rule 31(4).
[71] *Ante*, para. 11–023.
[72] Contrast *Charterers Mutual Assurance Assn Ltd. v. British & Foreign* [1998] I.L.Pr. 838, 855 (proceedings not excluded by Art. 1(4), but Art. 22 not applicable).
[73] [1997] 2 Lloyd's Rep. 98. See also *Phillip Alexander Securities and Futures Ltd. v. Bamberger* [1997] I.L.Pr. 73, at 92 and 101, *per* Waller J., affd. on other grounds *ibid.* 104 (C.A.).
[74] [1998] 1 Lloyd's Rep. 379 (C.A.).

21 is inapplicable irrespective of whether the defendant in the foreign proceedings has contested the jurisdiction of the foreign court.[75]

ILLUSTRATIONS

12–132   1. A, an English company, and X, an American company, enter into a contract which provides that the parties submit to the jurisdiction of the High Court and that N of London should be the agent of X to accept service of process on its behalf. A brings an action against X for breach of contract. Process is served upon N. The court has jurisdiction.[76]

2. A, a Japanese company, and X, a U.S. company, enter into a contract whereby A's tug will tow X's oil rig from the United States to Italy. The contract provides that "any dispute arising must be treated before the London Court of Justice," but does not make any provision for service. The tug and tow are forced to take refuge in Tampa, Florida, each alleging that this was the other's fault. X brings an action against A in Florida, and A brings an action against X in England. The court may assume jurisdiction and give permission to serve process on X in the United States.[77]

3. The facts are as in Illustration 2, except that A is a German company. The court has jurisdiction and permission to serve out of the jurisdiction is not required.[78]

4. A & Co. are the holders of bills of lading in respect of plywood shipped from Roumania to England on board a Turkish ship. The bills of lading provide that disputes shall be decided in Turkey in accordance with Turkish law. A & Co. bring an action *in rem* against the ship claiming damages for breach of contract. Most of the evidence is available in England; but Turkish law differs materially from English law in the relevant respects. The factors tending to rebut and reinforce the prima facie case for a stay are nicely balanced. The court stays the action.[79]

5. By a contract governed by Israeli law between A, an English company, and X, an Israeli company with a branch in London. A is appointed to be the sole distributor in the United Kingdom of wine produced by X. The contract contains a clause submitting all disputes to the exclusive jurisdiction of the courts of Tel Aviv. X purports to terminate the contract on the ground that A has not used proper efforts to market the wine in the United Kingdom, and appoints Y to be its distributor in place of A. A commences proceedings in England against X for breach of contract and conspiracy and against Y for unlawful interference with contract and conspiracy. The substance of the case is about the proper marketing of wine in the United Kingdom; all the essential witnesses are in the United Kingdom; Israeli law does not differ from English law in any material respect; the action is properly brought against Y and a stay would result in two sets of proceedings. The court declines to stay the action.[80]

12–133   6. Potatoes are shipped from Alexandria in Egypt to Liverpool on an Egyptian ship, The El Amria. A & Co., an English company controlled by an Egyptian businessman, are the holders of bills of lading. When the potatoes are unloaded, A & Co. allege that they have deteriorated as a result of the breach of contract and/or negligence of X & Co., the Egyptian owners of The El Amria, and bring an action *in rem* in England. Subsequently A & Co. also sue Y, the harbour authority, for damages for delay in discharging the cargo. The effect of the bills of lading is to provide that all claims against the carriers should be decided in Egypt according to Egyptian law. The connection of the parties and of the evidence with Egypt is closer than that with England, but similar issues are involved in the actions against X & Co. and against Y and there is a danger of conflicting decisions. The court refuses to stay the action against X & Co.[81]

---

[75] In Case C–391/95 *Van Uden Maritime BV v. Firma Deco-Line* [1998] E.C.R. I–7091, 7131, [1999] 2 W.L.R. 1181, 1208, the European Court said that where parties had validly excluded the jurisdiction of the courts in a dispute arising under a contract and had referred the dispute to arbitration, there were no courts of any state which had jurisdiction for the purposes of the 1968 Convention.

[76] CPR 6.15; *cf. Tharsis Sulphur Co. v. Société des Métaux* (1889) 58 L.J.Q.B. 435.

[77] Ord. 11, r. 1(1)(*d*)(iv); *cf. The Chaparral* [1968] 2 Lloyd's Rep. 158 (C.A.). For the sequel in the U.S. courts see *M/S Bremen v. Zapata Offshore Co.*, 407 U.S. 1 (1972), [1972] 2 Lloyd's Rep. 315; Collins, *Essays*, p. 253; Kahn-Freund (1977) 26 I.C.L.Q. 825, 845–848.

[78] 1968 Convention, Art. 17; Ord. 11, r. 1(2)(*a*).

[79] *Cf. The Eleftheria* [1970] P. 94, where the ship was Greek.

[80] These are the facts of *Evans Marshall & Co. Ltd. v. Bertola S.A.* [1973] 1 W.L.R. 349 (C.A.), except that the foreign company in that case did not have a branch in England. The court declined to set aside service out of the jurisdiction under Ord. 11.

[81] *The El Amria* [1981] 2 Lloyd's Rep. 119 (C.A.).

7. A, domiciled in England, sells goods to X, domiciled in France. The price is payable in England. X's purchase order, which A has seen in previous transactions, provides in printed conditions on the back that the French courts are to have exclusive jurisdiction over any disputes. X refuses to pay, claiming that the goods are not in conformity with the contract. A brings an action in England. The court has no jurisdiction.[82]

8. A & Co., an American bank with a branch in London, lends money to X and Y., one-ship Panamanian and Liberian companies, owned and managed by Greek nationals, who guarantee the loan. The loan agreement provides that the English court is to have jurisdiction over all disputes arising under it. X, Y and Z bring proceedings in Greece for damages for breach of business morality; A & Co. then institutes proceedings and applies for an anti-suit injunction from the English courts. The English court has jurisdiction by reason of Article 17 of the 1968 Convention, and grants the injunction.[83]

---

[82] 1968 Convention, Art. 17, as amended, reversing the effect of Case 24/76 *Salotti v. RÜWA* [1976] E.C.R. 1831.
[83] *Continental Bank N.A. v. Aeakos Compania Naviera S.A.* [1994] 1 W.L.R. 588 (C.A.).

CHAPTER 13

JURISDICTION IN ADMIRALTY CLAIMS *IN REM*[1]

13R–001   RULE 33—[2] **(1) Subject to the provisions of the Supreme Court Act 1981 and to Clause (2) of this Rule, the High Court has jurisdiction to entertain an Admiralty claim *in rem* if the process is served on the *res* in England.[3]**

(2)(a) Where the defendant is not domiciled in the United Kingdom, but is domiciled in a State party to the Brussels Convention on jurisdiction and the enforcement of judgments in civil and commercial matters ("the 1968 Convention"), the High Court does not have jurisdiction to entertain an Admiralty claim *in rem* (even if the process is served on the *res* in England) unless it has jurisdiction under the 1968 Convention or under a convention "on a particular matter" within the terms of Article 57 of the 1968 Convention.

(b) Where the defendant is not domiciled in the United Kingdom, but is domiciled in a State which is a party to the Lugano Convention on jurisdiction and the enforcement of judgments in civil and commercial matters (but not the 1968 Convention), the High Court does not have jurisdiction to entertain an Admiralty claim *in rem* (even if the process is served on the *res* in England) unless it has jurisdiction under the Lugano Convention or under a convention falling within the terms of Article 57(1) of the Lugano Convention.

(3) For the purposes of this Rule, the domicile of a party is to be determined according to Rule 23.[4]

COMMENT

13–002   **Introduction.** The only claim *in rem* which exists in English law is an Admiralty claim brought in the Queen's Bench Division of the High Court.[5]

---

[1] The Admiralty jurisdiction of the High Court comprises jurisdiction both *in rem* and *in personam*. Jurisdiction *in personam* is discussed in Chapter 11. This chapter deals only with claims *in rem*. On Admiralty jurisdiction and practice, see Jackson, *Enforcement of Maritime Claims* (2nd ed. 1996); McGuffie, *Admiralty Practice* (1964); Meeson, *Admiralty Jurisdiction and Practice* (1993); see also Civil Procedure Rules 1998, Part 49F, *Practice Direction–Admiralty* (in this Chapter referred to as CPR PD49F).

[2] This Rule must be read subject to Rules 19, 53 and 54 and to the provisions of Sections 5–9 of the 1968 and Lugano Conventions, in particular Art. 17 (jurisdiction agreements), Art. 18 (submission to jurisdiction), Art. 21 (*lis alibi pendens*) and Art. 22 (related actions). As to the power of the court to stay an action, see *ante*, Chap. 12. On the arrest of a ship as a means of securing satisfaction of a judgment or arbitration award, see paras. 8–031 *et seq.*

[3] *Castrique v. Imrie* (1870) L.R. 4 H.L. 414, 448; *The Nautik* [1895] P. 121; Supreme Court Act 1981, ss.20, 21; CPR PD49F, para. 2.2.

[4] *The Deichland* [1990] 1 Q.B. 361 (C.A.); *The Po* [1991] 2 Lloyd's Rep. 206 (C.A.); the 1968 and Lugano Conventions, Art. 3 and Art. 57, in Civil Jurisdiction and Judgments Act 1982, Scheds. 1 and 3C.

[5] The Admiralty jurisdiction of the High Court was transferred from the Probate, Divorce and Admiralty Division to the Queen's Bench Division in 1970. A special Admiralty court is constituted as part of the Queen's Bench Division: Supreme Court Act 1981, s.6(1)(b).

The *res* is normally a ship, though, as will be seen below, it can sometimes be something else. The precise nature of a claim *in rem* in English law has been a matter of controversy,[6] but it may be distinguished from a claim *in personam* on the basis of two characteristics. First, if the judgment is solely *in rem*, it may be enforced only against the *res*; consequently, it does not affect anyone who does not have an interest in the *res* and, if he does have such an interest, affects him only to the extent of that interest. Secondly, it is binding, to the extent of his interest in the *res*, on anyone who has such an interest, even if he was not served with process or otherwise informed of the proceedings, and even if he took no part in the proceedings. In view of these characteristics, it has sometimes been said that an action *in rem* is against the *res*, rather than against an individual.[7] Since the idea that a ship can be a defendant in legal proceedings was always a fiction,[8] this should be regarded as a metaphor rather than as a literal statement of the legal position.[9] In *Republic of India v. India Steamship Co. Ltd. (No. 2)*[10] the House of Lords rejected the personification theory, that an action *in rem* is brought against a ship, and held that the owners are parties to an action *in rem*. If the claim results in a judgment for a sum of money, such judgment (if not satisfied voluntarily) can be enforced only through the sale of the *res* by order of court. The *res* may be arrested by the court,[11] thus providing security for the claim, but (apart from the 1968 and Lugano Conventions) the jurisdiction of the court is not dependent on its arrest.

These characteristics of a claim *in rem* are obscured by the fact that the **13–003** owner of the *res* (or someone else with an interest in it) will almost invariably defend the claim. If he defends on the merits, he is considered by English law to have submitted to the jurisdiction *in personam* of the court.[12] The result is that the court can give a judgment *in personam* against him, provided that he is liable *in personam* on the claim.[13] That judgment is not then limited to the value of the *res* and can be enforced against him in the normal way.[14] Moreover, if the *res* has been arrested, the person defending the action will usually obtain its release by putting up security. However, the claimant will normally accept security only if the defendant submits to the jurisdiction *in personam* of the court, in which case the defendant's liability is not limited

---

[6] See *Republic of India v. India Steamship Co. Ltd. (No. 2)* [1998] A.C. 878; Teare [1998] L.M.C.L.Q. 33.

[7] See, for example, *The Burns* [1907] P. 137, 149–150; *The Nordglimt* [1988] Q.B. 183; *The Mawan* [1988] 2 Lloyd's Rep. 459, 460; *The Al Tawwab* [1991] 1 Lloyd's Rep. 201, 205 (C.A.).

[8] *Republic of India v. India Steamship Co. Ltd. (No. 2)* [1998] A.C. 878, 907, *per* Lord Steyn.

[9] *The Deichland* [1990] 1 Q.B. 361 (C.A.); *The Sylt* [1991] 1 Lloyd's Rep. 240, 244–245.

[10] [1998] A.C. 878.

[11] Although process may be served by the claimant, arrest is effected only by the marshal or his substitute (after the claimant has obtained a warrant of arrest from the court). Arrest may take place at the same time as service of process (in which case the marshal or his substitute may serve the process along with the warrant of arrest) or at a later date.

[12] *The Gemma* [1899] P. 285 (C.A.); see also *The August 8* [1983] 2 A.C. 450, 456 (P.C.); *The Dictator* [1892] P. 304. If process was properly served on the *res*, the court would also have jurisdiction *in rem*; the claim *in rem* is not merged in the action *in personam* and the two claims continue side by side: *The Nordglimt* [1988] Q.B. 183; *The Maciej Rataj* [1992] 2 Lloyd's Rep. 552 (C.A.). If process was never served on the *res* (for example, where solicitors accept service on behalf of the owner), the claim is *in personam* only: *The Tuyuti* [1984] 1 Q.B. 838, 842 (C.A.).

[13] *The Nordglimt* [1988] Q.B. 183, 200–201.

[14] *The Gemma, supra.*

either to the amount of the security or the value of the *res.*[15] For these reasons, the characteristic features of a claim *in rem* are apparent only if it is not defended, a rare occurrence. This, however, does not alter its essential nature.

13–004   **Admiralty jurisdiction.** The Admiralty jurisdiction of the High Court, whether *in rem* or *in personam*, is defined by section 20 of the Supreme Court Act 1981,[16] which lists "questions and claims" of a maritime nature in paragraphs (a) to (s) of subsection (2) and three further types of proceedings in subsection (3), together with the residuary jurisdiction of the former High Court of Admiralty. For example, the High Court has Admiralty jurisdiction in relation to claims for damage received by a ship,[17] for loss or damage to goods carried in a ship[18] and for damage done by a ship[19]; the High Court also has jurisdiction for any claim arising out an agreement relating to the carriage of goods in a ship or to the use or hire of a ship.[20] Some of the claims so listed are in practice obsolete, *e.g.* claims arising out of bottomry.[21] Although a claim *in personam* may be brought in all cases within the court's Admiralty jurisdiction,[22] the court's jurisdiction *in rem* is more limited.[23] For example, a claim *in rem* cannot be brought to enforce a claim for damage done by a ship falling within section 20(2)(e).

13–005   The *res* against which Admiralty claims *in rem* can be brought are as follows: ships[24]; cargo in or landed from a ship and still identifiable as cargo; freight; aircraft and their cargo; and the proceeds of sale of ships, cargo or aircraft. Not all the claims listed in the Act may be brought against all these *res*. For instance, a collision claim may be brought against a ship but not against cargo; a claim can only be brought against an aircraft[25] if the claim is for towage or pilotage while the aircraft is waterborne, or for salvage.[26] In practice, claims *in rem* against aircraft or their cargo are virtually unknown.

13–006   **Service of claim form and warrant of arrest.** The process by which a claim *in rem* is begun will be regarded as having been effectively served if the owner's solicitor indorses on the claim form a statement that he accepts

---

[15] *The Dictator* [1892] P. 304; *The Gemma* [1899] P. 285 (C.A.); *The Dupleix* [1912] P. 8; *The August 8* [1983] 2 A.C. 450 (P.C.). See also *The Good Herald* [1987] 1 Lloyd's Rep. 236; *The Linda* [1988] 1 Lloyd's Rep. 175. *Cf. The Dagmara* [1988] 1 Lloyd's Rep. 431. If the owner voluntarily gives bail to prevent the ship's arrest, or if he acknowledges the issue of the claim form, he is deemed to have submitted to the jurisdiction of the court: *The Prinsengracht* [1993] 1 Lloyd's Rep. 41.

[16] As amended by Merchant Shipping (Salvage and Pollution) Act 1994, s.1(6), Sched. 2, para. 6; Merchant Shipping Act 1995, s.314(2), Sched. 13, para. 59; Merchant Shipping and Maritime Security Act 1997, s.29(1), Sched. 6, para. 2.

[17] Supreme Court Act 1981, s.20(2)(d).

[18] *Ibid.*, s.20(2)(g).

[19] *Ibid.*, s.20(2)(e).

[20] *Ibid.*, s.20(2)(h).

[21] Bottomry (*respondentia*) bonds were originally given by the master of a ship as security for a loan needed when the ship was in distant parts of the world. Modern methods of communication have made them unnecessary.

[22] Supreme Court Act 1981, s.21(1).

[23] s.21(2)–(4). See *infra.* and paras. 13–009 *et seq.*

[24] The term "ship" as used in this chapter includes any description of vessel (including hovercraft) used in navigation, whether British or not and whether registered or not and wherever the residence or domicile of the owners may be: Supreme Court Act 1981, ss.20(7), 24(1).

[25] See *The Glider Standard Austria S.H. 1964* [1965] P. 463.

[26] Supreme Court Act 1981, s.20(2)(j)(k) and (l) and s.24(1).

service of it on behalf of the owner,[27] or if the owner acknowledges service before service has actually been effected,[28] or if there has been compliance with a contractually agreed method of service.[29] In the absence of one of these methods of service, process must normally be served on the property against which the claim is brought.[30] However, if the property is freight, process must be served on the cargo in respect of which the freight is payable or on the ship in which that cargo was carried[31] and, if the property has been sold and the proceeds of sale paid into court, process must be served by filing the claim form in the Admiralty and Commercial Registry.[32] Service[33] of an *in rem* claim form is made by fixing it on the outside of the property proceeded against in a position which may reasonably be expected to be seen. Where the property is freight, service may be made either on the cargo in respect of which the freight was earned or on the ship on which that cargo was carried. If the property to be served is in the custody of a person who will not permit access to it, service is effected by leaving the claim form with that person. The court has power to order an alternative method of service.[34] If the claim form is served in any other way, *e.g.* by leaving a copy with the master,[35] the service is invalid and will be set aside, because other persons with an interest in the ship would not be sufficiently notified of the proceedings.

A claim form may be served by the claimant or his solicitor, or by the   **13–007** Admiralty marshal[36]; but a warrant of arrest may be executed only by the marshal or his substitute.[37] No arrest of proceeds of sale in court is necessary or permitted.

Unlike process beginning a claim *in personam*, process beginning an action   **13–008** *in rem* cannot be served out of the jurisdiction.[38] Therefore, unless it is deemed to have been duly served on the defendant under the CPR Admiralty Practice Direction,[39] the *res* must be in England at the time when the process is served, though it need not be in England at the time when process is issued; and it is immaterial that the ship leaves the jurisdiction after the service of the claim form but before the execution of the warrant of arrest.[40]

Supreme Court Act 1981, s.21. Section 21(1) to (4) sets out the three   **13–009** types of case in which a claimant may invoke the court's Admiralty jurisdiction by bringing a claim *in rem*. The predecessor of section 21(4) of the

---

[27] CPR PD49F, para. 2.2(e).
[28] *Ibid.*, para. 2.4.
[29] *Ibid.*, para. 2.2(f). In these situations the action will be *in personam* and not *in rem*: *The Tuyuti* [1984] Q.B. 838, 842 (C.A.).
[30] CPR PD49F, para. 2.2(a).
[31] *Ibid.*
[32] *Ibid.*, para. 2.2(c).
[33] *Ibid.*, para. 2.2.
[34] *Ibid.*, para. 2.2(g), (but only if the *res* is in England).
[35] *The Prins Bernhard* [1964] P. 117, 130–132.
[36] The marshal or his substitute will normally serve the claim form only if the *res* is arrested at the same time.
[37] CPR PD49F, para. 6.4.
[38] *Aichorn & Co. K.G. v. The Talabut* (1974) 132 C.L.R. 449; *General Motors-Holdens v. The Northern Highway* (1982) 29 S.A.S.R. 138.
[39] CPR PD49F, paras. 2.2(e) (solicitor accepting service), 2.3 (acknowledgment of service, after issue but before service).
[40] *The Nautik* [1895] P. 121.

Supreme Court Act 1981 was enacted to implement the Brussels Convention of 1952 on the Arrest of Seagoing Ships.[41] In interpreting the Act recourse may be had not only to the Brussels Arrest Convention itself,[42] but also to its *travaux préparatoires*, the proceedings of the conference which led to it.[43]

13–010   Section 21(2) provides that in the cases mentioned in section 20(2)(*a*) to (*c*) and (*s*) an action *in rem* may be brought in the High Court against the ship or property in question.

Section 21(3) provides that in any case in which there is a maritime lien or other charge on any ship, aircraft or other property for the amount claimed, an action *in rem* may be brought in the High Court against that ship, aircraft or property.

13–011   A maritime lien permits a claim form to be served on the *res*, and the *res* to be arrested, no matter who is the owner at the time of the arrest or the issue or service of process.[44] A claimant who has a maritime lien on a ship may thus proceed under section 21(3) by a claim *in rem* against the ship, even though it may have changed hands since the cause of action arose.[45] In English law, a maritime lien arises for claims for collision damage, salvage, wages of the master and crew, and master's disbursements.[46] It attaches from the time the cause of action accrues. In English law, a claim supported by a maritime lien enjoys priority over certain other maritime claims, such as a mortgage, if the proceeds of the sale of the *res* are insufficient to meet all claims against it.[47]

13–012   The words "other charge" in section 21(3) are not defined in the Act and their meaning is not free from doubt. They do not refer to charges in the nature of a mortgage, because these are specifically referred to in section 21(2) above. They probably refer to certain charges imposed by the Merchant Shipping Acts. At any rate they do not include a possessory lien for repairs.[48]

13–013   Section 21(4) provides as follows: "In the case of any such claim as is mentioned in section 20(2)(*e*) to (*r*), where (a) the claim arises in connection with a ship; and (b) the person who would be liable on the claim in an action *in personam* ("the relevant person") was, when the cause of action arose, the owner or charterer of, or in possession or control of, the ship, an action *in rem* may (whether or not the claim gives rise to a maritime lien on that ship) be brought in the High Court against (i) that ship, if at the time when the action is brought the relevant person is either the beneficial owner of that ship as respects all the shares in it or the charterer of it under a charter by demise; or

---

[41] Text in Cmnd. 8954 (1953) and in Singh, *International Maritime Law Conventions* (1983), Vol. 4, pp. 3101–3107. It will be replaced by the International Convention on Arrest of Ships 1999 (not yet in force).

[42] *The Eschersheim* [1967] 1 W.L.R. 430 (H.L.). On resort to the French text see *The Antonis P. Lemos* [1985] A.C. 711, 731.

[43] *Gatoil International Inc. v. Arkwright-Boston Manufacturers Mutual Insurance Co.* [1985] A.C. 255. See also *The River Rima* [1988] 1 W.L.R. 758 (H.L.).

[44] A maritime lien will, however, be lost if the *res* is sold by order of the court.

[45] *The St. Merriel* [1963] P. 247, 251.

[46] There is also a maritime lien for claims on bottomry (*respondentia*) bonds, but these are now obsolete.

[47] Questions of priorities are decided by the *lex fori: The Union* (1860) Lush. 128; *The Colorado* [1922] P. 102. See, further, para. 7–032, *ante*.

[48] *The St. Merriel* [1963] P. 247.

(ii) any other ship of which, at the time when the action is brought, the relevant person is the beneficial owner as respects all the shares in it."

At first sight it might appear that section 21(4) has a restrictive effect on the **13–014** jurisdiction of the court and cuts down the unqualified right conferred by section 21(3). For section 21(3) says that a claimant with a maritime lien on a ship can proceed by action *in rem* against that ship, irrespective of a change of ownership; and then section 21(4), particularly the words in brackets "(whether or not the claim gives rise to a maritime lien on that ship)," seems to say that he cannot do so if the ship has changed hands after the cause of action arose and before the issue of process. But the effect of section 21(4) is in reality an enlarging and not a restricting one.[49] The two subsections have to be read disjunctively, so that a claimant who has a maritime lien on a ship and is content to proceed against that ship can do so under section 21(3). It is only when the claimant has no maritime lien, or (whether he has a maritime lien or not) when he wishes to proceed against some other ship than the one in respect of which the cause of action arose, that section 21(4) (which creates what is sometimes referred to as "the statutory lien") comes into operation. Before 1956 an action *in rem* could not be brought against any ship other than the one in respect of which the cause of action arose.[50] But under section 21(4) such an action may be brought against a sister ship owned (at the time of the issue of the claim form[51]) by the person who (at the time when the cause of action arose) would have been liable on the claim in an action *in personam*.[52] There is no requirement that the sister ship must have been owned by that person at the time when the cause of action arose. Section 21(4) does not allow a claim *in rem* to be brought against a ship owned by a "sister company", *i.e.* a company with the same shareholders and directors as the company owning the ship in relation to which the claim arises.[53]

Soon after the passing of the Administration of Justice Act 1956 (the **13–015** predecessor of the relevant provisions of the Supreme Court Act 1981) a practice grew up of issuing process against the ship in respect of which the cause of action arose and against sister ships in the same ownership, and serving it on one ship as soon as a suitable one (*i.e.* one whose value was sufficient to provide adequate security for the claim) came within the jurisdiction. The validity of this practice was approved (*obiter*) by a majority of the Court of Appeal in *The Banco*,[54] and confirmed by section 21(8) of the 1981 Act, which provides that once a ship has been served with a writ (now called a claim form) or arrested in an action *in rem* brought to enforce a claim within section 20(2)(*e*) to (*r*), no other ship may be served with a writ or arrested in that or any other action *in rem* brought to enforce that claim[55]; but this provision does not prevent the issue of process naming more than one ship or of two or more claim forms each naming a different ship.[56] In addition,

---

[49] *The St. Elefterio* [1957] P. 179, 185.

[50] *The Beldis* [1936] P. 51 (C.A.).

[51] *The Andria* [1984] Q.B. 477, 489 (C.A.).

[52] For the position under Irish law see *The Kapitan Labunets* [1995] I.R. 164.

[53] *The Evpo Agnic* [1988] 1 W.L.R. 1090 (C.A.). See also *The Mawan* [1988] 2 Lloyd's Rep. 459.

[54] [1971] P. 137, 153, 158–159.

[55] For the position in Scotland see *The Alfalfa* [1995] 2 Lloyd's Rep. 286 (O.H.).

[56] See also *The Stephan J.* [1985] 2 Lloyd's Rep. 344.

section 21(8) does not preclude a ship being arrested in England in connection with English proceedings *in rem* notwithstanding that the ship[57] or a sister ship[58] has previously been arrested and released in foreign proceedings involving the same maritime claim. However, the court has a discretion to order the ship's release if the arrest is vexatious or oppressive or otherwise an abuse of the process of the court.[59]

13–016   The relationship between the "relevant person" and the ship, which for convenience one may call "ownership", is not quite the same in the different provisions of section 21(4). When the cause of action arises, the relevant person must be either (a) the owner or (b) the charterer or (c) "in possession or in control" of the ship in relation to which the claim arises. Here "owner" means "registered owner".[60] When the claim is brought, if it is brought against the same ship, the relevant person must be either (a) the "beneficial owner" of the ship as respects all the shares in it or (b) the demise charterer[61]; if, on the other hand, it is brought against a sister ship, alternative (b) does not exist: it must be shown that the relevant person is the beneficial owner of the ship as respects all the shares in it. The statute does not define "beneficial owner". Under the predecessor of this section it was held by Brandon J. in *The Andrea Ursula*[62] that for the purposes of determining the beneficial ownership of the ship in respect of which the cause of action arose the expression included the interest of a charterer by demise and any other person with a similar complete possession and control over the ship who might thereby become liable on a claim within what are now paragraphs (*e*) to (*r*) of section 20(2) of the Act. But this decision was not followed by Robert Goff J. in *The I Congreso del Partido*,[63] where it was held that the expression means equitable ownership, whether or not accompanied by legal ownership, and does not include possession and control (however full and complete) without ownership. Robert Goff J.'s interpretation, which was made in the context of a case involving the determination of the beneficial ownership of a sister ship, where the question remains relevant, was followed by the Court of Appeal in *The Nazym Khikmet*.[64]

13–017   The onus of showing that the beneficial ownership is the same at the time when the claim is brought as it was when the cause of action arose rests on the claimant. The court will look behind the registered owner to determine the beneficial ownership.[65] Where a ship is transferred by the relevant person to a new owner after the cause of action has arisen but before the institution of proceedings *in rem*, the court may conclude that the transfer is a sham if,

---

[57] *The Tjaskemolen (No. 2)* [1997] 2 Lloyd's Rep. 477.
[58] *The Kommunar (No. 2)* [1997] 1 Lloyd's Rep 8.
[59] *The Tjaskemolen (No. 2), supra.*
[60] *The Evpo Agnic* [1988] 1 W.L.R. 1090 (C.A.).
[61] *The Giuseppe di Vittorio* [1998] 1 Lloyd's Rep. 136 (C.A.); *cf. Laemthong International Lines Co. Ltd. v. BPS Shipping Ltd.* (1997) 190 C.L.R. 181.
[62] [1973] Q.B. 265, not following *The St. Merriel* [1963] P. 247, 258. These decisions are obsolete since s.21(4) provides that the ship in respect of which the cause of action arose may be arrested if the person liable *in personam* is either the beneficial owner *or* the charterer by demise. See also *The Father Thames* [1979] 2 Lloyd's Rep. 364, 366–367.
[63] [1978] Q.B. 500, 537–542, revd. on other grounds [1983] 1 A.C. 244; applied in *The Father Thames* [1979] 2 Lloyd's Rep. 364; *The Permina 3001* [1979] 1 Lloyd's Rep. 327 (Singapore C.A.).
[64] [1996] 2 Lloyd's Rep. 362 (C.A.).
[65] *The Aventicum* [1978] 1 Lloyd's Rep. 184; *The Saudi Prince* [1982] 2 Lloyd's Rep. 255.

rather than serving a commercial purpose, it is designed simply to prevent the arrest of the ship in question.[66] In such a case, the relevant person remains the beneficial owner.

If the claimant has a statutory right of action *in rem* not amounting to a   **13–018** maritime lien (*i.e.* a statutory lien), and the ship is sold after the cause of action arose but before the issue of process, he cannot proceed *in rem* against the ship.[67] But he can do so if the ship is sold after the issue of process but before service thereof or arrest of the ship.[68]

In determining for the purposes of section 21(4) whether a person would be   **13–019** liable on a claim in an action *in personam*, it is to be assumed that he has his habitual residence or a place of business in England.[69] This statutory assumption is necessary because proceedings *in personam* for damage, loss of life or personal injury arising out of a collision or other like navigational incident between two or more ships lie only if that collision or incident occurred in English inland waters or in an English port, or is or has been the subject-matter of proceedings in the court, or if the defendant has his habitual residence or a place of business in England.[70] The effect of the assumption is to render the person who incurred the claim notionally liable in an action *in personam*, even if he habitually resides abroad and has no place of business in England, but only for the limited purposes of the court's jurisdiction in an action *in rem* under section 21(4). The reference to "the person who would be liable on the claim in an action *in personam*" does not mean that the claimant must prove at the outset that he has a cause of action sustainable in law[71]; as long as the claimant's case is not bound to fail he is entitled to proceed with it.[72] The purpose of the words is merely to identify the person whose ship may be arrested in relation to the right of arresting a sister ship.[73]

Section 21(5) provides that in the case of a claim in the nature of towage   **13–020** or pilotage in respect of an aircraft, the Admiralty jurisdiction of the court may be invoked by an action *in rem* against that aircraft if at the time when the action is brought it is beneficially owned by the person who would be liable on the claim in an action *in personam*. The same assumption applies as it does under section 21(4) that the person who would be liable on the claim in an action *in personam* has his habitual residence or a place of business in England.[74] But there is no provision for such claims against an aircraft when a mere charterer has incurred the claim, nor for such claims against another aircraft in the same ownership.

Section 22 of the Act, which defines the jurisdiction of the court in claims   **13–021** *in personam* for damage, loss of life or personal injury arising out of a collision between two or more ships,[75] does not apply to claims *in rem*. But section 23, which excludes the jurisdiction of the court in cases certified by the

---

[66] *The Tjaskemolen* [1997] 2 Lloyd's Rep. 465.
[67] *The Henrich Björn* (1886) 11 App.Cas. 270.
[68] *The Monica S.* [1968] P. 741; *The Helene Roth* [1980] Q.B. 273.
[69] Supreme Court Act 1981, s.21(7).
[70] *Ibid.* s.22; and see Rule 23.
[71] *The St. Elefterio* [1957] P. 179. See also *Ocean Industries Pty Ltd. v. Owners of the Ship M. V. "Steven C"* [1994] 1 Qd.R. 69.
[72] *The Yuta Bondarovskaya* [1998] 2 Lloyd's Rep. 357.
[73] *Ibid.* at p. 186; *The St. Merriel* [1963] P. 247, 258.
[74] s.21(7).
[75] See *post*, para. 15–028.

Secretary of State to fall within the provisions of the Rhine Navigation Convention,[76] applies equally to claims *in personam* and claims *in rem*.

13–022   **Effect of the 1968 Convention and Lugano Convention.** Admiralty claims *in rem* fall within the scope of the 1968 Convention[77] and the Lugano Convention; it follows, therefore, that an English court cannot take jurisdiction in such a claim if this is precluded by the provisions of either Convention. If the defendant is domiciled (in the Convention sense) in the United Kingdom, the court will have jurisdiction under Article 2 of the 1968 Convention. If the defendant is domiciled neither in the United Kingdom nor in any other Contracting State to either Convention, Article 4 of each Convention allows the English court to take jurisdiction under the provisions of English law. Where, however, the defendant is not domiciled in the United Kingdom and is domiciled in a State party to either Convention, the provisions of the applicable Convention must be satisfied. The Convention to be applied depends on the domicile of the defendant: if he is domiciled in a State party to the 1968 Convention, that Convention is to be applied; if, on the other hand, he is domiciled in a State which is a party to the Lugano Convention but not the 1968 Convention (*i.e.* one of the EFTA countries), the Lugano Convention is to be applied.[78]

13–023   Where the defendant is not domiciled in the United Kingdom, but is domiciled in another Contracting State, Article 3 provides that the English court may take jurisdiction only by virtue of the rules set out in Sections 2–6 of Title II of the relevant Convention (Articles 5–18). However, Article 57 of each Convention provides that it does not prevent the court of a Contracting State from assuming jurisdiction in accordance with a convention "on a particular matter" to which the Contracting State is a party, even where the defendant is domiciled in another Contracting State. Consequently, where the 1968 Convention or the Lugano Convention applies, the English court must have jurisdiction either under one of the provisions of Sections 2–6 or under one of the provisions of a convention on a particular matter.

13–024   **Meaning of "defendant".** It has not yet been definitively determined who would be regarded as a defendant in a claim *in rem* for the purposes of the 1968 and Lugano Conventions, but the owner of the *res* or anyone with an interest in it whose interest would be affected by the claim would probably be so regarded. In *The Deichland*,[79] which was approved by the House of Lords in *Republic of India v. India Steamship Co. Ltd. (No. 2)*[80] a company which was the demise charterer of the ship at the time when the process was issued (though the charter had ended by the time it was served) was regarded as the defendant for the purposes of the 1968 Convention.

13–025   **Sections 2–6 of the Conventions.** With two exceptions, none of these provisions is specifically concerned with Admiralty claims. The first exception is Article 6A, which deals with limitation claims. This has already been

---

[76] See *post*, para. 15–039.
[77] *The Deichland* [1990] 1 Q.B. 361 (C.A.). The scope of the Conventions as regards subject matter is defined by Art. 1, by which they apply in civil and commercial matters, whatever the nature of the court or tribunal. This is subject to certain exceptions, none of which concerns actions *in rem*.
[78] Lugano Convention, Art. 54B.
[79] [1990] 1 Q.B. 361 (C.A.).
[80] [1997] 3 W.L.R. 818 (H.L.).

discussed.[81] The second exception is Article 5(7), which deals with claims for remuneration for the salvage of cargo or freight, but not ships. It provides that such claims may be brought in the court under whose authority the cargo or freight (a) has been arrested or (b) could have been arrested, but bail or other security has been given. The reason why this very narrow head of jurisdiction was included in the Conventions is explained below.

Conventions on particular matters. The question of Admiralty jurisdiction *in rem* was discussed in the negotiations preceding the United Kingdom's accession to the 1968 Convention. The solution adopted was to rely on Article 57 of the 1968 Convention, as interpreted and expanded by Article 25(2) of the 1978 Accession Convention. Following the 1989 Accession Convention, Article 57 was amended and consolidated.[82] Article 57 of each Convention deals with conventions on "particular matters" to which States party to the 1968 or Lugano Conventions are, or will become, parties, and provides that the operation of such conventions will not be affected by the 1968 Convention or the Lugano Convention. Conventions on particular matters are conventions which fall within the general scope of the 1968 Convention and the Lugano Convention because they deal with jurisdiction or the enforcement of judgments, but which concern only particular issues (in contrast to the 1968 and Lugano Conventions, which deal with these matters in a general way).[83] Conventions dealing specifically with Admiralty actions *in rem* would fall into this category.   **13–026**

Article 57(2)(a) of the 1968 Convention and Article 57(2) of the Lugano Convention make clear that a court of a Contracting State which is a party to a convention on a particular matter may assume jurisdiction in accordance with that convention, even if the defendant is domiciled in another Contracting State (to the 1968 or Lugano Convention) and that State is not a party to the convention on a particular matter.[84] Moreover, it is not necessary for the claimant to be domiciled in, or a national of, a Contracting State, nor is it necessary (unless this is required by the convention on a particular matter) for him to be domiciled in, or a national of, a State party to the convention on a particular matter.[85] A judgment given by an English court in these circumstances must be recognised by all Contracting States (to the 1968 and Lugano Conventions), even if such State is not a party to the convention on a particular matter.[86]   **13–027**

This means that if the United Kingdom is a party to a convention on a particular matter, and if an English court assumes jurisdiction in a claim *in rem* in accordance with the provisions of that convention, the bar imposed by   **13–028**

---

[81] Rule 28(8).

[82] The differences between the relevant provisions of Art. 57 of the 1968 Convention (as amended) and those of Art. 57 of the Lugano Convention are only verbal.

[83] For a list, which is not necessarily complete, see Schlosser [1979] O.J. C59/71, para. 238, n. 59.

[84] Art. 20 must nevertheless be applied. This requires the court in certain cases to declare of its own motion that it has no jurisdiction; it also makes provision for the defendant to be served in sufficient time to enable him to arrange for his defence.

[85] *The Po* [1991] 2 Lloyd's Rep. 206 (C.A.).

[86] Art. 57(2)(b) of the 1968 Convention. For the Lugano Convention, see Art. 57(3); but see Art. 57(4), which provides that a Contracting State need not enforce such a judgment against a person domiciled in its territory if that state is not a party to the convention on a particular matter. See also the second paragraph of Art. 57(2)(b) of the 1968 Convention and Art. 57(5) of the Lugano Convention.

Article 3 of the 1968 and Lugano Conventions is lifted. Where there is conflict between conventions, the jurisdictional provisions of a convention on a particular matter prevail over those contained in the 1968 or Lugano Convention (as the case may be); and there is no reason for thinking that the convention on a particular matter should be interpreted narrowly in order that it should impinge as little as possible on the 1968 or Lugano Convention.[87] Article 57 does not, however, make the convention on a particular matter part of English law, nor does it positively grant jurisdiction to the English court.[88] It is not necessary that United Kingdom legislation should expressly provide that the convention on a particular matter is to have the force of law in England,[89] but, if it does not, the English court must have jurisdiction under some other provision of English law. In other words, the requirements of Rule 33(1) must be satisfied, in addition to those of the convention on a particular matter.

13–029   Two conventions on particular matters need to be considered. The first is the Brussels Arrest Convention of 1952.[90] This provides that a ship flying the flag of a Contracting State (to the Arrest Convention) may be arrested for a "maritime claim", but not for any other claim[91]; a ship flying the flag of a non-contracting State, on the other hand, may be arrested for a maritime claim or for any other claim for which it may be arrested under the law of the Contracting State in which the arrest takes place.[92] The Convention then provides that the courts of the country where the arrest took place will have jurisdiction to hear the action if they have such jurisdiction under their domestic law.[93] This means that, in the case of a ship flying the flag of a Contracting State, the court has jurisdiction only with regard to a "maritime claim". This is defined in the Convention[94]: the definition covers largely the same ground as section 20 of the Supreme Court Act 1981, but is not identical to it.

13–030   The result is that, where the English court has jurisdiction under Rule 33(1), it will normally have jurisdiction under the Arrest Convention. There are, however, two important exceptions. The first results from the fact that the Arrest Convention provides for the arrest only of ships; consequently, it grants jurisdiction *in rem* only against ships. Section 20 of the Supreme Court Act 1981, on the other hand, makes provision for claims *in rem* against certain other kinds of property. One such case is a salvage action against cargo or freight. Article 5(7) of the 1968 Convention (and later, the Lugano Convention) was adopted to allow such a claim.

13–031   The second exception is that the Arrest Convention grants jurisdiction only when the ship has been arrested. It is not sufficient that the ship *could have*

---

[87] *The Anna H* [1995] 1 Lloyd's Rep. 11 (C.A.).
[88] *The Po* [1991] 2 Lloyd's Rep. 206 (C.A.).
[89] *Ibid.*
[90] The International Convention Relating to the Arrest of Seagoing Ships, signed in Brussels on May 10, 1952. The text is set out in Cmnd. 8954 (1953) and in Singh, *International Maritime Law Conventions* (1983), Vol. 4, pp. 3101–3107. It is recognised as being a "convention on a particular matter" in terms of Art. 57: Schlosser [1979] O.J. C59/71, para. 238, n. 59; *The Deichland* [1990] 1 Q.B. 361 (C.A.).
[91] Art. 2.
[92] Art. 8(2).
[93] Art. 7(1). For the meaning of domestic law see *The Anna H* [1995] 1 Lloyd's Rep. 11 (C.A.). This also gives certain additional grounds of jurisdiction, but, since Art. 7(1) as a whole applies only if the ship has been arrested, and the jurisdictional requirements of English law must in any event be satisfied, these additional grounds appear to be of little relevance.
[94] Art. 1(1).

been arrested, but was not (because security was given).[95] Once the ship has been arrested within the jurisdiction of the English court, the court will not lose its jurisdiction if the ship is then released.[96] It is, therefore, necessary both to serve the process on the ship (to fulfil the requirements of English law) and to arrest it (to fulfil the requirements of the Arrest Convention).[97] Once this has been done, security may be accepted for its release. The court is able to claim jurisdiction under the Arrest Convention even if the defendant has put up security for the claim prior to the arrest and the ship is released immediately afterwards.[98] Although the Arrest Convention defines arrest as "the detention of a ship by judicial process to secure a maritime claim",[99] it has been held that to qualify as an arrest for the purposes of the Convention all that is required is that the legal consequence of judicial detention of the ship is that it becomes security for a maritime claim; there is no requirement that the claimant's motive for the arrest should be to obtain security.[1]

The second convention is the Brussels Collision Convention,[2] which concerns actions for collision between seagoing vessels or between seagoing vessels and inland navigation craft.[3] Article 1(1) confers jurisdiction in such actions on (a) the court where the defendant has his habitual residence or a place of business; (b) the court of the place where arrest has been effected of the defendant ship or of any other ship belonging to the defendant which can lawfully be arrested, or where arrest could have been effected and bail or other security has been furnished; or (c) the court of the place of collision when the collision has occurred within the limits of a port or in inland waters.[4] The most important of these grounds is that set out in Article 1(1)(b). To some extent it covers the same ground as the Arrest Convention[5]; however, it goes further in one important respect: it is sufficient if arrest could have been effected and bail or other security was furnished. This means that in collision cases the arrest of the defendant vessel is not essential.[6]

13–032

---

[95] *The Deichland* [1990] 1 Q.B. 361 (C.A.). The court will, however, have jurisdiction *in personam* over the defendant if he voluntarily submits to its jurisdiction, for example by giving bail to prevent the ship's arrest or by acknowledging the issue of the writ. See *The Prinsengracht* [1993] 1 Lloyd's Rep. 41.

[96] *The Anna H* [1995] 1 Lloyd's Rep. 11 (C.A.).

[97] If the defendant submits to the jurisdiction of the English court in terms of Art. 17 (jurisdiction agreements) or Art. 18 (defending on the merits) of the 1968 or Lugano Conventions, arrest will not of course be necessary.

[98] *The Anna H* [1995] 1 Lloyd's Rep. 11 (C.A.).

[99] Art. 1(2).

[1] *The Anna H, supra.*

[2] International Convention on Certain Rules Concerning Civil Jurisdiction in Matters of Collision, May 10, 1952. The text is set out in Cmnd. 8954 (1953). This is recognised as a convention on a particular matter: Schlosser [1979] O.J. C59/71, para. 238, n. 59; *The Po* [1991] 2 Lloyd's Rep. 206 (C.A.).

[3] It also concerns certain other actions: see Art. 4.

[4] At first sight, Art. 8 might be thought to limit the application of the Collision Convention to cases where all the vessels concerned fly the flag of a Contracting State, but this view was rejected by the Court of Appeal in *The Po, ante,* where it was held that the action before the court was covered by the Collision Convention, even though the plaintiff's vessel flew the flag of a non-contracting State. The correct interpretation of Art. 8 may perhaps be that it does no more than preclude additional grounds of jurisdiction where the vessels concerned fly the flag of a Contracting State.

[5] See Art. 1(1)(a) and Art. 7(1) of the Arrest Convention.

[6] *The Po, supra.*

13–033   **Jurisdictional issues not regulated by conventions on particular matters.** Although it is provided that the operation of conventions on particular matters is not to be affected by the 1968 and Lugano Conventions,[7] this principle has been glossed by the European Court in *The Tatry*.[8] The European Court ruled that the provisions of a convention on a particular matter prevail over the 1968 Convention only to the extent that there is a conflict; where a specific jurisdictional issue is not covered by a convention on a particular matter the provisions of the 1968 Convention continue to apply. So, even where the court has obtained jurisdiction *in rem* by virtue of an arrest under the Arrest Convention, Articles 21 and 22 of the 1968 Convention are applicable if there are concurrent proceedings in another 1968 Convention Contracting State.[9] This is because the Arrest Convention does not contain provisions dealing with *lis pendens* or related actions.

13–034   The European Court's decision in *The Tatry* was distinguished in *The Bergen*,[10] a case in which the defendant challenged the court's jurisdiction *in rem* on the basis that the parties had agreed to the exclusive jurisdiction of the German courts. The defendant argued that, since the Arrest Convention was silent as to the effect of a jurisdiction agreement, the case was governed by Article 17 of the 1968 Convention, according to which the English court had no jurisdiction. Clarke J. distinguished *The Tatry* on the ground that Article 17 (which has the effect of depriving all courts other than those chosen of the jurisdiction which they otherwise would have had) is different from Article 21 (which does not deprive courts of jurisdiction but merely requires them not to exercise it); if the court were required to give effect to Article 17 it would have been deprived of jurisdiction under the Arrest Convention, something which is expressly excluded by Article 57 of the 1968 Convention.[11]

13–035   **Defendant domiciled in Scotland or Northern Ireland.** As was said above, Article 2 of each of the 1968 and Lugano Conventions confers jurisdiction on the courts of the Contracting State in which the defendant is domiciled; consequently, if the defendant is domiciled in the United Kingdom, the courts of the United Kingdom have jurisdiction in terms of the 1968 Convention. It is provided by section 16 of the Civil Jurisdiction and Judgments Act 1982 that, where the defendant is domiciled in the United Kingdom, the provisions of Schedule 4 determine whether the courts of any part of the United Kingdom have jurisdiction in any given case. However, paragraph 6(a) of Schedule 5 (read with section 17) provides that Schedule 4 does not apply to proceedings brought in pursuance of a statutory provision which implements a convention on a particular matter or which makes provision with respect to jurisdiction in any field to which the convention relates. Under paragraph 6(b), the same applies to proceedings brought in pursuance of a rule of law which has the effect of implementing such a convention. If one regards the "field" to which the Brussels Arrest Convention relates as being Admiralty claims *in rem*, such claims would seem to be exempt from the require-

---

[7] Civil Jurisdiction and Judgments Act 1982, Sched. 1, Art. 57(1); Sched. 3C, Art. 57(1).
[8] Case C–406/92 [1994] E.C.R. I–5439; [1999] Q.B. 515.
[9] See *ante*, para. 11–037.
[10] [1997] 1 Lloyd's Rep. 380.
[11] The proceedings were subsequently stayed under the court's inherent jurisdiction: *The Bergen (No. 2)* [1997] 2 Lloyd's Rep. 710.

ments of Schedule 4.[12] It would seem, therefore, that, as long as the defendant is domiciled in some part of the United Kingdom, compliance with Rule 33(1) is all that is required.

ILLUSTRATIONS

1. By a contract of sale made in London, an English company, on behalf of the Russian **13–036** Government, purports to sell to an Italian company a Russian ship which, prior to the promulgation of a Russian decree nationalising the Russian mercantile marine, had belonged to A & Co., a Russian company. A & Co., which has removed its business to France, issues a writ *in rem* claiming possession of the ship and a declaration that it is the owner thereof. The writ is served on the ship in an English port. The court has jurisdiction, although the dispute is between foreigners and relates exclusively to a foreign ship.[13]

2. Y & Co., charterers by demise of X & Co.'s German ship, order repairs to be done to her by A. A issues a writ *in rem* against the ship claiming £5,180 in respect of the repairs. The writ is served on the ship in England. At the date of the service of the writ Y & Co. are still charterers by demise. The court has jurisdiction. There is no maritime lien, so the case is not within section 21(3) of the Supreme Court Act 1981.[14] But the requirements of section 21(4) are met, because at the time when the cause of action arose and at the time when the writ was issued, Y & Co. was the charterer by demise.[15]

3. The circumstances are the same as in Illustration 2, except that A brings a claim *in rem* against another ship beneficially owned at the time of the issue of the proceedings by Y & Co. The court has jurisdiction.[16]

4. The circumstances are the same as in Illustration 2, except that A brings a claim *in rem* against another ship of which Y & Co. is, at the time of issue of the proceedings, the charterer by demise. The court has no jurisdiction.[17]

5. A collision occurs on the high seas between A's ship and X's ship. After the collision, X's ship is transferred to Y. A then issues a claim form *in rem* against that ship and serves it on the ship in England. The court has jurisdiction.[18]

6. The circumstances are the same as in Illustration 5, except that A issues a claim form against **13–037** another ship beneficially owned at the time of the issue by X and serves it on that ship in England. The court has jurisdiction, even though X habitually resides abroad and has no place of business in England.[19]

7. A's Spanish ship collides with an oil jetty in the River Thames because of the negligent navigation of the *Banco*, a British ship belonging to X. The oil catches fire and A is faced with claims amounting to several million pounds from those who suffered damage in the collision. A brings an Admiralty action *in rem* against the *Banco* and six sister ships owned by X. The court sets aside the service of the writ on the six sister ships.[20]

8. A, the owner of cargo damaged while carried on a ship belonging to (or demise chartered by) X & Co., brings a claim *in rem* under the Supreme Court Act 1981. The claim form is served on the ship in an English port, but the ship is not arrested because contractual security is given by X & Co., a company domiciled in a Contracting State to the 1968 Convention. X & Co. challenges the jurisdiction of the court. On the facts of the case the court does not have

---

[12] The statutory provision would be s.20 of the Supreme Court Act 1981 together with such other statutory provisions as may be relevant. Common law rules which have the effect of implementing the Arrest Convention would be covered by para. 6(b). If the "field" to which the Convention relates is regarded as being restricted to actions *in rem* against ships, proceedings in which the *res* is something other than a ship would have to comply with the requirements of Sched. 4. In salvage cases, Art. 5(7) of Sched. 4 would be relevant; in other cases, Art. 5(8)(b) might possibly be applicable.

[13] *The Jupiter (No. 2)* [1925] P. 69 (C.A.). As to notifying the consul of the State to which the ship belongs, see CPR PD49F, para. 6.2(7).

[14] *The St. Merriel* [1963] P. 247.

[15] Supreme Court Act 1981, s.21(4).

[16] Supreme Court Act 1981, s.21(4).

[17] *The I Congreso del Partido* [1978] Q.B. 500, 537–542, revd. on other grounds [1983] 1 A.C. 244.

[18] Supreme Court Act 1981, s.21(3).

[19] *Ibid.* s.21(4)(7).

[20] *The Banco* [1971] P. 137 (C.A.).

jurisdiction under Articles 5–18 of the 1968 Convention. Since the ship was not arrested, the court has no jurisdiction to hear the action under the Brussels Arrest Convention.[21]

9. The circumstances are the same as in Illustration 8, but the ship is arrested. Although the court does not have jurisdiction under the 1968 Convention, it does have jurisdiction under the Brussels Arrest Convention.[22]

10. The circumstances are the same as in Illustration 8, but X & Co. puts up security by means of a bail bond. The court has jurisdiction to determine the claim because, by giving bail, X & Co. is deemed to have submitted to the court's jurisdiction.[23]

11. A ship owned by the United States is damaged in Rio de Janeiro harbour as a result of a collision with a ship owned by X & Co., a company domiciled in Italy (a Contracting State to the 1968 Convention). The United States Government brings proceedings *in rem* in England to obtain damages, serving the writ in an English port on the ship owned by X & Co. The ship could have been arrested, but is not, since security is given. On the facts of the case, the English court does not have jurisdiction under the provisions of Articles 5–18 of the 1968 Convention; nevertheless, it has jurisdiction to hear the proceedings, since it has jurisdiction under Article 1(1)(b) of the Brussels Collision Convention of 1952.[24]

12. A, the owners of cargo carried in a ship owned by X & Co., a Polish shipping company, alleges that in the course of the voyage the cargo was contaminated. X & Co. starts proceedings against A in the Netherlands for a declaration of non-liability. A issues English proceedings *in rem* under the Supreme Court Act 1981, the writ is served and the ship is arrested. Although the court's jurisdiction is derived from the Brussels Arrest Convention, the court must decline jurisdiction under Article 21 of the 1968 Convention.[25]

---

[21] *The Deichland* [1990] 1 Q.B. 361 (C.A.).
[22] *Ibid.*
[23] *The Prinsengracht* [1993] 1 Lloyd's Rep. 41.
[24] *The Po* [1991] 2 Lloyd's Rep. 206 (C.A.).
[25] Case C–406/92 *The Tatry* [1994] E.C.R. I–5439; [1999] Q.B. 515.

CHAPTER 14

FOREIGN JUDGMENTS[1]

1. INTRODUCTORY

RULE 34—**A judgment of a court of a foreign country (hereinafter**   14R–001
referred to as a foreign judgment) has no direct operation in England but
may

(1) **be enforceable by claim or counterclaim at common law or under**
    statute, or

(2) **be recognised as a defence to a claim or as conclusive of an issue**
    in a claim.

---

[1] See Patchett, *Recognition of Commercial Judgments and Awards in the Commonwealth* (1984),
Pt. I; Read, *Recognition and Enforcement of Foreign Judgments* (1938); Piggott, *Foreign Judgments* (1908); Briggs & Rees, *Civil Jurisdiction and Judgments* (2nd ed. 1997), Chap. 7;
Restatement, Chap. 5; Restatement Third, *Foreign Relations Law*, 1987, ss. 481–483; Scoles
and Hay, Chap. 24. This Chapter deals with judgments of foreign municipal courts. International tribunals set up by treaty are variously described as courts and arbitral tribunals, but
their judgments or awards do not fall within the scope of this chapter or of Chapter 16 on
arbitration. See *post*, Rule 66 (International Centre for Settlement of Investment Disputes); and
Schachter (1960) 54 A.J.I.L. 1, 12–14; Schreuer (1975) 24 I.C.L.Q. 153; Giardina (1979)
Recueil des Cours, IV, p. 233. On the Iran-U.S. claims tribunal see *Dallal v. Bank Mellat* [1986]
Q.B. 441, 457–458 (where it was treated as an arbitral tribunal under international law);
Ministry of Defense of Iran v. Gould Inc., 887 F. 2d 1357 (9th Cir. 1989), cert. den. 494 U.S.
1016 (1990) (where its award was enforced under the New York Convention, *post*, Rule 63);
cf. Bendone-Derossi International v. Iran, 6 Iran-U.S. C.T.R. 130, 132 (1984); *Housing and
Urban Services Int. Inc. v. Iran*, 9 Iran-U.S. C.T.R. 313, 330 (1985) ("an international forum,
established by a treaty"); *Anaconda-Iran, Inc. v. Iran*, 13 Iran-U.S. C.T.R. 199, 223 (1986); see
also Lewis (1988) 26 Col. J. Transn. L. 515; Caron (1990) 84 A.J.I.L. 104.

Comment

14–002   **The distinction between enforcement and recognition.** A foreign judgment has no direct operation in England. It cannot, thus, be immediately enforced by execution. This follows from the circumstance that the operation of legal systems is, in general, territorially circumscribed. Nevertheless, a foreign judgment may be recognised or enforced in England. It is plain that, while a court must recognise every foreign judgment which it enforces, it need not enforce every foreign judgment which it recognises.

14–003   Such questions may arise in various ways but may be grouped into three categories. In the first place, the person in whose favour such a judgment is pronounced may seek to have that judgment executed or otherwise carried out as against the person against whom it is given. The claimant is then seeking to *enforce* the judgment. The case is not different when the plaintiff in the original or foreign proceedings, being subsequently made a defendant in English proceedings in the same or a related matter, sets up the foreign judgment by way of counterclaim or other cross-proceedings of a positive sort. Not every type of judgment is capable of enforcement in this way. A judgment dismissing a claim or counterclaim is obviously not capable of enforcement, unless it orders the unsuccessful party to pay costs, as it frequently does; nor is a declaratory judgment, *e.g.* one declaring the status of a person or the title to a thing; nor is a decree of divorce. There may, however, be orders ancillary to a decree of divorce which, because they order the payment of money, are capable of enforcement. Examples are an order that the husband should pay maintenance to his wife, or vice versa, or that the unsuccessful party should pay the other's costs. A judgment *in rem* determining the title to a foreign immovable is equally obviously incapable of enforcement in England. A foreign judgment *in rem* decreeing the sale of a ship or other chattel to meet the claim does not normally require enforcement in England, because this can usually be satisfied out of the proceeds of sale of the *res*, or out of the bail or other security which the owner gave to avoid the arrest of the *res*. But if the security given in the foreign court is insufficient, it has been held that an action *in rem* may be brought in England against the ship to enforce the foreign decree if it is necessary to complete the execution of the judgment, provided that the ship remains the property of the judgment debtor at the time of arrest.[2]

14–004   Secondly, the person in whose favour a judgment is given in a foreign country may seek on its basis merely to resist a claim here in the same or a connected matter. In this case the type of judgment involved is largely immaterial. For instance, A may sue X in England for a debt and X successfully defend the action by showing that the matter has already been litigated in a foreign court, which has found that the alleged debt does not exist and has in consequence given judgment for X.[3] In such a case the situation indeed is that a party to English proceedings is relying directly upon a foreign judgment, but he is doing so merely to establish a negative proposition and seeks that *recognition* alone be accorded to that judgment. There is no question of *enforcement*. Again, if a foreign judgment *in rem* decrees the sale of a ship or other chattel in favour of A, A may resist proceedings in England by the

---

[2] *The Despina G.K.* [1983] Q.B. 214; see also *The City of Mecca* (1879) 5 P.D. 28, revd. on other grounds (1881) 6 P.D. 106 (C.A.). See *post*, para. 14–103.
[3] *Cf. Barber v. Lamb* (1860) 8 C.B. (N.S.) 95.

owner of the ship or chattel in reliance on the foreign judgment,[4] or he may bring a claim *in personam* for wrongful interference against one who denies his title. In neither case is he seeking to enforce the judgment; he is relying on the foreign judgment to prove his title, and the judgment is recognised *qua* an assignment of property rather than *qua* a judgment. For A is relying on the title created by the foreign judgment rather than on the judgment itself.[5]

Thirdly, the party against whom a judgment was given may seek to use that judgment, or the fact that he has satisfied that judgment, to resist a further claim by the party in whose favour the judgment was given. For example, a claimant may have brought proceedings in a foreign court but have obtained a judgment for less than he had sought. If he brings a second set of proceedings upon the same claim, the defendant may seek to rely on the foreign judgment in support of either of two answers to the claim. He may seek *recognition* of the judgment if it contained a discrete ruling in his favour dismissing part of the claim, just as in the previous example. But he may also rely upon the existence, or the satisfaction, of the judgment as a bar to further proceedings on the same claim,[6] or on a separate claim but which should have been advanced, if at all, in the proceedings in the foreign court.[7] This also involves *recognition* of a foreign judgment, but its effect is to treat the foreign judgment as a final adjudication of the issues which arose between the parties, and to preclude the bringing of further proceedings *ab initio*, as distinct from establishing that the findings in favour of the party relying on the foreign judgment are conclusive upon issues which will arise for adjudication in the English proceedings. **14–005**

The bases of enforcement and recognition. English courts have recognised and enforced foreign judgments from the seventeenth century onwards.[8] It was at one time supposed that the basis of this enforcement was to be found in the doctrine of comity. English judges believed that the law of nations required the courts of one country to assist those of any other, and they feared that if foreign judgments were not enforced in England, English judgments would not be enforced abroad.[9] But later this theory was superseded by what is called the doctrine of obligation, which was stated by Parke B. in *Russell v. Smyth*[10] and *Williams v. Jones*[11] and approved by Blackburn J. a generation later in *Godard v. Gray*[12] and *Schibsby v. Westenholz*[13] in the following words: "We think that . . . the true principle on which the judgments of foreign tribunals are enforced in England is . . . that the judgment of a court of competent jurisdiction over the defendant imposes a duty or obligation on the defendant to pay the sum for which judgment is given, which the courts in this country are bound to enforce; and consequently that anything which negatives **14–006**

---

[4] See *Castrique v. Imrie* (1870) L.R. 4 H.L. 414.
[5] See *post*, para. 14–101.
[6] *Cf.* Civil Jurisdiction and Judgments Act 1982, s.34; *Republic of India v. India Steamship Co. Ltd.* [1993] A.C. 410. See *post*, paras. 14–034 *et seq.*
[7] *Henderson v. Henderson* (1843) 3 Hare 100. See *post*, para. 14–035.
[8] See Sack in *Law, A Century of Progress, 1835–1935* (1937), Vol. 3, pp. 342, 382–384. *Cf.* Holdsworth, *History of English Law*, Vol. 11, pp. 270–273.
[9] See *Roach v. Garvan* (1748) 1 Ves.Sen. 157, 159; *Wright v. Simpson* (1802) 6 Ves. 714, 730; *Alves v. Bunbury* (1814) 4 Camp. 28.
[10] (1842) 9 M. & W. 810, 819.
[11] (1845) 13 M. & W. 628, 633.
[12] (1870) L.R. 6 Q.B. 139, 149–150.
[13] (1870) L.R. 6 Q.B. 155.

that duty, or forms a legal excuse for not performing it, is a defence to the action."[14] It followed that provided the foreign court had jurisdiction to give the judgment according to the English rules of the conflict of laws, the judgment is conclusive in England (unless it is impeachable for reasons of fraud, public policy or the like) and not merely prima facie evidence of the defendant's liability as had at one time been supposed.[15]

14–007   In *Adams v. Cape Industries plc*[16] Scott J. accepted Blackburn J.'s restatement of the obligation doctrine as being the basis on which English courts would recognise and enforce foreign judgments *in personam*.[17] The Court of Appeal, however, accepted that the obligation doctrine was purely theoretical, since it has no practical value in identifying the foreign judgments which give rise to the obligation. The Court of Appeal accepted that at common law foreign judgments were enforced, not through considerations of comity, but on the basis of the principle that a legal obligation arises to satisfy a judgment of a court of competent jurisdiction[18]; but in a later passage it also expressed the view that some notion of comity lay behind the recognition of judgments, but "this cannot be comity on an individual nation-to-nation basis, for our courts have never thought it necessary to investigate what reciprocal rights of enforcement are conceded by the foreign country, or to limit their exercise of jurisdiction to that which they would recognise in others. The most one can say is that the duty of positive law first identified in *Schibsby v. Westenholz* . . . must stem from an acknowledgement that the society of nations will work better if some foreign judgments are taken to create rights which supersede the underlying cause of action, and which may be directly enforced in countries where the defendant or his assets are to be found."[19]

14–008   In *Adams v. Cape Industries plc* the basis for the recognition of judgments was considered to be relevant by the Court of Appeal in deciding the issue whether the federal court in Texas had jurisdiction under Rule 36(1) by virtue of the alleged presence of the judgment debtor in another State of the American Union, Illinois: was the relevant "country", for the purposes of the enforcement of the Texas court, the United States (in which event presence in Illinois would be regarded as giving the court jurisdiction) or Texas (in which event it would not be so regarded)? Scott J. took as the starting point the suggestion in *Schibsby v. Westenholz*[20] that the basis of the jurisdiction of a foreign court over resident aliens was that they had the benefit of the protection of the laws of that country or owed temporary allegiance to it. Scott J. concluded that the relevant "country" was the United States because the source of authority of the Federal court was in the sovereign power which established it, namely the United States.[21] The Court of Appeal was sceptical about the application of the idea of "allegiance" as being the basis of the obligation, and saw the judgment debtor's duty to abide by the foreign judgment as deriving from the fact that "by going to a foreign place he invests himself by tacit consent with the rights and obligations stemming from the local laws as administered by the local court."[22] In the event, it was not

---

[14] (1870) L.R. 6 Q.B. 155, 159. For criticism, see Ho (1997) 46 I.C.L.Q. 443.
[15] See *post*, Rule 41.
[16] [1990] Ch. 433 (Scott J. and C.A.).
[17] *Ibid.* p. 457.
[18] [1990] Ch. 433, 513. See also *Owens Bank Ltd. v. Bracco* [1992] 2 A.C. 443, 484.
[19] [1990] Ch. 433, 552.
[20] (1870) L.R. 6 Q.B. 155, 161.
[21] [1990] Ch. 433, 490–491.
[22] *Ibid.* at p. 555.

necessary to decide this issue, because (like Scott J.) the Court of Appeal held that the judgment debtor had not been present or resident in Illinois; but the Court of Appeal indicated that if it had been necessary to decide the question, it would have agreed with Scott J. that the relevant "country" was the United States rather than Texas.

Enforcement at common law. A judgment creditor seeking to enforce a **14–009** foreign judgment in England at common law cannot do so by direct execution of the judgment. He must bring an action on the foreign judgment. But he can apply for summary judgment under what is now Part 24 of the Civil Procedure Rules 1998, previously Order 14 of the Rules of the Supreme Court, on the ground that the defendant has no real prospect of successfully defending the claim[23]; and if his application is successful, the defendant will not be allowed to defend at all. The speed and simplicity of this procedure, coupled with the tendency of English judges narrowly to circumscribe the defences that may be pleaded to a claim on a foreign judgment, mean that foreign judgments are in practice enforceable at common law much more easily than they are in many foreign countries.[24]

Enforcement under statute. A foreign judgment may be enforceable **14–010** under statute by a more direct process of registration. The first step in this direction was taken as long ago as 1801, when the Crown Debts Act provided for the reciprocal enrolment and enforcement of English and Irish Exchequer orders and Chancery decrees. This early innovation was broadened and applied also in relation to Scotland by the Judgments Extension Act 1868. This enactment dispensed with the necessity for an action upon a judgment to which it applied. A certificate of such a judgment obtained in one part of the United Kingdom was registrable as of right in another such part, and thereupon acquired exactly the force and effect of a local judgment.

The Judgments Extension Act 1868[25] was followed by the Administration **14–011** of Justice Act 1920 ("the 1920 Act") wherein provision is made for the reciprocal enforcement of the judgments of superior courts within the United Kingdom, on the one hand, and corresponding courts of other territories within the Commonwealth on the other.[26] Before the 1920 Act could be extended to a country in the Commonwealth Her Majesty had to be satisfied that reciprocal provisions had been made in the country concerned for the enforcement therein of United Kingdom judgments[27]; and it has been extended by Order in Council to very many such countries.[28] Registration of a foreign judgment under the 1920 Act is discretionary and not as of right, since it can be refused unless the registering court "in all the circumstances of the case . . . think it is just and convenient that the judgment should be

---

[23] *Grant v. Easton* (1883) 13 Q.B.D. 302 (C.A.); *Colt Industries Inc. v. Sarlie (No. 2)* [1966] 1 W.L.R. 1287 (C.A.). See *post*, para. 14–025.

[24] For a comparative study on the recognition and enforcement of foreign judgments see Delaume, *Law and Practice of Transnational Contracts* (1988), Chap. 7. See also Report of the Foreign Judgments (Reciprocal Enforcement) Committee, Cmd. 4213 (1932), paras. 2, 9, 10, 14.

[25] The Inferior Courts Judgment Extension Act 1882 provided for enforcement of judgments of lesser tribunals. The 1868 and 1882 Acts are replaced by the Civil Jurisdiction and Judgments Act 1982, Pt. II.

[26] See Rule 46.

[27] 1920 Act, s.14.

[28] See *post*, para. 14–161.

enforced in the United Kingdom."[29] Registration is, moreover, not to be ordered if the original court acted without jurisdiction (though no attempt is made to give a comprehensive definition of this term), or if the defendant establishes any of a limited number of defences which are very similar to those available at common law.[30] Where, however, a judgment has been duly registered it is to have the same force and effect as a judgment of the registering court.[31] Although the person entitled under a judgment registrable under the Act is not deprived of the possibility of suing thereon at common law, the employment of this alternative is discouraged by a provision that it should ordinarily involve sacrifice of the costs of the claim.[32] The Act still remains generally in force[33] but its application to territories to which it had not already been applied was excluded by an Order in Council made under the Foreign Judgments (Reciprocal Enforcement) Act 1933,[34] the intention being that the wider scheme elaborated in the latter enactment should ultimately replace that of the 1920 Act.

14–012   The basis of the system of enforcement of foreign judgments introduced by the Foreign Judgments (Reciprocal Enforcement) Act 1933 ("the 1933 Act") is still reciprocity of treatment. But the scheme of the 1933 Act is wider than that of the 1920 Act in that it is capable of application to countries completely foreign in the political sense. So far it has been applied only to Austria, Belgium, France, Germany, Israel, Italy, the Netherlands, Norway and Suriname among countries of this category and, of countries within the Commonwealth, only to Australia, Canada, India, Pakistan, Tonga, Guernsey, Jersey and the Isle of Man.[35] But as regards Austria, Belgium, France, Germany, Italy, the Netherlands and Norway, the 1933 Act is almost entirely superseded by enforcement and recognition under Part I of the Civil Jurisdiction and Judgments Act 1982.[36] The 1933 Act permits the registration of judgments of courts of countries to which it applies within a period of six years of their pronouncement.[37] Registration is available as of right instead of merely at discretion as under the 1920 Act, provided that any judgment sought to be registered has not been wholly satisfied and is enforceable by execution in the country of the original court.[38] Registration, however, may or must be set aside if the judgment debtor shows certain grounds and execution may not issue until the time has passed within which an application for setting it aside may be made.[39] The 1933 Act contains detailed rules[40] on when foreign courts are deemed to have jurisdiction for the purposes of its provisions; these rules are modelled very closely on those of the common law. The grounds for the setting aside of a registered judgment correspond, broadly, to those upon which a foreign judgment is impeachable at common law or upon which registration of a judgment under the 1920 Act is to be refused and are discussed in detail

---

[29] s.9(1).
[30] s.9(2).
[31] s.9(3).
[32] s.9(5).
[33] For the territories to which the Act applies, see *post*, para. 14–167.
[34] See the Foreign Judgments (Reciprocal Enforcement) Act 1933, s.7(1), and S.R. & O. 1933 No. 1073. And see para. 14–161, *post*.
[35] See Rule 47.
[36] See Rule 48.
[37] s.2(1).
[38] *Ibid.* proviso.
[39] ss.4(1), 2(2), proviso.
[40] s.4(2).

hereafter.[41] The effect of registration is in general, as under the earlier Acts, to assimilate a foreign judgment to a judgment of the registering court.[42] No proceedings upon the judgment itself other than proceedings for its registration may be brought in any court in the United Kingdom.[43]

The Civil Jurisdiction and Judgments Act 1982[44] provides for the recognition and enforcement of judgments emanating from Scotland and Northern Ireland,[45] and from the European Communities States which are parties to the Brussels Convention on jurisdiction and the enforcement of judgments in civil and commercial matters of 1968 ("the 1968 Convention") and the EFTA countries which are parties to the similar Lugano Convention.[46] As regards judgments from other parts of the United Kingdom it replaces and extends the Judgments Extension Act 1868 and the Inferior Courts Judgments Extension Act 1882, and, as under the legislation it replaces, the court in which registration of the judgment is made may not impeach the judgment for lack of jurisdiction or for any of the reasons for which judgments may be impeached at common law. As regards judgments of States which are parties to the 1968 Convention or the Lugano Convention it largely supersedes the system under the 1933 Act. The power of the United Kingdom to examine the jurisdiction of the foreign court is very limited. The scheme of the Conventions is that, in general, it is for the court in which the judgment is given to determine that it has jurisdiction under the relevant Convention. The judgment may be impeached only on a number of limited grounds. Enforcement under the 1982 Act is by way of registration only, and no proceedings may be brought at common law.[47] A striking innovation of the 1982 Act, both as regards enforcement of judgments of other parts of the United Kingdom and of the Convention States, is that it applies not only to money judgments but also to other types of non-money judgments, such as injunctions, and to interlocutory, as well as to final, judgments. **14–013**

The European Communities (Enforcement of Community Judgments) Order 1972[48] makes provision for the enforcement by registration in the United Kingdom of "community judgments," *i.e.* decisions or orders of the European Court of Justice and of certain other organs of the European Communities. **14–014**

The State Immunity Act 1978[49] makes provision for the recognition of judgments rendered against the United Kingdom in countries which are parties to the European Convention on State Immunity. **14–015**

Common law and statute. The statutes which deal with enforcement of foreign judgments are of limited geographical application and the judgments of very many foreign countries are not within their scope. There thus remains a considerable area within which enforcement at common law is the only process possible, and it remains of practical importance because several important foreign countries (including the United States) do not yet have **14–016**

---

[41] See paras. 14R–118 *et seq.*
[42] s.2(2).
[43] s.6.
[44] ss.18–19.
[45] See Rule 49.
[46] See Rule 48.
[47] See *post*, paras. 14–219 and 14–233.
[48] S.I. 1972 No. 1590; *post*, Rule 50.
[49] ss.18–19; *post*, Rule 51.

treaties with the United Kingdom for the reciprocal enforcement and recognition of judgments and thus do not come within the statutory schemes.

14–017   **Scope and arrangement of this chapter.** The arrangement of this chapter is as follows: it is divided into four sections. The first contains the present introductory rule. The second deals with enforcement and recognition of foreign judgments at common law, including the jurisdiction of foreign courts to pronounce judgments capable of enforcement (or recognition)[50] in England, and the extent to which a foreign judgment is conclusive in England and the extent to which it may be impeached in English proceedings in which its recognition or enforcement is sought.[51] The third section deals with enforcement and recognition under statute, the 1920, 1933 and 1982 Acts,[52] and enforcement of Community judgments and foreign judgments against the Crown.[53] The fourth section deals with the effect of the Protection of Trading Interests Act 1980 on the enforceability of foreign judgments for multiple damages.[54] The chapter does not deal, however, except incidentally, with the effect given in England to foreign judgments relating to the administration of estates, foreign decrees of dissolution or nullity of marriage, foreign adjudications in bankruptcy or orders for the winding up of companies, or foreign maintenance orders, which because of their special character are dealt with in the context of the matters to which they relate.[55]

2. ENFORCEMENT AND RECOGNITION AT COMMON LAW

A. *Enforcement and Recognition*

14R–018   **RULE 35—(1) Subject to the Exceptions hereinafter mentioned and to Rule 55 (international conventions), a foreign judgment[56] *in personam* given by the court of a foreign country with jurisdiction to give that judgment in accordance with the principles set out in Rules 36 to 39, and which is not impeachable under any of Rules 42 to 45, may be enforced by a claim or counterclaim for the amount due under it if the judgment is**

   (a) for a debt, or definite sum of money[57] (not being a sum payable in respect of taxes or other charges of a like nature[58] or in respect of a fine or other penalty[59]); and

---

[50] Rules 35 to 40.

[51] Rules 41 to 45.

[52] Rules 46 to 49.

[53] Rules 50 to 51.

[54] Rule 52.

[55] See Rules 78 to 81 (divorce and nullity); 88 (maintenance orders); 127 (administration of estates); 158 (winding up); 165–171 (bankruptcy).

[56] As to what is a judgment, see *Berliner Industriebank A.G. v. Jost* [1971] 2 Q.B. 463 (C.A.) (ascertainment of a debt in German bankruptcy proceedings); *Midland International Trade Services Ltd. v. Sudairy, Financial Times*, May 2, 1990 (judgment of court as distinct from administrative tribunal).

[57] *Sadler v. Robins* (1808) 1 Camp. 253. The historical explanation of this limitation is that the form of action appropriate for the enforcement of a foreign judgment was originally debt, though some authorities allow assumpsit.

[58] *Government of India v. Taylor* [1955] A.C. 491, 514; *Rossano v. Manufacturers' Life Insurance Co. Ltd.* [1963] 2 Q.B. 352, 376–378; *Att.-Gen. for Canada v. Schulze*, (1901) 9 S.L.T. 4; *U.S.A. v. Harden* (1963) 41 D.L.R. (2d) 721 (Sup.Ct.Can.); *Commissioner of Taxes v. McFarland*, 1965 (1) S.A. 470. See Stoel (1967) 16 I.C.L.Q. 663.

[59] *Huntington v. Attrill* [1893] A.C. 150 (P.C.); *U.S. v. Inkley* [1989] Q.B. 255 (C.A.). See Restatement, s.120.

(b) final and conclusive,[60]
but not otherwise.

Provided that a foreign judgment may be final and conclusive, though it is subject to an appeal, and though an appeal against it is actually pending in the foreign country where it was given.[61]

(2) A foreign judgment given by the court of a foreign country with jurisdiction to give that judgment in accordance with the principles set out in Rules 36 to 39, which is not impeachable under any of Rules 42 to 45 and which is final and conclusive on the merits,[62] **is entitled to recognition at common law and may be relied on in proceedings in England.**[63]

(3) No proceedings may be be brought by a person on a cause of action in respect of a judgment which has been given in his favour in proceedings between the same parties or their privies in a court in another part of the United Kingdom or in a court in an overseas country unless that judgment is not enforceable according to clause (1), or not entitled to recognition according to clause (2), of this Rule.[64]

This Rule must be read subject to Rule 52.

COMMENT

Introduction. Until after 1933 there was no mode of directly enforcing a foreign judgment in England (unless it were a Scottish or Northern Irish judgment or the judgment of a court of some country of the Commonwealth overseas[65]) by execution, but a foreign judgment for a debt or definite sum of money might be enforced by an action *in personam* on the part of the person in whose favour the judgment was given (generally the plaintiff in the foreign proceedings) for the sum due under the judgment. Enforcement was not dependent on the reciprocal treatment of English judgments in the foreign country, English policy being singularly generous in this regard. Nor was it necessary that the judgment should be given as the result of investigation of the merits of the case; if the court were one which in the view of English law had jurisdiction over the defendant, and he failed to defend, the court's judgment might be enforced in England as fully as if he had defended the case

14–019

[60] *Nouvion v. Freeman* (1889) 15 App.Cas. 1; *Plummer v. Woodburne* (1825) 4 B. & C. 625; *Paul v. Roy* (1852) 15 Beav. 433; *Patrick v. Shedden* (1853) 2 E. & B. 14; *Frayes v. Worms* (1861) 10 C.B.(N.S.) 149; *Blohn v. Desser* [1962] 2 Q.B. 116; *Berliner Industriebank A.G. v. Jost* [1971] 2 Q.B. 463 (C.A.); *Gauthier v. Routh* (1842) 6 U.C.Q.B.(O.S.) 602; *Graham v. Harrison* (1889) 6 Man.L.R. 210; Read, pp. 64–86; Restatement, ss.107–109.

[61] *Nouvion v. Freeman* (1889) 15 App.Cas. 1, 13; *Nouvion v. Freeman* (1887) 37 Ch.D. 244, 255 (C.A.); *Scott v. Pilkington* (1862) 2 B. & S. 11; *Colt Industries Inc. v. Sarlie (No. 2)* [1966] 1 W.L.R. 1287; *Barned's Banking Co. Ltd. v. Reynolds* (1875) 36 U.C.Q.B. 256; *Howland v. Codd* (1894) 9 Man.L.R. 435; *Wilcox v. Wilcox* (1914) 16 D.L.R. 491 (Man. C.A.); *Campbell v. Morgan* [1919] 1 W.W.R. 644 (Man.); *Pan American World Airways v. Varghese* (1984) 7 D.L.R. (4th) 499, app. dismissed (1985) 15 D.L.R. (4th) 768 (Ont. C.A.); *Four Embarcadero Center Venture v. Mr. Greenjeans* (1988) 64 O.R. (2d) 746, app. dismissed (1988) 65 O.R. (2d) 160 (C.A.).

[62] *Harris v. Quine* (1869) L.R. 4 Q.B. 653; *Black-Clawson International Ltd. v. Papierwerke Waldhof-Aschaffenburg A.G.* [1975] A.C. 591; *The Sennar (No. 2)* [1985] 1 W.L.R. 490 (H.L.); *Tracomin S.A. v. Sudan Oil Seeds Co. Ltd. (No. 1)* [1983] 1 W.L.R. 662, affd. [1983] 1 W.L.R. 1026 (C.A.); contrast *Charm Maritime Inc. v. Kyriakou* [1987] 1 Lloyd's Rep. 433, 441, 450 (C.A.); *Desert Sun Loan Corp. v. Hill* [1996] 2 All E.R. 847 (C.A.).

[63] See Read, pp. 101–106, and Gutteridge (1932) 13 B.Y.I.L. 49, 60–64.

[64] Civil Jurisdiction and Judgments Act 1982, s.34.

[65] See Rules 46, 49, *post*.

on the merits.[66] The foregoing remains the law in the sense that a foreign judgment is still enforceable by action, but since 1933 the more direct enforcement of certain foreign judgments has become possible under the 1933 and 1982 Acts.

14–020   **Clause (1) of the Rule.** For a claim to be brought to enforce a foreign judgment, the judgment must be for a definite sum of money, which expression includes a final order for costs, *e.g.* in a divorce suit.[67] It must order X, the defendant in the English action, to pay to A, the claimant, a definite and actually ascertained[68] sum of money; but if a mere arithmetical calculation is required for the ascertainment of the sum it will be treated as being ascertained[69]; if, however, the judgment orders him to do anything else, *e.g.* specifically perform a contract, it will not support an action,[70] though it may be *res judicata.*[71] The judgment must further be for a sum other than a sum payable in respect of taxes or the like, or in respect of a fine or other penalty. It is well settled[72] that an English court will not entertain an action for the enforcement, either directly or indirectly, of a penal[73] or revenue[74] law of a foreign country. Since "the essential nature and real foundation of a cause of action are not changed by recovering judgment upon it,"[75] it follows that the court cannot entertain an action for the enforcement, either directly or indirectly,[76] of a foreign judgment ordering the payment of taxes,[77] fines or other contributions or penalties. A penalty in this sense normally means a sum payable to the State, and not to a private claimant, so that an award of punitive or exemplary damages is not penal.[78] But it is possible that an award of multiple damages, *e.g.* in an anti-trust action, might nevertheless be regarded as penal at common law.[79] If the foreign judgment imposes a fine on the defendant and also orders him to pay compensation to the injured party (called the "*partie civile*" in French proceedings), the latter part of the judgment can be severed from the former and enforced in England.[80]

14–021   No foreign judgment will be recognised or enforced in England at common law unless it is "final and conclusive." The expression is repetitive but, having

---

[66] *Russell v. Smyth* (1842) 9 M. & W. 810; *Boyle v. Victoria Yukon Trading Co.* (1902) 9 B.C.R. 213.

[67] *Russell v. Smyth* (1842) 9 M. & W. 810; *cf. Ruf v. Walter* [1990] 6 W.W.R. 661 (Sask.).

[68] *Sadler v. Robins* (1808) 1 Camp. 253. Compare *Hall v. Odber* (1809) 11 East 118.

[69] *Beatty v. Beatty* [1924] 1 K.B. 807 (C.A.).

[70] *Cf. Church of Scientology of California v. Miller, The Times,* October 15, 1987, affd. *The Times,* October 23, 1987 (C.A.); *Re Resort Condominiums International Inc.* [1995] 1 Qd. 406 (interlocutory injunction not enforceable).

[71] Wolff, s.243; see *Duke v. Andler* [1932] 4 D.L.R. 529 (Sup.Ct.Can.). But see White (1982) 9 Sydney L.Rev. 630.

[72] See Rule 3.

[73] See, *e.g. Huntington v. Attrill* [1893] A.C. 150 (P.C.); *U.S. v. Inkley* [1989] Q.B. 255 (C.A.).

[74] See, *e.g. Government of India v. Taylor* [1955] A.C. 491.

[75] *Wisconsin v. Pelican Insurance Co.,* 127 U.S. 265, 292 (1888). See Scoles and Hay, pp. 984–986, for subsequent developments in the United States.

[76] *Rossano v. Manufacturers' Life Insurance Co. Ltd.* [1963] 2 Q.B. 352, 376–378.

[77] *Att.-Gen. for Canada v. Schulze,* (1901) 9 S.L.T. 4; *U.S.A. v. Harden* (1963) 41 D.L.R. (2d) 721 (Sup.Ct.Can.); *Commissioner of Taxes v. McFarland,* 1965 (1) S.A. 470.

[78] *Cf. S.A. Consortium General Textiles v. Sun & Sand Agencies Ltd.* [1978] Q.B. 279, 309, *per* Lord Denning M.R., *obiter* (a case on the 1933 Act).

[79] *Cf. Jones v. Jones* (1889) 22 Q.B.D. 425 (a case not involving a foreign judgment). The effect of the Protection of Trading Interests Act 1980 is that such judgments are not enforceable at common law or otherwise: see Rule 52.

[80] *Raulin v. Fischer* [1911] 2 K.B. 93; *cf. Black v. Yates* [1992] Q.B. 526.

been rendered familiar by many judicial statements, is reproduced in the 1933 Act.[81] The test of finality is the treatment of the judgment by the foreign tribunal as a *res judicata*. "In order to establish that [a final and conclusive] judgment has been pronounced, it must be shown that in the court by which it was pronounced, it conclusively, finally, and forever established the existence of the debt of which it is sought to be made conclusive evidence in this country, so as to make it *res judicata* between the parties."[82] A foreign judgment which is liable to be abrogated or varied by the court which pronounced it is not a final judgment.[83] But a default judgment may be final and conclusive, even though it is liable to be set aside in the very court which rendered it.[84] Otherwise, the clearer the claimant's case, the more useless his judgment would be.

If the judgment is given by a court of a law district forming part of a larger   **14–022** federal system, *e.g.* an American state, the finality and conclusiveness of the judgment in the law district where it was given are alone relevant in England; its finality and conclusiveness in other parts of the federal system, *e.g.* in other American states, are irrelevant.[85]

The class of foreign judgments in relation to which it is most difficult to   **14–023** decide whether or not they are "final and conclusive" are maintenance orders, providing for periodical payments. The principle applicable to such orders is, however, the same as that applying to all other foreign judgments. If they are incapable of alteration by the court which made them, then they are actionable in England.[86] But if they are capable of variation by the court which made them, as are orders for periodical payments made by the Family Division of the High Court, no action is maintainable upon them,[87] just as no action in the Queen's Bench Division will lie upon an order of the Family Division.[88] Yet an order variable in respect of future payments may be invariable in so far as arrears are concerned in which case an action may be brought for the recovery of the arrears.[89] Statutory means exist for the enforcement in England of

---

[81] s.1(2)(*a*), as substituted by 1982 Act, Sched. 10, para. 1.

[82] *Nouvion v. Freeman* (1889) 15 App.Cas. 1, 9.

[83] *Nouvion v. Freeman* (1889) 15 App.Cas. 1, 13; *Re Macartney* [1921] 1 Ch. 522, 531, 532; *Westfal-Larsen A.S. v. Ikerigi Naviera S.A.* [1983] 1 All E.R. 382, 389; *cf. Charm Maritime Inc. v. Kyriakou* [1987] 1 Lloyd's Rep. 433, 442, 450 (C.A.); see also *M'Donnell v. M'Donnell* [1921] 2 I.R. 148.

[84] *Vanquelin v. Bouard* (1863) 15 C.B.(N.S.) 341, 367–368; *Boyle v. Victoria Yukon Trading Co.* (1902) 9 B.C.R. 213; *Barclays Bank Ltd. v. Piacun* [1984] 2 Qd.R. 476; *Minkler and Kirschbaum v. Sheppard* (1991) 60 B.C.L.R. (2d) 360; *Re Dooney* [1993] 2 Qd.R. 362; *cf. Four Embarcadero Center Venture v. Mr. Greenjeans* (1988) 64 O.R. (2d) 746, app. dismissed (1988) 65 O.R. (2d) 160 (C.A.). For criticism of dicta in *Nouvion v. Freeman* see Read, pp. 85–86.

[85] *Colt Industries Inc. v. Sarlie (No. 2)* [1966] 1 W.L.R. 1287.

[86] *Cf. McLean v. McLean* [1979] 1 N.S.W.L.R. 620; *Holt v. Thomas* (1987) 38 D.L.R. (4th) 117 (Alb.).

[87] *Harrop v. Harrop* [1920] 3 K.B. 386; *Re Macartney* [1921] 1 Ch. 522; *M'Donnell v. M'Donnell* [1921] 2 I.R. 148; *Maguire v. Maguire* (1921) 64 D.L.R. 180 (Ont.C.A.); *Davis v. Davis* (1922) 22 S.R.N.S.W. 185; *Estate H. v. Estate H.*, 1952 (4) S.A. 168; *Ashley v. Gladden* [1954] 4 D.L.R. 848 (Ont.C.A.); *Smith v. Smith* [1955] 1 D.L.R. 229 (B.C.); *Re Paslowski and Paslowski* (1957) 11 D.L.R. (2d) 180 (Man.). The rule is criticised by Grodecki (1959) 8 I.C.L.Q. 18, 32–40, and has been rejected by some American state courts: see Restatement, s.109; Scoles and Hay, p. 537.

[88] *Bailey v. Bailey* (1884) 13 Q.B.D. 855 (C.A.); *Robins v. Robins* [1907] 2 K.B. 13.

[89] *Beatty v. Beatty* [1924] 1 K.B. 807 (C.A.); *G. v. G.* [1984] I.R. 368; *Splatt v. Splatt* (1889) 10 N.S.W.L.R. 227; *Hadden v. Hadden* (1898) 6 B.C.R. 340; *Robertson v. Robertson* (1908) 16 O.L.R. 170; *Wood v. Wood* (1916) 28 D.L.R. 367 (Ont.C.A.); *Patton v. Reed* (1972) 30 D.L.R. (3d) 494 (B.C.); *Lear v. Lear* (1974) 51 D.L.R. (3d) 56 (Ont.C.A.).

maintenance orders made by Scottish or Northern Irish courts, and by the courts of certain foreign countries outside the United Kingdom.[90]

14–024   **Proviso.** At common law, a foreign judgment may be final and conclusive even though an appeal is actually pending in the foreign country where it was given.[91] "In order to its receiving effect here, a foreign decree need not be final in the sense that it cannot be made the subject of appeal to a higher court; but it must be final and unalterable in the court which pronounced it; and if appealable the English court will only enforce it, subject to conditions which will save the interests of those who have the right of appeal."[92] So in a proper case a stay of execution would no doubt be ordered pending a possible appeal.[93]

14–025   **Enforcement.** Where the statement of case[94] in proceedings on a foreign judgment has been served on the defendant and the defendant has acknowledged service or filed a defence, the claimant may apply for summary judgment on the ground that the defendant has no real prospect of successfully defending the claim.[95] Unless the defendant satisfies the court that there is an issue or question in dispute which ought to be tried—for instance, on the ground that the judgment was obtained by fraud[96]—the court may give judgment for the claimant.[97] Where the defendant does not appear the claimant may enter judgment at once.[98] The proceedings upon such an action may thus have a largely formal character. The English court must have *in personam* jurisdiction over the judgment debtor, and the process in a claim to enforce a judgment at common law must be served on him in England, unless permission is obtained to serve him outside. But even where the judgment debtor has no connection with England process may be issued, with permission, for service outside the jurisdiction, solely on the basis that the claim is to enforce a foreign judgment.[99]

---

[90] See *post*, Rule 88.

[91] *Scott v. Pilkington* (1862) 2 B. & S. 11; *Colt Industries Inc. v. Sarlie (No. 2)* [1966] 1 W.L.R. 1287. Contrast the position under the 1920 Act, s.9(2)(*e*), the 1933 Act, ss.1(3), 5(1) and the 1982 Act, Scheds. 1 and 3C, Art. 38, and Scheds. 6 and 7, para. 3, *post*, paras. 14–163, 14–179, 14–196 and 14–234.

[92] *Nouvion v. Freeman* (1889) 15 App.Cas. 1, 13.

[93] *Scott v. Pilkington* (1862) 2 B. & S. 11, 41; *Colt Industries Inc. v. Sarlie (No. 2)* [1966] 1 W.L.R. 1287; *Four Embarcadero Center Venture v. Mr. Greenjeans, supra,* n. 84; *Arrowmaster Inc. v. Unique Farming Ltd.* (1993) 17 O.R. (3d) 407; *cf. The Varna (No. 2)* [1994] 2 Lloyd's Rep. 41, 46.

[94] Under the practice prior to the CPR, the statement of claim usually contained a specific assertion that the foreign court had jurisdiction: there is nothing in the CPR which requires any change in the practice.

[95] CPR 24.2, replacing R.S.C. Ord. 14, r. 1; *Grant v. Easton* (1883) 13 Q.B.D. 302 (C.A.); *Colt Industries Inc. v. Sarlie (No. 2)* [1966] 1 W.L.R. 1287 (C.A.).

[96] *Manger v. Cash* (1889) 5 T.L.R. 271; *Codd v. Delap* (1905) 92 L.T. 510 (H.L.); *Israel Discount Bank of New York v. Hadjipateras* [1984] 1 W.L.R. 137 (C.A.); *Jet Holdings Inc. v. Patel* [1990] 1 Q.B. 335, 347 (C.A.); *House of Spring Gardens Ltd. v. Waite* [1991] 1 Q.B. 241, 250 (C.A.); *Jacobs v. Beaver* (1908) 17 O.L.R. 496.

[97] CPR 24.2.

[98] CPR 12.

[99] Ord. 11, r. 1(1)(*m*) and Rule 27, clause (13), *ante*, para. 11R–204, reversing the effect of *Perry v. Zissis* [1977] 1 Lloyd's Rep. 607 (C.A.). For an example, see *Midland International Trade Services Ltd. v. Sudairy, Financial Times,* May 2, 1990. Ord. 11, r. 1(1)(*m*) will not apply, however, unless and until there is a judgment which has been rendered by the foreign court: *Mercedes Benz A.G. v. Leiduck* [1996] 1 A.C. 284, 298–299 (P.C.).

It is immaterial that the debtor dies before judgment is pronounced by the foreign court and that the judgment is pronounced against his personal representatives.[1]

14–026

Since *Miliangos v. George Frank (Textiles) Ltd.*[2] there is no reason why a claim for enforcement of a foreign judgment may not be for the amount of the judgment in the currency in which it was rendered.

A foreign judgment *in personam* cannot be enforced in England by a claim *in rem*.[3]

Clause (2) of the Rule. A foreign judgment may be relied on in English proceedings otherwise than for the purpose of its enforcement. A claimant who has brought proceedings abroad and lost may seek to bring a similar claim in England; or in proceedings on a different claim an issue may be raised which has been decided abroad. In such cases a foreign judgment entitled to recognition may give rise to *res judicata, i.e.* to a cause of action estoppel, which prevents a party to proceedings from asserting or denying, as against the other party, the existence of a cause of action, the nonexistence or existence of which has been determined by the foreign court, or to an issue estoppel, which will prevent a matter of fact or law necessarily decided by a foreign court from being re-litigated in England.

14–027

Thus a foreign judgment which is final and conclusive on the merits in favour of the defendant is at common law[4] a good defence to a claim in England for the same matter.[5] There is no cause of action estoppel against a different remedy,[6] although there may be an issue estoppel if a relevant issue has been decided directly in the foreign action. Where two conflicting foreign judgments, each of which would satisfy the criteria for recognition, have determined issues which arise in the English proceedings, the general rule is that the one given first in time is to be recognised, to the exclusion of the latter.[7]

14–028

It was established by a majority of the House of Lords in *Carl Zeiss Stiftung v. Rayner & Keeler Ltd. (No. 2)*[8] that a foreign judgment could give rise to an issue estoppel, *i.e.* prevent a party from denying any matter of fact or law necessarily decided by the foreign court. For there to be such an issue

14–029

---

[1] *Re Flynn (No. 2)* [1969] 2 Ch. 403.

[2] [1976] A.C. 443. See Rule 211. *Cf.* the position under the 1933 Act, *post*, para. 14–173.

[3] *The City of Mecca* (1881) 6 P.D. 106 (C.A.); *The Sylt* [1991] 1 Lloyd's Rep. 240, 244.

[4] See also 1933 Act, s.8 (*post*, para. 14–181), 1982 Act, s.19, and Scheds. 1 and 3C, Art. 26, (*post*, para. 14–221).

[5] *Ricardo v. Garcias* (1845) 12 Cl. & F. 368; *Jacobson v. Frachon* (1927) 138 L.T. 386 (C.A.). *Cf. Booth v. Leycester* (1837) 1 Keen 579. It is irrelevant which proceedings were commenced first. It used to be said that the foreign judgment only gave rise to the estoppel if the English proceedings were subsequent to the foreign judgment: but see *Lee v. Citibank N.A.* [1981] Hong Kong L.R. 470 (C.A.), following *Bell v. Holmes* [1956] 1 W.L.R. 1359 and *Morrison Rose & Partners v. Hillman* [1961] 2 Q.B. 266 (C.A.) and not following *The Delta* (1876) 1 P.D. 393; *Houstoun v. Sligo* (1885) 29 Ch.D. 448, 454.

[6] *Callandar v. Dittrich* (1842) 4 M. & G. 68. On the other hand, a mere change in form to proceedings *in rem* is immaterial: *The Griefswald* (1859) Swab. 430, 435. But the same relief may be asked based on a different case giving rise to a new equity: *Hunter v. Stewart* (1861) 4 De G.F. & J. 168; contrast *Henderson v. Henderson* (1843) 3 Hare 100, 115. See *Michado v. The Hattie and Lottie* (1904) 9 Exch.C.R. 11.

[7] *Showlag v. Mansour* [1995] 1 A.C. 431 (P.C.). But if the party holding the earlier judgment is himself estopped from relying on it, the general rule will be displaced.

[8] [1967] 1 A.C. 853, 917, 925, 967.

estoppel, three requirements must be satisfied[9]: first, the judgment of the foreign court must be (a) of a court of competent jurisdiction, (b) final and conclusive and (c) on the merits; secondly, the parties to the English litigation must be the same parties (or their privies) as in the foreign litigation[10]; and, thirdly, the issues raised must be identical. A decision on the issue must have been necessary for the decision of the foreign court and not merely collateral. But Lord Reid emphasised that special caution is required before a foreign judgment can be held to give rise to an issue estoppel: English courts are unfamiliar with modes of procedure in many foreign countries, and it may be difficult to see whether a particular issue has been decided or that a decision was a basis of a foreign judgment and not merely collateral or obiter; and it might be unjust for a litigant to be estopped from putting forward his case in England because he failed to do so in an earlier case of a trivial character abroad.[11]

14–030   The requirement that the judgment must be final and conclusive applies when it is relied on by the defendant as a defence,[12] just as it does when it is relied upon by the claimant seeking enforcement. The judgment must be "on the merits." In *The Sennar (No. 2)*[13] Lord Diplock seems to have thought this added nothing to the condition that the judgment must be final and conclusive, but Lord Brandon suggested that "a decision on the merits is a decision which establishes certain facts as proved or not in dispute; states what are the relevant principles of law applicable to such facts; and expresses a conclusion with regard to the effect of applying those principles to the factual situation concerned."[14] The issue determined by the foreign court in *The Sennar (No. 2)*, was that a jurisdiction agreement bound the claimant to bring his claim in Sudan, and as such may have been considered as being procedural in nature. But it was the final conclusion of the foreign court on the point which it had been asked to decide, namely, whether the exclusive jurisdiction agreement

---

[9] *The Sennar (No. 2)* [1985] 1 W.L.R. 490, 499 (H.L.) See also *Vervaeke v. Smith* [1983] 1 A.C. 145; *Tracomin S.A. v. Sudan Oil Seeds Co. Ltd. (No. 1)* [1983] 1 W.L.R. 662, 673, affd. [1983] 1 W.L.R. 1026 (C.A.); *The Jocelyne* [1984] 2 Lloyd's Rep. 569; *E.D. & F. Man (Sugar) Ltd. v. Haryanto (No. 2)* [1991] 1 Lloyd's Rep. 429; *cf. Westfal-Larsen A/S v. Ikerigi Compania Naviera S.A.* [1983] 1 All E.R. 382; *E.I. du Pont de Nemours v. Agnew (No. 2)* [1988] 2 Lloyd's Rep. 240 (C.A.); *Black v. Yates* [1992] Q.B. 526; *Desert Sun Loan Corp. v. Hill* [1996] 2 All E.R. 847 (C.A.).

[10] *Carl Zeiss Stiftung v. Rayner & Keeler Ltd. (No. 2)* [1967] 1 A.C. 853, 910–911, 928–929, 936–937, 944–946. But it may be an abuse of the process to attempt to relitigate in England an issue decided by a foreign court against one, but not both, of the parties to the English action: *Rayner v. Bank für Gemeinwirtschaft A.G.* [1983] 1 Lloyd's Rep. 462 (C.A.). In *House of Spring Gardens Ltd. v. Waite* [1991] 1 Q.B. 241 (C.A.) it was held that an Irish judgment was enforceable against a judgment creditor, who (unlike his co-defendants) had not applied in Ireland to set aside the judgment for fraud. Since he was aware of the proceedings, he would be regarded as "privy" to them, and was bound by the determination of the Irish court that there had been no fraud in the absence of fresh evidence. Even if he were not estopped it would be an abuse of process and contrary to justice and public policy for the issue of fraud to be relitigated in England after the issue had been decided by the foreign court. *Cf. Owens Bank Ltd. v. Etoile Commerciale S.A.* [1995] 1 W.L.R. 44 (P.C.). For discussion of whether judgments or settlements in U.S. class actions may be regarded as *res judicata* against class members resident outside the United States, see Dixon (1997) 46 I.C.L.Q. 134.

[11] [1967] 1 A.C. 853 at p. 918, *per* Lord Reid. But *cf. The Sennar (No. 2)* [1985] 1 W.L.R. 490, 500 (H.L.).

[12] *Plummer v. Woodburne* (1825) 4 B. & C. 625; *Frayes v. Worms* (1861) 10 C.B. (N.S.) 149; *Carl Zeiss Stiftung v. Rayner & Keeler Ltd. (No. 2)* [1967] 1 A.C. 853. See also *Charm Maritime Inc. v. Kyriakou* [1987] 1 Lloyd's Rep. 433 (C.A.).

[13] [1985] 1 W.L.R. 490, 494 (H.L.).

[14] *Ibid.* p. 499.

applied to a claim framed in tort; and it was on this account held capable of supporting an estoppel against the claimant[15] upon the issue. In *Desert Sun Loan Corp. v. Hill*[16] the Court of Appeal accepted in principle that issue estoppel could arise from an interlocutory judgment of a foreign court on a procedural, non-substantive issue where there was express submission of the issue in question to the foreign court, and the specific issue of fact was raised before and decided, finally and not just provisionally, by the court. It was emphasised that before according preclusive effect to any such finding by a foreign court the need for caution should be borne in mind.[17] Consequently, if the decision of the foreign court is a non-reviewable but clear decision upon an issue submitted to it for its determination,[18] it is unnecessary for the purposes of issue estoppel to characterise the issue so decided as being substantive rather than procedural.

It has been held that at common law and under the 1933 Act a judgment **14–031** given in favour of the defendant on the ground that the action is barred by a statute of limitation was not on the merits.[19] But the effect of these decisions is reversed by section 3 of the Foreign Limitation Periods Act 1984, by which a foreign judgment determining any matter by reference to limitation is deemed to be on the merits. A judgment in default or by consent may, however, be a judgment on the merits.[20]

By the Civil Liability (Contribution) Act 1978 "any person liable" in **14–032** respect of any damage may recover from any other person liable in respect of the same damage. It has been held that the equivalent provision in Scots law (which is in different terms and refers to liability found in an action) applies to the liability of the party seeking contribution established in an action in Scotland, and not in a foreign country.[21] The view has been expressed that a foreign judgment gives no right to seek contribution under the 1978 Act.[22] This question was left open in the Privy Council in *Soc. Nat. Ind. Aerospatiale v. Lee Kui Jak*,[23] but it indicated that the argument that the 1978 Act did not apply to foreign judgments had some substance.[24] It is suggested that these doubts are well-founded, unless a foreign judgment, in proceedings to which the person from whom contribution is sought is a party, has held him liable and is entitled to recognition.

A distinct question arises when a foreign judgment is relied on as the basis **14–033** of a consequential contractual claim. Where an insurer has been adjudged

---

[15] Who was necessarily taken to be bound by findings made by a court to the jurisdiction of which he had unquestionably submitted.

[16] [1996] 2 All E.R. 847 (C.A.).

[17] This represents the view of the majority, Evans and Stuart-Smith L.JJ; Roch L.J. dissented.

[18] For consideration of the separate question whether it is open to the losing party to contend that he did not submit to the jurisdiction of the foreign court, so that its ruling is not to be recognised as against him, notwithstanding that he sought a determination on the point in question, see *post*, para. 14–065.

[19] *Harris v. Quine* (1869) L.R. 4 Q.B. 653; *Black-Clawson International Ltd. v. Papierwerke-Aschaffenburg A.G.* [1975] A.C. 591.

[20] See Read, p. 101; but on the need for caution in the case of default judgments see *Carl Zeiss Stiftung v. Rayner & Keeler Ltd. (No. 2)* [1967] 1 A.C. 853, 916–917, 926, 946; Spencer-Bower, Turner and Handley, *Res Judicata* (3rd ed. 1996), pp. 74–75.

[21] *Comex Houlder Diving Ltd. v. Colne Fishing Co. Ltd.*, 1987 S.L.T. 443 (H.L.).

[22] Clerk and Lindsell, *Torts* (17th ed. 1995), para. 151.

[23] [1987] A.C. 871.

[24] *Ibid.* at p. 902, *per* Lord Goff of Chieveley, who was a party to both decisions, as was Lord Keith who delivered the leading speech in the former case.

liable to an insured, and claims reimbursement from his reinsurer, the judgment of the foreign court will be recognised as the foundation for the claim if the foreign court was one of competent jurisdiction in relation to the claim against the insurer; judgment was not obtained by the insured in breach of a jurisdiction agreement or other contractual obligation not to proceed in that court; the insured took all proper defences; and the judgment was not manifestly perverse. To this extent the reinsurer is bound by the findings of a court in proceedings to which he was not party,[25] provided that there is no express term to the contrary in the contract of reinsurance.

14–034   **Clause (3) of the Rule.** Clause (2) of the Rule deals with the case in which issues determined by a foreign court are recognised as being *res judicata* for the purpose of proceedings properly brought in an English court in which those issues also arise. The party in whose favour the relevant finding was made relies on the foreign judgment to prevent his being at risk for a second time. The situation is different when a claimant has succeeded in a foreign court, but, dissatisfied with the measure of his recovery, sues again on the original cause of action. In this case there may have been no finding in favour of the defendant which may be recognised in his defence,[26] and clause (2) will furnish no answer to the second claim. A foreign judgment in favour of a claimant was at one time no bar to a subsequent action in England based on the original cause of action. But section 34 of the 1982 Act provides that no proceedings may be brought by a person on a cause of action[27] in respect of which a foreign judgment has been given in his favour in proceedings between the same parties, or their privies,[28] unless the judgment is not enforceable or entitled to recognition in England. This displaces in part the rule of the common law that a foreign judgment does not extinguish the original cause of action in respect of which the judgment was given: a rule which was described by Lord Wilberforce as a rule "which, if surviving at all, is an illogical survival".[29]

14–035   Section 34 does not enact a statutory rule of merger[30] (by which the original cause of action would cease to exist), but provides that "no proceedings shall be brought". This form of words was held by the House of Lords in *Republic of India v. India Steamship Co. Ltd.*[31] to debar the claimant from bringing proceedings, as distinct from removing the jurisdiction of the court to hear the claim. Accordingly it would be open to the claimant to demonstrate that reasons existed, such as prior agreement between the parties to litigate a claim in two separate parts, or estoppel by representation, acquiescence or convention, why the claimant should not be prevented from proceeding in the

---

[25] *Commercial Union Assurance Co. plc v. NRG Victory Reinsurance Ltd.* [1998] 2 All E.R. 434 (C.A.). But if the insured's claim has been settled, this principle cannot be applied, and the reinsurer may require the insurer to demonstrate its legal liability to the insured.
[26] If there has been, and if the defendant succeeded in part and obtained a determination of certain issues in his favour, recognition of that part of the judgment under clause (2) of this Rule will provide him with the necessary defence.
[27] For the meaning of the same cause of action, see *Black v. Yates* [1992] Q.B. 526; *Republic of India v. India Steamship Co. Ltd.* [1993] A.C. 410, 419–421. It means the factual situation which confers a remedy, and not the evidence to support it, nor the nature of the remedy itself.
[28] *Cf. Black v. Yates, supra; House of Spring Gardens v. Waite* [1991] 1 Q.B. 241 (C.A.); para. 14–029, *ante.*
[29] *Carl Zeiss Stiftung v. Rayner & Keeler Ltd. (No. 2)* [1967] 1 A.C. 855, 966.
[30] [1993] A.C. 410, 423–424.
[31] [1993] A.C. 410.

circumstances of the particular case. In *Republic of India v. India Steamship Co. Ltd.*, cargo owners sued shipowners in India for damages for short delivery of a small part of a cargo which had been jettisoned en route; after the Indian proceedings had been commenced, but before judgment, the parties agreed that the claim for the total loss of the whole cargo would be subject to English law and jurisdiction. The cargo owners recovered damages in their action in India, but when they sued in England for damages for loss of the whole cargo, the shipowners succeeded in an argument that section 34 debarred the cargo owners' action. Though the House of Lords held that section 34 might not apply in the case of waiver, estoppel or agreement to exclude it, and remitted the matter to the Admiralty judge for his determination, it ruled in *Republic of India v. India Steamship Co. Ltd. (No. 2)*[32] that there was no basis on the facts for lifting the bar to proceedings constituted by section 34.

Where the proceedings in the foreign court were brought in the form of an **14-036** action *in personam*, but the subsequent English proceedings are brought as an Admiralty claim *in rem*, the two sets of proceedings are to be regarded as being between the same parties, for a claim *in rem* is a claim against the owners of the vessel from the moment the Admiralty Court is seised with jurisdiction.[33] The fact that the proceedings are differently constituted as a matter of procedural law is insufficient by itself to displace the operation of section 34. The section may also apply even though the foreign court has not given judgment by the date of institution of the English proceedings.[34] It is unclear what the position would be if the English proceedings were commenced first and the foreign action second, but the foreign court were to give judgment before the English court did. If the policy behind section 34 is to prevent the institution of a second set of proceedings, there is no reason why it should have any application to the proceedings which were commenced first.

Section 34 has no application when the English claim is in respect of a **14-037** different cause of action from that litigated in the foreign proceedings. But the principle in *Henderson v. Henderson*[35] may be applied to prevent the subsequent raising of a claim which could and should have been brought and included in the proceedings before the foreign court; alternatively (though to the same effect) it may be an abuse of process for the second action to brought.[36]

ILLUSTRATIONS

(1) ENFORCEMENT

1. A recovers judgment against X in a Jamaican court, that X should pay A £3,000, after first **14-038** deducting thereout X's costs, to be taxed by the proper officer. The costs have not been taxed. The judgment is not a judgment for a fixed sum. No claim is maintainable.[37]

2. A agrees with X in California to sell to X land situate in England. The land is conveyed to X in accordance with English law. A sues X in California to set aside the conveyance because of

---

[32] [1998] A.C. 878.

[33] *Ibid.*, at pp. 906–910.

[34] *Ibid.*, at p. 912.

[35] (1843) 3 Hare 100. See also *Desert Sun Loan Corp. v. Hill* [1996] 2 All E.R. 847, 863 (C.A.); the point was left open in *Republic of India v. India Steamship Co. Ltd. (No. 2), supra,* at p. 916.

[36] *Cf. Desert Sun Loan Corp. v. Hill, supra,* at pp. 859, 863–4.

[37] *Sadler v. Robins* (1808) 1 Camp. 253.

X's fraud. The Californian court orders X to reconvey the land to A and on X's refusal to do so the clerk of the court purports to reconvey in X's name. A cannot obtain in England a declaration that he is the owner of the land on the sole ground of the Californian decision.[38]

3. X, a British subject, is arrested in Florida on fraud charges. He is released on bail on condition that he enters into an "appearance bond". He is given permission to leave the United States for 30 days, but fails to return. The United States Government obtains a judgment on the bond in a civil action. No claim on the judgment is maintainable, because the purpose of the claim is the enforcement of the criminal process.[39]

14–039
4. X, while recklessly galloping her horse in a foreign country, ran into A, and seriously injured him. X was prosecuted for her criminal negligence by the foreign authorities, and A intervened in the prosecution and claimed damages from X as allowed by the foreign law. The court convicted X, fined her 100 francs, and ordered her to pay 15,000 francs to A by way of damages, and also costs. A was held entitled to recover the sterling equivalent of the damages and costs in England.[40]

5. A took certain summary or "executive" proceedings against X in a Spanish court for the recovery of a debt, and obtained a so-called *remate* judgment for £10,000. In these executive proceedings X could set up certain limited defences, but could not dispute the validity of the contract under which the debt arose. Either party, if unsuccessful in the executive proceedings, might in the same court and in respect of the same matter take ordinary or (so-called) plenary proceedings in which all defences might be set up, and the merits of the matter could be gone into. In the plenary proceedings a *remate* judgment could not be set up as *res judicata* or otherwise, and a plenary judgment rendered the *remate* judgment inoperative. The *remate* judgment was not final and conclusive. No action was maintainable on the *remate* judgment.[41]

14–040
6. A, in an action in New York, recovers judgment against X for the equivalent of £900,000. X appeals against the judgment to the New York Court of Appeals. An appeal under the law of New York is not a stay of execution. While the appeal is pending A brings a claim in England against X on the judgment. The claim is maintainable, and it is immaterial that the judgment may not be enforceable in other American states until the appeal has been dismissed.[42]

7. X, who resided in England, was a sleeping partner in a firm carrying on business in Vienna. A obtained judgment against the firm in Vienna on a bill of exchange. By Austrian law, although the firm had no separate legal personality, the judgment was not enforceable against the partners personally unless a further action was brought against them individually, when various personal defences not concluded by the judgment against the firm would be available. A brought an action in England against X on the judgment. The action was not maintainable because the Austrian judgment against the firm was not final and conclusive as against X.[43]

8. W obtains a maintenance order against H in a foreign court. The court has power under its law to vary the amount of the payments, both in respect of past and future instalments. W cannot bring a claim in England on the judgment of the foreign court, as that judgment is not final and conclusive.[44]

(2) Recognition

14–041
9. A brings an action in a Victorian court against X for breach of contract. X denies the breach. A judgment which is final and conclusive in Victoria is given in favour of X. The judgment is a defence to a claim in England against X by A for the same breach of contract.[45]

10. In 1865 A brought an action against X in the Isle of Man to recover a debt. Under a Manx statute no action could be brought to recover a debt more than three years after the cause of action accrued. The statute did not extinguish the debt. The Manx court gave judgment for X on the

---

[38] *Cf. Duke v. Andler* [1932] 4 D.L.R. 529 (Sup.Ct.Can.); *cf. Haspel v. Haspel* [1934] 2 W.W.R. 412 (Alta.): see *post*, para. 14–105.

[39] *U.S. v. Inkley* [1989] Q.B. 255 (C.A.).

[40] *Raulin v. Fischer* [1911] 2 K.B. 93.

[41] *Nouvion v. Freeman* (1889) 15 App.Cas. 1.

[42] *Colt Industries Inc. v. Sarlie (No. 2)* [1966] 1 W.L.R. 1287; *cf. Scott v. Pilkington* (1862) 2 B. & S. 11, 41.

[43] *Blohn v. Desser* [1962] 2 Q.B. 116. As to whether the Austrian court had jurisdiction over X, see *post*, para. 14–072.

[44] *Harrop v. Harrop* [1920] 3 K.B. 386; *cf. M'Donnell v. M'Donnell* [1921] 2 I.R. 148. Contrast *Beatty v. Beatty* [1924] 1 K.B. 807 (C.A.). Compare *Re Macartney* [1921] 1 Ch. 522.

[45] 1982 Act, s.34. *Cf. Plummer v. Woodburne* (1825) 4 B. & C. 625. See also *Ricardo v. Garcias* (1845) 12 Cl. & F. 368. Contrast *Frayes v. Worms* (1861) 10 C.B.(N.S.) 149.

ground that the action was statute-barred. A then sued X for the debt in England. The Manx judgment was not a defence to the action.[46] But today it would be a defence.[47]

11. A sued X in England for the return of a sum of money, and obtained judgment that X was constructive trustee of the money and liable to return it. A brought similar proceedings in Jersey; as the English judgment was recognised under Jersey law, X's defence was struck out. An Egyptian court later gave a judgment that X had received the money by way of gift and not as trustee; and X applied to amend his defence, contending that the Egyptian judgment was *res judicata*. Both judgments would in principle have qualified for recognition in Jersey. The Jersey court would recognise the first, and therefore not the second, judgment.[48]

12. In proceedings by the Zeiss Foundation of East Germany against X in England, X denies the authority of Zeiss' solicitors to bring the action, relying (in part) on a decision of a West German court in proceedings between Zeiss and X that Zeiss was not properly before the West German court because the East German organ which purported to act on its behalf had no authority. The decision of the West German court does not give rise to an issue estoppel because there is no identity of parties or identity of interest, since the relevant parties in England on the issue are X and Zeiss' solicitors and not X and Zeiss.[49]

14–042

13. A sues X in the Netherlands. The Dutch court decides that the parties have agreed that the dispute should be heard exclusively by the Sudanese courts. A then sues X in England. A is bound by the determination of the Dutch court on the issue of the applicability of the jurisdiction clause.[50]

14. H, an Englishman, was killed in Spain by the negligent driving of X, on whose motorcycle H was a passenger. W, his widow, gave a power of attorney to a Spanish lawyer to represent her and their children in Spanish criminal proceedings (in which civil damages may also be awarded). The Spanish lawyer failed to reserve the right under Spanish law to seek damages elsewhere than in Spain. The Spanish court ordered the defendant to pay damages. In a subsequent action in England, W could not sue on her own behalf because the English proceedings were brought on a cause of action in respect of which the Spanish judgment had been given; but she could sue on behalf of the estate, because no claim on behalf of the estate had been made in Spain, and she could sue on behalf of the children because the actions taken on their behalf in Spain were contrary to their interests, and there was no evidence that they were able to give informed consent to the power of attorney.[51]

(3) DEBARRING PROCEEDINGS

15. A brings an action in New York against X, a resident of New York, and recovers judgment for $100,000. Part of the judgment debt is paid by X. Thereupon A brings a claim in England against X for the same debt. The claim on the debt will fail[52]; A's remedy is to enforce the balance of the judgment.

14–043

16. A brings proceedings in New York against X, a resident of New York, and recovers judgment for $100,000, which is far less than he had claimed. He later brings a claim in England against X in respect of the same cause of action, giving credit for the $100,000 already recovered. In the absence of grounds for an estoppel or the like, the proceedings must be struck out.[53]

Exception 1—**No proceedings may be entertained by any court in the United Kingdom for the recovery of a sum payable under a foreign judgment capable of registration in accordance with the provision of**

14E–044

    (1) Part I of the Foreign Judgments (Reciprocal Enforcement) Act 1933;

    (2) Part I of the Civil Jurisdiction and Judgments Act 1982; and

    (3) Part II of the Civil Jurisdiction and Judgments Act 1982,

other than proceedings for registration in the manner described in Rules 47 to 49.

---

[46] *Harris v. Quine* (1869) L.R. 4 Q.B. 653.
[47] Foreign Limitation Periods Act 1984, s.3.
[48] *Showlag v. Mansour* [1995] 1 A.C. 431 (P.C.).
[49] *Carl Zeiss Stiftung v. Rayner & Keeler Ltd. (No. 2)* [1967] 1 A.C. 853.
[50] *The Sennar (No. 2)* [1985] 1 W.L.R. 490 (H.L.), a case on the law prior to the 1968 Convention.
[51] *Black v. Yates* [1992] Q.B. 526, a case on the law prior to the 1968 Convention.
[52] 1982 Act, s.34.
[53] 1982 Act, s.34. *cf. Republic of India v. India Steamship Co. Ltd.* [1993] A.C. 410.

Comment

14–045 Under the 1933 Act no action may be brought at common law upon a judgment capable of direct enforcement by registration under the Act.[54] Part I of the 1982 Act deals with judgments of States which are parties to the 1968 Convention and the Lugano Convention. Section 4 of the 1982 Act provides that enforcement of judgments under the Conventions shall be effected through registration. Although the Act does not expressly provide that no claim may be brought at common law, the Conventions, which have the "force of law,"[55] lay down a simplified procedure for the enforcement of judgments which is inconsistent with the continuance of other forms of enforcement.[56] As regards judgments of other parts of the United Kingdom, the 1982 Act provides expressly that they shall not be enforced otherwise than in accordance with the registration procedures of the Act.[57] Where a judgment is registrable under the 1920 Act[58] the judgment creditor is not deprived of the possibility of suing to enforce it at common law, but the employment of this alternative is discouraged by a provision that it should ordinarily involve sacrifice of the costs of the action.[59]

14E–046 *Exception 2*—**No proceedings may be entertained in any court in the United Kingdom for the recovery of any sum alleged to be payable under a judgment given in a court of a country to which section 9 of the Foreign Judgments (Reciprocal Enforcement) Act 1933 has been applied by Order in Council.**[60]

Comment

14–047 Section 9(1) of the 1933 Act provides that if it appears to Her Majesty that the treatment in respect of recognition and enforcement accorded by the courts of any foreign country to judgments given in the courts of the United Kingdom is substantially less favourable than that accorded by the courts of the United Kingdom to judgments of the courts of that country, Her Majesty may apply that section to that country, with the consequences stated in Exception 2 above. The object of this enactment was to strengthen the hand of H.M. Government in negotiating conventions with foreign countries for the reciprocal enforcement of foreign judgments.[61] No Order in Council has yet been made under the section. The section refers to "any foreign country." It is thus not limited to foreign countries to which Part I of the 1933 Act applies, but is of general application. However, the term "foreign country" is limited to

---

[54] 1933 Act, s.6. Nor can a claim be brought on the original cause of action: para. 14–112, *post*.
[55] 1982 Act, s.2(1).
[56] Case 42/76 *De Wolf v. Cox* [1976] E.C.R. 1759.
[57] 1982 Act, s.18(8).
[58] Rule 46.
[59] 1920 Act, s.9(5). But a claim on the original cause of action may not be brought: para. 14–112, *post*.
[60] 1933 Act, s.9, as amended by 1982 Act, Sched. 10, para. 2.
[61] See the Report of the Foreign Judgments (Reciprocal Enforcement) Committee, Cmd. 4213 (1932), Annex V, para. 14.

countries foreign in the political sense: it does not extend to countries forming part of the Commonwealth.[62]

B. *Jurisdiction of Foreign Courts at Common Law*

(1) JURISDICTION IN PERSONAM

RULE 36—Subject to Rules 37 to 39, a court of a foreign country outside the United Kingdom has jurisdiction to give a judgment *in personam* capable of enforcement or recognition in the following cases[63]:   **14R–048**

First Case[64]**—If the judgment debtor was, at the time the proceedings were instituted, present in the foreign country.**

Second Case[65]**—If the judgment debtor was claimant, or counterclaimed, in the proceedings in the foreign court.**

Third Case[66]**—If the judgment debtor, being a defendant in the foreign court, submitted to the jurisdiction of that court by voluntarily appearing in the proceedings.**

Fourth Case[67]**—If the judgment debtor, being a defendant in the original court, had before the commencement of the proceedings agreed, in**

---

[62] This is made clear in s.7.

[63] See generally *Adams v. Cape Industries plc* [1990] Ch. 433, 512–525 (C.A.). See also *Schibsby v. Westenholz* (1870) L.R. 6 Q.B. 155, 161; *Rousillon v. Rousillon* (1880) 14 Ch.D. 351, 371; *Emanuel v. Symon* [1908] 1 K.B. 302, 309 (C.A.).

[64] *Carrick v. Hancock* (1895) 12 T.L.R. 59; *Littauer Glove Corporation v. F.W. Millington (1920) Ltd.* (1928) 44 T.L.R. 746; *Vogel v. R. A. Kohnstamm Ltd.* [1973] Q.B. 133; *Adams v. Cape Industries plc* [1990] Ch. 433 (C.A.); *cf. Sfeir & Co. v. National Insurance Co. of New Zealand* [1964] 1 Lloyd's Rep. 330 (a case on the 1920 Act); Read, pp. 148–151.

[65] Cases cited in n. 63 *supra*, and *Burpee v. Burpee* [1929] 3 D.L.R. 18 (B.C.); Read, p. 160.

[66] *De Cosse Brissac v. Rathbone* (1861) 6 H. & N. 301, as explained in *Schibsby v. Westenholz* (1870) L.R. 6 Q.B. 155, 162; *Voinet v. Barrett* (1885) 55 L.J.Q.B. 39 (C.A.); *Guiard v. de Clermont* [1914] 3 K.B. 145; *S.A. Consortium General Textiles v. Sun & Sand Agencies Ltd.* [1978] Q.B. 279 (C.A.) (a case under the 1933 Act); *Jet Holdings Inc. v. Patel* [1990] 1 Q.B. 335, 341 (C.A.); *Re Overseas Food Importers & Brandt* (1981) 126 D.L.R. (3d) 422; (B.C.C.A.); *Canada Trustco Mortgage Co. v. Rene Management & Holdings Ltd.* (1988) 53 D.L.R. (4th) 222 (Man. C.A.); *575225 Saskatchewan Ltd. v. Boulding* [1988] 6 W.W.R. 738 (B.C.C.A.); *First National Bank of Houston v. Houston E. & C. Inc.* [1990] 5 W.W.R. 719 (B.C.); *Gourmet Resources International Inc. v. Paramount Capital Corp.* [1993] I.L.Pr. 583 (Ont.); and *cf. The Atlantic Emperor (No. 2)* [1992] 1 Lloyd's Rep. 624, 633 (C.A.); Read, pp. 161–171; Clarence Smith (1953) 2 I.C.L.Q. 510; on the effect of an appearance to protest the jurisdiction of the foreign court see 1982 Act, s.33, and paras. 14–063, *et seq., post.*

[67] *Feyerick v. Hubbard* (1902) 71 L.J.K.B. 509; *Copin v. Adamson* (1875) 1 Ex. D. 17 (C.A.); *Jeannot v. Fuerst* (1909) 25 T.L.R. 424; *Bank of Australasia v. Harding* (1850) 9 C.B. 661; *Bank of Australasia v. Nias* (1851) 16 Q.B. 717; *Kelsall v. Marshall* (1856) 1 C.B.(N.S.) 241; *Vallée v. Dumergue* (1849) 4 Exch. 290; *Blohn v. Desser* [1962] 2 Q.B. 116; *Vogel v. R. A. Kohnstamm Ltd.* [1973] Q.B. 133; *S.A. Consortium General Textiles v. Sun & Sand Agencies Ltd.* [1978] Q.B. 279 (C.A.) (a case on the 1933 Act); *First City Capital Ltd. v. Winchester Computer Corp.* (1987) 44 D.L.R. (4th) 301 (Sask. C.A.); *Bank of Credit & Commerce International (Overseas) Ltd. v. Gokal* [1995] 2 W.W.R. 240 (B.C.C.A.); Read, pp. 171–177; Restatement, ss.32, 43.

respect of the subject matter of the proceedings, to submit to the jurisdiction of that court or of the courts of that country.

COMMENT

14–049 A fundamental requirement for the recognition or enforcement of a foreign judgment in England at common law[68] is that the foreign court should have had jurisdiction according to the English rules of the conflict of laws. "All jurisdiction is properly territorial," declared Lord Selborne,[69] "and *extra territorium jus dicenti, impune non paretur.* . . . In a personal action, . . . a decree pronounced *in absentem* by a foreign court, to the jurisdiction of which the defendant has not in any way submitted himself, is by international law an absolute nullity. He is under no obligation of any kind to obey it; and it must be regarded as a mere nullity by the courts of every nation, except (when authorised by special local legislation) in the country of the forum by which it was pronounced." Thus, in an early leading case[70] upon the subject, the plaintiff brought an action in England on a judgment of a court in the island of Tobago. The defendant had never been in the island, nor had he submitted to its jurisdiction. There had been a substituted service, valid by the law of Tobago, effected by nailing a copy of the writ to the court-house door. In refusing to recognise the judgment, Lord Ellenborough said "Can the Island of Tobago pass a law to bind the rights of the whole world? Would the world submit to such an assumed jurisdiction?"

14–050 In *Adams v. Cape Industries plc*,[71] the leading modern authority, it was said that "in determining the jurisdiction of the foreign court. . . . , our court is directing its mind to the competence or otherwise of the foreign court to summon the defendant before it and to decide such matters as it has decided"[72] and "we would . . . regard the source of the territorial jurisdiction of the court of a foreign country to summon a defendant to appear before it as being his obligation for the time being to abide by its laws and accept the jurisdiction of its courts while present in its territory."[73]

14–051 It has already been seen[74] that the identification of the relevant "country" can present a problem in the case of a federal system, whose constituent states (like those in the United States) retain some degree of legislative sovereignty. But while not deciding the issue, the Court of Appeal inclined to agree with Scott J. that the relevant country (or law district) for the purposes of the recognition and enforcement of the judgment of a federal court sitting in Texas (and applying Texan substantive law) was the United States and not Texas.

14–052 In that case the Court of Appeal indicated, first, that foreign judgments were enforced in England only if the foreign court was one of "competent jurisdiction"[75]; second, in deciding whether the foreign court was one of competent jurisdiction, the English court would apply, not the law of the foreign court,

---

[68] And under the 1920 and 1933 Acts. The power of the English court to review the jurisdiction of the foreign court under the 1982 Act is more limited. See Rule 48, *post.*

[69] *Sirdar Gurdyal Singh v. Rajah of Faridkote* [1894] A.C. 670, 683–684 (P.C.).

[70] *Buchanan v. Rucker* (1808) 9 East 192, 194.

[71] [1990] Ch. 433, 517–518 (C.A.).

[72] Citing *Pemberton v. Hughes* [1899] 1 Ch. 781, 790 (C.A.).

[73] [1990] Ch. at pp. 517–519.

[74] *Williams v. Jones* (1845) 13 M. & W. 628, 633; *Godard v. Gray* (1870) L.R. 6 Q.B. 139, 147; *Schibsby v. Westenholz* (1870) L.R. 6 Q.B. 155, 159.

[75] *Ibid.*

but English rules of the conflict of laws.[76] Those rules were developed in the nineteenth century, and were restated in the frequently cited judgment of Buckley L.J. in *Emanuel v. Symon*[77]: "In actions *in personam* there are five cases in which the courts of this country will enforce a foreign judgment: (1) where the defendant is a subject of the foreign country in which the judgment has been obtained; (2) where he was resident in the foreign country when the action began; (3) where the defendant in the character of plaintiff has selected the forum in which he is afterwards sued[78]; (4) where he has voluntarily appeared; and (5) where he has contracted to submit himself to the forum in which the judgment was obtained." The actual issue in the case was whether the possession of property in the foreign country was sufficient to give jurisdiction to the foreign court,[79] and none of the heads of jurisdiction enumerated by Buckley L.J. was subjected to scrutiny in that case. As will be seen later,[80] the first case mentioned in Buckley L.J.'s statement can no longer be relied on. The second case was adopted in the 1933 Act, but was stated without reference to those cases which led to the conclusion that mere presence, without residence, would be sufficient to confer jurisdiction and which were approved by the Court of Appeal in *Adams v. Cape Industries plc.*[81] The other three cases are examples of the principle of submission and correspond respectively to the Second, Third and Fourth Cases of Rule 36. All four cases (including residence, rather than presence) were adopted (and slightly altered) in the 1933 Act, and in their altered and re-arranged form they are set out in Rule 47.

The provisions of the 1933 Act were deliberately framed so as to reproduce the rules of the common law as closely as possible,[82] though, as the Foreign Judgments (Reciprocal Enforcement) Committee conceded, it was found desirable to make one or two very slight departures from the common law rules in order to secure international agreements which would be likely to operate satisfactorily in practice.[83] The question therefore arises whether the provisions of the 1933 Act as to the jurisdiction of foreign courts, and as to the scope of the defences, can legitimately be invoked by a court which is asked to enforce a foreign judgment at common law, even though the 1933 Act has not been extended by Order in Council to the foreign country in question. Although the Act has been used[84] to negative arguments that there are additional bases for recognition at common law,[85] the Court of Appeal has

14–053

---

[76] See *post*, para. 14–119.
[77] [1908] 1 K.B. 302, 309 (C.A.), which (as he acknowledged) was taken verbatim from the judgment of Fry J. in *Rousillon v. Rousillon* (1880) 14 Ch.D. 351, 371. The Supreme Court of Canada has said that Buckley L.J.'s summary "bears a remarkable resemblance to a Code": *Morguard Investments Ltd. v. De Savoye* [1990] 3 S.C.R. 1077, 1087.
[78] *i.e.* where a counterclaim is brought.
[79] *Post*, para. 14–076.
[80] *Post*, para. 14–078.
[81] [1990] Ch. 433 (C.A.).
[82] Report of the Foreign Judgments (Reciprocal Enforcement) Committee, Cmd. 4213 (1932), paras. 2, 16, 18 and Annex V, para. 7.
[83] *Ibid.* para. 18 and Annex V, para. 7.
[84] See *Re Trepca Mines Ltd.* [1960] 1 W.L.R. 1273, 1282 (C.A.); *Rossano v. Manufacturers' Life Insurance Co. Ltd.* [1963] 2 Q.B. 352, 383.
[85] In *Owens Bank Ltd. v. Bracco* [1992] 2 A.C. 443, 489, it was held that, because the 1920 Act adopted the common law approach to fraud in relation to foreign judgments (*post*, para. 14–130), it would be wrong for the courts now to alter the common law rule.

held that it is wrong to use the Act to ascertain the common law "by arguing backwards from the provisions of the statute."[86]

14–054   **The first case. Presence.** There is divergence of authority on the question whether presence, as distinct from residence, is a sufficient basis of jurisdiction. The older cases acknowledge that the residence of a defendant in the country at the time when proceedings are commenced gives that court jurisdiction over him at common law.[87] The position is the same under the 1920 Act[88] and the 1933 Act,[89] except that the former requires "ordinary residence", which in this context probably does not differ much from residence simpliciter[90] and the latter contains special rules for corporations. But some of the older cases also suggest that presence, rather than residence, is a sufficient basis,[91] and presence as a basis of jurisdiction is strengthened by those authorities which suggested that "temporary allegiance" to the local sovereign was one of the reasons why a defendant might be under an obligation to comply with the judgments of its courts.[92] For this reasoning is no less applicable where a defendant is merely present within the foreign country concerned. It is also supported by the authorities on the jurisdiction of the English court over persons present in England: the temporary presence of an individual defendant in England gives the English court jurisdiction at common law[93] and the test for the presence of corporations in that context[94] is the same as that for corporations in the context of the jurisdiction of foreign courts, although in the latter context it is described as residence rather than presence.[95] It may be doubted, however, whether casual presence, as distinct from residence, is a desirable basis of jurisdiction if the parties are strangers and the cause of action arose outside the country concerned. For the court is not likely to be the *forum conveniens*, in the sense of the appropriate court most adequately equipped to deal with the facts or the law.[96] The 1920 and 1933 Acts adopted residence rather than presence as the basis of jurisdiction over individuals, and presence (at least as regards domiciliaries of Contracting States) is regarded as an exorbitant basis of jurisdiction over individuals for the purposes of the 1968 Convention and the Lugano Convention.[97] Whilst it is true that the test for corporations in relation to foreign judgments is

---

[86] *Henry v. Geoprosco International* [1976] Q.B. 726, 751. *Cf. Société Co-opérative Sidmetal v. Titan International Ltd.* [1966] 1 Q.B. 828, 845–846.

[87] *Schibsby v. Westenholz* (1870) L.R. 6 Q.B. 155, 161; *Emanuel v. Symon* [1908] 1 K.B. 302, 309 (C.A.). In *State Bank of India v. Murjani Marketing Group Ltd.* unrep., March 27, 1991 (C.A.), Sir Christopher Slade inclined to the view that residence (in the sense of principal home) would be a sufficient basis of jurisdiction, even if the judgment debtor was not present in the foreign country at the date of commencement of proceedings.

[88] s.9(2)(*b*).

[89] s.4(2)(*a*)(iv).

[90] *Cf. ante*, para. 6–118.

[91] *Carrick v. Hancock* (1895) 12 T.L.R. 59; *Herman v. Meallin* (1891) 8 W.N. (N.S.W.) 38; *Forbes v. Simmons* (1914) 20 D.L.R. 100 (Alta.); *cf. General Steam Navigation Co. v. Guillou* (1843) 11 M. & W. 377. Contrast *Australian Assets Co. Ltd. v. Higginson* (1897) 18 L.R. (N.S.W.) Eq. 189, 193.

[92] *Schibsby v. Westenholz* (1870) L.R. 6 Q.B. 155, 161; *cf. Sirdar Gurdyal Singh v. Rajah of Faridkote* [1894] A.C. 670, 683–684 (P.C.).

[93] *Colt Industries Inc. v. Sarlie* [1966] 1 W.L.R. 440 (C.A.); *Maharanee of Baroda v. Wildenstein* [1972] 2 Q.B. 283 (C.A.) *ante*, para. 11–082; *Cf.* Restatement, s.28.

[94] *Ante*, paras. 11–097 *et seq.*

[95] *Post*, para. 14–059.

[96] *Cf.* Dodd (1929) 23 Ill.L.Rev. 427, 437–438.

[97] *Ante*, para 11–233.

equivalent to that for the "presence" of corporations in the context of the jurisdiction of the English court, the test for "presence" of corporations involves some fixed place of business in the foreign country,[98] and is not comparable to what may be the fleeting presence of an individual, even in the extreme case where the place of business is established for a very short period.[99]

In *Adams v. Cape Industries plc*[1] the Court of Appeal reviewed the author- **14–055** ities on presence and residence in the context of the jurisdiction of foreign courts over corporations, but took the opportunity to express general views on the issue. The First Case of the Rule is now framed in terms of presence rather than residence in the light of this decision but the issue remains open in the House of Lords.

In *Carrick v. Hancock*[2] the plaintiff was an Englishman domiciled in **14–056** Sweden who had acted in Sweden as an agent on commission for the defendant, an Englishman. The defendant was served with Swedish proceedings during a short visit to Sweden, and he subsequently defended the Swedish proceedings. Accordingly, the case had a significant connection with Sweden, and in any event the defendant had clearly submitted to the jurisdiction of the Swedish courts. But in an unreserved judgment Lord Russell of Killowen C.J. decided that the Swedish judgment was enforceable because of the defendant's presence in Sweden, and "the question of the time the person was actually in the territory was wholly immaterial".[3]

This decision (among others[4]) was relied on by the Court of Appeal in **14–057** *Adams v. Cape Industries plc* as supporting the principle that, in the absence of submission to the jurisdiction of the foreign court, the competence of a foreign court to summon the defendant before it depended on the physical presence of the defendant in the country concerned at the time of suit: "So long as he remains physically present in that country, he has the benefit of its laws, and must take the rough with the smooth, by accepting his amenability to the process of its courts. In the absence of authority compelling a contrary conclusion, we would conclude that the voluntary presence of an individual in a foreign country, whether permanent or temporary and whether or not accompanied by residence, is sufficient to give the courts of that country territorial jurisdiction over him under our rules of private international law."[5]

The Court of Appeal referred to the "voluntary" presence of the defendant **14–058** as being one not induced by compulsion, fraud or duress, but it is clear from the context[6] that it was not finally decided that the presence of these factors

---

[98] *Post*, para. 14–059.
[99] As in *Dunlop Pneumatic Tyre Co. Ltd. v. A.G. Cudwell & Co.* [1902] 1 K.B. 342 (C.A.).
[1] [1990] Ch. 433 (C.A.).
[2] (1895) 12 T.L.R. 59.
[3] *Ibid.* at p. 60.
[4] *Sirdar Gurdyal Singh v. Rajah of Faridkote* [1894] A.C. 670, 683–684; *Employers' Liability Assurance Corp. v. Sedgwick Collins & Co. Ltd.* [1927] A.C. 95, 114–115.
[5] [1990] Ch. 433 at p. 519. The Court of Appeal indicated that dicta (in cases on the jurisdiction of the *English* court) indicated that the relevant time was *service* of proceedings, rather than *issue*, but expressed no final view. The Court of Appeal (at p. 518) also left open the question whether residence without presence would be a sufficient basis of jurisdiction, but *cf. State Bank of India v. Murjani Marketing Group Ltd.*, *ante*, para. 14–054.
[6] See *ibid.* pp. 518–519.

would negative jurisdiction. There is no decision in England on what the position is when the defendant is forcibly brought, or fraudulently induced to come, into the jurisdiction of the foreign court and there served with process.[7] But in the United States the view is held that in such a case jurisdiction exists but may or should be disclaimed by the court for reasons of equity if the plaintiff is privy to the force or fraud.[8] In this case also, it is clear, the defendant has the benefit of the laws of the State concerned and owes temporary allegiance thereto. The question whether at common law a foreign court has jurisdiction over an individual who is neither resident or present within the foreign jurisdiction but who carries on business regularly there through an agent has been raised but not decided,[9] although it is a basis of jurisdiction under the 1920 Act.[10]

14–059   Where a corporation is concerned neither residence nor presence has, of course, any real meaning. But there is a long line of cases dealing with the question whether a foreign corporation does or does not carry on business in England so as to render itself amenable to the jurisdiction of the English courts at common law.[11] The principle of these cases applies also to the question whether a corporation is present in a foreign country so as to give its courts jurisdiction over it.[12] In *Adams v. Cape Industries plc*[13] the Court of Appeal held that in the case of corporations the test of jurisdiction is satisfied if the corporation is carrying on business at a definite and fixed place. The basic principle is that a trading corporation will be regarded as present within the jurisdiction of the courts of a foreign country if (a) it has established and maintained a fixed place of business and for more than a minimal time has carried on its own business there, *or* (b) its representative has for more than a minimal period of time been carrying on the corporation's business in that country at or from some fixed place of business. In the latter case it will be necessary to consider a number of factors (already mentioned in connection with the jurisdiction of the English court[14]) to determine whether the business being carried on is that of the corporation or its representative. In deciding whether a company is present in a foreign country as a result of the acts of a subsidiary present there, the court must consider whether the subsidiary was acting as agent, and if so, on what terms; it may also treat the subsidiary as the *alter ego* of the parent if special circumstances exist which indicate that there

---

[7] See *Stein v. Valkenhuysen* (1858) E.B. & E. 65 and *Watkins v. North American Lands, etc., Co.* (1904) 20 T.L.R. 534 (H.L.), *ante*, para. 11–082, which suggest that in appropriate circumstances English process might be set aside if the defendant was fraudulently lured into the jurisdiction.

[8] Restatement, s.82, comments *b, d* and *f*.

[9] *Blohn v. Desser* [1962] 2 Q.B. 116, 123, on which see *post*, para. 14–072. The mere fact that the defendant contracted through an agent in the foreign country is not of itself sufficient: *cf. Seegner v. Marks* (1895) 21 V.L.R. 491.

[10] 1920 Act, s.9(2)(*b*). On the jurisdiction of the English court in such a case see *ante*, para. 11–083.

[11] *Ante*, paras. 11–097 *et seq.*

[12] *Littauer Glove Corporation v. F. W. Millington (1920) Ltd.* (1928) 44 T.L.R. 746; *Vogel v. R. A. Kohnstamm Ltd.* [1973] Q.B. 133; *Adams v. Cape Industries plc* [1990] Ch. 433 (C.A.); see also *Moore v. Mercator Enterprises Ltd.* (1978) 90 D.L.R. (3d) 590 (N.S.).

[13] [1990] Ch. 433, 530–544. *Cf. Akande v. Balfour Beatty Construction Ltd.* [1998] I.L.Pr. 110 (a case on the 1920 Act).

[14] *Ante*, para. 11–102.

is a "mere façade concealing the true facts".[15] If the local agent has authority to enter into contracts on behalf of the corporation without seeking the prior approval of the corporation, this is a powerful indicator that the corporation is present; if the agent does not have this authority, this fact points powerfully in the opposite direction.[16]

Under the 1920 Act the principle of the cases on the jurisdiction of the **14–060** English court applies also to the question whether a corporation carries on business in the jurisdiction of the original court within the meaning of the Act. Thus it has been held that a New Zealand insurance company does not carry on business in Ghana merely because it maintains agents there with limited powers to settle claims.[17] The 1933 Act[18] requires that the corporation must have its principal place of business (and not merely carry on business) in the foreign country.

The second case. Appearance as claimant or counter-claimant. It is **14–061** obvious that a person who applies to a tribunal himself is bound to submit to its judgment, should that judgment go against him, if for no other reason than that fairness to the defendant demands this. It is no less obvious that a claimant exposes himself to acceptance of jurisdiction of a foreign court as regards any set-off, counterclaim or cross-action which may be brought against him by the defendant.[19] By the same token, a defendant who resorts to a counterclaim or like cross-proceeding in a foreign court clearly submits to the jurisdiction thereof.

The third case. Appearance. This case rests on the simple and universally **14–062** admitted principle that a litigant who has voluntarily submitted himself to the jurisdiction of a court by appearing before it cannot afterwards dispute its jurisdiction. Where such a litigant, though a defendant rather than a claimant, appears and pleads to the merits without contesting the jurisdiction there is clearly a voluntary submission. The same is the case where he does indeed contest the jurisdiction but nevertheless proceeds further to plead to the merits,[20] or agrees to a consent order dismissing the claims and cross-claims,[21] or where he fails to appear in proceedings at first instance but appeals on the merits.[22] If the defendant takes no part in the proceedings and allows judgment to go against him in default of appearance, and later moves to set the default judgment aside, the application to set aside may be a voluntary appearance if it is based on non-jurisdictional grounds, even if the application

---

[15] [1990] Ch. at p. 539, citing *Woolfson v. Strathclyde Regional Council*, 1978 S.L.T. 159, 161 (H.L.) (a case not involving the conflict of laws).

[16] *F & K Jabbour v. Custodian of Israeli Absentee Property* [1954] 1 W.L.R. 139, 146; *Adams v. Cape Industries plc* [1990] Ch. 433, 531 (C.A.).

[17] *Sfeir & Co. v. National Insurance Co. of New Zealand* [1964] 1 Lloyd's Rep. 330.

[18] s.4(2)(*a*)(iv).

[19] *Schibsby v. Westenholz* (1870) L.R. 6 Q.B. 155, 161; *Burpee v. Burpee* [1929] 3 D.L.R. 18 (B.C.); Westlake, ss.324, 325.

[20] *Cf. Boissière v. Brockner* (1889) 6 T.L.R. 85, criticised by Clarence Smith (1953) 2 I.C.L.Q. 510, 517–520; *McFadden v. Colville Ranching Co.* (1915) 8 W.W.R. 163 (Alta.); *Richardson v. Allen* (1916) 28 D.L.R. 134 (Alta. C.A.).

[21] *Adams v. Cape Industries plc* [1990] Ch. 433, 461, *per* Scott J., affd. on other grounds *ibid.* p. 503 (C.A.).

[22] *S.A. Consortium General Textiles v. Sun & Sand Agencies Ltd.* [1978] Q.B. 279 (C.A.) (a case on the 1933 Act).

is unsuccessful.[23] There is no English[24] authority directly in point; in *Guiard v. De Clermont*[25] the defendant applied successfully to have a default judgment set aside and to have judgment entered in his favour at first instance, but the original judgment was restored by an appeal court; he was held to have voluntarily submitted.

14–063   Where the defendant contests the jurisdiction of a foreign court, the position is regulated by section 33 of the Civil Jurisdiction and Judgments Act 1982. If his challenge to the jurisdiction of the foreign court is successful, no question of submission arises. If it is unsuccessful and he goes on to contest the case on the merits, he will have submitted to the jurisdiction of the foreign court. But if he takes no further part in the proceedings and judgment in default is entered against him, will he be regarded as having voluntarily submitted? Common sense would suggest that a defendant who has been vigorously protesting that a court has no jurisdiction should not be regarded as having voluntarily submitted.[26] Under the 1933 Act an appearance for the purpose of (*inter alia*) contesting the jurisdiction is not to be regarded as a voluntary appearance.[27] But in *Harris v. Taylor*,[28] decided at common law, a defendant who had entered a conditional appearance in the Isle of Man court in order to set aside the proceedings on jurisdictional grounds was held to have submitted to the jurisdiction of the Manx Court, even though he took no further part in the proceedings after his application to set aside was unsuccessful. This decision was followed in *Henry v. Geoprosco International*,[29] where the Court of Appeal held that there was a voluntary appearance where the defendant appeared before the foreign court to invite that court in its discretion not to exercise a jurisdiction which it had under its local law; and that there was also a voluntary appearance if the defendant merely protested against the jurisdiction of the foreign court if the protest took the form of a conditional appearance which was converted automatically by operation of law into an unconditional appearance if the decision on jurisdiction went against the defendant. The court left open the question whether an appearance the sole purpose and effect of which was to protest against the jurisdiction of the foreign court would be a voluntary appearance. The criticism to which this

---

[23] Cheshire and North, p. 418; Read, pp. 168–170.

[24] There are two Canadian cases where there was held to be no voluntary appearance in the circumstances. In *McLean v. Shields* (1885) 9 O.R. 699 (C.A.) the application in the original court to set aside the default judgment was dismissed because it was made too late; it does not appear from the report what the grounds of the application were. In *Esdale v. Bank of Ottawa* (1920) 51 D.L.R. 485 (Alb. C.A.) there was a successful application to set aside a default judgment and for leave to defend; the defendant was granted leave to defend on condition that he made a payment into court; when he failed to make the payment judgment was again given against him, but he was nevertheless held not to have voluntarily submitted. These cases have been followed in Canada (*Re Carrick Estates Ltd. and Young* (1987) 43 D.L.R. (4th) 161 (Sask. C.A.)) but are of doubtful authority.

[25] [1914] 3 K.B. 145.

[26] *Re Dulles' Settlement (No. 2)* [1951] Ch. 842, 850 (C.A.), *per* Denning L.J. See also *Daarnhouwer & Co. N.V. v. Boulos* [1968] 2 Lloyd's Rep. 259.

[27] 1933 Act, s.4(2)(*a*)(i).

[28] [1914] 3 K.B. 145 (C.A.); followed in *Kennedy v. Trites* (1916) 10 W.W.R. 412 (B.C.); not followed in *Dovenmuehle v. Rocca Group Ltd.* (1981) 34 N.B.R. (2d) 444, app. dismissed (1982) 43 N.B.R. (2d) 359 (Sup.Ct.Can.). See also *Re McCain Foods and Agricultural Publishing Co. Ltd.* (1979) 103 D.L.R. (3d) 734 (Ont. C.A.); *Mid-Ohio Imported Car Co. v. Tri-K. Investments Ltd.* (1995) 129 D.L.R. (4th) 181 (B.C.C.A.).

[29] [1976] Q.B. 726 (C.A.), criticised by Collins (1976) 92 L.Q.R. 268 (reprinted in Collins, *Essays*, p. 313); Carter (1974–75) 47 B.Y.I.L. 379; Solomons (1976) 25 I.C.L.Q. 665.

decision was subjected led to considerable pressure for its reversal by legislation, and this was effected by section 33 of the 1982 Act.

Section 33 provides that a judgment debtor shall not be regarded as having **14–064** submitted by reason only of the fact that he appeared (conditionally or otherwise) in the foreign proceedings (a) to contest the jurisdiction of the court; (b) to ask the court to dismiss or stay the proceedings on the ground that the dispute in question should be submitted to arbitration[30] or to the determination of the courts of another country; or (c) to protect, or obtain the release of, property seized or threatened with seizure in the proceedings. If the defendant in the foreign court fails on any of these issues, but nevertheless goes on to defend the case on the merits, he will be regarded as having submitted.

If a defendant makes an appearance in order to argue that the court seised **14–065** has no international jurisdiction over him according to its law, the section plainly applies to protect him from the contention that he submitted by appearance. But if he appears to argue that the particular court has no local jurisdiction because the claim exceeds its internal competence, or because the court in a different judicial district alone has jurisdiction, it is less clear that an appearance to make this objection this would be protected by section 33(1)(*a*). Certainly it was not the problem which was presented by *Henry v. Geoprosco International*, and which the section was immediately designed to remedy. It is submitted that if the whole of the relief sought by the defendant from the foreign court is a decision by the court that it has no international jurisdiction, the appearance will be protected from being regarded as a submission by section 33(1)(*a*)[31]; but that a contention that a different court (but in the same country) has jurisdiction is not to be seen as contesting the jurisdiction within the meaning of s. 33(1)(*a*), for it is implicit in the contention that the courts of the country do not lack jurisdiction.

Some systems of law require or allow a defendant to plead to the merits at **14–066** the same time as, and as an alternative to, an objection to the jurisdiction. In *Boissière & Co. v. Brockner*[32] a plea on the merits put forward in this way was regarded as a submission at common law. But it should not now be so regarded, provided at least that, having lost on the issue of jurisdiction, the defendant does not put forward his case on the merits. This conclusion is supported by two decisions on submission as a basis of jurisdiction in the original court, and by two decisions on foreign judgments. In *Elefanten Schuh GmbH v. Jacqmain*[33] the European Court held, in the context of Article 18 of the 1968 Convention, that pleading to the merits as an alternative to an objection to the jurisdiction would not be a submission. The House of Lords has held, in the context of submission to the jurisdiction of the English court,[34] that a step in the proceedings only amounts to a submission when the defendant has taken some step which is only necessary or only useful if the

---

[30] As in *Tracomin S.A. v. Sudan Oil Seeds Co. Ltd. (No. 1)* [1983] 1 W.L.R. 662, affd. [1983] 1 W.L.R. 1026 (C.A.).

[31] In *Desert Sun Loan Corp. v. Hill* [1996] 2 All E.R. 847 (C.A.), the defendant appeared before the foreign court to contend that he had not authorised his attorney to accept service of the writ. The majority (Evans and Stuart-Smith L.JJ.) did not appear to consider s.33(1)(*a*) to be relevant to the case; by contrast, Roch L.J. interpreted such a contention as falling squarely within the section.

[32] (1889) 6 T.L.R. 85.

[33] Case 150/80 [1981] E.C.R. 1671.

[34] *Ante*, para. 11–110.

objection to the jurisdiction has been waived.[35] In *Adams v. Cape Industries plc*[36] defendants to United States proceedings objected to the jurisdiction of the court, but also participated in pre-trial discovery on the merits of the case. These steps were accompanied, expressly or impliedly, by a re-assertion of the jurisdictional objection, and under Federal law the steps taken did not amount to a submission. It was held that steps not regarded by the foreign court as a submission should not be regarded as a submission for the purposes of enforcement in England. In *Marc Rich & Co. AG v. Soc. Italiana Impianti P.A. (No. 2)*[37] it was held that Section 33 should not be construed narrowly: an objection to the jurisdiction of the Italian court, accompanied by a defence on the merits, did not amount to a submission, even though it was not necessary under Italian law for an alternative defence on the merits to be put forward. But after the Italian court had ruled that the parties had not agreed to arbitrate in London, and that it therefore had jurisdiction over the merits of the dispute, the defendants in the Italian proceedings lodged a defence on the merits. The consequence was that they thereby submitted to the jurisdiction of the Italian court, and were bound by the decision that the contract did not contain an arbitration clause.

14–067   Where the property of the defendant is attached in foreign proceedings and he intervenes to obtain its release, a similar question of submission arises. The 1933 Act provided, for cases within its scope, that an appearance for the purpose of protecting, or obtaining the release of, property seized or threatened with seizure in the foreign proceedings was not to be regarded as a voluntary appearance.[38] There was some doubt as to the extent to which this represented the common law rule,[39] but the 1982 Act[40] makes this principle one of general application. The common law authorities may still be helpful in considering the extent to which the defendant may go in taking steps to preserve his property. Thus it is clear that an appearance was not involuntary at common law merely because it was motivated by the fact that the defendant had property within the jurisdiction of the foreign court on which execution might be levied in the event of judgment going against him by default[41]; still less was an appearance involuntary when it was made because, although the defendant had no property within the jurisdiction of the foreign court, his business often took him there, so that the judgment might be made effective against him.[42] Secondly, an appearance is not involuntary when it is made after execution has been levied under the judgment in order to rescue the property which is the subject-matter of the execution.[43] Thirdly, if property is

---

[35] *Williams & Glyn's Bank v. Astro Dinamico* [1984] 1 W.L.R. 438 (H.L.), applied in *Akai Pty. Ltd. v. People's Insurance Co. Ltd.* [1998] 1 Lloyd's Rep. 90.

[36] [1990] Ch. 433, 461 *per* Scott J., affd. on other grounds *ibid.* p. 503 (C.A.); *The Eastern Trader* [1996] 2 Lloyd's Rep. 585, 600; *Akai Pty. Ltd. v. People's Insurance Co. Ltd., supra.* Cf. *Canada Trustco Mortgage Co. v. Rene Management & Holdings Ltd.* (1986) 32 D.L.R. (4th) 747 (Man.); *Gourmet Resources International Inc. v. Paramount Capital Corp.* [1993] I.L.Pr. 583 (Ont.).

[37] [1992] 1 Lloyd's Rep. 624 (C.A.); *The Eastern Trader, supra,* at pp. 598–602.

[38] 1933 Act, s.4(2)(a)(i).

[39] *Voinet v. Barrett* (1885) 55 L.J.Q.B. 39, 41 (C.A.); *Schibsby v. Westenholz* (1870) L.R. 6 Q.B. 155, 162 (C.A.); *Guiard v. De Clermont* [1914] 3 K.B. 145, 155; *Henry v. Geoprosco International* [1976] Q.B. 726, 746–747 (C.A.).

[40] 1982 Act, s.33(1)(c).

[41] *De Cosse Brissac v. Rathbone* (1861) 6 H. & N. 301 (the third plea).

[42] *Voinet v. Barrett* (1855) 55 L.J.Q.B. 39 (C.A.).

[43] *Guiard v. De Clermont* [1914] 3 K.B. 145; *Poissant v. Poissant* [1941] 3 W.W.R. 646, 650 (Sask.).

seized and the defendant appears and defends the case on the merits, the appearance is not involuntary.[44] But there may be cases in which the defendant may appear to oppose the seizure on jurisdictional grounds, *e.g.* where he denies he has property within the jurisdiction or where he challenges the validity of the seizure.[45] In such cases the effect of section 33 of the 1982 Act is that the appearance will not be voluntary.

The defendant, by an appearance which is voluntary in the sense explained, **14–068** renders himself subject to the jurisdiction of the foreign court with respect not only to the original claim but also to such further claims as the court allows to be added by the plaintiff. But this does not mean that he subjects himself also to claims by new claimants.[46] In principle, a submission will extend to claims concerning the same subject-matter, and to related claims which ought to be dealt with in the same proceedings, but (in either case) only if advanced by parties who were such at the date of the defendant's submission to the jurisdiction of the court; the decision of the foreign court to allow the new claim is not decisive.[47]

The fourth case. Agreement to submit. If a contract provides that all **14–069** disputes between the parties shall be referred to the exclusive jurisdiction of a foreign tribunal, not only will proceedings brought in England in breach of such agreement usually be stayed,[48] but also the foreign court is deemed to have jurisdiction over the parties.[49] A contractual submission to a particular court is not of itself a submission generally to the jurisdiction of all courts of that country[50]; the question is one of construction of the contract.

An agreement to submit may also take the form of an agreement to accept **14–070** service of process at a designated address. Thus, if a person takes shares in a foreign company, the articles of association or statutes of which provide that all disputes shall be submitted to the jurisdiction of a foreign court, and that every shareholder must "elect a domicile" at a particular place for service of process, and that in default the officers of the company may do so for him, then he is deemed to have agreed to submit to the jurisdiction of the foreign court, even if he never does elect a domicile.[51] And a member of a foreign company is bound by a statute enacted in the country of its incorporation providing that the particular company may sue and be sued in the name of its chairman and that execution on any judgment against the company may be issued against the property of any member in like manner as if the judgment

---

[44] *Clinton v. Ford* (1982) 137 D.L.R. (3d) 281 (Ont.C.A.); *cf. Re Low* [1894] 1 Ch. 147, 160 (C.A.).

[45] As he may do in the United States on constitutional grounds: see *Shaffer v. Heitner*, 433 U.S. 186 (1977).

[46] See Restatement, s.26, comment *e* and Illustration 8, and *Re Indiana Transportation Co.*, 244 U.S. 456 (1917) (submission to jurisdiction in respect of death of one passenger held not to involve submission in other claims). And see, by analogy, *Jordan Grand Prix Ltd. v. Baltic Insurance Group* [1999] 2 A.C. 127.

[47] *Murthy v. Sivajothi* [1999] 1 W.L.R. 467 (C.A.), in which the text to n. 46 was approved.

[48] Rule 33(2). A non-exclusive jurisdiction agreement (see *ante*, para. 12–078) will also be regarded as a submission: *First Capital Ltd. v. Winchester Computer Corp.* (1987) 44 D.L.R. (4th) 301 (Sask. C.A.).

[49] *Feyerick v. Hubbard* (1902) 71 L.J.K.B. 509; *Jeannot v. Fuerst* (1909) 25 T.L.R. 424.

[50] *S.A. Consortium General Textiles v. Sun & Sand Agencies Ltd.* [1978] Q.B. 279 (C.A.) (a case on the 1933 Act).

[51] *Copin v. Adamson* (1874) L.R. 9 Ex. 345; (1875) 1 Ex. D. 17 (C.A.) (the first replication).

had been obtained against him personally.[52] But English courts have stopped short of inferring an agreement to submit from a mere general provision in the foreign law (and not in the articles of association or in a statute specifically referring to the particular company) that the shareholder must "elect a domicile" for the service of process,[53] unless he does in fact elect such a domicile.[54]

14–071   It would seem that a judgment based on a "cognovit clause," which gives a claimant or his lawyer power to enter judgment against the defendant in a specified court in the event of a default in payment, would be enforceable on the basis that the defendant has agreed thereby to submit,[55] at any rate if the clause is valid by the law applicable to the contract. Such clauses are common in the United States, where they are subject to widespread criticism because of their potential abuse, and where their validity varies from state to state.[56]

14–072   It may be laid down as a general rule that an agreement to submit to the jurisdiction of a foreign court must be express: it cannot be implied.[57] If the parties agree, expressly or by implication, that their contract shall be governed by a particular foreign law, it by no means follows that they agree to submit to the jurisdiction of the courts which apply it.[58] Nor can any such agreement be implied from the fact that the cause of action arose within a foreign country or from the additional fact that the defendant was present there when the cause of action arose.[59] In *Emanuel v. Symon*,[60] the Court of Appeal held that a defendant did not submit to the courts of a foreign country merely because he became a member of a partnership firm which carried on business there. But in *Blohn v. Desser*,[61] Diplock J. held that where a person resident in England became a sleeping partner in an Austrian firm she did submit to the jurisdiction of the Austrian courts. These cases can perhaps be reconciled on the basis that *Emanuel v. Symon* was concerned with the liability of the partners *inter se*, while *Blohn v. Desser* was concerned with the liability of a partner to an outside creditor. In other words, there was an element of holding out in *Blohn v. Desser* which was absent from *Emanuel v. Symon*. It is submitted that on

---

[52] *Bank of Australasia v. Harding* (1850) 9 C.B. 661; *Bank of Australasia v. Nias* (1851) 16 Q.B. 717; *Kelsall v. Marshall* (1856) 1 C.B.(N.S.) 241.

[53] *Copin v. Adamson* (1874) L.R. 9 Ex. 345 (the second replication). The point was reserved in the Court of Appeal: see 1 Ex D. 17, 19. See also *Risdon Iron & Locomotive Works v. Furness* [1906] 1 K.B. 49, 57; *Allen v. Standard Trusts Co.* (1920) 57 D.L.R. 105 (Man. C.A.); *Veco Drilling v. Armstrong* [1982] 1 W.W.R. 177 (B.C.); *Jamieson v. Robb* (1881) 7 V.L.R. 170, on which see Read, pp. 176–177.

[54] *Vallée v. Dumergue* (1849) 4 Exch. 290.

[55] See *Re Hughes & Sharp* (1968) 70 D.L.R. (2d) 298, revd. on other grounds (1969) 5 D.L.R. (3d) 760 (B.C.C.A.); *Batavia Times Publishing Co. v. Davis* (1977) 82 D.L.R. (3d) 247, app. dismissed (1979) 102 D.L.R. (3d) 192 (Ont. C.A.); Read, p. 172.

[56] See Scoles and Hay, pp. 281–282; Restatement, s.32.

[57] *Sirdar Gurdyal Singh v. Rajah of Faridkote* [1894] A.C. 670 (P.C.); *Emanuel v. Symon* [1908] 1 K.B. 302 (C.A.); *Vogel v. R. A. Kohnstamm Ltd.* [1973] Q.B. 133 and *New Hampshire Insurance Co. v. Strabag Bau A.G.* [1992] 1 Lloyd's Rep. 361, 371–372 (C.A.), not following dicta in *Blohn v. Desser* [1962] 2 Q.B. 116, 123 and in *Sfeir & Co. v. National Insurance Co. of New Zealand* [1964] 1 Lloyd's Rep. 330, 339–340.

[58] *Sfeir & Co. v. National Insurance Co. of New Zealand* [1964] 1 Lloyd's Rep. 330, 340 (a case on the 1920 Act); *Mattar and Saba v. Public Trustee* [1952] 3 D.L.R. 399 (Alta. C.A.); *Dunbee Ltd. v. Gilman & Co.* (1968) 70 S.R.N.S.W. 219; also reported [1968] 2 Lloyd's Rep. 394.

[59] *Sirdar Gurdyal Singh v. Rajah of Faridkote* [1894] A.C. 670 (P.C.); *Emanuel v. Symon* [1908] 1 K.B. 302 (C.A.); *Mattar and Saba v. Public Trustee* [1952] 3 D.L.R. 399 (Alta. C.A.); *Gyonyor v. Sanjenko* [1971] 5 W.W.R. 381 (Alta.).

[60] [1908] 1 K.B. 302 (C.A.).

[61] [1962] 2 Q.B. 116, 123, criticised Lewis (1961) 10 I.C.L.Q. 910; Cohn (1962) 11 I.C.L.Q. 583; Carter (1962) 38 B.Y.I.L. 493.

this point *Blohn v. Desser* cannot be supported. It was not followed in *Vogel v. R. A. Kohnstamm Ltd.*,[62] and in *Adams v. Cape Industries plc*[63] Scott J. said that he did not think it was right that an agreement to submit could be implied: but he accepted that an alleged consent which was not contractually enforceable could be treated as a representation by the defendant of a willingness to submit to the jurisdiction if acted upon by the plaintiff, provided that the representation was intended to be acted upon, or at least be one which the plaintiff reasonably believed was intended to be acted upon. But in that case no such representation could be inferred.[64]

If the defendant agrees to submit to the jurisdiction of a foreign court, and agrees (or is deemed to agree) to a particular method of service, it is immaterial at common law that he does not receive actual notice of the proceedings if service is effected in the agreed manner.[65] It was suggested in earlier editions of this work[66] that, even if there is no agreement as to method of service, it is immaterial that the defendant did not receive sufficient notice of the proceedings to enable him to defend them; but it is submitted that there is no rule to this effect: the ultimate question is whether there has been substantial injustice, and the court may take into account (*inter alia*) whether the foreign law provides an opportunity for the judgment to be set aside.[67]   **14–073**

The 1920 and 1933 Acts both contain provisions, separate and distinct from their provisions as to jurisdiction, which require respectively that the defendant must have been duly served[68] or must have received notice of the proceedings in sufficient time to enable him to defend.[69]   **14–074**

What does not give jurisdiction. The rules of common law (by contrast with those under the 1933 Act, which are exhaustive[70]) as to jurisdiction are not necessarily exclusive. Like any other common law rules, they are no doubt capable of judicious expansion to meet the changing needs of society. However, English courts have decided that certain jurisdictional bases are inadequate, though some of them are quite commonly relied upon by foreign courts. These are as follows: **14–075**

(1) *Possession by the defendant of property in the foreign country.* This is relied upon in Scotland[71] but has been rejected in England.[72] As early as the   **14–076**

---

[62] [1973] Q.B. 133.

[63] [1990] Ch. 433, 465–466, *per* Scott J., affd. on other grounds *ibid.* p. 503 (C.A.).

[64] In particular, it was held that a submission in one set of proceedings could not be regarded as a submission in another set of (related) proceedings.

[65] *Vallée v. Dumergue* (1849) 4 Exch. 290; *Bank of Australasia v. Harding* (1850) 9 C.B. 661; *Bank of Australasia v. Nias* (1851) 16 Q.B. 509; *Copin v. Adamson* (1875) 2 Ex. D. 17 (C.A.). *Cf. Jamieson v. Robb* (1881) 7 V.L.R. 170.

[66] 11th ed., p. 446. *Cf. Feyerick v. Hubbard* (1902) 71 L.J. K.B. 509; and the Canadian cases on "cognovit clauses", *supra*, n. 55.

[67] *Adams v. Cape Industries plc* [1990] Ch. 433, 563–571; *cf. Jeannot v. Fuerst* (1909) 25 T.L.R. 424. See *post*, Rule 45.

[68] 1920 Act, s.9(2)(*c*).

[69] 1933 Act, s.4(1)(*a*)(iii).

[70] *Société Co-opérative Sidmetal v. Titan International Ltd.* [1966] 1 Q.B. 828; *Sharps Commercials Ltd. v. Gas Turbines Ltd.* [1956] N.Z.L.R. 819 (a decision on the identically worded New Zealand Act).

[71] See Anton, pp. 188–196.

[72] *Schibsby v. Westenholz* (1870) L.R. 6 Q.B. 155, 163; *Rousillon v. Rousillon* (1880) 14 Ch.D. 351, 371; *Sirdar Gurdyal Singh v. Rajah of Faridkote* [1894] A.C. 670 (P.C.); *Emanuel v. Symon* [1908] 1 K.B. 302 (C.A.).

Judgments Extension Act 1868 the registration in England or Northern Ireland of a Scottish judgment based on this ground was specifically excluded.

14–077   (2) *Presence of the defendant in the foreign country at the time when the cause of action arose.* Though a dictum of Lord Blackburn favours this head,[73] the Privy Council and the Court of Appeal have since rejected it.[74]

14–078   (3) *Defendant a national of the foreign country.* There is a long chain of dicta extending from 1828 to 1948 suggesting that the courts of a foreign country might have jurisdiction over a person if he was a subject or citizen of that country.[75] But there is no actual decision which supports this proposition. *Douglas v. Forrest*[76] goes nearest to a decision to this effect. But that is a very old case, and the judgment dwells also on the fact that the defendant retained property in the foreign country—an alternative basis of jurisdiction which would not now be acknowledged as adequate. It is evident that nationality is quite inappropriate as a basis of jurisdiction when the defendant is, *e.g.* a British citizen[77] or an American citizen,[78] or an Australian citizen since in these cases the political unit (or State) does not coincide with the law district (or country). Citizenship does not serve to identify them with any particular law district, such as England or New York or Victoria, within a composite State such as the United Kingdom, the United States or Australia. Moreover, the question whether a person is a national of a given state is a matter for the law of that state.[79] As a connecting factor, therefore, nationality is not subject to the control or definition of the *lex fori*; and as the law of the given state may deem a person to be a national, or deny nationality, on grounds which are objectionable in English eyes, nationality would constitute too unpredictable a basis for jurisdiction. Nationality as a basis of jurisdiction has been doubted by three High Court judges,[80] and definitely rejected by the Irish High Court.[81] It cannot therefore safely be relied upon today.[82] It is not mentioned as a basis of jurisdiction in the 1933 Act.

14–079   (4) *Defendant domiciled (but not resident or present) in the foreign country.* There are dicta in English cases[83] which suggest (though rather faintly) the

---

[73] *Schibsby v. Westenholz* (1870) L.R. 6 Q.B. 155, 161.
[74] *Sirdar Gurdyal Singh v. Rajah of Faridkote* [1894] A.C. 670 (P.C.); *Emanuel v. Symon* [1908] 1 K.B. 302 (C.A.); *cf. Mattar and Saba v. Public Trustee* [1952] 3 D.L.R. 399 (Alta. C.A.); *Gyonyor v. Sanjenko* [1971] 5 W.W.R. 381 (Alta.).
[75] *Douglas v. Forrest* (1828) 4 Bing. 686; *Schibsby v. Westenholz* (1870) L.R. 6 Q.B. 155, 161; *Rousillon v. Rousillon* (1880) 14 Ch.D. 351, 371; *Emanuel v. Symon* [1908] 1 K.B. 302, 309 (C.A.); *Gavin Gibson & Co. v. Gibson* [1913] 3 K.B. 379, 388; *Harris v. Taylor* [1915] 2 K.B. 580, 591 (C.A.); *Forsyth v. Forsyth* [1948] P. 125, 132 (C.A.). *Cf.* Restatement, s.31, comment c.
[76] (1828) 4 Bing. 686.
[77] See *Gavin Gibson & Co. v. Gibson* [1913] 3 K.B. 379.
[78] See *Dakota Lumber Co. v. Rinderknecht* (1905) 6 Terr.L.R. 210, 221–224.
[79] See *ante*, para. 6–128.
[80] *Blohn v. Desser* [1962] 2 Q.B. 116, 123; *Rossano v. Manufacturers' Life Insurance Co. Ltd.* [1963] 2 Q.B. 352, 382–383; *Vogel v. R. A. Kohnstamm Ltd.* [1973] Q.B. 133; see also *Patterson v. D'Agostino* (1975) 58 D.L.R. (3d) 63 (Ont.).
[81] *Rainford v. Newell-Roberts* [1962] I.R. 95. *Cf.* Cheshire and North, p. 419.
[82] The observations in *British Nylon Spinners Ltd. v. Imperial Chemical Industries* [1953] Ch. 19, 25 (C.A.) relate, it is submitted, to nationality as a basis of legislative rather than curial jurisdiction.
[83] *Turnbull v. Walker* (1892) 67 L.T. 767, 769; *Emanuel v. Symon* [1908] 1 K.B. 302, 308, 314 (C.A.); *Jaffer v. Williams* (1908) 25 T.L.R. 12, 13; *Gavin Gibson & Co. v. Gibson* [1913] 3 K.B. 379, 385.

recognition of domicile in the common law sense[84] as a basis of jurisdiction, but no English decision supports this, though one Canadian decision does.[85] It is not claimed as a ground of jurisdiction by the Scottish courts.[86] It is not mentioned in the 1933 Act. Despite the Canadian decision referred to above, Dean Read concluded that "domicile alone, unaccompanied by either residence or presence, will not yet suffice."[87]

(5) *Reciprocity.* Reciprocity is used in two distinct senses in connection **14–080** with the recognition and enforcement of foreign judgments. Firstly, it is used to describe the view, once espoused by the United States Supreme Court[88] but which has been largely abandoned in the United States,[89] that a judgment rendered by the court of a foreign country will not be enforced unless that country would enforce a comparable judgment of the requested court. That view of reciprocity forms part of the law of many civil law countries,[90] but has never been the law in England. Secondly, reciprocity is used to describe the view that the English court should recognise the jurisdiction of the foreign court if the situation is such that, *mutatis mutandis*, the English court might have exercised jurisdiction, *e.g.* under Order 11, r. 1(1) of the Rules of the Supreme Court.[91] On the present state of the authorities, the jurisdiction of the foreign court will not be recognised on such a basis.

In *Schibsby v. Westenholz*[92] the plaintiff brought an action in England on a **14–081** French judgment. The defendant was not in France when the writ was issued, nor did he appear or submit to the jurisdiction. The writ was served on him in England. The Court of Queen's Bench was much pressed with the argument that, under what were then sections 18 and 19 of the Common Law Procedure Act 1852 and is now Order 11, r. 1(1) in Schedule 1 to the Civil Procedure Rules 1998,[93] the English court would have had power to order service out of the jurisdiction on converse facts, and therefore it should enforce the French judgment. In rejecting this argument Lord Blackburn observed[94] that "if the principle on which foreign judgments were enforced was that which is loosely called 'comity,' we could hardly decline to enforce a foreign judgment given in France against a resident in Great Britain under circumstances hardly, if at all, distinguishable from those under which we, *mutatis mutandis*, might give judgment against a resident in France; but it is quite different if the principle be that which we have just laid down" (*i.e.* the doctrine of obligation quoted earlier in this chapter[95]). This was followed in *Turnbull v. Walker*,[96] where Wright J. refused to enforce a New Zealand judgment based on provisions for the service of writs out of the jurisdiction which were identical with the English provisions.

---

[84] Domicile in the sense of the 1982 Act would for most purposes be within the First Case.
[85] *Marshall v. Houghton* [1923] 2 W.W.R. 553 (Man. C.A.). *Cf.* Restatement, s.29.
[86] *Kerr v. Ferguson*, 1931 S.C. 736, overruling *Glasgow Corporation v. Johnston*, 1915 S.C. 555.
[87] Read, p. 160. *Cf.* Cheshire and North, pp. 419–420.
[88] *Hilton v. Guyot*, 159 U.S. 113 (1895).
[89] Restatement Third, *Foreign Relations Law*, s.481, Rep. Note 1.
[90] *e.g.* Germany: Code of Civil Procedure, para. 328.
[91] Now in CPR, Sched. 1. See Rule 27, *ante.*
[92] (1870) L.R. 6 Q.B. 155.
[93] *i.e.* Rule 27, *ante.*
[94] At p. 159.
[95] *Ante*, para. 14–006.
[96] (1892) 67 L.T. 767. *Cf. Phillips v. Batho* [1913] 3 K.B. 25, 29–30; *Wendel v. Moran*, 1993 S.L.T. 44 (fact that delict occurred in the U.S. insufficient to give jurisdiction).

14–082　　In spite of these decisions, it was suggested by Denning L.J.[97] that an English court would recognise that a court in the Isle of Man had jurisdiction to give a judgment based on service of the writ out of the jurisdiction if the English court would have assumed jurisdiction in converse circumstances. And in *Travers v. Holley*[98] the Court of Appeal recognised a New South Wales divorce granted in the absence of domicile on the ground that "it would be contrary to principle and inconsistent with comity if the courts of this country were to refuse to recognise a jurisdiction which *mutatis mutandis* they claimed for themselves." The width and generality of this statement led to suggestions being made extra-judicially[99] that the principle of reciprocity might be applicable to foreign judgments *in personam*. But it has since been held that this is not so and that English courts do not concede jurisdiction *in personam* to foreign courts merely because English courts would, in converse circumstances, have power to order service out of the jurisdiction.[1] "The decision in *Travers v. Holley* was a decision limited to a judgment *in rem* in a matter affecting matrimonial status, and it has not been followed in any case except a matrimonial case."[2] "Comity has never been the basis on which we recognise or give effect to foreign judgments."[3] "I am unwilling to accept . . . that the law of foreign divorce (still less other) jurisdiction must be a mirror image of our own law."[4] Indeed, in *Amin Rasheed Shipping Corp. v. Kuwait Insurance Co.*[5] (which was not a case involving foreign judgments) Lord Diplock went so far as to say that the jurisdiction exercised under Order 11, r. 1(1) is an exorbitant jurisdiction, in the sense that "it is one which, under general English conflict rules, an English court would not recognise as possessed by any foreign court in the absence of some treaty providing for such recognition." Although Lord Diplock was wrong to describe Order 11, r. 1(1) as an exorbitant jurisdiction,[6] he was certainly expressing the orthodox view on recognition of foreign judgments in cases where the debtor was neither within the foreign jurisdiction nor had submitted to it. Thus, none of the following facts by itself gives jurisdiction to the courts of a foreign country: that the cause of action arose out of a contract made or broken there or which was to be governed by the law thereof, or out of a tort committed there; or that the defendant is a necessary or proper party to an action properly brought against a person duly served. This means, of course, that in proceedings *in personam* English courts claim in this respect a wider jurisdiction than they are prepared to concede to foreign courts.

---

[97] *Re Dulles' Settlement (No. 2)* [1951] Ch. 842, 851 (C.A.).

[98] [1953] P. 246, 257, *per* Hodson L.J.

[99] Kennedy (1954) 32 Can.Bar Rev. 359, 373–383; (1957) 35 *ibid.* 123; Cheshire, 7th ed., pp. 557–558; contrast 13th ed., pp. 420–422.

[1] *Re Trepca Mines Ltd.* [1960] 1 W.L.R. 1273, 1280–1282 (C.A.); *Société Co-opérative Sidmetal v. Titan International Ltd.* [1966] 1 Q.B. 828; *Sharps Commercials Ltd. v. Gas Turbines Ltd.* [1956] N.Z.L.R. 819, 823; *Crick v. Hennessy* [1973] W.A.R. 74.

[2] *Re Trepca Mines Ltd., supra*, at pp. 1281–1282, *per* Hodson L.J., approved in *Henry v. Geoprosco International* [1976] Q.B. 726, 745 (C.A.). *Cf. Schemmer v. Property Resources Ltd.* [1975] Ch. 273, 287.

[3] *Indyka v. Indyka* [1969] 1 A.C. 33, 58, *per* Lord Reid, citing *Schibsby v. Westenholz* (1870) L.R. 6 Q.B. 155 at p. 159.

[4] *Ibid.*, at p. 106, *per* Lord Wilberforce.

[5] [1984] A.C. 50, 65.

[6] *Ante*, para. 11–123, n. 18.

(6) *Real and substantial connection.* In *Indyka v. Indyka*[7] the House of　**14–083**
Lords held that foreign divorce decrees should be recognised, not only on the
basis of reciprocity under the doctrine in *Travers v. Holley*, but also wherever
a real and substantial connection was shown between the petitioner and the
country whose court granted the decree. There is no authority in England
which suggests that this is the appropriate test for the recognition and enforcement of foreign judgments *in personam*. But in 1990 the Supreme Court of
Canada held in *Morguard Investments Ltd. v. De Savoye*[8] that, as regards the
enforcement of judgments between the Canadian provinces, it was no longer
appropriate to apply the nineteenth century rules developed in England for the
recognition and enforcement of wholly foreign judgments. It was held that
courts in one province should give full faith and credit (a phrase borrowed
from the United States Constitution) to judgments given by a court in another
province or territory "so long as that court has properly, or appropriately,
exercised jurisdiction in the action". That condition was met when the defendant was present in the foreign jurisdiction at the time of the action, or
submitted to its judgment by agreement or appearance: in other cases, the test
to be applied was not that of reciprocity in the sense discussed above,[9] but
whether the foreign jurisdiction had a real and substantial connection with the
claim.

The decision of the Supreme Court of Canada involved the enforcement of　**14–084**
an Alberta judgment in British Columbia, and rested in part on the federal
structure of the Constitution, including the strong need for the enforcement
throughout the country of judgments given in one province; the fact that there
were no concerns about differential quality of justice in the various provinces;
and the existence of the Supreme Court of Canada as a court of final review,
which could determine when the courts of one province have appropriately
exercised jurisdiction. The extent to which this development will also be
extended to judgments of foreign countries has not been the subject of final
decision, but several cases have applied the test of real and substantial
connection to foreign country judgments.[10]

(7) *Judgment in personam ancillary to divorce decree.* In *Phillips v.*　**14–085**
Batho,[11] it was held that a judgment of an Indian divorce court awarding
damages to a husband against a co-respondent could be enforced in England,
although the co-respondent had left India before the commencement of the
proceedings for divorce and did not submit to the jurisdiction. The decision is
in terms confined to a foreign country which is part of the Commonwealth. It
is submitted that this decision is wrong and that a foreign judgment for
damages or costs against a co-respondent cannot be enforced in England

---

[7] [1969] 1 A.C. 33.
[8] [1990] 3 S.C.R. 1077, on which see Black and Swan (1991) 12 Advocates' Q. 489. *Cf.* Briggs
(1987) 36 I.C.L.Q. 240.
[9] Which was the basis on which the judgment had been recognised in the lower court: [1988] 5
W.W.R. 650 (B.C.C.A.), on which see Blom (1989) 68 Can.B.Rev. 359; Black (1989) 4 Oxford
J. Leg. Stud. 547; Law Reform Commission, British Columbia, *The Enforcement of Judgments
Between Canadian Provinces* (1989).
[10] *Clarke v. Lo Bianco* (1991) 84 D.L.R. (4th) 244 (B.C.); *Minkler and Kirschbaum v. Sheppard*
(1991) 60 B.C.L.R. (2d) 360; *Federal Deposit Insurance Corp. v. Vanstone* (1992) 88 D.L.R.
(4th) 448 (B.C.); *Moses v. Shore Boat Builders Ltd.* (1993) 106 D.L.R. (4th) 654 (B.C.C.A.);
Clancey v. Beach [1994] 7 W.W.R. 332 (B.C.); *Webb v. Hooper* [1994] 7 W.W.R. 324 (Alta.);
Arrowmaster Inc. v. Unique Forming (1993) 17 O.R. (3d) 407.
[11] [1913] 3 K.B. 25.

unless the foreign court had jurisdiction over him under Rule 37. The decision has been severely criticised extra-judicially,[12] it has not been followed in New Zealand,[13] and there is a later English case which undermines its reasoning.[14]

ILLUSTRATIONS[15]

THE FIRST CASE

14–086   1. 462 Individuals bring personal injury actions in the federal court in Texas against (*inter alia*) X & Co., an English company which is the holding company of two other defendants: Y & Co., an English company, which is engaged in the worldwide marketing of asbestos, and Z & Co., an Illinois corporation, which is engaged in the marketing of asbestos in the United States. X & Co. and Y & Co. object to the jurisdiction of the federal court, but the actions are settled under a consent order by a payment to the plaintiffs to which X & Co. and its subsidiaries contribute. Subsequently a further 206 individuals commence similar proceedings in Texas. X & Co., Y & Co. and Z & Co. take no part in these proceedings. Z & Co. ceases to carry on business, and the United States marketing is carried on by two new subsidiaries of X & Co., one incorporated in Illinois and the other in Liechtenstein, whose shares are held by nominees. Subsequently default judgments are entered in the Texas court. The default judgments are not recognised because, among other reasons,[16] the federal court in Texas has no jurisdiction: the consent order in the first set of actions is a submission to the jurisdiction of the court in that set of actions, but not in the second set of actions; whether or not presence in Illinois was sufficient for the purposes of the enforcement of the judgment of a Federal court sitting in Texas, X & Co. and Y & Co. were not present in Illinois through their Illinois subsidiaries.[17]

2. X, an English traveller, is staying for a few days in an hotel in Massachusetts when there is issued and served upon him a summons commencing an action against him in the Massachusetts court. The Massachusetts court has jurisdiction.[18]

3. Y is the director of X & Co., an English company. Y visits New York and while he is there A, a New York firm, takes out a summons against X & Co. and serves process upon Y. X & Co. has no branch in New York and does not carry on business there. The New York court has no jurisdiction.[19]

4. X & Co., an English company, employs Y, a resident of Israel, as its representative there to elicit orders from customers for X & Co.'s goods. Y has no authority from X & Co. to make contracts on its behalf. Y introduces an Israeli customer, A, who contracts with X & Co. for the purchase of X & Co.'s goods. A sues X & Co. in Israel for damages for breach of contract. X & Co. takes no part in the proceedings and has no office or place of business in Israel. The Israeli court has no jurisdiction at common law.[20]

THE SECOND CASE

14–087   5. A, an Englishman residing in England, brings an action against X in Tel Aviv for breach of a contract made and broken in England. The court gives judgment for costs against A. The Israeli court has jurisdiction.

THE THIRD CASE

14–088   6. A brings an action in a New York court against X, an Englishman. X appears and defends the action because his business transactions frequently involve his presence in New York, so that judgment might be executed against him there. His appearance is voluntary and the New York court has jurisdiction over him.[21]

---

[12] Read, pp. 262–267.

[13] *Redhead v. Redhead* [1926] N.Z.L.R. 131 (costs).

[14] *Jacobs v. Jacobs and Ceen* [1950] P. 146, where dicta in *Phillips v. Batho* were dissented from. See *post*, para. 18–082.

[15] See also the Illustration to Rule 42, *post*, para. 14–126.

[16] See *post*, para. 14R–141, on natural justice.

[17] *Adams v. Cape Industries plc* [1990] Ch. 433 (C.A.).

[18] *Carrick v. Hancock* (1895) 12 T.L.R. 59.

[19] *Littauer Glove Corporation v. F.W. Millington* (1920) *Ltd.* (1928) 44 T.L.R. 746.

[20] *Vogel v. R.A. Kohnstamm Ltd.* [1973] Q.B. 133 (decided before the 1933 Act was extended to Israel).

[21] *Cf. Voinet v. Barrett* (1885) 55 L.J.Q.B. 39 (C.A.).

7. The circumstances are the same as in Illustration 6 save that X has valuable property in the United States upon which execution might be levied. X appears and defends the action in order to protect that property. The New York court has jurisdiction.[22]

8. The circumstances are the same as in Illustration 6 save that X does not appear until after judgment has been given against him in default and execution has been levied, when he appears and secures the reopening of the proceedings in order to recover property upon which execution has been levied. The New York court has jurisdiction.[23]

9. A brings an action in a foreign court against X and obtains a judgment against X in default of appearance. X's application to the foreign court for leave to appeal out of time is dismissed, but X also appeals to the Court of Appeal for the relevant district on the basis that he was not in fact out of time to appeal. The appeal is not expressed to be on jurisdictional grounds. The foreign court has jurisdiction.[24]

10. A brings an action in a foreign country against X, an Englishman, jurisdiction being founded solely upon the arrest of property of X in the country concerned. X appears in order to recover the property arrested. *Semble*, the foreign court has no jurisdiction.[25]

11. A brings an action against X in a foreign court. X enters a conditional appearance in order to contest the jurisdiction. The conditional appearance becomes unconditional automatically when X's application to contest the jurisdiction fails, but X takes no further part in the proceedings. The foreign court has no jurisdiction.[26]

12. A brings an action against X in a foreign court. X applies to the foreign court to set aside the proceedings on the grounds that the foreign court is not the *forum conveniens*. The foreign court has no jurisdiction.[27]

13. A brings an action against X in a foreign court. X merely contests the jurisdiction. The foreign court has no jurisdiction.[28]

THE FOURTH CASE

14. A is a New York firm carrying on business in New York. X is a British citizen resident in England. By a contract made in New York X agrees to assign certain patent rights to A, the contract providing *inter alia* that "all disputes as to the present agreement and its fulfilment shall be submitted to the New York jurisdiction." In an action by A in the appropriate New York court for breach of the contract, judgment is given for A for $1 million. The New York court has jurisdiction.[29]   **14–089**

15. X, who was resident in England, held shares in a French company. The statutes or articles of association of the company provided that every dispute should be subject to the jurisdiction of the French courts and that every shareholder must "elect a domicile" in France for service of process and that in default the officers of the company might do so for him. X never elected a domicile. The company went into liquidation and A brought an action in France against X for moneys not paid up on X's shares. Notice was duly served on X at his statutory domicile. X, however, had no knowledge of the proceedings. Judgment was given against X. The French court had jurisdiction.[30]

16. The circumstances are the same as in Illustration 15, except that the provisions about disputes being referred to the jurisdiction of the French courts and about "electing a domicile" were general provisions of French law applicable to all French companies. The French court had no jurisdiction.[31]

17. X, who is resident in England, is a member of an Australian company. By an Australian statute referring to this particular company the chairman of the company is capable of suing or being sued in place of the company and may act and be treated as the agent of the members. A

---

[22] *Cf. De Cosse Brissac v. Rathbone* (1861) 6 H. & N. 301 (the third plea).

[23] *Cf. Guiard v. De Clermont* [1914] 3 K.B. 145.

[24] *S.A. Consortium General Textiles v. Sun & Sand Agencies Ltd.* [1978] Q.B. 279 (C.A.) (a case on the 1933 Act).

[25] *Guiard v. De Clermont, supra*, at p. 155. *Cf. Re Low* [1894] 1 Ch. 147 (C.A.).

[26] 1982 Act, s.33(1)(*a*), reversing the effect of *Harris v. Taylor* [1915] 2 K.B. 580 (C.A.).

[27] 1982 Act, s.33(1)(*b*), reversing the effect of *Henry v. Geoprosco International, supra*.

[28] 1982 Act, s.33(1)(*a*).

[29] *Cf. Feyerick v. Hubbard* (1902) 71 L.J.K.B. 509. See also *Jeannot v. Fuerst* (1909) 25 T.L.R. 424.

[30] *Copin v. Adamson* (1874) L.R. 9 Ex. 345; 1 Ex. D. 17 (C.A.) (the first replication).

[31] *Copin v. Adamson, supra* (the second replication). Contrast *Vallée v. Dumergue* (1849) 4 Exch. 290, where X did "elect a domicile" though he had no notice of the proceedings. *Cf.* Case C–214/89 *Powell Duffryn plc v. Petereit* [1992] E.C.R. I–1745.

recovers judgment against the chairman, and therefore against, *inter alios*, X, in an action in an Australian court of which X has no notice. The Australian court has jurisdiction.[32]

18. X, a British citizen, when resident and carrying on business in Western Australia, there entered into partnership with A for the working of a gold mine there situate. The partnership was dissolved and an account was taken under decree of a Western Australian court. A deficiency appearing, A sued X therefor in the same court. X had ceased to be resident in Western Australia and the writ was served upon him in England. X did not appear. The Western Australian court had no jurisdiction.[33]

(2) WHERE JURISDICTION DOES NOT EXIST

14R–090   **RULE 37—A court of a foreign country outside the United Kingdom has no jurisdiction under the First Case of Rule 36 if the bringing of the proceedings in that court was contrary to an agreement under which the dispute in question was to be settled otherwise than by proceedings in the courts of that country and the judgment debtor did not agree to the proceedings being brought in that court nor counterclaim in the proceedings, or otherwise submit to the jurisdiction of that court.[34]**

COMMENT

14–091   This Rule is based on section 32 of the 1982 Act, which adopted and extended a similar provision in the 1933 Act[35] on which there was no authority at common law.[36] Section 32 provides that a judgment of a foreign court shall not be recognised or enforced in the United Kingdom if (a) the bringing of the proceedings in that court was contrary to an agreement under which the dispute in question was to be settled otherwise than by proceedings in the courts of that country; and (b) those proceedings were not brought in that court by or with the agreement of, the person against whom the judgment was given; and (c) that person did not counterclaim in the proceedings or otherwise submit to the jurisdiction of that court. Section 32 is therefore subject to the principle of submission. Consequently, where an action was brought in a foreign country in breach of an arbitration agreement and the defendant defended the action on the merits after the foreign court had dismissed an objection to its jurisdiction, the defendant was held to have submitted to the jurisdiction of the foreign court; it could not therefore rely on section 32.[37] The principal object of section 32 is to counteract those systems of law which disregard[38] arbitration clauses or clauses providing for the jurisdiction of the English courts on the ground (for example) that an exchange of telexes or faxes or printed forms incorporating an arbitration or jurisdiction clause is not in "writing." The section does not apply where the agreement was illegal,

---

[32] *Bank of Australasia v. Harding* (1850) 9 C.B. 661. See also *Bank of Australasia v. Nias* (1851) 16 Q.B. 717.

[33] *Emanuel v. Symon* [1908] 1 K.B. 302 (C.A.). Contrast *Blohn v. Desser* [1962] 2 Q.B. 116.

[34] 1982 Act, s.32.

[35] 1933 Act, s.4(3)(*b*).

[36] But for Canada, see *Old State Brewing Co. v. Newlands Service Inc.* (1998) 155 D.L.R. (4th) 250 (B.C.C.A.).

[37] *Marc Rich & Co. A.G. v. Soc. Italiana Impianti P.A. (No. 2)* [1992] 1 Lloyd's Rep. 624 (C.A.); see also *The Eastern Trader* [1996] 2 Lloyd's Rep. 585; *Akai Pty. Ltd. v. People's Insurance Co. Ltd.* [1998] 1 Lloyd's Rep. 90.

[38] For an extreme example see *Deutsche Schachtbau v. Shell International Petroleum Co. Ltd.* [1990] 1 A.C. 295, 310–311 (C.A.), revd. on other grounds, p. 329.

void or unenforceable or was incapable of being performed for reasons not attributable to the fault of the party bringing the proceedings in which the judgment was given, but in determining whether a judgment given by the foreign court should be recognised or enforced a court in the United Kingdom is not bound by any decision of the overseas court relating to any of these matters.[39] English law (including its rules of the conflict of laws) would apply to determine whether the agreement was illegal, void or unenforceable, etc., without regard to the determination of the foreign court.

Section 32(4) provides that section 32 does not apply to judgments which are required to be recognised under the 1968 or Lugano Conventions.[40] **14–092**

ILLUSTRATION

A New York company buys peanuts from a company connected with the Government of the Sudan. The contract form provides for English law to govern and for London arbitration. In breach of the arbitration clause the New York buyers bring an action in the New York courts because the sellers had some assets there whereas they had none in England. The sellers apply to the New York court for a stay on the ground that the parties had agreed to arbitration in London; the New York courts hold that the arbitration clause is not binding. In proceedings in England in which the buyers challenge the validity of the appointment of an arbitrator the English court will not recognise the New York judgment.[41] **14–093**

RULE 38—**A court of a foreign country outside the United Kingdom has no jurisdiction to give a judgment capable of enforcement or recognition in England against a person who under the rules of public international law was entitled to immunity from the jurisdiction of the courts of that country and did not submit thereto.** **14R–094**

COMMENT

This Rule is based on a provision of the 1933 Act,[42] which (although there is no direct authority) probably reflects the position at common law. Section 31 of the 1982 Act deals comprehensively with one class of defendant entitled to immunity under public international law, namely States. The effect of the section[43] is that a foreign judgment against a State, other than the United Kingdom or the State to which the court which pronounced the judgment belongs, is to be recognised and enforced in the United Kingdom if it would be so recognised and enforced if it had not been given against a State and the foreign court would have had jurisdiction in the matter if it had applied rules **14–095**

---

[39] 1982 Act, s.32(2), (3).

[40] That is, recognition and enforcement under Rule 48. For the question whether these Conventions require the recognition or enforcement of judgments rendered in breach of arbitration agreements, see *post*, paras. 14–187 *et seq.*

[41] *Cf. Tracomin S.A. v. Sudan Oil Seeds Co. Ltd. (No. 1)* [1983] 1 W.L.R. 662, affd. [1983] 1 W.L.R. 1026 (C.A.).

[42] 1933 Act, s.4(3)(c).

[43] 1982 Act, s.31(3) provides that s.31 is not to affect the recognition or enforcement in the United Kingdom of judgments to which the 1933 Act applies by virtue of the Carriage of Goods by Road Act 1965, s.4; Nuclear Installations Act 1965, s.17(4); Merchant Shipping Act 1995, s.166(4); Merchant Shipping Act 1995, s.314(2) and Sched. 13; Carriage by Railway Act 1972, s.5 (replaced by International Transport Conventions Act 1983, s.6); Carriage of Passengers by Road Act 1974, s.5 (not yet in force).

corresponding to those applicable to such matters in the United Kingdom in accordance with sections 2 to 11 of the State Immunity Act 1978.[44] For this purpose judgments against a State include judgments against a government, a department of the government, against the sovereign or head of State in his public capacity, but not judgments against an entity which is distinct from the executive organs or government, except in proceedings relating to anything done by it in the exercise of the sovereign authority of the State; in the case of a federal State, State includes any of its constituent territories. A foreign judgment against a State will be capable of enforcement in England, if both of the following conditions are fulfilled: first, that the foreign court would have had jurisdiction if it had applied the United Kingdom rules on sovereign immunity set out in Sections 2 to 11 of the State Immunity Act 1978, the effect of which is that a State is not immune (*inter alia*) where it submits to the jurisdiction or where the proceedings relate to a commercial transaction; second, that under United Kingdom law the State is not immune from the processes of execution. Section 31(4) of the 1982 Act gives to judgments against foreign States the benefit of (*inter alia*) the immunities from execution contained in sections 13 and 14(3), (4) of the 1978 Act; their effect is that there can be no execution against sovereign property without the written consent of the foreign State unless the property is in use or intended for use for commercial purposes.[45]

14–096   Section 31 does not deal with other persons entitled to immunity such as diplomats and international organisations. In these cases the general principle in this Rule will apply.

14R–097   **RULE 39—A court of a foreign country outside the United Kingdom has no jurisdiction to give a judgment in proceedings regulated by certain international conventions which have been given effect in the law of the United Kingdom unless the jurisdictional requirements of the convention concerned are fulfilled.**

COMMENT

14–098   The scope of this Rule extends to international conventions relating to such matters as carriage of goods by road, carriage by railway, third party liability in the field of nuclear energy, and oil pollution damage. The jurisdictional rules of these conventions, and their provisions relating to enforcement of judgments, are dealt with in Chapter 15.

(3) JUDGMENTS IN REM

14R–099   **RULE 40[46]—(1) A court of a foreign country has jurisdiction to give a judgment *in rem* capable of enforcement or recognition in England if the**

---

[44] Rule 19, Exceptions 1 to 11, *ante*, paras. 10E–024 *et seq.*
[45] *Ante*, paras. 10–012 *et seq.*
[46] *Castrique v. Imrie* (1870) L.R. 4 H.L. 414; *Meyer v. Ralli* (1876) 1 C.P.D. 358; *The City of Mecca* (1879) 5 P.D. 28, reversed on other grounds (1881) 6 P.D. 106 (C.A.); *Re Trufort* (1887) 36 Ch.D 600; *Minna Craig Steamship Co. v. Chartered, etc. Bank* [1897] 1 Q.B. 460; *McKie v. McKie* [1933] I.R. 464; Read, pp. 133–144; Restatement, ss.56, 59–65. See also 1933 Act, s.4(2)(*b*).

subject-matter of the proceedings wherein that judgment was given was immovable or movable property which was at the time of the proceedings situate in that country.

(2) A court of a foreign country has no jurisdiction to adjudicate upon the title to, or the right to possession of, any immovable situate outside that country.[47]

COMMENT

Introduction. A judgment *in rem* is a judgment whereunder either (1) **14–100** possession or property in a thing is adjudged to a person, or (2) the sale of a thing is decreed in satisfaction of a claim against the thing itself. The term is used also to describe (3) an adjudication as to status such as a decree of nullity or dissolution of marriage,[48] and (4) a judgment ordering property to be sold by way of administration in bankruptcy or on death, but judgments of these last two categories are outside the scope of this chapter. The question whether a foreign judgment is *in personam* or *in rem* is sometimes a difficult one on which English judges have been divided in opinion.[49]

Foreign judgments *in rem* are freely recognised in England but rarely call **14–101** for enforcement. If, for instance, a foreign judgment *in rem* determines the title to an immovable, either the immovable is within the country of the foreign court, in which case no question of enforcement can arise[50]; or it is elsewhere, in which case that court had no jurisdiction. Again, if the person entitled under a foreign judgment *in rem* vesting in him the title to some movable thing brings an action for wrongful interference in England against a person who denies that title, he is in reality relying on his title rather than the source of it—the judgment. He is, in other words, relying on the foreign judgment *qua* an assignment rather than *qua* a judgment. So also is the purchaser of a ship sold by foreign judicial sale who sets up the foreign judgment by way of defence to the original owner's proceedings for wrongful interference. All that is involved is, at most, recognition of the foreign judgment, and, at that, recognition *qua* an assignment. As Lord Blackburn put it,[51] "In the case of *Cammell v. Sewell*[52] a more general principle was laid down, *viz.* that 'if personal property is disposed of in a manner binding according to the law of the country where it is, that disposition is binding everywhere.' This, we think, as a general rule is correct, though no doubt it may be open to exceptions and qualifications; and it may very well be said that

---

[47] *Boyse v. Colclough* (1854) 1 K. & J. 124; *Re Hoyles* [1911] 1 Ch. 179, 185–186 (C.A.); *Re Trepca Mines Ltd.* [1960] 1 W.L.R. 1273, 1277 (C.A.); *Duke v. Andler* [1932] 4 D.L.R. 529 (Sup.Ct.Can.); *Haspel v. Haspel* [1934] 2 W.W.R. 412 (Alta.); *cf. Tezcan v. Tezcan* (1987) 46 D.L.R. (4th) 176 (B.C.C.A.); *Chapman Estate v. O'Hara* [1988] 2 W.W.R. 275 (Sask. C.A.); Read, pp. 135–137.

[48] *Von Lorang v. Administrator of Austrian Property* [1927] A.C. 641, 662.

[49] See *Cammell v. Sewell* (1858) 3 H. & N. 617 (*in rem*); (1860) 5 H. & N. 728 (*in personam*); *Castrique v. Imrie* (1860) 8 C.B.(N.S.) 1 (*in personam*); *Imrie v. Castrique* (1860) 8 C.B.(N.S.) 405 (*in rem*); *Castrique v. Imrie* (1870) L.R. 4 H.L. 414 (*in rem*).

[50] It has been held in New Zealand that an action *in personam* to recover instalments of purchase money due under a sale of land is not an action of which the subject-matter is immovable property within the meaning of the 1933 Act, s.4(2)(*b*): *Re a Judgment, McCormac v. Gardner* [1937] N.Z.L.R. 517.

[51] *Castrique v. Imrie* (1870) L.R. 4 H.L. 414, 429.

[52] (1860) 5 H. & N. 728, 746.

the rule commonly expressed by English lawyers, that a judgment *in rem* is binding everywhere, is in truth but a branch of that more general principle."

14–102   The degree of recognition to be accorded to such a judgment, therefore, falls to be determined not so much by the rules governing the recognition of foreign judgments as by the rules governing the validity of assignments of property.[53] The distinction is important because while a foreign judgment is in general impeachable for fraud,[54] the validity of an assignment of property depends almost entirely upon the *lex situs*[55]; though it is conceivable that recognition of a foreign judgment *qua* an assignment may be refused on grounds of public policy.

14–103   There are two reported cases of a foreign judgment *in rem* being enforced in England by an action *in rem*. In *The City of Mecca*,[56] a collision occurred on the high seas between a Spanish ship and a British ship. The owners of the Spanish ship brought an action in Portugal against the British ship, then lying in Lisbon, and obtained a judgment against the owners for damages. The ship returned to England before the judgment was satisfied. On the assumption that the Portuguese judgment was *in rem*, Sir Robert Phillimore allowed an action *in rem* in the Admiralty Division of the High Court against the ship on the unsatisfied judgment. His ground for doing so was that international law requires courts of admiralty to act in aid of each other,[57] although Blackburn J. had categorically denied in *Godard v. Gray*[58] that it was "an admitted principle of the law of nations that a State is bound to enforce within its territories the judgment of a foreign tribunal." On the production of further evidence to the effect that Portuguese law had abolished actions *in rem*, Sir Robert Phillimore's decision was reversed by the Court of Appeal.[59] In the *Despina G.K.*[60] Sheen J. applied Sir Robert Phillimore's decision in an action *in rem* in England in which cargo owners claimed the balance of a sum outstanding on a judgment which they had obtained in an action *in rem* in the Swedish admiralty court in respect of the cargo. It was held that a judgment creditor who has obtained a final judgment against a shipowner by proceedings *in rem* in a foreign admiralty court can bring an action *in rem* in England against the ship to enforce the decree of the foreign court if that is necessary to complete the execution of the judgment, provided that the ship is the property of the judgment debtor when she is arrested. The correctness of this decision was open to doubt, since nothing in the Supreme Court Act 1981, section 21, justified the exercise of jurisdiction *in rem* in relation to such a claim. There seemed to be no reason why a judgment *in rem* should not be registrable under the 1920 or 1933 Acts provided that a sum of money was payable thereunder, or under Parts I and II of the 1982 Act.

14–104   Clause (1) of Rule 40 reproduces almost exactly a provision of the 1933 Act[61]; and there is also ample support for it at common law. Hence it is essential to the recognition or enforcement in England of a foreign judgment

---

[53] See Rules 116–117.
[54] See Rule 43. *Cf. Ellerman Lines v. Read* [1928] 2 K.B. 144 (C.A.).
[55] See Rules 116–117.
[56] (1879) 5 P.D. 28.
[57] *Ibid.* p. 32.
[58] (1870) L.R. 6 Q.B. 139, 148.
[59] (1881) 6 P.D. 106.
[60] [1983] Q.B. 214. See also *Pacific Star v. Bank of America National Trust and Savings Association* [1965] W.A.R. 159.
[61] s.4(2)(*b*).

in rem that the *res* should have been situate in the foreign country concerned at the time of the proceedings. If it was, jurisdiction probably exists even though the owner of the *res* did not consent to its being there, *e.g.* when a ship puts into a foreign port through stress of weather, or a yacht is stolen and abandoned in a foreign port.[62]

Clause (2) of the Rule rests on a very slender basis of precedent, and its **14–105** exact scope is a matter of some doubt. It is a corollary of the principle that English courts have no jurisdiction to determine the title to, or the right to the possession of, any immovable situate outside England.[63] But though this principle is subject to exceptions,[64] Rule 40(2) is not; or, to put it more precisely, none have yet been formulated. It is therefore an illustration of the proposition that English courts sometimes claim for themselves a wider jurisdiction than they are prepared to concede to foreign courts. Thus, English courts do not admit the jurisdiction of any foreign court to determine a person's title, under a will or otherwise, to English immovables,[65] even though English courts sometimes determine the validity of wills dealing with foreign land.[66] Again, the Supreme Court of Canada has held that a foreign equitable degree *in personam* relating to land in British Columbia, though based on the fraud of a defendant personally subject to the jurisdiction of the foreign court and therefore within the rule in *Penn v. Lord Baltimore*,[67] will not be enforced in Canada.[68] In earlier editions of this work[69] it was suggested that a court of a foreign country would not have jurisdiction to grant damages for any injury in respect of an immovable situate outside that country. Section 30 of the 1982 Act abrogates the rule that an English court has no jurisdiction to entertain proceedings for torts to foreign land.[70] This change does not directly affect Rule 40(2) but its adoption makes it unlikely that a foreign court would be regarded as not having jurisdiction to entertain proceedings for torts to land outside the country in which it sits. The 1933 Act provides[71] that the courts of a foreign country shall not be deemed to have jurisdiction if the subject-matter of the proceedings is immovable property outside that country. The precise scope of this enactment is not very clear; but it is not likely that it affects this conclusion in cases within its scope.

The jurisdiction of the courts of the *situs* to give a judgment *in rem* affecting **14–106** a movable is not necessarily exclusive. For example, English courts recognise that the courts of a foreign country have jurisdiction to determine the succession to all movables wherever locally situate of a testator or intestate dying domiciled in such country.[72] For this reason clause (2) of Rule 40 is limited to immovables.

---

[62] *Cammell v. Sewell* (1860) 5 H. & N. 728, 745. Contrast Read, pp. 139–142.

[63] *British South Africa Co. v. Companhia de Moçambique* [1893] A.C. 602.

[64] See *post*, Rule 114.

[65] *Boyse v. Colclough* (1854) 1 K. & J. 124; *Re Hoyles* [1911] 1 Ch. 179, 185–186 (C.A.).

[66] *Nelson v. Bridport* (1846) 8 Beav. 547; *Re Piercy* [1895] 1 Ch. 83; *Re Stirling* [1908] 2 Ch. 344; *Re Ross* [1930] 1 Ch. 377; *Re Duke of Wellington* [1948] Ch. 118 (C.A.); *post*, paras. 23–049.

[67] (1750) 1 Ves.Sen. 444; see *post*, paras. 23–040 *et seq.*

[68] *Duke v. Andler* [1932] 4 D.L.R. 529 (Sup.Ct.Can.); *cf. Haspel v. Haspel* [1934] 2 W.W.R. 412 (Alta.); *Fall v. Eastin*, 215 U.S. 1 (1909). See Restatement, s.102, comment *d.*

[69] See 10th ed., p. 1071.

[70] *Post*, para. 23–038.

[71] s.4(3)(*a*).

[72] See Rule 130. *Cf.* Rule 167 (bankruptcy).

ILLUSTRATIONS

14–107   1. A, an Englishman, is owner of a British ship. Whilst the ship is at a foreign port, the foreign court, honestly exercising its jurisdiction, pronounces in a proceeding *in rem* a judgment under which the ship is ordered to be sold for the payment of necessaries supplied to M, the master, and is sold to X, a British citizen. The court has acted under a misconception of English law, and in consequence has not recognised the rights of A as owner. The foreign court has jurisdiction.[73]

    2. A foreign Admiralty court gives a judgment *in rem* against a British ship owned by A, an Englishman. The judgment is obtained by the fraud of B, the plaintiff. The ship is, under the judgment, sold to X, an innocent purchaser, and comes into an English port. A claims the vessel and seeks to show that the foreign judgment was obtained by fraud. *Semble*, X's title prevails.[74]

    3. A British ship is seized as prize by a Russian vessel, on the ground of attempted breach of blockade, and taken to a Russian port for adjudication as prize by a prize court. The goods on board the ship are sold under the order of the court to X. It is ultimately decided by the prize court that the ship was not lawfully captured. The Russian court has jurisdiction.[75]

    4. Cargo was consigned on a Greek vessel to A in Malta. It was damaged en route while the ship was in a Greek port, and a Greek court authorised the hypothecation of the cargo and the execution thereon of a bottomry bond to cover the cost of transhipment. The Greek court was held to have jurisdiction.[76]

14–108   5. A & Co., cargo-owners, bring an action *in rem* in the Admiralty Court of Stockholm against a Liberian ship, from which their cargo has been dumped at sea. A & Co. obtain judgment against X, the shipowners, who pay part of the sum awarded by the Swedish court. When the ship enters an English port, A & Co. issue proceedings *in rem* claiming the sum outstanding on the Swedish judgment and apply for a warrant of arrest of the ship. *Semble*, the proceedings may not be brought and A & Co. must proceed by enforcing their judgment by registration under Rule 48, or by proceedings on the judgment at common law.[77]

    6. T, by his will executed in 1842, devised all his real and personal estate to A. He had real estate in Ireland and also in England. The Irish courts, it was held, had no jurisdiction to adjudicate upon the validity of the will as related to the real estate in England; and a decree of the Irish Court of Chancery did not determine the validity or invalidity of the will so far as the lands in England are concerned, and could not be pleaded in bar to a suit in the English Court of Chancery.[78]

    7. A agrees with X in California to sell to X land in England. A and X are residents of California. The land is conveyed to X in accordance with English law. A sues X in California to set aside the conveyance because of X's fraud. The Californian court orders X to reconvey the land to A and on X's refusal to do so the clerk of the court purports to reconvey in X's name. A sues X in England for a declaration that he (A) is the owner of the land. The Californian decree will not be recognised in England.[79]

C. *Conclusiveness of Foreign Judgments: Defences*

14R–109   **RULE 41[80]—A foreign judgment which is final and conclusive[81] on the merits and not impeachable under any of Rules 42 to 45 is conclusive as**

---

[73] *Castrique v. Imrie* (1870) L.R. 4 H.L. 414.

[74] See *Castrique v. Imrie* (1870) L.R. 4 H.L. 414, 433; *Simpson v. Fogo* (1863) 1 H. & M. 195, 248. See also *Castrique v. Behrens* (1861) 30 L.J.Q.B. 163.

[75] See *Stringer v. English, etc., Insurance Co.* (1870) L.R. 5 Q.B. 599, esp. 606; *Hughes v. Cornelius* (1681) 2 Show.K.B. 232.

[76] *Messina v. Petrococchino* (1872) L.R. 4 P.C. 144; *Dent v. Smith* (1869) L.R. 4 Q.B. 414.

[77] 1982 Act, s.34, reversing *The Despina G.K.* [1983] Q.B. 214.

[78] *Boyse v. Colclough* (1854) 1 K. & J. 124.

[79] *Cf. Duke v. Andler* [1932] 4 D.L.R. 529 (Sup.Ct.Can.).

[80] *Godard v. Gray* (1870) L.R. 6 Q.B. 139; *Bank of Australasia v. Nias* (1851) 16 Q.B. 717; *Ellis v. M'Henry* (1871) L.R. 6 C.P. 228, 238; *Carl Zeiss Stiftung v. Rayner & Keeler Ltd.* (*No. 2*) [1967] 1 A.C. 853, 917, 925, 965–966; *Page v. Phelan* (1844) 1 U.C.Q.B. 254; *Kingsmill & Davis v. Warrener & Wheeler* (1852) 13 U.C.Q.B. 18; *Four Embarcadero Center Venture v. Kalen* (1988) 65 O.R. (2d) 551; Read, pp. 87–93. See also 1933 Act, s.8(1), *post*, para. 14–181.

[81] See Rule 35, where the meaning of this expression is elucidated, and *post*, para. 14–113.

to any matter thereby adjudicated upon, and cannot be impeached for any error either

> (1) of fact[82]; or
>
> (2) of law.[83]

COMMENT

During the eighteenth century and the first part of the nineteenth century it **14–110** was much debated whether a foreign judgment given by a court of competent jurisdiction could be re-examined on its merits when recognition or enforcement of that judgment was sought in England. As late as 1834 Lord Brougham said in the House of Lords "a foreign judgment is only prima facie, not conclusive, evidence of a debt."[84] And as late as 1863 Page Wood V.-C. refused to recognise a Louisiana judgment on the ground that it showed on its face "a perverse and deliberate refusal to recognise the law" of England.[85] But meanwhile it had been decided in a series of cases that a foreign judgment could not be re-examined on the merits provided the foreign court had jurisdiction according to the English rules of the conflict of laws.[86] And finally, in *Godard v. Gray*[87] it was held that this was so even if the foreign court made an obvious mistake of English law which appeared on the face of the judgment. Since that decision, the principle of Rule 41 has never been questioned. It is consistent with the maxims *interest reipublicae ut sit finis litium* (it is in the public interest that there should be an end to litigation) and *nemo debet bis vexari pro eadem causa* (no one should be sued twice on the same ground).

Rule 41 holds good whether the judgment is relied upon by the claimant[88] **14–111** or by the defendant.[89] It applies whether the judgment is *in personam* or *in rem*[90] (including a judgment affecting status[91]). The only difference in this respect between a judgment *in personam* and a judgment *in rem* is that the former is conclusive only between the parties and their representatives, while the latter is conclusive against all the world.[92] A foreign judgment *in rem* is

---

[82] *Henderson v. Henderson* (1844) 6 Q.B. 288; *De Cosse Brissac v. Rathbone* (1861) 6 H. & N. 301 (the third plea).

[83] *Castrique v. Imrie* (1870) L.R. 4 H.L. 414; *Godard v. Gray* (1870) L.R. 6 Q.B. 139; *Scott v. Pilkington* (1862) 2 B. & S. 11; *De Cosse Brissac v. Rathbone* (1861) 6 H. & N. 301 (the third plea); *Minna Craig Steamship Co. v. Chartered, etc., Bank* [1897] 1 Q.B. 460 (C.A.); *cf. Dallal v. Bank Mellat* [1986] Q.B. 441. See Restatement, s.106.

[84] *Houlditch v. Donegal* (1834) 2 Cl. & F. 470, 477. *Cf. Smith v. Nicolls* (1839) 5 Bing.N.C. 208, 221.

[85] *Simpson v. Fogo* (1863) 1 H. & M. 195, 247. The correctness of this decision was doubted in *Luther v. Sagor* [1921] 3 K.B. 532, 558 (C.A.) and in *Carl Zeiss Stiftung v. Rayner & Keeler Ltd. (No. 2)* [1967] 1 A.C. 853, 917–918, 922, 978, and it may be of only historical interest today.

[86] *Henderson v. Henderson* (1844) 6 Q.B. 288; *Bank of Australasia v. Harding* (1850) 9 C.B. 661; *Bank of Australasia v. Nias* (1851) 16 Q.B. 717; *De Cosse Brissac v. Rathbone* (1861) 6 H. & N. 301.

[87] (1870) L.R. 6 Q.B. 139. *Cf. Castrique v. Imrie* (1870) L.R. 4 H.L. 414.

[88] Cases *supra*.

[89] *Ricardo v. Garcias* (1845) 12 Cl. & F. 368. See Rule 35, *ante*.

[90] *Castrique v. Imrie* (1870) L.R. 4 H.L. 414.

[91] *Harvey v. Farnie* (1882) 8 App.Cas. 43 (divorce); *Von Lorang v. Administrator of Austrian Property* [1927] A.C. 641 (nullity).

[92] *Castrique v. Imrie, supra; Von Lorang v. Administrator of Austrian Property, supra.*

within the scope of Rule 41 even though there may be only one original party thereto.

14–112   Rule 41 in effect applies to foreign judgments the principles well known in English domestic law under the name of estoppel *per rem judicatam*. This doctrine has two branches: "cause of action estoppel," which precludes a party from relitigating the existence of the same cause of action, and "issue estoppel," which precludes a party from denying any matter of fact or law necessarily decided by the earlier judgment.[93] Most of the cases applying the doctrine to foreign judgments have been concerned with cause of action estoppel. A foreign judgment is *res judicata* whether it is given in favour of the claimant or defendant. The judgment of an English court of record extinguishes the original cause of action, which merges in the judgment.[94] If A in an English court recovers judgment for £10,000 against X for breach of contract or for a tort he can issue execution on the judgment, but he cannot bring proceedings against X for the breach of contract or for the tort. But at common law a foreign judgment did not extinguish the original cause of action, so that if A recovered judgment in a New York court for $10,000 against X he could bring an action in England on the judgment but he could also, if he chose, bring an action for the debt, in which case the foreign judgment would be merely evidence of the debt. This anomaly has been removed by section 34 of the 1982 Act, which has been discussed in connection with Rule 35, and which provides that no proceedings may be brought by a person in England on a cause of action in respect of which a judgment has been given in his favour in proceedings between the same parties, or their privies, in a foreign court,[95] unless the judgment is not enforceable or entitled to recognition in England.

14–113   In *Carl Zeiss Stiftung v. Rayner & Keeler Ltd. (No. 2)*,[96] a majority of the House of Lords held that issue estoppel can be based on a foreign judgment, and this decision was applied by a unanimous House in *The Sennar (No. 2)*.[97] Three conditions must be fulfilled before the doctrine can be applied[98]: (1) The judgment of the foreign court must be of a court of competent jurisdiction, and must be final and conclusive on the merits in the sense of Rule 35; (2) there must be identity of parties[99]; (3) there must be identity of subject-matter, that is to say, the issues must be the same. In the *Carl Zeiss* case it was not expressly laid down that the foreign judgment must not be impeachable on any of the grounds referred to in Rule 41, *i.e.* under any of Rules 42 to 45. But in *The Sennar (No. 2)* it was made clear that the foreign court must be competent and it can hardly be supposed that an estoppel could be based, *e.g.* on a foreign judgment which had been obtained by fraud.[1]

14–114   Closely parallel to the rule that a foreign judgment is conclusive is the rule that the defendant must take all available defences in the foreign court, and that, if he does not do so, he cannot be allowed to plead them afterwards in

---

[93] *Ante*, para. 14–027.
[94] Halsbury's *Laws of England*, 4th ed., Vol. 16, para. 1536.
[95] Or in a court of another part of the United Kingdom.
[96] [1967] 1 A.C. 853.
[97] [1985] 1 W.L.R. 490 (H.L.).
[98] [1967] 1 A.C. 853, 909–910, 935, 942, 967–971; [1985] 1 W.L.R. 490, 499. See *ante*, para. 14–029.
[99] Of course this condition does not apply to judgments *in rem*: see n. 92, *supra*.
[1] See, *e.g. Von Lorang v. Administrator of Austrian Property* [1927] A.C. 641, which does not appear to have been cited in *Carl Zeiss Stiftung v. Rayner & Keeler Ltd. (No. 2), supra.*

England.[2] But neither of these rules applies if the judgment was obtained by fraud.[3] It has even been held that it is no defence to plead that since the date of the judgment the defendant has discovered new evidence which he could not with reasonable diligence have discovered earlier and which shows that the judgment is erroneous.[4] But it would be a mistake to conclude from this one decision that in no circumstances can a foreign judgment be impeachable at common law on the ground that fresh evidence has been discovered. For the plea was much less precise than a statement of case would have to be in an action to review an English judgment on this ground[5]; it did not even allege that if the fresh evidence had been produced to the foreign court, it must have led to the opposite result. Since an English judgment can be set aside, even in the absence of fraud, if the unsuccessful party discovers new and material evidence after the trial,[6] there seems no reason why a foreign judgment should be in a different position.

The meaning of the word "conclusive" in Rule 41 must be carefully **14–115** distinguished from the meaning of the term "final and conclusive" in Rule 35. For clearly the word "conclusive" is used in these two Rules in two quite different senses. In this Rule the reference is to a rule of English law whereby a foreign judgment given by a court of competent jurisdiction, and not impeachable on a number of strictly limited grounds, is conclusive and not merely prima facie evidence of the matters therein decided. But in Rule 35 the reference is to a quality which the foreign judgment must possess by the law of the foreign country concerned, without which quality it cannot be recognised or enforced in England.

ILLUSTRATIONS

1. A sued X in a French court for breach of an English charterparty, in which was a clause, **14–116** "penalty for the non-performance of this agreement, estimated amount of freight." The foreign court, under an erroneous view of the English law, treated this clause as fixing the amount of damages recoverable, and therefore gave judgment in favour of A for £700, the amount of the freight. The judgment, though given under a mistaken view of English law, was conclusive.[7]

2. A brings an action in England for £200 due to A from X under a judgment of a New York court. The judgment is founded on a mistaken view of the law of New York. The judgment is conclusive.[8]

3. A obtains a judgment for a debt against X in a Canadian court. X, at the time when the action is brought in Canada, has been made bankrupt in England, and might have pleaded his discharge in the bankruptcy in defence to the action. The Canadian judgment is conclusive.[9]

---

[2] *Henderson v. Henderson* (1844) 6 Q.B. 288; *De Cosse Brissac v. Rathbone* (1861) 6 H. & N. 301; *Ellis v. M'Henry* (1871) L.R. 6 C.P. 228; *Israel Discount Bank of New York v. Hadjipateras* [1984] 1 W.L.R. 137 (C.A.).

[3] *Post*, Rule 43. Contrast *House of Spring Gardens Ltd. v. Waite* [1991] 1 Q.B. 241 (C.A.), where judgment debtors were estopped from raising fraud by a judgment in a separate action in the foreign court to set aside the original judgment.

[4] *De Cosse Brissac v. Rathbone* (1861) 6 H. & N. 301 (the fifth plea).

[5] *Boswell v. Coaks* (1894) 6 R. 167, 170–172; 86 L.T. 365n., 366n. (H.L.); D.M. Gordon (1961) 77 L.Q.R. 358, 533, especially at pp. 549–554.

[6] Halsbury's *Laws of England*, 4th ed., Vol. 26, para. 561; Gordon (1961) 77 L.Q.R. 358, 533 especially at pp. 371, 536.

[7] *Godard v. Gray* (1870) L.R. 6 Q.B. 139. See also *Castrique v. Imrie* (1870) L.R. 4 H.L. 414.

[8] *Scott v. Pilkington* (1862) 2 B. & S. 11. Cf. *De Cosse Brissac v. Rathbone* (1861) 6 H. & N. 301; and contrast *Meyer v. Ralli* (1876) 1 C.P.D. 358 which (*semble*) is wrongly decided, unless it can be sustained on the score of the consent of the parties to recognise the incorrectness of the foreign court's view of the law.

[9] *Ellis v. M'Henry* (1871) L.R. 6 C.P. 228.

14–117   4. A obtains a judgment on a guarantee against X and Y in a New York court. X seeks to resist enforcement in England on the ground that the guarantee was executed under the undue influence of Y, but X had deliberately refrained from making that allegation in the New York proceedings. The judgment is conclusive.[10]

5. A sues X for a debt in a foreign court. X pleads that he has paid the debt but lost the receipt. The court disbelieves him and gives judgment for A. Subsequently, X finds the missing receipt and applies to the foreign court for leave to appeal out of time against the judgment. The foreign court dismisses his application. A brings an action on the judgment against X in England. *Semble*, the action will fail.[11]

6. A Russian court awards salvage in respect of a Russian ship. The decision probably rests on a misinterpretation of maritime law. The judgment is conclusive in an English court in a claim by an owner who has paid against an insurance company.[12]

14R–118   **RULE 42—(1) A foreign judgment is impeachable if the courts of the foreign country did not, in the circumstances of the case, have jurisdiction to give that judgment in the view of English law in accordance with the principles set out in Rules 36 to 40 inclusive.[13]**

(2) A foreign judgment cannot, in general, be impeached on the ground that the court which gave it was not competent to do so according to the law of the foreign country concerned.[14]

COMMENT

14–119   **Clause (1) of the Rule.** Lack of jurisdiction on the part of the foreign court is the objection which can most frequently be raised in answer to a party who relies on a foreign judgment in English proceedings. It is not enough, it must be again emphasised, that the foreign court is duly invested with jurisdiction under the foreign legal system. It must also have jurisdiction according to the English rules of the conflict of laws. These rules have already been considered in Rules 36 to 40 and there is no need to repeat here what is there said. Clause (1) of the present Rule is thus in a sense merely mechanical, in that it merely refers to other Rules.

14–120   But a foreign judgment, whatever its jurisdictional basis, is prima facie capable of enforcement or, as the case may be, recognition in England.[15] In *Adams v. Cape Industries plc*[16] the Court of Appeal accepted that no specific assertion need be made that the foreign court was competent in terms of foreign law, because whether the foreign court was competent was irrelevant. But there was a legal burden on a claimant seeking to enforce a foreign

---

[10] *Israel Discount Bank of New York v. Hadjipateras* [1984] 1 W.L.R. 137 (C.A.).

[11] See para. 14–114, *ante.* Contrast *De Cosse Brissac v. Rathbone* (1861) 6 H. & N. 301 (the fifth plea).

[12] *Cf. Dent v. Smith* (1869) L.R. 4 Q.B. 414.

[13] *Buchanan v. Rucker* (1808) 9 East 192; *Schibsby v. Westenholz* (1870) L.R. 6 Q.B. 155; *Sirdar Gurdyal Singh v. Rajah of Faridkote* [1894] A.C. 670 (P.C.); *Emanuel v. Symon* [1908] 1 K.B. 302 (C.A.).

[14] *Vanquelin v. Bouard* (1863) 15 C.B. (N.S.) 341; *Pemberton v. Hughes* [1899] 1 Ch. 781 (C.A.); *Adams v. Cape Industries plc* [1990] Ch. 433, 513–514, 550 (C.A.); Read, pp. 93–100; *cf.* Restatement, s.105.

[15] *Alivon v. Furnival* (1834) 1 C.M. & R. 277; *Bank of Australasia v. Nias* (1851) 16 Q.B. 717; *Henderson v. Henderson* (1844) 6 Q.B. 288; *Robertson v. Struth* (1844) 5 Q.B. 941; *Taylor v. Ford* (1873) 29 L.T. 392.

[16] [1990] Ch. 433, 450 (C.A.).

judgment to prove that the foreign court was competent in the sense recognised by English law to assume jurisdiction over him: the evidentiary burden might shift at trial.

There is a rule similar to Rule 42 under the 1920 Act[17] and the 1933 Act.[18] **14–121**
But under Part I of the 1982 Act the right of the English court to examine the jurisdiction of the court of another State party to the 1968 Convention or the Lugano Convention is very limited, and under Part II of the 1982 Act the English court has no power to examine the jurisdiction of the Scottish or Northern Irish court.[19]

Clause (2) of the Rule. If a judgment is pronounced by a court of a foreign **14–122**
country whose courts have jurisdiction in the view of English law, but the particular foreign court is not the proper court in terms of the domestic rules of the foreign legal system, is the judgment capable of enforcement or recognition in England? This question must almost certainly be answered in the affirmative, at any rate so far as judgments *in personam* are concerned; but the authorities are at first sight in a state of some confusion.

In *Vanquelin v. Bouard*[20] the defendant was sued in England on a French **14–123**
judgment in respect of a bill of exchange. The French court had jurisdiction according to the English rules of the conflict of laws and the subject-matter of the action (bills of exchange) was within its internal competence. But the defendant pleaded that the particular French court had no internal competence over him because he was not a trader. This plea was held bad.

On the other hand, in *Castrique v. Imrie*[21] (a case on a foreign judgment *in* **14–124**
rem) Blackburn J. regarded it as material "whether the sovereign authority of that State has conferred on the court jurisdiction to decide as to the disposition of the thing, and the court has acted within its jurisdiction." This could be taken to mean that a foreign judgment *in rem*, in order to be recognised in England, must have been pronounced by a court having local competence as well as international jurisdiction. Further, in *Papadopoulos v. Papadopoulos*,[22] one reason for refusing to recognise a Cypriot decree of nullity of marriage was that the court had no internal competence to annul a marriage under the Order in Council which established it. And in *Adams v. Adams*,[23] a Rhodesian divorce was not recognised because the judge who pronounced it had not taken the oath of allegiance and the judicial oath in the prescribed form.

The difficulties of the question raised and the apparent differences of **14–125**
opinion between judges may be reduced by the following considerations. When, *e.g.* a New York court, which from an international point of view is a court of competent jurisdiction, delivers a judgment in excess of the authority conferred upon the court by New York law, the judgment, though obviously not pronounced by a court having local competence, may bear one of two characters. It may be irregular, but have validity in New York until it is set

---

[17] 1920 Act, s.9(2)(*a*).
[18] 1933 Act, ss.4(1)(*a*)(ii), 8(1)(2).
[19] *Post*, paras. 14–201 and 14–231.
[20] (1863) 15 C.B.(N.S.) 341, approved in *Pemberton v. Hughes* [1899] 1 Ch. 781, 791 (C.A.). See also *Brijlal Ramjidas v. Govindram Seksaria* [1943] I.L.R.(Bom.) 366; (1947) L.R. 74 Ind.App. 203, and Monroe (1950) 3 Int.L.Q. 444.
[21] (1870) L.R. 4 H.L. 414, 429. Blackburn J.'s statement was approved by Lord Chelmsford at p. 448.
[22] [1930] P. 55.
[23] [1971] P. 188.

aside; or it may be a complete nullity, and have no legal effect whatever in New York. In the former case the judgment ought to be held valid in England unless and until it is set aside in New York.[24] The latter case is doubtful, but most unlikely to occur in practice. A judgment pronounced by a foreign court is far more likely to be irregular than void. The practical result, therefore, is that such a judgment is generally unimpeachable in England, even though not pronounced by a court having local competence.[25]

ILLUSTRATION[26]

14-126   A, a Danish subject resident in France, obtained judgment in a French court for £460 against X, a Danish subject resident and carrying on business in England. X was not present in France when the writ was issued, nor did he appear or submit to the jurisdiction of the French court. He was served with the writ in England. The judgment was impeachable for lack of jurisdiction.[27]

14R-127   **RULE 43[28]—A foreign judgment relied upon as such in proceedings in England, is impeachable for fraud.**

Such fraud may be either

(1) fraud on the part of the party in whose favour the judgment is given; or

(2) fraud on the part of the court pronouncing the judgment.

COMMENT

14-128   Any judgment whatever, and therefore any foreign judgment, is, if obtained by fraud, open to attack. A party against whom an English judgment has been given may bring an independent action to set aside the judgment on the ground that it was obtained by fraud; but this is subject to very stringent safeguards, which have been found to be necessary because otherwise there would be no end to litigation and no solemnity in judgments.[29] The most

---

[24] *Cf. S.A. Consortium General Textiles v. Sun & Sand Agencies Ltd.* [1978] Q.B. 279 (C.A.) (a case on the 1933 Act).

[25] See further *Macalpine v. Macalpine* [1958] P. 35, 41, 45; *Merker v. Merker* [1963] P. 283, 297–299.

[26] See also the Illustrations to Rule 36, *ante*, paras. 14–086 *et seq.*

[27] *Schibsby v. Westenholz* (1870) L.R. 6 Q.B. 155.

[28] As to the effect of fraud upon judgments generally, see *Duchess of Kingston's Case* (1776) 2 Sm.L.C. (13th ed.) 644; upon foreign judgments *in personam, Ochsenbein v. Papelier* (1873) L.R. 8 Ch.App. 695; *Abouloff v. Oppenheimer* (1882) 10 Q.B.D. 295 (C.A.); *Vadala v. Lawes* (1890) 25 Q.B.D. 310 (C.A.); *Syal v. Heyward* [1948] 2 K.B. 433 (C.A.); *Blohn v. Desser* [1962] 2 Q.B. 116; *Jet Holdings Ltd. v. Patel* [1990] 1 Q.B. 335 (C.A.); *House of Spring Gardens Ltd. v. Waite* [1991] 1 Q.B. 241 (C.A.); *Owens Bank Ltd. v. Bracco* [1992] 2 A.C. 443; on foreign judgments *in rem, Castrique v. Behrens* (1861) 30 L.J.Q.B. 163; *Castrique v. Imrie* (1870) L.R. 4 H.L. 414, 433; *Ellerman Lines Ltd. v. Read* [1928] 2 K.B. 144 (C.A.); on foreign decrees of divorce and nullity, see *post*, para. 18–122; under statute, 1920 Act, s.9(2)(*d*); 1933 Act, s.4(1)(*a*)(iv). See, generally, Read, pp. 273–281; Restatement, s.115.

[29] See *Hunter v. Chief Constable of the West Midlands Police* [1982] A.C. 529; Halsbury's *Laws of England*, 4th ed., Vol. 26, para. 560; D. M. Gordon (1961) 77 L.Q.R. 358, 533.

important of these safeguards is that the second action will be summarily dismissed unless the claimant can produce evidence newly discovered since the trial, which evidence could not have been produced at the trial with reasonable diligence, and which is so material that its production at the trial would probably have affected the result, and (when the fraud consists of perjury) so strong that it would reasonably be expected to be decisive at the rehearing and if unanswered must have that result.[30] But it does not matter whether the fraud is extrinsic, *e.g.* consists in bribing witnesses, or intrinsic, *e.g.* consists in giving or procuring of perjured or forged evidence.[31]

A foreign judgment, on the other hand, can be impeached for fraud even **14–129** though no newly discovered evidence is produced and even though the fraud might have been, and was, alleged in the foreign proceedings. This was first laid down in *Abouloff v. Oppenheimer*,[32] where the Court of Appeal had some difficulty in reconciling its decision with the then recently established principle that foreign judgments are conclusive on the merits and cannot be impeached for any errors of fact or law.[33] Lord Coleridge C.J. and Brett L.J. solved the difficulty by holding that the issue whether a foreign court had been deliberately misled was not, and never could be, one on which that court had passed.[34] Hence to examine the judgment in subsequent English proceedings was not to re-open the merits of the judgment pronounced by the foreign court. The technical nature of this hypothesis was admitted in *Vadala v. Lawes*,[35] where the evidence necessary to establish the fraud was precisely the same as that which had been rejected by the foreign court. But Lindley L.J. refused to "fritter away" the judgment in *Abouloff v. Oppenheimer*; and he observed that "if the fraud upon the foreign court consists in the fact that the plaintiff has induced that court by fraud to come to a wrong conclusion, you can re-open the whole case even although you will have in this court to go into the very facts which were investigated and which were in issue in the foreign court."[36] It has even been held to be immaterial that the facts relied upon to establish a prima facie case of fraud were known to the party relying on them at all material times and could thus have been raised by way of defence in the foreign proceedings.[37] Thus, the rule that foreign judgments can be impeached for fraud stands in square opposition to the principle of conclusiveness and also to the principle that English judgments can only be impeached for fraud if new evidence of a decisive character has since been discovered. Objections to the doctrine as thus established have been advanced by various writers and

---

[30] Gordon (1961) 77 L.Q.R. 358, 376–377, and cases there cited.

[31] Gordon, *ibid.* at pp. 535–546, and cases there cited.

[32] (1882) 10 Q.B.D. 295 (C.A.), stated *post*, para. 14–139, Illustration 1. By demurring to the plea of fraud, the plaintiff conceded that the foreign judgment had been so obtained, and rendered it unnecessary to prove the fraud by evidence.

[33] See Rule 41.

[34] (1882) 10 Q.B.D. 295, 302, 306.

[35] (1890) 25 Q.B.D. 310 (C.A.); stated *post* para. 14–139, Illustration 2. *Cf. Ellerman Lines Ltd. v. Read* [1928] 2 K.B. 144 (C.A.); contrast *Blohn v. Desser* [1962] 2 Q.B. 116. The reasoning in *Abouloff v. Oppenheimer* was described as illogical in *Westacre Investments Inc. v. Jugoimport SDPR Holding Co. Ltd.* [1999] Q.B. 740, 782 (a case on arbitral awards).

[36] (1890) 25 Q.B.D. 310 at pp. 316–317. The principle laid down in these two cases was mentioned, with apparent approval, in *R. v. Humphrys* [1977] A.C. 1, 21, 30, 46.

[37] *Syal v. Heyward* [1948] 2 K.B. 443 (C.A.); stated *post*, para. 14–139, Illustration 4; *Svirskis v. Gibson* [1977] 2 N.Z.L.R. 4.

a different approach has been adopted in Canada.[38] It may be observed, however, that if fraud is alleged in relation to an English judgment, its effect will be to destroy the judgment and prevent its enforcement anywhere. By contrast, when fraud is alleged in relation to a foreign judgment, the effect is only to prevent enforcement in England; no impact will be felt in the State whose courts produced the judgment nor (issues of estoppel aside) in any third country. As such, the effect of a finding of fraud in relation to a foreign judgment is more limited than in the case of an English judgment, and it is not difficult to argue that the nature of the evidence required to justify these two discrete results need not be identical in quality.[39]

14–130   In *Keele v. Findley*[40] the New South Wales Commercial Division rejected the English authorities and preferred the Canadian authorities. It was held that the current state of English law reflected an historical error: the authorities had failed to take proper account of the developments in the law relating to domestic judgments. Consequently, fraud was a defence to an action on a foreign judgment only if there had been a new discovery of material evidence which would establish fraud and make it reasonably probable that the opposite result would have been reached. But the English authorities have now been reaffirmed by the Court of Appeal in *Jet Holdings Inc. v. Patel*[41] and by the House of Lords in *Owens Bank Ltd. v. Bracco*,[42] in each of which it was confirmed that the defence of fraud was not limited to fraud which was extraneous or collateral to the dispute which the foreign court determined, and applied equally to fraud which was intrinsic in the sense mentioned above. The latter decision was on section 9(2)(*d*) of the 1920 Act, under which no judgment can be registered if it was obtained by fraud. The House of Lords held it had to be construed with reference to the common law as understood when the 1920 Act was enacted. It was recognised that there was a strong case for according to overseas judgments the same finality as was accorded to English judgments, but the House of Lords considered that to overrule *Aboul-off v. Oppenheimer* and *Vadala v. Lawes* would produce the absurd result that a judgment creditor, denied statutory enforcement under the 1920 Act or the 1933 Act on the ground that he had obtained his judgment by fraud, could

---

[38] Cheshire (1st ed.), pp. 521–524; *cf.* Cheshire and North, pp. 442–446; Wolff, s.247; Read, pp. 279–293, and in (1930) 8 Can.Bar Rev. 231–237; Cowen (1949) 65 L.Q.R. 82. The view of the Canadian courts is different and is best indicated by the words of Garrow J. in *Jacobs v. Beaver* (1908) 17 O.L.R. 496, 506. "The fraud relied on must be something collateral or extraneous, and not merely the fraud which is imputed from alleged false statements made at the trial, which were met by counter-statements by the other side, and the whole adjudicated upon by the court and so passed on into the limbo of estoppel by the judgment. This estoppel cannot be disturbed except upon the allegation and proof of new and material facts, or newly discovered material facts which were not before the former court, and from which are to be deduced the new proposition that the former judgment was obtained by fraud." See also *Woodruff v. McLennan* (1887) 14 O.A.R. 242; *Hollender v. Ffoulkes* (1894) 26 O.R. 61 (Ont. C.A.); *Manolopoulos v. Pnaiffe* [1930] 2 D.L.R. 169 (N.S.C.A.); *Boga v. Chamberlen* [1936] 1 D.L.R. 660 (N.S.); *Union of India v. Bumper Development Corp.* [1995] 7 W.W.R. 80 (Alta.).

[39] See also *Soleimany v. Soleimany* [1999] Q.B. 785 (C.A.).

[40] (1991) 21 N.S.W.L.R. 444. See also *Wentworth v. Rogers (No. 5)* (1986) 6 N.S.W.L.R. 534, 541. But in *Close v. Arnot* (November 21, 1997, N.S.W.), the Common Law Division distinguished *Keele v. Findley* and applied the traditional English standard of fraud in respect of a foreign judgment in a case where the defendant had, for good reason, allowed foreign proceedings to go undefended.

[41] [1990] 1 Q.B. 335 (C.A.).

[42] [1992] 2 A.C. 443.

succeed in a common law action to enforce his judgment because the evidence on which the judgment debtor relied did not satisfy the English rule for domestic judgments. "Accordingly", said Lord Bridge (with whom all the other members concurred), "the whole field is effectively governed by statute and, if the law is now in need of reform, it is for the legislature, not the judiciary, to effect it."[43] This conclusion is, it is suggested, unconvincing: first, the whole field is *not* governed by statute, since the legislation applies to two countries only (Israel and Suriname) outside the Commonwealth and Western Europe[44]; secondly, as has been seen, under the 1933 Act no action may be brought at common law upon a judgment capable of direct enforcement by registration under the Act.[45]

In *Jet Holdings Inc. v. Patel* the Court of Appeal also reaffirmed that it was **14–131** irrelevant that in the view of the foreign court there was no fraud. But in *House of Spring Gardens Ltd. v. Waite*[46] some of the judgment debtors commenced a fresh action in the foreign country to set aside the original foreign judgment on the ground of fraud. That action failed after a 22 day trial. It was held that the judgment debtors (including one who had not been a party to the fresh action) were estopped by the decision of the foreign court that there had been no fraud. This decision has been held to lay down a general principle that a decision by a foreign court that a foreign judgment was, or was not, obtained by fraud can create an estoppel in English proceedings to enforce that judgment.[47]

The decision of the Court of Appeal in *House of Spring Gardens Ltd. v.* **14–132** *Waite*, that the decision of a foreign court on the allegation of fraud given in fresh proceedings instituted by the judgment debtor may found an estoppel upon that issue in subsequent English enforcement proceedings, is consistent with recent authority on issue estoppel.[48] The fact that the judgment debtor elected[49] to seise the foreign court[50] distinguishes the case from *Jet Holdings Inc. v. Patel*. But the court went on to hold[51] that if it was wrong in its analysis of fraud, it was nevertheless an abuse of the process of the court to raise for a second (or third) time an argument which had been raised and disposed of in the foreign court. Subsequent authorities support the suggestion that the concept of abuse of process may be capable of circumscribing the common

---

[43] [1992] 2 A.C. 443, 489.
[44] *Ante*, paras. 11–005 *et seq.*; *post*, paras. 14R–159 and 14–170 and see Collier [1992] C.L.J. 441 for very strong criticism on this ground (the criticism was noted, without dissent, in *Owens Bank Ltd. v. Etoile Commerciale S.A.* [1995] 1 W.L.R. 44, 50 (P.C.)).
[45] 1933 Act, s.6, Exception 1 to Rule 35, *ante*.
[46] [1991] 1 Q.B. 241 (C.A.).
[47] *Owens Bank Ltd. v. Bracco* [1992] 2 A.C. 443, 474 (C.A.) (where the foreign court in question was not in the country of the original judgment, but another country in which enforcement was sought). The point was not addressed by the House of Lords.
[48] For issue estoppel in relation to foreign judgments, see generally Rule 35, *ante*, paras. 14R–018 *et seq.*
[49] It should be noted that this may not be uncontroversial: the judgment debtor may not have had a free and unconstrained choice to bring the second action if, for example, he had assets within the jurisdiction of the foreign court which were threatened with seizure by way of execution. *Cf.* 1982 Act, s. 33(1)(*c*), and para. 14–067, *ante*, for the possibility that an appearance in such circumstances may not be a submission to the jurisdiction of the court applied to.
[50] With the consequence that he has submitted to the jurisdiction, and the court in the second action had, as a matter of the English rules of the conflict of laws, jurisdiction to bind him.
[51] [1991] 1 Q.B. 241, 254 (C.A.).

law rule that, as long as there can be shown to be a prima facie case[52] for investigation, a foreign judgment may be impeached for fraud. In *Owens Bank Ltd. v. Etoile Commerciale S.A.*[53] a French court had given judgment in favour of Etoile on a bank guarantee, rejecting the bank's allegation of fraud and forgery on the part of the plaintiff. A claim brought by the bank in St Vincent against Etoile for damages for fraud was struck out by the court; in subsequent proceedings in St. Vincent to enforce the French judgment, the Privy Council struck out, as an abuse of process, the bank's attempt to plead fraud as a defence.[54]

14–133   The fraud which vitiates a judgment must generally be fraud of the party in whose favour the judgment is obtained, but it may (conceivably, at any rate) be fraud on the part of the foreign court giving the judgment,[55] as where a court gives judgment in favour of A, because the judges are bribed by some person, not the plaintiff, who wishes judgment to be given against X, the defendant. In such a case the defence of fraud tends to merge with the defence that the proceedings were opposed to natural justice.[56]

14–134   The doctrine that fraud vitiates a judgment does not necessarily apply to foreign judgments of every class. It is clearly applicable to a judgment *in personam*,[57] where, be it noted, the rights in question are the rights of the litigants or of their representatives. Evidence raising a triable issue of fraud suffices for permission to be given to defend a claim if the claimant applies for summary judgment on the ground that the defendant has no real prospect of successfully defending the claim.[58] It has already been seen that the 1920 Act provides[59] that no judgment can be registered under that Act if it was obtained by fraud and that in *Owens Bank Ltd. v. Bracco*[60] it was held that the reference to fraud in the 1920 Act must be construed by reference to the common law principles. It has been assumed that the same is so under the 1933 Act,[61] which provides[62] that the registration of a judgment under that Act must be set aside if the registering court is satisfied that the judgment was obtained by fraud. And under that Act a foreign judgment, whether registered or not and whether registrable or not, will not be recognised as conclusive between the parties thereto in English proceedings founded on the same cause of action if it was obtained by fraud.[63]

14–135   But fraud as such is not a ground for refusal to enforce or recognise a judgment under Part I of the 1982 Act,[64] because the 1968 Convention and the Lugano Convention do not contain a defence of fraud. They do contain a defence of public policy. In continental European law fraud in this context

---

[52] The question is whether there is a prima facie that the particular foreign court was defrauded in the particular case.

[53] [1995] 1 W.L.R. 44 (P.C.). Lord Templeman stated that the Privy Council did not "regard the decision in *Aboulof*'s case ... with enthusiasm". *Cf. Desert Sun Loan Corp. v. Hill* [1996] 2 All E.R. 847, 859, 863–864 (C.A.).

[54] A submission that issue estoppel arose from the first St. Vincent action was not addressed.

[55] *Price v. Dewhurst* (1837) 8 Sim. 279.

[56] See Rule 45, *post*.

[57] *Vadala v. Lawes* (1890) 25 Q.B.D. 310 (C.A.).

[58] See para. 14–025, n. 95, *ante*.

[59] s.9(2)(*d*).

[60] [1992] 2 A.C. 443.

[61] *Syal v. Heyward* [1948] 2 K.B. 443 (C.A.).

[62] s.4(1)(*a*)(iv).

[63] s.8(1)(2).

[64] *Post*, para. 14–206.

generally falls within the exception of public policy,[65] and it is for this reason that international conventions on the recognition of judgments[66] and arbitration awards[67] commonly omit the defence of fraud as such. In *Interdesco S.A. v. Nullifire Ltd.*[68] and in *Société d'Informatique Service Réalisation Organisation v. Ampersand Software B.V.*[69] it was confirmed that the defence of fraud had only a very limited scope under the 1968 Convention. It was accepted that it could come within the public policy exception.[70] But if means of redress against the alleged fraud were available in the country of judgment, it would not be contrary to English public policy to recognise and register a judgment which was subject to those means of redress.

Because of the absolute terms of Part II of the 1982 Act,[71] no Scottish or   **14–136** Northern Irish judgment registrable in England can be impeached on the ground that it was obtained by fraud. In such a case the defendant's remedy would be to attack the judgment in Scotland or Northern Ireland by appeal out of time or by an application to set it aside.

The doctrine may apply as between the litigants to a judgment *in rem*.[72] But   **14–137** it is questionable whether the fraud which, as between the litigants, appears to vitiate a judgment *in rem* affects the rights of third persons, *e.g.* bona fide purchasers, who, in ignorance of the fraud, acquire under or in consequence of the judgment a title to the *res, e.g.* a ship, affected thereby.[73] The reason why there is a question in this last case is that such third persons are relying on the judgment merely *qua* an assignment rather than *qua* a judgment and are entitled to the benefit of the rule that an assignment of movables is wholly governed in its proprietary aspects by the *lex situs*.[74] As Blackburn J. put it,[75] "Fraud will indeed vitiate everything; though we may observe that there is much force in what [counsel] suggested in the course of his argument in this case, that even if there had been fraud on the part of the litigants, or even of the tribunal, it would be very questionable whether it could be set up against a bona fide purchaser who was quite ignorant of it." The recognition of foreign decrees affecting status is not within the scope of this chapter, and the position in relation to those decrees has been touched on merely because of the connection it has with the effect of fraud on judgments properly *in rem*. It may be that only foreign judgments *in personam* are impeachable for fraud.

---

[65] Batiffol and Lagarde, Vol. 1, pp. 409 *et seq.*

[66] *e.g.* Hague Convention on the Recognition of Divorces and Legal Separations (1968), implemented by the Family Law Act 1986, as to which see *post*, para. 18–121. In *Kendall v. Kendall* [1977] Fam. 208 it was held that recognition of a foreign divorce decree obtained by fraud would be refused because it was manifestly contrary to public policy within the meaning of what is now s.51(3) of the Family Law Act 1986, notwithstanding that there was no separate basis for non-recognition on the ground of fraud in the Act.

[67] Geneva Convention (1927) and New York Convention (1958), implemented by the Arbitration Act 1950, Part II, and the Arbitration Act 1975, as to which see Rules 62 and 63.

[68] [1992] 1 Lloyd's Rep. 180.

[69] [1994] I.L.Pr. 55 (C.A.).

[70] For approval of the reasoning in *Interdesco v. Nullifire S.A.*, but refusal to allow it to contradict the public policy of upholding the finality of arbitral awards, see *Westacre Investments Inc. v. Jugoimport SDPR Holding Co. Ltd.* [1999] Q.B. 740.

[71] *Post*, para. 14–232.

[72] *Messina v. Petrococchino* (1872) L.R. 4 P.C. 144, 157.

[73] *Castrique v. Behrens* (1861) 30 L.J.Q.B. 163, stated *post*, para. 14–140, Illustration 6; *Castrique v. Imrie* (1870) L.R. 4 H.L. 414, 433. See Rule 40.

[74] See Rule 116.

[75] *Castrique v. Imrie, supra*, at p. 433.

14–138   It is equally possible to adduce fraud in opposition to a claim based on a foreign judgment and to a defendant's defence based on a similar source.[76]

ILLUSTRATIONS

14–139   1. A obtains in a Russian court judgment against X that X shall either deliver to A certain goods of A's, then, as alleged, in X's possession, or pay A a sum equivalent to £1,050. The judgment, which is affirmed on appeal to a superior Russian court, is obtained by A's fraudulently concealing from the court that at the very moment when the action is brought the goods are in the possession of A. The judgment is impeachable in England.[77]

2. A brings an action in New York against X to recover money alleged to be due on certain bills of exchange. A obtains judgment against X by fraudulently representing to the New York court that the bills of exchange were given under the authority of X and for mercantile transactions, whereas they were given without X's authority for gambling debts. The judgment is impeachable in England.[78]

3. A, an Indian moneylender, obtains judgment against X for 20,000 rupees alleged to be due on a loan. The writ is served upon X in India, but he fails to appear. A registers his judgment in the High Court under the 1933 Act. X applies to set aside the registration of the judgment on the ground of fraud. He alleges that the amount of the loan was only 10,800 rupees and that A has concealed from the Indian court the possibility that X might have a defence under the Indian Usurious Loans Act. The court will direct the trial of an issue whether X's allegations are true and, if they are, will set aside the registration of the judgment.[79]

4. A & Co. sue X in California to recover sums allegedly misappropriated by X. X defends the proceedings on the ground that representatives of A & Co. had been violent towards him and that X had, under further threats from them, to pay substantial amounts to A & Co. X is too frightened to attend depositions in California, and judgment in default is given against him after A & Co.'s lawyers represent to the Californian court that X's account of violence and threats is untrue. X has an arguable defence that the judgment was obtained by fraud, and leave to defend is given.[80]

14–140   5. A & Co. sue X, Y and Z in the Republic of Ireland for misuse of confidential information and breach of copyright, and obtain judgment for £3 million. X, Y and Z appeal unsuccessfully to the Supreme Court of Ireland. X and Y (but not Z) bring a fresh action in Ireland to set aside the judgment on the ground of fraud. After a 22 day trial, the allegation of fraud is rejected. The original judgment is enforceable in England, not only against X and Y, but also against Z, who is estopped from alleging fraud: he is privy to the second Irish judgment because the original judgment was obtained against X, Y and Z jointly and severally and because he was well aware of the proceedings to set aside the original judgment.[81]

6. B. is the owner of a British ship. He mortgages her to A and later goes bankrupt. While the ship is at Melbourne M, the master, draws a bill of exchange on B for necessaries supplied to the ship by X. The bill is never accepted and is dishonoured at maturity. During the ship's return voyage to Europe X conspires with Y, and indorses the bill to Y (but not for value) in order that Y may take advantage of a provision of foreign law whereby the bona fide holder of such a bill can take proceedings *in rem* against the ship in the foreign court. When the ship is in the foreign port Y brings proceedings *in rem* against her which result in the court ordering the sale of the ship in order to pay the bill. In an action by A against X in England for conspiracy to defraud, A cannot impeach the foreign judgment for fraud.[82]

---

[76] See Westlake, s.335, though *Henderson v. Henderson* (1843) 3 Hare 100, 117 is not conclusive; *Manolopoulos v. Pnaiffe* [1930] 2 D.L.R. 169 (N.S.C.A.).

[77] *Cf. Abouloff v. Oppenheimer* (1882) 10 Q.B.D. 295 (C.A.).

[78] *Cf. Vadala v. Lawes* (1890) 25 Q.B.D. 310 (C.A.). Contrast *Blohn v. Desser* [1962] 2 Q.B. 116.

[79] *Syal v. Heyward* [1948] 2 K.B. 443 (C.A.).

[80] *Jet Holdings Inc. v. Patel* [1990] 1 Q.B. 335 (C.A.).

[81] *House of Spring Gardens Ltd. v. Waite* [1991] 1 Q.B. 241 (C.A.).

[82] *Castrique v. Behrens* (1861) 30 L.J.Q.B. 163; approved in *Bater v. Bater* [1906] P. 209, 219, 228 (C.A.). Compare *Castrique v. Imrie* (1870) L.R. 4 H.L. 414, 433.

RULE 44[83]—**A foreign judgment is impeachable on the ground that its enforcement or, as the case may be, recognition, would be contrary to public policy.**   14R–141

COMMENT

There are very few reported cases in which foreign judgments *in personam*[84] have been denied enforcement or recognition for reasons of public policy at common law.[85] In *Re Macartney*,[86] a foreign judgment awarding the mother on behalf of an illegitimate child perpetual maintenance against the estate of the deceased putative father was refused enforcement on three grounds: (1) it was contrary to public policy to enforce an affiliation order not limited to minority; (2) the cause of action—a posthumous affiliation order—was unknown to English law; and (3) the judgment was not final and conclusive.[87] Under the second head the court relied heavily on an American case[88] in which a French judgment awarding maintenance to a French son-in-law against his American father-in-law and mother-in-law was refused enforcement in the United States. Both these cases were disapproved or distinguished in *Burchell v. Burchell*[89] and *Phrantzes v. Argenti*.[90]   14–142

In *Burchell v. Burchell* an Ontario court enforced a judgment of an Ohio divorce court for a lump-sum payment by a wife for the support of her husband, although by the law of Ontario a husband could not have obtained alimony from his wife. In *Phrantzes v. Argenti* (which was not a case upon a foreign judgment), the English court refused to enforce a claim by a Greek daughter against her father for the provision of a dowry on her marriage as required by Greek law, not on the ground that the cause of action was unknown to English law, but on the ground that English law had no remedy for awarding a dowry, the amount of which in Greek law was within the discretion of the court and varied in accordance with the wealth and social position of the father and the number of his children. On the other hand, in *Mayo-Perrot v. Mayo-Perrot*[91] the Supreme Court of the Republic of Ireland   14–143

---

[83] *Re Macartney* [1921] 1 Ch. 552; *S.A. Consortium General Textiles v. Sun & Sand Agencies Ltd.* [1978] Q.B. 279 (C.A.); *Israel Discount Bank of New York v. Hadjipateras* [1984] 1 W.L.R. 137 (C.A.); *E.D. & F. Man (Sugar) Ltd. Haryanto (No. 2)* [1991] 1 Lloyd's Rep. 429 (C.A.); *Mayo-Perrott v. Mayo-Perrott* [1958] I.R. 336; *Holt v. Thomas* (1987) 38 D.L.R. (4th) 117 (Alb.); *Honolulu Savings and Loan Ass'n. v. Robinson* (1989) 64 D.L.R. (4th) 551, affd. (1990) 76 D.L.R. (4th) 103 (Man. C.A.); *Minkler and Kirschbaum v. Sheppard* (1991) 60 B.C.L.R. (2d) 360; *Resorts International Hotel Inc. v. Auerbach* (1991) 89 D.L.R. (4th) 688 (Que. C.A.); *Boardwalk Regency Corp. v. Maalouf* (1992) 88 D.L.R. (4th) 612 (Ont. C.A.); *Union of India v. Bumper Development Corp.* [1995] 7 W.W.R. 80 (Alta.); *Connor v. Connor* [1974] 1 N.Z.L.R. 632; Read, pp. 292–295; Restatement, s.117. In *Adams v. Cape Industries plc* [1990] Ch. 433, 496, affd. *ibid.* 503, Scott J. suggested that the principles in Rules 44 and 45 might overlap in the sense that, if a foreign judgment were obtained in breach of natural justice, it would also be contrary to public policy to enforce it.

[84] For non-recognition of foreign divorce and nullity decrees see *post*, Rule 82.

[85] There is also a public policy in favour of accepting the finality of litigation: *cf.*, in the context of arbitral awards, *Westacre Investments Inc. v. Jugoimport SDPR Holding Co. Ltd.* [1999] Q.B. 740.

[86] [1921] 1 Ch. 522.

[87] See Rule 35, *ante*. This third ground would clearly have been sufficient by itself to dispose of the case.

[88] *De Brimont v. Penniman* (1873) 10 Blatchford Circuit Court Reports 436.

[89] [1926] 2 D.L.R. 595 (Ont.).

[90] [1960] 2 Q.B. 19, 31–34.

[91] [1958] I.R. 336.

refused to enforce an English order for costs in favour of a wife against her husband which was ancillary to an English divorce decree. The grounds of this decision were partly that the cause of action was of such a character that it could not have supported an action in the Republic, where divorce was then not allowed, and partly that to enforce an order ancillary to a divorce decree was contrary to Irish public policy.

14–144   In *Israel Discount Bank of New York v. Hadjipateras*[92] it was suggested that it might be contrary to public policy to enforce a judgment based on a contract which had been executed as a result of undue influence. But the decision has been convincingly criticised[93] on the grounds that it is the recognition of the judgment which must be contrary to public policy, and not the underlying contract on which the cause of action is based[94]; and that as a matter of domestic English law the enforcement of a contract obtained by undue influence is not contrary to public policy, although it may be rescinded in equity.

14–145   It will be contrary to public policy to recognise or enforce a judgment which has been obtained in disobedience of an injunction not to proceed with the action in a foreign court.[95] It is now established that a foreign judgment will not be recognised if it is inconsistent with a previous decision of a competent English court in proceedings between the same parties (or their privies). In *Vervaeke v. Smith*[96] it was held that the principle of *res judicata* in English law was a rule of public policy, and that it would therefore be contrary to public policy to recognise a foreign decree of nullity which was inconsistent with an earlier decision of the English court that the marriage was valid. This principle was applied to a foreign judgment *in personam* in *E. D. & F. Man (Sugar) Ltd. v. Haryanto (No. 2)*,[97] where the English court had dismissed the defendant's action for a declaration that he was not bound by contracts for the purchase of sugar, and an Indonesian court had subsequently decided that the contracts were illegal and contrary to Indonesian public policy. The Indonesian judgment was denied recognition.

14–146   It would seem that the enforcement of a judgment for exemplary or punitive damages is not contrary to public policy[98]; and it has been held in New Zealand that, although the court will not directly or indirectly enforce a foreign public law,[99] the enforcement of a foreign judgment for costs is not contrary to public policy merely because the costs if recovered would be payable to a foreign legal aid fund.[1] The 1933 Act contains a separate provision[2] excluding from its registration provisions a foreign judgment for taxes or for a fine or other penalty.

---

[92] [1984] 1 W.L.R. 137 (C.A.).

[93] Collier [1984] C.L.J. 47.

[94] But *cf.* 1920 Act, s.9(2)(*f*).

[95] *Phillip Alexander Securities & Futures Ltd. v. Bamberger* [1997] I.L.Pr. 73, at p. 103 (Waller J.) affd. *ibid.* 104, at p. 115 (C.A.); *cf. Fakih Bros. v. A.P. Moller (Copenhagen) Ltd.* [1994] 1 Lloyd's Rep. 103.

[96] [1983] 1 A.C. 145. For a similar rule under the 1968 Convention and the Lugano Convention see *post*, para. 14–214.

[97] [1991] 1 Lloyd's Rep. 429 (C.A.), stated *post*, Illustration, para. 14–148.

[98] *S.A. Consortium General Textiles v. Sun & Sand Agencies Ltd.* [1978] Q.B. 279, 299–300, *per* Lord Denning M.R., *obiter; Four Embarcadero Center Venture v. Kalen* (1988) 65 O.R. (2d) 551. But see para. 14–020, *ante*, and *cf.* Rule 52, *post*.

[99] Rule 3.

[1] *Connor v. Connor* [1974] 1 N.Z.L.R. 632.

[2] s.1(2)(*b*).

The 1920 Act excludes from registration a judgment "which was in respect **14–147**
of a cause of action which for reasons of public policy or for some other
similar reason could not have been entertained by the registering court."[3] The
1933 Act provides that registration may be set aside if "the enforcement of the
judgment would be contrary to public policy in the country of the registering
court."[4] It will be observed that there is an important difference between the
1920 and 1933 Acts in this connection. The 1920 Act excludes enforcement
of a judgment on the basis that the original cause of action is contrary to
public policy. The 1933 Act lays down the more limited (and surely more
desirable) principle that enforcement or recognition must be withheld if
enforcement or recognition would be contrary to public policy. The effect of
Articles 27 and 34 of the 1968 Convention and the Lugano Convention is that
enforcement or recognition under Part I of the 1982 Act may be refused if
recognition is "contrary to public policy" in the United Kingdom.[5] Enforcement or recognition of Scottish or Northern Irish judgments cannot be refused
on the ground of public policy. Any such objection is precluded by the terms
of Part II of the 1982 Act.[6]

ILLUSTRATION

A & Co., sugar traders, sell sugar to X, an Indonesian citizen, for $200 million under contracts   **14–148**
governed by English law. Disputes arise and X seeks a declaration in England that he is not bound
by the contracts. His action is dismissed, and the judgment is confirmed by the Court of Appeal,
which also dismisses his application to raise an issue that the contracts are illegal by reason of a
prohibition on importation of sugar into Indonesia. Further English proceedings ensue which are
settled by an agreement governed by English law, under which X agrees to pay A & Co. $27
million. Subsequently, X commences proceedings in Indonesia against A & Co., and the Indonesian court decides that the settlement agreement is illegal because it arises out of illegal
contracts, and that it is contrary to Indonesian public policy to recognise the English judgment.
A & Co. then seek a declaration in England that the settlement agreement is valid and binding on
X. The Indonesian judgment is not recognised because the real issue in those proceedings was the
validity of the underlying agreements which had already been the subject of a decision of the
English court.[7]

RULE 45—A foreign judgment may be impeached if the proceedings in   **14R–149**
which the judgment was obtained were opposed to natural justice.[8]

COMMENT

In a celebrated passage in his judgment in *Pemberton v. Hughes*[9] (a case on   **14–150**
the recognition of a foreign divorce decree), Lord Lindley observed: "If a

---

[3] 1920 Act, s.9(2)(*f*).
[4] 1933 Act, ss.4(1)(*a*)(v), 8(1)(2).
[5] *Post*, para. 14–205.
[6] *Post*, para. 14R–230.
[7] *E. D. & F. Man (Sugar) Ltd. v. Haryanto (No. 2)* [1991] 1 Lloyd's Rep. 429 (C.A.).
[8] *Buchanan v. Rucker* (1808) 9 East 192; *Sheehy v. Professional Life Assurance Co.* (1857) 2
   C.B.(N.S.) 211; *Crawley v. Isaacs* (1867) 16 L.T. 529; *Pemberton v. Hughes* [1899] 1 Ch. 781,
   790 (C.A.); *Robinson v. Fenner* [1913] 3 K.B. 835; *Bergerem v. Marsh* (1921) 91 L.J.K.B. 80;
   Richardson v. Army, Navy and General Assurance Association Ltd. (1925) 21 Ll.L.R. 345;
   Jacobson v. Frachon (1927) 138 L.T. 386 (C.A.); *Adams v. Cape Industries plc* [1990] Ch. 433
   (C.A.); *Herzberg v. Manitoba* (1984) 38 R.F.L. (2d) 412 (Man.) (maintenance order); Read, pp.
   281–288; Restatement, s.25.
[9] [1899] 1 Ch. 781, 790 (C.A.).

judgment is pronounced by a foreign court over persons within its jurisdiction and in a matter with which it is competent to deal, English courts never investigate the propriety of the proceedings in the foreign court, unless they offend against English views of substantial justice." This passage refers to irregularity in the proceedings, for it is clear that a foreign judgment, which is manifestly wrong on the merits or has misapplied English law or foreign law, is not impeachable on that ground.[10] Nor is it impeachable because the court admitted evidence which is inadmissible in England[11] or did not admit evidence which is admissible in England[12] or otherwise followed a practice different from English law.[13] In *Jacobson v. Frachon*[14] Atkin L.J., after referring to the use of the expression "principles of natural justice,"[15] said: "Those principles seem to me to involve this, first of all that the court being a court of competent jurisdiction, has given notice to the litigant that they are about to proceed to determine the rights between him and the other litigant; the other is that having given him that notice, it does afford him an opportunity of substantially presenting his case before the court."[16]

14–151   *Adams v. Cape Industries plc*[17] appears to be the only English case in which the defence of breach of natural justice was established in relation to a judgment *in personam*.[18] The Court of Appeal held that the defence of breach of natural justice was not limited to the requirements of due notice of the hearing to a litigant and opportunity to put a case to the foreign court. It confirmed that the basic question was that stated in *Pemberton v. Hughes*,[19] namely whether there was a procedural defect which constituted a breach of the English court's view of substantial justice,[20] which would depend on the nature of the proceedings under consideration.

14–152   A mere procedural irregularity would not offend English concepts of substantial justice.[21] In *Adams v. Cape Industries plc* the foreign judgment was for damages in default of appearance, and notice was given to the defendants of the application for a default judgment on an unliquidated claim. Under United States law (as under English law) the assessment of damages is effected (even in cases of default) by the court, but the United States judge did not hold any form of hearing, and the judgment was not based on an objective assessment by the judge of the evidence. The Court of Appeal did not decide that a lack of judicial assessment of damages is *per se* a breach of natural justice; but it is a breach where the foreign legal system contains provision for

---

[10] See *Jacobson v. Frachon* (1927) 138 L.T. 386, 390, 393 (C.A.); *Adams v. Cape Industries plc* [1990] Ch. 433, 569 (C.A.).

[11] *De Cosse Brissac v. Rathbone* (1861) 6 H. & N. 301 (the sixth plea).

[12] *Scarpetta v. Lowenfeld* (1911) 27 T.L.R. 509; *Robinson v. Fenner* [1913] 3 K.B. 835.

[13] *Boissière v. Brockner* (1899) 6 T.L.R. 85.

[14] (1927) 138 L.T. 386 (C.A.).

[15] By Lord Hanworth M.R. *ibid.* at p. 390.

[16] *Ibid.* at p. 392.

[17] [1990] Ch. at 564–566. *Cf. Leaton Leather & Trading Co. v. Ngai Tak Kong* (1997) 147 D.L.R. (4th) 377 (B.C.).

[18] On foreign decrees of divorce and nullity see *post*, para. 18–120; *Shaw v. Att.-Gen.* (1870) L.R. 2 P. & D. 156; *Rudd v. Rudd* [1924] P. 72 (divorce); *Gray v. Formosa* [1963] P. 259 (C.A.); *Lepre v. Lepre* [1965] P. 52 (nullity). See also Family Law Act 1986, s.51(3).

[19] [1899] 1 Ch. 781; *Jacobson v. Frachon* (1927) 138 L.T. 386, 392 (C.A.), *per* Atkin L.J.

[20] The terms "natural justice" and "substantial justice" appear to be used interchangeably in this context.

[21] [1990] Ch. at 567, citing *Pemberton v. Hughes* [1899] 1 Ch. 781.

judicial assessment and the judgment debtor therefore has a reasonable expectation that there will be a judicial assessment.

The case is therefore an example of a breach of natural justice outside the **14–153** categories of notice and opportunity to be heard, because the judgment debtors were given notice and had an opportunity to contest the quantum of damages; they did not take the opportunity because they did not wish to submit to the jurisdiction of the foreign court. This decision also puts into context those decisions which were thought to the authority for the view that, if the defendant agrees to the jurisdiction of the foreign court, he cannot take the objection that he did not receive sufficient notice.[22] If the defendant has agreed, or is deemed to agree, a particular method of service (such as service at an address in the foreign country notified to a company of which he is a member) then it is immaterial that he did not receive actual notice.[23] If the defendant has agreed to submit to the jurisdiction of the foreign court, and service has been effected in accordance with the foreign law, but actual notice has not been given, then the question will be whether substantial injustice has been caused by the lack of notice, including consideration of whether the defendant had a remedy in the foreign court.[24] The objection that the defendant did not receive sufficient notice of the foreign proceedings to enable him to defend them tends to become confused with the objection that the foreign court had no jurisdiction. If the defendant is resident in the foreign country at the time when the proceedings were commenced, or if he voluntarily appears in the proceedings, it is difficult for him to take the objection that he did not receive sufficient notice, for in such circumstances any notice is sufficient which is in accordance with the law of the foreign country,[25] provided that the foreign procedure does not offend against English views of substantial justice.[26] If the defendant agrees in advance to submit to the jurisdiction of the foreign court and service is effected in accordance with the method of service to which he has agreed (or is deemed to have agreed) he cannot complain if he did not receive actual notice.[27] "It is not contrary to natural justice that a man who has agreed to receive a particular mode of notification of legal proceedings should be bound by a judgment in which that particular mode of notification has been followed, even though he may not have had actual notice of them."[28]

May the defence of breach of natural justice be raised before the English **14–154** court if the objection could have been taken before the foreign court? In *Jet Holdings Inc. v. Patel*[29] Staughton L.J. said, *obiter*, that logically the foreign court's view should be neither conclusive nor relevant as to the propriety of

---

[22] *Ante*, para. 14–073.
[23] *Vallée v. Dumergue* (1849) 4 Exch. 290; *Copin v. Adamson* (1875) 1 Ex.D. 17 (C.A.). *Cf. Bank of Australasia v. Harding* (1850) 9 C.B. 661; *Bank of Australasia v. Nias* (1851) 16 Q.B. 717 (chairman of company deemed agent of shareholders); *Jamieson v. Robb* (1881) 7 V.L.R. 170.
[24] [1990] Ch. at 570. *Cf. Jeannot v. Fuerst* (1909) 25 T.L.R. 424. Contrast *Feyerick v. Hubbard* (1902) 71 L.J.K.B. 509.
[25] Dicey, 3rd ed., p. 441.
[26] *Ante*, para. 14–073.
[27] *Ibid.*
[28] *Vallée v. Dumergue* (1849) 4 Exch. 290, 303.
[29] [1990] 1 Q.B. 335, 345 (C.A.), disagreeing with reliance in previous editions of this work (11th ed. p. 475) on *Jacobson v. Frachon* (1927) 138 L.T. 386 (C.A.) for the view that a foreign judgment could not be impeached if the objection could have been taken, and was taken, before the foreign court.

its own proceedings. In *Adams v. Cape Industries plc*[30] the evidence was that the judgment debtors had the right to apply in the United States to set aside the default judgment on the ground that the assessment of damages was irregular, and it was recognised that such an application would have been allowed if made in due time. The Court of Appeal thought that where the objection came within the two categories mentioned by Atkin L.J., want of notice or lack of opportunity to be heard, the judgment debtor may raise the objection in England even if there is a remedy in the foreign country.[31] But in other categories (as in the one under consideration in that case) the existence of a remedy in the foreign court is not wholly irrelevant in determining whether the proceedings in the foreign court, viewed as a whole, offend against English views of substantial justice: it would be anomalous if the English court were obliged to disregard the existence of a remedy under a foreign system of procedure in considering whether the defective operation of that procedure had led to a breach of natural justice. The judgment debtor cannot justify a failure to avail himself of the remedy by reference to his unwillingness to submit to the jurisdiction of a foreign court. But in that case the defendants had no way of knowing from the judgment served on them that the judgment had been entered without a judicial assessment of damages, since the recitals in the judgment indicated there had been a hearing.

14–155   The 1920 and 1933 Acts contain specific provisions dealing with service and notice. The 1920 Act provides[32] that registration of a foreign judgment must be refused if the defendant was not duly served with the process of the original court and did not appear, notwithstanding that he was ordinarily resident or was carrying on business within the jurisdiction of that court or agreed to submit to its jurisdiction. There is some doubt as to what "duly served" means in this connection. In one case[33] it was assumed that it means duly served according to the law of the original court. However, some limit must no doubt be imposed on the width of this principle. In *Buchanan v. Rucker*,[34] nailing a copy of the writ to the court-house door was no doubt "due service" according to the law of Tobago, but it could hardly constitute due service within the meaning of the 1920 Act. Probably due service must involve actual notice, but not necessarily service within the jurisdiction of the original court.[35] The 1933 Act provides[36] that registration of a foreign judgment must be set aside if the defendant did not receive notice of the proceedings (*i.e.* of the initiation of the action[37]) in sufficient time to enable him to defend and he did not appear, even if process may have been duly served on him in accordance with the applicable foreign law. And under the 1933 Act a foreign judgment, whether registered or not and whether registrable or not, will not be recognised as conclusive between the parties thereto in English proceedings founded on the same cause of action if the defendant did not

---

[30] [1990] Ch. 433, 569 (C.A.).
[31] Contrast *Jeannot v. Fuerst* (1909) 100 L.T. 816, 818. In *Leaton Leather & Trading Co. v. Ngai Tak Kong* (1997) 147 D.L.R. (4th) 1377 (B.C.) a failure to exercise a right to appeal was held not to make enforceable a judgment rendered contrary to natural justice.
[32] s.9(2)(*c*).
[33] *Sfeir & Co. v. National Insurance Co. of New Zealand* [1964] 1 Lloyd's Rep. 330, 341.
[34] (1809) 9 East 192; *ante*, para. 14–049.
[35] *Cf. Re Gacs and Maierovitz* (1968) 68 D.L.R. (2d) 345 (B.C.).
[36] s.4(1)(*a*)(iii).
[37] *Brockley Cabinet Co. Ltd. v. Pears* (1972) 20 F.L.R. 333.

receive such notice and did not appear.[38] This ground for setting aside the registration of a judgment is quite independent of and distinct from the ground that the foreign court had no jurisdiction. Hence it follows that the common law authorities suggesting that a defendant who agrees to submit to the jurisdiction of a foreign court also agrees to waive actual notice of the proceedings[39] have no application.

The effect of Article 27(2) of the 1968 Convention and of the Lugano Convention is that judgments in default of appearance, falling within the scope of Part I of the 1982 Act, will not be enforceable in the United Kingdom if the defendant was not duly served with the document instituting the proceedings in sufficient time to arrange for his defence.[40] Lack of notice or service, or failure to observe natural justice, are not grounds for refusal of recognition or enforcement of Scottish and Northern Irish judgments under Part II of the 1982 Act.[41]

    14–156

ILLUSTRATIONS

1. X, who was resident in England, held shares in a French company. The articles of association of the company provided that all disputes between the company and its shareholders should be subject to the jurisdiction of the French courts and that service of process on each shareholder should be at a designated address in France. The company went into liquidation and A brought an action against X in France for moneys not paid up on X's shares. Process was served on X at the designated address, but he received no notice of the proceedings. The French court gave judgment against X before 1937 (when the 1933 Act was extended to France). A brought an action on the judgment against X in England. The judgment was not impeachable.[42]

    14–157

2. The circumstances were the same as in Illustration 1, except that the French judgment was given after 1937, and that A registered the judgment in England under the 1933 Act. Registration would be set aside.[43]

3. X, a merchant of Lyons, contracted to sell silk to A, a merchant of London. A dispute having arisen about the quality of the silk, X brought an action against A in a court at Lyons. The court appointed an expert to examine the goods and report on their quality. The expert made no proper examination of the goods; he refused to listen to A's witnesses; and his report (described by the English court as "the erroneous and uncandid production of a biased and prejudiced mind") was wholly in favour of X. The French court gave judgment in favour of X. When A sued X in England, X pleaded the French judgment as a defence. The judgment was not impeachable because the French court was not obliged to accept the report, and because A attacked it unsuccessfully in France.[44]

    14–158

4. 206 plaintiffs sue X & Co. and Y & Co., both English companies, in an action for personal injuries, in the Federal Court in Texas. X & Co. and Y & Co., not wishing to submit to the jurisdiction of the United States court, take no part in the proceedings. X & Co. and Y & Co. are given notice of a hearing to assess damages in default of appearance, but again take no part. On the application of the plaintiffs the United States judge signs a default judgment for $15 million, but without holding any hearing. No evidence of damage or injury to the plaintiffs is placed before the judge; the judgment is signed before the judge has an opportunity to consider the medical records or summaries of each plaintiff's case; the damages awarded are quantified on a global basis or as an average per plaintiff, and are arbitrary. The judgment is not enforceable.[45]

---

[38] s.8(1), (2). See *post*, para. 14–177.
[39] *Ante*, para. 14–073.
[40] *Post*, para. 14–208.
[41] *Post*, para. 14–231.
[42] *Copin v. Adamson* (1875) 1 Ex.D. 17 (C.A.).
[43] 1933 Act, s.4(1)(*a*)(iii).
[44] *Jacobson v. Frachon* (1927) 138 L.T. 386 (C.A.).
[45] *Adams v. Cape Industries plc* [1990] Ch. 433 (C.A.).

3. ENFORCEMENT AND RECOGNITION UNDER STATUTE

(1) Administration of Justice Act 1920

14–159 **Rule 46—When Part II of the Administration of Justice Act 1920 is extended to any part of the Commonwealth outside the United Kingdom,[46] a judgment creditor who has obtained a judgment in a Superior Court in such part of the Commonwealth under which a sum of money is made payable, may apply to the High Court,[47] at any time within twelve months (or such longer period as may be allowed by the court) after the date of the judgment, to have the judgment registered in the court, and, if the court thinks it is just and convenient that the judgment should be enforced in the United Kingdom, it may order the judgment to be registered accordingly,[48] and from the date of registration the judgment will be of the same force and effect, and proceedings may be taken upon it,[49] as if it were a judgment of the court in which it is registered.**

Provided that no judgment will be ordered to be registered if the judgment debtor satisfies the High Court either that an appeal is pending, or that he is entitled and intends to appeal against the judgment.[50]

This Rule must be read subject to Rule 52.

COMMENT

14–160 This Rule, which closely follows the terms of the Administration of Justice Act 1920, is the outcome of proposals for the reciprocal enforcement of judgments and arbitration awards throughout the Empire which were brought forward at the Imperial Conference of 1911.[51] It was enacted in section 14 that the Act could come into operation only by the issue of an Order in Council extending it to some part of the Commonwealth outside the United Kingdom in which reciprocal provision had been made for the recognition of judgments obtained in the Superior Courts of the United Kingdom.

14–161 The 1933 Act empowers the Crown in Council to extend Part I of that enactment to all parts of the Commonwealth outside the United Kingdom. It is provided that upon the application of the later Act in this manner the 1920 Act shall cease to have effect except in relation to such territories to which it extends at the date of such Order.[52] The effect of this provision, which has been acted upon,[53] is merely to prevent the further extension of the system of enforcement envisaged by the 1920 Act. Its effect is not to apply instead the scheme of the 1933 Act. For Part I of the latter to come into operation in

---

[46] The Act has been extended to almost the whole of the Commonwealth. Apart from countries to which the 1933 Act has been extended (as to which see *post*, para. 14–170), the most important exceptions are South Africa and Bangladesh. The Act no longer applies to Hong Kong as it is no longer a member of the Commonwealth; and it no longer applies to Gibraltar if the judgment is given after February 1, 1998: see *post*, para. 14–235. For the countries to which the 1920 Act has been extended see *post*, para. 14–167.

[47] Or, as the case may be, the Court of Session in Scotland or the High Court of Northern Ireland.

[48] 1920 Act, s.9(1).

[49] *Ibid.* s.9(3)(*a*).

[50] *Ibid.* s.9(2)(*e*).

[51] See Sumner Committee Report, 1919, Cmd. 251.

[52] s.7(1).

[53] S. R. & O. 1933 No. 1073.

relation to any particular territory, a further and specific Order in Council is required.[54] The making of such an Order, which has occurred only in relation to India,[55] Pakistan,[56] Canada (apart from Quebec)[57] and Australia,[58] is, however, to revoke the application of the 1920 Act, if it has any application, in relation to the territory concerned.[59]

The judgments to which the Rule applies are any judgments or orders in any   **14–162** civil proceedings providing for the payment of a sum of money, and include awards in arbitration proceedings if these can, under the law in force where they are made, be enforced in the same manner as judgments.[60] Rules of court provide that an application for registration may be made without notice (*ex parte*). It must be supported by a verified or certified or otherwise duly authenticated copy of the judgment, and by evidence that the judgment does not fall within any of the cases in which a judgment may not be registered under the Act. The judgment may, and perhaps must, be registered for an amount expressed in the currency in which it was rendered.[61] Notice of registration must be served on the judgment debtor. If he is out of the jurisdiction, the notice can be served on him without special permission.[62] The High Court, moreover, has the same control and jurisdiction over the execution of the judgment as it has over judgments given by itself.[63] Registration is not to be ordered if "the original court acted without jurisdiction."[64] No attempt is made to give a comprehensive definition of this term, but section 9(2)(*b*) provides that a judgment shall not be registered under the Act if the judgment debtor was "neither carrying on business nor ordinarily resident within the jurisdiction of the original court, did not voluntarily appear or otherwise submit or agree to submit to the jurisdiction of that court." This differs from the common law principles in Rule 36[65] only in minor respects and there is little room for additional objection on jurisdictional grounds on the basis of section 9(2)(*a*). Under the 1920 Act "carrying on business" is used as an alternative to residence not only in the case of corporations but also in the case of individuals. The principle of the cases on the jurisdiction of the English court[66] applies also to the question whether a corporation carried on

---

[54] *Yukon Consolidated Gold Corporation v. Clark* [1938] 2 K.B. 241 (C.A.); *Jamieson v. Northern Electricity Supply Corporation Ltd.*, 1970 S.L.T. 113.

[55] S.I. 1958 No. 425.

[56] S.I. 1958 No. 141. The Act formerly applied also to Burma.

[57] S.I. 1987 No. 648, S.I. 1987 No. 2211, S.I. 1988 No. 1304, S.I. 1988 No. 1853, S.I. 1989 No. 987, S.I. 1991 No. 1724, S.I. 1992 No. 1731.

[58] S.I. 1994 No. 1901.

[59] s.7(2) of the 1933 Act. As to the status of a judgment already given upon the making of such an Order, see the Administration of Justice Act 1956, s.51; and see para. 14R–169, n. 93, *post*.

[60] 1920 Act, s.12(1); see Rule 65. It has been held in Scotland that an order of a Commonwealth court setting aside an assignment of property by a husband to his wife is not registrable under the Act: *Platt v. Platt*, 1958 S.C. 95.

[61] See para. 14–173, n. 26, *post*.

[62] Ord. 71, rr. 2, 3, 7 (in Civil Procedure Rules 1998, Sched.1).

[63] 1920 Act, s.9(3)(*b*).

[64] 1920 Act, s.9(2)(*a*).

[65] 1982 Act, s.33 (what constitutes a voluntary appearance) applies to judgments under the 1920 Act.

[66] *Ante*, paras. 11–096 *et seq*. See also *Akande v. Balfour Beatty Construction Ltd.* [1998] I.L.Pr. 110.

business in the jurisdiction of the original court within the meaning of the 1920 Act. Thus it was held that a New Zealand insurance company did not carry on business in Ghana merely because it maintained agents there with limited powers.[67] The 1920 Act includes, as a basis of jurisdiction additional to carrying on of business, ordinary residence, while under the 1933 Act residence simpliciter is required, but there is not likely to be any significant difference.[68] Rules 37 to 39 on where jurisdiction does not exist apply also to registration under the 1920 Act.[69]

14–163 The other grounds for non-registration are that (i) the judgment debtor was not duly served with the process of the original court and did not appear; (ii) the judgment was obtained by fraud; (iii) the judgment debtor satisfies the court that an appeal is pending, or that he is entitled and intends to appeal, against the judgment; or (iv) the judgment was in respect of a cause of action which for reasons of public policy or for some other similar reason could not have been entertained by the English court. The defence of fraud under the Act is to be decided by reference to the common law principles discussed in connection with Rule 43.[70] There is no general ground for impeachment on the basis of lack of natural justice. Instead, the 1920 Act provides[71] that registration must be refused if the defendant was not duly served with the process of the original court and did not appear, notwithstanding that he was ordinarily resident or was carrying on business within the jurisdiction of the foreign court or agreed to submit to its jurisdiction. As has been seen,[72] it was assumed in one case[73] that "duly served" meant served according to the law of the foreign court. At common law (and under the 1933 and 1982 Acts) the public policy exception relates to enforcement and recognition of the judgment itself, whereas the 1920 Act excludes from registration any judgment in respect of a cause of action which for reasons of public policy or some other similar reason could not have been entertained by the registering court.[74] Finally it should be noted that the pendency of an appeal is a ground for non-registration, even though at common law that does not prevent the judgment being "final and conclusive."[75]

14–164 The 1920 Act also provides that registration is within the discretion of the court and will only be allowed if the court thinks it just and convenient that the judgment should be enforced here.[76] The Act does not specifically provide that judgments for taxes or fines or other penalties are not registrable under its provisions. Since it is clear that a foreign judgment for fines or other penalties cannot be enforced at common law or under the 1933 and 1982 Acts, it seems safe to conclude that it would not be enforced under the 1920 Act, either because it would be contrary to public policy or because the court would exercise its discretion not to register the judgment.

---

[67] *Sfeir & Co. v. National Insurance Co. of New Zealand* [1964] 1 Lloyd's Rep. 330.
[68] *Ante*, paras. 14–057 *et seq.*; *cf. Re Duncan & Hirsch* [1952] 3 D.L.R. 850 (Alta.).
[69] *Ante*, paras. 14R–090 *et seq.*
[70] *Owens Bank Ltd. v. Bracco* [1992] 2 A.C. 443.
[71] s.9(2)(*c*).
[72] *Ante*, para. 14–155.
[73] *Sfeir & Co. v. National Insurance Co. of New Zealand, supra.*
[74] s.9(2)(*f*).
[75] *Ante*, para. 14–023.
[76] s.9(1).

The judgment creditor remains free to bring an action at common law on **14–165** the foreign judgment, subject to the rule that, unless the court otherwise orders, the claimant will not be entitled to recover any costs of the action, unless he has previously applied for registration of his judgment and has been refused, in any case in which such registration is permissible under the terms of the Act.[77]

The 1920 Act contains no provisions dealing with recognition, as opposed **14–166** to enforcement, of judgments within its scope. Recognition will, therefore, depend on common law principles.[78]

The list of states and territories to which the Act applies was consolidated **14–167** by statutory instrument,[79] and has since been amended by deletion. It now applies to many of the states of the Commonwealth, but it should be noted that it does not apply to Australia,[80] Bangladesh,[81] Canada,[82] Gibraltar,[83] Hong Kong,[84] India,[85] Pakistan[86] and South Africa.[87]

ILLUSTRATIONS

1. A & Co., who carry on business in Ghana, bring an action in Ghana against X & Co., a New **14–168** Zealand insurance company, for a loss under a policy of marine insurance issued by X & Co. in Beirut. X & Co. do not carry on business in Ghana or have any assets there or connection therewith except that they maintain agents there with limited power to settle claims. The policy contains a clause stating that claims are payable by X & Co.'s agents in Ghana to whom notice of loss must be given. The writ is served on X & Co. at their branch office in London by leave of the Ghana court. X & Co. take no part in the Ghana proceedings and judgment is given against them in default of appearance. A & Co. now seek to register their judgment in England under the Act of 1920. Although X & Co. were duly served with the process of the court under the law of Ghana, the judgment will not be registered in England, because X & Co. neither carried on business in Ghana nor submitted to the jurisdiction of the Ghana court.[88]

2. A & Co., bankers, bring proceedings against X, an Italian citizen, and Y & Co., an Italian company, in the courts of St. Vincent and the Grenadines, on agreements providing for a loan to Y & Co., to be guaranteed by X. X and Y & Co. allege that the agreements are forgeries, but their defence is rejected by the St. Vincent court. A & Co. bring enforcement proceedings in England (where the defendants have assets) and in Italy. Registration of the judgment is set aside because there is a prima facie case of fraud, and an issue is directed to be tried as to whether the judgment was obtained by fraud.[89]

---

[77] 1920 Act, s.9(5).

[78] *Ante*, paras. 14–027 *et seq.*

[79] S.I. 1985 No. 1994.

[80] S.I. 1994 No. 1901, which extends the 1933 Act to Australia and to the Australian states and territories.

[81] Enforcement of judgments from Bangladesh is governed by the common law.

[82] The 1933 Act applies to Canada and to all provinces and territories except Quebec; judgments from Quebec are recognised and enforced under the common law.

[83] S.I. 1997 No. 2601. Judgments from Gibraltar are enforced under regulations made under Part IV of the 1982 Act: Rule 49(4), *post*, para. 14–235.

[84] Which is no longer a member of the Commonwealth; judgments will be recognised and enforced in accordance with the common law.

[85] S.I. 1958 No. 425.

[86] S.I. 1958 No. 141.

[87] Judgments from South Africa are enforced under the common law.

[88] *Sfeir & Co. v. National Insurance Co. of New Zealand* [1964] 1 Lloyd's Rep. 330.

[89] *Owens Bank Ltd. v. Bracco* [1992] 2 A.C. 443. The European Court ruled (Case C–129/92 [1994] E.C.R. I–117; [1994] Q.B. 509) that as the enforcement of judgments from non-Contracting States was not within the scope of the 1968 Convention, Arts. 21 and 22 had no application to proceedings which were part of that process.

(2) FOREIGN JUDGMENTS (RECIPROCAL ENFORCEMENT) ACT 1933

14R–169   RULE 47[90]—(1) When Part I of the Foreign Judgments (Reciprocal Enforcement) Act 1933 is extended to any foreign country outside the United Kingdom, a judgment creditor under a judgment[91] to which the Act applies may apply to the High Court[92] at any time within six years[93] after the date of such judgment to have the judgment registered in the High Court, and on any such application the court will order the judgment to be registered.

Provided that no judgment will be ordered to be registered if—

(a) it has been wholly satisfied; or

(b) it could not be enforced by execution in the country of the original court.[94]

(2) Subject to the provisions of the 1933 Act with respect to the setting aside of registration, a registered judgment will be of the same force and effect as if the judgment had been a judgment originally given in the High Court and entered on the date of registration.[95]

(3) Any judgment of a recognised court of a country to which the Act applies given after the application of the Act to such country is capable of registration in accordance with this Rule if—

(a) it is final and conclusive as between the judgment debtor and the judgment creditor or requires the former to make an interim payment to the latter; and

(b) there is payable thereunder a sum of money (not being a sum payable in respect of taxes or other charges of a like nature or in respect of a fine or other penalty).[96]

This Rule must be read subject to Rule 52.

COMMENT

14–170   The scheme of direct enforcement of foreign judgments provided for in the 1933 Act upon which this Rule is based and the wording of which it follows closely, is designed to apply in relation not only to countries foreign in the political sense, but also to countries of the Commonwealth outside the United Kingdom. It would clearly be redundant as regards the latter to have two systems of enforcement of judgments, and the Act therefore provides for the restriction and replacement of the system set up earlier by the 1920 Act.[97] In

---

[90] See Report of the Foreign Judgments (Reciprocal Enforcement) Committee, 1932, Cmd. 4213. In case of ambiguity resort may be had to the Report of the Committee to determine the mischief the Act was intended to remedy: *Black-Clawson International Ltd. v. Papierwerke Waldhof-Aschaffenburg A.G.* [1975] A.C. 591.

[91] Including an arbitration award enforceable as a judgment in the place where it is given: 1933 Act, s.10A (added by 1982 Act, s.35(1), Sched. 10, para. 4). See Rule 65, *post.*

[92] For Scotland and Northern Ireland, see 1933 Act, ss.12 and 13.

[93] A judgment of a court of a country which forms part of the Commonwealth given before the application of the 1933 Act to that country is registrable within twelve months of the date thereof or within such longer period as the court may allow. And any judgment of any such country registered under the 1920 Act is to be deemed to have been registered under the 1933 Act: Administration of Justice Act 1956, s.51.

[94] 1933 Act, ss.1(2), 2(1).

[95] 1933 Act, s.2(2).

[96] *Ibid.* s.1(2), as amended by 1982 Act, s.35(1) and Sched. 10, para. 1.

[97] See *ante*, para. 14–161.

pursuance of this provision the later Act has been extended to India,[98] Pakistan,[99] Australia and the states and territories of Australia,[1] the Federal Court of Canada and the Canadian provinces except Quebec,[2] Tonga,[3] Guernsey,[4] Jersey,[5] and the Isle of Man.[6] Of countries foreign in the political sense, only Austria,[7] Belgium,[8] Germany,[9] France,[10] Israel,[11] Italy,[12] the Netherlands,[13] Norway,[14] and Suriname[15] so far come within the Act for general purposes. For almost all practical purposes the 1933 Act is superseded by Part I of the 1982 Act as regards Belgium, Germany, France, Italy and the Netherlands (which are parties to the 1968 Convention) and as regards Austria and Norway (which are parties to the Lugano Convention). In addition, the 1933 Act extends to any country which is a party to certain international conventions dealt with in connection with Rule 55, but only in relation to proceedings arising under those conventions.[16] The basis of the application of the 1933 Act in regard to any territory is the existence of a substantial measure of reciprocity.

A judgment is defined as meaning a judgment or order given or made by a **14–171** court in any civil proceedings[17] or a judgment or order given or made by a court in any criminal proceedings for the payment of a sum of money in respect of compensation or damages to an injured party.[18] Thus, under the Act, as at common law, it is possible to enforce a judgment of *e.g.* a French court awarding compensation to the "*partie civile*" or injured victim of a crime, even though the judgment also imposes a fine or penalty on the defendant which is not enforceable.[19]

As a result of amendments made by the 1982 Act, the 1933 Act applies to **14–172** judgments of "recognised courts" of the foreign country, *i.e.* courts to which the 1933 Act is extended by Order in Council, and not only, as before, to

---

[98] S.I. 1958 No. 425.

[99] S.I. 1958 No. 141; Pakistan Act 1990, Sched., para. 8.

[1] S.I. 1994 No. 1901.

[2] S.I. 1987 No. 468 (Federal Court, British Columbia, Manitoba, New Brunswick, Nova Scotia, Ontario) as amended by S.I. 1987 No. 2211 (Yukon Territory), S.I. 1988 Nos. 1304 (Prince Edward Island) and 1853 (Saskatchewan), S.I. 1989 No. 987 (Northwest Territories), S.I. 1991 No. 1724 (Newfoundland) and S.I. 1992 No. 1731 (Alberta). For amendment of the U.K.-Canada Convention, see S.I. 1995 No. 2708.

[3] S.I. 1980 No. 1523.

[4] S.I. 1973 No. 610.

[5] S.I. 1973 No. 612.

[6] S.I. 1973 No. 611.

[7] S.I. 1962 No. 1339.

[8] S.R. & O. 1936 No. 1169.

[9] S.I. 1961 No. 1199.

[10] S.R. & O. 1936 No. 609.

[11] S.I. 1971 No. 1039.

[12] S.I. 1973 No. 1894.

[13] S.I. 1969 No. 1063, as amended by S.I. 1977 No. 2149.

[14] S.I. 1962 No. 636.

[15] S.I. 1981 No. 735.

[16] See *post*, paras. 15R–041 *et seq.*

[17] But not "judgments on judgments," *i.e.* judgments given by foreign courts enforcing the judgments of third states: 1933 Act, s.1(2A), added by 1982 Act, s.35(1) and Sched. 10, para. 1(2).

[18] 1933 Act, s.11.

[19] s.1(2). For the meaning of penalty, see *ante*, para. 14–020. See also Rule 52, *post*. But see Isle of Man Act 1979, s.4.

superior courts of that country.[20] In the case of any country to which the 1933 Act had been extended before its amendment by the 1982 Act, superior courts of that country are deemed to be recognised courts. As from January 1, 1987 the 1933 Act has applied, not only to judgments which are "final and conclusive", but also to judgments for interim payments.[21]

14–173   As at common law, a judgment is deemed to be final and conclusive notwithstanding that an appeal is pending or that it may still be subject to appeal.[22] But the court has a discretionary power to set aside the registration of a judgment on such terms as it thinks fit, if the applicant satisfies the court that an appeal is pending or that he is entitled and intends to appeal.[23] And if upon an application for registration it appears that part or parts only of the judgment are capable of registration, then such part or parts may be registered alone.[24] Registration is for the sum payable under the original judgment, plus interest due under the law of the original court up to the date of registration, plus reasonable costs incidental to registration.[25] The judgment may, and perhaps must, be registered for an amount expressed in the currency in which it was rendered.[26] Where the judgment has been partially satisfied, registration is for the unsatisfied balance.[27]

14–174   An application for registration in accordance with the Act may be made without notice. It must be supported by a verified or certified or otherwise duly authenticated copy of the judgment, and by a certified translation thereof, as well as by a witness statement or affidavit stating that the applicant believes himself entitled to enforce the judgment and that registration is not liable to be set aside. Notice of registration must be served on the judgment debtor. If he is out of the jurisdiction, the notice can be served on him without permission.[28] There is no requirement that the judgment debtor be subject to the personal jurisdiction of the English court.[29] Enforcement is by registration, and not by action, and the judgment debtor need have no connection with England, although in practice registration will be of little value unless he has assets in England.

14–175   The effect of registration of a foreign judgment under the 1933 Act is to render it for purposes of execution of the same force and effect as if it were a judgment of the High Court. Thus, a stay of execution will not be ordered merely because an English action is pending between the same parties which raises similar issues.[30] Execution may not, however, issue so long as it is competent to any party to make an application for the setting aside of the judgment or until the final determination of any such application. The High Court has the same control over execution as it has over the execution of its own judgments. Proceedings may be taken upon a registered judgment exactly

---

[20] Judgments from courts which are not "recognised courts" will be capable of enforcement and recognition under the common law.

[21] s.1(2)(*a*), as amended by 1982 Act, s.35(1) and Sched. 10, para. 1(2).

[22] s.1(3).

[23] s.5. See *S.A. Consortium General Textiles v. Sun and Sand Agencies Ltd.* [1978] Q.B. 279 (C.A.); *Hunt v. B.P. Exploration Co. (Libya)* [1980] 1 N.Z.L.R. 104.

[24] s.2(5).

[25] s.2(6).

[26] Administration of Justice Act 1977. See *The Supreme Court Practice 1999*, 71/3/2.

[27] s.2(4).

[28] See Ord. 71, rr. 2, 3, 7 (Civil Procedure Rules 1998, Sched. 1).

[29] See in this sense *Hunt v. B.P. Exploration Co. (Libya) Ltd.* (1980) 144 C.L.R. 565; *Hunt v. B.P. Exploration Co. (Libya)* [1980] 1 N.Z.L.R. 104.

[30] *Wagner v. Laubscher Bros & Co.* [1970] 2 Q.B. 313 (C.A.).

as if it were a judgment of the High Court.[31] Thus a statutory demand under the Insolvency Act 1986 may be served upon it.[32] The sum for which a foreign judgment is registered carries interest in the same manner as an English judgment debt.[33]

Jurisdiction of the foreign court. Registration must be set aside under the   **14–176**
1933 Act if "the courts of the country of the original court had no jurisdiction in the circumstances of the case."[34] Except in the case of judgments within the scope of the international conventions referred to above,[35] the original court is deemed to have had jurisdiction in an action *in personam*[36]: (i) if the judgment debtor submitted by voluntarily appearing[37]; or (ii) if the judgment debtor was plaintiff in, or counterclaimed in, the proceedings in the original court; or (iii) if the judgment debtor had before the commencement of the proceedings agreed, in respect of the subject matter of the proceedings, to submit to the jurisdiction of that court or of the courts of the country of that court; or (iv) if the judgment debtor was at the time when the proceedings were instituted resident in, or being a body corporate, had its principal place of business in, the country of that court; or (v) if the judgment debtor had an office or place of business in the country of that court and the proceedings in that court were in respect of a transaction effected through or at that office or place. Rules 37 and 38 on where jurisdiction does not exist also apply to cases within the 1933 Act. The grounds of jurisdiction in the 1933 Act were deliberately framed so as to reproduce the rules of the common law as closely as possible,[38] though it was found desirable to make some slight departures from the common law rules in order to secure international agreements which would be likely to operate satisfactorily in practice.[39] The provisions of the 1933 Act as to the jurisdiction of foreign courts are exclusive, *i.e.* no judgment can be registered under the 1933 Act unless the jurisdiction of the foreign court can be brought under one of these heads.[40] The main differences between the common law and the 1933 Act are as follows: first, the 1933 Act does not treat the foreign court as having jurisdiction over an individual by virtue of the mere presence of the defendant, whereas the First Case of Rule 36[41] now states, on the authority of *Adams v. Cape Industries plc*,[42] that presence is a head of jurisdiction at common law. Secondly, under the 1933 Act there is jurisdiction over a corporation only if either (a) it has its principal place of business in the foreign country or (b) where it has an office or place

---

[31] s.2(2).

[32] *Re a Judgment Debtor (No. 2176 of* 1938) [1939] Ch. 601 (C.A.), a case under the Bankruptcy Act 1914; *Re McGilvray* (1986) 66 A.L.R. 181.

[33] s.2(2)(*c*); *cf.* Private International Law (Miscellaneous Provisions) Act 1995, s.1.

[34] s.4(1)(*a*)(ii).

[35] Text at n. 16, *ante.* In these cases the jurisdictional rules depend on the Conventions as incorporated by legislation discussed in connection with Rule 55.

[36] s.4(2)(*a*).

[37] See also 1982 Act, s.33, paras. 14–063 *et seq., ante,* which was derived from the original version of 1933 Act, s.4(2)(*a*)(i), and applies to judgments under the 1933 Act.

[38] Report of the Foreign Judgments (Reciprocal Enforcement) Committee, Cmd. 4213 (1932), paras. 2, 16, 18 and Annex V, para. 7.

[39] *Ibid.* para. 18, and Annex V, para. 7.

[40] *Société Co-opérative Sidmetal v. Titan International Ltd.* [1966] 1 Q.B. 828; *Sharps Commercials Ltd. v. Gas Turbines Ltd.* [1956] N.Z.L.R. 819 (a decision on the identically worded New Zealand Act).

[41] *Ante,* para. 14R–048.

[42] [1990] Ch. 433 (C.A.).

of business which is not its principal place of business and the cause of action arose from a transaction effected through that office. At common law it is sufficient that there be a place of business irrespective of its status or how the cause of action arose.[43] Thirdly, like the 1920 Act, the 1933 Act contemplates jurisdiction over an individual with a place of business in the foreign country, provided (in the case of the 1933 Act) that the cause of action is connected with that place.

14–177   Complete satisfaction of the foreign judgment, or the circumstance that it could not be enforced by execution in the place where it was given, are absolute bars to registration under the Act.[44] Registration is liable to be set aside on certain specified grounds upon the application of any party against whom it is enforceable made within a time specified in the registration order.[45] Registration *must* be set aside[46] if the court is satisfied (i) that the judgment is incapable of registration under the Act or has been registered in contravention of it; or (ii) that the courts of the country of the original court had no jurisdiction in the circumstances of the case; or (iii) that the judgment debtor, being the defendant in the original proceedings, did not receive sufficient notice to enable him to defend and he did not appear; or (iv) that the judgment was obtained by fraud; or (v) that the enforcement of the judgment would be contrary to English public policy; or (vi) that the rights under the judgment are not vested in the applicant for registration, which expression includes any person in whom the rights under the judgment have become vested by succession or assignment or otherwise.[47] Of these grounds (i) calls for no comment, and (ii) has been discussed in the previous paragraph. The provision with regard to notice of the proceedings has been mentioned in connection with the common law principle of natural justice.[48] where it was pointed out that under the 1933 Act a waiver of notice of proceedings by a defendant who submits to the jurisdiction of a foreign court will not be implied. The provisions with regard to fraud and public policy are the same as the common law rules.[49] In particular, the common law rule that a foreign judgment can be impeached for fraud even though no newly discovered evidence is produced, and even though the fraud was alleged in the foreign proceedings, applies to enforcement and recognition under the 1933 Act. In *Owens Bank Ltd. v. Bracco*[50] the House of Lords held that the fraud exception in the 1920 Act was subject to the same rule, and indicated (*obiter*) that the same must be so under the 1933 Act.

14–178   Registration *may* be set aside if the court is satisfied that the matter in dispute in the original proceedings had previously to the date of judgment in those proceedings been the subject of a final and conclusive judgment by a court having jurisdiction in the matter.[51]

14–179   Where registration is set aside on the ground that an appeal is pending or that the applicant is entitled and intends to appeal the right to apply again later

---

[43] *Ante*, para. 14–059.
[44] s.2(1), Proviso.
[45] ss.4, 5. For the practice, see *The Supreme Court Practice 1999*, notes to Ord. 71, and see *Re a Debtor (No. 11 of 1939)* [1939] 2 All E.R. 400 (C.A.).
[46] s.4(1)(*a*).
[47] s.11
[48] Rule 45.
[49] Rules 43 and 44.
[50] [1992] 2 A.C. 443. See also *Syal v. Heyward* [1948] 2 K.B. 443 (C.A.).
[51] s.4(1)(*b*). See Illustration 2, *post*, para. 14–182.

for registration is not prejudiced.[52] The same is the case where registration is set aside on the sole ground either that the judgment was not enforceable by execution in the country of the original court[52] or that, having been registered for the whole sum payable thereunder, it has been partially satisfied.[53] In all other cases the setting aside of registration would presumably be a bar to a second application for registration. An application to set aside registration is made under Part 23 of the Civil Procedure Rules 1998 supported by witness statement or affidavit.[54]

The 1933 Act introduced what was then a striking innovation in that it   **14–180** provided that no proceedings for the recovery of a sum payable under a foreign judgment capable of registration in accordance with its provisions, other than proceedings for such registration, might be entertained by any court.[55] This provision does not of course limit in any way the taking of proceedings upon a registrable judgment after its registration. For it is elsewhere specifically provided that proceedings may be taken upon a registered judgment as if it had been originally given by the High Court.[56] As has been seen above,[57] no proceedings may be brought on the original cause of action.

Recognition. The 1933 Act[58] saves the common law rule as to conclusive-   **14–181** ness which is discussed above.[59] But it also contains a tortuously drafted provision which states that a judgment to which Part I of the Act applies, or would have applied if a sum of money had been payable thereunder, whether it can be registered or not, and whether it is registered or not, "shall be recognised in any court in the United Kingdom as conclusive between the parties thereto in all proceedings founded on the same cause of action and may be relied on by way of defence or counterclaim in any such proceedings."[60] This provision, however, is expressed not to apply where the registration of a judgment has been set aside or could be set aside (whether it could have been registered or not) on any of the grounds on which registration under the 1933 Act must be set aside (*i.e.* lack of jurisdiction, fraud, lack of notice of the proceedings, public policy).[61] The expression "a judgment to which Part I of this Act . . . would have applied if a sum of money had been payable" is obscure. The House of Lords held by a majority in *Black-Clawson International Ltd. v. Papierwerke Waldhof-Aschaffenburg A.G.*[62] that the section applies to judgments in favour of a defendant dismissing the plaintiff's claim. Under the 1933 Act, as at common law, the judgment is only conclusive as regards the question adjudicated upon, so that a judgment which was not on the merits, because it was given in the defendant's favour on the ground that the action was time-barred, was not a bar to a subsequent action in England.[63]

---

[52] s.5(2).
[53] s.5(3).
[54] Ord. 71, r. 9.
[55] s.6. The position is the same under the 1982 Act, Parts I and II, Rules 48–49, *post.*
[56] s.2(2)(*b*).
[57] 1982 Act, s.34, *ante*, para. 14–034.
[58] s.8(3).
[59] *Ante*, paras. 14–028 *et seq.*
[60] s.8(1).
[61] s.8(2).
[62] [1975] A.C. 591 at pp. 619 (Lord Dilhorne), 635 (Lord Diplock), and 652 (Lord Simon). Lord Reid dissented.
[63] [1975] A.C. 591. But the result would be different under the Foreign Limitation Periods Act 1984, s.3. See *ante*, para. 14–031.

Whether the provision applies to judgments as to status is a question on which differing views have been expressed. The extrinsic material, namely the Report of the Foreign Judgments (Reciprocal Enforcement) Committee[64] and the Conventions which were negotiated prior to the enactment of the 1933 Act, suggests that section 8 was not intended to be confined to judgments *in personam*.[65] A literal interpretation of the sub-section, in conjunction with the definition of judgment in section 1(2), suggests that judgments as to status are within the scope of section 8(1), and this view had the support of Sir John Arnold, P. in *Vervaeke v. Smith*.[66] But in the same decision Eveleigh L.J.[67] (with whom Cumming-Bruce L.J. agreed) shared the doubts of Lord Reid[68] and thought that section 8(1) did not apply to decrees in matrimonial cases concerning status (as opposed to money judgments). In *Maples v. Maples*[69] Latey J. preferred the majority view that the 1933 Act in general, and s.8(1) in particular, did not apply to judgments relating to marital status.

Illustrations

14–182   1. A obtains a judgment for 1 million shekels against X from an Israeli Court. The judgment has not been registered. No action lies upon the judgment in England.

2. A, a French company, sells clothing from its Lille branch and its Paris branch to X & Co., an English company. The invoices for the goods from Lille provide for the jurisdiction of the Lille court and the invoices for the goods from Paris provide for the jurisdiction of the Paris court. When X & Co. refuses to pay for either sets of goods, A sues in the Lille court for the total amount outstanding, plus 10,000 francs as "résistance abusive," a head of claim for unreasonable refusal to pay. X & Co. initially ignores the Lille proceedings and judgment in default is awarded against it for the amount claimed. X & Co. subsequently applies to appeal out of time from the Lille judgment. The appeal proceedings are a submission to the jurisdiction of the Lille court, even for the Paris goods, although there has been no contractual submission to the Lille court in respect of those goods. The judgment for "résistance abusive" is not a fine or penalty, or contrary to public policy. The judgment is registrable.[70]

(3) Part I of the Civil Jurisdiction and
Judgments Act 1982[71]

14R–183   **Rule 48—A judgment given by a court in a State party to the Brussels Convention or the Lugano Convention on jurisdiction and the enforcement of judgments in civil and commercial matters and which falls within their scope has, on registration in the appropriate court[72] in the United**

---

[64] Cmd. 4213, para. 4.

[65] Patchett, at p. 179, *op. cit. supra*, para. 14R–001, n. 1. See also Lipstein [1981] C.L.J. 201.

[66] [1981] Fam. 77, 126 (C.A.). The point was left open in the House of Lords: [1983] 1 A.C. 145.

[67] [1981] Fam. at pp. 126–127.

[68] *Black-Clawson International Ltd. v. Papierwerke Waldhof-Aschaffenburg A.G.* [1975] A.C. 591, 617 (a dissenting judgment).

[69] [1988] Fam. 14.

[70] *S.A. Consortium Textiles v. Sun & Sand Agencies Ltd.* [1978] Q.B. 279 (C.A.). This case would now fall within Part I of the 1982 Act, Rule 48, *post.*

[71] Collins, pp. 105–125; Hartley, pp. 82–100; Anton, *Civil Jurisdiction*, pp. 128–155; Briggs & Rees, Chap. 7; Kaye, Pt. 8; O'Malley and Layton, Chaps. 26 to 30. For the Contracting States see *ante*, paras. 11–005 *et seq.*

[72] The High Court in England; the Court of Session in Scotland; the High Court in Northern Ireland: 1982 Act, Sched. 1, 1968 Convention, Art. 32; Lugano Convention, Art. 32, in 1982 Act, Scheds. 1 and 3C; 1982 Act, s.4(1). On the transitional provisions of the 1982 Act, see *The Volvox Hollandia* [1988] 2 Lloyd's Rep. 361 (C.A.); Case C–163/95 *Von Horn v. Cinnamond* [1997] E.C.R. I–5451; [1998] Q.B. 214; *Davy International Ltd. v. Voest Alpine Industrieanlagenbau GmbH* [1999] 1 All E.R. 103 (C.A.).

Kingdom, the same force and effect as a judgment of the court in which it is registered, and proceedings for or with respect to its enforcement may be taken, as if the judgment had been originally given by the registering court.[73]

COMMENT

Introduction. The jurisdictional provisions of the 1968 Convention and   **14–184** the Lugano Convention have been fully discussed in Chapter 11, and Rule 48 states the essence of the enforcement aspects of the Conventions, which are set out in Articles 25 and 31 to 46, as implemented by section 4 of the 1982 Act and the Civil Procedure Rules.[74] The most notable features of enforcement under the Conventions in which they differ from the régime established by the common law and the 1920 and 1933 Acts are that enforcement under the Conventions is not limited to money judgments, or to final judgments, and that in principle (but subject to certain limitations) the court in which enforcement is sought is not entitled to investigate the jurisdiction of the court which gave the judgment. It is also important to note that the effect of the Conventions is that the enforcement procedures apply to all judgments within their scope, whether or not they are against persons domiciled in a Contracting State. Thus an English default judgment against a New York resident in a case where the jurisdiction of the English court was based on the temporary presence of the defendant in England will be enforceable in France; and a French judgment against a New York resident in a case where the jurisdiction of the French court was based on the French nationality of the plaintiff under Article 14 of the Civil Code will be enforceable in England. But Article 59 allows a Contracting State to assume in relation to a non-Contracting State the obligation not to recognise judgments given in other Contracting States against defendants domiciled or habitually resident in the third state where the basis of jurisdiction could only be one of the "exorbitant" bases of jurisdiction set out in Article 3(2) (which include the jurisdiction in England based on temporary presence and the jurisdiction in France based on nationality).[75]

Judgments. Article 25 of each Convention provides that "judgment"   **14–185** means any judgment given by a court or tribunal of a Contracting State, whatever the judgment may be called, including a decree, order, decision, or writ of execution, as well as the determination of costs by an officer of the court.[76] It does not include judicially approved settlements, but does include

---

[73] 1982 Act, s.4(3). For the recognition of such judgments without the need for registration, see *post*, para. 14–221.

[74] Ord. 71, rr. 25 to 34, in Civil Procedure Rules 1998, Sched. 1.

[75] Negotiations for such a treaty between the United Kingdom and the United States ended unsuccessfully in 1980. Treaties have been concluded, and brought into effect, with Canada (S.I. 1986 No. 2027 as amended by S.I. 1995 No. 2708) and with Australia (S.I. 1994 No. 1901). There are negotiations in progress for the adoption of a worldwide Convention, under the auspices of the Hague Conference: see von Mehren (1994) 57 Law & Contemp. Prob. 271.

[76] s.15(1) of the 1982 Act provides that "judgment" in Part I of the Act (which deals with the Conventions) has the meaning given to it by Art. 25. *Cf.* s.50 of the 1982 Act, which provides that, subject to s.15(1), judgment means any judgment or order (by whatever name called) given or made by a court in any civil proceedings; that court includes a tribunal; and that tribunal means a tribunal of any description other than a court of law. For maintenance orders see Rule 88, *post*.

judgments by consent.[77] The expression includes not only judgments ordering the payment of money,[78] orders for costs[79] and for interest,[80] but also non-money judgments and judgments which are not final and which are interlocutory or provisional in nature.[81] This is because there is no requirement that the judgment be "final and conclusive": it may be an interim order providing for periodical payments or a provisional order freezing assets.[82] It may be an order made under Article 24 by a court which has no jurisdiction over the substance of the case, provided that it is not granted *ex parte* and intended to be executed without notice.[83] Thus, for example, the English court will be required to enforce German injunctions. But the mode of enforcement (*e.g.* sequestration or committal) will be a matter for English law,[84] which will determine the procedural requirements (such as the endorsement of a penal notice on the order) and also the extent of the court's discretion to commit or fine.

14–186   It is obvious that a judgment must fall within the scope of the Convention if it is to fall within Title III of the Convention and qualify for recognition and enforcement under this Rule.[85] The provisions of Title III do not extend to "judgments on judgments". Accordingly, a judgment from the courts of State A enforcing a judgment of State B would not be a judgment within Article 25.[86] A similar result is reached when the courts of a Contracting State A enforce the judgment of a non-Contracting State, and the judgment creditor then seeks to enforce the "judgment" of State A under Title III of the Convention in Contracting State B. The European Court held, in *Owens Bank Ltd. v. Bracco*,[87] that in such circumstances the judgment of State A falls outside the scope of the 1968 Convention altogether, because the merits of the

---

[77] *Landhurst Leasing plc v. Marcq* [1998] I.L.Pr. 822 (C.A.). On the enforcement of authentic instruments and of settlements approved by courts in the course of proceedings, see Arts. 50 and 51 of the Conventions, *post*, para. 14–223. For the distinction between court-approved settlements and judgments by consent see Case C-414/92 *Solo Kleinmotoren GmbH v. Boch* [1994] E.C.R. I-2237, 2255, and esp. at p. 2245, *per* Gulmann A.-G.

[78] Including the order to pay under the "Zahlungsbefehl" procedure of German law: Case 166/80 *Klomps v. Michel* [1981] E.C.R. 1593, and the order to pay made under the "*decreto ingiuntivo*" procedure of Italian law: Case C–474/93 *Firma Hengst Import BV v. Anna Maria Campese* [1995] E.C.R. I–2113.

[79] 1982 Act, s.7; Scheds. 1 and 3C, Art. 25.

[80] 1982 Act, s.7.

[81] *e.g. The Tjaskemolen (No. 2)* [1997] 2 Lloyd's Rep. 476, 478–479; *Normaco v. Lundman* [1999] I.L.Pr. 381.

[82] *Cf.* Case 143/78 *De Cavel v. De Cavel (No. 1)* [1979] E.C.R. 1055; Case 125/79 *Denilauler v. SNC Couchet Frères* [1980] E.C.R. 1553; *Babanaft International Co. S.A. v. Bassatne* [1990] Ch. 13, 31 (C.A.); *cf.* Case 258/83 *Brennero v. Wendel GmbH* [1984] E.C.R. 3971; *The Atlantic Emperor (No. 2)* [1992] 1 Lloyd's Rep. 624 (C.A.); *Barrett International Resorts Ltd. v. Martin*, 1994 S.L.T. 434.

[83] Case 125/79 *Denilauler v. SNC Couchet Frères* [1980] E.C.R. 1553; *E.M.I. Records Ltd. v. Modern Music GmbH* [1992] Q.B. 115. But orders for discovery and the taking of evidence are not within its scope: see *CFEM Façades v. Bovis Construction S.A.* [1992] I.L.Pr. 561; see also Schlosser, paras. 184–187; Collins, p. 106.

[84] Schlosser, paras. 212–213; Collins, p. 116.

[85] For the approach in cases where the judgment on a matter *prima facie* within the scope of the Convention is closely connected to matters which are excluded from the scope of the Convention, see Case 145/86 *Hoffmann v. Krieg* [1988] E.C.R. 645 (status); Case C–267/97 *Coursier v. Fortis Bank S.A.*, April 29, 1999 (insolvency). For cases where the judgment was given between parties who had agreed to arbitrate their differences, see *post*, paras. 14–187 *et seq.*

[86] Droz, para. 437; *cf.* 1982 Act, s.18(7).

[87] Case C–129/92 [1994] E.C.R. I–117; [1994] Q.B. 509; *Dubai Bank Ltd v. Abbas* [1998] I.L. Pr. 391.

dispute will have been adjudicated upon by a judge in a non-Contracting State, and that this is outside the framework of mutual recognition established by the Convention.

Effect of exclusion of arbitration. Article 1(4) of each of the Conventions   **14–187** excludes "arbitration" from its scope. This exclusion has been considered earlier,[88] and in the present context arises in relation to the recognition or enforcement of judgments of Contracting States rendered in connection with disputes which the parties have agreed, or are alleged to have agreed, should be resolved exclusively by arbitration.

It is clear from the Jenard Report[89] and the Schlosser Report[90] that the   **14–188** recognition and enforcement of arbitral awards are outside the scope of the Conventions. It has been held that a French judgment making a French award enforceable was not entitled to enforcement under the 1968 Convention for that reason.[91] There are two more controversial questions.

The first is whether a judgment of a Contracting State, deciding that an   **14–189** alleged arbitration agreement is invalid or non-existent, is entitled to recognition in other Contracting States. The Schlosser Report[92] expressed the view that the effect of Article 1(4) was that a judgment determining whether an arbitration agreement was valid was not covered by the 1968 Convention. One of the questions referred to the European Court in *Marc Rich & Co. A.G. v. Soc. Italiana Impianti PA*[93] was whether the exclusion in Article 1(4) applied to judgments where the initial existence of an arbitration agreement was in issue. Darmon A.-G.[94] was of the opinion that, where the main issue in a proceeding before a national court related to whether an arbitration agreement existed between the parties, the dispute did not fall within the 1968 Convention, since a dispute as to the existence of an arbitration agreement fell outside the scope of the Convention. The European Court did not rule expressly on this question: the actual ruling was the narrow one that the exclusion in Article 1(4) extended to litigation pending before a national court concerning the appointment of an arbitrator even if the existence or validity of the arbitration agreement was a preliminary issue in that litigation. But it did expressly reject the argument[95] that the exclusion in Article 1(4) did not apply where the existence or validity of an arbitration agreement was being disputed before

---

[88] *Ante*, paras. 11–233 *et seq.*
[89] p. 13, referred to with approval in Case C–190/89 *Marc Rich & Co. A.G. v. Soc. Italiana Impianti P.A.* [1991] E.C.R. I–3855, 3900.
[90] Para. 65(c), referred to with approval in Case C–391/95 *Van Uden Maritime BV v. Firma Deco-Line* [1998] E.C.R. I–7091, 7133; [1999] 2 W.L.R. 1181, 1209.
[91] *ABCI v. Banque Franco-Tunisienne* [1996] 1 Lloyd's Rep. 495, affd. on other aspects [1997] 1 Lloyd's Rep. 531 (C.A.). See Hascher (1996) 12 Arb. Int. 233, who suggests that the decision is supportable on the basis that the French order was not in fact a judgment on the award, but simply an execution order.
[92] Para. 64(b). But the Evrigenis-Kerameus Report on the 1989 Accession Convention suggested (para. 35) that where a court, which is seised of proceedings brought in alleged violation of an arbitration agreement, decides on the validity of the arbitration agreement in the course of proceedings to contest its jurisdiction, the judgment on validity must be considered as falling within the scope of the 1968 Convention.
[93] Case C–190/89 [1991] E.C.R. I–3855.
[94] [1991] E.C.R. I–3855, at 3876, citing the Schlosser Report and Kaye, p. 150.
[95] By the Italian sellers, supported by the Commission.

different courts, regardless of whether the issue was raised as a main issue or preliminary one.[96]

14-190   In *The Heidberg*,[97] however, it was held that a decision of a French court that a bill of lading did not incorporate an arbitration clause was entitled to recognition in England, and that the exclusion in Article 1(4) did not apply. In coming to that conclusion, Judge Diamond Q.C. (sitting as a High Court judge) relied particularly on the opinions given by Professor Schlosser and M. Jenard on behalf of the Italian sellers in the *Marc Rich* case[98] and expressed the view that conflicts would be avoided if the decision of the court which had jurisdiction over the substantive dispute were entitled to recognition. He also relied on section 32(4)(*a*) of the Civil Jurisdiction and Judgments Act 1982[99]; that sub-section provides that nothing in section 32(1) (the basic rule that a foreign judgment in breach of an arbitration agreement is not entitled to recognition or enforcement) "shall affect the recognition or enforcement in the United Kingdom of . . . a judgment which is required to be recognised or enforced" under the Conventions. He appears to have considered that the effect of the sub-section was to make judgments rendered in breach of an arbitration agreement enforceable. But it is submitted that it is a wholly neutral provision, the only effect of which is to ensure that there is no conflict between the rule in section 32(1) and any possible contrary rule under the Conventions, without in any way pre-judging whether there is any such contrary rule.

14-191   In *Phillip Alexander Securities and Futures Ltd. v. Bamberger*[1] Waller J. accepted the proposition that section 32(4)(*a*) was neutral and expressed "the strong inclination"[2] that a ruling of a foreign court on the validity of an arbitration agreement should not have to be recognised by the English court. The Court of Appeal would have referred the question to the European Court had it been material, on the basis that the European Court had refrained from answering it when it had the opportunity of doing so in the *Marc Rich* case.

14-192   It is suggested that, subject to the question of submission mentioned below,[3] a judgment of the court of a Contracting State on the existence or validity of an arbitration agreement is covered by the exception in Article 1(4) and is not entitled to recognition in England under the Conventions, and that *The Heidberg* was wrongly decided.

14-193   The second controversial question is whether the judgment of the court of a Contracting State which has given judgment on the substance of the dispute between the parties, notwithstanding an arbitration agreement between the parties, is entitled to recognition or enforcement under the Conventions. In the

---

[96] In *The Atlantic Emperor (No. 2)* [1992] 1 Lloyd's Rep. 624, 628 (C.A.) Neill L.J. said that the decision of the European Court gave no guidance on the question of the applicability of the exclusion where the challenge to the validity of the arbitration agreement constitutes the dispute. But for a contrary view see Hascher (1997) 13 Arb. Int. 33, 39–40. See also Audit (1993) 9 Arb. Int. 1.

[97] [1994] 2 Lloyd's Rep. 287. See also *Toepfer International GmbH v. Molino Boschi Srl* [1996] 1 Lloyd's Rep. 510.

[98] *Ante* para. 14–139. Darmon A.-G. said (at 3872) that Professor Schlosser "puts forward a view which in every aspect contradicts the official report signed by him concerning application of the Convention to disputes relating to arbitration before national courts".

[99] See *ante*, para. 14–091.

[1] [1997] I.L. Pr. 73, affd. on other grounds *ibid.* 104 (C.A.).

[2] At 100. See also *The Xing Su Hai* [1995] 2 Lloyd's Rep. 15, 21 for the view that *The Heidberg, supra* was a "borderline case".

[3] *Post*, para. 14–194.

course of the negotiations for the 1978 Accession Convention, the United Kingdom took the position that the court addressed could refuse recognition or enforcement of such a judgment on the basis that it was outside the scope of the 1968 Convention because the exclusion in Article 1(4) covered all disputes which the parties had effectively agreed should be settled by arbitration. But the question was not resolved in the negotiations.

It is suggested, however, that a judgment of the court of a Contracting State **14–194** on the merits of the dispute, notwithstanding that there is an arbitration agreement between the parties, is a Convention judgment.[4] But the view was expressed (correctly, it is submitted) by Waller J. in *Phillip Alexander Securities and Futures Ltd. v. Bamberger*[5] that such a judgment may be refused recognition on the ground of public policy. First, if there were an English injunction restraining the foreign proceedings,[6] enforcement of a foreign judgment obtained in breach of the injunction would be contrary to public policy under Article 27(1) (or, perhaps, not entitled to recognition on the basis that it was irreconcilable with the English injunction under Article 27(3))[7]; secondly, irrespective of whether there were an injunction, it may be contrary to public policy to enforce a Convention judgment obtained in breach of an arbitration provision, at least where there had been a blatant disregard of the arbitration agreement.[8]

Effect of Submission. If the defendant in the foreign proceedings chal- **14–195** lenges the jurisdiction of the foreign court (or its exercise), that will not amount to a submission to the jurisdiction of the foreign court: that is expressly provided by section 33 of the 1982 Act, and if (as is submitted above) the decision of the foreign court on the existence or validity of the arbitration agreement is outside the scope of the 1968 and Lugano Conventions, the decision is not entitled to recognition under the Conventions. But if the defendant in the foreign proceedings goes on to contest to merits of the disputes, and judgment is given against him, then the judgment of the foreign court will be entitled to recognition and enforcement. This is because he will have submitted to the jurisdiction of the foreign court, or waived the arbitration agreement. In the *Marc Rich* proceedings, prior to the ruling of the European Court, the effect of which was that Article 21 of the 1968 Convention did not prevent English proceedings for the appointment of arbitrators, the Italian Corte di Cassazione had decided that the Italian courts had jurisdiction and that there was no binding arbitration agreement. While the ruling of the European Court was pending, the Swiss buyers lodged a pleading on the merits in the Italian proceedings. On their application for an injunction to restrain the Italian proceedings, it was held by the English Court of Appeal that the effect of their pleading in the Italian court was that they had submitted

---

[4] This view has been expressed, *obiter*, in *The Heidberg* [1994] 2 Lloyd's Rep. 287, 301 and in *Phillip Alexander Securities and Futures Ltd v. Bamberger* [1997] I.L.Pr. 73, 98, affd. on other grounds *ibid.* 104 (C.A.). See also *Zellner v. Phillip Alexander Securities and Futures Ltd.* [1997] I.L.Pr. 730, 742–743.

[5] *Supra*, at 101–102.

[6] See *ante*, para. 14–145.

[7] The Court of Appeal agreed: see p. 115.

[8] Waller J. thought that the provision in Art. 28(3) that public policy may not be applied to the rules relating to jurisdiction was not a bar to this conclusion; it would not be a ruling on jurisdiction, but a mark of disapproval of breach of agreement: p. 101.

to the jurisdiction of the Italian court to deal with the merits of the claim; that submission covered the whole proceedings, including the prior interlocutory decision by the Italian court that there was a valid arbitration agreement.[9]

14–196   **Appeals.** The pendency of an appeal in the foreign court will not prevent registration of a judgment capable of enforcement,[10] but once it is registered the court may stay enforcement proceedings if an "ordinary" appeal has been lodged against the judgment in the State in which it was given[11]; enforcement may also be stayed if the time for appeal has not yet expired, and an appeal has not been lodged, subject to the power of the English court to specify the time within which the appeal must be lodged.[12] In seeking a stay, the judgment debtor is not entitled to rely on the likelihood of success of his pending appeal in the foreign court, since the enforcing court is not permitted to examine, directly or indirectly, the substance of the case.[13]

14–197   Article 38(4) provides that the court may also make *enforcement* conditional on the provision of such security as it shall determine.[14] This is primarily designed to ensure that the judgment *debtor* does not find that he is unable to recover the judgment debt from the judgment creditor if the original judgment is overturned. But it has been held that a *stay* of enforcement may be made conditional on the provision of security by the judgment debtor, so that the judgment *creditor* is not prejudiced by the delay.[15]

14–198   The distinction between ordinary and extraordinary appeals has no counterpart in the United Kingdom, and although the distinction is found in the civil law Contracting States it is not applied uniformly. The European Court, in *Industrial Diamond Supplies v. Riva*,[16] held that (a) whether an appeal was ordinary or extraordinary depended on a Convention interpretation rather than on the procedural law of the court of origin; (b) the expression "ordinary appeal" must be understood as meaning any appeal which forms part of the normal course of an action and which, as such, constitutes a procedural development which any party must reasonably expect; (c) any appeal bound by the law to a specific period of time which starts to run by virtue of the

---

[9] *The Atlantic Emperor (No. 2)* [1992] 1 Lloyd's Rep. 624 (C.A.).

[10] Art. 31 provides that a judgment may be enforced in a Contracting State when it is has been declared enforceable in the state of origin; for the meaning of "enforceable" see Case C–267/97 *Coursier v. Fortis Bank S.A.*, April 29, 1999.

[11] Art. 38. But only the first instance court has this power: there may be no appeal against its refusal to order a stay: Case C–183/90 *Van Dalfsen v. Van Loon* [1991] E.C.R. I–4743; nor may the court hearing an appeal on a point of law under the second paragraph of Art. 37 impose such a stay for itself: Case C–432/93 *Société d'Informatique Service Réalisation Organisation v. Ampersand Software BV* [1995] E.C.R. I–2269; [1996] Q.B. 127. Art. 30 contains corresponding provisions relating to recognition.

[12] *Cf.* 1933 Act, s.5, *ante*, para. 14–179.

[13] Case C–183/90 *Van Dalfsen v. Van Loon* [1991] E.C.R. I–4743.

[14] This order may only be made when, or after, the High Court confirms the registration: Case 258/83 *Brennero SAS v. Wendel GmbH* [1984] E.C.R. 3971.

[15] *Petereit v. Babcock International Ltd.* [1990] 1 W.L.R. 350. The inter-relationship of the powers conferred on the court by Arts. 38 and 39 was considered in *William Grant & Sons International Ltd. v. Marie-Brizard Espana S.A.*, 1998 S.C. 536, and various questions referred to the European Court. The reference was subsequently withdrawn. See also *post*, para. 14–220.

[16] Case 43/77 [1977] E.C.R. 2175, applied in *Interdesco S.A. v. Nullifire Ltd.* [1992] 1 Lloyd's Rep. 180 (*recours en révision* in France not an ordinary appeal; stay refused).

actual decision whose enforcement is sought constitutes such a development. Consequently, any appeal which might be dependent on events which were unforeseeable at the date of the original judgment or upon action taken by persons who were extraneous to the judgment would not be an "ordinary appeal." Thus an application for a re-trial after new evidence had come to light or an application for a re-hearing would not be an "ordinary appeal." Article 38(2) provides that where the judgment is given in the United Kingdom or the Republic of Ireland any form of appeal available under their law shall be treated as an ordinary appeal for the purposes of Article 38(1). The special provisions relating to the United Kingdom and Ireland apply only to the enforcement of their judgments in other Contracting States. Therefore the English court may still be required to consider whether an ordinary appeal is pending in another Contracting State in order to decide whether to grant a stay of enforcement proceedings.

No review of substance. Article 29 provides that "under no circumstances **14–199** may a foreign judgment be reviewed as to its substance."[17] The grounds for non-recognition or non-enforcement of judgments within the scope of the Conventions are very limited. The English court has no right, except within very confined limits, to investigate the jurisdiction of the court which gave the judgment. There are grounds, such as public policy or lack of notice, which bear some resemblance to the rules at common law and under the 1920 and 1933 Acts.[18]

It has not been finally determined whether the court in which recognition or **14–200** enforcement is sought would be precluded from deciding for itself whether the judgment fell within the scope of the Conventions (that is, was given in a civil or commercial matter and was not otherwise excluded from the scope of the Conventions), but it is submitted that it must have this right and duty.[19] Article 29 does not cover the point, for though it precludes jurisdictional review for judgments which are within the scope of the Convention, it does not apply to the distinct question whether a judgment is within the Convention (and, as such, subject to Article 29). The English court must be free to decide this question for itself, not being bound to accept the view of the adjudicating court upon whether the case fell within the scope of the Convention. If the judgment is outside the scope of the relevant Convention, recognition and enforcement may be sought under the common law or the 1933 Act.

Jurisdiction of the foreign court. The jurisdiction of the foreign court **14–201** may only be investigated by the English court if the case falls within Sections 3 (insurance), 4 (consumer contracts) or 5 (exclusive jurisdiction) of Title II of each Convention, but even in those cases the English court is bound by the

---

[17] But a court must be able to review the substance to the extent necessary to determine whether Art. 27 requires that the judgment be not recognised: *cf.* Case C–78/95 *Hendrickman v. Magenta Druck & Verlag GmbH* [1996] E.C.R. I–4943.

[18] See *ante*, paras. 14R–141 *et seq.* and *post*, paras. 14–204 *et seq.*

[19] *Cf.* Case 29/76 *LTU GmbH v. Eurocontrol* [1976] E.C.R. 1541; Case 133/78 *Gourdain v. Nadler* [1979] E.C.R. 733; and Case C–172/91 *Sonntag v. Waidmann* [1993] E.C.R. I–1963, where the court in which recognition was sought apparently undertook this inquiry for itself.

findings of fact on which the foreign court based its judgment.[20] In addition, if the order of which recognition is sought is one where the court which made it purported to base, or may have based, its jurisdiction on Article 24 of the Convention, the court asked to enforce the order is obliged to ascertain for itself whether the order is of the type which is authorised by Article 24.[21]

14–202   Because the English court cannot investigate the jurisdiction of the foreign court, it is no objection to enforcement that the foreign court took jurisdiction wrongly, *e.g.* where it is alleged that the parties had agreed to the exclusive jurisdiction of the English court or that the defendant had not voluntarily appeared before the foreign court.[22] These questions must be raised at the outset of proceedings before the foreign court and cannot be re-opened in England. It is for the court in which the proceedings are begun to rule on whether another court has exclusive jurisdiction by virtue of an agreement under Article 17.[23] If the foreign court decides that the agreement is invalid or inoperative, or for any other reason that the alleged jurisdiction agreement is inapplicable and that it has jurisdiction, then any resulting judgment will be enforceable in the United Kingdom. This is so notwithstanding the terms of section 32 of the 1982 Act (which would otherwise entitle the United Kingdom court to disregard a foreign judgment given in disregard of a jurisdiction agreement) since that section is expressly subject to the Conventions.[24]

14–203   Where the defendant has appeared to protest the jurisdiction of the court of another Contracting State, Article 18 provides that the appearance is not a submission. If the foreign court holds that it has jurisdiction under the relevant Convention (*i.e.* the defendant loses on the question of jurisdiction) and the defendant then contests the proceedings, a resulting judgment will be enforceable in England because the foreign court found that it had jurisdiction under the Convention and the defendant submitted to its jurisdiction; if, however, the defendant takes no further steps in the proceedings and the foreign court enters a judgment in default of defence, it should only do so if it finds that it has jurisdiction under the Convention[25] and should not do so merely on the basis of the appearance to contest the jurisdiction; but if it finds it has jurisdiction the resulting judgment will be enforceable in England. There will be no room for refusal to enforce the judgment on the basis of section 33 of

---

[20] Art. 28. For examples see German Federal Supreme Court, 1979, in *Digest* I–28–B3 (insurance); *Tonnoir v. Vanherf S.A.*, Ct.App. Douai, 1989 in 1991 *Clunet* 161 (consumer contract). The court may also investigate the jurisdiction of the foreign court over a defendant domiciled or habitually resident in a non-Contracting State with which there is a Treaty under Art. 59; see *post*, para. 14–204; and it may also do so if the judgment is to be recognised under the transitional provisions of Art. 54: Case C–163/95 *Von Horn v. Cinnamond* [1997] E.C.R. I–5451; [1998] Q.B. 214.

[21] *Cf.* Case C–99/96 *Mietz v. Intership Yachting Sneek B.V.* [1999] I.L.Pr. 541.

[22] Or that the foreign court misapplied the *lis alibi pendens* provisions of Art. 21: *cf. Société Brasserie du Pêcheur v. Kreissparkasse Main-Spessart* [1997] I.L.Pr. 173 (French Cour de Cassation, 1996).

[23] See generally Case C–351/89 *Overseas Union Insurance Ltd. v. New Hampshire Insurance Co.* [1991] E.C.R. I–3317; [1992] Q.B. 434. But if the English court is second seised, and concludes that the court first seised has accepted (or may accept) jurisdiction in breach of a jurisdiction agreement, it may restrain the plaintiff in those foreign proceedings by injunction: see *ante*, Rule 32.

[24] On 1982 Act, s.32, see *ante*, Rule 37; for further discussion of s.32 in this context, see *ante*, paras. 14–187 *et seq.*

[25] Art. 20.

the 1982 Act on the theory that the defendant submitted only for the purpose of contesting the jurisdiction.[26]

Grounds for refusal to recognise or enforce. The other grounds for non-recognition and non-enforcement are set out in Articles 27 and 28.[27] In addition, the effect of Article 28(1) is that the English court does not have to recognise or enforce a judgment of a Contracting State to the extent that it conflicts with an obligation of the United Kingdom assumed *vis-à-vis* a third state not to recognise "exorbitant" judgments given against domiciliaries or residents of that State.[28]   14–204

Public policy. The first ground is that the foreign judgment is contrary to public policy (*"contraire à l'ordre public"*) in the State where its recognition or enforcement is sought. The public policy exception is to operate only in exceptional circumstances,[29] and recourse to it is inappropriate when the issue must be resolved on the basis of another provision of Article 27,[30] such as Article 27(2)[31] or Article 27(3).[32] It is plain that a mere difference between the substantive law (or the rules of private international law[33]) of the original court and that of the court in which enforcement is sought is not sufficient to justify non-recognition or non-enforcement. In many countries, including England, a default judgment does not contain reasons, and the mere fact that a foreign judgment does not contain reasons should be insufficient for public policy to be invoked to deny recognition. But the French courts will not recognise a default judgment from another Contracting State if that judgment does not give reasons.[34] It was on the basis of evidence of a similar practice in other Contracting States that the Commercial Court[35] in effect conducted a   14–205

---

[26] s.33 (on which see *ante*, para. 14–064) is not intended to affect enforcement under the Convention: s.33(2).

[27] Other grounds not expressly mentioned include: (a) the judgment has been satisfied; (b) the judgment is not within the scope of the Convention; (c) the judgment is not enforceable in the State of the original court: see Jenard, p. 50; Schlosser, para. 220.

[28] Under Art. 59. See *ante*, para. 14–184. In addition, the combined effect of Arts. 28(2) and 54B(3) of the Lugano Convention is that an EFTA Member State court may refuse recognition or enforcement of a judgment delivered by a court in an E.C. Member State if the grounds on which the latter court has based its jurisdiction are not provided for in the Lugano Convention and if recognition or enforcement is being sought against a party domiciled in an EFTA Contracting State. This will rarely arise, because the 1968 Convention and the Lugano Conventions are almost identical: see Jenard-Möller, p. 68. See also Lugano Convention, Art. 57(4).

[29] Jenard, p. 44; Case 145/86 *Hoffmann v. Krieg* [1988] E.C.R. 645, 668; Case C–78/95 *Hendrickman v. Magenta Druck & Verlag GmbH* [1996] E.C.R. I–4943; *cf. Klopp v. Holder*, Cour de cassation, France, 1984, in 1985 *Rev. Crit.* 131, note Mezger; *Hupprichs v. Dorthu*, Supreme Court, Netherlands, 1986 in [1990] I.L. Pr. 180. Contrast *Vanclef v. Soc. TTI*, Cour de cassation, France, in 1979 *Clunet* 380, note Holleaux.

[30] Case C–78/95 *Hendrikman v. Magenta Druck & Verlag GmbH* [1996] E.C.R. I–4943, 4968, citing Jenard, p. 44. Proposed revisions to the Conventions (*ante*, para. 11–011) add the word "manifestly".

[31] *Ibid.*, *infra*, para. 14–208.

[32] Case 145/86 *Hoffmann v. Krieg* [1988] E.C.R. 645, *infra*, para. 14–214.

[33] Except for the special case in Art. 27(4), *post*, para. 14–217; *cf.* Case C–7/98 *Krombach v. Bamberski* (pending; relevance of nationality as a basis for jurisdiction over a criminal action in the course of which civil damages were claimed).

[34] *Sarl Polypetrol v. Soc. Gen. Routière* [1993] I.L.Pr. 107 (Cour de Cassation, 1991); *Soc. Transports Intenationaux Dehbashi v. Gerling* [1996] I.L.Pr. 104 (Cour d'App., Poitiers, 1991).

[35] Acting under the inherent jurisdiction.

trial (in the absence of the defendant) before giving judgment against a defendant who had not acknowledged service, so as to ensure that the judgment creditor would not be impeded in enforcing the judgment in other Contracting States.[36] Ultimately it is for the English court to apply its own rules of public policy to foreign judgments within the scope of the Conventions, subject to a possible check by the European Court on abuse.[37]

14-206   In England fraud is a ground for refusal of recognition or enforcement of a foreign judgment, and in this context fraud has a very wide meaning.[38] In civil law countries fraud is not a separate reason for non-recognition, and the Conventions do not contain a special provision for fraud. But in civil law countries a judgment procured by fraud may be refused recognition on grounds of public policy, and this is reflected in the United Kingdom bilateral treaties with France and Germany. Under the Conventions it is likely that the procurement of a judgment by fraud (at least where it is no longer possible to raise it in the court of origin[39]) may be held to offend against the public policy of the court in which enforcement is sought.[40] In *Interdesco S.A. v. Nullifire Ltd.*[41] it was held that the English court would not refuse enforcement of a French judgment on the ground of alleged fraud, even if there were newly discovered evidence, if the judgment debtor had a remedy in the French courts. That was because the public policy ground of recognition ought to operate only in exceptional circumstances,[42] and the court in the State in which enforcement was sought should always consider whether the judgment debtor could seek a remedy in the foreign court.[43]

14-207   Article 28 expressly provides that public policy cannot be used to re-open the question of jurisdiction of the original court. This would prevent, for example, an English court from invoking public policy in order to refuse to recognise a French judgment based on Article 14 of the Civil Code, in a case where the plaintiff was French, the defendant was domiciled in a non-Contracting State and the case had nothing to do with France.[44] But if the judgment has been obtained by the claimant in disobedience of an injunction ordering him not to institute or proceed with the foreign action, it will be contrary to public policy for the judgment to be recognised in England.[45]

14-208   **Right to defend.** Article 27(2), which requires non-recognition or non-enforcement, applies if the following conditions are met: (1) the judgment is

---

[36] *Berliner Bank v. Karageorgis* [1996] 1 Lloyd's Rep. 426.
[37] *Cf.* in the context of the EC Treaty, *Henn and Darby v. D.P.P.* [1981] A.C. 850; Case 34/79 *R. v. Henn* [1979] E.C.R. 3795.
[38] *Ante*, para. 14–129.
[39] See Schlosser, para. 192. *Cf. Artic Fish Sales Co. Ltd. v. Adam* (No. 2), 1996 S.L.T. 970.
[40] *Cf. ante*, para. 14–135 and *Kendall v. Kendall* [1977] Fam. 208 (foreign divorce obtained by fraud refused recognition on grounds of public policy).
[41] [1992] 1 Lloyd's Rep. 180; *Société d'Informatique Service Réalisation Organisation v. Ampersand Software B.V.* [1994] I.L.Pr. 55(C.A.).
[42] Jenard, p. 44; *cf.* Case C–78/95 *Hendrickman v. Magenta Druck & Verlag GmbH* [1996] E.C.R. I–4943.
[43] Schlosser, para. 192.
[44] *Cf.* Case C–7/98 *Krombach v. Bamberski* (pending; relevance on grounds of public policy of nationality of defendant as jurisdictional basis for criminal proceedings in which order for compensation was made). For a suggestion that a judgment given in breach of an agreement to arbitrate may be denied recognition on grounds of public policy, see *Phillip Alexander Securities & Futures Ltd. v. Bamberger* [1997] I.L.Pr. 73, 100–102, affd. without reference to this point, *ibid.* p. 104 (C.A.), and *ante*, paras. 14–187 *et seq.*
[45] *Phillip Alexander Securities & Futures Ltd. v. Bamberger* [1997] I.L.Pr. 73, affd. *ibid.* 104 (C.A.); *cf. Fakih Bros. v. A.P. Moller (Copenhagen) Ltd.* [1994] 1 Lloyd's Rep. 103.

in default of appearance, and either (2) the defendant was not duly served with the document instituting the proceedings (or an equivalent document), or (3) the defendant was not served in sufficient time to arrange for his defence. The purpose of Article 27(2) (which is particularly important in relation to default judgments entered following substituted service on a defendant) is to safeguard the interests of the defendant and to ensure that he has sufficient time to defend himself.[46]

According to the text of Article 27(2), it applies only to judgments in **14–209** default of appearance, but this expression has been held to have an autonomous meaning, and not to be defined by reference to the law of the adjudicating court. In *Hendrickman v. Magenta Druck & Verlag GmbH*[47] a German court gave judgment against a defendant in circumstances where a legal representative purported to be authorised to represent the defendant but where, according to the defendant, no such authorisation had been given.[48] As a matter of German law the judgment was not entered in default of appearance, but the European Court accepted that the judgment was to be seen as one in default of appearance, for the defendant had been "quite powerless to defend himself" and was on that account to be regarded as a defendant in default of appearance. It is unlikely that the consequent extension of the scope of Article 27(2) will be wide, but in some circumstances the argument that a defendant lacked a proper opportunity to be heard may now be accommodated under Article 27(2), whether or not the judgment was technically in default of appearance.

A judgment in default of appearance may retain this character even if the **14–210** defendant later seeks, unsuccessfully, to set it aside.[49] The availability of a legal remedy after the making of the order is not equivalent to having the right to be heard before the order is made, and is not therefore an adequate substitute; and the judgment will remain as one given in default of appearance.

Article 27(2) applies whether or not the defendant is domiciled or resident in the State of the court of origin.[50]

The court in which enforcement of a default judgment is sought must **14–211** consider whether service was duly effected, and whether, following service, the defendant had sufficient time to arrange for his defence.[51] It seems that the English court may re-open and consider for itself whether service was effected in accordance with the law of the court of origin, provided that the court of origin has not been seised of this question in adversary proceedings.[52] If

---

[46] Case 166/80 *Klomps v. Michel* [1981] E.C.R. 1593, 1605; Case 228/81 *Pendy Plastic Products v. Pluspunkt* [1982] E.C.R. 2723.

[47] Case C–78/95 [1996] E.C.R. I–4943.

[48] This will be a matter for the recognising court to determine for itself: see p. 4967.

[49] Case C–123/91 *Minalmet GmbH v. Brandeis Ltd.* [1992] E.C.R. I–5661; *Hendrickman v. Magenta Druck & Verlag GmbH* [1996] E.C.R. I–4943.

[50] Case 49/84 *Debaecker and Plouvier v. Bouwman* [1985] E.C.R. 1779; *cf.* Case 166/80 *Klomps v. Michel* [1981] E.C.R. at p. 1621, *per* Reischl A.-G.

[51] Case 166/80 *Klomps v. Michel* [1981] E.C.R. 1593, applied in Case 228/81 *Pendy Plastic Products v. Pluspunkt* [1982] E.C.R. 2733. Both conditions must be fulfilled: Case C–305/88 *Isabelle Lancray S.A. v. Peters und Sickert KG* [1990] E.C.R. I–2725; Case C–123/91 *Minalmet GmbH v. Brandeis Ltd.* [1992] E.C.R. I–5661. See also *Artic Fish Sales Co. Ltd. v. Adam (No. 2)*, 1996 S.L.T. 970; *Selco Ltd. v. Mercier*, 1996 S.L.T. 1247. Proposed revisions to the Conventions (*ante*, para. 11–011) omit the reference to "duly served" and will reverse the effect of these decisions.

[52] *Ibid.* See also Case 49/84 *Debaecker and Plouvier v. Bouwman* [1985] E.C.R. 1779. On service under the Hague Convention, see *Noirhomme v. Walklate* [1992] 1 Lloyd's Rep. 427.

service was not made in accordance with that law, it was not duly made, and it is not open to an English court to purport to cure by reference to its own procedural law, or to overlook, the defect in service.[53] Even if the defendant is well aware that there has been purported service, but it had not been *duly* made, Article 27 (2) still applies to deny recognition to the judgment. But if the defect in service may be, and has been, cured according to the law of the court of origin, service will be treated as duly made.[54]

14–212   The question whether service was effected in sufficient time is a question of fact, which is not to be determined on the basis of the law of the court of origin or of English law as the law of the court in which enforcement is sought. Thus the fact that service was properly effected under the law of the court of origin does not preclude re-examination of whether it was effected in sufficient time.[55] As a general rule the court in which enforcement is sought may confine its examination to ascertaining whether the period reckoned from the date on which service was duly effected allowed the defendant sufficient time to arrange for his defence. Nevertheless the court must consider whether, in the particular case, there are exceptional circumstances which warrant the conclusion that although service was duly effected, it was, however, inadequate for the purpose of enabling the defendant to take steps to arrange for his defence (because it did not in fact come to his notice until some time later) and accordingly could not cause the time stipulated by Article 27(2) to begin to run. In considering whether it is confronted with such a case, the English court may take account of all the circumstances (including those occurring after service is effected[56]) such as the means employed for effecting service, the relations between the claimant and the defendant or the nature of the steps which had to be taken in order to prevent judgment from being given in default. If, for example, the dispute concerns commercial relations and if the document which instituted the proceedings was served at an address at which the defendant carries on his business activities, the mere fact that the defendant was absent at the time of service should not normally prevent him from arranging his defence, especially if the action necessary to avoid a judgment in default may be taken informally and by a representative.

14–213   A question which arose in *Klomps v. Michel*[57] and which has considerable practical importance with regard to certain forms of judgment was whether a *Zahlungsbefehl*, or order to pay, under German law was the document instituting the proceedings for the purposes of enforcement. The European Court ruled that a measure such as the order for payment in German law, service of which on the defendant enables the plaintiff, where no objection to the order is made, to obtain an enforceable decision was to be understood as being covered by the words "the document which instituted the proceedings." The enforcement order, issued following service of an order for payment and

---

[53] Case C–305/89 *Isabelle Lancray S.A. v. Peters & Sickert K.G.* [1990] E.C.R. I–2725. Breaches of the law of the court of origin other than those relating to due service may not be relied on to impugn the quality or effectiveness of service: Case C–474/93 *Hengst Import B.V. v. Campese* [1995] E.C.R. I–2113.

[54] Case C–123/91 *Minalmet GmbH v. Brandeis Ltd.* [1992] E.C.R. I–5661.

[55] Case 49/84 *Debaecker and Plouvier v. Bouwman, supra.*

[56] For a list of possible circumstances see Verloren van Theemat A.–G. in Case 49/84, *supra*; see also *Re A Belgian Default Judgment* [1992] I.L.Pr. 528 (German Fed.Sup.Ct. 1991).

[57] Case 166/80 [1981] E.C.R. 1593; in Case C–474/93 *Hengst Import B.V. v. Campese* [1995] E.C.R. I–2113 it was held that the Italian *decreto ingiuntivo*, together with the application instituting the proceedings, was "the document which instituted the proceedings".

which is, in itself, enforceable under the Convention, is not the relevant document.

Incompatibility with a judgment already given in the State in which recognition is sought. Article 27(3) provides that a judgment[58] irreconcilable with a judgment given[59] in a dispute between the same parties in the State in which recognition is sought shall not be recognised. Its practical importance will be limited by Articles 21 to 23, which in substance give priority to the court first seised.[60] The second court seised must give up its jurisdiction or stay its proceedings, and must recognise the judgment of the first court under Article 26. It is not necessary under Article 22 for the same cause of action to be involved. But where (for whatever reason) there are irreconcilable judgments then the English court may refuse to recognise or enforce the foreign judgment even if it was rendered before the relevant English judgment, and even if the English judgment is outside the scope of the relevant Convention.[61] **14–214**

Judgments are irreconcilable when they entail consequences which are mutually exclusive.[62] A judgment awarding damages for breach of contract would be irreconcilable with one declaring that the contract had been rescinded; and a declaration of non-liability of one party to the other may[63] be irreconcilable with a judgment awarding damages. But a judgment awarding an unpaid seller the price would not be irreconcilable with a judgment awarding damages to the buyer for breach of warranty. **14–215**

If an English court has granted an injunction ordering the plaintiff in proceedings in the courts of another Contracting State not to continue with the action, but the plaintiff is defiant and obtains judgment, recognition of the judgment may be refused on grounds of public policy.[64] It is not clear whether it would also be permissible to refuse recognition under Article 27(3). As the injunction is formally an order made in proceedings not involving an adjudication on the merits of the underlying claim, there is no formal irreconcilability between the two judgments. Though a judgment on the merits in Contracting State X, and an order that the plaintiff not obtain that judgment, appear to be mutually irreconcilable in the sense that the one will not be enforced in the face of the other, the reason for the unenforceability will lie in the behaviour of the plaintiff in the foreign proceedings, not in the matters which have become *res judicata* by the two judgments. It is therefore suggested that Article 27(3) will not apply in such a case. But in the light of Article 27(1), however, the issue is not likely to arise in this context.[65] **14–216**

Preliminary questions as to status. Article 27(4) provides that a judgment shall not be recognised if the original court, in order to arrive at its judgment, **14–217**

---

[58] The rule applies to judgments, but not to authentic instruments or to settlements approved in the course of judicial proceedings: Case C–414/92 *Solo Kleinmotoren GmbH v. Boch* [1994] E.C.R. I–2237; see also Arts. 50, 51.

[59] If there are proceedings in England but no judgment which has yet been given, Art. 27(3) has no application: *Landhurst Leasing plc v. Marcq* [1998] I.L.Pr. 822 (C.A.).

[60] *Ante*, Rule 31(3).

[61] Case 145/86 *Hoffmann v. Krieg* [1988] E.C.R. 645.

[62] Case 145/86 *Hoffmann v. Krieg* [1988] E.C.R. 645; *Macaulay v. Macaulay* [1991] 1 W.L.R. 179.

[63] It will depend on the breadth or basis of the declaration and its compatibility with the basis for the damages award.

[64] Under Art. 27(1), *ante*, para. 14–205.

[65] But it is of importance in relation to Arts. 21 and 22; see *ante*, para. 12–039.

has decided a preliminary question concerning the status of legal capacity of natural persons, rights in property arising out of a matrimonial relationship, wills or succession in a way that conflicts with a rule of the private international law of the court in which recognition or enforcement is sought, unless the same result would have been reached by the application of the rules of private international law of the latter. In several systems application by the court of origin of a rule of private international law different from that of the state addressed is a ground for non-recognition. This is a very limited example of that practice; it will mainly be relevant in England in maintenance proceedings.[66]

14–218   **Conflicts with judgments given in non-Contracting States which qualify for recognition.** Article 27(5) of the 1968 Convention, as amended by the 1978 Accession Convention, and of the Lugano Convention provide that a judgment shall not be recognised if it is irreconcilable with an earlier judgment given in a non-Contracting State[67] involving the same cause of action and between the same parties, provided that this latter judgment fulfils the conditions necessary for its recognition in the State addressed. It applies, for example, in the case of a decision dismissing an action against a person domiciled in a Contracting State which is given in non-Contracting State A; Contracting State B is obliged to recognise the judgment under a bilateral convention; the plaintiff brings fresh proceeding in another Contracting State, C, which is not obliged to recognise judgments given in a non-Contracting State. A judgment given in a non-Contracting State takes priority where it has to be recognised not only by virtue of a multilateral or bilateral Convention, but also at common law.

14–219   **Procedure.** The combined effect of Article 31[68] of the Conventions and of section 4 of the 1982 Act is that enforcement of a judgment under the Conventions is by way of registration. The judgment creditor cannot bring an action on the original cause of action.[69] Nor, it seems, can he proceed by way of enforcement at common law; this follows from the decision in *De Wolf v. Cox*[70] where it was held that it would be incompatible with the enforcement provisions of the 1968 Convention to allow an action on the original cause of action, even though it might be cheaper to obtain summary judgment on the original cause of action than to enforce a foreign judgment. Interest is payable on a registered judgment debt at the rate applicable under the law of the court of origin, not only for the period prior to registration[71] but also until satisfaction of the judgment.[72] It is implicit in the Convention system that judgments should be registered in their original currency. The procedure for registration

---

[66] *Post*, paras. 18–219 *et seq*. Proposed revisions to the Conventions (*ante*, para. 11–011) include the deletion of Art. 27(4).

[67] For the position where there are conflicting judgments of two Contracting States (other than the State in which enforcement or recognition is sought), which is not covered by Art. 27(3) or (5), see Jenard-Möller, p. 79; *cf. Showlag v. Mansour* [1995] 1 A.C. 431 (P.C.); *ante*, para. 14–028.

[68] Art. 31 of the 1968 Convention was amended by the 1989 Accession Convention to take account of a minor adjustment effected in the Lugano Convention, Art. 31.

[69] Case 42/76 *De Wolf v. Cox* [1976] E.C.R. 1759; 1982 Act, s.34.

[70] *Supra*.

[71] As under the 1933 Act.

[72] 1982 Act, s.7.

is regulated by the Civil Procedure Rules.[73] Registration of the judgment is made on an *ex parte* application, and the judgment debtor is notified only after registration is effected.[74]

The judgment debtor may appeal[75] to a judge against registration of the   **14–220**
judgment. Before the time for appealing has expired or before the appeal has been determined, execution of the judgment is not possible,[76] although protective measures may be taken.[77] An applicant for registration has a similar right of appeal against refusal to register.[78] There is a further right of appeal on a point of law,[79] to the Court of Appeal or the House of Lords.[80]

Recognition. Article 26 distinguishes between recognition and enforce-   **14–221**
ment and provides that: (a) a judgment given in a Contracting State shall be recognised in the other Contracting States without any special procedure being required.[81] This was designed to abolish special procedures for recognition existing in some countries, such as Italy; (b) any interested party who raises the recognition of a judgment as the principal issue in a dispute may apply for a decision that the judgment be recognised.[82] This is designed to deal with a situation where a person who is not a party to the action in which a judgment was given wishes to raise the judgment as a defence, *e.g.* a bank

---

[73] Ord. 71, rr. 25–34 (CPR, Sched. 1); see also 1982 Act, s.11 (proof of judgments of courts of other Contracting States). On Art. 33(2) (put into effect by Ord. 71, r. 28(*c*)) see Case 198/85 *Carron v. Germany* [1986] E.C.R. 2437; *Rhatigan v. Textiles Confecciones Europeas S.A.* [1990] I.L.R.M. 825.

[74] Art. 35; Ord. 71, r. 32(1). For the documents required to make the application, see Arts. 46–49. For defects in the documents, and the power of the recognising court to cure the defect, see Case C–275/94 *Van der Linden v. BFE* [1996] E.C.R. I–1393. For failure to make proper service, see *Barnaby (London) Ltd. v. Mullen* [1997] 2 I.L.R.M. 341 (Sup.Ct.).

[75] See Arts. 36, 37; Ord. 71, r. 33. Only the judgment debtor has standing: see Case 148/84 *Deutsche Genossenschaftsbank v. Brasserie du Pêcheur S.A.* [1985] E.C.R. 1981; Case C–172/91 *Sonntag v. Waidmann* [1993] E.C.R. I–1963. Arts. 36 and 37 are concerned with appeals against the authorisation of enforcement, and do not authorise an appeal from a decision refusing a stay of enforcement under Art. 38: Case C–183/90 *Van Dalfsen v. Van Loon* [1991] E.C.R. I–4743; see also Case 258/83 *Brennero SAS v. Wendel GmbH* [1984] E.C.R. 3971; Case C–432/93 *Société d'Informatique Service Réalisation Organisation v. Ampersand Software B.V.* [1995] E.C.R. I–2269.

[76] Art. 39; Ord. 71, r. 34(1).

[77] Art. 39(2); Ord. 71, r. 34(4). These protective measures depend on national procedural law, subject to the overriding principle of Art. 39, that the judgment creditor has a means of preventing the judgment debtor from disposing of his property so as to frustrate enforcement: Case 119/84 *Capelloni v. Pelkmans* [1985] E.C.R. 3147 (where it was also held that national law cannot require a separate judicial proceeding for protective measures; or require them to be taken before the appeal procedure under Art. 36 is exhausted; or make an order for protective measures subject to a confirmatory hearing). See also *Elwyn (Cottons) Ltd. v. Pearle Designs Ltd.* [1989] I.R. 9 (further proceedings: *Elwyn (Cottons) Ltd. v. Master of the High Court* [1989] I.R. 14). See generally Lipstein (1987) 36 I.C.L.Q. 873. *Cf.* the position under Art. 38(4) (enforcement pending appeal in foreign court): Case 258/83 *Brennero SAS v. Wendel GmbH* [1984] E.C.R. 3971; *Petereit v. Babcock International Ltd.* [1990] 1 W.L.R. 350.

[78] Art. 40. Notice of the appeal must be given to the judgment debtor; R.S.C., Ord. 71, r. 33 and see also Case 178/83 *Firma P. v. Firma K.* [1984] E.C.R. 3033.

[79] Arts. 37, 40. This is the exclusive remedy: Case 145/86 *Hoffmann v. Krieg* [1988] E.C.R. 645.

[80] 1982 Act, s.6. For references to the European Court on the interpretation of the 1968 Convention see *ante*, paras. 11–043 *et seq.*

[81] Recognition involves according to the judgment the same effects in the State in which enforcement is sought as it does in the State in which the judgment was given: Case 145/86 *Hoffmann v. Krieg* [1988] E.C.R. 645. See also *Berkeley Administration Inc. v. McClelland* [1995] I.L.Pr. 201 (C.A.).

[82] See, Ord. 71, r. 35 for the procedure.

in State B presented with a bill of exchange which has already been declared invalid in State A. In this case the jurisdiction of the court which gave the original judgment does not have to be verified by the court of the State in which the recognition is sought unless the matter in question falls within the scope of provisions relating to insurance, consumer contracts, or exclusive jurisdiction; (c) if the outcome of the proceedings in a court of a Contracting State depends on the determination of an incidental question of recognition that court shall have jurisdiction over the question.

14–222   The object of Article 26 is to confer on judgments the authority and effectiveness accorded to them in the State in which they were given,[83] and accordingly a foreign judgment which is to be recognised under Article 26 must in principle have the same effect in the State in which recognition is sought as it does in the State in which it is given.[84] The grounds for non-recognition are the same as those for refusal to enforce.[85] The effect of Article 26 is that the English court will have to recognise judgments of Contracting States within the scope of the Conventions and will have very limited power to examine the jurisdiction of the foreign court.[86] Neither the Conventions nor the Official Reports give an answer to the difficult question of the scope of the estoppel which arises when the foreign judgment dismisses a case on grounds which are regarded in some countries as procedural and in others as substantive.[87]

14–223   **Authentic instruments and court-approved settlements.** Title III of the 1968 Convention and the Lugano Convention deals with the recognition and enforcement of judgments. Though the Title III category is broad enough to include, and does encompass, judgments by consent,[88] it does not extend to certain other procedural measures, found under the law of certain other Contracting States, by which a dispute may be terminated. The recognition and enforcement of two such measures is dealt with in Title IV.

14–224   An authentic instrument is a document which has been formally drawn up or registered as such. It must be drawn up by a public official, usually a civil law notary.[89] Under the law of certain Contracting States, such as Germany, the instrument takes effect as an express, conclusive, and enforceable, statement of a party's indebtedness, but which is obtained without the institution of court proceedings. Authentic instruments may be enforced in another

---

[83] Jenard, p. 43.

[84] Case 145/86 *Hoffmann v. Krieg* [1988] E.C.R. 645, 666 (an enforcement case); *Boss Group Ltd. v. Boss France SA* [1997] 1 W.L.R. 351 (C.A.) (finding in provisional proceedings in France not binding).

[85] Art. 27.

[86] See, *e.g. The Atlantic Emperor (No. 2)* [1992] 1 Lloyd's Rep. 624 (C.A.) (judgment of Italian court that contract did not incorporate arbitration clause).

[87] See Schlosser, para. 191. This is not likely to arise frequently in practice since the Foreign Limitation Periods Act 1984, *ante*, para. 14–031.

[88] *Cf.* Case C–414/92 *Solo Kleinmotoren GmbH v. Boch* [1994] E.C.R. I–2237, at 2245, *per* Gulmann A.-G., drawing a distinction between this and a court-approved settlement.

[89] For examples, see German Code of Civil Procedure, Art. 794; *Office de Prévoyance v. Grand*, 1991 *Clunet* 162 (Cour d'App. Paris, 1990), *Tonon v. Office Cantonal de la Jeunesse de Tutlingen* [1995] I.L.Pr. 23 (French Cour de cassation, 1991). But if the law of the state in question does not require the participation of, and authentication by, a public official, the document drawn up will not be an authentic instrument for the purposes of the Conventions: Case C–260/97 *Unibank A/S v. Christensen*, June 17, 1999: promissory note formally drawn up and enforceable under Danish law not authentic instrument as authentication by public official, even though this was not required by Danish law for the instrument to be enforceable.

Contracting State in accordance with the procedures in Articles 31 *et seq.* of the Conventions; the application for enforcement may be refused only if enforcement of the instrument is contrary to the public policy of the State in which enforcement is sought.

A settlement which has been approved by a court in the course of proceed-   **14–225** ings is not regarded as a judgment within the scope of Title III, for it derives its authority from the parties' agreement, and not from the adjudication of a court; for this reason it does not enjoy the authority of *res judicata*.[90] But if it is enforceable in the State in which it was concluded it may be enforced under the same conditions as govern the enforcement of authentic instruments.

ILLUSTRATIONS

1. A, a Frenchman, obtains a judgment against X, an Englishman, for 100,000 francs in a   **14–226** French court. The judgment is registrable in England under Part I of the 1982 Act.

2. A obtains a final order from the French court ordering X to return a chattel to A. X brings the chattel to England. The order is registrable.

3. The facts are as in Illustration 2, except that the order is a provisional one pending trial of the merits in France. The provisional order is registrable.

4. A, a Frenchman, sues in France X, who is resident in New York, for 100,000 francs for breach of a contract to be performed in New York. X does not appear in the French court, which assumes jurisdiction on the basis of A's French nationality under Article 14 of the Civil Code. A obtains a default judgment. The judgment is registrable in England. The position would be different if the United Kingdom and the United States were to enter into a treaty requiring non-enforcement of judgments rendered by third states on the basis of exorbitant provisions such as Article 14 of the French Civil Code.[91]

5. A & Co., a German company, obtains an *ex parte* injunction in a German court against X   **14–227** & Co., an English company, which restrains X & Co. from various acts in relation to tapes made by a pop music group. The order is not registrable in England.[92]

6. A, a French public authority, obtains a default judgment in France against X, an Englishman who is not present or resident in France, and who has not submitted to the French jurisdiction. The judgment is registrable under Part I of the 1982 Act if the matter is a "civil or commercial matter" but not otherwise.[93]

7. A, a Frenchman, sues in France X, an Englishman, who is not resident in France, for breach of contract. X does not submit to the French jurisdiction. The French court assumes jurisdiction on the mistaken view that the contract was to be performed in France, and A obtains a default judgment. The judgment is registrable.

8. The facts are as in Illustration 7 except that X appears in the French proceedings to contest the jurisdiction but his objection fails and he takes no further part in the proceedings and judgment is entered in default of appearance. The judgment is registrable, not because of the appearance but because the French court has found that it has jurisdiction.

9. The facts are as in Illustration 7, except that service on X under French law is not effected.   **14–228** The judgment is not registrable.[94]

10. A, a Frenchman, obtains a judgment in France against X, an Englishman. X appeals in France. A is entitled to register the judgment under Part I of the 1982 Act, but the English court may stay enforcement pending the appeal.[95]

---

[90] An English judgment by consent, though not an adjudication, has the authority of *res judicata*: *Landhurst Leasing plc v. Marcq* [1998] I.L.Pr. 822 (C.A.). See *loc. cit.*, *supra*, n. 88, *per* Gulmann A.-G. Contrast the English "Tomlin order", whereby proceedings are stayed except for the purpose of putting into effect the terms of settlement scheduled to the order: that is not a judgment.

[91] Art. 59.

[92] *E.M.I. Records Ltd. v. Modern Music GmbH* [1992] Q.B. 115.

[93] Case 29/76 *LTU GmbH v. Eurocontrol* [1976] E.C.R. 1851.

[94] Art. 27(2).

[95] Art. 38.

11. A Frenchman obtains a judgment in France against X, a Frenchman with assets in England. X appeals to the judge in chambers against the registration. Pending the appeal, A cannot execute the judgment, but the English court may order X not to remove his assets from the jurisdiction.[96]

12. A & Co., a French company, obtain a judgment in France for damages to be assessed against X & Co., an English company. X & Co.'s appeal fails, and judgment is entered for 7 million francs. A & Co. register the judgment in England. X & Co. institute a special form of procedure before the Court of Appeal in Paris to set aside the judgment on the ground that it was obtained by fraud. X & Co. also seek to set aside the registration in England on the ground that recognition would be contrary to public policy. Registration is confirmed because X & Co. have a remedy in the French court, and no stay of enforcement can be ordered because the application to the Court of Appeal in Paris is not an "ordinary appeal" within the meaning of Article 30.[97]

14–229
13. A, the receiver of a German company, obtains a judgment in Germany against X & Co., an English company. X & Co. appeal against the judgment. A registers the judgment in England. The court stays execution conditionally on X & Co. providing security pending the outcome of the appeal in Germany.[98]

14. A, a Belgian, sues in Belgium X, an Englishman, who has left his residence without leaving a forwarding address. Substituted service pursuant to Belgian law is effected on X at a Belgian police station. Subsequently X informs A's lawyer of his new address, but service is not effected at the new address, and A obtains a judgment in default. In considering whether service was effected on X in sufficient time for him to arrange for his defence, the English court may take into account the fact that A was informed of X's new address, and also the fact that X contributed to the failure of the document originating the proceedings to reach him.[99]

15. The facts are as in Illustration 14, except that the substituted service was not in accordance with Belgian law. The judgment is not registrable.[1]

(4) Parts II and IV of the Civil Jurisdiction and Judgments Act 1982

14R–230
Rule 49—(1) A money judgment of a court in any part of the United Kingdom has, on a certificate being duly registered in a Superior Court of any other part of the United Kingdom, the same force and effect as a judgment of the court in which the certificate is registered, and proceedings for or with respect to its enforcement may be taken, as if the certificate had been a judgment originally given in the court in which the certificate is registered.[2]

(2) A non-money judgment of a court in any part of the United Kingdom has, on being duly registered in a Superior Court of any other part of the United Kingdom, the same force and effect as a judgment of the court in which it is registered, and proceedings for or with respect to its enforcement may be taken, as if it had been a judgment originally given in the court in which the judgment is registered.[3]

The term "Superior Court"[4] means in this Rule,

(a) as applied to England, the High Court of Justice in England;

(b) as applied to Northern Ireland, the High Court of Justice in Northern Ireland;

(c) as applied to Scotland, the Court of Session in Scotland.

---

[96] Art. 39.
[97] *Interdesco S.A. v. Nullifire Ltd.* [1992] 1 Lloyd's Rep. 180.
[98] *Petereit v. Babcock International Ltd.* [1990] 1 W.L.R. 350.
[99] Case 49/84 *Debaecker and Plouvier v. Bouwman* [1985] E.C.R. 1779.
[1] Case C–305/89 *Isabelle Lancray S.A. v. Peters und Sickert KG* [1990] E.C.R. I–2725.
[2] 1982 Act, s.18 and Sched. 6.
[3] 1982 Act, s.18 and Sched. 7.
[4] Scheds. 6 and 7, para. 5(2).

(3) A judgment from a territory in respect of which provision has been made for the recognition and enforcement of judgments on grounds corresponding to those of the 1968 Convention may be enforced or, as the case may be, recognised, according to the terms of that provision.[5]

COMMENT

Clauses (1)–(2) of the Rule. Until the 1982 Act came into force the enforcement of judgments of the courts of a part of the United Kingdom in other parts was regulated by the antiquated and limited procedure of the Judgments Extension Act 1868 and the Inferior Courts Judgments Extension Act 1882. The main defect of the dual system under the 1868 and 1882 Acts was that enforcement was limited to money judgments. An important difference between the 1868 Act and the 1920 and 1933 Acts was that, subject to one exception, under the 1868 Act the enforcing court was not entitled to investigate the jurisdiction of the original court and could not disregard its judgment on the ground that it lacked international jurisdiction. The exception was where a Scots judgments was founded on arrestment and entered in default. Under the 1882 Act there were stringent jurisdictional requirements. The 1982 Act makes the international jurisdiction of the original court irrelevant. If the judgment has been pronounced by a court in the United Kingdom, a court in another part of the United Kingdom cannot question the exercise of its jurisdiction. **14–231**

Section 18 applies the provisions of Schedules 6 and 7 to the enforcement in one part of the United Kingdom of money and non-money judgments given by a court in another part. Judgments are widely defined.[6] The extension of the enforcement system to non-money judgments is novel.[7] But it does not apply to interlocutory orders.[8] "Judgments on judgments" cannot be enforced,[9] at least where they are judgments registered under the statutory provisions for enforcement of foreign judgments, including the 1982 Act itself. So that if a French judgment is registered in Scotland under the 1982 Act, it will be the French judgment which the judgment creditor will have to register in England and not the Scottish registration. **14–232**

The procedure by way of registration is the exclusive procedure.[10] In the case of money judgments, the party who wishes to enforce applies for a certificate from the original court, and, in the case of non-money judgments, for a certified copy of the judgment. Once registered, the judgment of the original court has effect as a judgment of the court in which it is registered. A certificate (or certified copy) is not to be issued unless under the law of the part of the United Kingdom in which the judgment was given two conditions are fulfilled: first, either (i) the time for bringing an appeal against the judgment has expired, no such appeal having been brought within that time; **14–233**

---

[5] 1982 Act, s. 39.

[6] See s.18(2), (4) for a full list of the judgments to which it applies. See also Drug Trafficking Offences Act 1986, s.39(4).

[7] For the procedure in the High Court see Ord. 71, rr. 37 and 38, especially in the case of non-money judgments, the power of the court to direct the issue of a claim form: Ord. 71, r. 38(1).

[8] 1982 Act, s.18(5)(*d*).

[9] 1982 Act, s.18(7).

[10] 1982 Act, s.18(8). See *Clarke v. Fennoscandia Ltd.*, 1998 S.C.L.R. 568 (no injunction to restrain enforcement of English costs order).

or (ii) such an appeal having been brought within that time, that appeal has finally been disposed of; and, secondly, enforcement of the judgment is not for the time being stayed or suspended, and the time available for its enforcement has not expired. If the conditions are fulfilled, the officer of the original court issues a certificate, in the case of a money judgment, stating the sum or aggregate of sums (including any costs or expenses) payable under the money provisions contained in the judgment, the rate of interest, if any, payable thereon and the date or time from which any such interest began to accrue; and stating that the conditions concerning the absence of an appeal or enforce-ability of a judgment are satisfied. In the case of a non-money judgment he issues a certified copy of the judgment. Where a certificate (or certified copy of a judgment) has been issued any interested party may, within six months from the date of its issue, in the case of money judgments (there is no time limit for non-money judgments) apply to the proper officer of the Superior Court in any other part of the United Kingdom for the certificate (or judgment) to be registered. Where application is made to the proper officer, he registers the certificate in court. Where a certificate or judgment is registered the reasonable costs of obtaining the certificate and its registration are recover-able. In the case of money judgments, provision is made for interest from registration at the rate, if any, stated in the certificate.

14–234   The registering court may, if it is satisfied that any person against whom it sought to enforce the certificate is entitled and intends to apply under the law of the part of the United Kingdom in which the judgment was given for any remedy which would result in the setting aside or quashing of the judgment, stay proceedings for the enforcement of the certificate (or judgment). A certificate or registered judgment must be set aside by the registering court if it is satisfied that registration was contrary to the provisions of Schedule 6 or 7; and may set aside the registration if it is satisfied that the matter in dispute in the proceedings in which the judgment in question was given had pre-viously been the subject of a judgment by another court or tribunal having jurisdiction in the matter. But fraud is not a ground for setting registration aside.

14–235   **Clause (3) of the Rule.** Section 39 of the 1982 Act provides that provision may be made corresponding[11] to that in the 1968 Convention for the recogni-tion and enforcement of judgments from certain British territories, namely the Isle of Man, any of the Channel Islands, Gibraltar, and the Sovereign Base Areas of Akrotiri and Dhekelia. Provision has been made under the section for judgments from Gibraltar[12]; these will be treated for the purposes of English law[13] as if Gibraltar were a Contracting State to the 1968 Convention. Such a judgment may therefore be registered for enforcement under section 4 of the 1982 Act,[14] and the only permitted grounds of objection to the registration will be those set out in Rule 48.

---

[11] Modifications are permitted: s.39(1).
[12] S.I. 1997 No. 2602 (in force February 1, 1998). As a result of S.I. 1997 No. 2601, the 1920 Act will no longer apply to Gibraltar. Judgments from the Isle of Man, Jersey, and Guernsey are at present governed by the 1933 Act; those from Akrotiri and Dhekelia by the 1920 Act.
[13] This will have no effect in other Contracting States.
[14] It is not expressly so provided by the Order. But if Gibraltar is to be regarded as if Article 31 of the 1968 Convention applied to it, section 4(1) of the 1982 Act will mean that the judgment may be registered for enforcement.

(5) COMMUNITY JUDGMENTS

RULE 50—A Community judgment to which the Secretary of State has   14R–236
appended an order for enforcement must be registered in the High Court,
whereupon it has for all purposes of execution the same force and effect
as if it had been a judgment or order made by the High Court.[15]

COMMENT

The European Communities (Enforcement of Community Judgments) Order   **14–237**
1972 provides that a Community judgment[16] to which the Secretary of State
has appended an order for enforcement[17] shall, upon application duly made by
the person entitled to enforce it, be registered in the High Court.[18] A "Community judgment" means a judgment of the European Court of Justice or of
the Arbitration Committee of the European Atomic Energy Community, or a
decision of the Council or Commission of the European Communities imposing a pecuniary obligation on persons other than States, or a decision of the
High Authority of the European Coal and Steel Community which includes a
pecuniary obligation on undertakings.

If the judgment has been partly satisfied, the judgment is registered only for   **14–238**
the unpaid balance.[19] The effect of registration is that the judgment has for all
purposes of execution the same force and effect as if it had been a judgment
or order given or made by the High Court; and proceedings may be taken on
it and any sum payable under it carries interest accordingly.[20] The Order in
Council is not confined to judgments under which a sum of money is
payable.

An order of the European Court that the enforcement of a registered   **14–239**
Community judgment be suspended must be registered and has the same force
and effect as if the order had been made by the High Court staying the
execution of the judgment.[21] No steps to enforce the judgment can then be
taken while the order remains in force.

If a Euratom inspection order[22] is registered, the High Court may make   **14–240**
such order as it thinks fit against any person for the purpose of ensuring that
effect is given to the order.[23]

---

[15] European Communities (Enforcement of Community Judgments) Order, S.I. 1972 No. 1590, amended by Administration of Justice Act 1977, Sched. 5, Pt. I. See Ord. 71, rr. 15–24.

[16] Defined as any decision, judgment or order which is enforceable under Art. 187 or 192 of the E.E.C. Treaty (now Arts. 244 and 256 of the E.C. Treaty); Art. 18, 159 or 164 of the Euratom Treaty; Art. 44 or 92 of the E.C.S.C. Treaty; or Art. 82 of Regulation 40/94 of December 20, 1993 on the community trade mark: S.I. 1972 No. 1590, Art. 2(1) as amended by S.I. 1998 No. 1259.

[17] Defined as an order by or under the authority of the Secretary of State that the Community judgment to which it is appended is to be registered for enforcement in the United Kingdom: *ibid.*

[18] *Ibid.* Art. 3(1): or in the Court of Session or the High Court in Northern Ireland: *ibid.* Art. 2(1).

[19] *Ibid.* Art. 3(4).

[20] *Ibid.* Art. 4.

[21] *Ibid.* Art. 5.

[22] Defined as an order made by or in the exercise of the functions of the President of the European Court or by the Commission of the European Communities under Art. 81 of the Euratom Treaty: *ibid.* Art. 2(1).

[23] *Ibid.* Art. 6.

(6) Judgments Against the United Kingdom

14R–241   **Rule 51—A judgment given against the United Kingdom by a court in a State which is a party to the European Convention on State Immunity will be recognised in the United Kingdom, if it was given in proceedings in which the United Kingdom was not entitled to immunity by virtue of provisions corresponding to sections 2 to 11 of the State Immunity Act 1978 and if it is final in the sense that it is not subject to appeal or liable to be set aside.[24]**

> **Provided that no judgment will be recognised under this Rule if**
>
> **(a)   it would be manifestly contrary to public policy or if any party to the proceedings in which the judgment was given had no adequate opportunity to present his case[25]; or**
>
> **(b)   the judgment was given without proper notice having been given to the United Kingdom and the United Kingdom has not entered an appearance or applied to have the judgment set aside[26]; or**
>
> **(c)   prior proceedings between the same parties are pending in the United Kingdom or another State party to the Convention[27]; or**
>
> **(d)   the judgment is inconsistent with a prior judgment of a court in the United Kingdom or of a court in another State party to the Convention[28]; or**
>
> **(e)   the judgment is in respect of proceedings relating to an interest of the United Kingdom in movable or immovable property arising by way of succession, gift or *bona vacantia*, and either (i) the foreign court would not have had jurisdiction if it had applied rules of jurisdiction corresponding to those applicable to such matters in the United Kingdom; or (ii) the foreign court applied a law other than that indicated by the United Kingdom rules of private international law and would have reached a different conclusion if it had applied the law so indicated.[29]**

Comment

14–242   Sections 18 and 19 of the State Immunity Act 1978 are designed to give effect, in part, to Articles 20–22 of the European Convention on State Immunity of 1972,[30] which set out the circumstances in which a Contracting State is bound to give effect to a judgment given against it in another Contracting State in circumstances where it is not immune from the jurisdiction. The broad effect of sections 18 and 19 is to provide for *recognition* (but not enforcement[31]) of judgments given in other Contracting States against the United Kingdom in circumstances where a foreign government would not have been immune

---

[24] State Immunity Act 1978, s.18(1).

[25] s.19(1)(*a*).

[26] s.19(1)(*b*).

[27] s.19(2)(*a*).

[28] s.19(2)(*b*).

[29] s.19(3). There are no unified rules of jurisdiction and choice of law in these matters in the United Kingdom, but English and Scots law are similar.

[30] For Text see Cmnd. 7742. See Sinclair (1973) 22 I.C.L.Q. 254, 266–267, 273–276. A certificate of the Secretary of State is conclusive as to whether a State is party to the Convention: State Immunity Act 1978, s.21(*c*).

[31] Presumably an action on a relevant foreign judgment could be brought against the Crown as for a debt, although process of execution would not lie: Crown Proceedings Act 1947, ss.1, 25.

from similar proceedings in the United Kingdom.[32] Recognition may be refused on grounds of public policy, but only where it is manifestly contrary to public policy. Proviso (e) is concerned with judgments relating to interests in movable or immovable property arising by way of succession, gift or *bona vacantia*, and follows closely the wording of Article 20(3) of the Convention.

4. PROTECTION OF TRADING INTERESTS ACT 1980

RULE 52—No judgment given in a court of a country outside the United Kingdom will be enforced under any of Rules 35, 46 or 47 if it is   14R–243
    (a) a judgment for multiple damages, or
    (b) a judgment based on a provision or rule of law specified by the Secretary of State as concerned with the prohibition of restrictive trade practices.

COMMENT

This Rule is based upon section 5 of the Protection of Trading Interests Act 1980, which prohibits the enforcement under the common law, and under the 1920 and 1933 Acts,[33] of foreign judgments for multiple damages and other foreign judgments specified by statutory instrument as concerned with restrictive trade practices. It was enacted in order to counteract what was perceived by the United Kingdom to be an excessive exercise of jurisdiction by United States courts in anti-trust actions.[34] Similar legislation has been enacted in Australia, Canada, and South Africa.[35]   14–244

A judgment for multiple damages is defined as a judgment for an amount arrived at by doubling, trebling or otherwise multiplying a sum assessed as compensation for the loss or damage sustained by the judgment creditor.[36] The scope of judgments whose enforcement is prohibited may be extended by the Secretary of State to any judgment based on a provision or rule of law which appears to him to be concerned with the prohibition or regulation of agreements, arrangements or practices designed to restrain, distort or restrict competition in the carrying on of business of any description or to be otherwise concerned with the promotion of such competition.[37]   14–245

---

[32] See Exceptions to Rule 19, *ante*.

[33] See Ord. 71, r. 3(1)(*e*) (CPR, Sched. 1).

[34] The exercise of anti-trust jurisdiction by United States courts has given rise to misgivings in the United Kingdom for many years: see, *e.g.* *British Nylon Spinners Ltd. v. Imperial Chemical Industries* [1953] Ch. 19 (C.A.); *Re Westinghouse Uranium Contract Litigation M.D.L. Docket No. 235* [1978] A.C. 547; *cf. British Airways Board v. Laker Airways Ltd.* [1985] A.C. 58, 78; *Midland Bank plc v. Laker Airways Ltd.* [1986] Q.B. 689 (C.A.). See also Lowe (1981) 75 A.J.I.L. 257, *Extraterritorial Jurisdiction* (1983), pp. 176–192; Lowenfeld (1981) 75 A.J.I.L. 629; and generally Jennings (1957) 33 B.Y.I.L. 153; F. A. Mann, *Studies in International Law* (1973), pp. 82–94; Collins [1986] J.B.L. 372 and 542 (reprinted in Collins, *Essays*, Chap. 8).

[35] Foreign Proceedings (Excess of Jurisdiction) Act 1984 (Aus.); Foreign Extraterritorial Measures Act 1984 (Can.) (amended 1996 Statutes, Ch. 28); Protection of Businesses Act 1978 (S.A.).

[36] s.5(3).

[37] s.5(4). The power of the Secretary of State is exercisable by statutory instrument: s.5(5).

14–246   The judgments most likely to be affected by the Act are judgments in United States anti-trust actions,[38] but the Act applies to judgments of all overseas countries[39] whether rendered before or after the passage of the Act.[40] Judgments caught by section 5 are wholly unenforceable, and not merely as regards that part of the judgment which exceeds the damages actually suffered by the judgment creditor.

14–247   Section 6 of the Protection of Trading Interests Act 1980 goes further and gives British citizens, corporations incorporated in the United Kingdom, and persons carrying on business in the United Kingdom against whom multiple damages have been awarded the right to recover from persons in whose favour the judgment was rendered so much of the damages as exceeds the sum assessed by the foreign court as compensation for the loss or damage sustained. This section does not apply in favour of an individual who was ordinarily resident, or of a corporation which had its principal place of business, in the foreign country where the proceedings in which the judgment was given were instituted; nor does it apply to judgments concerned with activities exclusively concerned with a branch or establishment carried on by the defendant in the foreign proceedings in that country.[41] The section contains the unusual provision that proceedings under it may be brought notwithstanding that the plaintiff in the foreign proceedings is not within the jurisdiction of the United Kingdom court.[42] Permission to serve the proceedings is not required.[43]

14–248   The effect of section 6 is that where a United States corporation obtains a judgment for treble damages against an English company and is able to execute the judgment in the United States against the English company's assets there, the English company may sue in England to recover the punitive element. English proceedings in these circumstances will only be of assistance to the English company if either the United States corporation has assets in the United Kingdom (*e.g.* a branch or shares in a subsidiary) or in a country which will recognise the English judgment. The Australian, Canadian and South African legislation goes further. The Australian Foreign Proceedings (Exercise of Jurisdiction) Act 1984 provides[44] that any corporation which is related to the foreign plaintiff is liable to repay the relevant part of the judgment given in the foreign anti-trust proceedings. The Canadian Foreign Extraterritorial Measures Act 1984 provides[45] that the Canadian court which gives judgment for the recovery of damages paid under a foreign anti-trust judgment may order the seizure and sale of shares of any Canadian corporation in which the foreign plaintiff has a direct or indirect beneficial interest. The South African

---

[38] For claims under the U.S. Racketeer Influenced and Corrupt Organisations Act (RICO), see also *Société Commerciale de Réassurance v. Eras International Ltd. (No. 2)* [1995] 2 All E.R. 278, 307–312; *Simon Engineering plc v. Butte Mining plc* [1996] 1 Lloyd's Rep. 104n, at 111.

[39] Defined by s.7(2) to mean any country outside the United Kingdom other than one for whose international relations the United Kingdom Government is responsible.

[40] But it does not apply to judgments which had actually been registered under the 1920 or 1933 Acts, or where judgment had been obtained at common law on the foreign judgment, before its passage: s.5(6).

[41] s.6(3), (4).

[42] s.6(5).

[43] This is because proceedings under the Act are now within Ord. 11, r. 1(2)(*b*), Rule 26, whereas formerly they were within Ord. 11, r. 1(1).

[44] s.10(5).

[45] s.9(2).

Protection of Businesses Act 1978,[46] as amended in 1984, makes corporations which control, or are controlled by, the foreign plaintiff jointly and severally liable to repay damages.

By section 7 of the 1980 Act[47] provision may be made by Order in Council **14–249** for the reciprocal enforcement in the United Kingdom of foreign judgments which are given pursuant to foreign laws designed to counteract multiple damages awards. This power may be exercised if the following conditions are met: (a) the law of the foreign country provides for the enforcement of United Kingdom judgments given under section 6 of the 1980 Act; (b) the foreign judgment is given under a provision of the foreign law relating to the recovery of sums paid or obtained pursuant to a judgment for multiple damages within the meaning of the 1980 Act. The Australia-United Kingdom Agreement of 1990 provides for the reciprocal recognition and enforcement of such "clawback" judgments.[48]

---

[46] s.1B(4).

[47] As amended by Civil Jurisdiction and Judgments Act 1982, s.38. This amendment made it unnecessary for the foreign law to "correspond" with s.6.

[48] S.I. 1994 No. 1901, Art. 6 (*cf.* Foreign Proceedings (Excess of Jurisdiction) Act 1980, s.10 (Aus.)). No such provision is to be found in the Canada-United Kingdom Agreement 1984, S.I. 1987 No. 468.

CHAPTER 15

JURISDICTION AND ENFORCEMENT OF JUDGMENTS UNDER MULTILATERAL CONVENTIONS

15R–001   RULE 53—The High Court has jurisdiction to entertain a claim under enactments giving effect in the law of the United Kingdom to certain international conventions if and only if the respective jurisdictional requirements of those enactments are fulfilled.

COMMENT

15–002   **Introduction.** There are a number of international conventions which, in relation to the particular subject-matter of the convention, establish special rules as to the courts which are to have jurisdiction to hear and determine disputes. Many of these conventions also contain provisions as to the recognition and enforcement of judgments.[1] The special jurisdictional rules derived from these conventions and given effect by statutory enactment in the law of England are examined in the present Rule. The enactments concerned are the Carriage by Air Act 1961, the Carriage by Air (Supplementary Provisions) Act 1962, the Carriage of Goods by Road Act 1965, the Carriage by Air Acts (Application of Provisions) Order 1967,[2] the Consular Relations Act 1968 (in respect of certain proceedings relating to members of the crew of aircraft and ships), the Carriage of Passengers by Road Act 1974 (which is not yet in force), the Carriage by Air and Road Act 1979 (the relevant provisions of which are not yet in force), the Carriage of Passengers and their Luggage by Sea (Interim Provisions) Order 1980,[3] section 22 of the Supreme Court Act 1981 (dealing with certain claims arising out of collisions at sea), certain provisions of the Civil Aviation Act 1982[4] dealing with claims in respect of air navigation services, the Merchant Shipping (Liner Conference) Act 1982, the International Transport Conventions Act 1983[5] (dealing with carriage by rail), sections 151 to 171 of the Merchant Shipping Act 1995 (dealing with oil pollution), section 182B of the Merchant Shipping Act 1995 (which concerns claims for damage arising from the carriage of hazardous and noxious substances by sea)[6] and section 183(1) of the Merchant Shipping Act 1995 (which deals with the carriage of passengers and their luggage by sea). They are examined below, grouped by subject-matter.

---

[1] See *post*, Rule 55.
[2] S.I. 1967 No. 480, as amended by S.I. 1969 No. 1083, S.I. 1979 No. 931, S.I. 1981 No. 440, S.I. 1998 No. 1058, S.I. 1998 No. 1751, and S.I. 1999 No. 1737.
[3] S.I. 1980 No. 1092 as amended by S.I. 1987 No. 670.
[4] As amended by the Civil Aviation (Eurocontrol) Act 1983.
[5] As amended by S.I. 1992 No. 237.
[6] No order has yet been made under this section to give effect to the convention in question.

In principle, these jurisdictional rules are not affected by either the Brussels   **15–003**
Convention ("the 1968 Convention") or the Lugano Convention on jurisdic-
tion and the enforcement of judgments in civil and commercial matters.
Article 57(1) of each Convention provides that it is not to affect any conventions to which the Contracting States are or will be parties and which, in
relation to particular matters, govern jurisdiction or the recognition or enforcement of judgments.[7] In *The Tatry*,[8] however, the European Court held that the
effect of Article 57 is not to exclude the 1968 Convention entirely in cases
falling within the scope of a convention which, in relation to particular
matters, governs jurisdiction. The 1968 Convention is excluded only to the
extent that it conflicts with a convention on a particular matter; if the latter
does not cover a specific jurisdictional issue the provisions of the 1968
Convention continue to apply. Accordingly, in a case where the court has
jurisdiction under an international convention which does not contain provisions dealing with *lis pendens* or related actions, the court should apply
Articles 21 and 22 of the 1968 (or Lugano) Convention if there are concurrent
proceedings in another Brussels (or Lugano) Contracting State.[9] Similarly,
jurisdictional rules derived from international conventions are not affected by
those provisions of the Civil Jurisdiction and Judgments Act 1982 based upon
the 1968 Convention which regulate the allocation of jurisdiction between the
various parts of the United Kingdom.[10] Where a special jurisdictional rule
derived from an international convention confers jurisdiction on the courts of
the United Kingdom without specifying the relevant part whose courts are to
have jurisdiction, the allocation of jurisdiction as between the various parts of
the United Kingdom has to be resolved by traditional jurisdiction rules
(including the doctrine of *forum non conveniens*).[11]

It is provided in the 1968 Convention that it is not to apply to provisions   **15–004**
which, in relation to particular matters, govern jurisdiction or the recognition
or enforcement of judgments and which are or will be contained in acts of the
institutions of the European Communities or in national laws harmonised in
implementation of such acts.[12] The Lugano Convention has an annexed
Protocol which provides that provisions which, in relation to particular matters, govern jurisdiction or the recognition or enforcement of judgments and
which are or will be contained in acts of the institutions of the European
Communities are to be treated in the same way as the conventions referred to
in Article 57(1).[13]

In many of the cases here examined, service of process out of the jurisdic-   **15–005**
tion will be permissible without the permission of the court by virtue of Order
11, rule 1(2)(*b*) of the Rules of the Supreme Court,[14] the claims being claims
which, by virtue of an enactment, the High Court has power to hear and
determine notwithstanding that the person against whom the claim is made is

---

[7] For the interpretation of this provision, see Art. 57(2) of the 1968 Convention, added by the
  1989 Accession Convention but based upon Art. 25(2) of the 1978 Accession Convention; and
  Art. 57(2), (3), (5) of the Lugano Convention, and *ante*, paras. 11–034—11–036.
[8] [1994] E.C.R. 1–5439; [1999] Q.B. 515. Contrast *The Bergen* [1997] 1 Lloyd's Rep. 380. See
  ante, paras. 13–033—13–034.
[9] *Cf. Deaville v. Aeroflot Russian International Airlines* [1997] 2 Lloyd's Rep. 67.
[10] Civil Jurisdiction and Judgments Act 1982, ss.16 and 17, Sched. 4, and Sched. 5, para. 6.
[11] See *Abnett v. British Airways plc.*, 1996 S.L.T. 529 (O.H.): for further proceedings not
  involving this point see *ibid.* (I.H.) and *Sidhu v. British Airways plc.* [1997] A.C. 430.
[12] Art. 57(3).
[13] Protocol No. 3, para. 1.
[14] In Civil Procedure Rules 1998, Sched. 1.

not within the jurisdiction of the Court or that the wrongful act, neglect or default giving rise to the claim did not take place within the jurisdiction.[15]

15–006   **Carriage by air.** The Carriage by Air Act 1961 gives binding force in the United Kingdom to an international convention on carriage by air known as the Warsaw Convention 1929 as amended at The Hague in 1955.[16] The Convention applies to the carriage of passengers, baggage and cargo,[17] provided that it falls within the definition of "international carriage," that is carriage in which, according to the agreement between the parties, the place of departure and the place of destination, whether or not there be a break in the carriage or a transhipment, are situated either within the territories of two High Contracting Parties, or within the territory of a single High Contracting Party, if there is an agreed stopping place within the territory of another State.[18] The United Kingdom and its dependencies are a single High Contracting Party; thus while a flight between London and Dublin, or between London and Paris, will be "international carriage" for the purposes of the Act, a flight between London and Gibraltar will not be (in the absence of an agreed stopping place in, *e.g.* France or Spain).

15–007   An Order in Council made under the Carriage by Air Act 1961[19] gives binding force in the United Kingdom both to the unamended text of the Warsaw Convention 1929 in respect of international carriage within the terms of that unamended Convention and to the Warsaw Convention as amended by additional Protocol No. 1 of Montreal 1975.[20] Whether the carriage falls within the scope of the amended or unamended texts is a matter largely determined by the identity of the High Contracting Parties concerned. So, the United States is a party to the unamended text only, never having ratified the 1955 Hague Protocol; a flight London-New York does not, therefore, fall within the amended text as given effect by the Carriage by Air Act 1961, but does fall within the provisions of the unamended Convention given effect by the Order in Council.

The High Contracting Parties to both versions of the Convention are certified from time to time by Order in Council, which is conclusive evidence of the matters certified.[21]

15–008   Under the different versions of the Convention, the same special jurisdictional rules are prescribed.[22] These rules are designed to provide a claimant with a limited choice of competent and appropriate jurisdictions in which to bring his claim. An action for damages must be brought, at the option of the plaintiff, in the territory of one of the High Contracting Parties either before

---

[15] See *ante*, Rule 26.

[16] For a full account of "the Warsaw system," see Shawcross and Beaumont, *Air Law* (4th ed., Re-Issue) Division VII.

[17] But not of mail or postal packets. Such carriage is governed for the purposes of English law by Schedule 1 to the Carriage by Air Acts (Application of Provisions) Order 1967, S.I. 1967 No. 480: *American Express Co. v. British Airways Board* [1983] 1 W.L.R. 701.

[18] Carriage by Air Act 1961, Sched. 1, Art. 1(2).

[19] Carriage by Air Acts (Application of Provisions) Order 1967, S.I. 1967 No. 480, Arts. 3, 5 and 5A; Scheds. 2 and 3.

[20] See *infra*.

[21] Carriage by Air Act 1961, s.2(1)(3). The current Order is the Carriage by Air (Parties to Convention) Order 1999, S.I. 1999 No. 1313. See *Philippson v. Imperial Airways Ltd.* [1939] A.C. 332 for the position where the text of the Warsaw Convention is incorporated by contractual term.

[22] Carriage by Air Act 1961, Sched. 1, Art. 28(1); Carriage by Air Acts (Application of Provisions) Order 1967, S.I. 1967 No. 480, Sched. 2, Art. 28(1); Sched. 3, Art. 28(1).

the court having jurisdiction where the carrier is ordinarily resident, or has his principal place of business, or has an establishment by which the contract has been made, or before the court having jurisdiction at the place of destination. The court's inherent jurisdiction to stay proceedings on the basis of *forum non conveniens* in favour of the courts of another High Contracting Party is inconsistent with the option conferred on the claimant by the Convention; once the claimant has chosen the courts of a particular Contracting Party as his forum the defendant has no basis on which to challenge that choice.[23] However, since the Convention's jurisdictional rules identify the High Contracting Parties whose courts are to have jurisdiction without addressing the allocation of jurisdiction as between various parts of a Contracting Party (*e.g.* as between England and Scotland),[24] it is not inconsistent with the Convention for proceedings commenced in England under the Convention to be stayed on the ground that the courts of Scotland or Northern Ireland provide a more appropriate forum. Any clause in the contract of carriage, and all special agreements entered into before the damage occurred by which the parties purport to alter the rules as to jurisdiction are null and void; but in the carriage of cargo arbitration clauses are allowed if the arbitration is to take place within one of the jurisdictions referred to.[25] It would seem that an agreement as to jurisdiction made after the occurrence of the damage would be valid, and that submission by the defendant would also give the court jurisdiction.[26] Where the claimant has a claim for damages which falls within the scope of the Warsaw Convention, the Convention provides the claimant with his only remedy. If recovery is not available under the Warsaw Convention, *e.g.* because of the limitation provisions contained in Article 29, the claimant cannot rely on any alternative cause of action.[27]

Carriers by air are almost invariably corporations, and their ordinary residence will generally coincide with their principal place of business; the mere existence of a branch office within the jurisdiction will not support a finding of ordinary residence.[28] There is no English authority on the precise relationship which need exist between the carrier and the "establishment by which a contract has been made." It is submitted that the establishment need not be in the exclusive ownership of the carrier, but that more than a mere agency is required; a sales organisation maintained by the carrier, even if in co-operation with another carrier, would suffice.[29] The "place of destination" in the case of a round trip will be identical with the place of departure.[30]

15–009

---

[23] *Milor S.r.l. v. British Airways plc.* [1996] Q.B. 702 (C.A.). *Cf. Re Aircrash Disaster near New Orleans, Louisiana, on 9 July 1982*, 821 F.2d 1147 (5th Cir. 1987).

[24] *Abnett v. British Airways plc*, 1996 S.L.T. 529 (O.H.).

[25] Carriage by Air Act 1961, Sched. 1, Art. 32; Carriage by Air Acts (Application of Provisions) Order 1967, S.I. 1967 No. 480, Sched. 2, Art. 32; Sched. 3, Art. 32.

[26] *Rothmans of Pall Mall (Overseas) Ltd. v. Saudi Arabian Airlines Corporation* [1980] 3 All E.R. 359, *per* Mustill J.

[27] *Sidhu v. British Airways plc.* [1997] A.C. 430. See also *Emery Air Freight Corporation v. Nerine Nurseries Ltd.* [1997] 3 N.Z.L.R. 723 (C.A.).

[28] *Rothmans of Pall Mall (Overseas) Ltd. v. Saudi Arabian Airlines Corporation* [1981] Q.B. 368 (C.A.); *Roberts v. Guyana Airways Corporation* (1998) 41 O.R. (3d) 653 (Ont.).

[29] See *Qureshi v. K.L.M. Royal Dutch Airlines* (1979) 102 D.L.R. (3d) 205 (N.S.); *Berner v. United Airlines Inc.*, 3 A.D. 2d 9, 157 N.Y.S. 2d 884 (1956), affd. 3 N.Y. 2d 1003, 147 N.E. 2d 732 (1957). *Cf. Eck v. United Arab Airlines Inc.*, 360 F. 2d 804 (2d Circ. 1966); *Orchestre Symphonique de Vienne v. T.W.A.* (1972) 35 R.G.A.E. 202.

[30] *Grein v. Imperial Airways Ltd.* [1937] 1 K.B. 50; *Qureshi v. K.L.M. Royal Dutch Airlines* (1979) 102 D.L.R. (3d) 205 (N.S.).

15–010   Further amendments to the Warsaw Convention were agreed in a series of Protocols drawn up at Montreal in 1975. The new text creates an additional basis for jurisdiction: in respect of damage resulting from the death, injury or delay of a passenger, or the destruction, loss, damage or delay of baggage, the action may also be brought in the territory of one of the High Contracting Parties before the court within the jurisdiction of which the carrier has an establishment if the passenger has his ordinary or permanent residence in that territory.[31] Provisions are made in the Carriage by Air and Road Act 1979 to give binding force in the United Kingdom to the Convention as so amended, but the provision introducing the additional basis of jurisdiction is not yet in force.[32]

15–011   The Carriage by Air Act 1961 (and the corresponding provisions in the Carriage by Air and Road Act 1979) are enactments within Order 11, r. 1(2)(*b*),[33] and permission is not required to serve process out of the jurisdiction. The Act contemplates that the defendant carrier may itself be a High Contracting Party, that is a foreign government.[34] A High Contracting Party is deemed to have submitted to the jurisdiction of the court, and section 12 of the State Immunity Act 1978 provides for serving process upon the foreign government with the assistance of the Secretary of State[35]; these provisions do not, however, authorise the issue of execution against the property of any High Contracting Party.[36]

15–012   The Carriage by Air (Supplementary Provisions) Act 1962 gives binding force in the United Kingdom to a supplementary convention known as the Guadalajara Convention 1961. It deals with the problems which arise when, as is very frequently the case, the "actual carrier" who performs carriage by air is not the carrier with whom the original contract of carriage was made (the "contracting carrier").[37] An action for damages in relation to carriage performed by the actual carrier may be brought, at the option of the plaintiff, against that carrier or the contracting carrier, or against both together or separately.[38] Such an action must be brought, again at the option of the plaintiff, either before a court in which an action may be brought against the contracting carrier as provided by Article 28 of the different versions of the Warsaw Convention, or before the court having jurisdiction at the place where the actual carrier is ordinarily resident or has his principal place of business.[39] Permission of the court is not required

---

[31] Carriage by Air and Road Act 1979, Sched. 1, Art. 28(2) (not yet in force).

[32] Additional Protocols Nos. 1 and 2 (which, *inter alia*, establish a new unit of account for the Warsaw Convention) are implemented by S.I. 1998 No. 1058 and S.I. 1997 No. 2565 (which brings into force various provisions of the Carriage by Air and Road Act 1979). S.3(1) of the 1979 Act was brought into force by S.I. 1998 No. 2562 to allow for the implementation of Additional Protocol No. 4, which was brought into force by S.I. 1999 No. 1312.

[33] In CPR, Sched. 1. See *ante*, Rule 26.

[34] Carriage by Air Act 1961, s.8. This is applied to carriage within the Second Schedule to the Carriage by Air Acts (Application of Provisions) Order 1967, S.I. 1967 No. 480 by Art. 5(3) of the Order.

[35] See also Ord. 11, r. 7 which is however limited to cases in which permission to serve the process has been obtained from the court.

[36] Carriage by Air Act 1961, s.8.

[37] The Act is also applied to carriage falling within Schedules 2 and 3 to the Carriage by Air Acts (Application of Provisions) Order 1967, S.I. 1967 No. 480, *i.e.* carriage under the unamended Warsaw Convention.

[38] Carriage by Air (Supplementary Provisions) Act 1962, Sched., Art. VII.

[39] *Ibid.* Sched., Art. VIII.

for service of process out of the jurisdiction when a claim is brought under this Act.[40]

The provisions of the Carriage by Air Act 1961 as to actions against foreign governments are applied equally to actions under the 1962 Act.[41]

Carriage by rail. The Berne Convention concerning International Car-   15–013
riage by Rail 1980 (COTIF) is designed to replace the earlier international conventions on carriage by rail which it consolidates with amendments.[42] It is given the force of law in the United Kingdom by the International Transport Conventions Act 1983. The COTIF Convention was modified by a Protocol[43] in 1990 and the Act was amended[44] to implement it.[45] States which are parties to the Convention may be certified by Order in Council, which is conclusive for the purposes of English law.[46] The Convention incorporates two sets of Uniform Rules, one dealing with the carriage of passengers and their luggage (CIV) and forming Appendix A to the COTIF Convention, the other dealing with carriage of goods (CIM) and forming Appendix B to the COTIF Convention. Both sets of Rules apply in certain cases of international through traffic using road, sea or inland waterways as well as railway lines.[47]

The CIV Uniform Rules concerning the contract for international carriage   15–014
of passengers and luggage by rail apply, subject to certain exceptions,[48] to any carriage of passengers and luggage under international transport documents made out for a journey over the territories of at least two States and exclusively over lines or services in a list of CIV lines compiled in accordance with the Convention by the Intergovernmental Organisation for International Carriage by Rail (OTIF).[49] The term "international transport documents" is not formally defined, but refers to tickets and luggage registration vouchers.[50] An action based on the liability of the railway in case of the death of, or personal injury to, passengers may only be brought against the railway which operates the line on which the accident occurred; in the case of joint operations, the plaintiff may elect to sue either of the operating railways.[51] The action must be instituted in the courts of the State in whose territory the accident happened, subject (as are all the Convention's jurisdictional rules) to different provisions in "agreements between States or acts of concession."[52] In the case of a fatal accident, the existence of a right of action under the Convention precludes the bringing of an action under the Fatal Accidents Act 1976, other than in respect of damages for bereavement.[53] An action under the CIV Uniform Rules for the recovery of a sum paid under the contract of carriage may be brought against the railway which collected the sum or against the

---

[40] Ord., 11, r. 1(2)(*b*); *ante*, Rule 26.
[41] Carriage by Air (Supplementary Provisions) Act 1962, s.3(3).
[42] For the text of the Convention, see Cmnd. 8535 (1982).
[43] Cm. 1689 (1991).
[44] S.I. 1992 No. 237.
[45] For the consolidated text of the Convention as amended by the 1990 Protocol see Cm. 2312 (1993).
[46] International Transport Conventions Act 1983, s.2. No Order has been made.
[47] Convention, Arts. 2(2), 3(3).
[48] Set out in App. A, Arts. 2, 3 and 33.
[49] Convention, Arts. 3, 10; App. A, Art. 1.
[50] For these documents, see App. A, Arts. 11, 20.
[51] App. A, Arts. 26(4), 51(1).
[52] App. A, Art. 52(1).
[53] International Transport Conventions Act 1983, s.3.

railway on whose behalf it was collected.[54] Other actions under these Rules may be brought against the railway of departure, the railway of destination or the railway on which the event giving rise to the proceedings occurred.[55] All such actions must be instituted in the courts of the State having jurisdiction over the defendant railway.[56]

15–015   The CIM Uniform Rules concerning the contract for international carriage of goods by rail apply, subject to certain exceptions,[57] to all consignments of goods for carriage under a through consignment note made out for a route over the territories of at least two States and exclusively over lines or services included in a list of CIM lines compiled in accordance with the Convention by OTIF.[58] An action under the CIM Uniform Rules for the recovery of a sum paid under the contract of carriage may be brought against the railway which collected the sum or against the railway on whose behalf it was collected; but an action in respect of cash on delivery payments may only be brought against the forwarding railway.[59] Other actions under the CIM Rules may be brought against the forwarding railway, the railway of destination or the railway on which the event giving rise to the proceedings occurred.[60] All actions under the CIM Rules must be instituted in the courts of the State having jurisdiction over the defendant railway.[61]

The Convention also provides for the use, by agreement between the parties concerned, of an arbitral tribunal as an alternative to the ordinary courts, and regulates the composition and procedure of such a tribunal.[62]

15–016   **Carriage by road.** The Carriage of Goods by Road Act 1965 gives binding force in the United Kingdom to the Geneva Convention on the Contract for the International Carriage of Goods by Road, of May 19, 1956, generally known as the CMR Convention.[63] The Convention applies to every contract for the carriage of goods by road in motor vehicles for reward, when the place of taking over the goods and the place designated for delivery, as specified in the contract, are situated in two different countries, of which at least one is a Contracting country.[64] It also applies if part of the journey is by sea, rail, inland waterways or air, provided that the goods are not unloaded from the vehicle.[65] It does not apply to traffic between the United Kingdom and the Republic of Ireland.[66] High Contracting Parties are specified from time to time by Orders in Council which are conclusive for the purposes of English law.[67]

---

[54] App. A, Art. 51(2).

[55] App. A, Art. 51(3).

[56] App. A, Art. 52(2).

[57] Set out in App. B, Art. 2.

[58] Convention, Arts. 3, 10; App. B, Art. 1. For the consignment note, see App. B, Arts. 11–13 and 18.

[59] App. B, Art. 55(1)(2).

[60] App. B, Art. 55(3).

[61] App. B, Art. 56.

[62] Convention, Arts. 12–16.

[63] For text see Cmnd. 3455; for commentary see Hill and Messent, *CMR: Contracts for the International Carriage of Goods by Road* (1984).

[64] Carriage of Goods by Road Act 1965, Sched., Art. 1(1). See *Gefco (U.K.) Ltd. v. Mason* [1998] C.L.C. 1468.

[65] *Ibid.* Sched., Art. 2.

[66] Protocol of Signature.

[67] Carriage of Goods by Road Act 1965, s.2. The current Order is the Carriage of Goods by Road (Parties to Convention) Order 1967, S.I. 1967 No. 1683, as amended by S.I. 1980 No. 697.

Any legal proceedings arising out of carriage under the Convention[68] must be brought in a court or tribunal of a Contracting country designated by agreement between the parties, or in the courts or tribunals of a country within whose territory (a) the defendant is ordinarily resident, or has his principal place of business, or the branch or agency through which the contract of carriage was made; or (b) the place where the goods were taken over by the carrier or the place designated for delivery is situated.[69] The designation of a court by agreement can take place in the contract, or after the cause of action has arisen; if the designation is in the original contract it would seem to be binding on the consignee of the goods the subject of the contract as the consignee's rights are those "arising from the contract."[70] An arbitration clause is permitted, so long as it expressly provides that the arbitral tribunal must apply the Convention.[71] Where jurisdiction is based upon the presence in England of a "branch or agency" through which the contract was made, it must be shown that it was "his," *i.e.* the defendant's, branch or agency; but the precise meaning of this requirement, especially in the agency case, is far from clear. If the goods were "taken over" by a carrier in England the English court will have jurisdiction, even if the defendant carrier was the actual carrier only in respect of a later stage of the journey, provided that the carrier can be regarded as a carrier for the purposes of the contract as a whole.[72]

Permission of the court is not required for service of process out of the **15–017** jurisdiction when the claim is brought under this Act.[73] The Act contemplates that the defendant carrier may itself be a High Contracting Party, that is a foreign government.[74] A High Contracting Party is deemed to have submitted to the jurisdiction of the court, and section 12 of the State Immunity Act 1978 provides for serving process upon the foreign government with the assistance of the Secretary of State[75]; these provisions do not, however, authorise the issue of execution against the property of any High Contracting Party.[76]

The Carriage of Passengers by Road Act 1974 gives the force of law in the **15–018** United Kingdom to the Geneva Convention on the Contract for the International Carriage of Passengers and Luggage 1973 (CVR), but the Act is not yet in force.[77] The Convention applies to every contract for the carriage of passengers and of their luggage by road in motor vehicles when the contract provides that the carriage shall take place in the territory of more than one State and that the place of departure or the place of destination, or both these places, shall be situated on the territory of a State that is a party to the Convention, irrespective of the place of residence and the nationality of the parties.[78] Contracting States are to be specified from time to time by Orders

---

[68] Including "extra-contractual claims" under Art. 28.
[69] Carriage of Goods by Road Act 1965, Sched., Art. 31(1). For actions between carriers, see *ibid.*, Sched., Art. 39 and *Cummins Engine Co. Ltd. v. Davis Freight Forwarding (Hull) Ltd.* [1981] 1 W.L.R. 1363 (C.A.).
[70] *Ibid.*, Sched., Art. 13(1).
[71] *Ibid.*, Sched., Art. 33; *A.B. Bofors-UVA v. A.B. Skandia Transport* [1982] 1 Lloyd's Rep. 410 (where the court recognised the existence of divergent views on the point in foreign courts).
[72] *Moto Vespa S.A. v. M.A.T. (Britannia Express) Ltd.* [1979] 1 Lloyd's Rep. 175.
[73] Ord. 11, r. 1(2)(*b*); *ante*, Rule 26.
[74] Carriage of Goods by Road Act 1965, s.6.
[75] See also Ord. 11, r. 7 which is however limited to cases in which permission to serve the claim form has been obtained from the court.
[76] Carriage of Goods by Road Act 1965, s.6.
[77] Carriage of Passengers by Road Act 1974, s.1(1).
[78] *Ibid.*, Sched., Art. 1(1).

in Council, which will be conclusive for the purposes of English law.[79] Where carriage by road is interrupted and another mode of transport is used, the Convention applies to the portions of carriage which are performed by road, even if they are not international within the meaning of Article 1, provided that they are not ancillary to the other mode of transport.[80] Where the vehicle itself is carried over part of the journey by another mode of transport, the Convention applies to loss or damage caused by an accident connected with the carriage by the vehicle and which occurs either while the passenger is inside the vehicle or is entering or alighting from the vehicle, or in connection with the fact that luggage is on or in the vehicle or is being loaded or unloaded.[81] Legal proceedings arising out of carriage under the Convention may be brought at the option of the claimant in any court or tribunal of a Contracting Party designated by agreement between the parties, or in the courts or tribunals of the country within whose territory is situated (a) the place where the defendant has his principal place of business, is habitually resident, or has the place of business through which the contract of carriage was made; or (b) the place where the loss or damage occurred; or (c) the place of departure or of destination of the carriage; and in no other court or tribunal.[82] Any stipulation which would directly or indirectly derogate from the provisions of the Convention is null and void; this applies also to any arbitration clause agreed to before the event that caused the damage[83]; but there is no prohibition on the making of an agreement to the same effect after that event, and it would seem that submission to the jurisdiction of a court would give that court jurisdiction.[84]

15–019   Permission of the court is not required for service of process out of the jurisdiction when the claim is brought under this Act.[85] The Act contemplates the possibility of actions against Contracting States.[86] A Contracting State is deemed to have submitted to the jurisdiction of the court and section 12 of the State Immunity Act 1978 provides for service of process upon the foreign government with the assistance of the Secretary of State[87]; these provisions do not, however, authorise the issue of execution against the property of any state.[88]

15–020   **Carriage of passengers and luggage by sea.** Section 183(1) of the Merchant Shipping Act 1995 (which replaced section 14(1) of the 1979 Act) gives the force of law in the United Kingdom to the Athens Convention relating to the Carriage of Passengers and their Luggage by Sea 1974. The Convention, which is reproduced in Part I of Schedule 6 to the Act, applies to any international carriage (defined as meaning any carriage in which, according to the contract of carriage, the place of departure and the place of destination are situated in two different States, or in a single State if, according to the contract of carriage or the scheduled itinerary, there is an intermediate

---

[79] *Ibid.*, s.2.
[80] *Ibid.*, Sched., Art. 2.
[81] *Ibid.*, Sched., Art. 3.
[82] Carriage of Passengers by Road Act 1974, Sched., Art. 21(1).
[83] *Ibid.*, Sched., Art. 23(1)(3).
[84] *Cf.* the position under the Carriage by Air Act 1961; *ante*, para. 15–008.
[85] Ord. 11, r. 1(2)(*b*); *ante*, Rule 26.
[86] Carriage of Passengers by Road Act 1974, s.6.
[87] See also Ord. 11, r. 7, which is however limited to cases in which permission to serve process has been obtained from the court.
[88] Carriage of Passengers by Road Act 1974, s.6.

port of call in another State[89]) if the ship is flying the flag of or is registered in a State which is a party to the Convention, or if the contract of carriage has been made in such a State, or if the place of departure or destination according to the contract of carriage is in such a State.[90] Carriage which is not for reward is excluded.[91] The Act makes provision for Orders in Council declaring States to be contracting parties to the Convention,[92] but such an Order does not preclude evidence that additional States are in fact parties.[93]

Any action arising under the Convention must be brought, at the option of **15–021** the claimant, in one of the following courts, provided that the court is located in a State which is a party to the Convention. The courts are (a) the court of the place of permanent residence or principal place of business of the defendant; (b) the court of the place of departure or that of the destination according to the contract of carriage; (c) a court of the State of the domicile or permanent residence of the claimant, if the defendant has a place of business and is subject to jurisdiction in that State; or (d) a court of the State where the contract of carriage was made, if the defendant has a place of business and is subject to jurisdiction in that State.[94] However, after the occurrence of the incident which has caused the damage, the parties may agree that the claim for damages shall be submitted to any jurisdiction or to arbitration.[95] Any contractual provision concluded before the occurrence of the incident which has caused the death of or personal injury to a passenger or the loss of or damage to his luggage purporting to restrict the claimant's choice of forum under Article 17(1) is null and void.[96]

Section 184(1) of the Merchant Shipping Act 1995 (replacing section 16(2) **15–022** of the 1979 Act) enables a modified version of the Convention to be applied by Order in Council to domestic carriage, *i.e.* carriage where the place of departure and the place of destination under the contract are within the British Islands and there is no intermediate port of call outside those Islands. The power conferred by section 16(2) of the 1979 Act was exercised.[97] The jurisdictional requirements under the modified text are as in the Convention itself, but without the requirement that the court chosen must be located in a State which is party to the Convention.[98]

---

[89] Merchant Shipping Act 1995, Sched. 6, Part I, Art. 1(9).

[90] *Ibid.*, Sched. 6, Part I, Art. 2(1).

[91] *Ibid.*, s.183(2) and Sched. 6, Part II, para. 9. The provisions of the Convention are also excluded in two further situations: (*a*) by its own terms in certain cases of combined transport, where an international convention relating to another mode of transport has mandatory effect (Art. 2(2)), and (*b*) by virtue of the Merchant Shipping Act 1995, s.183(2) and Sched. 6, Part II, para. 2, if such other convention is declared to be mandatory in the contract of carriage.

[92] *Ibid.*, Sched. 6, Part II, para. 10. See Carriage of Passengers and their Luggage by Sea (Parties to Convention) Order 1987, S.I. 1987 No. 931.

[93] *Cf.* the more usual formula, found, *e.g.* in the Carriage by Air Act 1961, s.2(1)(3).

[94] Merchant Shipping Act 1995, Sched. 6, Part I, Art. 17(1).

[95] *Ibid.*, Sched. 6, Part I, Art. 17(2).

[96] *Ibid.*, Sched. 6, Part I, Art. 18.

[97] Carriage of Passengers and their Luggage by Sea (Interim Provisions) Order 1980, S.I. 1980 No. 1092 as amended by S.I. 1987 No. 670. Merchant Shipping Act 1979, s.16(1) (which was repealed by the 1995 Act) also enabled a modified version of the Convention to be applied, in respect of contracts made during the period before the relevant provisions of the 1979 Act came into force, to any contract of carriage for international carriage which was made in the United Kingdom, or under which a place in the United Kingdom was the place of departure or destination. This power was exercised by Carriage of Passengers and their Luggage by Sea (Interim Provisions) Order 1980, S.I. 1980 No. 1092.

[98] Art. 17(1) as modified by S.I. 1980 No. 1092, Sched., para. 3.

15–023   Permission is not required for the service of process out of the jurisdiction when the claim is brought under the Convention as given effect by section 183(1) of the Merchant Shipping Act 1995 or (in its modified form) by Order in Council.[99]

15–024   **Claims in respect of air navigation services.** The Civil Aviation Act 1982, as amended, contains provisions as to the recovery of charges payable in respect of air navigation services. The supply of air navigation services is an obligation imposed upon Contracting States by the Chicago Convention on International Civil Aviation 1944.[1] It is discharged through agencies such as the Civil Aviation Authority in the United Kingdom, through international arrangements applying to particular routes, and through international agencies such as Eurocontrol. The latter, known more formally as the European Organisation for the Safety of Air Navigation, was established by the Brussels Convention relating to Co-operation for the Safety of Air Navigation of December 13, 1960,[2] which was extensively revised by a Protocol of 1981.[3]

15–025   Under section 73 of the Civil Aviation Act 1982, the Secretary of State for Transport has power to make regulations establishing charges to be paid in respect of air navigation services. The regulations may provide for charges to be payable elsewhere than in the United Kingdom and to be recoverable in the United Kingdom whenever they are payable.[4] Liability may be imposed upon the operator or owner of any aircraft whether or not it is registered in the United Kingdom, whether or not it is in or over the United Kingdom at the time the services are provided, and whether or not the services are provided from a place in the United Kingdom.[5] Section 74(6) provides that a court in any part of the United Kingdom shall have jurisdiction to hear and determine a claim for charges or interest payable to the Secretary of State or the Civil Aviation Authority or Eurocontrol notwithstanding that the person against whom the claim is made is not resident within the jurisdiction of the court. Permission of the court is not required for the service of process out of the jurisdiction in respect of such a claim.[6] Claims for the payment of charges due to Eurocontrol are not within the Brussels Convention on jurisdiction and the enforcement of judgments in civil and commercial matters of 1968.[7]

15–026   Although made within the context of international agreements, these provisions are strictly only within this Rule so far as charges payable to Eurocontrol are concerned; it is only in that case that jurisdictional rules are contained in the relevant international instrument. The Multilateral Agreement Relating to Route Charges (1981)[8] provides that proceedings for the recovery of such

---

[99] Ord. 11, r. 1(2)(*b*); *ante*, Rule 26.

[1] Cmd. 8742. See, in particular, Art. 28.

[2] For text, see Cmnd. 1373 (1962).

[3] For text, see Cmnd. 8662 (1982).

[4] Civil Aviation Act 1982, s.73(4).

[5] *Ibid.* as amended by Civil Aviation (Eurocontrol) Act 1983, s.3(2). Various sets of Regulations have been made, each set applying to services provided by a particular organisation or under a particular international arrangement; see Shawcross and Beaumont, *Air Law* (4th ed. Re-Issue) para. VI(16).

[6] Ord. 11, r. 1(2)(*b*); *ante*, Rule 26.

[7] Case 29/76 *LTU GmbH & Co. v. Eurocontrol* [1976] E.C.R. 1541. See *ante*, para. 11–014.

[8] Provisions is made to give effect to the Agreement in respect of the enforcement of judgments in the Civil Aviation (Eurocontrol) Act 1983, s.1; effect can be given to its jurisdictional provisions by amendment to Regulations made under Civil Aviation Act 1982, s.74(6).

charges shall be instituted in the territory of the Contracting State where the debtor has his residence or registered office; or, if there is no such residence or office in a Contracting State, in the territory of a Contracting State where the debtor has a place of business; or if none of the preceding grounds of jurisdiction are available, in the territory of a Contracting State in which the debtor has assets; or, if no other ground is available, in Belgium, the country in which Eurocontrol has its headquarters.[9]

Schedule 4 to the Civil Aviation Act 1982 provides[10] that a court in any part of the United Kingdom shall have jurisdiction to hear and determine a claim against Eurocontrol for damages in respect of any wrongful act, neglect or default, notwithstanding that the act, neglect or default did not take place within the jurisdiction of the court or that Eurocontrol is not present within the jurisdiction of the court; but a court does not have jurisdiction under this provision in respect of damage or injury sustained wholly within or over a country to which the provisions of the Act relating to Eurocontrol do not extend.[11] Permission of the court is not required for the service of process out of the jurisdiction in respect of claims brought against Eurocontrol under these provisions.[12]   **15–027**

Collisions at sea. Section 22 of the Supreme Court Act 1981 contains provisions based upon those of the Brussels International Convention on Certain Rules concerning Civil Jurisdiction in Matters of Collision, 1952.[13] The provisions apply to any claim, whether or not it is within the Admiralty jurisdiction of the High Court,[14] for damage, loss of life or personal injury, arising out of a collision between ships, or the carrying out of, or omission to carry out, a manoeuvre in the case of one or more of two or more ships, or non-compliance on the part of one or more such ships, with the collision regulations. The High Court has jurisdiction to entertain an action to enforce such a claim if, but only if, the defendant has his habitual residence or place of business in England, or the cause of action arose within inland waters of England or within the limits of a port of England, or an action arising out of the same incident or series of incidents is proceeding in the court or has been heard and determined in the court,[15] or if the defendant submits or has agreed to submit to the jurisdiction of the court.[16] Permission is required for the service of process out of the jurisdiction in claims brought under these provisions.   **15–028**

Disputes as to liner conferences. The Geneva Convention on a Code of Conduct for Liner Conferences 1974 was negotiated under the auspices of UNCTAD (the United Nations Conference on Trade and Development). The United Kingdom has acceded to the Convention with reservations made in   **15–029**

---

[9] Art. 13.

[10] Para. 3(1), as amended by Civil Aviation (Eurocontrol) Act 1983, s.2.

[11] Civil Aviation Act 1982, Sched. 4, para. 3(2). See also para. 1(4B)(4C) inserted by Civil Aviation (Eurocontrol) Act 1983, s.2.

[12] Ord. 11, r. 1(2)(*b*); *ante*, Rule 26.

[13] For text see Cmd. 8954 (1952); Singh, *International Maritime Law Conventions* (1983), Vol. 4, pp. 3107–3111.

[14] Supreme Court Act 1981, s.22(8).

[15] *Ibid.* s.22(1)(2)(6). "Inland waters" and "port" are defined in s.22(2). See *The World Harmony* [1967] P. 341.

[16] Supreme Court Act 1981, s.22(5).

accordance with the agreed policy of the E.C. Member States.[17] The Merchant Shipping (Liner Conferences) Act 1982 enables the Secretary of State to make by regulation such provision as appears appropriate to give effect to the Code, having regard in particular to the reservations made by the United Kingdom.[18] The Code contains provisions for the settlement of disputes,[19] one of which is that disputes between shipping lines of the same flag, as well as those between organisations belonging to the same country, shall be settled within the framework of the national jurisdiction of that country, unless this creates serious difficulties in the fulfilment of the provisions of the Code.[20] The Act provides that proceedings arising out of a dispute to which this provision applies shall not be entertained by the High Court except as permitted by that provision.[21]

15–030   **Employment of crew of aircraft and ships.** An Order in Council made under section 4 of the Consular Relations Act 1968 may exclude or limit the jurisdiction of any court in the United Kingdom to entertain proceedings relating to the remuneration or any contract of service of the master or commander or a member of the crew of any ship or aircraft belonging to a State specified in the Order, except where a consular officer of that State has been notified of the intention to invoke the jurisdiction of the court and does not object within a period of two weeks from the date of such notification.[22] A provision of this nature is included in the European Convention on Consular Functions 1967,[23] but can also be included in bilateral arrangements between the United Kingdom and other States.

15–031   **Oil pollution by ships.** Sections 152 to 171 of the Merchant Shipping Act 1995 give effect to the International Convention on Civil Liability for Oil Pollution Damage, 1992.[24] Civil liability is imposed on the owner of a ship from which persistent oil has been discharged or has escaped[25] and, where there is a grave and imminent threat of damage being caused if oil were to be discharged or to escape from a ship, the owner is liable for the cost of measures taken to prevent or minimise such damage and for any damage caused by such measures.[26] The Act provides for compulsory insurance against liability for oil pollution damage[27] and for direct action against the insurer.[28] Under the Convention,[29] actions can be brought only in the courts of the contracting State or States in which the damage occurred. This is reflected in section 166(2) of the Act in its negative aspect: no court in the United Kingdom is to entertain an action (whether *in rem* or *in personam*) to enforce

---

[17] Council Regulation 954/79 of May 15, 1979 [1979] O.J. L121/1.
[18] See S.I. 1985 Nos. 405, 406. See Ord. 71, rr. 40–44 (in CPR, Sched. 1) for procedure.
[19] Chapter VI (Arts. 23 to 46).
[20] Art. 23, para. 2.
[21] Merchant Shipping (Liner Conferences) Act 1982, s.7(1)(2).
[22] For Orders in Council under s.4, see *Halsbury's Laws of England*, Vol. 18, para. 1594.
[23] Art. 35(3).
[24] The 1992 Convention is the Brussels International Convention on Civil Liability for Oil Pollution Damage 1969 (Cmnd. 4403 (1970)) as amended by the Protocols of November 19, 1976 and December 2, 1992. For a composite text see Brown, *International Law of the Sea, Volume II: Documents: Cases and Materials* (1994), pp. 260–273.
[25] s.153(1).
[26] s.153(2).
[27] s.163.
[28] s.165.
[29] Art. IX(1).

any claim arising from damage caused in another Convention country by contamination resulting from the discharge or escape of persistent oil from a ship or arising from the cost of measures taken in another Convention country to prevent or minimise such damage if no damage is caused or no measures are taken in the United Kingdom. Convention countries may be certified from time to time by Orders in Council, which are conclusive for the purposes of English law.[30]

Permission of the court is required for the service of process outside the jurisdiction in respect of a claim under section 153 of the Act.[31] The Act contemplates the possibility of actions against Convention states.[32] A Convention state is deemed to have submitted to the jurisdiction of the court, and section 12 of the State Immunity Act 1978 and Order 11, r. 7 provide for service of process upon the foreign government with the assistance of the Secretary of State; these provisions do not, however, authorise the issue of execution against the property of any state.[33]   **15–032**

Claims for damage arising from the carriage of hazardous and noxious substances by sea. Section 182B of the Merchant Shipping Act 1995 (inserted by the Merchant Shipping and Maritime Security Act 1997) makes provision for the implementation of the International Convention on Liability and Compensation for Damage in Connection with the Carriage of Hazardous and Noxious Substances by Sea 1996.[34] The text of the 1996 Convention is set out in Schedule 5A to the 1995 Act.[35] It is expressly provided that the 1996 Convention has no application to pollution damage as defined in the International Convention on Civil Liability for Oil Pollution Damage.[36]   **15–033**

Where a person has a claim, other than a claim arising out of a contract for the carriage of goods and passengers,[37] as a result of damage arising from the carriage of hazardous and noxious substances (HNS) by sea, the Convention imposes liability on the owner of the ship carrying the HNS[38] and requires the owner to maintain insurance or other financial security for such claims.[39] A claim may be brought against the owner only in accordance with the Convention.[40] The Convention also establishes the International Hazardous and Noxious Substances Fund (HNS Fund),[41] the purpose of which is to pay compensation to any person who suffers damage and who is unable to obtain adequate compensation from the owner.[42] Accordingly, the Convention contemplates claims being brought against either the owner of the ship carrying the HNS or, in appropriate circumstances, the HNS Fund.   **15–034**

Where a claim against an owner arises out of an incident which causes damage in the territory (including the territorial sea) of a State Party or which leads to the taking of preventative measures in the territory of a State Party,   **15–035**

---

[30] Merchant Shipping Act 1995, s.152(2).
[31] CPR PD49F, para. 3.1(1).
[32] s.167(3).
[33] Merchant Shipping Act 1995, s.167(3).
[34] No order has yet been made under s.182B to implement the 1996 Convention.
[35] Inserted by Merchant Shipping and Maritime Security Act 1997, s.14(2); Sched. 3.
[36] Art. 4(3)(a).
[37] Art. 4(1).
[38] Arts. 7–11.
[39] Art. 12.
[40] Art. 7(4).
[41] Arts. 13–36.
[42] Art. 14(1).

an action for compensation may be brought against the owner only in the courts of that State; if damage is caused in more than one State Party, the plaintiff may sue the owner in the courts of any of the State Parties concerned.[43] If the incident causing damage (or leading to the taking of preventative measures) does not cause damage in the territory of any State Party (or does not cause preventative measures to be taken in any State Party), an action may be brought against the owner in (i) the State Party in which the ship is registered (or, if unregistered, the State Party whose flag the ship is entitled to fly), or (ii) the State Party where the owner is habitually resident or in which his principal place of business is established, or (iii) the State Party in which the owner has established a limitation fund.[44] Where a limitation fund has been established in a State Party the courts of that State have exclusive jurisdiction over the apportionment and distribution of the fund.[45] Where a claim for compensation is brought against the HNS Fund the action must be brought in the court which had jurisdiction in respect of the action against the owner (or which would have had jurisdiction in respect of an action against an owner if an owner had been liable).[46]

ILLUSTRATIONS

15–036   1. A makes a contract with X & Co. in Stockholm for a return air flight Stockholm—London—Stockholm. X & Co. is a Swedish company with a branch office in London. A is injured in an accident as the aircraft lands in London. He wishes to claim damages from X & Co. The English courts have no jurisdiction; London is not the place of destination, nor does the presence of a branch office render X & Co. ordinarily resident in England.[47]

2. A makes a contract with B & Co., a Spanish company, for the carriage of goods by road from Birmingham to Madrid. B & Co. sub-contracts the carriage of the goods from Birmingham to Paris to C & Co., and only carries the goods itself from Paris to Madrid. The goods are damaged during the Paris—Madrid carriage, and A claims damages from B & Co. The English court has jurisdiction as the goods were taken over by the carrier in England. The sub-contracting of the first part, or the whole, of the actual carriage is immaterial.[48]

3. A makes a contract in England with X & Co., a French company, for the carriage of himself and his luggage from Cork to Bordeaux. The luggage is damaged during the carriage. A wishes to claim damages from X & Co. The English court has jurisdiction if X & Co. has a place of business in England and the writ is served upon the person authorised to accept service on behalf of the company in accordance with the Companies Act 1985.[49]

15R–037   RULE 54—English courts have no jurisdiction to determine any claim or question certified under statutory powers by the Secretary of State to be a claim or question which under an international convention falls to be determined by a court in some foreign country.[50]

---

[43] Art. 38(1).

[44] Art. 38(2). Limitation of liability is governed by Art. 9, which provides that the fund may be established only in a State Party where an action against the owner has been (or could be) brought under Art. 38.

[45] Art. 38(5).

[46] Art. 39(1).

[47] Carriage by Air Act 1961, Sched. 1, Art 28(1); *Grein v. Imperial Airways Ltd.* [1937] 1 K.B. 50; *Qureshi v. K.L.M. Royal Dutch Airlines* (1979) 102 D.L.R. (3d) 205 (N.S.); *Rothmans of Pall Mall (Overseas) Ltd. v. Saudi Arabian Airlines Corp.* [1981] Q.B. 368 (C.A.).

[48] Carriage of Goods by Road Act 1965, Sched., Art. 31(1); *Moto Vespa S.A. v. M.A.T. (Britannia Express) Ltd.* [1979] 1 Lloyd's Rep. 175; *Ulster-Swift Ltd. v. Taunton Meat Haulage Ltd.* [1977] 1 W.L.R. 625 (C.A.).

[49] Merchant Shipping Act 1995, Sched. 6, Part I, Art. 14(1); Carriage of Passengers and their Luggage by Sea (Interim Provisions) Order 1980, S.I. 1980 No. 1092 as amended by S.I. 1987 No. 670.

[50] Supreme Court Act 1981, s.23; Nuclear Installations Act 1965, s.17(1).

Comment

The jurisdictional requirements of international conventions to which the   **15–038**
United Kingdom is a party are commonly incorporated in the enactment
giving the convention the force of law in the United Kingdom; these cases
were examined in Rule 53. In certain cases, however, a different technique is
used, the enactment merely providing for the exclusion of jurisdiction by the
grant of a certificate by the Secretary of State that the claim is one which falls,
in accordance with the relevant convention, to be determined by the courts of
some foreign country.

Thus, section 23 of the Supreme Court Act 1981 provides that the High   **15–039**
Court[51] shall not have jurisdiction to determine any claim or question certified
by the Secretary of State to be a claim or question which, under the Rhine
Navigation Convention,[52] falls to be determined in accordance with the
provisions thereof. The United Kingdom is not a party to that Convention. But
Part I of the Administration of Justice Act 1956 (since replaced by sections 20
to 24 of the Supreme Court Act 1981) was passed in order to implement two
Conventions signed at Brussels in 1952,[53] to which the United Kingdom is a
party, and which contain savings for the Rhine Navigation Convention. The
section is unlikely to be invoked very often, partly because of its restricted
scope and partly because various British shipping and insurance associations
have stated that they will not seek the Secretary of State's certificate in claims
for death or personal injuries brought by British citizens against the owners of
British ships owned or insured by members of those associations.[54]

Again, section 17(1) of the Nuclear Installations Act 1965 provides that no   **15–040**
court in the United Kingdom or any part thereof shall have jurisdiction to
determine any claim or question under that Act certified by the Secretary of
State to be a claim or question which, under any relevant international
agreement,[55] falls to be determined by a court of some other country which is
bound by that agreement or of some other part of the United Kingdom. The
Act gives effect to various international conventions (to which the United
Kingdom is a party) on civil liability for nuclear "occurrences."[56] The Act
imposes absolute liability on the operators (including certain foreign operators) of nuclear installations for nuclear occurrences which cause injury to any

---

[51] For Scotland, see Administration of Justice Act 1956, s.46; for Northern Ireland, see Sched. 1,
Pt. I, para. 6. For county courts, see County Courts Act 1984, s.27(9).
[52] Defined in Supreme Court Act 1981, s.24(1) as the Convention of October 7, 1868 as revised
by any subsequent convention. See *British and Foreign State Papers*, Vol. 59, p. 470. The 7th
October, is evidently a mistake for 17th October. An amending Convention (to which the
United Kingdom is a party) was signed at Strasbourg on November 20, 1963, and came into
force on April 14, 1967. See Cmnd. 3371 (1967).
[53] Convention on Certain Rules Concerning Civil Jurisdiction in Matters of Collision, and
Convention Relating to the Arrest of Sea-going Ships, Cmnd. 8954 (1952); reprinted in Singh,
International Maritime Law Conventions (1983), Vol. 4, pp. 3107, 3101.
[54] Marsden, *Collisions At Sea* (1961), s.256.
[55] A "relevant international agreement" is one with respect to third-party liability in the field of
nuclear energy (excluding liability in respect of nuclear reactors comprised in means of
transport): s.26(1).
[56] The Paris Convention on Third Party Liability in the Field of Nuclear Energy (1960) (as
amended), Cmnd. 2514 (1964); and the Convention (1963) Supplementary to the Paris
Convention, Cmnd. 2515 (1964). *Cf.* the Vienna Convention (1963), Cmnd. 2333 (1964), not
yet ratified by the U.K. and the Joint Protocol relating to the Application of the Vienna
Convention and the Paris Convention (1988), Cm. 774, signed but not yet ratified by the U.K.
See *ante*, para. 11–209 and *post*, paras. 15–052—15–055.

person or damage to any property of any person other than the operator.[57] Under the Conventions,[58] jurisdiction prima facie lies only with the courts of the Contracting Party within whose territory the nuclear incident occurred. But if the nuclear incident occurred outside the territory of any Contracting Party, or if the place of the nuclear incident cannot be determined with certainty, jurisdiction lies with the courts of the Contracting Party in whose territory the nuclear installation of the operator liable is situated. If jurisdiction lies with the courts of more than one Contracting Party, then if the nuclear incident occurred partly outside the territory of any Contracting Party and partly within the territory of a single Contracting Party, jurisdiction lies with the courts of the latter; in any other case jurisdiction lies with the courts of one of the relevant Contracting Parties, under the Vienna Convention that chosen by agreement between the Contracting Parties and under the Paris Convention that identified by an arbitral tribunal as being the Contracting Party most closely related to the case in question. The Secretary of State's certificate will in appropriate cases reflect the agreement reached, or the ruling of the arbitral tribunal, as to the proper forum.

The certificate of the Secretary of State under section 17(1) of the Nuclear Installations Act 1965 is conclusive,[59] and the same is no doubt true under section 23 of the Supreme Court Act 1981.

15R–041 **RULE 55—A judgment of a court of a foreign country outside the United Kingdom in proceedings regulated by certain international conventions which have been given effect in the law of the United Kingdom will be recognised and enforced if the jurisdictional requirements of the convention concerned are fulfilled.**

COMMENT

15–042   A number of international conventions dealing with particular matters contain provisions as to the recognition and enforcement of judgments, and these are reflected in the United Kingdom legislation giving effect to the conventions. The United Kingdom legislation concerned is the Carriage of Goods by Road Act 1965, sections 152 to 171 of the Merchant Shipping Act 1995, section 182B of the Merchant Shipping Act 1995,[60] the Carriage of Passengers by Road Act 1974 (which is not yet in force), certain provisions of the Civil Aviation Act 1982 dealing with air navigation charges, and the International Transport Conventions Act 1983. The legislation commonly provides for the application to judgments given in accordance with the relevant convention of a modified version of Part I of the Foreign Judgments (Reciprocal Enforcement) Act 1933. Where the judgment is given by a court in a Contracting State to the 1968 or Lugano Conventions on jurisdiction and the enforcement of judgments in civil and commercial matters, the position is affected by Article 57 of each Convention. If both the United Kingdom and the Contracting State in which the judgment was given are parties to a convention on a particular matter, and that convention lays down conditions

---

[57] ss.7–10, 12. See Street and Frame, *Law Relating to Nuclear Energy* (1966).
[58] Vienna Convention, Art. XI; Paris Convention, Art. 13(a)(b) and (c).
[59] s.17(2).
[60] See *supra*, n. 34.

for the recognition or enforcement of judgments, those conditions continue to apply.[61] In any event the procedures of the 1968 Convention or the Lugano Convention (as the case may be) may be applied.[62]

Certain conventions, *e.g.* the Warsaw Convention of 1929 dealing with **15–043** carriage by air, contain no express provisions as to the recognition and enforcement of judgments but do contain provisions as to the allocation of jurisdiction. If a judgment is given in another Contracting State to the 1968 Convention or the Lugano Convention in the exercise of jurisdiction provided for in such a convention, *e.g.* as being the court having jurisdiction at the place of destination in carriage by air, its recognition and enforcement will be governed in the United Kingdom by the 1968 Convention or the Lugano Convention.[63] It follows that a judgment given by the courts of a 1968 Convention or Lugano Convention Contracting State under the Warsaw Convention may be denied recognition or enforcement only on the grounds set out in the 1968 Convention or Lugano Convention (as the case may be). When a judgment is given in a Lugano Convention Contracting State under a particular convention, recognition or enforcement may be refused not only on the grounds provided for in Articles 27 and 28,[64] but also if the State addressed is not a contracting party to the convention in question and the person against whom recognition or enforcement is sought is domiciled in that State, unless the judgment may otherwise be recognised or enforced under any rule of the State addressed.[65] If such a judgment is given in a foreign court to whose judgments Part I of the Foreign Judgments (Reciprocal Enforcement) Act 1933 applies, it is submitted that the foreign court will be deemed to have jurisdiction, this exercise of jurisdiction being one recognised by the United Kingdom legislation; but there seems no clear authority to this effect. If recognition and enforcement is sought at common law a similar argument can be advanced, that the jurisdiction of the foreign court is recognised in English law; again, there is no clear authority.[66] United Kingdom legislation to which these arguments apply includes the Carriage by Air Act 1961, the Carriage by Air (Supplementary Provisions) Act 1962, the Carriage by Air Acts (Application of Provisions) Order 1967,[67] section 183(1) of the Merchant Shipping Act 1995, and the Carriage of Passengers and their Luggage by Sea (Interim Provisions) Order 1980.[68]

The various cases falling within the scope of the Rule are examined below, grouped by subject-matter.

Carriage by Air. There are no provisions as to the recognition and **15–044** enforcement of judgments in any version of the Warsaw Convention 1929 nor

---

[61] Civil Jurisdiction and Judgments Act 1982, Sched. 1, Art. 57(1), (2); Sched. 3C, Art. 57(1)(5).

[62] *Ibid.*

[63] Civil Jurisdiction and Judgments Act 1982, Sched. 1, Art. 57(1), (2); Sched. 3C, Art. 57(1), (3).

[64] See *ante*, paras. 14–201—14–218.

[65] Civil Jurisdiction and Judgments Act 1982, Sched. 3C, Art. 57(4).

[66] This is not an argument based upon "reciprocity" (see paras. 14–080—14–082); it does not rest upon the assertion of jurisdiction by the English courts but upon its allocation to the courts of various countries by a convention having effect in English law.

[67] S.I. 1967 No. 480 (as amended).

[68] S.I. 1980 No. 1092 as amended by S.I. 1987 No. 670.

in the supplementary Guadalajara Convention 1961, nor in the United Kingdom legislation giving effect to those Conventions.[69] There are however provisions as to jurisdiction enabling actions to be brought only in certain courts[70] and, for the reasons stated above,[71] it is submitted that a judgment given in a foreign court under these provisions is entitled to recognition and enforcement in England.

15–045   **Carriage by rail.** Part I of the Foreign Judgments (Reciprocal Enforcement) Act 1933, with the omission of section 4(2) and (3), applies to any judgment given by a court in a country which is a party to the Berne Convention concerning International Carriage by Rail (COTIF) in accordance with the jurisdictional rules of the Convention and its related Uniform Rules,[72] and which has become enforceable under the law applied by that court.[73] The effect of the omission of section 4(2) and (3) is that while the registration of the foreign judgment must be set aside if the courts of the country concerned had no jurisdiction in the circumstances of the case,[74] the existence of jurisdiction is to be gathered from the terms of the Convention.

15–046   **Carriage by road.** Part I of the Foreign Judgments (Reciprocal Enforcement) Act 1933, with the omission of section 4(2) and (3), applies to any judgment given by a court or tribunal in a country which is a party to the Geneva Convention on the Contract for the International Carriage of Goods by Road 1956 (the CMR Convention),[75] which was given in accordance with the jurisdictional provisions of the Convention, and which has become enforceable in the country in which it was given; this is the case whether or not that Part has been extended to the country concerned, and whether or not the judgment is given by a court specified for the purposes of that Part.[76] In effect jurisdiction will exist if, and only if, the courts of the foreign country were designated by agreement between the parties, or the defendant was ordinarily resident in that country or had his principal place of business there or the branch through which the contract was made was situated there, or the place where the goods were taken over by the carrier or the place designated for delivery was situated there.[77]

15–047   When the Carriage of Passengers by Road Act 1974 is brought into force, similar provisions will apply in respect of the Geneva Convention on the Contract for the International Carriage of Passengers and Luggage (the CVR

---

[69] For the Conventions and the legislation (the Carriage by Air Act 1961, the Carriage by Air (Supplementary Provisions) Act 1962, and the Carriage by Air Acts (Application of Provisions) Order 1967, S.I. 1967 No. 480 as amended), see *ante*, paras. 15–006—15–012.

[70] See Carriage by Air Act 1961, Sched. 1, Art. 28(1), Carriage by Air (Supplementary Provisions) Act 1962, Sched., Art. VIII, and Carriage by Air Acts (Application of Provisions) Order 1967, S.I. 1967 No. 480. Sched. 2, Art. 28(1); Sched. 3, Art. 28(1).

[71] *Ante*, para. 15–043.

[72] For the Convention, and parties to it, see *ante*, paras. 15–013—15–015.

[73] International Transport Conventions Act 1983, s.6; Convention, Art. 18(1). See also Civil Jurisdiction and Judgments Act 1982, ss.31(3) and 32(4)(*b*) both as amended by International Transport Conventions Act 1983, s.11(2).

[74] Foreign Judgments (Reciprocal Enforcement) Act 1933, s.4(1)(*a*)(ii).

[75] For the Convention, and parties to it, see *ante*, para. 15–016.

[76] Carriage of Goods by Road Act 1965, s.4. See also the exclusion of judgments to which this provision applies from the scope of Civil Jurisdiction and Judgments Act 1982, ss.31 (judgments against States) and 32 (judgments in breach of agreement for settlement of disputes).

[77] Carriage of Goods by Road Act 1965, Sched., Art. 31(1) and (3). See *ante*, para. 15–016.

Convention).[78] Part I of the Foreign Judgments (Reciprocal Enforcement) Act 1933 is applied with the same modifications as in the case of the CMR Convention.[79] The effect is that a court or tribunal in another Contracting State will be deemed to have jurisdiction if, and only if, it was designated by agreement between the parties, or if there is situated in the foreign country concerned (a) the place where the defendant has his principal place of business, is habitually resident, or has the place of business through which the contract of carriage was made; or (b) the place where the loss or damage occurred; or (c) the place of departure or destination of the carriage.[80]

Carriage of passengers and luggage by sea. There are no provisions as   **15–048** to the recognition and enforcement of judgments in the Athens Convention relating to the Carriage of Passengers and their Luggage by Sea 1974, nor in section 183(1) of the Merchant Shipping Act 1995 (which gives effect to the Convention), nor in the Carriage of Passengers and their Luggage by Sea (Interim Provisions) Order 1980.[81] There are however provisions as to jurisdiction enabling actions to be brought only in certain courts,[82] and, for the reasons stated above,[83] it is submitted that a judgment given in a foreign court under these provisions is entitled to recognition and enforcement in England.

Claims in respect of air navigation services. The Civil Aviation (Euro-   **15–049** control) Act 1983 contains provisions as to the recognition and enforcement of determinations by a relevant authority in a Contracting State to the Multilateral Agreement relating to Route Charges 1981 as to whether or not any sum is due to Eurocontrol in respect of air navigation services.[84] Certain provisions of the Foreign Judgments (Reciprocal Enforcement) Act 1933[85] are applied, but there are more elaborate further provisions than in the other cases considered in this Rule. "Relevant authority" includes courts and tribunals, and also administrative authorities if their determinations are subject to appeal to or review by a court or tribunal.[86] The relevant authority has jurisdiction for the purposes of recognition and enforcement if the proceedings are brought (a) in the Contracting State (if any) in which there is situated the residence or, as the case may be, the registered office of the person liable to pay the charges; (b) if his residence or registered office is not situated in a Contracting State, in any Contracting State in which he has a place of business; (c) if his residence or registered office is not situated in a Contracting State and he has no place of business in any Contracting State, in any Contracting State in which he has assets; (d) if his residence or registered office is not situated in a Contracting State and he has neither a place of business nor any assets in a

---

[78] For the Convention and the designation of parties to it, see *ante*, para. 15–018.

[79] Carriage of Passengers by Road Act 1974, s.5 (not yet in force). See also Civil Jurisdiction and Judgments Act 1982, ss.31(3) (as amended by Merchant Shipping Act 1995, s.314(2), Sched. 13, para. 66) and 32(4)(*b*).

[80] Carriage of Passengers by Road Act 1974, s.5(1) and Sched., Art. 21(1) (not yet in force).

[81] S.I. 1980 No. 1092 (amended by S.I. 1987 No. 670).

[82] Convention, Art. 17(1), applied by the 1980 Order with the omission of the requirement that the court be located in a Contracting State.

[83] *Ante*, para. 15–043.

[84] Civil Aviation (Eurocontrol) Act 1983, s.1 adding a new s.74A to the Civil Aviation Act 1982. For the Multilateral Agreement and Eurocontrol, see *ante*, paras. 15–024—15–027.

[85] ss.2, 3, 5(3), with modifications to s.5(2).

[86] Civil Aviation Act 1982, s.74A(8) as inserted by Civil Aviation (Eurocontrol) Act 1983, s.1.

Contracting State, in Belgium (being the country in which Eurocontrol has its headquarters).[87]

15–050   **Oil pollution by ships.** Part I of the Foreign Judgments (Reciprocal Enforcement) Act 1933 applies, with the omission of section 4(2) and (3), to any judgment given by a court in a country which is a party to the International Convention on Civil Liability for Oil Pollution Damage 1992[88] to enforce a claim in respect of liability incurred under any provision of foreign legislation corresponding to section 153 of the Merchant Shipping Act 1995; this is the case whether or not that Part has been extended to the country concerned, and whether or not the judgment is of a court specified for the purposes of that Part.[89] The effect of omitting Section 4(2) and (3) of the 1933 Act is that while the registration of the foreign judgment must be set aside if the courts of the country concerned had no jurisdiction in the circumstances of the case,[90] the existence of jurisdiction is to be gathered from the terms of the Convention. In effect, jurisdiction will exist if damage was caused or preventive or remedial measures were taken in the foreign country, including its territorial waters.[91] The International Convention on Liability and Compensation for Damage in Connection with the Carriage of Hazardous and Noxious Substances by Sea 1996, which may be implemented by Order in Council under section 182B of the Merchant Shipping Act 1995,[92] deals with the recognition and enforcement of judgments.[93] Where the courts of a Contracting State assume jurisdiction in accordance with the Convention, the ensuing judgment is entitled to recognition and enforcement in other Contracting States provided that the judgment is enforceable in the State of origin and is "no longer subject to ordinary forms of review".[94] The only exceptions to recognition and enforcement countenanced by the Convention are where the judgment was obtained by fraud and where the defendant was not given reasonable notice and fair opportunity to present his case. In no circumstances may the merits of the case be reopened.[95]

15R–051   **RULE 56—(1) A court in a foreign country outside the United Kingdom which is a party to the Paris Convention on Third Party Liability in the Field of Nuclear Energy (1960) (as amended in 1964)[96] has no jurisdiction to give judgment in proceedings in which the plaintiff claims damages for injury to his person or for damage to his property in respect of a nuclear occurrence unless the Secretary of State certifies that the judgment is a relevant foreign judgment for the purposes of the Nuclear Installations Act 1965.[97]**

---

[87] *Ibid.* s.74A(5) as inserted by 1983 Act, s.1.
[88] For the Convention, see *ante*, para. 15–031.
[89] Merchant Shipping Act 1995, s.166(4).
[90] Foreign Judgments (Reciprocal Enforcement) Act 1933, s.4(1)(*a*)(ii).
[91] See *ante*, para. 15–031.
[92] See *supra*, n. 34.
[93] Art. 40.
[94] Art. 40(1). For Consideration of the analogous wording in Art. 30 of the 1968 Convention see *ante*, para. 14–196.
[95] Art. 40(2).
[96] Cmnd. 2514 (1964).
[97] Nuclear Installations Act 1965, s.17(4).

(2) **No judgment given in a court of a country outside the United Kingdom will be enforced in England against a person who shows that—**

   (a)   **the sum payable under the judgment was awarded in respect of injury or damage which is the subject of an international convention with respect to liability in the field of nuclear energy to which the United Kingdom is a party; and**

   (b)   **the country of the foreign court is not a party to such convention; and**

   (c)   **the sum was not awarded in pursuance of any international convention referred to in the Carriage by Air Act 1932,[98] the Carriage by Air Act 1961, the Carriage by Air (Supplementary Provisions) Act 1962, or the Carriage of Goods by Road Act 1965,[99]**

unless the judgment in question is enforceable in the United Kingdom in pursuance of an international agreement.[1]

COMMENT

Clause (1) of the Rule. The Nuclear Installations Act 1965 gives effect to   15–052
various international conventions (to which the United Kingdom is a party) on civil liability for nuclear occurrences.[2] Section 17(4) of the Act provides that Part I of the Foreign Judgments (Reciprocal Enforcement) Act 1933 shall apply to any judgment given in a court of any foreign country which is certified by the Secretary of State to be a relevant foreign judgment for the purposes of the Act, and shall have effect as if in section 4 of that Act subsections (1)(*a*)(ii), (2) and (3) were omitted. A "relevant foreign judgment" means a judgment of a court of a relevant territory other than the United Kingdom which, under a relevant international agreement, is to be enforceable anywhere within the relevant territories. A "relevant international agreement" means an international agreement with respect to third-party liability in the field of nuclear energy to which the United Kingdom is a party. A "relevant territory" means a country for the time being bound by a relevant international agreement.[3]

The effect of omitting parts of section 4 of the 1933 Act is that the court   15–053
cannot address itself to the question whether the foreign court had jurisdiction. The matter is determined by the Secretary of State, whose certificate is presumably conclusive. He will base his decision on the jurisdictional rules in the Conventions, which are not set out in the Nuclear Installations Act 1965.[4]

Clause (2) of the Rule. This clause is based upon section 17(5) of the   15–054
Nuclear Installations Act 1965,[5] which provides that it shall be a sufficient defence to proceedings in the United Kingdom against any person for the recovery of a sum alleged to be payable under a judgment given in a country

---

[98] Now repealed.
[99] Nuclear Installations Act 1965, s.17(5) as amended by Energy Act 1983, s.31.
[1] Nuclear Installations Act 1965, s.17(5A), inserted by Energy Act 1983, s.31.
[2] See *ante*, para. 15–040.
[3] s.26.
[4] For these jurisdictional rules, see *ante*, para. 15–040.
[5] As amended by Energy Act 1983, s.31.

outside the United Kingdom for that person to show the three things mentioned in sub-clauses (a), (b) and (c) of the Rule. However this provision does not apply where the judgment in question is enforceable in the United Kingdom in pursuance of an international agreement.[6] "International agreement" will include any bilateral or multilateral convention to which the United Kingdom is a party; the phrase is not to be confused with "relevant international agreement" which has a special meaning for the purposes of the Nuclear Installations Act 1965.[7]

15–055   The 1965 Act and the Conventions aim to channel all liability to the operator of the nuclear installation in which the occurrence happened, and to limit his liability.[8] Both these objects would have been frustrated, and a plaintiff suing in a country which is not a party to the Conventions might be in a better position than a plaintiff suing in a country which is such a party had it not been for section 17(5). For the plaintiff could have brought his action in a non-contracting country against a person who would be under no liability to him under the Conventions, or might have recovered a sum in excess of the upper limit imposed by the Act, and could then have enforced his judgment in England. Section 17(5) therefore provides that no such judgment shall be enforceable here. This principle cannot, however, prevail against treaty obligations of the United Kingdom requiring the enforcement of judgments, and this was recognised by an amendment made to the Act in 1983.[9] The original text of the 1965 Act made it clear that the principle did not affect the application of certain international conventions in the field of transport. These are listed in the Rule; the Carriage of Goods by Road Act 1965 is there specified, the Nuclear Installations Act 1965 (which was passing through Parliament at the same time) referring to "any Act which may be passed to give effect to" the CMR Convention.[10] Recent international transport conventions expressly save the provisions of conventions dealing with nuclear damage.[11]

---

[6] Nuclear Installations Act 1965, s.17(5A) inserted by Energy Act 1983, s.31.

[7] s.26(1); see *ante*, para. 15–040.

[8] The original limit of £5 million has since been raised; the current limit is £140 million, except for licensees for whom it is £10 million: Energy Act 1983, s.27; S.I. 1994 No. 909.

[9] *i.e.* the insertion of s.17(5A), *supra*.

[10] The future tense in the words cited in the text is not thought to preclude reference to the Carriage of Goods by Road Act 1965 which has an earlier chapter number than the Nuclear Installations Act 1965.

[11] *e.g.* Carriage of Goods by Sea Act 1971, Sched., Art. IX; Merchant Shipping Act 1995, Sched. 6, Art. 20.

CHAPTER 16

ARBITRATION AND FOREIGN AWARDS[1]

1. ARBITRATION: GOVERNING LAW

RULE 57—(1) The validity, effect and interpretation of an arbitration agreement are governed by its applicable law.[2]   16R–001

---

[1] Mustill and Boyd, *Commercial Arbitration* (2nd ed. 1989), Chap. 4; Patchett, *Recognition of Commercial Judgments and Awards in the Commonwealth* (1984), pp. 193–308; Lorenzen, Chaps. 19 and 20; F. A. Mann, in *International Arbitration: Liber Amicorum for Martin Domke* (ed. Sanders, 1967), p. 157, reprinted in (1986) 2 Arb.Int. 241; Fouchard, *L'Arbitrage Commercial International* (1965); Wetter, *The International Arbitral Process* (1979), Chaps. 5 and 6; Collins, in *Contemporary Problems in International Arbitration* (ed. Lew, 1986), p. 126; Rubino-Sammartano, *International Arbitration Law* (1990), Chaps. 8 and 14; Redfern and Hunter, *Law and Practice of International Commercial Arbitration* (3rd ed. 1999), Chap. 2; Berger, *International Economic Arbitration* (1993), Chaps. 2 and 5; Thomas [1984] L.M.C.L.Q. 141, 304, 491; Hill (1997) 46 I.C.L.Q. 274. See also Grigera Naon, *Choice of Law Problems in International Commercial Arbitration* (1992); Maniruzzaman (1992) 9 Arb.Int. 371.

[2] The relevant authorities continue to be the common law authorities, since the Rome Convention on the Law Applicable to Contractual Obligations (Contracts (Applicable Law) Act 1990, Sched. 1) does not apply to "arbitration agreements" (Art. 1(2)(d)), *post*, paras. 32–034 *et seq.* See *Hamlyn & Co. v. Talisker Distillery* [1894] A.C. 202; *Norske Atlas Insurance Co. Ltd. v. London General Insurance Co. Ltd.* (1927) 28 Ll.L.R. 104; *Kianta Osakeyhtio v. Britain and Overseas Trading Co. Ltd.* [1953] 2 Lloyd's Rep. 569; *The Elizabeth H.* [1962] 1 Lloyd's Rep. 172; *Dalmia Dairy Industries Ltd. v. National Bank of Pakistan* [1978] 2 Lloyd's Rep. 223 (C.A.); *International Tank & Pipe S.A.K. v. Kuwait Aviation Fuelling Co. K.S.C.* [1975] Q.B. 224 (C.A.); *Nova (Jersey) Knit Ltd. v. Kammgarn Spinnerei* [1977] 1 W.L.R. 713, 718, 730 (H.L.); *Black-Clawson International Ltd. v. Papierwerke Waldhof-Aschaffenburg A.G.* [1981] 2 Lloyd's Rep. 446; *Qatar Petroleum v. Shell International Petroleum* [1983] 2 Lloyd's Rep. 35, 43 (C.A.); *The Marques de Bolarque* [1984] 1 Lloyd's Rep. 652; *Naviera Amazonica Peruana S.A. v. Cia Internacional de Seguros del Peru* [1988] 1 Lloyd's Rep. 116 (C.A.); *Deutsche Schachtbau v. Shell International Petroleum Co. Ltd.* [1990] 1 A.C. 295, 309–310 (C.A.), revd. on other grounds *ibid.*, p. 329; *Paul Smith Ltd. v. H & S International Holding Inc.* [1991] 2 Lloyd's Rep. 127, 130; *Channel Tunnel Group Ltd. v. Balfour Beatty Construction Ltd.* [1993] A.C. 334, 357; *Union of India v. McDonnell Douglas Corporation* [1993] 2 Lloyd's Rep. 48; *Sumitomo Heavy Industries Ltd. v. Oil and Natural Gas Commission* [1994] 1 Lloyd's Rep. 45; *Grupo Torras v. Sheikh Fahad Mohammed Al-Sabah* [1995] 1 Lloyd's Rep. 374, 451; *cf. Dallal v. Bank Mellat* [1986] Q.B. 441, 455.

591

(2) In general, and subject to the mandatory rules of the law of the seat of the arbitration, the law chosen by the parties governs arbitral proceedings; in the absence of agreement, arbitral proceedings are governed by the law of the seat of the arbitration.[3]

COMMENT

16–002   **Introductory: scope of this chapter.** Recent years have seen a large growth in private[4] arbitration with a foreign element, or international commercial arbitration as it is frequently called. Certain types of contract in use in international trade customarily provide for arbitration (very often in London). Thus contracts for the sale of commodities often provide for arbitration by a trade association, such as the Grain and Feed Trade Association (GAFTA). In other cases, parties may wish to provide for the resolution of disputes by an independent tribunal, and where they are of equal bargaining power, each may be reluctant to submit disputes to the courts of the other party, or of a third country, but may be prepared to provide for arbitration. Sometimes the arbitration will be an *ad hoc* one, sometimes it will be under the auspices of institutional arbitration, such as the London Court of International Arbitration or the International Chamber of Commerce.[5] Questions may arise before, during and after the arbitration as to the validity of the submission to arbitration, the procedure to be applied in the arbitration, and the scope of the court's power of supervision. Or one party may, in breach of the arbitration agreement, bring proceedings in a court, and the other party may seek to enforce the arbitration agreement by applying for a stay. Where arbitration takes place in a country in which neither party has its place of business, the losing party may be dissatisfied with the award, and refuse to comply with it. The successful party may therefore need to enforce the award in other countries. This chapter deals with the following aspects of international commercial arbitration in

---

[3] Arbitration Act 1996, ss.2, 4, 103(2)(*e*) and Sched. 1. For the common law position prior to the entry into force of the 1996 Act see *Whitworth Street Estates (Manchester) Ltd. v. James Miller & Partners Ltd.* [1970] A.C. 583; *Compagnie Tunisenne de Navigation S.A. v. Compagnie d'Armement Maritime S.A.* [1971] A.C. 572, 604; *Dalmia Dairy Industries Ltd. v. National Bank of Pakistan* [1978] 2 Lloyd's Rep. 223, 270 (C.A.); *International Tank & Pipe S.A.K. v. Kuwait Aviation Fuelling Co. K.S.C.* [1975] Q.B. 224, 232 (C.A.); *Bank Mellat v. Helliniki Techniki S.A.* [1984] Q.B. 291, 301 (C.A.); *President of India v. La Pintada Compania Navigacion* [1985] A.C. 104, 119; *Paul Smith Ltd. v. H & S International Holding Inc.* [1991] 2 Lloyd's Rep. 127, 129–130; *Hiscox v. Outhwaite* [1992] 1 A.C. 562, 597–598; *Channel Tunnel Group Ltd. v. Balfour Beatty Construction Ltd.* [1993] A.C. 334, 357; *Union of India v. McDonnell Douglas Corporation* [1993] 2 Lloyd's Rep. 48; *The Star Texas* [1993] 2 Lloyd's Rep. 445, 449, 452 (C.A.); *Sumitomo Heavy Industries Ltd. v. Oil and Natural Gas Commission* [1994] 1 Lloyd's Rep. 45, 57.

[4] This Chapter is concerned with private or consensual arbitration. In some countries there are statutory or permanent tribunals which are called arbitral tribunals, but which are really courts. This chapter is only concerned with those tribunals if their jurisdiction depends on the consent of the parties: *cf.* Cmnd. 1515, p. 24, discussing Art. I(2) of the New York Convention. See also Rule 66, *post*, on awards of the International Centre for the Settlement of Investment Disputes (ICSID). For the status of awards of the Iran-U.S. Claims Tribunal, which was set up as a standing body with access by private parties, *cf. Dallal v. Bank Mellat* [1986] Q.B. 441 (where it was treated as an arbitral tribunal under international law) with *Ministry of Defense of Iran v. Gould, Inc.*, 887 F.2d 1357 (9th Cir. 1989), cert. den. 494 U.S. 1016 (1990) (where its award was enforced under the New York Convention).

[5] For a general description see *Bank Mellat v. Helliniki Techniki S.A.* [1984] Q.B. 291, 314–315, *per* Robert Goff L.J. See also Craig, Park and Paulsson, *International Chamber of Commerce Arbitration* (2nd ed., 1990).

English law: (1) the law applicable to arbitration agreements[6]; (2) the extent to which English law regulates procedural questions in relation to arbitrations with a foreign element[7]; (3) the law to be applied by the arbitral tribunal[8]; (4) the duty of the English court to stay proceedings brought in England in disregard of an agreement to refer the dispute to arbitration[9]; (5) the recognition and enforcement in England of foreign arbitral awards.[10]

It is firmly established that more than one national system of law may bear **16–003** upon an international arbitration.[11] First, there is the law which regulates the substantive rights of the parties. Secondly, there is the law governing the agreement to submit the dispute to arbitration. Thirdly, there is the law which regulates the conduct of the arbitration. Rule 57 deals with two general principles, clause (1) with the law governing the agreement itself and clause (2) with the law governing the conduct of the arbitration including the determination of the law (or other considerations) applicable to the merits of the dispute.

An arbitration agreement may assume one of two forms, in that it may **16–004** submit present or future disputes to arbitration.[12] A contract may contain an arbitration clause by which the parties agree that if disputes arise under the contract they shall be referred to arbitration. Or parties may agree to submit a particular dispute between them (which need not necessarily stem from a contract) to the decision of a particular arbitrator. According to English law an arbitration clause in a contract constitutes a self-contained contract collateral or ancillary to the main contract of which it forms a part.[13] The arbitration clause sometimes designates the place where the arbitration is to be held or (as is sometimes said) to have its seat; sometimes it leaves the identity of the arbitrator or arbitrators and the place of the arbitration to be chosen by, *e.g.* the President of a Chamber of Commerce or of a trade or professional association, or through the machinery of institutional arbitration such as the London Court of International Arbitration (L.C.I.A.) or the Court of Arbitration of the International Chamber of Commerce (I.C.C.).

In the second half of the twentieth century the law relating to international **16–005** commercial arbitration has been transformed by developments on the international plane. Perhaps most importantly, the New York Convention of 1958,

---

[6] Rule 57(1).

[7] Rule 57(2).

[8] *Ibid.*

[9] Rule 58.

[10] Rules 59 to 66.

[11] *Channel Tunnel Group Ltd. v. Balfour Beatty Construction Ltd.* [1993] A.C. 334, 357, *per* Lord Mustill.

[12] See Mustill and Boyd, Chaps. 6 and 7.

[13] Arbitration Act 1996, s.7 provides that, unless otherwise agreed by the parties, an arbitration agreement which formed or was intended to form part of another agreement (whether or not in writing) shall not be regarded as invalid, non-existent or ineffective because that other agreement is invalid, or did not come into existence or has become ineffective, and it shall for that purpose be treated as a distinct agreement. See also Arbitration Act 1996, s.30, which provides that, unless otherwise agreed by the parties, the arbitral tribunal may rule on its own substantive jurisdiction, including the question whether there is a valid arbitration agreement. For the position at common law see *Heyman v. Darwins Ltd.* [1942] A.C. 356; *Bremer Vulkan Schiffbau und Maschinenfabrik v. South India Shipping Corp. Ltd.* [1981] A.C. 909; *Harbour Assurance Co. (U.K.) Ltd. v. Kansa General International Insurance Co. Ltd.* [1993] Q.B. 701 (C.A.).

which is implemented in England by various provisions of the Arbitration Act 1996,[14] has gone a long way towards ensuring the international enforcement of arbitration agreements[15] and arbitral awards.[16] More recently, a Model Law on International Commercial Arbitration was adopted in 1985 by the United Nations Commission on International Trade Law (UNCITRAL). It is designed to apply to arbitrations where (a) the parties to an arbitration agreement have, at the time of the conclusion of that agreement, their places of business in different States; or (b) one of the following places is situated outside the State in which the parties have their place of business: (i) the place of arbitration, if it is determined in, or pursuant to, the arbitration agreement; (ii) any place where a substantial part of the obligations of the commercial relationship is to be performed or the place with which the subject-matter of the dispute is most closely connected; or (c) the parties have expressly agreed that the subject-matter of the arbitration agreement relates to more than one country. The UNCITRAL Model Law contains rules relating to the definition and form of the arbitration agreement; the duty of the courts to stay proceedings brought in breach of an arbitration agreement; the power of the court to grant interim measures in support of an arbitration; the composition of the tribunal (including appointment; grounds for challenge); the competence of the arbitral tribunal to rule on its jurisdiction, and to order interim measures; the procedure of the arbitration; the grounds for setting aside awards; recognition and enforcement of awards.

16–006   Although the UNCITRAL Model Law has been substantially adopted by a number of countries, including Scotland,[17] Canada, India and Australia, and some of the States in the United States (including California)[18] it seemed at first that it would not have a significant impact in England. In 1989 a Departmental Advisory Committee on Arbitration Law (under the chairmanship of Lord Justice Mustill), which had been established by the Secretary of State for Trade and Industry, recommended against the adoption in England of the UNCITRAL Model Law.[19] The principal reason was that some of the provisions in the Model Law were thought to be unsatisfactory, particularly those relating to the form of arbitration agreements and the number and appointment of arbitrators. However, the Departmental Advisory Committee ("the D.A.C.") recommended that there should be new improved legislation relating to arbitration. The Arbitration Act 1996 ("the 1996 Act") was the result of that recommendation.[20] It would appear that during the course of the process of reform the Model Law's influence increased. As the D.A.C. Report

---

[14] ss. 5, 9, 100–104. These sections replace the equivalent provisions of the Arbitration Act 1975.

[15] See Rule 58, *post.*

[16] See Rule 63, *post.*

[17] Law Reform (Miscellaneous Provisions) (Scotland) Act 1990, s.66 and Sched. 7 (which applies to arbitrations commenced after January 1, 1991).

[18] See Sanders (1995) 11 Arb. Int. 1.

[19] Reprinted in (1990) 6 Arb. Int. 3. *Cf.* the recommendations of the Scottish Advisory Committee (under the chairmanship of Lord Dervaid) which led to the adoption of the Model Law in Scotland: (1990) 6 Arb. Int. 63.

[20] A guide to the provisions of the 1996 Act is to be found in two reports prepared by the D.A.C.: *Report on the Arbitration Bill* (1996) ("D.A.C. Report"), paras. 1 to 276 of which are reprinted in (1997) 13 Arb. Int. 257 and *Supplementary Report on the Arbitration Act 1996* (1997) ("D.A.C. Supplementary Report"), reprinted in (1997) 13 Arb. Int. 317.

makes clear,[21] although the Act does not adopt wholesale the UNCITRAL Model Law, very close regard was paid to it, and the structure and content of the Act owe much to it. The 1996 Act, which came into force on January 31, 1997,[22] superseded Part I of the Arbitration Act 1950 ("the 1950 Act") and all of the Arbitration Act 1975 ("the 1975 Act"), the Arbitration Act 1979 ("the 1979 Act") and the Consumer Arbitration Agreements Act 1988.

The aim of the 1996 Act was not only to make English arbitration law more accessible and comprehensible, but also to bring it more up to date. One of the fundamental principles enshrined by the Act is the principle of party autonomy, which is restricted only to the extent that it is necessary to protect the public interest.[23] Although parties to an arbitration agreement are largely free to determine the process by which their disputes are to be resolved, the Act contains a number of mandatory provisions which may not be excluded by the parties' agreement.[24]   **16–007**

The country in which an arbitration is to take place is often referred to as the "seat" of the arbitration, a term which is adopted by the 1996 Act. The seat is an important concept within the structure of the Act in that the scope of the legislation is largely determined by reference to it: the general principle is that Part I of the Act (which effectively deals with all aspects of arbitration law other than the recognition and enforcement of foreign awards) applies where the seat of the arbitration is in England.[25] The seat is defined by section 3 of the 1996 Act to mean the juridical seat of the arbitration designated (a) by the parties to the arbitration agreement, or (b) by any arbitral or other institution or person vested by the parties with powers to fix the seat, or (c) by the arbitral tribunal if so authorised by the parties, or determined, in the absence of any such designation, having regard to the parties' agreement and all the relevant circumstances. These provisions are more complex and comprehensive than the corresponding provision of the Model Law, which states simply that the parties are free to agree on the place of arbitration and that, in the absence of such agreement, the place of arbitration shall be determined by the arbitral tribunal.[26] In practice, the choice of a place of arbitration by contract is common. In the absence of choice by the parties, arbitral rules may provide for its determination by the arbitral institution (as in the I.C.C. Rules) or by the tribunal (as in the UNCITRAL and L.C.I.A. Rules).   **16–008**

The legal "seat" must not be confused with the geographically convenient place for holding hearings.[27] Although the seat will usually be the place where the arbitration is actually conducted, this is not necessarily so, particularly if different parts of the proceedings are held in different countries. There is no legal requirement that any part of the arbitral proceedings should take place at the seat of the arbitration.[28] Particularly in large arbitrations, hearings may be   **16–009**

---

[21] (1997) 13 Arb. Int. 257, 276.

[22] S.I. 1996 No. 3146.

[23] 1996 Act, s.1(*b*).

[24] *Ibid.*, s.4 and Sched. 1.

[25] *Ibid.*, s.2. See further paras. 16–020 *et seq., post.*

[26] Art. 20(1).

[27] *Naviera Amazonica Peruana S.A. v. Cia Internacional de Seguros del Peru* [1988] 1 Lloyd's Rep. 116, 117 (C.A.).

[28] 1996 Act, s.34(2)(a). This is also the position under the UNCITRAL Model Law, Art. 20(2).

held in a variety of countries, but the seat of the arbitration will remain (unless there is agreement to the contrary) the place designated in the arbitration agreement, or the place nominated by the appointing authority or by the arbitrators as the seat.

16–010   The 1968 Convention and the Lugano Convention on jurisdiction and the enforcement of judgments in civil and commercial matters exclude arbitration from their scope.[29] The European Court confirmed in *Marc Rich & Co. A.G. v. Soc. Italiana Impianti P.A.*[30] that Article 1(4) of the 1968 Convention is intended to exclude arbitration in its entirety, including proceedings brought before national courts, and in particular, proceedings relating to the appointment of an arbitrator, even if there were a preliminary issue as to the existence or validity of the arbitration agreement. More recently, in *Van Uden Maritime B.V. v. Firma Deco-Line*,[31] the European Court referred, with apparent approval, to the passage in the Schlosser Report,[32] in which it is stated that the 1968 Convention does not apply (*inter alia*) to judgments determining whether an arbitration agreement is valid or not, or to proceedings concerning the recognition and enforcement of arbitration awards, or to proceedings ancillary to arbitration proceedings. There have been several English decisions on the scope and effect of Article 1(4),[33] and there remain a number of important questions which are not finally settled, including the questions whether the English court may enjoin proceedings in another Contracting State which have been brought in breach of an arbitration agreement[34] and whether a decision of the court of a Contracting State on the existence or validity of an arbitration agreement is entitled to recognition under the Conventions, and whether a decision on the merits in disregard of an arbitration agreement is entitled to recognition or enforcement.[35]

16–011   **Clause (1) of the Rule.** Questions relating to the governing law of an arbitration agreement arise in a variety of contexts. A respondent may seek to restrain the continuance of an arbitration,[36] or may resist enforcement of a foreign award,[37] on the ground that the agreement to arbitrate, or the contract of which it forms a part, is invalid. Or a question may arise as to the jurisdiction of the arbitrator to decide a particular issue between the parties,[38] or as to whether the arbitration agreement has been frustrated.[39] These, and related issues, fall to be determined by the law governing the arbitration agreement.

---

[29] Art. 1, *ante*, paras. 11–023 *et seq.*
[30] Case C–190/89 [1991] E.C.R. I–3855.
[31] Case C–391/95 [1998] E.C.R. I–7091; [1999] 2 W.L.R. 1181.
[32] Paras. 64 and 65.
[33] *Ante*, paras. 11–028 *et seq.*
[34] See para. 15–056.
[35] See paras. 14–187 *et seq.*
[36] *The Marques de Bolarque* [1984] 1 Lloyd's Rep. 652.
[37] *e.g. Dalmia Dairy Industries Ltd. v. National Bank of Pakistan* [1978] 2 Lloyd's Rep. 223 (C.A.); *Deutsche Schachtbau v. Shell International Petroleum Co. Ltd.* [1990] 1 A.C. 295 (C.A.), revd. on other grounds, *ibid.* p. 329.
[38] *Ibid.*
[39] See *Black-Clawson International Ltd. v. Papierwerke Waldhof-Aschaffenburg A.G.* [1981] 2 Lloyd's Rep. 446, 455.

There is no uniform international practice on the determination of the   **16–012**
governing law of the arbitration agreement[40] and the question has not received
detailed scrutiny in England.

The governing law of the arbitration agreement is normally the same as the
law governing the contract of which it forms a part, but there may be
exceptional cases where the arbitration agreement will be governed by a
different law.[41]

The principles on which the governing law of the contract is determined are   **16–013**
considered in detail elsewhere in this book.[42] They depend on the Rome
Convention on the Law Applicable to Contractual Obligations, which is given
the force of law by the Contracts (Applicable Law) Act 1990. The rules in the
Rome Convention, however, do not apply to "arbitration agreements".[43] The
United Kingdom Government proposed the inclusion of arbitration agreements in the Rome Convention, on the ground that they did not differ from
other agreements with regard to their contractual aspects; but other governments (especially those of Germany and France) opposed the proposal, on the
grounds (*inter alia*) that the arbitration clause was severable and independent,
and that it would be difficult to apply the choice of law rules to arbitration
clauses. Accordingly, it was decided to exclude arbitration agreements and to
study the question further with a view to the conclusion of a separate
Protocol.[44] There is no prospect of such a Protocol.

If, which is rare, there is an express choice of law to govern the arbitration   **16–014**
agreement, that choice will be effective, irrespective of the applicable law of
the contract as a whole.[45]

If there is an express choice of law to govern the contract as a whole, the   **16–015**
arbitration agreement will also be governed by that law: this is so whether or
not the seat of the arbitration is stipulated, and irrespective of the place of the
seat.[46] If there is no express choice of law, and no choice of the seat of the
arbitration, the applicable law of the contract will normally be determined in

---

[40] See Craig, Park and Paulsson, pp. 72–74. One of the grounds for refusal to recognise or enforce
an award under the New York Convention (Article V(1)(*a*)) is that the arbitration agreement
was not valid under " . . . the law to which the parties subjected it or, failing any indication
thereon, under the law of the country where the award was made.": 1996 Act, s.103(2)(*b*). The
Swiss Private International Law Act provides that an arbitration agreement is valid if it
conforms to the law chosen by the parties, or to the law governing the substance of the dispute,
or to Swiss law: see decision of Swiss Federal Tribunal in (1997) 22 Yb. Comm. Arb. 800.

[41] See *Deutsche Schachtbau v. Shell International Petroleum Co. Ltd.* [1990] 1 A.C. 295, 309–310
(C.A.), revd. on other grounds *ibid.* p. 329 (arbitration agreement governed by Swiss law;
Swiss arbitrators applied general principles of law as substantive law); *Naviera Amazonica
Peruana S.A. v. Cia Internacional de Seguros del Peru* [1988] 1 Lloyd's Rep. 116, 119
(C.A.).

[42] Chap. 32, *post.*

[43] 1990 Act, Sched. 1, Art. 1(2)(d). See *post*, paras. 32–034 *et seq.*

[44] Giuliano-Lagarde Report on the Rome Convention [1980] O.J. C282/11 (in Plender, *European
Contracts Convention* (1991), p. 243).

[45] *Naviera Amazonica Peruana S.A. v. Cia Internacional de Seguros del Peru* [1988] 1 Lloyd's
Rep. 116, 119 (C.A.).

[46] *International Tank & Pipe S.A.K. v. Kuwait Aviation Fuelling Co. K.S.G.* [1975] Q.B. 224
(C.A.); *Qatar Petroleum v. Shell International Petroleum* [1983] 2 Lloyd's Rep. 35 (C.A.); *The
Marques de Bolarque* [1984] 1 Lloyd's Rep. 116; *Paul Smith Ltd. v. H & S International
Holdings Inc.* [1991] 2 Lloyd's Rep. 127, 130; *Union of India v. McDonnell Douglas Corpora-
tion* [1993] 2 Lloyd's Rep. 48; *Sumitomo Heavy Industries Ltd. v. Oil and Natural Gas
Commission* [1994] 1 Lloyd's Rep. 45.

accordance with the principles in the Rome Convention, and the arbitration agreement will be governed by the law so determined.[47] If there is no express choice of the law to govern either the contract as a whole or the arbitration agreement, but the parties have chosen the seat of the arbitration, the contract will frequently (but not necessarily) be governed by the law of that country on the basis that the choice of the seat is to be regarded as an implied choice of the law governing the contract.[48] In each of these cases, the contract and the arbitration agreement will be governed by the same law.

16–016   If there is no choice of law to govern the contract as a whole, but the selection of the seat of the arbitration is not treated as an implied choice of the law of that place to govern the contract,[49] the question arises whether the arbitration agreement is governed by the law applicable to the contract or by the law of the seat of the arbitration. It has been held that to determine the governing law, it is not permissible to look at the arbitration agreement in isolation; regard should be had to the surrounding circumstances, including the law governing the substantive contract.[50] Nevertheless, the law of the seat of the arbitration will apply if the circumstances point to an implied intention to choose the law of that place to govern the arbitration agreement. In such cases the law governing the arbitration agreement will be different from the law governing the substantive contract. In *Deutsche Schachtbau v. Shell International Petroleum Co. Ltd.*[51] it was held that an arbitration agreement providing for arbitration in Geneva under the auspices of the International Chamber of Commerce was governed by Swiss law, notwithstanding that the contract, which was to be performed in R'As Al Khaimah, had been held by the arbitral tribunal to be governed by general principles of law. Even if the choice of the seat does not point to an implied intention to choose the law governing the arbitration agreement, there is an argument for saying that the arbitration agreement should nonetheless be governed by the law of the seat[52]; an arbitration agreement is severable from the contract of which it forms a part and is normally more closely connected with the country of the seat than with any other country.

---

[47] A similar passage in the 11th edition was quoted with approval in *The Star Texas* [1993] 2 Lloyd's Rep. 445, 448 (C.A.).

[48] *Egon Oldendorff v. Libera Corporation* [1995] 2 Lloyd's Rep. 64; (*No. 2*) [1996] 2 Lloyd's Rep. 380. See also the cases decided at common law: *Hamlyn & Co. v. Talisker Distillery* [1894] A.C. 202; *N.V. Kwik Hoo Tong Handel Maatschappij v. James Finlay Co. Ltd.* [1927] A.C. 604; *The Njegos* [1936] P. 90; *N.V. "Vulcaan" v. A/S J. Ludwig Mowinckels Rederi* [1938] 2 All E.R. 152 (H.L.); *The SLS Everest* [1981] 2 Lloyd's Rep. 389 (C.A.); *The Parouth* [1982] 2 Lloyd's Rep. 351 (C.A.); *The Mariannina* [1983] 1 Lloyd's Rep. 12 (C.A.); *Steel Authority of India Ltd. v. Hind Metals Inc.* [1984] 1 Lloyd's Rep. 405; *The Elli 2* [1985] 1 Lloyd's Rep. 107 (C.A.).

[49] See, *e.g. Atlantic Underwriting Agencies Ltd. v. Compagnie di Assicurazione di Milano* [1979] 2 Lloyd's Rep. 240 (arbitration in Geneva, contract governed by Italian law); *The Castle Alpha* [1989] 2 Lloyd's Rep. 383 (arbitration in London, contract governed by Japanese law).

[50] *Deutsche Schachtbau v. Shell International Petroleum Co. Ltd.* [1990] 1 AC 295 (C.A.), revd. on other grounds *ibid.*, p. 329.

[51] At p. 310. *Cf. Black-Clawson International Ltd. v. Papierwerke Waldhof-Aschaffenberg A.G.* [1981] 2 Lloyd's Rep. 446, 456. In *Hamlyn & Co. v. Talisker Distillery* [1894] A.C. 202 only Lord Herschell L.C. (at pp. 207–208) treated the question of the law governing the arbitration agreement as a question separate from that of the law governing the contract; see Lorenzen, pp. 479–480. See also Mustill and Boyd, p. 63.

[52] See Lorenzen, pp. 497–498.

All questions relating to the formation of an arbitration agreement are   **16–017**
governed by the law which would govern if it were validly concluded, *i.e.* by
its putative applicable law.[53] The law governing the arbitration agreement will
determine its validity, effect and interpretation. The question whether the
arbitration clause is wide enough to cover the dispute between the parties is
a question of interpretation and therefore depends on the law governing the
arbitration agreement.[54] That law will normally[55] determine whether
the clause remains binding on the parties although one of them alleges that the
contract is void, voidable or illegal,[56] or that it has been discharged by breach
or frustration.[57] The governing law will also determine whether an arbitration
clause can be imported by implication into a different contract between the
same parties, or between one of them and a third party.[58]

Prior to the entry into force of the 1996 Act there were potential problems   **16–018**
concerning the borderline between issues of substance determined by the law
governing the arbitration agreement and issues of procedure governed by the
procedural law of the arbitration.[59] Such problems are avoided under the 1996
Act, which clearly determines the scope of each of the various provisions of
Part I.[60] Although the general rule is that Part I applies in cases where England
is the seat of the arbitration,[61] it is also expressly provided[62] that, where the

---

[53] *The Heidberg* [1994] 2 Lloyd's Rep. 287.

[54] *Nova (Jersey) Knit Ltd. v. Kammgarn Spinnerei* [1977] 1 W.L.R. 713 (H.L.); *Dalmia Dairy Industries Ltd. v. National Bank of Pakistan* [1978] 1 Lloyd's Rep. 223 (C.A.); *The Marques de Bolarque* [1984] 1 Lloyd's Rep. 652, 660.

[55] Subject to overriding legislation which applies irrespective of the governing law, such as the Carriage of Goods by Road Act 1965: *A/B Bofors v. A/B Skandia Transport* [1982] 1 Lloyd's Rep. 410.

[56] *Dalmia Dairy Industries Ltd. v. National Bank of Pakistan, supra*; *cf. Mackender v. Feldia* [1967] 2 Q.B. 590 (C.A.); Kahn-Freund (1977) 26 I.C.L.Q. 825, 838–841. On the important practical question whether, and under what law, a foreign State may invoke its incapacity under its own law to submit to international arbitration see Van Den Berg, pp. 278–282; Delaume, *Law and Practice of Transnational Contracts*, 1988, pp. 354–359; Paulsson (1986) 2 Arb.Int. 90. The Swiss Private International Law Act of 1987, Art. 177(2), provides that a State cannot rely on its own law to contest its capacity to be a party to arbitration. The point has not arisen in England. The answer should depend on the law governing the arbitration agreement, rather than the law of the State concerned, but the Arbitration Act 1996, s.103(2)(*a*) (and the corresponding provision in the New York Convention) suggest otherwise in the context of enforcement: *post*, para. 16–133.

[57] *Black-Clawson International Ltd. v. Papierwerke Waldhof-Aschaffenburg A.G.* [1981] 2 Lloyd's Rep. 446. In this decision Mustill J. showed that the obligations of the parties concerning the conduct of the arbitration, which arise only when the arbitral machinery is put into operation, may be governed (although only in exceptional circumstances) by a law different from that of the arbitration clause itself; see also Mustill and Boyd, pp. 61–62.

[58] *Kianta Osakeyhtio v. Britain and Overseas Trading Co. Ltd.* [1953] 2 Lloyd's Rep. 569, 576; *The Elizabeth H.* [1962] 1 Lloyd's Rep. 172; *Datronics Engineers Inc. v. Hardeman-Monier-Hutcherson* [1966] W.A.R. 55.

[59] The problem became acute where the court was asked to exercise its powers in a case which had connections with England but in which no place of arbitration had been stipulated or determined: the solution adopted by the courts was to treat the power as dependent on the law governing the arbitration agreement: see, *e.g. International Tank & Pipe S.A.K. v. Kuwait Aviation Fuelling Co. K.S.G.* [1975] Q.B. 224 (C.A.) (power to extend contractual time for commencement of arbitration); *The Mariannina* [1983] 1 Lloyd's Rep. 12 (C.A.) (power to appoint arbitrators).

[60] See D.A.C. Supplementary Report (1997) 13 Arb. Int. 317, 318–322.

[61] 1996 Act, s.2(1).

[62] *Ibid.*, s.2(5).

seat is outside England or where the seat has not been determined or designated, section 7 (which provides, subject to the parties' contrary agreement, that an arbitration agreement is to be treated as distinct from any contract of which it forms a part) and section 8 (which provides that, unless the parties agree otherwise, an arbitration agreement is not discharged by the death of a party) are applicable if English law is the law governing the arbitration agreement.

16–019   **Clause (2) of the Rule.** The position prior to the 1996 Act was that the law governing arbitral proceedings was the law chosen by the parties, or, in the absence of agreement, the law of the country in which the arbitration was held. This principle, which was applicable both to English arbitrations and to those which were held abroad,[63] was by no means absolute since it is clear that, at common law, parties to an English arbitration were not able to exclude various aspects of English arbitration law (such as the court's power to set aside or remit an English award for misconduct) simply by choosing the law of a foreign country as the procedural law of the arbitration.[64]

16–020   The 1996 Act delimits the circumstances in which English procedural law applies; it does not address the more general question, what procedural law applies to an international arbitration? This is unlikely to pose any problems as it is only in unusual circumstances that this question might require an answer. In essence, issues relating to the procedural aspects of an arbitration arise in English courts in only three types of situation. The first is a where a dispute concerns the way in which English arbitral proceedings ought to be (or ought to have been) conducted. The second concerns the powers of the English court to intervene in an arbitration, whether the seat is in England or abroad. Both of these situations are comprehensively dealt with by the statutory provisions which determine the scope of Part I of the 1996 Act. The third issue is whether a foreign award can be refused recognition or enforcement on the basis that the arbitral procedure was defective. This is addressed primarily by provisions of the New York Convention of 1958, which are implemented in England by Part III of the 1996 Act.[65]

16–021   Section 2 of the 1996 Act determines the scope of Part I of the Act. The basic rule in section 2(1) is that the provisions contained in Part I apply where the seat of the arbitration is in England. Since the parties may choose the seat of the arbitration,[66] either at the time of contracting or subsequently, they may effectively choose the application of English arbitration law to govern the procedural aspects of their arbitration.

16–022   If the seat of the arbitration is in England, the provisions of the 1996 Act determine *inter alia* how the arbitrators are to be appointed, whether an

---

[63] See *Whitworth Street Estates (Manchester) Ltd. v. James Miller & Partners Ltd.* [1970] A.C. 583; *Naviera Amazonica Peruana S.A. v. Cia Internacional de Seguros del Peru* [1988] 1 Lloyd's Rep. 116 (C.A.).

[64] *Union of India v. McDonnell Douglas Corporation* [1993] 2 Lloyd's Rep. 48.

[65] See Rule 63, *post.* For the different considerations which apply to an international claims tribunal set up by States see *Dallal v. Bank Mellat* [1986] Q.B. 441 (a case concerning the Iran-U.S. Claims Tribunal whose procedure is not subject to Dutch law, although it sits in the Netherlands) and para. 16–002, n. 4, *ante.*

[66] 1996 Act, s.3. See *ABB Lummus Global Ltd. v. Keppel Fels Ltd.* [1999] 2 Lloyd's Rep. 24.

arbitrator may be appointed by the court, whether the authority of an arbitrator may be revoked, what law the arbitrators are to apply (and whether they are expected or allowed to decide *ex aequo et bono* or as *amiables composi-teurs*),[67] the procedural powers and duties of the arbitrators, including questions of evidence (but not their jurisdiction to decide the dispute, which is governed by the arbitration agreement and the law applicable to it), the powers of the court to support arbitral proceedings, whether the court has the power to extend agreed time limits, and whether the award may be remitted or set aside for serious irregularity.

The general principle in section 2(1) is subject to four qualifications which **16–023** extend the scope of various statutory provisions to cases where the seat of the arbitration is outside England or where no seat has been designated or determined. First, certain provisions apply regardless of the seat of the arbitration,[68] namely those relating to the stay of proceedings[69] and the enforcement of arbitral awards.[70] Secondly, some powers are exercisable by the English court in relation to foreign arbitrations and in cases where the seat of the arbitration has not been determined.[71] The specific powers are the power to secure the attendance of witnesses who are in the United Kingdom in cases where the arbitral proceedings are being conducted in England[72] and powers exercisable in support of arbitral proceedings[73] (in particular, the power to grant interim injunctions[74]). These powers are discretionary and the court may refuse to exercise any of them if, in the opinion of the court, the fact that the seat of the arbitration is outside England makes it inappropriate to do so. The court must be careful to avoid coming into conflict with the courts of other countries, in particular the courts of the seat. In a case where another country is the seat of the arbitration, the courts of that country are the natural forum for the granting of interim relief; if, in such a case, an application for interim relief is made in English proceedings, it is for the plaintiff to show why the English court should prefer itself to the natural forum.[75] Thirdly, the English court may exercise any other power under the Act for the purpose of supporting the arbitral process where the seat of the arbitration has not been designated or determined and, by reason of a connection with England, the court is satisfied that it is appropriate to do so.[76] For example, in a case where the seat of the arbitration has yet to be determined, the court may exercise its power to extend agreed time limits or to appoint an arbitrator if the arbitration agreement is governed by English law or if it is likely that, once determined,

---

[67] *Ibid.*, s.46. For further discussion see paras. 16–031 *et seq. infra*. See also Lorenzen, pp. 465–466; Mezger, in Domke, *International Trade Arbitration* (1958), p. 229 at pp. 239–243; Klein, in *The Art of Arbitration: Liber Amicorum for Pieter Sanders* (ed. Schultz and Van Den Berg, 1982), p. 189.

[68] 1996 Act, s.2(2).

[69] *Ibid.*, ss.9–11 (because the power to stay proceedings is exercisable wherever the arbitration is being, or is to be, held).

[70] *Ibid.*, s.66 (because the powers are exercisable in relation to foreign awards).

[71] *Ibid.*, s.2(3).

[72] *Ibid.*, s.43.

[73] *Ibid.*, s.44.

[74] *Ibid.*, s.44(2)(e).

[75] *Channel Tunnel Group Ltd. v. Balfour Beatty Construction Ltd.* [1993] A.C. 334, 368, *per* Lord Mustill.

[76] 1996 Act, s.2(4).

the seat will be in England.[77] Fourthly, as already noted, the provisions relating to the separability of the arbitration agreement and the death of a party[78] also apply where English law is the law applicable to the arbitration agreement, regardless of the seat of the arbitration.[79]

16–024   Although section 2 determines the circumstances in which the various provisions of Part I of the 1996 Act are prima facie applicable, it is important to note that a number of these provisions may be excluded by the agreement of the parties.[79a] The scheme of the Act is to divide the provisions of Part I into two groups: those which are mandatory and those which are non-mandatory.[80] To the extent that they are rendered applicable by the terms of section 2, the mandatory provisions cannot be excluded. Some of the most important of the mandatory provisions relate to the court's powers of supervision (in particular, the power to set aside or remit an award for lack of jurisdiction or serious irregularity and the power to remove an arbitrator). It is a fundamental principle that, where England is the seat of the arbitration, the parties cannot contract out of the supervisory role of the court. However, section 69 the 1996 Act, which provides that a party to arbitral proceedings may appeal to the court on a question of law arising out of an award, and section 45, which allows questions of law arising out of arbitral proceedings to be referred to the court, are non-mandatory provisions which may be excluded by the parties' agreement. By contrast with the provisions of the 1979 Act which it replaces, the 1996 Act does not limit the parties' freedom to exclude the right to appeal on a point of law in cases falling within the so-called special categories; nor does it draw a distinction between domestic and non-domestic arbitration agreements.[81] Some of the provisions which relate to the court's support of the arbitral process (for example, the duty to stay proceedings brought in breach of an arbitration agreement, the power to extend agreed time limits and the power to secure the attendance of witnesses) are mandatory. Certain of the mandatory provisions relate to the general duties of the parties, the duty of the arbitral tribunal to act fairly and impartially and the immunity of the arbitral tribunal and arbitral institutions. It should also be noted that section 13, which provides that the English Limitation Acts (including the Foreign Limitation Periods Act 1984[82]) apply to any arbitration whose seat is in England, is a mandatory provision.

16–025   The non-mandatory provisions are in effect "fall-back" provisions, which apply only to the extent that the parties have not made their own arrangements.[83] Parties may make their own arrangements in one of a number of ways. As regards specific provisions—such as section 69, which enables parties to appeal to the court on a question of law arising out of an award—the parties may simply exclude them by an agreement in writing and not put anything else in their place. More generally, the parties may enter into an *ad*

---

[77] For the position under the 1950 Act see *International Tank & Pipe S.A.K. v. Kuwait Aviation Fuelling Co. K.S.C.* [1975] Q.B. 224 (C.A.).
[78] 1996 Act, ss. 7, 8.
[79] *Ibid.*, s.2(5).
[79a] See *Re Q's Estate* [1999] 1 Lloyd's Rep. 931.
[80] *Ibid.*, s.4 and Sched. 1.
[81] The restrictions in the 1979 Act were intended as a temporary measure and the responses to the D.A.C.'s consultation exercise led to the conclusion that the restrictions should not be preserved.
[82] 1996 Act, s.13(4).
[83] *Ibid.*, s.4(2).

hoc arbitration agreement which regulates many of the issues covered by the non-mandatory provisions or they may incorporate a set of arbitration rules (such as the Rules of the London Court of International Arbitration or the UNCITRAL Arbitration Rules) into their arbitration agreement, with the consequence that the non-mandatory provisions of the 1996 Act are replaced by the corresponding arbitration rules agreed by the parties.[84] It is also possible, although it will rarely (if ever) occur in practice, for parties to agree that England should be the seat of the arbitration but to choose the law of another country to govern the procedure of the arbitration. The choice of foreign law is effective as regards those matters which are not regulated by the mandatory provisions of the 1996 Act; the non-mandatory provisions are displaced by the equivalent provisions of the law chosen by the parties.[85]

Just as parties to an English arbitration might choose a foreign law as the   **16–026**
procedural law, parties to a foreign arbitration may choose English law as the procedural law. In this type of situation, apart from the provisions relating to the stay of legal proceedings and the enforcement of awards,[86] the only provisions in the 1996 Act which are capable of applying directly (as distinct from by operation of the parties' agreement, which will in turn be subject to the mandatory provisions of the law of the seat) are those relating to the attendance of witnesses and to the powers of the court exercisable in support of arbitral proceedings,[87] *i.e.* the provisions which are applicable to any arbitration whose seat is outside England. Even where English law governs the contract and the arbitration agreement, the court has no jurisdiction to exercise its supervisory powers over a foreign arbitration or in relation to a foreign award.[88] Although a choice of English law as the law to govern foreign arbitral proceedings does not have the effect of extending the scope of the provisions of the 1996 Act, it may be supposed that the court will be more inclined to exercise its powers under section 43 (to secure the attendance of witnesses) and section 44 (to support foreign arbitral proceedings) in cases where the parties have agreed that English law should govern procedural aspects of the arbitration; if the parties have chosen English law as the procedural law the exercise of the court's powers to support a foreign arbitration is less likely to be inappropriate.

With regard to the powers of the court, it should be noted that the 1996 Act   **16–027**
determines only the framework; many of the statutory provisions are open-textured in that they simply set out the powers which, unless effectively excluded by the parties' agreement, the court *may* exercise. On the basis of cases decided prior to the 1996 Act, the court should, when exercising its discretion, have regard to the degree of connection that the parties or the

---

[84] *Ibid.*, s.4(3). An agreement to arbitrate under Rules of the Court of Arbitration of the International Chamber of Commerce (I.C.C.) has the effect of excluding the right to appeal to the court on a point of law because the rules provide that the parties waive their right to any form of recourse: *Arab African Energy Corporation Ltd. v. Olieprodukten Nederland B.V.* [1983] 2 Lloyd's Rep. 419; *Marine Contractors Ltd. v. Shell Petroleum Development Co. of Nigeria Ltd.* [1984] 2 Lloyd's Rep. 77.

[85] *Ibid.*, s.4(5).

[86] *Ibid.*, ss.9–11, 66.

[87] *Ibid.*, ss.43, 44.

[88] For the position at common law see *Whitworth Street Estates (Manchester) Ltd. v. James Miller & Partners Ltd.* [1970] A.C. 583.

arbitration have with England and its legal system and to the kind of arbitral procedure which the parties envisaged.[89]

16–028   The Civil Procedure Rules 1998, Practice Direction–Arbitrations,[90] regulate proceedings under the 1996 Act (such as applications for the appointment of an arbitrator, or for the setting aside of an award)[91] and deal with service of the process (the arbitration claim form) on the respondent. If the process cannot be served in England,[92] the court may give permission for service of an arbitration claim form out of the jurisdiction.[93] The court shall not give permission unless the case is a "proper one".[94] The relevant test is that which is applied in the context of applications for permission for service out of the jurisdiction under Order 11.[95] Accordingly, the applicant must satisfy the court not only that any conditions laid down in the Practice Direction – Arbitrations are satisfied, but also that England is the *forum conveniens* (which will normally be the case if England is the seat of the arbitration).[96]

16–029   **"De-localised" arbitration.** In recent years there has developed a theory (mainly in continental Europe) that it is possible and desirable to have a system of "de-localised" (or "floating" or "de-nationalised") arbitration.[97]

---

[89] *Bank Mellat v. Helliniki Techniki S.A.* [1984] Q.B. 291, 303, *per* Kerr L.J.; *S.A. Coppée Lavalin N.V. v. Ken-Ren Chemicals and Fertilizers Ltd.* [1995] 1 A.C. 38, 63, *per* Lord Mustill. One of the effects of the 1996 Act is to alter the position in relation to orders for security for costs. Under the 1950 Act, s.12(6)(a) the court had the power to make such orders; see, in particular, *S.A. Coppée Lavalin N.V. v. Ken-Ren Chemicals and Fertilizers Ltd.* [1995] 1 A.C. 38. Under the 1996 Act, s.38(3) it is the tribunal, rather than the court, which may order a claimant to provide security for the costs of the arbitration (though this power may be excluded by the parties' agreement).

[90] CPR PD49G.

[91] For the definition of "arbitration application" see CPR PD49G, para. 2.1. An application for an anti-suit injunction to restrain foreign proceedings brought in breach of an arbitration agreement falls within Ord. 11, r.1(1)(*d*) (CPR, Sched. 1) if the arbitration agreement is governed by English law: *Schiffahrtgesellschaft Detlev von Appen GmbH v. Voest Alpine Intertrading G.m.b.H.* [1997] 2 Lloyd's Rep. 279 (C.A.); *cf. Sokana Industries Inc. v. Freyre Co. Inc.* [1994] 2 Lloyd's Rep. 57.

[92] In accordance with CPR Part 6 or CPR PD49G, para. 7.

[93] CPR PD49G, para. 8.1. This rule applies only to applications by and against parties to an arbitration; it does not allow service out of the jurisdiction on a non-party: *The Cienvik* [1996] 2 Lloyd's Rep. 395; *cf. Tate & Lyle Industries Ltd. v. Cia Usina Bulhoes* [1997] 1 Lloyd's Rep. 355 (Hobhouse L.J., as a single judge of C.A.).

[94] para. 8.2(2).

[95] *The Atlantic Emperor* [1989] 1 Lloyd's Rep. 548, 553 (C.A.); *Sokana Industries Inc. v. Freyre & Co. Inc.* [1994] 2 Lloyd's Rep 57, 64. For consideration of Ord. 11 see Rule 27.

[96] *The John C Helmsing* [1990] 2 Lloyd's Rep. 290 (C.A.). Where the case falls within the scope of Ord. 11 as well as the Practice Direction the application should be made under the latter: *The John C Helmsing, ibid.*, at p. 293.

[97] The literature is very considerable. See especially Goldman (1963) *Recueil des Cours*, II, p. 347; Fragistas, *Rev.Crit.* 1960, 1; Lalive (1967) *Recueil des Cours*, I, p. 571; Lew, *Applicable Law in International Commercial Arbitration* (1978); Fouchard, *op. cit. supra* n. 1, Vol. 2, pp. 401 *et seq.*; Paulsson (1981) 30 I.C.L.Q. 358, (1983) 32 I.C.L.Q. 53; and for criticism see F. A. Mann, *op. cit. supra* n. 1; Wetter, *op. cit. supra* n. 1, Vol. 2, pp. 403–404, 526–531; Park (1983) 32 I.C.L.Q. 21; Collins, in *Basle Symposium on the Law Governing Contractual Obligations* (ed. Klein & Vischer, 1983), pp. 70–79; Mustill in *Liber Amicorum for Lord Wilberforce* (1987), pp. 149–184, reprinted in (1988) 4 Arb.Int. 86; *Lex Mercatoria and Arbitration*, ed. Carbonneau, 1990; Strenger (1991) *Recueil des Cours*, II, p. 207; Kerr (1993) 2 Am. Rev. Int. Arb. 377; Rivkin (1993) 9 Arb. Int. 67; Gaillard, 1995 *Clunet* 5. See also *S.A. Coppée Lavalin N.V. v. Ken-Ren Chemicals and Fertilizers Ltd.* [1995] 1 A.C. 38, 51–52, *per* Lord Mustill. Art. 28(1) of UNCITRAL Model Law allows a choice of "*rules* of law", which is intended to allow the choice of a non-national system: UNCITRAL, *Yearbook*, vol. 16, 1985, pp. 132–133.

According to this theory it serves the aims and interests of party autonomy in international contracts for the parties to be able to stipulate in their contract for arbitration which is not to be subject to the procedural rules of any particular country, or to the rules of the conflict of laws of any particular country, or to the substantive rules of any particular legal system.[98] Instead the arbitration will be subject to the procedural rules chosen by the parties (but not to the mandatory procedural rules of the place of arbitration); the arbitrators will not necessarily apply the rules of conflict of laws of the seat of arbitration, but those rules of conflict of laws which they "deem appropriate"[99] and they may apply, not the substantive rules of any particular legal system, but the general principles of law or "*lex mercatoria.*"

With regard to procedural rules, the theory of de-localisation has found   **16–030** little support in England. At common law it was well established that English law "does not recognise the concept of arbitral procedures floating in the transnational firmament, unconnected with any municipal system of law."[1] The 1996 Act provides that the provisions of Part I are applicable to arbitrations whose seat is in England. Although parties are free to exclude many of the provisions of Part I by a specific agreement or to displace them by the adoption of a set of institutional rules or by the choice of the law of another country as the procedural law, there is a core of mandatory provisions which cannot be excluded. Regardless of the parties' express intentions, an arbitrator in England is subject to the mandatory provisions of the 1996 Act. There can be no doubt that where an arbitration takes place in England under the rules of the International Chamber of Commerce (which has a body, called a Court of Arbitration, which administers from Paris arbitrations conducted under its auspices) it is an English arbitration and not a supra-national arbitration.[2] The rejection of the theory of de-localisation also has the consequence that by English law a foreign arbitration is subject to the procedure of the foreign

---

[98] Arbitrations between states and private parties raise special problems: in several such cases arbitrators have applied the procedural law of the place of arbitration, but not its conflict of laws rules: see, *e.g. Sapphire International Petroleum Ltd. v. National Iranian Oil Co.* (1967) 35 I.L.R. 136; *B.P. v. Libya* (1979) 53 I.L.R. 297. But *cf. Saudi Arabia v. Aramco* (1963) 27 I.L.R. 117; *Texaco Overseas Petroleum Co. Ltd. v. Libya* (1979) 53 I.L.R. 389; *LIAMCO v. Libya* (1982) 62 I.L.R. 140; *Kuwait v. Aminoil* (1984) 66 I.L.R. 518.

[99] Variants of this phrase appear in a number of institutional procedural rules (UNCITRAL, UN Economic Commission for Europe, International Chamber of Commerce) influenced by the European Convention on International Commercial Arbitration (1961) (not ratified by the United Kingdom): see Klein, in *The Art of Arbitration: Liber Amicorum* for *Pieter Sanders* (1982), at p. 201. The UNCITRAL Model Law provides that, failing a choice of law by the parties, the arbitral tribunal shall apply "the law determined by the conflict of law rules which it considers applicable": Art. 28(2). This provision was intended to have the effect that the tribunal must apply conflict of law *rules*, but not necessarily those of the seat of arbitration: see *e.g.* Delaume, *Law and Practice of Transnational Contracts*, 1988, p. 321. But it does not have the effect of permitting the arbitral tribunal to apply the "*lex mercatoria*" to the exclusion of any national law: see Mustill (1988) 4 Arb.Int. 86, 96–97.

[1] *Bank Mellat v. Helliniki Techniki S.A.* [1984] Q.B. 291, 301 (C.A.). See also *Naviera Amazonica Peruana S.A. v. Compania International de Seguros del Peru* [1988] 1 Lloyd's Rep. 116, 119 (C.A.); *The Star Texas* [1993] 2 Lloyd's Rep. 445, 452 (C.A.); Mustill [1984] Curr. Legal Problems 133, 150.

[2] *Cf. Bremer Vulkan Schiffbau und Maschinenfabrik v. South India Shipping Corp. Ltd.* [1981] A.C. 909, 940–941 (Lord Denning M.R.), 949 (Roskill L.J.). This aspect is not affected by the reversal of the Court of Appeal's decision by the House of Lords, the effect of which has in turn been reversed by what is now 1996 Act, s.41(3). See also *Naviera Amazonica Peruana S.A. v. Cia International de Seguros del Peru* [1988] 1 Lloyds Rep. 116, 120 (C.A.).

seat[3] and a foreign award which has not been made in conformity with the law governing the arbitral procedure may be refused recognition and enforcement.[4]

16–031 With regard to the application of choice of law rules, it used to be thought that an English arbitrator could neither apply any conflict of laws rules other than English rules nor apply any substantive law other than that of a fixed and recognisable system. The traditional common law position was substantially altered by the 1996 Act, which gives the parties (and the arbitral tribunal) much greater freedom in the determination of the standards by which the merits of the dispute are to be judged. Section 46 of the 1996 Act provides:

> "(1) The arbitral tribunal shall decide the dispute—
>
> > (a) in accordance with the law chosen by the parties as applicable to the substance of the dispute, or
> >
> > (b) if the parties so agree, in accordance with such other considerations as are agreed by them or determined by the tribunal. . . .
>
> (3) If or to the extent that there is no such choice or agreement, the tribunal shall apply the law determined by the conflict of laws rules which it considers applicable."

Section 46 reflects, to some extent, Article 28 of the UNCITRAL Model Law. Its effect is that the parties may agree the applicable law[5] (which signifies substantive law and not conflict of laws rules[6]) but may also agree that their dispute is to be decided not in accordance with a recognised system of law but in accordance with "such other considerations as are agreed by them or determined by the tribunal."[7] This means that the parties may adopt "what in this country may often be called 'equity clauses' or arbitration '*ex aequo et bono*', or '*amiable composition*', *i.e.* general considerations of justice and fairness etc."[8] Similarly, parties may agree that the substance of the dispute should be decided by reference to a set of rules or principles which fall short of a fixed and recognisable system of law; the parties can employ an open-textured expression in their agreement (such as "internationally accepted principles of law governing contractual relations" or the *lex mercatoria*) or they may expressly adopt an established body of non-national principles (such as the 1994 UNIDROIT *Principles of International Commercial Contracts*[9]). It is also clear that parties may choose public international law to govern the substance of their contract.[10]

---

[3] *Whitworth Street Estates (Manchester) Ltd. v. James Miller & Partners Ltd.* [1970] A.C. 583.

[4] *Post*, Rules 59, 62, 63. On enforcement of "de-localised" awards see Van Den Berg, *The New York Arbitration Convention of 1958* (1981), pp. 34–43; *cf. Ministry of Defense of Iran v. Gould, Inc.*, 887 F. 2d 1357 (9th Cir. 1989), cert. den. 494 U.S. 1016.

[5] 1996 Act, s.46(1)(a).

[6] *Ibid.*, s.46(2).

[7] *Ibid.*, s.46(1)(b).

[8] D.A.C. Report (1997) 13 Arb. Int. 275, 310.

[9] For the application of the UNIDROIT *Principles* by arbitrators, see Berger (1998) 46 Am. J. Comp. Law 129.

[10] For the position at common law see *Orion Compania Espanola de Seguros v. Belfort* [1962] 2 Lloyd's Rep. 257; *cf. Dallal v. Bank Mellat* [1986] Q.B. 441. See also Schwebel, in International Council for Commercial Arbitration, 12th International Arbitration Congress, 1994, p. 562.

If there is no choice of the applicable law, and no agreement to the **16–032** application of other considerations, the tribunal is to "apply the law determined by the conflict of laws rules which it considers applicable."[11] This formulation is identical to that found in Article 28(2) of the UNCITRAL Model Law and Article 33(1) of the UNCITRAL Arbitration Rules.[12] Its effect is that, in the context of an arbitration whose seat is in England, an arbitral tribunal is not bound to apply English conflict of laws rules. For example, if the dispute is between parties neither of whom has any connection with Europe, it may not be appropriate for the tribunal to apply the Contracts (Applicable Law) Act 1990 in order to determine the applicable law.[13] Although in cases falling within the scope of section 46(3) considerable discretion is conferred on the arbitrators, it should be observed that, unless the parties have agreed to the application of other considerations, the arbitral tribunal is obliged to apply the *law* determined by the applicable conflict of laws rules. In the absence of agreement by the parties, there is no scope for the arbitrators to apply the *lex mercatoria* or general principles of law, because neither constitutes "law", which can mean only a specific system of law.[14]

Section 46 is not made mandatory under the 1996 Act; it applies only to the **16–033** extent that the parties have not made their own arrangements by agreement. If the parties have agreed to arbitration in accordance with a set of arbitration rules (such as the I.C.C. Rules or the UNCITRAL Arbitration Rules) which includes a choice of law provision, the arbitral tribunal should have regard to the rules agreed by the parties rather than to section 46. Since the basic framework of section 46 mirrors that of the choice of law provisions to be found in many of the leading sets of arbitration rules, the exclusion of section 46 by the parties' agreement will often have little or no practical significance.

Although the 1996 Act is generally applicable to arbitrations commenced **16–034** on or after January 31, 1997, section 46(1)(*b*) is applicable only in cases where the arbitration agreement was concluded on or after that date.[15]

ILLUSTRATIONS

1. A, a Scottish firm, enters into a contract with X, an English firm, to be performed in Scotland. **16–035** The contract provides for arbitration in London, but without naming the arbitrator. At that time under Scots law an arbitration clause which did not name the arbitrator was invalid. A sues X in the Scots court. The action is stayed because the arbitration agreement is governed by English law under which it is valid.[16]

2. A, a Kuwaiti company, enters into a contract with X, another Kuwaiti company, whereby A is to construct a fuelling depot for X in Kuwait. The contract incorporates general conditions

---

[11] 1996 Act, s.46(3).

[12] *Cf.* I.C.C. Rules, Art. 13(3).

[13] Although s.2(1) of the 1990 Act provides that the Conventions to which it gives effect are to have "the force of law in the United Kingdom" there seems no reason in principle why arbitrators should not exercise the discretion conferred by the later 1996 Act.

[14] See D.A.C. Report (1997) 13 Arb. Int. 275, 310; *cf.* Shackleton (1997) 13 Arb. Int. 375.

[15] S.I. 1996 No. 3146, Sched. 2, para. 4. As regards arbitrations arising from agreements concluded before January 31, 1997 the effect of an equity clause or a clause expressly adopting the *lex mercatoria* continues to be governed by the common law, under which it is generally assumed that an English arbitrator is bound to apply the choice of law rules which would be binding on an English court: see pp. 584–585 of the 12th edition. *Cf. Deutsche Schachtbau v. Shell International Petroleum Co. Ltd.* [1990] 1 A.C. 295 (C.A.), revd. on other grounds, *ibid.* p. 329; Lando (1998) 47 I.C.L.Q. 394, 403–404.

[16] *Hamlyn & Co. v. Talisker Distillery* [1894] A.C. 202.

which provide for disputes to be decided by an engineer, and, if a party is dissatisfied with his decision, by arbitration provided the dispute is referred to arbitration within 90 days of the engineer's decision. The contract is expressed to be governed by English law but does not specify the place of arbitration. A dispute arises and A fails to give notice of arbitration within 90 days of the engineer's decision. A applies to the English court under section 12 of the 1996 Act for an extension of time in which to begin arbitral proceedings. Because the seat of the arbitration has not been designated or determined, the court may grant the extension; the fact that the arbitration agreement is governed by English law means that there is a connection with England which makes it not inappropriate for the court to exercise its power.[17]

3. A contract concluded by a A, a Japanese corporation, and X, an Indian entity, provides that disputes arising out of the contract shall be subject to the laws of India and that such disputes shall be referred to arbitration, the proceedings of which shall be held in London. Although England is the seat of the arbitration, as a consequence of which English law governs the arbitration, the arbitration agreement is governed by Indian law.[18]

16–036

4. A & Co., a Scottish firm of builders, agree to carry out conversion work at the factory in Scotland of X & Co., an English company. The contract contains an arbitration clause providing for the appointment of an arbitrator by the President of the Royal Institute of British Architects. The President appoints a Scottish architect as arbitrator and the arbitration proceedings take place in Scotland. Although the law governing the contract is English law, the seat of the arbitration is in Scotland. The parties to the arbitration may not appeal to the High Court on a question of law arising out of the award.[19]

5. An insurance policy between a Peruvian insurance company and a Peruvian ship-owning company provides in printed conditions that the latter accepts the jurisdiction and competence of the Lima, Peru, court but also contains standard insurance conditions which provide for "Arbitration under the conditions and laws of London". The arbitration clause overrides the printed conditions, and the effect of the arbitration clause is that the seat of any arbitration is to be in London. Accordingly the English court has jurisdiction to appoint an arbitrator.[20]

6. A employs X to build a tunnel under the English Channel. The contract provides for disputes to be referred initially to a panel of experts and then to arbitration in Belgium. When a dispute arises, X threatens to suspend work on the tunnel. In proceedings in England A applies for an injunction to restrain X from suspending the work. The High Court has the power to grant the relief sought by A, though it may refuse to exercise it if the fact that the seat of the arbitration is in Belgium makes it inappropriate to do so.[21]

7. A contract which includes an arbitration clause expressly provides that it is governed by the law of India. The arbitration clause states both that any arbitration shall be conducted in accordance with the procedure provided in the Indian Arbitration and Conciliation Ordinance 1996 and that the seat of the arbitration shall be London. A dispute arises and is referred to arbitration. Although the provisions of Part I of the 1996 Act are prima facie applicable (because London is the seat of the arbitration), the effect of the parties' choice of Indian law is that the corresponding rules of Indian law apply instead of the non-mandatory provisions of Part I.[22]

8. A contract between A & Co., a company incorporated in Nigeria, and X & Co., a company incorporated in Delaware, provides that X & Co. shall lay a pipeline in Nigeria for A & Co. The contract provides for arbitration in London according to the Rules of the International Chamber of Commerce. The Rules exclude the right of recourse to any court. The right to appeal to the court on a question of law under s. 69 of the 1996 Act, a non-mandatory provision, is excluded by the parties' agreement; the right to challenge the award for lack of jurisdiction or serious irregularity under ss. 67 and 68, which are mandatory provisions, is not.[23]

---

[17] 1996 Act, s.2(4); *cf. International Tank & Pipe S.A.K. v. Kuwait Aviation Fuelling Co. K.S.C.* [1975] Q.B. 224 (C.A.) (a case at common law).

[18] *Sumitomo Heavy Industries Ltd. v. Oil and Natural Gas Commission* [1994] 1 Lloyd's Rep. 45.

[19] 1996 Act, s.2; *cf. Whitworth Street Estates (Manchester) Ltd. v. James Miller & Partners Ltd.* [1970] A.C. 583 (a case at common law).

[20] 1996 Act, s.2(1); *cf. Naviera Amazonica Peruana S.A. v. Cia Internacional de Seguros del Peru* [1988] 1 Lloyd's Rep. 116 (C.A.) (a case at common law).

[21] 1996 Act., ss.2(3), 44; *cf. Channel Tunnel Group Ltd. v. Balfour Beatty Construction Ltd.* [1993] A.C. 334 (a case at common law).

[22] 1996 Act., ss.2(1), 4(2) and Sched. 1; *cf. Union of India v. McDonnell Douglas Corporation* [1993] 2 Lloyd's Rep. 48 (a case at common law).

[23] 1996 Act, ss.2(1), 4(1) and Sched. 1; *cf. Marine Contractors Ltd. v. Shell Petroleum Development Co. of Nigeria Ltd.* [1984] 2 Lloyd's Rep. 77 (a case under the 1979 Act).

2. STAYING OF ENGLISH ACTIONS

RULE 58[24]—Upon application by a party to an arbitration agreement[25]   **16R–037**
against whom legal proceedings are brought (whether by way of claim or
counterclaim) in respect of a matter which under the agreement is to be
referred to arbitration, the court shall grant a stay of the proceedings so
far as they concern that matter unless satisfied that the arbitration
agreement is null and void, inoperative, or incapable of being
performed.

COMMENT

This Rule states the effect of section 9 of the 1996 Act. Section 9, which   **16–038**
replaced section 1 of the 1975 Act, gives effect (with some modifications) to
Article II of the New York Convention on the Recognition and Enforcement
of Arbitral Awards of June 10, 1958.[26] Article I limits the Convention's scope
to awards made in another State and to those which are regarded as non-
domestic awards under the law of the forum, but there is no equivalent
provision which expressly limits the scope of the rules which deal with
arbitration agreements to cases with a foreign element. Nevertheless, it is
generally accepted that it was not intended that Contracting States should be
required to enforce arbitration agreements in wholly domestic cases.[27] The
legislation which the 1996 Act replaced drew a distinction between domestic
arbitration agreements (which were governed by section 4(1) of the 1950 Act)
and non-domestic agreements[28] (which fell within the scope of section 1 of the
1975 Act); whereas a stay of proceedings brought in breach of a domestic
arbitration agreement was discretionary, in non-domestic cases the stay was
mandatory. During the reform process which led to the enactment of the 1996
Act, the D.A.C. recommended that consideration should be given to abolishing the distinction between domestic and non-domestic agreements. However,
because there had not been adequate opportunities to take soundings, special
provisions relating to domestic arbitration agreements were included in the
1996 Act.[29] Shortly before the Act received the Royal Assent, the Court of
Appeal decided, in the context of the Consumer Arbitration Agreements Act
1988 (repealed by the 1996 Act), that the distinction between domestic and

---

[24] 1996 Act, s.9.
[25] A party to an arbitration agreement includes any person claiming under or through a party to
the agreement: 1996 Act, s.82(2).
[26] For the text of the Convention, see Mustill and Boyd, pp. 725–729. On the Convention see Van
den Berg, *The New York Arbitration Convention of 1958* (1981); Patchett, *Recognition of
Commercial Judgments and Awards in the Commonwealth* (1984), Chap. 8; Contini (1959) 8
Am. J. Comp. L. 283. The Convention (and its *travaux préparatoires*) may be referred to in aid
of the interpretation of the Act in so far as the provisions of the latter are ambiguous: see
Government of Kuwait v. Sir Frederick Snow and Partners [1984] A.C. 426, 436; *The Tuyuti*
[1984] Q.B. 838, 852 (C.A.); *Hiscox v. Outhwaite* [1992] 1 A.C. 562, 593; *ante*, paras. 1–024
et seq. International arbitration practice is documented in the volumes of *Yearbook Commercial
Arbitration* (Yb. Comm. Arb.), the first of which was published in 1975; a special section of
each volume since 1982 (Vol. 7) is devoted to court decisions on the Convention and includes
a consolidated commentary (by Van den Berg) on the developing case law of the Contracting
States.
[27] See Cohn (1962) 25 M.L.R. 449, 451.
[28] Defined by 1975 Act, s.1(4).
[29] ss.85–87.

non-domestic arbitration agreements was incompatible with European Community law because it amounted to a restriction on the freedom to provide services contrary to Article 59 (now Article 49) of the Treaty of Rome and/or unlawful discrimination contrary to Article 6 (now Article 12).[30] After a short consultation exercise it was decided to abolish the distinction and the special provisions of the 1996 Act relating to non-domestic arbitration agreements were not brought into force.[31] As a result, a mandatory stay is in principle available in any case where proceedings are brought in breach of an agreement to refer a dispute to arbitration.[32]

16–039   Rule 58 applies only to arbitration agreements "in writing", an expression which is exhaustively defined by section 5 of the 1996 Act. The effect of section 5 is considerably wider than that of the equivalent Article 7 of the UNCITRAL Model Law. The 1989 D.A.C. Report recommended against the adoption of Article 7, because it would have excluded most bills of lading, many brokers' contract notes and many other important categories of contract.[33] Although the definition in the 1996 Act goes beyond the UNCITRAL Model Law, the D.A.C. considered that it was consistent with Article II(2) of the New York Convention.[34]

16–040   For the purposes of the 1996 Act there is an agreement in writing (a) if the agreement is made in writing (whether or not it is signed by the parties), (b) if the agreement is made by exchange of communications in writing, or (c) if the agreement is evidenced in writing.[35] So, an oral acceptance of a written quotation containing an arbitration clause constitutes an agreement in writing.[36] Where parties agree otherwise than in writing by reference to terms which are in writing, they make an agreement in writing.[37] This is designed to cover extremely common situations such as salvage operations where parties orally agree to a set of written terms (such as Lloyd's Open Form) which include an arbitration agreement.[38] An agreement is evidenced in writing if an agreement made otherwise than in writing is recorded by one of the parties, or by a third party, with the authority of the parties to the agreement.[39] An exchange of written submissions in arbitral or legal proceedings in which the existence of an agreement otherwise than in writing is alleged by one party against another party and not denied by the other party in his response constitutes as between those parties an agreement in writing to the effect alleged.[40] Although based on Article 7(2) of the UNCITRAL Model Law, this

---

[30] *Phillip Alexander Securities and Futures Ltd. v. Bamberger* [1997] I.L.Pr. 73 (Waller J. and C.A.).
[31] S.I. 1996 No. 3146.
[32] Although the 1996 Act does not generally apply to proceedings pursuant to the Washington Convention for the Settlement of Investment Disputes (ICSID), it is expressly provided that legal proceedings brought in breach of an agreement to arbitrate under the auspices of ICSID shall be stayed in accordance with s.9 of the 1996 Act: Arbitration (International Investment Disputes) Act 1966, s.3 (as amended by Arbitration Act 1996, s.107(1) and Sched. 3, para. 24). For special provision for consumer arbitration agreements see Arbitration Act 1996, ss.89–91 (the effect of which is to apply the Unfair Terms in Consumer Contracts Regulations 1999, S.I. 1999 No. 2083 to arbitration clauses) and S.I. 1996 No. 3211.
[33] (1990) 6 Arb. Int. 3, 52. See also Kaplan (1996) 12 Arb. Int. 27.
[34] D.A.C. Report (1997) 13 Arb. Int. 275, 282.
[35] 1996 Act, s.5(2).
[36] See *Zambia Steel & Building Supplies Ltd. v. Clark & Eaton Ltd.* [1986] 2 Lloyd's Rep. 225 (a case decided under the 1975 Act).
[37] 1996 Act, s.5(3).
[38] D.A.C. Report (1997) 13 Arb. Int. 275, 282–283.
[39] 1996 Act, s.5(4).
[40] *Ibid.*, s.5(5).

rule is more stringent in that an agreement in writing cannot arise where one party alleges an arbitration agreement and the other party fails to respond at all.[41] References to anything being written or in writing, include its being recorded by other means,[42] though it is doubtful whether this extends to recorded speech as opposed to recorded text.[43]

Under the 1996 Act an application for a stay may be made only by a party to an arbitration agreement against whom legal proceedings are brought.[44] The duty to grant a stay applies both to claims and counterclaims.[45] It is quite possible for a situation to arise in which, although the defendant's counterclaim falls within the terms of the parties' arbitration agreement, the claim made by the claimant does not. In these circumstances only the counterclaim will be referred to arbitration. The court's duty to grant a stay does not depend on the parties being able to proceed to arbitration as soon as the proceedings are stayed; a stay must be granted even where other dispute resolution procedures must be followed before reference of the parties' dispute to arbitration.[46] Although it is not necessary that the arbitration agreement should have been entered into before the court proceedings were commenced,[47] the party wishing to enforce the arbitration agreement loses the right to a stay if he takes a step in the proceedings to answer the substantive claim.[48] Where, however, a party to an alleged arbitration agreement brings proceedings for a declaration that the arbitration agreement is non-existent, the right to a stay is not lost if the proceedings are unsuccessful.[49] The duty to grant a stay under section 9 applies in cases where the arbitration agreement takes the form of a *Scott v. Avery* clause (*i.e.* a contractual provision which makes an award a condition precedent to the bringing of legal proceedings); if, however, the court refuses to stay proceedings brought in breach of a *Scott v. Avery* clause (for example, because the arbitration clause is unworkable) it is provided that the clause ceases to have effect,[50] thereby permitting the parties' dispute to be litigated.

16–041

Once the party seeking the stay has established that the parties agreed to arbitration and that their dispute falls within the scope of that agreement, the court must grant a stay unless the other party satisfies the court that there is a good reason why a stay should be refused (for example, because the arbitration agreement is null and void). The question whether an arbitration agreement is wide enough to cover the dispute between the parties depends on

16–042

---

[41] See D.A.C. Report (1997) 13 Arb. Int. 275, 283.

[42] 1996 Act, s.5(6).

[43] *Cf.* UNCITRAL Model Law, Art. 7(2).

[44] 1996 Act, s.9(1). Although s.1 of the 1975 Act referred simply to "any party" this was interpreted as meaning a party to the arbitration agreement: *Etri Fans Ltd. v. N.M.B. (U.K.) Ltd.* [1987] 1 W.L.R. 1110 (C.A.); *cf. Marine Expeditions Inc. v. The Ship Akademik Shuleykin* [1995] 2 N.Z.L.R. 743.

[45] 1996 Act, s.9(1).

[46] 1996 Act, s.9(2). This subsection resolves doubts in dicta of Lord Mustill in *Channel Tunnel Group Ltd. v. Balfour Beatty Construction Ltd.* [1993] A.C. 334 at p. 354, on which see Reymond (1993) 109 L.Q.R. 337.

[47] *The Tuyuti* [1984] Q.B. 838, 852 (C.A.).

[48] 1996 Act, s.9(3). See *Patel v. Patel* [1999] 3 W.L.R. 322; *Queensland Sugar Corp. v. The Hanjin Jedda* [1995] 7 W.W.R. 237 (B.C.) (a case concerning UNCITRAL Model Law, Art. 8).

[49] See *Metal Scrap Trade Corp. v. Kate Shipping Co. Ltd.* [1990] 1 W.L.R. 115 (H.L.).

[50] 1996 Act, s.9(5).

the principles of interpretation of the law applicable to the arbitration agreement.[51]

16–043　　Neither Article II of the Convention nor section 9 of the 1996 Act indicates what law is to decide whether the arbitration agreement is null and void, inoperative or incapable of being performed. Presumably, the validity of the arbitration agreement would be a matter for its governing law.[52] But in practice the English court is likely to determine the other matters mentioned for itself, uninfluenced by foreign law. The words "incapable of being performed" presumably refer to cases where there is no mechanism for constituting the arbitral tribunal or putting the arbitral procedure in motion. For example, if it is impossible for a party to find a person who has the necessary qualifications to act as arbitrator in the case and who is prepared to act at the place where the parties have agreed that the arbitration is to be conducted, it is arguable that the arbitration agreement is incapable of being performed.[53] An arbitration agreement however, is not inoperative or incapable of being performed simply because it fails to specify the seat of the arbitration or the method by which the arbitral tribunal is to be appointed. An arbitration agreement should be regarded as incapable of being performed only if gaps in the parties' agreement cannot be filled by any arbitral institution chosen by the parties or by a court of competent jurisdiction exercising its powers. If, for example, a named arbitrator refuses to act, there will normally be a court with the power to appoint a replacement. Also, an arbitration agreement is not incapable of being performed because it refers to a non-existent arbitral institution or to non-existent arbitration rules. In such a case the law of the seat of the arbitration will furnish the applicable procedural rules and, in the event of the parties failing to reach agreement, the local courts will normally be competent to appoint an arbitrator and to exercise other powers to support the arbitral process. The fact that the claimant cannot afford the deposit for the costs of the arbitration,[54] or that the defendant would be financially incapable of satisfying the award in full[55] is no reason for refusing a stay. Moreover, the mere fact that if the dispute goes to arbitration, the claimant will be met by a plea that his claim is out of time, is no reason for regarding the arbitration agreement as "inoperative."[56] Otherwise, the claimant could avoid a stay by waiting until the time for arbitration had expired and then bringing an action. But an arbitration agreement may become inoperative by reason of some further agreement between the parties (for example, by a contractual agreement settling the dispute[57] or by a jurisdiction agreement which supersedes the

---

[51] See, *e.g. The Paola d'Alesio* [1994] 2 Lloyd's Rep. 366. This principle is supported by analogous cases concerning the interpretation of jurisdiction clauses: see para. 12–080, *ante*.

[52] See *ante*, para. 16–017. *Cf. A/B Bofors v. A/B Skandia* [1982] 1 Lloyd's Rep. 410 (where a mandatory rule of English law invalidated an arbitration agreement governed by foreign law).

[53] *Gatoil International plc v. National Iranian Oil Co.* (1992) 17 Yb. Comm. Arb. 587 (Gatehouse J.); *The Independent*, March 13, 1990 (C.A.).

[54] *Paczy v. Haendler and Natermann GmbH* [1981] 1 Lloyd's Rep. 302 (C.A.).

[55] *The Rena K* [1979] Q.B. 377, 391–393.

[56] *The Merak* [1965] P. 223, 239. Nor is the fact that there is a risk of inconsistent findings as a result of other pending litigation: *Lonrho Ltd. v. Shell Petroleum Co. Ltd., The Times*, February 1, 1978.

[57] *Shanghai Foreign Trade Corp. v. Sigma Metallurgical Co. Pty Ltd.* (1996) 133 F.L.R. 417 (N.S.W.).

original arbitration clause). There is also no room for the argument which was unsuccessfully raised in *The Merak*,[58] that there is no obligation to stay the proceedings unless and until arbitrators have been appointed.

The mere fact that some issues between the parties fall outside the scope of the arbitration agreement does not render the agreement inoperative or incapable of being performed.[59] In this type of case the court must grant a stay in respect of the part of the claim which is covered by the arbitration agreement.[60] Also, an arbitration agreement can still be performed even if some parties to the dispute are not parties to the agreement[61]; as between the parties to the agreement the dispute must be referred to arbitration even though, in the interest of the efficient administration of justice, it might well be preferable if related issues were resolved in a single set of proceedings.[62] In a case involving multiple parties, only some of whom are bound by the arbitration agreement, the court may, under its inherent jurisdiction, stay proceedings against litigants who are not parties to the arbitration agreement.[63]

16–044

The 1975 Act qualified the defendant's right to a stay by providing that the court need not order a stay if satisfied that "there [was] not in fact any dispute between the parties with regard to the matter agreed to be referred."[64] The 1975 qualification, which does not appear in Article II of the Convention, was successfully relied upon by plaintiffs to enable them to resist a stay of English proceedings in cases where, although the defendant did not admit the plaintiff's claim, the defendant had no real defence.[65] By contrast, in those countries which implemented Article II of the Convention (or the similar Article 8 of the UNCITRAL Model Law) without the addition of an equivalent of the 1975 qualification, it is well established that the court has no power to investigate the reality of the dispute with a view to refusing a stay in cases where there is no answer to the claim.[66]

16–045

The 1975 qualification was not reproduced in section 9 of the 1996 Act. In *Halki Shipping Corp. v. Sopex Oils Ltd.*,[67] the first reported case decided under section 9, the question arose whether this omission necessarily entailed a change in the practice of the courts. The plaintiffs claimed demurrage which was allegedly due under a charterparty which included an arbitration clause. The defendants did not admit liability. When the plaintiffs applied for summary judgment under R.S.C. Order 14 (now Part 24 of the Civil Procedure Rules 1998), the defendants sought a stay under section 9 of the 1996 Act. The crucial question facing the court was the meaning to be attached to the word "dispute" in the arbitration agreement.

16–046

---

[58] *Supra.*
[59] *Kaverit Steel and Crane Ltd. v. Kone Corp.* (1992) 87 D.L.R. (4th) 129 (Alta. C.A.).
[60] *The Tuyuti* [1984] Q.B. 838, 849 (C.A.).
[61] *BWV Investments Ltd. v. Saskferco Products Inc.* [1995] 2 W.W.R. 1 (Sask. C.A.).
[62] See *Wealands v. CLC Contractors Ltd.* [1998] C.L.C. 808.
[63] *Roussel-Uclaf v. G. D. Searle Ltd.* [1978] 1 Lloyd's Rep. 225.
[64] s. 1(1). The words are taken from Arbitration (Foreign Awards) Act 1930, s.8 which amended Arbitration Clauses (Protocol Act) 1924. They were reproduced in the 1975 Act on the recommendation of the Private International Law Committee: Fifth Report, Cmnd. 1515 (1961).
[65] For a review of the position under the 1975 Act see *Channel Tunnel Group Ltd. v. Balfour Beatty Construction Ltd.* [1993] A.C. 334.
[66] See *e.g. Baltimar Aps Ltd. v. Nalder & Biddle Ltd.* [1994] 3 N.Z.L.R. 129 (C.A.).
[67] [1998] 1 W.L.R. 726 (C.A.).

16–047   The majority, Henry and Swinton Thomas L.JJ., adopted a broad view of what constitutes a dispute. The word "dispute" should not be narrowly and artificially construed so as to be restricted to those disputes which cannot be resolved by the summary judgment procedure (*i.e.* cases in which there is an arguable defence to the claim)[68]; there is a dispute wherever a claim is made by one party against another and the claim has not been admitted.[69] In the words of Swinton Thomas L.J.: "if a party has refused to pay a sum which is claimed or has denied that it is owing then in the ordinary use of the English language there is a dispute between the parties."[70] The majority refused to accept the argument that the 1975 qualification had been superfluous and therefore that its omission from section 9 of the 1996 Act left the previous law unchanged.[71]

16–048   Hirst L.J. dissented on the ground that a "dispute" cannot be said to exist unless there is a genuine dispute, *i.e.* one party advances a claim to which the other party has an arguable defence.[72] It follows from this that the 1975 qualification was superfluous and its omission did not involve any change in the law: if the defendant does not have an arguable defence there is no dispute which can be referred to arbitration; the value of the court's jurisdiction to order summary judgment in cases where a party to an arbitration agreement has no arguable defence to the claim has been judicially recognised at the highest level[73]; if the D.A.C. had intended to bring about a revolutionary change in the law, the D.A.C. Report would have spelled it out more explicitly.

16–049   Although the decision in the *Halki Shipping* case has been criticised on the ground that arbitrators are less well equipped than courts to decide disputes summarily,[74] there is no reason to doubt the correctness of the majority's decision, which is consistent with the principle of party autonomy, one of the cornerstones of the 1996 Act.[75]

16–050   May a party who has agreed to arbitration retain a form of security, or obtain interlocutory relief, from the court pending the outcome of the arbitration and satisfaction of the award? If the claim is *in personam*, the question will normally arise in the context of an application for a *Mareva* injunction or other form of interim remedy. If the claim is *in rem*, it will arise in the context of retention of the arrested property. The modern trend is to recognise that, whether or not the seat of the arbitration is within its jurisdiction, a court which grants a mandatory stay of proceedings on the basis of an arbitration

---

[68] At p. 746, *per* Henry L.J. Under CPR 24 the question is whether the defendant has a real prospect of successfully defending the claim: CPR 24.2(a)(i).

[69] At p. 761, *per* Swinton Thomas L.J. See, *e.g. Ellerine Bros. (Pty) Ltd. v. Klinger* [1982] 1 W.L.R. 1375; *Hayter v. Nelson* [1990] 2 Lloyd's Rep. 265.

[70] At p. 761. See also *Wealands v. CLC Contractors Ltd.* [1998] C.L.C. 808 (a domestic case).

[71] In reaching its decision the majority did not overlook the fact that the D.A.C. was chaired by Saville L.J. (who had decided *Hayter v. Nelson* [1990] 2 Lloyd's Rep. 265): see Swinton Thomas L.J. at pp. 762–763.

[72] See *Nova (Jersey) Knit Ltd. v. Kammgarn Spinnerei G.m.b.H.* [1977] 1 W.L.R. 713 (H.L.) (the leading authority supporting this proposition).

[73] *Channel Tunnel Group Ltd. v. Balfour Beatty Construction Ltd.* [1993] A.C. 334, 356, *per* Lord Mustill.

[74] Duncan Wallace [1998] I.C.L.R. 371, 395–397; *cf. Halki Shipping Corp. v. Sopex Oils Ltd.* [1998] 1 W.L.R. 726, 752, 755.

[75] s.1(*b*).

agreement between the parties is entitled to grant interim measures of protection[76] including pre-award attachments to secure the eventual award.[77]

Prior to the 1996 Act English law was in a somewhat unsatisfactory and fragmentary state.[78] The court's power to grant interim injunctions under the 1950 Act[79] was limited to cases involving English arbitrations,[80] though it had been held that the court could grant injunctions in support of foreign arbitrations under the general law[81] if the defendant was amenable to the *in personam* jurisdiction of the court.[82] No legislative action was taken to bring into force section 25(3) of the Civil Jurisdiction and Judgments Act 1982, which would have provided for the grant of interim relief in relation to any arbitral proceedings.[83]

   16–051

The 1996 Act adopts the modern position and does away with the distinctions which disgraced the old law. Where there is a mandatory stay under the 1996 Act, *i.e.* Rule 58, the court has the power to make orders in support of arbitral proceedings, in particular the power to grant interim injunctions under section 44(2)(e), which replaces section 12(6)(*h*) of the 1950 Act. The 1996 Act seeks to ensure that the court is not able to interfere with or usurp the arbitral process.[84] It is provided that, unless the case is one of urgency, the court shall act under section 44 only where the application is made with the permission of the tribunal or the written agreement of the other parties.[85] Furthermore, the court is permitted to act only to the extent that the arbitral tribunal has no power or is unable for the time being to act effectively.[86]

   16–052

Subject to the contrary agreement of the parties, the powers conferred by section 44 may be exercised not only in cases where England is the seat of the arbitration, but also where the seat is abroad or even if no seat has been determined or designated; the court may, however, refuse to exercise the power if the fact that the seat is outside England (or when designated or determined it is likely to be outside England) makes it inappropriate to do so.[87] If the grant of the injunction sought by the claimant would largely pre-

   16–053

---

[76] *Guinea v. Atlantic Triton Co.* (1987) 26 I.L.M. 373 (Cour de cassation, France, 1986); *Katran Shipping Co. Ltd. v. Kenven Transportation Ltd.* [1992] 1 H.K.C. 538; *Trade Fortune Inc. v. Amalgamated Mill Supplies Ltd.* (1994) 113 D.L.R. (4th) 116 (B.C.). For the position in the United States see *Borden Inc. v. Meiji Milk Products Co. Ltd.*, 919 F. 2d 822 (2d Cir. 1990), cert. denied, 500 U.S. 953 (1991); *cf. Pilkington Bros. plc v. AFG Industries Inc.*, 581 F. Supp. 1039 (D.Del. 1984). On (ultimately unsuccessful) attempts to obtain U.S. discovery in connection with arbitrations conducted outside the United States see Rivkin and Legum (1998) 14 Arb. Int. 213; *ante*, para. 8–064.

[77] See Van den Berg, pp. 139–144; Art. 9 of the UNCITRAL Model Law and Holtzmann & Neuhaus, *A Guide to the UNCITRAL Model Law of International Commercial Arbitration* (1989), pp. 332–333. There has been considerable discussion in the United States in relation to whether it is incompatible with the New York Convention for a court to grant pre-judgment attachments: see McDonnell (1984) 22 Col. J. Trans. L. 273; Becker (1985) 1 Arb. Int. 40; Brower and Tupman (1986) 80 A.J.I.L. 24; and many cases, especially *McCreary Tire and Rubber Co. v. CEAT SpA*, 501 F. 2d 1032 (3d Cir. 1974) (attachment incompatible with Convention); *Carolina Power and Light Co. v. Uranex*, 451 F. Supp. 1044 (N.D. Cal. 1977) (attachment compatible with Convention).

[78] See, in particular, Collins (1992) 108 L.Q.R. 175. *Cf.* paras. 8–028 *et seq.*, *ante*.

[79] s.12(6)(h).

[80] *Channel Tunnel Group Ltd. v. Balfour Beatty Construction Ltd.* [1993] A.C. 334.

[81] Supreme Court Act 1981, s.37.

[82] *Channel Tunnel Group Ltd. v. Balfour Beatty Construction Ltd.*, *supra*.

[83] This provision was repealed by the 1996 Act, which superseded it.

[84] D.A.C. Report (1997) 13 Arb. Int. 275, 308–309.

[85] 1996 Act, s.44(4).

[86] *Ibid.*, s.44(5).

[87] *Ibid.*, s.2(3).

empt any decision to be made by the arbitrators, it would not be appropriate for the court to exercise the power conferred by section 44.[88] In addition, the European Court has ruled that, in a case where the court does not have jurisdiction over the substance of the dispute between the parties, the grant of provisional measures is conditional on the existence of a real connecting link between the subject-matter of the measures and the territorial jurisdiction of the court.[89]

16–054   In Admiralty proceedings *in rem*, the question whether the arrested property or security may be retained even if proceedings are stayed under Rule 58 is regulated by section 11 of the 1996 Act (which, as regards cases which are stayed on the basis of an arbitration agreement replaced section 26 of the Civil Jurisdiction and Judgments Act 1982[90]). Section 11(1) provides that where proceedings are stayed on the ground that the dispute should be referred to arbitration (whether in England or abroad), the court may (a) order that property arrested be retained as security for the satisfaction of any award, or (b) order that the stay of proceedings be conditional on the provision of equivalent security. Potential problems surround the second alternative form of order in cases falling within the scope of the New York Convention. The wording of section 11(1)(*b*) suggests that, if a defendant who is ordered to provide equivalent security fails to do so, the proceedings *in rem* will proceed, a result which would be inconsistent with the mandatory nature of the stay under section 9 of the 1996 Act and with the New York Convention. For this reason, in *The World Star*[91] Sheen J. indicated that only the first form of order is available in case where a stay is mandatory. But the same result is reached by the exercise of the power to release a vessel from arrest. That power is normally exercised only if security is provided by guarantee or otherwise for the claim, interest and costs.[92]

16–055   It has been held that the High Court has an inherent power to stay proceedings brought in disregard of an arbitration agreement if for some reason the statutory requirements are not met.[93] For example, the court may stay proceedings brought in breach of an oral arbitration clause under its inherent jurisdiction.[94]

16–056   Given that more than one hundred States are parties to the New York Convention, it is to be expected that, in most cases where legal proceedings are brought in another country in breach of the terms of an arbitration agreement, the foreign court will grant a stay of the proceedings under Article II of the Convention (or the applicable implementing legislation). Nevertheless, the English court has an inherent power to grant an injunction restraining a party from prosecuting proceedings in a foreign court in breach

---

[88] *Cf. Channel Tunnel Group Ltd. v. Balfour Beatty Construction Ltd.* [1993] A.C. 334.
[89] Case C–391/95 *Van Uden Maritime B.V. v. Firma Deco-Line* [1998] E.C.R. I–7091; [1999] 2 W.L.R. 1181.
[90] See *The Tuyuti* [1984] Q.B. 836 (C.A.); *The Bazias 3* [1993] Q.B. 673 (C.A.).
[91] [1986] 2 Lloyd's Rep. 274.
[92] CPR PD49F, para. 6.6(1); *The Bazias 3* [1993] Q.B. 673 (C.A.): see *ante*, paras. 8–031—8–034.
[93] *Roussel-Uclaf v. G. D. Searle Ltd.* [1978] 1 Lloyd's Rep. 25; *Etri Fans Ltd. v. N.M.B. (U.K.) Ltd.* [1987] 1 W.L.R. 1110 (C.A.); *Nissan (U.K.) Ltd. v. Nissan Motor Co. Ltd.*, 1991, unreported (C.A.); *Channel Tunnel Group Ltd. v. Balfour Beatty Construction Ltd.* [1993] A.C. 334; *Kaverit Steel and Crane Ltd. v. Kone Corp.* (1992) 87 D.L.R. (4th) 129 (Alta. C.A.). Contrast *Mount Cook (Northland) Ltd. v. Swedish Motors Ltd.* [1986] 1 N.Z.L.R. 720.
[94] The common law as to the effect of oral arbitration agreements is expressly preserved by the 1996 Act, s.81(1)(*b*).

of an arbitration agreement governed by English law or an agreement to arbitrate in England.[95]

ILLUSTRATIONS

1. A contract between A & Co. and X & Co., two English companies, provides for arbitration in Switzerland. The English court must stay proceedings brought in England, if the requirements of Rule 58 are met.　　**16–057**

2. A contract between A & Co., Greek company, and X & Co., a French company, provides for arbitration in England. A & Co. applies for summary judgment against X & Co. in English proceedings under the Civil Procedure Rules 1998, Part 24. When X & Co. applies for a stay of the proceedings, A & Co. seeks to resist the stay on the ground that X & Co. has no real defence to the claim. The English court must stay the proceedings.[96]

3. ENFORCEMENT OF FOREIGN AWARDS

A. *At Common Law*

RULE 59—**Subject to the Exception hereinafter mentioned and to the effect of Rule 61, a foreign arbitration award[97] will be enforced in England, or recognised as a defence to a claim, if the award is**　　**16R–058**

(1) **in accordance with an agreement to arbitrate which is valid by its applicable law; and**

(2) **valid and final according to the law governing the arbitration proceedings.[98]**

The award will be enforced by a claim or, by leave of the High Court, under the more summary procedure of section 66 of the Arbitration Act 1996.[99]

COMMENT

Foreign arbitration awards are usually based on a contract to arbitrate, but they are not themselves contracts. They are decisions, but they are not judgments: they cannot be enforced without the assistance of a court. They can be enforced in England in various ways. First, they can be enforced at common law.[1] Secondly, if they come within the Geneva Convention for the Execution of Foreign Arbitral Awards (1927), they can be enforced under Part II of the Arbitration Act 1950 under conditions very similar to, though not precisely　　**16–059**

---

[95] The limits of this power are discussed *ante*, paras. 12–128 *et seq.*

[96] *Halki Shipping Corp. v. Sopex Oils Ltd.* [1998] 1 W.L.R. 726 (C.A.).

[97] In this chapter a "foreign arbitration award" means generally one which is made outside England. But in s.35 of the Arbitration Act 1950 the term "foreign award" is used in the special sense of an award falling within the Geneva Convention of 1927, *i.e.* Rule 62.

[98] *Norske Atlas Insurance Co. Ltd. v. London General Insurance Co. Ltd.* (1927) 43 T.L.R. 541, 542; 28 Ll.L.R. 104, 106; *Oppenheim & Co. v. Mahomed Haneef* [1922] 1 A.C. 482 (P.C.); *Bankers and Shippers Insurance Co. of New York v. Liverpool Marine and General Insurance Co. Ltd.* (1926) 24 Ll.L.R. 85 (H.L.); *Dalmia Cement Ltd. v. National Bank of Pakistan* [1975] Q.B. 9; *Dalmia Dairy Industries Ltd. v. National Bank of Pakistan* [1978] 2 Lloyd's Rep. 223 (C.A.); *cf. Union Nationale des Coopératives Agricoles v. Catterall* [1959] 2 Q.B. 44 (C.A.).

[99] *Dalmia Cement Ltd. v. National Bank of Pakistan, supra; post*, paras. 16–073 *et seq.* In view of this decision, enforcement at common law must be taken to mean "as reinforced by s.66 of the Arbitration Act 1996."

[1] Rules 59–61.

identical with, those obtaining at common law.[2] Thirdly, if they come within the New York Convention on the Recognition and Enforcement of Foreign Arbitral Awards (1958), they can be enforced under Part III of the Arbitration Act 1996 under similar conditions.[3] Fourthly, an arbitration award made in one part of the United Kingdom can be enforced in other parts of the United Kingdom under Part II of the Civil Jurisdiction and Judgments Act 1982.[4] Fifthly, arbitration awards made in countries to which Part II of the Administration of Justice Act 1920 or Part I of the Foreign Judgments (Reciprocal Enforcement) Act 1933 have been extended can be enforced in England as if they were judgments, by registration under those Acts.[5] Sixthly, arbitration awards made in pursuance of a contract for the international carriage of goods by road can sometimes be enforced by registration under the Foreign Judgments (Reciprocal Enforcement) Act 1933.[6] Seventhly, arbitration awards made in pursuance of the International Convention for the Settlement of Investment Disputes between Contracting States and nationals of other Contracting States can be enforced by registration under the Arbitration (International Investment Disputes) Act 1966 as if they were judgments.[7] And eighthly, if the arbitration award has been made enforceable by a judgment in a foreign country, the judgment creditor can enforce the judgment in England in the same way as any other foreign judgment can be enforced.[8]

16–060   Very often the claimant can choose between different methods of enforcement. Thus, if the award is one to which the Geneva Convention applies, the claimant may enforce it under Part II of the Arbitration Act 1950 or, if he prefers, by proceedings at common law[9]; if the award is one to which the New York Convention applies, he may enforce it under the Arbitration Act 1996 or by proceedings at common law[10]; if the award is made in a country to which the Administration of Justice Act 1920 or the Foreign Judgments (Reciprocal Enforcement) Act 1933 applies it may be enforced by registration under those Acts; if the award is registrable as a judgment under the Administration of Justice Act 1920 or the Foreign Judgments (Reciprocal Enforcement) Act 1933 or Part II of the Civil Jurisdiction and Judgments Act 1982, the claimant is not prevented from enforcing it by proceedings at common law[11]; if the award has been made enforceable by a foreign judgment, the claimant may enforce the judgment as a judgment or, in certain circumstances, enforce the award by proceedings at common law.[12]

16–061   The first mode of enforcing foreign arbitration awards (that at common law) is always available, but the others are all restricted in their application. Thus, the second mode applies only between parties and in relation to States to which the Geneva Convention of 1927 applies; the third only applies if the award is made in a State which is a party to the New York Convention;

---

[2] Rule 62.
[3] Rule 63.
[4] Rule 64.
[5] 1933 Act, s.10A (added by Civil Jurisdiction and Judgments Act 1982, Sched. 10, para. 4).
[6] Rule 65.
[7] Rule 66.
[8] Rule 60(2).
[9] Arbitration Act 1950, s.40(*a*), which saves the right to enforce such awards at common law.
[10] Arbitration Act 1996, s.104, which saves the right to enforce such awards at common law.
[11] Administration of Justice Act 1920, s.9(5). But he may not get his costs. 1933 Act, s.6, does not apply to arbitration awards (1933 Act, s.10A), nor does 1982 Act, s.18(8): see *ante*, paras. 14E–044 *et seq.*
[12] *Post*, paras. 16–068 *et seq.*

the fourth only applies if the award is made in Scotland or Northern Ireland; the fifth only applies to awards made in certain Commonwealth and foreign countries; the sixth applies only to awards made in States which are parties to the Geneva Convention on International Carriage of Goods by Road (1956); and the seventh only applies to awards made in respect of an investment dispute between a State which is a party to the international Convention for the settlement of such disputes and a national of another State which is a party to that Convention.

Enforcement at common law. The enforcement of foreign arbitration   16–062
awards may be required more frequently than the enforcement of foreign judgments. This is because proceedings *in personam* are very often brought in the country where the defendant resides and keeps his assets, so that the need for enforcement elsewhere is the exception rather than the rule. But nowadays many contracts between parties carrying on business in different countries provide for arbitration in a third or "neutral" country, where neither carries on business or holds assets. The vast majority of these contracts are no doubt performed without serious dispute between the parties, and where disputes are referred to arbitration, most are settled, and (if not settled) result in an award with which the parties comply. But in a significant minority of cases, the award of the tribunal will not be complied with, and it may therefore become necessary to enforce it in a country where the party in default has assets.[13] At the enforcement stage, the losing party may seek to question the award and it is not uncommon for a party resisting enforcement to argue for example, that the arbitral procedure was defective. Often such arguments are designed primarily to put off the day of reckoning, and the law reports contain examples of enforcement cases where the points taken by the defendant are singularly lacking in merit or substance.[14]

Although English courts have enforced foreign judgments from the sev-   16–063
enteenth century onwards,[15] it is only since 1927[16] (so far as one can judge from reported cases) that they have enforced foreign arbitration awards, and so authority is relatively scanty. This is no doubt because arbitration is so ancient and well-developed an institution in England that for many years most disputes that had any connection with England, and many that had none,[17] were referred to arbitration in England.

What is it which is enforced? It is sometimes necessary to determine the   16–064
nature of the claim to enforce a foreign arbitration award, and, in particular, whether a party who seeks to enforce a foreign award is suing on the award,

---

[13] For modern examples see *Deutsche Schachtbau v. Shell International Petroleum Co. Ltd.* [1990] 1 A.C. 295 (contract for oil exploration in Middle East; Swiss award); *Rosseel N.V. v. Oriental Commercial & Shipping Co. (U.K.) Ltd.* [1991] 2 Lloyd's Rep. 625 (sale of oil by English company to Belgian company; New York award); *Westacre Investments Inc. v. Jugoimport-SDPR Holding Co.* [1999] Q.B. 740 (consultancy contract between Panamanian corporation and Yugoslav entities; Swiss award).

[14] See *e.g. Dalmia Dairy Industries Ltd. v. National Bank of Pakistan* [1978] 2 Lloyd's Rep. 223; *China Agribusiness Development Corp. v. Balli Trading* [1998] 2 Lloyd's Rep. 76.

[15] *Ante*, para. 14–006.

[16] *Norske Atlas Insurance Co. Ltd. v. London General Insurance Co. Ltd.* (1927) 28 Ll.L.R. 104.

[17] For a striking and well-known example, see *Gilbert v. Burnstine*, 255 N.Y. 348, 174 N.E. 706 (1931), where the New York Court of Appeals enforced an English award made in pursuance of an arbitration clause in a contract made and to be performed in New York between two residents of that state. See also Kerr (1978) 41 M.L.R. 1, 5, 6.

or on the contract containing the arbitration agreement, or on the arbitration agreement itself. The question has arisen in decisions (involving both English and foreign awards) in several different contexts, and there is a clear tendency to give the answer which will make the award enforceable. Thus in *Norske Atlas Insurance Co. Ltd. v. London General Insurance Co. Ltd.*[18] the unsuccessful respondents to an arbitration in Norway arising out of a reinsurance contract made in London sought to resist enforcement of the Norwegian award on the ground that the action was brought to enforce a reinsurance contract which had not been validly stamped. It was held that the plaintiffs were suing not on the reinsurance contract, but on the award, and the action was therefore maintainable. In *Bremer Oeltransport v. Drewry*[19] the defendants, who were unsuccessful respondents to an award made in Hamburg arising out of a charterparty made in London, sought to set aside proceedings served on them outside the jurisdiction to enforce the award. Leave to serve the proceedings abroad had been granted on the basis that the action was for the enforcement of a contract made within the jurisdiction, *i.e.* the submission to arbitration contained in the charterparty. In this case, therefore, by contrast with *Norske Atlas Insurance*, it was the defendant who argued that the action was on the award, for in that event there would at that time[20] have been no basis for service outside the jurisdiction. The Court of Appeal, however, held that for this purpose the plaintiffs were suing "on the agreement to submit the difference of which the award is the result" or "on the charterparty made in London and more particularly on the submission to arbitration therein contained" or on the "agreement containing a term to refer disputes."[21] It was therefore an action for the enforcement of a contract made within the jurisdiction and accordingly an appropriate case for service outside the jurisdiction. The Court of Appeal left open the question whether the action could also be regarded as being solely on the award.

16–065   More recently, in *Agromet Motoimport Ltd. v. Maulden Engineering Co. (Beds.) Ltd.*[22] the unsuccessful respondents to a Zurich arbitration resisted enforcement of the award on the ground that the limitation period (six years from the date on which the cause of action accrued) had expired; they argued that the relevant cause of action was the breach of the underlying contract on which the award was based and that the breach had occurred more than six years before the action to enforce the award. This unmeritorious argument was rejected on the ground that the action was an action on the award or on an implied term in the submission agreement that the award would be honoured. Accordingly, the action was not time-barred.[23] The effect of these authorities is that the claimant must plead and prove both the arbitration agreement and

---

[18] (1927) 28 Ll.L.R. 104.
[19] [1933] 1 K.B. 753 (C.A.). See also *Brali v. Hyundai Corp.* (1988) 84 A.L.R. 176.
[20] See now Ord. 11, r. 1(1)(*m*), *ante*, paras. 11R–204 *et seq.*
[21] At pp. 764–765, *per* Slesser L.J.
[22] [1985] 1 W.L.R. 762. See also *Northern Sales Co. Ltd. v. Compania Maritima Villa Nova S.A.* [1992] 1 F.C. 550 (Fed. C.A.)
[23] A further illustration of the tendency to classify the proceedings in such a way as to uphold the enforceability of the award is *The St. Anna* [1983] 1 W.L.R. 895, where it was held that an action to enforce an English award made pursuant to a dispute under a charterparty was within the Admiralty jurisdiction *in rem* on the basis that the claim was one "arising out of any agreement relating to the carriage of goods in a ship or to the use or hire of a ship" (Supreme Court Act 1981, s.20(2)(*h*)). This is inconsistent with *The Beldis* [1936] P. 51, 61–62, 83 (C.A.). See also Mustill and Boyd, p. 418.

the award[24] and that depending on the context, the proceedings may be classified as a claim on the award itself or on the submission agreement.

The definition of that which is being enforced, *i.e.* the choice between the view that the claimant is seeking to enforce the agreement to arbitrate and the view that he is seeking to enforce the award, is in England exclusively a matter of English law as the *lex fori*.[25] The attitude to this question of the law governing the submission is irrelevant and so is the attitude of the law governing the arbitration proceedings. The question, however, whether the claimant may, instead of suing on the submission agreement or on the award, go back to the original cause of action and sue on the contract itself is, it is submitted, determined by the law which governs the arbitration proceedings. This includes the question whether the claim made before the arbitrators is merged in the award.[26]
16–066

An English award may give rise to a cause of action estoppel or an issue estoppel,[27] and if the award is a final award under the law governing the arbitration proceedings the claimant in the arbitration should not be entitled to sue on the original cause of action.[28] There is no reason of legal policy why the same should not be true in the case of a foreign award. In relation to foreign judgments the non-merger rule has been abolished by statute,[29] and there is no reason of policy or principle why the obsolete and anomalous rule of non-merger in relation to foreign judgments should be extended to foreign awards. Indeed the consensual and contractual character of arbitration means that parties to an arbitration agreement impliedly promise to perform a valid award,[30] and it should follow that they also promise not to take any action inconsistent with their submission to arbitration. Bringing proceedings on the original cause of action would be wholly inconsistent with the obligation under the submission and the subsequent award. If, therefore, under the law governing the arbitration proceedings the original cause of action is merged in the award, a claimant should not be entitled to rely on the original contract.
16–067

This question should not be confused with the very different question whether, in the event of a judgment having been obtained abroad on the award, the award is merged in that judgment: as in other cases of enforcement of foreign judgments this is a matter for the *lex fori* of the court asked to enforce it. In England a local award may be enforced under section 66 of the Arbitration Act 1996, under which leave of the court may be obtained to enforce the award in the same manner as a judgment, and also, if the claimant applies, to enter judgment in terms of the award. In most countries a local award may be enforced by a similar or analogous procedure, varying from mere deposit of the award with the court which gives it executory effect, to a formal order giving the award executory effect or entering judgment in terms of the award. If enforcement measures of this kind are taken in the foreign country, is it the award or the foreign judgment which is to be enforced in
16–068

---

[24] Mustill and Boyd, p. 417.

[25] *Cf.* Kahn (1930) 12 Jo.Comp.Leg. (3rd series), 228, 245; Lorenzen, pp. 520–524.

[26] Mustill and Boyd, p. 409.

[27] *Ibid.*; *cf. Ayscough v. Sheed, Thomson & Co. Ltd.* (1924) 40 T.L.R. 707; *Fidelitas Shipping Co. Ltd. v. V/O Exportchleb* [1966] Q.B. 630, 643 (C.A.).

[28] In *The Rena K.* [1979] Q.B. 377, 405, Brandon J. assumed (without deciding) that this was so in the case of an English award. *East India Trading Co. Inc. v. Carmel Exporters and Importers Ltd.* [1952] 2 Q.B. 439 has been taken to suggest the contrary in the case of a foreign award, but the decision does not bear this out.

[29] Civil Jurisdiction and Judgments Act 1982, s.34, *ante*, paras. 14–034 *et seq.*

[30] See *Bremer Oeltransport v. Drewry* [1933] 1 K.B. 753 (C.A.).

England, or does the claimant have an option? There is no doubt that, provided it fulfils the requirements for enforcement, a foreign judgment on a foreign award is regarded as a judgment for the purposes of the rules relating to enforcement of foreign judgments.[31] Nor, where the foreign order has merely the effect of rendering the award executory, is there any reason why the award should not be enforced as such.[32]

16–069   A doubt, however, arises whether an award can be enforced as such after entry of judgment on it in the foreign country. The mere fact that the claimant has taken enforcement proceedings involving entry of judgment abroad should as a matter of policy be no bar to enforcement of the award, but it is possible that the abolition of the doctrine of non-merger in relation to foreign judgments[33] may have had the unintended result that, provided the judgment is enforceable in England, then it will be the foreign judgment, and not the award, which will be enforceable in England. This anomalous result could only apply to enforcement at common law, since (it is suggested) the provision in section 101 of the Arbitration Act 1996 that Convention awards "shall" be recognised as binding on the parties would apply even if judgment on the award had been entered abroad.[34]

16–070   **Conditions for enforcement.** The cases support the proposition, stated in the Rule, that a foreign award can be enforced or recognised in England, provided that it fulfils two fundamental requirements. These are (1) that the parties have submitted to the arbitration by an agreement which is valid by its governing law; and (2) that the award is valid and final according to the law which governs the arbitration proceedings. The principles governing those questions have been discussed in Rule 57. The jurisdiction of the tribunal to render the award is governed by the law governing the arbitration agreement, and the validity of the award depends on the law governing the arbitration proceedings.

16–071   The English court will not refuse to recognise or enforce a foreign award merely because the arbitrators (in its view) applied the wrong law to the dispute, or misapplied the right law. There is no authority to this effect, but it

---

[31] *East India Trading Co. Inc. v. Carmel Exporters and Importers Ltd.* [1952] 2 Q.B. 439; *International Alltex Corp. v. Lawler Creations Ltd.* [1965] I.R. 264; *Union Nationale des Coopératives Agricoles v. Catterall* [1959] 2 Q.B. 44, 54 (C.A.); *cf. Stolp & Co. v. Browne & Co.* [1930] 4 D.L.R. 703 (Ont.); see Rule 60(2).

[32] *Cf.* Lorenzen, p. 523; Kahn (1930) 12 Jo.Comp.Leg. (3rd series) 228, 246; Hascher (1996) 12 Arb. Int. 233; *cf. ABCI v. Banque Franco-Tunisienne* [1996] 1 Lloyd's Rep. 485, affd. on other aspects [1997] 1 Lloyd's Rep. 531 (C.A.).

[33] 1982 Act, s.34, *supra*, n. 29. In England a domestic award is merged in a judgment entered on it. The prior non-merger rule prevailing in relation to foreign judgments was used to justify the ability to enforce the award: Mustill and Boyd, p. 423; *Brali v. Hyundai Corp.* (1988) 84 A.L.R. 176, 178–181; *Oilcakes and Oilseeds Trading Co. v. Sinason-Teicher Inter American Grain Corp.*, 170 N.Y.S. 2d 378, affd. 8 N.Y. 2d 852, 203 N.Y.S. 2d 904 (1960). See also Van Den Berg, *op. cit.*, para. 16–038, n. 26; Patchett, *ibid.*, pp. 233, 296; Note (1975) 124 U.Pa.L.Rev. 223. In Canada it was held that where a foreign judgment was entered on a foreign award, only the judgment was enforceable: *Stolp & Co. v. Browne & Co.* [1930] 4 D.L.R. 703 (Ont.), not followed in *Schreter v. Gasmac Inc.* (1992) 7 O.R. (3d) 608, a case on the enforcement provisions of the UNCITRAL Model Law. The question was left open in *Oppenheim & Co. v. Mahomed Haneef* [1922] 1 A.C. 482 (P.C.). 1920 Act, s.12(1) and 1933 Act, s.10A (added by 1982 Act, Sched. 10, para. 4) *post*, para. 16–135, strongly suggest that the award remains enforceable as such under those Acts, even if judgment has been entered on it in the foreign country.

[34] See *post*, para. 16–111, for the position under the Arbitration Act 1996 and U.S. decisions on the New York Convention.

is a reasonable deduction from the similar rule applicable to the recognition and enforcement of foreign judgments.[35] Nor should it be of any concern to the English court that the arbitrators applied no law at all if this is permissible under the law governing the arbitration proceedings.

To be enforceable in England, the award must be final and binding on the parties in the English sense, *i.e.* it must fulfil one of the conditions for the enforcement of foreign judgments.[36] This is one of the most important requirements for the recognition or enforcement of foreign awards in England. Whether the award is final in the English sense must, it is submitted, depend on the law governing the arbitration proceedings. The question to be answered is "Has it become final, as we understand that phrase, in the country in which it was made? Of course the question whether it is final in [that country] will depend no doubt upon [the foreign] law, but the [foreign] law is directed to showing whether it is final as that word is understood in English."[37] These remarks were made in a case where the award was enforced under Part II of the Arbitration Act 1950 (*i.e.* under Rule 62); but it is submitted that they are equally applicable to the enforcement of awards at common law. However, whereas under Part II of the Act an award is not deemed to be final "if any proceedings for the purpose of contesting the validity of the award are pending in the country in which it was made,"[38] it is far from clear whether the pendency of such proceedings prevents the enforcement of a foreign award at common law. On the analogy of the enforcement of foreign judgments at common law,[39] it is suggested that it would not. However, it is reasonable to suppose that, in appropriate circumstances, enforcement proceedings in England may be stayed[40] pending the outcome of any foreign proceedings challenging the award. **16–072**

Mode of enforcement. In order to enforce an arbitration award it is always necessary to obtain an enforcement title from a court. This applies to foreign, as it applies to English, awards. The party seeking to enforce the award has the choice between bringing proceedings on it and applying for permission to enforce it by a summary procedure under section 66 of the Arbitration Act 1996. An application to enforce an award under section 66 may be made without notice,[41] though the court may direct that the application is to be served on the relevant parties.[42] Service of the application out of the jurisdiction may be effected with the permission of the court, whether the award is made in England or abroad.[43] The summary procedure is available for the enforcement of awards provided that the arbitration agreement is in writing as required by section 5 of the 1996 Act. The summary procedure can be **16–073**

---

[35] See *ante*, para. 14–110.
[36] See Rule 35. The difference between finality and enforceability under the foreign law is discussed in the Comment to the next Rule, *post*, paras. 16–078 *et seq.*
[37] *Union Nationale des Coopératives Agricoles v. Catterall* [1959] 2 Q.B. 44, 53 (C.A.).
[38] s.39; see Rule 62(3), proviso.
[39] Rule 35, proviso.
[40] For the position under the 1996 Act see *Soleh Boneh International Ltd. v. Government of Uganda* [1993] 2 Lloyd's Rep. 208, which is discussed at para. 16–121, *post*.
[41] CPR PD49G, para. 31.2.
[42] *Ibid.*, para. 31.3.
[43] *Ibid.* Permission to serve out of the jurisdiction on a foreign defendant may be given even if there is no jurisdictional connection with England (*e.g.* assets in England): *Rosseel N.V. v. Oriental Commercial & Shipping Co. (U.K.) Ltd.* [1991] 2 Lloyd's Rep. 625; *cf. ABCI v. Banque Franco-Tunisienne* [1996] 1 Lloyd's Rep. 485, affd. [1997] 1 Lloyd's Rep. 531 (C.A.).

employed unless there is a real ground for doubting the validity of the award[44]; but it should be borne in mind that the enforcement of foreign awards may sometimes involve more difficult questions than does the enforcement of English awards.

If the award provides for payment of money out of the jurisdiction, it cannot be enforced under section 66, though it can be enforced by action on the award.[45]

16–074   An award may be expressed in foreign currency, and such an award can be enforced under section 66.[46] But, whether enforced by proceedings or under section 66, it must be converted into sterling before it can be enforced in England by any process of execution. The date for conversion will be the date when the court authorises enforcement of the judgment or when permission to enforce the award in sterling under section 66 is given.[47]

16–075   **Recognition of foreign awards in England.** The conditions under which a foreign award may be enforced in England at common law apply, it is submitted, also to its recognition otherwise than by enforcement.[48] A valid English award duly made in pursuance of a valid agreement to arbitrate is a defence to proceedings on the original cause of action,[49] and there seems no reason why the same should not be true of a valid foreign award.[50] More difficult questions arise if the foreign award was not based on the underlying merits, *e.g.* because the notice to arbitrate was out of time. There is a tendency in cases not involving a foreign element for the English court to construe contractual time-barring provisions as barring the claim if the arbitral machinery is not invoked in time.[51] Thus it was held that an action on the same cause of action was barred by an award holding that the arbitration was out of time.[52] In that case the arbitrators held that they had jurisdiction and the claim

---

[44] *Re Boks & Co. and Peters, Rushton & Co. Ltd.* [1919] 1 K.B. 491 (C.A.), as explained in *Middlemiss & Gould v. Hartlepool Corporation* [1972] 1 W.L.R. 1643, 1647 (C.A.). In *Union Nationale des Coopératives Agricoles v. Catterall* [1959] 2 Q.B. 44, 52 (C.A.), the same test was adopted and applied to the enforcement of a foreign award under Part II of the Arbitration Act 1950 (*i.e.* Rule 62). s.36 of the 1950 Act makes the summary procedure under s.66 of the 1996 Act applicable to the enforcement of foreign awards which come within Part II of the 1950 Act and the same summary procedure is available in cases involving the enforcement of New York Convention awards under s.101 of the 1996 Act (CPR PD49G, para. 31.2). See *post*, para. 16–123.

[45] *Dalmia Cement Ltd. v. National Bank of Pakistan* [1975] Q.B. 9, 23–27; *cf. Bank Mellat v. G.A.A. Development and Construction Co.* [1988] 2 Lloyd's Rep. 44.

[46] *Jugoslavenska Oceanska Plovidba v. Castle Investment Co. Inc.* [1974] Q.B. 292 (C.A.). See Rule 211.

[47] In the *Jugoslavenska* case, *supra*, the date of the award was chosen: see at pp. 300, 302, 305, 306. But in *Miliangos v. George Frank (Textiles) Ltd.* [1976] A.C. 443, 469, Lord Wilberforce could see no reason why this date should not be adjusted so as to allow conversion to be made at the date stated in the text. See also s.4 of the Administration of Justice Act 1977, repealing s.1(3) of the Arbitration (International Investment Disputes) Act 1966 (which made the date of the award the date for conversion).

[48] For the analogous question under Part II of the Arbitration Act 1950 and under the Arbitration Act 1996, see Rule 62(2) and Rule 63(2), *post*.

[49] *Ayscough v. Sheed, Thomson & Co. Ltd.* (1924) 40 T.L.R. 707 (H.L.). It is sometimes said that this is because the submission to arbitration contains an implied promise by each party to abide by the award: see Mustill and Boyd, p. 413.

[50] But see Mustill and Boyd, p. 415.

[51] See Mustill and Boyd, pp. 202–204.

[52] See *Ayscough v. Sheed, Thomson & Co. Ltd.* (1924) 40 T.L.R. 707 (H.L.). *Cf.* the position with regard to foreign judgments, *ante*, para. 14–031, and the Foreign Limitation Periods Act 1984, s.3, which does not apply to foreign awards.

was dismissed on the basis that the claim (as opposed to the remedy) was barred by the claimant's failure to invoke the arbitral machinery in time. A foreign award to the effect that a claim was barred by a contractual time limitation would be entitled to recognition in England, for the decision would be "on the merits."[53]

ILLUSTRATIONS

1. A, a Norwegian company, and X, an English company, enter into a reinsurance contract **16–076** containing an agreement to arbitrate in Oslo. The reinsurance contract (but not the arbitration clause) is void according to English law because it is not embodied in a stamped policy. A dispute arises, and A appoints an arbitrator, but X refuses to do so. In accordance with the agreement to arbitrate a second arbitrator is appointed by a Norwegian judge at A's request. The arbitrators make an award in favour of A which is valid by Norwegian law. A can enforce the award by proceedings in England.[54]

2. A, a New York company, and X, an English company, enter into a reinsurance contract containing an agreement to arbitrate in New York. A dispute arises, and A appoints an arbitrator, but X fails to do so and revokes the submission. In accordance with the agreement to arbitrate A appoints a second arbitrator and the arbitrators appoint an umpire. An award is made in favour of A. According to a New York statute an order of the New York court is required to allow the arbitration to proceed without an arbitrator appointed by X. This statute is interpreted by the New York Court of Appeals as establishing a condition for the validity of the award. The award is a nullity and A cannot in England recover the amount of the award.[55]

3. A contract for the sale of skins made between A, a foreign buyer, and X, an English seller, provides for arbitration in the foreign country. A dispute having arisen as to the quality of the skins, A proceeds to arbitration and appoints an arbitrator, but X, although he has notice of the proceedings, fails to do so. The arbitrator appointed by A proceeds with the arbitration in the absence of X and makes an award in favour of A. This award is valid and final according to the law of the foreign country. A can enforce it by proceedings in England.[56]

4. The circumstances are the same as in Illustration 3, except that the award contains on its face an error of fact or law. *Semble*, if this prevents the award from being final in the English sense according to the law of the foreign country, A cannot enforce the award in England; but if it does not, he can.

RULE 60—(1) A foreign arbitration award will be enforced in England **16R–077** whether or not the law governing the arbitration proceedings requires a judgment or order of a court to make the award enforceable.[57]

(2) If a party obtains a foreign judgment by which a foreign arbitration award is made enforceable, he may enforce that judgment in England in accordance with Rules 35, 46, 47 and 49.[58]

---

[53] *Cf. The Sennar (No. 2)* [1984] 2 Lloyd's Rep. 142 (C.A.), affd. [1985] 1 W.L.R. 490 (H.L.). If the foreign arbitral tribunal decides merely that it has no jurisdiction because notice of arbitration was not given within the contractual time, the unsuccessful claimant may be able to bring proceedings in England on the original cause of action: *cf. Pinnock Brothers v. Lewis & Peat Ltd.* [1923] 1 K.B. 690, a case involving an English arbitration. But in some circumstances the defendant may be entitled to a stay, for otherwise a claimant could avoid arbitration in such a case by waiting until the time for arbitration had expired. The respondent to the arbitration would be in a dilemma if the claimant purports to give notice of arbitration; if the respondent does not object he will have waived the time bar; if he objects and relies on the time bar he may be faced with court proceedings.

[54] *Norske Atlas Insurance Co. Ltd. v. London General Insurance Co. Ltd.* (1927) 28 Ll.L.R. 104.

[55] *Bankers and Shippers Insurance Co. of New York v. Liverpool Marine and General Insurance Co. Ltd.* (1926) 24 Ll.L.R. 85 (H.L.).

[56] *Cf. Oppenheim & Co. v. Mahomed Haneef* [1922] 1 A.C. 482 (P.C.).

[57] *Union Nationale des Coopératives Agricoles v. Catterall* [1959] 2 Q.B. 44 (C.A.).

[58] *East India Trading Co. Inc. v. Carmel Exporters and Importers Ltd.* [1952] 2 Q.B. 439; *International Alltex Corp. v. Lawler Creations Ltd.* [1965] I.R. 264; see also *ante*, para. 16–069.

Comment

16–078   **Clause (1) of the Rule.** The enforcement in England of foreign awards, like the enforcement of foreign judgments, is governed by English law. Foreign law regulating the enforcement of awards and in particular the need for obtaining judgments thereon does not apply in England. Hence a foreign award may be enforced in England though it has not been made enforceable by judgment in its country of origin and though the law of that country requires a judgment of a court to make the award enforceable. If the English court insisted on a foreign judgment in order to make the award enforceable in England, it would "not be enforcing the award but the judgment,"[59] *i.e.* the foreign award as such might be deprived of all effect in England. The English technique of enforcing an award applies to all proceedings for the enforcement of arbitral awards in England, whether the awards are English or foreign. How the award can be made enforceable under its own law is of no concern to the English court. All doubts concerning this important principle were removed by the decision of the Court of Appeal in *Union Nationale des Coopératives Agricoles v. Catterall*.[60] This case was decided under the provisions of Part II of the Arbitration Act 1950 (*i.e.* under Rule 62), but it is submitted that the principles applied by the court apply with equal force to cases arising at common law. As Lord Evershed M.R. pointed out,[61] the opposite view leads to the result that a foreign award as such would never be enforceable in an English court, a conclusion clearly incompatible with the rule established at least since the decision in the *Norske Atlas Insurance* case.[62] This must be emphasised because the decision in *Merrifield Ziegler & Co. v. Liverpool Cotton Association*[63] is to the opposite effect, *viz.* that, in order to be enforced in England, the foreign award must be actually and not only potentially enforceable in the country in which it was rendered. This decision was not considered either in the *Norske Atlas Insurance* case or in *Union Nationale des Coopératives Agricoles v. Catterall*.[64] It is submitted that it cannot stand with these two cases and that it cannot now be considered as expressing the law.[65]

16–079   Since, to be enforced in England, a foreign arbitration award must be valid and final in accordance with the law which governs the arbitration proceedings, a distinction must be made between conditions which under that law must be fulfilled to render the award valid and final, and conditions which must be fulfilled to render it enforceable. This line may sometimes be difficult to draw.[66] But the distinction between "validity" and "finality" on the one

---

[59] *Union Nationale des Coopératives Agricoles v. Catterall* [1959] 2 Q.B. 44, 54 (C.A.).

[60] [1959] 2 Q.B. 44.

[61] *Ibid.*, p. 54; see also *per* Pearce L.J. at p. 56.

[62] *Norske Atlas Insurance Co. Ltd. v. London General Insurance Co. Ltd.* (1927) 28 Ll.L.R. 104.

[63] (1911) 105 L.T. 97. For critical discussions of the case, see Lorenzen, pp. 521 *et seq.*; Kahn (1930) 12 Jo.Comp.Leg. (3rd series), 228, 244 *et seq.*

[64] [1959] 2 Q.B. 44 (C.A.); stated *post*, para. 16–083, Illustration 1.

[65] See, to this effect, *Dalmia Dairy Industries Ltd. v. National Bank of Pakistan* [1978] 2 Lloyd's Rep. 223, 249. There was no appeal from this part of Kerr J.'s judgment.

[66] For a succinct formulation of the problem, see *Bankers and Shippers Insurance Co. of New York v. Liverpool Marine and General Insurance Co. Ltd.* (1924) 19 Ll.L.R. 335, 338. This decision was affirmed by the House of Lords: (1926) 24 Ll.L.R. 85, stated *ante*, para. 16–076, Illustration 2. For a discussion of the case from an American point of view, see Domke (1952) 17 *Law and Contemporary Problems* 545, 555.

side and "enforceability" on the other is, it is submitted, familiar in English domestic law and the difficulties which arise are not insuperable.

Clause (2) of the Rule. Where the award has in fact been reduced to a judgment in the country in which it was rendered, or, perhaps, in another country, the judgment may be enforced in England.[67] This does not mean, however, that the party who has obtained a foreign award in his favour and subsequently a court order rendering it enforceable in its country of origin is compelled to enforce the judgment in England.   **16–080**

Where, as is often the case, the foreign judgment upon the award has the character of an *exequatur*,[68] a formal order giving leave to enforce the award comparable to an order under section 66 of the Arbitration Act 1996,[69] that which is enforced in England will probably always be the award and not the order. It has been seen above that where a foreign judgment has been obtained on the award it is a matter of some doubt whether the award may be enforced.[70] But the distinction between enforcing the award and enforcing the order declaring an award enforceable may be insubstantial.   **16–081**

By submitting to arbitration the parties also submit to the jurisdiction of the court which, in accordance with the law governing the arbitration proceedings, is called upon to declare the award enforceable.[71] That, in the eyes of the English courts, that court has jurisdiction to pronounce on the enforcement of the award, seems never to have been doubted. If, however, in a very unusual situation, the facts of the case show that a party, whilst submitting to the arbitration, did not submit to the enforcement proceedings, it may be of importance that the party who has obtained the award is able to enforce it in England irrespective of its enforceability abroad.   **16–082**

ILLUSTRATIONS

1. A contract for the sale of wheat seed made between A, French buyers, and X, English sellers, contains a clause referring all disputes to the Arbitration Chamber of Copenhagen. A dispute having arisen, A obtains an award from the committee of the Copenhagen Arbitration Chamber ordering X to pay £183,000. Under the rules of the Chamber, awards made by the committee are final. But by Danish law, the award is not enforceable in Denmark until a judgment of a Danish court has been obtained. However, only objections of a formal nature can be taken in the proceedings to obtain a judgment, which are in no sense a rehearing. *Semble*, A can enforce the award by proceedings in England at common law or under section 66 of the Arbitration Act 1996, even though no judgment has been obtained in Denmark, because the award is by Danish law final and binding in the English sense.[72]   **16–083**

2. A obtains an arbitration award in New York ordering X to pay a sum of money. A obtains a judgment against X in New York to enforce the award. A can bring proceedings in England

---

[67] *East India Trading Co. Inc. v. Carmel Exporters and Importers Ltd.* [1952] 2 Q.B. 439, stated *infra*, Illustration 2; *International Alltex Corp. v. Lawler Creations Ltd.* [1965] I.R. 264; *cf. Stolp & Co. v. Browne & Co.* [1930] 4 D.L.R. 703 (Ont.).

[68] See *ante*, para. 16–068; Lorenzen, pp. 514–520.

[69] *Ante*, para. 16–068.

[70] *Ante*, para. 16–069.

[71] *International Alltex Corp. v. Lawler Creations Ltd.* [1965] I.R. 264. See Rule 36, *Fourth Case*, and paras. 14–069 *et seq., ante*.

[72] *Cf. Union Nationale des Coopératives Agricoles v. Catterall* [1959] 2 Q.B. 44 (C.A.). This case was decided under Part II of the Arbitration Act 1950, *i.e.* under Rule 62, but it is submitted that the result would have been the same at common law. The right to proceed at common law is preserved by s.40(*a*) of the Act.

against X on the judgment.[73] *Quaere*, whether A could, had he so chosen, have sued X on the award instead of suing on the judgment.[74]

3. A, a Dutch firm, obtains an arbitration award in Holland against X, a Canadian firm. A deposits the award in the competent court at Amsterdam which, by endorsing the award, gives it executory force. No notice of these proceedings is given to X, nor is this required by Dutch law. Although notice of analogous proceedings would have been required according to the law of Ontario, the Dutch award, as endorsed by the Dutch court, can be enforced in Ontario as a foreign judgment.[75]

16R–084   RULE 61—A foreign arbitration award which complies with Rule 59 will (*semble*) not be recognised or enforced in England if

(1) under the submission agreement and the law applicable thereto the arbitrators had no jurisdiction to make it[76]; or

(2) it was obtained by fraud[77]; or

(3) its recognition, or as the case may be enforcement, would be contrary to public policy[78]; or

(4) the proceedings in which it was obtained were opposed to natural justice.[79]

COMMENT

16–085   There is very little authority on the circumstances in which a foreign award can be challenged in England, notwithstanding that it was made in accordance with a valid agreement to arbitrate as required by Rule 59(1), and is valid and final according to the law governing the arbitration proceedings as required by Rule 59(2). Rule 61 must therefore be regarded as somewhat speculative. But it will be observed that it follows closely the grounds on which a foreign judgment can be impeached in England at common law. It can hardly be supposed that foreign arbitration awards will be more readily enforced or recognised in England than are foreign judgments. Hence the existence at least of these grounds of opposition can, it is submitted, be taken for granted.

16–086   In one sense the jurisdiction of the arbitrators raises less complicated problems than does the jurisdiction of a foreign court to give a judgment capable of recognition or enforcement in England.[80] This is because the agreement of the parties to submit their dispute to arbitration is the sole ground of the arbitrators' jurisdiction, and not one of several grounds as is an

---

[73] *East India Trading Co. Inc. v. Carmel Exporters and Importers Ltd.* [1952] 2 Q.B. 439.

[74] See *ante*, para. 16–069 and *cf. Oppenheim & Co. v. Mahomed Haneef* [1922] 1 A.C. 482 (P.C.).

[75] *Stolp & Co. v. Browne & Co.* [1930] 4 D.L.R. 703 (Ont.).

[76] See *Kianta Osakeyhtio v. Britain and Overseas Trading Co. Ltd.* [1954] 1 Lloyd's Rep. 247 (C.A.); *Dalmia Dairy Industries Ltd. v. National Bank of Pakistan* [1978] 2 Lloyd's Rep. 223 (C.A.). Compare Rule 42(1), and Rule 62(3)(a), (b) (which reproduces s.37(1)(*a*), (*b*) of the Arbitration Act 1950) and Rule 63(4)(d), (e) (which reproduces s.103(2)(*d*), (*e*) of the Arbitration Act 1996).

[77] *Oppenheim & Co. v. Mahomed Haneef* [1922] 1 A.C. 482, 487 (P.C.) Compare Rule 43. This is not a ground under which an award can be refused enforcement under the Geneva Convention (Rule 62) or the New York Convention (Rule 63). Nor is it supported by any actual decision.

[78] Compare Rule 44, and Rule 62(3) *ad finem* (which reproduces s.37(1) *ad finem* of the Arbitration Act 1950) and Rule 63(5) (which reproduces s.103(3) of the Arbitration Act 1996).

[79] Compare Rule 45, and the more limited provisions of Rule 62(4)(b) (which reproduces s.37(2)(*b*) of the Arbitration Act 1950) and Rule 63(4)(c) (which reproduces s.103(2)(*c*) of the Arbitration Act 1996).

[80] See Rule 36.

agreement to submit to the jurisdiction of a foreign court. But a court which is asked to enforce or recognise an award will require to be satisfied that the arbitrators acted within the terms of the agreement to arbitrate. It is for the claimant seeking enforcement to prove that the award is covered by the terms of the submission agreement. It is a "fundamental principle which is . . . equally applicable to the case of English law and of foreign law that it is for the party who is setting up the award to prove that the arbitrators acted within the terms of the authority which was given to them."[81] If, however, the claimant produces "a document which appears to be regular and made with jurisdiction, . . . the onus may pass to the defendant to prove, if he can do so, that the award which appeared to be regular is defective in that it deals with matters beyond the scope of the agreement for arbitration."[82]

There are very few reported cases in which foreign judgments *in personam*   **16–087** have been denied recognition or enforcement in England on grounds of public policy,[83] no doubt because this concept is narrowly interpreted in the English conflict of laws[84]; and the refusal to recognise or enforce a foreign arbitration award on this ground is likely to be an equally rare event. Nor can there be any doubt that the rule that a foreign judgment may be denied recognition or enforcement because the proceedings in which it was obtained were opposed to natural justice[85] applies also to foreign awards.[86]

ILLUSTRATIONS

1. A, Finnish sellers, contract with X, English buyers, for the sale of timber. The contract   **16–088** contains an arbitration clause for disputes to be settled in Helsinki. Part delivery only is made under the contract and a compromise "compensation" agreement without an arbitration clause is entered into. No deliveries are made under the latter agreement and A institute arbitration proceedings in Finland, X refusing to participate. An award is made in favour of A. *Semble*, A cannot enforce the award by action in England at common law, because under the "compensation" agreement the arbitrators had no jurisdiction to make it.[87]

2. Arbitration proceedings take place in a foreign country between A, a foreign buyer, and X, an English seller. The arbitrator admits evidence which is inadmissible by the law of the foreign country. He refuses to adjourn the proceedings in order to give X an opportunity of rebutting this evidence. Throughout the proceedings he shows bias against X. His award is in favour of A. In these circumstances an English arbitrator could have been removed by the court for misconduct,[88] but there is no such power of removal under the foreign law, according to which the award is valid and final. *Semble*, it will not be enforced in England, for the proceedings were opposed to natural justice.

---

[81] *Kianta Osakeyhtio v. Britain and Overseas Trading Co. Ltd.* [1953] 2 Lloyd's Rep. 569, 573, affd. [1954] 1 Lloyd's Rep. 247 (C.A.). *Cf. Dalmia Dairy Industries Ltd. v. National Bank of Pakistan* [1978] 2 Lloyd's Rep. 233 (C.A.).

[82] [1954] 1 Lloyd's Rep. 247, 250–251 (C.A.). *Cf.* Rule 63(4)(d), (e) (which reproduces s.103(2)(*d*), (*e*) of the Arbitration Act 1996).

[83] *Ante*, Rule 44.

[84] See Rule 2; *Westacre Investments Inc. v. Jugoimport-SDPR Holding Co.* [1999] Q.B. 740; *Soinco SACI v. Novokuznetsk Aluminium Plant* [1998] C.L.C. 730 (C.A.).

[85] *Ante*, Rule 45.

[86] *Cf. Dalmia Dairy Industries Ltd. v. National Bank of Pakistan* [1978] 2 Lloyd's Rep. 223, 270 (where it was argued, unsuccessfully, that the arbitrator's refusal to hear witnesses was contrary to public policy or to principles of natural justice).

[87] *Cf. Kianta Osakeyhtio v. Britain and Overseas Trading Co. Ltd.* [1954] 1 Lloyd's Rep. 247 (C.A.). This case was decided under Part II of the Arbitration Act 1950, *i.e.* under Rule 62, but it is submitted that the result would have been the same at common law. The right to proceed at common law is preserved by s.40(*a*) of the Act.

[88] *Re Enoch and Zaretsky, Bock & Co.* [1910] 1 K.B. 327 (C.A.).

3. Arbitration proceedings take place in a foreign country between A, an English buyer, and X, a foreign seller. The dispute relates to the quality of the goods sold. The arbitrator (who is a relative of X) hurriedly examines some (but not all) of the goods, and refuses to listen to A's witnesses. He makes an award in favour of X which, in the opinion of the English court, is "the erroneous and uncandid production of a biased and prejudiced mind." The award is valid and final by the law of the foreign country. When A sues X in England on the contract, X pleads the award as a defence. *Semble*, the award will not be recognised in England, because the proceedings were opposed to natural justice.[89]

16–089   4. Arbitration proceedings arising out of a collision on the high seas between a Norwegian and a Portuguese ship take place in a foreign country. During the course of the proceedings the arbitrator makes remarks indicating that he holds preconceived ideas about the veracity of Portuguese witnesses. In such circumstances an English arbitrator would be removed by the court for misconduct.[90] The owners of the Portuguese ship apply to the foreign court to remove the arbitrator, but the court declines to interfere. The arbitrator makes an award in favour of the owners of the Norwegian ship. *Semble*, it will not be enforced in England.

5. A, an Indian company, sells a cement factory in Pakistan to B, a resident of Pakistan. The contract (which is governed by Indian law) provides for arbitration in Geneva under the rules of the International Chamber of Commerce. X, a Pakistan bank, unconditionally and irrevocably guarantees the payment of the price. Before the price can be paid, war breaks out between India and Pakistan. Under the Rules of the International Chamber of Commerce, the arbitrator can determine his own jurisdiction. The arbitrator makes his award in favour of A, who seeks enforcement against X in England. The Court of Appeal holds that though the arbitrator cannot determine his own jurisdiction, by Indian law the arbitration clause was not abrogated by the outbreak of war, and it was not contrary to English public policy to enforce the award.[91]

B. *Under Part II of the Arbitration Act 1950*

16R–090   RULE 62[92]—(1) A foreign award made—

    (a)   **in pursuance of an agreement, other than an arbitration agreement governed by the law of England, to which the Protocol set out in the First Schedule to the Arbitration Act 1950 is applicable;**

    (b)   **between parties who are respectively subject to the jurisdiction of different States which are declared by Order in Council[93] to be parties to the Geneva Convention on the Execution of Foreign Arbitral Awards of September 26, 1927[94];**

    (c)   **in a territory to which the Convention is declared to apply;**

is enforceable by action, or under the provisions of section 66 of the Arbitration Act 1996, *i.e.* by leave of the High Court, in the same manner as a judgment or order to the same effect.

(2) Such an award will be treated as binding for all purposes on the persons between whom it is made, and may be relied on by way of defence, set-off or otherwise in any legal proceedings.

---

[89] *Cf. Jacobson v. Frachon* (1927) 138 L.T. 386 (C.A.), stated *ante*, para. 14–158, Illustration 3. In that case the proceedings in which the French judgment was obtained were held not to be contrary to natural justice, because the expert's report was not binding on the French court. But in this case the arbitrator is appointed not by the court but by the parties; and it is assumed that his decision is final by the foreign law.

[90] *Catalina (Owners) v. Norma (Owners)* (1938) 61 Ll.L.R. 360.

[91] *Dalmia Dairy Industries Ltd. v. National Bank of Pakistan* [1978] 2 Lloyd's Rep. 223 (C.A.).

[92] Arbitration Act 1950, Part II and First and Second Schedules, substantially re-enacting the Arbitration Clauses (Protocol) Act 1924 and the Arbitration (Foreign Awards) Act 1930. Patchett, *Recognition of Commercial Judgments and Awards in the Commonwealth* (1984), Chap. 7.

[93] For a list of States which have been declared to be parties to the Convention, see S.I. 1984 No. 1168.

[94] The Convention is reproduced in Arbitration Act 1950, Sched. 2.

(3) To be enforceable an award must have—

(a) been made in pursuance of an agreement for arbitration which was valid under the law by which it was governed;

(b) been made by the tribunal provided for in the agreement or constituted in manner agreed upon by the parties;

(c) been made in conformity with the law governing the arbitration procedure;

(d) become final in the country in which it was made;

(e) been in respect of a matter which may lawfully be referred to arbitration under the law of England;

and the enforcement thereof must not be against the public policy or the law of England.

Provided that an award will not be deemed final if any proceedings for the purpose of contesting the validity thereof are pending in the country in which it was made.

(4) An award will not be enforceable if the court dealing with the case is satisfied that—

(a) the award has been annulled in the country in which it was made; or

(b) the party against whom it is sought to enforce the award was not given notice of the arbitration proceedings in sufficient time to enable him to present his case, or was under some legal incapacity and was not properly represented; or

(c) the award does not deal with all the questions referred or contains decisions on matters beyond the scope of the agreement for arbitration.

Provided that, if the award does not deal with all the questions referred, the court may, if it thinks fit, either postpone the enforcement of the award or order its enforcement subject to the giving of such security by the person seeking to enforce it as the court may think fit.

(5) If a party seeking to resist the enforcement of such an award proves that there is any ground other than the non-existence of the conditions specified in paragraphs (a), (b) and (c) of clause (3) of this Rule, or the existence of the conditions specified in paragraphs (b) and (c) of clause (4) of this Rule, entitling him to contest the validity of the award, the court may, if it thinks fit, either refuse to enforce the award or adjourn the hearing until after the expiration of such period as appears to the court to be reasonably sufficient to enable that party to take the necessary steps to have the award annulled by the competent tribunal.

(6) A foreign award which is also a New York Convention award under Rule 63 is not enforceable under Rule 62.[95]

COMMENT

Introductory: the Geneva Convention. Efforts to promote the inter-national recognition and enforcement of commercial arbitration awards have on a number of occasions been made by means of multilateral international conventions.[96] The United Kingdom is a party to the Protocol on Arbitration Clauses of 1923 and to the Geneva Convention on the Execution of Foreign   **16–091**

---

[95] Arbitration Act 1996, s.99. See *post*, para. 16–126.
[96] See Nussbaum (1942) 56 Harv.L.R. 219.

Arbitral Awards of 1927. The Geneva Convention has been largely (but not wholly) superseded by the New York Convention of 1958, which is dealt with in Rule 63. The Geneva Convention does not apply to any award which is a New York Convention award, *i.e.* an award made in a State which is a party to the New York Convention.[97] Since very few States which are parties to the Geneva Convention have not also become parties to the New York Convention[98] the earlier Convention has no more than a residual role.

16–092   Rule 62 reproduces the principal provisions of Part II of the Arbitration Act 1950, which enacts the Protocol of 1923 as supplemented by the Convention on the Execution of Arbitral Awards of 1927.

16–093   The procedure under Part II of the Act is optional. Even within its scope of application the Convention, and therefore the Act, does not prejudice any rights which any person has to seek enforcement at common law.[99]

16–094   **Scope of application.** The scope of application of Part II is limited to awards made between persons who are subject to the jurisdiction of two different States, both of which are parties to the Protocol of 1923 and both of which have, by reason of reciprocity, been declared by Order in Council "to be parties to the Convention" of 1927.[1] The meaning of the somewhat obscure phrase "subject to the jurisdiction" occasioned much speculation.[2] In England it was held to mean not that the parties must have different nationalities, but that they must reside or carry on business in two different Contracting States, and that the contract containing the submission to arbitration must have resulted from business so conducted.[3] To come within the scope of Part II the award must further have been made in the territory of a Contracting State.[4] No award can be enforced under Rule 62 if it was made in pursuance of an arbitration agreement governed by English law.[5]

16–095   **Conditions of enforceability.** The Act requires that the award must have been made by the tribunal agreed upon or constituted in manner agreed upon by the parties, that the award must have been made in conformity with the law governing the arbitration procedure, and that it must have become final in the country in which it was made.[6] There is no authority on the questions whether the law of the country where the award was made governs the arbitration procedure or whether the parties may determine the law which does.

16–096   **Finality of the award.** One of the conditions for the enforcement of the award is that it must have "become final in the country in which it was made."[7] The word "final" in Rule 62 means the same thing as at common law. This is the gist of the decision of the Court of Appeal in *Union Nationale des Coopératives Agricoles v. Catterall*.[8] Hence, the proviso to Rule 62(3) may

---

[97] Rule 62(6).
[98] *e.g.* Malta.
[99] Arbitration Act 1950, s.40(*a*). See Second Schedule, Art. 5.
[1] *Ibid.*, s.35(1)(*b*).
[2] See Nussbaum (1942) 56 Harv.L.R. 219, 234–235, and references there given.
[3] *Brazendale & Co. Ltd. v. Saint Frères S.A.* [1970] 2 Lloyd's Rep. 34. *Cf. Union Nationale des Coopératives Agricoles v. Catterall* [1959] 2 Q.B. 44, 50 (C.A.).
[4] Arbitration Act 1950, s.35(1)(*c*).
[5] *Ibid.*, s.40(*b*).
[6] *Ibid.*, s.37(1)(*b*), (*c*), (*d*).
[7] *Ibid.*, s.37(1)(*d*).
[8] [1959] 2 Q.B. 44 (C.A.).

not be read as a definition of the term "final." By section 39, which is reproduced in the proviso an award shall not, for the purposes of Part II, be "deemed final if any proceedings for the purpose of contesting the validity of the award are pending in the country in which it was made." The section merely means that, in the presence of such proceedings, an award may not be treated as final, not that in their absence it is necessarily final.[9] In other countries the condition that the award be final has been regarded as requiring a "double exequatur," *i.e.* a court order both in the country where the award is made and in the country where it is to be enforced. The interpretation placed on section 39 of the Act by the Court of Appeal is not in accordance with the definition of the term "final" for the purpose of the corresponding provision of the Convention.[10]

Enforcement contrary to public policy. No award may be enforced under Part II if its enforcement would be "contrary to the public policy or the law of England."[11] "Contrary to the law of England" (the corresponding term in the Convention is "principles of law"[12]) connotes that the legal rule involved is of a mandatory character, such as those contained in English revenue law, or import or export control.   **16–097**

It is apparently no defence that the award was obtained by fraud, nor that the proceedings were opposed to natural justice (except to the extent mentioned in clause (4)(b) of the Rule). But in continental European law fraud in this context generally falls within the exception of public policy.[13]   **16–098**

Jurisdiction of the arbitrators. According to Rule 62(3)(a), to be enforceable, a foreign award must have been made in pursuance of an arbitration agreement valid by its own law, and according to Rule 62(4)(c) the award is not enforceable if the court is satisfied that the award contains decisions on matters beyond the scope of the agreement for arbitration. It was held in *Kianta Osakeyhtio v. Britain and Overseas Trading Co. Ltd.*[14] that the first provision deals with a situation in which no part of the dispute was ever within the arbitration clause and the arbitrators had no jurisdiction at all, whereas the second provision covers the not uncommon situation where the arbitrators have jurisdiction, but exercise it so as to include in their decision matters which are raised in the proceedings but are outside their authority.   **16–099**

Mode of enforcement. A party who has obtained a foreign award which is within the terms of the Rule may, at his option, enforce it by proceedings at common law or by application for leave to enforce the award under section 66 of the Arbitration Act 1996.   **16–100**

ILLUSTRATIONS

1. A, Finnish sellers, contract with X, English buyers, for the sale of timber. The contract contains an arbitration clause for disputes to be settled in Helsinki. Part delivery only is made   **16–101**

---

[9] *Ibid.*, at p. 51.
[10] Arbitration Act 1950, Sched. 2, Art. 1(*d*).
[11] *Ibid.*, s.37(1) *ad finem*.
[12] *Ibid.*, Sched. 2, Art. 1(*e*). In the French text it is "principes du droit public." *Cf. Masinimport v. Scottish Mechanical Light Industries Ltd.*, 1976 S.C. 102.
[13] See *ante*, para. 14–206.
[14] [1953] 2 Lloyd's Rep. 569, 573.

under the contract and a compromise "compensation" agreement without an arbitration clause is entered into. No deliveries are made under the latter agreement and A institute arbitration proceedings in Finland, X refusing to participate. An award is made in favour of A. In enforcement proceedings in England, A fails as the "compensation" agreement does not satisfy the conditions of Rule 62(4)(c) in that the "award . . . contains decisions on matters beyond the scope of the agreement for arbitration." Alternatively (*semble*) the award is not one "made in pursuance of an agreement for arbitration which was valid under the law by which it was governed" under Rule 62(3)(a).[15]

2. A contract for the sale of wheat seed made between A, French buyers, and X, English sellers, contains a clause referring all disputes to the Arbitration Chamber of Copenhagen. A dispute having arisen, A obtain an award from the committee of the Copenhagen Arbitration Chamber ordering X to pay £183,000. Under the rules of the Chamber, awards made by the committee are final. But by Danish law, the award is not enforceable in Denmark until a judgment of a Danish court has been obtained. However, only objections of a formal nature can be taken in the proceedings to obtain a judgment, which are in no sense a rehearing. A can enforce the award in England under section 66 of the Arbitration Act 1996, even though no judgment has been obtained in Denmark, because the award is final within the meaning of Rule 62(3)(d).[16]

C. *Under Part III of the Arbitration Act 1996*

16R–102   **RULE 63—(1) A New York Convention award, that is an award made in pursuance of an arbitration agreement in the territory of a State, other than the United Kingdom, which is a party to the New York Convention on the Recognition and Enforcement of Foreign Arbitral Awards of June 10, 1958,[17] shall be recognised as binding on the persons as between whom it was made, and may accordingly be relied on by those persons by way of defence, set-off or otherwise in any legal proceedings in England.[18]**

(2) A New York Convention award may be enforced either by proceedings at common law or under the provisions of section 66 of the Arbitration Act 1996, *i.e.* by leave of the High Court, in the same manner as a judgment or order of the court to the same effect.[19]

(3) A party seeking the recognition or enforcement of a New York Convention award must produce

(a)   the duly authenticated original award or a duly certified copy of it; and

(b)   the original arbitration agreement or a duly certified copy of it; and

(c)   if the award or agreement is in a foreign language, a translation of it certified by an official or sworn translator or by a diplomatic or consular agent.[20]

(4) Recognition or enforcement of a New York Convention award may be refused if the person against whom it is invoked proves

(a)   that a party to the arbitration agreement was (under the law applicable to him) under some incapacity; or

---

[15] *Kianta Osakeyhtio v. Britain and Overseas Trading Co. Ltd.* [1954] 1 Lloyd's Rep. 247 (C.A.). In this and the next Illustration the awards would now be enforceable under Rule 63.

[16] *Union Nationale des Coopératives Agricoles v. Catterall* [1959] 2 Q.B. 44 (C.A.).

[17] For parties to the Convention see S.I. 1984 No. 1168, S.I. 1989 No. 1348 and S.I. 1993 No. 1256.

[18] 1996 Act, ss. 100(1),(4), 101(1). These provisions apply to Northern Ireland as well as England.

[19] *Ibid.*, s.101(2).

[20] *Ibid.*, s.102.

(b) that the arbitration agreement was not valid under the law to which the parties subjected it or, failing any indication thereon, under the law of the country where the award was made; or

(c) that he was not given proper notice of the appointment of the arbitrator or of the arbitration proceedings or was otherwise unable to present his case; or

(d) that the award deals with a difference not contemplated by or not falling within the terms of the submission to arbitration or contains decisions on matters beyond the scope of the submission to arbitration; provided that an award which contains decisions on matters not submitted to arbitration may be recognised or enforced to the extent that it contains decisions on matters submitted to arbitration which can be separated from those on matters not so submitted; or

(e) that the composition of the arbitral authority or the arbitral procedure was not in accordance with the agreement of the parties or, failing such agreement, with the law of the country in which the arbitration took place; or

(f) that the award has not yet become binding on the parties, or has been set aside or suspended by a competent authority of the country in which, or under the law of which, it was made.[21]

(5) Recognition or enforcement of a New York Convention award may also be refused if the award is in respect of a matter which is not capable of settlement by arbitration, or if it would be contrary to public policy to recognise or enforce the award.[22]

(6) Recognition or enforcement of a New York Convention award may not be refused except in the cases mentioned above.[23]

COMMENT

This Rule states the effect of sections 100 to 103 of the Arbitration Act 1996, the language of which it closely follows. These sections replace the equivalent provisions of the Arbitration Act 1975, which was passed to enable the United Kingdom to accede to the New York Convention on the Recognition and Enforcement of Foreign Arbitral Awards of June 10, 1958.[24]   **16–103**

Comparison between New York and Geneva Conventions. The main differences between the New York and the Geneva Convention (as to which, see Rule 62) are as follows: **16–104**

(1) The definition of awards to which the former applies is much simpler. The award need only be made in a State, other than the United Kingdom,   **16–105**

---

[21] *Ibid.*, s.103(2), (4).

[22] *Ibid.*, s.103(3).

[23] *Ibid.*, s.103(1). See, however, *Far Eastern Shipping Co. v. AKP Sovcomflot* [1995] 1 Lloyd's Rep. 520 (in which it was held that, where the plaintiff has obtained leave to enforce an award under the summary procedure provided by what is now Arbitration Act 1996, s.66, the court may stay execution of the judgment in accordance with the procedural rules and conditions applicable to English judgments; but the court will rarely, if ever, make such an order in respect of a New York Convention award).

[24] For the text of, and literature on, the New York Convention see *ante*, para. 16–038, n. 26 and, particularly on enforcement under the Convention, Van Den Berg, *The New York Arbitration Convention of 1958* (1961), Chap. 3; Patchett, *Recognition of Commercial Judgments and Awards in the Commonwealth* (1984), Chap. 8; Brotons (1984) *Recueil des Cours*, I, p. 169.

which is a party to the New York Convention. There is no requirement that the parties to the award must be respectively "subject to the jurisdiction" of different Contracting States—a phrase used in the Geneva Convention which has caused much difficulty of interpretation.[25] Nor is there any requirement that the arbitration agreement should not be governed by English law.[26] The New York Convention also applies to "arbitral awards not considered as domestic awards" in the enforcing State.[27] This provision, which is not incorporated in the 1996 Act, was intended to apply to arbitrations conducted in the enforcing state under the law of another State, but in the United States it has been interpreted to mean any award with an international element.[28]

16–106   (2) The burden of proof is differently distributed. The party seeking recognition or enforcement merely has to prove the formal matters mentioned in clause (3) of the Rule. The burden is on the party resisting recognition or enforcement to establish the substantive grounds mentioned in clause (4) of the Rule. The New York Convention separates the two matters mentioned in clause (5) of the Rule from those mentioned in clause (4) in order to make clear that the former can be taken either by the party resisting recognition or enforcement or by the court on its own motion.

16–107   (3) The grounds on which recognition and enforcement may be refused are, generally speaking, drafted with greater precision than they are in the Geneva Convention. Thus, they provide fewer opportunities for obstruction by a defendant resisting enforcement. For example, it is a defence that enforcement of the award would be contrary to the public policy of the enforcing State, but not (as it is under the Geneva Convention) that it is contrary to its law.

16–108   (4) If the party resisting recognition or enforcement establishes any of the grounds in clauses (4) or (5) of the Rule, refusal to recognise or enforce the award is within the discretion of the court[29] and not mandatory as it generally is under the Geneva Convention. Thus even if one of the grounds is established, the court may recognise or enforce the award if the rights of the party resisting the award were not substantially violated or where the degree of prejudice is not substantial. Nevertheless, in a case coming within clause (5) it would be most surprising for the court to recognise or enforce an award if to do so would be contrary to public policy.[30]

16–109   **Definition of Convention award.** A Convention award is defined[31] as "an award made in pursuance of an arbitration agreement[32] in the territory of a State, other than the United Kingdom, which is a party to the New York Convention". For this purpose an award made in a Contracting State before it

---

[25] See *ante*, para. 16–094.

[26] Contrast Arbitration Act 1950, s.40(*b*).

[27] Art. I(1).

[28] *Bergeson v. Joseph Müller Corp.*, 701 F. 2d 928 (2d Cir. 1983), criticised by Van Den Berg (1986) 2 Arb.Int. 191. See also *Lander Co. Inc. v. MMP Investments Inc.*, 107 F. 3d 476 (7th Cir. 1997) (a case involving two U.S. corporations).

[29] *China Agribusiness Development Corp. v. Balli Trading* [1998] 2 Lloyd's Rep. 76; Paulsson (1998) 14 Arb. Int. 227.

[30] See *Hebei Import & Export Corporation v. Polytak Engineering Co. Ltd.* [1998] H.K.L.R.D. 287 (H.K.C.A.).

[31] 1996 Act, s.100(1).

[32] Which must be in writing as defined by s.5: s.100(2)(a). On the requirement of an arbitration agreement see *Peter Cremer GmbH v. Co-operative Molasses Traders Ltd.* [1985] I.L.R.M. 564.

became a party to the Convention is a Convention award.[33] To be entitled to recognition and enforcement under Rule 63 the decision of the arbitrator must constitute an arbitral award. An interlocutory order made by an arbitrator is not an award for these purposes.[34] Whether awards granted under the Italian form of arbitration known as *arbitrato irrituale* fall within the scope of the Convention has yet to be considered by the English courts,[35] though it is suggested that they do.[36]

In *Hiscox v. Outhwaite*[37] the House of Lords had to consider where an   **16–110** award was "made" for these purposes, albeit in very unusual circumstances. Although England was the seat of the arbitration and the hearings before a sole arbitrator took place in England, the arbitrator signed his award in Paris (where he resided and carried on his professional practice). It was held that the award was "made" in France, because a document was made when and where it was perfected, and an award was perfected when it was signed. The House of Lords accepted that it was "anomalous and regrettable that the fortuitous circumstance of signature in Paris should stamp what was clearly intended to be an award subject to all the procedural regulations of an English arbitration with the character of a Convention award", but rejected the theory that the expression "award ... made in the territory of a State" (which derives from Article I of the New York Convention) should not be construed as a geographical concept, but as a reference to the place where the arbitration has its seat, irrespective of where the actual hearings take place or where the award is physically signed.[38] This decision was reversed, however, by the Arbitration Act 1996, which provides that, as a matter of law, an award is made at the seat of the arbitration: where the seat of the arbitration is located in a State which is a party to the New York Convention the award is a New York Convention award[39]; if England is the seat of the arbitration the award is treated as made in England, regardless of where it was signed.[40]

Effect of foreign judgment. It has been seen[41] that there is controversy   **16–111** whether, when a foreign judgment has been entered on an award, it is the judgment or award which is enforceable. Courts in other countries have regularly enforced awards under the New York Convention which have been declared enforceable by judgments in the country in which they were made, and it is suggested that in such cases the award may be enforced under the

---

[33] *Government of Kuwait v. Sir Frederick Snow and Partners* [1984] A.C. 426. *Cf. Dallal v. Bank Mellat* [1986] 1 Q.B. 441 (award of international claims tribunal sitting in the Netherlands under Iran-U.S. treaty not a New York Convention award) with *Ministry of Defense of Islamic Republic of Iran v. Gould Inc.*, 887 F. 2d 1357 (9th Cir. 1989), cert. denied 494 U.S. 1016 (1990) (award enforced under New York Convention).

[34] *Re Resort Condominiums International Inc.* [1995] 1 Qd. 406.

[35] It is an informal method of arbitration; it results in an award which is enforceable as a contract. See Patocchi and Schiavello [1998] Arb. & Dispute Res. L.J. 132. See *Europcar Italia S.P.A. v. Maiellano Tours Inc.*, 156 F. 3d 310 (2d Cir. 1998), for an inconclusive discussion of Italian and German decisions on the application of the New York Convention to this form of arbitration.

[36] But see Sanders and Van den Berg (1979) 4 Yb. Comm. Arb. 231, 232–233.

[37] [1992] 1 A.C. 562, criticised by Reymond (1992) 108 L.Q.R. 1; F. A. Mann, *ibid.* 6; Davidson (1992) 41 I.C.L.Q. 637; Montare (1993) 4 Am. Rev. Int. Arb. 311.

[38] The view of Van Den Berg, pp. 294–295; F. A. Mann (1985) 1 Arb.Int. 107; Reymond (1992) 108 L.Q.R. 1.

[39] s.100(2)(*b*).

[40] s.53.

[41] *Ante*, para. 16–069.

1996 Act,[42] or the judgment may be enforced under whatever régime applies to it.[43]

16–112 **Defences.** The grounds on which recognition and enforcement may be refused, listed in clauses (4) and (5) of the Rule, are exhaustive.[44] So, the court before which recognition or enforcement of a New York Convention award is sought may not review the merits of the award because a mistake of fact or law by the arbitrator is not one of the available grounds of review.

(1) The first ground under clause (4) of the Rule is that a party to the arbitration agreement was (under the law applicable to him) under some incapacity. The Convention does not state what that law is, and therefore the court is thrown back on its own conflict rule for capacity to contract. This is by no means an easy question in the English conflict of laws. The Rome Convention on the Law Applicable to Contractual Obligations, enacted by the Contracts (Applicable Law) Act 1990, does not apply to arbitration agreements, and its general choice of law rules do not apply to the legal capacity of natural persons or of corporations.[45] Consequently the common law rules of the conflict of laws on capacity will apply, but the content of these rules is controversial.[46] It is to be noted that the defence is not limited to cases where the defendant was under some incapacity. It extends to cases where a party to the arbitration agreement (including apparently the claimant seeking enforcement) was so incapable.

16–113 (2) The second ground is that the arbitration agreement was not valid under the law to which the parties subjected it or, failing any indication thereon, under the law of the country where the award was made.[47]

16–114 (3) The third ground is in substance a defence of absence of natural justice, that there was no proper notice of the appointment of the tribunal or of the arbitration proceedings, or that otherwise the party resisting recognition or

---

[42] *ABCI v. Banque Franco-Tunisienne* [1996] 1 Lloyd's Rep. 485, 489, affd. on other aspects [1997] 1 Lloyd's Rep. 531 (C.A.).

[43] This has been decided by the German Federal Supreme Court, 1984 (1985) 10 Yb. Comm.Arb. 427, in relation to the New York Convention, and in Ontario in relation to the UNCITRAL Model Law: *Schreter v. Gasmac Inc.* (1992) 7 O.R. (3d) 608. The trend in the United States is in a similar direction, although there is no clear decision in this sense: *Island Territory of Curacao v. Solitron Devices, Inc.* 489 F. 2d 1313 (2d Cir. 1973); *Fotochrome Inc. v. Copal Co. Ltd.*, 517 F. 2d 512, 518 (2d Cir. 1975); *Waterside Ocean Navigation Co., Inc. v. International Navigation Ltd.*, 737 F. 2d 150 (2d Cir. 1984); *Victrix Steamship Co. v. Salen Dry Cargo AB*, 825 F. 2d 709 (2d Cir. 1987); *Seetransport Wiking Trader v. Navimprex Cetrala Navara*, 29 F. 3d 79 (2d Cir. 1994). *Cf. Oriental Commercial & Shipping Co. (UK) Ltd. v. Rosseel N.V.*, 769 F. Supp. 514 (S.D.N.Y. 1991). See also Delaume, *Law and Practice of Transnational Contracts*, 769 F. Supp. 514 (1988), pp. 342–343. In *ABCI v. Banque Franco-Tunisienne*, n. 42 *ante*, it was held that a French judgment making a French award enforceable was not entitled to enforcement under the 1968 Convention because the enforcement of arbitral awards is outside its scope. Hascher (1996) 12 Arb. Int. 233, 239–240 supports the result, but on the basis that the French order was not a judgment on the award, but an execution order.

[44] Rule 63(6); *Rosseel N.V. v. Oriental Commercial & Shipping Co. (U.K.) Ltd.* [1991] 2 Lloyd's Rep. 625. See also *M & C Corp. v. Erwin Behr G.m.b.H. & Co. K.G.*, 87 F. 3d 844 (6th Cir. 1996).

[45] 1990 Act, Sched. 1, Art. 1(2)(a)(e). *Post*, paras. 32–031 *et seq*. On the capacity of foreign states see *ante*, para. 16–017, n. 56.

[46] *Post*, paras. 32–215 *et seq*.

[47] See *Deutsche Schachtbau v. Shell International Petroleum Co. Ltd.* [1990] 1 A.C. 295 309–310 (C.A.), revd. on other grounds, *ibid.* p. 329.

enforcement was unable to present his case.[48] This ground for refusing recognition or enforcement essentially sanctions the application of the standards of due process of the forum in which recognition or enforcement is sought.[49] Although parties to an arbitration are often entitled to a hearing, it does not follow from the fact that the arbitral tribunal determines the dispute solely on the basis of the parties' documentary evidence that there has been a procedural irregularity.[50] A party who resists recognition or enforcement of an award on the ground of inability to present its case must point to matters outside its control and cannot rely on its own failure to take advantage of an opportunity to participate in the arbitral proceedings.[51]

(4) The fourth ground is that the award deals with a difference not contem-　**16–115** plated by or not falling within the terms of the submission to arbitration or contains decisions on matters beyond the scope of the submission to arbitration. But it is expressly provided that matters properly submitted may be separated from matters not so submitted.[52]

(5) The fifth ground is that the composition of the arbitral authority or the　**16–116** arbitral procedure was not in accordance with the agreement of the parties, or, failing such agreement, with the law of the country where the arbitration took place.[53] The wording of the New York Convention represented a compromise between those countries who wished arbitration to be subject to the procedural law of the place of arbitration and those countries who wished the parties to be free from legal control.[54] The parties are free to choose the law governing the arbitral proceedings, and, in the absence of such choice, the proceedings are governed by the law of the country where the arbitration takes place. It follows that for the purposes of clause (4)(e) it is no defence that the award was not rendered in accordance with the law of the country where the arbitration was conducted, provided that it was rendered in accordance with the procedural law chosen by the parties. Potential problems arise, however, if there is a conflict between the procedure chosen by the parties and the mandatory requirements of the procedural law of the seat. If the arbitrator applies the former, thereby failing to comply with the latter, the award may be set aside by the courts of the country in which it was made, as a consequence of which recognition or enforcement may be refused under clause (4)(f) of the Rule. Although the arbitrator's failure to follow the agreed procedure provides a ground on which recognition or enforcement may be refused under clause (4)(e), the parties' freedom to choose the arbitral procedure must be understood as being subject to the mandatory rules of the law of the seat.[55] If the arbitrator diverges from the procedure agreed by the parties in order to comply with the mandatory procedural rules of the law of the seat the court should, in the exercise its discretion, not refuse to recognise or enforce the award under

---

[48] *Cf. Parsons & Whittemore Overseas Co. Inc. v. RAKTA*, 508 F. 2d 969 (2d Cir. 1974) where it was held that breach of natural justice outside the scope of this defence may justify invocation of the public policy defence.

[49] *Parsons & Whittemore Overseas Co. Inc. v. RAKTA*, 508 F. 2d 969 (2d Cir. 1974).

[50] *Dalmia Dairy Industries Ltd. v. National Bank of Pakistan* [1978] 2 Lloyd's Rep. 223 (a case decided at common law).

[51] *Minmetals Germany GmbH v. Ferco Steel Ltd.* [1999] C.L.C. 647.

[52] 1996 Act, s.103(2)(d), (4). See *Deutsche Schachtbau v. Shell International Petroleum Co. Ltd.*, *supra*, at pp. 311–312.

[53] See, *e.g. China Agribusiness Development Corp. v. Balli Trading* [1998] 2 Lloyd's Rep. 76.

[54] See Contini (1959) 8 Am.J.Comp. L. 283, 301–303; Quigley (1961) 70 Yale L.J. 1049, 1068–1069.

[55] *Cf.* Rule 57(2); 1996 Act, s.4.

clause (4)(e).[56] Where the agreed arbitral procedure has not been complied with, a party who has waived the procedural irregularity is not able to rely on clause (4)(e).[57]

16–117   (6) The sixth ground is that the award has not yet become binding on the parties,[58] or has been set aside or suspended by a competent authority of the country in which, or under the law of which, it was made. The wording of this ground omits the word "final" which appears in the Geneva Convention and caused difficulty in interpretation.[59] It is clear that the Conference which approved the New York Convention chose the word "binding" rather than "final" in order to avoid a double *exequatur* of arbitral awards, one in the country where the award was made and the other in the country where it is sought to be enforced. The Private International Law Committee in its Fifth Report[60] suggested that an award is to be regarded as "binding" if no further recourse may be had to another arbitral tribunal (*e.g.* an appeals tribunal); and the fact that recourse may be had to a court of law does not prevent the award from being binding.[61]

16–118   Although under clause (4) of the Rule the court has a discretion to recognise or enforce an award in cases where one of the grounds has been established, it is to be expected that the court will refuse recognition or enforcement in cases where the award has been set aside in the country in which it was made.[62]

16–119   The paradigm case which brings clause (4)(f) into play is one where an award is set aside in the country where the seat of the arbitration was located. In addition, this ground is intended to encompass the exceptional cases where, an arbitration having been conducted in one country under the law of another country, the award is set aside by the courts of the latter. The reference to the law of the country under which the award was made signifies the procedural law of the arbitration not the substantive law governing the contract out of which the dispute arose nor the law governing the arbitration agreement.[63] So, where a dispute arising out of a contract governed by Pakistani law is referred to arbitration in Switzerland, if the resulting award were set aside by the Pakistani courts,[64] the English court would not be able to refuse recognition or enforcement under clause (4)(f).

---

[56] See Van den Berg (1989) 5 Arb. Int. 2, 9–10.

[57] *Minmetals Germany GmbH v. Ferco Steel Ltd.* [1999] C.L.C. 647.

[58] See *Rosseel N.V. v. Oriental Commercial & Shipping Co. (U.K.) Ltd.* [1991] 2 Lloyd's Rep. 625 (agreement that any proceedings to confirm or vacate New York award would be brought in the U.S. did not prevent enforcement in England; it was not an agreement which deprived the award of its binding character, and it did not amount to an agreement not to enforce).

[59] See *ante*, para. 16–069.

[60] Cmnd. 1515 (1961), para. 14.

[61] See, *e.g. Fertilizer Corp. of India v. IDI Management Inc.*, 517 F. Supp. 948 (S.D. Ohio 1981).

[62] For exceptional cases where awards which had been set aside in the country where they were made were enforced abroad see *Hilmarton Ltd. v. Omnium de Traitement et de Valorisation* (1995) 20 Yb. Comm. Arb. 663 (Cour de cassation, France, 1994); *Arab Republic of Egypt v. Chromalloy Aeroservices Inc.* (1997) 22 Yb. Comm. Arb. 691 (Cour d'appel, Paris, 1997); *Chromalloy Aeroservices Inc. v. Arab Republic of Egypt*, 939 F. Supp. 907 (D.D.C. 1996).

[63] Decisions to this effect in several countries are discussed in *International Standard Electric Corp. v. Bridas Sociedad Anonima Petrolera, Industrial y Comercial*, 745 F. Supp. 172 (S.D.N.Y. 1990).

[64] See *Rupali Polyester Ltd. v. Bunni* [1995] 3 L.R.C. 617 (in which the Supreme Court of Pakistan held that the Pakistani courts have supervisory jurisdiction over an award made in another country if the arbitration agreement is governed by the law of Pakistan).

A question arises whether the court may refuse to enforce a New York   **16–120**
Convention award in a case where, as a result of the bringing of proceedings
to have the award set aside in the country where it was made, the award is
automatically suspended. Since the ground provided by clause (4)(f) refers to
an award being suspended *by a competent authority*, it would seem that
automatic suspension under the law of the country where the award was made
does not entitle the courts of other countries to refuse to recognise or enforce
the award.[65] This analysis is consistent with the framework of the Convention
which draws a distinction between grounds on which recognition or enforcement may be *refused* and circumstances in which proceedings for the recognition or enforcement of an award may be *adjourned*: although a court may
refuse to recognise or enforce an award which has been suspended by a
competent authority, it may adjourn proceedings in which an award is relied
upon if the award is automatically suspended as a result of proceedings
challenging the award being brought in the country in which the award was
made. It is provided that where an application for setting aside or suspension
of a New York Convention award has been made to a competent authority of
the country in which, or under the law of which, it was made, the court which
is asked to recognise or enforce the award may adjourn the proceedings and
may, on the application of a party seeking recognition or enforcement of the
award, order the other party to give security.[66]

In *Soleh Boneh International Ltd. v. Government of Uganda*[67] it was held   **16–121**
that there are two important factors in the exercise of the discretion to order
security in enforcement cases. The first is the strength of the argument that the
award is invalid, as perceived on a brief consideration by the court which is
asked to enforce the award while proceedings to set aside are pending
elsewhere. If the award is manifestly invalid there should be an adjournment
and no order for security; if it is manifestly valid there should either be an
order for immediate enforcement or else an order for substantial security. In
between there are various degrees of plausibility in the argument for invalid-
ity; and the judge must be guided by his preliminary conclusion on the point.
The second factor is that the court must consider the ease or difficulty of
enforcement of the award, and whether it will be rendered more difficult, for
example, by movement of assets or improvident trading, if enforcement is
delayed. If this is likely to occur the case for security is stronger; if, on the
other hand, there are and always will be insufficient assets within the jurisdiction, the case for security is necessarily weakened.

Public policy. In clause (5) of the Rule, it is for the law of England to   **16–122**
decide what matters are capable of settlement by arbitration,[68] and it is
English public policy which is meant. This is not explicit in section 103(3) of
the Act, but it is explicit in Article V.2 of the Convention. In *Deutsche*

---

[65] Van den Berg, p. 352. *Cf. AB Götaverken v. General National Maritime Transport Co.* (1981)
6 Yb. Comm. Arb. 237 (Swedish Sup.Ct., 1979) with *Creighton Ltd. v. Government of Qatar*
(1996) 21 Yb. Comm. Arb. 751 (D.D.C. 1995).

[66] 1996 Act, s.103(5). See Tupman (1987) 3 Arb. Int. 209.

[67] [1993] 2 Lloyd's Rep. 495 (C.A.).

[68] This is made clear by the wording of the Convention, Art. V(5)(a). As to what matters are
capable of settlement by arbitration by the law of England, see Mustill and Boyd, pp. 149–150.
See also *Mitsubishi Motors Corp. v. Soler Chrysler-Plymouth, Inc.*, 473 U.S. 614 (1985);
Shearson/American Express Inc. v. McMahon, 482 U.S. 220 (1989); *Rodriguez de Quijas v.
Shearson/American Express Inc.*, 490 U.S. 477 (1989); *PPG Industries Inc. v. Pilkington plc*,
825 F. Supp. 1465 (D.Ariz. 1993).

Schachtbau v. Shell International Petroleum Co. Ltd.[69] it was held that it was not contrary to English public policy to enforce a Swiss award, valid under Swiss law, in which the arbitrators applied general principles of law; the arbitrators' choice of the governing law (in the absence of a choice by the parties) was not outside the scope of the choice which the parties left to the arbitrators. Sir John Donaldson M.R. emphasised that public policy could never be exhaustively defined, and that it should be approached with extreme caution: for an argument based on public policy to succeed it has to be shown that there is some element of illegality or that recognition or enforcement of the award would be clearly injurious to the public good, or, possibly, that recognition or enforcement would be wholly offensive to the ordinary reasonable and fully informed member of the public on whose behalf the powers of the State are exercised.[70] In two recent cases[71] it was held that it was not contrary to public policy to enforce a foreign award, notwithstanding that it was argued that the underlying contract involved a conspiracy to break the laws of a foreign State.[72] In each of these cases the arbitrators had heard and rejected the respondent's defence of illegality. The position may be different if the arbitral tribunal has not ruled on the question of illegality or if the contract is indisputably illegal.[73] Even in cases which do not fall within clause (4)(c) or (e), recognition or enforcement of an award may be refused on the ground of public policy if it is established that the award is contrary to English requirements of substantial justice.[74] Where, however, an award has been challenged on procedural grounds before the courts of the seat of arbitration, and the challenge has been dismissed, the court must, when deciding whether or not to refuse to recognise or enforce the award on grounds of public policy, give appropriate weight to the policy of upholding New York Convention awards; normally, the English court will not re-investigate an alleged procedural defect which has been ruled on by the courts of the seat of arbitration.[75]

16–123   **Mode of enforcement.** A party who has obtained a New York Convention award may, at his option, enforce it either by action or by an application for leave to enforce the award summarily under section 66 of the Arbitration Act 1996, as if it were a judgment or order of the court.[76]

16–124   Article III of the New York Convention provides that "there shall not be imposed substantially more onerous conditions or higher fees or charges on the recognition or enforcement of arbitral awards to which this Convention applies than are imposed on the recognition or enforcement of domestic

---

[69] [1990] 1 A.C. 295 (C.A.), revd. on other grounds, *ibid.* p. 329.

[70] At p. 316. It is widely accepted that the public policy ground should be given a restrictive application: see, *e.g. Waterside Ocean Navigation Co. Inc. v. International Navigation Ltd.*, 737 F. 2d 150, 152 (2d Cir. 1984); *Inter Maritime Management S.A. v. Russin & Vecchi* (1997) 22 Yb. Comm. Arb. 789 (Swiss Federal Tribunal, 1995); *Renusager Power Co. Ltd. v. General Electric Co.* (1995) 20 Yb. Comm. Arb. 681 (Indian Sup.Ct.); *Paklito Investment Ltd. v. Klöckner (East Asia) Ltd.* [1993] 2 H.K.L.R. 39.

[71] *Westacre Investments Inc. v. Jugoimport-SDPR Holding Co.* [1999] Q.B. 740; *Soinco SACI v. Novokuznetsk Aluminium Plant* [1998] C.L.C. 730 (C.A.).

[72] See para. 16–087, *ante* and paras. 32R–226 *et seq, post.*

[73] *Soleimany v. Soleimany* [1999] Q.B. 785 (C.A.) (a case concerning an English award).

[74] *Adams v. Cape Industries plc* [1990] Ch. 433 (C.A.) (a case concerning the enforcement of a foreign judgment at common law).

[75] *Minmetals Germany GmbH v. Ferco Steel Ltd.* [1999] C.L.C. 647.

[76] See *ante*, para. 16–073.

arbitral awards." There is no corresponding provision in the legislation implementing the Convention. Parliament must have regarded it as inconceivable that any court would discriminate against foreign awards in this way.

Recognition of New York Convention award as defence. Any New York   **16–125**
Convention award must be recognised as binding on the persons as between whom it was made, and may accordingly be relied upon by way of defence, set-off or otherwise in any legal proceedings in England.[77] Hence, a valid New York Convention award in favour of the defendant is a defence to an action on the original cause of action.[78]

Supersession of Geneva Convention.   Article VII.2 of the New York   **16–126**
Convention provides that the Geneva Convention (*i.e.* Rule 62) shall cease to have effect between Contracting States on their becoming bound by the later Convention. This provision is implemented not by the repeal of Part II of the Arbitration Act 1950 (because it may still be required as between the United Kingdom and States which are parties to the Geneva Convention but not to the New York Convention), but by section 99 of the 1996 Act which provides that Part II of the 1950 Act applies to foreign awards within the meaning of that Part only if they are not also New York Convention awards.[79]

Saving for common law.   A party seeking to enforce a New York Conven-   **16–127**
tion award may do so by proceedings at common law (*i.e.* under Rule 59) if he so prefers. Section 104 of the 1996 Act provides that nothing in Part III affects any right to rely upon or enforce a New York Convention award at common law or under section 66.[80] This is in accordance with Article VII.1 of the New York Convention.

ILLUSTRATIONS

1. A & Co. enters into a contract, on behalf of a consortium of oil companies, with the R'as   **16–128**
Al Khaimah National Oil Company (Raknoc) for exploration for oil in R'as Al Khaimah, one of the United Arab Emirates. The contract provides for arbitration in Geneva under the Rules of the International Chamber of Commerce, but contains no choice of law to govern the contract. When disputes arise, A & Co. commences an arbitration. Raknoc takes no part in the proceedings. The arbitral tribunal makes a substantial award of damages. In arriving at their award, the arbitrators decide that the law governing the contractual relations of the parties is "internationally accepted principles of law". The award is valid under Swiss law. Raknoc fails to comply with the award. Some years later A & Co. discovers that Raknoc has sold a quantity of oil to Shell Petroleum, London, and that consequently Shell Petroleum owes a large sum of money to Raknoc. A & Co. is granted leave to enforce the award, and obtains an injunction restraining Raknoc from removing outside the jurisdiction the proceeds of the debt due to it from Shell Petroleum. Raknoc applies to set aside the leave to enforce the award, on the ground (*inter alia*) that it is contrary to English public policy to enforce an award based on general principles of law. The award is held to be enforceable, because the parties intended to create legally enforceable rights and liabilities, and the arbitrators' choice of law was not outside the scope of the choice left to the arbitrators. Subsequently A & Co. obtains a garnishee order nisi in relation to the debt owed by Shell Petroleum to Raknoc. But the Government of R'as al Khaimah sues Shell Petroleum in the courts of R'as Al Khaimah for the same debt (in breach of an agreement providing for arbitration in London), and arrests a ship belonging to an affiliated company. The garnishee order absolute is

---

[77] 1996 Act, s.101(1).
[78] See *ante*, para. 16–075 for the question whether the award must be on the merits.
[79] See Rule 62(6).
[80] s.40(a) of the 1950 Act contains a similar saving.

discharged, because it would be unjust to subject Shell Petroleum to the risk of having to pay twice.[81]

2. A Corp., a Chinese corporation, and X & Co., an English company, enter a contract which provides for arbitration in China under the provisional rules of procedure of FETAC (Foreign Trade Arbitration Commission). A dispute is referred to arbitration; the arbitration is conducted under the auspices of FETAC's successor, CIETAC (China International Economic and Arbitration Commission) and the arbitration is conducted in accordance with CIETAC's new arbitration rules. An award is made in A Corp.'s favour. X & Co. has no defence to enforcement of the award in England under clause (4)(e) of the Rule because, as a matter of construction, the parties agreed that the arbitration would be conducted under the rules of the relevant institution (*i.e.* CIETAC) at the time when arbitration was invoked; even if the defence under clause (4)(e) were established, enforcement of the award would be ordered as the difference between FETAC's provisional rules of procedure and CIETAC's new rules is insubstantial.[82]

3. A Inc., a Panamanian company, and X & Co., a Yugoslav entity, enter a consultancy contract which includes an arbitration clause. The contract anticipates that A Inc. will bribe Kuwaiti officials. A dispute is referred to arbitration in Geneva under I.C.C. Rules. The arbitral tribunal, having decided that the arbitration agreement is valid and that the consultancy contract is not invalid due to an infringement of bona mores, makes an award ordering X & Co. to pay sums due to A Inc. under the consultancy contract. When A Inc. seeks enforcement of the award in England, X & Co. argues that enforcement should be refused under clause (5) of the Rule on the basis of public policy. It is not contrary to public policy for the award to be enforced in England.[83]

D. *Under Part II of the Civil Jurisdiction and Judgments Act 1982*

16R–129   **RULE 64—An arbitration award which has become enforceable in one part of the United Kingdom in the same manner as a judgment given by a court of law in that part is enforceable by registration in other parts of the United Kingdom under Schedules 6 or 7 to the Civil Jurisdiction and Judgments Act 1982.**

COMMENT

16–130   This Rule stems from the definition of "judgment" in section 18(2)(*e*) of the Civil Jurisdiction and Judgments Act 1982. It means that an arbitration award made, *e.g.* in Scotland or Northern Ireland, which has become enforceable there in the same manner as a judgment given there by a court of law can be registered in England as a judgment under Schedule 6 of the 1982 Act (if it orders payment of a sum or sums of money) or under Schedule 7 (if it orders any relief or remedy not requiring payment of a sum of money) and then enforced accordingly. The provisions of Schedules 6 and 7 have been discussed above[84] and here it is only necessary to state that the application for a certificate (which is the necessary prerequisite to registration) must be made to the court which gave the judgment or made the order by virtue of which the award has become enforceable as a judgment.[85]

16–131   Registration of a Scottish or Northern Irish judgment in England is normally the only way in which it can be enforced there. But this does not apply to arbitration awards within this Rule,[86] and accordingly such an award may be enforced in England at the option of the claimant either by registration or

---

[81] *Deutsche Schachtbau v. Shell International Petroleum Co. Ltd.* [1990] 1 A.C. 295 (C.A. and H.L.).
[82] *China Agribusiness Development Corp. v. Balli Trading* [1999] 2 Lloyd's Rep. 76.
[83] *Westacre Investments Inc. v. Jugoimport-SDPR Holding Co.* [1999] Q.B. 740.
[84] *Ante*, paras. 14R–230 *et seq.*
[85] Scheds. 6 and 7, para. 2(2)(*e*).
[86] 1982 Act, s.18(8).

by the summary procedure of section 66 of the Arbitration Act 1996, where it is available.

Section 19 of the 1982 Act provides that a judgment within section 18 given   **16–132**
in one part of the United Kingdom shall not be refused recognition in another part of the United Kingdom solely on the ground that the court which gave the judgment was not a court of competent jurisdiction according to the rules of private international law in force where it is sought to be registered. But this does not apply to arbitration awards falling within section 18(2)(*e*).

E. *Under Part II of the Administration of Justice Act 1920 or Part I of the*
Foreign Judgments (Reciprocal Enforcement) Act 1933

RULE 65—(1) An arbitration award made in a country outside the United   **16R–133**
Kingdom to which Part II of the Administration of Justice Act 1920 or
Part I of the Foreign Judgments (Reciprocal Enforcement) Act 1933
applies is enforceable in the same manner as a judgment given by a court
in that country, provided that the award has, in pursuance of the law in
force in the country where it was made, become enforceable in the same
manner as a judgment given by a court in that country.[87]

(2) An arbitration award made in a country outside the United King-
dom which is a party to the Geneva Convention on the International
Carriage of Goods by Road of May 19, 1956, is enforceable by registra-
tion under the Foreign Judgments (Reciprocal Enforcement) Act 1933,
if

(a) **the award has become enforceable in that country**[88]**; and**
(b) **the clause in the contract of carriage conferring competence on the**
      arbitration tribunal provided that the tribunal should apply the
      Convention.[89]

COMMENT

Clause (1) of the Rule. As we have seen,[90] the Administration of Justice   **16–134**
Act 1920 provides for the direct enforcement in the United Kingdom of judgments of superior courts of countries of the Commonwealth overseas to which the Act has been extended by Order in Council.[91] The Act provides that any such judgment may be registered in the High Court in England, if that court thinks it is just and convenient that the judgment should be enforced in the United Kingdom[92]; and that a judgment so registered shall be of the same force and effect as if it had been a judgment of the High Court.[93] The Act defines a judgment so as to include an arbitration award if the award has, in pursuance of the law in force in the place where it was made, become enforceable in the same manner as a judgment given by a court in that place.[94]

---

[87] Administration of Justice Act 1920, s.12(1); Foreign Judgments (Reciprocal Enforcement) Act 1933, s.10A (added by Civil Jurisdiction and Judgments Act 1982, Sched. 10, para. 4). *Cf. Brali v. Hyundai Corp.* (1988) 84 A.L.R. 176.
[88] Carriage of Goods by Road Act 1965, ss.4(1), 7(1).
[89] *Ibid.* Schedule, Art. 33.
[90] See Rule 46.
[91] For those countries, see *ante*, para. 14R–159, n. 46.
[92] Administration of Justice Act 1920, s.9(1).
[93] *Ibid.*, s.9(3)(*a*).
[94] *Ibid.* s.12(1).

The judgment creditor remains free to bring an action on the award in accordance with Rule 59, but he may be deprived of his costs.[95]

16–135   It was the intention of Parliament that the system introduced by the Administration of Justice Act 1920 should gradually be replaced by that introduced by the Foreign Judgments (Reciprocal Enforcement) Act 1933,[96] since it would clearly be redundant to have two different systems of registration of judgments, one for countries of the Commonwealth and one for politically foreign countries. Accordingly, no further extension of the 1920 Act to countries of the Commonwealth can now take place[97]; and the 1933 Act has been extended to India,[98] Pakistan,[99] Australia,[1] Canada,[2] Tonga,[3] Guernsey,[4] Jersey[5] and the Isle of Man.[6] It was found that the replacement of the 1920 Act by the 1933 Act was impeded by various circumstances, one of which was that in the 1920 Act the definition of judgments includes arbitration awards, while in the 1933 Act it did not. The 1933 Act was therefore amended so that it also applies to awards which are made enforceable in the same manner as a judgment by an order of the court of the country in which the award was made.[7]

16–136   To be registrable under the 1920 Act or the 1933 Act the award must have become enforceable in the same manner as a judgment according to the law in force in the place where it was made. This requirement would appear to be satisfied if leave to enforce has been given in terms equivalent to those in section 66 of the Arbitration Act 1996.[8] It would seem that all the provisions of Part II of the 1920 Act and of Part I of the 1933 Act as to what judgments are registrable and as to the setting aside of registration[9] apply *mutatis mutandis* to arbitration awards registrable as judgments under those Acts. In addition, the English court which is asked to register the award as a judgment would no doubt require to be satisfied that the agreement to arbitrate was valid by its applicable law and that the arbitration tribunal acted within the terms of the agreement.

16–137   Where an award is enforceable by registration under the 1933 Act, it will remain enforceable at common law or under section 66 of the Arbitration Act 1996. This is because section 10A of the 1933 Act provides that section 6 of the 1933 Act, which makes registration the exclusive method of enforcement, is not to apply to the enforcement of awards under the 1933 Act.

---

[95] *Ibid.* s.9(5).
[96] See *ante*, para. 14–170.
[97] Foreign Judgments (Reciprocal Enforcement) Act 1933, s.7(1); S.R. & O. 1933 No. 1073.
[98] S.I. 1958 No. 425.
[99] S.I. 1958 No. 141.
[1] S.I. 1994 No. 1901.
[2] S.I. 1987 No. 468, as amended.
[3] S.I. 1980 No. 1523.
[4] S.I. 1973 No. 610.
[5] S.I. 1973 No. 612.
[6] S.I. 1973 No. 611.
[7] Civil Jurisdiction and Judgments Act 1982, Sched. 10, para. 4. which added s.10A to the 1933 Act. For an earlier extension of the 1933 Act to arbitral awards made in Commonwealth countries see Administration of Justice Act 1956, s.51(a).
[8] If the award has actually been entered as a judgment in the country where it was made, the judgment itself will be enforceable under the 1920 and 1933 Acts, since the parties would be regarded as having submitted to the jurisdiction of the foreign court: see *ante*, Rule 60(2) and also para. 16–069.
[9] See *ante*, Rules 46 and 47.

Clause (2) of the Rule. The Carriage of Goods by Road Act 1965, which   **16–138**
(as we have seen[10]) enacts as part of the law of the United Kingdom the
provisions of the Geneva Convention on the International Carriage of Goods
by Road (1956), provides in section 4(1) that Part I of the Foreign Judgments
(Reciprocal Enforcement) Act 1933[11] shall apply to any judgment given by
any court or tribunal of a foreign country which is a party to the Convention[12]
in proceedings arising out of carriage under the Convention, provided that the
judgment has become enforceable in that country. Section 7(1) of the Act
provides that any reference in the preceding provisions of the Act to a court
includes a reference to an arbitration tribunal acting by virtue of Article 33 of
the Convention. Article 33 provides that the contract of carriage may contain
a clause conferring competence on an arbitration tribunal if the clause provides that the tribunal shall apply the Convention. It would appear, therefore,
that if the above conditions are satisfied, an arbitration award is registrable as
a judgment under the Foreign Judgments (Reciprocal Enforcement) Act
1933.

F. *Under the Arbitration (International Investment Disputes) Act 1966*

RULE 66—An arbitration award made by the International Centre for the   **16R–139**
Settlement of Investment Disputes, being an award made in respect of
any legal dispute arising directly out of an investment, between a Con-
tracting State and a national of another Contracting State, may be
registered in the High Court, and thereupon will be of the same force and
effect for the purposes of execution as if it had been a judgment of the
High Court given when the award was rendered and entered on the date
of registration.[13]

COMMENT

A Convention (to which the United Kingdom is a party) was entered into in   **16–140**
Washington on March 18, 1965, for the settlement of investment disputes
between Contracting States and nationals of other Contracting States. More
than 100 States have signed the Convention. The Convention is scheduled to
the Arbitration (International Investment Disputes) Act 1966, which provides
the machinery for enforcing arbitration awards made in pursuance of the
Convention. The Convention sets up an International Centre for the settlement
of investment disputes (ICSID), with an administrative council, secretariat
and panels of conciliators and arbitrators. Its jurisdiction extends to "any legal
dispute arising directly out of an investment, between a Contracting State and
a national of another Contracting State, which the parties to the dispute

---

[10] *Ante*, para. 15–046.
[11] Except s.4(2) and (3) thereof, which relate to jurisdiction: Carriage of Goods by Road Act 1965, s.4(2).
[12] S.I. 1967 No. 1683, as amended by S.I. 1980 No. 697, states who are parties to the Convention.
[13] Arbitration (International Investment Disputes) Act 1966, ss.1, 2. See Delaume, *Law and Practice of Transnational Contracts* (1988), Chap. 10; Broches (1993) 18 Yb. Comm. Arb. 627–717i and for enforcement of ICSID awards in France and New York see Delaume (1983) 77 A.J.I.L. 784; Van Den Berg (1989) 5 Arb.Int. 2, 11 *et seq.*; and the decision in *Soc. SOABI v. Senegal*, Cour de cassation, France, 1991, in 1992 *Rev.Crit.* 331, (1991) 30 I.L.M. 1169.

consent in writing to submit to the Centre."[14] The arbitration tribunal must decide the dispute in accordance with the law agreed by the parties, or in the absence of such agreement, in accordance with the law of the Contracting State party to the dispute and such rules of international law as may be applicable, or (if the parties so agree) *ex aequo et bono*.[15] Provision is made for the annulment of the award on certain grounds specified in the Convention.[16]

16–141   A person seeking recognition or enforcement of such an award is entitled to have the award registered in the High Court in England.[17] If any pecuniary obligation imposed by the award is expressed in a foreign currency, it can (and perhaps must) be registered for an amount expressed in foreign currency.[18] An award so registered has, as respects the pecuniary obligation which it imposes, the same force and effect for the purposes of execution as if it had been a judgment of the High Court given when the award was rendered pursuant to the Convention and entered on the date of registration. Accordingly, proceedings may be taken on the award, the sum for which it is registered carries interest, and the High Court has the same control over the award as if it had been a judgment of the High Court.[19]

16–142   The Act provides similar machinery for the enforcement of awards within its scope in Scotland,[20] Northern Ireland,[21] the Isle of Man, the Channel Islands and any colony.[22]

---

[14] 1966 Act, Sched., Art. 25.

[15] *Ibid.* Art. 42.

[16] *Ibid.* Art. 52. The use of applications for annulment has been controversial: see *Klöckner Industrie A.G. v. Cameroon*, 1985, in (1986) 1 ICSID Rev.–F.I.L.J. 89; *Amco Asia Corp. v. Indonesia* (1986) 25 I.L.M. 1439, 12 Yb. Comm. Arb. 129; *MINE v. Guinea* (1991) 16 Yb. Comm. Arb. 41. See Broches (1991) 6 ICSID Rev.–F.I.L.J. 32.

[17] *Ibid.* s.1(2). See CPR PD49G, para. 34.

[18] This appears to be the effect of s.4(2)(*b*)(ii) of the Administration of Justice Act 1977, which repealed s.1(3) of the Arbitration (International Investment Disputes) Act 1966. See *post*, para. 36–076, n. 11.

[19] 1996 Act, s.2(1).

[20] s.7.

[21] s.8.

[22] s.6.

INDEX

References to the Brussels Convention and the Lugano Convention are to the Brussels Convention of 1968 and the Lugano Convention of 1988 on jurisdiction and the enforcement of judgments in civil and commercial matters.
References to the Rome Convention are to the Rome Convention on the Law Applicable to Contractual Obligations 1980.

I

III